SIMS INDEX

To

LAND GRANTS

In

West Virginia

GENEALOGICAL PUBLISHING Co., Inc

Originally published 1952
Supplement published 1956[?]
Reprinted: Genealogical Publishing Co., Inc.
Baltimore, 2003
Library of Congress Catalogue Card Number 2002114473
International Standard Book Number 0-8063-1714-0
Made in the United States of America

The land grants listed herein were made by Lord Fairfax prior to the creation of the Virginia Land Office; by the Commonwealth of Virginia, of lands now embracing the State of West Virginia; and, by the State of West Virginia, under its first Constitution. Preparation of this index was made pursuant to Chapter 120, Acts of the 1951 Session of the West Virginia Legislature.

The information contained herein was compiled after an exhaustive and careful page-by-page examination of the copies of land grants filed in my office, and no effort has been spared to assure that the spellings of the names of grantees, location and descriptions of tracts, are accurate as herein listed. Many variations of spellings of grantees' names were encountered, and required indexing under each spelling, or as a repetition of the names in a different spelling as shown in parentheses. In case of doubt as to correct spellings, due to illegibility of some of the penmanship, careful comparisons were made with the land books of the Commissioner of Revenue, now the Assessor, of the county in which the tract is located.

The editorial work and preparation of this index was done by Mary F. Tessiatore, Mary E. Easton, Spurgeon H. White, and Keith Clark, under the supervision of James M. Hardman, Chief of the Land Department of my office.

Edgar B. Sims
State Auditor.

Charleston, West Virginia, 1952.

ERRATA

The following errors in the final printing of the book occurred too late to be corrected.

Page 359, Line 16—Delete "Likins" from **"Likins,** Lickens, Likens, Lykens."

Page 367, Line 56—Stewart, Alexander, **"300** acres," should read, "500 acres."

Page 367, Line 57—Stewart, Alexander, "500 acres," should read "300 acres."

Page 761, Line 15—Change "Pryor, see Perine" to read, "Pryon, see Perine."

CONTENTS

INDEX TO COUNTIES

DATE OF FORMATION OF WEST VIRGINIA COUNTIES
and
COUNTIES FROM WHICH FORMED

County	Date of Formation	Counties From Which Formed
Barbour	1843	Harrison, Lewis, Randolph
Berkeley	1772	*Frederick*
Boone	1847	Cabell, Kanawha, Logan
Braxton	1836	Kanawha, Lewis, Nicholas
Brooke	1796	Ohio
Cabell	1809	Kanawha
Calhoun	1856	Gilmer
Clay	1858	Braxton, Nicholas
Doddridge	1845	Harrison, Lewis, Ritchie, Tyler
Fayette	1831	Greenbrier, Kanawha, Logan, Nicholas
Gilmer	1845	Kanawha, Lewis
Grant	1866	Hardy
Greenbrier	1777	*Bpteourt, Montgomery*
Hampshire	1753	*Augusta, Frederick*
Hancock	1848	Brooke
Hardy	1785	Hampshire
Harrison	1784	Monongalia
Jackson	1831	Kanawha, Mason, Wood
Jefferson	1801	Berkeley
Kanawha	1788	Greenbrier, *Montgomery*
Lewis	1816	Harrison
Lincoln	1867	Boone, Cabell, Kanawha, Putnam
Logan	1824	Cabell, *Giles*, Kanawha, *Tazewell*
Marion	1842	Harrison, Monongalia
Marshall	1835	Ohio
Mason	1804	Kanawha
Mercer	1837	*Giles, Tazewell*
Mineral	1866	Hampshire
Mingo	1895	Logan
Monongalia	1776	*West Augusta District*
Monroe	1799	Greenbrier
Morgan	1820	Berkeley, Hampshire
McDowell	1858	*Tazewell*
Nicholas	1818	Greenbrier, Kanawha, Randolph
Ohio	1776	*West Augusta District*
Pendleton	1787	*Augusta*, Hardy, *Rockingham*
Pleasants	1851	Ritchie, Tyler, Wood
Pocahontas	1821	*Bath*, Pendleton, Randolph
Preston	1818	Monongalia
Putnam	1848	Cabell, Kanawha, Mason
Raleigh	1850	Fayette
Randolph	1786	Harrison
Ritchie	1843	Harrison, Lewis, Wood
Roane	1856	Gilmer, Jackson, Kanawha
Summers	1871	Fayette, Greenbrier, Mercer, Monroe
Taylor	1844	Barbour, Harrison, Marion
Tucker	1856	Randolph
Tyler	1814	Ohio
Upshur	1851	Barbour, Lewis, Randolph
Wayne	1842	Cabell
Webster	1860	Braxton, Nicholas, Randolph
Wetzel	1846	Tyler
Wirt	1848	Jackson, Wood
Wood	1798	Harrison
Wyoming	1850	Logan

Italics denotes Virginia Counties.

Sims Index

BARBOUR COUNTY

Name of Grantee	Acres	Local Description	Year	Book	Page
Alexander, Francis et al	10	Anglin's Run	1854	1	153
Allen, John M. et al	22	Brushy Fork	1853	1	143
Arnold, Jesse W.	50	Gnatty Creek	1854	1	149
Auvil, Anglina & Amanda	55	Brushy Fork	1852	1	107
Auvil, D. M.	7	Teter's Creek	1852	1	128
Auvil, Daniel M.	25	Brushy Fork	1849	1	65
Auvil, Daniel M.	45	Wts. Valley River	1854	1	176
Auvil, Daniel M.	8	Raccoon Creek	1854	1	177
Auvil, Daniel M.	55	Raccoon Creek	1859	1	238
Auvil, Daniel M. et al	50	Barker's Mill Cr.	1861	1	254
Auvil, Henry D.	58	Brushy Fork	1853	1	131
Auvil, Lewis	6½	Brushy Fork	1850	1	78
Auvil, William	103	Brushy Fork	1850	1	79
Baker, Jacob Sr. et al	19	Brushy Fork	1854	1	179
Baker, Jacob Sr. et al	25	Brushy Fork	1854	1	180
Baldwin, Israel	400	Brushy Fork	1854	1	165
Barnhouse, Solomon	200	Wolf Run	1845	1	7
Bartlett, Nathan E.	75	Pleasant Creek	1857	1	208
Bartlett, Thomas F.	150	Bartlett's Run	1854	1	172
Bartlett, William P.	60	Simpson's Creek	1858	1	231
Bennett, Asa H.	20	Teter's Creek	1852	1	112
Bennett, Henry P.	100	Teter's Creek	1852	1	106
Bennett, Henry P.	63	Teter's Creek	1856	1	197
Bennett, Jacob S.	400	Laurel Fork	1854	1	166
Bennett, John C.	93	Laurel Creek	1858	1	209
Bennett, Levi	60	Wts. Buckhannon River	1859	1	237
Berlin, Frederick	18	Teter's Creek	1851	1	96
Berlin, Frederick	353	Clapboard Run	1851	1	97
Berlin, Frederick	17	Brushy Fork	1851	1	98
Berlin, Frederick	310	Teter's Creek	1852	1	127
Berlin, Frederick	140	Brushy Fork	1854	1	163
Berlin, Frederick	250	Teter's Creek	1854	1	164
Berlin, Frederick	14	Big Sandy Creek	1857	1	200
Berlin, Frederick	900	Teter's Creek	1861	1	253
Berlin, Frederick et al	120	Brushy Fork	1849	1	69

Name of Grantee	Acres	Local Description	Year	Book	Page
Berlin, Frederick et al	340	Teter's Creek	1851	1	89
Berlin, Frederick et al	23	B. & M. Turnpike	1851	1	101
Berlin, Frederick et al	400	Wts. Tygert's Valley	1852	1	113
Berlin, Frederick et al	420	Teter's Creek	1852	1	114
Berlin, Frederick et al	835	Teter's Creek	1852	1	115
Berlin, Frederick et al	200	Mill Run	1852	1	122
Berlin, Frederick et al	200	Big Sandy Creek	1854	1	168
Berlin, Frederick et al	914	Beaver Creek	1854	1	169
Berlin, Frederick et al	28	Beaver Creek	1854	1	170
Berlin, Frederick et al	3,000	Sandy Creek	1855	1	182
Black, Athile M. et al Hrs.	100	Laurel Creek	1850	1	70
Black, Eliza M. et al Hrs.	100	Laurel Creek	1850	1	70
Black, John D. et al Hrs.	100	Laurel Creek	1850	1	70
Booth, Isaac	259	Mill Creek	1852	1	117
Booth, Isaac	23	Wts. Valley River	1852	1	118
Bowman, Henry V.	4	Adj. Levi Garner	1860	1	251
Braddee, Hannah	100	Cove Settlement	1847	1	24
Broddee, Hannah	100	Cove Settlement	1847	1	24
Bryan, John	215	Cove Settlement	1849	1	63
Burner, Jacob H.	8½a.20p.	Buckhannon River	1851	1	80
Byrne, John P.	300	Brushy Fork	1858	1	232
Callihan, William W. R.	48½	Elk Creek	1860	1	250
Camden, G. D.	283	Swamp Run	1847	1	22
Car, David	36	Teter's Creek	1849	1	59
Carlile, John S.	40	Brushy Fork	1846	1	15
Clevenger, Edmund	119	Brushy Fork	1860	1	246
Coontz, Adam	8	Hunter's Fork	1852	1	119
Coontz, Frederick et al	450	Hunter's Fork	1852	1	120
Corley, N. E. et al	351	Laurel Fork	1849	1	64
Corder, William Sr. et al	108½	Hacker's Creek	1850	1	76
Cox, William	9	Raccoon Creek	1854	1	178
Dayton, Spencer	80	Wts. Valley River	1853	1	137
Dayton, Spencer	30	Wts. Valley River	1853	1	139
Dayton, Spencer	2	Wts. Valley River	1853	1	140
Dayton, Spencer	7	Wts. Valley River	1853	1	141
Dayton, Spencer	214	Ford's Run	1854	1	171
Dayton, Spencer	1,063	Laurel Creek	1857	1	205
Dayton, Spencer	27	Ford Run	1858	1	222
Dayton, Spencer et al	400	Wts. Tygert's Valley	1852	1	113
Despard, Burton	104	Big Sandy Creek	1847	1	19
Despard, Burton	38½	Big Sandy Creek	1847	1	20
Despard, Burton	68	Gnatty Creek	1847	1	23
Digman, George K.	390	Jennie's Run	1854	1	152
Digman, Samuel	59½	Laurel Creek	1851	1	99
Digman, Samuel	19	Laurel Creek	1858	1	225
Elliott, Samuel	157	Ford's Run	1857	1	206
Elliott, Samuel	166	Laurel Creek	1857	1	207
Elliott, William et al	155	Brushy Fork	1856	1	191
Elliott, William & Samuel	50	Adj. Wm. Norris	1847	1	25
Elliott, William & Samuel	200	Laurel Hill	1851	1	93
Gainer, Jack B.	121	Laurel Creek	1858	1	210
Gainer, John	317	Sugar Creek	1852	1	126
Gainer, Nicholas	91	Brushy Fork	1854	1	154
Gainer, Nicholas et al	155	Brushy Fork	1856	1	191
Gainer, Samuel M.	10	Teter's Creek	1855	1	185
Goff, David et al	1,277	Zebb's Creek	1848	1	46
Goff, David et al	41½	Sandy Creek	1851	1	88
Golden, George et al	10	Anglin's Run	1854	1	153
Golden, Richama et al Hrs.	100	Laurel Creek	1850	1	70
Grose, Peyton, H.	100	Brushy Fork	1852	1	121
Hall, Charles B.	179	Laurel Creek	1858	1	221
Hall, David	24	Adj. David Hall	1847	1	26
Haller, Michael T.	20	Teter's Creek	1857	1	201

Name of Grantee	Acres	Local Description	Year	Book	Page
Harris, Abner J.	500	Wts. Middle Fork	1847	1	40
Hawley, Massalona et al Hrs.	100	Laurel Creek	1850	1	70
Heatherly, Samuel Jr.	35	Spaw Lick Run	1853	1	133
Hoffman See Huffman					
Hoffman, Anna et al Heirs	100	Laurel Creek	1850	1	70
Hoffman, Israel P.	17½	Adj. Loushbaugh Surv.	1848	1	48
Hoffman, John	33	Mosquito Run	1858	1	211
Hoffman, John	20	Maiden Glade Run	1858	1	212
Hoffman, John	14	Maiden Glade Run	1858	1	213
Hoffman, John S. et al	3,000	Sandy Creek	1855	1	182
Holtsberry, Samuel	10	Laurel Creek	1858	1	214
Holtsberry, William	700	Teter's Creek	1856	1	192
Hoatter, Melker J. (Hovatter)	20	Raccoon Creek	1854	1	181
Hovatter See Hoatter, Hoveatter					
Hovatter, Melker J. (Hoatter)	20	Raccoon Creek	1854	1	181
Hovatter, Michael (Hovvater)	19½	Cove Settlement	1847	1	27
Hovatter, Christopher C.	114	Raccoon Creek	1857	1	203
Huff, Levi	200	Elk Creek	1844	1	1
Huffman, Israel P.	100	Laurel Creek	1844	1	2
Jarvis, G. E.	117	Adj. D. Sluss	1849	1	60
Jarvis, G. E. et al	23	B. & M. Turnpike	1851	1	101
Jarvis, Granville Assignee	106	Wts. Buckhannon River	1850	1	71
Jarvis, Granville E.	49	Sugar Creek	1857	1	198
Johnson, Alexander	8a.1r.	Laurel Creek	1858	1	226
Johnson, Isaac	168	Simpson's Creek	1848	1	45
Johnson, Isaac	14	Adj. Alexander Jones	1860	1	241
Johnson, John G.	118	Teter's Creek	1861	1	258
Johnson, John G. et al	475	Mill Run	1857	1	199
Johnson, Levi	300	Teter's Creek	1846	1	14
Johnson, Levi & William	470	Laurel Hill	1850	1	72
Johnson, Martin	481	Brushy Fork	1853	1	142
Johnson, Peter	464	Teter's Creek	1854	1	155
Johnson, Peter	50	Teter's Creek	1856	1	196
Johnson, William	24	Teter's Creek	1851	1	85
Johnson, William	35	Teter's Creek	1861	1	259
Johnson, William et al	125	Teter's Creek	1852	1	111
Keller, Samuel et al	450	Hunter's Fork	1852	1	120
Kelley, John	60	Ford Run	1846	1	13
Kelley, John	72	Ford's Run	1848	1	49
Kittle, Martin	45	Teter's Creek	1851	1	102
Kittle, Nester H.	2½	Adj. Alsy Coffman	1855	1	183
Kittle, Nester H.	85	Big Sandy Creek	1858	1	219
Kittle, Nester H.	187	Big Sandy Creek	1858	1	220
Kurkendall, Prudence	8	Adj. Isaac Booth	1847	1	28
Leonard, John A.	18¼	Big Sandy Creek	1848	1	50
Lewis, Abraham E.	20	Brushy Fork	1847	1	29
Lough, Zebulon	12½	Big Laurel Run	1858	1	229
Lowther, William	395	Little Laurel Run	1854	1	148
Male, William	175	Laurel Creek	1854	1	175
Marsh, C. & E. S. D. et al	22	Brushy Fork	1853	1	143
Marteney, Daniel	25	Laurel Creek	1844	1	3
Marteney, Daniel et al	275	Laurel Creek	1844	1	4
McCamy, Robert A. et al	93	Big Run	1847	1	38
McCamy, Robert et al	11	Grass Run	1847	1	30
McLane, William	47½	Tom's Run	1848	1	51
Middleton, Henry C. (or O.)	1,000	Wts. Tygert's Valley	1848	1	43
Middleton, Henry C. (or O.)	1,000	Wts. Tygert's River	1848	1	44
Middleton, Henry O.	602	Wts. Middle Fork	1845	1	11
Middleton, Henry O.	200	Wts. Buckhannon River	1846	1	16
Middleton, Henry O.	6,000	Big Sand Run	1846	1	17
Middleton, Henry O.	1,629	Handy Camp Branch	1847	1	21
Middleton, Henry O.	465	Hacker's Creek	1850	1	77
Middleton, Henry O.	400	Buckhannon R.	1851	1	82

Name of Grantee	Acres	Local Description	Year	Book	Page
Middleton, Henry O.	170	Brushy Fork	1851	1	83
Middleton, Henry O.	313	Brushy Fork	1851	1	84
Middleton, Henry O.	1,153	Stone Coal	1852	1	109
Middleton, Henry O.	384	Elk Creek	1854	1	156
Middleton, Henry O. et al	2,078	Wts. Middle Fork	1848	1	41
Miller, Andrew	150	Laurel Creek	1858	1	215
Miller, Syntha	60	Stoney Run	1857	1	202
Moats, Allen	29	Maiden Glade Run	1860	1	248
More, Eli	83	Teter's Creek	1856	1	195
Morgan, David J.	300	Middle Fork	1845	1	9
Morrall, L. D. et al	1,277	Zebb's Creek	1848	1	46
Morrall, Lair D.	162½	Laurel Creek	1844	1	5
Morrall, Lair D.	298	Mud Gut Branch	1845	1	8
Morrall, Lair D.	400	Wts. Middle Fork	1846	1	12
Morrall, Lair D.	28	Bill's Creek	1851	1	86
Morrall, Lair D.	64½	Tom's Run	1851	1	87
Morrall, Lair D.	945	Adj. Henry D. Martin	1860	1	249
Morrall, Lair D. et al	2,078	Middle Fork	1848	1	41
Morrall, Lair D. et al	275	Laurel Creek	1844	1	4
Morrall, Lair D. et al	482	Wts. Buckhannon River	1848	1	47
Morrall, Lair D. et al	120	Brushy Fork	1849	1	69
Morrall, Lair D. et al	41½	Sandy Creek	1851	1	88
Morrall, Lair D. et al	340	Teter's Creek	1851	1	89
Morrall, Lair D. et al	420	Teter's Creek	1852	1	114
Morrall, Lair D. et al	835	Teter's Creek	1852	1	115
Morrall, Lair D. et al	200	Mill Run	1852	1	122
Morrall, Lair D. et al	914	Beaver Creek	1854	1	169
Morrall, Lair D. et al	28	Beaver Creek	1854	1	170
Nester, David	49	Brushy Fork	1847	1	31
Nester, George	45	Teter's Creek	1850	1	75
Nester, George	45	Teter's Creek	1851	1	92
Nester, Hardin	39	Cove Run	1851	1	100
Nester, Jacob J.	15	Teter's Creek	1851	1	104
Neville, Harriet et al Heirs	100	Laurel Creek	1850	1	70
Nichola, Jacob B.	50	Adj. D. Cline	1860	1	242
Nicola or Nichola					
Nicola, Jacob B.	159	Glade Run	1861	1	255
Nicola, John	115	Wts. Valley River	1854	1	147
Norris, William	18	Clapboard Run	1854	1	157
O'Brine, Daniel	765	Middle Fork	1854	1	151
Peppers, Parker	26	Adj. W. Wright	1861	1	256
Phillips, Abraham et al	475	Mill Run	1857	1	199
Phillips, Black et al	18½	Glady Creek	1860	1	247
Phillips, Job	18	Glady Creek	1858	1	224
Phillips, William	45	Adj. A. Miller	1860	1	245
Pitzer, John M.	25	Brushy Fork	1851	1	94
Pitzer, John M. & R. S.	69	Adj. M. E. Poling	1859	1	239
Poling, David	40	Laurel Run	1859	1	236
Poling, George	164	Ford Run	1856	1	188
Poling, Martin B.	11	Wts. Valley River	1854	1	167
Poling, Martin D.	95	Brushy Fork	1854	1	150
Poling, Roger	115	Glady Creek	1856	1	193
Price, William	60	Bill's Creek	1860	1	240
Reeves, Josiah W. et al	200	Big Sandy Creek	1854	1	168
Right, William J. et al	50	Barker's Mill Cr.	1861	1	254
Ryan, Felix	21¼	Teter's Creek	1852	1	105
Ryan, James W.	100	Brushy Fork	1852	1	123
Ryan, John B.	33	Mill Run	1854	1	173
Sargent, James	30	Raccoon Creek	1848	1	52
Sargent, James	19	Raccoon Creek	1861	1	257
Shanabarger, Shornbarger					
Shanabarger, Christopher H.	8½	Laurel Creek	1858	1	223
Shaver, Jacob	220	Mill Run	1854	1	158

Namo of Grantee	Acres	Local Description	Year	Book	Page
Shaw, William	2½	Adj. A. O'Neal	1860	1	243
Shornbarger See Shanabarger					
Shornbarger, Christopher H.	60	Laurel Creek	1857	1	204
Simpson, William M.	70	Wts. Valley River	1853	1	132
Skidmore, Collins	15	Brushy Fork	1853	1	144
Smith, Hiram	84¼	Teter's Creek	1850	1	73
Smith, Hiram et al	124	Teter's Creek	1852	1	111
Smith, Hiram et al	18½	Glady Creek	1860	1	247
Smith, John F.	8½	Big Sandy Creek	1858	1	228
Snodgrass, John W.	186	Laurel Creek	1853	1	145
Stalnaker, Andrew V.	500	Glady Creek	1850	1	74
Stalnaker, James	163	Brushy Fork	1852	1	124
Stalnaker, James	57	Mill Run	1852	1	125
Stalnaker, James	400	Teter's Creek	1855	1	186
Stalnaker, James	3½	Teter's Creek	1858	1	227
Stalnaker, James	20	Adj. B. K. Gainer	1860	1	244
Stalnaker, John	114	Wts. Valley River	1853	1	134
Stalnaker Margaret et al Hrs.	100	Laurel Creek	1850	1	70
Stalnaker, William et al	75	Teter's Creek	1847	1	35
Stalnaker, William W.	156	Laurel Creek	1848	1	53
Stalnaker, William W.	558	Laurel Creek	1848	1	54
Stemple, Andrew J.	150	Bennica Run	1855	1	184
Stemple, Isaac	38	Lick Run	1849	1	61
Sterm or Sturm					
Sterm, Henry	204	Laurel Creek	1844	1	6
Stewart, John	300	Raccoon Creek	1853	1	135
Streets, George	21	Laurel Creek	1861	1	252
Stump, Michael	38	Peck's Run	1851	1	95
Sturm or Sterm					
Sturm, Brian	16¼	Sugar Creek	1847	1	32
Sturm, Henry	31	Glady Creek	1847	1	34
Sturm, Jacob	35	Sugar Creek	1847	1	33
Swecker, Absolom H.	46	Big Run	1848	1	42
Talbott, E. D.	160	Hunter's Fork	1858	1	230
Teter, Alva	17	Wts. Buckhannon Riv.	1847	1	37
Vequesney, Emile	29	Wts. Valley River	1858	1	216
Vequesney, Emile	10	Wts. Valley River	1859	1	235
Walter, William	25½	Big Cove Run	1852	1	108
Ward, Anthony	6½	Gnatty Creek	1859	1	234
Ward, James	100	Wts. Buckhannon Riv.	1845	1	10
Ward, James	368	Buckhannon Riv.	1849	1	68
Ward, James	42½	Cotrel's Run	1851	1	103
Ward, James	925	Gnatty Creek	1856	1	189
Ward, James	9	Gnat's Creek	1856	1	190
Ward, James	2½	Gnatty Creek	1859	1	233
Wells, Granville et al Hrs. of John Black Decd.	100	Laurel Creek	1850	1	70
Whitman, William et al	19	Brushy Fork	1854	1	179
Whitman, William et al	25	Brushy Fork	1854	1	180
Williamson, John R.	385	Banica Run	1856	1	187
Williamson, John R.	355	Buckhannon River	1851	1	81
Wilson, A. P.	38	Anglin's Run	1848	1	56
Wilson, A. P.	75½	Tygert's V. Riv.	1848	1	57
Wilson, A. P.	4	Big Sandy	1849	1	66
Wilson, A. P.	85	Tygert's Valley	1849	1	67
Wilson, A. P. et al	351	Laurel Fork	1849	1	64
Wilson, Alpheus P.	56	Brushy Fork	1847	1	36
Wilson, Alpheus P.	149½	Brushy Fork	1847	1	39
Wilson, Alpheus P. et al	11	Grass Run	1847	1	30
Wilson, Alpheus P. et al	93	Big Run	1847	1	38
Wilson, Alpheus P. et al	482	Wts. Buckhannon Riv.	1848	1	47
Wilson, Henry	37	Teter's Creek	1848	1	55
Wilson, Henry	178	Raccoon Creek	1849	1	62

Name of Grantee	Acres	Local Description	Year	Book	Page
Wilson, Isiah	8½	Bill's Creek	1851	1	91
Wilson, Joseph	275	Mill Run	1854	1	159
Wilson, Solomon	77	Mill Run	1854	1	161
Wilson, Solomon & Thomas	145	Teter's Creek	1854	1	162
Wilson, Thomas	145	Mill Run	1854	1	160
Wilson, William F.	125	Bill's Creek	1851	1	90
Wilson, William F.	57	Glady Creek	1852	1	136
Wilson, William F.	8	Sugar Creek	1853	1	138
Wilson, William F.	549	Ford Run	1854	1	174
Wilson, William F. et al	75¼	Teter's Creek	1847	1	35
Woodley, Willis H.	800	Wts. of Middle Fork	1847	1	18
Woods, Samuel	180	Big Sandy Creek	1854	1	146
Wright, Willis	130	Elk Creek	1858	1	217
Yeager, Daniel	9	Tygerts Valley	1848	1	58
Yeager, Daniel	41	Adj. his own	1852	1	129
Yeager, Daniel	32	Adj. Banks Line	1852	1	130
Yeager, James L.	250	Adj. David Poling	1852	1	110
Yeager, Solomon	233	Mill Creek	1852	1	116
Yock, Jeremiah	52	Tom's Run	1858	1	218
Zinn, Peter et al	108½	Hacker's Creek	1850	1	76
Zinn, William B. & Charles	105	Big Sandy Creek	1856	1	194

BERKELEY COUNTY

Abernathy, James et al	898	Sleepy Creek	1799	1	461
Albright, Moses	161	Tilhance's Branch	1860	2	294
Aldridge, Robert	262	Bear Garden Ridge	1775	1	527
Aldridge, Robert	262	Bear Garden Ridge	1776	1	542
Alexander, Josiah H.	3a.3r.20p.	North Mountain	1857	2	291
Alexander, William	330	Sleepy Creek	1800	1	233
Anderson, Colbert	22	Opequon Creek	1799	1	226
Anderson, George	555	Lick Branch	1789	1	41
Anderson, James et al	2,380	Sleepy Creek Mt.	1809	1	478
Askew, William	4	Opequon Creek	1792	1	123
Ayle, Valentine	12	Opequon Creek	1814	1	363
Bacon—See Bakin					
Bailey See Baley					
Bailey, Andrew	64	Back Creek	1789	1	73
Bailey, John	460	Sleepy Creek	1789	1	453
Bailey, John et al	890	Timber Ridge	1788	1	451
Bailey, John Jr.	206	Sleepy Creek	1777	1	589
Bailey, John Jr.	321	Sleepy Creek	1794	1	150
Bailey, Silas	390	Sleepy Creek	1789	1	76
Bailey, William	777	Sleepy Creek	1773	1	501
Bailey, William	323	Jenkin's Ridge	1780	2	531
Bailey, William	88	Back Creek	1780	2	537
Bailey, William	400	Sleepy Creek	1776	1	552
Bailey, William	200	Sleepy Creek	1777	1	560
Bailey, William et al	281	Sleepy Creek	1788	1	9
Baker, Henry W.	270	Short Hill Mt.	1789	1	37
Baker, Walter	6½a.19p.	Adj. G. Smallwood	1788	1	18
Bakin, Jonathan	100	Tilehauzey Branch	1791	1	110
Baldwin, William	364	North Mountain	1778	2	487
Baley See Bailey					
Baley, John	400	Mill's Gap	1794	1	148
Baley, John	120	So. Side Third Hill	1794	1	149
Barnes—See Burns					
Barnes, Henry (Barns)	12a.2r.16p.	Adj. W. Jones	1848	2	268

Name of Grantee	Acres	Local Description	Year	Book	Page
Barnes, Joseph	39½	Wts. Potomac	1774	1	512
Barnes, Joseph	55	Wts. Potomac	1774	1	511
Barnes, Teter (Peter)	50	Tilhance's Branch	1796	1	183
Barnes, William	206	Sleepy Creek	1778	2	483
Barns, Peter	21½	Mill Creek	1801	1	263
Bate, John	8	Adj. John Grantham	1797	1	196
Bedinger, Henry	8a.3r.	Opequon Creek	1797	1	189
Beeler, Benjamin	125¾	Wts. Shenandoah	1796	1	178
Beeson, Edward	1	Tuscarora Branch	1806	1	342
Beeson, Edward	24a.34p.	Back Creek	1806	1	343
Beeson, Edward	341	Back Creek	1778	2	479
Beeson, Edward	336	Shepherd's Corner	1778	2	481
Beeson, Edward	107	Tuscarorah Creek	1778	2	482
Beeson, Edward et al	300	Meadow Branch	1823	1	428
Beeson, Richard	258	Back Creek	1788	1	15
Beeson, Richard	292	Sleepy Creek	1789	1	36
Bell, Joseph Sr.	19	Bear Garden Ridge	1801	1	270
Bergmon, Jacob	47	North Mountain	1788	1	14
Bishop, Henry	230	North Mountain	1789	1	68
Bitzer, Michael	22¼	Adj. George Myles	1794	1	165
Blake, John C.	6a.43p.	Adj. E. Ryneal's	1861	2	295
Blue, James	26	Adj. John Marks	1798	1	216
Blue, Nathaniel	7	Opequon Creek	1815	1	369
Boarer, Adam	402	Adj. A. Stevens	1794	1	143
Boarer, Adam	80	Buffalo Lick Run	1803	1	307
Boarer, Adam	30	Sleepy Creek	1803	1	308
Boarer, Adam	20	Sleepy Creek	1803	1	309
Boarer, Adam	143	Sleepy Creek	1815	1	382
Boarer, Adam	122½	Sleepy Creek	1815	1	383
Boarer, Adam	23½	Sleepy Creek	1815	1	384
Boarer, Adam	41	Middle Fork	1819	1	397
Boggess, Thomas	434	Sleepy Creek	1788	1	8
Boggs, William	22	Back Creek	1798	1	214
Boley, John	300	Formerly John Cook land	1787	1	2
Bond, John Jr.	185	Back Creek	1777	1	588
Bonner, Gasper	365	Wts. Potomac	1779	2	494
Bourne, Morton (Alias Bourn)	55a.lr.2p.	Back Creek	1824	1	431
Bowman, Andrew	80¾	Great Lick Tract	1789	1	74
Bowman, Andrew et al	16a.lr.	Back Creek	1776	1	547
Bowman, Andrew et al	129	Back Creek	1776	1	548
Boyd, Elisha	409	Warm Spring Run	1796	1	179
Boyd, Elisha	368	Sleepy Creek	1796	1	180
Boyd, Elisha	261	Sleepy Creek	1796	1	181
Boyd, Elisha	110	North Mountain	1797	1	194
Boyd, Elisha	210	Back Creek	1797	1	195
Boyd, Elisha	228	Adj. Stephen Ross	1798	1	217
Boyd, Elisha	354	Short Hill Mountain	1802	1	278
Boyd, Elisha	27½	North Mountain	1819	1	399
Boyd, Elisha	7	North Mountain	1819	1	403
Boyd, Elisha	1,207	North Mountain	1797	1	457
Boyd, George	100	Wts. Potomac	1779	2	503
Boyd, John	53	Wts. of Opequon	1778	2	470
Boyd, John	137	Opequon Creek	1778	2	471
Boyle, William & Henry	372	Spring Ridge	1773	1	495
Boyle, William & Henry	74	Warm Spring Run	1773	1	498
Brent, George	365a.2p.	Cherry Run	1772	1	491
Brouce, Andrew	737	Wolf Hill	1780	2	562
Bruin, Peter	21½	Mill Creek	1801	1	263
Bryerley, Thomas	4	Adj. Robt. Stewart	1815	1	377
Buckles, Robert Sr.	404	Adj. Henry Stroap	1790	1	95
Bunn, Peter	21½	Mill Creek	1801	1	263
Burcham, Samuel	442	Tilehanzey Branch	1789	1	65
Burin, Peter	21½	Mill Creek	1801	1	263

Name of Grantee	Acres	Local Description	Year	Book	Page
Burn, Peter	21½	Mill Creek	1801	1	263
Burnes, Robert	62¾	Opequon Creek	1798	1	218
Burns, William Jr.	17½	Opequon Creek	1798	1	209
Burns, William Jr.	14	Wts. Opequon	1802	1	292
Bush, Philip	418	Sleepy Creek	1779	2	507
Butt, William	25	North Mountain	1848	2	270
Caldwell, Andrew	484	Adj. John Boyles	1778	2	474
Caldwell, Andrew	340	Mill Creek	1778	2	475
Campbell, Dugal	151	North Mountain	1825	1	433
Campbell, Duncan	206¾	Middle Creek	1787	1	5
Campbell, James	287	Middle Creek	1787	1	4
Campbell, Thomas	6a.3r.17p.	Opequon Branch	1792	1	125
Capp, Joseph & John	375	Sleepy Creek	1803	1	468
Cartwright, Robert (Cartright)	160	Meadow Branch	1789	1	47
Catlett, Alexander	66½	Lick Run	1799	1	246
Catlett, Alexander	157	Back Creek	1779	2	522
Catlett, Alexander	82	Back Creek	1780	2	538
Catlett, William	145	Sleepy Creek	1779	2	512
Catlett, William	41	Middle Fork	1818	1	391
Chaffin, John (Chalfin)	367	Back Creek	1779	2	497
Chaffin, John (Chalfin)	276	Baldwin's Branch	1780	2	551
Chaffin, Solomon (Chalfin)	428	Back Creek	1781	2	574
Chalfin—See Chaffin					
Champion, James et al	309	Tilhauzey's Branch	1777	1	566
Champion, John Sr.	110	Back Creek	1791	1	108
Chapman, William	147	Sleepy Creek	1777	1	562
Chenoweth, Chennoeth, Chinnoeth, Chinnoweth, Chinworth					
Chenoweth, Isaac	23a.2r.	Mill Creek	1788	1	21
Cheny, Thomas & William	132	Wts. Potomac	1775	1	534
Cherry, Thomas & William	132	Wts. Potomac	1775	1	534
Cherry, William	412½	Black Lick Run	1790	1	87
Chinnoeth, William	16	Mile Creek	1799	1	248
Chinnoweth, Absolom et al	650	Back Creek	1803	1	306
Chinworth, Absolom	59	Wts. Opequon	1779	2	515
Cockran, James	802	Back Creek	1778	2	476
Cockran, James	122	Back Creek	1778	2	478
Collett, Alexander	66½	Lick Run	1799	1	246
Collins, Edmund	220	Sleepy Creek	1779	2	500
Collins, Moses et al	300	Meadow Branch	1803	1	318
Colston, Edward et al	1,891	Sleepy Creek	1835	1	481
Connan, George	304	Sleepy Creek Mt.	1777	1	577
Connan, George	420	Sleepy Creek	1776	1	544
Conwell, John	132	North Mountain	1803	1	303
Cornwall, Samuel Sr.	36	Back Creek	1789	1	40
Courtney, Jacob	10¾	Sleepy Creek	1819	1	395
Crabb, Edward	432	Sleepy Creek	1778	2	463
Crane, James	106	Opequon Creek	1790	1	81
Crane, James	34	Adj. John Dawkins	1790	1	82
Creamer, George	22½	Warm Springs Run	1804	1	331
Crisman, Philip	208	Sleepy Creek	1780	2	554
Cromwell, Margaret	400	Adj. J. Chalfin	1789	1	46
Crosley, Robert	385	Back Creek	1776	1	553
Crouchman, Benedict	72	Wts. Opequon	1775	1	541
Curtis, James	149	Tilhanny's Branch	1840	2	261
Daniel, Robert	4a.2r.12p.	Adj. R. Evans	1815	1	368
Davenport, Abraham	400	Sleepy Creek Mt.	1772	1	485
Davenport, Abraham	400	Dry Run	1775	1	525
Davenport, Adrian	26	Adj. John Marks	1796	1	188
Davis, Jacob	3a.lr.27p.	Tullipes Branch	1805	1	337
Dawson, Jacob	145	Meadow Branch	1792	1	139
Deakins, William et al	386	Warm Springs Run	1778	2	485
Dixon, John	139	Sleepy Creek	1798	1	236
Dobbins, Thomas	243	Sugar Loaf Mt.	1777	1	569
Doster, William	400	Lit North Mt.	1806	1	341

Name of Grantee	Acres	Local Description	Year	Book	Page
Douglass, Hugh	755	Back Creek	1792	1	117
Douglass, William (or Hugh)	690	Back Creek	1792	1	116
Douglass, William (or Hugh)	168	Robertson's Run	1792	1	118
Duckwall or Duckwalt					
Duckwall, Lewis	104	Sleepy Creek	1798	1	215
Duckwall, Lewis	29	Sleepy Creek	1803	1	296
Duckwalt, Frederick	155	Adj. Capt. Stephens	1789	1	83
Duckwalt, Frederick	490	Sleepy Creek	1778	2	472
Duckwalt, Frederick	400	Dirt Hill Mt.	1780	2	564
Duckwalt, Joseph	80	Sleepy Creek	1799	1	244
Duncan, John	400	Adj. Samuel Jones	1791	1	134
Dunham, Samuel Sr.	11a.3r.	Back Creek	1799	1	237
Dunn, Robert	115	Back Creek	1778	2	452
Eastburn, Robertson	400	Sleepy Creek	1789	1	63
Edmondson, Edmonson					
Edmondson, James (Edmonson)	449	Morgan's Run	1777	1	582
Edmonson, James	190	Sleepy Creek	1776	1	555
Ellis, John	22	Adj. Elijah Harland's	1793	1	159
Ellzey, Thomazin (Elzay)	160	Stoney Ridge	1794	1	144
Ellzey, Thomazin (Elzay)	115	Warm Springs Run	1794	1	145
Ellzey, Thomazin (Elzay)	397	Adj. Wm. Wither	1794	1	146
Embly, Thomas	162	Warm Spring	1775	1	524
Erving, Thomas	145	Middle Creek	1773	1	503
Eskew—See Askew					
Evans, John	190	Tilehauzey's Br.	1772	1	487
Evans, Joseph	5a.1r.30p.	Opequon Creek	1801	1	268
Evans, Joseph	37	Wts. Opequon	1777	1	568
Evans, Thomas et al	281	Sleepy Creek	1788	1	9
Evans, Thomas et al	346	Sleepy Creek	1788	1	10
Everhard, Henry	50	Back Creek	1806	1	345
Everhart, Henry	23	Elk Lick Run	1851	2	284
Everhart, Nathan	464	3rd Hill Mountain	1851	2	282
Everhart, Nathan	213a.3r.30p.	Adj. Walker Lands	1858	2	293
Everhart, Teter	105	3rd Hill Mountain	1848	2	266
Everheart, George	100	Mill Creek	1836	1	448
Everheart, Henry	188	Third Hill Mt.	1820	1	417
Everheart, Henry	27	Rock Spring Run	1820	1	418
Ewing, Thomas	145	Middle Creek	1773	1	503
Eyre, Robert	25	Mill Creek	1789	1	77
Fairis See Faris					
Fairis, William	23	Back Creek	1790	1	86
Fairis, William	40	Back Creek	1773	1	506
Faris See Fairis					
Faris, Arthur	202	Back Creek	1779	2	493
Faris, David	353	Cor S. Harris	1775	1	531
Faris, William	108	Back Creek	1804	1	325
Faulkner, James	500	Short Hill Mt.	1803	1	295
Fenner, Stephen	382	Sleepy Creek	1779	2	523
Fenner, Wendle	400	Sleepy Creek	1777	1	590
Fernoe, John	110	Sleepy Creek	1804	1	328
Fernoe, John	21	Sleepy Creek	1815	1	372
Fernoe, John	9a.2r.20p.	Sleepy Creek	1815	1	373
Fields, Simon	337	Sleepy Creek	1779	2	508
Fletcher, Peter	210	North Mountain	1788	1	29
Fletcher, Peter	75	Back Creek	1788	1	30
Fletcher, Peter	407	Sleepy Creek	1778	2	466
Forbes, Nancy Hrs. of	11a.23p.	Adj. D. Kennedy	1825	1	432
Foreman, James	2a.3r.20p.	Wts. Opequon	1814	1	365
Foreman, Joseph	420	Ambrose Branch	1789	1	80
Foreman, Joseph	17	Back Creek	1803	1	315
Foreman, Joseph	5a.2r.14p.	Island in Potomac	1803	1	316
Forman, Benjamin	416	Sleepy Creek	1791	1	102
Forman, James	10	Island Potomac River	1804	1	334

Name of Grantee	Acres	Local Description	Year	Book	Page
Forman, Joseph	8a.3r.20p.	Wts. Potomac River	1815	1	380
Forman, William et al	16a.1r.	Back Creek	1776	1	547
Forman, William et al	129	Back Creek	1776	1	548
Foster, Isaac	100	Sleepy Creek	1789	1	56
Foster, Isaac	23a.2r.	Sleepy Creek	1792	1	135
Foster, Jacob	180	Back Creek	1794	1	166
Foster, Thomas	239	Back Creek	1780	2	550-A
Foudy, George (Fouty)	318	Sleepy Creek	1780	2	573
Fouty, George (Foudy)	318	Sleepy Creek	1780	2	573
Fraushour or Freshover, Freshour, Froshour, Froushour					
Fraushour, Wendle	298	Sleepy Creek	1789	1	79
Freeman, Joseph	420	Ambrose Branch	1789	1	80
French, John	5	Adj. H. French	1851	2	281
Fritz, Michael	147	Wts. Opequon	1778	2	457
Froshour, Wendle	371	Sleepy Creek	1777	2	449
Froshour, Wendle	405	Sleepy Creek	1777	2	451
Froushour, Windle (Wendle)	141	Sleepy Creek	1773	1	496
Fryatt, Bartholomew	315	Sleepy Creek	1779	2	517
Fryatt, John	10a.3r.	Middle Creek	1779	2	502
Fryatt, Robert	148	Elk Lick	1779	2	499
Gibbons, Morgan	226	Tilhauzey's Branch	1792	1	113
Gibbons, Morgan	65	Tilhauzey's Branch	1792	1	114
Gibbons, Morgan	106	Adj. James Orr	1792	1	115
Gilbreath, Hugh	16	Wts. Opequon	1780	2	566
Gill, Joseph et al	600	Sleepy Cr. Mt.	1803	1	304
Gill, Joseph et al	200	Sleepy Cr. Mt.	1803	1	305
Gosset, Mathias	190	Back Creek	1789	1	54
Gossett, Mathias	4½	Back Creek	1797	1	205
Grantham, Lewis	42a.1r.	Adj. N. Everhart	1848	2	271
Grantham, Moses S.	291	North Mountain	1849	2	275
Grantham, Moses S.	91	Adj. A. Fry	1851	2	279
Gray, John	8	Mill Creek	1802	1	283
Gray, John	3a.2r.	Adj. Wm. Baldwin	1812	1	362
Gray, William	92	Adj. John Reed	1789	1	43
Gray, William	65½	Warm Springs	1789	1	44
Gray, William	528	Back Creek	1789	1	452
Grier, John	187	Sleepy Creek	1776	1	545
Grundy, Elizabeth et al	400	Sleepy Creek	1772	1	488
Guffin, George & Thomas	280	Cherry's Branch	1778	2	467
Gustin, John	255	Wts. Potomac	1791	1	99
Gustin, John	255	Warm Springs	1796	1	174
Gustin, Robert	88½	Crooked Branch Ridge	1798	1	210
Gustin, Robert	244	Sleepy Creek	1801	1	271
Gustin, Robert	19	Sleepy Creek	1803	1	310
Gustin, Robert	166	Sleepy Creek	1803	1	311
Gustin, Robert	49	Sleepy Creek	1805	1	338
Gustin, Robert	705½	Sleepy Creek	1798	1	458
Gustin, Robert	179	Sleepy Creek	1805	1	476
Hain—See Ham					
Haines, Benjamin	120	Back Creek	1779	2	492
Haines, Joseph	19a.36p.	Swan Pond	1830	1	437
Hair, James Jr.	39½	North Mountain	1796	1	182
Ham, Nicholas (Hain-Horn)	281	Back Creek	1792	1	124
Hancher, John	110	Wts. Opequon	1780	2	567
Hannison, James	15	Wts. Potomac	1815	1	381
Harcourt, Peter	91½	Brush Run	1799	1	249
Harcourt, Peter	458	3rd. Hill Mountain	1799	1	250
Harlin, Stephen	5	Cherry Branch	1794	1	155
Harmanson, William	5¼	Sleepy Creek	1820	1	415
Harmison, James	15	Wts. Potomac	1815	1	381
Harper, Alexander	69a.3r.	Tilhance's Branch	1819	1	406
Harper, Alexander et al	15	Tilhance's Branch	1819	1	404
Harper, Alexander et al	15	Tilhance's Branch	1819	1	405

Name of Grantee	Acres	Local Description	Year	Book	Page
Harper, John	61	Cabin Branch	1788	1	13
Harper, William	16a.2r.	Tilhouse's Branch	1803	1	312
Harrison, James	15	Wts. Potomac	1815	1	381
Hart, Thomas	5½	Cabin Run	1790	1	91
Harting, John	16	Back Creek	1797	1	200
Haskinson, Basil	216	Warm Springs Run	1789	1	35
Hays, John Jr.	122	Middle Creek	1779	2	510
Hays, John Jr.	31a.3r.	Middle Creek	1779	2	511
Hays, William	288	Middle Creek	1795	1	170
Hedges, John R.	80	Dirt Hill Mountain	1802	1	273
Hedges, John R.	237	Stony Lick Run	1802	1	279
Hedges, Jonas	120	Meadow Branch	1822	1	423
Hedges, Jonas	63a.7p.	Adj. Robt. Pinkerton	1836	1	445
Hedges, Jonas	86a.3r.33p.	Adj. Palmer	1836	1	446
Hedges, Joseph	50	North Mountain	1797	1	197
Hedges, Joseph & John	300	Meadow Branch	1800	1	255
Hedges, Samuel	50	North Mountain	1790	1	94
Hedges, Samuel (the 4th)	4a.3r.28p.	Back Creek	1823	1	426
Hedges, William	41	Tilehanny's Branch	1841	2	262
Henderson, Alexander	63	Adj. Robt. Buckles	1790	1	93
Hess, Jacob	6a.2r.25p.	Wts. Opequon	1806	1	344
Higgins, John	404	Harding's Place	1789	1	51
Hite, George	52½	Adj. J. Strode	1794	1	161
Hogain, John	400	Lick Branch	1781	2	578
Holland, Jacob	19¼	Back Creek	1797	1	191
Hollis, Joseph W.	16½	North Mountain	1851	2	280
Hood, John	248	Sleepy Creek	1773	1	508
Hoover, Martin	164	Lick Run	1789	1	72
Horn—See Ham					
Hoskinson See Haskinson					
Houseman, Martin	130	Wts. Potomac	1779	2	504
Hoyle, Andrew	326	Brush Creek	1789	1	71
Huck, Christian	412	Wts. Potomac	1773	1	509
Hufman, George	365	Sleepy Creek	1780	2	560
Hulse, Robert	367	Sleepy Creek	1792	1	454
Hunter, David	178	Back Creek	1799	1	247
Hunter, David	158	Jerrardstown	1804	1	333
Hunter, David	400	Wts. Potomac	1810	1	356
Hunter, David	1,500	Wts. Potomac	1810	1	357
Hunter, David	1,050	Wts. Potomac	1810	1	358
Hunter, David	54p.	Opequon Creek	1820	1	407
Hunter, David	439	Meadow Branch	1803	1	467
Hunter, David	19a.3r.16p.	Falling Waters	1776	1	556
Hunter, David et al	2,380	Sleepy Creek Mt.	1809	1	478
Hunter, Elizabeth et al	3,980	Sleepy Creek Mt.	1803	1	470
Hunter, John	183	Warm Springs Run	1800	1	261
Hunter, John	184	Sleepy Cr. Mt.	1803	1	302
Hunter, John	22¾	Sleepy Creek	1810	1	360
Hylton, William	332	Warm Spring Ridge	1800	1	228
Hylton, William	332	Warm Spgs. Run	1800	1	592
Jack, James	21½	Adj. Capt. J. White	1794	1	160
Jackson, Capt. Robert	178	Back Creek	1777	1	571
Jackson, Robert	58	Back Creek	1773	1	505
Jenkins, See Jinkins					
Jenkins, Andrew	1a.2r.15p.	Wts. Potomac	1814	1	364
Jenkins, John	235	Elk Lick	1779	2	518
Jenkins, John	343	Elk Lick	1779	2	519
Jinkins, John	270	Stony Lick	1789	1	42
Johns, Richard et al	386	Warm Springs Run	1778	2	485
Johnson, Frank (the Younger)	108	Adj. Jacob French	1827	1	434
Johnston, George	204	Sleepy Creek	1794	1	151
Jones, Robert	101	Elk Ridge	1789	1	53
Jones, Robert	100	Back Creek	1796	1	184
Kearney—See also Kerny					
Kearney, James (Kerney)	4½	Adj. John Duke	1792	1	121

Name of Grantee	Acres	Local Description	Year	Book	Page
Keesacker, See Keyseeker, Keesaker					
Keesacker, George	7	Adj. Jonas Hedges	1850	2	278
Keesacker, Henry	8¾	Adj. Robt. Johnson	1852	2	286
Kelly, Cornelius	1,000	Wts. Potomac	1802	1	277
Kenneday, Samuel	126	Back Creek	1791	1	105
Kennedy, Nancy C. et al	3,980	Sleepy Creek Mt.	1803	1	470
Kennedy, Robert Jr.	29	Back Creek	1804	1	324
Kennedy, Robert Sr.	27	Back Creek	1804	1	323
Kerns, Michael	3	Mill Creek	1856	2	290
Kerny—See Kearney					
Kerny, Anthony	38	Adj. Van Bennett	1827	1	435
Keyes, Humphrey	370	Sleepy Creek	1774	1	514
Keyseeker, John (Keesaker)	8a.43p. (43) a.	Sleepy Creek	1819	1	396
Kilmer, John et al	50	North Mountain	1847	2	265
Koughel, John G.	400	Back Creek	1796	1	177
Koughee, John G.	400	Back Creek	1796	1	177
Lawson, Thomas	479	Cabin Branch	1790	1	88
Lawson, Thomas	42	Dirt Hill Mt.	1780	2	54[illegible]
Ledman, James	1a.3r.8p.	North Mountain	1834	1	440
Lee, Charles	330	Sleepy Creek	1793	1	152
Lee, Charles	330	Sleepy Creek	1793	1	153
Lee, Charles	460	Warm Springs	1793	1	154
Lee, Colonel Richard	245	Dry Run	1780	2	527
Lemon, Thomas	26a.3r.23p.	Big Run	1836	1	447
Lemon, William	262	Sleepy Creek	1797	1	190
Leonard, Nicholas	111	Adj. S. Lozier	1789	1	49
LeRue, Isaac	343	Adj. T. Rutherford	1772	1	484
LeRue, Samuel	202	Adj. Lofton's	1775	1	540
Lewis, John	951	Swan Ponds	1775	1	536
Light, John S.	2a.2r.22p.	Opequon	1835	1	442
Light, Peter Sr.	70	Big Lick Branch	1790	1	85
Light, Samuel	6a.1r.17p.	Opequon Creek	1816	1	385
Littlejohn, John	195	Back Creek	1789	1	45
Littlejohn, John	400	Back Creek	1789	1	52
Lodman, Conrad	200	Sleepy Creek	1803	1	300
Lowman, Ephraim	100	Sleepy Creek	1801	1	264
Lowman, Ephraim	268	Sleepy Creek	1802	1	276
Lowman, George	18	Falling Waters	1791	1	98
Lowrey, James	50	North Mountain	1797	1	198
Lyle, John	120	North Mountain	1823	1	427
Lyle, Robert	80	North Mountain	1822	1	424
Lyle, Robert	65	North Mountain	1822	1	425
Magowen—or McGowen					
MaGowen, James	460	Brush Creek	1798	1	212
Magowen, James	205	Dark Lick Run	1789	1	64
Martin, Ephraim	334	Sleepy Creek	1772	1	483
Martin, Thomas B.	480	Warm Springs Run	1777	1	585
Martin, Thomas B.	510	Wts Potomac	1777	1	586
Mason, Elenor	107	Middle Creek	1800	1	260
Maund, John James	790	Opequon Creek	1788	1	19
McCleane, John	116½	Adj. J. Miller	1796	1	185
McCleary, John	435	Stony Lick Run	1802	1	288
McCleary, John	370	White's Branch	1802	1	289
McCleary, John	500	Cherry Branch	1803	1	317
McCoy, Daniel	12a.2r.	Wts. Potomac	1817	1	388
McDonald, Allan	183	9 Mile House	1775	1	529
McDonald, Allan	111	Sleepy Creek	1777	1	564
McDonald, Allen	216	Indian Field	1788	1	12
McFeeley, Joseph et al	300	Meadow Branch	1823	1	428
McGill, Charles	23	Mile Creek	1788	1	17
McGowen, See Magowen					
McGowen, James	277	Springer's Run	1789	1	62
McGowen, James	460	Brush Creek	1798	1	212

Name of Grantee	Acres	Local Description	Year	Book	Page
McIntire, Nicholas	1¾	Adj. James Varder	1792	1	136
McIntire, Thomas	306	Sleepy Creek	1780	2	541
McKay, John	409	Clay Lick	1780	2	552
McKenny, Catherine et al	400	Sleepy Creek	1772	1	488
McKearnan, Laurence	35½	Sleepy Creek	1800	1	257
McKearnan, Laurence Jr.	38	Sleepy Creek	1800	1	258
McKernan, Lawrence Jr.	361	Sleepy Creek	1800	1	232
McKewan, Charles	22	Adj. Benjamin Chandler	1793	1	156
McKewan, Michael	380	Back Creek	1800	1	229
McKewan, Michael	11½	Sleepy Creek	1799	1	241
McKewan, Michael	56	Adj. J. Strode	1799	1	242
McKewan, Michael	44½	Sleepy Creek	1799	1	243
McKewan, Michael	63a.3r.	Sleepy Creek	1799	1	245
McKewan, Michael	365½	Dry Run	1802	1	466
McKewan, Michael	101	North Mountain	1824	1	429
McKewan, Michael et al	199	Adj. M. Caster	1792	1	128
McKewan, Michael et al	333	Warm Springs	1792	1	129
McKewan, Michael et al	890	Timber Ridge	1788	1	451
McKewan, Michael et al	898	Sleepy Creek	1799	1	461
McKoun, John	3a.1r.31p.	Cor. to Jacob Rees	1818	1	393
McManus, Luke	6a.	Back Creek	1815	1	376
McSherry—or McTheny					
McSherry, Richard	56½	Back Creek	1797	1	202
McSherry, Richard	93	North Mountain	1797	1	203
McSherry, Richard	858	Meadow Branch	1804	1	474
McTheny—or McSherry					
Merchant, Isaac	48a.31r.	Opequon Creek	1794	1	162
Michael, Peter	40	Sleepy Creek	1802	1	285
Millar, Stephen	429	Middle Fork	1775	1	530
Miller, Elon	53¾	Back Creek	1799	1	220
Miller, Elon	9¼	Back Creek	1799	1	254
Miller, Elon	320	Back Creek	1800	1	462
Miller, George D.	¾	Adj. S. C. West	1844	2	263
Miller, Henry	21	Adj. Jones' Land	1850	2	277
Miller, Henry	349	Adj. Edw. Beeson	1779	2	514
Miller, John	400	Sleepy Creek	1791	1	100
Miller, John	245	Wts. of Potomac	1791	1	112
Miller, John	232	Mountain Sinks	1792	1	131
Miller, John	10	Tilhance's Branch	1815	1	374
Miller, John	62	Tilhance's Branch	1806	1	477
Miller, William S.	4a.12p.	Adj. J. L. Campbell	1849	2	274
Miller, Zachariah	306	Back Creek	1779	2	489
Miller, Zachariah	263	Adj. L. O'Neel	1779	2	490
Mitchell, Joseph	470	Sleepy Creek	1778	2	468
Monrow, George	500	Poplar Spring	1787	1	6
Moore, Lewis	250	Adj. Wm. Masters	1780	2	545
Moore, Lewis	71	Mill Creek	1780	2	549
Moore, Lewis	57	Mill Creek	1780	2	550
Morgan, Richard	3r.29p.	Swan Ponds	1809	1	348
Morris, Richard et al	281	Sleepy Creek	1788	1	9
Morris, Richard et al	346	Sleepy Creek	1788	1	10
Morris, Richard et al	450	Sleepy Creek	1788	1	11
Morris, Richard et al	256	Sleepy Creek	1788	1	450
Mound See Maund					
Murphy, John	38a.2r.	Back Creek	1781	2	579
Murphy, John W.	195	Tilhanny's Branch	1846	2	264
Murphy, Robert	1a.2r.15p.	Back Creek	1822	1	422
Murphy, Valentine	197	Back Creek	1777	1	579
Myers, Archibald	102	3rd Hill Mt.	1849	2	276
Myers, Jacob	10	Opequon Creek	1832	1	439
Myers, John	60	Opequon Creek	1800	1	230
Myers, John et al	300	Meadow Branch	1823	1	428
Myles, George	546	Davis Run	1775	1	522

Name of Grantee	Acres	Local Description	Year	Book	Page
Neale See Neil					
Neale, William (Neil)	98a.2r.	Sleepy Creek	1802	1	284
Neeley, William et al	199	Adj. M. Caster	1792	1	128
Neeley, William et al	333	Warm Springs	1792	1	129
Neely, William	450	Sleepy Creek	1777	2	450
Neil, William (Neale)	71	Sleepy Creek	1781	2	575
Newkirk, George et al	40	North Mountain	1801	1	265
Newkirk, George et al Heirs	251	Goff's Run	1801	1	463
Nicholas, Amos (Nichols)	164¾	Wts. Opequon	1789	1	75
Nichols, Amos (Nicholas)	40	Adj. George Williams	1791	1	132
Nichols, Amos (Nicholas)	145	Opequon Creek	1791	1	133
Nichols, Amos (Nicholas)	25	Opequon Cr.	1804	1	326
Noland, Thomas	4	Back Creek	1803	1	319
Nowland, Philip	220	Back Creek	1789	1	60
Nowland, Thomas	676	Back Creek	1789	1	59
Nowland, William	198	Back Creek	1789	1	61
Oden, Elias	2½	Adj. R. Butts	1815	1	378
O'Ferrall, John	143	Back Creek	1803	1	301
Overley, Peter	58	Sleepy Creek	1780	2	558
Overton, John	669	Sleepy Creek	1791	1	104
Overton, John et al	281	Sleepy Creek	1788	1	9
Overton, John et al	346	Sleepy Creek	1788	1	10
Overton, John et al	450	Sleepy Creek	1788	1	11
Overton, John et al	256	Sleepy Creek	1788	1	450
Paul, Andrew	50	Back Creek	1798	1	206
Paul, Andrew	10	Lick Run	1798	1	207
Paul, Andrew	24¼	North Mountain	1798	1	211
Paul, William	58	North Mountain	1788	1	34
Payne, Jane	370	Cherry Branch	1792	1	130
Payne, Thomas	50	Cove of T. Hill Mt.	1799	1	222
Payne, Thomas	235	Cherry's Branch	1799	1	223
Pearce, Andrew	228	Wts. Potomac	1777	1	584
Pendleton, Philip	327	Formerly John Cook Prop.	1787	1	3
Pendleton, Philip	800	Adj. M. Shrively	1790	1	90
Pendleton, Philip	65	Lick Run	1795	1	171
Pendleton, Philip	99	Back Creek	1795	1	172
Pendleton, Philip	115	Back Creek	1796	1	187
Pendleton, Philip	336	Sleepy Creek	1798	1	213
Pendleton, Philip	129	Warm Springs Run	1800	1	262
Pendleton, Philip C.	144a.2r.38p.	Third Hill Mt.	1836	1	444
Pendleton, Philip C. et al	3,980	Sleepy Creek Mt.	1803	1	470
Pendleton, Philip C. et al	1,891	Sleepy Creek	1835	1	481
Pennybacker, William et al	94	Tilhance's Branch	1802	1	275
Penteney, James	7	North Mountain	1858	2	292
Pentoney, Michael	52a.1r.26p.	Sleepy Creek	1819	1	402
Pentoney, Michael	420	Sleepy Creek	1820	1	419
Perkle, George	236	Opequon Creek	1773	1	507
Peters, Isaac	31	Sleepy Creek	1806	1	340
Pinkerton, Robert	270	Tilhauzey's Branch	1792	1	119
Pinkerton, Robert	131	Short Hill Mt.	1792	1	120
Pinkerton, Robert	81	Stoney Lick Branch	1792	1	122
Pitzer, James S.	5a.34p.	North Mountain	1852	2	285
Plotner, John	145	Adj. John Gray	1789	1	66
Plotner, John	73	Back Creek	1791	1	101
Plotner, Morris	29	Sleepy Creek	1789	1	67
Poffenberger See Povenberger					
Poole, William et al	221	North Mountain	1791	1	106
Povenberger, John	806	Brush Creek	1788	1	16
Powell, John	3½	Adj. N. Ross	1820	1	410
Powell, John	8½	Adj. Obed Noland	1820	1	411
Powell, John	73	North Mountain	1820	1	412
Powell, John	598	Brush Creek	1821	1	420
Powell, John	90	Back Creek	1821	1	421

Name of Grantee	Acres	Local Description	Year	Book	Page
Sharff, See Sheriff					
Sharff, Jacob & John	1,405	Meadow Branch	1835	1	479
Sharff, John & Jacob	202a.10p.	Third Hill Mt.	1835	1	443
Sharp, Thomas	332	Back Creek	1780	2	534
Shearer, Archibald	336	Wts. Potomac	1778	2	454
Sheriff See Sharff					
Sheriff, John	317	Stillwater Branch	1788	1	20
Sheriff, John Sr.	137	Sleepy Creek	1788	1	33
Shields, John (Shield)	201	Back Creek	1777	1	576
Shields, John	128	Adj. John Champion	1789	1	39
Shields, John	118	Gilliland's Run	1777	1	574
Shields, William	18½	Tilehauzey Branch	1791	1	107
Shields, William	22	Adj. Robt. Jackson	1791	1	111
Shields, William	16a.2r.	Back Creek	1802	1	272
Shields, William	11a.2r.19p.	Back Creek	1829	1	436
Shimp, Mahala J.	73	Tilehouze's Branch	1848	2	269
Shockey, Jacob	100	Middle Fork	1799	1	253
Shockey, Jacob	60	Middle Fork	1807	1	346
Shockey, John	262	Middle Fork	1775	1	526
Silar See Sylar					
Silar, Jacob	199	Back Creek	1804	1	332
Siler, Jacob	126	Back Creek	1780	2	540
Silkwood, Solomon	220	Back Creek	1788	1	32
Small, John	18	Opequon Cr.	1804	1	327
Small, John M. et al	50	North Mountain	1847	2	265
Smith, James	9	Sleepy Creek	1819	1	398
Smith, John	212	Sleepy Creek	1776	1	551
Smith, John et al	15	Tilhance's Branch	1819	1	404
Smith, John et al	15	Tilhance's Branch	1819	1	405
Smith, Mary & James	400	Mill Creek	1795	1	169
Smith, William	127	Stoney Lick Run	1776	1	543
Smoot, Edward	265	White Gap	1789	1	48
Smyth, Alexander	200	Cherry Branch	1801	1	464
Smyth, Isaac & John	285	Stony Lick Run	1804	1	329
Snider See Snyder					
Snider, Jacob	54	Back Creek	1787	1	7
Snider, Jacob	44	Back Creek	1789	1	38
Snider, Jacob	140	Back Creek	1773	1	493
Snively, Henry	400	Meadow Branch	1792	1	127
Snively, Henry	400	Glady Meadows	1776	1	549
Snodgrass, Robert	19a.38p.	Adj. James Winning	1799	1	221
Snodgrass, Robert	290	Back Creek	1774	1	513
Snodgrass, Robert	46	Back Creek	1774	1	516
Snodgrass, Robert	300	Elk Hill	1774	1	518
Snodgrass, Robert Jr.	85	Back Creek	1802	1	293
Snodgrass, Robert Jr.	50	Back Creek	1820	1	414
Snodgrass, Robert V.	2a.3r.16p.	Adj. H. G. Kitchen	1849	2	272
Snodgrass, Robert V.	10	Back Creek	1849	2	273
Snodgrass, Robert V.	210	Rock Gap Run	1819	1	400
Snodgrass, Stephen	30	Back Creek	1799	1	227
Snodgrass, Stephen	86	Back Creek	1816	1	389
Snodgrass, Stephen	48	Wts. Potomac	1818	1	390
Snodgrass, Stephen	472½	Amberson Branch	1798	1	459
Snyder See Snider					
Snyder, Abraham	107	North Mountain	1830	1	438
Snyder, Gasper	234a.2r.22p.	Back Creek	1800	1	256
Snyder, William	22	North Mountain	1854	2	287
Soder, John R.	150	Wts. Potomac	1789	1	78
Southood, See Southwood					
Southood, Edward	102	Adj. A. Throckmorton	1793	1	158
Southood, Edward	20	Wts. Opequon Cr.	1802	1	291
Southwood See Southood					
Southwood, Edward (Southood)	23	Opequon Creek	1792	1	137

Name of Grantee	Acres	Local Description	Year	Book	Page
Trayer, George	100	Wts. Potomac	1777	1	559
Tucker, Henry St. George	110	Adj. A. Vanmeter	1819	1	394
Turner, E.	1a.1r.22p.	Swan Pond	1834	1	441
Turner, John	50	North Mountain	1795	1	173
Turner, John	597¼	White's Branch	1802	1	274
Turner, John & Ruth	345	Back Creek	1791	1	103
Turner, Joseph	33a.1r.33p.	Adj. T. Turner	1802	1	290
Turner, Simeon	72a.1r.	Adj. J. S. Lane	1824	1	430
Turner, Thomas	7½	Vanmeter's Branch	1792	1	126
Turner, Thomas	183¾a.20p.	Wts. Potomac	1794	1	163
Turner, Thomas	46	Adj. John Turner	1802	1	287
Turner, Thomas	61	Wts. Potomac	1773	1	504
Vanmeter, Henry	360a.3r.	Tuscaroh Branch	1776	1	557
Vincenheller or Vincentheller, Vinsonhillar					
Vincentheller, John	70	North Mountain	1791	1	109
Vinsonhillar, Philip	37	North Mountain	1800	1	234
Waggoner, Andrew	69a.2r.	Woodfin's Branch	1799	1	251
Waggoner, Andrew	38	Opequon Creek	1799	1	252
Warner, George	100	Sleepy Creek	1780	2	571
Warner, Zebulon	83	North Mountain	1799	1	238
Washington, Charles	445	Bullskin	1774	1	521
Watson, Arthur	63	Adj. John Fletcher	1788	1	31
Watson, John Jr.	130	Wts. Opequon	1780	2	559
Watson, Joseph	423	Warm Springs Run	1773	1	492
Watson, William	16a.2r.2p.	Opequon Creek	1837	2	260
Weaver, Jacob	6a.3r.23p.	Adj. G. Myers	1815	1	370
Weaver, Jacob	5a.16p.	Opequon Creek	1815	1	371
Welch, James	303¾	Sleepy Creek	1802	1	294
Welchance, Henry	8½	Opequon Cr.	1804	1	330
Wheat, James M.	86	Warm Spring Run	1816	1	387
White, Christian et al	393a.3r.	Sleepy Creek	1775	1	528
White, Nathaniel	72¾	Adj. N. Bull	1805	1	339
Whiting, Henry	951	Jones' Mill Run	1775	1	538
Whitmire See Witmire, Widmyer, Wydmire					
Whitmire, Michael	194	Sleepy Creek	1807	1	347
Whitmire, Michael	27	Sleepy Creek	1814	1	367
Widmyer, Michael	240	Sleepy Creek	1802	1	280
Wilcox, Robert	358	Adj. Wm. Bailey	1794	1	456
Williams, Edward O.	355	Adj. G. Williams	1809	1	354
Williams, Edward O.	316	Wts. Opequon	1810	1	359
Williams, Edward O.	19a.36p.	Swan Pond	1819	1	401
Williams, Jerom	412	Sleepy Creek	1778	2	456
Willson See Wilson					
Willson, Thomas	16a. 2r.	Island in Shenandoah	1800	1	259
Wilson, Edward	25½	Opequon Creek	1777	1	581
Wilson, John	11	Opequon Waters	1775	1	535
Wilson, William	264	Wts. Opequon	1780	2	547
Withers, William	108	Sleepy Creek	1778	2	486
Withers, William	253½	Dry Run	1772	1	489
Withers, William	253½	Dry Run	1772	1	490
Withers, William	229	Adj. Wm. Maxfield	1780	2	528
Withers, William	463	Sleepy Creek	1777	1	578
Witmire, John F.	412	Sleepy Creek	1780	2	570
Wolf, Lewis	200	Little Muddy Creek	1788	1	24
Wood, Richard	250	Sleepy Creek	1788	1	25
Wood, Richard	207	Timber Ridge	1788	1	26
Wood, Richard	431	Sleepy Creek	1788	1	27
Wood, Richard	244	Jacob Johnson's Run	1788	1	28
Wydmire See Whitmire, Witmire, Widmyer					
Wydmire, Michael	100	Warm Spring Ridge	1802	1	281
Wynekoop, Garrett	4a.3r.10p.	Adj. Levi Martin	1820	1	413
Yates, Andrew	243	Back Creek	1774	1	520
Yates, William	404	Baldwin Branch	1789	1	50
Yoal, Ann Eve	100	Back Creek	1780	2	536

BOONE COUNTY

Name of Grantee	Acres	Local Description	Year	Book	Page
Adkins, Alexander	136	Parsoner's Creek	1851	1	63
Adkins, Anderson	22	Mud River	1858	1	240
Adkins, Andrew J.	45	Cane Bottom Br.	1849	1	1
Adkins, Cumberland et al	1,177	Sycamore Fork	1852	1	449
Adkins, David	256	Mud River	1852	1	103
Adkins, Elisha	66	Mud River	1853	1	124
Adkins, Elisha	62	Parson's Creek	1858	1	257
Adkins, Goldsberry	53	Mud River	1849	1	18
Adkins, Goldsberry	104	Big Creek	1850	1	55
Adkins, Goldsberry	79	Slash Branch	1857	1	210
Adkins, Goldsberry	30	Big Creek	1857	1	211
Adkins, Hamilton	148	Laurel Creek	1855	1	169
Adkins, Hamilton	58	Adj. his own	1859	1	282
Adkins, Hamilton	54	Unknown	1859	1	281
Adkins, Hiram	114	Big Creek	1850	1	56
Adkins, Hiram	50	Mud River	1850	1	61
Adkins, James W.	157	Mud River	1858	1	241
Adkins, John	171	Mud River	1851	1	62
Adkins, John	21	Mud River	1858	1	221
Adkins, Joshua Jr.	50	Mud River	1852	1	96
Adkins, Luke	252	Mud River	1856	1	173
Adkins, Luke G.	256	Dry Fork	1855	1	161
Adkins, Mark	67	Mud River	1850	1	22
Adkins, Matthew	63	Mud River	1852	1	95
Adkins, Parker	107	Big Creek	1850	1	54
Allen, Albert	170	Pond Fork	1851	1	65
Allen, Albert	58	Pond Fork	1851	1	66
Allen, Albert	35	Pond Fork	1852	1	85
Allen, Albert	180	Laurel Branch	1859	1	285
Allen, Albert	104	Pond Fork	1860	1	298
Allen, Albert et al	110	Hunter's Branch	1855	1	170
Allen, Albert et al	231	Hunter's Branch	1855	1	171
Allen, John et al	1,136	Ballard's Fork	1858	1	242
Allen, John et al	678	Rush Patch Branch	1859	1	263
Allen, John et al	1,229	Pond Fork	1859	1	273
Averell, Oscar J. et al	397	Laurel Branch	1860	1	297
Avrel See Averell					
Avrel, John H. (Avrell)	178	Pond Fork	1850	1	37
Avrel, John H.	230	Hewitt's Creek	1855	1	156
Avrel, John H.	145	Hewitt's Creek	1856	1	194
Ball, Augustus A.	23	Hewitt's Creek	1849	1	2
Ball, James A.	45	Ant's Fork	1859	1	275
Ball, John F.	233	Philip's Br.	1854	1	154
Ball, Joseph Jr.	48	Adj. O. Bias	1860	1	290
Ball, Joseph Sr.	42	Ant's Fork	1852	1	141
Ballard, St. Clair	160	Stanley Camp Fork	1851	1	64
Ballard, St. Clair	189	Spruce Fork	1852	1	119
Ballard, St. Clair	282	Cor. Peter Price	1857	1	217
Ballard, St. Clair	17	Little Coal	1857	1	218
Ballard, William	600	Fuquas Fork	1853	1	122
Barker, Anderson	78	Hewitt's Creek	1861	1	312
Barker, R. T. & Noah	391	Big Creek	1861	1	311
Bennett, Martin	55	Low Gap Creek	1854	1	134
Bennett, Martin	77	Low Gap Creek	1854	1	135
Bennett, Perry	26	Pond Fork	1849	1	14
Bias, Armstrong	12	Hewitt's Creek	1851	1	67
Bias, Evermont	78	Six Mile Creek	1859	1	277
Bias, Obadiah	145	Branch not given	1858	1	237
Bias, Simeon	25	Bias Branch	1851	1	68
Bias, Simeon	461	Spruce Fork	1857	1	204
Bias, William	257	Hewitt's Creek	1854	1	132
Bias, William	32	Hewitt's Creek	1854	1	133

Name of Grantee	Acres	Local Description	Year	Book	Page
Bowe, Cornelius	85	Tony's Branch	1853	1	125
Bragg, George W.	36	Stinson Creek	1852	1	97
Breedlove, Lindsey	100	Big Horse Creek	1850	1	27
Brown, James	52	West Fork	1858	1	246
Brown, Thomas L.	2,000	Joe's Creek	1860	1	455
Brown, William	30	Pond Fork	1849	1	13
Brown, William	45	West Fork	1851	1	81
Canterberry, John Sr.	140	Rich Hollow	1850	1	28
Chambers, Burwell	150	Spruce Fork	1860	1	291
Chandler, Thomas et al	246	Smith's Branch	1857	1	214
Clark, Samuel	20	Big Laurel	1852	1	104
Clay, M. C.	58	Adj. Z. Elkins	1859	1	289
Cole, Augustus W. et al	883	Big Coal River	1859	1	453
Collins, Levi	333	On Connally	1856	1	186
Conley, Sylvester	15	Hewitt's Creek	1852	1	126
Coon, Lorenzo D.	33	Pond Fork	1849	1	3
Coon, Lorenzo D.	348	Adj. B. Green	1861	1	307
Coon, Lorenzo D.	80	Pond Fork	1861	1	309
Coon, Lorenzo D.	47	Adj. E. Jarrell	1861	1	310
Cooper, Francis	25	Parson's Creek	1853	1	121
Cooper, Francis	95	Parson's Creek	1854	1	153
Cooper, William	65	Laurel Creek	1855	1	157
Cummings, Adam	253	Laurel Fork	1850	1	31
Cummings, William	142	Turtle Creek	1856	1	183
Cummins, Adam	50	Mud River	1855	1	172
Davis, Alexander	63	Blue Ridge	1855	1	160
Dingess, Guy et al	242	Laurel Fork	1850	1	24
Dingess, John M.	280	Sycamore	1857	1	206
Eastep, Sherwood	354	Lick Branch	1858	1	251
Egnor, John W.	232	Dry Fork	1855	1	162
Elkin, Elijah	190	Mud River	1855	1	167
Elkin, Elijah	81	Sand Lick Branch	1855	1	168
Elkin, Robert	75	Unknown	1859	1	258
Elkin, Robert	31	Adj. James Ball	1859	1	259
Elkins, Nathaniel	190	Big Creek	1858	1	248
Elkins, Zacheus	46	Hewitt's Fork	1851	1	69
Fauver, George	255	Tony's Branch	1858	1	254
Ferrell, Chapman	126	West Fork	1858	1	245
Ferrell, James et al	1,510	Upton Creek	1856	1	451
Fipps, John	31	Hewitt's Creek	1854	1	136
Fisher, Henry	145	Tony's Branch	1859	1	271
Foster, James & Thomas	37	Joe's Creek	1851	1	82
Gore, George W.	104	Old Camp Fork	1849	1	6
Gore, George W.	520	Pond Fork	1849	1	19
Gore, George W.	210	Bull Creek	1852	1	120
Gore, George W.	147	Jack's Branch	1852	1	127
Gore, George W.	44	Bull Creek	1853	1	128
Green, Andrew	110	Joe's Creek	1858	1	231
Green, George	59	Keaton's Branch	1849	1	4
Green, George	13	John's Creek	1849	1	5
Green, George	100	Pond Fork	1859	1	266
Hager, Andrew Sr.	8	Unknown	1858	1	252
Hager, Andrew Sr.	80	Parson's Branch	1858	1	253
Hager, James Jr.	89	Mud River	1850	1	42
Hager, James Jr.	172	Mud River	1850	1	43
Hager, James Jr.	718	Mud River	1850	1	58
Hager, James Sr.	261	Mud River	1850	1	44
Hager, John (Hagar)	276	Mud River	1856	1	195
Hager, John (Hagar)	324	Horse Creek	1856	1	193
Hager, John (Hagar)	241	Big Creek	1856	1	192
Hager, John (Hagar)	697	Big Creek	1856	1	191
Hager, John	91	Parshner's Creek	1856	1	178
Hager, John	890	Mud River	1856	1	181

Name of Grantee	Acres	Local Description	Year	Book	Page
Hager, John	361	Spruce Pine	1856	1	196
Hager, John	185	Stinson Branch	1856	1	197
Hager, Joseph	100	Spruce Fork	1852	1	86
Hager, Joseph	170	Spruce Fork	1852	1	115
Hager, Lewis	150	Branch not given	1858	1	238
Hager, Robert	151	Bear Branch	1849	1	7
Hager, Robert	125	Bear Branch	1849	1	25
Hager, Robert	41	Mud River	1852	1	98
Hager, Robert	286	Bear Branch	1852	1	99
Hager, Robert	50	Six Mile Cr.	1854	1	137
Hager, Robert	50	Stone Coal Br.	1854	1	138
Hager, Robert	136	Six Mile Creek	1854	1	139
Hager, Robert	165	Six Mile Creek	1854	1	140
Hager, Robert	254	Six Mile Creek	1854	1	142
Hager, Robert	98	Mud River	1856	1	174
Hager, Robert	58	Coal Branch	1859	1	267
Hager, Robert	783	Big Creek	1859	1	268
Hager, Robert	380	Mud River	1859	1	270
Hager, Robert	248	Adj. Zadock Miller	1859	1	272
Hager, Robert	19	Bee Branch	1859	1	278
Hager, Robert	71	Bear Branch	1859	1	279
Hager, Robert	164	Adj. M. Adkins	1859	1	280
Hager, Robert	12	Adj. J. Tony	1860	1	293
Hager, Robert	283	Spruce Fork	1860	1	296
Hager, Russell (Hagar)	20	Cor. to Wm. Gonoe	1856	1	182
Hart, Stephen	233	Flat Creek	1850	1	57
Hatfield, Calvery	106	Big Branch	1854	1	143
Hatfield, Calvery	164	Big Branch	1855	1	163
Hatfield, Calvery	75	Adj. John Hager	1858	1	235
Hatton, Hotton, Holton					
Hatton, Allen	48	Road Fork	1852	1	106
Hatton, Allen	316	Laurel Fork	1852	1	105
Hill, Andrew	36	Big Horse Creek	1850	1	40
Hill, Andrew	41	Big Horse Creek	1850	1	41
Hill, B. & H.	116	Mud River	1852	1	100
Hill, B. & H.	242	Mud River	1852	1	102
Hill, Bradford	108	Old House Branch	1856	1	188
Hill, Henry	50	Big Horse Creek	1850	1	39
Hill, Spencer	13	Rattlesnake Fork	1853	1	123
Himes, George W.	158	Bear Creek	1855	1	166
Himes, George W.	490	Mud River	1856	1	175
Himes, George W.	820	Conley Branch	1856	1	201
Himes, George W.	582	Simeon Bias Branch	1857	1	207
Himes, George W.	2,679	Mud River	1856	1	450
Hinchman, Burwell S.	217	Unknown	1858	1	247
Hinchman, John K.	39	Spruce Fork	1850	1	33
Hinchman, John K.	101	Spruce Fork	1850	1	34
Hinchman, John K.	60	Philip's Branch	1851	1	80
Holdren, Bartholomew	60	Hewitt's Cr.	1860	1	292
Hunter, Samuel	25	Trace Fork	1860	1	301
Hunter, Samuel et al	110	Hunter's Branch	1855	1	170
Hunter, Samuel et al	231	Hunter's Branch	1855	1	171
Hunter, Thomas	73	Jack's Branch	1860	1	303
Huffman, Charles	45	Horse Creek	1850	1	38
Jarrell, Benjamin	35	Pond Fork	1854	1	144
Jarrell, Benjamin	35	Pond Fork	1857	1	208
Jarrell, Daniel	40	Pond Fork	1852	1	108
Jarrell, Elijah Sr.	41	Casey's Branch	1852	1	107
Jarrell, John Jr.	62	Pond Fork	1850	1	60
Jarrell, John Jr.	218	Adj. his own	1859	1	260
Jarrell, Landon (London)	181	Pond Fork	1850	1	45
Jarrell, Madison	218	Big Elk Run	1851	1	75
Jarrell, Preston	17	Little Coal River	1858	1	232

Name of Grantee	Acres	Local Description	Year	Book	Page
Jarrell, Simeon	25	Skin Poplar Fork	1850	1	46
Jarrell, Simeon	26	Big Laurel	1850	1	47
Jarrell, Simeon	85	Dennison Fork	1850	1	48
Jarrell, Simeon	56	Laurel Branch	1850	1	59
Jarrell, Simeon	111	Casey's Creek	1852	1	87
Jarrell, Simeon	590	Trough Fork	1859	1	283
Jarrell, Simeon	746	Bean Hollow	1859	1	287
Jarrell, Simeon et al	296	Trough Fork	1860	1	294
Jones, John G.	115	Hewitt's Fork	1853	1	130
Kessinger, Wilson	164	Brushy Fork	1852	1	109
Lake, Nicholas	95	Spruce Fork	1856	1	203
Lawson, Anthony et al	1,510	Upton Creek	1856	1	451
Lawson, James et al	242	Laurel Fork	1850	1	24
Lilly, John	90	Middle Fork	1855	1	158
Linville, P. P.	59	Bull Creek	1851	1	76
Linville, P. P.	60	Red Horse Shoals	1851	1	77
Linville, Preston P.	59	West Fork	1849	1	8
Lovejoy, Anderson	135	Big Creek	1857	1	213
Lovejoy, Richard	860	Lf. Hd. Fork Mud	1857	1	205
Lovejoy, Richard Jr.	200	Sanging Branch	1856	1	184
Lovejoy, William	391	Spruce	1856	1	185
Lovejoy, William P.	35	Left Hd. Fork Mud	1859	1	269
Lovejoy, William P.	41	Rich's Branch	1859	1	276
Lovejoy, William P.	117	Adj. H. Smith	1860	1	295
Martin, William	137	Mud River	1850	1	49
Martin, William	193	Left Hand Fork	1854	1	145
McComas, Patrick K.	92	Pond Fork	1849	1	15
McNeely, Alexander	28	Vanatter's Br.	1858	1	222
McNeely, Alexander	86	Cor. of Old Surv.	1858	1	223
McNeely, Joseph	47	Spruce Fork	1850	1	50
McNeely, Joseph	8	Spruce Fork	1850	1	51
McNeely, Joseph	50	Laurel Branch	1850	1	52
Meadows, Joseph	44	Big Coal River	1857	1	216
Miller, Benton J.	200	Cor. Cummings' Line	1858	1	226
Miller, Benton J.	344	Camp Creek	1858	1	227
Miller, Benton J.	690	Pigeon Roost	1858	1	228
Miller, Benton J.	425	Turtle Creek	1858	1	229
Miller, Benton J.	212	Ballard's Fork	1859	1	286
Miller, Daniel	171	Cor Miller's Old Sur.	1858	1	224
Miller, Daniel Jr.	134	Turtle Creek	1858	1	225
Miller, Ezekiel S.	80	Ballard Fork	1852	1	116
Miller, Ezekiel S.	28	Mud River	1852	1	117
Miller, Ezekiel S.	81	Turtle Creek	1852	1	118
Miller, George	50	Low Gap Creek	1859	1	261
Miller, Col. John	107	Big Branch	1852	1	93
Miller, Col. John	118	Big Branch	1852	1	94
Miller, Col. John	100	Stable Branch	1854	1	152
Miller, Joshua	150	Conley Fork	1851	1	78
Miller, Joshua	205	Left Hand Fork	1854	1	146
Miller, Moses	40	Wolf Branch	1854	1	131
Miller, Preston J.	1,157	Lick Creek	1858	1	452
Miller, William	132	Houchins Fork	1849	1	12
Miller, Zadock	192	Mud River	1851	1	70
Mitchell, Joshua	111	Mud River	1858	1	243
Mitchell, Joshua	600	Mud River	1858	1	244
Nelson, Thomas & Elijah	55	Jack's Branch	1851	1	79
Parsons, William	53	Adj. James Hager	1859	1	288
Pauley, Daniel	71	Bennett's Branch	1849	1	10
Pauley, Daniel	387	Pond Fork	1849	1	20
Pauley, Joseph	174	Roaches' Branch	1851	1	71
Pauley, Preston	65	Pond Fork	1849	1	9
Payne, Thornton	100	Big Horse Creek	1851	1	72
Plumley, Isaac	71	Mud River	1857	1	215

Name of Grantee	Acres	Local Description	Year	Book	Page
Plumley, Mathias	86	Laurel Fork	1852	1	88
Plumley, Mathias	175	Laurel Fork	1852	1	89
Plumley, Mathias	239	Laurel Fork	1852	1	90
Plumley, Mathias	172	Laurel Creek	1858	1	220
Plumley, Sylvester	131	Laurel Creek	1858	1	219
Powell, John	190	Spruce Fork	1855	1	155
Powell, John	188	Spruce Fork	1856	1	176
Powell, John	24	Philip's Branch	1856	1	177
Powell, John	216	Stable Branch	1861	1	313
Price, Peter	193	Lick Branch	1850	1	23
Price, Thomas	947	Big Horse Creek	1850	1	30
Reynolds, S. H. et al	397	Laurel Branch	1860	1	297
Smith, Ezekiel	146	Left Hand Fork	1854	1	150
Smith, Henry	97	Parson's Creek	1852	1	91
Smith, Henry	85	Left Hand Fork	1854	1	147
Smith, Henry	126	Laurel Creek	1854	1	148
Smith, Henry	93	Parson's Creek	1854	1	149
Smith, Henry	87	Parson's Fork	1860	1	304
Smith, William	249	Parsoner's Creek	1857	1	209
Smith, William Jr.	89	Parson's Creek	1852	1	92
Smoot, Alexander	156	Joe's Branch	1849	1	11
Smoot, Alexander	30	Meadow Branch	1859	1	264
Smoot, John et al	1,177	Sycamore Fork	1852	1	449
Smoot, Samuel	500	Laurel Creek	1859	1	265
Smoot, William	100	Slash Branch	1850	1	29
Smoot, William	186	Bear Branch	1850	1	32
Smoot, William	178	Lick Creek	1850	1	36
Smoot, William	108	Little Coal	1852	1	110
Spurlock, Burwell	80	Bearin-She Run	1856	1	189
Spurlock, Eliphaz	273	Mud River	1851	1	73
Spurlock, Eliphaz	72	Upton Creek	1856	1	187
Spurlock, Eliphaz	557	Mud River	1859	1	262
Spurlock, Ely	85	Mud River	1856	1	190
Spurlock, John	194	Mud River	1852	1	101
Spurlock, John	178	Riches' Branch	1853	1	129
Spurlock, John	421	Parcener's Creek	1856	1	202
Spurlock, Robertson	261	Mud River	1852	1	111
Spurlock, Robertson	249	Mud River	1852	1	112
Spurlock, Seth & John	604	Mud River	1849	1	16
Spurlock, Thomas	32	Wild Cat Branch	1849	1	17
Spurlock, Thomas	63	Turtle Creek	1849	1	26
Stollings, Granville	90	Spruce Fork	1860	1	299
Stone, Samuel S.	55	Horse Creek	1856	1	198
Stone, Samuel S.	121	Horse Creek	1856	1	199
Stone, Samuel S.	202	Smith Branch	1856	1	200
Stone, Sameul S.	123	Little Blue Knob	1860	1	302
Stone, Samuel S. et al	246	Smith's Branch	1857	1	214
Thompson, Francis	50	Turtle Creek	1858	1	230
Thompson, James B.	72	Sleepy Branch	1855	1	159
Toney, B. & S.	277	Big Creek	1851	1	83
Toney, John	45	Adj. B. S. Hinchman	1859	1	274
Toney, Robert & P.	122	Toney's Branch	1851	1	84
Vance, Isaac	92	Big Branch	1858	1	233
Vance, Isaac	84	Big Branch	1858	1	234
Vance, Isaac	46	Big Branch	1861	1	308
Vannater, John	86	Vanater's Branch	1854	1	179
Vannater, John	85	Vanater's Branch	1854	1	180
Vannatter, Allen	158	Mud River	1859	1	284
Vannatter, John	340	Berry Branch	1858	1	250
Vannatter, John	384	Dog Bone	1858	1	255
Vannatter, John	110	Left Hand Fork	1860	1	300
Vannatter, John	200	Hager's Branch	1858	1	249
Vickers, Elias P.	300	Brushy Fork	1852	1	113

Name of Grantee	Acres	Local Description	Year	Book	Page
Vickers, Simeon C.	32	Brushy Fork	1855	1	164
Vickers, Simeon C.	188	Horse Creek	1855	1	165
Wall, Augustus	1,000	Laurel	1858	1	239
Wall, Augustus	957	Laurel & Spruce	1858	1	236
Ward, Evermont	981	Mud River	1850	1	35
Ward, Evermont	61	Hager's Branch	1850	1	53
Ward, Evermont	600	Mud River	1851	1	74
Ward, Evermont et al	1,136	Ballard's Fork	1858	1	242
Ward, Evermont et al	678	Rush Patch Branch	1859	1	263
Ward, Evermont et al	1,229	Pond Fork	1859	1	273
Watson, Daniel	35	Trace Fork	1852	1	114
Watt, William H. et al	883	Big Coal River	1859	1	453
White, Benjamin W. et al	296	Trough Fork	1860	1	294
White, Russell	54	Brown's Br.	1854	1	151
Woodrum, Balt	700	Pond Fork	1850	1	21
Workman, George	53	Laurel Branch	1858	1	256
Workman, Jane	15	Pond Fork	1861	1	305
Workman, William	157	Pond Fork	1861	1	306

BRAXTON COUNTY

Adams, P. B.	672	Laurel Run	1860	2	177
Adams, P. B.	170	Bear Run	1860	2	178
Adams, P. B.	120	Wts of Lit Birch	1860	2	182
Adams, P. B. et al	190	Big Otter	1857	2	75
Adams, P. B. et al	1,560	Wts. Big Sandy	1858	2	124
Adams, P. B. et al	530	Whetstone	1858	2	125
Adams, P. B. et al	735	Big Laurel	1858	2	126
Adams, P. B. et al	100	Wts. Elk	1858	2	127
Adams, P. B. et al	135	Wts. of Elk	1858	2	128
Adams, P. B. et al	990	Big Otter	1858	2	135
Adams, P. B. et al	2,800	West Fork	1860	2	189
Adams, P. B. et al	2,700	Little Laurel	1858	2	452
Adams, Pearson B. et al	220	O'Brien's Fork	1857	2	74
Adams, Pearson B. et al	60	Tague Fork	1856	2	67
Adams, Pearson B. et al	170	Grannie's Creek	1856	2	66
Adams, Pearson B. et al	200	Triplett's Fork	1856	2	63
Adams, Pierson B.	194	Wolfe Creek	1857	2	77
Albert, Henry	100	Cedar Creek	1850	1	195
Albert, Henry	100	Cedar Creek	1854	1	442
Alkire, David	786	Wts. of Lit Kanawha	1856	2	60
Anawalt, Ananias et al	742	Raccoon Creek	1856	2	44
Arnold, George I. (or J.)	484	Wts. Lit Kanawha	1850	1	205
Arnold, George I. (or J.)	325	Oil Creek	1850	1	451
Arnold, George I. (or J.) et al	439	Wts. Lit. Kanawha	1850	1	211
Arnold, George I. (or J.) et al	224	Grass Run	1851	1	268
Arnold, George I. (or J.) et al	400	Byrne's Run	1851	1	269
Arnold, George I. (or J.) et al	200	Grass Run	1852	1	304
Arnold, George I. (or J.) et al	65	Bickle's Fork	1852	1	305
Arnold, George I. (or J.) et al	264	Byrne's Run	1852	1	306
Arnold, George I. (or J.) et al	50	Bickle's Fork	1852	1	307
Arnold, George I. (or J.) et al	220	Clout Run	1852	1	308
Arnold, George I. (or J.) et al	380	Salt Lick	1850	1	191
Arnold, James W. et al	190	Walnut Fork	1851	1	267
Arters, William R.	100	Wts. of Holley	1856	2	59
Arthur, Richard A.	220	Big Run	1850	1	158

Name of Grantee	Acres	Local Description	Year	Book	Page
Arthur, Richard A.	1,000	Grassy Creek	1850	1	159
Arthur, Richard A.	241	Grassy Creek	1850	1	160
Arthur, Richard A.	1,100	Grassy Creek	1851	1	265
Arthur, Richard A.	155	Big Grassy Creek	1854	1	393
Arthur, William R.	200	Big Grassy Creek	1853	1	355
Arthur, Wilson	38	Adj. Thomas Miller	1850	1	157
Bail, Jane	238	Little Otter Cr.	1854	1	416
Bail, John	100	Little Otter Cr.	1854	1	415
Baldwin, Israel et al	990	Copen Run	1851	1	454
Ball, Augustian F. (or T.)	200	Copen Run	1850	1	196
Ball, Augustian T.	12	Copen's Run	1854	1	395
Barber, John	100	Bogg's Fork	1850	1	218
Barker, Edmund	167	Crooked Fork	1851	1	249
Barker, Edmund	100	Westfall Fork	1852	1	302
Barker, Edmund	100	Cedar Creek	1852	1	303
Barker, Edmund	180	Wts. Steer Creek	1852	1	310
Barker, Edmund	225(245)	Salt Lick Creek	1852	1	324
Barker, Edmund	225	Cedar Creek	1852	1	325
Barker, Edmund	100	Scott Camp Fork	1855	2	3
Barker, Edmund	190	Piper's Fork	1855	2	4
Barker, Edmund et al	190	Tague Fork	1855	1	444
Barnett, James M.	150	Laurel Run	1858	2	96
Beirne See Bierne					
Beirne, Duffy & Company et al	325	O'Brien's Fork	1853	1	347
Belknap, James	83	Big Trace Run	1850	1	173
Belknap, James	350	Trace Run	1853	1	379
Belknap, Thomas	175	Grass Lick	1853	1	377
Belknap, William	50	Grass Lick	1850	1	172
Belknap, William	125	Bender's Run	1850	1	171
Belknap, William	75	Adj. T. Belknap	1850	1	178
Belknap, William	75	Grass Lick Fork	1858	2	107
Bender, John	180	Steer Creek	1848	1	95
Bender, John	245	Straight Fork	1851	1	271
Bender, John	30	Wts. Steer Creek	1851	1	278
Bender, John	700 (900)	Wts. Steer Creek	1851	1	455
Berry, Allen S.	72	Salt Lick Creek	1850	1	229
Berry, Joel	200	Oil Creek	1849	1	152
Berry, Joel	28	O'Brien's Fork	1854	1	406
Betts, John	50	Grannie's Creek	1842	1	15
Bierne—See Beirne					
Bierne, Duffy & Company et al	950	Polemic Run	1858	2	95
Boggs, Francis C.	43	Wts. Elk	1847	1	70
Boggs, Francis C.	154	Wts of Elk	1847	1	72
Boggs, Francis C.	200	Lick Fork	1855	2	31
Boggs, Hezekiah	66	2 Mile Run	1850	1	203
Boggs, Hezekiah	45	Steer Creek	1850	1	214
Boggs, Hezekiah	37	Adj. T. Keener	1850	1	217
Boggs, Hezekiah	25	Wts. Steer Creek	1850	1	221
Boggs, James A.	152	Wts. Elk	1847	1	71
Boggs, James A.	85	Big Otter	1848	1	90
Boggs, James A.	176	Big Otter	1848	1	91
Boggs, James A.	250	Wts. Elk	1850	1	185
Boggs, James A.	30	Big Run	1853	1	340
Boggs, James A.	120	Wts. Steer Creek	1856	2	48
Boggs, James A.	50	O'Brien's Fork	1857	2	81
Boggs, James A.	25	O'Brien's Fork	1857	2	82
Boggs, James A.	20	Dobbin's Fork	1859	2	151
Boggs, John E.	100	Rock Camp	1849	1	101
Boggs, Norman	200	West Fork	1849	1	449
Boggs, William M.	127	Francis Fork	1838	1	3
Boggs, William M.	166	Big Otter	1850	1	176
Boggs, William M. et al	400	Big Otter	1851	1	263
Boggs, William M. et al	35	Big Otter	1850	1	154

Name of Grantee	Acres	Local Description	Year	Book	Page
Boggs, William M. et al	185	O'Brien's Creek	1850	1	155
Boggs, William M. et al	60	O'Brien's Creek	1850	1	156
Boon, Robert	50	Limestone	1848	1	83
Bosley, Peter L.	125	Cedar Creek	1855	2	20
Bosley, Peter L. et al	128	Spring Run	1852	1	316
Bourn, Warren	116	Shock's Mill Run	1858	2	132
Brady, John	75	Steer Creek	1845	1	30
Bragg, Adam	150	O'Brien's Fork	1856	2	64
Bragg, Jesse	120	Salt Lick Creek	1852	1	296
Brock, Robert	50	Big Otter	1851	1	266
Brown, George et al	1,100	Big Laurel	1854	1	398
Brown, Jeremiah et al	1,100	Big Laurel	1854	1	398
Burnes, Hugh	150	Shock's Mill Run	1858	2	136
Butcher, Gibson J.	970	Flat Run	1849	1	134
Butler, Jeremiah	227	Big Otter	1848	1	84
Butler, Jeremiah	118	Big Otter	1853	1	342
Butler, Jeremiah	675	Big Otter Creek	1854	1	401
Butler, Margaret B.	100	Big Otter	1853	1	343
Butler, Oliver	56	Big Otter	1850	1	227
Butler, Oliver	175	Big Otter	1853	1	341
Butler, William F.	45	Big Otter	1850	1	225
Byrne, B. W. et al	1,560	Wts. Big Sandy	1858	2	124
Byrne, B. W. et al	530	Whetstone	1858	2	125
Byrne, B. W. et al	735	Big Laurel	1858	2	126
Byrne, B. W. et al	100	Wts. Elk	1858	2	127
Byrne, B. W. et al	135	Wts. of Elk	1858	2	128
Byrne, B. W. et al	2,700	Little Laurel	1858	2	452
Byrne, John P.	200	Salt Lick	1838	1	8
Byrne, John P.	900	Wts. Lit. Kanawha	1850	1	180
Byrne, John P.	410	Wts. Lit. Kanawha	1851	1	230
Byrne, John P. et al	602½	Salt Lick	1849	1	146
Byrne, John P. et al	990	Copen Run	1851	1	454
Byrne, John P. et al	1,280	Cedar Creek	1850	1	457
Byrne, Marcellus	218	Wts. Little Kanawha	1854	1	431
Byrne, Marcellus et al	1,030	Cedar Creek	1857	2	80
Byrne, Peyton B.	229	Salt Lick Creek	1838	1	12
Byrne, Peyton B.	70	G. White's Run	1838	1	13
Byrne, T. et al	100	Bickles Fork	1850	1	212
Byrne, Thaddeus	233	Bickle's Fork	1855	2	19
Byrne, Thadeus et al	500	Crooked Fork	1854	1	432
Byrne, Thadeus et al	240	Little Buffalo	1853	1	352
Byrne, Thadeus et al	80	Bear Run	1853	1	356
Byrne, Thadeus et al	320	Raccoon Creek	1853	1	357
Byrne, Thadeus et al	100	Long Run	1853	1	358
Byrne, Thadeus et al	125	Buffalo Creek	1854	1	413
Byrne, Thadeus et al	445	Raccoon Creek	1855	2	10
Camden, Gideon D.	305	Buffalo Creek	1844	1	22
Camden, Gideon D.	250	Grassy Fork	1844	1	23
Camden, Gideon D.	176	Wts. Little Birch	1844	1	24
Camden, Gideon D.	70	Crooked Fork	1844	1	25
Camden, Gideon D.	179	Pistol Fork	1844	1	26
Camden, J. N.	256	Raccoon Creek	1852	1	292
Camden, J. N.	180	Big Otter Creek	1853	1	334
Camden, J. N.	555	Wolf Creek	1859	2	152
Camden, J. N. et al	49	Wts. Little Birch	1847	1	54
Camden, J. N. et al	300	Little Buffalo	1847	1	80
Camden, J. N. et al	240	Little Buffalo	1853	1	352
Camden, J. N. et al	125	Buffalo Creek	1854	1	413
Camden, J. N. et al	500	Crooked Fork	1854	1	432
Camden, John S.	1,184	Old Woman's Run	1857	2	83
Camden, John S.	390	Grannie's Creek	1859	2	146
Camden, John S. et al	100	Wts. Elk	1847	1	51
Camden, John S. et al	400	Rush Fork	1850	1	165

Name of Grantee	Acres	Local Description	Year	Book	Page
Camden, John S. et al	100	Rush Fork	1851	1	232
Camden, Johnson N.	175	Horse Fork	1854	1	409
Camden, Johnson N.	120	Little Otter	1850	1	168
Camden, Johnson N.	57	O'Brien's Fork	1854	1	412
Camden, Johnson N. et al	209	Bear Run	1847	1	62
Camden, Johnson N. et al	220	Bear Run	1847	1	63
Camden, Johnson N. et al	145	Sandy Fork	1847	1	64
Camden, Johnson N. et al	126	Big Laurel	1847	1	65
Camden, Johnson N. et al	143	Joe's Spring Knob	1847	1	66
Camden, Johnson N. et al	138	Sandy Fork	1847	1	67
Camden, Johnson N. et al	112	Bear Run	1847	1	68
Camden, Johnson N. et al	450	Long Run	1847	1	69
Camden, Johnson N. et al	148	Little Birch	1849	1	111
Camden, Johnson N. et al	320	Raccoon Creek	1853	1	357
Camden, Johnson N. et al	100	Long Run	1853	1	358
Camden, Johnson N. et al	445	Raccoon Creek	1855	2	10
Camden, L. D.	100	Wts. of Elk	1851	1	259
Camden, L. D.	50	Wts. Elk	1851	1	273
Camden, L. D.	20	Wts. Elk	1851	1	279
Camden, L. D.	25	Wts. of Elk	1851	1	280
Camden, L. D. et al	145	Log Shoal Run	1851	1	234
Camden, L. D. et al	105	Lit Rouel's Creek	1851	1	245
Camden, Lorenzo D. et al	260	Long Run	1847	1	61
Canfield, John S. et al	1,100	Big Laurel	1854	1	398
Carr, Andrew et al	190	Tague Fork	1855	1	444
Carr, James C.	85	Tague Fork	1850	1	220
Carr, John	75	Triplett's Fork	1850	1	219
Carpenter, John L.	200(2,000)	White Oak Run	1851	1	231
Chapman, Andrew J.	107	Laurel Creek	1848	1	81
Chapman, Andrew J.	75	Laurel Creek	1850	1	161
Chapman, James	50	Wts. Elk	1845	1	37
Chapman, James	43	Elk River	1849	1	109
Chapman, John	100	Wts. Elk	1847	1	48
Chapman, John	100	Laurel Creek	1848	1	86
Chapman,William	75	Wts. Elk	1845	1	38
Chapman, William	50	Whetstone Run	1848	1	85
Chapman, William C.	150	Wts. Elk	1851	1	253
Chapman, William Sr.	18	Wts. Elk.	1851	1	241
Chenoweth, David W.	140	Stinson Fork	1854	1	417
Chenoweth, David W.	140	West Fork	1855	2	33
Clifton, Esra	125	Big Grassy Creek	1856	2	51
Clifton, Esra	135	Big Grassy Creek	1856	2	52
Clifton, Ezra B.	70	Wts Holly	1858	2	108
Clifton, Jesse	115	Cow Run	1855	2	21
Clifton, William W.	137	Howell's Run	1855	2	24
Cocke, John S. Tr.	185	Shrieve's Run	1850	1	181
Cocke, John S. Tr.	220	Oil Creek	1850	1	182
Cocke, John S. Tr.	97	Wts. Lit. Kanawha	1854	1	391
Cocke, John S. Tr.	300	Oil Creek	1854	1	392
Cocke, John S. Tr.	508	Wts. Lit. Kanawha	1849	1	450
Coger, Asa	60	Wts. Salt Lick	1855	2	22
Coger, Asa et al	90	Shrieve's Run	1854	1	407
Coger, Asa et al	140	Copen's Run	1854	1	408
Coger, James	185	Salt Lick Creek	1854	1	411
Coger, John	50	Salt Lick	1838	1	11
Coger, Silas	186	Big Grassy Creek	1854	1	399
Coger,Tubal Cane et al	80	Hughes Fork	1855	2	15
Conrad, Currence B. et al	200	Jerry's Fork	1838	1	5
Cool, Henry	97	Butcher's Run	1849	1	133
Cool, John C.	50	Wts. Holly	1855	2	25
Cool, John C.	65	Wts. of Holly	1855	2	39
Cool, Walter	110	Holly River	1837	1	1
Cool, Walter	100	Holly River	1851	1	243

Name of Grantee	Acres	Local Description	Year	Book	Page
Cool, Walter	50	Waters of Holly	1855	1	448
Cool, Walter	50	Desert Fork	1855	2	5
Cool, Walter	96	Wts. of Holly	1855	2	6
Corley, James M. et al	390	Wts. Elk River	1852	1	309
Corley, James M.	310	Wts. Little Birch	1847	1	52
Corley, James M.	15	Laurel Fork	1855	2	35
Corley, William L. J.	925	Wts. Little Birch	1856	2	46
Corley, William L. J.	246	Wts. of Elk	1858	2	103
Corley, William L. J.	100	Middle Run	1860	2	161
Corley, William L. J.	100	Laurel Run	1860	2	176
Corley, William L. J.	125	Strange Creek	1860	2	181
Corley, William L. J. et al	274	Wts. Little Birch	1859	2	141
Cotteral—See Cottrel, Cottrill					
Cotteral, Andrew	100	Rush Fork	1851	1	242
Cotteral, George W.	97	Walker's Fork	1851	1	281
Cotteral, George W.	130	Shock's Mill Run	1853	1	351
Cotteral, George W.	100	Sleath Fork	1853	1	381
Cotteral, Thomas	50	Mound's Run	1852	1	297
Cottrel, George W.	200	Shock's Mill Run	1857	2	88
Cottrill, Cotteral, Cottrel					
Cottrill, George W.	50	West Fork	1858	2	139
Coulter, George & J. C.	150	Wts. Elk	1847	1	49
Cox, Thomas	93	Wts. Big Birch	1857	2	87
Crites, John et al	550	Wts. Little Birch	1857	2	68
Culp, John	100	Mill Creek	1853	1	335
Cutlip, George W.	30	Wts. of Little Birch	1860	2	159
Cutlip, John	50	Wts. Little Birch	1847	1	56
Cutlip, John	50	Little Birch	1849	1	113
Cutlip, Samuel	800	Cedar Creek	1850	1	453
Cutlip, Samuel	500	Wts. of Cedar	1855	2	38
Cutlip, Samuel	1,300	Wts. Cedar	1858	2	94
Cutlip, Samuel	165	Wts. Cedar	1856	2	180
Cutlip, William	380	Wts. of Little Kanawha	1852	1	300
Davis, Jesse	162	Raccoon Creek	1849	1	145
Dobbins, Benjamin	349½	Triplett Fork	1837	1	2
Dobbins, Benjamin	150	Triplett Fork	1847	1	73
Dobbins, Benjamin	93	O'Brien's Fork	1848	1	87
Dobbins, Benjamin	336	Triplett Fork	1854	1	433
Dobbins, Joel	40	O'Brien's Fork	1850	1	167
Dobbins, John	20	Steer Creek	1849	1	102
Dobbins, Peter	40	O'Brien's Fork	1849	1	114
Dobbins, Peter	80	O'Brien's Fork	1849	1	124
Dobbins, Samuel et al	325	O'Brien's Fork	1853	1	347
Dobbins, Samuel Jr.	71	Wts. Elk	1846	1	41
Dobbins, Samuel Sr.	70	O'Brien's Fork	1849	1	110
Dobbins, Samuel Sr.	20	O'Brien's Fork	1853	1	329
Dobbins, Sarah	55	Shock's Mill Run	1847	1	74
Dobbins, Thomas	150	Triplett Fork	1853	1	346
Dobbins, Thomas et al	130	Mound Run	1853	1	348
Duffield, George	112	Middle Run	1855	2	9
Duffield, George et al	200	Elk River	1849	1	125
Duffield, George et al	410	Diatia Run	1858	2	104
Duffield, William M.	70	Wts. of Elk	1859	2	156
Duffy, Philip	650	Crooked Fork	1853	1	345
Duffy, Philip	235	Wts. Cedar	1859	2	142
Duffy, Philip	500	Raccoon Creek	1859	2	148
Duffy, Philip et al	130	Mound Run	1853	1	348
Duffy, Philip et al	550	Wts. Lit Birch	1857	2	68
Dyer, Morgan	200	Salt Lick Creek	1849	1	148
Dyer, Morgan	140	Little Buffalo	1851	1	233
Dyer, Morgan	157	Wts. Lit Birch	1851	1	244
Dyer, Morgan et al	900	Wts. Little Birch	1844	1	21
Edwards, William H.	7,327	Wts. Elk	1850	1	206

Name of Grantee	Acres	Local Description	Year	Book	Page
Green, Thomas et al	500	Road Run	1860	2	173
Gregory, Adam	100	Wts. of Holly	1859	2	150
Gregory, Joseph	184	Grassy Fork	1844	1	32
Gregory, Joseph	203	Buck Fork	1845	1	33
Griffin, Leroy A. et al	990	Big Otter	1858	2	135
Griffin, Leroy A.	520	Wts. Little Kanawha	1858	2	110
Griffin, Leroy et al	742	Raccoon Creek	1856	2	44
Griffin, Leroy et al	200	Triplett's Fork	1856	2	63
Griffin, Leroy et al	60	Tague Fork	1856	2	67
Griffin, Leroy et al	170	Grannie's Creek	1856	2	66
Griffith, Hugh	70	Wts. Elk	1848	1	89
Hall, Joseph	50	West Fork	1859	2	155
Hamrick, Allen	100	Back Fork	1846	1	40
Hamrick, Allen	215	Big Grassy Creek	1855	2	41
Hamrick, Isaac G.	132	Triplett Fork	1843	1	18
Hamrick, Nathan Mc.	95	Middle Run	1854	1	423
Hamrick, Nathan Mc.	120	Diatia Run	1858	2	99
Hamrick, Seth F.	47	O'Brien's Fork	1850	1	174
Hamrick, Seth F.	130	O'Brien's Fork	1852	1	321
Hamrick, Seth F. et al	220	O'Brien's Fork	1857	2	74
Hanna, Nathan et al	250	Wts Elk	1841	1	14
Harley See Hurley					
Harley, Cornelius C. et al	1,799	Wts. Lit. Kan.	1853	1	331
Harmon, Aves (Avis)	35	Lit. Laurel	1849	1	126
Harmon, Aves (Avis)	115	Big Sandy	1849	1	127
Harmon, Aves	150	Lit. Laurel Creek	1850	1	179
Harmon, Aves	75	Log Shoal Run	1852	1	291
Haymond, Benjamin W.	47	Wts. Salt Lick	1851	1	282
Haymond, Benjamin W.	60	Wilson Haymond's Run	1851	1	283
Haymond, Benjamin W.	90	Wts. Lit. Kanawha	1853	1	354
Haymond, L. D. et al	120	O'Brien's Fork	1858	2	115
Haymond, Luther et al	1,560	Wts. Big Sandy	1858	2	124
Haymond, Luther et al	530	Whetstone	1858	2	125
Haymond, Luther et al	735	Big Laurel	1858	2	126
Haymond, Luther et al	100	Wts. of Elk	1858	2	127
Haymond, Luther et al	135	Wts. of Elk	1858	2	128
Haymond, Luther et al	2,700	Lit Laurel	1858	2	452
Haymond, M. P.	149	Oil Creek	1862	2	192
Haymond, M. P. et al	90	Oil Creek	1862	2	191
Haymond, Miranda P.	160	Copen Run	1853	1	383
Haymond, Miranda P.	535	Stone Run	1853	1	384
Hays, Benjamin G. (Hayse)	140	Wts. of Elk	1850	1	163
Hays, Benjamin G.	40	Wts. of Elk	1852	1	298
Hays, Peregrine et al	190	Walnut Fork	1851	1	267
Heater, John (Heatter)	98	Salt Lick Creek	1851	1	236
Heater, John	60	O'Brien's Fork	1849	1	139
Heater, William	75	Clout Run	1851	1	274
Hefner, Jacob	229	Cedar Creek	1855	1	447
Hefner, William S.	150	Adj. M. R. Haymond	1858	2	137
Hicks, Washington	20	Laurel Creek	1849	1	104
Hoffman—See Huffman					
Hoffman, John S.	2,000	Laurel Creek	1859	2	149
Holt, H. A.	1,700	Wts. of Elk	1855	2	32
Holt, H. A.	200	Raccoon Creek	1858	2	93
Holt, H. A.	135	Coon Creek	1860	2	175
Holt, H. A. et al	2,800	West Fork	1860	2	189
Holt, Homer A.	2,820	Big Otter Cr	1855	2	450
Holt, Homer A. et al	1,031	Cedar Creek	1857	2	80
Hoover, John	75	Buffalo Shoal Run	1848	1	98
Hopkins, Andrew J.	70	Paddy's Run	1851	1	250
Hopkins, Andrew J.	77	Salt Lick Creek	1851	1	251
Hopkins, Andrew J.	440	Salt Lick Creek	1855	2	26
Howel, Zachariah R.	50	Back Fork	1854	1	434

Name of Grantee	Acres	Local Description	Year	Book	Page
Long, James	80	Long Run	1850	1	190
Long, James	135	Raccoon Creek	1853	1	344
Lynch, Adam G.	100	Elk River	1849	1	130
Lynch, Adam G.	70	Big Grassy Creek	1854	1	428
Lynch, Isaac G.	155	Widow Miller's Run	1854	1	426
Lyons, William S.	70	Salt Lick Creek	1852	1	336
Matthews, David	200	Laurel Fork	1850	1	188
Matthews, David	200	Duck Creek	1850	1	189
Matthews, David	72	West Fork	1853	1	359
Matthews, George I.	195	Duck Creek	1852	1	326
McClure, Jacob D.	454	Wts. Elk	1838	1	4
McCoy, William H.	50	Wts. Salt Lick	1858	2	106
McCoy, William H.	192	Salt Lick Creek	1855	1	443
McElwain, George	80	Laurel Creek	1853	1	337
McElwain, Thomas (McLewain)	50	Wts. of Elk	1847	1	77
McElwain, Thomas	50	Steer Creek	1845	1	31
McElwain, Thomas	100	Grannie's Creek	1850	1	166
McLaughlin, Addison	235	Wolf Pen Run	1850	1	177
McLaughlin, Addison	500	Cedar Creek	1851	1	261
McLaughlin, Addison	345	Salt Lick Creek	1851	1	262
McLaughlin, Addison	86	Wts. Lit Kanawha	1856	2	61
McLaughlin, Addison et al	35	Big Otter	1850	1	154
McLaughlin, Addison et al	185	O'Brien's Creek	1850	1	155
McLaughlin, Addison et al	60	O'Brien's Creek	1850	1	156
McLaughlin, Addison et al	400	Big Otter	1851	1	263
McLaughlin, Addison et al	1,799	Wts. Lit Kanawha	1853	1	331
McLaughlin, Addison et al	100	Cedar Creek	1855	2	11
McLaughlin, Duncan	50	Wts Lit Kanawha	1858	2	133
McLewain See McElwain					
McNamar, Joseph C.	50	O'Brien's Fork	1860	2	167
McNemar, Elijah	50	Wts Lit Kanawha	1838	1	10
McNemar, Elijah	50	Wts. of L. Kanawha	1850	1	198
Meadows, David	50	Big Otter	1850	1	223
Meadows, David	50	Big Otter Creek	1854	1	429
Miller, Samuel	300	Grassy Creek	1852	1	460
Miller, Samuel C.	100	Wts. of Elk	1855	2	30
Miller Samuel F.	160	Back Fork	1855	2	36
Miller, Samuel F.	40	Big Grassy Creek	1855	2	37
Miller, Thomas	40	Milburn Glade	1849	1	120
Miller, Thomas	100	Spilman Mt.	1849	1	121
Modes, Christian	50	Steer Creek	1849	1	105
Mollohan—See Mollohon					
Mollohan, Charles	6	Wts. Holly	1844	1	20
Mollohan, Charles	175	Salt Lick	1849	1	150
Mollohan, Charles	215	Wts. Salt Lick	1852	1	290
Mollohan, Charles	190	Wts. Little Kan.	1853	1	368
Mollohan, George D.	165	Laurel Patch Run	1851	1	277
Mollohan, George D.	260	Wts. of Holly	1857	2	92
Mollohan, Nathan	280	Duck Creek	1853	1	375
Mollohan, William	71	Walnut Fork	1846	1	44
Mollohan, William	97	Walker Fork	1846	1	46
Mollohan, William	100	West Fork	1847	1	76
Mollohan, William	135	West Fork	1848	1	96
Mollohan, William	30	Big Otter	1848	1	97
Mollohan, William	100	Stinson's Fork	1850	1	208
Mollohan, William	79	Walker Fork	1850	1	209
Mollohan, William	286	West Fork	1853	1	330
Mollohon, George D.	346	Wts. of Holly	1861	2	187
Mollohon, George D.	380	Wt. Lit. Kanawha	1859	2	145
Mollohon, William	200	Big Otter Creek	1851	1	252
Monk, Henry B.	200	Wts. Steer Creek	1851	1	284
Moore, John	100	Crooked Fork	1851	1	255
Morgan, Charles S. et al	900	Wts. Lit. Birch	1844	1	21

Name of Grantee	Acres	Local Description	Year	Book	Page
Morrison, John	10	Flat Woods Run	1852	1	289
Morrison, John	10	Flat Woods Run	1855	2	40
Newlon, William	600	Crooked Fork	1844	1	28
O'Brien, Timothy (O'Brian)	400	Camp Fork	1854	1	425
O'Brien, Timothy	62	Camp Fork	1847	1	50
O'Brien, Timothy	50	Big Otter	1849	1	106
Parker, William W. et al	100	Wts. Elk	1847	1	51
Parker, William W. et al	49	Wts. Little Birch	1847	1	54
Parker, William W. et al	260	Long Run	1847	1	61
Parker, William W. et al	209	Bear Run	1847	1	62
Parker, William W. et al	220	Bear Run	1847	1	63
Parker, William W. et al	145	Sandy Fork	1847	1	64
Parker, William W. et al	126	Big Laurel	1847	1	65
Parker, William W. et al	143	Joe's Spring Knob	1847	1	66
Parker, William W. et al	138	Sandy Fork	1847	1	67
Parker, William W. et al	112	Bear Run	1847	1	68
Parker, William W. et al	450	Long Run	1847	1	69
Parker, William W. et al	300	Little Buffalo	1847	1	80
Parker, William W. et al	148	Little Birch	1849	1	111
Parker, William W. et al	400	Rush Fork	1850	1	165
Parker, William W. et al	100	Rush Fork	1851	1	232
Perkins, Elijah	117	Crooked Fork	1851	1	239
Perkins, Elijah	116	Crooked Fork	1851	1	240
Perkins, Elijah	200	Cedar Creek	1851	1	272
Perkins, Elijah	900	Wts. Cedar Creek	1857	2	91
Perkins, Elijah et al	1,280	Cedar Creek	1850	1	457
Perkins, William	102½	Little Otter Creek	1855	2	27
Perkins, William	110	Little Otter	1860	2	183
Perrine, Andrew	200	Laurel Creek	1855	2	12
Perrine, Henry	120	Back Fork	1853	1	327
Perrine, Henry et al	90	Shrieve's Run	1854	1	407
Perrine, Henry et al	140	Copen's Run	1854	1	408
Perrine, Lewis	63	Grass Lick	1844	1	29
Perrine, Lewis	100	Grass Lick	1845	1	36
Persinger, Martin	16	Wts Lit Kanawha	1859	2	153
Phares, John	75	Adj. C. Bickle	1855	2	29
Phares, John	39	Wts. of Elk	1852	1	288
Pierson, Albert	100	Wts. Little Birch	1857	2	76
Pierson, Elizabeth et al	950	Polemic Run	1858	2	95
Pierson, George W.	50	Wts. Big Birch	1859	2	144
Pierson, Henry	420	Laurel Run	1854	1	396
Pierson, Henry	100	Middle Run	1854	1	397
Pierson, Henry	90	Middle Run	1858	2	98
Pierson, Henry	20	Diatia Run	1860	2	160
Pierson, Jonathan	160	Bear Run	1847	1	58
Pierson, Jonathan	30	Middle Run	1847	1	59
Pierson, Jonathan	103	Hungary Springs	1852	1	315
Pierson, Johnathan et al	410	Diatia Run	1858	2	104
Pierson, Jonathan & Henry et al	200	Elk River	1849	1	125
Pierson, Washington	95	Middle Run	1854	1	424
Pierson, William G.	76	Big Buffalo	1847	1	53
Pierson, William G.	89	Big Buffalo	1852	1	299
Pierson, William G.	70	Wts. of Elk	1856	2	50
Pierson, William G.	190	Mill Creek	1858	2	113
Pierson, William G.	50	Lit. Otter	1858	2	129
Posey, Alfred et al	90	Oil Creek	1862	2	191
Posey, William	70	Oil Creek	1849	1	142
Posey, William	50	Oil Creek	1849	1	143
Pritt, James	122	Grassy Creek	1843	1	17
Pritt, James	175	Grassy Creek	1854	1	404
Pritt, James	75	Grassy Creek	1854	1	405
Rainer, John G. et al	273	Elk River	1854	1	427
Reap, Peter	125	Mill Creek	1853	1	338

Name of Grantee	Acres	Local Description	Year	Book	Page
Reap, Peter Sr.	30	Big Run	1853	1	339
Riffle, Jacob	85	O'Brien's Fork	1849	1	144
Riffle, William A.	190	O'Brien's Creek	1853	1	369
Riling, William	80	Wts. of Elk River	1853	1	349
Ritchy, Leonard	70	Walker's Fork	1855	2	28
Roberts, Jeremiah M.	15	Wts. Birch	1858	2	138
Roberts, Jeremiah M. et al	80	Bear Run	1853	1	356
Roberts, John	170	Buffalo	1849	1	135
Roberts, John	130	Buffalo Creek	1849	1	136
Roberts, John	125	Buffalo Creek	1851	1	285
Roberts, John	70	Buffalo Creek	1851	1	286
Roberts, John et al	500	Road Run	1860	2	173
Rogers, A. M.	135	Grass Lick	1853	1	360
Rogers, Alfred M.	45	Steer Creek	1849	1	137
Rogers, James A.	118	Rush Fork	1846	1	45
Rogers, James A.	100	Road Fork	1856	2	53
Rogers, James A.	508	Rush Fork	1856	2	54
Rogers, James A.	80	Rush Fork	1856	2	55
Rogers, James A.	37	Middle Fork	1858	2	112
Rogers, James A.	62½	West Fork	1851	1	256
Rogers, John	167	Little Otter	1847	1	78
Rogers, John	229	Little Otter	1858	2	114
Rogers, John A.	100	Bender's Run	1854	1	430
Rogers, Levi	80	Wts. of Elk	1851	1	275
Rogers, Philip Jr.	11	Salt Lick Creek	1855	1	445
Rogers, William F.	285	Little Otter	1849	1	112
Rogers, William F.	120	West Fork	1850	1	164
Rollyson, John	50	Duck Creek	1850	1	199
Rollyson, John	180	Duck Creek	1853	1	361
Rollyson, Martin	125	Otter Creek	1857	2	90
Rollyson, Martin	50	Triplett Fork	1850	1	207
Rollyson, Samuel E.	70	Shock's Mill Run	1853	1	372
Rose, Andrew M.	200	O'Brien's Creek	1852	1	287
Rose, Charles	50	Big Laurel	1848	1	94
Rose, Isaac	100	Grove's Creek	1854	1	441
Rose, Isaac	38	Wts. of Elk	1854	1	439
Rose, William	100	Middle Run	1858	2	100
Rose, William	100	Wts. Birch	1858	2	122
Rose, William	30	Diadda Run	1861	2	184
Rose, William	50	Sugar Camp Run	1861	2	185
Rose, William	20	Wts. of Birch	1861	2	186
Salsberry, John	50	Persimmon Hollow	1842	1	16
Sands, Matthew	84	Salt Lick	1838	1	9
Shaver, Jacob	180	Cedar Creek	1850	1	170
Shields, John M.	65	Cedar Creek	1854	1	436
Shields, John M.	80	Cedar Creek	1854	1	437
Shields, John M.	130	Wts. of Salt Lick	1856	2	58
Shock, Jacob	150	Steer Creek	1850	1	204
Shock, Jacob	88	Steer Creek	1850	1	215
Shock, Jacob	145	Shock's Barn Run	1851	1	216
Shock, Jacob	46	Bogg's Fork	1857	2	86
Shock, Jacob	230	Anthony Fork	1858	2	131
Siers, Isaac	70	Mud Lick Fork	1850	1	194
Siers, Isaac	80	West Fork	1853	1	350
Siers, John	50	West Fork	1849	1	122
Siers, John	80	Shock's Mill Run	1851	1	237
Siers, John	100	Shock's Mill Run	1851	1	248
Siers, John	106	West Fork	1853	1	374
Siers, John	50	West Fork	1858	2	123
Singleton, C. E. et al	224	Grass Run	1851	1	268
Singleton, C. E. et al	400	Byrne's Run	1851	1	269
Singleton, Charles E.	75	Salt Lick Creek	1852	1	311
Singleton, Charles E.	96	Salt Lick	1850	1	213

Name of Grantee	Acres	Local Description	Year	Book	Page
Singleton, Charles E.	1,000	Wts. Little Kanawha	1853	1	367
Singleton, Charles E.	100	Flat Woods Run	1859	2	147
Singleton, Charles E.	33	Cedar Branch	1860	2	166
Singleton, Charles E. et al	380	Salt Lick	1850	1	191
Singleton, Charles E. et al	50	Bickel's Fork	1852	1	307
Singleton, Charles E. et al	220	Clout Run	1852	1	308
Singleton, Charles E. et al	100	Cedar Creek	1855	2	11
Singleton, Charles E. et al	300	Bickle's Fork	1855	2	14
Singleton, Charles E. et al	80	Hughes' Fork	1855	2	15
Singleton, Charles E. et al	800	Hughes's Fork	1856	2	45
Singleton, F. F. et al	100	Bickle's Fork	1850	1	212
Singleton, French F.	110	Salt Lick Creek	1855	2	1
Singleton, French F.	35	Salt Lick Creek	1855	2	2
Singleton, French F.	303	Salt Lick Creek	1855	2	17
Singleton, French F.	100	Byrne's Run	1859	2	140
Singleton, French F.	190	Wts. of Elk	1860	2	163
Singleton, French F.	65	Rebecca Run	1862	2	190
Singleton, French F. et al	439	Wts. Lit. Kanawha	1850	1	211
Singleton, French F. et al	200	Grass Run	1852	1	304
Singleton, French F. et al	65	Bickle's Fork	1852	1	305
Singleton, French F. et al	264	Byrne's Run	1852	1	306
Singleton, French F. et al	128	Spring Run	1852	1	316
Singleton, French F. & U. W.	370(390)	Long Run	1855	2	13
Singleton, Samuel J.	45	Wts. O'Brien's Fork	1857	2	72
Singleton, Uriah W.	350	Salt Lick	1849	1	132
Singleton, Uriah W.	120	Grass Run	1859	2	158
Singleton, Uriah W.	100	Bickle's Fork	1860	2	165
Singleton, William K.	300	Right Hand Fork	1849	1	151
Singleton, William K.	100	Cedar Creek	1851	1	264
Singleton, William K.	100	Salt Lick Creek	1853	1	328
Singleton, William K.	175	Wts. of Salt Lick	1856	2	56
Singleton, William K.	200	Copen Run	1860	2	170
Singleton, William K.	120	Slab Camp Run	1860	2	171
Singleton, William K.	150	Salt Lick Creek	1860	2	172
Singleton, William K.	1,014	Wts. Salt Lick	1855	2	449
Skidmore, Andrew	50	Wts. Elk	1847	1	79
Skidmore, Thomas et al	155	Flat Woods Run	1848	1	100
Skinner, Alexander Trustee	300	Salt Lick Creek	1854	1	385
Skinner, Alexander Tr.	141	Wts. Lit. Kanawha	1854	1	414
Skinner, Alexander Tr.	1,080	Salt Lick Creek	1854	1	461
Smith, Michael	91	Cedar Creek	1849	1	107
Squires, Elijah	265	Salt Lick Creek	1852	1	301
Squires, Elijah	75	Salt Lick Creek	1853	1	332
Stephenson, John D. et al	550	Wts. Lit. Birch	1857	2	68
Stewart, George W.	150	Road Run	1856	2	43
Stout, John W.	275	Cedar Creek	1853	1	380
Stout, Michael	125	Westfall Fork	1858	2	121
Stout, Michael	200	Westfall Fork	1858	2	134
Stout, Sylvester	80	Copen Run	1849	1	147
Stout, Sylvester	97	Copen Creek	1850	1	200
Stout, Sylvester	96	Copen Run	1850	1	201
Stout, Sylvester	86	Copen Run	1854	1	389
Stout, Sylvester	376	Copen Run	1854	1	390
Stout, Thomas B.	84	O'Brien's Fork	1856	2	62
Stout, William	89	Wts. Little Kanawha	1850	1	169
Stout, William	240	Copen Run	1850	1	202
Stout, William	102	Hyer's Run	1851	1	247
Stout, William	102	Wts. Lit. Kanawha	1852	1	294
Stout, William	210	Copen Run	1854	1	386
Stout, William	404	Hyer's Run	1854	1	387
Stout, William	190	Cedar Creek	1854	1	388
Stout, William	453	Cedar Creek	1851	1	458
Stout, William	50	Wts. Lit. Kanawha	1858	2	120

Name of Grantee	Acres	Local Description	Year	Book	Page
Stout, William	110	Wts. Little Kanawha	1860	2	162
Stump, Jesse	100	Copen Run	1853	1	382
Stump, Miranda H.	516	Wts. Lit. Kanawha	1854	1	402
Stump, Miranda H.	220	Copen Run	1854	1	403
Tharp, Samuel	125	Elk River	1849	1	131
Tharp, Samuel	130	Wts. of Elk	1855	2	16
Tomblinson, Isaac	200	Laurel Fork	1851	1	257
Truman, Shederick	95	Sleath Creek	1853	1	333
Westfall, Jacob W.	100	Scott's Camp Fork	1854	1	440
White, John W.	312	Wts. Lit. Kanawha	1860	2	164
Williams, Bazel L.	105	Log Shoal Run	1848	1	88
Williams, Elizabeth	50	Big Run	1838	1	6
Williams, Jane	180	Back Fork	1856	2	42
Williams, Margaret	100	Wts. Holly River	1851	1	258
Williams, Samuel S.	50	Big Run	1838	1	7
Williams, Thomas O.	60	Lime Kiln Run	1859	2	143
Wilson, William M. et al	150	Mill Creek	1860	2	169
Wood, James	17	Wts. of Elk	1855	2	34
Wyatt, John H.	65	Steer Creek	1849	1	108
Wyatt, John H.	380	Grass Lick	1853	1	364
Yancey, Charles	45	Kanawha River	1849	1	141
Yancey, Charles	127	Oil Creek	1850	1	184
Yancey, James M.	342	Oil Creek	1854	1	394
Young, Henry	40	Elk River	1849	1	123
Young, Henry	83	Rose's Run	1851	1	276
Young, Henry	100	Strange Creek	1852	1	295
Young, Johnathan	35	Big Run	1858	2	101
Young, Johnathan	186	Wts. Big Birch	1858	2	102

BROOKE COUNTY

Adams, William	65	Buffalo Creek	1805	1	500
Alexander, James Adm.	41	Holbert's Run	1816	1	320
Allison, James	424	Tomlinson's Run	1804	1	496
Aten, William	19a.3r.37p.	Harden's Run	1845	1	372
Atkinson, George	384	Adj. R. Wells	1800	1	470
Atkinson, Joseph	34a.3r.39p.	Harmon's Creek	1842	1	353
Baker, Catherine et al	430	Buffalo Creek	1802	1	468
Baker, Nathan	20	Adj. D. McLead	1810	1	510
Baxter, William	400	Harmon's Creek	1798	1	456
Beard, John	691	Cor. to Richard Wells	1801	1	469
Beard, John	128	McMahan's Run	1804	1	497
Beaver, John	13	Island Ohio River	1799	1	458
Beck, John W.	18a.119p.	Long Run	1860	1	376
Blair, Runnel	8a.56p.	Newland's Run	1809	1	509
Boner, George	4a.2r.22p.	Hoglan's Run	1840	1	347
Brown, Jacob	23a.1r.12p.	2-Islands Ohio River	1842	1	352
Brown, James W.	5a.3r.10p.	King's Creek	1843	1	363
Brown, James W.	5a.24p.	Island in Ohio R.	1843	1	364
Brown, John	5a.3r.29p.	Island Ohio River	1842	1	354
Burgoyne, Joshua R.	9	Island in Ohio R.	1848	1	375
Cain, Walter	360	Buffalo Creek	1803	1	487
Calendine, Daniel	53a.8prchs.	Buffalo Creek	1817	1	516
Cameron, Joseph	24a.1r.14p.	Adj. J. Bane	1843	1	368
Campbell, James	400	Harmon's Creek	1810	1	511
Cantwell, Nancy et al	430	Buffalo Creek	1802	1	468
Cellor, Jas. (or Jos.)	80	West's Mill Dam	1802	1	473

Name of Grantee	Acres	Local Description	Year	Book	Page
Cochran, Jacob	33	Adj. J. Farris	1809	1	506
Cochran, Jacob	20	Adj. Charles Blackmore	1809	1	507
Cochran, Jacob	43¾	Adj. Cochran & McGovern	1810	1	512
Cochran, John	6a.17p.	Adj. D. Benward's	1841	1	350
Connell, John (Lots)	No. 26 & No. 70	Wellsburg	1821	1	516
Connell, Solomon	7a.64p.	Pierce's Run	1812	1	315
Connell, Solomon	53a.80p.	Panther's Run	1812	1	316
Connell, Solomon	62	Hermon's Creek	1816	1	319
Crider, John	8a.1r.13p.	Adj. S. Elliott	1836	1	336
Dodridge, Philip et al	129	McMachan's Run	1802	1	483
Downing, James	380	White Oak Run	1802	1	472
Durben, John	44	Adj. E. Hart	1808	1	504
Edgington, Jesse (Edington)	9a.3r.16p.	Buffalo Creek	1835	1	330
Edie, John	86	Robert's Run	1809	1	508
Edie, John	38½	Island Ohio River	1803	1	480
Edington or Edgington					
Edington, George	32	Cor. Wm. Griffith	1802	1	467
Faris, John	70½	Adj. Jacob Cochran	1810	1	513
Fowler, Daniel	5a.3r.22p.	Cross Creek	1836	1	333
Freshwater, Reuben	13a.2r.13p.	Herman's Creek	1835	1	325
Freshwater, Reuben	18a.59p.	Adj. Wm. Adams	1809	1	506
Freshwater, Reuben Sr.	30a.75p.	Harmon's Creek	1835	1	328
Frue, Alexander (Frew)	11a.2r.36p.	Adj. J. McCormack	1811	1	515
Gallagher, David	46a.1r.14p.	White Oak Run	1841	1	349
Greathouse, John	465	Muckmore's Bottom	1805	1	499
Griffith, James	200	Adj. J. Swearingen	1803	1	484
Griffith, James	13½	Adj. Sam'l Robinson	1803	1	487
Griffith, James	10a.37p.	Adj. J. Campbell	1804	1	495
Griffith, William	14a.55p.	Island Ohio River	1808	1	502
Hartford, Robert	118½	Buffalo Creek	1803	1	482
Hedges, Joseph	300	Buffalo Creek	1800	1	460
Hedges, Joseph Sr.	70	Short Creek	1800	1	462
Hibbitt, William	14¾	White Oak Run	1833	1	324
Hunter, John et al	11a.3r.35p,	Harmon's Creek	1836	1	334
Hunter, John et al	43½	Harmon's Creek	1836	1	335
Jarrett—See Jarrard					
Jarrard, Thomas (Jarrett)	931½	Tomlinson's Run	1804	1	493
Jarrard, Thomas (Jarrett)	110a.60p.	Tomlinson's Run	1807	1	501
Johnson, Abel	11	Cross Creek	1799	1	457
Johnson, Joseph	22a.24p.	Harmon's Creek	1835	1	329
Johnston, Benjamin	22a.87p.	Cross Creek	1838	1	345
Jones, Isaac et al	11a.3r.35p.	Harmon's Creek	1836	1	334
Jones, Isaac et al	43½	Harmon's Creek	1836	1	335
Jones, Isaac Sr.	6a.2r.17p.	Adj. J. Wiggins	1836	1	331
Jones, Isaac Sr.	18a.7p.	Cross Creek	1836	1	332
Jones, William	9a.3r.7p.	Cross Creek	1843	1	361
Jones, William	21a.6p.	Grog Run	1843	1	362
Jones, William	2a.109p.	Mill Creek	1845	1	370
Kerr, John	400	Adj. Wm. Baxter	1804	1	491
Kerr, John	60½	Adj. John Relf	1804	1	495
Kincade, James	11a.100p.	Adj. Wm. Adams	1809	1	511
Lee, Joshua	2a.5p.	Cross Creek	1810	1	514
Marks, Samuel E.	41a.3r.8p.	Adj. Col. W. Chambers	1843	1	358
Marks, Samuel E.	46a.35p.	Adj. Squire Scott's Hrs.	1843	1	359
Marsh, James	11a.150p.	Harmon's Creek	1846	1	374
Marshall, Aaron	75a.114p.	Tomlinson's Run	1809	1	505
McConnell, John	222a.3r.17p.	Buffalo Creek	1835	1	326
McConnell, Richard	8a.3r.18p.	Buffalo Creek	1835	1	327
McCullock, George Jr.	400	Buffalo Creek	1800	1	463
McCurdy, William	26	Tomlinson's Run	1830	1	323
McGovern, Mark	38	Adj. J. Cochran	1803	1	486
Meek, Garrett C.	16a.18p.	Cross Creek	1845	1	371
Meeks, Samuel	82p	Cross Creek	1818	1	321
Moore, David et al	35	Buffalo Creek	1815	1	318

Name of Grantee	Acres	Local Description	Year	Book	Page
Moore, John	14	Buffalo Creek	1803	1	489
Moore, Robert	Lot No. 239	Wellsburg	1821	1	517
Moore, Robert T.	60	Cor. George Cox	1807	1	501
Moorehead, Alexander	58a.9p.	King's Creek	1844	1	369
Moorehead, Alexander (Morehead)	156prchs.	King's Creek	1842	1	351
Murphy, Elizabeth et al Hrs.	400	Tomlinson's Run	1804	1	491
Murray, James	33a.1r.35p.	Cor. J. Blackbourn	1845	1	373
Nesley, Jacob	2,674	Tomlinson's Run	1802	1	464
Newhouse, Benjamin et al	1 Lot	Federal St. (Charlestown) now Wellsburg	1837	1	338
Owings, Asa	15	Adj. J. Hunter	1803	1	479
Parkinson, George	8a.3r.30p.	Mingo Run	1837	1	339
Parkinson, George	3a.8p.	Wells Run	1837	1	340
Parkinson, George	8a.1r.6p.	Mingo Run	1837	1	341
Patterson, John	113	Castleman's Run	1803	1	490
Patton, A. J.	3a.2r.30p.	Pierce's Run	1843	1	355
Patton, William	13a.9pchs.	Buffalo Creek	1843	1	356
Patton, William	4a.2r.20p.	Buffalo Creek	1843	1	357
Patton, William	7a.3r. 15p.	Buffalo Creek	1843	1	365
Patton, William	4a.3r.24p.	Adj. DeLong & Peter Keller	1843	1	366
Patton, William	53a.22p.	Buffalo Creek	1843	1	367
Priest, Henry	18a.62p.	Cross Creek	1810	1	513
Ralston, Samuel	42	Adj. Robt. Parks	1809	1	509
Reeves, Josiah	35a.153p.	Cross Creek	1819	1	322
Reeves, Josiah	222	King's Creek	1803	1	485
Russell, James et al Hrs.	1 Lot	Federal St. (Charlestown) now Wellsburg	1837	1	338
Silvers, Edward M.	8a.1r.16p.	Ogle's Run	1837	1	342
Silvers, Edward M.	4a.22p.	Buffalo Creek	1837	1	343
Silvers, Edward M.	1a.3r.38p.	Ogle's Run	1837	1	344
Sinclair, William	74	Tomlinson's Run	1800	1	458
Sinclair, William	541	Harmon's Creek	1800	1	459
Sinclair, William	85	Tomlinson's Run	1800	1	461
Smith, Edward	3a.26p.	Pierce's Run	1843	1	360
Strain, Catherine et al Hrs.	I Lot	Federal St. (Charlestown) now Wellsburg	1837	1	338
Sutherland, William et al	129	McMachan's Run	1802	1	483
Swearingen, Daniel	88a.20p.	King's Creek	1840	1	348
Swearingen, Daniel	37	Adj. Samuel Swearingen	1802	1	475
Swearingen, Daniel	504	Adj. William Barnes	1802	1	476
Talbot, Elisha (Talbott)	12¾	Buffalo Creek	1840	1	346
Talbot, Richard	4a.2r.29p.	Buffalo Creek	1811	1	314
Thorp, William	6a.	Pierce's Run	1808	1	503
Walker, Jacob	400	Adj. McMahon's Line	1808	1	503
Wallace, William	6A.21p.	Harmon's Creek	1836	1	337
Wells, Alexander Sr.	5	Buffalo Creek	1810	1	514
Wells, Caleb	5	Pierce's Run	1813	1	317
Wells, Caleb	350	Buffalo Creek	1804	1	493
Wiggins, Thomas	50	Cross Creek	1800	1	463
Wilcoxon, Anthony	180	Adj. John Wilcoxon	1803	1	478
Wilcoxon, Anthony	54	Adj. Roger Hill	1808	1	505
Wilcoxon, John	235	Adj. Joakim Wickoff	1802	1	475
Williams, Catherine et al	430	Buffalo Creek	1802	1	468
Williams, John et al	430	Buffalo Creek	1802	1	468
Williamson, John et al	35	Buffalo Creek	1815	1	318
Willson, Samuel	9a.1r.34p.	Buffalo Creek	1829	1	518
Wilson, James	15	Island Ohio River	1803	1	481
Work, David	145½	Tomlinson's Run	1804	1	498
Wyckoff, Joakim	294	Adj. Wm. Hedgson	1802	1	474
Wylie, John	111	Adj. J. Campbell	1803	1	477
Wylie, John	93	Adj. J. McMillian	1803	1	481
Young, John G.	200	Adj. D. Greathouse	1802	1	471
Young, John G.	9a.63p.	King's Creek	1809	1	507

CABELL COUNTY

Name of Grantee	Acres	Local Description	Year	Book	Page
Acres—See Aken, Akers					
Acres, Robert	115	Hurricane Cr.	1838	3	346
Acres, Stephen	40	Hurricane Cr.	1843	4	11
Adams, Nathaniel S.	100	Fall Creek	1845	4	49
Adams, Robert	120	Wts. of Ohio	1812	1	45
Adams, William et al	100	Mill Creek	1823	2	238
Adkins, Alexander	65	Wts. of Mud	1850	4	422
Adkins, Anderson	32	Wts. of Mud	1851	4	460
Adkins, Anderson	88	Main Fork	1857	5	373
Adkins, Anderson	64	Main Fork	1857	5	374
Adkins, Archibald	240	Beech Fork	1838	3	153
Adkins, Bartlett	44	Wts. of Mud	1833	2	414
Adkins, Calvin	175	Raccoon Fork	1861	5	441
Adkins, Charles	50	Beech Fork	1827	2	314
Adkins, Charles	135	Beech Fork	1838	3	152
Adkins, Charles	75	Rock Camp Br.	1842	3	498
Adkins, David	1,000	Big Creek	1851	4	442
Adkins, Elias	100	Beech Fork	1816	2	85
Adkins, Elisha	95	Beech Fork	1838	3	211
Adkins, Goldsberry	92	Wts. of Mud	1845	4	48
Adkins, Henry	250	Sulphur Spg. Fork	1845	4	72
Adkins, Hezekiah	105	12 Pole Creek	1812	1	32
Adkins, Hezekiah	80	Wts. Guyan	1834	2	487
Adkins, Hezekiah Jr.	60	Beech Fork	1825	2	288
Adkins, Hezekiah Jr.	165	Beech Fork	1838	3	155
Adkins, Hezekiah Jr.	70	Beech Fork	1838	3	156
Adkins, Hezekiah & L.	100	Beech Fork	1813	1	99
Adkins, Hiram	125	Beech Fork	1836	2	510
Adkins, Hiram	20	Mill Seat Br.	1841	3	440
Adkins, Hiram	325	Big Creek	1855	5	282
Adkins, Hiram	315	Big Creek	1859	5	427
Adkins, Isaac	250	Trace Fork	1813	1	55
Adkins, Isaac	60	Beech Fork	1824	2	256
Adkins, Isaiah	90	Beech Fork	1834	2	478
Adkins, Isaiah	50	Smith's Br.	1843	4	14
Adkins, Isiah	50	Beech Fork	1838	3	154
Adkins, Jacob	300	Beech Fork	1812	1	44
Adkins, Jacob	150	Lick Creek	1837	3	75
Adkins, Jacob Jr.	40	Beech Fork	1838	3	212
Adkins, Jacob Jr.	105	Cor to G. Rogers	1838	3	273
Adkins, Jacob Jr.	250(350)	Wts. Guyandotte	1838	3	275
Adkins, Jacob Jr.	90	12 Pole Cr.	1843	4	13
Adkins, Jacob Jr. & Jesse	100	Wts. of Guyandotte	1838	3	274
Adkins, Jacob Sr.	30	Mill Seat Br.	1842	3	464
Adkins, James A.	90	Beech Fork	1848	4	195
Adkins, Jesse	110	Wts. of Guyandotte	1838	3	270
Adkins, Jesse	35	Beech Fork	1838	3	272
Adkins, John	15	Beech Fork	1838	3	320
Adkins, John	60	Beech Fork	1838	3	321
Adkins, John	25	Right Hand Fork	1838	3	381
Adkins, John C.	60	Trace Fork	1850	4	348
Adkins, John G.	25	Stone Coal Br.	1851	4	440
Adkins, John R.	25	Beach Fork	1838	3	345
Adkins, John T.	100	10 Mile Creek	1851	4	457
Adkins, John T.	37	4 Mile Creek	1858	5	406
Adkins, John T. et al	160	10 Mile Creek	1850	4	344
Adkins, Joseph	205	6 Mile Creek	1849	4	234
Adkins, Joseph	50	Pheasant Cr.	1851	4	441
Adkins, Joseph & John	50	Six Mile Cr.	1849	4	235
Adkins, Lewis	50	Wts. of Guyandotte	1845	4	52
Adkins, Lewis	350	Wts. of Guyandotte	1848	4	177

Name of Grantee	Acres	Local Description	Year	Book	Page
Adkins, Lewis	75	Wts. of Guyand.	1848	4	184
Adkins, Lewis	95	Wts. of Guyand.	1849	4	266
Adkins, Lewis	100	Wts. of Guyand.	1849	4	267
Adkins, Lewis	116	14 Mile Creek	1856	5	354
Adkins, Lewis et al	325	Sulphur Spring Fork	1855	5	307
Adkins, Little B.	60	Raccoon Fork	1817	2	91
Adkins, Little B.	25	Laurel Creek	1838	3	344
Adkins, Little B. Jr.	40	12 Pole Creek	1838	3	296
Adkins, Little B. Sr.	44	12 Pole Cr	1843	4	15
Adkins, Littleberry	70	Stephenson's Fk	1813	1	100
Adkins, Luke	80	Laurel Creek	1838	3	376
Adkins, Luke	25	Right Hand Fork	1838	3	378
Adkins, Luke	37	Big Creek	1838	3	379
Adkins, Luke	108	Big Laurel	1846	4	79
Adkins, Luke	41	Wts. of Mud	1846	4	80
Adkins, Luke	325	Wts. of Mud	1849	4	257
Adkins, Mark	42	Left Hand Fork	1838	3	377
Adkins, Mark	72	Wts. of Mud	1845	4	53
Adkins, Millington	325	Smith's Creek	1846	4	109
Adkins, Milington et al	148	Guyandotte River	1854	5	254
Adkins, Parker	130	Beech Fork	1834	2	484
Adkins, Parker Jr.	50	Raccoon Fork	1838	3	392
Adkins, Parker & Richard	25	10 Mile Creek	1838	3	382
Adkins, Price	57	Fall Creek	1845	4	46
Adkins, Price	50	Fall's Branch	1845	4	51
Adkins, Price	27	Fall Creek	1854	5	274
Adkins, Price	10	Straley Branch	1853	5	227
Adkins, Randal	20	Four Mi Cr	1836	2	508
Adkins, Randal	45	Raccoon Fork	1848	4	208
Adkins, Randall	45	Raccoon Creek	1845	4	50
Adkins, Randolph	45	Raccoon Fork	1813	1	76
Adkins, Randolph	50	Ten Mile Cr	1838	3	271
Adkins, Randolph	150	10 Mile Creek	1838	3	380
Adkins, Richard	25	Stout's Branch	1836	3	30
Adkins, Richard	86	10 Mile Cr	1850	4	418
Adkins, Richard	300	Stout's Creek	1856	5	339
Adkins, Richard & Alfred	164	Stout's Creek	1859	5	432
Adkins, Richard et al	41	10 Mile Creek	1857	5	357
Adkins, Samuel	230	Ten Mile Cr.	1850	4	310
Adkins, Samuel	48	4 Mile Creek	1858	5	396
Adkins, Samuel	34	Low Gap Branch	1859	5	425
Adkins, Samuel	92	10 Mile Creek	1859	5	431
Adkins, Samuel	2	Stout's Creek	1859	5	435
Adkins, Samuel et al	106	10 Mile Creek	1855	5	293
Adkins, Samuel et al	402	10 Mile Creek	1856	5	342
Adkins, Samuel & G. S.	61	10 Mile Creek	1859	5	429
Adkins, Sherod	200	Beech Fork	1812	1	39
Adkins, Sherod	85	Beech Fork	1813	1	89
Adkins, Sherod	115	Lick Creek	1823	2	235
Adkins, Sherod	115	12 Pole Creek	1823	2	236
Adkins, Sherod	20	12 Pole Cr.	1823	2	246
Adkins, Sherod	62	Beech Fork	1823	2	247
Adkins, Sherod	12	Beech Fork	1828	2	323
Adkins, Sherod	25	Cove Creek	1834	2	422
Adkins, Sherod	8	12 Pole	1834	2	428
Adkins, Sherod	70	12 Pole Cr	1838	3	157
Adkins, Sherod Jr.	100	Beech Fork	1838	3	394
Adkins, Sherod Jr. et al	80	Beech Fork	1838	3	388
Adkins, Sylvester	50	Lick Fork	1853	5	224
Adkins, Thomas T.	110	Trace Creek	1851	4	451
Adkins, William	60	12 Pole Creek	1837	3	66
Adkins, William	105	Beech Fork	1838	3	322
Adkins, William	325	Cove Cr.	1838	3	323

Name of Grantee	Acres	Local Description	Year	Book	Page
Adkins, William	32	Trace Fork	1846	4	81
Adkins, William	50	Trace Fork	1846	4	82
Adkins, William	140	4 Mile Cr.	1850	4	311
Adkins, William	14	Four Mile Creek	1850	4	312
Adkins, William	53	Trace Fork	1856	5	316
Aken, Acres Akers					
Aken, Stephen (Akers)	275	Hurricane Cr.	1843	4	12
Akers, Stephen (Aken)	275	Hurricane Cr.	1843	4	12
Alford, James	90	Middle Fork	1848	4	185
Alford, James	75	Middle Fork	1850	4	292
Alford, James	70	Middle Fork	1856	5	350
Alford, James	30	Wts. of Mud	1857	5	364
Alford, John	100	Camp Creek	1849	4	268
Alford, John	150	Merrit's Creek	1852	5	203
Alford, Mary	42	Wts. of Mud	1836	2	509
Alford, Mary	50	Middle Fork	1838	3	396
Alford, Robert	250	Straight Fork	1838	3	395
Alford, Wm. et al Heirs	105	Middle Fork	1838	3	397
Alford, Wm. et al Heirs	130	Middle Fork	1838	3	398
Anderson, Jackson et al	150	12 Pole Cr.	1830	2	344
Ansel, Martin	165	Goose Run	1838	3	295
Ansel, Martin	137	9 Mile Creek	1848	4	209
Armstrong, John	23	Adj. E. Daniel	1811	1	13
Arthur, Isaac	23	Lower Creek	1838	3	393
Arthur, Thomas	24	Cabell Creek	1833	2	395
Arthur, Thomas	20	Cabell Creek	1838	3	297
Artrip or Autrip					
Artrip, William et al	100	Left Hd. Fk	1815	2	24
Artrip, William	25	Tug Fork	1833	2	413
Ashworth, Isaac	133	Big Creek	1834	2	489
Ashworth, Isaac et al	220	Trace Fork	1832	2	350
Ashworth, James	170	Bee Branch	1850	4	309
Ashworth, James A.	50	Trace Fork	1845	4	47
Ashworth, John	125	Trace Fork	1838	3	209
Ashworth, Jonathan	58	Trace Fork	1838	3	210
Ashworth, Michael J.	95	Big Creek	1850	4	308
Ausben or Ausborn, Osborne, Osburn					
Ausben, Edmund	33	12 Pole Cr.	1830	2	331
Ausborn, John	50	12 Pole Cr.	1821	2	197
Ausborn, John	22	12 Pole Creek	1823	2	240
Austin, Alexander	38	Buffalo Cr.	1825	2	270
Autrip—See Artrip					
Baker, John L.	20	Wts. of Guyand.	1848	4	221
Baker, John L.	40	Wts. of Guyandotte	1848	4	222
Baker, John L. et al	225	Ten Mile Cr.	1850	4	368
Baker, John L. et al	135	Ten Mile Creek	1853	5	212
Baker, John L. et al	173	Wts. Guyandotte	1855	5	308
Baker, Nathaniel	17	Meeting House Br.	1842	3	494
Baker, Nathaniel	12½	Adj. John Pratt	1843	4	10
Ball, George et al	95	Joe's Branch	1842	3	482
Ball, James	50	Mill Creek	1866	2	77
Ball, James	130	Mill Creek	1818	2	139
Ball, James	70	Mill Cr.	1818	2	140
Ball, James	25	Mill Creek	1825	2	287
Ball, John	85	Camp Creek	1815	2	12
Ball, Robert	44	12 Pole Cr.	1827	2	305
Ball, Sarah	70	Left Hand Fork	1838	3	347
Ball, Sarah	12½	Sycamore Cr.	1847	4	119
Ball, Zachariah	200	Kilgore's Cr.	1838	3	327
Ballard, James & John W.	800	Sugar Tree Fork	1850	4	384
Ballard, Perry	55	Middle Fork	1850	4	351
Ballard, Perry et al	330	Middle Fork	1850	4	349
Ballard, Perry et al	1,260	Bear Fork	1850	4	350

Name of Grantee	Acres	Local Description	Year	Book	Page
Ballard, Philip Sr.	50	Spruce Fork	1822	2	234
Ballard, St. Clair et al	850	Wts. of Mud	1850	4	389
Ballard, St. Clair et al	1,400	Big Creek	1850	4	390
Ballard, St. Clair et al	525	Trace Fork	1850	4	391
Barner or Barnet					
Barner, John	150	Davis Creek	1813	1	62
Barner, John	25	Fudge's Creek	1813	1	64
Barner, John	60	Fudge's Creek	1818	2	129
Barnet—See Barner					
Barnhart, Jacob	100	Wts. Guyandotte	1813	1	94
Barnhart, Peter	125	Ocley's Gap	1819	2	153
Barret, See Barrett, Barritt, Barrott					
Barret, Edward	150	Wts. of Mud	1812	1	23
Barret, John et al	200	Middle Fork	1812	1	26
Barret, Joseph	25	Wts. Guyandotte	1812	1	22
Barrett, Andrew	100	Wts. of Mud	1836	3	17
Barrett, Andrew	140	Middle Fork	1838	3	399
Barrett, Andrew	200	Big Creek	1838	3	400
Barrett, Andrew	25	Wts. of Mud	1842	3	501
Barrett, Andrew	40	Big Laurel Cr.	1842	3	523
Barrett, Andrew	161	Merritt's Cr.	1844	4	24
Barrett, Andrew	100	Middle Fork	1816	2	65
Barrett, Andrew	80	Middle Fork	1817	2	99
Barrett, Andrew	125	Sugar Tree Fk.	1817	2	101
Barrett, Andrew	46	Rt. Hd. Fork	1822	2	224
Barrett, Andrew	80	Middle Fork	1836	2	527
Barrett, Andrew	170	Middle Fork	1836	2	534
Barrett, Andrew et al	145	Wts. of Guyandotte	1837	3	106
Barrett, Andrew et al	450	Wts. of Mud	1817	2	102
Barrett, Andrew et al	120	Trace Fork	1820	2	171
Barrett, Andrew J. & J. A.	79	Merritt's Creek	1857	5	381
Barrett, Blackburn E.	128	Sycamore Fork	1838	3	415
Barrett, Blackburn E.	30	Wts. of Mud	1843	4	16
Barrett, Blackburn E.	58	Sugar Tree Fork	1843	4	17
Barrett, Blackburn E. et al	850	Wts. of Mud	1850	4	389
Barrett, Blackburn E. et al	1,400	Big Creek	1850	4	390
Barrett, Blackburn E. et al	525	Trace Fork	1850	4	391
Barrett, Harvey (or Hervey)	200	Trace Creek	1850	4	387
Barrett, Harvey et al	28	Wts. of Mud	1850	4	388
Barrett, Henry	380	Wts. of Mud	1850	4	385
Barrett, Hervey (Harvey)	3	Trace Creek	1850	4	386
Barrett, James & Andrew	250	Middle Fork	1816	2	69
Barrett, John	100	Scary Creek	1820	2	172
Barrett, John & Joseph	100	Middle Fork	1816	2	58
Barrett, Joseph & Andrew	100	Middle Fork	1817	2	98
Barrett, Joseph et al	330	Middle Fork	1850	4	349
Barrett, Joseph et al	1,260	Bear Fork	1850	4	350
Barrett, Samuel	235	Middle Fork	1816	2	59
Barrett, Samuel	130	Big Buffalo	1818	2	143
Barritt, Andrew	200	Middle Fork	1814	1	138
Barritt, Andrew & John	100	Middle Fork	1815	2	55
Barritt, Edward	50	Wts. of Mud	1815	2	53
Barritt, John	50	Fall Creek	1815	2	54
Barritt, John & Joseph	100	Middle Fork	1815	2	33
Barrott, Edward	388	4 Mile Creek	1813	1	81
Bartrum, David	50	Beech Fork	1817	2	97
Bartrum, David	150	12 Pole Cr.	1822	2	225
Bartrum, William	40	Bartrum's Br.	1837	3	96
Bauer, Joseph	82	Huett's Fork	1818	2	121
Bays, Henry	25	Poplar Fork	1859	5	422
Bean, Stephen (Been)	50	Wts. of Sandy	1812	1	51
Beckett, Andrew L.	25	Fudge's Cr.	1847	4	118
Beckett, James	100	Fudge's Creek	1837	3	118

Name of Grantee	Acres	Local Description	Year	Book	Page
Beckett, James	120	Hervey's Cr.	1843	4	2
Beckett, James Jr.	35	Trace Creek	1837	3	119
Beckett, Moses	25	Charlie's Cr.	1834	2	461
Beckett, Moses	20	Charlie's Cr.	1838	3	245
Beckett, Thomas	75	Trace Fork	1838	3	277
Beckett, Thomas	250	Trace Fork	1847	4	117
Beckett, William	125	Trace Fork	1838	3	276
Beckett, William	240	Trace Fork	1850	4	405
Beckett, William	95	Sycamore Cr.	1832	2	355
Beckett, William	52	Trace Fork	1834	2	456
Belcher, Ali	10	Rt Hd Fork	1838	3	137
Bellamy, Mathew S.	345	Wts. of Sandy	1841	3	441
Bench See Bunch					
Bench, Lewis	75	12 Pole Creek	1842	3	497
Beuhring or Buhering					
Beuhring, F. G. L.	32	Adj. J. Savage	1835	2	496
Bias, Daniel	370	Merritt's Cr.	1846	4	86
Bias, James	100	Fall Creek	1848	4	225
Bias, James F.	233	Trace Creek	1854	5	255
Bias, John	30	9 Mile Creek	1838	3	299
Bias, Obadiah	45	14 Mile Cr.	1835	2	501
Bias, Obadiah Sr.	100	Tyler's Creek	1815	2	7
Bias, Obadiah Sr. et al	75	Wts. of Guyandotte	1815	2	20
Bias, Roland	145	Merritt's Cr.	1831	2	336
Bias, Roland	100	Wts. of Mud	1836	2	517
Bias, Roland	57	Merritt's Cr.	1847	4	159
Bias, Roland et al	65	Scary Creek	1848	4	178
Bias, Rolen	82	Stinson's Cr.	1842	3	492
Bias, Rolen	42	Left Hand Fork	1842	3	493
Bias, Rolen	48	Right Hand Fk.	1842	3	500
Bias, Rowland S.	8	Trace Creek	1856	5	351
Billips, William	200	Hurricane Creek	1837	3	69
Billups, Peter	180	Teas Valley	1838	3	401
Billups, Peter	100	Sycamore Creek	1854	5	258
Billups, William	175	Big Hurricane	1831	2	332
Billups, William	125	Hurricane Cr.	1834	2	454
Billups, William	75	Teas Valley	1834	2	455
Billups, William	20	Mill Seat Br.	1838	3	218
Billups, William	205	Hurricane Cr.	1838	3	219
Black, Adam	90	Adj. J. Black	1838	3	207
Black, Adam et al	2½	Adj. A. Jordan	1838	3	326
Black, Jacob	90	Sander's Cr.	1820	2	173
Black, James C.	48	Wts. of Mud	1837	3	94
Black, James C.	27	Main Fork	1859	5	424
Black, James C. et al	850	Wts. of Mud	1838	3	158
Black, James C. et al	754	Main Fork	1855	5	302
Black, James C. et al	650	Big Creek	1856	5	459
Black, James C. et al	3,350	Nine Mile Cr.	1856	5	460
Black, James C. et al	1,970	Trace Fork	1856	5	461
Black, John (Brock) et al	100	Dry Creek	1852	5	445
Black, John et al	575	Sander's Cr.	1848	4	183
Blair, John	100	Wts. of Sandy	1825	2	268
Blake, Jeremiah	30	Cabell Creek	1838	3	298
Blake, Jeremiah	20	Cabell Creek	1833	2	394
Blake, Morris	100	Wts. of Mud	1838	3	151
Blake, Penal	50	Cabell Cr.	1838	3	246
Blake, Peter	22	Adj. P. Danting	1833	2	369
Blankenship, William P.	50	Wts. Guyandotte	1854	5	232
Blenner, Daniel et al	700	Tabour's Cr.	1820	2	180
Blenner, Daniel et al	320	Wts. Sandy	1820	2	181
Blenner, Daniel et al	2,500	Tabour's Creek	1818	2	537
Blevins, Levi	90	Blue Lick Br.	1842	3	495
Bloomer, See Blumer, Blenner					

Name of Grantee	Acres	Local Description	Year	Book	Page
Bloomer, Daniel et al (Blumer)	700	Tabour's Cr.	1820	2	180
Bloomer, Daniel et al (Blumer)	320	Wts. of Sandy	1820	2	181
Bloomer, Daniel et al	2,500	Tabour's Creek	1818	2	537
Bloss, Hiram	22	Laurel Creek	1842	3	496
Boatright, James	40	Rocket Creek	1825	2	286
Boner, Joseph	82	Huett's Fork	1818	2	121
Booten, See Booton					
Booten, Asa	60	Beech Fork	1834	2	437
Booten, Reuben	118	Beech Fork	1813	1	71
Booton, Laban	150	Beech Fork	1812	1	20
Bostick, Manoah	150	Four Pole Cr.	1819	2	150
Bostick, Manoah	450	Adj. John Savage	1819	2	151
Bowen, Abner	26	Wts. Guyandotte	1837	3	120
Bowen, Alderson	25	12 Pole	1841	3	449
Bowen, Alderson	325	Beech Fork	1848	4	203
Bowen, Alderson	55	Madison Creek	1850	4	352
Bowen, Alderson	100	Raccoon Fork	1854	5	234
Bowen, Ann F.	18	12 Pole Creek	1858	5	405
Bowen, Hugha	35	Beech Fork	1815	2	48
Bowen, Hugha	140	Beech Fork	1815	2	49
Bowen, Hugha	30	Beech Fork	1820	2	175
Bowen, Hugha	25	Beech Fork	1820	2	176
Bowen, Hugha	100	12 Pole Cr	1833	2	400
Bowen, Hugha	33	Beech Fork	1836	3	44
Bowen, Hugha	25	12 Pole Creek	1838	3	348
Bowen, Hugha	50	Francis Br.	1843	4	1
Bowen, Hugha et al	350	Wts. Guyandotte	1813	1	108
Bowen, Jefferson	150	Enoch's Br.	1843	4	8
Bowen, Jefferson	10	Long Branch	1843	4	9
Bowen, Jefferson	32	Long Branch	1850	4	314
Bowen, Jefferson B.	13	Beech Fork	1848	4	186
Bowen, Jefferson B.	7	Beech Fork	1848	4	187
Bowen, Jefferson B.	75	Beech Fork	1848	4	204
Bowen, Jefferson B.	22	Beech Fork	1848	4	210
Bowen, Jefferson B.	125	Francis's Branch	1856	5	348
Bradshaw, Moses	100	Raccoon Fork	1815	2	1
Bragg, Jacob	150	Wts. of Mud	1833	2	412
Bragg, Jacob	37	Wts. of Mud	1836	3	20
Brammer, John	75	Charlie's Creek	1815	2	22
Brewer, William H.	151	Mill Fork	1856	5	345
Brewer, William H.	514	Sugar Tree Fork	1856	5	346
Brock, John (Black) et al	100	Dry Creek	1852	5	445
Brown, Charles et al	200	Middle Fork	1812	1	26
Brown, James	50	Wts. of Mud	1812	1	24
Brown, James	40	Wts. of Mud	1834	2	476
Brown, James	4	Trace Fork	1858	5	413
Brown, Richard	100	12 Pole Creek	1812	1	52
Brown, Richard	100	Adj. J. Savage	1820	2	182
Brown, Thomas	85	Wts. of Mud	1838	3	402
Brown, Thomas S.	72	Trace Fork	1852	5	199
Brown, Thomas S. et al	46	Wts. of Mud	1846	4	102
Brown, Thomas S. et al	240	Wts. of Mud	1852	5	443
Brumfield, John H.	255	Big Ugly Cr.	1838	3	300
Brumfield, John H.	100	Ugly Creek	1850	4	303
Brumfield, John H. et al	230	Wts. Guyandotte	1850	4	304
Brumfield, John H. et al	700	14 Mile Creek	1855	5	294
Brumfield, John H. et al	696	Little Ugley	1855	5	455
Brumfield, William	75	Wts. Guyandotte	1819	2	167
Brumley, John	25	Mill Creek	1838	3	227
Brumley, John	40	Grassy Branch	1841	3	457
Brumley, John	25	12 Pole Creek	1841	3	458
Brumley, John	260	Mill Creek	1841	3	460
Brumley, John	30	Lick Branch	1842	3	490

Name of Grantee	Acres	Local Description	Year	Book	Page
Brumley, John	12½	Adj. his own	1842	3	491
Brumley, William et al	150	Mill Creek	1823	2	244
Bryan, William et al	500	Rt. Hd. Fk.	1816	2	68
Bryant, Gabriel	35	Wts. of Mud	1838	3	242
Bryant, Gabriel	30	Wts. of Guyan	1838	3	383
Bryant, Jacob	115	Lower Creek	1838	3	159
Bryant, Jacob	25	Lower Creek	1838	3	325
Bryant, John	100	Lower Creek	1818	2	120
Bryant, John	175	Middle Fork	1836	3	13
Bryant, John	23	Mill Creek	1836	3	58
Bryant, John	95	Wts. Guyandotte	1838	3	324
Bryant, William	100	Wts. of Mud	1838	3	414
Buffington, James	35	12 Pole Creek	1814	1	124
Buffington, James H.	70	12 Pole Cr.	1838	3	241
Buffington, James H.	250	12 Pole Creek	1853	5	220
Buffington, John	120	Wts. Guyandotte	1838	3	229
Buffington, Peter C.	40	Rt. Hd. Fork	1838	3	228
Buffington, Peter C.	135	Wts. of Mud	1838	3	303
Buffington, Peter C.	500	Wts. of Guyand.	1838	3	304
Buffington, Peter C.	70	Grapevine Fork	1838	3	305
Buffington, Peter C.	200(2,000)	Four Pole Cr.	1846	4	88
Buffington, Peter C.	35	Long Branch	1852	5	202
Buffington, Peter C. et al	100	Wts. of Guyandotte	1833	2	407
Buffington, Peter C. et al	195	12 Pole Cr.	1836	2	506
Buffington, Peter C. et al	1,380	7 Mi. Creek	1847	4	158
Buffington, P. C. et al	75	4 Pole Creek	1851	4	427
Buffington, Peter C. & T. J.	93	4 Pole Creek	1840	3	416
Buffington, Thomas	75	Right Hand Fork	1812	1	29
Buffington, Thomas	25	Wts. of Guyandotte	1816	2	60
Buffington, Thomas et al	100	Big Buffalo	1818	2	111
Buffington, Thomas J.	50(20)	12 Pole Creek	1838	3	302
Buffington, Thomas J.	50	Milam's Cr.	1843	4	3
Buffington, Thomas J.	50	12 Pole Cr.	1843	4	4
Buffington, Thomas J.	100	4 Mile Cr.	1845	4	54
Buffington, Thomas J.	40	R. Hand Fork	1838	3	230
Buffington, Thomas J.	50	Mill Cr.	1843	4	5
Buffington, Thomas J.	50	Big Branch	1843	4	6
Buffington, Thomas Jr.	50	12 Pole Cr.	1813	1	68
Buffington, Thomas Jr. et al	120	Big Buffalo	1818	2	109
Buffington, William	50	12 Pole Cr.	1812	1	37
Buffington, William	50	12 Pole Cr.	1812	1	38
Buffington, William	100	12 Pole Cr.	1812	1	41
Buffington, William	75	Wts. Guyandotte	1812	1	49
Buffington, William	45	Left Hand Fork	1813	1	74
Buffington, William	50	Pigeon Creek	1813	1	77
Buffington, William	255	Pigeon Creek	1812	1	82
Buffington, William	125	Big Lynn Cr.	1825	2	283
Buffington, William	100	12 Pole Cr.	1825	2	284
Buffington, William	90	Wts. of Guyandotte	1834	2	495
Buffington, William	250	12 Pole Cr.	1835	2	497
Buffington, William	400	Beech Fork	1836	3	21
Buffington, William	40	Left Hd. Fork	1837	3	107
Buffington, William et al	100	Left Hand Fork	1812	1	48
Buffington, William et al	50	Left Hand Fork	1812	1	53
Buffington, William et al	350	Wts. of Guyandotte	1813	1	108
Buffington, William et al	100	Taber's Creek	1815	2	39
Buffington, William et al	60	Left Hand Fork	1815	2	40
Buffington, William et al	100	Left Hand Fork	1815	2	41
Buffington, William et al	50	Left Hand Fork	1815	2	42
Buffington, William et al	20	Wts. of Sandy	1815	2	43
Buffington, William et al	60	Wts. of Sandy	1815	2	44
Buffington, William et al	450	Wts. of Mud	1817	2	102
Buffington, William et al	190	14 Mile Cr.	1833	2	382

Name of Grantee	Acres	Local Description	Year	Book	Page
Chapman, John & J. B.	75	Wts. of Guyand.	1848	4	192
Chapman, John M.	125	Cabell Creek	1837	3	92
Chapman, Martha	9	Carter Creek	1856	5	317
Chapman, Thomas	50	Pigeon Creek	1818	2	112
Childers, Benjamin	22	Trace Fork	1838	3	162
Childers, Benjamin	50	Smith Creek	1847	4	131
Childers, Melville	235	Heath's Creek	1846	4	83
Childers, Melville et al	171	Raccoon Fork	1855	5	299
Childers, Melville et al	37	14 Mile Creek	1856	5	353
Childers, Royal	65	Alford's Cr.	1833	2	409
Childers, Royal	25	Hart's Creek	1838	3	161
Childers, Royal	60	Merritt's Cr.	1846	4	84
Childers, Royal	260	Heath's Cr.	1846	4	85
Childers, Royal	80	Heath's Creek	1848	4	190
Childers, Royal	50	Merritt's Cr.	1848	4	191
Childers, Thomas	50	Merritt's Cr.	1833	2	367
Childers, Thomas	25	Merritt's Creek	1838	3	249
Childers, Thomas A. et al	350	14 Mile Creek	1855	5	303
Childers, Thomas et al	700	14 Mile Creek	1855	5	294
Childers, William L.	15	Merritt's Cr.	1851	4	452
Cites—See Ceits, Scitz, Sites					
Cites, Christopher	40	9 Mile Cr.	1848	4	189
Clark, William	250	12 Pole Creek	1813	1	66
Clark, William	110	Beech Fork	1814	1	127
Collins, Harrison	65	Seven Mile Cr.	1857	5	385
Conley, Bailey et al	584	14 Mile Creek	1856	5	330
Conner, Andrew	22	Wts. of Mud	1832	2	352
Conner, James	33	Tease Valley	1836	3	32
Conner, James	60	Hurricane Cr.	1836	3	40
Conner, James	65	2 Mile Creek	1850	4	355
Conner, James Jr. et al	88	2 Mile Creek	1850	4	346
Conner, James Jr. & William Sr.	100	Madison Creek	1838	3	251
Conner, William	25	Wts. of Mud	1851	4	428
Conner, William	6	Wts. of Mud	1851	4	429
Conner, William	25	Wts. of Mud	1851	4	430
Conner, William	75	2 Mile Creek	1851	4	431
Conner, William Jr.	85	Wts. of Mud	1847	4	121
Conner, William Jr.	25	Wts. of Mud	1850	4	318
Conner, William Jr.	43	Wts. Mud River	1854	5	260
Conner, William Jr. et al	190	Wts. of Mud	1847	4	122
Conner, William Sr. et al	24	Wts. of Mud	1838	3	252
Conrad—Coonrod					
Conrad, David	125	Lower Creek	1833	2	415
Conrad, John	115	Bear Branch	1838	3	163
Coonrod, David et al Heirs	75	Lower Creek	1838	3	385
Cooper, Silas	50	Wts. of Mud	1834	2	442
Cooper, Thomas	95	Sugar Tree Fork	1850	4	406
Cooper, William	80	Laurel Creek	1838	3	328
Cooper, William	50	Big Laurel Cr.	1845	4	55
Copley, James	25	Left Hand Fork	1838	3	208
Copley, James Sr.	17	Tug Fork	1842	3	488
Copley, William	45	Left Hd. Fork	1821	2	188
Copley, William	29	Drag Creek	1837	3	124
Copley, William Sr. & James Jr.	25	Drag Creek	1842	3	487
Corbin, Anderson et al	200	Booth's Creek	1837	3	529
Corlein, Anderson et al	200	Booth's Creek	1837	3	529
Cornell See Cornwell					
Cornell, Lemuel G.	75	9 Mile Cr.	1838	3	306
Cornell, Lemuel G.	38	9 Mile Creek	1838	3	384
Cornell, Zilpha	9	9 Mile Creek	1836	3	26
Cornwell, Samuel (or Lemuel) G.	38	9 Mile Creek	1838	3	384
Cowens, Thomas J.	25	Old Field Br.	1849	4	269
Cox, James	50	Wts. of Mud	1833	2	398

Name of Grantee	Acres	Local Description	Year	Book	Page
Cox, John	20	Tug Fork	1813	1	86
Cox, John	75	Left Hand Fork	1813	1	87
Cox, William	40	Mill Creek	1815	2	35
Cox, William	150	Mill Creek	1816	2	67
Cox, William	50	Mill Creek	1818	2	108
Cox, William	50	Adj. his own	1822	2	231
Cox, William	50	9 Mile Cr.	1834	2	474
Cremeans, Higgins & Nathan	25	Slab Camp Fork	1838	3	307
Cremeans, Hiram	190	Wts. of Guyandotte	1845	4	56
Cremeans, Lewis	75	Fall Creek	1853	5	215
Cremeans, Moses	600	Wts. of Mud	1845	4	57
Cremeans, Sanders (Cremeens)	50	Madison Cr.	1851	4	425
Cremeans, Saunders	50	Madison Creek	1847	4	155
Cremeans, Saunders	35	Madison Creek	1853	5	226
Cremeans, Winchester (Cremeens)	30	Madison Cr.	1851	4	424
Crum, Adam et al	80	12 Pole Creek	1841	3	445
Crum, Frederick	10	Coon Branch	1841	3	426
Crum, Frederick	50	Left Hand Fork	1841	3	427
Crum, Frederick	90	Bull Creek	1841	3	454
Crum, Frederick	60	Bull Creek	1841	3	456
Crum, Frederick	15	Adj. his own	1842	3	502
Crum, James	90	7 Mile Cr.	1834	2	425
Crum, James	70	7 Mile Creek	1838	3	349
Crum, James or John	20	7 Mile Cr.	1838	3	350
Crum, Reuben	75	Tug Fork	1836	3	11
Crum, William Jr.	78	Tug Fork	1841	3	451
Crum, William Jr.	50	Silver Creek	1841	3	452
Crum, William Sr.	20	Tug Fork	1841	3	442
Cummins, William	23	Wts. of Mud	1843	4	18
Currie See Curry					
Currie, William	5	Main Fork	1858	5	397
Currie, William	50	Little Laurel Cr.	1858	5	398
Currie, William	3	Main Fork	1858	5	399
Curry See Currie					
Curry, Andrew N. et al	457	Coon Creek	1850	4	317
Curry, William	35	Main Fork	1858	5	404
Curry, William	15	Wts. of Mud	1858	5	415
Curry, William et al	308	Wts. of Mud	1858	5	403
Curry, William et al	26	9 Mile Creek	1860	5	439
Cyrus—See Sires, Sirus, Syrus					
Cyrus, James	40	Everett's Cr.	1838	3	330
Damrill—See Damron					
Damron, Augustin (Damrill)	68	Greystone Cr.	1818	2	110
Damron, Augusta	50	Wts. of Sandy	1813	1	57
Damron, George	125	12 Pole Cr.	1831	2	337
Damron, George	75(25)	12 Pole Creek	1838	3	231
Damron, George	70	Wolf Pen Ridge	1842	3	483
Damron, Lazarus et al	150	Mill Creek	1823	2	244
Damron, Moses	75	12 Pole Cr.	1831	2	334
Damron, Richard	50	12 Pole Cr.	1842	3	484
Damron, Samuel	200	12 Pole Creek	1831	2	338
Damron, Samuel	120	12 Mile Cr.	1836	3	5
Damron, Samuel	50	12 Pole Creek	1841	3	431
Damron, Samuel et al	50	12 Pole Cr.	1836	2	518
Damron, Samuel et al	65	Rich Creek	1836	2	521
Damron, Samuel et al	50	12 Pole Cr.	1836	2	522
Damron, Samuel et al	90	Milam's Cr.	1836	2	529
Damron, Samuel Jr.	130	12 Pole Cr.	1841	3	432
Damron, Samuel Jr.	40	12 Pole Cr.	1841	3	433
Damron, Samuel Jr.	35	12 Pole Cr.	1842	3	485
Damron, Samuel Jr.	70	12 Pole Cr.	1842	3	486
Damron, Samuel Sr.	98	12 Pole Creek	1841	3	434
Darting, See Darton, Dirton, Dirting, Durting					

Name of Grantee	Acres	Local Description	Year	Book	Page
Darting, Philip	155	Wts. of Mud	1833	2	410
Darton, Philip (Dirton)	300	Wts. of Mud	1837	3	73
Davis, Achillis M. C. et al	100	4 Mile Creek	1850	4	356
Davis, Benjamin	50	Beech Fork	1815	2	4
Davis, Benjamin	50	Long Branch	1816	2	71
Davis, Benjamin	152	Camp Branch	1828	2	321
Davis, Benjamin	40	Cain Branch	1828	2	322
Davis, Benjamin	280	Four Mile Cr.	1850	4	320
Davis, Benjamin & Daniel	150	Beech Fork	1811	1	11
Davis, Daniel	300	12 Pole Creek	1850	4	321
Davis, James M. C.	24	Four Mile Cr.	1845	4	59
Davis, James M. C.	83	4 Mile Creek	1858	5	408
Davis, James M. C.	116	Kentucky Fork	1858	5	409
Davis, James M. C.	169	4 Mile Creek	1857	5	355
Davis, Paul	5	12-Pole Cr.	1836	2	533
Davis, Paul	30	Beech Fork	1816	2	74
Davis, Paul	50	Left Hand Fork	1838	3	278
Davis, Paul	160	Davis Creek	1838	3	279
Davis, Paul	190	Davis Creek	1848	4	212
Davis, Paul	35	Davis Creek	1850	4	407
Davis, Paul H.	150	12 Pole Creek	1836	3	63
Davis, Paul H.	40	Beech Fork	1838	3	280
Davis, William	125	Bear Creek	1819	2	165
Davis, William	40	Beech Fork	1828	2	319
Davis, William	75	Beech Fork	1836	3	29
Davis, William G.	100	Davis Creek	1838	3	138
Davis, William G.	50	Davis Creek	1845	4	58
Davis, William G.	25	Price's Cr.	1846	4	89
Davis, William G.	50	Davis Cr.	1848	4	174
Davison, George (Daveson)	100	Adj. John Savage	1816	2	87
Deal, Henry	250	Wts. of Mud	1847	4	123
Dean, Benjamin	100	Davisson's Br.	1813	1	59
Dean, John	80	12 Pole Creek	1833	2	386
Dean, John	18	12 Pole Cr.	1836	3	48
Dean, John Sr.	25	12 Pole Cr.	1838	3	232
Dean, Jonathan	25	12 Pole Cr.	1843	3	528
Deboy, John	240	Long Branch	1846	4	87
Deboy, John	70	Beech Fork	1847	4	124
Defoe—or Defore					
Defoe, Harrison	75(25)	Fudge's Creek	1838	3	253
Defoe, John	100	Beech Fork	1834	2	471
Defoe, Polly	75	Beech Fork	1836	3	36
Dempsey See Demsey					
Dempsey, John et al	50	14 Mile Cr.	1845	4	43
Dempsey, Joseph	50	Pigeon Creek	1825	2	276
Demsey, John & Thomas	100	Mud Fork	1816	2	62
Dial, Elisha	200	Trace Fork	1859	5	430
Dial, John	40	Kentucky Fork	1837	3	131
Dial, John M.	400	Kentucky Fork	1850	4	394
Dial, Thomas	110	Four Mile Cr.	1837	3	104
Dial, Thomas	100	4 Mile Creek	1838	3	308
Dial, Thomas	10	4 Mile Cr.	1844	4	26
Dial, Thomas	150	4 Mi. Cr.	1848	4	193
Dingess, Captain Peter et al	120	Big Buffalo	1818	2	109
Dingess, Captain Wm.	200	Main Island Cr.	1818	2	133
Dingess, Peter	112	Wts. Mud River	1814	1	143
Dingess, Peter	100	Buffalo Cr.	1816	2	63
Dingess, Peter	100	Buffalo Cr.	1816	2	64
Dingess, Peter	50	Island Creek	1824	2	265
Dingess, Peter	50	Main Island Cr.	1824	2	266
Dingess, Peter	170	Hart's Creek	1824	2	267
Dingess, Peter	90	Island Creek	1825	2	273
Dingess, Peter	50	12 Pole Cr.	1825	2	274

Name of Grantee	Acres	Local Description	Year	Book	Page
Dingess, Peter	100	Dingess Cr.	1825	2	275
Dingess, Peter	100	Buffalo Cr.	1825	2	285
Dingess, Peter et al	100	Big Buffalo	1818	2	111
Dingess, William	160	Island Creek	1814	1	140
Dingess, William	100	Wts. of Guyandotte	1814	1	141
Dingess, William	100	Middle Fork	1814	1	142
Dingess, William	50	Rum Creek	1818	2	137
Dingess, William	100	Wts. of Guyandotte	1818	2	138
Dingess, William	50	Wts. of Guyand	1820	2	170
Dingess, William et al	28	Dry Fork	1815	2	32
Dingess, William et al	630	Spruce Fork	1818	2	136
Dirting—See Darting etc.					
Dirting, William	45	Wild Cat Br.	1844	4	27
Dirton—See Darting					
Dirton, Philip (Darton)	300	Wts. of Mud	1837	3	73
Dodd, James	141(141½)	Trace Fork	1856	5	325
Dodd, James et al	2,700	Wts. of Mud	1859	5	472
Dodd, Lewis	418	4 Pole Creek	1834	2	481
Donathan, Elijah	25	Wts. of Sandy	1815	2	45
Donathan, Elijah	90	Wts. of Sandy	1823	2	243
Donathan, Elijah	50	Adj. Wm. Cox	1822	2	232
Doolittle, Ambrose L.	350	Cabell Creek	1838	3	164
Doolittle, Ambrose L.	90	Cabell Creek	1838	3	254
Doolittle, Ambrose L.	50	Cabell Creek	1831	2	333
Douglas, George	90	Four Mile Cr.	1850	4	412
Douglas, George	70	Lick Branch	1844	4	25
Douglass, George	165	4 Mile Creek	1848	4	179
Douglass, George	218	4 Mile Cr.	1850	4	392
Douglass, George	135	4 Mile Cr.	1850	4	393
Douglass, George	122	4 Mile Creek	1854	5	242
Drake, Henderson	60	Luster's Br.	1836	3	60
Drake, Henderson	150	Wts. of Guyan	1850	4	319
Drake, Henderson	440	Cor. to J. Campbell	1855	5	309
Drake, Henderson	9	9 Mile Creek	1858	5	410
Drake, Henderson	8½	Betty's Branch	1858	5	411
Drake, Henderson et al	825	Laurel Hill Creek	1855	5	301
Draper, William F.	89	Sycamore Fork	1856	5	331
Draper, William F.	100	Sycamore Fork	1856	5	332
Draper, William F.	200	Sycamore Fork	1856	5	341
Draper, William F.	37	Sycamore Fork	1859	5	426
Draper, William F.	33	Sycamore Fork	1859	5	428
Drown, Benjamin	7¼	Beech Fork	1838	3	220
Drown, Benjamin	7¾	Long Branch	1838	3	221
Drown, Benjamin (Drowen)	75	Low's Branch	1834	2	440
Duke, James	185	Charlie's Cr.	1837	3	136
Durting or Darting, etc.					
Durting, William	25	Wts. of Mud	1834	2	444
Dusenberry, William F.	45	Smith's Creek	1857	5	382
Dyer, Calvin F. et al	275	4 Mile Creek	1856	5	464
Egnor, Archibald	300	Sugar Tree Fork	1850	4	284
Egnor, Archibald	150	Middle Fork	1850	4	285
Egnor, Archibald	164	Middle Fork	1855	5	289
Elkins, Archibald	87½	14 Mile Cr.	1848	4	196
Elkins, Darby K.	175	12 Pole Creek	1838	3	165
Elkins, Harvey	105	Hart's Branch	1850	4	283
Elkins, Joel	50	14 Mile Creek	1853	5	222
Elkins, Rees W.	37	9 Mile Creek	1852	4	463
Elkins, Reese W.	125	14 Mile Creek	1857	5	383
Elkins, Richard	168	Wts. of Guyan.	1848	4	180
Elkins, Richard	125	14 Mile Cr.	1848	4	194
Elkins, Richard et al	230	Wts. of Guyandotte	1850	4	304
Elkins, William	50	Beech Fork Spruce	1815	2	27
Ellis, Philip	50	Mill Creek	1819	2	149

Name of Grantee	Acres	Local Description	Year	Book	Page
Ellis, Spencer	55	Wts. Guyan	1813	1	110
Elmore, Edward	70	Fudge's Creek	1834	2	433
Elmore, Edward	33	Price's Creek	1850	4	322
Elmore, William	75	Mill Creek	1833	2	392
Elmore, William	15	Wts. of Mud	1834	2	429
Endicott, Joshua	15	Camp Creek	1846	4	108
Eplin, Henry	215	Fall Creek	1845	4	60
Eplin, John	90	4 Mile Creek	1838	3	386
Eplin, John	20	4 Mile Creek	1838	3	387
Eplin, William	65	4 Mile Cr.	1850	4	413
Eplin, William & Frederick	225	12 Pole Cr.	1842	3	477
Eskew, Elisabeth M. et al Hrs.	100	Porter's Fork	1850	4	277
Estep, Corbin	68	Camp Creek	1838	3	233
Estep, Corbin	82	4 Mile Creek	1856	5	347
Estes, Joel	115	Madison Creek	1812	1	36
Estes, Joel Sr.	75	Tom's Creek	1815	2	15
Evans See Ivins					
Evans, Ferril	80	Tug Fork	1815	2	25
Everett, John	100	Wts. of Mud	1814	1	128
Everett, Nathan	50	Cabell Creek	1833	2	357
Everett, Nathan	95	Fudge's Creek	1833	2	358
Everett, Nathan	250	Wts. of Mud	1835	2	494
Everett, Nathan	50	Fudge's Creek	1838	3	166
Everett, Nathan	30	Fudge's Creek	1838	3	167
Failes, John (Foiles)	70	7 Mile Cr.	1838	3	234
Fannan See Fanning					
Fannan, John	45	Four Pole Cr.	1813	1	114
Fanning or Fannan					
Fanning, John	75	Buffalo Creek	1813	1	115
Farley, Henry	100	Buffalo Creek	1821	2	215
Farley, Henry	50	Pigeon Creek	1821	2	216
Farley, Henry	25	Davis Branch	1821	2	217
Farley, Henry (Farler)	100	Wts. Guyandotte	1814	1	123
Farrier—See Ferrier					
Feasel, W. E.	300	Trace Fork	1858	5	395
Feasel, William E.	834	Nine Mile Cr.	1857	5	372
Feasel, William E. et al	250	9 Mile Cr.	1850	4	300
Feasel, William E. (Feazel)	350	9 Mile Cr.	1851	4	439
Ferguson, Furguson, Forguson, Fulkerson					
Ferguson, James	125	Rich Creek	1838	3	168
Ferguson, James	300	Beech Branch	1838	3	169
Ferguson, James	68	Mill Creek	1841	3	435
Ferguson, James	90	12 Pole Cr.	1841	3	436
Ferguson, James	90	Greenbrier Br.	1838	3	437
Ferguson, James	90	Big Lynn	1841	3	438
Ferguson, James	50	2 Mile Creek	1841	3	439
Ferguson, James	100	2 Mile Creek	1842	3	478
Ferguson, James et al	225	12 Pole Creek	1842	3	479
Ferguson, James et al	195	Taber's Creek	1842	3	517
Ferguson, James et al	75	12 Pole Cr.	1842	3	519
Ferguson, Joel	80	12 Pole Creek	1821	2	186
Ferguson, Joel	80	12 Pole Cr.	1838	3	201
Ferguson, Joseph	35	Seven Mi. Cr.	1836	3	39
Ferguson, Milton	25	12 Pole Creek	1842	3	480
Ferguson, Milton	45	Cyntha's Branch	1842	3	481
Ferguson, Milton	220	Camp Creek	1842	3	503
Ferguson, Milton	100	Lick Creek	1842	3	504
Ferguson, Milton	85	Coon Branch	1842	3	505
Ferguson, Milton	58	Brush Creek	1842	3	506
Ferguson, Milton	320	10 Mi. Creek	1846	4	112
Ferguson, Milton et al	95	Joe's Branch	1842	3	482
Ferguson, Samuel Jr.	150	12 Pole Creek	1819	2	147
Ferguson, William	25	12 Pole Creek	1838	3	332

Name of Grantee	Acres	Local Description	Year	Book	Page
Hatton, Allen	40	Wts. of Mud	1838	3	371
Hatton, Asa	160	Graystone Cr.	1812	1	17
Hatton, Asa	50	Greystone Cr.	1818	2	131
Hatton, Charles	20	Wts. of Mud	1833	2	370
Hatton, Charles	95	Wts. of Mud	1837	3	76
Hatton, George	75	Big Laurel	1826	2	302
Hatton, George A.	42	Maning's Branch	1850	4	377
Hatton, James	52	Laurel Creek	1837	3	123
Hatton, John	175	Wts. Sandy	1818	2	123
Hatton, Joseph	60	Wts. of Mud	1833	2	389
Hayden, Jeremiah	70	Four Mile Cr.	1813	1	58
Hayner, See Haner					
Hazlett, Alexander	50	Mill Creek	1815	2	28
Heath, Israel	15	Wts. of Guyan.	1815	2	56
Heath, James	50	Wts. of Mud	1836	2	526
Heath, James (or Jonas)	70	Middle Fork	1837	3	77
Hensley, Fretwell G.	31	Rock Camp Br.	1849	4	245
Hensley, John	5	Heath's Creek	1850	4	411
Hensley, Stephen	120	Big Fork	1817	2	94
Hicks, Ahas	220	Trace Fork	1844	4	38
Hill, Henry et al	185	Fall Creek	1845	4	65
Hill, John	120	Wolf Pen Fork	1850	4	357
Hinchman, William	22	Wts. of Guyan.	1816	2	76
Hinchman, William	78	Rich Creek	1817	2	104
Hinkle, George (Hincle)	90	10 Mile Creek	1854	5	261
Hisey, John	100	4 Mile Cr.	1812	1	50
Hite, Jacob	410	Wts. Guyandotte	1833	2	544
Hite, John W.	400	Wts. Guyandotte	1833	2	545
Hodgerson, See Hodgeson					
Hodgeson, John	110	Wts. of Mud	1818	2	106
Hodgeson, John	35	Charlies Cr.	1823	2	248
Holderbey, William et al	100	Left Hand Fork	1812	1	48
Holderby, Absolom	60p.	Barboursville	1829	2	541
Holderby, Absolom	50	Wts. of Guyandotte	1836	3	59
Holderby, Absolom et al	125	2 Mile Creek	1847	4	161
Holderby, Absolom et al	350	10 Mile Cr.	1852	4	464
Holderby, James	200	Adj. Wm. Buffington	1833	2	363
Holderby, James	2½	4 Pole Creek	1849	4	240
Holderby, Robert	456	Wts. Guyandotte	1829	2	542
Holderby, Robert	25	Russell's Cr.	1836	2	503
Holdright—See Holdride, Holdryde					
Holdright, Elizabeth	100	Cabell Creek	1847	4	129
Holdright, John D.	100	Cabell Cr.	1833	2	365
Holdright, John D.	30	Cabell Creek	1838	3	334
Holdright, John D.	75	Cabell Cr.	1847	4	128
Holdryde, Holdright, Holdride					
Holdryde, John D.	100	Cabell Creek	1847	4	127
Holdryde, Olivia	125	Cabell Creek	1847	4	126
Holley, Andrew	100	Laurel Creek	1850	4	375
Holley, Francis	75	Turkey Creek	1837	3	122
Holley, Francis	25	Turkey Creek	1838	3	404
Holley, James A.	62	Wts. of Mud	1850	4	376
Holley, James A. et al	336	Trace Creek	1855	5	310
Holley, James A. et al	158	Big Creek	1856	5	334
Holley, James A. et al	556	Ten Mile Creek	1856	5	343
Holley, James A. et al	100	Wts. of Mud	1857	5	367
Holley, James A. et al	300	Sulphur Spgs. Fk.	1858	5	393
Holley, James A. et al	500	Merritt's Cr.	1859	5	433
Holley, James A. et al	674	Wts. Mud River	1855	5	457
Holley, James A. et al	650	Big Creek	1856	5	459
Holley, James A. et al	3,350	9 Mile Cr.	1856	5	460
Holley, James A. et al	1,970	Trace Fork	1856	5	461
Holley, James A. et al	830	Lit. Cabell Cr.	1857	5	466

Name of Grantee	Acres	Local Description	Year	Book	Page
Holley, William	78	Trace Creek	1850	4	395
Holly, James A. et al	150	Sugar Tree Fork	1855	5	296
Holly, James A. et al	248	Main Fork	1856	5	322
Holstein or Holston					
Holstein, William A.	100	Wts. of Mud	1850	4	396
Holstein, William A.	130	Sycamore Creek	1850	4	397
Holston or Holstein					
Holston, William A.	62	Middle Fork	1857	5	379
Holston, William A. (Holstein)	53	Sycamore Fork	1856	5	320
Holt, Nathan	55	Mill Creek	1836	2	524
Holt, Nathan	13	Mill Creek	1837	3	82
Holt, Nathaniel	125	12 Pole Cr.	1827	2	312
Holt, William et al	35	12 Pole Cr.	1831	2	340
Holton, Hatton, Hotton					
Holton, Allen	30	Wts. of Mud	1845	4	61
Holton, Allen	108	Big Laurel Cr.	1846	4	94
Holton, Allen	52	Big Laurel Cr.	1846	4	95
Holton, Charles	185	Wts. of Mud	1846	4	96
Holton, James	38	Wts. of Mud	1846	4	97
Holton, James	125	Wts. of Mud	1846	4	98
Hooser—See Huser					
Hooser, Rudolph	50	Hurricane Cr.	1832	2	354
Hotton, Hatton, Holton					
Howard, Clabourn	50	Fudge's Creek	1833	2	384
Hudson, Lewis	21	Charlie's Cr.	1833	2	427
Hudson, Lewis	50	Charlie's Cr.	1837	3	111
Hugart, Andrew (Hugard) et al	150	Fudge's Creek	1818	2	107
Hull, Martin	35	Big Fork	1822	2	221
Hull, Martin	110	Adj. E. Goodwin	1826	2	293
Hunter, Samuel	60	Raccoon Fork	1834	2	482
Hunter, Samuel	65	Beech Fork	1836	2	516
Hunter, Samuel	60	Bowen's Creek	1838	3	213
Hunter, Samuel	170	Raccoon Creek	1846	4	93
Hunter, Samuel	100	4 Mile Creek	1849	4	251
Hunter, Samuel	120	Fall Branch	1856	5	329
Huser—See Hooser					
Huser, Rudolph	65	Wts. of Sandy	1819	2	162
Ivins See Evans					
Ivins, Ferril	80	Tug Fork	1815	2	25
Jackson, Thomas W.	50	Beech Fork	1834	2	434
Jarrell, Harrison	35	12 Pole Creek	1841	3	459
Jarrell, John	100	Mill Creek	1842	3	508
Jefferson, John W.	69	9 Mile Creek	1853	5	219
Jefferson, John W.	60	Two Mile Creek	1853	5	221
Jenkins, Bennett	280	Merritt's Creek	1813	1	83
Jenkins, Cary	50	Trace Fork	1837	3	85
Jenkins, Cary	65	Wts. Guyandotte	1837	3	108
Jenkins, Cary	75 (25)	Wts. Guyandotte	1838	3	310
Johnson, Alexander	40	Smith's Cr.	1846	4	74
Johnson, Alexander	340	Smith's Cr.	1846	4	75
Johnson, Alexander	30	Smith's Cr.	1846	4	76
Johnson, Alexander	35	Smith's Cr.	1846	4	77
Johnson, Alexander	75	Smith's Cr.	1846	4	110
Johnson, Alexander	50	Smith's Cr.	1848	4	170
Johnson, Benjamin	160	Trace Fork	1836	3	10
Johnson, Benjamin	75	Trace Fork	1836	3	37
Johnson, Benjamin	175	Turkey Creek	1838	3	405
Johnson, Eps	25	Wts. Guyandotte	1844	4	30
Johnson, Eps	2¾	Smith's Creek	1854	5	262
Johnson, John	50	Raccoon Fork	1838	3	174
Johnson, John	20	Raccoon Fork	1852	5	205
Johnson, John	117	Raccoon Fork	1857	5	356
Johnson, John	6½	Raccoon Fork	1857	5	358
Johnson, Margaret	70	Madison Cr.	1848	4	175

Name of Grantee	Acres	Local Description	Year	Book	Page
Johnson, Margaret	24	Madison Cr.	1848	4	176
Johnson, Maxwell	100	Trace Fork	1857	5	387
Johnson, Merrit	24	Raccoon Fork	1838	3	173
Johnson, Merrett	80	Raccoon Creek	1855	5	279
Johnson, Merrett	36	Beech Fork	1855	5	280
Johnson, Merritt	25	Raccoon Branch	1841	3	446
Johnson, Merritt	120	Beech Fork	1848	4	214
Johnson, Merritt	100	Raccoon Fork	1853	5	217
Johnson, Sugar	65	Trace Creek	1819	2	166
Johnson, William	25	Sulphur Spg. Fork	1846	4	78
Johnson, William	280	14 Mile Creek	1849	4	242
Johnson, William	1,514	14 Mile Creek	1850	4	301
Johnson, William	180	14 Mile Cr.	1850	4	370
Johnson, William et al	650	Wts. Guyandotte	1849	4	229
Johnson, William et al	600	14 Mile Creek	1850	4	302
Johnson, William et al	185	14 Mile Creek	1853	5	228
Johnson, William et al	100	Ten Mile Creek	1854	5	273
Jordan, Jorden, Jourdan, Jourden					
Jordan, Andrew	125	Kilgore Creek	1855	5	278
Jorden, John	40	John's Creek	1815	2	13
Jourdan, Jordan, Jorden, Jourden					
Jourdan, John	145	Cow Hide Branch	1850	4	327
Jourden, Andrew	25	Wts. of Mud	1833	2	372
Jourden, Andrew	125	Cor. to T. Kilgore	1837	3	91
Jourden, John Jr.	75	Cow Hide Cr.	1848	4	197
Joy, Thomas	140	7 Mi .Creek	1838	3	309
Keaton See Keyton					
Keaton, Rilen	60	10 Mile Creek	1850	4	328
Keaton, Rilen	42	Wts. of Mud	1850	4	408
Keaton, Rilen et al	190	Wts. of Mud	1847	4	122
Keaton, Ryland	25	2 Mile Cr.	1832	2	351
Keaton, Ryland	33	2 Mile Creek	1833	2	359
Keenan, Patrick	100	Four Mile Creek	1852	5	206
Keesee, Richard	77	Tug Fork	1813	1	103
Kessinger, Wilson	100	Straight Fork	1850	4	400
Ketchum, Alonzo F.	293	10 Mile Creek	1855	5	292
Ketchum, Alonzo F.	450	10 Mile Creek	1857	5	366
Ketchum, Alonzo F.	300	10 Mile Creek	1858	5	388
Ketchum, Alonzo F. et al	106	Ten Mile Creek	1855	5	293
Keyton, See Keaton					
Keyton, Ryland	35	Wts. of Mud	1838	3	258
Keyton, Ryland et al	24	Wts. of Mud	1838	3	252
Kile, James C. et al	37	9 Mile Creek	1856	5	326
Kilgore, George	60	Mile Branch	1851	4	461
Kilgore, George	22	Kilgore Creek	1854	5	281
Kilgore, George	26½	Davis Creek	1855	5	285
Kilgore, George et al	54	Wts. Mud	1854	5	268
Kilgore, George et al	1,020	Big Creek	1854	5	269
Kilgore, George et al	12	Wts. Guyandotte	1854	5	270
Kilgore, George et al	93	Wts. of Mud	1854	5	271
Kilgore, George et al	16	Wts. of Mud	1854	5	272
Kilgore, George et al	19	Wts. of Mud	1855	5	276
Kilgore, George et al	150	Raccoon Fork	1855	5	277
Kilgore, George et al	1,165	Wts. of Mud	1855	5	283
Kilgore, George et al	336	Trace Creek	1855	5	310
Kilgore, George et al	556	Ten Mile Creek	1856	5	343
Kilgore, George et al	830	Lit. Cabell Cr.	1857	5	466
Kilgore, Thomas	25	Kilgore's Cr.	1833	2	374
Kilgore, Thomas	50	Lee's Creek	1833	2	379
Kilgore, Thomas	140	Charlie's Creek	1833	2	391
Kilgore, Thomas	30	Adj. his own	1816	2	61
Kilgore, Thomas	20	Kilgore's Cr.	1818	2	125
Kilgore, Thomas	185	Charlie's Creek	1837	3	70

Name of Grantee	Acres	Local Description	Year	Book	Page
Kilgore, Thomas	170	Tease Valley	1837	3	84
Kilgore, Thomas	530	Wts. of Mud	1838	3	406
King, John	75	McComas Branch	1838	3	257
King, John & S. S.	90	McComas Branch	1850	4	329
King, Sampson S.	47½	Wts. Guyandotte	1854	5	240
Kinnason, W. G.	25	Adj. T. McComas	1854	5	265
Kirk, James	150	Marrowbone Cr.	1825	2	269
Kirk, James	25	Jenney's Cr.	1838	3	200
Kirk, John	350	Wts. Sandy	1824	2	262
Kirk, John	25	Wts. of Sandy	1825	2	281
Kirk, John	36	Left Hand Fork	1836	3	31
Kirk, John	150	Three Mile Creek	1853	5	210
Kirtley, Jeremiah S.	313	Charlie's Cr.	1847	4	132
Kirtley, Joseph	145	Charlie's Cr.	1834	2	467
Kirtley, Joseph	100	Trace Fork	1844	4	35
Knapper, Thomas	118	12 Pole Cr.	1828	2	324
Knight, See Night					
Knight, Abner	100	9 Mile Creek	1848	4	198
Knotts, Thomas et al	200	Booth's Creek	1837	3	529
Knowls, Thomas et al	200	Booth's Creek	1837	3	529
Kyle, John	30	7 Mile Cr.	1838	3	351
Kyle, John	75	Nine Mile Cr.	1838	3	352
Kyle, John	50	7 Mile Creek	1832	2	353
Kyle, Robert	19	9 Mile Creek	1838	3	226
Kyle, Samuel	25	7 Mile Creek	1837	3	134
Lake, Nicholas	600	Big Creek	1850	4	383
Lake, Nicholas	65	Big Creek	1851	4	453
Lamay, James et al (Lama)	150	Fudge's Creek	1818	2	107
Lambert, Elijah	60	12 Pole Creek	1838	3	353
Lambert, Isaac	30	12 Pole Cr.	1836	2	514
Lambert, William	75	Left Hd. Fork	1822	2	226
Lambert, William	50	12 Pole Cr.	1828	2	327
Lansford, John	50	Smith's Creek	1819	2	160
Large, William	75	Four Mile Creek	1849	4	258
Large, William	50	Four Mile Cr.	1850	4	401
Lattin, Charles	75	9 Mile Creek	1854	5	233
Lattin, Charles	50	4 Mile Creek	1857	5	359
Lattin, Charles	378	14 Mile Creek	1859	5	434
Lattin, Charles	405	2 Mile Creek	1860	5	471
Lattin, Charles et al	54	Wts. of Mud	1854	5	268
Lattin, Charles et al	1,020	Big Creek	1854	5	269
Lattin, Charles et al	12	Wts. of Guyandotte	1854	5	270
Lattin, Charles et al	93	Wts. of Mud	1854	5	271
Lattin, Charles et al	16	Wts. of Mud	1854	5	272
Lattin, Charles et al	19	Wts. of Mud	1855	5	276
Lattin, Charles et al	150	Raccoon Fork	1855	5	277
Lattin, Charles et al	1,165	Wts. of Mud	1855	5	283
Lattin, Charles et al	700	14 Mile Creek	1855	5	294
Lattin, Charles et al	150	Sugar Tree Fork	1855	5	296
Lattin, Charles et al	171	Raccoon Fork	1855	5	299
Lattin, Charles et al	754	Main Fork	1855	5	302
Lattin, Charles et al	350	14 Mile Creek	1855	5	303
Lattin, Charles et al	365	Merritt's Creek	1855	5	304
Lattin, Charles et al	286	Middle Fork	1855	5	305
Lattin, Charles et al	325	Sulphur Spring Fork	1855	5	307
Lattin, Charles et al	336	Trace Creek	1855	5	310
Lattin, Charles et al	248	Main Fork	1856	5	322
Lattin, Charles et al	37	9 Mile Creek	1856	5	326
Lattin, Charles et al	584	14 Mile Creek	1856	5	330
Lattin, Charles et al	158	Big Creek	1856	5	334
Lattin, Charles et al	556	10 Mile Creek	1856	5	343
Lattin, Charles et al	37	14 Mile Creek	1856	5	353
Lattin, Charles et al	100	Wts. of Mud	1857	5	367

Name of Grantee	Acres	Local Description	Year	Book	Page
Lusher, Irvin	750	Wts. of Guyan	1850	4	378
Lusher, Irvin	200	9 Mile Creek	1850	4	379
Lusher, Irvin	5	9 Mile Creek	1857	5	376
Lusher, Irvin	300	Big Creek	1857	5	377
Lusher, Irvin	2,568	2 Mile Creek	1857	5	468
Lusher, Irvin et al	150	Pheasant Cr.	1851	4	443
Lusher, Irvin et al	170	10 Mile Cr.	1851	4	444
Lusher, Irvin et al	170	10 Mile Creek	1851	4	445
Lusher, Irvin et al	900	Laurel Creek	1851	4	446
Lusher, Irvin et al	650	6 Mile Cr.	1851	4	447
Lusher, Irvin et al	240	10 Mi. Cr.	1851	4	448
Lusher, Irvin et al	250	Pheasant Cr.	1851	4	449
Lusher, Irvin et al	250	9 Mile Cr.	1851	4	450
Mainard, Jesse	100	12 Pole Creek	1838	3	235
Malcolm, John M. et al	955	Wts. of Mud	1848	4	206
Malcomb, John M.	50(30)	Adj. his own	1838	3	181
Mansfield, Isaac	50	Charle's Creek	1819	2	168
Marcum, Markum, Markim					
Marcum, Jacob	17	Silver Creek	1842	3	461
Marcum, John	100	Jenney's Creek	1836	3	43
Marcum, John	20	Silver Creek	1841	3	450
Marcum, John C.	40	Jenny's Creek	1841	3	448
Marcum, John & Josiah	100	Jenny's Cr.	1834	2	465
Marcum, Joseph	25	Jenny's Cr.	1838	3	236
Marcum, Moses	25	Jenny's Cr.	1836	2	525
Marcum, Moses	50	12 Pole Cr.	1844	4	23
Marcum, Stephen	100	Mill Creek	1838	3	356
Markim, Jacob	75	Left Hand Fork	1821	2	213
Markim, Joseph	20	Jenny's Cr.	1822	2	218
Markim, Josiah	40	Bull Creek	1822	2	220
Markim, Josiah & Moses	75	Left Hd. Fork	1818	2	117
Markim, Moses	25	Left Hand Fork	1815	2	36
Markim, Stephen	45	Left Hand Fork	1813	1	79
Marrs, Andrew	185	Madison Creek	1845	4	41
Martin, Benjamin	50	Mill Creek	1819	2	152
Martin, Benjamin	50	Wts. of Sandy	1821	2	194
Martin, Benjamin	25	Lowe's Branch	1826	2	297
Martin, Benjamin et al	700	Tabour's Creek	1820	2	180
Martin, Benjamin et al	320	Wts. Sandy	1820	2	181
Martin, Benjamin et al	170	Wts. of Sandy	1827	2	306
Martin, Benjamin et al	70	Tug Fork	1833	2	380
Martin, Benjamin et al	2,500	Tabour's Cr.	1818	2	537
Martin, Jesse	75	Taber's Creek	1821	2	195
Maupin, Addison & C. W.	400	Wts. of Mud	1847	4	136
Maupin, Addison & C. W.	138	Fudge's Creek	1848	4	216
Maupin, Beverly W.	120	Wts. of Mud	1838	3	206
Maupin, William et al	470	Clymer's Cr.	1849	4	256
Maupin, William et al	500	Clymer's Creek	1849	4	264
May, Jacob W.	30	Middle Fork	1850	4	286
May, Jacob W.	6	Middle Fork	1850	4	287
May, Jacob W.	18	Middle Fork	1856	5	321
Mayo, James	150	Four Pole Creek	1813	1	65
Mayo, James	175	Lick Branch	1823	2	237
Mays, George	40	Mill Creek	1833	2	405
Mays, James	30	Steer Branch	1838	3	177
Mays, Lewis	80	Turkey Creek	1848	4	199
Mays, Willis	41	Mill Creek	1836	3	56
McAlister, McAllister, McCalister, McCallister					
McAlister, Sylvester et al	210	Trace Fork	1857	5	375
McCallister, Andrew W.	10	Charlie's Cr.	1847	4	135
McCallister, Isaac & John	135	Trace Creek	1845	4	67
McCallister, James	50	Teas Valley	1836	2	519
McCallister, James	147	Trace Fork	1836	3	55

Name of Grantee	Acres	Local Description	Year	Book	Page
McCallister, James	100	Rock House Fork	1838	3	282
McCallister, John & Isaac	140	Trace Creek	1851	4	455
McCallister, Perry	103	Trace Fork	1854	5	236
McCallister, Richard	270	Turkey Creek	1837	3	78
McCallister, Richard	50	Trace Creek	1837	3	109
McCallister, Richard	100	Turkey Creek	1838	3	284
McCallister, Richard	56½	Turkey Creek	1854	5	237
McCallister, Richard & John	170	Trace Creek	1849	4	246
McCallister, Robert A. et al	457	Coon Creek	1850	4	317
McCallister, Sylvester	154½	Turkey Creek	1854	5	246
McCallister, Thomas	75	Charlie's Creek	1815	2	23
McCallister, Thomas	535 (537)	Charlie's Creek	1820	2	179
McCallister, Thomas	70	Charlie's Creek	1834	2	453
McCallister, Thomas	70	Charlie's Cr.	1847	4	133
McCallister, Thomas	210	Charlie's Cr.	1847	4	134
McCallister, Thomas	170	Charlie's Cr.	1850	4	332
McCann, Richard W.	40	12 Pole Cr.	1842	3	473
McClaskey John	30	Big Creek	1834	2	452
McClasky, John	60	Trace Fork	1832	2	349
McComas, Ballard S.	206	4 Mile Creek	1855	5	298
McComas, Ballard S. et al	275	4 Mile Creek	1856	5	464
McComas, Blackburn et al	63	9 Mile Cr.	1848	4	167
McComas, David	300	Wts. of Mud	1811	1	14
McComas, David	200	Tyler's Creek	1814	1	136
McComas, David	150	Madison's Creek	1815	2	5
McComas, David	200	2 Mile Creek	1850	4	331
McComas, David et al	75	2 Mile Cr	1842	3	509
McComas, Elisha	20	Fall Creek	1812	1	25
McComas, Elisha	112	Wts. Guyandotte	1838	3	144
McComas, Elisha	195	4 Mile Creek	1838	3	145
McComas, Elisha	40	4 Mile Creek	1838	3	146
McComas, Elisha	50	Low Gap Branch	1851	4	432
McComas, Elisha et al	178	Wts. of Guyan.	1815	2	30
McComas, Elisha et al	300	Sulphur Spgs. Fk.	1858	5	393
McComas, Elisha et al	433	4 Mile Creek	1856	5	465
McComas, Elisha Jr.	25	4 Mile Cr.	1818	2	144
McComas, Elisha Jr.	15	4 Mile Cr.	1818	2	145
McComas, Elisha Jr.	180	Wts. Guyandotte	1818	2	146
McComas, Elisha Jr.	60	4 Mile Cr.	1838	3	147
McComas, Elisha Jr.	190	Wts. of Guyand	1845	4	66
McComas, Elisha Jr.	33	4 Mile Creek	1848	4	171
McComas, Elisha Jr.	25	4 Mile Cr.	1848	4	173
McComas, Elisha M. Jr.	40	4 Mile Creek	1848	4	172
McComas, Elisha M. (or W.)	135	10 Mile Creek	1853	5	212
McComas, Elisha & Thomas I.	70	4 Mile Creek	1851	4	433
McComas, Elisha W.	240	10 Mile Creek	1850	4	298
McComas, Elisha W.	105	10 Mile Creek	1850	4	299
McComas, Elisha W.	50	Wts. of Guyan.	1850	4	366
McComas, Elisha W.	78	Stout Creek	1850	4	367
McComas, Elisha W.	212	9 Mile Creek	1850	4	369
McComas, Elisha W. et al	225	10 Mile Cr.	1850	4	368
McComas, Elisha W. et al	150	Pheaasnt Cr.	1851	4	443
McComas, Elisha W. et al	170	10 Mile Cr.	1851	4	444
McComas, Elisha W. et al	170	10 Mile Cr.	1851	4	445
McComas, Elisha W. et al	900	Laurel Creek	1851	4	446
McComas, Elisha W. et al	650	Six Mile Cr.	1851	4	447
McComas, Elisha W. et al	240	10 Mile Cr.	1851	4	448
McComas, Elisha W. et al	250	Pheasant Cr.	1851	4	449
McComas, Elisha W. et al	250	9 Mile Creek	1851	4	450
McComas, George	50	4 Mile Creek	1835	2	500
McComas, Harrison	180	Wts. of Guyan	1849	4	238
McComas, Harrison	50	Dry Branch	1851	4	437
McComas, Harrison	50	6 Mile Cr.	1858	5	414

Name of Grantee	Acres	Local Description	Year	Book	Page
McComas, Hiram	11½	Wts. of Guyan	1836	2	536
McComas, Hiram	25	Wts. Guyan	1836	3	51
McComas, Hiram	12½	Wts. Guyandotte	1838	3	410
McComas, Hiram et al	145	Wts. Guyandotte	1837	3	106
McComas, Isaac	34	9 Mile Cr.	1811	1	12
McComas, James et al	65	Scary Creek	1848	4	178
McComas, James et al	250	9 Mile Creek	1850	4	300
McComas, James et al	148	Guyand. River	1854	5	254
McComas, James et al	173	Wts. Guyandotte	1855	5	308
McComas, James M.	210	McComas Branch	1852	5	207
McComas, John	50	Big Creek	1851	4	426
McComas, John	35¼	Big Creek	1856	5	340
McComas, Moses	450	Wts. of Guyand.	1817	2	103
McComas, Patrick K.	90	Chapman's Br.	1848	4	215
McComas, Sanders	25	Fall Creek	1838	3	283
McComas, Thomas	97	Wts. of Guyand.	1843	4	19
McComas, Thomas I.	140	4 Mile Creek	1851	4	434
McComas, Thomas I.	230	4 Mile Cr.	1851	4	435
McComas, Thomas I. & Elisha	80	4 Mile Creek	1851	4	436
McComas, Thomas J. et al	100	10 Mile Creek	1854	5	273
McComas, Thomas Jr.	70	Wts. of Guyand.	1836	3	25
McComas, Thomas Jr.	200	Wts. Guyand.	1838	3	143
McComas, Thomas Jr.	18	Trace Fork	1854	5	241
McComas, William	50	Madison Creek	1812	1	34
McComas, William	35	Fall Creek	1812	1	35
McComas, William	360	Wts. of Guyand.	1816	2	72
McComas, William	53	9 Mile Creek	1836	2	532
McComas, William	300	9 Mile Creek	1850	4	330
McCorkle, Alexander	80	Fudges's Big Creek	1857	5	386
McCullough, Patrick H. et al	1,025	Davis Creek	1847	4	115
McDonald, Joseph & Lewis	250	Big Bend	1817	2	105
McGinnis, Allen	179	Davis Creek	1838	3	222
McGinnis, Allen	321	Russell's Cr.	1840	3	419
McGinnis, Allen	370	4 Mile Creek	1852	5	201
McGinnis, Allen	100	Rusell's Creek	1855	5	295
McGinnis, Allen	1,004	10 Mile Creek	1858	5	470
McGinnis, Allen et al	180	Turkey Creek	1850	4	272
McGinnis, Allen et al	250	Turkey Creek	1850	4	273
McGinnis, Allen et al	260	Turkey Creek	1850	4	274
McGinnis, Edmund	200	Graystone Cr.	1813	1	63
McGinnis, Edmund & Allen	200	Merritt's Cr.	1819	2	156
McGinnis, Edmund et al	500	Rt. Hd. Fk.	1816	2	68
McGinnis, Edward	144	Wts. Guyandotte	1829	2	542
McGinnis, James	25	4 Pole Creek	1834	2	436
McGinnis, Oliver A.	90	4 Mile Creek	1853	5	218
McGinnis, Pyrrhus	50	Graystone Creek	1812	1	47
McGinnis, Pyrrus	40	Fudge's Cr.	1816	2	82
McGinnis, Pyrrus	50	Wts. of Mud	1816	2	83
McGinnis, Samuel	350	4 Mile Creek	1813	1	78
McHenry, John	170	Mill Creek	1838	3	358
McKeand, Willis	340	Davis Creek	1835	2	498
McKeand, Willis	160	4 Mile Creek	1838	3	148
McKeand, Willis	22	Wts. of Mud	1838	3	149
McKeand, Willis et al	414	Wts. of Guyand.	1835	2	493
McKendree, A. F. et al	185	14 Mile Creek	1853	5	228
McKenney, James	100	Teas Valley	1832	2	348
McNeeley, Benjamin	100	McCarty's Fork	1857	5	384
McWhorter, James (McWherter)	50	Wts. of Mud	1823	2	250
Merritt, Lerose	25	Wts. Guyandotte	1813	1	84
Merritt, Melchor	410	Reece's Creek	1857	5	365
Merritt, Obediah	110	14 Mile Creek	1816	2	75
Merritt, Obadiah	220	Wts. Guyandotte	1823	2	239
Merritt, Obadiah	85	Wts. of Guyandotte	1833	2	368

Name of Grantee	Acres	Local Description	Year	Book	Page
Merritt, Obadiah	25	Smith's Creek	1833	2	387
Merritt, Obadiah	140	Tom's Creek	1833	2	404
Merritt, Obadiah	65	Merritt's Cr.	1833	2	417
Mesinger or Messinger					
Mesinger, Nicholas	33	Tom's Creek	1838	3	176
Mesinger, Nicholas	200	Tom's Creek	1838	3	180
Messinger or Mesinger					
Meyer, Charles	14	Big Creek	1860	5	437
Midkiff, Lewis	24	Guyandotte River	1854	5	238
Midkiff, Spencer	82	Fall Creek	1844	4	31
Midkiff, Spencer	50	Long Branch	1850	4	414
Midkiff, Spencer	22	Fall Creek	1850	4	415
Midkiff, Spencer	13	Wts. Guyandotte	1854	5	229
Midkiff, Spencer	36	Wts. Guyandotte	1854	5	230
Midkiff, Spencer	55	Fall Creek	1859	5	419
Midkiff, Spencer et al	185	Fall Creek	1845	4	65
Miller, Eliza J.	60	Calf Branch	1842	3	462
Miller, George R.	22	Mill Creek	1838	3	237
Miller, Hugh	200	Wts. of Mud	1813	1	85
Miller, James	10	Fudge's Cr.	1833	2	408
Miller, John	22	Fudge's Creek	1833	2	361
Miller, John	75	Lick Fork	1837	3	102
Miller, John	25	Fudge's Creek	1838	3	175
Miller, John	40	Fudge's Cr.	1838	3	179
Miller, John	24	Fudge's Cr.	1845	4	64
Miller, John	275	Wts. of Mud	1850	4	333
Miller, Maria Luisa	38	Beech Fork	1842	3	463
Miller, W. C.	185	Merritt's Creek	1848	4	223
Miller, W. C. et al	50	Two Mile Creek	1848	4	166
Miller, William C. et al	1,380	7 Mile Cr.	1847	4	158
Miller, William C. et al	125	2 Mile Cr.	1847	4	161
Miller, William C. et al	775	Wts. of Guyand.	1849	4	265
Miller, William C. et al	350	10 Mile Cr.	1852	4	464
Miller, William C. et al	675	Scary Creek	1852	4	466
Miller, William C. et al	170	Middle Fork	1852	4	467
Miller, William C. et al	600	Middle Fork	1852	4	468
Miller, William C. et al	280	Middle Fork	1852	4	469
Miller, William C. et al	825	Laurel Hill Creek	1855	5	301
Miller, William C. et al	1,924	Middle Fork	1852	5	448
Mines, or Mynes					
Mines, Martin et al	170	Wts. of Sandy	1827	2	306
Mins, Martin et al	170	Wts. of Sandy	1827	2	306
Moore—See More					
Moore, Grandison B.	100	Wts. of Mud	1850	4	275
Moore, Grandison B.	180	Sulphur Spgs. Fk.	1850	4	276
Moore, Grandison B. et al Hrs.	100	Porter's Fork	1850	4	277
Moore, Thomas (More)	4	Lick Creek	1837	3	132
More, See Moore					
More, Frederick	500	Big Hurricane Cr.	1824	2	253
More, Frederick	350	Lick Branch	1827	2	313
Morehead, Benedict et al	70	Tug Fork	1833	2	380
Morgan, Simon	650	12 Pole Cr.	1810	1	2
Morgan, Simon	650	Mth. Big Sandy	1810	1	3
Morgan, Simon	400	Wts. Guyandotte	1810	1	4
Morris, John	70	Adj. Lewis Hudson	1836	2	504
Morris, John	500	Hurricane Cr.	1836	3	15
Morris, John	400	Adj. Jas. Young	1843	3	527
Morris, John	2,300	Charlie's Creek	1837	3	530
Morris, John	170	Charlie's Cr.	1850	4	358
Morris, John et al	135	Wts. of Mud	1813	1	98
Morrison, James	94	Heath Creek	1838	3	215
Morrison, James	115	Heath's Cr.	1846	4	100
Morrison, John et al	120	Cabell Creek	1856	5	349

Name of Grantee	Acres	Local Description	Year	Book	Page
Morrison, Patrick	300	Wts. of Guyan	1833	2	411
Morrison, Thompson	50	Tom's Creek	1838	3	178
Morrison, Thompson	75	Cabell Creek	1853	5	214
Morrison, Washington	75	Cabell Creek	1838	3	259
Morrison, Washington	225	Tom's Creek	1850	4	382
Morrison, William	125	Cabell Creek	1838	3	260
Mounts, David	185(125)	Left Hd. Fork	1821	2	190
Mullins, Nathaniel	40	Buffalo Cr.	1825	2	271
Mullins, Spencer A.	228	14 Mile Creek	1854	5	252
Mullins, Spencer A.	200	14 Mile Creek	1854	5	253
Muncey, James	150	Pigeon Cr.	1821	2	191
Muncey, James	50	Pigeon Cr.	1821	2	192
Murphy, John	150	Mate's Creek	1821	2	189
Mynes, See Mines					
Mynes, Isaac	75	Sycamore Cr.	1833	2	421
Mynes, Isaac	20	Sycamore Creek	1838	3	407
Mynes, Isaac	30	Sycamore Creek	1838	3	408
Mynes, Isaac	70	Sycamore Creek	1845	4	68
Napier, Moses	10	12 Pole Creek	1836	3	46
Napier, Moses F.	18	Lick Creek	1844	4	36
Newman, Joseph	60	Everet's Creek	1838	3	340
Newman, Leroy	25	Mill Creek	1826	2	300
Newman, Leroy	125	Mill Creek	1833	2	377
Newman, Leroy et al	135	Wts. of Mud	1813	1	98
Newman, Payton	75	Adj. Wm. Walker	1818	2	113
Newman, Russell	60	Wts. of Mud	1833	2	373
Newman, Russell	20	Mill Creek	1833	2	375
Newman, Russell	105	Wts. of Mud	1833	2	390
Newman, Russell	200	Mill Creek	1848	4	205
Newman, Russell & Vincent	160	Mill Creek	1838	3	204
Newman, Russell & Vincent	30	Mill Creek	1838	3	205
Newman, Vincent	45	Mill Creek	1848	4	217
Newman, William	50	Big Sandy	1820	2	169
Nicholas, John S.	103	Middle Fork	1837	3	87
Nicholas, John S.	6½	Middle Fork	1837	3	125
Nicholas, John S.	63	Mud River	1838	3	285
Nicholas, Solomon	50	Turkey Creek	1838	3	286
Night, Abner	50	9 Mile Creek	1834	2	485
Night, Abner	23	Nine Mile Cr.	1836	3	4
Night, Abner	50	Nine Mi Creek	1838	3	311
Night, Henry	25	Nine Mile Creek	1836	3	38
Night, William	81	9 Mile Creek	1848	4	200
Osborne or Ausben, Ausborn, Osburn					
Osburn, Edmond	100	12 Pole Cr.	1842	3	472
Osburn, Edmund	24	Trace Fork	1834	2	430
Osburn, John	27½	12 Pole Creek	1836	3	27
Osburn, John	50	12 Pole Creek	1838	3	357
Osburn, John	50	12 Pole Creek	1838	3	359
Osburn, John	38	12 Pole Cr.	1842	3	510
Osburn, Thomas	60	Wolf Creek	1842	3	511
Osburn, Thomas	175	Wolf Creek	1838	3	182
Otts, Simeon	337	Middle Fork	1856	5	336
Otts, Simeon	500	Bear Fork	1857	5	368
Paine See Payne					
Paine, Harrison	100	Fall Creek	1852	5	208
Paine, Simeon	110	2 Mile Creek	1850	4	306
Park, George Jr.	20	Tug Fork	1837	3	133
Parker, Henry I. (or J.)	75	Cabell Creek	1838	3	261
Parks, James S.	72	Big Hurricane Cr.	1847	4	114
Parsons, George	80	Beech Fork	1837	3	113
Parsons, George	60	Raccoon Br.	1844	4	33
Parsons, George	90	Four Mile Cr.	1845	4	69
Parsons, George W.	150	4 Mile Cr.	1838	3	187

Name of Grantee	Acres	Local Description	Year	Book	Page
Pore, Robert	40	Wts. of Mud	1815	2	18
Pore, Robert	45	Mill Creek	1815	2	19
Pore, Robert	112	Mill Creek	1833	2	383
Pore, Robert et al	100	Wts. Guyandotte	1833	2	407
Porter, Amacetta et al Heirs	222	Raccoon Fork	1860	5	438
Porter, David	250	Wts. of Mud	1833	2	416
Porter, David	25	Wts. of Mud	1836	2	511
Porter, David	110	Wts. of Mud	1837	3	90
Porter, David	35	Wts. of Mud	1837	3	97
Porter, David	80	Wts. of Mud	1837	3	98
Porter, David	90	Two Mile Cr.	1844	4	32
Porter, David	160	Trace Creek	1847	4	130
Porter, David	125	Wts. of Mud	1847	4	137
Porter, David	10	Wts. of Mud	1848	4	218
Porter, David	200	Wts. of Mud	1849	4	230
Porter, David	130	Wts. of Mud	1850	4	336
Porter, David	700	Wts. of Mud	1850	4	337
Porter, David	125	Peter Cave Branch	1850	4	338
Porter, David	½	Adj. M. Jordan	1850	4	359
Porter, David	118	Little Buffalo	1850	4	409
Porter, J.	90	Madison Creek	1853	5	211
Porter, John Jr.	300	Trace Fork	1836	3	12
Porter, John W.	500	Raccoon Fork	1856	5	344
Porter, John W. Heirs	222	Raccoon Fork	1860	5	438
Porter, Samuel	60	Mill Branch	1853	5	223
Porter, William	50	Trace Creek	1818	2	134
Porter, William	50	Trace Creek	1832	2	356
Porter, William	180	Wts. of Mud	1834	2	488
Porter, William	25	Mud Trace	1838	3	412
Porter, William	375	Trace Creek	1853	5	225
Porter, William Jr.	45	Trace Creek	1836	2	512
Poteet, James	100	Wts. of Guyand.	1829	2	541
Poteet, James et al	220	Wts. of Guyand.	1812	1	42
Powell, John	65	Trace Creek	1847	4	164
Powell, Philip	1	Main Fork	1858	5	416
Pratt, John	50	Mill Creek	1838	3	238
Pratt, John	25	Mill Creek	1842	3	471
Pratt, John	50	Mill Creek	1842	3	513
Preston, John	3,525	Wts. Guyand.	1821	2	538
Preston, Thomas	25	12 Pole Cr.	1838	3	239
Preston, Thomas	57	12 Pole Cr.	1842	3	470
Preston, Thomas	12½	12 Pole Cr.	1843	3	526
Price, Sampson	45	Wts. Sandy	1815	2	8
Proctor, James	32	Dry Creek	1861	5	442
Queen, Absolom	70	12 Pole Creek	1840	3	417
Queen, Absolom	150	12 Pole Creek	1841	3	428
Queen, Absolom	70	12 Pole Creek	1841	3	429
Queen, Absolom	100	12 Pole Creek	1841	3	430
Queen, John	165	Lick Creek	1841	3	447
Queen, John et al	195	12 Pole Cr.	1836	2	506
Ratcliff, William	50	Lft. Hd. Fk.	1838	3	361
Ratcliff, William	54	Bear Creek	1838	3	362
Ratcliff, William	35	Lost Creek	1838	3	363
Ratliff See Ratcliff					
Ratliff, William et al	610	Wts. of Sandy	1834	2	492
Ray, Luke	50	4 Pole Cr.	1837	3	86
Ray, Luke	95	4 Pole Creek	1837	3	89
Rece or Reece					
Rece, Joseph	50	Cabell Cr.	1833	2	364
Reece or Rece					
Reece, Edmund C.	100	Wts. of Mud	1834	2	480
Reece, James H.	265	Wts. of Mud	1850	4	380
Reece, James H. (Rece)	33	Wts. of Mud	1845	4	39

Name of Grantee	Acres	Local Description	Year	Book	Page
Reynolds, Ezekiel	90	Wts. of Mud	1849	4	231
Reynolds, Isaiah	50	Wts. of Mud	1838	3	264
Reynolds, James	100	Ivy Creek	1836	2	530
Reynolds, James	75	Lower Creek	1836	3	3
Reynolds, James	90	Dry Creek	1838	3	390
Reynolds, James	20	Dry Creek	1838	3	391
Reynolds, James	135	2 Mile Creek	1852	5	444
Reynolds, James et al	575	Sander's Cr.	1848	4	183
Reynolds, James et al	955	Wts. of Mud	1848	4	206
Reynolds, James et al	100	Dry Creek	1852	5	445
Reynolds, Simon et al	46	Wts. of Mud	1846	4	102
Reynolds, Simon et al	240	Wts. of Mud	1852	5	443
Riddle, Charles J.	50	Charles's Cr.	1847	4	139
Riddle, Charles J.	80	Charlie's Cr.	1847	4	140
Ritchie, Luther et al	195	Merritt's Cr.	1838	3	341
Roberts, Alexander	75	Bob's Branch	1836	3	6
Roberts, Anderson & James	95	Trace Fork	1842	3	514
Roberts, Barthalomew & Henry	50	Ball's Branch	1833	2	378
Roberts, Charles	90	Raccoon Creek	1848	4	182
Roberts, Gabriel	170	Trace Fork	1834	2	491
Roberts, Gabriel	215	Trace Fork	1846	4	103
Roberts, Green	60	Trace Fork	1829	2	329
Roberts, Green	40	Trace Fork	1834	2	458
Roberts, Harrison	100	Big Creek	1837	3	80
Roberts, Harrison	60	Rose's Run	1847	4	160
Roberts, Henry & B.	100	Charlie's Cr.	1847	4	138
Roberts, James	56	Wts. of Mud	1850	4	339
Roberts, John	50	Tug Fork	1842	3	469
Roberts, John L.	25	Wts. of Mud	1849	4	243
Roberts, John L.	25	Mulberry Br.	1849	4	244
Roberts, Jones	75	Trace Fork	1850	4	360
Roberts, Michael G. et al	220	Trace Fork	1832	2	350
Roberts, Pleasant	25	Trace Fork	1834	2	457
Roberts, Pleasant	100	Trace Fork	1838	3	372
Roberts, William	28	Raccoon Creek	1834	2	438
Roberts, William	80	Raccoon Creek	1836	3	2
Roberts, William	50	Rock Camp Cr.	1848	4	202
Robertson, Joseph	75	Mill Creek	1815	2	46
Robertson, Joseph	15	Mill Creek	1821	2	200
Robertson, Joseph	45	Mill Creek	1822	2	219
Roffe, C. L.	65	Beech Fork	1854	5	231
Roffe, Charles L.	170	Long Branch	1847	4	154
Roffe, Charles L.	1,000	Wts. of 2 Mi. Cr.	1847	4	157
Roffe, Charles L.	1,400	Cabell Creek	1849	4	247
Rogers, George	75	9 Mile Creek	1811	1	10
Rogers, George	22	Wts. Guyandotte	1813	1	92
Rogers, George et al	178	Wts. of Guyand.	1815	2	30
Rogers, James D.	50	Sugar Tree Fork	1850	4	341
Rogers, James D.	75	Sycamore Fork	1850	4	342
Rogers, John	270	Sugar Tree Fk.	1850	4	417
Rogers, John C. et al	365	Merritt's Creek	1855	5	304
Rogers, John C. et al	286	Middle Fork	1855	5	305
Rogers, Michael	150	Middle Fork	1850	4	340
Rogers, Michael	114	Sugar Tree Creek	1855	5	315
Rogers, Michael	263	Sugar Tree Fork	1859	5	423
Rogers, Michael et al	29	Sugar Tree Fork	1857	5	362
Rogers, William et al	120	Cabell Creek	1856	5	349
Ross, Covington	65	12 Pole Cr.	1834	2	468
Ross, Covington	90	Little Lynn	1842	3	468
Ross, John	50	Wts. of Sandy	1818	2	132
Ross, John	180	Beech Fork	1838	3	192
Ross, Madison	150	Beech Fork	1833	2	388
Ross, Madison	135	Lynn Creek	1838	3	190

Name of Grantee	Acres	Local Description	Year	Book	Page
Sires, Thomas	100	Prise's Mill Cr.	1813	1	96
Sirus, Cyrus, Sires, Syrus					
Sirus, Abraham	12	Mill Creek	1818	2	116
Sirus, Abraham	25	Buffalo Cr.	1818	2	118
Sites, See Ceits, Cites, Scitz					
Sites, Christopher Jr.	67	9 Mile Cr.	1850	4	363
Sites, Christopher et al	63	9 Mi. Cr.	1848	4	167
Skelton, Henry et al	225	12 Pole Cr.	1842	3	479
Skelton, Henry et al	195	Taber Creek	1842	3	517
Skelton, Henry et al	75	12 Pole Creek	1842	3	519
Sly, Benjamin,et al	75	4 Pole Creek	1851	4	427
Smiley, Samuel et al	700	Mill Creek	1811	1	6
Smiley, Samuel et al	50	Mill Creek	1812	1	30
Smiley, Samuel et al	50	Left Hand Fork	1812	1	53
Smiley, Samuel et al	100	Tabor's Creek	1815	2	39
Smiley, Samuel et al	60	Left Hand Fork	1815	2	40
Smiley, Samuel et al	100	Left Hand Fork	1815	2	41
Smiley, Samuel et al	50	Left Hand Fork	1815	2	42
Smiley, Samuel et al	20	Wts. Sandy	1815	2	43
Smiley, Samuel et al	60	Wts. of Sandy	1815	2	44
Smith, Adam	50	Camp Creek	1818	2	127
Smith, Ballard	85	Wts. of Guyand.	1849	4	237
Smith, Eldridge Jr.	135	10 Mile Cr.	1836	3	54
Smith, Ezekiel	50	Wts. Guyandotte	1814	1	122
Smith, Ezekiel	50	Dingess Run	1816	2	88
Smith, Henry	22	12 Pole Creek	1838	3	223
Smith, Henry	90	12 Pole Creek	1845	4	44
Smith, Henry	35	Sycamore Cr.	1845	4	45
Smith, Henry	90	Passenger Cr.	1846	4	104
Smith, Henry	26	Beech Fork	1847	4	144
Smith, Henry	110	Beech Fork	1847	4	145
Smith, Henry	120	Long Branch	1848	4	219
Smith, Jackson et al	650	Wts. of Guyand.	1849	4	229
Smith, Jacob	45	12 Pole Cr.	1847	4	142
Smith, Jacob Jr.	25	Mud Lick	1849	4	241
Smith, James	100	Smith's Creek	1813	1	101
Smith, James	70	Big Ugly Creek	1824	2	252
Smith, James	28	Big Ugly Cr.	1824	2	255
Smith, James	25	Wts. of Mud	1834	2	473
Smith, James	25	Sycamore Cr.	1846	4	111
Smith, James	50	14 Mile Creek	1849	4	232
Smith, James	17	Sycamore Creek	1849	4	248
Smith, James	250	Trace Fork	1850	4	410
Smith, James & Harvey	200	14 Mile Creek	1849	4	233
Smith, John	50	Wts. of Guyand.	1816	2	57
Smith, John	100	Mill Creek	1819	2	155
Smith, John	35	Hurricane Cr.	1823	2	245
Smith, John et al	65	Trace Creek	1823	2	249
Smith, John et al	975	Lick Creek	1836	3	14
Smith, Moses	45	12 Pole Cr.	1850	4	345
Smith, Peter	300	Wts. of Mud	1815	2	29
Smith, Peter	37	Rt. Hd. Fk.	1816	2	89
Smith, Peter	50	Wts. of Mud	1819	2	148
Smith, Peter	120	Trace Fork	1837	3	105
Smith, Peter	50	Trace Fork	1838	3	268
Smith, Peter	165	Trace Fork	1838	3	374
Smith, Peter	28	Middle Fork	1841	3	455
Smith, Peter	190	Trace Fork	1850	4	419
Smith, Peter	187	Trace Fork	1856	5	333
Smith, Robert G.	60	Camp Creek	1840	3	418
Smith, Thomas	50	Left Hand Fork	1821	2	203
Smith, Thomas	15	Left Hand Fork	1821	2	204
Smith, Thomas	50	John's Creek	1828	2	320

Name of Grantee	Acres	Local Description	Year	Book	Page
Smith, Thomas	12	Mill Creek	1833	2	399
Smith, Thomas	9	Mill Creek	1833	2	401
Smith, Thomas	85	John's Creek	1836	2	515
Smith, Thomas	175	Mill Creek	1836	3	7
Smith, William	50	Mill Creek	1815	2	17
Smith, William	50	14 Mile Cr.	1826	2	295
Smith, William et al	62	Wts. of Guyand.	1838	3	224
Snidow, William	40	Wts. of Sandy	1834	2	459
Snidow, William et al	610	Wts. of Sandy	1834	2	492
Snodgrass, James	65	Wts. of Mud	1815	2	10
Snodgrass, James	15	Lick Creek	1815	2	11
Snodgrass, James	40 (50)	Laurel Creek	1836	3	41
Snodgrass, James B.	100	Big Creek	1851	4	454
Snodgrass, James B.	9	Wts. of Mud	1854	5	263
Snodgrass, James B.	65	Wts. of Mud	1854	5	266
Snodgrass, James Jr.	550	Wts. of Mud	1838	3	289
Snodgrass, Robert	50	Main Fork	1815	2	2
Snodgrass, Samuel	50	Main Fork	1815	2	21
Softis, Parmelia et al Heirs	100	Porter's Fork	1850	4	277
Spaulding, Flemman	25	Jenny's Creek	1841	3	420
Spears—See Speers					
Spears, Benjamin	50	Nine Mile Creek	1852	5	209
Spears, James	68	9 Mile Creek	1856	5	324
Spears, John (Speers)	100	Alford's Creek	1814	1	135
Spears, Paul (Speers)	65	Alford's Creek	1813	1	97
Spears, Payton	100	9 Mile Creek	1855	5	314
Spears, Thomas H.	50	9 Mile Creek	1856	5	323
Spears, William	175	9 Mile Cr.	1851	4	438
Speers, George	300	Wts. of Guyand.	1815	2	51
Sperry, Abijah	25	Wts. of Sandy	1813	1	56
Sperry, Abijah	15	Adj. his own	1818	2	126
Sperry, Benjamin	53	Tug Fork	1818	2	124
Sperry, Benjamin	50	Wts. Sandy	1837	3	139
Sperry, Benjamin et al (Speery)	100	Left Hand Fork	1815	2	24
Sprouse, Elijah	70	Trace Fork	1816	2	86
Sprouse, Robert	50	Davison's Br.	1813	1	75
Spurlock, Alexander	115	Middle Fork	1850	4	288
Spurlock, Alexander	100	Middle Fork	1850	4	289
Spurlock, Alexander	111	Middle Fork	1857	5	370
Spurlock, Alexander	66	Middle Fork	1857	5	371
Spurlock, Charles	50	Hart's Creek	1821	2	202
Spurlock, Charles	172	Wts. Guyandotte	1837	3	129
Spurlock, Charles & Robertson	70	Wt. of Mud	1838	3	267
Spurlock, Daniel	75	Wts. of Guyand.	1833	2	371
Spurlock, Daniel	70	Cow Fork	1833	2	396
Spurlock, Daniel	20	Cow Fork	1838	3	314
Spurlock, Daniel	680	Wts. of Guyandotte	1838	3	315
Spurlock, Eliphas	120	Wts. of Mud	1847	4	162
Spurlock, Harrison R.	50	Road Fork	1850	4	282
Spurlock, Harrison R.	104	Bear Fork	1856	5	335
Spurlock, Harvey	40	Wts. of Guyandotte	1838	3	316
Spurlock, Harvey	60	Wts. of Guyandotte	1838	3	317
Spurlock, Jesse	350	Right Fork	1812	1	21
Spurlock, Jesse	100	Beech Fork	1838	3	355
Spurlock, Robinson & Charles	50	Wts. of Mud	1844	4	37
Spurlock, Thomas	90	Lick Branch	1838	3	313
Spurlock, William	500	Wts. of Sandy	1828	2	540
Stafford, John	100	Left Hd. Fork	1818	2	119
Stallings See Stollings					
Stallings, Jacob	60	Wts. of Guyandotte	1813	1	106
Stallings, Jacob	185	Hart's Cr.	1813	1	111
Stallings, Jacob	318	Crawley's Cr.	1813	1	112
Stanley, Robert	141	Tom's Creek	1854	5	264

Name of Grantee	Acres	Local Description	Year	Book	Page
Walker, Daniel	25	Tug Fork	1813	1	95
Walker, John	75	Hurricane Cr.	1838	3	366
Walker, Patent (Patton)	40	Big Cabell Cr.	1821	2	214
Walker, William	100	12 Pole Creek	1811	1	9
Walker, William	100	Adj. J. Chenoweth	1813	1	116
Walker, William	50	12 Pole	1825	2	289
Walker, William et al	150	Wts. of Sandy	1812	1	16
Walker, William et al	35	12 Pole Cr.	1831	2	340
Wallis, John	50	Sycamore Creek	1815	2	6
Walton, Nancy	105	Wts. of Mud	1816	2	84
Walton, William	40	Wts. of Mud	1812	1	40
Walton, William	90	Main Fork	1817	2	100
Ward, Evermont et al	1,125	Wts. Guyandotte	1854	5	267
Ward, Evermont et al	1,930	Wts. Guyandotte	1855	5	456
Ward, Thomas	100	Beech Fork	1811	1	7
Ward, Thomas	150	Wts. Guyandotte	1811	1	8
Ward, Thomas	50	Heath's Creek	1812	1	27
Ward, Thomas	75	Wts. of Guyandotte	1812	1	28
Ward, Thomas	80	Wts. of Guyand.	1817	2	96
Ward, Thomas et al	700	Mill Creek	1811	1	6
Ward, Thomas et al	50	Mill Creek	1812	1	30
Ward, Thomas et al	100	Wts. Guyandotte	1812	1	31
Ward, Thomas et al	100	Wts. of Guyandotte	1812	1	46
Warden, Albert et al	448	Little Trace	1855	5	300
Warden, James	125	Hurricane Creek	1834	2	463
Warden, James M.	32	Adj. T. Lewis	1838	3	269
Washington, Samuel F.	50	4 Pole Cr	1837	3	100
Watts, Ambrose	30	Hurricane Cr.	1843	4	20
Watts, Ely et al	100	Mill Creek	1823	2	238
Weathro, Witherow, Withrow					
Weathro, William	25	12 Pole Cr.	1824	2	257
Webb, Edward	325	Wts. of Mud	1847	4	147
Webb, Edward	70	Trace Fork	1847	4	148
Webb, Edward	130	Sycamore Cr.	1847	4	149
Webb, Edward	40	Sycamore Cr.	1849	4	253
Webb, James	100	Charles's Creek	1821	2	208
Webb, James	90	Charlie's Cr.	1834	2	466
Webb, James	80	Charlie's Cr.	1834	2	483
Webb, Robert	20	Wts. of Sandy	1816	2	70
Webb, Samuel	45	Wilson's Br.	1827	2	304
Webb, Samuel	85	Mill Creek	1827	2	311
Webb, Samuel	180	Taber's Creek	1827	2	316
Webb, Samuel	90	Mill Creek	1836	3	42
Webb, Samuel	90	Mill Creek	1838	3	367
Webb, Samuel	25	Mill Creek	1838	3	368
Webb, Samuel	20	Mill Cr.	1830	2	342
Webb, Seabird	187	Charlie's Cr.	1837	3	110
Webb, William W.	100	Charlie's Creek	1834	2	431
Webb, William W.	175 (195)	Wts. of Mud	1838	3	198
Webb, William W.	100	Big Creek	1845	4	70
Wellman, James	110	Left Hand Fork	1822	2	222
Wellman, James	10	Lick Branch	1837	3	81
Wellman, James	150	Hurricane Cr.	1837	3	93
Wellman, Jeremiah	25	Mill Creek	1815	2	37
Wellman, John	110	Wts. of Sandy	1827	2	308
Wellman, John	30	Mill Creek	1827	2	309
Wellman, John	100	12 Pole Cr.	1830	2	345
Wellman, John	50	Wts. of Sandy	1836	2	535
Wellman, John et al	50	12 Pole Cr.	1836	2	518
Wellman, John et al	65	Rich Creek	1836	2	521
Wellman, John et al	50	12 Pole Cr.	1836	2	522
Wellman, John et al	90	Milam's Creek	1836	2	529
Wellman, Madison	200	Wts. of Sandy	1838	3	365

Name of Grantee	Acres	Local Description	Year	Book	Page
Wellman, Robert	110	Big Hur. Creek	1827	2	315
Wellman, Robert	28	Mill Creek	1841	3	444
Wents—See Wentz, Wince, Wints, Wintz					
Wentz, William	75	Smith Creek	1838	3	290
Wheeler, Edward	74	Straight Fork	1838	3	373
Wheeler, Edward	20	Middle Fork	1850	4	364
Wheeler, Eli	50	Porter Fork	1838	3	291
Wheeler, Eli	412	Porter's Fork	1850	4	290
Wheeler, James	58 (50)	Straight Fork	1838	3	292
Wheeler, James	40	Middle Fork	1850	4	291
Wheeler, John	16	Trace Fork	1836	3	35
Wheeler, John	53	Trace Fork	1836	3	49
Wheeler, John	14	Trace Fork	1836	3	50
Wheeler, John	38	Trace Fork	1836	3	52
Wheeler, John	50	Clymer's Creek	1838	3	293
Wheeler, John	125	Trace Fork	1850	4	347
Wheeler, Joseph	90	Trace Fork	1834	2	451
Wheeler, William	100	Clymer's Cr.	1833	2	420
Wheeler, William	55	Climer's Creek	1837	3	130
Wheeler, William	100	Clymer's Creek	1838	3	294
Wheeler, William & Joseph	545	Wts. Mud River	1854	5	251
Wheeler, William et al	130	Clymer's Cr.	**1837**	**3**	**101**
White, Charles	16	Stone Coal Cr.	1836	3	23
White, James	75	Mill Creek	1818	2	135
White, James	100	9 Mi. Creek	1845	4	71
Williams, Archelous N.	25	2 Mile Creek	1847	4	116
Williams, Archelous N.	62½	Fudge's Creek	1849	4	239
Williams, William M.	10	Trace Creek	1847	4	163
Williamson, Elias	85	Jenny's Cr.	1836	2	531
Wilson, Alexander	50	Mill Creek	1823	2	241
Wilson, Alexander	50	Mill Creek	1842	3	518
Wilson, Alexander	75	12 Pole Cr.	1842	3	520
Wilson, Alexander & Charles	60	Mill Creek	1826	2	299
Wilson, Allen et al	150	12 Pole Cr.	1830	2	344
Wilson, Anderson	25	12 Pole Cr.	1846	4	107
Wilson, Charles	100	Mill Creek	1821	2	205
Wilson, Charles	25	Adj. J. Wilson	1842	3	521
Wilson, James	75	Wts. of Sandy	1815	2	50
Wilson, James	40	Smiley's Br.	1820	2	174
Wilson, James	70	Left Hand Fork	1821	2	210
Wilson, James	25	Left Hand Fork	1821	2	211
Wilson, James	45	Camp Creek	1821	2	212
Wilson, James	25	Adj. his own	1823	2	242
Wilson, James	50	12 Pole	1826	2	301
Wilson, James	50	12 Pole Creek	1831	2	335
Wilson, James	90	Wts. of Mud	1834	2	443
Wilson, James	48	Wts. of Mud	1837	3	64
Wilson, James	45	Wts. of Mud	1838	3	196
Wilson, James et al	190	14 Mile Cr.	1833	2	382
Wilson, James et al	175	12 Pole Cr.	1836	2	505
Wilson, Robert	50	12 Pole Creek	1814	1	126
Wilson, Samuel	85	Wts. of Mud	1838	3	197
Wilson, Samuel E. O.	100	Wts. of Mud	1847	4	146
Wilson, Samuel E. O.	50	Wts. of Mud	1850	4	381
Wilson, Samuel O.	60	Wts. of Mud	1833	2	360
Wilson, Samuel O.	40	Wts. of Mud	1833	2	406
Wince, Wents, Wentz, Wints, Wintz					
Wince, Joseph	50	Wts. of Mud	1834	2	470
Wince, Philip	25	9 Mile Creek	1819	2	161
Wince, William et al	75	4 Pole Creek	1851	4	427
Wince, Windle	100 (400)	Above 9 Mi. Cr.	1821	2	206
Winters, Benjamin	87	Blue Hollow	1847	4	165
Wints, Wents, Wentz, Wince, Wintz					

Name of Grantee	Acres	Local Description	Year	Book	Page
Wints, Philip et al	50	Long Hollow	1838	3	266
Wints, Windle	25	9 Mile Creek	1834	2	445
Wints, Windle	25	9 Mile Cr	1834	2	446
Wintz, Wents, Wentz, Wince, Wints					
Wintz, Jacob	60	Wts. of Mud	1837	3	67
Wintz, Jacob	60	Wts. of Mud	1838	3	150
Wishan, John (Wishon)	100	6 Mile Creek	1814	1	125
Wishon, John	250	Wts. Guyandotte	1821	2	184
Witcher, Daniel	60	Laurel Fork	1841	3	421
Witcher, Daniel	35	12 Pole Cr.	1841	3	422
Witcher, Daniel	15	12 Pole Creek	1841	3	423
Witcher, Daniel	32	12 Pole Creek	1841	3	424
Witcher, Daniel Jr.	80	Heath's Creek	1816	2	90
Witcher, Daniel Sr.	165	Wts. Guyand.	1833	2	385
Witcher, Jeremiah	28	Wts. of Guyand.	1849	4	271
Witcher, Jeremiah	4½	Middle Fork	1858	5	391
Witcher, Jeremiah	872	Wts. Mud River	1854	5	454
Withrow, Weathro, Witherow					
Withrow, John	70	12 Pole Cr.	1828	2	326
Woods, John	37	12 Pole Cr.	1834	2	426
Wooten, Winston	25	Saunder's Creek	1852	5	200
Workman, Jesse	70	Bull Creek	1842	3	465
Workman, Joseph	40	12 Pole Cr.	1834	2	450
Workman, Stephen	22	Wolf Pen Br.	1838	3	318
Wyatt, Thomas et al	120	Trace Fork	1820	2	171
Yates, John T.	25	Porter's Fork	1850	4	365
Yates, William B.	90	Fudge's Creek	1847	4	150
Yates, William B.	125	Fudge's Creek	1847	4	151
Young, George	65	Lower Creek	1838	3	319
Young, James	50	Charlie's Cr.	1834	2	419

CALHOUN COUNTY

Arnold, James W.	300	Wts Lit. Kanawha	1861	1	499
Ball, John	185	Wts Lit. Kanawha	1860	1	484
Barr, Samuel	185	Wts Lit. Kanawha	1860	1	485
Bennett, John & William	86	Bennett's M. Run	1860	1	489
Bennett, Jonathan M.	1,000	Wts. Lit. Kanawha	1858	1	481
Betts, Collins, et al	160	Big Root Cr.	1860	1	483
Chenoweth, R. J.	59	3-Lick Run	1860	1	488
Elison, Madison T.	68	Stinson Fork	1860	1	487
Farnsworth, Isaac P. et al	160	Big Root Cr.	1860	1	483
Fell, Thomas B.	100	Stinson Fork	1859	1	482
Ferrell, Valentine, et al	160	Big Root Cr.	1860	1	483
Greathouse, Samuel	318	Rowel's Run	1860	1	491
Greer, John M.	350	Rowel's Run	1858	1	475
Greer, John M.	100	Panther Run	1858	1	477
Hays, Peregrine	700	West Fork	1861	1	494
Hays, Peregrine	857	Wts Lit. Kanawha	1861	1	495
Hays, Peregrine	867	West Fork	1861	1	496
Hoffman—Huffman					
Huffman, Alexander	600	Wts of Lit. Kanawha	1860	1	486
Huffman, John S., et al	453	Rowel's Run	1861	1	497
Huffman, John S., et al	923	Pine Creek	1861	1	498
Jackson, Minter, et al	580	Lemuel's Run	1857	1	470
McCoy, George W.	35	West Fork	1858	1	474
Norris, Milton	150	Lemuel's Run	1858	1	471

Name of Grantee	Acres	Local Description	Year	Book	Page
Norris, Milton	60	Pine Creek	1858	1	472
Norris, Milton, et al	453	Rowel's Run	1861	1	497
Norris, Milton, et al	923	Pine Creek	1861	1	498
Norris, Milton, et al	580	Lemuel's Run	1857	1	470
Nutter, Levi	180	Barren's Run	1860	1	492
Rafferty, Patrick	300	Laurel Creek	1860	1	500
Robinson, James	291	Sycamore Cr.	1858	1	473
Starcher, Adam & Thomas	200	Barren's Run	1858	1	476
Starcher, William	350	Rowel's Run	1860	1	490
Sterm, Peter	400	Sycamore Fork	1858	1	479
Stump, Michael	868	Pine Creek	1858	1	478
Sturm—See Sterm					
Witte, Charles	300	Pine Cr	1858	1	480
Wolverton. James S.	100	Coal Fork	1860	1	493

CLAY COUNTY

Brown, James H., et al	816½	Wts of Elk	1860	1	503
Campbell, Christopher C.	200	Wts of Elk	1860	1	505
Goshorn, William F., et al	816½	Wts of Elk	1860	1	503
Lewis, Charles L.	148¾	Big Laurel	1859	1	502
Paxton, Thomas	100	Wts of Elk	1860	1	504
Rogers, Allen S.	100a. (100 poles)	Granny She Fork	1860	1	506
Sinnet, Abel P., et al	816½	Wts of Elk	1860	1	503
Smith, Benjamin H. & G. W.	5537½	Sandy & Elk	1859	1	501
Swann, Thomas B., et al	816½	Wts of Elk	1860	1	503

DODDRIDGE COUNTY

Adams, Jonathan	150	Sugar Camp Run	1849	2	5
Adams, Josias	2,000	Robinson's Fork	1855	2	205
Adams, Josias	1,100	Flint Run	1855	2	206
Adams, Preston M.	400	Flint Run	1859	2	214
Allen, Joshua	40	Frank's Run	1859	2	216
Allen, Osbern	22¾	Elk Lick Run	1860	2	223
Ashburn, Josephus	45	Flint Run	1856	2	209
Austin, A. M. & P. S., et al	608¼	Meathouse Fork	1860	2	228
Barnett, Allison	65	South Fork	1851	2	118
Barnett, Allison, et al	100	South Fork	1851	2	117
Bee, Amaziah	225	Meathouse Fork	1850	2	44
Bee, Amaziah	12	Meathouse Fork	1851	2	87
Bee, Amaziah	90	Tom Hickman's Run	1852	2	147
Bee, Amaziah	146	Meat House Fk	1849	1	555
Bee, Ephraim	150	Lick Run	1849	2	24
Bee, Ephraim	9¼	Lick Run	1850	2	32
Bee, Ephraim	196	Meathouse Fork	1850	2	33
Bee, Ephraim	34	Little Flink's Run	1850	2	35
Bee, Ephraim	47	Nutter's Fork	1850	2	36
Bee, Ephraim	500	M. Island Creek	1850	2	50
Bee, Ephraim	183½	Long Run	1851	2	88

Name of Grantee	Acres	Local Description	Year	Book	Page
Davis, Joel H.	15	Lick Run	1856	2	212
Davis, Joshua J.	50	Morgan's Run	1848	1	546
Davis, Lewis S.	50	Arnold's Creek	1850	2	45
Davis, Lewis S.	43½	Arnold's Cr.	1848	2	547
Davis, Lodawick H.	182	Buckeye Fork	1847	1	520
Davis, Milton S.	68	Sugar Camp Run	1853	2	165
Davis, Nathan J.	92	Mid. Island	1851	2	92
Davis, Nathan J.	120	Middle Island	1850	2	52
Davis, Nathan J.	40	Mid. Island	1850	2	56
Davis, Peter	124	Greenbrier Run	1851	2	73
Davis, Peter W.	82	Mid. Island	1850	2	57
Davis, Peter W.	50	Buckeye Fork	1848	1	540
Davis, Stephen T.	375	Flint Run	1847	1	522
Davis, William J.	40	Nutter's Fork	1848	1	538
Davisson, D. D.	2¼	Long Run	1860	2	221
Davisson, Devictmen D.	3¾	Long Run	1860	2	220
Davisson, Josia, et al	128	Buffalo Calf Run	1859	2	215
Dent, Nimrod, et al	608¼	Meathouse Fork	1860	2	228
Despard, Richard	150	Meat House Fork	1851	2	101
Dis Debar, Joseph H.	3,300	Cove Creek	1855	2	188
Doak, Davis	99½	Long Run	1846	1	511
Dotson, Henry F.	152	Lick Run	1852	2	134
Dotson, Henry F. (Dodson)	97½	Long Run	1847	1	526
Dotson, James	50	Arnold's Cr.	1851	2	72
Dotson, John	10	Arnold's Cr.	1854	2	176
Dotson, John	200	Sugar Camp Run	1854	2	177
Dotson, John, et al	102	Arnold's Creek	1849	2	17
Dotson, Mathias	57	Long Run	1846	1	512
Dotson, Mathias & Asbury	90	Long Run	1846	1	517
Dotson, William B.	9	Dotson's Run	1849	2	2
Dotson, William B.	24	Dotson's Run	1849	2	3
Dotson, William B.	33	Dotson's Run	1851	2	121
Dotson, William B.	66	Jefferson's Run	1854	2	179
Dotson, William, Sr.	47½	Dotson's Run	1856	2	200
Duckworth, Wellington	10½	Long Run	1858	2	193
Eliason, Elias (Eleason)	1,050	Arnold's Creek	1856	2	207
Engle — See Ingle					
Engle, John J., et al	200	Arnold's Creek	1847	1	521
Ford, Albert	230	Morgan's Run	1850	2	40
Ford, Albert	30	Buckeye Run	1848	1	541
Ford, Thomas	335	Buckeye Fork	1847	1	523
Foreman, Henry	36½	Dotson's Run	1854	2	172
Fleming, James	150	Arnold's Creek	1848	1	534
Fox, John & William	25	Snake Run	1853	2	163
Gain, Adam S.	100	Dotson's Run	1850	2	58
Gain, Christopher R., et al	270	Frank's Run	1860	2	229
Gapen, John	590	Flint Run	1850	2	53
Garner, Delila	32	Arnold's Creek	1850	2	59
Garrett, Addison P.	50	Long Run	1848	1	545
Gatrell, Thomas, et al	200	Arnold's Creek	1847	1	521
Gray, Thomas S.	300	South Fork	1859	2	213
Hall, Smith C., et al	617	South Fork & Sugar Camp	1860	2	567
Haney, Harriet	104	Watson's Run	1858	2	194
Harrison, Thomas, et al	950	Arnold's Cr.	1860	2	224
Haymond, Luther	32	Lick Run	1849	2	10
Haymond, Luther	276	Tom's Fork	1849	2	20
Haymond, Mary Anne	2,000	Big Battle	1855	2	187
Herald, Willis	76½	Morgan's Run	1849	2	16
Hess, A.	265	Mid. Island	1851	2	69
Hess, A.	200	Buckeye Fork	1851	2	70
Hickman, F. D.	375	Sandy Run	1857	2	202
Holliday, James R.	155	Morgan's Run	1849	2	27
Holliday, John W.	45	Riggin's Run	1849	2	18

Name of Grantee	Acres	Local Description	Year	Book	Page
Horner, James Y.	740	Hd. Wts. Mud Lick Run	1846	2	568
Hoskins, J. C. C.	2¼	Long Run	1855	2	185
Hughes, Martin	40	M. Island Creek	1850	2	48
Hughes, Martin, et al	181	Buckeye Fork	1850	2	43
Hutson, Eiven	88	Buckeye Fork	1848	1	542
Hutson, Minter (or Winter)	89	Elkhorn Run	1849	2	23
Ice, Isaac	100	Archer's Fork	1851	2	102
Ingle—See Engle					
Ingle, John J.	119	Arnold's Cr.	1849	2	28
Jackson, Benjamin W.	228	Buckeye Fork	1851	2	81
Jackson, Benjamin W., et al	140	Indian Fork	1851	2	114
Jackson, George A., et al	145	South Fork	1854	2	175
Jarvis, Granville D.	10½	Wilhem's Run	1852	2	139
Jeffrey, Joseph	100	Red Lick	1850	2	60
Jeffrey, Joseph	(158)150	Bluestone Br.	1847	1	524
Jeffrey, Joseph	52	Meathouse Fork	1848	1	539
Jeffrey, William	360½	Flint Run	1849	2	29
Johnston, Robert	715	Meathouse Fk.	1852	2	140
Johnston, Robert	2,065	Middle Fork	1858	2	195
Johnston, Robert, et al	275	Meathouse Fork	1851	2	74
Johnston, Robert, et al	260	Buckeye Fork	1851	2	75
Johnston, Robert, et al	42	South Fork	1851	2	76
Johnston, Robert, et al	380	Morgan's Run	1851	2	77
Johnston, Robert, et al	290	Middle Fork	1851	2	78
Johnston, Robert, et al	1,125	Meathouse Fork	1851	2	79
Johnston, Robert, et al	610	Flint Run	1851	2	80
Johnston, Robert, et al	70	Tom's Fork	1851	2	124
Keller, Fealdon F.	100	Sycamore Fork	1851	2	120
Kelley, James F.	26	Doyle Run	1853	2	166
Kelley, James F. (Kelly)	51	Long Run	1854	2	180
Kelley, James F., et al	950	Arnold's Cr.	1860	2	224
Kinney, Israel	940	Flint's Run	1851	2	122
Lefever, Jesse W.	490	Wolf Pen Run	1849	2	26
Lefever, Jesse W.	455	Meathouse Fork	1853	2	168
Lefever, Jesse W.	400	Big Dry Fork	1853	2	169
Lefever, Jesse W.	255	Meat House Fork	1853	2	170
Lewis, Charles S.	200	Ralph's Run	1857	2	201
Lewis, Charles S.	2,535	Flint Run	1860	2	560
Lynn, John C.	100	Watson's Run	1859	2	217
Lynn, Michael, et al	270	Frank's Run	1860	2	229
Maxon—See Maxson					
Maxson, John	100	Sugar Camp Run	1849	2	7
Maxson, John	100	Bridge Run	1848	1	543
Maxson, John	25	Buckeye Fork	1848	1	544
Maxwell, Abner	112	Tom's Fork	1849	2	11
Maxwell, Abner	48	Tom's Fork	1849	2	12
Maxwell, Abner	40	Tom's Fork	1851	2	115
Maxwell, Abner	130	Tom's Fork	1851	2	116
Maxwell, Abner, et al	228	Tom's Fork	1849	2	13
Maxwell, Abner, et al	100	South Fork	1851	2	117
Maxwell, Franklin	550	Bluestone Run	1849	2	6
Maxwell, Franklin	26	Blue Stone	1851	2	93
Maxwell, Lewis	250	Paten Lick	1851	2	65
Maxwell, Lewis	90	Middle Island	1851	2	66
Maxwell, Lewis	550	Middle Fork	1852	2	142
Maxwell, Lewis	1,640	Robert's Fork	1852	2	143
Maxwell, Lewis	2,030	Indian Fork	1852	2	144
Maxwell, Lewis	2,032½	Cabin Run	1860	2	227
Maxwell, Lewis	140	Thomas Fork	1848	1	535
Maxwell, Lewis	94	Bear Run	1848	1	536
Maxwell, Lewis	200	Lick Run	1848	1	537
Maxwell, Lewis	2,000	Meathouse Fork	1851	2	549
Maxwell, Lewis	1,400	Meathouse Fork	1851	2	552

Name of Grantee	Acres	Local Description	Year	Book	Page
Maxwell, Lewis	4,820	Cove Creek	1852	2	554
Maxwell, Nathaniel	110	Panther Lick Run	1854	2	182
McClain, David	56	Snake Run	1850	2	41
McClain, David	65	Beech Lick	1850	2	54
McReynolds, Maria C.	33½	Ralph's Run	1860	2	222
Meeks, Montecue	60	Buckeye Fork	1851	2	82
Meline, James F.	1,000	Bear Fork	1853	2	164
Michel, Jesse (Mitchell)	125	Camp Run	1849	2	8
Mitchell see Michel					
Neely, Floyd	100	Middle Fork	1857	2	203
Neely, Floyd et al	191	Wolf Pen	1851	2	85
Neely, Floyd, et al	140	Mid. Island	1851	2	94
Neely, Floyd, et al	360	Trough Fork	1851	2	111
Neely, Floyd, et al	540	Flint Run	1851	2	112
Neely, Floyd, et al	617	South Fork & Sugar Camp	1860	2	567
Neely, Mathew	76	Shingle Tree Run	1851	2	113
Nutter, Anda Jr.	100	South Fork	1852	2	132
Nutter, Anda Jr.	18	Tom's Fork	1852	2	133
Nutter, Anda Jr.	100	Tom's Fork	1852	2	138
Orr, John P.	100	Waldo's Run	1850	2	63
Pearcy, Joshua	130	Tom's Fork	1849	2	14
Pearcy, Joshua	60	Tom's Fork	1852	2	137
Pigott, Edward	75	Rush Run	1852	2	145
Powell, Reuben & Ralph	260	Wiseman's Run	1850	2	61
Randolph, Isaac F.	25	Buckeye Fork	1849	2	9
Randolph, Isaac F.	112	M. Island Creek	1850	2	47
Randolph, Isaac F.	220	Hunter's Fork	1848	1	550
Randolph Jeptha F.	135	Buckeye Fork	1851	2	83
Randolph, Jeptha F.	135	Patterson's Fork	1851	2	127
Randolph, Jeptha F.	52	Wolf Pen Run	1856	2	208
Randolph, Jeptha F.	78	Buckeye Fork	1848	1	532
Randolph, Jeptha F.	80	Buffalo Calf Run	1848	1	533
Randolph, Jeptha F.	160	Meat House Fk.	1849	1	557
Randolph, Samuel P. F.	125	Rock Run	1850	2	46
Randolph, William F.	60	Greenbrier Run	1851	2	68
Randolph, William F.	275	Mid. Island	1851	2	95
Randolph, William F.	100	Greenbrier Run	1851	2	96
Randolph, William F.	40	Buckeye Fork	1848	1	530
Randolph, William F.	150	Laurel Run	1848	1	531
Robinson, Alfred N.	50	Snake Run	1853	2	167
Sandy, William et al Heirs	375	Adj. V. A. Sandy	1856	2	199
Sayre, Squire	100	Rush Run	1851	2	86
Sayre, Squire	120	Arnold's Creek	1851	2	131
Scott, Thomas D.	12	Sugar Camp Run	1852	2	150
Scott, Thomas D.	32	Wilhem's Creek	1854	2	181
Scott, Thomas D., et al	102	Arnold's Creek	1849	2	17
Sherwood, Daniel	240	Buckeye	1851	2	100
Sherwood, Daniel	18½	Long Run	1851	2	128
Sherwood, Daniel et al	275	Meathouse Fork	1851	2	74
Sherwood, Daniel et al	260	Buckeye Fork	1851	2	75
Sherwood, Daniel et al	42	South Fork	1851	2	76
Sherwood, Daniel et al	380	Morgan's Run	1851	2	77
Sherwood, Daniel et al	290	Middle Fork	1851	2	78
Sherwood, Daniel et al	1,125	Meathouse Fork	1851	2	79
Sherwood, Daniel et al	610	Flint Run	1851	2	80
Sherwood, Daniel et al	191	Wolf Pen	1851	2	85
Sherwood, Daniel et al	635	Meat House	1851	2	89
Sherwood, Daniel et al	688½	Meat House	1851	2	90
Sherwood, Daniel et al	440	Long Run	1851	2	107
Sherwood, Daniel et al	360	Long Run	1851	2	108
Sherwood, Daniel et al	140	Indian Fork	1851	2	114
Sherwood, Daniel et al	70	Tom's Fork	1851	2	124
Shinn, Josiah H.	334	Lick Run	1850	2	34

Name of Grantee	Acres	Local Description	Year	Book	Page
Shinn, Josiah H.	132	Long Run	1851	2	129
Shinn, Josiah H.	42	Lick Run	1852	2	149
Shinn, Josiah H.	428	Arnold's Cr.	1852	2	151
Shinn, Josiah H.	96	Long Run	1858	2	191
Shinn, Josiah H.	58	Rush Run	1860	2	219
Shinn, Levi	62	Arnold's Cr.	1852	2	141
Smith, James W.	68¾	Arnold's Cr.	1860	2	225
Smith, John H.	174½	Middle Run	1860	2	226
Smith, Thomas	840	Flint Run	1850	2	49
Sommerville, Alexander L.	310	Clay Lick	1860	2	218
Sommerville, William M.	25	Lick Run	1848	1	552
Stout, Abner	50	Red Lick	1850	2	62
Stout, James M.	100	Jim's Run	1853	2	160
Stout, James M.	100	Trap Fork	1853	2	162
Stout, Job B.	170	Wts. Hughes River	1849	2	21
Stout, Job B.	30	Tom Hickman's Run	1849	2	22
Stout, Job B., et al	228	Tom's Fork	1849	2	13
Stout, Joseph et al	145	South Fork	1854	2	175
Strunk, Hiram C.	50	Long Run	1854	2	183
Stutler, Abraham P.	112	Cole Run	1849	2	15
Stutler, Isaac	49	Buckeye Run	1849	1	558
Stutler, Isaac	78	Trough Fork	1849	2	1
Stutler, Isaac	245	Buckeye Fork	1851	2	84
Stutler, Isaac	275	Buckeye Fork	1851	2	130
Stutler, Isaac	30½	Morgan's Run	1854	2	184
Stutler, Robert	54	Buckeye Fork	1850	2	42
Stutler, Robert et al	181	Buckeye Fork	1850	2	43
Sutton, Reuben D.	32	Buckeye Fork	1848	1	548
Swiger, Alfred	186	McElroy's Cr.	1851	2	119
Swiger, Thomas	45	Sycamore Fork	1852	2	159
Swiger, Thomas	400	McElroy's Cr.	1852	2	161
Swiger, Thomas	740	Sycamore Fork	1854	2	178
Tate, Hugh	232	Big Battle	1849	2	4
Tate, Hugh	62	Skelton's Run	1852	2	154
Tate, Hugh	168	Big Battle	1848	1	554
Thomas, George	2	Dotson's Run	1856	2	198
Traugh, Jacob et al	128	Buffalo Calf Run	1859	2	215
Trough, Jacob et al	128	Buffalo Calf Rn.	1859	2	215
Tucker, Mary	76¼	Gum Run	1851	2	67
Weekly, James	24	McElroy's Fork	1855	2	186
Weekly, William	172	Persimmon Lick	1856	2	210
Williams, John A.	164	Flint Run	1850	2	64
Williams, William W.	161	Meadow Run	1859	2	196
Wilson, Benjamin	62	Buckeye Run	1851	2	103
Wilson, Benjamin	120	Buckeye Run	1851	2	104
Wilson, Benjamin	70	Indian Fork	1851	2	105
Wilson, Benjamin	200	East Run	1851	2	106
Wilson, Benjamin	4,000	Flint Run	1852	2	155
Wilson, Benjamin et al	150	Flint Run	1851	2	97
Wilson, Benjamin et al	440	Long Run	1851	2	107
Wilson, Benjamin et al	360	Long Run	1851	2	108
Wilson, Benjamin & J. D.	295	Buckeye Fork	1851	2	109
Wilson, Benjamin & J. D.	215	Buckeye Fork	1851	2	110

FAYETTE COUNTY

Name of Grantee	Acres	Local Description	Year	Book	Page
Abbott, Wilson	50	Marsh Fork	1838	2	118
Abbott, Wilson	45	Marsh Fork	1838	2	127
Alderson, George	94	Wts. of New River	1834	2	74
Amick, Jacob Sr.	200	Wts. Meadow R.	1846	2	199
Anderson, Alexander	178	Walnut Knob	1854	2	267
Anderson, Alexander	150	Adj. J. Anderson	1856	2	321
Anderson, John	14	Wts. New River	1836	2	62
Anderson, John	100	Wts. of New River	1838	2	120
Anderson, John	15	Wts. of New River	1838	2	121
Anderson, John	73	New River Cliffs	1838	2	122
Anderson, John	115	Wts. New River	1838	2	123
Anderson, John	170	Wts. of New River	1850	2	240
Anderson, Micajah	425	Armstrong Cr.	1845	2	192
Anthony, Abner Jr.	450	Rich Creek	1843	2	171
Anthony, Mark	1,000	Wts. Gauley	1842	2	151
Anthony, Mark	2,940	Rich Creek	1842	2	568
Arbough, Price	40	Turkey Creek	1852	2	312
Armstrong, Nancy	35	Clear Fork	1849	2	231
Armstrong, Stuard (Stuart)	241½	Bishop's Fork	1861	2	378
Armstrong, Thomas	59	Mossy Creek	1861	2	379
Backhouse, Rhoda	50	Bell Creek	1858	2	350
Bailey, John (Baily)	150	Paint Creek	1834	2	66
Ballenger—See Bollinger					
Bays, William	135	Wts. Meadow River	1847	2	211
Beckley, Alfred	196	Wts. of Piney R.	1844	2	190
Blake, Adam	70	Cabin Creek	1861	2	370
Blume, G. M. & J. L.	77	Keeney's Creek	1853	2	257
Blume, Jacob L.	70	Short Creek	1854	2	265
Blume, Jacob L.	120	Keeney's Cr.	1855	2	293
Blume, Jacob L.	170	Keeney's Creek	1856	2	315
Blume, Jacob L.	100	Short Creek	1856	2	324
Blume, Jacob L. et al	250	Keeney's Creek	1855	2	280
Blume, Jacob L. et al	45	Keeney's Creek	1854	2	264
Blume, Jacob L. et al	18	Keeney's Creek	1853	2	258
Blume, Jacob L. & G. L. (or M.)	32	Cliffs of New River	1855	2	286
Blume, Jacob L. & G. M.	33	Keeney's Creek	1855	2	287
Bollinger, Bolen (Bolenger)	185	Keeney's Cr.	1842	2	166
Bowyer, Lewis	40	Keesy Creek	1840	2	141
Bowyer, William	775	New River Cliffs	1839	2	129
Bradley, Joshua (Bradly)	8¼	Marsh Fork	1834	2	72
Bradley, Joshua	8	Marsh Fork	1834	2	76
Bradley, Joshua	13	Marsh Fork	1834	2	77
Bragg, Adam	94	Wts. of New River	1841	2	145
Bragg, Thomas	40	Wts. of New River	1851	2	297
Brannon, Lawrence H.	32½	Adj. G. Richards	1834	2	82
Brannon, Lawrence H.	506	Wts. of New River	1857	2	332
Burdett, David C.	180	Wts. of M. River	1859	2	353
Busby, William	68	Long Branch	1835	2	52
Busby, William	130	Paint Creek	1835	2	54
Buster, George W.	100	Morris B. Ground	1851	2	309
Buster, James R.	97	Armstrong Cr.	1847	2	215
Buster, James R.	57	Armstrong Cr.	1847	2	216
Buster, William B. et al	440	Big Creek	1859	2	356
Caldwell, James R. et al	5,000	Sewell Creek	1858	2	580
Campbell, David H. et al	785	Mann's Creek	1855	2	289
Caperton, Allen T.	275	Wts. of N. River	1854	2	274
Carrick, Samuel	420	Cotton Hill	1854	2	266
Chafin, C. O. et al	14,696	Cabin Creek	1859	2	581
Chapin, C. O. et al	14,696	Cabin Creek	1859	2	581
Chapman, C. O. et al	14,696	Cabin Creek	1859	2	581
Clay, John T. (or F.) et al	168	Miller's Camp Br.	1834	2	71
Clay, John T. et al	82	Paint Creek	1834	2	79

Name of Grantee	Acres	Local Description	Year	Book	Page
Claypole, Eli	196	Glade Creek	1833	2	14
Clopton, John B. et al	1,183¼	Wts. of New River	1848	2	225
Coffman, Michael	170	War Ridge	1836	2	90
Coffman, Michael & John	925	War Ridge	1836	2	91
Coffman, Samuel	200	War Ridge	1846	2	206
Coffman, Samuel	185	War Ridge	1846	2	207
Cole, James B.	25	Cain Branch	1835	2	51
Cole, James B.	2½	Cane Branch	1834	2	78
Coleman, J. J. et al	665	Wts. New River	1856	2	586
Coleman, John J. et al	535	Wts. of New River	1856	2	319
Coleman, Mason	78¾	Loup Creek	1860	2	369
Coleman, Mason et al	790	Loup Creek	1848	2	224
Coleman, Seaton	70	Mill Creek	1843	2	172
Cook, David	280	Marsh Fork	1838	2	113
Cook, Wilson	98½	Rockhouse Fork	1838	2	114
Cooke, John	86	Marsh Fork	1838	2	593
Copland, Anthony B.	236	Big Creek	1855	2	288
Craig, James	72	Armstrong Cr.	1842	2	158
Craig, James	75	Armstrong Cr.	1842	2	159
Craig, James	53	Armstrong Cr.	1848	2	220
Craig, James	93	Armstrong Cr.	1848	2	221
Craig, James	120	Armstrong Cr.	1848	2	222
Creigh, David S.	1,000	Buffalo Creek	1850	2	577
Creigh, David S.	450	Ephriam's Creek	1851	2	578
Curry, Leonard	63	(Loop) Coop Creek	1836	2	89
Curry, Thomas	32	Loup Creek	1842	2	162
Darlington, James	50	Loup Creek	1847	2	217
Davis, John	100	Wts. of New River	1851	2	241
Davis, Joseph	200	Glade Creek	1860	2	363
Dean, Samuel	50	Ephriam's Cr.	1856	2	325
Deets, Garrison et al	34	Pine Spgs. Run	1859	2	354
Dennis, Robert F. et al	5,000	Sewell Creek	1858	2	580
Dequasie See Duquisie					
Dequasie, Thomas	50	Adj. his own	1850	2	238
Dick, William	35	Wts. of New River	1840	2	140
Dickins, Thomas	40	Drew's Creek	1837	2	98
Dickins, Thomas	135	Peach Tree Fork	1838	2	115
Dickinson, Hudson et al	665	Wts. New River	1856	2	586
Dickinson, Hudson M. et al	535	Wts. New River	1856	2	319
Duquisie See Dequasie					
Duquisie, Thomas	50	Adj. his own	1850	2	238
Ellison, Amos	135	Sand Lick Fork	1843	2	183
Farry, Hugh et al (Ferry)	143	Mum's Creek	1838	2	134
Feamster, John	100	Adj. John Guinn	1849	2	228
Ferry, Hugh et al (Farry)	143	Mum's Creek	1838	2	134
Fipps See Fips					
Fips, Fielding	50	Sand Lick Fork	1835	2	57
Fips, Fielding	76	Sand Lick Fork	1836	2	60
Fisher, Meredith	400	Mossy Creek	1858	2	342
Fleashman or Fleshman					
Fleashman, Samuel	173	Big Sewell Mt.	1851	2	36
Fleashman, Samuel	250	Glade Creek	1851	2	37
Fleshman or Fleashman					
Fleshman, Charles	181	Glade Creek	1838	2	130
Foster, E. C. et al	1,183¼	Wts. of New River	1848	2	225
Foster, Turley	115	Loup Creek	1847	2	214
Foulke, William Parker	268½	Wts. Meadow River	1849	2	236
Foulke, William Parker	64½	Adj. J. Sturgeon	1850	2	237
Fox, James M.	91	Spring Branch	1846	2	198
Fox, William M.	15	New River Cliffs	1851	2	298
French, William H.	500	Glade Creek	1847	2	213
Fugate, Francis	20	Laurel Creek	1852	2	248
Garland, William V.	35	Horseshoe Creek	1836	2	63

Name of Grantee	Acres	Local Description	Year	Book	Page
Gill, Samuel	10	Adj. Mason and Matthew's	1860	2	364
Green, John et al	50	Wts. of New River	1838	2	119
Grinstead, William H.	42	Paint Creek	1835	2	49
Grinstead, William H.	175	Paint Creek	1835	2	55
Guinn or Gwinn					
Guinn, John	450	Glade Creek	1852	2	242
Guinn, John	434	Big Sewell Mt.	1852	2	243
Guinn, John	444	Wts. Meadow River	1852	2	244
Guinn, John	1,470	Laurel Cr.	1852	2	245
Guinn, John	360	Laurel Creek	1855	2	281
Guinn, John	1,461	War Ridge	1855	2	282
Guinn, John	36	Buffalo Hump	1855	2	283
Guinn, John	992	Laurel Creek	1855	2	285
Guinn, John	535	War Ridge	1855	2	284
Gwinn or Guinn					
Gwinn, Andrew	75	War Ridge	1836	2	85
Gwinn, Andrew	130	Wts. of New River	1836	2	87
Gwinn, John	40	Wallow Hole Ridge	1838	2	131
Gwinn, John	400	Glade Creek	1852	2	239
Gwinn, John & Andrew	2,100	Wts. New River	1842	2	161
Gwinn, John et al	50	Wts. of New River	1838	2	119
Gwinn, William	100	War Ridge	1846	2	200
Hamilton, Thomas B.	10	Mill Creek	1841	2	149
Hamilton, Thomas B.	10	Adj. R. Hicks	1841	2	150
Hamilton, Thomas B.	225	Wts. New River	1842	2	156
Hamilton, Thomas B.	10	Turnpike Road	1847	2	212
Hamilton, Thomas B.	165	Mill Creek	1849	2	233
Hamilton, Thomas B.	10	Mill Creek	1855	2	278
Hamilton, Thomas B.	84	Turkey Creek	1851	2	308
Hamilton, Thomas B.	12	Turkey Creek	1844	2	186
Haner, David et al	50	Wts. New River	1838	2	119
Hannah, David (Hanna) et al	50	Wts. New River	1838	2	119
Hannah, Samuel	190	Paint Creek	1838	2	126
Hannah, Thomas (Hana)	120	War Ridge	1851	2	22
Hannah, Thomas	45	War Ridge	1846	2	204
Hansford, Felix G. (Hanford)	400	Boomer's Br.	1835	2	44
Hansford, Felix G.	124	Boomer Branch	1834	2	64
Hanson, William R.	100	Glade Creek	1851	2	307
Harper, Joseph	90	Paint Creek	1837	2	96
Harper, Joseph (or John) et al	168	Miller's Camp Br.	1834	2	71
Harper, Joseph et al	82	Paint Creek	1834	2	79
Harrah, David (Hara) et al	50	Wts. New River	1838	2	119
Harrah, Thomas (Harra)	120	War Ridge	1851	2	22
Harrah, Thomas	45	War Ridge	1846	2	204
Hawkins See Hockins					
Hawkins, Nicholas	50	Cliffs of Gauley	1854	2	272
Heffner, Daniel et al	785	Mann's Creek	1855	2	289
Hess, Hiram	19	Laurel Creek	1852	2	249
Hill, Franklin R.	24	Bell Creek	1854	2	271
Hill, John	540	Wts. of New River	1843	2	173
Hill, John	700	Bell Creek	1852	2	252
Hill, John	1,300	Wts. Rich Creek	1838	2	567
Hill, John et al	320	Laurel Branch	1835	2	45
Hill, Moses	174	Bill's Creek	1838	2	109
Hill, Robert	50	Pritt Fork	1835	2	58
Hill, William	260	Wts. of Gauley	1833	2	17
Hockins See Hawkins					
Hockins, Pleasant et al	95	Cane Branch	1837	2	107
Hockins, Pleasant et al	200	Laurel Branch	1838	2	136
Holliday, Israel E.	80	Keeney's Cr.	1853	2	261
Holliday, Noah M.	167	Keeney's Creek	1859	2	357
Holliday, Robert	174	Adj. G. Alderson	1856	2	317
Holliday, Robert	24	Keeney's Creek	1856	2	318

Name of Grantee	Acres	Local Description	Year	Book	Page
Holliday, Robert	50	Keeney's Creek	1859	2	358
Holliday, Robert	120	Keeney's Creek	1859	2	359
Honaker, Samuel S.	232	Paint Creek	1861	2	383
Hopkins, Henry S.	30	Sandy Lick Fork	1846	2	208
Hopkins, Henry S.	70	Rock Creek	1846	2	209
Huddleston, George P. et al	657	Wts. of Kanawha	1856	2	320
Huddleston, Joseph et al	458	Wts. New River	1834	2	83
Hughart, Charles et al	787	Ephraim's Cr.	1855	2	291
Hughart, George	60	Wts. New River	1838	2	132
Hughart, George	25	Adj. J. Anderson	1845	1	230
Hughart, George	40	Big Bend	1845	1	231
Hughes, Robert Jr.	150	Wts. Gauley	1838	2	133
Hughes, Thomas	34	Rock Camp Hollow	1835	2	47
Humphrey or Humphries					
Humphrey, William	175	Willis Branch	1852	2	251
Humphrey, William	103	Town Creek	1852	2	253
Humphrey, William	205	Paint Creek	1858	2	346
Humphries See Humphrey					
Humphries, William et al	370	Paint Creek	1852	2	246
Hutcheson—See Hutchinson, Hutchison					
Hutchison, Andrew	159	Laurel Creek	1849	2	234
Hutchison, Andrew (Hutcheson)	230	Burnt Creek	1836	2	86
Hutchison, Michael et al	190	Adj. Wm. Miller	1855	2	290
Ingram, Robert & Mathew	120	Loup Creek	1843	2	184
Jarrel, Lemuel	70	Horse Creek	1833	2	19
Jarrel, Lemuel	77	Clear Fork	1834	2	68
Jarrel, Lemuel	103	Sand Lick Fork	1834	2	73
Johnson, Andrew	32	Loup Creek	1837	2	102
Johnson, James	48	Loup Creek	1837	2	103
Johnson, James	42	Loup Creek	1844	2	163
Johnson, John	37	Loup Creek	1843	2	174
Johnson, John Jr.	40	Loup Creek	1842	2	167
Johnson, Jonathan	63	Loup Creek	1842	2	164
Johnson, William	11	Loup Creek	1843	2	175
Keeney—See Kinney					
Keeney, Nicholas C.	1,000	Adj. P. Lykins	1855	2	276
Kelly, William	11	Loup Creek	1842	2	176
Kelly, William	96	Loup Creek	1843	2	177
Kincade or Kincaid					
Kincade, James	100	Sand Lick Run	1832	2	7
Kincade, William	46	Unknown	1835	2	46
Kincaid, Diana	180	Laurel Creek	1861	2	372
Kincaid, Manser	98	Laurel Creek	1851	2	299
Kinney—See Keeney					
Kinney, Nicholas C.	1,000	Adj. P. Lykins	1855	2	276
Kinney, Nicholas C.	350	Smither's Cr.	1855	2	294
Koontz, Jacob	300	Wts. of Gauley	1856	2	326
Lafferty, John	75	Paint Creek	1858	2	347
Lewis, Zachary et al	1,183¼	Wts. New River	1848	2	225
Lively, Elias	372	Town Creek	1858	2	339
Lively, Rufus	350	Paint Creek	1858	2	340
Lively, Rufus	36	Paint Creek	1861	2	381
Lively, Rufus	200	Adj. Wm. Humphreys	1861	2	382
Lively, Rufus	100	Paint Creek	1861	2	384
Lykins, James	17	Mill Creek	1844	2	189
Lykins, James	14	Adj. J. B. Westlake	1852	2	255
Lykins, James et al	170	Wts. of New River	1842	2	155
Mann, Thomas	170	War Ridge	1849	2	229
Mann, William T.	480	War Ridge	1851	2	25
Mann, William T.	40	War Ridge	1851	2	26
Mann, William T.	240	War Ridge	1851	2	27
Mann, William T.	280	Laurel Creek	1851	2	28
Mann, William T.	40	War Ridge	1851	2	29

Name of Grantee	Acres	Local Description	Year	Book	Page
Mann, William T.	200	Laurel Creek	1851	2	30
Mann, William T.	160	War Ridge	1851	2	34
Mann, William T.	786	War Ridge	1849	2	230
Mann, William T.	926	Laurel Creek	1852	2	254
Mann, William T.	1,310	Laurel Creek	1853	2	262
Mann, William T.	393	Laurel Creek	1854	2	275
Mann, William T.	162	Wts of New River	1856	2	328
Mann, William T.	258	War Ridge	1857	2	334
Mann, William T.	850	Slater's Creek	1857	2	335
Mann, William T.	540	Wts. of New River	1857	2	336
Mann, William T.	4,700	Laurel Creek	1849	2	571
Mann, William T.	2,100	Buffalo Creek	1851	2	575
Mann, William T.	1,147	Wts. New River	1856	2	584
Mann, William T. et al	787	Ephraim's Cr.	1855	2	291
Mann, William T. et al	1,000	Laurel Creek	1851	2	574
Manser, Miles (Mansor)	250	Rich Creek	1841	2	144
Martin, William	6½	Horseshoe Creek	1861	2	373
McCoy, Samuel	8	Paint Creek	1835	2	50
McCoy, Samuel	64	Paint Creek	1835	2	53
McGinnis, Pyrrhus	351	Bailey Creek	1846	2	197
McGraw, George	50	Turkey Creek	1842	2	157
McGraw, Samuel	90	Honey Creek	1842	2	165
McGraw, Samuel	50	Pine Creek	1856	2	327
McGriffin, Abram S.	125	Wts. of M. River	1837	2	106
McGriffin, Thomas	37	Adj. T. A. Terry	1851	2	295
McGuffin, Abram S.	125	Wts. Meadow River	1837	2	106
McGuffin, Thomas	37	Adj. T. A. Terry	1851	2	295
McMullen, William A. et al	657	Wts. of Kanawha	1856	2	320
McVey, Alexander	152(150)	Short Creek	1852	2	40
McVey, Alexander	100	Ferren Spgs. Run	1841	2	147
McVey, Alexander et al	250	Keeney's Creek	1855	2	280
McVey, William S.	300	Keeny's Creek	1841	2	148
Metsker, Philip	50½	Cor. to Mansor	1834	2	75
Metsker, Philip et al	300	Wts. of Meadow River	1834	2	65
Metzker or Metsker					
Middleton, Henry O.	2,000	Pine Spg. Run	1851	2	35
Middleton, Henry O.	850	Wts. of New River	1838	2	110
Middleton, Henry O.	400	Wts. Meadow River	1838	2	124
Middleton, Henry O.	3,109	Arrowood Run	1852	2	250
Middleton, Henry O.	961	Mill Creek	.1857	2	329
Middleton, James E.	154	Old State Road	1858	2	343
Miller, John	120	War Ridge	1851	2	23
Miller, John	1,100	Lick Creek	1851	2	24
Miller, John	445	Laurel Creek	1851	2	31
Miller, John	120	Mann's Creek	1851	2	32
Miller, John	47	Laurel Creek	1851	2	33
Miller, John	868	Walnut Knob	1851	2	573
Miller, John et al	143	Man's Creek	1838	2	134
Miller, John et al	1,000	Laurel Creek	1851	2	574
Miller, John Jr. et al	1,300	Laurel Creek	1848	2	218
Mins, H. B. et al	14,696	Cabin Creek	1859	2	581
Montgomery, Henry et al	300	Wts. Meadow River	1834	2	65
Montgomery, Henry et al	458	Wts. New River	1834	2	83
Montgomery, Henry et al	95	Cane Branch	1837	2	107
Montgomery, Henry et al	200	Laurel Branch	1838	2	136
Montgomery, James	500	Wts. of Kanawha	1838	2	117
Montgomery, Michael	45	Loup Creek	1838	2	135
Moore, James	200	Marsh Fork	1843	2	178
Morris, William	2,300	Scrabble Creek	1832	2	565
Muncey, James	8¼	Wts. New River	1836	2	88
Muncey, James B.	41¾	Cane Branch	1838	2	125
Neal, James	99	Cliffs of Gauley	1839	2	128
Neal, Samuel	31	Wts. of Gauley	1842	2	168

Name of Grantee	Acres	Local Description	Year	Book	Page
Slaughter, Alfred	100	Laurel Creek	1854	2	263
Smails, George	47	Laurel Creek	1844	2	187
Smails, George	171	Laurel Creek	1851	2	301
Smails, George et al	300	Laurel Creek	1851	2	304
Smails, John	110	Laurel Creek	1851	2	300
Smith, Alexander	380	Bell Creek	1855	2	277
Smith, Alexander	10	Adj. A. B. Smith	1859	2	351
Smith, Allen B.	213	Bell Creek	1856	2	313
Smith, Henry	23	Mth. of Piney	1837	2	99
Smith, John	18	Bell Creek	1836	2	59
Smith, John	225	Bell Creek	1838	2	116
Smith, John	40	Wts. of New River	1853	2	260
Smith, Moletas	110	Bell Creek	1855	2	279
Smith, William & Theopolis	300	Auzborn Creek	1833	2	10
Snuffer, Cyrus	275	Stephen's Branch	1849	2	227
Snuffer, George	120	Breckenridge Fork	1833	2	20
Snuffer, George	220	Breckenridge Fork	1837	2	100
Snuffer, George	110	Adj. C. Snuffer	1846	2	205
Stockton, Aaron	200	Sand Branch	1838	2	108
Stockton, Aaron	590	Rock Camp	1843	2	179
Stockton, Aaron	200	Sand Branch	1843	2	180
Stockton, Aaron et al	630	Bridge Fork	1838	2	139
Stockton, Aaron et al	790	Loup Creek	1848	2	224
Stockton, Aaron et al	1,183¼	Wts. of New River	1848	2	225
Stockton, William T. et al	320	Laurel Branch	1835	2	45
Stover, Jacob	18	White Oak Fork	1832	2	9
Stover, John	130	Clear Fork	1832	2	1
Stover, John	130	Clear Fork	1833	2	21
Sturgeon, James	250	Wts. of Meadow R.	1835	2	56
Taylor, James	100	Turkey Creek	1833	2	16
Taylor, Oliver	91	Turkey Creek	1844	2	188
Taylor, Oliver & John W.	60	Turkey Creek	1834	2	69
Taylor, William	500	Wts. of Kanawha	1856	2	316
Terry, James	100	Wts. of N. River	1833	2	18
Terry, Thomas	170	Horseshoe Cr.	1833	2	13
Terry, Thomas	48	Horseshoe Cr.	1837	2	93
Terry, William	80	Mill Creek	1846	2	194
Thomas, Jesse	240	Adj. L. Rodgers	1859	2	352
Tincher, James	53	Laurel Creek	1860	2	361
Tincher, James	31	Laurel Creek	1860	2	362
Tully, Landon	6	Adj. Geo. Alderson	1854	2	273
Tully, Landon	174	Keeney's Creek	1856	2	314
Tyree, Francis	47	Marsh Fork	1836	2	92
Tyree, Francis	589	Wts. New River	1842	2	160
Tyree, Francis	180	Glade Creek	1851	2	302
Tyree, Francis	450	Laurel Creek	1851	2	303
Tyree, Francis	220	Glade Creek	1848	2	349
Tyree, Francis et al	1,300	Laurel Creek	1848	2	218
Tyree, Francis et al	300	Laurel Creek	1851	2	304
Tyree, Richard F.	50	Ephraim's Cr.	1834	2	80
Tyree, Samuel et al	440	Big Creek	1859	2	356
Tyree, Samuel et al	14,696	Cabin Creek	1859	2	581
Tyree, William	9	Mill Creek	1843	2	185
Tyree, William	52	Adj. T. A. Teery	1851	2	296
Tyree, William	129¾	Adj. J. Ellis	1861	2	323
Tyree, William	287	Gauley Mountain	1861	2	374
Tyree, William	56	Horseshoe Cr.	1861	2	375
Tyree, William	13½	Horseshoe Run	1861	2	376
Tyree, William et al	170	Wts. New River	1842	2	155
Tyree, William et al	370	Paint Creek	1852	2	246
Tyree, William et al	110	Gauley Mt.	1851	2	305
Viney, G. Harrison et al	34	Pine Spgs. Run	1859	2	354
Viney, George	64	Pine Spg. Branch	1833	2	15

Name of Grantee	Acres	Local Description	Year	Book	Page
Viney, George	36	Pine Creek	1834	2	81
Viney, George	50	Pine Spgs. Run	1841	2	146
Viney, Nathaniel	55	Horse Shoe Cr.	1837	2	101
Wage See Wedge					
Wage, Cyrus et al	90	Wts. Gauley	1835	2	61
Walker, Archibald B.	232	Wts. Piney River	1849	2	232
Walker, H. L.	87	Wts. New River	1852	2	247
Walker, H. L.	158	Laurel Creek	1855	2	292
Walker, Hezekiah L.	120	Walnut Knob	1848	2	219
Walker, Hezekiah L.	125	Laurel Creek	1851	2	306
Ward, Thomas	50	War Ridge	1846	2	203
Warren, James C.	390	Arrowood Run	1845	2	191
Warren, James C.	20	Adj. W. B. Foulks	1852	2	310
Warren, James C.	837	Adj. Wm. Bilbow	1852	2	311
Wedge—See also Wage					
Wedge, Cyrus	78	Adj. Keenan & Stockton	1835	2	48
Whalen, Nancy R.	100	Adj. H. Zimmerman	1860	2	367
White, James	965	Adj. J. Hamilton	1854	2	268
White, James	386 (380)	Big Sewell Cr.	1857	2	330
White, William	30	Wts. of M. River	1858	2	368
Williams, Isaac	120	Paint Creek	1861	2	380
Williams, John	135	Paint Creek	1832	2	2
Williams, John	22	Clear Fork	1832	2	3
Williams, John	103	Adj. Moore & Beckley	1852	2	256
Wood, Amos	50	Wts. of New River	1832	2	4
Wood, Amos	258	Wts. of New River	1842	2	152
Wood, Bailey & Eli	145	Spring Creek	1840	2	143
Wood, Bailey & Eli	20	Cliffs New River	1847	2	210

GILMER COUNTY

Arnold, Benjamin B.	100	Camp Run	1852	2	346
Arnold, Benjamin B.	25	Big Crooked Run	1857	2	527
Arnold, George I. et al	1,000	Stuart's Creek	1857	2	543
Arnold, George I. (or J.)	1,000	Rocky Fork	1848	1	451
Arnold, George I (or J.) et al	234	Pigeon Run	1858	3	4
Arnold, Jacob R.	20	Owen's Ridge	1859	3	47
Arnold, Jacob R. et al Heirs	428	Wts. Steer Cr.	1856	2	484
Arnold, Jacob R. et al Heirs	178	Owen's Fork	1856	2	511
Arnold, James I.	66	Grass Run	1856	2	499
Arnold, James I. (or J.)	16	Grand Camp Run	1856	2	504
Arnold, James I. (or J.)	500	Crooked Run	1857	3	2
Arnold, Jas. I. (or J.)	48	Crooked Run	1856	2	502
Arnold, John E.	150	Grand Camp Run	1852	2	345
Arnold, Maranda	50	Wts. of L. Kanawha	1851	2	339
Arnold, William E.	125	Raccoon Run	1849	1	533
Arnold, William E. et al	150	Leading Creek	1849	1	531
Arnold, William E. et al	350	Leading Cr.	1850	2	334
Ayres, Moses	29	Lick Run	1859	3	52
Ayers, Salem V.	100	Laurel Creek	1856	2	488
Baldwin, Israel et al	150	West Fork	1851	2	301
Baldwin, Israel et al	225	Rock Camp Run	1851	2	302
Ball, George E.	155	Leading Cr.	1854	2	437
Ball, John	166	Bennett's M. Run	1852	2	349
Ball, Robert J. et al	300	Yellow Creek	1856	2	487
Ball, Robert J. et al	120	Laurel Lick Run	1859	3	41
Ball, Robert J. et al	190	Bush Camp	1859	3	42

Name of Grantee	Acres	Local Description	Year	Book	Page
Barr, James	200	Bennett's M. Run	1852	2	359
Beall, G. N. et al	18	Wts. Lit. Kanawha	1853	2	398
Beall, G. N. et al	543	Myer's Run	1853	2	400
Beall, George H.	50	Stinking Cr.	1854	2	426
Beall, George I.	68	Third Run	1856	2	518
Beall, George I.	91	Stinking Creek	1856	2	519
Beall, Hamilton C.	50	Wts. L. Kanawha	1860	3	60
Beall, Henderson et al	256	Bee Run	1855	2	479
Beall, Henry	200	Wts. Lit. Kanawha	1849	1	544
Beall, Henry M.	4½	Stinking Cr.	1861	3	73
Beall, James T.	6	Stinking Creek	1856	2	506
Beirne, Duffy & Co. et al	71	Lowther Ridge	1853	2	385
Bennett, J. M. et al	574	Cedar Creek	1850	1	564
Bennett, J. M. et al	1226	West Fork	1855	2	480
Bennett, J. M. et al	382	West Fork	1855	2	481
Bennett, John	50	Adj. E. C. Wilson	1851	2	334
Bennett, John	133	Wts. of Steer Cr.	1851	2	335
Bennett, John	120 (128)	Bennett's Mill Run	1850	1	552
Bennett, John & William	598	Bennett's Mill Run	1850	1	549
Bennett, Jonathan M.	170	Tanner's Fork	1847	1	393
Bennett, Jonathan M.	184	Bull Fork	1854	2	424
Bennett, Jonathan M.	766	Crooked Fork	1849	1	546
Bennett, Jonathan M. et al	114	Wts. L. Kanawha	1846	1	392
Bennett, Jonathan M. et al	53	Wts. of Lit. Kanawha	1847	1	395
Bennett, Jonathan M. et al	351	Laurel Creek	1847	1	406
Bennett, Jonathan M. et al	399	Trace Fork	1847	1	407
Bennett, Jonathan M. et al	241	Spring Fork	1847	1	408
Bennett, Jonathan M. et al	210	Leaf Bank	1847	1	409
Bennett, Jonathan M. et al	690	Yellow Creek	1847	1	410
Bennett, Jonathan M. et al	491	Yellow Cr.	1847	1	411
Bennett, Jonathan M. et al	95	West Fork	1847	1	413
Bennett, Jonathan M. et al	50	Horn Creek	1847	1	414
Bennett, Jonathan M. et al	75	Steer Run	1848	1	425
Bennett, Jonathan M. et al	396	Wts. Steer Cr.	1848	1	426
Bennett, Jonathan M. et al	144	Left Hand Fork	1848	1	427
Bennett, Jonathan M. et al	288	Road Fork	1848	1	436
Bennett, Jonathan M. et al	212	Grass Run	1848	1	437
Bennett, Jonathan M. et al	100	Wts. Lit. Kanawha	1848	1	444
Bennett, Jonathan M. et al	99	West Fork	1848	1	445
Bennett, Jonathan M. et al	50	Adj. M. Brannon	1848	1	446
Bennett, Jonathan M. et al	200	Wild Cat	1848	1	460
Bennett, Jonathan M. et al	300	Lick Run	1848	1	461
Bennett, Jonathan M. et al	100	Cherry Fork	1849	1	478
Bennett, Jonathan M. et al	200	Grass Run	1849	1	479
Bennett, Jonathan M. et al	100	Peach Tree Fork	1849	1	480
Bennett, Jonathan M. et al	560	Bear Fork	1849	1	488
Bennett, Jonathan M. et al	238	Camp Run	1849	1	489
Bennett, Jonathan M. et al	110	Yellow Creek	1849	1	490
Bennett, Jonathan M. et al	300	Laurel Creek	1849	1	526
Bennett, Jonathan M. et al	500	Fish Pot Run	1849	1	538
Bennett, William	170	Tanner's Fork	1847	1	405
Bennett, William G.	225	Tanner's Fork	1852	2	367
Bennett, William G.	55	Wild Cat Run	1856	2	503
Bird, John	100	Stewart's Creek	1849	1	534
Boggs, John C.	290	Wolf Pen Run	1854	2	420
Boggs, John C.	120	Steer Run	1854	2	421
Boggs, William et al	380	Triplet's Run	1851	2	337
Booker, J. G. & G. W.	500	Wts. of L. Kanawha	1856	2	498
Boon, Jacob	280	Bear Fork	1852	2	350
Boyd, John J.	200	Road Run	1848	1	491
Boyd, John J.	3325	Wts. Leading Cr.	1849	1	588
Brady, James B.	238	Crooked Fork	1856	2	523
Burk, Jacob	50	Cedar Creek	1854	2	418

Name of Grantee	Acres	Local Description	Year	Book	Page
Burk, Jacob	75	Wts. L. Kanawha	1848	1	474
Burk, Jonathan H.	25	Cedar Creek	1852	2	351
Burk, Jonathan H.	74	Cedar Creek	1854	2	444
Burk, William	83	Wts. of L. Kanawha	1850	2	272
Burrass, John	362	Trace Fork	1856	2	485
Burrass, William H.	150	Laurel Creek	1853	2	379
Bush, Abraham	102	Stinking Cr.	1852	2	372
Bush, Abraham	35	Stinking Cr.	1857	3	3
Bush, Adam et al	640	Buck Horn Fork	1855	2	461
Bush, Adam et al	190	Flat Run	1858	3	40
Bush, Adam et al	35	Mound Run	1861	3	81
Bush, Adam et al	140	Bull Run	1861	3	82
Bush, Eli	32½	Horn Creek	1850	2	239
Bush, Eli	17½	Cox's Camp Fork	1850	2	240
Bush, Eli	100	Tanner's Fork	1855	2	457
Bush, Eli	68¾	Tanner's Fork	1857	2	546
Bush, George F.	60	Stinking Cr.	1847	1	404
Bush, George F.	46	Stinking Cr.	1853	2	399
Bush, George F. et al	405	Stinking Creek	1849	1	523
Bush, George F. et al	400	Horn Creek	1850	2	245
Bush, George F. et al	227	Tanner's Fork	1856	2	495
Bush, Henry F.	225	Leading Creek	1849	1	495
Bush, Henry F.	30	Leading Cr.	1852	2	370
Bush, Henry F.	159	Horn Creek	1855	2	466
Bush, Jacob	182	Horn Creek	1848	1	452
Bush, Jacob	210	Frame's Fork	1850	2	269
Bush, Jacob Sr.	115	Lower Big Run	1856	2	510
Bush, John W. et al	346	Panther Fork	1858	3	27
Bush, John W. et al	672	Tanner's Fork	1858	3	36
Bush, Peter	300	Big Run	1852	2	374
Bush, Peter	220	Upper Big Run	1858	3	23
Bush, Silas F.	32	Horn Creek	1858	3	20
Butcher, Henry et al	640	Buck Horn Fork	1855	2	461
Butcher, Henry et al	346	Panther Fork	1858	3	27
Butcher, Henry et al	672	Tanner's Fork	1858	3	36
Butcher, Henry et al	190	Flat Run	1858	3	40
Butcher, Henry et al	35	Mound Run	1861	3	81
Butcher, Henry et al	140	Bull Run	1861	3	82
Byrne, John P. et al	150	West Fork	1851	2	301
Byrne, John P. et al	225	Rock Camp Run	1851	2	302
Camden, G. D.	30	Road Fork	1851	2	298
Camden, G. D. et al	351	Laurel Creek	1847	1	406
Camden, G. D. et al	399	Trace Fork	1847	1	407
Camden, G. D. et al	241	Spring Fork	1847	1	408
Camden, G. D. et al	210	Leaf Bank	1847	1	409
Camden, G. D. et al	690	Yellow Creek	1847	1	410
Camden, G. D. et al	491	Yellow Cr.	1847	1	411
Camden, G. D. et al	95	West Fork	1847	1	413
Camden, G. D. et al	99	West Fork	1848	1	445
Camden, Gideon D.	62	Middle Run	1850	2	241
Camden, Gideon D.	192	Road Run	1851	2	299
Camden, Gideon D.	268	Barns Run	1851	2	300
Camden, Gideon D.	200	Wts. L. Kanawha	1849	1	539
Camden, Gideon D. et al	53	Wts. Little Kanawha	1847	1	395
Camden, Gideon D. et al	100	Wts. Lit. Kanawha	1848	1	444
Camden, Gideon D. et al	50	Adj. M. Brannon	1848	1	446
Camden, Gideon D. et al	500	Fish Pot Run	1849	1	538
Camden, Richard P.	250	Laurel Creek	1849	1	524
Camden, Richard P.	140	Road Run	1852	2	368
Camden, Richard P. et al	75	Steer Run	1848	1	425
Camden, Richard P. et al	396	Wts. Steer Cr.	1848	1	426
Camden, Richard P. et al	144	Left Hand Fork	1848	1	427
Chapman, Henry D. et al	440	West Fork	1857	2	529

Name of Grantee	Acres	Local Description	Year	Book	Page
Chapman, Henry D. et al	700	Sinking Spg. Run	1857	2	530
Chapman, Henry D. et al	50	Barnes Run	1857	2	531
Chenoweth, David W.	137	Farmer's Fork	1854	2	435
Chenoweth, David W.	238	Slab Camp Fork	1855	2	476
Chenoweth, David W. & R. J.	134	Standing Stone	1854	2	428
Chenoweth, David W. & R. J.	142	Big Frozen Run	1854	2	429
Chenoweth, David W. et al	93	Big Lick Fork	1854	2	447
Chenoweth, R. J. et al	860	Big Run	1854	2	436
Connolly, Anthony	152	Upper Nighcut Run	1856	2	500
Connolly, Thomas C.	200	Cedar Creek	1846	1	390
Connolly, Thomas C.	84	Grand Camp Run	1846	1	391
Connolly, Thomas C.	100	Grand Camp Run	1847	1	396
Connolly, Thomas C.	56	Leading Cr.	1858	3	17
Connolly, Thomas C. et al	1632½	Wts. Steer Creek	1848	1	454
Conrad, C. B.	30	Indian Fork	1851	2	315
Conrad, C. B.	810	Sleeth's Run	1855	2	455
Conrad, Currence B.	50	Ellis Fork	1848	1	428
Conrad, Currence B.	90	Sand Fork	1848	1	429
Conrad, Currence B.	193	Ellis Fork	1848	1	475
Conrad, Currence B.	100	Bush Run	1849	1	503
Conrad, Currence B.	100	Sand Fork	1850	1	553
Conrad, Currence B.	180	Sand Fork	1850	1	554
Conrad, Currence B.	362	Sand Fork	1850	1	559
Conrad, Currence B.	200	Indian Fork	1851	2	303
Conrad, Currence B.	1,000	Spruce Fork	1856	2	494
Conrad, Currence B.	200	Ellis Fork	1856	2	512
Conrad, Currence B.	37	Ellis Fork	1856	2	513
Conrad, Currence B.	61	Sand Fork	1857	2	528
Conrad, Currence B.	498	Indian Fork	1858	3	29
Conrad, Currence B.	30	Indian Fork	1858	3	38
Conrad, Currence B.	30	Stewart's Creek	1861	3	75
Conrad, Currence B. et al	333	Wts. L. Kanawha	1848	1	476
Conrad, Currence B. et al	1,334	Pine Creek	1856	2	514
Conrad, Currence B. et al	70	Crooked Run	1858	3	37
Conrad, Currence B. et al	34	Grand Camp Run	1861	3	76
Cooper, James H.	116	Tanner's Fork	1849	1	515
Cooper, James H.	387	Jesse's Run	1856	2	521
Cooper, James H.	370	Brushy Fork	1856	2	522
Cottrel, Thomas	220	West Fork	1854	2	416
Cottrell, Even T.	30	Brushy Run	1857	2	538
Cox, Isaac N.	50	Stone Lick Run	1854	2	417
Cox, Isaac N.	200	Tanner's Fork	1854	2	423
Cox, Isaac N.	490	Tanner's Fork	1854	2	427
Cox, Isaac N.	350	Horn Creek	1854	2	431
Cox, L. R. & J. B.	113	Yellow Creek	1856	2	520
Cox, Leonard R. et al	300	Yellow Creek	1856	2	487
Cox, Oliver P.	250	Old Improvement Run	1858	3	21
Cox, Oliver P.	290	Big Cove Creek	1858	3	22
Cox, Oliver P.	140	Tanner's Fork	1860	3	66
Cox, Philip D.	50	Spruce Fork	1855	2	473
Cox, Philip D.	290	2 Run	1849	1	528
Cox, Philip D.	50	Spruce Fork	1849	1	529
Cox, Philip et al	50	Horn Creek	1847	1	414
Cox, William M.	100	Trace Run	1854	2	434
Cox, William M.	10	Indian Fork	1859	3	45
Depue, Jonathan	137	Wts Little Kanawha	1855	2	450
Depue, Jonathan	220	Leading Creek	1855	2	451
Despard, Burton	320	Grand Camp Run	1849	1	540
Despard, Burton	21½	Stinking Cr.	1853	2	396
Despard, Burton	250	Laurel Cr.	1853	2	397
Despard, Burton et al	351	Laurel Creek	1847	1	406
Despard, Burton et al	399	Trace Fork	1847	1	407
Despard, Burton et al	241	Spring Fork	1847	1	408

Name of Grantee	Acres	Local Description	Year	Book	Page
Despard, Burton et al	210	Leaf Bank	1847	1	409
Despard, Burton et al	690	Yellow Creek	1847	1	410
Despard, Burton et al	100	Wts Lit. Kanawha	1848	1	444
Despard, Burton et al	99	West Fork	1848	1	445
Despard, Burton et al	50	Adj. M. Brannon	1848	1	446
Despard, Burton et al	110	Yellow Creek	1849	1	490
Despard, Burton et al	150	Leading Creek	1849	1	531
Despard, Burton et al	500	Fish Pot Run	1849	1	538
Despard, Burton et al	350	Leading Cr.	1850	2	234
Divine, Patrick et al	300	Leaf Bank Run	1857	2	541
Dobbins, William et al	71	Lowther Ridge	1853	2	385
Dobbins, William et al	296	Steer Creek	1851	2	386
Downey, Alexander	25	West Fork	1852	2	373
Downey, Alexander et al	860	Big Run	1854	2	436
Duffy, Beirne & Company et al	71	Lowther Ridge	1853	2	385
Duffy, Philip et al	296	Steer Creek	1853	2	386
Dusky, Daniel	440	West Fork	1855	2	467
Dusky, Daniel	343	West Fork	1855	2	468
Dye, Benjamin	590	Coal Fork	1849	1	506
Ellis, Phanuel (Ellius)	110	Tanner's Fork	1854	2	438
Ellis, Phanuel et al	190	Bush Camp	1859	3	42
Farnsworth, Isaac P.	364	Sugar Camp Run	1856	2	505
Farnsworth, Moses	74	Adj. J. Farnsworth	1856	2	524
Farnsworth, Moses	100	Leading Cr.	1856	2	525
Fell, James W.	190	Stewart's Cr.	1859	3	51
Fisher, Adam & W. H.	106	Pike Fork	1853	2	392
Fisher, Adam et al	640	Buckhorn Fork	1855	2	461
Fisher, Charles	100	Horn Creek	1851	2	293
Fisher, Charles & J. M.	58	Panther Fork	1851	2	294
Fisher, Elias	147	Wts Lit. Kanawha	1849	1	542
Fisher, Jacob M.	360	Tanner's Fork	1849	1	511
Fisher, Jacob M. & Charles	350	Tanner's Fork	1856	2	489
Fisher, Philip	20	Tanner's Fork	1848	1	447
Fling George	105	Tanner's Fork	1850	1	558
Fling, George	81	Tanner's Fork	1860	3	67
Fling, John	245	Tanner's Fork	1849	1	494
Fling, John	18	Tanner's Fork	1850	1	560
Fling, Levi	255	Tanner's Fork	1849	1	496
Fling, Levi	50	Tanner's Fork	1850	1	563
Fling, Levi	31¾	Tanner's Fork	1861	3	80
Frame, Lewellen	50	Left Hand Fork	1848	1	430
Gainer—See Garner					
Gainer, Brian	50	Adj. Levi Fling	1852	2	364
Gainer, Brian Jr.	17	Tanner's Fork	1858	3	18
Gainer, Brian Jr.	62	Tanner's Fork	1861	3	77
Gainer, Cornelius	26	Adj. B. G. Vannoy	1851	2	336
Gainer, Cornelius	200	Tanner's Fork	1848	1	433
Gainer, Cornelius	104	Sycamore Run	1858	3	19
Gainer, Sylvester et al	35	Tanner's Fork	1848	1	448
Garner—See Gainer					
Garner, Cornelius	200	Tanner's Fork	1848	1	433
Garner, Sylvester et al	35	Tanner's Fork	1848	1	448
Gary—See Geary					
Gary, Mathew	100	White Oak Fork	1856	2	508
Geary—See Gary					
Geary, Mathew (Gary)	25	Turkey Fork	1856	2	507
Goff, Benjamin S.	146	Tanner's Fork	1860	3	65
Goff, Hiram A.	50 (60)	Leading Cr.	1847	1	397
Goff, Hiram A.	124	Stinking Cr.	1847	1	417
Goff, Hiram A.	100	Leading Creek	1849	1	512
Goff, Hiram A.	169	Leading Cr.	1849	1	522
Goff, Hiram A.	100	Stinking Cr.	1850	1	556
Goff, S. G. et al	280	Tanner's Fork	1859	3	54

Name of Grantee	Acres	Local Description	Year	Book	Page
Goff, Strawther G.	47	Big Run	1847	1	394
Goff, Strawther G.	160	Big Run	1851	2	304
Goff, Thomas R. et al	200	Tar Kiln Fork	1860	3	74
Goff, Waldo P.	133	Owen's Ridge	1849	1	520
Goff, Waldo P.	150	Owen's Fork	1849	1	521
Goff, Waldo P.	482	Grass Run	1849	1	525
Goff, Waldo P.	10,380	Dusk Camp Run	1850	2	233
Goldsmith, James	50	Beech Fork	1856	2	486
Hall, John	37	Horn Creek	1850	2	242
Hall, John	46	Horn Creek	1850	2	243
Haverty, Michael H. et al	200	Big Root Run	1849	1	505
Haverty, William P.	61	Adj. P. Stallman	1847	1	420
Haverty, William P. et al	395	Big Root	1857	2	539
Hayden, John	375	Buckhorn Fork	1847	1	412
Hayden, John	625	Horn Creek	1847	1	416
Hays, Peregrine	1,000	West Fork	1857	2	544
Hays, Peregrine	90	West Fork	1859	3	53
Hays, Peregrine	83	Pond Run	1859	3	55
Hays, Peregrine et al	1,021	West Fork	1850	2	279
Hays, Peregrine et al	200	West Fork	1853	2	393
Hays, Peregrine et al	170	Big Nighcut	1855	2	462
Hays, Peregrine et al	58	Walnut Fork	1855	2	463
Hays, Peregrine et al	200	Butcher's Fork	1858	3	39
Hays, Samuel L.	335	Cherry Tree Fork	1849	1	516
Heckert, Adam	167	Leading Creek	1848	1	453
Heckert, Adam	185	Leading Cr.	1856	2	491
Heckert, Daniel E.	25	Leading Creek	1860	3	64
Hews, David T.	546	Leading Creek	1856	2	501
Hicks, Stephen B.	100	Stinson Fork	1859	3	43
Hoffman See Huffman					
Hoffman, John S.	40	Wts. L. Kanawha	1848	1	462
Hoffman, John S.	250	Lower Run	1848	1	463
Hoffman, John S.	200	Middle Run	1848	1	464
Hoffman, John S. et al	578	Tanner's Fork	1857	2	535
Hoffman, John S. et al	22	Leading Cr.	1858	3	16
Hoffman, John S. et al	74	Wolf Pen Run	1859	3	48
Hoffman, John S. et al	105	Mud Lick Run	1859	3	49
Hoffman, John T. et al Heirs	264	Wts. L. Kanawha	1849	1	548
Holbert, Jerome B.	244	Cool Fork	1857	2	526
Holbert, William	40	Stinking Creek	1856	2	490
Hollman, John S. et al	578	Tanner's Fork	1857	2	535
Holt, J. F. W. et al	280	Tanner's Fork	1859	3	54
Holt, John F. W.	100	Paddy's Run	1849	1	485
Holt, John F. W.	118	Cedar Creek	1849	1	486
Holt, John F. W.	22	Cedar Creek	1849	1	487
Holt, John F. W.	600	Rowel's Run	1850	2	256
Holt, M. & J. F. W.	100	Wts. of Cedar	1851	2	338
Holt, M. & J. F. W.	607	Michael's Run	1850	2	258
Holt, M. & J. F. W. et al	560	Bear Fork	1849	1	488
Holt, M. & J. F. W. et al	238	Camp Run	1849	1	489
Holt, M. & John F. W.	200	Rowel's Run	1850	2	247
Holt, M. & John F. W.	300	Rowel's Run	1850	2	257
Hoover, Able	100	Wts. Tanner's Fk.	1855	2	452
Hoover, Abel et al	120	Laurel Lick Run	1859	3	41
Holyman, John J.	200	Big Run	1853	2	407
Huffman, See Hoffman					
Huffman, Alexander et al	364	Wts. Lit. Kanawha	1848	1	470
Huffman, John S.	95	Third Run	1849	1	541
Huffman, John S.	500	Spruce Run	1851	2	305
Huffman, John S. et al	1,000	Stuart's Creek	1857	2	543
Huffman, John S. et al	190	Spruce Run	1858	3	10
Huffman, John S. et al	58	Horn Creek	1858	3	11
Hughes See Hews					

Name of Grantee	Acres	Local Description	Year	Book	Page
Hurst, Samuel	15	Fink's Creek	1850	2	237
Hurst, Samuel	185	Little Cove Cr.	1850	2	238
Hurst, Samuel	140	Cove Creek	1857	2	548
Jackson, George A.	68½	Stuart's Cr.	1850	2	235
Jackson, George A.	201	Big Root	1850	2	236
Jackson, George A.	305	Lick Run	1848	1	438
Jackson, George A. et al	114	Wts. Lit. Kanawha	1846	1	392
Jackson, Minter	36	Stuart's Creek	1855	2	472
Jackson, Minter	41	Cedar Creek	1859	3	58
Jackson, Minter	42	Adj. Aaron Halbert	1853	2	409
Jackson, Minter	45	Dry Fork	1860	3	71
Jackson, Minter	50	Laurel Creek	1849	1	517
Jackson, Minter	52	Stuart's Creek	1855	2	471
Jackson, Minter	54	Cedar Creek	1849	1	481
Jackson, Minter	78	Stinking Cr.	1850	2	232
Jackson, Minter	80	Sugar Camp Run	1861	3	83
Jackson, Minter	95	Sycamore Fork	1850	2	246
Jackson, Minter	97	Tanner's Fork	1860	3	68
Jackson, Minter	100	Level Run	1857	2	540
Jackson, Minter	130	Stewart's Cr.	1849	1	482
Jackson, Minter	135	Upper Big Run	1853	2	395
Jackson, Minter	143	Tanner's Fork	1859	3	57
Jackson, Minter	150	Adj. B. Riddle	1851	2	306
Jackson, Minter	150	Road Run	1851	2	311
Jackson, Minter	152	Cedar Creek	1859	3	59
Jackson, Minter	153	George Lynch Run	1849	1	547
Jackson, Minter	166	Wts. Lit. Kanawha	1852	2	354
Jackson, Minter	285	Stuart's Cr.	1851	2	282
Jackson, Minter	320	Leading Cr.	1857	2	534
Jackson, Minter	373	Stuart's Creek	1849	1	483
Jackson, Minter	400	Stinking Creek	1849	1	587
Jackson, Minter	420	Stinking Cr.	1856	2	496
Jackson, Minter	500(525)	Stinking Creek	1849	1	484
Jackson, Minter	590	Bull Fork	1859	3	56
Jackson, Minter	670	Sycamore Run	1851	2	281
Jackson, Minter	700	Trace Fork	1860	3	72
Jackson, Minter et al	1,632½	Wts. Steer Creek	1848	1	454
Jackson, Minter et al	405	Stinking Creek	1849	1	523
Jackson, Minter et al	250	Stewart's Creek	1849	1	530
Jackson, Minter et al	400	Horn Creek	1850	2	245
Jackson, Minter et al	770	Crooked Fork	1851	2	283
Jackson, Minter et al	210	Adj. John Wolf	1851	2	312
Jackson, Minter et al	227	Tanner's Fork	1856	2	495
Jackson, Minter et al	578	Tanner's Fork	1857	2	535
Jackson, Minter et al	190	Spruce Run	1858	3	10
Jackson, Minter et al	58	Horn Creek	1858	3	11
Jackson, Minter et al	22	Leading Creek	1858	3	16
Jackson, Minter et al	74	Wolf Pen Run	1859	3	48
Jackson, Minter et al	105	Mud Lick Run	1859	3	49
Jackson, Minter et al	245	Steer Run	1859	3	50
James, David V.	100	Crooked Fork	1850	2	278
James, David V.	160	Shock's Run	1853	2	380
Jarvis, Jane et al Heirs	100	Upper Nighcut	1849	1	532
Jarvis, Thomas	172	Beech Fork	1849	1	535
Johnson, Alexander	75	Pine Creek	1848	1	471
Johnson, Alexander	11	Wts. L. Kanawha	1848	1	477
Johnson, James W.	5	Adj. Robt. Johnson	1851	2	342
Johnson, John H. et al	364	Wts. L. Kanawha	1848	1	470
Johnson, Levi	612	Wts. of L. Kanawha	1851	2	340
Johnson, Levi	53	Lade's Run	1851	2	341
Johnson, Levi	422	Wts. L. Kanawha	1848	1	469
Johnson, Levi et al	140	Bull Run	1861	3	82
Johnson, Levi N. & J. (M. or W.)	790	Pine Creek	1854	2	443

Name of Grantee	Acres	Local Description	Year	Book	Page
Keister, George	130	Big Cove Creek	1850	1	550
Keister, George	60	Little Cove Cr.	1850	1	551
Keister, George	129	Fink's Creek	1852	2	355
Keister, George	680	Crane Run	1857	3	1
Keister, Jacob C.	404	Big Cove Creek	1859	3	44
Keller, George	50	Stuart's Creek	1851	2	314
Kendal, Joseph C.	200	Left Hand Fork	1848	1	431
Kimble, Peter	89	Wts. L. Kanawha	1852	2	365
Kirkpatrick, Andrew J.	13	Stewart's Cr.	1854	2	432
Knight, Amanuel	133	Laurel Creek	1853	2	375
Knight, Joshua L.	306	5 Mile Run	1854	2	445
Knight, Joshua L.	603	Cole Fork	1854	2	446
Knight, Joshua L.	345	Sycamore Run	1854	2	448
Knight, Joshua L.	100	Buckhorn Run	1854	2	449
Knotts, John	50	West Fork	1851	2	323
Knotts, John (Knots)	226	West Fork	1856	2	497
Knotts, Joseph et al	170	Big Nighcut	1855	2	462
Knotts, Joseph et al	58	Walnut Fork	1855	2	463
Linn See Lynn					
Linn, Robert	100	Wts. L. Kanawha	1848	1	455
Linn, Robert	300	Steer Creek	1851	2	320
Linn, Robert et al	134	Lynn Camp	1847	1	401
Linn, Robert et al	1334	Pine Creek	1856	2	514
Long, Christian	531	Wts. Steer Cr.	1853	2	377
Long, Christian	380	Crooked Fork	1854	2	422
Lowther, Alexander Jr. et al	238	Horn Creek	1854	2	411
Lowther, Alexander Jr. et al	623	Horn Creek	1854	2	412
Lowther, Daniel S. et al Heirs	264	Wts. L. Kanawha	1849	1	548
Lynch, George	50	Bear Run	1851	2	324
Lynch, George Jr.	130	Crummy's Creek	1850	2	244
Lynch, George Jr.	142	West Fork	1851	2	316
Lynch, George Jr.	87	West Fork	1851	2	317
Lynch, George Jr.	75	West Fork	1851	2	325
Lynch, George Jr.	50	Adj. Wm. Lynch	1851	2	326
Lynch, George Jr.	50	West Fork	1851	2	327
Lynch, George Jr.	389	West Fork	1851	2	387
Lynch, George Jr.	855	Daniel's Run	1857	2	532
Lynch, George Jr. et al	1,021	West Fork	1850	2	279
Lynch, George Jr. et al	200	West Fork	1853	2	393
Lynch, George Jr. et al	1,226	West Fork	1855	2	480
Lynch, George Jr. et al	382	West Fork	1855	2	481
Lynch, George Jr. et al	440	West Fork	1857	2	529
Lynch, George Jr. et al	700	Sinking Spg. Run	1857	2	530
Lynch, George Jr. et al	50	Barnes Run	1857	2	531
Lynch, William	50	Wts. Lit. Kanawha	1848	1	449
Lynch, William	75	Wts. Lit. Kanawha	1849	1	493
Lynch, William	35	Wts. Lit. Kanawha	1852	2	358
Lynch, William	100	Lynch's Run	1857	2	533
Lynn or Linn					
Lynn, Benjamin et al	675	Big Two Run	1851	2	275
Marks, Evan et al	100	Lower Level Run	1851	2	292
Marks, Evan et al	147	Cedar Creek	1851	2	296
Marks, Heirs	25	Big 2 Run	1851	2	307
Marks, John	100	Bull Run	1856	2	515
Maze, Joseph	451	Wts. Lit. Kanawha	1855	2	478
McKinley, Anna et al Heirs	264	Wts. L. Kanawha	1849	1	548
McQuain, Hugh	500	Big Cove Creek	1859	3	549
Meline, James F.	2,321	Horn Creek	1853	2	381
Messenger, Henry	200	Wolf Pen Run	1854	2	442
Metcalf, Elliott et al	200	Tar Kiln Fork	1860	3	74
Middleton, Henry O.	75	Adj. J. Riddel	1846	1	386
Middleton, Henry O.	100	Sinking Creek	1846	1	387
Middleton, Henry O.	200	Stinking Creek	1846	1	388

Name of Grantee	Acres	Local Description	Year	Book	Page
Sinn—See Linn					
Sinnett, Joseph et al	380	Triplet's Run	1851	2	337
Smarr, Daniel B.	126	Grass Run	1854	2	439
Smith, Jonathan	290	Wts. of L. Kanawha	1852	2	344
Smith, Joshua	15	Wts. Lit. Kanawha	1852	2	352
Smith, Joshua	300	Yellow Cr.	1853	2	406
Smith, Joshua et al	18	Wts. Lit. Kanawha	1853	2	398
Smith, Joshua et al	543	Myer's Run	1853	2	400
Smith, Joshua et al	256	Bee Run	1855	2	479
Smith, Nathan	50	Leading Cr.	1849	1	519
Snodgrass, Elisha L.	153	Upper Big Run	1858	3	7
Snodgrass, Elisha L.	225	Horn Creek	1858	3	8
Sperry, Charles M.	185	Bear Fork	1848	1	439
Sperry, Charles M.	414½	Owen's Fork	1851	2	290
Sperry, P. G. et al	329	Spruce Fork	1849	1	536
Springston, John G.	500	Leading Creek	1856	2	492
Springston, John G.	230	Leading Creek	1856	2	493
Stallman, Henry	25	Wts. of L. Kanawha	1853	2	378
Stallman, Peter	48	Pine Creek	1853	2	394
Stalnaker, S. G.	310	Third Run	1850	1	557
Stalnaker, S. G. et al	200	Wild Cat	1848	1	460
Stalnaker, S. G. et al	300	Lick Run	1848	1	461
Stalnaker, S. G. et al	300	Michael's Run	1849	1	537
Stalnaker, S. G. et al	400	Third Run	1850	1	555
Stalnaker, S. G. et al	260	Wts. L. Kanawha	1850	1	561
Stalnaker, S. G. et al	260	Wts. L. Kanawha	1850	2	260
Stalnaker, S. G. et al	6½	Adj. J. Riddle	1852	2	347
Stalnaker, S. G. et al	185	Job's Run	1853	2	405
Stalnaker, S. G. et al	777	Laurel Creek	1852	2	562
Stalnaker, S. G. et al	194	Tanner's Fork	1858	3	24
Stalnaker, William	183	Wts. Little Kanawha	1848	1	457
Starcher, Adam	200	West Fork	1851	2	319
Starcher, Philip (Startcher)	200	Barnes Run	1854	2	430
Starcher, Thomas	200	Sinking Creek	1855	2	458
Starcher, William	100	West Fork	1852	2	356
Stevens, William O. (or Q.)	50	Sycamore Fork	1851	2	318
Stinchcomb, T. et al	238	Horn Creek	1854	2	411
Stinchcomb, T. et al	623	Horn Creek	1854	2	412
Stout, Absolom L.	558	Dusk Camp	1856	2	517
Stout, E. T.	108	Low Gap Run	1851	2	309
Stout, E. T.	47	Wts. Lit. Kanawha	1853	2	408
Stout, E. T.	983	Rocky Fork	1861	3	78
Stout, E. T.	226	Dusk Camp Run	1861	3	79
Stout, Ezekiel T.	170	Dusk Camp	1849	1	504
Stout, Ezekiel T.	410	Wts. Lit. Kanawha	1850	1	590
Stout, Ezekiel T.	55	Wts. Lit. Kanawha	1853	2	403
Stout, Ezekiel T.	290	Dusk Camp Run	1858	3	26
Stout, Ezekiel T.	128	Little Bull Run	1858	3	28
Stout, Ezekiel T. et al	333	Wts. L. Kanawha	1848	1	476
Stout, Ezekiel T. et al	200	Big Root Run	1849	1	505
Stout, Ezekiel T. et al	200	Butcher's Fork	1858	3	39
Stout, William	75	Wts. Little K.	1848	1	468
Stout, William	75	Cedar Cr.	1851	2	288
Stout, William	310	Cedar Creek	1851	2	289
Stringer, John G.	500	West Fork	1851	2	333
Stringer, John G. et al	1,000	Rowel's Run	1851	2	331
Stringer, John G. et al	500	West Fork	1851	2	332
Stringer, John G. et al Heirs	264	Wts. Lit. Kanawha	1849	1	548
Stump, Absolom	560	Butcher's Run	1852	2	366
Stump, Alfred	97	Sycamore Fork	1858	3	5
Stump, Archibald	200	Wts. Steer Cr.	1849	1	502
Stump, Archibald	150	Wts. Steer Cr.	1849	1	508
Stump, Archibald	156	Bear Fork	1850	2	273

Name of Grantee	Acres	Local Description	Year	Book	Page
Stump, Archibald	105	Wts. of Steer Cr.	1850	2	275
Stump, Archibald	290	Philip's Run	1850	2	277
Stump, Archibald	70	Wts. of Steer Cr.	1851	2	287
Stump, Archibald	200	Wts. Steer Cr.	1851	2	343
Stump, Archibald	330	Bear Fork	1852	2	353
Stump, Archibald	242	Camp Run	1852	2	369
Stump, Archibald	375	Big Run	1854	2	413
Stump, Archibald	403	Horn Creek	1854	2	414
Stump, Jacob	195	Adj. E. Shock	1855	2	456
Stump, Jacob	260	Crooked Fork	1855	2	465
Stump, Jacob J.	274	Raccoon Run	1847	1	415
Stump, Jacob J.	275	Wolf Run	1851	2	313
Stump, Jacob M.	53	Wts. of Steer Cr.	1850	2	274
Stump, Jesse	470	Wts. L. Kanawha	1850	2	280
Stump, Jesse	55	Wts. of Lit. Kanawha	1853	2	391
Stump, John Sr.	360	Wts. Steer Cr.	1852	2	357
Stump, Lemuel	40	Buck Lick Run	1849	1	543
Stump, Lemuel	197	Pine Creek	1849	1	545
Stump, Lemuel	210	Pine Creek	1851	2	297
Stump, Lemuel	118	Crooked Fork	1853	2	389
Stump, Lemuel	175	Pine Creek	1853	2	390
Stump, Maranda H. et al	70	Crooked Run	1858	3	37
Stump, Margaret	60	Adj. A. Stump	1850	2	276
Stump, Martin	275	Daniel's Run	1855	3	6
Stump, Michael	50	Cherry Tree Fork	1848	1	450
Stump, Michael	880	Wts. Steer Cr.	1848	1	458
Stump, Michael	560	Wts. Steer Cr.	1849	1	501
Stump, Michael	170	Wts. L. Kanawha	1856	2	516
Stump, Simon P.	100	Wts. L. Kanawha	1857	2	545
Taylor, James M. et al	1,000	Philip's Run	1858	3	12
Taylor, James M. et al	1,000	Leading Creek	1858	3	13
Taylor, James M. et al	1,000	Wts. of Steer Cr.	1858	3	14
Taylor, James M. et al	854	Wts. Steer Creek	1858	3	15
Taylor, James M. et al	850	Lynch's Run	1858	3	30
Taylor, James M. et al	550	Big Run	1858	3	31
Taylor, James M. et al	796	Leading Cr.	1858	3	32
Taylor, James M. et al	975	Wts. Lit. Kanawha	1858	3	33
Taylor, James M. et al	530	Road Run	1858	3	34
Taylor, James M. et al	399	Straight Creek	1858	3	35
Tharp, Timothy	115	Horn Creek	1847	1	403
Tharp, Timothy	46	Cain Run	1848	1	434
Tharp, Timothy et al	238	Horn Creek	1854	2	411
Tharp, Timothy et al	623	Horn Creek	1854	2	412
Thompson, Pamela R.	75	Owens Fork	1853	2	404
Townsend, Ezekiel T.	78	Wts. Lit. Kanawha	1849	1	514
Townsend, Ezekiel T.	50	Cedar Creek	1851	2	291
Townsend, Ezekiel T. et al	100	Lower Level Run	1851	2	292
Townsend, Ezekiel T. et al	147	Cedar Creek	1851	2	296
Townsend, John B.	40	Cedar Creek	1851	2	322
Trotter, Preston	1,000	Triplett's Run	1848	1	424
Turner, Robert R.	100	Dusk Camp Run	1851	2	310
Unger See Onger					
Vannoy, Benjamin G.	25	Adj. A. Holbert	1850	2	263
Vannoy, Benjamin G.	190	Tanner's Fork	1848	1	435
Vannoy, Benjamin G.	195	Wts. Lit. Kanawha	1848	1	459
Vannoy, Benjamin G.	220	Middle Run	1850	2	264
Vannoy, Benjamin G.	685	Wts. of L. Kanawha	1850	2	262
Wagoner, Anthony	100	Tanner's Fork	1854	2	433
Wagoner, Michael	65	Tanner's Fork	1855	2	464
Waint See Wiant, Wyant					
Waint, N. C.	50	Cedar Creek	1850	1	562
Waint, Nicholas C. et al	80	Crooked Run	1848	1	467
Walden, John	500	Wts. of L. Kanawha	1848	1	432

Name of Grantee	Acres	Local Description	Year	Book	Page
Watson, James O.	400	Adj. Wm. Stalnaker	1847	1	421
Watson, James O.	400	Stinking Creek	1847	1	422
Watson, James O.	200	Stone Lick Run	1849	1	492
Watson, William A. et al	234	Pigeon Run	1858	3	4
West, John	79	Pike Run	1854	2	441
West, John	137	Pike Run	1860	3	70
White, Weeden	100	Little Bull Run	1858	3	25
Whiting, Samuel	100	Paddy's Run	1848	1	423
Whiting, Samuel	100	Wts. Steer Creek	1848	1	466
Whiting, Samuel	145	Little 2 Run	1848	1	472
Whiting, Samuel	50	Cedar Creek	1848	1	473
Whiting, Samuel	45	Cedar Creek	1854	2	440
Whiting, Samuel et al	80	Crooked Run	1848	1	467
Whiting, Samuel et al	60	Lynn Camp Fork	1850	2	259
Wiant, Waint, Wyant					
Wiant, N. C.	50	Cedar Creek	1850	2	261
Wiant, Nicholas C.	4	Cedar Creek	1852	2	348
Wilson, Edgar C.	147	Straight Cr.	1850	2	249
Wilson, Edgar C.	274	Leading Cr.	1850	2	250
Wilson, Edgar C.	130	Yellow Cr.	1850	2	251
Wilson, Edgar C.	100	Laurel Creek	1850	2	252
Wilson, Edgar C.	103	Wts. of L. Kanawha	1850	2	253
Wilson, Edgar C.	60	Wts. of L. Kanawha	1850	2	254
Wilson, Edgar C.	155	Wts. of L. Kanawha	1850	2	255
Wilson, Josiah F. et al	34	Grand Camp Run	1861	3	76
Wolf, Oliver P.	178	Stewart's Cr.	1853	2	410
Wolverton, James S.	98	Leading Cr.	1857	2	537
Wolverton, Joab	50	3-Mile Run	1857	2	536
Wyant See Waint, Wiant					
Yoak, Robert J.	50	Leaf Bank Run	1857	2	542
Yoak, Robert J.	85	Leaf Bank Run	1855	2	460
Yoak, Robert J. et al	300	Leaf Bank Run	1857	2	541

GREENBRIER COUNTY

Abbott, James	320	Adj. J. Hughart	1791	2	363
Abell, Jeremiah	45	Adj. T. Stewart	1796	3	341
Abernathy, James	1,000	Wts New River	1795	3	220
Abernathy, James	1,000	Wts New River	1795	3	221
Abernathy, James	1,000	Wts of New River	1795	3	222
Abernathy, James	1,720	Beaver Creek	1795	3	223
Abernathy, James	5,939	Wts Meadow River	1795	´3	224
Abernathy, James	1,000	Wts of New River	1795	3	226
Abernathy, James	1,000	Wts New River	1795	3	225
Abernathy, James	7,596	Wts Meadow R.	1795	3	227
Abernathy, James	2,080	Big Clear Cr.	1795	3	228
Abernathy, James	1,000	Wts. New River	1795	3	229
Adair, Robert	1⅛	Irish Corner	1859	6	467
Adkins, Lewis	70	River Ridge	1797	4	133
Adkinson, Mary et al Heirs	200	Spring Creek	1828	6	101
Ahárra—See Oharra					
Aharra, Charles	200	Sinking Creek	1797	3	529
Aharra, Charles et al	1,250	Muddy Creek	1800	5	552
Aharra, Daniel Jr.	365	Muddy Creek	1789	2	217
Aharra, William	135	Muddy Cr. Mt.	1799	4	253
Airy, Joseph	156	Hopkins Mt.	1834	6	174
Akers, Simon	226	Greenbrier R.	1793	3	119

Name of Grantee	Acres	Local Description	Year	Book	Page
Akers, Simon	226	Greenbrier R.	1793	3	120
Alderson,—See Olderson					
Alderson, Curtis	207	Lick Creek	1815	5	305
Alderson, David	100	2 Mile Creek	1798	4	103
Alderson, Franklin	100	Laurel Cr.	1838	6	231
Alderson, George	500	Morris's Fork	1824	2	548
Alderson, George	1,000	Glade Creek	1797	4	62
Alderson, George	200	Wts. Meadow River	1797	4	176
Alderson, George	525	Wts. of Elk	1800	4	446
Alderson, George	182	Wts. of Elk	1800	4	445
Alderson, George	186	Lick Creek	1825	6	78
Alderson, George	15½	Wts. Meadow River	1830	6	141
Alderson, George et al	1,206	Wts. Gr. Kanawha	1792	2	380
Alderson, George et al	3,225	Laurel Creek	1826	6	561
Alderson, George et al	402	Gauley Mt.	1795	3	274
Alderson, George et al	428	Burning Springs Bot.	1792	2	423
Alderson, John	72½	Alderson's Br.	1800	5	55
Alderson, John	150	Muddy Cr. Mt.	1844	6	271
Alderson, John	420	Wts. Greenbrier	1785	1	102
Alderson, John	114	Wts. Greenbrier	1792	2	426
Alderson, Joseph	55	Muddy Creek	1821	6	519
Alderson, Joseph et al	33	Wts. Greenbrier	1830	6	136
Alderson, Lina Mims	500	Lick Creek	1849	6	322
Alderson, Thomas	320	Wts. Greenbrier	1793	3	7
Alderson, Thomas	86	Lick Creek	1798	4	104
Alexander, Andrew	115	Sewell Cr.	1827	6	120
Alexander, Hugh Jr.	109	Spring Cr.	1801	5	15
Alexander, James	80	Adj. F. Tincher	1795	3	189
Alexander, James et al	250	Hurricane Cr.	1799	4	289
Alexander, Mathew	192	The Sinks	1791	2	365
Alford—See Allford					
Alford, Henry	120	Wts. Meadow R.	1820	6	504
Alford, John	86	Wolf Creek	1796	3	491
Allen, Hancock	600	Sinking Cr.	1800	4	427
Allen, James	300	Turkey Cr.	1787	1	503
Allen, Samuel	195	Indian Draught	1800	4	414
Allen, Thomas	124	Swope's Knob	1805	3	544
Allen, William	170	Wts. New River	1796	3	493
Allford—See Alford					
Allford, Henry	200	Anthony's Cr.	1799	4	226
Allison, Elizabeth	270	Second Cr.	1791	2	390
Allison, Esa	62	Indian Creek	1792	2	496
Allison, James Jr.	60	Sinking Creek	1789	2	201
Altharr, Jacob	268	Muddy Creek	1816	1	606
Althear, Jacob	268	Muddy Creek	1816	1	606
Amick, Henry	64	Anglin's Cr.	1830	6	145
Amick, Jacob	202	Anglin's Cr.	1831	6	146
Amick, Jacob	120	Anglin's Cr.	1831	6	147
Amick, Jessie et al	2,013	Anglin's Cr.	1857	6	454
Amick, John	50	Anglin's Cr.	1823	6	5
Amick, John	46	Anglin's Cr.	1823	6	6
Anderson, Alexander H.	1	Muddy Creek	1848	6	313
Anderson, George et al	1,000	Wts. Meadow River	1804	3	542
Anderson, James	70	Slash Lick	1806	5	202
Anderson, John	194	Adj. S. Moore	1786	1	220
Anderson, John	700	Howard's Cr.	1786	1	227
Anderson, John	560	Wts. Greenbrier	1786	1	251
Anderson, John	151	Glade Creek	1832	6	167
Anderson, John	1,076	Anthony's Cr.	1786	1	508
Anderson, John	450	Anthony's Cr.	1787	1	325
Anderson, John	400	Meadow Cr.	1792	2	415
Anderson, John	920	Howard's Creek	1799	4	288
Anderson, John	93	Anthony's Creek	1792	2	370

Name of Grantee	Acres	Local Description	Year	Book	Page
Anderson, John B. et al	1,000	Spring Creek	1823	6	4
Anderson, Joseph Jr.	2½	Anthony's Cr.	1860	6	472
Anderson, Robert	146	Anthony's Cr.	1799	4	251
Anderson, William	38	Adj. T. Carraway	1833	6	172
Anderson, William	5¾a9p.	Muddy Creek	1834	6	178
Anderson, William Dr.	147	Howard's Cr.	1853	6	391
Anglin, Isaac	300	Meadow River	1785	1	69
Anthony, Christopher	180	Campbell's Cr.	1790	2	322
Anthony, James C.	112	Rich Creek	1805	5	181
Anthony, James C.	152	Rich Creek	1805	5	182
Anthony, James C.	113	Rich Creek	1805	5	183
Arbaugh—See Arbough					
Arbaugh, John	140	Muddy Creek	1802	5	154
Arbough—or Arbaugh					
Arbough, Michael	444	Muddy Cr. Mt.	1838	6	229
Arbough, Michael	171	Muddy Creek	1819	1	532
Arbough, Michael	80	Muddy Cr. Mt.	1785	3	240
Arbough, Michael Sr.	120	Muddy Cr.	1838	6	220
Arbuckle, Charles	100	Sewell Creek	1798	4	98
Arbuckle, Charles	310	Adj. J. Davis	1801	5	116
Arbuckle, Charles	62	Wolf Creek	1800	4	319
Arbuckle, Charles et al	700	Sewell Cr.	1797	4	167
Arbuckle, James	114	Muddy Creek	1800	4	501
Arbuckle, James & Matthew	570	Welch's Glades	1796	3	496
Arbuckle, James & Matthew	1,000	Lick Fork	1787	1	272
Arbuckle, John	500	Peter's Creek	1799	4	112
Arbuckle, Mathew	450	Bracken's Cr.	1801	5	46
Arbuckle, Mathew	1,160	Howard's Creek	1801	5	75
Arbuckle, Mathew	200	Howard's Cr.	1801	5	74
Arbuckle, Mathew	50	Anthony's Creek	1801	5	73
Arbuckle, Matthew	260	Carpenter's Run	1801	5	38
Arbuckle, Matthew	136	Wts. of Greenbrier	1801	5	39
Arbuckle, Matthew	46	Anthony's Cr.	1801	5	37
Arbuckle, Matthew	114	Wts. of Greenbrier	1801	5	36
Arbuckle, Thomas	60	Burnes Cr.	1800	4	375
Arbuckle, Thomas et al	200	Spring Creek	1806	5	190
Arbuckle, Thomas & Samuel	1,550	Glade Creek	1796	4	127
Arbuckle, William	320	Gr. Levels	1787	2	27
Arbuckle, William	150	Wts. of Elk	1791	2	386
Arbuckle, William	1,239	Wts. of Elk	1787	1	323
Arbuckle, William	1,112	Wts. Kanawha	1786	1	170
Arbuckle, William	950	McCoy's Creek	1786	1	137
Arbuckle, William	150	Wts. of Elk	1787	1	290
Arbuckle, William	293	Wts. of Elk	1787	1	289
Arbuckle, William	99	Wts. of Elk	1787	1	287
Archer, John et al	630½	Wts. of Elk	1787	1	465
Argabright, John	6	Muddy Creek	1850	6	343
Argabright, John	2r.19p.	Mill Creek	1834	6	183
Argabright, John	2r. 4p.	Mill Creek	1834	6	182
Argabright, John et al	679	Muddy Cr.	1837	6	210
Argabright, John et al	5¼	Mill Creek	1838	6	228
Armstrong, John	27	Wts. Greenbrier	1817	1	579
Armstrong, Robert	140	Great Levels	1788	2	184
Armstrong, Robert	40	Adj. P. Lockhart	1788	2	60
Armstrong, Robert	658	Wts. Greenbrier	1794	3	205
Armstrong, Robert	753	Honning Block	1786	1	114
Armstrong, Robert et al	500	Anthony's Cr.	1801	5	35
Armstrong, Robert et al	1,300	Anthony's Creek	1801	5	34
Armstrong, Robert Jr.	65	Anthony's Cr.	1792	2	427
Armstrong, Robert Sr.	753	Anthony's Cr.	1792	2	414
Arnet, John	150	Second Cr.	1795	3	235
Atkeson—See Atkison, Atkinson					
Atkeson, John	228	Adj. P. Murphy	1796	3	414

Name of Grantee	Acres	Local Description	Year	Book	Page
Atkinson, George	100	Adj. J. Erwin	1796	3	426
Atkison—See Atkeson, Atkinson					
Atkison, John	300	Adj. A. Donnally	1800	4	302
Austin, John	180	Burns Creek	1799	4	227
Bailey, Edward B. et al	620	Anthony's Cr.	1848	6	314
Bails, Thomas	240	Adj. P. Hoover	1793	3	6
Baker, Abraham	100	Wts. Kanawha	1787	1	275
Baker, Abraham	200	Wts. of Kanawha	1800	4	447
Baker, Michael	3¼	Adj. J. Rambo	1819	4	540
Ballard, Curtis	669	Hand's Creek	1799	4	287
Ballard, Elijah (Eliza) et al	970	Hand's Creek	1800	4	315
Ballard, Johnson	100	Blue Lick Run	1800	4	419
Ballard, T. W.	100	Big Clear Cr.	1845	6	282
Ballard, William	600	Indian Creek	1802	5	95
Ballard, William	195	Blue Lick Run	1799	4	276
Ballengee, Jean	300	Wts. New River	1800	5	56
Ballenger, Isaac	184	Sheep Rock Br.	1787	2	25
Banhart, Peter	224	Adj. P. Hoover	1800	4	325
Banks, Henry	1,410	Wts. Gr. Kanawha	1786	1	223
Banks, Henry	1,000	Wts. Gr. Kanawha	1786	1	222
Banks, Henry	1,000	Wts. Gr. Kanawha	1786	1	212
Banks, Henry	1,000	Laurel Creek	1786	1	213
Banks, Henry	1,000	Wts. of Gr. Kanawha	1786	1	214
Banks, Henry	1,000	Wts. Gr. Kanawha	1786	1	211
Banks, Henry	1,000	Wts. Gr. Kanawha	1786	1	209
Banks, Henry	1,000	Adj. his No. 5	1786	1	210
Banks, Henry	1,000	Glade Creek	1786	1	208
Banks, Henry	130	Howard's Cr.	1820	1	521
Banks, Henry	600	Howard's Creek	1820	1	519
Banks, Henry	800	Howard's Cr.	1820	1	518
Banks, Henry	560	Muddy Creek	1820	1	515
Banks, Henry	850	Anthony's Cr.	1820	1	516
Banks, Henry	420	Anthony's Cr.	1820	1	513
Banks, Henry	380	Howard's Cr.	1820	1	512
Banks, Henry	50	Adj. J. Carrel	1786	1	174
Banks, Henry	1,000	Laurel Creek	1786	1	175
Banks, Henry	1,000	Wts. Gr. Kanawha	1786	1	178
Banks, Henry	1,000	Wts. Gr. Kanawha	1786	1	177
Banks, Henry	1,000	Wts. of Kanawha	1786	1	176
Banks, Henry	1,120	War Ridge	1786	1	146
Banks, Henry	1,000	Wts. of Kanawha	1786	1	144
Banks, Henry	1,000	Wts. Kanawha	1786	1	145
Banks, Henry	1,000	Wts. of Kanawha	1786	1	143
Banks, Henry	1,000	Wts. of Kanawha	1786	1	142
Banks, Henry	1,000	Wts. of Kanawha	1786	1	141
Banks, Henry	1,000	Wts. of Kanawha	1786	1	140
Banks, Henry	1,050	Rich Creek	1796	3	472
Banks, Henry	765	Wts. Meadow River	1796	3	470
Banks, Henry	3,752	10 Mile Cr.	1796	3	499
Banks, Henry	440	Smithers' Creek	1796	3	500
Banks, Henry	500	Wts. of New River	1796	3	503
Banks, Henry	1,000	Wts. of Kanawha	1786	1	139
Banks, Henry	200	McCoy Creek	1785	1	96
Banks, Henry	400	Pocatalico	1784	1	80
Banks, Henry	300	Pocatalico	1784	1	79
Banks, Henry	500	Pocatalico	1784	1	78
Banks, Henry	1,900	Elk Creek	1784	1	77
Banks, Henry	200	Pocatalico	1784	1	54
Banks, Henry	5,875	Town Creek	1784	1	55
Banks, Henry	1,400	Indian Creek	1822	6	537
Banks, Henry	1,000	Indian Creek	1822	6	542
Banks, Henry	200	Indian Creek	1822	6	543
Banks, Henry	150	Rich Creek	1822	6	545

Name of Grantee	Acres	Local Description	Year	Book	Page
Banks, Henry	120	Jonnycake Fork	1822	6	544
Banks, Henry	115	Rich Creek	1822	6	546
Banks, Henry	137	Rich Creek	1822	6	547
Banks, Henry	100	Wts. New River	1822	6	550
Banks, Henry	120	Rich Creek	1822	6	549
Banks, Henry	96	Irish Creek	1822	6	548
Banks, Henry	1,300	Wts. Gr. Kanawha	1786	1	207
Banks, Henry	1,000	Wts. Gr. Kanawha	1786	1	206
Banks, Henry	1,000	Wts. Gr. Kanawha	1786	1	205
Banks, Henry	1,000	Wts. Gr. Kanawha	1786	1	204
Banks, Henry	1,000	Wts. Gr. Kanawha	1786	1	203
Banks, Henry	1,000	Wts. Gr. Kanawha	1786	1	202
Banks, Henry	1,000	Wts. Gr. Kanawha	1786	1	201
Banks, Henry	1,000	Glade Creek	1786	1	200
Banks, Henry	1,000	Adj. his No. 9	1786	1	199
Banks, Henry	1,000	Wts. Gr. Kanawha	1786	1	198
Banks, Henry	1,000	Wts. Gr. Kanawha	1786	1	197
Banks, Henry	1,000	Wts. Gr. Kanawha	1786	1	196
Banks, Henry	1,000	Wts. Gr. Kanawha	1786	1	195
Banks, Henry	1,000	Wts. of Gr. Kanawha	1786	1	194
Banks, Henry	1,000	Laurel Creek	1786	1	192
Banks, Henry	1,000	Wts. of Gr. Kanawha	1786	1	193
Banks, Henry	1,000	Laurel Creek	1786	1	191
Banks, Henry	8,580	Wts. Greenbrier	1802	5	569
Banks, Henry	3,793	Meadow River	1789	2	285
Banks, Henry	154	Adj. Wm. Morris	1797	4	107
Banks, Henry	3,360	Howard's Cr.	1797	4	67
Banks, Henry	2,385	Anthony's Cr.	1797	4	66
Banks, Henry	32,300	Wts. Williams R.	1797	4	68
Banks, Henry	265	Wts. New River	1795	4	48
Banks, Henry	1,450	Howard's Cr.	1797	4	9
Banks, Henry	58	Spring Creek	1797	4	24
Banks, Henry	220	Sinking Creek	1797	4	8
Banks, Henry	135	Brush Cr.	1797	4	7
Banks, Henry	110	Lit. Wolf Cr.	1797	4	5
Banks, Henry	109	Adj. Wm. Gilliland	1797	4	6
Banks, Henry	3,466	Anthony's Cr.	1798	4	190
Banks, Henry	1,100	Brackin's Cr.	1797	4	160
Banks, Henry	114	Howard's Cr.	1797	4	161
Banks, Henry	815	Sinking Creek	1797	4	159
Banks, Henry	210	Wts. Meadow River	1797	4	158
Banks, Henry	360	Sinking Creek	1797	4	156
Banks, Henry	2,000	Sewell Creek	1797	4	157
Banks, Henry	180	Rich Creek	1797	4	154
Banks, Henry	475	Sinking Creek	1797	4	155
Banks, Henry	44	Adj. his 66 acres	1820	4	592
Banks, Henry	85	Howard's Creek	1820	4	593
Banks, Henry	132	Tinker's Mill Pl.	1820	4	594
Banks, Henry	66	Howard's Creek	1820	4	590
Banks, Henry	80	Howard's Creek	1820	4	591
Banks, Henry	2,915	Wts. Greenbrier	1798	4	561
Banks, Henry	28,280½	Muddy Creek	1798	4	562
Banks, Henry	135	Howard's Cr.	1820	4	534
Banks, Henry	1,300	Wts. Greenbrier	1796	3	413
Banks, Henry	900	Wts. Meadow River	1796	3	383
Banks, Henry	990	Brush Creek	1796	3	382
Banks, Henry	335	Rock Castle Cr.	1796	3	381
Banks, Henry	190	Brackin's Creek	1796	3	380
Banks, Henry	223	Big Clear Cr.	1796	3	379
Banks, Henry	880	Rich Creek	1796	3	507
Banks, Henry	270	Glade Creek	1796	3	505
Banks, Henry	2,000	15 Mi. Creek	1796	3	497
Banks, Henry	1,727	10 Mi. Creek	1796	3	462

Name of Grantee	Acres	Local Description	Year	Book	Page
Banks, Henry	1,940	15 Mi. Creek	1796	3	463
Banks, Henry	230	Man's Creek	1796	3	465
Banks, Henry	2,273	15 Mile Creek	1796	3	461
Banks, Henry	2,000	10 Mi. Creek	1796	3	372
Banks, Henry	3,687	15 Mi. Creek	1796	3	374
Banks, Henry	1,076	Pine Spring Run	1796	3	371
Banks, Henry	1,443	15 Mi. Creek	1796	3	370
Banks, Henry	250	10 Mile Creek	1796	3	369
Banks, Henry	4,390	10 Mi. Creek	1796	3	368
Banks, Henry	1,812	15 Mi. Creek	1796	3	367
Banks, Henry	1,698	18 Mi. Creek	1796	3	366
Banks, Henry	2,000	15 Mi. Creek	1796	3	459
Banks, Henry	10,350	15 Mi. Creek	1794	3	16
Banks, Henry	100	Adj. Morris Battleground	1796	3	460
Banks, Henry	360	E. Fork Suell	1794	3	75
Banks, Henry	166	Meadow River	1794	3	74
Banks, John	1,800	Adj. West's, Wts. Ohio	1787	1	312
Banks, John	400	Matt's Creek	1787	1	313
Banks, John	4,535	Wts. Meadow River	1792	2	383
Banks, William B. et al	4,340	Wts. Meadow River	1802	5	92
Banks, William B. et al Trustees	2,147	15 Mi. Creek	1805	5	179
Banks, William B., Trustee et al	1,000	Big Levels	1798	4	237
Barber—See Barger					
Barber, Joseph	200	Wts. Gauley	1800	4	352
Barclay, John	7,570	Wts. New River	1795	3	574
Bard, David	680	Gauley River	1803	5	160
Barger, Jacob	69	Burns Creek	1800	4	437
Bargor, John	200	Keeny's Knob	1808	5	213
Barler, Joseph	200	Wts. Gauley	1800	4	352
Barnes, Adam	200	Wts. Greenbrier	1794	3	141
Barnett, John	600	Mill Creek	1789	2	234
Barnhart, Peter	224	Adj. P. Hoover	1800	4	325
Barns, Adam	50	Wolf Creek	1793	2	540
Barret, Edward	280	Peter's Creek	1790	2	294
Barrett, Edward	200	Wts. Greenbrier	1790	2	290
Bartlett, Nicholas	235	Sinking Cr.	1785	1	97
Bartley, Lazarus	146	Adj. A. Smith	1793	3	157
Bartley, Lazarus	600	Adj. J. Bumgarner	1793	3	14
Barton, Seth	900	2nd Creek	1799	4	216
Beam, Christian	44	Second Creek	1820	6	497
Beane, Christian	44	Second Creek	1820	6	497
Beard, Andrew	119	Big Levels	1851	6	344
Beard, Christopher	12	Big Levels	1835	6	187
Beard, Christopher	8½	Great Levels	1840	6	239
Beard, John	143	Clovervale Run	1793	2	532
Beard, John	307	Droop Mt.	1792	2	502
Beard, John	200	Culberson's Cr.	1793	3	87
Beard, John	320	Spring Creek	1787	1	322
Beard, John	315	Spring Lick	1783	1	29
Beard, John	50	Bushy Mt.	1801	5	76
Beard, John	80	Spring Cr.	1801	5	78
Beard, John & Thomas	350	Adj. his own	1787	1	326
Beard, Joseph	2a.29p.	Spring Creek	1859	6	463
Beard, Joseph	766	Spring Creek	1851	6	567
Beard, Samuel	38	Spring Cr.	1813	5	282
Beard, Samuel	305	Spring Cr.	1813	5	283
Beard, Samuel	520	Hendrick's Run	1817	1	584
Beard, Thomas	235	Spring Cr.	1813	5	281
Beard, William R.	4	Adj. John Roberts	1819	1	530
Beard, William R.	442	Wts. Spring Creek	1848	6	312
Beard, William R.	50	Spring Cr.	1828	6	124
Beckett, Thomas	400	Wolf Creek	1787	2	26
Beckley, John et al	3,000	Cranberry Glades	1787	2	98

Name of Grantee	Acres	Local Description	Year	Book	Page
Bowen, James H.	500	Big Clear Cr.	1846	6	300
Bowen, James H.	124	Lit. Cl. Creek	1848	6	302
Bowen, James H.	460	Big Clear Cr.	1848	6	301
Bowen, James H.	2,650	Hominy Cr.	1846	6	585
Bowen, Moses H.	38	Anthony's Creek	1848	6	311
Bowger—See Bougher, Bowyer, Boyer					
Bowger, John	743	Mann's Creek	1815	2	566
Bowin—See Bowen					
Bowin, Anthony	20	Wts. Greenbrier	1829	6	132
Bowman, John	100	Adj. G. Myers	1799	4	230
Bowman, John	235	Muddy Creek Mt.	1795	3	213
Bowyer—See Bougher, Bowger, Boyer					
Bowyer, Adam (Boyer)	15	2nd Creek	1793	2	473
Bowyer, Adam	143	2nd Creek	1795	3	187
Bowyer, Adam	300	Second Cr.	1784	1	48
Bowyer, Adam	283	Second Cr.	1784	1	49
Bowyer, John	743	Mann's Creek	1815	2	566
Bowyer, John	534	Keeney's Cr.	1824	6	49
Bowyer, John	17	Wts. New River	1818	1	550
Bowyer, John	43	Wts. New River	1818	1	551
Bowyer, J hn	1,017	Wts. New River	1818	1	552
Bowyer, Jonn	806	Mann's Cr.	1817	1	594
Bowyer, Lewis	446	Keeny's Cr.	1832	6	159
Bowyer, Michael	8¾	Howard's Cr.	1786	1	254
Bowyer, Michael	950	Howard's Cr.	1784	1	36
Bowyer, Peter	97	Mann's Creek	1826	6	94
Bowyer, Peter	55	Mann's Cr.	1809	5	238
Bowyer, Peter	402	Mann's Cr.	1818	1	568
Bowyer, Peter	187	Cliff's New R.	1817	1	577
Bowyer, Philip	21	Wts. of Greenbrier	1815	5	310
Bowyer, William	105	Mann's Creek	1819	1	535
Boyd—See Boid					
Boyd, Patrick et al	52	Wolf Creek	1809	5	229
Boyer—See Bougher, Bowger, Bowyer					
Boyer, Michael	170	Howard's Cr.	1788	2	153
Bragg, Jacob	197	Laurel Run	1850	6	334
Branamon, John	120	Little Creek	1864	6	492
Branham, Sarah	100	Howard's Creek	1849	6	319
Brattin, Wallace et al	1,000	Big Levels	1798	4	237
Bredin, John	500	Adj. A. Dozier	1790	2	291
Bredin, John	390	Millican's Cr.	1793	2	536
Briant, Martin	62½	Anthony Cr.	1800	4	420
Bridwell, Marcus	100	Sewell Mt.	1823	6	18
Bright, Frances	980	Hungates Cr.	1789	2	260
Bright, Frances	1,000	Unknown	1789	2	259
Bright, Francis	1,000	Hungates Creek	1789	2	245
Brindley, James Jr.	617	Adj. J. McNeil	1793	3	3
Brindley, William	150	Droop Mt.	1796	3	509
Brown, E. M.	6	Muddy Cr.	1849	6	321
Brown, James	433	Mann's Creek	1795	3	296
Brown, John	40	Wts. Greenbrier	1829	6	131
Brown, John G.	12,208	Wts. Greenbrier	1797	4	553
Brown, Samuel	240	Big Levels	1795	3	311
Brown, Samuel	25	Wts. Greenbrier	1822	6	536
Brown, Samuel	920	Big Levels	1785	1	101
Brown, Samuel	7	Spring Creek	1818	1	562
Brown, Samuel	5	Big Levels	1816	1	571
Brown, Samuel	150	Sims Run	1849	6	329
Brown, Samuel	1,000	Howard's Cr.	1794	3	150
Brown, Samuel	1,344	Wts. Meadow River	1787	2	19
Brown, Samuel	1,592	Adj. J. McClintick	1788	2	55
Brown, Samuel	150	The Sinks	1788	2	133
Brown, Samuel	56	Meadow River	1800	4	328

Name of Grantee	Acres	Local Description	Year	Book	Page
Brown, Thomas	60	Adj. Robt. McClintic	1820	6	502
Brown, William	100	Second Cr.	1792	2	505
Brown, William	181	Brush Creek	1797	4	143
Brown, William	192	Wts. Greenbrier	1798	4	95
Brown, William	230	Adj. P. Boid	1792	2	372
Brown, William	230	Bradshaw Run	1789	2	222
Brown, William et al	300	Wts. Greenbrier	1799	4	232
Bryan, Benjamin	109	Muddy Creek	1799	4	111
Bryan, Christopher	500	Horseshoe Bottom	1787	2	127
Bryan, Christopher	300	Adj. Wm. McClung	1788	2	99
Bryan, Christopher	194	Great Levels	1787	2	18
Buckley, Joshua	349	Wts. of Greenbrier	1783	1	21
Buckley, Joshua	70	Maze's Lick	1794	3	145
Bullet, Cuthbert	1,030	Wts. of Elk	1779	1	4
Bumgarnor, Jacob	164	Adj. Henison	1794	3	122
Bunger, Henry	7a.3r.	Millican's Cr.	1840	6	248
Burbridge, Roland et al	698	Anthony's Cr.	1787	1	324
Burns, Andrew	150	Adj. M. Kissinger	1800	4	317
Burnsides—See Byrnsides					
Burnsides, James	1,000	Indian Creek	1780	1	9
Burnsides, James	360	Wts. Greenbrier	1783	1	26
Burnsides, John	300	Wts. Greenbrier	1784	1	45
Burnsides, John et al	4,000	Wts. of Gauley	1795	3	295
Burr, Aaron	813	Snodgrass Run	1857	6	443
Burr, Aaron	35	Spring Creek	1821	6	523
Burr, Aaron	40	Spring Creek	1823	6	9
Burr, Adam et al	95	Wts. Greenbrier	1815	5	297
Burr, John	24	Sinking Creek	1844	6	266
Burr, John	7	Sinking Cr.	1844	6	263
Burr, John	2½	Crooked Run	1844	6	264
Burr, John	3¼	Sinking Cr.	1844	6	265
Burr, John	310	Wts. of Meadow R.	1791	2	401
Burr, Peter & Stephen	253	Spring Creek	1804	5	175
Buster, Claudius	1,000	Wts. Meadow River	1825	6	84
Butler, James	148	Muddy Creek	1787	1	403
Butler, James	102	Adj. Wm. Griffith	1800	4	347
Butler, James	2¾	Muddy Creek	1819	1	536
Butler, James	130	Flagg Fork	1810	5	244
Butler, James	200	Lick Creek	1798	4	200
Butler, John	240	Ephraim's Cr.	1811	5	268
Butts, Thomas	100	Anthony's Creek	1797	4	44
Buzzard, Henry S.	136	Anthony's Cr.	1855	6	403
Buzzard, Solomon	200	Anthony's Cr.	1852	6	379
Byers, Peter	50	New River	1808	5	218
Byers, Peter	130	Mann's Creek	1808	5	220
Byers, Peter	40	New River	1808	5	219
Byers, Peter	70	Adj. H. Kerry	1798	4	201
Byrne—See Beirne (Beers)					
Byrnside—See Burnside, Byrnsides					
Byrnside, James	150	Brush Creek	1787	1	311
Byrnside, John	150	Wts. Greenbrier	1796	3	337
Byrnside, John	3,000	Laurel Creek	1798	4	191
Byrnside, John	5,000	Mann's Creek	1798	4	192
Byrnside, John	140	Wts. Meadow River	1797	4	52
Byrnside, John et al	730	Wts. Pocatalico	1787	1	241
Byrnsides, James	1,180	Indian Creek	1786	1	489
Byrnsides, James	340	Indian Creek	1787	1	493
Byrnsides, James	131	Wts. New River	1784	1	66
Byrnsides, James Sr.	331	Wts. New River	1785	1	98
Byrnsides, John	1,500	Pocatalico	1786	1	190
Byrnsides, John	82	Indian Creek	1796	3	474
Byrnsides, John	200	Indian Creek	1800	4	335
Byrnsides, John	110	Indian Creek	1800	4	340

Name of Grantee	Acres	Local Description	Year	Book	Page
Carr, Thomas	50	Sinking Cr.	1801	5	16
Carr, Thomas	115	Sinking Cr.	1801	5	62
Carrawa—See Carraway, Carriway, Carroway					
Carrawa, John	23	Mill Creek	1811	5	271
Carrawa, John	160	Mill Creek	1811	5	272
Carraway—See Carrawa, Carriway, Carroway					
Carraway, Carson (Carroway)	12	Muddy Cr.	1850	6	335
Carraway, Carson	3	Muddy Cr.	1857	6	478
Carraway, George	¾	Muddy Cr.	1858	6	434
Carraway, Samuel (Carroway)	14	Muddy Creek	1849	6	323
Carraway, Thomas	24	Muddy Cr.	1835	6	188
Carraway, Thomas & Wm.	270	Wts. of Meadow R.	1801	5	43
Carrel—See Carrell, Carrill, Carroll, Connell, Cornwell, Correll					
Carrel, Joseph	360	Wts. Gr. Kanawha	1787	1	373
Carrell, Angell	100	Adj. Wm. Young	1792	2	457
Carrell, John	6	Culbertson's Cr.	1819	1	546
Carrell, Samuel	315	Wolf Hollow	1796	3	394
Carrill, Joseph et al	514	Mann's Creek	1791	2	360
Carriway—See Carrawa, Carraway, Carroway					
Carriway, Thomas	500	Wts. Muddy Cr.	1788	2	112
Carroll—See Carrel, Carrell, Carrill					
Carroll, John	240	Adj. A. Boggs	1799	4	281
Carroll, Samuel	68	Spring Cr.	1813	5	285
Carroll, Samuel	175	Howard's Cr.	1798	4	524
Carroway—See Carrawa, Carraway, Carriway					
Carry—See Karry, Kerry					
Carson, George	100	Kert's Mt.	1797	4	3
Cart, William	100	Adj. J. Anderson	1800	4	405
Carven, James	516	12 Pole Creek	1796	3	415
Cash—See Kash					
Cassle, Henry	85	Muddy Creek	1809	5	250
Caul—See Call					
Caul, Elizabeth	42	Big Levels	1823	6	11
Caul, Hugh et al	115	Big Levels	1816	1	608
Caul, Hugh (Call) et al	115	Big Levels	1816	2	556
Cavendish, W. H.	400	Adj. A. Donnally	1787	1	292
Cavendish, William	100	Culbertson's Cr.	1795	3	287
Cavendish, William	100	Muddy Creek	1795	3	201
Cavendish, William H.	19½	Muddy Creek	1804	3	540
Cavendish, William H.	275	Sinking Creek	1782	1	13
Cavendish, William H.	120	Adj. Wm. Blake	1791	2	348
Cavendish, William H.	140	Sinking Cr.	1791	2	343
Cavendish, William H. et al	250	Little Clear Cr.	1801	5	59
Cavendish, William H. et al	400	Roaring Cr.	1801	5	58
Cavendish, William H. et al	400	Roaring Cr.	1801	5	23
Cavendish, William H. et al	2,085	Lit. Clear Cr.	1800	4	306
Cawen, James	516	12 Pole Creek	1796	3	415
Chambers, James	250	Wts. Greenbrier	1787	2	17
Chambers, James	247	The Sinks	1800	4	484
Chambers, Robert	116	Wolf Creek	1787	1	310
Chambers, Robert	245	Indian Creek	1801	5	13
Chambers, Robert	120	Dropping Lick Cr.	1793	2	537
Chambers, Robert	90	Wolf Creek	1793	2	533
Chambers, Robert	100	Wolf Creek	1797	4	180
Chambers, William et al	1,000	Meadow Creek	1796	3	506
Chapman, Jacob	192	Muddy Creek	1795	3	204
Chapman, John	368	Wts. Greenbrier	1786	1	221
Charlton, Thomas	651	Wts. Greenbrier	1787	1	477
Charlton, Thomas	651	Wts. Greenbrier	1787	1	476
Charlton, Thomas	793	The Sinks	1799	4	578
Childers, William	30	Little Cr.	1837	6	215
Childress, Joseph (Childry)	400	Wts. Kanawha	1787	1	405
Chisholm, Arc(h)ibald	1,000	Wts. Greenbrier	1787	1	359

Name of Grantee	Acres	Local Description	Year	Book	Page
Cobb, William	127	Sandy Creek	1799	4	282
Cobb, William	148	The Sinks	1792	2	499
Cochran—See Cockran					
Cochran, Jesse et al	412½	Wts. Greenbrier	1851	6	370
Cockburn, Robert	116	Jordan's Sugar Camp	1801	5	70
Cockburn, Robert	400	Sinking Creek	1792	2	444
Cockran—See Cochran					
Cockran, Alexander et al	100	2nd Creek	1800	4	418
Cockran, William et al	300	2nd Creek	1800	4	357
Cockran, William et al	940	2nd Creek	1800	4	358
Cockran, William et al	100	Second Creek	1800	4	355
Cockran, William et al	500	2nd Creek	1800	4	356
Cockran, William et al	24½	Turkey Creek	1800	4	354
Coffman, Michael	320	Meadow River	1825	6	85
Coffman, Samuel	1a.2r.13p.	Bunches' Hill	1848	6	308
Coggin, William (Cogin)	50	Big Clear Cr.	1815	5	295
Cole, Richard	264	Anthony's Cr.	1833	6	171
Collings, James	22	Swobe's Knob	1795	3	316
Collings, James	168	Swoob's Knob	1795	3	191
Collings, James	210	Swoab's Branch	1787	1	481
Collins—See Collings					
Collison—See Callison					
Collison, James Jr.	58	Wts. Greenbrier	1801	5	105
Comber—See Comer					
Comber, John	185	Greenbrier River	1803	5	174
Comber, John	1,000	Wts. Greenbrier	1795	3	321
Comer—See Comber					
Comer, Frederick	150	Greenbrier River	1793	3	84
Conaugh, Adam	150	Wts. Meadow R.	1795	3	184
Connell—See Carrel, Carrell, Carrill, Carroll, Cornwell, Correll					
Connell, Angell	100	Adj. Wm. Young	1792	2	457
Conner, John	7	Muddy Creek	1818	1	569
Conner, John (Connar)	243	Muddy Creek	1792	2	495
Conrod, George	1,000	Second Creek	1792	2	384
Cook, John	184	Muddy Creek Mt.	1799	4	273
Cook, Valentine	141	Savage Run	1800	4	349
Cook, Valentine	116	Indian Creek	1793	3	47
Cooper, Barnabus	220	Muddy Creek	1796	4	116
Cooper, John	100	Wts. of Rich Creek	1797	4	54
Cooper, Philip	165	Indian Creek	1793	2	513
Cooper, Leonard	200	Wts of Kanawha	1791	2	397
Cooper, Leonard et al	630½	Wts of Elk	1787	1	465
Cooper, Leonard et al	131½	Wts of Elk	1787	1	466
Cooper, Leonard et al	286	Wts of Elk	1788	2	134
Cooper, Leonard et al	103	Wts Potacalico R.	1788	2	135
Cooper, Philip	175	Fork Run	1793	2	517
Cooper, Philip	370	Dropping Lick	1792	2	449
Cooper, William	380	Turkey Creek	1787	1	314
Corner, Frederick	150	Greenbrier River	1793	3	84
Cornwell—See Carrel, Carrell, Carrill, Carroll, Connell, Correll					
Cornwell, Angell	100	Adj. Wm. Young	1792	2	457
Cornwell, Edmund	168	Adj. A. Hozack	1795	3	211
Cornwell, Edmund	245	Samuel Black's Run	1794	3	132
Cornwell, Edmund	100	2nd Creek	1784	1	52
Cornwell, Edward	100	Big Devil's Cr.	1800	4	313
Cornwell, Edward	375	2nd Creek	1787	2	6
Cornwell, Edward	300	Big Devil's Cr.	1795	3	210
Cornwell, Edward	472	Second Cr.	1795	3	209
Cornwell, Edward	500	Adj. D. McMullen	1787	1	475
Cornwell, Edward	100	Wts. Greenbrier	1787	1	474
Cornwell, Edward	348	Big Levels	1785	1	83
Cornwell, Eliza	442	Howard's Cr.	1837	6	218
Cornwell, Eliza	42	Dry Fork	1837	6	219

Name of Grantee	Acres	Local Description	Year	Book	Page
Correll—See Carrel, Carrell, Carrill, Carroll, Connell, Cornwell					
Correll, Angell	100	Adj. Wm. Young	1792	2	457
Correll, John	6	Culbertson's Cr.	1819	1	546
Correll, Samuel	175	Howard's Cr.	1798	4	524
Corven, James	516	12 Pole Creek	1796	3	415
Coulter, James	383	Slab Camp Run	1856	6	433
Coulter, John	96	Spring Cr.	1824	6	42
Cowen, James	516	12 Pole Creek	1796	3	415
Cox, John	190	Cherry Tree R.	1803	5	150
Cox, John	196	Laurel Creek	1803	5	151
Coyser, Martin	78	Adj. Keeney's	1787	1	484
Craig, Robert	595	Adj. P. Lockhart	1789	2	231
Craig, Robert	232	Spring Creek	1786	1	116
Craig, Robert	1,0[illegible]	Greenbrier R.	1793	3	80
Craig, William	264	Spring Creek	1789	2	199
Craig, William	391	Adj. A. Wilson	1786	1	135
Craig, William	86	Spring Creek	1796	3	517
Crawford, James	62½	Irish Corner	1851	6	346
Crawford, James	270	Wts. Greenbrier	1783	1	35
Crawford, Robert	540	Sewell Creek	1801	5	126
Crawford, Robert	810	Wts. Meadow River	1796	3	388
Crawford, Robert	225	Sewell Creek	1796	3	410
Crawford, Samuel	317	Adj. Craig	1787	2	7
Crawford, William E.	84	Sewell Creek	1815	2	569
Creed, Matthew	100	Indian Creek	1800	4	350
Creed, Matthew	170	Indian Creek	1791	2	329
Creek, John	120	Robert's Fork	1805	5	201
Creek, Joseph	120	Robert's Fork	1805	5	197
Creek, Joseph	40	Robert's Fork	1805	5	198
Creigh, Thomas	7a1r.24p.	Big Levels	1798	4	199
Creigh, Thomas	600	Mann's Creek	1797	4	46
Creigh, Thomas	42	Wts. Greenbrier	1821	6	521
Creigh, Thomas	6,000	Kent's Mt.	1796	3	417
Creigh, Thomas	615	Big Laurel Cr.	1816	1	599
Creigh, Thomas	70	Adj. P. Kelly	1811	5	269
Crenshaw, John	1,000	Witcher's Cr.	1787	1	302
Cristal—See Christal					
Cristal, William	235	Wts. Greenbrier	1787	1	482
Cromwell, Edward	100	Big Devil's Creek	1800	4	313
Croughton, Charles	300	Indian Creek	1799	4	261
Cunningham, John et al	3,000	2nd Creek	1800	5	561
Cunningham, John et al	1,630	Peter's Mt.	1800	5	559
Currie, William & James et al	3,000	Pocatalico	1797	4	132
Currie, William & James et al	3,000	Wts. L. Kanawha	1797	4	78
Currie, Wm. & James et al	3,000	Cor. to his 2nd Survey	1797	4	77
Currie, William & James et al	3,000	Wts. of L. Kanawha	1797	4	79
Currie, William & James et al	3,000	Wts. L. Kanawha	1797	4	80
Currie, William & James et al	3,000	Wts. L. Kanawha	1797	4	82
Currie, William & James et al	3,000	Pocatalico	1797	4	83
Curry, Benjamin A	54a 29p.	Wts. Greenbrier	1840	6	242
Curry, John	100	Wts. Wolf Cr.	1787	2	1
Curry, Robert	280	Second Cr.	1791	2	328
Cutlip, David	250	Spring Creek	1800	4	314
Cutlip, David et al	240	Spring Creek	1796	3	354
Cutlip, George	300	Spring Cr.	1783	1	20
Daniel, Hugh	200	Williams Creek	1797	4	140
Dannel, Hugh	200	Williams Creek	1797	4	140
Davis, A. W. G.	39	Muddy Cr. Mt.	1838	6	241
Davis, A. W. G.	40	Wts. Greenbrier	1836	6	207
Davis, A. W. G.	2a.3r.	Muddy Cr. Mt.	1838	6	240
Davis, Aaron	135	Wts. of Muddy Cr.	1791	2	399
Davis, John	363	Big Levels	1789	2	200
Davis, Richard	80	Wts. Greenbrier	1795	3	307

Name of Grantee	Acres	Local Description	Year	Book	Page
Davis, Walter	165	Wts. Greenbrier	1801	5	127
Davis, Walter	400	Wts. Greenbrier	1787	1	501
Davis, William	60	Howard's Creek	1791	2	402
Davis, William	105	Adj. Adam Barnes	1788	2	139
Davis, William & Belfield	30	Kate's Mt.	1845	6	287
Davis, Wm. & Belfield	70	Kate's Mt.	1845	6	288
Day, John	560	Lit. Levels	1783	1	22
Dean, Charles	15¾	Howard's Cr.	1850	6	336
Dean, George	93	Howard's Cr.	1854	6	397
Dean, John B.	80	Howard's Cr.	1858	6	399
Dearing, Conrad et al	130	Adj. A. Hamilton	1809	5	241
Deboy, John	110	Wts. of Greenbrier	1797	4	64
Deboy, John	309	Wolf Creek	1800	5	553
Deboy, John	215	Swope's Knob	1796	3	391
Decamp, Zachariah	270	Indian Creek	1801	5	576
Deckard, Richard	100	Pond Lick	1802	5	156
Deem, A. P.	105	Lit. Sewell Cr.	1861	6	482
Defoor, Zachariah	500	Adj. J. Ahovia	1785	1	99
Dempsey, James	295	2nd Creek	1787	2	13
Dempsey, James et al	180	Second Creek	1793	3	43
Dequazer—See Dequasia, Duquasie					
Dequazer, Thomas	139	Laurel Creek	1828	6	112
DeValcoulon, Savery	905	Mill Creek	1788	2	164
DeValcoulon, Savery et al	7,000	Silver Creek	1787	2	95
DeValcoulon, Savery et al	10,900	Big Sandy Cr.	1788	2	53
DeValvoulon, Savery et al	7,103	Big Sandy Cr.	1788	2	52
DeValcoulon, Savery et al	16,800	Wts. Big Sandy	1788	2	51
Devalt, Daniel	188	Stamping Cr.	1796	3	373
Dick, David	112	Indian Creek	1793	3	48
Dick, John & David	226	Laurel Creek	1846	6	294
Dick, Joseph	110	Laurel Creek	1857	6	445
Dick, Joseph	27½	Laurel Creek	1857	6	446
Dick, Joseph	58	Laurel Cr.	1859	6	469
Dick, Joseph	200	Laurel Creek	1850	6	337
Dick, William	150	Little Stony Cr.	1797	4	175
Dickenson—See Dickeson, Dickinson, Dickison					
Dickenson, John	268	Elk River	1793	3	117
Dickenson, John et al	600	Wts of Elk	1793	3	12
Dickeson, John	100	Peter's Mt.	1800	4	456
Dickinson, John	444	15 Mi. Creek	1793	3	77
Dickinson, John	1,050	Sandy Creek	1789	2	211
Dickison—See Dickeson, Dickenson, Dickinson					
Dickison, John	704	Wts of Kanawha	1790	2	292
Dickison, John	502	Campbell's Cr.	1792	2	433
Dickson—See Dixon					
Dickson, George	100	Wts Greenbrier	1822	6	539
Dickson, Joseph	80	Howard's Creek	1795	3	276
Dickson, Richard	103	Howard's Cr.	1812	5	275
Dickson, Richard	500	Howard's Cr.	1818	1	564
Divier—See Dwier, Dwyer					
Divier, James	540	Big Levels	1788	2	111
Dixon—See Dickson					
Dixon, George	80	Adj. Richard Davis	1800	4	377
Dixon, Henry	100	Wolf Creek	1800	4	502
Dixon, John	244	Big Levels	1800	4	509
Dixon, John	363	Cove Creek	1792	2	371
Dixon, John	116	Kelly's Cr.	1787	1	280
Dixon, John	370	Howard's Cr.	1785	1	103
Dixon, John	60	Dutch Draught	1796	3	384
Dixon, John	53	Pollie's Creek	1792	2	377
Dixon, John et al	240	Howard's Cr.	1799	4	229
Dixon, John Sr.	150	Adj. S. Brown	1800	4	336
Dixon, John (Dixson) Sr.	61	Howard's Creek	1796	3	385

Name of Grantee	Acres	Local Description	Year	Book	Page
Dunscomb, Andrew	1,025	Meadow Creek	1797	4	153
Dunwoody, William Sr.	530	Great Levels	1790	2	309
Dupriest, Thomas et al	127	Muddy Creek	1856	6	419
Dupriest, Thomas et al	299	Muddy Cr.	1856	6	418
Duquasie—See Dequazer					
Duquasie, Thomas (Duquasia)	343	Indian Grave Ridge	1834	6	176
Duval, William	1,000	Wts. of New R.	1795	3	258
Duval, William	1,000	Wts. of New River	1795	3	256
Duval, William	1,000	Wts. New River	1795	3	257
Duval, William	1,000	Wts. New River	1795	3	255
Duval, William	1,000	Mann's Cr.	1795	3	254
Duval, William	1,000	Mann's Creek	1795	3	253
Duval, William	1,000	Wts. New River	1795	3	244
Duval, William	1,000	Mann's Creek	1795	3	245
Duval, William	1,000	Glade Cr.	1795	3	248
Duval, William	1,000	Wts. of N. River	1795	3	246
Duval, William	1,000	Wts. New River	1795	3	251
Duval, William	1,000	Glade Cr.	1795	3	249
Duval, William	1,000	Wts. New River	1795	3	250
Duval, William	1,000	Wts. New River	1795	3	252
Duval, William	1,000	Glade Cr.	1795	3	243
Dwier—See Divier, Dwyer					
Dwier, James	540	Big Levels	1788	2	111
Dwyer—See Divier, Dwier					
Dwyer, Mark	113	Muddy Creek	1815	2	572
Dyer, John	370	Sinking Cr.	1787	1	454
Dysard, Jacob	650	Anthony's Cr.	1851	6	361
Eagan, John	242	Swope's Knob	1800	4	511
Eagle, George et al	112	The Sinks	1790	2	298
Eagle, Joseph	1,260	Lick Creek	1796	3	510
Eathel, Henry	350	Adj. H. Dychess	1812	5	586
Echols—or Eckhols					
Eckhols,William	352	Wts. of Kanawha	1787	1	388
Edgar, James	218	Cherry T. Bot.	1792	2	462
Edgar, James	83	Cherry T. Run	1792	2	463
Edgar, James	220	Bet. Cherry T. Bot. & Lau. Cr.	1792	2	460
Edgar, James	195	Cherry T. Bot.	1792	2	461
Edgar, Thomas	142	Burn's Creek	1797	3	528
Edgar, Thomas	83	Spring Cr.	1809	5	237
Edgar, Thomas	930	Adj. B. Jones	1801	5	564
Edgar, Thomas (Edger)	400	Rich Creek	1785	1	84
Edgar, Thomas (Edger)	270	Rich Creek	1785	1	85
Edgar, Thomas et al	510	Adj. J. Neal	1787	2	4
Edminston—See Edmondson					
Edminston, James	363	Adj. C. Clendenin	1787	1	472
Edminston, John (or James) et al	412½	Wts. Greenbrier	1851	6	370
Edmondson—See Edminston					
Edmondson, David et al	1,000	Old Town Creek	1787	1	473
Edwards, Arthur	200	Stony Creek	1797	4	165
Eleanor, John et al	350	Wts. of Greenbrier	1800	4	329
Eleon, Marcus et al (Eleau)	2,530	Brush Creek	1787	1	457
Elliott, James	89	Anthony's Cr.	1820	6	501
Elliott, Peter	1,000	Wts. Greenbrier	1797	4	85
Elliott, William	203	Adj. John Gilkerson	1786	1	108
Ellis, John	389	Little Levels	1789	2	227
Ellis, Owen	290	Wolf Creek	1794	3	153
Ellis, Owing	100	Wolf Creek	1804	3	530
Ellison, Esaw	150	Fitze's Run	1799	4	279
Ellison, James	600	Indian Creek	1792	2	373
Ellison, James Jr.	223	Wts. New River	1792	2	493
Ellison, James Jr.	233	Wts. Kanawha	1790	2	307
Ellison, James Sr.	511	Hand's Creek	1790	2	310
Ellison, John	60	Han's Creek	1797	4	179

Name of Grantee	Acres	Local Description	Year	Book	Page
Fenton, William	10½	Adj. S. Lewis	1809	5	236
Fife, Thomas	75	Dropping Lick Cr.	1800	4	310
Fifer, John	324	Adj. Wm. Craig	1791	2	407
Filson, William	254	Anthony's Creek	1789	2	248
Finie—See Fenney, Finney, Finnie					
Finie, James	320	Wts. Meadow River	1796	3	418
Finie, James	330	Meadow River	1796	3	436
Finie, John	200	Cherry Tree River	1792	2	494
Finie, John et al	500	Wts. Kanawha	1787	2	50
Finney—See Fenney, Finie, Finnie					
Finney, James (Fenney)	4,350	Wts. of Ohio	1787	1	278
Finney, James	2,000	Wts. of Ohio	1787	1	316
Finton, John	93	Sinking Creek	1789	2	230
Fipher—or Fisher					
Fisher, Peter (Fipher)	300	Great Levels	1794	3	149
Fitzpatrick, James	187	Indian Creek	1785	1	94
Fleashers, Edward	155	Adj. P. Keenan	1787	1	267
Fleathers, Edward	155	Adj. P. Keenan	1787	1	267
Fleathers, Edward	225	The Sinks	1800	4	587
Flemming, James	236	2nd Creek	1796	3	439
Fleshman, John	10	Adj. his own	1807	5	207
Fleshman, John	250	Greenbrier River	1807	5	209
Fleshman, John	185	Keeney's Knob	1864	6	490
Fleshman, John	890	Sewell Cr.	1817	1	578
Fleshman, Moses	70	Glade Creek	1816	2	559
Fleshman, Samuel	378	Glade Creek	1816	1	601
Fleshman, Samuel	60	Glade Creek	1817	1	585
Fleshman, Simeon	350	Mann's Cr.	1818	1	555
Fleshman, William	470	Muddy Cr.	1860	6	505
Flinn, John	400	Adj. his own	1789	2	258
Flinn, William Sr.	400	Mill Creek	1789	2	232
Flopees, David	400	Spring Creek	1824	6	47
Foard—See Ford					
Foard, Francis	68	Sinking Creek	1804	3	539
Foltz, Frantz J. et al	8,712	Wts. Meadow River	1789	2	550
Foltz, Frantz J. et al	2,166	Lit. Clear Cr.	1789	2	269
Foltz, Frantz J. et al	2,472	Meadow River	1789	2	268
Foltz, Frantz J. et al	4,478	Meadow River	1789	2	267
Foltz, Frantz J. et al	6,477	Adj. his No. 8	1789	2	266
Foltz, Frantz J. et al	4,214	Muddy Creek	1789	2	265
Foltz, Frantz J. et al	5,790	Brackin's Cr.	1789	2	264
Foltz, Frantz J. et al	4,050	Meadow River	1789	2	263
Foltz, Frantz Jacob et al	3,483	Meadow River	1789	2	262
Ford—See Foard					
Ford, Arnab	110	Spring Creek	1798	4	212
Ford, Francis et al	30	Adj. W. H. Cavendish	1800	4	311
Foster, Bedford	50	Wolf Creek	1797	4	53
Foster, Grigsby	293	Wts. Greenbrier	1799	4	236
Foster, Isaac	209	Swobe's Knob	1796	3	365
Foster, James	93	The Sinks	1800	4	351
Fox, David	9	Adj. J. Miller	1858	6	451
Foy—See Fay					
Frazer—See Frazier, Frasher					
Frazer, Thomas	48	Adj. Moses Keeney	1810	5	259
Frazer, Thomas	75	Muddy Creek	1824	6	46
Frazer, Thomas	73	Muddy Creek	1828	6	100
Frazer, James	105	Nr. Lewisburg	1816	1	600
Frazier—Frasher, Frazer					
French, George	346	Sinking Creek	1794	3	135
Friend, Abraham	237	Fork Run	1787	2	92
Friend, Charles	100	Turkey Creek	1787	1	420
Friend, Charles	71	Indian Cr.	1801	5	60
Friend, Charles	160	Turkey Cr.	1793	2	466
Frier—See Fryer					
[illegible]	[illegible]	[illegible]	[illegible]	[illegible]	[illegible]

Name of Grantee	Acres	Local Description	Year	Book	Page
Frogg, William	68	Adj. P. Hoover	1800	4	434
Frogg, William	130	Stony Lick	1800	4	436
Frogg, William	380	Adj. J. Miller	1800	4	460
Frogg, William	160	Stony Lick	1800	4	430
Frogg, William	235	Burn's Creek	1796	3	378
Frogg, William et al	606⅛	Muddy Creek	1786	1	156
Fry, William Adam et al	400	Wts. Meadow River	1794	3	162
Fryer, John (Frier)	84	Culbertson's Cr.	1805	5	186
Fryer, John (Frier)	100	Culbertson's Cr.	1795	3	236
Fullerton, William	40	Adj. his own	1797	4	138
Fullerton, William	150	Sinking Creek	1789	2	226
Fullerton, William Jr.	170	Sinking Cr.	1800	4	520
Fulton, Thomas, & Lizzie, his wife et al	350 (348)	Wts. Greenbrier	1799	4	579
Fulwider, Albert & Anthony	100	Hugart's Cr.	1851	6	373
Fulwider, Jacob	120	Donnally's Ridge	1823	6	2
Fulwider, Ulrick	400	Donally's Ridge	1792	2	432
Gainer—See Garner					
Gainer, John	87	Wts. Greenbrier	1797	4	41
Gainer, William F.	300	Cranberry Cr.	1798	4	568
Gaines, William F.	285	Cranberry Cr.	1798	4	101
Gaines, William F.	300	Cranberry Cr.	1798	4	568
Gaiton—See also Gratton					
Gaiton, Daniel	310	Wts. Greenbrier	1798	4	206
Galahan, Edward	18½	The Sinks	1801	5	82
Gallatin, Albert et al	7,000	Silver Creek	1787	2	95
Gallatin, Albert et al	10,900	Big Sandy Cr.	1788	2	53
Gallatin, Albert et al	7,103	Big Sandy Cr.	1788	2	52
Gallatin, Albert et al	16,800	Big Sandy Cr.	1788	2	51
Gamble, Robert	200	Wts. New River	1792	2	508
Gammons, John	220	Howard's Creek	1800	4	304
Gardner, James	64	Lit. Creek	1851	6	345
Gardner, John (Gardnor)	100	2nd Creek	1802	5	104
Garlund, Overton et al (Garland)	275	Glade Creek	1820	4	589
Garner—See Gainer					
Garner, John	96	Wts. Greenbrier	1795	3	314
Garner, John	300	Wts. Greenbrier	1783	1	31
Garrad—See also Jarret, Jarrett					
Garrad, Jacob (or David)	246	Wts. Greenbrier	1799	4	266
Garrad, James	277	Muddy Cr.	1800	4	394
Gartin, Elisha	226	Laurel Creek	1795	3	172
Gartin, Griffey	55	Indian Creek	1800	4	344
Gartin, Griffy	100	Indian Draught	1793	2	470
Gartin, Nathaniel	74	Laurel Creek	1795	3	175
Gartin, Richard	76	Indian Creek	1800	4	401
Gartin, Richard	289	Big Stony Creek	1800	4	291
Gartin, Richard	77	Indian Creek	1800	4	471
Gartin, William	107	Swobe's Knob	1793	2	471
Gartin, William	57	Indian Creek	1797	4	177
Gartin, William	150	Lick Run	1793	3	50
Gartin, William	39	Swope's Knob	1793	3	49
Garvin, John	50	2nd Creek	1800	4	478
Gatlett—Gotlett, Gutlett					
Gatliff, Charles	43	Wts. New River	1793	2	465
Gawin, John	50	2nd Creek	1800	4	478
Gentry, William	300	Adj. J. Moorehead	1802	5	91
George, John	14½	Wts. Meadow River	1855	6	410
George, John	100	Morris Fork	1855	6	385
George, Thomas	105	Muddy Creek	1816	2	555
George, Thomas	204	Lick Creek	1825	6	59
George, W. F. & R. D.	195	Long Draught	1787	2	14
Gibson, John	88	Adj. Colton	1789	2	215
Gibson, John	150	Howard's Cr.	1817	1	589
Gibson, Levin	100	Howard's Creek	1795	3	277

Name of Grantee	Acres	Local Description	Year	Book	Page
Gibson, Levin	125	Anthony's Cr.	1795	3	286
Gibson, William et al Heirs	100	Howard's Creek	1815	5	311
Gilaspy—See Gillaspie					
Gilaspy, John	50	Wolf Creek	1796	3	504
Gilbert, William	200	2nd Cr.	1787	1	277
Gilkerson—See Gilkeson, Gilkinson, Gilkison					
Gilkeson—See Gilkerson					
Gilkinson—See Gilkerson					
Gilkinson, Ebenezer	390	Adj. J. Stuart	1797	4	40
Gilkison—See Gilkerson					
Gilkison, Isaac	400	Sewell Creek	1819	1	538
Gillaspie—See Gilaspy					
Gillaspie, John K.	145	Howard's Cr.	1851	6	374
Gillaspie, Thomas	248	The Levels	1789	2	219
Gillbro—See Billbroe					
Gillbro, William (Billbroe)	1,000	Crossing Laurel Cr.	1798	4	209
Gillelan—Gilleland, Gillilan Gilliland, Gillilan					
Gillelan, James	205	Adj. R. Clendenin	1785	1	92
Gillelan, Nathan	580	Adj. Wm. Poage	1785	1	105
Gilleland, James	148	Spring Creek	1796	3	389
Gilleland, James	50	Spring Cr.	1809	5	232
Gilleland, Samuel (Gilliland)	560	Spring Cr.	1787	1	371
Gilleland, Samuel	284	L. Levels	1795	3	214
Gilleland, Samuel et al	387	Spring Cr.	1788	2	180
Gilleland, Samuel et al	840	Sinking Cr.	1788	2	181
Gilliland, James	300	Adj. George Clendenen	1793	3	81
Gilliland, James	350	Adj. James Armstrong	1787	2	15
Gilliland, James (Gillilan)	450	Adj. C. Wahab	1787	2	63
Gilliland, Robert	45	Wts. Greenbrier	1823	6	34
Gilliland, Samuel et al	712	Sinking Creek	1788	2	179
Gillilan, William (Gillilaw)	490	Meadow River	1799	4	570
Giroud, Honore	7,103	Big Sandy Cr.	1788	2	61
Given—See Givens					
Given, James	400	Little Wolf Cr.	1787	2	23
Given, John	31	Lick Creek	1822	2	543
Given, Joseph	75	Kelly's Creek	1796	3	481
Given, Matthew	350	2nd Creek	1787	2	21
Given, Morris	1,080	Muddlethepeg	1791	2	333
Given, Morris et al	500	Wts. Gauley	1788	2	65
Given, Morris et al	250	Wts. Gauley	1788	2	66
Given, Morris et al	130	Wts. of Gauley	1787	2	108
Given, Samuel	489	Stoney Cr.	1795	3	299
Given, Samuel	138	Blue Lick	1794	3	163
Given, Samuel	400	Wts. Greenbrier	1787	1	464
Givens, James	96	Wts. of Greenbrier	1787	1	408
Glackin, William	270	Spring Run	1795	3	313
Glenn, James	140	Indian Creek	1796	3	485
Glenn, James	246	Bradshaw Run	1796	3	483
Gold, Pricilla	200	Hand's Creek	1794	3	134
Goodman, John	340	Wts. of Elk	1787	1	462
Gordon, Griffy & Katerene his wife et al Heirs	350(348)	Wts. Greenbrier	1799	4	579
Gordon, Charles	110	2nd Creek	1799	4	277
Gordon, Thomas	4,703	Wts. Meadow River	1790	2	321
Gotlett—or Gatlett, Gutlett					
Gotliff, Charles	43	Wts. New River	1793	2	465
Gowin, John	50	2nd Creek	1800	4	478
Grace, Margaret	19	Muddy Creek	1825	6	87
Graham, David	130	Anthony's Cr.	1801	5	40
Graham, David	81	Wts. Greenbrier	1801	5	115
Graham, David	151	Laurel Creek	1801	5	117
Graham, David	120	Indian Cr.	1801	5	118
Graham, David	1,060	Hungert's Creek	1801	5	563

Name of Grantee	Acres	Local Description	Year	Book	Page
Graham, David	130	Hungar's Creek	1795	3	312
Graham, David & William	284	Blue Lick	1805	5	178
Graham, James	465	Wts. Greenbrier	1799	4	231
Graham, James	448	Wts. Greenbrier	1799	4	572
Graham, James	153	Hungales Cr.	1787	1	469
Graham, James	220	Wts. of Greenbrier	1787	1	468
Graham, James	286	Wts. of Greenbrier	1787	1	467
Graham, James	286	Hungales Creek	1787	1	422
Graham, James	240	Wts. of Kanawha	1787	1	421
Graham, James	191	Wts. Greenbrier	1802	5	94
Graham, John	400	Big Meadow Cr.	1855	6	402
Graham, John	453	Laurel Creek	1851	6	372
Graham, John	200	Wts. Meadow River	1851	6	371
Graham, John	197	Wts. Meadow R.	1861	6	481
Graham, William	251	Wts. of Greenbrier	1795	3	280
Graham, William	225	Lit. Meadow Cr.	1798	4	211
Graham, William	275	Lick Branch	1793	2	481
Grant, Cornelius	34	Sinking Cr.	1800	4	435
Grass, John	53	Anthony's Cr.	1826	6	98
Gratton—See also Gaiton					
Gratton, Daniel	310	Wts. Greenbrier	1796	3	355
Gratton, Daniel	130	Burn's Creek	1800	4	503
Gratton, Daniel	250	Big Levels	1787	1	329
Gratton, Daniel	45	Wts. Greenbrier	1810	5	248
Gratton, Thomas	650	Big Levels	1787	1	328
Gratton, Thomas et al	1,680	Adj. S. Brown	1794	3	148
Gratz, Michael et al	3,000	Adj. his 2nd Surv.	1787	1	264
Gratz, Michael et al	3,000	Adj. his 3rd	1787	1	265
Gratz, Michael et al	3,500	Below Letart Falls	1787	1	262
Gratz, Michael et al	4,000	Letart's Falls	1787	1	263
Gratz, Michael et al	4,000	Letart Falls	1787	1	181
Graves—See also Groves					
Graves, Francis	1,000	New River	1794	3	72
Graves, Francis	1,000	Wts. of New River	1794	3	71
Graves, Francis	1,000	Wts. New River	1794	3	68
Graves, Francis	1,000	Wts. New River	1794	3	69
Graves, Francis	1,000	Wts. New River	1794	3	70
Graves, Francis	1,000	Wts. New River	1794	3	67
Graves, Francis	1,000	Wts. New River	1794	3	66
Graves, Francis	1,000	Wts. New River	1794	3	65
Graves, Francis	1,000	Wts. New River	1794	3	64
Graves, Francis	1,000	Wts. New River	1794	3	63
Graves, Francis	1,000	Wts. New River	1794	3	62
Gray, John Sr.	246	Wts. Greenbrier	1800	4	513
Gray, John Jr.	100	Laurel Run	1800	4	451
Green, Gabriel	464	Byrnes' Cr.	1786	1	258
Green, Garret	103	Sink Holes	1785	1	100
Green, Jesse	100	Indian Creek	1797	4	173
Greenley, James	460	Sinking Cr.	1794	3	139
Greenwood, Bailey	150	Campbell's Cr.	1796	3	449
Griffith, Abraham	441	Muddy Creek	1802	5	137
Griffith, John	134	Fish Water Fork	1800	4	483
Griffith, Thomas	368	Greenbrier River	1793	3	78
Griffith, William	3	Muddy Creek	1851	6	375
Griffith, William	429	Wts. of Elk	1787	1	402
Griffith, William	185½	Muddy Creek	1787	1	414
Griffith, William	271	Wts. of Elk	1787	1	471
Griffits, William	70	Muddy Creek	1793	3	92
Grigsby, Benjamin	1,050	Wts. Greenbrier	1804	5	579
Grigsby, Benjamin	550	Howard's Cr.	1810	5	257
Gromer, Frederick	218	Second Cr.	1793	2	530
Groves—See Graves					
Groves, John	100	Otter Creek	1797	4	147

Name of Grantee	Acres	Local Description	Year	Book	Page
Grovner, Frederick	218	Second Cr.	1793	2	530
Guin—Guinn, Gwin, Gwinn—See also Gum					
Guin, James Jr.	132	Lit. Wolf Cr.	1800	4	321
Guinn, Ephraim	21	Lick Creek	1842	6	253
Guinn, John	11	Lick Creek	1828	6	108
Guinn, John	140	Coon Creek	1828	6	104
Guinn, John	354	Lick Creek	1843	6	261
Guinn, John	20	Lick Creek	1858	6	417
Guinn, John	882½	Lick Creek	1837	6	216
Gum—See Guin, Guinn, Gwin, Gwinn					
Gum, John	73	Anthony's Cr.	1832	6	162
Gum, John	88	Anthony's Cr.	1832	6	161
Gutlett—or Gatlett, Gotlett					
Gutlett, William	460	Sink Hole Land	1787	2	20
Gwin—Guin, Guinn, Gwinn—See also Gum					
Gwin, James	60	Kelley's Creek	1789	2	282
Gwin, James Sr.	104	Wts. Greenbrier	1800	4	326
Gwin, Matthew	350	2nd Creek	1787	2	21
Gwin, Morris	1,080	Muddlethepeg	1781	2	333
Gwin, Morris et al	500	Wts. Gauley	1788	2	65
Gwin, Morris et al	130	Wts. of Gauley	1787	2	108
Gwin, Morris et al	250	Wts. Gauley	1788	2	66
Gwin, Robert	30	Pollies Creek	1799	4	275
Gwin, Samuel	50	Lick Creek	1800	5	7
Gwin, Samuel	220	Gwin's Branch	1798	4	70
Gwin, Samuel (Gwinn)	112	Kelley's Creek	1798	4	88
Gwin, Samuel (Gwinn)	207	Wts. Greenbrier	1798	4	86
Gwinn, Andrew	109	Little Meadow Cr.	1815	5	302
Gwinn, James	96	Wts. of Greenbrier	1787	1	408
Gwinn, James	400	Lit. Wolf Cr.	1787	2	23
Gwinn, John	31	Lick Creek	1822	2	543
Gwinn, Joseph	75	Kelly's Creek	1796	3	481
Gwinn, Samuel	138	Blue Lick	1794	3	163
Gwinn, Samuel	489	Stoney Cr.	1795	3	299
Gwinn, Samuel	95	Lick Creek	1825	6	61
Gwinn, Samuel	400	Wts. Greenbrier	1787	1	464
Hackley, Richard C. (or S.)	2,000	Wts. Greenbrier	1796	3	291
Hackley, Richard S.	2,000	Sinking Cr.	1795	3	330
Hafner—Hefner, Heffner, Heifner, Hevnor, Hofner					
Hafner, John	60	Anthony's Cr.	1836	6	201
Hagan, William	265	Wts. Greenbrier	1784	1	41
Hall, John	314	Wolf Creek	1787	1	428
Hall, Moses	150	Wolf Creek	1787	1	425
Hall, Philip	450	William's Run	1797	4	50
Hall, William	196	Wts. Meadow River	1826	6	97
Hall, William et al	128	Mann's Creek	1823	6	27
Halstead—See Holstead					
Hamilton, Andrew (Hambleton)	1,584	Old Town Cr.	1786	1	256
Hamilton, Andrew	1,466	Adj. his own	1787	1	461
Hamilton, Andrew	1,000	Muddy Cr. Mt.	1787	1	460
Hamilton, Andrew	1,277	Anthony's Cr.	1787	1	459
Hamilton, Andrew	650	Adj. his own	1787	1	392
Hamilton, Andrew	700	Anthony's Cr.	1787	1	393
Hamilton, Andrew	666	Muddy Cr.	1787	1	387
Hamilton, Andrew	600	Wts. of Greenbrier	1787	1	385
Hamilton, Andrew	1,100	Wts. Greenbrier	1783	1	32
Hamilton, Andrew	40	Burn's Creek	1801	5	54
Hamilton, Andrew	38	Muddy Creek	1825	6	62
Hamilton, Andrew	590	Wts. Greenbrier	1792	2	497
Hamilton, Andrew	400	Big Levels	1795	3	310
Hamilton, Andrew	275	Wts. Greenbrier	1794	3	165
Hamilton, Andrew et al	316¾	Snake Run	1856	6	429
Hamilton, Andrew et al	46	Muddy Creek	1856	6	416

Name of Grantee	Acres	Local Description	Year	Book	Page
Hamilton, Andrew or James	400	Wts. of Greenbrier	1787	1	389
Hamilton, John	520	Mumbelthepeg	1791	2	409
Hamilton, John et al	130	Wts. Gauley	1787	2	108
Hamilton, John et al	250	Wts. Gauley	1788	2	66
Hamilton, John et al	500	Wts. Gauley	1788	2	65
Hamilton, William	340	Meadow River	1800	4	493
Hamilton, William	50	Muddy Cr.	1800	4	492
Hamilton, William	580	Muddy Creek	1788	2	155
Hamilton, William	300	Muddy Creek	1796	3	431
Hamilton, William et al Heirs	500	Adj. J. Boggs	1831	6	149
Hamilton, William et al Heirs	600	Sandy Cr.	1831	6	148
Hamilton, William Sr.	2¾	Muddy Creek	1825	6	57
Hamrick, John	240	Culbertson's Cr.	1819	4	539
Hand—See Hinds, Hines					
Hand, Christopher	282	Second Cr.	1800	4	470
Handley—See Handly, Hundley					
Handley, Archibald	300	Indian Cr.	1787	2	34
Handley, Austin	250	Bogg's Knob	1859	6	437
Handley, Harvey et al	2,013	Anglin's Creek	1857	6	454
Handley, James	260	Jeter's Mt.	1799	4	110
Handley, John	4	Adj. T. Hughes	1840	6	243
Handley, John	336	Indian Creek	1787	2	24
Handley, John	218	Spring Creek	1797	4	137
Handley, John	25	Weaver's Knob	1824	6	43
Handly—See Handley, Hundley					
Handly, John	150	Turkey Creek	1787	1	407
Hanger, George	3¼	Mill Cr.	1820	6	503
Hanger, George et al	112	The Sinks	1790	2	298
Hanger, John	127	The Sinks	1793	3	5
Hank, William (Hanks)	80	Lit. Mountain	1797	4	146
Hanna, Alice et al Heirs	494	Sinking Creek	1818	1	558
Hanna, Andrew	23	Spring Cr.	1825	6	75
Hanna, Andrew	310	Spring Creek	1823	6	10
Hanna, David	22	Sewell Mt.	1858	6	453
Hanna, David	278	Wts. Meadow River	1835	6	189
Hanna, David	152	Muddy Cr.	1835	6	190
Hanna, David	83	Muddy Creek	1836	6	192
Hanna, David	660	Huggart's Mt.	1837	6	211
Hanna, David	50	Huggart's Cr.	1838	6	235
Hanna, David	200	Greenbrier River	1793	3	112
Hanna, David	100	Spring Creek	1822	2	546
Hanna, David	262	Sewell Cr.	1825	6	91
Hanna, David	500	Morris Cr.	1825	6	90
Hanna, David	1,000	Sewell Creek	1825	6	88
Hanna, David	40	Wts. Meadow River	1848	6	306
Hanna, David	738	Hominy Creek	1844	6	279
Hanna, David et al	33	Charley's Creek	1814	5	289
Hanna, David et al	660	Lit. Sewell Cr.	1846	6	293
Hanna, David et al	215	Hominy Creek	1844	6	278
Hanna, David et al (Daniel)	577	Hominy Creek	1846	6	292
Hanna, David et al	265	Lit. Clear Cr.	1844	6	274
Hanna, David et al	395	Roaring Cr.	1844	6	272
Hanna, David et al	28	Wts. Meadow River	1848	6	305
Hanna, David et al Heirs	395	Spring Cr.	1821	6	524
Hanna, David & William	130	Spring Cr.	1822	2	544
Hanna, George	31	Dry Run	1851	6	376
Hanna, James	317	Spring Lick	1784	1	46
Hanna, James	230	Spring Creek	1792	2	492
Hanna, James	22	Spring Creek	1796	3	451
Hanna, James	80	Spring Cr.	1795	3	329
Hanna, James et al	82	Culbertson's Cr.	1802	5	98
Hanna, James et al	110	Spring Creek	1802	5	99
Hanna, James et al	120	Spring Creek	1802	5	100
Hanna, James et al	240	Spring Creek	1796	3	359

Name of Grantee	Acres	Local Description	Year	Book	Page
Hanna, James et al	515	Indian Creek	1796	3	358
Hanna, James Jr.	26	Spring Cr.	1815	2	564
Hanna, James Sr.	38	Spring Cr.	1818	1	554
Hanna, John	293	Spring Creek	1836	6	206
Hanna, John	140	Spring Cr.	1810	5	266
Hanna, William	168	Spring Cr.	1832	6	160
Hanna, William	63	Spring Creek	1849	6	320
Hanna, William	36	Dry Run	1851	6	348
Hanna, William	55	Spring Creek	1823	6	33
Hannah, Abraham	150	Swobe's Knob	1795	3	275
Hannah, David	175	Spring Creek	1792	2	442
Hannah, James et al Heirs	150	Spring Cr.	1791	2	327
Hannah, John	1,000	Hungard (Hungale's) Cr.	1787	1	383
Hannah, John	1,000	Hungales Cr.	1787	1	510
Hannah, Nicholas	1,050	Second Cr.	1787	1	350
Hannah, Nicholas	752	Wts. of Elk	1787	1	390
Hannah, William & Michael	1,000	Wts. of Greenbrier	1787	1	397
Haponsall, Haponstall, Hapensall, Hapenstall, Hempensall, Hempenstall					
Haptenstall—See Haponsall					
Haptenstall, A.	300	Ohio River	1790	2	288
Haptenstall, Abraham (Haponstall)	330	Morris Cr.	1790	2	320
Hargrove, Jeany (Jenny)	56	Rich Creek	1800	4	320
Harper, Henry	532	Meadow Fork	1851	6	363
Harper, Henry	46	Anthony's Cr.	1830	6	137
Harra, Charles & Robert	1,300	Wts. New River	1816	2	561
Harra, Charles & Thomas	200	Mann's Creek	1816	1	596
Harra, Robert	113	Wts. Meadow River	1817	1	593
Harra, Robert	239	Glade Creek	1815	2	574
Harra, Robert	239	Glade Cr.	1815	2	582
Harriman, John	400	3 Mile Creek	1814	5	291
Harriman, Shadrack	140	Campbell's Cr.	1787	1	423
Harriman, Shadrack	450	Swobe's Knob	1787	2	62
Harriman, Shadrack	127	Campbell's Cr.	1787	2	33
Harriman, Shadrack	170	Witcher's Cr.	1787	2	31
Harriman, Shadrack	95	Witcher's Cr.	1787	2	32
Harriman, Shadrack	542	Indian Creek	1787	2	30
Harriman, Shadrack	1,600	Old Town Cr.	1787	2	22
Harriman, Shadrack	400	18 Mile Creek	1787	2	16
Harris, John et al	106	Byrnes Creek	1800	4	476
Harris, John et al	205	Byrnes Creek	1800	4	475
Harrison, Reuben & Joseph	320	2nd Creek	1800	4	426
Harrow, Robert	155¾	Muddy Cr.	1841	6	249
Hart, Patrick	125	Hand's Creek	1800	5	47
Harvey—or Harvie					
Harvey, Benjamin	210	Hand's Creek	1800	4	459
Harvey, Daniel	57	Droop Mt.	1796	3	464
Harvie, Benjamin	512	Hand's Creek	1800	4	586
Harvie, Benjamin	380	Hand's Creek	1800	5	51
Harvie, John et al	235	Rich Creek	1799	4	218
Harvie, Nicholas	433	Rich Creek	1799	4	386
Harvie, Nicholas	152	Indian Creek	1800	4	413
Hawk, Jacob	165	Lit. Sinking Cr.	1793	3	96
Hawthorn, James	666	12 Mile Creek	1799	4	217
Hawthorne, James	1,000	Old Town Cr.	1787	1	396
Hay—See Hays					
Hay, James	570	18 Mile Creek	1787	1	376
Hay, James	500	3 Mile Creek	1787	1	377
Hay, James	720	18 Mile Cr.	1787	2	49
Haynes, Joseph	90	The Sinks	1800	4	307
Haynes, Joseph	250	Swobe's Knob	1800	4	305
Haynes, William	50	Turkey Creek	1800	4	439
Haynes, William	135	Second Creek	1796	3	508
Haynes, William	200	2nd Creek	1793	3	88

Name of Grantee	Acres	Local Description	Year	Book	Page
Hays—See Hay					
Hays, Patrick	12	Anthony's Cr.	1820	6	509
Hays, Patrick	12	Anthony's Cr.	1820	6	508
Hays, Patrick	26	Anthony's Cr.	1820	6	507
Heath, John	1,395	Wts. Meadow River	1789	2	209
Hederick—or Hedrick					
Hederick, Christopher	150	Muddy Creek	1793	3	20
Hederick, Henry Sr.	300	Rich Hollow	1793	3	113
Hedges, J. K.	4¼	Charlie's Run	1861	6	530
Hedrick, Henry	190	Droop Mountain	1783	1	17
Hedrick, Henry Jr.	220	Adj. J. Hughart	1801	5	21
Hedrick, John	59	Slab Camp Mt.	1825	6	89
Hefner, Hafner, Heffner, Heifner, Hevnor, Hofner					
Heffner, Harvey	924	Mid. Mountain	1859	6	462
Heifner,—Hafner, Heffner, Hefner, Hevnor, Hofner					
Heifner, James	100	Anthony's Cr.	1851	6	350
Heifner, James	35	Wts. Anthony's Cr.	1851	6	349
Heifner, Samuel	870	Anthony's Cr.	1851	6	362
Helpinstine, Philip	95	Howard's Cr.	1800	4	372
Hempenstall, Haptonsall, Haponsall, Haptonstall, Hempensall					
Hempenstall, Abraham (Hempengstall)	275	Howard's Cr.	1801	5	69
Hempenstall, Abraham (Hempensall)	492	Wts. Greenbrier	1787	1	266
Hempenstall, Abraham (Hempinstal)	40	Adj. E. Luddington	1800	4	464
Hempenstall, Abraham	630	Howard's Creek	1795	1	122
Hempenstall, Isaac	50	Howard's Creek	1798	4	205
Hempenstall, Isaac et al	240	Howard's Cr.	1799	4	229
Hempinstall, Charles Jr.	168	Dutch Draft	1853	6	389
Hempinstall, John (Hempingstall)	100	Howard's Cr.	1823	6	15
Henderson, James	200	Rich Creek	1787	1	424
Henderson, James	116	Turkey Creek	1787	1	455
Henderson, James	100	Rich Creek	1787	1	351
Henderson, James	220	Indian Creek	1786	1	130
Henderson, James	380	Indian Creek	1785	1	93
Henderson, James	350	Turkey Creek	1787	2	93
Henderson, James	243	2nd Creek	1787	2	29
Henderson, John	90	Wts. New River	1797	4	55
Henderson, John	350	Wts. of Kanawha	1787	2	28
Henderson, John	1,215	Brush Creek	1796	3	597
Henderson, Samuel	340	Rich Creek	1787	1	500
Henderson, Sarah	100	Turkey Creek	1801	5	8
Henderson, Sarah	167	Dropping Lick	1797	4	12
Henderson, Sarah	190	Wts. Greenbrier	1799	4	240
Hendrix, Henry	400	Adj. John Davis	1787	1	391
Hening—See Henning, Hennings					
Hening, William W. et al, Trustees	2,147	15 Mi. Creek	1805	5	179
Henkle—See Hinkle					
Henkle, Philip et al	130	Adj. A. Hamilton	1809	5	241
Henning, Thomas Sr.	106	Wts. Greenbrier	1823	6	1
Henning, Thomas Sr. et al	683	Adj. Wm. Neal	1858	6	450
Henning, William W. et al, Trustee	1,000	Big Levels	1798	4	237
Hennings, William W. et al	4,340	Wts. Meadow River	1802	5	92
Henry, Abraham	200	Keeny's Mill Run	1789	2	205
Henry, Peter	400	The Levels	1789	2	204
Henshaw, William	1,000	Wts. Gauley	1787	1	300
Henshaw, William	1,000	Teter's Cr.	1787	1	299
Henshaw, William	1,000	Cherry Tree	1787	1	295
Henshaw, William	1,000	Beaver Cr.	1787	1	306
Henshaw, William	1,000	Wts. Gauley	1787	1	307

Name of Grantee	Acres	Local Description	Year	Book	Page
Henshaw, William	1,000	Beaver Cr.	1787	1	327
Henshaw, William	1,000	Wts. of Gauley	1787	1	369
Henshaw, William	1,000	Beaver Creek	1787	1	294
Henson, William	12a.3r.	Muddy Creek	1860	6	480
Henson, William	144	Muddy Cr. Mt.	1855	6	414
Henton—See Hinton					
Henton, Thomas	39	Indian Creek	1797	4	19
Herd, John	1,000	Cooper's Cr.	1787	1	502
Heron, James	1,150	Big Level	1793	2	541
Heron, William	340	Spring Creek	1808	5	217
Hevnor—Hafner, Hefner, Heffner, Heifner, Hofner					
Hevnor, Daniel	500	Anthony's Cr.	1838	6	226
Hevnor, John	250	Anthony's Cr.	1829	6	125
Hickenbottom—See Higginbotham					
Hickenbottom, Joseph	220	Little Devil's Cr.	1793	2	520
Hickenbottom, Moses	228	Lit. Devil's Creek	1793	2	523
Hickenbottom, Moses	194	Second Creek	1793	2	522
Hickenbottom, Moses	236	Big Devil's Cr.	1793	2	524
Hickenbottom, Moses	192	Laurel Creek	1793	2	525
Hickenbottom, Moses	330	2nd Creek	1793	2	526
Hickenbottom, Moses	400	2nd Creek	1793	2	529
Hickenbottom, Moses	400	Big Run	1793	2	521
Hickman, John	104	Wts. Meadow River	1820	4	535
Hickman, Lewis	50	Sewell Cr.	1825	6	56
Hickman, Thompson	50	Sewell Cr.	1825	6	58
Hicks, John et al	3,000	Cor. to his 2nd Survey	1797	4	77
Hicks, John et al	3,000	Wts. L. Kanawha	1797	4	78
Hicks, John et al	3,000	Wts. L. Kanawha	1797	4	79
Hicks, John et al	3,000	Wts. L. Kanawha	1797	4	80
Hicks, John et al	3,000	Wts. of L. Kanawha	1797	4	82
Hicks, John et al	3,000	Pocatalico	1797	4	83
Hicks, John et al	3,000	Pocatalico	1797	4	132
Hicks, Richard et al	148	Laurel Creek	1817	1	583
Higginbotham—See Hickenbottom					
Higginbotham, Moses	500	2nd Creek	1786	1	164
Higgins, John	280	Clear Creek	1800	4	384
Higgins, John	220	Clear Creek	1800	4	383
Hillman, Thomas	143	Bradshaw Run	1794	3	164
Hinchman, John	144	Kelly's Creek	1799	4	280
Hinchman, John	100	Adj. Wm. Cavendish	1796	3	422
Hinchman, William	425	Kelly's Creek	1799	4	286
Hinchman, William	175	Wolf Creek	1794	3	143
Hinchman, William	70	Adj. J. Given	1794	3	128
Hinchman, William	64	Greenbrier R.	1793	3	121
Hinchman, William	200	Kelly's Creek	1793	3	42
Hinds—See Hand, Hines					
Hinds, Edward	200	Clear Creek	1800	4	374
Hines, Charles	50	Pollie's Creek	1792	2	376
Hinkle—See Henkle					
Hinkle, Abraham	100	Spring Creek	1828	6	102
Hinkle, Abraham	40	Spring Cr.	1831	6	152
Hinton—See Henton					
Hinton, John	47	Wts. New River	1838	6	232
Hockman, Jacob	8	Mill Cr. of Muddy Cr.	1820	6	495
Hoffman—See Huffman					
Hoffman, Enos	¾	Muddy Creek	1845	6	283
Hofner—Hafner, Hefner, Heifner, Hevnor					
Hogan, William	265	Wts. Greenbrier	1784	1	41
Hogan, William	280	Levels	1789	2	247
Hogshead, John	400	Second Cr.	1785	1	73
Hoke, Christopher G.	12	Second Cr.	1852	6	386
Holcomb, Samuel	137	Muddy Creek	1825	6	63
Holcomb, Timothy	300	Beaver Cr.	1791	2	346

Name of Grantee	Acres	Local Description	Year	Book	Page
Hollan, Frank	260	Peter's Mt.	1800	4	398
Holley, Israel	166	Anthony's Cr.	1799	4	252
Hollingsback, Daniel	210	Adj. Wm. Long	1787	1	497
Hollingsworth—See Hollinsworth					
Hollingsworth, John	98½	Adj. Anderson	1800	4	404
Hollingsworth, Samuel (Hollinsworth)	2,100	Wts. Greenbrier	1798	4	90
Hollingsworth, Samuel	397	Muddy Creek	1799	4	223
Hollingsworth, Samuel	100	Anthony's Creek	1799	4	224
Hollingsworth, Samuel	254	Spring Creek	1799	4	225
Hollingsworth, Samuel	265	Wts. of Sandy	1796	3	502
Hollingsworth, Stephen et al	400	Adj. John Stewart	1788	2	163
Hollinsworth—See Hollingsworth					
Hollinsworth, Samuel	440	Lick Creek	1798	4	94
Hollinsworth, Samuel	2,280	Meadow Creek	1798	4	93
Hollinsworth, Samuel	1,200	Lick Creek	1798	4	182
Hollinsworth, Samuel	442	Wts. Greenbrier	1798	4	181
Hollinsworth, Samuel	1,480	Wts. Greenbrier	1798	4	184
Hollinsworth, Samuel	1,755	Lick Creek	1798	4	183
Hollinsworth, Samuel	5,718	Laurel Creek	1798	4	186
Hollinsworth, Samuel	1,920	Little Stony Cr.	1798	4	185
Hollinsworth, Samuel	3,390	Lick Creek	1798	4	188
Holly, Joel	70	Muddy Creek	1853	6	390
Holmes, Richard (Homes)	110	Adj. A. Donnally	1791	2	341
Holsaple, Henry	290	Wts. of Greenbrier	1792	2	454
Holsaple, Phillip (Holsapple)	150	Second Creek	1800	4	452
Holsaple, Philip	600	Carpenter's Run	1793	2	519
Holstead, John	96	Indian Creek	1793	3	158
Homes, Richard (Holmes)	110	Adj. A. Donnally	1791	2	341
Honaker, Frederick	57	Lick Run	1800	4	443
Hooch, Henry	100	Adj. S. Williams	1800	5	4
Hook, Henry	100	Adj. S. Williams	1800	5	4
Hoover—See Hover, Howver					
Hoover, George	94	Anthony's Cr.	1830	6	144
Hoover, Henry	68	Anthony's Cr.	1820	4	528
Hoover, Henry	90	Anthony's Cr.	1829	6	129
Hoover, Henry	50	Anthony's Cr.	1832	6	163
Hoover, Henry	137	Anthony's Creek	1851	6	347
Hoover, Henry	160	Anthony's Cr.	1836	6	204
Hoover, Joseph et al	35	Adj. Wm. Baker	1813	5	288
Hoover, Palser (Hover)	390	Adj. John Miller	1791	2	336
Horton, Joseph	145	Byers Knob	1808	5	222
Horton, Joseph	50	Culbertson's Cr.	1804	5	167
Hover—See Hoover, Howver					
Hover, Palser	390	Adj. John Miller	1791	2	336
Howland, Joseph (or James) et al	9,800	Wts. of New River	1797	4	545
Howver—See Hoover etc.					
Howver, George et al (Hoover)	35	Adj. M. Baker	1813	5	288
Hoxey, William	200	Laurel Creek	1797	4	171
Hoxey, William	129	Wts. of Elk	1800	4	343
Hozack, Alexander	400	2nd Creek	1786	1	151
Huddleston, Daniel (Hudleston)	308	Wts. of Kanawha	1791	2	400
Huff, Joseph	252	Laurel Creek	1803	5	173
Huffman—See Hoffman					
Huffman, Enos et al	316¾	Snake Run	1856	6	429
Hull, Jesse	405	Lit. Creek	1864	6	489
Hugart—See Huggart					
Hugart, George	160	Glade Cr.	1825	6	72
Hugart, George	173	Glade Creek	1831	6	156
Hugart, George	49	Wts. New River	1825	6	74
Hugart, James	400	Hugart's Cr.	1787	1	479
Hugart, William	344	Sinking Cr.	1787	1	478
Huggart, George	200	Keeny's Cr.	1823	6	17

Name of Grantee	Acres	Local Description	Year	Book	Page
Huggart, George	110½	Keeny's Cr.	1826	6	92
Huggart, George et al	128	Mann's Creek	1823	6	27
Huggart, William et al	48	Adj. R. Renick	1804	5	168
Hughes, Peter Grant	500	Rockcastle Cr.	1789	2	250
Hughes, William	240	Adj. Wm. & G. Clendenen	1793	3	93
Humes, James et al Heirs	200	Spring Creek	1805	5	200
Humes, James et al Heirs	400	Cherry Tree River	1805	5	199
Humphreys—or Humphries					
Humphreys, James	390	Adj. R. Armstrong	1792	2	412
Humphreys, James	195	Anthony's Cr.	1792	2	413
Humphreys, John Jr.	32	Adj. J. Humphreys Sr.	1800	4	341
Humphreys, John Jr.	125	Adj. J. Humphreys Sr.	1800	4	342
Humphreys, Richard	18	Meadow River	1807	5	206
Humphreys, Samuel	210	Anthony's Creek	1792	2	368
Humphreys, Samuel	400	Cherry Tree Bot.	1800	4	371
Humphreys, Samuel	100	Anthony's Cr.	1796	3	515
Humphries—or Humphreys					
Humphries, Andrew C.	200	Anthony's Cr.	1849	6	330
Humphries, John	815	Second Creek	1789	2	277
Humphries, Richard (or Robert)	279	Mill Creek	1787	1	411
Humphries, Richard	330	Mill Creek	1798	4	197
Humphries, Richard	300½	Muddy Creek	1787	1	416
Humphries, Robert (Humphrys)	160	Second Cr.	1796	3	433
Humphries, Robert W. et al	192	Anthony's Cr.	1847	6	296
Hundley—See Handley, Handly					
Hundley, James	76	Wts Greenbrier	1799	4	221
Hundley, James	300	Stony Creek	1799	4	577
Hunt, Jesse	390	Adj. J. Patterson	1800	4	330
Hunter, Henry	860	Birch River	1787	1	319
Hunter, Henry	264	Adj. G. Blackburn	1786	1	219
Hunter, Henry	200	Old Town Cr.	1786	1	218
Hunter, Henry	328	Old Town Creek	1793	3	101
Hunter, Henry	318	Old Town Creek	1793	3	102
Hunter, Henry B.	159	Wts. Greenbrier	1815	2	568
Hunter, Henry F.	860	Anthony's Cr.	1849	6	326
Hunter, Henry F.	120	Anthony's Cr.	1853	6	392
Hunter, Henry F.	892	Howard's Cr.	1863	6	487
Hunter, John	400	Wts. Birch River	1796	4	124
Hunter, John	700	Wts. Kanawha	1796	4	123
Hunter, John	150	Morris Cr.	1790	2	323
Hunter, John	330	Wts. Meadow River	1796	3	353
Hunter, John A.	500	Muddy Creek	1852	6	380
Hunter, John A.	13a.3r.25p.	Adj. Wm. Montgomery	1861	6	484
Hunter, John et al	1,430	Wills Cr.	1795	3	198
Hunter, John et al	1,000	Wills Creek	1790	2	289
Hunter, Moses	2,760	Beaver Creek	1786	1	179
Hunter, Nathaniel	170	Culbertson's Creek	1805	5	196
Hunter, Nathaniel	19	Culbertson's Creek	1805	5	195
Hutcheson—Hutchinson, Hutchison					
Hutcheson, Adam	177	Meadow River	1828	6	105
Hutchinson, Alexander	400	Elk Lick	1791	2	351
Hutchinson, Archibald	50	Wts. Greenbrier	1823	6	30
Hutchinson, John	50	Brush Creek	1792	2	498
Hutchinson, John	210	Dropping Lick Cr.	1791	2	350
Hutchinson, John	37	3 Mile Cr.	1791	2	345
Hutchison, Alexander	190	Valley Springs	1795	3	173
Hutchison, Andrew	210	Brush Creek	1800	4	523
Hutchison, John	400	Brush Creek	1788	2	144
Hutchison, John	135	Rich Creek	1797	4	172
Hutchison, William	890	Hand's Creek	1788	2	142
Hutchison, William Jr.	100	Dropping Lick Cr.	1795	3	237
Hutsinpillar—See Hutsonpiller					
Hutsinpillar, Anthony	69	Sinking Creek	1817	1	587

Name of Grantee	Acres	Local Description	Year	Book	Page
Hutsinpillar, Benjamin	46	Millican's Creek	1816	2	555
Hutsinpillar, Jacob	95	Adj. J. McVey	1801	5	90
Hutsinpillar, Jacob	220	Adj. Henry Sholtz	1801	5	88
Hutsinpillar, Jacob	400	Spring Cr.	1801	5	85
Hutsinpillar, Jacob	25	Sinking Creek	1799	4	257
Hutsinpillar, Jacob	50	Brushy Run	1799	4	256
Hutsonpiller—Hutsinpillar, Hutsonpillar					
Hutsonpiller, Anthony	12	Sinking Creek	1819	1	529
Hutsonpiller, Anthony	312	Sinking Cr.	1819	1	529
Hutsonpiller, Benjamin	145	Milam's Creek	1838	6	237
Hyde, Benjamin, et al	1,260	Wts. of Gauley	1792	2	487
Hyde, Benjamin et al	1,000	Wts. of Gauley	1792	2	485
Hyde, Benjamin et al	1,000	Wts. of Gauley	1792	2	486
Hyde, Benjamin et al	1,000	Wts. of Gauley	1792	2	484
Hynes, William	53	Peter's Mt.	1796	3	356
Ieacock, David	370	L. Sinking Cr.	1793	3	110
Ingram, Ester	95	Muddy Creek	1795	3	315
Irwin, William	418	2nd Creek	1796	3	392
Israel, Isaac	400	Spring Creek	1807	5	210
Israel, Isaac	400	Spring Creek	1812	5	273
Israel, Isaac (In Trust)	400	Spring Creek	1795	3	304
Israel, Isaac (In Trust)	400	Spring Creek	1795	3	305
James, David	200	Droop Mt.	1793	3	155
James, David	91	Droop Mt.	1795	3	203
James, Richard B.	480	Anthony's Cr.	1857	6	449
Jameson, David	500	Beaver Creek	1787	1	394
Jameson, David	750	Adj. John Jones	1789	2	284
Jarrett—See Garrad, Jarret					
Jarrett, David (Jarret)	623	Wts. of Elk	1791	2	398
Jarrett, David	220	Wolf Creek	1787	1	401
Jarrett, James (Jarrat)	400	Muddy Creek Mountain	1800	4	316
Jarrett, James	550	Muddy Creek	1787	1	412
Jarrett, James et al	600	Wts. of Elk	1793	3	12
Jarrett, James et al	428	Burning Spgs. Bottom	1792	2	423
Jarrett, James Jr. (Jerrett)	23	Muddy Creek	1818	1	557
Jarrett, James & David	600	Gauley Mt.	1793	3	11
Jarrett, Owen	172	Muddy Creek	1787	1	271
Jarrett, Owin	26	Muddy Creek	1801	5	130
Jeacock, David	370	L. Sinking Cr.	1793	3	110
Jeffries, William	184	Huggart's Cr.	1838	6	236
Jeiser, See Yeiser					
Jenkins, Azariah	163	Culbertson's Cr.	1795	3	174
Johnson or Johnston					
Johnson, Andrew D.	560	Meadow Creek	1856	6	422
Johnson, Robert	44	Swobe's Knob	1795	3	303
Johnson, Stephen	100	Cherry Tree Bot.	1798	4	71
Johnson, Stephen	150	Slippery Rock	1798	4	198
Johnson, William	150	Indian Creek	1796	3	340
Johnston or Johnson					
Johnston, Andrew D.	96	Wts. Greenbrier	1843	6	258
Johnston, Andrew D.	300	Sewell Mt.	1831	6	154
Johnston, Barnabus	150	Wolf Creek	1787	2	87
Johnston, Barnabus	180	Peter's Mt.	1801	5	18
Johnston, David	349	2nd Creek	1787	1	435
Johnston, James	58	Wts. Greenbrier	1804	3	533
Johnston, Robert	56	Wolf Creek	1796	3	489
Johnston, Thomas P. et al	400	Adj. John Stewart	1788	2	163
Johnston, William	341	Adj. S. Brown	1787	2	84
Johnston, William	300	Anthony's Creek	1792	2	436
Jonas, James et al	2,085	Lit. Clear Cr.	1800	4	306
Jones, Abel	42	Adj. G. Ellis	1860	6	528
Jones, Abel	90	Adj. T. A. Bell	1857	6	447
Jones, Abel	120	Laurel Run	1854	6	411

Name of Grantee	Acres	Local Description	Year	Book	Page
Jones, Abel	142	Anthony's Cr.	1853	6	393
Jones, James	240	The Sinks	1790	2	299
Jones, John	1,000	Turkey Creek	1794	3	19
Jones, John	400	Gauley Mountain	1792	2	425
Jones, John J.	3,300	Anthony's Cr.	1853	6	592
Jones, Masias	130	Big Levels	1789	2	225
Jones, William	200	Wts. Greenbrier	1796	3	406
Jones, William	150	Cuthbert's Cr.	1797	4	1
Joplin—See Jopling					
Jopling, Thomas	1,813	15 Mi. Creek	1787	1	374
Jordan, James (Jordon)	345	Sinking Cr.	1791	2	337
Jordan, James Sr.	220	Hugart's Cr.	1800	4	467
Jordan, James et al	2,085	Lit. Clear Cr.	1800	4	306
Jordon, Isaac	300	Wts. Williams R.	1825	6	67
Jordon, James	25	Sinking Cr.	1804	3	538
Karry, Henry	170	Gr. Levels	1787	2	80
Kash, James	318	Wts. Indian Cr.	1795	3	171
Kean, David	300	Sewell Cr.	1795	3	288
Keatley, Francis	300	Brush Creek	1787	1	304
Keeble—See Kibbee, Kibble					
Keeble, James	66	Howard's Cr.	1813	5	286
Keelar, Michael	100	Lick Creek	1823	6	16
Keen, Mathas	45	Wts. Greenbrier	1797	4	39
Keenan—See Kenan					
Keenan, Edward	316	Adj. T. Stuart	1792	2	506
Keenan, Edward	400	Wts. Greenbrier	1787	1	447
Keenan, Edward	27½	Lick Run	1800	4	339
Keeney—See Keeny, Kenney, Kenny					
Keeney, Moses	1¼	Muddy Cr.	1821	6	515
Keeney, Moses	13	Muddy Creek	1821	6	514
Keeney, Moses	20	Muddy Creek	1821	6	513
Keeney, Moses	50	Muddy Cr.	1821	6	512
Keeney, Nancy et al	320	Muddy Creek	1810	5	247
Keennon—See Keenan					
Keeny—See Keeney, Kenney, Kenny					
Keeny, John	115	Muddy Creek	1789	2	193
Keeny, John	353	Muddy Creek	1789	2	189
Keeny, John	50	Muddy Creek	1789	2	221
Keeper—See Kepper, Kippers					
Keeper, John	320	Muddy Settlement	1787	1	279
Kees—Keese, Keyes, Keyse, Keys					
Kees, Isaac	218	Tuckahoe Draught	1849	6	325
Keese—See Kees, Keyes, Keyse, Keys					
Keese, John U.	282	Tuckahoe Draft	1851	6	351
Keese, Thomas	259	Adj. B. Reed	1851	6	352
Keisel, George	200	Muddy Creek	1796	3	511
Keister—or Kester					
Keister, John	386	Wts. Meadow River	1838	6	234
Kelley, Thomas	17	Muddy Creek	1819	1	537
Kenan—See Keenan					
Kenan, Patrick	316	Indian Cr.	1786	1	224
Kennedy, James Dr.	110	Anthony's Cr.	1791	2	352
Kennedy, James Dr.	186	Anthony's Cr.	1791	2	353
Kenneer, Andrew	80	Wts. Greenbrier	1787	1	348
Kenney—See Keeney, Keeny, Kenny					
Kenney, James et al	500	Anthony's Cr.	1801	5	35
Kenney, James et al	1,300	Anthony's Creek	1801	5	34
Kenny—See Keeney, Keeny, Kenney					
Kenny, James	50	Anthony's Creek	1793	2	515
Kenny, John et al	206	Great Levels	1791	2	389
Kenard, Thomas	100	Carpenter's Run	1791	2	367
Kepper—Keeper, Kippers					
Kepper, William et al	33	Wts. Greenbrier	1830	6	136

Name of Grantee	Acres	Local Description	Year	Book	Page
Kerand, Thomas	100	Carpenter's Run	1791	2	367
Kerns, Alexander	123	Droop Mt.	1801	5	109
Kerns, Frederick	200	Muddy Creek	1800	4	474
Kerry—See Karry					
Kesinger—See Kishinger, Kisinger, Kissinger					
Kesinger, Mathias	100	Indian Creek	1797	4	17
Kesler—See Kisler					
Kesler, George	2	Adj. T. Kreigh	1811	5	270
Kester—See Keister					
Kester, John	100	Brushy Creek	1828	6	107
Kester, John	120	Wts. Gauley	1828	6	109
Keyes—See Kees, Keese, Keys, Keyse					
Keyes, Gursham	50	Tuckahoe Creek	1856	6	420
Keyes, John H.	165	Tuckahoe Cr.	1856	6	427
Keyes, Joseph	210	Tuckahoe Cr.	1856	6	425
Keyes, Joseph & Gursham	274	Tuckahoe Cr.	1856	6	426
Keyes, Thomas	236	Tuckahoe Cr.	1856	6	424
Keys—See Kees etc.					
Keys, Isaac	490	Tuckahoe Cr.	1856	6	421
Keys, Joseph	745	Howard's Creek	1851	6	354
Keyse, See Kees, Keese, Keyes, Keys					
Keyse, Joseph	40	Howard's Cr.	1836	6	205
Kiah, Augusteen	235	Roaring Creek	1798	4	527
Kibbee—See Keeble, Kibble					
Kibble—See Keeble					
Kibble, Charlotte et al Heirs	100	Howard's Creek	1815	5	311
Kibble, James Sr.	66	Howard's Cr.	1813	5	286
Kidd, David et al	1,875	18 Mi. Creek	1788	2	57
Kigar, John	190	Culbertson's Cr.	1804	3	536
Kilpatrick, Roger	56	Kilpatrick's Run	1796	3	404
Kilpatrick, Roger	206	Indian Creek	1796	3	399
Kilpatrick, Roger	237	Han's Creek	1796	3	398
Kincade—See Kincaid					
Kincaid—See Kinkaid, Kinkead, Kinkhead					
Kincaid, Andrew	170	Anthony's Cr.	1793	3	111
Kincaid, Andrew	215	Adj. J. Madison	1796	4	128
Kincaid, Francis	250	12 Mi. Creek	1797	4	178
Kincaid, George	233	Muddy Creek	1807	5	208
Kincaid, James	1a.17 pchs.	Sinking Cr.	1836	6	193
Kincaid, John	215	Slaty Run	1800	4	522
Kincaid, John	100	Anthony's Cr.	1801	5	44
Kincaid, John	194	Swobe's Knob	1789	2	210
Kincaid, John	100	Meadow's Fork	1800	4	521
Kincaid, Samuel	37	Anthony's Cr.	1825	6	53
Kincaid, Samuel	21	Anthony's Cr.	1825	6	52
Kincaid, Samuel	355	Anthony's Cr.	1809	5	239
Kincaid, Samuel	18	Anthony's Cr.	1825	6	51
Kincaid, Samuel	3	Muddy Creek	1825	6	76
Kincaid, Samuel	320	Anthony's Cr.	1792	2	552
Kincaid, Samuel	220	Anthony's Cr.	1792	2	419
Kincaid, Samuel	200	Lit. Meadow Cr.	1800	4	466
Kincaid, Samuel et al	460	Lit. Meadow R.	1827	6	565
Kincaid, Samuel Jr.	75	Lit. Meadow R.	1821	6	516
Kincaid, Samuel Sr.	80	Anthonys Cr.	1851	6	353
Kincaid, Thomas (Kinkaid)	88	Peter's Mt.	1788	2	106
Kincaid, Thomas	440	Adj. J. Mesey	1788	2	143
Kincaid, Thomas	120	Turkey Creek	1784	1	61
Kincaid, Thomas (Kincade)	42	Glade Creek	1825	6	55
Kincaid, Thomas	150	Adj. his own	1791	2	342
Kincaid, Thomas	315	Muddy Creek	1791	3	347
Kincaid, Thomas	1,334	Lit. Meadow River	1800	4	499
Kincaid, Thomas Sr.	42	Muddy Creek	1816	2	559

Name of Grantee	Acres	Local Description	Year	Book	Page
Kinder, Peter	194	Second Cr.	1787	2	91
Kinder, Peter	50	2nd Creek	1795	3	177
King, Andrew	71	Peter's Mt.	1800	4	296
King, George	210	Adj. J. King	1787	1	449
King, John	75	Adj. James Chambers	1787	1	440
Kinison, Charles	334	Adj. Wm. Hughes	1790	2	287
Kinison, David	300	Fryor Hole	1793	3	2
Kinison, Nathaniel	235	Little Levels	1789	2	280
Kinkaid—See Kincaid, Kinkead, Kinkhead					
Kinkaid, John	105	Meadow Run	1796	3	479
Kinkead—Kincaid, Kinkaid, Kinkhead					
Kinkead, John	320	Muddy Creek	1800	4	494
Kinkhead, William	400	Wts. Greenbrier	1784	1	43
Kippers—See Keeper, Kepper					
Kippers, John	17	Muddy Creek	1819	1	542
Kirkpatrick, George & Thomas	50	Anthony's Creek	1808	5	224
Kirkpatrick, John et al	1,250	Muddy Creek	1800	5	552
Kirkpatrick, Thomas	52	Anthony's Creek	1828	6	106
Kishinger—See Kesinger, Kisinger, Kissinger					
Kishinger, Mathias (Kisinger)	133	Wts. of Greenbrier	1790	2	304
Kisinger, Andrew	267	Cook's Run	1791	2	339
Kisinger, Andrew et al Hrs.	350 (348)	Wts. of Greenbrier	1799	4	579
Kisinger, Mathias	348	Wts. of Greenbrier	1789	2	207
Kisinger, Mathias	309	Indian Creek	1800	4	455
Kisler—See Kesler					
Kisler, Jacob	60	Adj. Wm. Newton	1816	1	603
Kitchen—See Kitcheon					
Kitchen, Margaret	18	Second Cr.	1799	4	109
Kitcheon, James	400	Wts. Meadow R.	1792	2	448
Knap—or Knapp					
Knap, Caleb	45½	Adj. M. Bunger	1825	6	73
Knapp, Caleb	70	Spring Creek	1802	5	153
Knapp, Caleb	49	Adj. James Boggs	1797	4	170
Knapp, James C. & Moses	6	Millican's Cr.	1828	6	103
Knight, Cavendish	1,300	Lit. Clear Cr.	1846	6	582
Knight, Cavendish	610	Lit. Clear Cr.	1846	6	583
Knox, Robert	300	2nd Creek	1793	2	479
Knox, Robert et al	220	Second Creek	1796	3	411
Krause, Daniel (Krouse)	140	Muddy Creek	1796	3	494
Kridor, Jacob	400	Adj. W. H. Cavendish	1799	4	235
Kughn—See Kuhn					
Kughn, Jacob	200	Clear Creek	1790	2	316
Kuhn—See Kughn					
Kuhn, Jacob	137	Wts. Greenbrier	1794	3	56
Kuhn, Jacob	150	Wts. Greenbrier	1794	3	59
Kuhn, Jacob	159	Wts. Greenbrier	1795	3	268
Kuhn, Jacob	100	Adj. G. Stewart	1795	3	267
Kuhn, Jacob	80	Wts. Greenbrier	1794	3	57
Kuhn, Jacob	120	Wts. Greenbrier	1794	3	58
Kuhn, Jacob	80	Adj. A. Donnally	1791	2	340
Kuhn, Jacob	150	Wts. Greenbrier	1791	2	326
Kuhn, Jacob	245	Clear Creek	1790	2	317
Kuhn, Jacob	344	Clear Creek	1790	2	318
Kuhn, Jacob	155	Spring Creek	1790	2	319
Kuhn, Jacob	1,149	Adj. P. Murphy	1790	2	315
Kuhn, Jacob	375	Clear Creek	1790	2	314
Kular, Michael	100	Lick Creek	1823	6	16
Kyle, John	163	Wts. Meadow River	1798	4	525
Lacey—Lacy, Lecy, Leacy					
Lacey, Mark (Lacy)	182	Crooked Run	1797	4	163
Lacey, William	220	Rich Creek	1793	2	468
Lacy—Lacey, Lecy, Leacy					

Name of Grantee	Acres	Local Description	Year	Book	Page
Lewis, Hezekiah	101	Adj. J. Chapman	1814	5	292
Lewis, John	700	Adj. J. Huston	1787	1	286
Lewis, John	278	Adj. J. Gilliahan	1784	1	62
Lewis, John	333	Old Town Cr.	1791	2	349
Lewis, John	380	Clear Creek	1790	2	311
Lewis, John	300	Wts. Meadow River	1796	4	115
Lewis, John	120	Muddy Cr. Mt.	1793	3	82
Lewis, John E. et al	620	Anthony's Cr.	1848	6	314
Lewis, Peggy	698½	Culbertson's Cr.	1800	4	428
Lewis, Samuel	200	Indian Creek	1796	3	338
Lewis, Samuel	300	Indian Creek	1795	3	339
Lewis, Samuel	1,058	Hazel Patch	1787	1	452
Lewis, Samuel G.	92	Miller's Mt.	1848	6	315
Lewis, Thomas	1,000	2nd Creek	1784	1	51
Lewis, William et al	228	Pine Springs	1817	1	588
Lewis, Wilson	128	Muddy Creek	1787	1	410
Lewis, Wilson	300	Muddy Creek	1789	2	228
Lewis, Wilson	100	Muddy Creek	1804	3	534
Liars, Joseph (Siers)	225	Indian Cr.	1792	2	464
Likens, James	237	Adj. G. Viney	1819	1	540
Lindsay, John	411	Sinking Cr.	1787	1	233
Lindsay, John	386	Big Levels	1787	1	395
Littlepage, John C.	415	Glade Creek	1796	3	375
Littlepage, John C.	2,060	Glade Creek	1796	3	376
Littlepage, John C.	1,085	Glade Creek	1796	3	377
Littlepage, John D.	523	The Levels	1792	2	375
Littlepage, John D.	770	Wts. of Gauley	1789	2	261
Littlepage, John D.	1,500	Meadow River	1789	2	274
Lively, Coteral	292	Brush Creek	1794	3	61
Loab—See Swobe					
Loat, John (See Swobe)	371	Wolf Creek	1787	1	239
Lockbridge—See Lockridge					
Lockbridge, Samuel	256	Blue Lick Run	1794	3	146
Lockhart, Levi et al	500	Wts. of Kanawha	1787	2	50
Lockhart, Patrick	500	Muddy Creek	1805	3	546
Lockhart, Patrick	340	Muddy Creek	1795	3	230
Lockhart, Patrick	400	Adj. J. Stuart	1787	1	495
Lockridge—See also Lockbridge					
Lockridge, John	220	Spring Creek	1786	1	169
Lockridge, John	92½	Spring Creek	1787	1	450
Lockridge, Samuel	256	Blue Lick Run	1794	3	146
Lockridge, Samuel	350	L. Meadow Cr.	1794	3	144
Lockridge, William	100	Anthony's Cr.	1800	4	323
Lohr, Peter et al	500	Wts. New River	1815	5	307
Long, Frances	397	Scott's Run	1787	1	507
Long, Philip	100	Wolf Cr. Mt.	1800	4	515
Long, William	364	Culbertson's Cr.	1786	1	255
Long, William P. et al	400	Anthony's Cr.	1850	6	338
Longacre, See Longaker					
Longaker, Jacob	480	Second Creek	1791	2	385
Lorentz, See Lorenz					
Lorentz, Stephen J. et al	2,166	Lit. Clear Cr.	1789	2	269
Lorentz, Stephen J. et al	2,472	Meadow River	1789	2	268
Lorentz, Stephen J. et al	4,478	Meadow River	1789	2	267
Lorentz, Stephen J. et al	6,477	Adj. his No. 8	1789	2	266
Lorentz, Stephen J. et al	4,214	Muddy Creek	1789	2	265
Lorentz, Stephen J. et al	4,050	Meadow River	1789	2	263
Lorentz, Stephen J. et al	3,483	Meadow River	1789	2	262
Lorentz, Stephen J. et al	5,790	Brackin's Cr.	1789	2	264
Lorenz or Lorentz					
Lorenz, Stephen J. et al	8,712	Wts. Meadow R.	1789	2	550
Louderback, David (Lowdenback)	150	2nd Creek	1787	2	40
Loudermilk, David	178	Wts. Greenbrier	1834	6	184

Name of Grantee	Acres	Local Description	Year	Book	Page
Low—See Lowe					
Low, Zodock	220	Swobe's Knob	1788	2	105
Lowance, John (Lawrence)	58	Lowance Creek	1815	5	298
Lowdenback, David (Louderback)	150	2nd Creek	1787	2	40
Lowe—See Low					
Lowe, Nehemiah	74	Indian Creek	1793	2	531
Lowe, Zadock	217	Swope's Knob	1801	5	42
Lowe, Zadock	22	Swope's Knob	1800	5	67
Lowe, Zadock	285	Wts. of Indian Cr.	1803	5	149
Lowe, Zedekiah	200	Laurel Creek	1797	4	15
Lowe, Zodock (Lowes)	100	Bradshaw Run	1797	4	74
Lowin, John	50	2nd Creek	1800	4	478
Ludington—See also Luddington					
Ludington, Esaw	40	Anthony Creek	1796	3	424
Ludington, Francis (Luddington)	822	Anthony's Cr.	1833	6	569
Ludington, Francis	50	Wts. Greenbrier	1800	4	504
Ludington, Francis	400	Wts. Greenbrier	1799	4	262
Ludington, Francis	20½	Big Levels	1827	6	122
Ludington, Francis	10	Big Levels	1827	6	123
Ludington, Francis	425	Wts. Greenbrier	1845	6	574
Ludington, Francis	9	Adj. John Carroll	1814	5	290
Ludington, Francis	280	Spring Cr.	1839	6	238
Ludington, Francis	128	Spring Cr.	1819	1	547
Ludington, Francis	3¾	Spring Cr.	1819	1	548
Ludington, Francis	310	Big Levels	1801	5	120
Lusher—See Lesher					
Lusher, John	113	Muddy Cr.	1810	5	261
Mabbit, Joseph (or James) et al	9,800	Wts. of New River	1797	4	545
Maddox—See Mattics					
Maddox, John	150	Bush Creek	1800	4	457
Maddy—See Mady					
Maddy, John	82	Indian Creek	1800	4	469
Maddy, William	100	Dropping Lick Cr.	1800	4	516
Maddy, William	385	Indian Creek	1786	1	136
Madison, Richard	750	Wts. of Greenbrier	1784	1	47
Mady—or Maddy					
Mady, James & Ann, his wife et al Heirs	350 (348)	Wts. Greenbrier	1799	4	579
Mady, William	421	Indian Cr.	1791	2	344
Mady, William	58	Indian Creek	1793	3	51
Mady, William	321	Indian Cr.	1786	1	225
Magert, David	25	Cove Hill	1800	5	66
Magert, David	103	Cove Springs	1795	3	178
Magnet, Henry	62	Swope's Knob	1800	5	49
Magnet, Henry	110	Howard's Cr.	1792	2	437
Magnet, Henry	105	Swope's Knob	1796	3	492
Mahoney, Timothy	59	Brush Mountain	1849	6	328
Mallow, John	2,390	Anthony's Cr.	1851	6	596
Mallow, John	1,130	Anthony's Cr.	1852	6	387
Mann, Adam	300	Indian Creek	1788	2	148
Mann, Adam	51	Indian Creek	1793	2	475
Mann, Jack & Mary, his wife, et al Heirs	350(348)	Wts. Greenbrier	1799	4	579
Mann, Jacob	80	Indian Creek	1788	2	140
Mann, Jacob	100	Bounds Run	1797	4	20
Mann, Jacob	238	Indian Creek	1800	4	508
Mann, Jacob Jr.	300	Indian Creek	1788	2	145
Mann, Jacob Jr.	299	Blue Lick Run	1799	4	264
Mann, Jacob Jr.	300	Wts. of New River	1799	4	265
Mann, Jacob Jr.	100	Indian Cr.	1788	2	113
Mann, Jacob Jr.	10	Indian Cr.	1800	4	500
Mann, James	100	Dropping Lick Cr.	1800	4	293
Mann, Moses H.	155	Anthony's Cr.	1836	6	571

Name of Grantee	Acres	Local Description	Year	Book	Page
Mann, Moses H. Jr. & William et al	134	Anthony's Cr.	1818	1	549
Mann, Moses Jr. et al Heirs	600	Sandy Cr.	1831	6	148
Mann, Moses Jr. et al Heirs	500	Adj. J. Boggs	1831	6	149
Mann, Thomas	140	Muddy Creek	1792	2	378
Mann, Thomas	990	Adj. James Scott	1792	2	379
Mann, William T.	32½	Wts. Greenbrier	1844	6	269
Mann, William T.	42½	Wts. Greenbrier	1844	6	270
Mann, William T.	5	Adj. J. Ellis	1831	6	155
Mannon, Michael	240	Spring Cr.	1796	3	438
Marrow, Francis	300	Culbertson's Cr.	1790	2	286
Martin, Henry et al	46	Muddy Creek	1856	6	416
Martin, Henry et al	299	Muddy Creek	1856	6	418
Martin, Henry et al	127	Muddy Cr.	1856	6	419
Martin, Henry et al	316¾	Snake Run	1856	6	429
Martin, Hudson et al	4,000	Wts. of Gauley	1795	3	295
Martin, Job (or Jacob)	90	Short Cr.	1834	6	181
Martin, Joseph et al	28	Wts. Meadow River	1848	6	305
Mashbarger—See Mushbarger					
Mashbarger, Jacob	135	Culbertson's Cr.	1818	1	563
Mashbarger, Jacob	10	Wts. Greenbrier	1818	1	566
Massey, Jeptha (or Joseph)	380	Wts. Greenbrier	1794	3	137
Massey, Joseph	2,725	Sewell Creek	1797	4	552
Massey, Joseph	1,450	Howard's Cr.	1797	4	61
Massey, Joseph (Massy)	2,400	Anthony's Creek	1797	4	73
Massey, Joseph (Massy)	1,000	Wts. Meadow River	1797	4	75
Massey, Joseph (Massy)	6,000	Griffiths Br.	1797	4	81
Massingbird, George	413	Little Levels	1790	2	293
Massingbird, George et al	800	Sinking Creek	1789	2	273
Masters, Thomas	150	Howard's Creek	1799	4	284
Masters, Thomas	115	Howard's Creek	1796	3	386
Mathews, See Mathias, Matthews					
Mathews, Archer	400	McCoy's Creek	1786	1	149
Mathews, James W.	165	Milican's Cr.	1817	1	595
Mathews, Townsend	200	Big Levels	1791	2	403
Mathias, Mathews, Matthews					
Mathias, Sampson	400	Lick Creek	1788	2	161
Mathias, Sampson (Matthews)	175	Wts. of Kanawha	1788	2	138
Matthew, Sampson	41	Wts. Greenbrier	1809	5	230
Matthews, See Mathews, Mathias					
Matthews, Archer	275	Pocatalico	1787	1	330
Matthews, Archer	253	Mill Creek	1787	1	375
Matthews, Archer	900	Adj. S. Brown	1786	1	109
Matthews, Archer	1,000	McCoy's Cr.	1786	1	107
Matthews, Archer	200	Wts. of Kanawha	1786	1	106
Matthews, Archer et al	850	18 Mi. Cr.	1787	1	282
Matthews, Archer et al	200	Wts. of Kanawha	1787	1	426
Matthews, Joseph	100	Wts. of Elk	1795	3	232
Matthews, Joseph	29	Adj. his own	1803	5	164
Matthews, Richard	250	Wts. of Elk	1801	5	11
Matthews, Richard	250	Wts. of Elk	1801	5	20
Matthews, Richard	200	Wts. of Elk	1801	5	19
Matthews, Richard	400	Adj. J. Elkins	1787	2	89
Matthews, Richard Sr .	300	Culbertson's Cr.	1791	2	325
Matthews, Sampson (Mathias)	99	Wts. of Kanawha	1788	2	110
Matthews, Sampson	400	Wts. Greenbrier	1782	1	14
Matthews, Sampson	20	Wts. Greenbrier	1809	5	233
Matthews, Sampson	196	Riburn's Mt.	1796	3	450
Matthews, Sampson Jr.	400	Wts. Greenbrier	1794	3	167
Matthews, Sampson Jr.	400	Wts. Greenbrier	1796	3	360
Matthews, Townsend	92	Adj. his own	1815	5	303
Mattics—See Maddox					
Mattics, Schofield (Matics)	7	Muddy Creek	1857	6	448
May—See Mays, Maze					

Name of Grantee	Acres	Local Description	Year	Book	Page
McCoy, James et al	5¼	Mill Creek	1838	6	228
McCoy, James et al	400	Roaring Cr.	1801	5	23
McCoy, James et al	400	Roaring Cr.	1801	5	58
McCoy, James et al	250	Little Cl. Creek	1801	5	59
McCoy, James et al	185	Big Clear Cr.	1796	3	514
McCoy, James et al	70	Big Clear Cr.	1796	3	513
McCoy, Joseph	196	Sinking Cr.	1844	6	276
McCoy, Nancy, et al Heirs	500	Adj. J. Boggs	1831	6	149
McCoy, Nancy, et al Heirs	600	Sandy Cr.	1831	6	148
McCoy, William	13½	Adj. E. Parkins	1822	2	545
McCoy, William	533	Sinking Cr.	1787	1	293
McCoy, William	363	Sinking Creek	1795	3	281
McCoy, William	326	Adj. Joseph McClung	1800	4	300
McCoy, William	1,021	Lit. Clear Cr.	1846	6	580
McCoy, William	190	Sinking Cr.	1836	6	202
McCoy, William	70	Sinking Cr.	1851	6	358
McCoy, William	76	Sinking Cr.	1820	6	494
McCoy, William	76	Spring Cr.	1823	6	35
McCoy, William et al	200	Big Cain Cr.	1848	6	307
McCoy, William et al	33	Charley's Creek	1814	5	289
McCoy, William et al	568	Roaring Cr.	1844	6	275
McCoy, William et al	265	Lit. Clear Cr.	1844	6	274
McCoy, William et al	395	Roaring Cr.	1844	6	272
McCoy, William et al	250	Lit. Clear Cr.	1844	6	277
McCoy, William et al Heirs	494	Sinking Creek	1818	1	558
McCue, David	36	Spring Cr.	1801	5	17
McCue, David	14½	Culbertson's Cr.	1806	5	203
McCue, John	369	Adj. S. Brown	1785	1	155
McCue, John	100	Elk River	1793	3	104
McCullock, McCollough, McCullough					
McCullock, Thomas (McCollock)	400	Adj. M. Guian	1787	1	498
McCullough, William	254	Muddy Creek	1793	3	124
McDaniel—McDannel, McDonnel, McDowell					
McDaniel, Henry	260	Crooked Run	1793	2	518
McDaniel, James	400	Wts. New River	1789	2	218
McDannel—McDaniel, McDonnel, McDowell					
McDannell—See McDannel, etc.					
McDannell, Henry	91	Rich Creek	1797	4	14
McDonnel, McDannel, McDaniel, McDowell					
McDonnel, Henry	89	Rich Creek	1787	2	86
McDonnell, Henry	219	Wts. of New River	1790	2	300
McDonnell, Henry Sr.	150	Wts. New River	1800	4	472
McDonnell, Henry Sr.	360	Rich Creek	1800	4	518
McDonnell, James	133	Brush Creek	1787	1	451
McDougal, John	430	Indian Creek	1796	3	352
McDougall, John	162	Little Mt.	1800	4	417
McDougall, John et al	83	Turkey Creek	1801	5	41
McDowell, McDaniel, McDannel, McDonnel					
McDowell, Archibald	142	Second Creek	1796	3	362
McDowell, Archibald	367	Adj. A. Donally	1785	1	64
McDowell, Archibald	380	Second Creek	1791	2	392
McDowell, John	219	Wts. of New River	1790	2	300
McDowell, John	50	Little Wolf Cr.	1799	4	274
McDowell, John	10	Wts. Greenbrier	1837	6	212
McDowell, John Jr.	37	Muddy Cr.	1823	6	8
McDowell, John Jr. (McDowel)	31	Muddy Creek	1823	6	7
McDowell, William	361	Adj. J. Stuart	1787	2	79
McDowell, William et al	220	Second Creek	1796	3	411
McFarren—or McFarvin, McFerren					
McFarren, John	300	Jones' Creek	1789	2	195
McFerran, John et al	48	Adj. R. Renick	1804	5	168
McFerren, James (alias McFarvin)	220	Hugart's Creek	1824	6	45
McGeehee—See McGhee					
McGeehee, Lively	126	Rich Creek	1801	5	29

Name of Grantee	Acres	Local Description	Year	Book	Page
McGhee—See McGeehee					
McGhee, Lively	185	Blue Lick Run	1796	4	30
McGlamary, McGlamy, McGlanny					
McGlamary, Mathias	100	2nd Creek	1800	5	6
McGlamary, Mathias	200	Dropping Lick	1795	3	185
McGlanny—McGlamy, McGlamary					
McGlanny, Mathias	75	Dropping Lick	1787	2	94
McGlanny, Mathias	300	Lick Creek	1787	2	74
McGraw, Henry	82	Ferren Spring Br.	1829	6	130
McGraw, Henry	200	Wts. New River	1839	6	233
McKee, Robert	500	Mumblethepeg	1792	2	421
McKee, William	495	Wts. Gauley	1788	2	132
McKee, William	1,000	Teter's Cr.	1788	2	131
McKee, William et al	672	Wts. Kanawha	1786	1	257
McLaughlin, Dennis	235	Adj. Ballentine's	1799	4	285
McMillan—See McMillian, McMillion, McMullen, McMullian, McMullin					
McMillan, John Sr.	44	Spring Cr.	1802	5	155
McMillian, James	55	Spring Creek	1830	6	140
McMillian, James	180	Spring Cr.	1829	6	127
McMillian, Ralph	18½	Adj. S. Watts	1843	6	259
McMillican, James (McMillian)	180	Spring Cr.	1829	6	127
McMillion—or McMillan, McMillian, McMullen, McMullian, McMullin					
McMillion, Daniel	96	Roaring Cr.	1823	6	37
McMillion, Daniel	4	Culbertson's Cr.	1856	6	474
McMillion, James	600	Spring Creek	1829	6	566
McMillion, James	190	William's River	1825	6	64
McMillion, James	100	Clear Creek	1825	6	65
McMillion, James	2,772	Wts. Meadow River	1832	6	169
McMillion, James (or Joseph)	128	Spring Creek	1798	4	526
McMillion, John	137	Spring Cr.	1819	4	538
McMillion, John	43¼	Robin's Fork	1851	6	368
McMillion, John	151	Robin's Fork	1851	6	369
McMillion, John	172	Culbertson's Cr.	1823	6	28
McMillion, John	500	Culbertson's Cr.	1791	2	338
McMillion, John	50	Spring Creek	1798	4	202
McMillion, John et al	320	Culbertson's Cr.	1820	6	496
McMillion, John et al	377	Spring Cr.	1820	6	506
McMillion, John Sr.	235	Culbertson's Cr.	1796	3	519
McMillion, Joseph	378	Dry Run	1820	4	532
McMillion, William	465	Culbertson's Cr.	1819	1	525
McMullen, John	133	Second Creek	1785	1	104
McMullian, James	180	Spring Cr.	1829	6	127
McMullin, Daniel	196	Adj. E. Wyatt	1788	2	85
McMullin, John	360	Culbertson's Cr.	1787	2	43
McMullin, Joseph	193	Culbertson's Cr.	1787	2	41
McMullin, Ralph	18½	Adj. S. Watts	1843	6	259
McNatt, or McNutt					
McNeal—See McNeil					
McNeal, Abraham	37	Buckeye Mt.	1795	3	319
McNeal, John	397	Adj. A. Smith	1797	4	36
McNeal, John et al	3,338	Beaver Creek	1788	2	54
McNeal, John et al	3,000	Cranberry Glades	1787	2	98
McNeal, John et al	2,000	Beaver Creek	1787	2	96
McNeil—See McNeal					
McNeil, John	322	L. Levels	1783	1	18
McNish, David	444	Wts. Meadow R.	1794	3	142
McNutt, Francis	250	Indian Creek	1795	1	72
McNutt, Francis et al	380	Indian Creek	1787	1	268
McNutt, James	571	Red House Shoals	1787	1	259
McNutt, James	250	Indian Cr.	1787	2	81
McPherson, Joel	735	Anthony's Cr.	1855	6	412
McPherson, Joel et al	620	Anthony's Cr.	1848	6	314
McPherson, Joel et al	1,100	Wts. New River	1848	6	304
McVey, Alexander	450	Ferrin Cr.	1832	6	164

Name of Grantee	Acres	Local Description	Year	Book	Page
Miller, John	109	Briary Run	1793	2	469
Miller, John	190	Burgan's Run	1800	4	411
Miller, John & Alexander	350	War Ridge	1827	6	115
Miller, John et al	1,100	Wts. New River	1848	6	304
Miller, John Jr.	1,730	Wts. Hungert's Cr.	1850	6	333
Miller, John Jr.	50	Indian Creek	1799	4	245
Miller, John Sr.	220	Great Levels	1787	1	180
Miller, Joseph	150	Adj. P. Miller	1785	1	86
Miller, Michael	63	Indian Creek	1799	4	255
Miller, Nancy et al Heirs	494	Sinking Creek	1818	1	558
Miller, Robert	27	Lick Creek	1810	5	246
Miller, Robert et al	700	Laurel Creek	1827	6	563
Miller, Robert & John	173	Lick Creek	1810	5	245
Miller, Thomas	115	Dropping Lick Cr.	1800	4	407
Miller; West	142	Indian Creek	1791	2	355
Miller, William	14¼	Meadow River	1859	6	466
Miller, William et al	700	Laurel Creek	1827	6	563
Minnis, Robert	45	Huggart's Cr.	1832	6	157
Mollihan, George	352	Sinking Creek	1797	4	37
Molton—See also Mullin					
Molton, Richard (Multin)	49	Muddy Creek	1787	1	415
Monerean, Joseph	10,899	Big Sandy Cr.	1789	2	271
Moody, John	1,210	Spring Cr.	1796	3	445
Moody, John	290	Spring Creek	1796	3	444
Moore, Andrew	5,867	Gauley River	1795	3	554
Moore, Andrew	43,417	Gauley & Meadow Rivers	1795	3	552
Moore, Andrew	11,300	Hominy Creek	1795	3	556
Moore, Andrew	5,000	Wts. of Gauley	1794	3	17
Moore, Andrew	20,000	Wts. of Gauley	1794	3	18
Moore, Andrew	562	Beaver Creek	1789	2	279
Moore, Andrew	400	Adj. W. Meadows	1792	2	482
Moore, Andrew	1,035	Wts. Gauley	1795	3	219
Moore, Andrew	1,570	Wts. Gauley	1795	3	218
Moore, Andrew et al	2,040	Hominy Creek	1795	3	266
Moore, Andrew et al	286	Wts. of Elk	1788	2	134
Moore, Andrew et al	103	Wts. Potalico R.	1788	2	135
Moore, Moses	250	Adj. J. Blair	1810	5	264
Moore, Samuel et al	250	Hurricane Cr.	1799	4	289
Moore, Simon	90	Wts. Meadow River	1801	5	81
Moorehead, Mooreheed					
Moorehead, John	7	Second Cr.	1821	6	520
Mooreheed, John	235	Mth. 2nd Creek	1793	3	97
Mordah—See Mordak, Murdock					
Mordah, James	355	Sink Hole Lands	1787	2	42
Mordak, David	200	Adj. J. Miller	1787	1	441
Mordak, James	355	Sinkhole Lands	1787	2	42
Morris, Henry	600	Peter's Creek	1793	3	10
Morris, Robert	9,300	Wts. Gauley	1795	3	241
Morris, Robert	12,170	Wts. Clear Cr.	1795	3	242
Morris, Robert	24,630	Wts. Birch River	1795	3	206
Morris, Robert	153,900	Wts. Greenbrier & Gauley	1795	3	547
Morris, Warder	1,421	Howard's Cr.	1857	6	475
Morris, William	934	Kelly's Bottom	1787	1	463
Morris, William	525	Adj. A. Lewis	1787	1	470
Morris, William	237	Wts. Meadow River	1797	4	76
Morris, William	1,000	Sewell Mt.	1797	4	60
Morris, William	400	Morris Creek	1787	1	480
Morris, William	110	Muddy Creek	1793	3	103
Morris, William	160	Rich Creek	1793	3	13
Morris, William	70	Wts. of Gauley	1796	3	466
Morris, William	260	Wts. of Gauley	1787	1	400
Morris, William et al	223	Wts. Gauley	1791	2	361
Morris, William et al	600	Wts. of Gauley	1797	4	10

Name of Grantee	Acres	Local Description	Year	Book	Page
Morris, William et al	1,206	Wts. Gr. Kanawha	1792	2	380
Morris, William et al	300	Mill Creek	1792	2	429
Morris, William et al	45	Wts. of Kanawha	1792	2	430
Morris, William et al	300	Mill Creek	1792	2	431
Morris, William et al	1,500	Mill Creek	1791	2	362
Morris, William et al	514	Mann's Cr.	1791	2	360
Morris, William et al	402	Gauley Mt.	1795	3	274
Morris, William et al	131½	Wts. of Elk	1787	1	466
Morris, William et al	630½	Wts. of Elk	1787	1	465
Morris, William et al	700	Sewell Creek	1797	4	167
Morrison, Andrew	100	Adj. Henry Perkins	1800	4	338
Morrison, Andrew	140	Roaring Creek	1800	4	510
Morrison, William	100	Anthony's Cr.	1815	5	308
Morrow, Francis	300	Culbertson's Cr.	1790	2	286
Morrow, James	133	Spring Cr.	1787	1	305
Morrow, William	370	Adj. J. Matthews	1803	5	163
Morton, David	1,100	Wts. New River	1798	4	89
Morton, David	640	Big Stony Cr.	1798	4	87
Morton, David	2,458	Laurel Creek	1798	4	92
Mossbarger, Jacob	40	Wts. Greenbrier	1826	6	93
Mossingbird—See Massingbird					
Moyars or Moyers					
Moyars, George	130	Wts. Greenbrier	1789	2	229
Moyars, George	380	Wts. Greenbrier	1789	2	192
Moyers or Moyars					
Moyers, George	155	Wts. Greenbrier	1789	2	196
Mullin—See also Molton					
Mullin, Richard	100	Muddy Creek	1789	2	190
Multon—See Molton					
Murdock—See Mordah, Mordak					
Murdock, James	91	Adj. S. Fleshman	1816	2	557
Murdock, James	100	Adj. B. Miller	1785	1	89
Murphy, Patrick	329	Adj. Wm. Mann	1789	2	275
Mushbarger—See Mashbarger					
Mushbarger, John	67	Culbertson's Cr.	1796	3	435
Mushbarger, John	33	Culbertson's Cr.	1796	3	428
Mushbarger, John	126	Wts. Meadow River	1809	5	240
Mushbarger, John	178	Burns Creek	1793	3	123
Mustoe, Anthony et al	1,000	Meadow Creek	1796	3	506
Nanna, Reese	111	Davie Run	1857	6	479
Neal, Daniel	70	Carpenter's Run	1798	4	97
Neal, John	200	Lewis Branch	1787	2	82
Neal, John	131	Millican's Cr.	1841	6	247
Neal, John	15a.2r.	Millican's Cr.	1841	6	246
Neal, John	13¼	Big Levels	1838	6	227
Neal, Owen	168	2nd Creek	1796	3	416
Neal, Walton	60	Dropping Lick Cr.	1800	4	489
Neal, William	45	Burns Creek	1825	6	83
Neal, William et al	200	Flagg Run	1788	2	175
Nealy, James	200	Wts. New River	1802	5	142
Nelson or Nilson					
Nelson, David	150	Wolf Creek	1805	5	187
Nelson, David	140	Wolf Creek	1801	5	57
Nesbit, David et al	2,530	Brush Creek	1787	1	457
~~Nettles, Abraham~~	~~140~~	~~Scott's Run~~	~~1797~~	~~4~~	169
Nevins, John	220	Adj. Capt. S. McClung	1800	4	496
Newton, Joseph	335	Wts. Greenbrier	1784	1	42
Newton, Joseph	165	Wts. Greenbrier	1802	5	140
Newton, William	28¾	Wts. Greenbrier	1824	6	48
Nicely, Adam	94	Big Levels	1800	4	438
Nichol—See Nicholas, Nichols, Nickel, Nickle, Nickols, Nicolas					
Nichol, Joseph	244	Wts. New River	1800	4	440
Nicholas—Nichol, Nichols, Nickel, Nickle, Nickols, Nicolas					

Name of Grantee	Acres	Local Description	Year	Book	Page
Nicholas, Andrew	222	Adj. Humphries	1787	1	448
Nicholas, George	477	Gr. Levels	1786	1	189
Nicholas, Isaac	270	Near ——— Cave	1787	2	78
Nicholas, John	123	Swope's Knob	1800	5	52
Nicholas, Joseph	165	Adj. Humphreys	1787	2	83
Nicholas, William	180	Anthony's Cr.	1838	6	230
Nicholas, Wilson C.	900	Anthony's Cr.	1795	3	289
Nicholas, Wilson C.	4,050	Wts. of Elk	1795	3	328
Nicholas, Wilson C.	10,785	Big Laurel Cr.	1795	3	563
Nicholas, Wilson C.	32,045	Wts. of Elk	1795	3	560
Nicholas, Wilson C.	2,220	Anthony's Creek	1795	3	558
Nichols—Nichol, Nicholas, Nickel, Nickols, Nicolas					
Nichols, Joseph (Nickols)	184	Indian Creek	1797	4	35
Nichols, Joseph	200	Indian Creek	1797	4	134
Nickel—Nichol, Nicholas, Nichols, Nickle, Nickols, Nicolas					
Nickel, Andrew	151	2nd Creek	1799	4	243
Nickel, Madison et al	48½	Muddy Cr.	1859	6	436
Nickel, Robert	200	The Sinks	1787	1	443
Nickel, William N.	44	Sewell Mt.	1859	6	464
Nickle—Nichol, Nicholas, Nichols, Nickel, Nickols, Nicolas					
Nickle, James	68	2nd Creek	1837	6	213
Nickle, John	44	2nd Creek	1821	6	511
Nickle, Robert	328	Swope's Knob	1804	3	537
Nickle, Robert P.	85	Wts. Meadow R.	1851	6	357
Nickle, Thomas	50	Adj. R. & T. Patton	1804	5	169
Nickle, Thomas	500	2nd Creek	1787	2	115
Nickols—See Nichol, Nicholas, Nichols, Nickel, Nickle, Nicolas					
Nickols, Joseph	168	Big Stony Creek	1797	4	129
Nicolas—See Nichol, Nicholas, Nichols, Nickel, Nickle, Nickols					
Nicolas, George	477	Gr. Levels	1786	1	189
Nilson—See Nelson					
Nilson, James	148	Indian Creek	1797	4	142
North, John A.	436	Muddy Cr.	1836	6	200
North, John A. et al	679	Muddy Creek	1837	6	210
Ocheltree—See Okeltree					
Ocheltree, Michael	150	Sinking Cr.	1788	2	56
O'Dell, Jeremiah	56	Anglin's Cr.	1817	1	581
O'Harra—See Aharra					
Oharra, Charles (Oharrow)	81	Mill Creek	1849	6	332
Oharra, Charles (Oharrow)	53¾	Mill Creek	1849	6	331
Oharra, Charles	385	Muddy Creek	1795	3	309
Oharra, Charles	145	Muddy Creek	1795	3	318
Okeltree—See Ocheltree					
Okeltree, James	230	Sinking Cr.	1801	5	72
Olderson—See Alderson					
Olderson, John	214	Wolf Creek	1787	1	453
Oldham, William	185	Wts. Greenbrier	1793	3	169
Oler, Henry	180	Sinking Creek	1796	3	475
Oliver, David	1,000	Lit. Meadow Cr.	1794	3	85
Oliver, Thomas	100	Indian Creek	1800	4	497
Oneal, Joseph	200	Burnes' Run	1792	2	504
Osborn, Osborne, Osburn, Ozburn					
Osborne, George et al	500	Wts. New River	1815	5	307
Osborne, John	20	Mill Creek	1800	4	312
Osborne, Josiah	685	Wts. New River	1812	5	279
Osborne, Josiah	170	Wts. New River	1812	5	280
Osborne, Leonard	19	Wts. Meadow River	1834	6	177
Osburn, Osborn, Osborne, Ozburn					
Osburn, Isaac	70	Muddy Creek Mt.	1796	3	421
Osburn, Isaac	31	Muddy Cr. Mt.	1802	5	158
Osburn, Levi	112	Wts of Elk	1791	2	393
Ott, Michael	166	Wts. Greenbrier	1830	6	135
Ozburn, or Osborn, Osborne, Osburn					

Name of Grantee	Acres	Local Description	Year	Book	Page
Ozburn, Elijah	216	Laurel Creek	1802	5	138
Ozburn, John	92	Wts. of Elk	1788	2	109
Ozburn, John	120	Lick Creek	1793	3	98
Ozburn, John	244	Lick Creek	1789	2	194
Ozburn, John	639	Mill Creek	1787	2	48
Ozburn, John	68	New River	1793	3	94
Ozburn, John	250	Lick Creek	1795	3	278
Page, Charles	105	Pine Spring Br.	1825	6	82
Pane, James	50	Muddy Cr. Mt.	1799	4	269
Pane, James	100	Wts. Meadow River	1802	5	136
Pargher, Jacob	160	Adj. Wm. Frogg	1796	3	440
Parker, Henry	263	Kitchen's Creek	1859	6	461
Parker, Jeremiah & Richard et al	750	Meadow River	1789	2	253
Parker, Jeremiah & Richard et al	1,500	Meadow River	1789	2	254
Parker, Jeremiah & Richard et al	1,395	Meadow River	1789	2	255
Parker, Jeremiah & Richard et al	388	Meadow River	1789	2	256
Parker, Jeremiah & Richard et al	900	Adj. Wm. Morris	1789	2	257
Parker, Jeremiah & Richard et al	930	Marsh Creek	1789	2	233
Parker, Jeremiah & Richard et al	1,090	Spring Creek	1789	2	235
Parker, Jeremiah & Richard et al	1,000	Marsh Creek	1789	2	236
Parker, Jeremiah & Richard et al	1,700	Matthews Cr.	1789	2	237
Parker, Jeremiah & Richard et al	1,225	Beaver Cr.	1789	2	238
Parker, Jeremiah & Richard et al	1,350	Marsh Creek	1789	2	239
Parker, Jeremiah & Richard et al	1,250	Meadow River	1789	2	240
Parker, Jeremiah & Richard et al	1,200	Deer Creek	1789	2	241
Parker, Jeremiah & Richard et al	937	Adj. J. Robinson	1789	2	242
Parker, Jeremiah & Richard et al	1,000	Meadow River	1789	2	243
Parker, Jeremiah & Richard et al	4,000	Wts. Gauley	1787	1	296
Parker, Jeremiah & Richard et al	4,000	Beaver Cr.	1787	1	297
Parker, Jeremiah & Richard et al	4,000	Wts. of Gauley	1787	1	298
Parker, Jeremiah & Richard et al	2,000	Forks of Gauley	1787	1	367
Parker, Jeremiah & Richard et al	4,000	Wts. of Gauley	1787	1	368
Parker, Jeremiah & Richard et al	480	Muddy Creek	1788	2	166
Parker, Joseph	378	Laurel Cr.	1800	4	392
Parker, Joseph	88	Swope's Knob	1800	4	408
Parker, Joseph	378	Swoopes Knob	1801	5	65
Parker, Joseph	130	Swobe's Knob	1801	5	112
Parker, Joseph	122	The Sinks	1795	3	284
Parker, Joseph	266	Wolf Creek	1800	4	298
Parker, Joseph	1,000	Cherry Tree	1788	2	173
Parker, Joseph	242	Frie's Run	1788	2	174
Parker, Joseph	489	Adj. T. Charlton	1788	2	170
Parker, Thomas	35	Sinking Cr.	1801	5	61
Parsons, Ezekiel & Eliz. his wife et al Heirs	350 (348)	Wts. Greenbrier	1799	4	579
Patterson, James	490	Muddy Creek	1789	2	223
Patterson, John (Paterson)	301¾	Adj P. Hoover	1796	3	423
Patterson, John	230	Lockhart's Fork	1792	2	374
Patterson, John	500	Muddy Creek	1804	5	172
Patterson, John et al	600	Muddy Cr.	1800	4	416
Patterson, William	98	Wts. Meadow River	1838	6	224
Patton, James et al	200	Big Cain Creek	1848	6	307
Patton, James et al	275	Big Clear Cr.	1844	6	273
Patton, James et al	250	Lit. Cl. Creek	1844	6	277
Patton, John	452	Sinking Creek	1800	4	402
Patton, John	252	Sinking Cr.	1787	1	364
Patton, John	157	Sinking Creek	1797	4	130
Patton, Matthew	136	Anthony's Cr.	1802	5	141
Patton, Robert	380	Greenbrier River	1806	5	188
Patton, Tristram & Robert	900	Second Creek	1801	5	577
Paul, Hugh	37	Indian Creek	1796	3	488
Payne, George W.	100	Wts. Greenbrier	1817	1	590
Pearcy—See Piercy					

Name of Grantee	Acres	Local Description	Year	Book	Page
Pearcy, John	140	Muddy Creek	1821	6	518
Pearson—See Peirson					
Pease, Josiah	260	Wts. Meadow River	1796	3	420
Pease, Josiah	280	Hominy Creek	1810	5	265
Peck, Samuel	50	River Ridge	1799	4	248
Peebles, See Peobles, Peoples					
Peebles, James	334	Old Town Cr.	1795	3	199
Peebles, James et al	185	Big Clear Cr.	1796	3	514
Peebles, James et al	70	Big Clear Cr.	1796	3	513
Peebles, Samuel	200	Muddy Creek	1800	4	463
Peebles, Thomas	4,455	Anthony's Cr.	1796	3	565
Peebles, Thomas	2,560	Spring Creek	1795	3	567
Peirson, Joseph	105	Kelly's Cr.	1797	4	149
Pence, John	1,000	12 Mile Creek	1795	3	247
Pendawfe, Michael	308	2nd Creek	1794	3	154
Penson, Joseph	105	Kelly's Cr.	1797	4	149
Peobles—See Peebles, Peoples					
Peobles, James et al (Peoples)	2,200	Spring Creek	1805	5	185
Peoples See Peebles, Peobles					
Peoples, James	124	Adj. H. Miller	1793	3	90
Peoples, James	230	Adj. G. Clendenen	1788	2	107
Perkins, Charles T.	83	Anthony's Cr.	1851	6	359
Perkins, Ely	95	Big Levels	1800	4	378
Perkins, Henry	190	Wts. Greenbrier	1789	2	186
Perkins, James	2½	Culbertson's Cr.	1823	6	14
Perkins, James	50	Wts. Greenbrier	1800	4	498
Perkins, James	300	Adj. John Stuart's	1800	4	584
Perkins, Samuel	12	Adj. John Wilson	1819	1	528
Perkins, Samuel	24	Wts. Greenbrier	1819	4	544
Perkins, Samuel	50	Wts. Greenbrier	1825	6	60
Perkins, Samuel	50	Wts. Greenbrier	1819	4	543
Perry, David (or Daniel)	380	Adj. Douglas	1787	1	429
Perry, John	100	Swope's Knob	1787	2	76
Perry, Joseph	240	Adj. Wm. Armstrong	1860	6	500
Perry, Joseph	13¼	Dry Creek	1861	6	529
Perry, Joseph	46	Sweet Springs	1851	6	360
Perry, Joseph	560	Howard's Cr.	1846	6	579
Perry, Moses H.	134	Anthony's Cr.	1855	6	409
Perry, Swift	607	Unknown	1787	1	444
Peters, Christian	213	Rich Creek	1799	4	254
Peters, Christian	385	Rich Creek	1794	3	129
Peters, Christian et al	235	Rich Creek	1799	4	218
Peters, John	48	Second Cr.	1801	5	119
Peters, John	280	Wts. New River	1808	5	227
Phelps, Isaac	25	Anthony's Cr.	1808	5	215
Phelps, Isaac	25	Anthony's Cr.	1808	5	214
Phillips, Zachariah	204	Indian Creek	1800	4	507
Piercy—See Pearcy					
Piercy, John Sr.	2	Muddy Cr.	1848	6	316
Pierson—See Peirson					
Pine, James	100	Wts. New River	1795	3	195
Pleasants, Thomas E.	1,000	Wts. Wms. River	1800	4	331
Plyman, John	75	Lick Creek	1796	3	476
Poage, John	400	L. Levels	1783	1	28
Poage, William	400	Adj. Joseph Cullon	1787	1	270
Poage, William	400	Wts. of Greenbrier	1782	1	11
Pollard, Benjamin	1,125	Bradshaw Run	1788	2	68
Pollard, Benjamin	1,390	Bradshaw Run	1788	2	67
Pollard, Benjamin	2,500	Bradshaw Run	1788	2	114
Pope, Henry	4¾	Big Levels	1815	5	309
Pope, Henry	47	Weaver's Big Knob	1796	4	28
Pope, Henry	193	Big Levels	1791	2	354
Porter, Alexander	1,350	Howard's Cr.	1797	4	4

Name of Grantee	Acres	Local Description	Year	Book	Page
Prescot, Roger	832	Adj. Wm. Clendenen	1788	2	167
Prescot, Roger	1,048	Adj. Pat Murphy	1788	2	165
Preston, Roger	832	Adj. Wm. Clendenen	1788	2	167
Price, Abram	4	Irish Corner	1851	6	377
Price, Jacob et al	400	Beaver Creek	1787	1	456
Price, Jacob et al	400	Beaver Creek	1787	2	46
Price, James et al	115	Big Levels	1816	2	556
Price, James et al	115	Big Levels	1816	1	608
Price, Samuel	615	Gr. Levels	1804	5	170
Price, Samuel	340	Beaver Creek	1786	1	132
Price, Samuel et al	580	Wts. M. River	1786	1	121
Props, Christian (Proaps)	60	Anglin's Cr.	1823	6	3
Pursel, Richard et al	170	Adj. T. Edgar	1790	2	303
Raider, Anthony et al	463	Muddy Creek	1818	1	574
Raider, J. et al Heirs	494	Sinking Creek	1818	1	558
Rambo, Joseph	300	Adj. R. Craig	1810	5	262
Rambo, Joseph et al	35	Adj. M. Baker	1813	5	288
Ransbarger, William	1½a.10p.	Miller's Mt.	1852	6	378
Rawlings, Roberts	1,036	Brushy Creek	1787	1	309
Ray, Edward (Rea)	500	Lit. Clear Cr.	1801	5	572
Rea—See Ray, Read, Red					
Read—Reed, Reid					
Read, Benjamin	380	Adj. R. Read	1796	3	526
Read, Edward (Rea-Red)	235	Sinking Creek	1801	5	107
Read, Robert	400	2nd Creek	1787	2	88
Reburn—See Ryburn					
Reburn, Henry	46	The Sinks	1793	2	528
Reburn, Henry	154	Wts. Greenbrier	1796	3	484
Reburn, John	400	2nd Creek	1787	1	436
Reburn, John	100	Indian Creek	1787	1	438
Reburn, John	145	Plank Cabin Drft.	1794	3	131
Red, Edward (Rea)	235	Sinking Creek	1801	5	107
Reed—Read, Reid					
Reed, Benjamin	200	Second Creek	1786	1	150
Reed, James	455	Adj. S. Price	1795	3	202
Reed, James	900	Campbell's Creek	1787	1	458
Reed, Robert	325	Millican's Cr.	1800	4	505
Reed, Robert	290	Sinking Creek	1793	3	4
Reid—Read, Reed					
Reid, James	1,000	Muddlethepeg	1791	2	356
Reid, James	560	Muddlethepeg	1790	2	302
Reid, James	450	Hopkins Creek	1800	4	517
Reid, James	500	Cooper's Creek	1787	1	378
Reid, James	540	Gr. Levels	1784	1	44
Reid, Robert	141	2nd Creek	1799	4	244
Renick—Rennick, Renix					
Renick, B. F.	291	Spring Creek	1851	6	365
Renick, Robert	150	Millican's Cr.	1822	6	534
Renick, Robert	50	Anthony's Cr.	1820	4	533
Renick, Robert	400	Adj. Robt. Stevenson	1815	2	563
Renick, Robert et al	600	Muddy Cr.	1800	4	416
Renick, William	480	Spring Cr.	1823	6	29
Renick, William	350 (340)	Adj. R. Armstrong	1787	1	276
Renick, William	400	Spring Cr.	1787	1	274
Renick, William	25	Spring Cr.	1800	4	389
Renick, William	100	Tuckahoe Draught	1800	4	345
Renick, William	150	Adj. J. Wooden	1800	4	346
Renick, William	240	Sinking Creek	1791	2	357
Renick, William	200	Spring Creek	1815	2	570
Renick, William	132	Spring Creek	1792	2	491
Renick, William	50	Adj. J. Kuhn	1801	5	125
Renick, William	95	Spring Cr.	1810	5	260
Renick, William	400	Spring Cr.	1812	5	276

Name of Grantee	Acres	Local Description	Year	Book	Page
Scothorn, Lewis	220 (320)	Devil's Creek	1800	4	290
Scothorn, Lewis	113	Wolf Creek	1800	4	444
Scott, James	20	Anthony's Cr.	1854	6	395
Scott, James	350	Adj. S. Hariman	1785	1	90
Scott, James	57	Anthony's Cr.	1825	6	69
Scott, James	38	Anthony's Cr.	1825	6	70
Scott, James	95	Adj. Wm. Craig	1796	4	125
See, George (Lee)	465	Muddy Creek	1792	2	443
Seebert, Jacob	200	Stamping Cr.	1795	3	231
Seebrow, William	300	Turkey Cr.	1786	1	152
Semple, William	2,000	Below Letart Falls	1786	1	171
Semple, William	2,000	Below Letart Falls	1786	1	172
Semple, William	2,000	Below Letart Falls	1786	1	125
Semple, William	2,000	Below Letart Falls	1786	1	126
Semple, William	2,000	Below Letart Falls	1786	1	124
Semple, William	2,000	Below Letart Falls	1786	1	123
Semple, William	2,000	Below Letart Falls	1786	1	127
Semple, William	2,000	Below Letart Falls	1786	1	128
Settington, Andrew	205	Donally's Ridge	1795	3	297
Sevey—See Sivey					
Sevey, George	150	Anthony's Cr.	1830	6	142
Shaffer, Shuffer, Snuffer					
Shank—or Shanks					
Shank, Christian	290	Adj. J. Rife	1788	2	69
Shank, Daniel	114	Wolf Cr.	1800	4	397
Shank, Michael (or William)	350	Adj. J. Lewis	1787	1	321
Shank, Michael	150	Muddy Creek	1796	3	419
Shank, Michael	46	Adj. Geo. Lewis	1800	5	68
Shanklin, Joseph	25	Adj. R. Shanklin	1800	4	450
Shanklin, Joseph	11	Adj. John Stuart	1801	5	71
Shanklin, Josiah et al	82	Osburn's Cr.	1820	4	531
Shanklin, Josias	376	Sewell Mt.	1823	6	19
Shanklin, Josias	842	Man's Creek	1823	6	21
Shanklin, Josias	372	Meadow River	1823	6	20
Shanklin, Josias	409	Sewell Cr.	1823	6	22
Shanklin, Josias	346	Bracken's Cr.	1823	6	23
Shanklin, Josias	26	Wts. Greenbrier	1823	6	24
Shanklin, Josias	20	Mellican's Creek	1823	6	26
Shanklin, Josias	9	Mill Creek	1823	6	25
Shanklin, Josias	204	Keeny's Creek	1825	6	80
Shanklin, Josias	520	Mann's Creek	1825	6	79
Shanklin, Josias	7	Big Levels	1818	1	572
Shanklin, Josias	82	Second Creek	1846	6	291
Shanklin, Josias et al	3,225	Laurel Creek	1826	6	561
Shanklin, Robert	368	Big Levels	1787	1	248
Shanks—See Shank					
Shanks, William	100	Indian Creek	1795	3	271
Shanks, William	444 (400)	Indian Creek	1787	1	245
Shannon, John	95	Bushy Run	1806	5	205
Shannon, Patrick	360	Sinking Creek	1792	2	435
Shannon, Patrick	400	Sinking Creek	1792	2	434
Shannon, William	395	Turkey Creek	1787	1	250
Sharp, William	355	Wts. Greenbrier	1787	1	261
Sharp, William R.	2¾	Walker Meadow	1861	6	483
Shaugh—See Shaw, Strough					
Shaugh, Moses	81	Muddy Creek	1818	1	561
Shaugh, Moses	139	Muddy Creek	1818	1	560
Shaugh, Moses	50	Greenbrier River	1807	5	211
Shaw—See Shaugh					
Sheaves, John (Sheves)	137	Sewell Creek	1826	6	96
Sheaves, John	160	Adj. J. Welch	1815	2	568
Sheeley—or Shely					
Sheeley, David	2,140	Elk & Birch River	1795	3	320

Name of Grantee	Acres	Local Description	Year	Book	Page
Smith, Jacob	57	Laurel Creek	1827	6	118
Smith, James	142	Swoob's Knob	1791	2	408
Smith, James	200	Wolf Creek	1800	5	27
Smith, John	40	Anthony's Creek	1792	2	369
Smith, Richard (Smythe)	1,000	Wts. of New River	1796	3	458
Smith, Richard	4½	Irish Corner	1845	6	284
Smith, Thomas a	5,393 (5398)	Pocatalico	1786	1	182
Smith, William et al	400	Wts. Meadow River	1794	3	162
Smitson, Thomas	72½	George's Branch	1800	5	3
Smyth—See Smith, Smythe					
Smyth, Richard	1,000	Wts. New River	1796	3	361
Smythe—See Smith, Smyth					
Smythe, Richard (Smith)	1,000	Wts. New River	1796	3	457
Smythe, Richard	1,000	Wts. of New River	1796	3	455
Smythe, Richard	1,000	Wts. New River	1796	3	456
Smythe, Richard	1,000	Wts. of New River	1796	3	453
Smythe, Richard	1,000	Wts. of New River	1796	3	454
Snodegar, Joshua	130	Anthony Creek	1797	4	45
Snodgrass, James	199	Wts. Greenbrier	1799	4	113
Snuffer, Shaffer, Shuffer					
Snuffer, George	400	Elk River	1787	1	332
Snuffer, George	384	Wts. of Elk	1787	1	432
Snyder, Philip	1⅜	Walker's Meadows	1859	6	465
Soat, John	371	Wolf Creek	1787	1	239
Sowards, Isaac	300	Peter's Mt.	1795	3	300
Sowards, Isaac Sr.	159	Dropping Lick	1787	1	349
Sowards, James	62	Dropping Lock	1800	5	28
Sowards, Thomas	360	Rich Creek	1794	3	130
Sowards, Thomas	137	Dropping Lick Cr.	1787	1	430
Sparre, John	100	Swope's Knob	1798	4	69
Spencer, James	130	Wts. Greenbrier	1830	6	138
Spore—Sparre					
Sprowle, Alexander	95	Turkey Creek	1791	2	358
Staples, John	1,703	Cherry Tree River	1795	3	208
Steel, James	48	2nd Creek	1819	1	543
Steel, Robert	280	Wts. Meadow River	1798	4	96
Steel, Robert	200	Meadow River	1803	5	171
Steele, Robert	4,975	Big Clear Cr.	1804	5	176
Stephen, Robert	40	Spring Creek	1797	4	139
Stephens, Robert	2	Spring Cr.	1812	5	278
Stephens, Robert	40	Spring Cr.	1797	4	187
Stephens, Robert	27	Adj. R. Wilson	1821	6	517
Stephenson—See Stevenson					
Stevenson—See Stephenson					
Stevenson, Robert et al	463	Muddy Creek	1818	1	574
Stewart or Stuart					
Stewart, Alexander	95	Adj. Wm. Wilson	1793	3	127
Stewart, Alexander	395	Rich Creek	1791	2	404
Stewart, George	400	Adj. his own	1796	3	397
Stewart, John	1,167	12 Mi. Creek	1786	1	229
Stewart, John	458	Greenbrier River	1806	5	191
Stewart, John	350	Muddy Creek	1794	3	126
Stewart John et al	135	Middle Fork	1786	1	117
Stewart, John et al	490	Middle Fork	1786	1	118
Stewart, John et al	374	Wts. Meadow R.	1786	1	120
Stiff, John	75	Adj. J. Gray	1786	1	112
Stiner, Frederick	165	Wts. Greenbrier	1795	3	290
Stockdell, John	160	Wts. of Greenbrier	1788	2	151
Stockley, Jacob	192	Butcher's Run	1793	3	53
Stockwell, Henry	75	Wts. Meadow River	1796	3	405
Stockwell, Henry	380	Wts. of Kanawha	1796	3	408
Stockwell, Henry	420	Wts. of Kanawha	1797	4	58
Stockwell, Mark, Executor	300	Sewell Cr.	1803	5	146

Name of Grantee	Acres	Local Description	Year	Book	Page
Stockwell, Mark, Executor	500	Wts. Gauley & Williams Rivers	1803	5	147
Stockwell, Mark, Executor	250	Lick Creek	1803	5	148
Stodgehill—See Stodghill, Stodgill					
Stodgehill, John (Stodghill)	777	Hand's Creek	1799	4	580
Stodghill, Joel	64	Wts. Hand's Cr.	1804	5	165
Stodghill, John	400	Hand's Creek	1787	1	249
Stroud, James	375	Muddy Creek	1795	3	176
Stroud, James	340	2 Mile Creek	1795	3	181
Strough—See Shaugh					
Strough, Moses	50	Greenbrier River	1807	5	211
Stuart—or Stewart					
Stuart, Alexander	40	Wts. New River	1801	5	113
Stuart, Alexander	632	Wts. of New River	1801	5	574
Stuart, Alexander	590	Wts. New River	1801	5	573
Stuart, Alexander	100	Butcher's Run	1800	4	519
Stuart, Archibald	360	Sinking Creek	1800	4	367
Stuart, Archibald	330	Muddy Creek	1800	4	364
Stuart, Archibald	320	Anthony Creek	1800	4	362
Stuart, Archibald	270	Wts. Greenbrier	1800	4	365
Stuart, Archibald	310	Wts. Greenbrier	1800	4	363
Stuart, Archibald	216	Muddy Creek	1800	4	361
Stuart, Archibald	300	Wts. Greenbrier	1800	4	359
Stuart, Archibald	480	Wts. Greenbrier	1800	4	360
Stuart, Archibald	385	Wts. Greenbrier	1800	4	423
Stuart, Archibald	90	Wts. Greenbrier	1800	4	421
Stuart, Archibald	375	Muddy Creek	1800	4	422
Stuart, Archibald	390	Spring Lick Cr.	1800	4	370
Stuart, Archibald	130	Muddy Creek	1800	4	369
Stuart, Archibald	400	Wts. Greenbrier	1800	4	368
Stuart, Archibald	40	Muddy Creek	1800	4	366
Stuart, Charles A.	54	Burns Creek	1840	6	244
Stuart, Charles A.	34	Big Levels	1816	2	556
Stuart, George	75	Wts. Greenbrier	1800	4	490
Stuart, George	150	Wts. Greenbrier	1800	4	462
Stuart, George	96	Wts. Greenbrier	1800	4	461
Stuart, George	90	Wts. Greenbrier	1817	1	586
Stuart, George	200	Wts. Greenbrier	1787	1	439
Stuart, John	583	Adj. J. Carroll	1821	6	510
Stuart, John	820	Big Levels	1786	1	131
Stuart, John	100	Lick Creek	1787	1	288
Stuart, John	1,560	Wts. Greenbrier	1786	1	487
Stuart, John	2,500	Wts. of Greenbrier	1799	4	575
Stuart, John	427	Adj. S. Carroll	1813	5	287
Stuart, John Capt.	56	Byrn's Creek	1854	6	413
Stuart, Lewis	68½	Muddy Creek	1829	6	128
Stuart, Lewis	19	Weaver's Knob	1818	1	539
Stuart, Lewis et al	858	Wts. Meadow River	1818	1	572
Stumbo, John	30½	Culbertson's Cr.	1816	1	607
Stump, Christopher	1,000	Wts. Greenbrier	1798	4	189
Sullivan, Sulaphan, Sylaphan					
Surbough, Henry	7½	Meadow River	1830	6	139
Surbough, Henry	36	Big Meadow Cr.	1842	6	256
Surgeon, Andrew et al	48½	Muddy Creek	1859	6	436
Swaab—Swobe, Swoop, Swope					
Swaab, Michael	445	Hand's Creek	1787	1	231
Swan, James	1,000	Howard's Cr.	1803	5	159
Sweet, Stephen	1,000	Howard's Cr.	1797	4	162
Sweet, Stephen	2,500	Anthony's Creek	1797	4	11
Swobe—Swaab, Swoop, Swope					
Swobe, John	520	Pocatalico	1786	1	153
Swobe, John	371	Wolf Cr.	1787	1	239
Swobe, Michael	65	Han's Creek	1787	1	308

Name of Grantee	Acres	Local Description	Year	Book	Page
Swoop—Swaab, Swobe, Swope,					
Swoop, Adam	200	Muddy Creek	1800	5	53
Swoop, Joseph	600	Wolf Creek	1786	1	230
Swoope, Joseph (Swope)	120	Wolf Creek	1792	2	418
Swope—Swaab, Swobe, Swoop					
Swope, Adam	780	Laurel Creek	1793	2	474
Swope, Adam	300	Spring Cr.	1792	2	417
Swope, Adam	350	Laurel Creek	1793	2	477
Swope, Adam	260	Laurel Cr.	1793	2	478
Swope, Adam	238	Wolf Creek	1793	2	480
Swope, Joseph	400	Wolf Creek	1792	2	507
Swope, Michael	200	Han's Creek	1796	3	400
Swope, Michael	58	Rich Creek	1796	3	401
Swords, James	62	Dropping Lick	1800	5	28
Sydenstricker—Sydenstriker					
Sydenstricker, Henry	52	Wts. Greenbrier	1819	1	544
Sydenstricker, Lewis	23	Howard's Creek	1850	6	339
Sydenstricker, Michael	375	Howard's Cr.	1857	6	477
Sydenstriker, Henry (Sydenstricker)	340	Adj. J. Longacre	1812	5	274
Sylaphan—or Sulaphan, Sullivan					
Sylaphan, Timothy	152	Laurel Creek	1790	2	308
Sylaphan, Timothy	373	Horse Creek	1789	2	202
Tacket or Tackett					
Tacket, Nimrod	275	Turkey Creek	1787	2	71
Tacket, Nimrod	150	Turkey Creek	1796	3	432
Tacket, Nimrod	150	Indian Cr.	1796	3	425
Tackett, John	120	Sewell Mt.	1801	5	108
Tackett, Nimrod	175	Turkey Creek	1799	4	260
Tackett, Nimrod	150	Turkey Creek	1799	4	215
Talman, Isaac I.	1,200	Wolf Creek	1797	4	164
Talman, Isaac I.	287	Laurel Creek	1800	4	333
Tate, David	90	Second Creek	1789	2	249
Taylor, Matthew	518	Spring Creek	1797	4	22
Taylor, Samuel	360	Spring Cr.	1792	2	455
Taylor, Thomas A.	2,091	Pocatalico	1786	1	188
Taylor, Thomas A.	642	Pocatalico	1786	1	187
Taylor, Thomas A.	7,923	Pocatalico	1786	1	186
Taylor, Thomas A.	808	Pocatalico	1786	1	185
Taylor, Thomas A.	6,124	Old Campaign Rd.	1786	1	183
Taylor, Thomas A.	1,000	Pocatalico	1786	1	184
Taylor, Thomas A.	(5398) 5,393	Pocatalico	1786	1	182
Taylor, Thomas A.	3,125	Pocatalico	1786	1	163
Taylor, Thomas A.	2,000	15 Mi. Creek	1786	1	162
Taylor, Thomas A.	1,165	Pocatalico	1786	1	161
Taylor, Thomas A.	3,051	Pocatalico	1786	1	160
Taylor, Thomas A.	1,000	Pocatalico	1786	1	159
Taylor, Thomas A.	1,040	Pocatalico	1786	1	158
Taylor, Thomas A.	1,014	Pocatalico	1786	1	157
Taylor, Thomas et al	200	Wts. of Kanawha	1787	1	426
Taysse—See Teas, Teays					
Taysse, Thomas (Teays)	221	12 Mile Cr.	1793	3	106
Teas, Thomas et al	850	18 Mi. Cr.	1787	1	282
Terry, Thomas (Tarry)	67	Shades of Death	1816	2	558
Tharp, John	129	Haddins Run	1789	2	220
Think, Daniel	114	Wolf Creek	1800	4	397
Thomas, David	233	Muddy Creek	1787	1	442
Thompson—See Thomson					
Thompson, Isaac	138	Howard's Cr.	1800	4	324
Thompson, James	606	Lit. Clear Cr.	1856	6	431
Thompson, James	200	Adj. J. Warren	1787	2	72
Thompson, James	215	Adj. R. Thompson	1787	2	90
Thompson, James	391	Above 3 Mi. Creek	1793	2	535

Name of Grantee	Acres	Local Description	Year	Book	Page
Thompson, James	80	Muddy Cr. Mt.	1811	5	267
Thompson, John	300	Rich Creek	1791	2	410
Thompson, John	25	The Sinks	1796	3	446
Thompson, John	582	Lit. Wolf Cr.	1796	3	447
Thompson, John	100	Muddy Cr. Mt.	1795	3	323
Thompson, John	1,390	Wts. Greenbrier	1795	3	322
Thompson, John	591	Culbertson's Cr.	1795	3	326
Thompson, John	100	Rich Creek	1795	3	179
Thompson, John	1,009	Pine Spg. Run	1796	4	126
Thompson, John et al	1,000	Wills Creek	1790	2	289
Thompson, John Jr.	100	Rich Creek	1796	4	117
Thompson, Robert	95	Lit. Sewell Cr.	1848	6	310
Thompson, Robert	73	Sewell Creek	1823	6	13
Thompson, Robert	227	Wolf Pen Run	1825	6	66
Thompson, Robert	200	Rich Creek	1786	1	173
Thompson, Robert	284	The Sinks	1787	2	38
Thompson, Robert	340	Rich Creek	1787	2	70
Thompson, Robert	225	Adj. R. Nickle	1787	2	73
Thompson, Robert & John	495	2nd Creek	1799	4	268
Thompson, Samuel S.	129	Howard's Cr.	1852	6	384
Thompson, Samuel S.	300	Laurel Cr.	1845	6	576
Thompson, William	25	Rich Creek	1800	4	514
Thomson—or Thompson					
Thomson, John	159	Adj. T. Charlton	1793	3	60
Tincher, Francis	100	Lick Creek	1797	4	34
Tincher, Frances	600	Muddy Creek	1789	2	212
Tindsley, Thomas et al	606⅛	Muddy Creek	1786	1	156
Tinsley, Thomas	1,860	Glade Creek	1796	3	512
Tipher, Peter (Fisher)	300	Gr. Levels	1794	3	149
Toney, William	400	Wts. of New River	1789	2	208
Toothman, John	125	Mellon's Cr.	1798	4	210
Towles, Oliver Jr. (Toles) et al	1,000	Wts. Meadow River	1804	3	542
Treason, Jacob	147	Lit. Levels	1783	1	16
Trent, Henry & J. B.	4,290	Muddy Creek	1788	2	171
Trotter, James	300	Turkey Creek	1786	1	133
Trueheart, William	1,500	Glade Creek	1796	3	363
Truhart, Daniel	1,140	Wts. Meadow River	1802	5	93
Tryer, John (Fryer)	100	Culbertson's Cr.	1795	3	236
Tucker, John R.	160	Big Clear Cr.	1831	6	151
Tuckwell, John	200	Wts. Greenbrier	1787	1	434
Tuckwillae, John (Tuckwiller)	239	Muddy Cr. Mt.	1789	2	187
Tuckwiller, Tuckwillae, Tuckwillow					
Tuckwillow, Daniel	48	Adj. C. Piercy	1834	6	173
Turner, James	94	New River	1789	2	276
Turpin, Solomon	400	2nd Creek	1787	1	269
Tutt, Elizabeth	80	Wts. L. Meadow	1810	5	243
Tyree, Richard F.	13	Muddy Creek	1804	3	531
Tyree, Richard F.	43	Wts. New River	1819	1	531
Tyree, Richard F.	107	Glade Creek	1817	1	592
Tyree, Richard F.	1,664	Wts. New River	1816	1	604
Tyree, Richard F.	861	Mann's Creek	1816	1	605
Tyree, Richard F.	785	Glade Creek	1820	4	537
Tyree, Richard F.	125	Wts. New River	1815	2	562
Tyree, Richard F.	35	Wts. Greenbrier	1802	5	139
Tyree, Richard F.	50	Ephriam's Cr.	1815	5	306
Underwood, John	138	Sinking Creek	1825	6	77
Vahab—See Wahab					
Vanbibber, John	345	Wts. Greenbrier	1787	1	283
Vanker, William Z. (or J.)	373½	Wts. of Elk	1792	2	509
Vanosdal—Vanosdle					
Vanosdal, Cornelius	76	Sinking Creek	1800	4	301
Vanosdle, Caleb	168	Howard's Creek	1796	3	403

Name of Grantee	Acres	Local Description	Year	Book	Page
Welch, Alexander	400	Elk River	1793	3	99
Welch, Alexander	400	Old Town Cr.	1784	1	81
Welch, Alexander	400	Wts. of Kanawha	1785	1	165
Welch, Alexander	495	3 Mile Cr.	1787	1	284
Welch, Alexander	540	Laurel Creek	1800	4	468
Welch, Alexander	600	Laurel Creek	1800	4	380
Welch, Alexander	900	Birch River	1787	1	281
Welch, Alexander et al	730	Wts. Pocatalico	1787	1	241
Welch, Alexander et al	4,000	Wts. of Gauley	1795	3	295
Welch, Ebenezer	400	Meadow River	1804	5	166
Welch, Ebenezer	1,000	Mann's Creek	1808	5	216
Welch, Ebenezer et al	2,200	Spring Creek	1805	5	185
Welch, James	45	Adj. Wolfinbarger	1808	5	223
Welch, James	90	Wts. Meadow River	1802	5	143
Welch, James	100	Carpenter's Run	1797	4	2
Welch, James	100	William's Creek	1800	4	297
Welch, James	100	Wts. Greenbrier	1802	5	144
Welch, James	120	Wts. Greenbrier	1800	4	424
Welch, James	247	Droop Mt.	1802	5	145
Welch, James	300	2nd Creek	1796	3	396
Welch, James	1,000	Howard's Creek	1805	3	543
Welch, James	1,000	Indian Creek	1797	3	586
Welch, James	1,020	Muddy Creek	1797	4	38
Welch, James	1,270	Bracken's Cr.	1797	4	65
Welch, James	1,300	Sand Creek	1798	4	238
Welch, James	1,096	Second Creek	1797	4	31
Welch, James	2,000	Indian Cr.	1797	3	579
Welch, James	2,723	Big Clear Cr.	1805	5	580
Welch, James	3,215	Lit. Devil's Cr.	1797	4	29
Welch, James	3,277	Big Clear Cr.	1805	3	545
Welch, James	3,277	Big Clear Cr.	1805	5	193
Welch, James	4,500	Gauley River	1805	5	192
Welch, James	4,830	Walk & Kelly's Cr.	1797	3	588
Welch, James	5,425	Wts. New River	1797	3	581
Walch, James	5,680	Howard's Creek	1797	4	547
Welch, James	7,000	Anthony's Creek	1797	4	550
Welch, James	12,714	Howard's Creek	1797	3	583
Welch, John	136	Laurel Creek	1796	4	119
Welch, John	170	Wts. of Gauley	1796	4	120
Welch, John	195	Welches' Glades	1796	3	495
Welch, John	500	Glade Creek	1796	4	121
Wells, James	220	Laurel Creek	1801	5	128
Wendleblake, Henry	50	The Sinks	1797	4	21
West, George	100	Lit. Wolf Cr.	1800	4	465
Wetzel, George	5	Adj. Thomas Creigh	1844	6	262
Whanger, John	15	Adj. Hamilton	1809	5	251
Wheeler, Joseph	400	Adj. J. Archer	1787	1	315
White, D. O. & J. O.	50	Lick Creek	1831	6	153
White, George et al	1,680	Adj. S. Brown	1794	3	148
White, George G.	1,610	Anthony's Cr.	1861	6	533
White, James	234	Anthony's Creek	1814	5	294
White, James	30	Anthony's Cr.	1813	5	284
White, James	200	Anthony's Creek	1800	4	477
White, James	132	Anthony..s Creek	1816	1	602
White, James Sr.	431	Anthony's Cr.	1820	2	577
White, John	93	Turkey Creek	1796	3	357
White, William	427	Howard's Cr.	1790	2	324
White, William	502	Tuckahoe Draught	1815	2	570
White, William Jr.	100	Kate's Mt.	1848	6	317
Whitecraft—See Whitecroft					
Whitecroft, William	1,000	Hungales Cr.	1787	1	510
Whitecroft, William	7,100	Wts. Meadow R.	1787	1	505
Whitecroft, William	1,000	Laurel Cr.	1787	1	511

Name of Grantee	Acres	Local Description	Year	Book	Page
Willis, Henry	186	Rich Creek	1790	2	295
Willis, Henry	320	Rut Creek	1789	2	272
Willis, James	270	Locust Creek	1785	1	70
Wilson, Andrew	200	Rich Creek	1787	1	365
Wilson, James	100	Carpenter's Run	1799	4	283
Wilson, James	155	Indian Creek	1786	1	217
Wilson, John	177	Muddy Creek	1795	3	308
Wilson, John	100	Muddy Creek	1802	5	101
Wilson, John	420½	Muddy Creek	1787	1	413
Wilson, John	500	Muddy Creek	1797	4	47
Wilson, Ralph	80	Anthony's Creek	1789	2	283
Wilson, Richard	180	Adj. B. Lewis	1795	3	197
Wilson, Richard	25	Wts. Greenbrier	1801	5	110
Wilson, Sampson	180	Sinking Creek	1787	1	291
Wilson, William	177	Wts. Gr. Kanawha	1786	1	228
Windle, John	220	Muddy Creek	1819	4	542
Windsor, Jonathan	240	Gauley R. below Ford	1792	2	381
Wirt, William	390	Muddy Cr.	1808	5	221
Wise, Adam	250	Second Cr.	1810	5	249
Wiseman, Isaac	94	Dropping Lick Cr.	1800	4	410
Wiseman, Samuel	148	Adj. J. Likens	1819	1	545
Withrow, Able	178	Lick Creek	1823	6	31
Withrow, Isaac	40	Pine Springs Run	1827	6	121
Withrow, Samuel	150	Lick Creek	1797	4	144
Withrow, Samuel	154	Lick Creek	1815	2	565
Withrow, Samuel	160	Wts. New River	1815	2	565
Wolf, Henry	28	Big Levels	1801	5	32
Wolf, Henry	172	Big Levels	1815	5	304
Wood—or Woods					
Wood, Bailey	69(95)	Pine Springs Br.	1820	4	530
Wood, Bailey	450	Wts. of Greenbrier	1788	2	160
Wood, John	100	Adj. T. Wright	1795	3	188
Wood, William	109	Peter's Mt.	1800	4	481
Woodden, John	500	Mumblethepeg	1795	3	282
Woodden, John	200	Beaver Creek	1797	4	145
Woods—or Wood					
Woods, William R.	2,207	Lick Creek	1857	6	440
Woods, William R.	127	Lick Creek	1857	6	441
Woods, William R.	268	Muddy Creek	1857	6	442
Woods, William R.	4¼	Adj. Wm. Spotts	1844	6	267
Woods, William R.	311	Adj. C. A. Stuart	1845	6	289
Woods, William R.	5	Adj. Wm. Spotts	1844	6	268
Woolfinbarger, Frederick	8½	Big Levels	1826	6	95
Woolfinbarger, John	340	Great Levels	1789	2	224
Woolford, Daniel	600	Muddy Creek	1791	2	406
Wright, Isaac et al	1,430	Wills Creek	1795	3	198
Wright, Thomas	385	Indian Cr.	1787	1	234
Wyatt—Wayte, Wiatt, Wyett					
Wyatt, Major et al	377	Spring Cr.	1820	6	506
Wyett, Major	215	Culbertson's Cr.	1820	1	522
Wyett, Major et al (Wyette)	320	Culbertson's Cr.	1820	6	496
Wyley—See Wileigh, Wiley, Wilie, Willey, Wylie					
Wyley, Robert Sr.	230	Wts. of New River	1788	2	157
Wylie—See Wileigh, Wiley, Wilie, Willey, Wyley					
Wylie, James	50	Long Draught	1797	4	59
Wylie, Robert	250	Wts. Greenbrier	1797	4	23
Yammons, John	220	Howard's Creek	1800	4	304
Yeacock—See Ieacock					
Yeates, Ralph et al	180	2nd Creek	1793	3	43
Yeiser, Frederick	1,000	Wts. of New River	1795	3	263
Yeiser, Frederick	1,000	Wts. of New River	1795	3	264
Yeiser, Frederick	1,000	Wts. New River	1795	3	265
Yeiser, Frederick	1,000	Wts. of New River	1795	3	261

Name of Grantee	Acres	Local Description	Year	Book	Page
Yeiser, Frederick	1,000	Wts. of New River	1795	3	260
Yeiser, Frederick	1,000	Wts. of New River	1795	3	262
Yeiser, Frederick	1,000	Wts. New River	1795	3	217
Yeiser, Frederick	1,000	Wts. of New River	1795	3	259
Yeiser, Frederick	1,000	Wts. New River	1795	3	216
Yeiser, Frederick	1,000	Wts. New River	1795	3	215
Yeiser, Frederick	500	Muddy Creek	1796	3	525
Young, Conrad	286	Muddy Creek	1787	1	235
Young, Edward	1,500	Howard's Creek	1795	3	269
Young, Edward	2,514	Big Laurel Cr.	1795	3	270
Young, Edward	250	Wts. of Elk	1795	3	292
Young, Edward	1,500	Howard's Cr.	1795	3	293
Young, Edward	250	Spies Rock	1795	3	294
Young, James	45	Wts. Greenbrier	1816	1	597
Young, James	52	2nd Creek	1816	1	598
Young, James	332	Wts. Greenbrier	1822	6	538
Young, James	236	2nd Creek	1796	3	486
Young, James	90	Wts. Greenbrier	1796	3	480
Young, James	197	2nd Creek	1796	3	482
Young, John	218	Tuckahoe Cr.	1856	6	473
Young, John	180	Tuckahoe's Draught	1848	6	318
Young, John Capt.	90	Muddy Creek	1823	6	40
Young, Mathias	109	Keeny's Creek	1825	6	86
Young, Mathias	127	Keeny's Cr.	1820	4	536
Young, Robert	400	Kelly's Fork	1796	3	524
Young, Robert	400	Spring Creek	1796	3	523
Young, Robert	4,075	Hedrick's Cr.	1796	3	343
Young, Robert	386	Pine Spring Run	1796	3	342
Young, Robert	470	Wts. Meadow River	1796	3	344
Young, Robert	600	Slab Camp Mt.	1795	3	334
Young, Robert	193	Cove Creek	1796	3	335
Young, Robert	425	Sinking Cr.	1795	3	336
Young, Robert	1,007	Pine Spring Run	1795	3	333
Young, Robert	555	Big Laurel Creek	1795	3	332
Young, Robert	470	Wts. Meadow River	1796	3	442
Young, Robert	165	Wts. New River	1796	3	443
Young, Robert	1,000	Lick Creek	1796	3	441
Young, Robert	75	Sinking Creek	1796	3	521
Young, Robert	150	Spring Creek	1796	3	522
Young, Robert	800	Slab Camp Run	1796	3	346
Young, Robert	9,000 (2,000)	Laurel Creek	1796	3	345
Young, Robert	200	Gauley Mt.	1796	3	348
Young, Robert	200	Wts. Meadow River	1796	3	347
Young, Robert	455	Adj. James Jordan	1796	3	349
Young, Robert	540	Sinking Cr.	1796	3	350
Young, Robert	13	Howard's Cr.	1857	6	476
Young, Robert	121	Wts. New River	1820	6	498
Young, Robert	585	Spring Creek	1819	1	523
Young, Robert	563	Roaring Creek	1797	4	131
Young, Robert	270	Peter's Cr.	1793	2	514
Young, Robert	390	Culbertson's Cr.	1801	5	25
Young, Robert	150	Anthony's Cr.	1800	5	5
Young, Robert	400	Culbertson's Cr.	1801	5	122
Young, Robert	360	Adj. Martin	1801	5	121
Young, Robert	247	Droop Mt.	1802	5	134
Young, Robert et al	1,000	Wts. of Gauley	1792	2	484
Young, Robert et al	1,000	Wts. of Gauley	1792	2	485
Young, Robert et al	1,260	Wts. Gauley	1792	2	487
Young, Robert et al	1,000	Wts. of Gauley	1792	2	486
Young, Samuel	260	Wts. Greenbrier	1788	2	136
Young, Samuel et al	800	Sinking Creek	1789	2	273
Young, William	100	Adj. E. Conrad	1787	1	240
Young, William	60	Adj. Angel Connell	1799	4	278

HAMPSHIRE COUNTY

Name of Grantee	Acres	Local Description	Year	Book	Page
Abernathy, James	50	South Br. Mt.	1836	7	527
Abernathy, James	86	Swisher's Run	1836	7	526
Abernathy, James	122	Swisher's Mt.	1834	3	372
Abernathy, James	15	Campbell's Mt.	1841	7	72
Abernathy, James	197	South Branch	1843	7	125
Abernathy, James	400	South Branch	1836	7	520
Abernathy, James	133	South Branch	1858	7	463
Abernathy, John	114½	Adj. Widow Riley	1819	5	252
Abernathy, John	386	Allegheny Mt.	1791	6	109
Abernathy, John	20	Adj. Old Tract	1791	6	94
Abernathy, John	5	North Branch	1800	9	247
Abernathy, Thomas	23	Stony Run	1836	7	524
Abernathy, Thomas	41	Stony Run	1834	3	371
Abernathy, William (of Samuel)	48	South Branch	1836	3	435
Abernathy, William	23½	Wts. Potomac	1856	7	404
Acton, John	54	Adj. S. Kite	1792	6	215
Acton, Richard	373	Bear Camp Drains	1779	2	154
Acton, Richard	187	Adj. E. Poston	1779	2	155
Acton, Richard	110	North Branch	1791	6	158
Adams, Jacob Sr.	10¾	Patterson's Cr.	1858	7	471
Adams, William	369	Timber Ridge	1789	8	242
Adams, William	481	South Br.	1789	8	241
Adams, William et al	400	Patterson's Cr.	1797	9	139
Airson, Jacob	464	South Branch	1789	8	430
Airson, John	414	Green Spring Run	1789	8	429
Airson, John	317	South Branch	1789	8	428
Akers, Ann	93	Knobly Mt.	1812	5	101
Alban, James W.	2a.3r.22p.	Bush's Run	1840	7	40
Albright, Jonathan W. et al	1½	Sandy Ridge	1854	7	369
Albright, Samuel	1a.1r.32p.	Lit. Cacapon	1859	7	488
Alderton, William	13½	Potomac River	1816	5	185
Alderton, William	67	Easter Run	1812	5	81
Alderton, William	100	Wts. Potomac	1820	5	288
Alderton, William	40	Gr. Cacapon	1796	9	52
Alderton, William	73½	Alderton Mt.	1855	7	553
Alender—See Allender					
Alexander, Robert	267	Lit Cacapon	1789	8	183
Alexander, William	268½	Cacapon Mt.	1794	6	412
Alger, Abraham J.	21¾	Lit. Cacapon	1853	7	349
Alkier—See Alkire					
Alkier, Maunis	294	Wts. Potomac	1765	1	243
Alkire—See Alkier					
Alkire, Maunus (Maurus)	304	South Branch	1788	8	102
Alkire, Nimrod	10	North Branch	1860	7	509
Allaback, John	9¾	Chestnut Spg. Run	1812	5	83
Allaback, John	18½	Gr. Cacapon	1817	5	197
Allen, James	107	Patterson's Cr.	1832	3	289
Allen, James	54	Patterson's Cr.	1848	7	256
Allen, John	50	Big Cacapon	1820	5	311
Allen, John Sr.	74	Sand Creek	1800	9	281
Allen, Robert	39	Town Hill	1803	9	433
Allen, Thomas	110	Patterson's Cr.	1816	5	196
Allender, James	90	Lit. Cacapon	1823	5	377
Allender, Thomas	6a.3r.11p.	South Branch	1853	7	356
Allender, William	285	Wts. Potomac	1789	8	477
Alverson, A. M.	110	Knobly Mt.	1859	7	495
Ambler, John	99	Pine Cabin Run	1838	7	34
Amory—See Emery, Emmery, Emory					
Amory, Edward	150	Knobly Mt.	1793	6	359

Name of Grantee	Acres	Local Description	Year	Book	Page
Anderson, Daniel	389	Trout Run	1789	8	491
Anderson, James	302	Wts. Cacapon	1796	6	554
Anderson, James Sr.	85a.2r.29p.	High Knob	1821	5	354
Anderson, Jesse	100	Loomis Branch	1821	5	351
Anderson, Thomas	187	North Branch	1793	6	413
Anderson, William	327	Indian Run	1789	8	278
Anderson, William	187	Wts. Potomac	1762	1	149
Anderson, William	412	Crooked Run	1777	2	78
Anderson, William	337	Crooked Run	1780	2	268
Arbanathy—See Abernathy					
Armstrong, Edward, Adm.	40½	Island Hill	1853	7	359
Armstrong, William	959	Green Spg. Run	1790	8	572
Armstrong, William	400	Patterson Cr.	1800	9	265
Armstrong, William	400	North River	1800	9	324
Armstrong, William	959	Green Spg. Run	1790	6	2
Armstrong, William	1,110	Green Spg. Run	1790	6	3
Armstrong, William	1,227	Green Spg. Run	1790	6	4
Armstrong, William	510	Broad Run	1819	5	256
Arnold, Andrew	400	North River	1764	1	214
Arnold, David	45	South Br. Mt.	1848	7	239
Arnold, David	49	Break Neck Mt.	1853	7	354
Arnold, David	4⅜	Lit. Cacapon	1853	7	353
Arnold, John (of Jachariah)	43a.14p.	Mill Creek	1827	3	105
Arnold, John (son of Samuel)	139½	Mill Run	1822	5	370
Arnold, John	96	Chestnut Ridge	1833	3	341
Arnold, John	4	Wallon Run	1848	7	238
Arnold, John	100	Lit. Cacapon	1825	5	441
Arnold, Jonathan	400	North River	1762	1	153
Arnold, Joseph	127¾	Patterson's Cr.	1854	7	393
Arnold, Joseph	221	Mike's Run	1843	7	124
Arnold, Joseph	84	Patterson's Cr.	1836	7	528
Arnold, Samuel	19½	New Creek	1848	7	240
Arnold, Samuel	19	New Creek Mt.	1845	7	167
Arnold, Zachariar	3	Mill Cr.	1822	5	369
Asberry—or Asbury					
Asberry, Henry	4½	Adj. T. Slone	1814	5	140
Asberry, Henry	136¾	Sidling Hill	1812	5	80
Asberry, Isaac	100	North River	1807	9	567
Asberry, Joseph	680	North River	1791	6	103
Asbury—See Asberry					
Asbury, Henry	30	North River	1797	9	138
Ashbey—or Ashby					
Ashbey, Jeremiah	50	Allegheny Mt.	1807	9	568
Ashbrook, Aaron	400	North River	1777	2	59
Ashbrook, Aaron	110	Buffalo Lick Run	1777	2	60
Ashbrook, Aaron	75	Tear Coat	1807	9	569
Ashbrook, Eli	91	Tear Coat Cr.	1809	5	27
Ashbrook, Elizabeth et al	400	Gr. Cacapon	1762	1	158
Ashbrook, John	72	North River	1792	6	199
Ashbrook, Thomas	355	Town Run	1791	6	105
Ashby—See also Ashbey					
Ashby, Benjamin	211	North Branch	1789	8	297
Ashby, Benjamin Sr.	192	Wts. Potomac	1778	2	130
Ashby, John Jr.	61	North Branch	1787	8	10
Ashby, Nimrod Capt.	424	Luney's Creek	1763	1	208
Asters, William	50	Gr. Cacapon	1796	9	59
Athey, John W.	22⅜	Mill Creek	1856	7	413
Athey, Thomas	106	Mill Gap	1792	6	281
Atkins, Thomas	377½	Trout Run	1789	8	492
Atwell, Thomas	406½	Thorn Bottom	1790	8	544
Atwill or Atwell					
Babb, Archibald	110 poles	South Branch	1838	7	32
Babb, John	100	Lick Run	1796	6	499

Name of Grantee	Acres	Local Description	Year	Book	Page
Babb, Joseph	100	Tear Coat Cr.	1800	9	256
Bacorn, Job	255	Buck Island Run	1789	8	267
Bacorn, Job	428	Cabin Run	1779	2	215
Bacorn, Job	400	Cabin Run	1779	2	214
Badgley, David	345	Looney's Creek	1788	8	144
Bailess, Edward	25	New Creek	1794	6	381
Bailey, Edward	21½	Patterson's Cr.	1858	7	467
Bailey, William	25	Cabin Run	1833	3	311
Bails, Henry	3	Adj. T. Williams	1810	5	59
Baker, George H.	16¼	North Branch	1860	7	507
Baker, George H.	90	Fairley Run	1860	7	508
Baker, Henry	334	Lit. Cacapon	1787	8	14
Baker, Henry	430	Sandy Ridge	1787	8	15
Baker, Henry	458	Lit. Cacapon	1788	8	152
Baker, Henry	182	North River	1788	8	153
Baker, Henry	420	Lit. Cacapon	1788	8	163
Baker, Henry	158	North River	1789	8	259
Baker, Henry	267	North River	1796	6	546
Baker, Henry	114	North River	1779	2	200
Baker, Henry	300	Cacapon	1779	2	201
Baker, Henry	252	Gr. Cacapon	1779	2	202
Baker, Henry	190	North River	1788	8	151
Baker, Isaac et al	124	Devil's Nose Mt.	1843	7	126
Baker, Jacob	180	Hanging Rock Run	1796	6	559
Baker, Jacob	70	North River	1796	9	97
Baker, Jacob et al	60	Wts. Potomac	1831	3	243
Baker, James	220	Lost River	1762	1	154
Baker, John	354	North Branch	1790	8	508
Baker, John	430	New Creek	1793	6	356
Baker, John	41¾	North River	1824	5	389
Baker, John	212	New Creek	1776	2	40
Baker, John	30¼	North River	1815	5	161
Baker, John Y.	26⅜	Spring Valley	1858	7	478
Baker, Joseph et al	200	South Branch	1799	9	197
Baker, Joseph et al	300	South Branch	1799	9	199
Baker, Joseph et al	400	Patterson's Cr.	1797	9	139
Baker, Michael	21	George's Run	1820	5	314
Baker, Nicholas et al	177	Lit. Cacapon	1806	9	543
Baker, Richard	139	Knobly Mt.	1852	7	307
Baker, Richard	57a.1r.	Knobly Mt.	1837	7	545
Baker, Samuel	34	Cacapon	1788	8	65
Baker, Samuel	142	Lost River	1762	1	155
Baker, Thomas	198	Green Spgs. Run	1843	7	127
Baker, William	242	Gr. Cacapon	1789	8	280
Baker, William	200	New Creek	1809	5	22
Baldwin, William	77	North River	1762	1	145
Ball, William	400	New Creek	1788	8	43
Ball, William	400	Adj. John Parker	1788	8	114
Ball, William	400	Patterson's Cr.	1788	8	126
Bane, George & Abner Jr.	100	Wts. Patterson Cr.	1828	3	128
Bane, Jesse	100	Patterson Cr.	1800	9	302
Barcley, Thomas	400	So. Branch	1792	6	129
Barcley, Thomas	395	Nor. Branch	1792	6	130
Barcley, Thomas	185	Patterson Cr.	1792	6	131
Bare, John	330	Lost River	1775	4	486
Barnhouse, John	400	Adj. his own	1789	8	446
Barnhouse, John	408	Near Decker's Line	1789	8	447
Barrett, Jonathan	65½	Park's Hollow	1841	7	56
Barrick, George	89	Abram's Ridge	1837	7	544
Barricks, Henry	140	Montgomery Run	1831	3	268
Barricks, Henry	32¾	Montgomery Run	1830	3	206
Barricks, Henry	44	Adj. J. Sharp	1828	3	130
Barricks, William	200	Stony Hill	1794	6	402

Name of Grantee	Acres	Local Description	Year	Book	Page
Battin, Henry	77	Gr. Cacapon	1778	2	110
Battin, Henry	168	Bean's Branch	1766	1	317
Battin, Simon	174	Gibson Run	1766	1	318
Baugh Henry	200	Gr. Cacapon	1803	9	430
Beal, Bazel	47	Allegheny Mt.	1805	9	502
Beal, Baziel	44	North Branch	1802	9	383
Beall, Eli	55	North River	1795	6	474
Beall, Eli	533	North River	1792	6	193
Beall, Elisha	250	North River	1800	9	257
Beall, Elisha	167	Camp Branch	1777	2	54
Beall, Elisha	127	North River	1794	6	475
Beall, Elisha	281	Lit. Cacapon	1788	8	92
Beall, Elisha	248	Tear Coat Cr.	1788	8	91
Beall, Elisha	214	Lit. Cacapon	1788	8	90
Beall, George	274a.1r.	Viney Run	1777	2	55
Beall, George	52	North River	1795	6	471
Beall, George	160	North River	1795	6	470
Beall, Samuel (The Third) et al	65	Stoke's Cabin	1779	2	182
Beall, William M.	94	Spring Run	1777	2	50
Beall, William M.	248	3 Spring Run	1777	2	51
Beall, William M.	186	Camp Branch	1777	2	52
Beall, William M.	320a.2r.	North River	1777	2	53
Bean, James	412	North River	1789	8	453
Bean, Jesse	300	Staggs Run	1791	6	84
Bean, Joseph	125	Sandy Lick Br.	1766	1	373
Bean, Thomas	453	Gr. Cacapon	1788	8	104
Beard, George	47	Mike's Run	1804	9	484
Beard, George Jr (or Sr.)	13¾	Cor. to G. Taylor	1806	9	549
Beatty—See Betty					
Beatty, George	320	Mill Cr. Knob	1802	9	388
Beatty, George	397	Mill Run	1789	8	452
Beatty, George	400	Foxcamp Run	1789	8	451
Beaver, Peter	176	Mike's Run	1789	8	317
Beaver, Peter	225	Lick Run	1762	1	122
Beaver, Peter	107	Lick Run	1762	1	123
Beaver, Peter	165	Mike's Run	1792	6	192
Beavers, Robert	37	Wts. Potomac	1830	3	210
Beckett, John	250	Patterson's Cr.	1766	1	350
Beckner, Henry	40	Adj. Philip Christman	1795	6	465
Beckwith, Marmaduke B.	194	Knobly Mt.	1791	6	72
Beckwith, Newman	262	Adj. Martin's Line	1795	6	433
Beckwith, Newman	536	Adj. Wm. Mechesny	1795	6	430
Beckwith, Newman	200	New Creek	1794	6	340
Beckwith, Newman	1,000	New Creek	1794	6	339
Beckwith, Newman	100	Stony Run	1792	6	211
Beckwith, Newman	200	New Creek	1792	6	210
Been—or Bean					
Been, Christopher	321 (326)	Patterson's Cr.	1777	2	62
Beeler, Benjamin	400	Elk Lick	1789	8	441
Beeler, Benjamin	402	Pine Swamps	1789	8	326
Beeler, Benjamin	400	Abraham's Cr.	1789	8	325
Beelor, Benjamin	152	New Creek	1788	8	82
Beery—See Berry					
Beery, David	39¾	Lit. Cacapon	1859	7	494
Begly, Henry	100	Patterson's Cr.	1770	5	564
Bell, William	100	Cabin Run	1795	6	450
Bell, William	402	Muddy Run	1792	6	157
Belsford—See Brelsford					
Belyes, Edward	25	New Creek	1794	6	381
Bennett, Isabella	21	North River	1854	7	400
Bennett, William	49	North River	1833	3	339
Bennett, William	50	Potomac	1798	9	165
Berkeley, John	252	Spring Gap Run	1779	2	188

Name of Grantee	Acres	Local Description	Year	Book	Page
Berry—See Beery					
Berry, Anna	30	Patterson's Cr.	1857	7	443
Berry, Enoch	476	Wts. Cacapon	1790	8	540
Berry, Enoch	468	Burrell's Run	1790	8	541
Berry, Enoch	162	Grassy Lick	1790	8	543
Berry, James	425	George's Run	1857	7	442
Berry, Reuben	173	Adj. G. Snicker	1778	2	131
Bethel, Joshua	39	North River	1825	5	427
Bettis—See Beatty, Betty					
Bettis, George	79	South Branch	1789	8	320
Betty—See Beatty					
Betty, George	291	South Branch	1791	6	61
Betty, George	20	South Branch	1791	6	60
Betty, George	269a.12r.	South Branch	1789	8	319
Bickerstaff—Biggerstaff					
Bickerstaff, William	84	Potomac River	1791	6	115
Bier, Thomas	100	So. Branch	1792	6	298
Biggerstaff, Samuel	49	Potomac	1796	9	113
Billingsley, Clement	404	Gr. Cacapon	1788	8	98
Bills, William	81	Gr. Cacapon	1789	8	479
Bills, William	326	Gr. Cacapon	1768	5	519
Bird, Stephen	219	So. Branch	1831	3	270
Bird, Stephen	46	South Br.	1843	7	150
Bird, Stephen	83	South Branch	1841	7	93
Bird, Stephen	17	So. Branch	1843	7	151
Bird, Stephen et al	144	South Branch	1841	7	92
Biser, Jacob	120	Patterson's Cr.	1829	3	175
Biser, Nicholas	66	Middle Ridge	1831	3	265
Bishop, George	246	Grassy Lick	1804	9	473
Bishop, George	300	Grassy Lick	1804	9	474
Bishop, John	450	Mill Creek	1792	6	241
Bizer, See Biser					
Blackburn, Edward	418	Maple Run	1777	2	71
Blackburn, Edward	408	Maple Run	1777	2	96
Blackburn, Joseph	300	Dry Run	1841	7	76
Bland, John	100	Knobly Mt.	1796	9	65
Blough, John	100	South Branch	1797	9	146
Bloxham, Thomas	19	Pine Draught Run	1836	3	429
Blue, Garrett J.	37 perches	South Branch	1854	7	364
Blue, Garrett W. Jr.	146	South Branch	1818	5	237
Blue, Isaac	282	South Branch	1829	3	155
Blue, John	225	So. Branch	1800	9	323
Blue, John	50	Hanging Rock Ridge	1817	5	219
Blue, John	203	Hanging Rock	1774	4	460
Blue, John W.	51½	Rock Mountain	1838	7	33
Blue, Richard	170⅛	So. Branch	1813	5	118
Blue, Richard	52	South Branch	1809	5	48
Blue, Richard	271½	Sugar Run	1825	5	424
Blue, Richard	147	So. Branch	1843	7	152
Blue, Richard	205	South Br. Mt.	1832	3	301
Blue, Thomas et al	144	South Branch	1841	7	92
Bodkin, Richard	112	Looney's Cr.	1788	8	115
Bogell—See Bogle					
Bogell, Andrew	100	New Creek	1796	9	41
Bogell, James	384	Stony River	1792	6	160
Bogle, or Bogell					
Bogle, Andrew	67	Adj. Nathanial Kuykendall	1842	7	107
Bogle, James	372	New Creek	1789	8	279
Bomcruts, Leonard (Boncrats)	50	Mill Creek	1804	9	476
Boncrats, Leonard	58	Mill Cr.	1819	5	240
Boncrats, Leonard Jr.	13a.20p.	Mill Cr.	1825	5	408
Boncratz, Leonard	50	Mill Creek	1804	9	476
Bonham, Samuel	10¼	River Hill	1854	7	383

Name of Grantee	Acres	Local Description	Year	Book	Page
Bonham, Samuel	24¾	Town Hill	1854	7	381
Bonham, Samuel	17	Baker's Run	1846	7	207
Bookless, David	80	Castleman's Run	1805	9	500
Bordman, Joseph	306	Patterson's Cr.	1789	8	196
Borer, Thomas	112	North Fork	1792	6	242
Boseley, Elizabeth et al	40	New Creek	1815	5	145
Boseley, William	248	Deep Run	1841	7	55
Boseley, William	61	New Creek	1838	7	31
Boseley, William	76	Sugar Camp Run	1831	3	250
Bower, Henry	55	Brushy Run	1796	6	525
Bower, Henry	255	Brushy Run	1789	8	298
Bower, Jacob	195	Gr. Cacapon	1799	9	208
Bowers, Jacob	50	Dilling's Run	1800	9	243
Bowman, Alfred	110	Wts. of Potomac	1831	3	223
Bowman, George (Bauman)	50	Cabin Run	1796	9	47
Bowman, George	100	George's Run	1796	6	521
Boyce, Nicholas	328	Mill Cr.	1795	6	441
Boyd, Alexander	478	Gibbon's Run	1789	8	299
Boyd, Samuel	381	Gr. Cacapon	1789	8	281
Boyd, Samuel	430	Gr. Cacapon	1789	8	271
Boyd, Samuel	411	Adj. John Largent	1789	8	270
Boyd, Samuel	342	North Branch	1789	8	387
Boyd, Samuel	20	North Branch	1789	8	385
Boyd, Samuel	446	North Branch	1789	8	386
Boyle, Andrew	133a.1r.	New Creek	1821	5	333
Brady, John	98½	Swisher's Run	1822	5	357
Brady, John	221	Middle Ridge	1845	7	168
Brady, John	15	Wts. Potomac	1835	3	407
Brak, Jacob (Barrick)	134	Boundary Line of Northern Neck	1789	8	467
Brand, Thomas	50	Spring Gap	1798	9	153
Bransford, Bernard	418	Edgington Gap	1789	8	475
Brant, John	1½	North Branch	1833	3	328
Brant, John	39	Wts. Potomac	1834	3	378
Brant, John	100	Allegheny Mt.	1834	3	379
Brant, John	49	Adj. L. L. Cundiff	1836	7	525
Brant, John	35a.3r.	No. Br. Potomac	1825	5	425
Brant, John	14¼	Wts. Potomac	1825	5	426
Brant, John	616	Wts. Potomac	1825	5	440
Brelsford, Bernard	418	Edgington Gap	1789	8	475
Brelsford, Marjoram (Belsford)	114	North Run	1831	3	227
Brelsford, Nathan B.	50	Knob Ridge	1831	3	224
Brewster—See Bruster					
Brill, Frederick W.	395	Spring Run	1850	7	292
Brill, Henry	28¾	Dry Run	1825	5	430
Brill, Henry	225	Gr. Cacapon	1851	7	301
Brill, Henry	50	Gr. Cacapon	1850	7	294
Brill, Henry	57	Timber Ridge	1849	7	263
Brill, Henry	15	Timber Ridge	1849	7	262
Brill, Henry et al	200	Gr. Cacapon	1850	7	295
Brill, Isaac	7¾	Lonan's Branch	1854	7	389
Brill, John	10	Gr. Cacapon	1850	7	293
Bringman, Henry	50	Sidling Hill	1815	5	156
Brown, Isaac	152	Chestnut Spg. Run	1788	8	35
Brown, John	496	Gr. Cacapon	1800	9	301
Brown, John	156	Gr. Cacapon	1800	9	261
Brown, John	198	Wiggin's Run	1809	5	36
Brown, John	640	Wiggin's Run	1809	5	13
Brown, John	392½	Lit. Cacapon	1770	5	568
Brown, John	402	Sidling Hill	1769	5	549
Brown, John	368	Gr. Cacapon	1768	5	531
Brown, Martin	590	Lit. Mountain	1792	6	161
Brown, Nathan	420	Lit. Cacapon	1791	6	102

Name of Grantee	Acres	Local Description	Year	Book	Page
Bute, Joseph (Buts)	375	Patterson Cr.	1788	8	45
Butler, Joseph Sr.	127	Potomac	1802	9	374
Buzzard, Edmund	161	Lit. Cacapon Mt.	1842	7	106
Buzzard, Frederick	18½	Owen's Ridge	1809	5	33
Buzzard, Frederick	40¾	Bear Garden Ridge	1809	5	35
Buzzard, Frederick	159	Adj. J. Slone	1812	5	82
Buzzard, Frederick	12a.3r.30p.	Adj. J. Buzzard	1812	5	86
Buzzard, Frederick	109	Bear Garden Ridge	1809	5	34
Buzzard, Jacob	10½	Tear Coat Cr.	1842	7	105
Byrn, Richard (Byron)	100	Parson's Run	1772	3	577
Byron, Richard	100	Parson's Run	1772	3	577
Cabrick—See Kabrick					
Cabrick, Peter	173	Dry Run	1815	5	168
Caldwell, Samuel	150	Wts. Potomac	1832	3	291
Cale, George	50	Big Cacapon	1823	5	376
Cale, George	150	Big Cacapon	1819	5	258
Calmes, William	47¼	South Branch	1821	5	326
Calvin—See Colvan					
Calvin, Joshua	363	So. Branch	1794	6	384
Calvin, Luther et al	173	Spring Gap Mt.	1821	5	353
Calvin, Robert	300	Lit. Cacapon	1809	5	31
Camblet—See Cramblet					
Campbell, John	439	Fairfax's Mill Lot	1789	8	292
Campbell, John	118	Mill Creek	1789	8	230
Campbell, John et al	388	South Branch	1788	8	68
Campbell, John et al	348	South Branch	1788	8	67
Candy or Caudy, Condy					
Candy, Evan et al	100	Adj. J. Candy	1813	5	128
Candy, James	75	Cacapon Mt.	1835	3	394
Candy, James	111	Timber Ridge	1766	1	313
Candy, John	60½	North River	1816	5	182
Candy, John	45	North River	1816	5	180
Candy, Michael	36½	Dillon's Run	1825	5	431
Candy, Michael	39½	Park Mountain	1825	5	421
Candy, Michael	69	Dillon's Run	1822	5	366
Cannon, George	109	Tear Coat	1822	5	359
Caplenner, John	1¼	Elswick's Run	1767	5	472
Caplenner, John	16	Adj. J. Mauzy	1767	5	471
Caplinger—See Caplenner					
Capper, John	47½	Isaac's Creek	1800	9	306
Capper, John	198½	Gr. Cacapon	1792	6	149
Capper, John	400	Broad Run	1789	8	378
Capper, John	250	Timber Ridge	1771	3	562
Carder, Abbot et al	77	Woodrow's Run	1828	3	124
Carder, William	14¼	Lit. Cacapon	1847	7	232
Carder, William	382	Meadow Run	1790	8	511
Carlin, Andrew	420	Spring Gap. Mtn.	1779	2	198
Carlin, Andrew et al	241	Lit. Cacapon	1800	9	298
Carlin, John	200	Lit. Cacapon	1798	9	155
Carlyle, Charles	9½	Gr. Cacapon	1833	3	319
Carlyle, Charles	6a.3r.	Gr. Cacapon	1833	3	315
Carlyle, John Col.	300	George's Run	1765	1	238
Carlyle, John et al	415	South Branch	1773	4	452
Carlyle, William	400	Lit. Mountain	1790	8	555
Carlyle, William	491	Adj. G. Horn	1789	8	381
Carlyle, William	210	Edward's Run	1789	8	379
Carlyle, William	50	Dillon's Run	1795	6	458
Carlyle, William	93½	Dillon's Run	1791	6	48
Carmichael, Daniel	12a.12p.	North River	1803	9	425
Carmichael, Robert	7¼	North River	1844	7	155
Carscadon—or Carskadon					
Carscadon, Thomas	150	Knobby Mt.	1836	3	434
Carscadon, Thomas	250	Stagg's Run	1809	5	9

Name of Grantee	Acres	Local Description	Year	Book	Page
Carscadon, Thomas (Carskaddon)	200	Middle Ridge	1822	5	358
Carskadon—Carscaden, Carscadon, Kerscadden					
Carskadon, Arthur & Thomas	122¼	Patterson's Cr.	1820	5	306
Carskadon, James	31	New Creek	1858	7	465
Carskadon, James	102	Middle Ridge	1856	7	411
Carskadon, James & I. H.	27	Mill Run	1860	7	515
Carter, Henry	124	N. River Mt.	1831	3	231
Carter, James	3a.20 pchs.	Pine Draught Run	1845	7	169
Caruthers—See Carruthers					
Caruthers, James	149	Adj. James Slater	1794	6	408
Caruthers, James	135	North River	1800	9	242
Carruthers, James	449	Adj. Lord Dunsmore	1789	8	463
Cary, Joseph	1,000	Gr. Cacapon	1796	6	553
Casey, Nicholas	79	Town Run	1789	8	434
Casey, Nicholas	132	South Branch	1789	8	433
Castleman, Jacob	106	So. Branch	1766	1	356
Castler, John	72	Cacapon Mt.	1799	9	195
Castler, John	16	Adj. his own & Johnson's	1799	9	189
Castler, Michael	179	Capt. John's Run	1765	1	271
Cathers, James	201	North River	1789	8	272
Cathers, Jasper	437	Patterson's Cr.	1789	8	273
Cathers, Jasper	400	North River	1789	8	276
Cathers, Jasper	266	Spring Gap Run	1789	8	277
Cathers, Jasper	250	Mike's Run	1789	8	282
Catlett, Hanson	255½	Patterson's Cr.	1820	5	312
Catterman—See Ketterman					
Catterman, Jacob	198	Mill Creek	1791	6	76
Caudy—See Candy, Condy					
Caudy, James	52	Gr. Cacapon	1799	9	221
Caudy, James	50	Gr. Cacapon	1806	9	558
Caudy, James	138	Dilling's Run	1806	9	557
Cavender, Garret	50	South Br. Mt.	1800	9	260
Caylor, Josiah	6¾	Spring Gap. Mt.	1854	7	390
Caylor, Nicholas	35	L. Cacapon	1834	3	375
Cerley, Thomas	154	Rocky Ridge	1791	6	16
Chadwick—See Chedwick					
Chamberlain, Jonas	14a.35p.	Patterson's Cr.	1823	5	382
Chamberline—See Chamberlain					
Chambers, Benjamin	36,000	New, Patterson, Looney's, Jordan Crs., and Stoney R.	1796	8	602
Champ, John	258	Abraham's Cr.	1779	2	226
Champ, John	162	Mike's Gap	1791	6	34
Chandler, Stephen	50-2/3	Patterson's Cr.	1796	6	513
Chapman, William	12	Town Hill	1798	9	176
Chapman, William	22	Lit. Cacapon	1794	6	407
Chedwick, Eli D.	82¼	Lit. Cacapon	1841	7	68
Chenoweth—See Chinoweth					
Chenoweth, John	238	North Branch	1792	6	135
Chenoweth, John	242	Cacapon Mt.	1789	8	406
Cheshir, or Cheshire					
Cheshir, John (of Obadiah)	22a.3r.	North River	1847	7	236
Cheshir, Obadiah	100	Hammack's Mt.	1852	7	341
Cheshire—See Cheshir					
Cheshire, John (Cheshir)	79	Tear Coat Creek	1831	3	246
Cheshire, John et al	100	Adj. J. Candy	1813	5	128
Cheshire, Samuel	151	Tear Coat Cr.	1789	8	455
Cheshire, Samuel	220	Tear Coat	1796	9	54
Chinoweth—See Chenoweth					
Chinoweth, John	70	Adj. his own	1800	9	305
Chisholm, Alexander	221	Gibbon's Run	1791	6	51
Chrisman, Jacob	270	Wts. Potomac	1789	8	380
Chrisman, Jacob	299	Sidling Hill	1789	8	483
Chritchfield, Benjamin	198¼	Plumb Run	1777	2	100

Name of Grantee	Acres	Local Description	Year	Book	Page
Coosick, Peter	200	Dry Run	1794	6	375
Copass, Thomas	40	Gr. Cacapon	1795	6	460
Copsey, John	37	Gr. Cacapon	1796	9	55
Corban, William	157	Lit. Cacapon	1789	8	493
Corbin, Benjamin	180	North River	1841	7	66
Corbin, Daniel	25	Cove Mt.	1800	9	241
Corbin, Daniel	83	Lit. Cacapon	1805	9	537
Corbin, Daniel	145	North River	1792	6	186
Corbin, Daniel	112	Grassy Lick Run	1809	5	7
Corbin, David	125	Lit. Cacapon	1800	9	319
Corbin, David	100	Lit. Cacapon	1800	9	295
Corbin, David	241	North River	1792	6	164
Corbin, David	440	Lit. Cacapon	1792	6	163
Corbin, David	103	Near Capper's and Scott	1792	6	162
Corbin, David	390	Tear Coat Cr.	1796	9	38
Corbin, David	2	Lit. Cacapon	1820	5	281
Corbin, David	446	Lit. Cacapon	1789	8	355
Corbin, David	580	Lit. Cacapon	1790	8	506
Corbin, David	393	Cacapon Wts.	1829	3	180
Corbin, Isaiah	186	Buck Mtn.	1850	7	281
Corbly, John	52	Gr. Cacapon	1765	1	279
Corder, John	361¾	Beaver Run	1767	5	505
Cornell, Cornwall, Cornwell					
Cornell, John	14½	Mill Creek	1858	7	469
Cornwall, Cornell, Cornwell					
Cornwell, William	100	Adj. M. Wheeler	1796	9	117
Cosick—See Coosick, Kooset, Koset					
Cossey—See Copsey....					
Covert, Burgin	352	Knobly Mt.	1791	6	42
Cowan, Robert (Cowin)	75	Adj. M. Colson	1796	6	523
Cowan, Robert	25	Adj. T. Johnson	1796	6	522
Cowden, James	60	Sidling Hill	1797	9	137
Cowden, James	135	Sidling Hill	1797	9	136
Cowden, James Sr.	394	Sidling Hill	1800	9	267
Cowden, James Sr.	64	Sidling Hill	1799	9	206
Cowgill, Elisha	80	Near J. Demoss's	1796	9	95
Cowgill, Henry	50	Town Hill	1843	7	128
Cowgill, Henry	3¾	Town Hill	1846	7	200
Cox, David	77½	Wts. Potomac	1772	3	585
Cox, Friend	240	Lit. Cacapon	1762	1	100
Cox, Friend	295 (195)	Wts. Potomac	1762	1	102
Cox, Gabriel	162	Wts. Potomac	1764	1	212
Cox, Isaac	78	Lit. Cacapon	1766	1	326
Cox, John	30	Lit. Cacapon	1765	1	231
Cracraft—See Crecroft					
Cracraft, Joseph	340	Gr. Cacapon	1777	2	88
Cracraft, Joseph Sr.	376	Gr. Cacapon	1792	6	253
Cracraft, William (Craicraft)	135	Gr. Cacapon	1768	5	532
Crain, John	200	Bear Wallow	1792	6	304
Cramblet—or Camblet					
Cramblet, Jacob	200	Sandy Ridge	1796	9	87
Crane—See Crain					
Crawfice, Margaret	100	Plum Run	1809	5	17
Crawfies, Margaret (Crawfice)	100	Plum Run	1809	5	17
Craigen, Robert	115	Walnut Thicket	1773	4	445
Craigen, Robert	315	Sidling Hill	1773	4	444
Craik, James	129	Parris Gap Run	1766	1	365
Craik, James Dr.	23	Gr. Cacapon	1761	1	75
Craik, James Dr.	400	North River	1771	3	556
Craik, James Dr.	131	Wts. Cacapon	1771	3	560
Craik, James et al	31	Daniel Wood's Run	1766	1	366
Craik, James et al	219	Dillon's Run	1766	1	367
Creamer, Mary	203	Adj. D. Vance	1761	1	60

Name of Grantee	Acres	Local Description	Year	Book	Page
Cunningham, James	300	South Branch	1806	9	560
Cunningham, John	436	Tear Coat Creek	1789	8	472
Cunningham, William	93½	Adj. R. Byrn	1790	8	535
Cunningham, William	135	Brand Mountain	1757	1	35
Cunningham, William	200	North River	1757	1	36
Cunningham, William	248	Mills Branch	1757	1	37
Cunningham, William	184	Cacapon	1757	1	38
Cupp—See Culp					
Cupp, David	10¾	Lit. Cacapon	1857	7	449
Cupp, David	11½	Lit. Cacapon	1857	7	450
Curtis, Edward	133	Chenoweth Run	1779	2	245
Cuthright, Peter	168	Sawmill Run	1792	6	279
Dailey—Daley, Dalley, Dayley					
Dailey, James et al	521	Muddy Run Mt.	1818	5	231
Dailey, James et al	86	Patterson's Cr.	1817	5	218
Dailey, James et al	15	Patterson's Cr.	1817	5	217
Dailey, James et al	645	Patterson's Cr.	1817	5	216
Dailey, James et al	26½	Patterson's Cr.	1817	5	215
Daley—Dailey, Dalley, Dayley					
Daley, Samuel (Dayley)	142	Adj. J. Champs	1789	8	351
Dall—See Doll					
Dall, Jacob	115½	Knobley	1812	5	104
Dalley—Dailey, Daley, Dayley					
Dalley, Philip	198	Tear Coat Cr.	1790	8	524
Dalton, John et al	415	South Branch	1773	4	452
Darby, Benjamin F.	78¾	Sandy Ridge	1853	7	358
Darby, John	4a.3r.	Big Cacapon	1825	5	417
Dasher, Christian	19	So. Branch	1794	6	338
Daton—See Dayton					
Daton, Isaac	300	South Branch	1794	6	398
Daugherty—See Dougherty					
Daugherty, William	460	L. Cacapon	1828	3	122
Davis—See Davise, Davey, also Drais					
Davis, Ebenezer	50	North Branch	1809	5	8
Davis, Jacob	145	South Branch	1788	8	105
Davis, John	5,000	Gr. Cacapon	1795	6	446
Davis, Joseph	100	North River	1802	9	393
Davis, Joseph	50	North River	1801	9	345
Davis, Joseph	85	Lick Run	1842	7	111
Davis, Joseph	62a.1r.	Adj. Robt. Sherrard	1842	7	94
Davis, Joseph	50	North Branch	1789	8	234
Davis, Joseph et al	740	North Branch	1842	7	114
Davis, Joseph & Reuben	150	Abram's Cr.	1852	7	306
Davis, Rachael	100	Deep Run	1796	9	129
Davis, Reuben	449	New Creek Mt.	1840	7	551
Davis, Reuben	49	Abraham's Cr.	1857	7	446
Davis, Reuben	251	Abram's Cr.	1852	7	305
Davis, Reuben	60	New Creek Mt.	1842	7	116
Davis, Reuben	40	New Creek	1829	3	141
Davis, Reuben	81a.2r.28p.	New Creek	1821	5	335
Davis, Reuben	88	New Creek	1842	7	100
Davis, Reuben	16a.10p.	New Creek	1829	3	149
Davis, Reuben et al	136a.3r.13p.	Adj. Blackburn, Cooper	1829	3	176
Davis, Samuel	50	Abram's Ridge	1810	5	62
Davis, Samuel	153	Knobly Mt.	1793	6	401
Davis, Samuel	100	Knobly Mt.	1798	9	175
Davis, Samuel B.	49¼	Frank's Gap	1827	3	107
Davis, Samuel B. Jr.	201½	Mill Run	1833	3	308
Davis, Theodore	236	Patterson's Cr.	1762	1	178
Davis, Thomas	130	Sidling Mt.	1815	5	167
Davis, Thomas	372	North River	1789	8	401
Davis, Walter	228	South Branch	1789	8	500
Davis, Walter	50	South Branch	1796	6	487

Name of Grantee	Acres	Local Description	Year	Book	Page
Doll, Abraham	19	Mike's Run	1843	7	144
Doll, Abraham	61	Mike's Run	1843	7	143
Doll, Abraham	105	Mike's Run	1833	3	335
Doll, Jacob	100	New Creek	1798	9	177
Doll, Daniel & George W.	56½	Knobly Mt.	1840	7	42
Dollahan, Daniel	100	Mill Creek	1801	9	336
Dolohon—See Dollahan					
Doman, Jacob	176	Branch Mt.	1800	9	258
Doman, John	30	Town Hill	1834	3	376
Doman, William	30	L. Cacapon	1831	3	222
Donald, Mary	50	Gr. Cacapon	1796	6	552
Donaldson, James	70	Green Spgs.	1800	9	288
Donaldson, John	222	Gr. Spgs. Run	1843	7	129
Donaldson, John	100	Green Spg. Valley	1792	6	165
Donaldson, William	97	Green Spgs. Run	1805	9	497
Donaldson, William	320	Gr. Spring Valley	1859	7	487
Donaldson, William et al	62½	Spring Valley	1859	7	486
Doran, Alexander	100	North River	1804	9	471
Doran, Alexander et al	300	North River	1819	5	248
Doran, David	14	Clay Lick Run	1852	7	327
Doran, William	167	North River	1824	5	393
Doran, William	29¾	Brushy Ridge	1824	5	399
Doran, William	88½	North River Mt.	1824	5	400
Dougherty—See Daugherty					
Dougherty, Hugh	460	Patterson's Cr.	1775	4	488
Douglass—See Duglas					
Douglass, James	219	So. Branch	1794	6	423
Douthat—See Douthit, Douthart					
Douthat, John (Douthart)	311½	Patterson's Cr.	1802	9	401
Douthit, Thomas	108	Mike's Run	1789	8	174
Dowdell, James G. et al	377	George's Run	1791	6	44
Dowdell, James G. et al	252½	Knobly Mt.	1791	6	43
Dowden, John	296	Adj. P. Cossick	1791	6	77
Dowden, John	337	Adj. G. Taylor	1791	6	82
Dowden, John	198	Beaver's Run	1791	6	87
Downey, Thomas	82	North Branch	1839	7	35
Doyle, Terence	326	North Branch	1779	2	237
Drais—See Davis					
Drais, Jacob	145	South Branch	1788	8	105
Drew, Betsy Ann et al	154¼	Lit. Cacapon	1833	3	316
Drew, Perez	407	Lit. Cacapon	1788	8	100
Drew, Perez	316	Lit. Cacapon	1788	8	101
Drew, Perez	433	Lit. Cacapon	1788	8	155
Drew, Perez	406	Swinburn's Run	1789	8	221
Drew, Perez	133	Lit. Cacapon	1796	9	73
Duckwalt, Lewis	410	Water Lick Run	1789	8	494
Duglas—See Douglas, Douglass					
Duglas, James	83	Near Trough	1791	6	90
Duling, William	192	New Creek	1849	7	265
Duling, William	21	Abram's Ridge	1841	7	63
Duling, William	82	New Creek	1835	3	416
Duncan—Dunkin					
Duncan, William Jr.	400	Adj. Elias Poston	1779	2	170
Duncan, William Jr.	408	Williamson's Run	1779	2	169
Dunkin, William	424	South Branch	1801	9	333
Dunmore, John Earl of	400	North River	1774	4	458
Dunmore, John Earl of	229	North River	1774	4	459
Dunmore, John Earl of	100a.3r.9p.	Short A. Mt.	1774	4	461
Dunmore, John Earl of	2,323	Pine Cabin Lick	1774	4	462
Dunmore, John Earl of	284	South Branch	1774	4	472
Dunmore, John Earl of	129	South Branch	1774	4	473
Dunn, Lewis T.	674	Patterson's Cr.	1856	7	403
Dye, John	107	Knobly Mt.	1838	7	28
Edgington—See Edginton					

Name of Grantee	Acres	Local Description	Year	Book	Page
Ellzey, Thomazin	494½	Patterson's Cr.	1792	6	225
Ellzey, Thomazin	448½	North Branch	1792	6	224
Ellzey, Thomazin	550	Loonie's Cr.	1792	6	223
Ellzey, Thomazin	450½	Lunies Creek	1792	6	222
Ellzey, Thomazin	411½	Lunies Creek	1792	6	221
Ellzey, Thomazin	276	Spring Gap Mt.	1791	6	39
Ellzey, Thomazin	449½(?)	Beaver Run	1773	4	446
Elmore, Mathias	400	Dillon's Run	1766	1	352
Elswick, Thomas	203	Mill Branch	1790	8	513
Elswick, Thomas	162	Clay Lick	1791	6	111
Ely—See Eley, Eli					
Ely, Benjamin	91	Lit. Cacapon	1841	7	62
Ely, William Sr. et al	154¼	Lit. Cacapon	1833	3	316
Elzey—See Ellzey					
Elzey, Thomazin	403	Abram's Cr.	1789	8	399
Elzey, Thomazin	406½	South Br. Mt.	1789	8	400
Elzey, Thomazin	517¾	Corn Run	1789	8	418
Elzey, Thomazin	445¾	Beaver Run	1789	8	419
Elzey, Thomazin	400	New Creek	1789	8	420
Elzey, Thomazin	400½	Great Run	1789	8	421
Elzey, Thomazin	448¼	Stony Lick Run	1789	8	422
Elzey, Thomazin	400¼	Abraham's Creek	1789	8	423
Elzey, William	308	Gr. Cacapon	1788	8	87
Emeory—(Amory) Emery, Emory					
Emeory, Edward	306	Patterson's Cr.	1778	2	140
Emeory, Edward	166	Wts. Potomac	1778	2	141
Emerson—See Emmerson					
Emerson, Thomas	50	Adj. J. Brookhart	1792	6	152
Emert—Emet, Emmitt, Emmert					
Emert, Jacob (Emmert)	120	North River	1774	4	482
Emery—(Amory) Emeory, Emory					
Emery, Edward	400	Allegheny Mt.	1805	9	495
Emet, Emert, Emmert, Emmitt					
Emet, Jacob	77	Cor. to Baker	1812	5	91
Emmerson—See Emerson					
Emmerson, Thomas	159	Turner's Mill Run	1788	8	116
Emmert—See Emet, Emert, Emmitt					
Emmert, George	189	North Fork	1780	8	593
Emmitt—Emet, Emert, Emmert					
Emmitt, Abraham	4½	North River	1845	7	170
Emory—Amory, Emery, Emeory					
Emory, Edward	400	Maple Run	1789	8	233
Emory, Edward	274	North Branch	1789	8	222
Engle, Isaac	67	Cacapon	1796	6	496
Engle, William	171	Dillon's Run	1787	8	7
Enoch, Henry	271½	Lit. Cacapon	1761	1	58
Enoch, Henry	278	Gr. Cacapon	1763	1	196
Enoch, Henry	100	Gr. Cacapon	1763	1	197
Enoch, Henry	57	North River	1764	1	225
Enoch, Henry Jr.	308	Lit. Cacapon	1765	1	277
Enoch, Henry Sr.	38	Enoch's Hollow	1762	1	176
Ernhalt, Andrew (Ernholt)	75	New Creek	1816	5	186
Eskridge, William & Elizabeth	405	North River	1789	8	301
Eskridge, William & Elizabeth	144	South Branch	1789	8	302
Ester, John	50	Grants Run	1804	9	477
Evans, Abel	50	North River	1854	7	365
Evans, Benjamin et al	40	New Creek	1815	5	145
Evans, Caleb	25a.20p.	Stack's Gap Run	1827	3	104
Evans, Mary	424	Tear Coat Cr.	1777	2	80
Evans, Peter	50	Dillion's Run	1853	7	362
Everman, Michael	71	South Branch	1791	6	95
Ewan, See Ewing					
Ewing, Thomas	367	Gr. Cacapon	1777	2	72

Name of Grantee	Acres	Local Description	Year	Book	Page
Ewing, Tristram (Ewan)	450	Grind Stone Ridge	1792	6	229
Ewing, Tristram (Ewan)	230	Grindstone Ridge	1792	6	187
Fahs, Philip	5¼	2 Lick Run	1845	7	171
Fahs, Philip Sr.	56¾	North River	1813	5	127
Fairfax, Ferdinand	26½	Potomac	1804	9	454
Fairfax, George William Col.	400	Wts. Potomac	1754	2	25
Fairfax, George Wm. Col.	400	Wts. Potomac	1754	1	14
Fairley, John (Fairly)	307	Patterson's Cr.	1796	9	5
Falkhimer—See Folkhimer					
Fankhouser, Funkhouser					
Fann, John	109	Elkhorn	1766	1	368
Farmer, Frances	100	Spring Gap Mt.	1830	3	185
Farr, John	109	Elkhorn	1766	1	368
Fathergill, Thomas	85	New Creek Mt.	1789	8	303
Fauber—See Fauver, Fawver					
Fauver—See Fauber, Fawver					
Fauver, Henry	50	Sidling Hill	1820	5	296
Fauver, Nicholas	100	Sidling Hill	1820	5	300
Fawver—See Fauber, Fauver					
Fawver, Henry	100	Bennett's Run	1809	5	18
Ferree, Cornelius	37	Cacapon	1799	9	220
Ferree, Cornelius	35½	Gr. Cacapon	1796	6	516
Ferree, Cornelius	789	Lit. Cacapon	1796	6	547
Ferree, Cornelius	200	Wiggin's Run	1796	6	550
Ferrill, William Henry	162	Hogs Lick Run	1791	6	25
Ferrill, William Henry	395	Wts. Potomac	1791	6	26
Fife, John	352	Patterson's Cr.	1769	5	542
Fink—See Finks					
Fink, Daniel et al	129½	Patterson Cr.	1818	5	242
Fink, Frederick	246	Patterson's Cr.	1789	8	304
Fink, Henry	100	Sugar Run	1804	9	444
Finks, Frederick	50	Middle Ridge	1798	9	157
Fisher, Adam	189	Middle Mountain	1787	8	1
Fisher, George	118	North Mill Cr.	1785	9	515
Flake—See Fleck, Fleek, Flick					
Flanagin—See Flaningham, Flenaghan					
Flanagin, Samuel (Flannegin)	149¾	Middle Ridge	1830	3	198
Flanagin, Samuel	73	Patterson Creek	1827	3	100
Flaningham—See Flanagin, Flenaghan					
Fleck—See Fleek, Flick					
Fleck, Henry	18½	Cabin Run	1806	9	548
Fleck, Jacob (Flake)	50	Plum Run	1792	6	280
Fleck, John	274	Cabin Run	1809	5	16
Fleek—See Fleck, Flick					
Fleek, Jacob	72	Knobby Mt.	1830	3	220
Fleet, Jacob	127a.3r.	Patterson Creek	1830	3	208
Fleming, James	107	Adj. Henry Naffle	1789	8	343
Fleming, James	12	Adj. S. Welch	1790	6	7
Fleming, James	354	Adj. H. Lightner	1791	6	8
Fleming, James	201	Patterson's Cr.	1791	6	54
Fleming, John	71	Tear Coat Cr.	1810	5	55
Fleming, Patrick	9¼	Adj. his own	1806	9	547
Flenaghan—See Flanagin, Flaningham					
Fletcher, Aaron	183	Mill Creek	1765	1	298
Fletcher, George	43½	Crooked Run	1829	3	181
Fletcher, Uriah	8¼	Bear Garden Ridge	1856	7	438
Flick—See Fleck, Fleek					
Flood, John	99	Plumb Run	1821	5	330
Flood, John	57	Patterson Cr.	1819	5	244
Flood, John	136	Plumb Run	1792	6	202
Flood, John	400	Plumb Run	1800	9	290
Flora, Thomas	91	Potomac	1800	9	317
Flowance, William Jr. (Florence)	243	Cabin Run	1805	9	504

Name of Grantee	Acres	Local Description	Year	Book	Page
Foley, Isaac et al	275	Long Lick Mt.	1843	7	142
Foley, Jasper et al Heirs	50	Mill Creek	1830	3	205
Foley, John	343	Tucker's Run	1789	8	360
Foley, John	342	Patterson's Cr. Mt.	1789	8	454
Foley, John	250	Mill Creek	1804	9	475
Folkhimer, John M.	100	Dillon's Run	1795	6	459
Foreman—See Forman					
Foreman, Benjamin	249	Lit. Cacapon	1789	8	348
Foreman, Benjamin	295	Gr. Cacapon	1806	9	546
Foreman, David et al	89¾	Parks Hollow	1829	3	136
Foreman, David et al	77½	Sandy Ridge	1826	3	87
Foreman, John	120	Wts. Potomac	1779	2	164
Foreman, John Jr.	58	South Br. Mt.	1792	6	297
Foreman, Samuel	15¼	Edward's Mt.	1820	5	270
Foreman, William	345	South Branch	1789	8	195
Forman—See Foreman					
Forman, Aaron	448	South Branch	1791	6	18
Forman, George	86	Adj. T. Edwards	1800	9	262
Forman, John	780	South Branch	1790	8	566
Forman, John	398½	The Branch	1790	8	567
Forman, John	208	Lit. Cacapon	1790	8	568
Forman, John	353	South Branch	1790	8	569
Forman, John	236	Sugar Tree Run	1790	6	5
Forman, William	195	Castleman's Run	1766	1	369
Forman, William	154a.2r.6p.	Wts. Potomac	1761	1	57
Forman, William	353	South Branch	1790	8	565
Forman, William et al	198	Patterson's Cr.	1788	8	137
Forman, William et al	200	South Branch	1788	8	136
Forman, William et al	180	New Creek	1788	8	134
Forster—or Foster					
Forster, Isaac	114	Spruce Run	1779	2	185
Foster, John et al	569	North Branch	1796	6	542
Foster, John et al	475	Knobly Mt.	1796	6	538
Foster, John et al	309	Plumb Run	1796	6	532
Foster, John et al	219	Plumb Run	1796	6	530
Foster, John et al	72	Knobly Mt.	1796	6	529
Foster, John et al	15	Knobly Mt.	1796	6	528
Foster, Nathaniel	91	Farmer's Run	1792	6	168
Fought—See Stephenfought					
Fout, Jacob & William	37	New Creek	1825	5	429
Fowler, Zachariah	100	Mill Cr.	1802	9	395
Fox, Absolam	276	Buffalo Lick Run	1780	2	272
Fox, Gabriel	90	Castleman Run	1831	3	252
Fox, Gabriel	400	Castleman's Run	1780	7	559
Fox, Gabriel & George	91	Castleman Run	1831	3	253
Fox, Jemima (Widow), et al Hrs.	980	Castleman's Run	1824	5	465
Fox, Vanse	268	Middle Ridge	1832	3	272
Fox, Vanse	100	South Branch	1820	5	320
Fox, William	1,173	Castleman's Run	1800	9	244
Fox, William	150	Castleman's Run	1800	9	245
Fox, William	278	Abraham's Cr.	1793	6	307
Fox, William	671	Abram's Creek	1797	9	131
Fox, William	101	Potomac	1797	9	134
Fox, William	77	Dry Run of Pat. Cr.	1799	9	202
Fox, William	10	South Branch	1811	5	68
Fox, William et al	404	North Branch	1792	6	166
Foxcraft—See Foxcroft					
Foxcraft, John et al	97	Pine Draught	1765	1	284
Foxcraft, John et al	175	Enoch's M. Run	1765	1	281
Foxcroft—See Foxcraft					
Foxcroft, John (James) et al	1,920	Enoch's Mill Run	1767	5	479
Foxcroft, John et al	243	Ross's Run	1773	3	593
Foxcroft, John et al	458	Enoch's M. Run	1773	3	592

Name of Grantee	Acres	Local Description	Year	Book	Page
Foxcroft, John et al	345	Enoch's M. Run	1771	3	567
Foxcroft, John et al	432	Tear Coat Run	1771	3	566
Foxcroft, John et al	24	Tear Coat Cr.	1771	3	555
Foxcroft, John et al	168	So. Branch	1769	5	539
Foxcroft, John et al	195	Gr. Cacapon	1767	5	481
Foxcroft, John et al	164	So. Branch	1767	5	480
Foxcroft, John et al	242(224)	Cor. to Mannor line	1767	5	478
Foxcroft, John et al	160	South Branch	1767	5	476
Foxcroft, Thomas	127	Bear Garden Ridge	1767	5	482
Frank, Michael	157	Spring Run	1770	5	580
French, James	65	Lit. Cacapon	1767	5	489
French, James	225	Lit. Cacapon	1767	5	485
French, Robert	38	Grassy Lick	1796	9	39
French, Robert	360	Grassy Lick	1796	9	37
French, Robert	400	Hairy Mountain	1796	9	31
French, Thomas et al	96	Stony Run	1859	7	502
French, William (of Robert)	13	Lit. Cacapon	1850	7	296
French, William	148⅝	South Branch	1812	5	105
French, William	51	Lit. Cacapon	1837	7	547
French, William	34	Stony Mt.	1845	7	172
French, William Jr.	50	Wts. of Potomac	1836	3	426
Friend, Andrew	252	Wts. Potomac	1763	1	198
Friend, Charles	126	Allegheny Mount.	1772	3	586
Friend, John	110	Wts. Potomac	1766	1	314
Friend, John	194	Wts. Potomac	1763	1	199
Friend, Nicholas	142	Wts. Potomac	1761	1	87
Friend, Nicholas & John	150	Wts. Potomac	1768	5	518
Fry—See Frye					
Fry, Christopher	210	Gr. Cacapon	1792	6	285
Fry, Henry	142	Adj. Thos. Little	1796	6	548
Fry, Henry	18	Gr. Cacapon	1795	6	481
Fry, Henry	53	Wts. Cacapon	1780	8	579
Fry, Henry	353	Gr. Cacapon	1780	8	580
Fry, Henry	53	Cacapon River	1765	1	311
Fry, Henry	213	Gr. Cacapon	1762	1	186
Fry, Henry	46	Cacapon River	1765	1	312
Fry, Joseph	138	Cacapon River	1766	1	348
Fryback, George	176	Wts. Potomac	1792	6	167
Fryback, John	258	Lit. Cacapon	1779	2	168
Frye—or Fry					
Frye, Benjamin	209	Gr. Cacapon	1789	8	407
Fuller, Stephen	50	Mill Cr.	1819	5	255
Fuller, William	50	South Branch	1819	5	263
Funkhouser, Daniel Jr. (Fankhouser)	214	Cacapon Mt.	1829	3	170
Gallant, James	200	Tear Coat	1767	5	483
Gallaway, Zorobable	17a.3r.	L. Cacapon	1829	3	173
Gardner, Elizabeth	135	Lit. Cacapon	1767	5	490
Garther, Elijah (Gather)	200	Romney Run	1800	9	237
Geelick—See Gulick					
Geno—Ganoe, Gunnoe					
Geno, Stephen	278	Stuart's Run	1800	9	274
George, Ellis	247	Sandy Ridge	1796	9	9
George, Joseph	30	Patterson's Cr.	1788	8	95
Gerstell, A.	122	Knobly Mt.	1860	7	517
Gibson, David	121	Patterson' Cr.	1843	7	131
Gibson, David	14	Patterson's Cr.	1845	7	173
Gibson, John	202	Lit. Cacapon	1780	6	603
Gibson, John	284	Lit. Cacapon	1780	6	602
Gick—See Glick, Guck					
Gick, Daniel (Glick)	100	Mill Creek	1805	9	499
Gick, Daniel	93½	Mill Creek	1828	3	120
Gilbert, George	52	Middle Ridge	1846	7	199

Name of Grantee	Acres	Local Description	Year	Book	Page
Hammock, or Hammack					
Hammock, Samuel	400	Gibbons Run	1828	3	127
Hand, James	191	Indian Run	1789	8	458
Hanes—See Haines, Haynes					
Hanes, Isaac	1½	Barton's Meadow	1856	7	414
Hanes, William	10a.28p.	Lewis's Run	1860	7	511
Hanes, William et al	634	Lewis Run	1854	7	378
Hannah, John	58	Lit. Cacapon Mt.	1845	7	175
Hannah, Stephen (Hannahs)	66	Wts. of Potomac	1834	3	367
Hannah, Stephen	10	Lit. Cacapon	1841	7	82
Hannah, Stephen	151	Lit. Cacapon	1841	7	81
Hannah, Stephen	67	South Branch	1840	7	44
Hannah's—See Hannah					
Hannum, Joseph	48½	Timber Ridge	1850	7	291
Hannum, Joseph	25½	Timber Ridge	1850	7	290
Hannum, Joseph	57	Timber Ridge	1850	7	289
Hannum, Joseph	107½	Big Cacapon	1842	7	95
Hansbrough—See Herbaugh					
Hansbrough, John	2¾	Rush Run	1852	7	331
Hardeman—Hardman, Hartman					
Hardin, John Sr.	100	McCracken's Run	1773	3	599
Hardin, John Sr.	44	Patterson's Cr.	1778	2	103
Hardin, John Sr.	211	Bird's Run	1778	2	116
Hardman—or Hartman					
Hardy, Israel	10¾	Gr. Cacapon	1852	7	319
Harlan—or Harland, Harlin					
Harlan, Aaron	100	Gr. Cacapon	1817	5	213
Harlan, Jesse	95	Gr. Cacapon	1815	5	146
Harland, Jesse	25	Gr. Cacapon	1796	9	61
Harland, Jesse	61	Gr. Cacapon	1796	9	57
Harlin, Aaron	18	Big Cacapon	1821	5	325
Harman, Adam	178	Mike's Run	1789	8	305
Harman, Thomas	100	High Knob	1772	3	578
Harness—See also Harris					
Harness, Adam	125	Loony's Cr.	1777	2	74
Harness, Adam	202½	Loony's Cr.	1777	2	75
Harness, Adam	143	Loony's Cr.	1777	2	76
Harness, George	198	Looney Cr.	1788	8	99
Harness, Leonard	89	Looney's Cr.	1788	8	162
Harness, Leonard	216	Looney's Cr.	1789	8	192
Harris—See also Harness					
Harris, George	125	Adj. J. Harris	1794	6	414
Harris, John	135	Lost River	1773	4	448
Harris, Nehemiah	336	Patterson's Cr.	1788	8	32
Harrison, Ann et al Heirs	34a.6p.	Mike's Run	1825	5	418
Harrison, Henry	50	New Creek	1847	7	223
Harrison, Henry	61	New Creek Mt.	1833	3	309
Harrison, Henry	11	New Creek	1832	3	278
Harrison, Mary	44a.	Mike's Run	1823	5	372
Harrison, Matthew	400	Middle Ridge	1768	5	529
Harrison, Robert	35½	Big Cacapon	1820	5	290
Harsell, Peter Jr.	17½	Patterson's Cr.	1848	7	258
Hartley, John	67	Patterson's Cr.	1764	1	226
Hartman—Hardman, Hardeman					
Hartman, George	20	Tear Coat Cr.	1852	7	318
Hartman, Henry (Hardeman)	164	Mill Creek	1789	8	170
Hartman, Henry	139	Mill Creek	1804	9	480
Hartman, Henry	163¼	Mill Creek	1812	5	107
Hartman, Henry	302	Mill Cr.	1789	8	190
Hartman, Jacob	100	Mill Creek	1806	9	552
Hartman, Peter	216	Mike's Run	1781	8	588
Hartman, Peter	75	Mill Creek	1831	3	264
Hartman, Peter et al	32a.1r.	Mill Creek	1831	3	263
Hartman, Peter et al	54¾	Mill Cr.	1831	3	261

Name of Grantee	Acres	Local Description	Year	Book	Page
Hartman, Peter & George	50	Mill Creek	1831	3	249
Hartshorn, William	412¾	Elkhorn Run	1776	2	41
Harvey, Elijah	145	Abram's Creek	1835	3	406
Harvey, Elijah	25	Abram's Creek	1835	3	391
Harvey, Reason	5½	Adj. E. L. Blackburn	1831	3	247
Harvey, Reason	22¾	No. Br. Potomac	1841	7	83
Harvey, Reason et al	136a.3r.13p.	Adj. Blackburn & Cooper	1829	3	176
Harvey, Reason et al	44¼	Adj. E. Smith	1841	7	86
Harvey, Reazin	31¾	North Branch	1821	5	346
Harvey, Samuel	50	North Branch	1837	7	3
Harvey, William	100	Abraham's Cr.	1829	3	152
Hatzenbeler—or Hotzenbeler					
Hawk—See Hawke, Hawks					
Hawk, Henry	340	Mill Creek	1789	8	328
Hawk, John	404	North River Mt.	1789	8	286
Hawk, John	386	Looney's Cr.	1789	8	178
Hawk, John	410	Oldacre's Run	1788	8	81
Hawke, Henry	22a.1r.28p.	Mill Creek	1830	3	204
Hawkins, John	280	North River	1789	8	476
Hawkins, John Sr.	90	North River	1810	5	60
Hawkins, William	40¾	North River Mt.	1829	3	137
Hawks—See Hawk, Hawke					
Hawks, Isaac & Mary	184	Cacapon	1791	6	71
Haws, Hawse (See also House, Howse)					
Haws, George	20	Lit. Cacapon	1852	7	328
Haws, George	25½	Tear Coat Cr.	1851	7	299
Haws, George	175	Lit. Cacapon	1838	7	27
Haws, George et al	100	Tear Coat Cr.	1836	3	418
Hawse, or Haws (See also House, Howse)					
Hawse, John	41	Clay Lick Run	1845	7	174
Hawse, John	105	Tear Coat Run	1835	3	390
Hayden, Belemas	437	Gr. Cacapon	1792	6	154
Hayden, William	950	Gr. Cacapon	1789	8	185
Haynes—See Haines, Hanes					
Haynes, Joseph	47½	Lit. Cacapon	1842	7	108
Hays, Gabriel	600	Gr. Cacapon	1803	9	418
Heare, Elisha P.	100	South Br.	1845	7	176
Hearsman—See Hersman, Hesman					
Hearsman, Casper	237	Beaver Run	1789	8	445
Hearsman, Christopher	171	Beaver's Run	1789	8	359
Heath—See Hieth, etc.					
Heath, Henry (Heth)	256	Cacapon River	1766	1	364
Heath, Henry	206	Maple Bottom	1762	1	129
Heath, Henry	131	Tear Coat Cr.	1762	1	128
Heath, Henry	115	North River	1762	1	127
Heath, Henry	161	Cacapon River	1762	1	126
Heath, Henry	246	Tearcoat Creek	1762	1	125
Heath, Jonathan	209	South Branch	1780	7	558
Heath, Jonathan	206	Timber Ridge	1792	6	200
Hedge, Solomon	250	New Creek	1762	1	164
Hedges, Silas	300	Patterson's Cr.	1761	1	62
Hegirty—Hagarty, Hagerty, Haggarty					
Hegirty, John	418	Crooked Run	1777	2	86
Heinzman, Henry	611	So. Branch	1817	5	202
Heitt—Hiat, Hiatt, Hiet, Hieth, Hiett, Hyatt, etc.					
Henderson, Alex, Attorney-in-Fact	576	Gibbon's Run	1789	8	391
Henderson, Alexander	306	Lit. Cacapon	1780	7	584
Henderson, Alexander	344	Lit. Cacapon	1780	7	585
Henderson, Alexander	400	Indian Camp Run	1780	7	586
Henderson, Alexander	400a.2r.	Town Hill	1780	7	587
Henderson, Alexander	404	Indian Camp Run	1780	7	588
Henderson, Alexander	400	Lit. Cacapon	1780	7	589
Henderson, Alexander	256	Lit. Cacapon	1780	7	590

Name of Grantee	Acres	Local Description	Year	Book	Page
Higgins, John	37	Crooked Run	1817	5	206
Higgins, John	440	Little Cacapon	1811	5	67
Higgins, John	134	Adj. P. Pendleton	1811	5	66
Higgins, John	77	Lit. Cacapon	1809	5	40
Higgins, John	22½	South Br. Mt.	1822	5	361
Higgins, John	373	Abraham's Cr.	1792	6	216
Higgins, John	90	South Br. Mt.	1800	9	315
Higgins, John	404	Warm Spring Ridge	1789	8	284
Higgins, John	370	Warm Spring Ridge	1789	8	410
Higgins, John	115	Wts. Potomac	1775	4	485
Higgins, John et al	400	Gr. Spring	1800	9	312
Higgins, John & James	359	Lit. Cacapon	1800	9	313
Higgins, John Jr.	122	Potomac River	1794	6	411
Higgins, Judiah	7	Potomac River	1796	9	120
Higgins, Robert	240	Lick Run	1777	2	73
Higgins, Robert	52	Tucker's Creek	1789	8	285
Higgins, Thomas (Higgans)	52	Wts. Potomac	1756	1	25
High, Elijah	42½	Mill Creek	1849	7	280
High, Elijah	46	Mill Cr.	1836	9	528
High, Frederick	25	Mill Creek	1832	3	298
High, Frederick	32	Mill Creek	1837	7	4
High, Frederick	150	Mill Creek	1804	9	487
High, Frederick	1,110	Mill Creek	1793	6	302
High, Frederick	100¾	Adj. H. Hawk	1812	5	78
High, Henry	39½	Mill Creek	1832	3	300
High, Henry	21½	Mill Creek	1830	3	183
High, Henry M.	43	Fodder House Knob	1856	7	408
High, Henry M.	13¼	Mill Creek	1856	7	410
High, John	100	Mill Cr.	1789	8	311
High, John	213	Stone Lick Run	1789	8	293
High, John	400	Mill Creek	1789	8	176
High, John	84	Mill Cr.	1788	8	50
Hill, Charles	170	Johnson's Run	1801	9	340
Hill, Daniel	122	Lost River	1778	2	133
Hill, George	281½	Putnam's Run	1819	5	450
Hill, Leroy	9½	Mill Run	1802	9	363
Hill, William	73	Patterson's Cr.	1802	9	362
Hilley, Frederick (Hieley)	100	Town Gap	1797	9	145
Himmelwright, Joseph (Himelwright)	267½	North River	1779	2	244
Himmelwright, Joseph	198	North Mountain	1779	2	191
Hines—Hynes					
Hinkle, Paul	12	Wts. Elkhorn	1794	6	418
Hire, Peter	79	Indian Creek	1790	8	517
Hite, Abraham Col.	324	Mill Creek	1765	1	237
Hite, Abraham Col.	360	Van Meter's Run	1765	1	236
Hite, Abraham	400	Mill Creek	1768	5	527
Hite, Abraham	398	Hickory Bottom	1776	2	34
Hite, Abraham Major	200	Van Meter's Run	1762	1	112
Hite, Abraham Major	110	South Branch	1762	1	113
Hite, Isaac	380	North River	1770	5	573
Hite, Isaac	399	Wts. Patterson Cr.	1776	2	33
Hite, Isaac	7¾	Bear Garden Ridge	1859	7	490
Hite, Isaac Jr. et al	35	Wts. Potomac	1793	6	362
Hite, John Col.	212	Cacapon	1762	1	109
Hite, John Col.	207	Cacapon	1762	1	108
Hite, John Col.	151	Cacapon Creek	1762	1	107
Hitts, Jacob (Mitts)	87	Cedar Swamp	1762	1	181
Hoddy—or Haddy					
Hoddy, Richard	100	Georges' Run	1797	9	152
Hoff—See Huff					
Hoff, Luke	4a.3r.	Potomac River	1791	6	101
Hoffman—See Huffman					

Name of Grantee	Acres	Local Description	Year	Book	Page
Hoffman, Conrad	219	South Branch	1789	8	200
Hoffman, Henry	210	Bear Wallow	1780	7	564
Hoffman, Henry K. et al	62½	Spring Valley	1859	7	486
Hoffman, John	104	Stony Run	1780	7	577
Hogan, William	137	Mike's Run	1796	9	35
Hogan, William	131	Abram's Ridge	1796	9	33
Hogan, William	162	Knobly Mt.	1799	9	183
Hoge, Solomon	75	South Branch	1804	9	459
Hoge, Solomon	25	South Branch Mt.	1804	9	460
Hogland, Cornelius	100	Patterson's Cr.	1791	6	80
Holdmand—See Halmand					
Holdmand, Peter	266	Gr. Cacapon	1771	3	557
Hole, Hanna et al	272	Patterson's Cr.	1779	2	217
Holenback—Hallenback, Hollenback, Hollinback, Hollingback					
Holenback, Thomas (Hollenback)	470	Patterson's Cr.	1794	6	377
Hollenback—Hallenback, Holenback, Hollinback, Hollingback					
Hollenback, Daniel	29½	Middle Ridge	1833	3	331
Hollenback, Isaac	54	Patterson's Cr.	1856	7	435
Hollenback, Thomas	441½ (441¼)	Knobly Mt.	1805	9	472
Hollenback, Thomas	100	Knobly Mt.	1798	9	173
Hollenback, Thomas	168	Patterson's Cr.	1794	6	383
Holliday, John	480	Patterson's Cr.	1767	5	508
Holliday, Richard	50	Patterson's Cr. Mt.	1823	5	374
Hollinback—Hallenback, Holenback, Hollenback, Hollingback					
Hollinback, Daniel (Hollingback)	17	Patterson's Cr.	1825	5	437
Hollinback, Daniel (Hollingback)	250¼	Patterson's Cr.	1825	5	438
Hollinback, Daniel	100	Patterson's Cr.	1809	5	42
Hollowell, Thomas	247	Mill's Branch	1764	1	213
Holmand, Peter	266	Gr. Cacapon	1771	3	557
Holme—See Holmes					
Holme, Ebenezer	400	New Creek	1764	1	224
Holmes, David	790	Dillon's Run	1790	8	532
Holmes, David	1,200	North River	1790	8	531
Holmes, David	122	Adj. G. Martin	1790	8	530
Holmes, David	220	Wagon Road	1792	6	120
Holmes, Ebenezer	400	Patterson's Cr.	1765	1	257
Holmes, Ebenezer	400	Patterson Cr.	1755	1	22
Holmes, Hugh	840	Winchester Road	1801	9	328
Holmes, Hugh	3,550	South Br. Mt.	1801	9	327
Holmes, Hugh	2,600	South Br. Mt.	1801	9	326
Holmes, Joseph	400	Murphy's Run	1774	4	471
Holtz—See Hultz					
Homan, Sethman	56	Potomac River	1784	9	510
Homan, Sethman	43	South Branch	1784	9	511
Hoober—See Hubar					
Hoober, Jacob	57	Gr. Cacapon	1800	9	300
Hook, Samuel	69	Stony Mt.	1858	7	477
Hook, Samuel	90	Bear Garden Ridge	1858	7	472
Hook, Thomas	18	Timber Ridge	1825	5	439
Hopkins, James	166	Patterson's Cr.	1811	5	445
Horn, George	191	Dillon's Run	1791	6	108
Horn, George	183	Gr. Cacapon	1791	6	99
Horn, George	83	Gum Spgs. Hollow	1833	3	337
Horn, George Jr.	50	Tear Coat Cr.	1792	6	153
Horn, Henry	144	Tear Coat	1796	9	12
Horn, John	5½	Tear Coat Cr.	1843	7	147
Horn, John	5½	Tear Coat Cr.	1843	7	146
Hornback, Isaac	222	South Branch	1778	2	111
Hornback, Simon & James	135	South Branch	1779	2	183
Horner, Stephen	292	North River	1766	1	360
Hott, David	124	Piney Mt.	1849	7	266
Holt—See Hott					
Hott, Conrod	32	Sandy Ridge	1829	3	154
Hott, David & George	49	Stony Mt.	1840	7	43

Name of Grantee	Acres	Local Description	Year	Book	Page
Hott, David	65	Hairy Mt.	1844	7	165
Hott, David & George	250	Hairy Mt.	1835	3	412
Hott, George & David	418	Piney Mt.	1842	7	121
Hott, Samuel	200	Adj. McBride	1811	5	71
Hottle—See also Huddle					
Hottle, George	400	Fry's Run	1825	5	409
Hotzenbeler, Hotzenpiller, Hutzenpeller					
Hotzenbeler, Peter	220½	Pond Branch	1773	4	450
Hotzenbeler, Peter	193	Dry Run	1777	2	70
Hotzenbeler, Peter	268	Warm Spgs. Run	1796	6	551
Hotzenbeler, Stephen	181	Pond Branch	1773	3	598
Hotzenbeler, Stephen	127	Dry Run	1777	2	68
Hotzenbeler, Stephen Jr.	68½	Pond Branch	1773	4	449
Hotzenpiller, Hotzenbeler, Hutzenpeller					
Hotzenpiller,Henry	194	Cacapon	1800	9	269
Hough, John	77	Patterson's Cr.	1796	6	502
Hough, John	91	Thompson Run	1794	6	393
Hough, John	200	South Branch	1774	4	480
House—Howse (See also Haws, Hawse)					
House, Andrew	223	North Branch	1788	8	75
House, George	14	Knobby Mtn.	1830	3	211
House, George	67	Knobby Mt.	1831	3	251
House, Jacob	162	South Fork	1791	6	46
House, Jacob	150	South Br.	1791	6	45
House, James	315¼	Sidling Hill	1812	5	100
House, John	15	Bird's Run	1810	5	52
House, John	24	Potomac River	1815	5	163
House, John	408	North Branch	1779	2	246
House, John	74	Wts. Potomac	1792	6	278
House, John	14a.3r.	Potomac	1799	9	216
House, John	50	Adj. his own	1796	9	112
House, Joseph	419	Patterson's Cr.	1791	6	93
House, Samuel	90	Knobly Mt.	1814	5	138
House, Samuel Jr.	32½	North Branch	1852	7	329
House, William	177	Dillon's Run	1789	8	480
Howard, John	43	Gr. Cacapon	1804	9	453
Howard, John	80	Gr. Cacapon	1807	5	1
Howard, Reason	441	Gibbon's Run	1779	2	173
Howe—See Hough					
Howse—See Hawse, Haws, House					
Hoye, John	118	Myer's Run	1847	7	231
Hoye, John	326½	Knobly Mt.	1848	7	244
Hoye, John	80½	North Branch	1820	5	316
Hoye, William W.	145	Potomac River	1796	9	100
Hoye, William W.	555	Potomac River	1796	9	99
Hubar, Jacob	213	Gr. Cacapon	1796	6	519
Hubbard, Jacob	40	North River	1789	8	474
Huddle—See also Hottle					
Huddle, George	409	Trout Run	1772	3	579
Huddle, George	404	Trout Run	1772	3	580
Huddle, George	200	Trout Run	1772	3	581
Huddle, George	220	Trout Run	1772	3	582
Huddle, George	220	Trout Run	1772	3	583
Huff—See Hoff					
Huff, Abraham	279	Gr. Cacapon	1789	8	497
Huff, Cornelius	73	Wts. Potomac	1790	8	570
Huff, John	60	Big Cacapon	1820	5	310
Huffman—See Hoffman					
Huffman, Christian	44	High Knob	1840	7	54
Huffman, Joseph	8½	North River	1846	7	201
Huffman, Joseph	80	Marshall Ridge	1841	7	85
Hugh—See Hughes, Hughs					
Hugh, Sethman	43	South Branch	1784	9	511

Name of Grantee	Acres	Local Description	Year	Book	Page
Jacobs, John J.	61½	Prater's Run	1825	5	432
Jacobs, John J.	5½	Potomac River	1796	9	123
Jacobs, John J.	6	Adj. his own	1796	9	122
Jacobs, John J.	8-1/10	Adj. his own	1804	9	440
Jacobs, John J.	106	Lick Run	1790	8	521
Jacobs, Joseph	27	Knobly Mt.	1802	9	364
Jacobs, Samuel	406	Mike's Run	1781	8	591
James, Evan	15¾	North Branch	1804	9	482
Jefferson, Luke	209	Cacapon Mt.	1789	8	218
Jenkins—See Junkins					
Jenkins, Jacob	252	Cacapon	1766	1	370
Jenkins, Jacob	353 (355)	Huntsman's Branch	1766	1	372
Jenkins, Jacob	19	Owen's Ridge	1796	9	124
Jenkins, Jacob	233¾	Ivory Run	1817	5	198
Jenkins, Jacob	42⅞	Bear Garden	1815	5	165
Jenkins, Jacob	128½	Sidling Hill	1812	5	110
Jenkins, Jacob	106½	Keyth's Run	1812	5	90
Jenkins, Jacob	24a.3r.	Gr. Cacapon	1780	6	594
Jenny—See Jenney					
Jenny, William (Jeney)	100	New Creek	1789	8	501
Jenny, William (Jenney)	6	New Creek	1850	7	283
Jenny, William	71	New Creek	1789	8	366
Jenny, William	12½	North Branch	1800	9	309
Jenny, William	400	New Creek	1791	6	21
Jenny, William	390a.6p.	New Creek	1792	6	195
Job, Jacob	181	South Br.	1788	9	534
Johnson—or Johnston					
Johnson, Abraham	46	Cabin Run	1777	2	67
Johnson, Abraham	36½	Patterson's Cr.	1852	7	332
Johnson, Abraham Jr.	275	Patterson's Cr.	1789	8	245
Johnson, Abraham Jr.	206	Patterson's Cr.	1789	8	244
Johnson, Abraham Jr.	219	Patterson's Cr.	1789	8	443
Johnson, Abraham Jr.	58	Adj. Job Bacorn	1789	8	444
Johnson, Isaac	5¼	Green Springs V.	1812	5	111
Johnson, Isaac	119½	Green Springs	1804	9	489
Johnson, Jacob	154 (154½)	Patterson's Cr.	1854	7	399
Johnson, John	268	Lit. Cacapon	1762	1	101
Johnson, John	45	Lit. Cacapon	1779	2	238
Johnson, John	58	Lit. Cacapon	1779	2	239
Johnson, John	400	Patterson's Cr.	1768	5	534
Johnson, John	250	Patterson's Cr.	1768	5	536
Johnson, John	60	Rock Gap Run	1809	5	47
Johnson, John et al	173	Spring Gap. Mt.	1821	5	353
Johnson, John W. et al	14⅝	Gr. Cacapon	1852	7	320
Johnson, Joseph (of John)	100	Lit. Cacapon	1816	5	193
Johnson, Joseph	166	Bloomery Run	1820	5	283
Johnson, Joshua	7	Potomac River	1796	9	125
Johnson, Okey	128	Sheet's Run	1828	3	118
Johnson, Okey	316	Sheetz Run	1836	7	519
Johnson, Okey	72	Rows Run	1828	3	131
Johnson, Okey	200	Patterson's Cr.	1767	5	487
Johnson, Okey	200	Middle Ridge	1820	5	318
Johnson, Thomas	70	Big Cacapon	1820	5	309
Johnson, Thomas	18¼	Big Cacapon	1820	5	287
Johnson, Thomas	51¾	Gr. Cacapon	1820	5	267
Johnson, Thomas	212	Gr. Cacapon	1837	7	540
Johnson, Thomas	85	Bloomery Run	1837	7	539
Johnson, William	122	Wolf Run	1834	3	365
Johnson, William	81	G. Cacapon	1834	3	356
Johnson, William	200	Capt. John's Run	1775	4	490
Johnson, William	150	Patterson's Cr.	1789	8	171
Johnston—or Johnson					
Johnston, Ephriam	50	Gr. Cacapon	1796	9	2

Name of Grantee	Acres	Local Description	Year	Book	Page
Keller, George	222	Trout Run	1788	8	47
Keller, John	300	Patterson's Cr.	1779	2	197
Keller, John	400	Patterson's Cr.	1796	6	543
Keller, John	309	Clay Lick Run	1796	6	497
Keller, John	177	Lit. Cattail Run	1800	9	255
Kelso, James	300	Lemon's Br.	1821	5	328
Kennedy, Samuel	130	Patterson's Cr.	1768	5	537
Kennedy, Samuel	113	Stradler's Run	1768	5	538
Kennedy, Samuel	408	Parker's Run	1787	8	29
Kennedy, Thomas	297(279)	Adj. Evan Hyatt	1789	8	388
Kennedy, William et al	377	George's Run	1791	6	44
Kennedy, William et al	252½	Knobly Mt.	1791	6	43
Kent, John	25	Patterson's Cr.	1797	9	151
Kent, John	48	Cabin Run	1798	9	147
Keran, Kearnes, Kearns, Kerns					
Keran, Patrick & Peter	245	Adj. his own	1789	8	431
Keran, Patrick	406	Tear Coat Cr.	1788	8	160
Keran, Peter	329	Cabin Lick Run	1788	8	71
Keran, William	50	Tear Coat	1800	9	282
Kerns, Kearns, Kearnes, Keran					
Kerns, Frederick	82	Spring Gap Mt.	1843	7	133
Kerns, Nathan	5½	Timber Ridge	1838	7	26
Kerns, Nathan (of George)	175	Timber Ridge	1833	3	306
Kerscadden, Carskadon, Carscaden, Carscadon.					
Kerscadden, Arthur	62	Patterson's Cr.	1816	5	175
Kerscadden, Arthur	70	Patterson's Cr.	1815	5	149
Kesler, John S.	573	L. Cacapon	1832	3	302
Kesler, John S.	80	Potomac River	1819	5	246
Kesler, John S.	538½	Lit. Cacapon	1823	5	461
Ketterman—See Catterman					
Key, James	32	Gr. Cacapon	1794	6	410
Keyes, Humphrey	123	Hanging Rock Run	1778	2	128
Keyes, Humphrey	1,244	Hanging Rock Run	1778	2	127
Keyes, Humphrey	213	Tear Coat Cr.	1778	2	126
Keys, Humphrey (Keyes)	400	Hanging Rock Run	1771	3	565
Keys, Humphrey (Keyes)	170	Enoch's Mill Run	1771	3	564
Kidner, George	130	Lost River	1789	8	265
Kidner, Nicholas	108	Baker's Run	1793	6	350
Kidwell, John	10a.1r.25p.	Big Cacapon	1826	3	97
Kidwell, John S.	71¼	North River Mt.	1854	7	367
Kiger—See Kyger					
Kiger, John	280	Chestnut Ridge	1779	2	152
Kiger, John	173	Chestnut Ridge	1779	2	153
Kight, John M.	355¼	North Branch	1854	7	385
Kight, John M.	6½	Wts. Potomac	1854	7	384
Kight, John M. (Joseph)	265¼	North Branch	1854	7	386
Kile—See Kyle					
Kile, Robert	346a.19p.	Knobly Mt.	1789	8	262
Kimball, John (Kimbill)	169	Clay Lick Run	1779	2	254
Kincheloe, Daniel	384	Gr. Cacapon	1789	8	371
Kincheloe, Daniel	192	Spring Gap Run	1789	8	370
Kincheloe, Daniel	398	Wts. Cacapon	1789	8	376
Kincheloe, Daniel	404	Gr. Cacapon	1789	8	375
King, Alexander	50	Adj. D. Black	1809	5	41
King, Alexander	1,200	Deep Run	1795	6	439
King, Alexander	136	Cabin Run	1795	6	436
King, Alexander	583	North Branch	1792	6	209
King, Alexander	1,090	North River	1798	9	158
King, Reasin	5a.3r.20p.	North River	1857	7	459
King, Reasin	4¾	North River	1856	7	441
King, Valentine	362	Wts. Potomac	1791	6	57
Kinsey, William	66	Lost River	1762	1	144
Kirk, Patrick	168	Patterson's Cr.	1788	8	33

Name of Grantee	Acres	Local Description	Year	Book	Page
Lane, William	169	Howell's Run	1794	6	342
Lane, William	200	Elk Garden	1794	6	341
Langham, Elias	391	Wts. Potomac	1796	6	518
Langham, Elias	300	Potomac River	1796	9	105
Lantz, Daniel	35	Green Spring	1802	9	371
Laramore—See Larrimore					
Laramore, James (Laramon)	76	Lit. Cacapon	1801	9	343
Laramore, James et al	241	Lit. Cacapon	1800	9	298
Lare, Nathan	19a.1r.23p.	North River	1827	3	106
Larew—Larue, LaRue, Lerue, LeRue					
Larew, John	26	Gr. Cacapon	1798	9	169
Larew, Lambert	495	Big Cacapon	1823	5	458
Larew, Peter	70	Gr. Cacapon	1796	9	46
Larew, Peter	425	Tear Coat Cr.	1830	3	221
Largent—See Sargent					
Largent, Aaron	173	Gr. Cacapon	1838	7	25
Largent, James	93	North River	1799	9	219
Largent, James	80	Adj. T. Daugherty	1792	6	138
Largent, James	152½	Gr. Cacapon	1792	6	133
Largent, James	184	Adj. J. Prunty	1787	8	6
Largent, James	102	Gr. Cacapon	1780	7	580
Largent, John (of Lewis)	73	North River Mt.	1836	3	427
Largent, John (of Lewis) et al	39½	North River Mt.	1829	3	177
Largent, John	14	Gr. Cacapon	1810	5	56
Largent, John	76	Big Cacapon	1828	3	109
Largent, John et al	400	Wts. Cacapon	1789	8	269
Largent, John et al	430	Drains of Cacapon	1789	8	268
Largent, John H.	11½	Cedar Hill	1853	7	350
Largent, John W. (Sargent)	112	Gr. Cacapon	1841	7	88
Largent, John W.	120	Little Mtn.	1834	3	361
Largent, John W.	17½	North River	1852	7	339
Largent, Joseph	18½	Jerry's Run	1841	7	58
Largent, Joseph & John	73	North River Mt.	1841	7	57
Largent, Lewis Jr.	78¾	Gr. Cacapon	1836	3	421
Largent, Randolph et al	124	Devil's Nose Mt.	1843	7	126
Largent, William	144	North River	1832	3	293
Largent, William	100	North River	1834	3	382
Largent, William	113	North River Mt.	1836	3	432
Larrimore—See Laramore					
Larrimore, Samuel	115	South Branch	1844	7	159
LaRue, Larew, Larue, LeRue, Lerue					
Larue, John	511	Gr. Cacapon	1796	9	42
Larue, John	205	Lit. Mtn.	1789	8	412
Laubenger—See Labinger, Lovinger					
Laubenger, Michael	63	Green Spg.	1802	9	400
Laubenger, Michael	247	South Branch	1802	9	405
Laubinger, George M.	100	Sugar Camp	1804	9	463
Laubinger, Michael	294	Mill's Branch	1789	8	465
Laubinger, Michael et al	400	Gr. Springs	1800	9	312
Laughlin, James	166	Cox's Run	1790	8	549
Laugham—See Langham					
Laurence—See Lawrence					
Lawrence, Michael (Laurence)	80	Gr. Cacapon	1780	8	600
Lawson, James	400	Farley's Run	1788	8	53
Lawson, Moses	14a.1r.20p.	Adj. J. Keller	1791	6	29
Lawson, Thomas	434	Patterson's Cr.	1779	2	235
Lawson, Thomas	190	Young's Run	1779	2	234
Lawson, Thomas	458	Patterson's Cr.	1779	2	195
Lawson, Thomas	6½	Ashby's Fort	1788	8	44
Lawton, John W.	13¼	North Branch	1856	7	416
Lay—Leigh (See also Loy, Say)					
Lazenby—Leazenby, Lezenby					
Lazenby, Thomas (Lazenbe)	50	Middle Ridge	1795	6	476

Name of Grantee	Acres	Local Description	Year	Book	Page
Lyons, Elijah	66	George's Run	1820	5	315
Lyons, Elisha	211(207)	Horse Shoe Ridge	1819	5	259
Lyons, Elisha	100	Cabin Run	1816	5	191
Macker, James	358	North Branch	1794	6	366
Macker, James	25	Wts. Potomac	1794	6	365
Macker, James	500	North Branch	1794	6	364
Mackey, Robert Dr.	430	Wms. Run	1778	2	104
Macracken—McCracken					
Macracken, William	69	Wts. Potomac	1779	2	218
MacRae, Ann	198	Maple Bot. Br.	1768	5	523
Maddox, Thomas	192	Great Cacapon	1765	1	333
Magill, Archibald	500	South Branch	1790	8	510
Mahan, William	341	Lit. Timber Ridge	1766	1	380
Mahany, Stephen	105	Deer Lick	1796	6	495
Malick—See Melick					
Malick, David	7½(47½)	North River	1845	7	181
Malick, James	128	Short A Mt.	1849	7	271
Malick, James et al	108	Tear Coat Cr.	1849	7	272
Malick, John (Malic)	29½	Tear Coat Cr.	1818	5	227
Malick, John	185	Tear Coat	1811	5	74
Malick, John	16½	Tear Coat	1842	7	104
Malick, Philip	131½	North River	1845	7	182
Malick, Philip	73	Tear Coat Cr.	1834	3	384
Malone, Hugh	260a.10p.	Mill Creek	1789	8	201
Manifee, Gerrard	227	Cacapon	1762	1	111
Manifee, Jonas	333	Maple Branch	1762	1	110
Mansar—See Mousar					
Marquis, Richard	355	Warm Spring	1763	1	209
Marquis, Richard	413	Capt. John's Run	1763	1	210
Marquis, Richard	659	Warm Spring Ridge	1792	6	288
Marshall, Benjamin H.	40	South Br. Mt.	1792	6	248
Marshall, John	100	North Branch	1828	3	108
Marshall, Thomas	288	North River	1789	8	333
Marshall, Thomas	377	Scagg's Run	1789	8	364
Marshall, Thomas	377	Skaggs Run	1792	6	246
Marshall, Thomas	400	North River	1792	6	247
Martin, Christopher	412	Mill Cr.	1789	8	346
Martin, George	282¾	North River	1794	6	406
Martin, George Jr.	182	Gibbon's Run	1800	9	314
Martin, James	103	Adj. Wm. Poole	1794	6	394
Martin, James	179	Lit. Cacapon	1794	6	395
Martin, James	550	North River	1800	9	249
Martin, James	200	Cor. Joseph Johnson	1800	9	268
Martin, James	100	North River	1800	9	277
Martin, James	104	Rocky Branch	1800	9	289
Martin, James	200	North Branch	1800	9	304
Martin, John	98a.1r.22p.	North Br. Mt.	1824	5	396
Martin, John	17½	North Branch	1820	5	323
Martin, John	160	North Branch	1790	8	534
Martin, John	4a.2r.9p.	Wts. of Potomac	1830	3	203
Martin, Joseph	32½	North River	1841	7	64
Martin, Joseph	9	North River	1846	7	220
Martin, Joseph	8a.25p.	North River	1824	5	398
Martin, Joseph et al	200	North River	1816	5	184
Martin, Luther Jr.	337	Wts. Potomac	1817	5	210
Martin, Nehemiah	304	Wts. Potomac (Lot 6)	1766	1	376
Martin, Philip Esq.	10,000	Patterson's Cr.	1767	5	501
Martin, Samuel	157	Patterson's Cr.	1789	8	214
Martin, Thomas B.	750	Trout Pond	1768	5	530
Martin, Thomas B.	1,550	Wappacome & Mud Lick Run	1767	5	502
Martin, Thomas B.	54,596	Gr. So. Fork	1767	5	499
Martin, Thomas B.	332	Patterson's Cr.	1792	6	184
Martin, Thomas B.	275	North Br.	1792	6	183

Name of Grantee	Acres	Local Description	Year	Book	Page
McBride, John et al	30	Adj. James Powell	1797	9	130
McBride, Joseph	15½	Lit. Cacapon	1854	7	379
McBride, Peter	103	Lit. Cacapon	1841	7	78
McBride, Robert	69	Tear Coat	1802	9	396
McBride, Thomas et al	53-¾	Big Cacapon	1813	5	114
McBride, Wilson	40	Lit. Cacapon Mt	1845	7	196
McCalley, See McCawley					
McCarroll, Nathianel	174	Lit. Cacapon	1762	1	184
McCarty, Edward (Macarty)	50	Adj. his own	1796	9	103
McCarty, Edward	192	Knobly Mt.	1788	8	49
McCarty, Edward	401	Limestone Run	1789	8	173
McCarty, Edward	66	Knobly Mt.	1815	5	166
McCarty, Edward	63	Knobly Mt.	1818	5	224
McCarty, Edward	9	North Branch	1800	9	233
McCarty, Edward	29	North Branch	1800	9	236
McCarty, Edward	650	Mill Creek	1800	9	291
McCarty, Edward et al	26½	Patterson's Cr.	1817	5	215
McCarty, Edward et al	645	Patterson's Cr.	1817	5	216
McCarty, Edward et al	15	Patterson's Cr.	1817	5	217
McCarty, Edward et al	86	Patterson's Cr.	1817	5	218
McCarty, Edward et al	521	Muddy Run Mt.	1818	5	231
McCarty, Patrick	70	Wts. Potomac	1762	1	175
McCarty, Thomas	108	Mud Lick	1788	8	93
McCarty, Thomas	31	South Branch	1788	8	124
McCarty, Thomas	405	Adj. Neville	1789	8	460
McCarty, Thomas	35	Mud Lick	1795	6	425
McCave, Ross	404	Luney's Creek	1780	2	271
McCave, Ross	400	Luney Creek	1780	2	269
McCawley, George (McCalley)	71-¾	North River	1812	5	88
McConkey, See McKonkey					
McConkey, Samuel	50	South Branch	1794	6	368
McConkey, Samuel	93	South Branch	1792	6	239
McCracken, See Macracken					
McCracken, Jane et al	201	Patterson's Cr.	1766	1	378
McCracken, Jane et al	306	Patterson's Cr.	1766	1	379
McCracken, William	69	Wts. Potomac	1779	2	218
McCracken, Virgil	200	Potomac River	1796	9	109
McCrae, Ann	198	Maple Bottom Branch	1768	5	523
McDevit, James	60	Mill Run	1792	6	287
McDonald, Allen et al	434	Wts. Potomac	1788	8	119
McDonald, Allen et al	455	Wts. Potomac	1788	8	109
McDonald, Angus W. Jr.	40½	North Branch	1859	7	501
McDonald, Ann, Executrix	370	Potomac	1802	9	384
McDonald, Ann, Executrix	445	PawPaw Ridge	1802	9	385
McDonald, Ann, Executrix	110	North Branch	1802	9	386
McDonald, Ann, Executrix	452	Potomac	1802	9	387
McDonald, Archibald et al	35	Wts. Potomac	1793	6	362
McDonald, Benjamin (McDonal)	34	North River	1816	5	174
McDonald, Benjamin	127	North River	1829	3	148
McDonald, Benjamin	90	North River	1829	3	147
McDonald, Benjamin	46¾	North River	1835	3	392
McDonald, Benjamin	65¼	North River	1816	5	177
McDonald, Daniel	322	Wts. Potomac	1791	6	32
McDonald, Daniel	286	Wts. Potomac	1789	8	296
McDonald, Eleanor	609	Potomac River	1796	9	107
McDonald, Evan	5	North River	1856	7	437
McDonald, James	96	Town Hill	1843	7	138
McDonald, Jared	8	Sandy Ridge	1841	7	60
McDonald, Jared	8	Gr. Cacapon	1841	7	59
McDonald, Dr. John (or Thomas)	35	Wts. Potomac	1791	6	19
McDonald, John	128	Sidling Hill	1796	9	108
McDonald, John	195	Lick Branch	1772	3	584
McDonald, John	440	Brier Bottom	1791	6	30

Name of Grantee	Acres	Local Description	Year	Book	Page
McDonald, John	211	Wts. Potomac	1791	6	31
McDonald, John	191	Lit. Cacapon	1794	6	399
McDonald, Marshall	43¾	Abram's Cr.	1859	7	483
McDonald, Peter	100	South Branch	1792	6	170
McDonald, William	7¼	Lit. Cacapon	1842	7	103
McDougan, William	115	Sandy Ridge	1837	7	543
McDougan, William	52½	North River	1837	7	541
McDowell, John	123⅜	Mike's Run	1815	5	171
McDowell, John et al	26½	Patterson's Cr.	1817	5	215
McDowell, John et al	645	Patterson's Cr.	1817	5	216
McDowell, John et al	15	Patterson's Cr.	1817	5	217
McDowell, John et al	86	Patterson's Cr.	1817	5	218
McGraw, Morris	276a.48p.	Gr. Cacapon	1791	6	37
McGraw, Thomas	81	Adj. Morris McGraw et al	1801	9	334
McGuire, Edward	403	Patterson's Cr.	1793	6	351
McGuire, Edward	400	Patterson's Cr.	1792	6	197
McGuire, Edward	280	Rowlick's Run	1792	6	196
McGuire, Edward	180	Patterson's Cr.	1792	6	182
McGuire, Edward	342	Mill Run	1791	6	33
McGuire, Edward	400	Lit. Cacapon	1790	8	529
McGuire, Edward	400	Lit. Cacapon	1789	8	322
McGuire, Edward	503	Patterson's Cr.	1788	8	125
McGuire, Edward	129	Patterson's Cr.	1788	8	42
McGuire, Edward	421	Patterson's Cr.	1788	8	41
McGuire, Edward	400	Patterson's Cr.	1788	8	40
McGuire, Edward	400	Patterson's Cr.	1788	8	39
McGuire, Edward	400	Patterson's Cr.	1788	8	38
McGuire, Edward	307	Cabbin Run	1766	1	338
McGuire, Edward	174	New Creek	1766	1	337
McGuire, Edward	91	Patterson Cr.	1766	1	329
McGuire, Edward	393	Cabin Run	1766	1	328
McGuire, Edward	350	Mill Creek	1766	1	327
McGuire, Edward et al	377	George's Run	1791	6	44
McGuire, Edward et al	252½	Knobly Mt.	1791	6	43
McGuire, James	295	Crow's M. Run	1791	6	79
McGuire, Thomas	400	Mike's Run	1799	9	204
McHendry, John	58	Lost River	1765	1	309
McIlwee, Jacob	303	Gr. Cacapon	1851	7	300
McKeever—McKever, McKiver					
McKeever, Paul	500	Gr. Cacapon	1800	9	311
McKeever, Paul	114	Cacapon Mt.	1796	9	22
McKenley, Hugh	100	Sawmill Run	1796	9	16
McKever—McKeever, McKiver					
McKever, Paul	372	Gr. Cacapon	1788	8	247
McKewen, Michael	333	Wts. Potomac	1789	8	261
McKewen, Michael	421	Wts. Potomac	1789	8	260
McKewan, Michael et al	455	Wts. Potomac	1788	8	109
McKewan, Michael et al	434	Wts. Potomac	1788	8	119
McKiver—McKever, McKeever					
McKiver, Jacob (McKeever)	26¼	Capon Spgs.	1854	7	398
McKonkey—See McConkey					
McLaughlin, Daniel	50	Dobson Knob	1835	3	405
McLaughlin, Daniel	77	South Banch	1843	7	137
McMahan—McMachon, McMahon					
McMahan,William	400	Wts. Potomac	1792	6	244
McMahan, William	245	Wts. Potomac	1792	6	231
McMahan, William	305	Wts. Potomac	1792	6	230
McMahon—McMachon, McMahan					
McMachon, William	149	Wts. Potomac	1789	8	264
McMachon, William	420	Sidling Hill	1789	8	263
McMeeken, John	203	North River	1801	9	353
McMeeken, John	42	Adj. Robt. French	1800	9	275
McMeekin, John	688	Lit. Cacapon	1797	9	141

Name of Grantee	Acres	Local Description	Year	Book	Page
McMeekin, John	477	South Branch	1797	9	140
McMeekin, John	438	Patterson's Cr.	1794	6	343
McMeekin, John	400	Lit. Cacapon	1800	9	321
McMeekin, John	120	Patterson's Cr.	1801	9	349
McMunn, George	450	Cacapon Mt.	1799	9	212
McNaman, Philip	324	Knobly Mt.	1789	8	216
McNamar, Philip	324	Knobly Mt.	1789	8	216
McNamara—See McNamarrow					
McNamarrow, Joseph	106	Town Fort	1792	6	136
McNary, Ebenezer	4a.1r.29p.	Pearsall's Run	1829	3	142
McNary, Ebenezer	59	Patterson Creek	1827	3	102
McNary, Ebenezer	4a.3r.29p.	Patterson Cr.	1826	3	98
McNary, Ebenezer	1a.1r.4p.	Patterson's Cr.	1826	3	89
McNary, Ebenezer	1,288a.3r.7p.	Patterson's Cr.	1829	3	551
McNeil, John (McNeill)	120	Gr. Cacapon	1771	3	569
McPherson, William	201	Adj. his own	1789	8	392
McPowell, William	62	Lit. Cacapon	1816	5	190
McVey, John et al	4⅞	North Branch	1856	7	436
McVicar, Duncan	74	Adj. his own	1796	9	23
McVicar, Duncan	26	Crooked Run	1796	9	24
McVicar, Duncan	258	Adj. his own Survey	1805	9	486
McVicker, John et al	94¼	Loonam's Cr.	1825	5	435
Meal, William	100	Adj. J. Critton	1794	6	387
Means, Isaac	300	Mill Creek	1802	9	370
Means, Isaac	47½	So. Branch	1796	6	490
Means, Isaac	361	Mill Creek	1791	6	36
Means, Isaac	321	Mill Creek	1779	2	216
Means, Robert	80	Adj. his Survey	1796	9	104
Meekins, James	25a.1r.	Lick Run	1831	3	262
Meekins, James	14½	Town Hill	1836	3	437
Meekins, Joseph & James	250	Town Hill	1820	5	319
Meenier—Mineer					
Meenier, John	47	Adj. J. Johnson	1794	6	385
Melick—See Malick					
Melick, John	63	Adj. Watford	1806	9	544
Melton, Isaac	355	Gr. Cacapon	1789	8	240
Melton, John	244	Looney's Cr.	1766	1	386
Menser, Conrad	1a.18p.	Maple Run	1820	5	274
Mentser—See Menser					
Mercer, George	260	Wts. Potomac	1773	3	596
Mercer, George	155	Hickory Bot. Run	1773	3	597
Mercer, George Col.	312	Thompson's Run	1762	1	121
Mercer, George Col.	342	Mill Run	1762	1	92
Mercer, George Col.	363	Timber Ridge	1762	1	91
Mercer, George Col.	100	Adj. N. Sampson	1762	1	90
Mercer, George Col.	145a.25p.	Hickory Bottom	1761	1	56
Metheny, Frederick	100	Limestone Run	1794	6	416
Michael, Daniel	40	Elk Ridge	1852	7	311
Michael, Frederick	40	Gr. Cacapon	1802	9	377
Michael, Frederick	60	Gr. Cacapon	1802	9	378
Milburn—See Millbourn					
Milburn, William	273	Wts. Cacapon	1779	2	166
Miles, David	411	Big Spring	1789	8	362
Mileson—Milleson, Millison					
Mileson, John	10¼	Spring Gap Mt.	1844	7	160
Mileson, John	74	Sidling Hill	1836	7	521
Mileson, William	165	Sidling Hill	1836	7	522
Millbourn—See Milburn					
Millbourn, William	464	Deep Run	1795	6	463
Miller, Anthony	348	Lost River	1780	7	581
Miller, George	194	Mill Run	1805	9	538
Miller, George	335	Patterson's Cr.	1789	8	469
Miller, George	76	North Fork	1789	8	456

Name of Grantee	Acres	Local Description	Year	Book	Page
Miller, George	226	Cabin Run	1796	9	32
Miller, Henry	225	Knobly Mt.	1791	6	62
Miller, Henry	25	New Creek	1791	6	63
Miller, Henry	280	Knobly Mt.	1791	6	64
Miller, Henry	127	Hughes Run	1795	6	466
Miller, Isaac	98½	So. Branch	1792	6	134
Miller, Isaac	166	Shop Run	1789	8	213
Miller, Jacob	150	Patterson's Cr.	1796	9	110
Miller, Jacob Jr.	28	Cabin Run	1842	7	115
Miller, Jacob Jr.	144	Knobby Mt.	1832	3	283
Miller, James	184	Wts. Potomac	1768	5	521
Miller, John B. et al	19	Lit. Cacapon	1839	7	36
Miller, John H.	85	Rock Lick Run	1789	8	238
Miller, Michael (Millar)	444	Saw Mill Run	1828	3	123
Miller, Michael (Millar)	60	Adj. I. Pancake	1828	3	119
Miller, Michael (Millar)	118½	Saw Mill Run	1828	3	117
Miller, Michael	237	Knobly Mt.	1794	6	379
Miller, Michael	605	South Fork	1847	7	229
Miller, Michael	1,322	Lit. Mountain	1845	7	183
Miller, Michael	82	South Branch	1789	8	459
Miller, Michael	158a.2r.30p.	Stony Run	1824	5	395
Miller, Michael	50	South Branch	1824	5	394
Miller, Michael	124½	Stony Run	1822	5	368
Miller, Reuben (Millar)	50	Mill Creek	1802	9	391
Miller, William	80	Adj. his own	1799	9	223
Miller, William	411	Lit. Cacapon	1789	8	202
Milleson—Mileson, Millison					
Milleson, Silas	11	Lit. Cacapon	1848	7	246
Milleson, Silas	16½	Lit. Cacapon	1848	7	245
Milleson, Silas	5½	Lit. Cacapon	1846	7	216
Milleson, Silas	102	Spring Gap Mt.	1846	7	215
Milleson, Silas	50	Spring Gap Mt.	1846	7	212
Mills, Mitchell	50	South Branch	1841	7	91
Mills, William	525	South Branch	1824	5	462
Mills, William	15	South Branch	1817	5	220
Mills, William	78	South Branch	1817	5	221
Mills, William	50	Mill Creek	1802	9	376
Millslagle—See Milslagle					
Millslagle, Andrew	107	Gr. Cacapon	1774	4	476
Millslagle, Jacob	148½	North River	1802	9	375
Millslagle, George	85	Tear Coat	1800	9	318
Millslagle, George	155	Tear Coat	1800	9	285
Milslagle—See Millslagle					
Milslagle, Abraham et al	1½	Sandy Ridge	1854	7	369
Milslagle, Jacob	43	North River	1815	5	160
Mineer—See Meenier					
Mineer, John	59	Wts. Potomac	1792	6	207
Mineer, John	153	Adj. his own	1792	6	206
Mircer—See Mercer					
Mitchell, David	333	North River	1787	8	17
Mitchell, David	332½	North River	1787	8	18
Mitchell, David	346	Buffalo Gap	1787	8	19
Mitchell, John	100	New Creek	1796	9	64
Mitchell, John	420	Patterson's Cr.	1789	8	306
Mitchell, John	148	Stony Lick	1788	9	535
Mitchell, John et al	400	Mill Creek	1766	5	525
Mitchell, John et al	165	So. Branch	1768	5	526
Mitchell, John Jr.	80	Frankfort Road	1799	9	193
Mitchell, John Jr.	100	Abraham's Ridge	1799	9	194
Mitchell, John Jr.	260	Rock Gap	1799	9	198
Mitchell, John Jr.	90	Wiggin's Run	1802	9	373
Mitchell, John Jr.	146	Wiggin's Run	1803	9	419
Mitchell, John Jr.	411	Gr. Cacapon	1803	9	420
Mitchell, John Jr.	150	Sidling Hill	1804	9	447

Name of Grantee	Acres	Local Description	Year	Book	Page
Mitchell, John Jr.	20	Patterson's Cr.	1804	9	448
Mitchell, John Jr.	450	Mill Creek	1804	9	449
Mitchell, John Jr.	24a.28p.	Great Cacapon	1804	9	492
Mitchell, John Jr.	33½	Cabin Run	1806	9	554
Mitchell, Joseph	400	Lit. Cacapon	1770	5	569
Mitchell, Joseph	400	Mill Creek	1789	8	327
Mitchell, Joseph	463	Gr. Cacapon	1773	4	451
Mitts, Jacob	87	Cedar Swamp	1762	1	181
Moffett, John	400	Mill Creek	1779	2	184
Moffett, John	157a.2r.	South Branch	1779	2	210
Moffett, John	298	Patterson's Cr.	1779	2	211
Moffett, John	325	Cabin Run	1779	2	212
Monroe, A. et al	300	Pot Lick Run	1758	7	466
Monroe, Alexander	25	Maple Run	1829	3	172
Monroe, Alexander	700	North River	1803	9	426
Monroe, Alexander	1,150	Lit. Cacapon	1803	9	424
Monroe, James	80½	Lit. Cacapon	1791	6	104
Monroe, Jeremiah	463	Tear Coat Cr.	1815	5	155
Monroe, John	50	North River Mt.	1818	5	225
Monroe, Robert	50	Knobly Mt.	1796	9	49
Monroe, Robert	11	Knobly Mt.	1796	9	101
Monroe, Robert	16	Knobly Mt.	1796	9	111
Monroe, Marquis	450	Plum Lick Run	1836	3	419
Moon, Abraham	15	Dixon's Run	1800	9	235
Moor,—See Moore, More					
Moor, Henry	304	Oldacre's Run	1780	7	583
Moor, James	184	Hughes Mill Run	1769	5	552
Moore—Moor, More					
Moore, Anthony	67	So. Branch	1792	6	299
Moore, Eli	23	Mike's Run	1825	5	415
Moore, James	121	Hughes Run	1772	3	576
Moore, Joseph	179	Lit. Cacapon	1789	8	215
Moore, Joseph	328	Lit. Cacapon	1792	6	181
Moore, Joseph	329	Lit. Cacapon	1786	9	519
Moore, Joseph	137	Lit. Cacapon	1786	9	518
Moore, Joseph	250	Lit. Cacapon	1786	9	516
Moore, Josias	37	Dry Run	1833	3	330
Moore, Juduthan	50	Adj. Wm. Clark	1799	9	213
Moore, Milly et al Heirs	50	Mill Creek	1830	3	205
Moore, Philip	25	Mill Creek	1834	3	385
Moore, Philip	373	Wts. Potomac	1762	1	182
Moorehead—See Muirheid					
Moorehead, James	47	So. Branch	1840	7	51
Moorehead, James	34	Lit. Cacapon	1840	7	50
More—Moor, Moore					
More, Josias	29½ (22½)	Mike's Run	1815	5	147
More, Philip	124½	Mill Creek	1828	3	116
Moreland, David	200	Spring Gap Mt.	1852	7	313
Moreland, George	200	Town Hill	1843	7	136
Moreland, Margery et al Hrs.	73	Lit. Cacapon	1854	7	371
Moreland, Richard	16¼	Taylor's Run	1837	7	8
Moreland, Richard	103¾	Lit. Cacapon	1830	3	190
Moreland, William	100	Park Mt.	1845	7	180
Moreland, William	46 6/10	Dillon's Mt.	1822	5	367
Moreland, William	72	Cacapon Mt.	1856	7	440
Moreland, William	315	Dillon's Mt.	1854	7	370
Moreland, William H.	32	Dillon's Run	1845	7	179
Moreland, William H.	182	L. Cacapon	1830	3	191
Moreland, William H.	209¾	L. Cacapon	1830	3	188
Moreland, William H.	118	Dellins Run	1835	3	388
Morgan, John	308	Bennett's Run	1781	8	581
Morris, Richard et al	110	Wts. of Potomac	1788	8	36
Morris, Richard et al	386	Morgan's Run	1788	8	37

Name of Grantee	Acres	Local Description	Year	Book	Page
Neal, William (Meal)	100	Adj. J. Critton	1794	6	387
Neale—Neall, Neil, Neill					
Neale, Thomas	312	Adj. A. Hite	1774	4	477
Neall, William	157½	Cox's Mill Run	1780	6	597
Neavil, Joseph et al	65	Stoke's Cabin	1779	2	182
Neely, William	24	Big Cacapon	1820	5	302
Neely, William	146	Long Hollow	1820	5	301
Neff, Abraham	50	New Creek	1796	6	517
Neff, Abraham	400	Corn Run	1796	6	515
Neff, Abraham	56	Adj. S. Houqe	1796	6	511
Neff, Abraham	300	New Creek	1796	9	43
Neff, Adam	155	Mill Creek	1790	8	550
Neff, Adam, Executor	200	South Branch	1790	8	552
Neff, John	200	Abram's Creek	1832	3	294
Neil—Neale, Neall, Neill					
Neill, William	232	Gr. Cacapon	1766	1	362
Neilson, James	311	Clay Lick Run	1794	6	382
Nelson, John	250	North River	1764	1	221
Nelson, John	314	North River	1764	1	220
Nelson, John G.	128	Stony Lick	1803	9	423
Nelson, Richard	47	Stony Lick	1803	9	422
Nelson, Richard	283	Horn Camp Run	1803	9	408
Nelson, Robert	52¼	Mill's Branch	1823	5	378
Newbanks, John	172	North River	1796	9	106
Newbanks, John	78	Dilling's Run	1800	9	263
New Creek Company	8a.2r.30p.	North Branch	1856	7	407
Newman, David	101	South Branch	1791	6	212
Newman, Isaac	288	Lit. Cacapon	1789	8	191
Newman, John	294	So. Branch	1789	8	182
Newman, John	198	South Branch	1789	8	181
Newman, Salman	200	South Branch	1801	9	342
Newton, John	315	North River	1754	1	21
Nicholas, Amos	357	Cacapon	1791	6	38
Nicholas, John	150	Plumb Run	1762	1	143
Nichols, Amos	357	Cacapon	1791	6	38
Nickson—See Nixon					
Nickson, George	79	Dillon's Run	1769	5	555
Nidy, David	215	Gr. Cacapon	1780	7	569
Nisewanger, Mary	400	Adj. J. Woodfin	1757	1	34
Nixon—See Nickson					
Nixon, George	82(82½)	Dillon's Mt.	1789	8	395
Nixon, William	54¾	Big Cacapon	1829	3	146
Noble, Anthony	144½	Gr. Cacapon	1777	2	63
Noble, Anthony	361	Timber Ridge	1777	2	64
Noble, Anthony	412	Bear Garden Ridge	1777	2	65
Noble, Anthony	415	Bear Garden Ridge	1777	2	66
Noble, Anthony	402	Isaac's Cr.	1779	2	250
Nourse, Gabriel	281	Hughes' Run	1795	6	437
Nourse, Gabriel	247	Adj. J. Alexander	1795	6	438
Oaks, George et al	25¼	Edward's Run	1830	3	212
Oats, George et al	25¼	Edward's Run	1830	3	212
Obannon, Joseph	400	Mt. Run	1792	6	249
Obannon, Joseph	28	So. Br. Mt.	1792	6	198
Ogan—or Ougan					
Ogan, Peter	324	Gr. Cacapon	1789	8	470
Ogan, Peter	233	Gr. Cacapon	1792	6	145
Ogan, Peter	97	Wts. Cacapon	1792	6	146
Ogan, Peter	216	Gr. Cacapon	1789	8	466
Ogden, Joseph et al	130	Pleasant Mill Run	1767	5	510
Ogden, Joseph et al	409	Stony Run	1767	5	511
Ogden, Joseph et al	374	Patterson's Cr.	1767	5	512
Ohaver, Christopher	144	Elk Hill	1781	8	598
Ohaver, Christopher	358	Big Ridge	1789	8	288

Name of Grantee	Acres	Local Description	Year	Book	Page
Ohaver, George	50	Gr. Cacapon	1802	9	381
Oldacre, John	248	Lost River	1787	8	25
Orr, John	346	Rodgers' Run	1779	2	232
Orr, John	350	South Br. Mt.	1779	2	233
Orrick, Nicholas	30	Wts. Potomac	1810	5	54
Orton, Robert	279	Lost River	1790	8	514
Ougan—See Ogan					
Ougan, Peter	175	Gr. Cacapon	1800	9	279
Overly, Peter	352	Sidling Hill	1789	8	485
Overseers of the Poor	6¼	South Br. Mt.	1845	7	184
Overton, John et al	386	Morgan's Run	1788	8	37
Overton, John et al	110	Wts. Potomac	1788	8	36
Osburn, George	93	Mill Creek	1762	1	169
Page, Alexander	93½	Grape Knob	1832	3	297
Painter—See Panther					
Palmer, Joseph	58½	Cabin Run	1837	7	12
Pancake, Isaac	744¾	Buffalo Run	1830	3	184
Pancake, John	109	So. Branch	1789	8	175
Pancake, John	175	Cacapon	1792	6	213
Pancake, John	234	So. Branch	1792	6	218
Pannell—See Parrell, Parrill					
Pannell, Edward (Parrill)	19½	Dilling's Run	1809	5	20
Panther, Benjamin	279	New Creek	1789	8	309
Panther, Benjamin	238	Abraham's Cr.	1789	8	198
Paris—See also Parris					
Paris, James	114	Abram's Ridge	1841	7	89
Paris, James	36	New Creek	1841	7	90
Park—or Parke, Parks					
Park, George	74½	Sandy Ridge	1826	3	92
Park, Harbert	18	Tear Coat Cr.	1842	7	118
Park, Harbert et al	97	Black Lick Run	1837	7	18
Park, John	224	Edward's Run	1796	9	27
Park, John	38	Grassy Lick Mt.	1852	7	333
Park, John	135	Cacapon	1769	5	554
Park, John et al	153	Lit. Cacapon	1800	9	266
Park, Samuel	50	Tear Coat	1796	9	56
Park, Solomon (Parks)	98½	Sandy Ridge	1804	9	493
Parke, George et al	400	Great Cacapon	1762	1	158
Parke, John	182	Edwards Mill Br.	1771	3	571
Parke, John	250	Wts. Cacapon	1762	1	159
Parker, Abraham	200	Mill Creek	1831	3	242
Parker, Benjamin	214	Patterson's Cr.	1765	1	230
Parker, Benjamin	100	Mill Creek	1798	9	174
Parker, Benjamin	119	Patterson's Cr.	1777	2	69
Parker, Benjamin	227	Mill Cr.	1763	1	194
Parker, Isaias	107	Cacapon River	1762	1	132
Parker, Jacob	400	Mill Creek	1830	3	201
Parker, Jacob	50	Mill Creek	1830	3	195
Parker, Jacob	326	Mill Creek	1820	5	452
Parker, Jacob	100	Mill Creek	1810	5	58
Parker, Job	421	Mill Creek	1762	1	118
Parker, John	209	Abram's Cr.	1788	8	72
Parker, John	113	New Creek	1757	1	26
Parker, John	350	Buck's Island	1757	1	27
Parker, John	150	Wts. Potomac	1757	1	28
Parker, John	200	Cacapon	1757	1	29
Parker, John	300	New Creek	1768	5	517
Parker, John	50	Mill Creek	1829	3	157
Parker, John	50	Mill Cr.	1829	3	162
Parker, John	54	Middle Ridge	1830	3	216
Parker, John	56	Middle Ridge	1830	3	218
Parker, John	69	Mill Creek	1833	3	344
Parker, John	27½	Middle Ridge	1830	3	219
Parker, John	69	Middle Ridge	1833	3	345

Name of Grantee	Acres	Local Description	Year	Book	Page
Parker, John	401¼	Emrie's Hunting C. Run	1771	3	561
Parker, John	29	Mill Creek	1843	7	141
Parker, Jonathan (Parkin)	422	Mill's Br.	1792	6	284
Parker, Jonathan	50	Mill Cr.	1805	9	539
Parker, Jonathan (Parkin)	422	Timber Ridge	1780	6	595
Parker, Nathaniel Jr.	300	Patterson's Cr.	1790	8	562
Parker, Robert	40	So. Branch	1788	8	132
Parker, Robert	377	So. Br. Mt.	1788	8	133
Parker, Robert	33	South Branch	1788	8	135
Parker, Robert	211	Raccoon Run	1789	8	219
Parker, Robert	72	Lit. Cacapon	1762	1	98
Parker, Robert	210	South Branch	1789	8	495
Parker, Robert	50	Mick's Run	1830	3	196
Parker, Robert	86a.1r.4p.	Cor. to R. Parker	1798	9	161
Parker, Robert	25	Chestnut Spg. Run	1796	9	121
Parker, Robert	227	Wts. Potomac	1792	6	139
Parker, Robert	237	South Branch	1792	6	140
Parker, Robert Jr.	150	South Branch	1809	5	4
Parkin, Jonathan (Parker)	422	Mill's Br.	1792	6	284
Parkin, Jonathan (Parker)	422	Timber Ridge	1780	6	595
Parks, Samuel	80	Tear Coat	1806	9	559
Parrel, Panel, Pannell, Pannill, Parrell, Parrill					
Parrell, Edward (Panel)	19½	Dilling's Run	1809	5	20
Parrell, John	177	Lonams Branch	1794	6	390
Parrell, John (Perral)	113	Gr. Cacapon	1796	9	15
Parrell, John (Perrel)	360	Gr. Cacapon	1801	9	351
Parrell, John & William (Perral)	35	Gr. Cacapon	1796	9	17
Parrill, Joseph	37	Dillon's Run	1854	7	372
Parris—See also Paris					
Parris, James	85	New Creek Mt.	1845	7	185
Parson, David Jr.	152	South Branch	1829	3	143
Parsons, David	7a.3r.29p.	South Branch	1821	5	334
Parsons, David	264	South Br. Mt.	1809	5	6
Parsons, Isaac Col.	67a.3r.	Green Spgs. Valley	1857	7	451
Parsons, Isaac Col.	42¼	Valley Mt.	1858	7	462
Parsons, James	4	South Branch	1809	5	19
Parsons, Thomas	45½	Richardson's Mill Run	1766	1	323
Passmore, Levis	325	Gr. Cacapon	1846	7	204
Passmore, Levis	20½	Gr. Cacapon	1846	7	206
Patten, See Patton					
Patterson, James	81½	Lit. Cacapon	1804	9	446
Patton, James (Patten)	100	Mill Creek	1772	3	591
Patton, James (Patten)	157	Mill Creek	1772	3	590
Paulson—See Poulison, Powelson					
Paulson, Anderson	200	Gr. Spgs.	1761	1	86
Payne, Adam	337	Wts. Potomac	1762	1	163
Pear, Isaac	123¼	Adj. Joseph Johnson	1852	7	334
Pearcall, Pearsall, Pierceall, Purcall					
Pearcall, John	124a.3r.8p.	Adj. H. Harrell	1789	8	228
Pearsall, Pearcall, Pierceall, Purcall					
Pearsall, John	200	Patterson Cr.	1793	6	361
Pearsall, John	230	Patterson's Cr.	1771	3	559
Pearsall, John	100	Sugar Camp	1800	9	322
Peck, George	400	North River	1775	4	483
Peepyat, William	50	Mill Creek	1796	9	119
Peerce—See Pierce					
Pendleton, Philip	1,586	South Br. Mt.	1801	9	329
Pendleton, Philip	1,300	Wts. South Br.	1801	9	330
Pendleton, Philip	1,200	South Br. Mt.	1801	9	331
Pendleton, Philip	266	Hopkins Lick	1801	9	332
Pennington, Abraham	23	Lit. Cacapon	1818	5	238
Pennington, Abraham	84½	Lit. Cacapon	1807	9	565
Pennington, Abraham et al	97	Lit. Cacapon	1822	5	362

Name of Grantee	Acres	Local Description	Year	Book	Page
Pennington, Enoch	12¾	Lonan's Branch	1841	7	61
Pennington, James	10a.34p.	Big Cacapon	1825	5	434
Pepper, Benjamin F.	100	Short A Mt.	1858	7	481
Pepper, Henry & John Jr.	21a.2r.22p.	Bear Wallow	1820	5	275
Perry, Daniel	276	Walnut Bot. Run	1770	5	558
Peters—See Petters, Pettit					
Peters, Abraham	126	Myers Run	1788	8	159
Peters, Branson	113	Tear Coat Cr.	1841	7	84
Peters, Branson et al (Petters)	146	Tear Coat	1834	3	377
Peters, Branson et al	104	Tear Coat	1834	3	366
Peters, John	43	Stony Lick Run	1810	5	50
Peters, John (or Jacob)	45	Lit. Cacapon	1809	5	26
Peters, Tunis	56	Tear Coat Cr.	1798	9	160
Peterson, Michael	58	North Fork	1791	6	110
Petters, Branson et al	104	Tear Coat Run	1834	3	366
Petters, Branson et al	146	Tear Coat	1834	3	377
Pettit, Branson et al	104	Tear Coat Run	1834	3	366
Pettit, Branson et al	146	Tear Coat	1834	3	377
Pettit, Moses	2a. 3r.13p.	Town Gap Run	1823	5	375
Philips, Jesse	335	Stony Ridge	1788	8	97
Philips, John	92	Plum Run	1794	6	352
Pierceall—See (Pearcall), Pearsall, Purcall					
Pierceall, John	174	Wts. Potomac	1762	1	162
Pierce, John T.	3a.2r.30p.	Cor. D. Vanmeter's Parker Tract	1859	7	484
Pierce, John T.	1a.2r. 8p.	Cor. David Vanmeter's Parker Tract	1859	7	485
Pigman, Bene S.	22	North Branch	1842	7	99
Pigman, Bene S.	160	North Branch	1842	7	110
Pigman, Matthew	400	Clay Lick	1801	9	361
Pigman, Moses	420	Tear Coat Cr.	1778	2	119
Pigman, Moses	390	Tear Coat Cr.	1778	2	118
Pigman, Moses	373	Tear Coat Cr.	1778	2	117
Pigman, Moses	400	New Creek	1790	8	542
Pike—See Pyke					
Pilcher, Stephen	70	Patterson Cr.	1801	9	357
Pilcher, Stephen	50	Mill & Dry Run	1801	9	359
Pilcher, Stephen	300	Cabin Run	1801	9	360
Pilcher, William	148	Dry Run	1804	9	450
Piper, Harry	200	South Branch	1770	5	577
Piper, Harry	396	South Branch	1770	5	578
Piper, Harry	357	South Branch	1770	5	579
Plough, Jacob	386	So. Branch	1792	6	255
Plum, See Plumb					
Plum, John	163	Coon's Branch	1781	8	586
Plum, John	65	Corn's Run	1769	5	550
Plumb, See Plum					
Plumb, Abraham	50	Falling Run	1821	5	331
Plumb, John	200	Corn Run	1789	8	342
Plumb, John	395	Adj. Chas. Linch	1789	8	341
Plumb, John	103	Patterson's Cr.	1789	8	340
Plumb, John Sr.	114	Mill Creek	1806	9	551
Plumb, Samuel	160	Bird's Run	1766	1	391
Poage, Robert	22	Poage's Run	1785	9	514
Poland—See Polin, Poling					
Poland, Aaron	219	Saw Mill Run	1837	7	10
Poland, Amos	49½	South Branch	1857	7	452
Poland, Amos	116	Saw Mill Run	1828	3	111
Poland, Amos	80	Piney Mtn.	1803	9	416
Poland, Amos	50	Kuykendall's M. Run	1803	9	414
Poland, Amos	90½	Piney Mtn.	1814	5	137
Poland, Amos	113½	So. Branch	1814	5	136
Poland, Amos	102½	South Branch	1814	5	135

Name of Grantee	Acres	Local Description	Year	Book	Page
Poland, John	112	Piney Mt.	1804	9	465
Poland, John	70	Lit. Cacapon	1816	5	176
Poland, John Sr.	92½	Keykendall's Run	1792	6	296
Poland, Peter	89	North River	1849	7	275
Poland, Peter	16	Plum Lick Ridge	1849	7	274
Poland, Peter	131	Marshall Ridge	1841	7	87
Polard, Peter	131	Marshall Ridge	1841	7	87
Polin—See Poland, Poling					
Polin, John Jr.	129	Kuykendall's Run	1796	9	45
Poling, William B.	183½	Haunted Lick Run	1855	7	402
Poners, Valentine	47	So. Branch	1784	9	509
Pool, Henry	92	Corns Run	1820	5	322
Pool, John & Jeremiah	75	Town Hill	1844	7	153
Pool, William	375¾	L. Cacapon	1829	3	166
Pool, William	150	South Branch	1807	9	570
Pool, William	9	So. Branch	1818	5	233
Pool, William et al	97	Lit. Cacapon	1822	5	362
Pootman—See also Putman					
Pootman, Peter (Putman)	410	Lick Run	1779	2	165
Popenjoy, John (Popenjay)	260 (200)	Mike Gap's	1781	8	599
Portmess, John	28	Lit. Cacapon	1843	7	140
Portmess, John (or James)	142	Town Hill	1843	7	139
Posten—See Poston					
Posten, Elias	460	North River	1796	9	76
Poston, Alexander	33	North River Mt.	1844	7	162
Poston, Alexander	64	Kinsman's Mt.	1824	5	402
Poston, Alexander	100	Tear Coat Cr.	1818	5	236
Poston, Branson	97	Hammock's M. Run	1826	3	84
Poston, Branson	93a.1r.	Craigs' Run	1833	3	310
Poston, Branson	4a.3r.	North River	1833	3	313
Poston, Branson	40	North River Mt.	1833	3	314
Poston, Elias	127	Dillon's Mt.	1800	9	308
Poston, Elias	125	North River	1796	9	83
Poston, Elias	71	Cacapon	1789	8	394
Poston, Elias	105	North River	1789	8	389
Poston, Samuel	30	Adj. D. Shire	1809	5	43
Poston, William	92	North River Mt.	1846	7	213
Poulison—See Paulson, Powelson					
Poulison, John	40	Lit. Cacapon	1804	9	490
Powell—See Pownall					
Powell, Dade et al	35a.1r.19p.	Big Cacapon	1820	5	289
Powell, Elisha	62½	Diamond Ridge	1858	7	470
Powell, James	348	Lit. Cacapon	1789	8	197
Powell, Jonathan	157	South Branch	1807	5	2
Powell, Robert M.	7a.36p.	Rocky Ridge	1820	5	295
Powell, Robert M. (3rd)	5a.	Jerry's Run	1858	7	473
Powell, Robert M. (the Third)	9	North River Mt.	1844	7	163
Powell, William M.	62	Lit. Cacapon	1816	5	190
Powelson—Poulison, Paulson					
Powelson, Cloe Ann	79a.3r.	L. Cacapon	1828	3	115
Powelson, James	18a.30p.	Lit. Cacapon	1856	7	412
Powelson, James	8⅝	Lit. Cacapon	1853	7	352
Powelson, John	22¼	Winchester Road	1807	9	571
Powelson, John	186½	Lit. Cacapon	1816	5	172
Powers, Valentine	47	South Branch	1784	9	509
Pownall—See Powell					
Pownall, Isaac	50	Town Hill	1846	7	198
Pownall, Isaac	48½	Town Hill	1837	7	9
Pownall, Isaac	74	South Br. Mt.	1837	7	11
Pownall, Isaac (Pownel)	264	Philip's Run	1789	8	236
Pownall, John	79⅜	Town Hill	1813	5	126
Pownall, John J.	257	South Branch	1845	7	186
Prather, See Preather					

Name of Grantee	Acres	Local Description	Year	Book	Page
Purget, Henry	100	Mill Creek	1796	9	118
Purget, Henry Jr.	52½	Mill Creek	1831	3	241
Purget, Henry Sr.	50	Mill Creek	1830	3	207
Purget, Jacob	125	Knobly Mt.	1796	6	510
Purget, Jacob	125	Adj. J. Spencer	1796	9	8
Purget, Jacob	75	Knobly Mt.	1796	9	7
Purget, Jacob	50	Knobly Mt.	1796	9	6
Purget, Jacob	93a.1r.6p.	Cabin Run	1789	8	235
Purget, Jacob	413	Cabin Run	1792	6	172
Purget, Sidney et al Hrs.	50	Mill Creek	1830	3	205
Putman—See also Pootman					
Putman, Jacob	200	Putman's Run	1799	9	182
Putman, Mary et al	63	North Branch	1799	9	179
Putman, Peter	63	North Branch	1793	6	306
Putman, Peter Jr.	369	Stagg Run	1789	8	461
Putman, Peter	136	Putman's Run	1789	8	336
Putman, Peter	283	Patterson's Cr.	1789	8	337
Putman, Peter	410	Lick Run	1779	2	165
Putman, Peter	100	Adj. J. Spiker	1799	9	180
Putman, Peter	109 (190)	Knobly Mt.	1791	6	20
Putman, Peter	100	North Branch	1793	6	305
Putman, Philip	142	Knob Mt.	1802	9	398
Pyke, Michael	300	Adj. C. Burkham	1760	1	47
Quarrier, Alexander et al	66¼	North Branch	1803	9	412
Quarrier, Alexander et al	381¾	Adj. Abernathy	1803	9	411
Quick, John	296	Scragg's Run	1794	6	421
Racey, Margaret et al Heirs	25¾	Big Cacapon	1825	5	436
Racey, Thomas	75	Timber Ridge	1821	5	350
Ramsey, Andrew	429½	Patterson's Cr.	1767	5	506
Ramsey, William (Ramsay)	400	Big Spgs. Run	1777	2	48
Ramsey, William et al	415	South Branch	1773	4	452
Randall—See Randoll					
Randoll, Abel	371	Brushy Run	1788	8	89
Randoll, Abel	404	Abram's Creek	1788	8	88
Rankin, John	49a.3r.35p.	Sheet's Run	1825	5	411
Rankin, John	100	Sheetz's Run	1821	5	329
Rankin, John et al	129½	Patterson Cr.	1818	5	242
Rannells—See Reynolds					
Rannells, John	1⅞	Town Hill	1846	7	208
Rannells, John et al	19	Lit. Cacapon	1839	7	36
Ratcliff, Stephen	75	Looney's Cr.	1789	8	232
Ravenscraft—See Ravenscroft					
Ravenscraft, James	120a. (120P.)	Knobby Mt.	1831	3	267
Ravenscraft, John	25	Wts. Potomac	1792	6	147
Ravenscraft, John D.	66½	Knobby Mt.	1829	3	156
Ravenscroft, See Ravenscraft					
Ravenscroft, John	172	Abram's Creek	1809	5	23
Ravenscroft, John	195	Cabin Run	1789	8	179
Ravenscroft, John	400	Patterson's Cr.	1800	9	248
Ravenscroft, John	41	North Branch	1795	6	469
Ravenscroft, John	36	Copper Spring	1795	6	472
Ravenscroft, Samuel	114	New Creek	1792	6	203
Ravenscroft, Samuel	150	Sugar Camp Run	1792	6	204
Ravenscroft, Samuel	27	North Branch	1794	6	415
Ravenscroft, Samuel	264	Maple Swamp	1796	6	494
Ravenscroft, Samuel Jr.	30	North Branch	1804	9	469
Ravenscroft, William	313	Knobly Mt.	1814	5	142
Rawlings, Peter	150	Steven's Run	1825	5	442
Rawlings, Peter	162	Stover's Run	1845	7	187
Rawlings, Santford	196	Patterson's Cr.	1860	7	514
Ray—See Roy					
Read, Jacob	250	Patterson's Cr.	1802	9	403
Reasau—See Rousaw, Roussau					
Reasau, Henry	418	Patterson's Cr.	1789	8	384

Name of Grantee	Acres	Local Description	Year	Book	Page
Reasner, Jacob (Reasoner)	127	Patterson's Cr.	1781	8	584
Reasoner, Jacob	118	North Branch	1789	8	383
Reasoner, Jacob	113	Patterson's Cr.	1789	8	382
Rector, Conway	38	South Branch	1809	5	5
Rector, Wharton	200	Cold Run	1802	9	365
Redtrock, Redtruck, Rotruck					
Redtrock, Andrew	449	Patterson's Cr.	1789	8	315
Redtruck, Redtrock, Rotruck					
Redtruck, Daniel	50	Adj. Wm. Duggan	1795	6	429
Reece, Reese, Rees					
Reed, Abraham	76	Patterson's Cr.	1833	3	318
Reed, James	370	Lanam's Br.	1802	9	366
Reed, Jeremiah	17½	Cor. to Jesse Anderson	1809	5	46
Reed, Jeremiah	178	Luna's Branch	1777	2	95
Reed, Jeremiah	150	Timber Ridge	1777	2	94
Reed, Jeremiah	262	Loman's Branch	1789	8	502
Reed, Jeremiah	95	Adj. his own	1800	9	310
Reed, Jeremiah	124	Gr. Cacapon	1800	9	303
Reed, Jeremiah	239	Back Creek	1798	9	164
Reed, John	118	Veal's Run	1771	3	563
Reed, John	100	Wts. Potomac	1762	1	170
Reed, John Sr. et al	180	New Creek	1788	8	134
Reed, John Sr. et al	200	So. Branch	1788	8	136
Reed, John Sr. et al	198	Patterson's Cr.	1788	8	137
Reeder, William	127	Gr. Cacapon	1790	8	564
Reeder, William Jr.	60	Lit. Cacapon	1800	9	273
Rees, Reece, Reese					
Rees, Ashford	280	Middle Ridge	1832	3	299
Rees, Silas et al	22-¾	No. Br. Potomac	1841	7	83
Rees, Silas et al	44¼	Adj. E. Smith	1841	7	86
Rees, Thomas	50	Patterson's Cr.	1825	5	414
Rees, Thomas et al	25	Dry Fork	1829	3	161
Rees, William D. et al	200	Middle Ridge	1846	7	205
Reese, Reece, Rees					
Reeve—See Reeves					
Reeve, Peter	100	Wts. Potomac	1765	1	308
Reeve, Peter	440	Walnut Run	1765	1	268
Reeve, Peter	402	Adj. John Moffitt	1765	1	264
Reeve, Peter	412	Patterson's Cr.	1765	1	256
Reeve, Peter	396	Looney's Cr.	1775	4	492
Reeve, Peter	400	Grass Lick	1775	4	491
Reeve, Peter	400	Patterson's Cr.	1765	1	255
Reeve, Peter	208	Loony's Cr.	1765	1	254
Reeves, Benjamin	60	South Branch	1788	8	56
Relfe—or Rolfe					
Relfe, James	408	Mill Creek	1790	8	548
Relfe, James	150	Mill Creek	1765	1	280
Relfe, John	295	Gr. Cacapon	1767	5	493
Relfe, John	367	Gr. Cacapon	1767	5	492
Relfe, John	156	Cacapon River	1766	1	383
Relfe, John	88	Cacapon River	1766	1	332
Relfe, John	212	Sandy Ridge	1766	1	331
Relfe, John	154	Cacapon	1766	1	330
Relfe, John	15	Lick Branch	1765	1	288
Relfe, John	191	Cacapon	1765	1	287
Relfe, John	195	Gr. Cacapon	1765	1	286
Relfe, John	202	Stony Lick Run	1765	1	285
Relfe, John	125	Wts. Potomac	1765	1	282
Relfe, John	316	North River	1765	1	270
Relfe, John	400	Cacapon River	1765	1	269
Relfe, John	447	Adj. J. Moffitt	1765	1	265
Relfe, John	132	Patterson's Cr.	1790	8	547
Relfe, John	158	Wts. Potomac	1790	8	546

Name of Grantee	Acres	Local Description	Year	Book	Page
Relfe, John	204	Patterson's Cr.	1765	1	253
Relfe, John	350	North River	1765	1	252
Relfe, John	123	North River	1765	1	251
Relfe, John	196	Enoch's Mill R.	1765	1	249
Relfe, John	283 (285)	North River	1765	1	248
Rennock, George	200	Trough Hill Run	1766	1	384
Rensaw, Henry	418	Patterson's Cr.	1789	8	384
Rentfro, James	348	Wts. Potomac	1766	1	319
Reyle—or Riley					
Reyle, Martin	161	Warm Spring Ridge	1787	8	16
Reynolds—Also Rannells					
Reynolds, William	285	South Branch	1778	2	120
Reynolds, William	151	So. Branch	1792	6	173
Rhodes, Joseph	135	Hawk's Tree	1754	1	19
Rice, John	264	Lit. Cacapon	1777	2	93
Richards, William	285	North River	1799	9	187
Richards, William	865	North River	1799	9	186
Richardson, William	110	Lost River	1792	6	142
Richmond, James	97	White Rock Mt.	1837	7	542
Ricketts, John T. et al	219	Plumb Run	1796	6	530
Ricketts, John T. et al	309	Plumb Run	1796	6	532
Ricketts, John T. et al	475	Knobly Mt.	1796	6	538
Ricketts, John T. et al	569	North Branch	1796	6	542
Ricketts, John T. et al	15	Knobly Mt.	1796	6	528
Ricketts, John T. et al	72	Knobly Mt.	1796	6	529
Ridgeway, John	18¾	Big Cacapon	1845	7	166
Ridgeway, Joseph	14¼	Gr. Cacapon	1826	3	95
Ridgeway, Thomas S. (Rigway)	4⅞	North Branch	1856	7	436
Riley—See Reyle					
Riley, George	37¼	North Branch	1854	7	373
Rinehart, Abraham	352	Edward's Run	1788	8	106
Rinehart, Abraham	206	Edward's Run	1796	6	491
Rinehart, Elijah	42	Patterson's Cr.	1840	7	52
Rinehart, Stephen C.	150	Middle Ridge	1856	7	432
Rinker, Casper	338	Crooked Run	1778	2	123
Rinker, Casper	279	Crooked Run	1778	2	122
Rinker, Casper	800	Dillon's Run	1762	1	133
Rinker, Casper	275	Brook Run	1788	8	46
Rinker, Casper	150	Gr. Cacapon	1791	6	73
Rinker, Casper et al	430	Drains of Cacapon	1789	8	268
Rinker, Casper et al	400	Wts. Cacapon	1789	8	269
Rinker, Jacob	75	Crooked Run	1819	5	251
Roberts, Benjamin N.	185	Mike's Run	1833	3	325
Roberts, David (3rd)	346	Lost River	1780	7	570
Roberts, Edward	148	North Branch	1781	8	578
Roberts, Edward	275	New Creek	1781	8	576
Roberts, Elijah	30	Murphy Run	1804	9	467
Roberts, Gersham	58½	Mike's Run	1806	9	555
Roberts, Thomas	300	Spring House Br.	1776	2	36
Robertson, Amos (Roberson)	71¼	Piney Mt.	1858	7	479
Robertson, David et al Executor of Duncan McRae	66¼	North Branch	1803	9	412
Robertson, David et al Executor of Duncan McRae	381-¾	Adj. Abernathy	1803	9	411
Robinson, Nicholas	400	Gr. Cacapon	1754	2	26
Robinson, Nicholas	400	Gr. Cacapon	1754	1	15
Roby, Pryor S.	250	Stony River	1792	6	234
Rogers, Evan	320	Isaac's Cr.	1780	7	568
Rogers, Ezekiel	240	2 Lick Run	1788	8	146
Rogers, Ezekiel	404	2 Lick Run	1788	8	130
Rogers, Ezekiel	90	Stuart's Run	1789	8	212
Rogers, George	165	Lit. Cacapon	1789	8	211
Rogers, George	193	Lit. Cacapon	1789	8	210
Rogers, John	252	Sleepy Creek	1787	8	22

Name of Grantee	Acres	Local Description	Year	Book	Page
Rogers, John	276	Bear Garden Ridge	1789	8	275
Rogers, John	406	Stuart's Run	1788	8	131
Rogers, John	114	Lick Branch	1777	2	99
Rogers, John	167	Lit. Cacapon	1786	9	517
Rogers, Mathew	115	Patterson's Cr.	1762	1	130
Rogers, Owen	121	Sleepy Creek	1787	8	23
Rogers, Robert	100	Adj. L. Throckmorton	1796	9	11
Rogers, Robert	100	Sidling Hill	1796	9	114
Rogers, Robert	93	Big Cacapon	1791	6	15
Rogers, Robert	76¼	Blumery Run	1812	5	112
Rogers, Robert	3½	Stair Run	1799	9	215
Rogers, Robert	100	Potomac	1800	9	283
Rogers, Robert et al	900	Gr. Cacapon	1804	9	445
Rohrbaugh—or Rohrbough, Rorabaugh, Rorabau, Roraboh, Rosebough, Rosbrough					
Roll, John	308	New Creek	1789	8	313
Rolls, John	129	New Creek	1789	8	177
Rorabaugh—See Rohrbough, Rorabough, Roraboh, Rorahbau, Rosebough, Rosbrough					
Rosbrough, John	929	Gr. Cacapon	1800	9	228
Rosbrough, John	72	Gr. Cacapon	1800	9	229
Rosbrough, John	200	Gr. Cacapon	1800	9	320
Rosbrough, John	143	North Mountain	1803	9	437
Rosbrough, John	90	Gr. Cacapon	1798	9	167
Rose, Robert	9	Wts. Potomac	1775	4	489
Rosebrough, Rohrbaugh, Rohrbough, Rorabaugh, Roraboh, Rorabau, Rosbrough					
Rosebrough, John	200	Gr. Cacapon	1819	5	247
Ross, John	150	Lit. Cacapon	1766	1	343
Ross, John	100	Hoge's Lick	1766	1	342
Ross, Philip	129	Patterson's Cr.	1762	1	117
Ross, Philip	408	Wts. Potomac	1765	1	258
Ross, Philip	151	Wts. Potomac	1765	1	307
Ross, Robert	233	Adj. his own	1799	9	201
Ross, Robert	400	Morgan's Run	1792	6	191
Ross, Stephen	183	Patterson's Cr.	1789	8	312
Rotruck, Redtrock, Redtruck					
Rousaw, Henry	418	Patterson's Cr.	1789	8	384
Roussau, John	353	Timber Ridge	1766	1	377
Roy, Joseph (Ray)	153	South Branch	1787	9	533
Roy, Joseph (Ray)	120	South Branch	1787	9	521
Royce—or Royse					
Royce, Daniel	300	Keithes Gap	1796	9	115
Royce, Daniel	33	Falling Spring	1796	9	116
Royce, Daniel	25	Gr. Cacapon	1795	6	480
Royce, Daniel	7a.3r.	Great Cacapon	1796	6	488
Royce, Frederick	345	Spring Gap Run	1789	8	490
Royce, Frederick et al	14⅝	Gr. Cacapon	1852	7	320
Royce, John	142	Gr. Cacapon	1773	4	443
Royce, John	357	Spring Gap Mt.	1766	1	344
Royse, Daniel	416	Sidling Hill	1795	6	468
Royse, John Sr.	254	Spring Gap Mt.	1787	8	5
Rozener, Gideon	116	Middle Ridge	1789	8	314
Ruckman, Gibson et al	283	Tear Coat Creek	1835	3	415
Ruckman, Gibson et al	108	Tear Coat Cr.	1849	7	272
Ruckman, Jacob	52	Lit. Cacapon	1813	5	133
Ruckman, Jacob	100	Lit. Cacapon	1800	9	287
Ruckman, John	305	Stony Mt.	1845	7	189
Ruckman, John	11a.11p.	L. Cacapon	1833	3	320
Ruckman, Joseph	46	Lit. Cacapon	1845	7	188
Ruckman, Peter	39¼	Lit. Cacapon	1818	5	223
Ruckman, Samuel (of John) et al	104	Tear Coat Run	1834	3	366
Ruckman, Samuel (of John) et al	146	Tear Coat	1834	3	377
Ruckman, Samuel (of John)	12	Cove Mt.	1852	7	317
Ruckman, Samuel (of John)	28½	Lit. Cacapon	1853	7	363
Ruckman, Samuel	20½	Lit. Cacapon	1794	6	396
Ruckman, Samuel	50	Cove Mt.	1858	7	476

Name of Grantee	Acres	Local Description	Year	Book	Page
Ruckman, Samuel	10a.3r.30p.	Lit. Cacapon	1842	7	322
Ruckman, Samuel	125	L. Cacapon	1831	3	240
Ruckman, Samuel	40	Stony Mt.	1804	9	456
Ruckman, Samuel	59	Lit. Cacapon	1800	9	292
Ruckman, Samuel C.	75	Lit. Cacapon	1842	7	102
Ruckman, Samuel C.	239	Piney Mt.	1844	7	164
Ruckman, Samuel C.	100	Piney Mt.	1853	7	361
Ruckman, Samuel C.	112	Stone Lick Fork	1859	7	491
Ruckman, Samuel et al	153	Lit. Cacapon	1800	9	266
Ruckman, Susanna	90a.2r.36p.	Lit. Cacapon	1822	5	363
Ruckman, Thomas	75	Stony Mt.	1842	7	112
Ruckman, Thomas	315	Lit. Cacapon	1804	9	479
Ruckman, Thomas	158	Lit. Cacapon	1800	9	316
Ruckman, Thomas	52	Nr. John Dowden	1800	9	284
Ruckman, Thomas	50	Lit. Cacapon	1800	9	259
Ruckman, Thomas	100	Lit. Cacapon	1800	9	246
Rudale, Stephen	237	Gr. Cacapon	1788	8	120
Rudolph, Adam	2	Lit. Cacapon	1841	7	75
Rudolph, Adam	14	Lit. Cacapon	1847	7	225
Rupell, David	210	Gr. Cacapon	1790	8	560
Rush, John	36	New Creek Mt.	1792	6	282
Russell, David	210	Gr. Cacapon	1790	8	560
Rutherford, Benjamin	83	Patterson's Cr.	1762	1	94
Rutherford, Benjamin et al	306	Patterson's Cr.	1766	1	379
Rutherford, Benjamin et al	201	Patterson's Cr.	1766	1	378
Rutherford, Robert	391	Enoch's Mill Run	1778	2	108
Rutherford, Robert	231	Wts. Potomac	1766	1	385
Rutherford, Robert	208	Chestnut Spgs.	1765	1	300
Rutherford, Robert	400	Lit. Cacapon	1787	8	31
Rutherford, Robert	400	Enoch's Mill Run	1772	3	575
Rutherford, Thomas	152	Bean's Branch	1762	1	185
Ryan, James	361½	Stone Lick Run	1792	6	205
Ryan, James	84	Patterson's Cr.	1778	2	121
Ryan, James	300	Patterson's Cr.	1765	1	305
Ryan, James	359¼	Patterson Cr.	1789	8	186
Ryan, James	150	Patterson's Cr.	1788	8	96
Ryan, John	22½	Patterson's Cr.	1792	6	132
Salt, Thomas	132	Lost River	1789	8	295
Salt, Thomas	71	Gr. Cacapon	1789	8	294
Salyards, John J.	100	Feritan's Br.	1859	7	493
Sampson, Richard	210	Gr. Cacapon	1788	8	157
Sands, Othniel	215	North Branch	1790	8	509
Sanduskey, Samuel	59	North Fork So. Br.	1786	9	520
Sapp, George	76	Green Spring Run	1779	2	249
Sargent, See Largent					
Sargent, John	348	North River	1803	9	435
Saunders, Alexander	46	South Branch	1853	7	357
Saunders, Alexander	94	Wts. Potomac	1857	7	447
Saunders, Joseph	370	Tear Coat Run	1779	2	213
Savage, John	178	Knobly Mountain	1778	2	142
Savage, John	183	Knobly Mt.	1794	6	400
Savage, Dr. William	400	Gr. Cacapon	1774	4	463
Savage, Dr. William	229	Gr. Cacapon	1774	4	464
Savage, Dr. William	169½	Gr. Cacapon	1774	4	465
Say, Lay, Loy					
Schullar, Benjamin	408	Farrington Branch	1774	4	478
Scott, Adonijah & David	400	Liney's Creek	1754	1	18
Scott, David & Adonijah (Brothers)	400	Looney's Cr.	1754	2	30
Scott, Isiah	91	Ft. Pleasant Road	1796	6	489
Scott, James	400	Looney's Cr.	1773	4	457
Scott, Robert	180	Patterson's Cr.	1779	2	156
Scott, Robert	151	Patterson's Cr.	1779	2	157
Scott, Robert	292	Clay Lick Br.	1779	2	158

Name of Grantee	Acres	Local Description	Year	Book	Page
Shellhorn, Bolsor	239	Adj. Clinton	1792	6	175
Shener, George	287	Flat Mountain	1793	6	357
Shepard—or Shepherd					
Shepard, Job	750	North Branch	1796	6	537
Shepard, Job	800	Tear Coat Run	1796	6	535
Shepard, Job	158	Constant's Run	1796	9	70
Shepherd, Benjamin	40	Adj. Jonathan Shepherd	1796	9	128
Shepherd, Job	480	Jackson's Mill	1794	6	420
Sherrard, Robert	166½	3 Spring Mt.	1820	5	269
Sherrard, Robert	17a.3r.	Bloomery Run	1821	5	349
Sherrard, Robert	97¼	Ivy Run	1830	3	186
Sherrard, Robert	50	Falling Spgs. Run	1831	3	225
Sherrard, Robert et al	35a.1r.19p.	Big Cacapon	1820	5	289
Sherrard, Robert B.	9⅜	Bear Garden Ridge	1856	7	417
Sherrard, Robert B.	21a.60p.	Bear Garden Ridge	1856	7	418
Sherrard, Robert B.	69¼	Bear Garden Ridge	1856	7	419
Sherrard, Robert B.	51	Owen's Ridge	1856	7	420
Sherrard, Robert B.	9a.20p.	Bloomery Run	1857	7	458
Sherrard, William	58	Bloomery Run	1820	5	282
Shields, John	40	Emmery's Run	1834	3	357
Shields, John	18	Abraham's Creek	1834	3	354
Shillhorn—See Shellhorn					
Shingleton—See Singleton					
Shingleton, Absolom	34	Lit. Cacapon	1817	5	214
Shingleton, John	52¾	South Branch	1852	7	335
Shinholt, Jacob	103½	Gibbons Run	1828	3	121
Shinholt, Peter	85½	Sandy Ridge	1832	3	275
Shinholt, Peter	84½	Sandy Ridge	1828	3	113
Shinholt, Peter	40a. 1r.	Sandy Ridge	1828	3	112
Shinn, Samuel	23	Gr. Cacapon	1817	5	201
Ship, Godfrey	19¼	Plum Run	1812	5	102
Ship, Godfrey	18¼	Plum Run	1812	5	99
Shipler, John & Henry	140	South Branch	1780	7	563
Shivers, John et al	25¼	Edward's Run	1830	3	212
Shockey, Joseph	58 (158)	Saw Mill Run	1833	3	305
Shockey, Joseph	66	Mill Creek	1831	3	274
Shocky, Joseph (Shockey)	122	Wts. Mill Cr.	1831	3	269
Shoemaker, George	302	Kempsey's Run	1789	8	457
Shoemaker, George	51½	Mill Creek	1831	3	239
Shoemaker, George	63	Mill Creek	1833	3	326
Shoemaker, George	4⅞	Mud Run	1857	7	444
Shoemaker, George et al	275	Long Lick Mt.	1843	7	142
Shoemaker, Peter	124	Gr. Cacapon	1795	6	478
Shore, Thomas	50	Allegheny Mt.	1802	9	369
Shores, Lander	245	South Branch	1833	3	327
Shores, Thomas	22½	Allegheny Mt.	1836	3	430
Shores, Thomas Jr.	50	Adj. J. McCormick	1836	7	534
Short, Isaac	345	Baker's Run	1780	6	598
Short, Jacob	278	Baker's Run	1779	2	172
Short, Jacob	15½	Grapevine Ridge	1854	7	376
Short, Michael	11a.3r.6p.	Crooked Run	1820	5	276
Short, Richard	74	Brackenridge Mt.	1833	3	321
Shrieve, Joseph	224	South Branch	1784	9	508
Sibole—See Sybole					
Simcock, Samuel	107	Round Bottom	1779	2	251
Simmons, Thomas	199a.3r.	Wts. Potomac	1779	2	175
Simons, Asa	25	Lit. Cacapon	1837	7	14
Simpson, John	226	Gr. Cacapon	1834	3	381
Simpson, John	53	North River	1835	3	387
Simpson, Joseph S.	122	Marshall Ridge	1849	7	277
Sims, Thomas	50	Gr. Cacapon	1796	9	28
Singleton—See Shingleton					
Singleton, John	150	Patterson's Cr.	1819	5	250

Name of Grantee	Acres	Local Description	Year	Book	Page
Smith, John L. et al	200	Gr. Cacapon	1850	7	295
Smith, Nathaniel	141	Knobly Mt.	1789	8	397
Smith, Nathaniel	40	Knobly Mt.	1789	8	404
Smith, Richard	400	Capt. John's Run	1777	2	98
Smith, Richard	349	Warm Spring	1792	6	291
Smith, Solomon (of Benjamin)	50	Adj. G. R. Tasker	1839	7	37
Smith, Solomon (of Benjamin) et al	300	Pine Swamp Run	1839	7	38
Smith, Stephen	55¾	Tear Coat Cr	1852	7	340
Smith, Timothy	200	Short Mountain	1801	9	344
Smith, William	41	Branch Mt.	1792	6	295
Smith, William	82	South Branch	1790	8	545
Smith, William	100	New Creek	1762	1	172
Smith, William	400	Wts. Potomac	1761	1	59
Smoot, Thomas	53	Adj. his own	1796	9	20
Smyth—See Smith					
Snapp, Joseph	125	Crooked Run	1832	3	273
Snickers, Edward	223	Lost River	1767	5	486
Snickers, Edward	90	Wts. Potomac	1762	1	168
Snyder, Levi	30	Town Hill	1853	7	355
Sollars, Thomas	50	New Creek	1825	5	413
Spade, George	3½	Gr. Cacapon	1854	7	395
Spade, John	2a.	Gr. Cacapon	1854	7	394
Speake, Thomas Capt.	196	Lit. Cacapon	1762	1	166
Speake, Thomas Capt.	115	Lit. Cacapon	1762	1	165
Spencer, J. H.	13¾	Cabin Run	1860	7	518
Spencer, John	322	Cabin Run	1792	6	177
Spencer, John	50	Knobbly Mt.	1832	3	295
Spencer, John	44½	Knobly Mt.	1803	9	421
Spencer, John Jr.	34	Knobly Mt.	1837	7	16
Spencer, John M.	150	Knobly Mt.	1852	7	324
Sphor—See Spore					
Spiker, Jacob	260	Mid Run	1789	8	345
Spore, John	264	Lit. Cacapon	1767	5	494
Spore, John	410	Lit. Cacapon	1767	5	495
Sprigg, Osburn	94	Green Spg. Valley	1796	6	544
Spurling, Jesse	53	Mill Creek	1847	7	219
Stafford, Richard	100	Knobly Mt.	1796	9	67
Stafford, Richard	108	Adj. T. Lawton	1792	6	137
Stafford, Richard	33	Patterson's Cr.	1792	6	126
Stagg—or Staggs					
Stagg, George	400	Parker's Run	1791	6	55
Stagg, George	44	Patterson's Cr.	1815	5	151
Stagg, George	13¾	Patterson's Cr.	1815	5	150
Staggs, Christopher	44a.2r.30p.	Stagg's Run	1828	3	125
Staggs, George	29	Patterson's Cr.	1819	5	262
Staggs, William	50	Cabin Run	1833	3	338
Staggs, William	230¼ (230¾)	Stagg's Run	1829	3	163
Stalcup, Emmor Jr.	246	North Branch	1847	7	237
Stalcup, Israel	64	Plum Run	1813	5	121
Stallcup—or Stalcup					
Stallcup, Emmor	112	Nobly Mt.	1854	7	374
Stallcup, Emmor Jr.	23	North Branch	1854	7	375
Stallman, Lewis	250	Staggs Run	1791	6	83
Stalnaker—See Stonaker					
Starkey, Frederick	257	Adj. George Nixon	1789	8	503
Starkey, John	65	Tear Coat Cr.	1848	7	249
Starkey, John et al	283	Tear Coat Creek	1835	3	415
Starky—See Starkey					
Starn—See Stern					
Starn, James (Starne)	6	Spring Gap Mt.	1848	7	248
Starn, John	506	North River	1816	5	178
Starn, John	57⅞	Adj. his own	1814	5	141
Starn. John	184	North River	1812	5	92

Name of Grantee	Acres	Local Description	Year	Book	Page
Starn, Joseph	95⅝	Adj. John Starn	1812	5	87
Starnes, John et al	634	Lewis Run	1854	7	378
Starr, James	300	Green Spg. Run	1792	6	174
Starr, John	251	Jurdin's Run	1791	6	35
Starr, Moses	103	Green Spgs. Run	1800	9	276
Steed, Aaron	400	Wts. Potomac	1791	6	74
Steel, John	235	Lit. Cacapon	1764	1	228
Steel, John	363	Lit. Cacapon	1764	1	229
Steel, John	233	Clay Lick Br.	1765	1	275
Steel, John	275	Lit. Cacapon	1765	1	276
Steel, John	111	Clay Lick Br.	1765	1	283
Stembel, Jost (Stemmel)	35	Mill Creek	1803	9	428
Stephen, Adam	542	Patterson's Cr.	1771	3	553
Stephen, Adam Col.	137	Bear Garden Mt.	1762	1	156
Stephenfought, John	100	Gr. Cacapon	1800	9	238
Stephens, Christian	326	Patterson's Cr.	1789	8	289
Stephens, David	150	Bear Ridge	1796	9	89
Stephens, Peter	206	North River	1762	1	148
Stephens, William	354	New Creek Mt.	1767	5	513
Stern—See Starn					
Stern, Jacob	236	Lit. Cacapon	1789	8	172
Stern, Jacob et al	213	Lit. Cacapon	1797	9	132
Stern, Jacob et al	30	Adj. J. Powell	1797	9	130
Stern, Jacob & John	40	South Br. Mountain	1797	9	135
Stern, Joseph et al	177	Lit. Cacapon	1806	9	543
Sterrett, William	400	Hopkins Lick	1800	9	231
Sterrett, William M.	400	Lanam's Br.	1801	9	352
Stevenbergen, Peter	185	Adj. J. Carroll	1760	1	40
Steward—See Stewart, Stuart					
Steward, James	240	Cacapon	1761	1	67
Stewart, David	7	North Branch	1795	6	431
Stewart, David	510	Adj. Alexander King	1795	6	432
Stewart, David	300	North Branch	1795	6	434
Stewart, David	1,300	Adj. Thomas B. Martin	1795	6	435
Stewart, David	480	Gr. Cacapon	1796	6	555
Stewart, David	405	Spring Gap Mt.	1796	6	556
Stewart, James Jr.	32	Tear Coat Cr.	1841	7	73
Stewart, James Jr.	50	Bare Knob	1841	7	74
Stewart, James Sr.	24½	Brushy Ridge	1835	3	409
Stewart, Thomas	57	Cabin Run	1799	9	196
Stickley, Tobias	28	Mike's Run	1837	7	15
Stingly, Jacob	198	Looney's Cr.	1789	8	189
Stoker—or Stokes					
Stoker, John	258	Mill Run	1780	6	596
Stoker, John	100	Lit. Cacapon	1820	5	321
Stoker, John	84	Lit. Cacapon	1818	5	235
Stoker, John	70	Lit. Cacapon	1818	5	234
Stokes—or Stoker					
Stokes, Palsor	232	Lit. Cacapon	1776	2	44
Stollaberger, Mathias	107½	Cabin Run	1830	3	217
Stonaker, Richard M.	3a.2r.13p.	Park's Valley	1854	7	391
Stonaker, Richard M.	116	Dillon's Mt.	1852	7	323
Stone, Benjamin	62	North River	1796	9	126
Stone, Benjamin	152½	North River	1791	6	78
Stone, Benjamin	1,103	North River	1791	6	81
Stone, Elijah	208	North River	1796	9	71
Stone, James	317	Branch Mt.	1788	8	148
Stone, Richard	100	Mill Creek	1809	5	21
Stradford, Jonathan	393	Lit. Cacapon	1791	6	97
Streit, Philip B.	10⅛	Deep Run	1858	7	461
Streit, Philip B.	19½	Abram's Creek	1858	7	460
Stricker, George	195	Adj. D. Vance	1764	1	223
Strode, John	398	Lit. Cacapon	1780	7	579

Name of Grantee	Acres	Local Description	Year	Book	Page
Strode, John	357	Lit. Cacapon	1780	7	578
Strode, John	190	Breakneck Run	1787	8	24
Stroud, Adam	235	North Branch	1788	8	158
Stuart—See Steward, Stewart					
Stuart, James	126	Adj. John McDonald	1789	8	256
Stump, Adam	24	Mill Cr. Mt.	1859	7	505
Stump, Adam	70¼	Wts. Potomac	1859	7	506
Stump, Augustus I.	57	Lit. Cacapon	1842	7	119
Stump, Benjamin	69	Lit. Cacapon	1820	5	294
Stump, George W. et al	96	Stony Run	1859	7	502
Stump, John	220	L. Cacapon	1830	3	189
Stump, John	240	Lit. Cacapon	1812	5	89
Stump, John	80	Town Hill	1844	7	154
Stump, Joseph	65	L. Cacapon	1833	3	348
Stump, Samuel J.	250	L. Cacapon	1831	3	229
Stump, Samuel J.	12½	North River Mt.	1856	7	427
Stump, Samuel J.	36½	North River Mt.	1848	7	247
Stump, William P.	148	North Br.	1848	7	255
Stump, William P.	488	North Branch	1848	7	254
Stump, William P.	54	South Br. Mt.	1845	7	193
Stump, William P.	15¼	South Br. Mt.	1845	7	192
Stump, William P.	160	Middle Ridge	1845	7	191
Stump, William P.	28½	So. Branch Mt.	1842	7	101
Stump, William P. et al	235	North Branch	1845	7	190
Sulser, Henry (Lutser)	100	Mill Creek	1833	3	347
Sultzer, Adam	100	Mill Creek	1832	3	282
Summers, John T. (L.)	34	North River	1816	5	195
Summerville, James	14a.31p.	Bloomery Run	1820	5	297
Summerville, James	145½	Bloomery Run	1828	3	135
Summetts, Jacob	154	Hughes Run	1778	2	115
Surbough—See Serbough					
Sutton, Samuel et al	562	Big Mountain	1835	3	414
Sutton, Zachariah	80	North River	1802	9	389
Swick, Benjamin	231	Adj. Ersom	1791	6	116
Swim, John	464	Gr. Cacapon	1788	8	112
Swires, Jacob (Swyer)	33	Bear Wallow	1822	5	360
Swisher Jacob	6a.	Lit. Cacapon	1854	7	388
Swisher Jacob	7½	Lit. Cacapon	1854	7	387
Swisher, John	330	Adj. his own land	1788	8	79
Swisher, John	154	North River Mt.	1809	5	15
Swisher, John	124	Hughes Mill Run	1815	5	164
Swisher, John	100	Dilling's Mt	1802	9	367
Swisher, John	809	Adj. S. Hinkle	1804	9	439
Swisher, John Sr.	263½	Hughes Run	1816	5	173
Swisher, Valentine	222	Gr. Cacapon	1792	6	176
Switzer, John	239	Dillon's Run	1789	8	287
Swyer—See Swires					
Sybole, or Sibole					
Sybole, Bazel	61	Little Mountain	1847	7	233
Syler, Jacob (Sylor)	100	Gr. Cacapon	1800	9	294
Taggart, Francis	428	Lit. Cacapon	1779	2	242
Taggart, Francis	425	Palmer's Run	1779	2	243
Tarpley, James	120	Rocky Branch	1790	8	553
Tarpley, James	20	Wts. Potomac	1780	7	573
Tarry, Stephen I.	50	Knobly Mt.	1802	9	372
Tarvin—See also Tervin					
Tarvin, George	417	Wts. Potomac	1790	8	520
Tasker, George G.	11½	North Branch	1829	3	160
Tasker, George G.	33¼	Abram's Ridge	1841	7	69
Tasker, George G.	56⅞	Montgomery Run	1852	7	338
Tasker, George G. & Benjamin	76	North Branch	1836	7	529
Tasker, George G. & Benjamin	525	Stoney Run	1832	3	303
Tasker, George G. & Benjamin et al	110	Howell's Run	1836	7	531

Name of Grantee	Acres	Local Description	Year	Book	Page
Tharp, Solomon	69¼	Hairy Mountain	1852	7	337
Tharp, Solomon	200	North River	1852	7	336
Tharp, Solomon	40	Horn Camp Run	1835	3	400
Tharp, Solomon et al	300	Pot Lick Run	1858	7	466
Thomas, Daniel	329	George's Run	1790	8	527
Thomas, Daniel	408	George's Run	1790	8	528
Thomas, Enoch D.	309	Sugar Camp	1787	9	522
Thomas, John	272	Brushy Run	1796	9	10
Thomas, Morris	16	Adj. D. Myles	1779	2	176
Thomas, Morris	276	Hutton's Run	1779	2	177
Thomas, Morris	86½	Hutton's Run	1779	2	178
Thomas, Moses	50	New Creek	1798	9	159
Thomas, Moses	84	New Creek	1796	9	69
Thomas, Moses	16	New Creek	1797	9	144
Thomas, William	142	Spring Gap Mt.	1846	7	209
Thompson—See Thomson					
Thompson, Andrew	302a.2r.	Hughes Run	1778	2	107
Thompson, Charles et al	175	Enoch's Mill Run	1765	1	281
Thompson, Charles et al	97	Pine Draught	1765	1	284
Thompson, George	184	Chestnut Ridge	1842	7	123
Thompson, George	17	Lit. Cacapon Mt.	1850	7	286
Thompson, George	5,000	Gr. Cacapon	1795	6	449
Thompson, James	50	North River	1828	3	114
Thompson, James	15½	North River	1806	9	545
Thompson, Jeremiah	98	Gr. Cacapon	1796	6	505
Thompson, Jeremiah	95	Gr. Cacapon	1796	6	503
Thompson, Jeremiah	74¼	Cacapon	1792	6	148
Thompson, Jeremiah	100	Constant's Run	1796	6	507
Thompson, Jeremiah	42	Gr. Cacapon	1796	6	506
Thompson, Jeremiah	38	Gr. Cacapon	1796	9	79
Thompson, Jeremiah	25½	Gr. Cacapon	1796	9	80
Thompson, Jeremiah	53	Gr. Cacapon	1804	9	478
Thompson, Jeremiah	136	Gr. Cacapon	1804	9	462
Thompson, Jeremiah et al	60	Constant Run	1804	9	461
Thompson, John	100	North River Mt.	1792	6	141
Thompson, John	150	North River	1795	6	164
Thompson, John	100	Sugar Run	1857	7	448
Thompson, John	100	Lit. Cacapon	1801	9	346
Thompson, John	212	Lit. Cacapon	1800	9	280
Thompson, John	200	South Branch	1811	5	447
Thompson, John	5	North River	1816	5	187
Thompson, John	226	Limestone Run	1778	2	145
Thompson, John	239	Limestone Run	1789	8	481
Thompson, John	233	Lit. Cacapon	1789	8	223
Thompson, John & Joseph	130	North River	1796	5	582
Thompson, Joseph	100	North River	1796	9	127
Thompson, Joseph	403	North River	1791	6	52
Thompson, Joseph	57	North R. Mt.	1807	9	562
Thompson, Joseph	100	Tear Coat	1804	9	491
Thompson, Joseph	120	North River	1809	5	12
Thompson, Joseph et al	200	North River	1816	5	184
Thompson, Samuel et al	300	North River	1819	5	248
Thompson, William	485	North River	1792	6	208
Thompson, William	184	So. Branch	1776	2	38
Thomson—or Thompson, Tompson					
Thomson, Charles	186	So. Branch	1769	5	541
Thomson, Charles et al	432	Tear Coat Run	1771	3	566
Thomson, Charles et al	345	Enoch's M. Run	1771	3	567
Thomson, Charles et al	458	Enoch's M. Run	1773	3	592
Thomson, Charles et al	243	Ross's Run	1773	3	593
Thomson, Charles et al	24	Tear Coat Creek	1771	3	555
Thomson, Charles et al	160	So. Branch	1767	5	476
Thomson, Charles et al	242 (224)	Cor. to Mannor line	1767	5	478

Name of Grantee	Acres	Local Description	Year	Book	Page
Thomson, Charles (Thompson) et al	1,920	Enoch's Mill Run	1767	5	479
Thomson, Charles (Thompson) et al	195	Gr. Cacapon	1767	5	481
Thomson, Charles et al	164	So. Branch	1767	5	480
Thomson, Charles et al	168	So. Branch	1768	5	539
Thorn, Michael	202	Wts. Potomac	1765	1	242
Thornton, John	127	North Branch	1788	8	117
Thorp—See Tharp					
Throckmorton, Daniel	275	Gr. Cacapon	1789	8	471
Throckmorton, Gabriel et al	900	Gr. Cacapon	1804	9	445
Throckmorton, Gabriel et al	135	Gr. Cacapon	1804	9	441
Throckmorton, Lewis	361	Yancey Run	1790	8	516
Throckmorton, Lewis	75	Wts. Potomac	1789	8	478
Throckmorton, Warner	12½	North Branch	1820	5	317
Throckmorton, Warner	106½	Wts. Potomac	1813	5	113
Thrush, David	68½	Abram's Ridge	1837	7	17
Thrush, John	68a.1r.30p.	Rawling Run	1822	5	364
Thrush, John	33	Stagg's Run	1829	3	164
Thrush, John	50	Stagg Run	1831	3	238
Thrush, John	147	Abram's Ridge	1836	7	523
Thrush, Michael	57½	Knobly Mt.	1855	7	401
Thrush, Michael	97	Stagg's Run	1829	3	159
Thrush, Peter M.	17a.3r.	Patterson's Cr.	1858	7	480
Thrush, Richard	49¼	Rawlings Run	1858	7	475
Tidball, James	251	Wts. Potomac	1812	5	95
Tiler, Jacob	20	Gr. Cacapon	1817	5	203
Tivepan, Daniel (Tevebaugh)	155	Spring Run	1788	8	103
Tompson—See Thompson, Thomson					
Tompson, John	297	Lit. Cacapon	1805	9	541
Totten, Samuel	100	Cabin Run	1795	6	467
Totten, Samuel	47	Patterson's Cr.	1820	5	271
Topper, Henry	125	Bear Garden	1820	5	272
Topper, Henry	12	Big Cacapon	1820	5	273
Toy—See Joy, Lay, Loy					
Triplet, Thomas	233	Cacapon	1761	1	76
Triplett, Joseph	28	North River	1797	9	133
Triplett, Thomas	245	Sidling Hill	1792	6	217
Trout, Henry	43	Knobly Mt.	1848	7	250
Trout, Henry	41	Knobly Mt.	1848	7	251
Trouten, William	12	Crooked Run	1848	7	252
Tucker, James	1,122	Potomac	1803	9	409
Tucker, James	600	South Branch	1803	9	410
Turk, Andrew	160	Mill's Br.	1776	2	45
Turner, William	178	Turner's Mill R.	1781	8	585
Tutterer, John	50	Patterson's Cr.	1796	9	72
Twigg, James	150	North Branch	1852	7	303
Twigg, James	245	North Br.	1848	7	253
Twigg, James	200	North Branch	1852	7	304
Tyler—See Tiler					
Ullery, Jacob	16¼	Lit. Cacapon	1854	7	392
Umstol—See Umstott					
Umstot, John	96½	Knobly Mt.	1852	7	325
Umstott—or Unstot					
Umstott, Conrad (Umstol)	1a.1r.	Beaver Run	1838	7	21
Umstott, Jacob & Conrad	3¾	Patterson's Cr.	1815	5	153
Umstott, John	9	Patterson's Cr.	1817	5	208
Umstott, Philip	15½	Horseshoe Ridge	1833	3	334
Umstott, Philip	12¾	Cabin Run	1833	3	333
Umstott, Philip	40	Knobby Mt.	1833	3	332
Umstott, Philip	50	Knobby Mt.	1828	3	110
Unstot—See Umstott					
Urias—See Urice					

Name of Grantee	Acres	Local Description	Year	Book	Page
Urias, Philip	274	Deep Run	1837	7	538
Urice—Also Urias, Urise					
Urice, George	60½	Knobly Mt.	1812	5	96
Urice, George et al	43¼	Cabin Run	1819	5	254
Urice, John & Peter	50	Knobby Mt.	1832	3	279
Urice, Peter	100	Knobly Mt.	1852	7	302
Urice, Philip	93½	Knobby Mountain	1828	3	132
Urise—See Urice					
Utt, Catherine	50	Dry Run	1835	3	403
Utt, Catherine (Utta)	16a.24p.	Mike's Run	1824	5	405
Utta, Christopher	27¼	Mike's Run	1856	7	424
Utta, Christopher	50	Mike's Run	1856	7	425
Utta, Christopher	65	Mike's Run	1856	7	426
Vanbibber, John	271	Wts. Potomac	1766	1	320
Van Buskirk, Elijah	213	Deep Run	1835	3	408
Van Buskirk, William	74	Dry Run	1833	3	342
Van Buskirk, William	74½	Johnson's Run	1833	3	340
Vance—See Vanse, Vause					
Vance, David	288	Wts. Potomac	1762	1	115
Vance, David	456	Patterson's Cr.	1762	1	116
Vance, James	564	North Mountain	1825	5	410
Vance, William	100	Fork Knob	1857	7	445
Vandever—See Vanderver, Vandiver					
Vandever, Vincent	232	Abraham's Cr.	1831	3	260
Vandiver—See Vandever					
Vandiver, Jacob	189	Cabin Run	1810	5	61
Vandiver, John	22	Decker's Glade Run	1836	3	431
Vandiver, John	93	Dry Run	1841	7	79
Vandiver, Lewis	400	Amory Run	1796	6	486
Vandiver, Lewis	150	North Branch	1796	6	492
Vandiver, Samuel	105½	Abraham's Creek	1833	3	322
Vandiver, Samuel	30	Hogeland's Glade Run	1833	3	312
Vandiver, Samuel	175	New Creek	1833	3	307
Vandiver, Samuel	260	Vandiver's Run	1823	5	371
Vandiver, Vincent	66	Patterson Creek	1833	3	324
Vandiver, Vincent	312	Patterson Creek	1833	3	323
Vandiver, Vincent	366	Wts. Potomac	1831	3	236
Vandiver, Vincent	299½	Adj. Reason Harvy	1831	3	235
Vandiver, Vincent	80	Mill Creek	1831	3	234
Vandiver, Vincent	273¾	Wts. Potomac	1831	3	233
Vandiver, Vincent	287	New Creek	1831	3	232
Vandiver, Vincent	17a.2r.18p.	Middle Run	1827	3	103
Vandiver, Vincent	179	Knobby Mt.	1825	5	419
Vandiver, Vincent	150	Knobly Mt.	1823	5	380
Vandiver, Vincent	75	Patterson's Cr.	1823	5	379
Vandiver, Vincent et al	94¼	Loonam's Cr.	1825	5	435
Vanesdal—or Vannosdall, Vanorsdall					
Vanesdal, Cornelius & Jeremiah	136	Gr. Cacapon	1846	7	202
Vanmeter, Abraham	22	Mill Run	1788	8	122
Vanmeter, Abraham	152¼	Stony Run	1826	3	93
Vanmeter, David	277	Abram's Creek	1845	7	195
Vanmeter, Garrett	237	Patterson's Cr. Mt.	1787	8	26
Van Meter, Garret	200	Flagg Meadow Run	1761	1	73
Van Meter, Garret	89	Patterson's Cr.	1762	1	97
Vanmeter, Garrett Col.	260	Patterson's Cr.	1780	6	604
Van Meter, Henry Col.	105	Patterson's Cr.	1765	1	296
Van Meter, Henry Col.	192	Flagg Meadow	1765	1	295
Van Meter, Henry Col.	360	Patterson's Cr.	1765	1	292
Van Meter, Henry Col.	122	Wts. So. Branch	1765	1	294
Vanmeter, Isaac	190	Adj. John Hufman	1789	8	496
Vanmeter, Isaac	686	High Knob Mt.	1798	9	178
Vanmeter, Isaac	162	South Br.	1791	6	75
Vanmeter, Isaac	200	Low Mill Run	1791	6	88

Name of Grantee	Acres	Local Description	Year	Book	Page
Watson, Joseph	70	North River	1765	1	250
Watson, Joseph	424	Enoch's Mill Run	1771	3	558
Watson, Joseph	366	Lit. Cacapon	1773	3	595
Watts, Archibald	59	Mill Creek	1804	9	443
Watts, James	225	Mile's Run	1796	9	19
Watts, James	50	Beaver Run	1794	6	397
Watts, James	50	Cor. to his Survey	1794	6	389
Watts, James	120	Mill Creek	1789	8	349
Watts, James	390	Patterson's Cr.	1789	8	338
Watts, James	180	Adj. F. Fink & his own	1803	9	407
Weatherton, John	187	Wts. Potomac	1788	8	147
Weetz, Joseph (Wertz)	100	Patterson's Cr.	1792	6	179
Welch—or Welsh					
Welch, Isaac	21	Patterson Cr.	1816	5	192
Welch, James	1,100	South Branch	1800	9	230
Welch, Sylvester	75	Cabin Run	1829	3	169
Welch, Thomas	280a.1r.	Cabin Run	1820	5	305
Welch, Thomas	98¾	Cabin Run	1836	9	529
Welch, William	57	Knobly Mt.	1839	7	39
Welsh, Demcy Sr.	20½	New Creek	1829	3	158
Welsh, William	50	Knobby Mt.	1834	3	383
Welsh, William, Ex.	100	Knobbly Mt.	1834	3	368
Welsh, William, Ex.	50	Knobley Mt.	1834	3	358
Welton—See Walton					
Welton, Jesse	104	Laurel Creek	1778	2	138
Welton, Jesse	68	Looney's Cr.	1788	8	127
Welton, Job	52	Patterson's Cr.	1762	1	136
Welton, John	340	Wts. Potomac	1762	1	135
Welton, William	53	Patterson's Cr.	1777	2	77
Welton, William	126	Patterson's Cr.	1787	8	27
Wertz, Joseph (Weetz)	100	Patterson's Creek	1792	6	179
West, Stephen	280	Spring Gap Mt.	1774	4	481
Westell, Humphrey	112	Cabin Run	1761	1	71
Westfall, Jacob	140	Looney's Creek	1761	1	72
Wetzel—See also Witzel					
Wetzel, Christopher	160	So. Branch	1777	2	56
Wharton, Joseph Jr.	319	Patterson's Cr.	1772	3	587
Wharton, Joseph Jr.	409	Ice's Gap	1772	3	589
Wharton, Joseph Jr.	448	Horseshoe Ridge	1772	3	588
Wharton, Thomas	164 (146)	Patterson's Cr.	1767	5	497
Wharton, Thomas	390	North Fork	1776	4	496
Wharton, Thomas & Joseph	467	Gibbons Run	1769	5	543
Wharton, Thomas & Joseph	310¾	Mud Lick	1769	5	545
Wharton, Thomas & Joseph	409½	Buffalo Lick Br.	1768	5	524
Wharton, Thomas & Joseph	401	Buffalo Lick Br.	1767	5	503
Wharton, Thomas & Joseph	82½	So. Branch	1767	5	498
Wharton, Thomas & Joseph	406	Patterson's Cr.	1765	1	306
Wharton, Thomas & Joseph	400	Patterson's Cr.	1765	1	266
Wharton, Thomas & Joseph	220	Patterson's Cr.	1765	1	263
Wharton, Thomas & Joseph	312	Looney's Cr.	1774	4	470
Wharton, Thomas & Joseph	422	Patterson's Cr.	1774	4	469
Wharton, Thomas & Joseph	344	Saw Mill Run	1774	4	468
Wharton, Thomas & Joseph	402	South Branch	1774	4	467
Wharton, Thomas & Joseph	272	Patterson's Cr.	1774	4	466
Wharton, Thomas & Joseph	400	Gr. Cacapon	1773	4	456
Wharton, Thomas & Joseph	426	Pond Lick Run	1773	4	455
Wharton, Thomas & Joseph	308	New Creek	1767	5	496
Wharton, Thomas & Joseph	189	Patterson's Cr.	1765	1	247
Wharton, Thomas & Joseph	198	Patterson's Creek	1765	1	246
Wharton, Thomas & Joseph	200	Patterson's Cr.	1765	1	245
Wharton, Thomas & Joseph	200	Patterson's Cr.	1765	1	244
Wharton, Thomas & Joseph	351	Patterson's Cr.	1764	1	218
Wharton, Thomas & Joseph	265	Kuykend. Saw Mill Run	1764	1	217

Name of Grantee	Acres	Local Description	Year	Book	Page
Williams, Thomas	22	Adj. A. Woodrow	1794	6	363
Williams, Thomas	25	Kanahaway Hill	1795	6	479
Williams, Thomas C.	113	Montgomery Run	1856	7	406
Williams, Vincent	195	Patterson's Cr.	1789	8	164
Williams, Vincent	377	Patterson's Cr.	1789	8	168
Williams, Vincent	23	Patterson's Cr.	1789	8	187
Williams, Vincent	504	Patterson's Cr.	1754	1	2
Williams, Vincent	504	Patterson's Cr.	1754	2	3
Williams, William	257	Wts. Potomac	1790	8	526
Williamson, Benjamin	203a.2r.	Sideling Hill	1831	3	228
Williamson, Benjamin	158	Sidling Hill	1856	7	433
Williamson, Cornelius	108	Crooked Run	1825	5	423
Williamson, John	120	North River	1826	3	99
Williamson, John	275	Lit. Cacapon	1789	8	248
Williamson, Mary et al	139¼	Lit. Cacapon	1804	9	457
Williamson, Samuel	128	Lit. Cacapon	1789	8	432
Williamson, Samuel	19¾	Crooked Run	1825	5	422
Williamson, Samuel	75	North River Mt.	1826	3	85
Williamson, Samuel	367	Tear Coat Cr.	1792	6	254
Williamson, Thomas	30	Lit. Cacapon	1800	9	299
Williamson, Thomas	150	Lit. Cacapon	1802	9	404
Williamson, Thomas	70	Adj. G. Morton	1792	6	251
Williamson, Thomas	92	Lit. Cacapon	1794	6	404
Williamson, William	168	Lit. Cacapon	1798	9	172
Williamson, William	9	Lit. Cacapon	1801	9	354
Williamson, William	260	Chestnut Spg. Run	1789	8	226
Williamson, William Jr.	306½	Tear Coat Cr.	1801	9	335
Williamson, Wm. et al	143	Lit. Cacapon	1801	9	339
Wilson, Isaac N.	1a.2r.32p.	North River	1831	3	266
Wilson, James	400	Indian Run	1800	9	224
Wilson, James	400	Deep Run	1800	9	225
Wilson, Richard	100	North Branch	1801	9	356
Wilson, Thomas	391	Wts. Potomac	1762	1	179
Wilson, Walter	361	Timber Ridge	1778	2	105
Wilson, William	280½	Gr. Cacapon	1788	8	66
Wilson, William	227	Trout Run	1788	8	64
Wilson, William	60	Trout Run	1788	8	63
Wilson, William	194	Carr's Gap	1789	8	334
Wilson, William	212a.12p.	Pine Swamp	1789	8	361
Wilson, William	120	Trout Run	1766	1	336
Winchester, William Jr.	333	Buffalo Run	1791	6	13
Winterton, William et al	135	Gr. Cacapon	1804	9	441
Winterton, William et al	900	Gr. Cacapon	1804	9	445
Wise, Abram	100	Patterson's Cr.	1792	6	180
Wise, Boston	67	Mill Creek	1787	9	530
Wise, Jacob	110	North M. Creek	1791	6	96
Wise, John	131	Mill Creek	1789	8	316
Witmire, John F.	412	Sleepy Creek	1780	8	595
Witzel—See also Wetzel					
Witzel, Christopher	413	Pine Cabin Lick	1780	2	263
Witzel, Christopher	235	Timber Ridge	1780	2	264
Witzel, Christopher	249	Lick Run	1780	2	265
Wodrow—See also Woodrow					
Wodrow, Alexander	114	Gr. Cacapon	1768	5	528
Wolf, Christopher	200	Thompson's Run	1791	6	112
Wolf, George et al	100	Tear Coat Cr.	1836	3	418
Wolfe, George	6½	Tear Coat Cr.	1847	7	235
Wolford—See Walford, Woolford					
Wolford, David	9	Tear Coat Cr.	1856	7	430
Wolford, Elijah	10¼	North River	1856	7	409
Wolford, Henry	25½	Tear Coat Creek	1857	7	455
Wolford, Henry	9⅜	Tear Coat Cr.	1857	7	456
Wolford, John	50	North River	1809	5	24
Wolverton, Isaac	110	North River	1794	6	388

HANCOCK COUNTY

Name of Grantee	Acres	Local Description	Year	Book	Page
Brown, Jacob N.	7a.3r.	Nessley's Cluster of Islands	1854	1	503
McHenry, Neil	17a.1r.39p.	Island Ohio R.	1861	1	502

HARDY COUNTY

Alexander, Samuel H.	34	Town Fort Run	1855	4	396
Alfree—or Alfrey					
Alfree, James	176	Patterson's Cr.	1792	1	219
Alfree, John	92	Patterson's Cr.	1796	1	390
Alfrey, Joseph	384	Patterson's Cr.	1792	1	191
Alkire, Michael	108	South Branch	1790	1	122
Allen, J. W. F. et al	119½	Hayes Ridge	1850	4	313
Allman, William	128	Shenandoah River	1793	1	292
Alt—See Ault					
Alt, Michael	50	Mill Creek	1793	1	290
Armentrout—Also Harmentrout, Hermantrout					
Armentrout, Christopher	6	Mill Creek	1854	4	377
Armentrout, Christopher	25	North Mill Cr.	1850	4	325
Armentrout, Job (Armontrout)	27	N. Mill Creek	1837	3	402
Arnold, Daniel	560	Patterson Cr. Mt.	1857	4	413
Arnold, Emanuel	22	Abram's Creek	1834	3	320
Arnold, Joseph	31¾ (30¾)	Mud Lick Run	1845	4	198
Arnold, Joseph	130	Patterson's Cr.	1842	4	121
Arnold, Joseph	90	Patterson Cr. Mt.	1842	4	101
Arnold, Joseph	50	Patterson Cr. Mt.	1842	4	100
Arnold, Joseph	110	Patterson's Cr.	1842	4	96
Arnold, Joseph	220	Patterson Cr. Mt.	1841	4	87
Arnold, Joseph	292	Patterson Cr. Mt.	1835	3	358
Arnold, Joseph	108	Patterson's Cr.	1835	3	351
Arnold, Moses	102½	Patterson's Cr. Mt.	1848	4	282
Arnold, Samuel & Zachariah	9⅝	My Lord's Meadow	1851	4	329
Arrohood—See Arrowhood, Orrowhood					
Arrohood, Joshua (Arrowhood)	80	Norman's Run	1829	3	260
Arrowhood, Alexander	389	Looney's Cr.	1789	1	67
Ault—See Alt					
Ault, Henry	21	Mill Creek	1789	1	47
Ault, Henry	45	Mill Creek	1789	1	78
Ault, Michael	4	N. Mill Creek	1820	3	215
Ault, Michael	100	South Branch	1791	1	129
Ayres, John	120	Middle Mt.	1847	4	262
Ayres, John	189½	Island Ridge	1847	4	265
Babb, Peter	100	Patterson Cr.	1844	4	159
Babs, Thomas	320	Mud Lick Run	1800	3	33
Bacorn—or Bakhorn					
Bacorn, John	3½	Patterson Cr.	1839	4	14
Badgley, David	45	Adj. his Fleming tract	1797	1	510
Badgley, David	146	Looney's Creek	1797	1	511
Badgley, David	352	Lunie's Creek	1788	1	4
Badgley, David	483	Stony River	1789	1	87
Baker, Aaron	3¼	Thorn Run	1847	4	242
Baker, Anthony	182	Allegheny	1791	1	158
Baker, Anthony Jr.	300	Wts. Stoney River	1800	3	34
Baker, Anthony Sr.	500	Wts. Stoney River	1800	3	35
Baker, Benjamin F.	160	Lost River	1845	4	200
Baker, Henry	175	Lost River	1836	3	377

Name of Grantee	Acres	Local Description	Year	Book	Page
Baker, Jacob	335	Baker's Run	1796	1	386
Baker, Jacob	165	Lost River	1796	1	385
Baker, Jacob	65	Bald Knob	1796	1	384
Baker, James	86	Lost River	1796	1	501
Baker, James	60	Lost River	1789	1	83
Baker, James	96	Lost River	1789	1	75
Baker, Joseph	130	Big Ridge	1796	1	365
Baker, Joseph	112	Baker's Run	1795	1	353
Baker, Nicholas	28a.103p.	Hutton's Run	1846	4	226
Baker, Nicholas	297	Big Run	1860	4	453
Baker, Nicholas	1a.1r.14p.	Fort Mt.	1860	4	452
Baker, Nicholas et al	600	Middle Mt.	1836	3	366
Baker, Samuel	234	Adj. his own	1798	1	544
Baker, Samuel	23	Adj. his own	1798	1	543
Baker, Samuel	234	Adj. his own	1797	1	515
Baker, Samuel	107	Gr. Cacapon	1796	1	502
Baker, Samuel et al	608	Lost River	1852	4	355
Baker, William	56¾	Baker's Run	1848	4	283
Baker, William	165¾	Lost River	1848	4	284
Baker, William	53½	Lost River	1849	4	296
Baker, William	24⅝	Lost River	1849	4	298
Baker, William	37	Lost River	1846	4	230
Baker, William	42½	Lost River	1846	4	225
Baker, William	88	North River	1840	4	57
Baker, William	99	Lost River	1796	1	377
Bakhorn—or Bacorn					
Bakhorn, Job & John (Bacorn)	490	Patterson's Cr.	1789	1	105
Barb, Abram	120	Beech Mt.	1842	4	114
Barb, Abram	47	Cacapon	1842	4	115
Barb, John M.	51	Trout Run	1850	4	303
Barkdall—See Barkdoll, Bergdoll, Berkdoll, Berkdull					
Barkdall, Aaron (Abraham)	22	Middle Mt.	1836	3	375
Barkdall, Jacob	39	S. Mill Cr.	1838	3	428
Barkdall, John	100	S. Mill Cr.	1836	3	376
Barkdoll, Jacob	800	South Fork	1826	3	249
Barkdoll, Jacob	206	S. Mill Cr.	1830	3	275
Barkdoll, Jacob	5	S. Mill Creek	1837	3	391
Barret, Mary	304	Walker's Ridge	1791	1	169
Barrett—See Barret					
Basher, Berker, Besher, Bishor					
Basore, Benjamin	136¾	Cove Run	1853	4	373
Basore, Conrad	1⅞	Lost River	1853	4	372
Basore, Conrad	6⅞	North Mt.	1853	4	371
Baughman—See Bauhman, Boughman, Bowman					
Baughman, Henry	15	Lost River	1831	3	288
Baughman, Henry	105	Lost River	1837	3	395
Baughman, Henry	22	Flat Ridge	1850	4	306
Baughman, Henry et al	52a.71p.	Lost River	1846	4	224
Baughman, John	39¼	Lost River	1846	4	223
Bauhman—See Baughman, Boughman, Bowman					
Bauhman, Andrew	29	Adj. Cockarall	1804	3	95
Baysore—or Basore, Bosore					
Beall, George	303	North River	1792	1	194
Bean, Bennett	100	North River	1837	3	404
Bean, Bennett	371	North River	1798	1	525
Bean, Bennett (1st)	51	North River	1837	3	405
Bean, Bennett (Secundus)	116	Bolner's Run	1848	4	278
Bean, Bennett (the 3rd)	95	South River	1836	3	382
Bean, Elizabeth et al Heirs	63	Scaggs Run	1820	3	220
Bean, Erasmus	276	Tucker's Run	1854	4	386
Bean, Ezekiel	224	Tucker's Run	1854	4	383
Bean, George	90	North River	1837	3	403
Bean, George	50	North River	1842	4	94

Name of Grantee	Acres	Local Description	Year	Book	Page
Bean, Horatio & Richard	100	Lick Run	1854	4	380
Bean, James	32	North River	1837	3	414
Bean, James	250	Vannell's Ridge	1842	4	104
Bean, James	300	Adj. J. Birch	1837	3	415
Bean, James	366	North River	1792	1	235
Bean, Masham	19⅝	Tucker's Run	1854	4	382
Bean, Peter	13¼	North River	1854	4	390
Bean, Samuel	50	Scagg's Run	1854	4	385
Bean, Samuel	104	Lick Run	1860	4	450
Bean, Samuel	10	Sagg's Run (Skaggs)	1841	4	90
Bearly—Beasley, Burley					
Bearly, Nicholas (Beasley)	35	Cove Run	1796	1	500
Bearly, Nicholas (Beasley)	42	Lost River	1797	1	518
Bearly, Nicholas	128	Cove Run	1800	3	22
Bearly, Nicholas	216	Lost River	1791	1	166
Beasley—See Bearly					
Beasley, Nicholas	35	Cove Run	1796	1	500
Been—See Bean					
Bergdoll—See Barkdall, Barkdoll, Berkdoll, Berkdull					
Bergdoll, Gideon	36	Westfall Knob	1852	4	356
Bergdoll, Hannah	137	South Mill Cr.	1858	4	429
Bergdoll, Jacob	56	N. Mill Creek	1825	3	245
Berkdoll, George	39	Middle Mt.	1858	4	436
Berkdull—See Barkdall, Barkdoll, Bergdoll, Berkdoll					
Berkdull, Jacob	80	Sugar Run	1796	1	362
Berker—See Basher, Besher, Bishor					
Berkley, Joseph H.	94	North River	1840	4	48
Berry, John	20	Lost River	1796	1	503
Besher—See Basher, Berker, Bishor					
Birch—See Burch					
Birch, John	26	Lick Spring	1837	3	396
Birch, Thomas	207	Branch Mt.	1800	3	26
Birch, Thomas	222	Skaggs Run	1800	3	25
Bishop, George	300	North River	1829	3	259
Bishop, George	167	Hunting Ridge	1798	1	558
Bishop, George	306	Skagg's Run	1798	1	555
Bishop, John	360	Looney's Cr.	1792	1	218
Bishop, John	355	Patterson's Cr.	1792	1	217
Bishop, John Jr.	350	Looney's Cr.	1792	1	238
Bishor—or Basher, Berker, Besher					
Bishor, Benjamin	27	Cove Run	1818	3	199
Bishor, Benjamin	60	Lost River	1817	3	196
Bixler, Elias	175	Baker's Run	1800	3	32
Bixler, Henry	204	Lost River	1796	1	421
Bland, Jonah	43	Looney's Cr.	1847	4	245
Bobo, Henry	353	Paine's Run	1860	4	445
Bobo, Thomas	320	Mud Lick Run	1800	3	33
Bodkin, Richard	75	New Creek	1797	1	513
Bogard, Ezekel et al	1,000	Fork Mtn.	1797	1	493
Bogard, Ezekiel et al	234	Allegheny Mt.	1789	1	48
Boger, John et al (Roger)	90	South Branch	1795	1	344
Bogle, James	120	Allegheny Mt.	1789	1	33
Bogle, James	48	New Creek	1789	1	40
Bogle, James	68	New Cr. Mt.	1789	1	34
Bolinger, Adam (Boliner)	200	Beech Mt.	1838	4	12
Bond, William O.	500	North River	1852	4	362
Boot—Boots					
Boot, Garret	128	South Br. and Mill Cr.	1793	1	279
Boot, George	32	Mill Creek	1789	1	108
Boots, Adam et al	130	N. Mill Creek	1825	3	244
Borah—See Borrer, (Bower)					
Borer—See Borah, (Bower)					
Borer, Thomas	139	Patterson's Cr.	1792	1	252

Name of Grantee	Acres	Local Description	Year	Book	Page
Boseley, Jacob (Bosley)	2	Adj. J. Ryan	1840	4	44
Boseley, John (Bosley)	300	Patterson Cr. Mt.	1838	4	1
Boseley, John	32	Patterson's Cr.	1842	4	111
Bosley, John	32	Patterson Cr. Mt.	1839	4	15
Bosore—or Basore, Baysore					
Boughman—See Baughman, Bauhman, Bowman					
Boughman, Andrew	48	Lost River	1793	1	268
Bower—See Borah, Borer, Borrer					
Bower, Jacob	25	Elkhorn Run	1795	1	345
Bowman—See Boughman					
Bowman, Martin	470	North Branch	1800	3	430
Bradfield—See Bradford					
Bradfield, George	406	Warden's Run	1804	3	102
Bradford—See Bradfield					
Bradford, George (Bradfield)	86	Patterson's Cr.	1840	4	47
Bradford, Elizabeth et al Heirs	130	Stony River	1839	4	37
Bradigum, Benjamin (Bradgum)	77	Lost River	1828	3	236
Bradigum, Benjamin	15a.30p.	Big Cove Run	1827	3	255
Brake, Isaac	90	Adj. W. Radcliff	1809	3	117
Brake, Isaac	90	Adj. Wm. Radcliff	1809	2	167
Brake, Jacob	114	North Branch	1793	1	288
Brake, John	129	So. Branch	1792	1	224
Brake, Michael	40	South Branch	1825	3	246
Branson, Jonathan	61	Cove Run	1812	3	140
Branson, Jonathan	19	Mill Run	1816	3	183
Branson, Lionel	52	Cove Run	1810	3	125
Branson, Lionel	23	Adj. Mat Wilkins	1810	3	124
Branson, Lionel	51	Lost River	1791	1	141
Branson, Lionel	156	Lost River	1794	1	317
Branson, Lionel	74	Lost River	1794	1	311
Branson, Lionel F. et al	1,700	Fork Mt.	1849	4	563
Branson, William	100	Lost River	1839	4	13
Branson, William	137½	Lost River	1844	4	161
Branson, William	278¼	Lost River	1844	4	162
Breathed, Edward	43,440	North Fork So. Br.	1795	1	337
Breathed, James	3,600	North & So. Mill Creek	1798	1	523
Brill, Isaac W.	416	Tucker's Run	1860	4	451
Brink, Philip	81	South Branch	1789	1	63
Brock, Jonas	103	Hunting Ridge	1851	4	330
Bromback—or Broomback					
Bromback, Samuel	120	Stony River	1854	4	375
Bromback, Samuel	84	Stony River	1854	4	374
Bromback, Samuel	172	Stony River	1849	4	288
Broomback—or Bromback					
Broomback, Samuel	172	Stony River	1849	4	288
Brown, Charles	39½	Tucker's Run	1854	4	379
Brown, Charles	88	Branch Mt.	1860	4	446
Brown, John	141	Little Mt.	1791	1	154
Bruce, Normand	141	Allegheny Mt.	1792	1	239
Bruce, Normand	150	Allegheny Mt.	1792	1	241
Bruce, Normand	216	North Branch	1792	1	240
Bruce, Upton	186	Jonnycake Run	1800	3	23
Bruce, Upton	400	Stony River	1792	1	223
Bruce, Upton	400	Adj. R. Seymore	1800	3	24
Bruce, Upton	1,086	Stony River	1792	1	222
Bucker—or Bucher, Butcher					
Bucker, Philip (Butcher)	36	Mike's Run	1794	1	325
Bucker, Philip (Butcher)	198	Mike's Run	1788	1	10
Buckley, Joseph	83	North River	1820	3	216
Buckley, Joseph H.	94	North River	1840	4	48
Buffenburg — See Buffenberg, Buffinberger, Buffinberry, Buffinburger					
Buffenburg, Peter	142	North Fork	1800	3	31
Buffinberger—See Buffinburg					

Name of Grantee	Acres	Local Description	Year	Book	Page
Buffington, William	40	Adam's Creek	1812	3	137
Bullet, William et al	50	Adj. P. Lynch	1800	3	46
Burch—See Birch					
Burch, Covington	90⅝	North River	1845	4	199
Burley—Bearly, Beasley					
Burley, Nicholas	128	Cove Run	1800	3	22
Bush, Gasper	305	North River	1798	1	537
Butcher, Philip (Bucher)	36	Mike's Run	1794	1	325
Byrns, Philip	100	Adj. Sink. Spg. Tr.	1797	1	517
Campbell, William	1,043	Big Cacapon	1832	3	302
Campbell, William	614	Big Cacapon	1832	3	303
Campbell, William	143	Chestnut Ridge	1835	3	335
Canter, Henry et al	424	Thorn Run	1789	1	42
Canter, Henry et al	75	Thorn Run	1789	1	41
Carr, Conrad	58	South Branch	1804	3	92
Carter, Henry et al	75	Thorn Run	1789	1	41
Carter, Henry et al	424	Patterson's Cr.	1789	1	42
Cassell, Michael	128	Powder Mill Run	1794	1	299
Cassin, John H. et al	18,557	Stony River	1860	4	443
Caterman—or Catterman, Ketterman					
Caterman, George	46	Mill Creek	1791	1	130
Catterman—or Caterman, Katterman, Ketterman					
Catterman, Daniel	44	South Branch	1798	1	554
Catterman, Jacob	33	Middle Mt.	1796	1	361
Chambers, Benjamin	36,000	New, Patterson, Looneys, Jordan Crks. & Stoney R.	1796	1	561
Champ, John	340	Abram's Creek	1796	1	359
Childs, Cephus	17	Lost River	1841	4	89
Childs, Cephus	112	Lost River	1851	4	331
Childs, Edward	110	Lost River	1789	1	106
Chrisman, George	413	Stony River	1793	1	260
Chrisman, Isaac	36	Lost River	1811	3	129
Chrisman, Jacob	73	Lost River	1791	1	142
Chrisman, Jacob A.	34¼	Lost River	1850	4	308
Claget, Hezekiah	27	Baker's Run	1836	3	381
Claget, Hezekiah	(233⅞)133⅞	Wait's Run	1846	4	228
Claget, Hezekiah	175	Sandy Ridge	1848	4	286
Clark, Abraham	108	Looney's Creek	1796	1	445
Clark, Abraham	299	Patterson's Cr.	1789	1	66
Clark, Ezra	38	Big Ridge	1839	4	16
Clark, Hendricks	115	Abraham's Cr.	1834	3	318
Clark, Henry	95	Looney's Creek	1798	1	547
Claypool, George	43	Big Ridge	1798	1	542
Claypool, George	217	Lost River	1797	1	512
Claypool, George	83	Scott's Run	1796	1	454
Claypool, Jacob	75	South Br. Mt.	1796	1	419
Claypool, James	50	Lost River	1796	1	392
Claypool, James	100	Lost River	1802	3	73
Claypool, James (or John)	106	Lost River	1796	1	423
Claypool, Philip	93	Cove Mt.	1811	3	134
Cline, George	8	Gr. Cacapon	1852	4	347
Cline, Jacob (Clein)	85	Capon Waters	1831	3	289
Cline, Jacob	21½(20½)	Big Ridge	1833	3	309
Cline, William	102	South Branch	1796	1	400
Coby, John	65	Fravel's Run	1844	4	163
Coby, John	78	Fravel's Run	1844	4	164
Coby, John	257¼	William's Run	1846	4	231
Coby, William	125	Lost River	1845	4	201
Cock, Thomas	323	Looney's Creek	1796	1	439
Coffman, Michael	56	South Mill Cr.	1797	1	509
Coffman, Michael	300	Fork Mountain	1829	3	271
Coler, David	50	Loonie's Cr.	1842	4	107
Coler, Henry	312	Patterson's Cr.	1815	3	165

Name of Grantee	Acres	Local Description	Year	Book	Page
Coler, Henry W. &. G. W.	7	Looney's Cr.	1843	4	146
Collins, David	97	Fork Mt.	1798	1	528
Collins, David	40	Middle Mountain	1793	1	272
Colp—or Kolp, Culp					
Colp, John	89	Lost River	1793	1	269
Combs, Francis I.	260	Gr. Cacapon	1789	1	100
Combs, Francis I.	250	Patterson's Cr.	1789	1	98
Combs, Francis I.	230	North River	1792	1	236
Combs, Francis I.	195	North River	1792	1	237
Combs, Francis J. (I)	93	Mt. Run	1800	3	37
Combs, Francis J. (I)	132	Hunting Ridge	1800	3	36
Combs, Pius	315	Big Ridge	1844	4	165
Conrad, Jacob	76	South Branch	1788	3	439
Conrad, Jacob	67	Lost River	1796	1	449
Conrad, Jacob	76	South Branch	1788	2	150
Conrad, John	176	South Branch	1789	1	22
Constable, Abraham	98	Lick Run	1840	4	56
Constable, Annanias	76 (96)	North River	1839	4	17
Cooper, Enos	50	Johny Cake Run	1857	4	415
Cooper, John	67	Mill Creek	1840	4	45
Cooper, Valentine	57	So. Fork Mt.	1821	3	225
Cooper, Valentine	10	South Mill Cr.	1821	3	224
Cooper, Valentine	100	S. Mill Creek	1805	3	104
Cooper, Valentine	45	Mill Creek	1792	1	246
Cooper, Valentine	19	Mill Creek	1792	1	245
Cooper, Valetine	33	Mill Creek	1792	1	206
Cooper, Valentine	81	Mill Creek	1792	1	207
Corby—See also Curby					
Corby, Thomas	55	Rocky Ridge	1796	1	427
Cornel, John (Cornell)	262	Oak Ridge	1829	3	270
Cornell—See Cornel, Cornwall, Cornwell					
Cornell, Archibald	150	Patterson's Cr.	1837	3	397
Cornell, Jacob	13	Patterson's Cr.	1829	3	258
Cornell, Jacob	50	Patterson's Cr.	1836	3	389
Cornell, Jacob	5	Powder Lick Dr.	1854	4	381
Cornell, Jacob	15	Patterson Cr. Mt.	1854	4	387
Cornell, John (Cornwall)	202	Patterson Cr.	1846	4	218
Cornell, William	200	Patterson's Cr.	1811	3	132
Cornwall—See Cornell, Cornwell					
Cornwall, Archibald	348	Patterson's Cr.	1850	4	305
Cornwell—See Cornell, Cornwall					
Cornwell, Jacob	27½	Patterson Cr.	1854	4	389
Cosner—See Costner					
Cosner, Benjamin	37¾	Mill Run	1861	4	455
Cosner, Christian	103	Abram's Cr.	1856	4	409
Cossin, John H. et al	18,557	Stony River	1860	4	443
Costner, Adam & Henry	48	Coon Creek	1839	4	18
Covanovan, Johnson	122 (722)	Top of Allegheny	1840	4	43
Craigen, George	146	Fork Mountain	1829	3	268
Crites, Jacob	23	Elk Horn	1796	1	373
Crites, Joel	76	Spring Run Ridge	1838	4	2
Crites, Joseph	245	Elkhorn Run	1843	4	122
Crites, Philip	416	Mill Cr.	1792	1	185
Crites, Philip & Jonathan	352	Black Oak Levels	1849	4	295
Critsinger—See Kritsinger					
Croce, Christian	45	Patterson's Cr.	1796	1	393
Cross, Richard	390	North Branch	1792	1	215
Crow, David	92	So. Branch	1798	1	539
Cunningham, Benjamin	5	South Fork	1843	4	145
Cunningham, Charles L. et al	7,470	Middle Mt.	1849	4	557
Cunningham, James	50	Sugar Leaf Run	1798	1	533
Cunningham, James et al	168	Patterson's Cr.	1802	3	75
Cunningham, Jesse	78	Adj. James Cunningham	1820	3	209

Cunningham, William	56	Looney's Creek	1793	1	267
Cunningham, William	246	Sees Run	1792	1	187
Cunningham, William	155	Middle Mt.	1798	1	540
Cunningham, William	120	Middle Mountain	1838	3	422
Cunningham, William Jr.	47	Patterson's Cr. Mt.	1821	3	227
Culp—or Colp, Kolp					
Curby—or Corby					
Curby, Thomas	45	Lost River	1793	1	274
Custard, Joseph	64	Cave Run	1789	1	120
Daggs, Hezekiah	50	Adj. D. Welton	1801	3	64
Daily, James & Co. et al	521	Muddy Run	1818	3	202
Danner, William	16	North River	1842	4	98
Danner, William	30	Short House Mt.	1842	4	99
Dasher, Isaac	127	Middle Mt.	1850	4	321
Dasher, Leonard	110	Adj. Abraham House	1830	3	276
Davidson—or Davison, Davisson					
Davidson, George P.	350	North River	1846	4	220
Davidson, George P. et al	300	North River	1846	4	222
Davidson, Jacob A.	124(624)	Branch Mt.	1845	4	204
Davidson, James	163¾	Mud Lick	1844	4	190
Davis—See Drais					
Davis, Henry M.	155	Stone Lick Run	1831	3	291
Davis, Henry M.	301	Mt. Run	1827	3	256
Davis, Jacob	177	Middle Mt.	1796	1	504
Davis, James	39	South Fork	1800	3	58
Davis, Jesse	12	New Creek	1854	4	384
Davis, Jesse	200	New Creek	1841	4	97
Davis, Jesse	51	New Creek	1811	3	138
Davis, Joseph	152	New Creek	1825	3	241
Davis, Joseph	70	North River	1796	1	371
Davis, Joseph	6	New Creek	1812	3	145
Davis, Reuben	95	Walker's Ridge	1839	4	19
Davis, Samuel	96	North River	1797	1	508
Davis, Samuel	200	North River	1798	1	536
Davis, Samuel	76	North River	1792	1	201
Davis, Thomas	148	Looney Cr.	1792	1	226
Davis, Thomas	181	New Creek	1792	1	230
Davis, William	23	Adj. C. Wilson	1801	3	72
Davis, William	175	Lost River	1790	1	125
Davis, William	300	North Mountain	1790	1	126
Davison—or Davidson, Davisson					
Davisson, Thomas S.	196	North River	1837	3	408
Dawson, Dan C.	140	Mill Creek	1836	3	386
Day, Samuel	120	North Fork	1790	1	124
Deakins, Frances	2,000	Stony River & Potomac	1799	1	576
Deakins, Francis	1,800	Stony River	1801	3	432
Deakins, Francis	740	Abraham's Cr.	1801	3	65
Deakins, Francis	660	Stoney River	1800	3	52
Deakins, Francis & William	240	Stony River	1796	1	412
Deakins, Francis & William	113	North Branch	1796	1	495
Deakins, Francis & William	290	Abram's Cr.	1796	1	496
Deakins, Francis & William	627	North Br.	1796	1	497
Deakins, Francis & William	510	Stony River	1796	1	498
Deakins, Francis & William	1,000	Abraham's Creek	1798	1	524
Deakins, Francis & William	25,500	North Br. & Stoney Riv.	1796	1	563
Dean, Benjamin	147	Wait's Run	1798	1	541
Delauder—Also Delawder					
Delauder, John	9	Lost River	1842	4	117
Delawder, Abraham	30	Upper Cove Run	1849	4	285
Delawder, John	27½	Upper Cove Run	1851	4	328
Delinger—See Dillinger					
Detrick, Jacob	108	Mill Creek	1840	4	61
Detrick, Simon	14	Fork Mt.	1840	4	60
Detrick, Simon et al	200	Deep Spring Run	1852	4	345

Name of Grantee	Acres	Local Description	Year	Book	Page
Dew, Samuel	140	Allegheny Mt.	1791	1	172
Dillinger, Martin	60	Break Neck Mt.	1834	3	333
Dodson, George P. et al	300	North River	1846	4	222
Douglas, James	83	Trough	1791	1	163
Drais, Jacob (Davis)	177	Middle Mt.	1796	1	504
Dull, Jacob	88	Knobly Mt.	1794	1	326
Dull, John	30	Patterson's Cr.	1796	1	391
Dye, David	164(264)	Patterson's Cr.	1796	1	414
Dyer, Herbert & Andrew	17	Mill Cr.	1840	4	59
Dyer, John	240	Adj. A. Smith	1840	4	58
Elswick, Thomas	80	Lost River	1794	1	324
Elswick, Thomas	87	Lost River	1798	1	532
Elswick, Thomas	100	Lost River	1795	1	354
Emmery, John	354	Littler's Run	1798	1	546
Evans, Alexander	33¼	Stone Lick Run	1852	4	349
Evans, Alexander	7⅝	North River	1852	4	352
Evans, Alexander et al	400	Mt. Run	1834	3	321
Evans, Caleb et al	143	Adj. B. Marshall	1800	3	45
Evans, Calop	100	North River	1796	1	369
Evans, John	227	Branch Mt.	1854	4	388
Extine, Leonard	226	Cornwell's Run	1792	1	211
Eyman, Christopher	30	South Branch	1793	1	273
Eyman, Christian	347	Deep Spring Run	1791	1	164
Eyman, Christian	248	Hurst's Spg. Run	1791	1	165
Feaster, Henry	85	Little Mt.	1848	4	268
Feaster, Henry	17a.112p.	Wolf Thicket	1845	4	196
Feaster, Henry	100	Lit. Mountain	1840	4	62
Feaster, Henry Jr.	123¼	New Creek Mt.	1848	4	267
Fidler, Edward	300	Walnut Bottom	1796	1	394
Fisher, Adam	34	Adj. his own from Byrn's	1796	1	484
Fisher, Adam	50	Byrn's Run	1796	1	483
Fisher, Adam	108	Middle Mt.	1792	1	209
Fisher, Adam	387	Adj. Wm. Cunningham	1792	1	208
Fisher, Adam et al	234	Allegheny Mt.	1789	1	48
Fisher, Adam & John	353	Parson's Run	1796	1	485
Fisher, George	101¾	Bodkin's Run	1852	4	358
Fisher, George	161	New Creek Mt.	1850	4	307
Fisher, George	100	Walker's Ridge	1844	4	168
Fisher, George	250	Cattail Run	1841	4	83
Fisher, George & Adam	70	Elkhorn	1825	3	248
Fisher, George et al	250	Abram's Creek	1844	4	178
Fisher, George M.	(18¾) 183¼	Looney's Creek	1844	4	167
Fisher, Jacob	330	Middle Mountain	1836	3	383
Fisher, Jacob	235	S. Mill Cr.	1835	3	357
Fisher, Jacob	400	Maxwell Run	1830	3	286
Fisher, Jacob H.	85	Looney's Cr.	1839	4	20
Fisher, John et al	1,000	Fork Mountain	1797	1	493
Fleming, James	140	Looney's Cr.	1789	1	116
Foley, John	407	Powder Lick	1789	1	79
Foley, John	59	Trough	1792	1	212
Foley, John	193	Vanmeter's Mill	1792	1	214
Foley, John	70	Adj. S. Vanmeter	1794	1	264
Foley, John	70	Mud Creek	1794	1	265
Foley, John	138	Elk Pound (Pond)	1794	1	266
Foley, John	406	South Br.	1789	1	111
Foley, John Sr.	710	Vanmeter's Mill Run	1809	2	158
Foley, John Sr.	710	Mill Run	1809	3	433
Foley, William	208	Patterson's Cr.	1794	1	262
Foley, William	318	Walnut Bottom	1794	1	263
Fout, John	241	Cove Run	1826	3	250
Fout, Sarah	200	Lost River	1843	4	128
Fout, William et al	600	Abram's Creek	1844	4	160
Fox, William	156	Mike's Run	1792	1	195

Name of Grantee	Acres	Local Description	Year	Book	Page
Fravel, George	50	Trout Run	1796	1	429
Frederick, Lewis	44½	Looney's Cr	1852	4	364
Frederick, Lewis	26	Tear Coat Run	1844	4	166
French, Thomas et al	2,528	Branch Mt.	1858	4	421
Frigill, Evin et al (Frizzell)	304	Patterson's Cr	1789	1	49
Frizel—or Frigill					
Fry—or Frye					
Fry, Henry	45	Fry's Run	1795	1	348
Fry, Henry	45	Fry's Run	1795	1	350
Fry, Henry W.	100	North Mt.	1856	4	412
Fry, Henry W.	99½	Moore's Run	1849	4	291
Fry, Henry W.	350	Baker's Mt.	1838	4	3
Fry, Henry W. et al	350	Adj. Switzer	1849	4	297
Fry, Isaac S. (or L.)	75	Fry's Run	1852	4	353
Fry, J. L. et al	46½	Fry's Run	1856	4	414
Fry, Thomas	74	Gr. Cacapon	1795	1	352
Fry, Thomas	21	Gr. Cacapon	1795	1	349
Frye, Samuel	500	Big Cacapon	1832	3	298
Frygill—Frigill, Frizzell					
Funkhouser, Henry	17¼	Little Ridge	1850	4	316
Funkhouser, Henry	67	Ruddle's Run	1850	4	318
Gale, George et al	17,518	Stony River	1796	1	383
Gale, George et al	7,500	Loony's Creek	1796	1	382
Garber, Martin	71	S. Mill Cr.	1812	3	148
Garbo—See Jarboe, Jerber					
Gardner, John P. & M. P.	100	Saw Mill Mountain	1856	4	403
Garret, Conrad	17⅛	Lick Run	1858	4	437
Garrett, Andrew	140	Lost River	1836	3	387
Garvin, Thomas	250	Loonies Cr.	1789	1	69
Gavin, Thomas	250	Loonis Creek	1789	1	69
Gemes, Robert (James)	68	Powder Spg. Ridge	1843	4	123
George, Joseph Jr. et al	304	Patterson's Cr.	1789	1	49
George, Thomas	20	Patterson Cr.	1840	4	50
Getts, Jacob (Sites)	234	Fork Mt.	1834	3	326
Getts, Jacob	133	Middle Mountain	1834	3	323
Getts, Jacob et al	43	Adj. A. Sites	1844	4	188
Gillett, Wheeler	14	Trout Run	1816	3	193
Gillett, Wheeler et al	197	Great Cacapon	1816	3	194
Gilpin, George	94	Patterson's Cr.	1801	3	67
Gilpin, George	1,280	Patterson's Cr.	1799	3	18
Gilpin, George	3,085	New Creek	1800	3	429
Gochenour, Samuel	90	North River	1842	4	103
Gochenour, Samuel	64	North River	1842	4	112
Godfrey, John	258	Cor. Vanmeter	1789	1	30
Godlop—and Godlove					
Godlop, Francis	78	North River	1820	3	208
Godlove, Francis	77	Cacapon River	1847	4	253
Graham, John	82	South Fk. & Mill Cr.	1796	1	448
Gray, James	206	North Fork	1823	3	235
Gray, James	12½	N. Mill Creek	1828	3	252
Gray, James	50	North Fork	1830	3	280
Gray, James	190	Charles's Knob	1835	3	340
Gray, James	40	Frenchmans' Run	1835	3	341
Gray, James	391	Radcliff Run	1836	3	372
Gray, James	32	North Mill Cr.	1838	4	4
Gray, James	10	North Mill Cr.	1838	4	5
Green, James W.	9,549	Stony River	1854	4	317
Green, James W.	763	Stony River	1855	4	394
Green, James W.	71	Stony River	1855	4	397
Green, Jones	1,000	Middle Mountain	1836	3	378
Greenwood, William et al	157	Fork Mountain	1830	3	274
Grooves, Solomon	16	Looney's Cr.	1816	3	181
Groves, Isaac	62	Looney's Cr.	1846	4	216

Name of Grantee	Acres	Local Description	Year	Book	Page
Groves, Solomon (Grooves)	16	Looney's Cr.	1816	3	181
Hacker, Daniel	200	Frye's Run	1835	3	338
Hackney, William	254	South Branch	1789	1	104
Hackney, William	233	Looney's Cr.	1789	1	103
Hackney, William	232	Looney's Cr.	1789	1	102
Hagarty—or Hagerty					
Hagarty, Paul	186	Patterson's Cr.	1789	1	58
Hagarty, Paul	55	Patterson Cr.	1796	1	466
Hagarty, Paul	48	Horn Run	1796	1	467
Hagarty, Paul	95	Sugar Run	1796	1	480
Hager, William	99	South Branch	1794	1	328
Hager, William J.	713	North River	1792	1	178
Hager, William J.	8	North River	1801	3	69
Hager, William J.	196	North River	1801	3	70
Hager, William J.	100	Secret Lick Run	1803	3	83
Hagerty—or Hagarty					
Hagerty, John	104	Thorn Run	1821	3	223
Hall, Adam	389	South Branch	1792	1	213
Hall, Thomas	75	South Branch	1790	2	152
Hall, Thomas	75	So. Branch	1790	3	441
Hall, William	28¼	Stony River	1858	4	424
Halleman—See Halterman, Hatterman					
Halleman, Jacob	194	Lost River	1789	1	76
Halterman—See Halleman, Hatterman					
Halterman, Christian	85	Cove Run	1809	3	111
Halterman, Christian	85	Cove Run	1809	2	161
Halterman, Christopher	72	Wts. Lost River	1809	2	171
Halterman, Christopher	72	Lost River	1810	3	121
Halterman, Christopher	75	Big Cove Run	1810	3	122
Halterman, Christopher	24	Big Cove Run	1810	3	123
Halterman, Jacob	183	Big Cove Run	1809	2	170
Halterman, Jacob	183	Big Cove Run	1810	3	120
Hammons, Jacob	95	Trout Run	1800	3	61
Hammons, Jacob	95	Trout Run	1799	3	1
Harmentrout—See Armentrout, Hermantrout					
Harmentrout, Christopher	40	No. Mill Cr.	1796	1	444
Harmontrout, Christopher	50	Mill Creek	1792	1	228
Harmontrout, Chrisopher	63	Mill Creek	1792	1	225
Harness—See Harris					
Harness, Adam	140	Looney's Cr.	1840	4	65
Harness, George	270	Fork Mountain	1831	3	287
Harness, George	180	Lewnie's Cr.	1799	3	9
Harness, George	11,000	South Br. & No. Mill Creek	1796	1	574
Harness, George	200	Looney's Cr.	1789	1	115
Harness, George	96	Lost River	1796	1	490
Harness, George C. & J. G.	204	Town Fort Run	1843	4	129
Harness, George C. & J. G.	446	Town Fort Run	1843	4	130
Harness, George et al	116	Abram's Cr.	1796	1	478
Harness, George et al	17,518	Stony River	1796	1	383
Harness, George et al	7,500	Looney's Creek	1796	1	382
Harness, George et al	160	Stony River	1794	1	327
Harness, George Sr.	400	Welton's Knob	1792	1	198
Harness, John G.	2a.29p.	Patterson's Cr.	1845	4	203
Harness, John G.	247	Sugar Leaf Mt.	1847	4	251
Harness, John G. Jr. et al	1,700	Fork Mt.	1849	4	563
Harness, Peter	72	Adj. his own	1796	1	374
Harper, Robert N. et al	18,557	Stony River	1860	4	443
Harper, Samuel	28	Lost River	1852	4	354
Harper, Samuel	162	Lost River	1847	4	260
Harper, Samuel	79¾	Still Run	1847	4	258
Harpold, Adam	28	Mill Creek	1796	1	389
Harris—See Harness					
Harris, James	125 (128)	Patterson's Cr.	1812	3	146

Name of Grantee	Acres	Local Description	Year	Book	Page
Himes, John	63	Lost River	1792	1	254
Hinckle—or Henkel, Henkle, Hinkel, Hinkle					
Hinckle, Felix	67	Mill Creek	1839	4	21
Hinckle, Felix	350	Mill Creek	1840	4	64
Hinckle, Jacob	16	Mill Creek	1796	1	376
Hinckle, John	56	Lick Run	1796	1	415
Hinegarner, John	182	Lost River	1852	4	357
Hines—See also Himes					
Hinkle—or Henkel, Henkle, Hinckle, Hinkel					
Hinkle, Abraham	40	South Mill Creek	1835	3	364
Hinkle, Nathan & Caleb	155	Mid. Mountain	1834	3	327
Hishman—or Hershman					
Hishman, George	6¾	Lost River	1854	4	392
Hishman, George (Hershman)	40½	Cacapon River	1854	4	391
Hister, Philip	35	Lost River	1793	1	291
Hite, Casper	165	Patterson's Cr.	1812	3	141
Hite, Casper	70	New Creek	1816	3	187
Hite, Mathias	90	So. Branch	1792	1	229
Hite, Mathias	448	South Branch	1792	1	227
Hodges, Stephen	132	Mill Creek	1791	1	145
Holmes, Hugh	4,000	North Mountain	1810	3	435
Holmes, John et al	17,518	Stony River	1796	1	383
Holmes, John et al	7,500	Looney's Creek	1796	1	382
Homan, John	162	Limestone Ridge	1825	3	242
Honeyuse, Anthony	22⅜	Fox Lick Run	1847	4	256
Hopewell, John	166	Laurel Run	1841	4	80
Horrobough, Philip (Horobah)	139	Looney's Cr.	1792	1	186
Horse—or Hose, Hosse, House, Husse					
Horseman, William	18	North River	1840	4	42
Hose, William	18	Lost River	1846	4	227
Hosse—or Horse, Hose, House, Husse					
Hottle, George (Hottel)	780	Cor. to M. Ohaver	1834	3	317
House—or Horse, Hosse					
House, John	2½	Adj. Alex Scott	1843	4	131
House, Peter	112	South Branch	1796	1	404
House, Peter	120	Cow's Run	1800	3	54
House, Peter	79	So. Branch	1800	3	55
Howdyshell, Adam	390	Lost River	1837	3	392
Hoy, John et al	1,000	Wram's Creek	1803	3	85
Hughes, John	15a.127p.	Diamond Lick Run	1848	4	279
Hughes, Samuel	154	Tucker's Run	1800	3	57
Huffman, Amos	16	South Fork	1849	4	290
Hull, Benjamin	76	Patterson's Cr.	1829	3	267
Hull, Jacob	115	Patterson Cr.	1840	4	63
Hulver, George	283	Adj. A. Boughman	1803	3	81
Hulver, George	64	Lost River	1803	3	80
Hulver, John	4a.142p.	Lost River	1846	4	232
Hume, John	70	Lost River	1796	1	450
Hungarden, John	182	Lost River	1852	4	357
Hunnous, Anthony	22⅜	Fox Lick Run	1847	4	256
Hupp, George F.	267	Trout Run	1852	4	340
Hupp, George F.	150	Waite's Run	1852	4	337
Hushman—See Hishman					
Husse—See Hosse, etc.					
Husse, John	253	Allegheny Mt.	1791	1	139
Hutton, Abraham et al	310	Allegheny Mt.	1794	1	293
Hutton, Cyrus	5	South Fork	1845	4	202
Hutton, Jesse et al	240	North Fork	1840	4	46
Hutton, Isaac	64	Middle Mt.	1798	1	545
Hutton, Peter	9¾	Patterson's Cr.	1844	4	169
Idleman, Conrad	373	Loony's Creek	1811	3	135
Idleman, Conrod	323	Bushy Run	1801	3	71
Idleman, Frances	85	Stony River	1835	3	339

Name of Grantee	Acres	Local Description	Year	Book	Page
Idleman, Francis	17	Stony River	1835	3	354
Idleman, Francis	129½	Oil Run	1852	4	348
Idleman, Jacob R. & L. S.	13½	Mill Run	1858	4	422
Idleman, Lewis S.	1a.3r.18p.	Oil Run	1858	4	434
Idleman, William	4½	Patterson's Cr.	1850	4	310
Idleman, William	133¼(133)	Bald Ridge	1845	4	214
Idleman, William et al	73	Patterson Cr. Mt.	1838	4	8
Inskeep, Abraham	11½	Lost River	1796	1	492
Inskeep, Abraham	12	Ruddle Run	1796	1	491
Inskeep, Abraham	200	Timber Ridge	1834	3	319
Inskeep, Abraham A.	29⅝	Lost River	1847	4	241
Inskeep, Abraham A.	95	Lost River	1848	4	269
Inskeep, Abraham & Isaac	14	Stony River	1837	3	400
Inskeep, Jeremiah	21	Lost River	1838	4	6
Inskeep, John et al	46½	Fry's Run	1856	4	414
Jackson, Peter	422	Looney's Cr.	1792	1	188
James, Robert	68	Powder Spgs. Ridge	1843	4	123
Jarboe—See also (Garbo), Jerber					
Jarboe, Benedict (Garbo)	384	North River	1789	1	85
Jefferson, Luke	385	Middle Mt.	1789	1	113
Jefferson, Luke	227	Middle Mt.	1789	1	112
Jefferson, Luke	100	Middle Mt.	1792	1	190
Jerber—See also (Garbo), Jarboe					
Jerber, Benedict (Garbo)	129	North River	1789	1	114
Job, Leonard	55	South Branch	1792	1	249
Job, Leonard	122	Stillhouse Rn.	1792	1	232
Job, Rudolph Jr.	59	Cor. to Harmontrout	1792	1	248
Job, Rudolph Sr.	108	Cor. to Harmontrout	1792	1	247
Johnson, John	176	Allegheny Mt.	1789	1	15
Johnson, John	133a.15p.	Lost River	1834	3	330
Johnston, Charles	21	Welton's Knob	1794	1	301
Johnston, Charles	47	Welton's Knob	1794	1	300
Johnston, George	106	Kinsey's Run	1804	3	103
Judy, Elijah	111	Middle Mt.	1845	4	192
Judy, Elijah	93¾	Middle Mt.	1847	4	247
Judy, Elijah	100	Fort Mt.	1840	4	66
Judy, George	17	S. Mill Creek	1816	3	178
Judy, Jacob	54	Mill Creek	1840	4	67
Judy, John	12	S. Mill Cr.	1816	3	180
Judy, Nimrod	48	S. Mill Creek	1835	3	355
Kelly, Larkin C.	184	Patterson Cr.	1860	4	454
Kelly, William	65	Middle Mt.	1794	1	295
Kelterman,—See Ketterman					
Keplinger, Jonathan	18	Looney's Creek	1842	4	116
Keplinger, Jonathan	33	Loonie's Cr.	1842	4	108
Keplinger, Solomon	20⅛	Looney's Cr.	1856	4	404
Ketterman—or Catterman, Katterman					
Ketterman, Abraham	301½	Middle Mt.	1847	4	259
Ketterman, Abraham	28	N. Mill Creek	1836	3	374
Ketterman, Adam	138	South Fork	1844	4	189
Ketterman, Clay et al	52	S. Mill Creek	1835	3	352
Ketterman, Jacob	52	Elkhorn Run	1806	2	156
Ketterman, Jacob	148	South Fork	1835	3	363
Ketterman, Jacob	85	S. Mill Cr.	1835	3	362
Ketterman, Jacob	52	Elk Horn	1806	3	107
Ketterman, Jacob Jr.	16¼	South Mill Cr.	1858	4	427
Ketterman, Jacob Jr.	29¼	Long Run	1858	4	428
Ketterman, Jacob Jr.	140	Mill Cr.	1842	4	118
Ketterman, Joel	12	Mill Creek	1843	4	124
Kidner, George	157	Lost River	1796	1	378
Kidner, Nicholas	50	Baker's Run	1796	1	435
Kile, William	208½	Big Cove Run	1847	4	248
Kimble, John	47	Patterson's Cr.	1796	1	406

Name of Grantee	Acres	Local Description	Year	Book	Page
Michael, Solomon	67¾	Patterson's Cr.	1844	4	172
Michael, Solomon	7½ (7¼)	Patterson's Cr.	1845	4	208
Milburn, William	160	Adj. G. Bush	1799	3	16
Miles, Adam F. et al	323	Patterson Cr. Mt.	1856	4	410
Miles, David	380	South Br.	1788	1	8
Miles, David	187	South Branch	1788	1	9
Miles, David	150	Hutton's Run	1799	3	14
Miles, David	132	Brushy Run	1799	3	15
Miles, James	62	Timber Ridge	1796	1	432
Miles, James	272	Patterson's Cr.	1796	1	476
Miles, James	1,000	Patterson's Cr.	1823	3	233
Miles, James	9¾	Hutton's Run	1844	4	175
Miles, John D.	250	Patterson's Cr.	1837	3	393
Miles, Weston	12⅝	Timber Ridge	1856	4	400
Miller, Anthony	145	Lost River	1793	1	289
Miller, Charles	25	Mud Run Mt.	1859	4	442
Miller, George	143	Kinsey's Run	1830	3	279
Miller, George	37	Lost River	1835	3	348
Miller, George	175	Mud Lick Run	1835	3	361
Miller, George	120	Keeney's Run	1843	4	134
Miller, Isaac C. & C. W.	186	Lost River	1835	3	337
Miller, Jacob	68	Cove Run	1810	3	126
Miller, Jacob	192	Lost River	1791	1	138
Miller, Jacob	37	Lost River	1796	1	366
Miller, Jacob	19	Lost River	1794	1	316
Miller, John	232¾	Patterson's Cr.	1852	4	365
Miller, John	55	Patterson's Cr.	1852	4	366
Miller, John & Henry	117	Mill Creek	1789	1	43
Miller, Martin	173½	Kinsey's Run	1832	3	301
Miller, Martin	57	Lost River	1843	4	133
Miller, Michael	1,322	Little Mt.	1845	4	519
Miller, Michael	101	Howell's Run	1789	1	16
Miller, Stephen	255	Rough Run	1790	1	121
Miller, William	240	Saw Mill Mt.	1842	4	92
Mills, David	150	Huttons Run	1799	3	14
Mitts, Adam	90	South Branch	1792	1	255
Mooney, Hannah	226	Trout Run	1791	1	144
Moore, Benjamin	60	Big Ridge	1833	3	308
Moore, Nicholas	287	North River	1792	1	199
Moore, Thomas	60	Gr. Cacapon	1820	3	219
Moore, Thomas	105	Gr. Cacapon	1820	3	218
Moorland, Elisha	27	Patterson's Cr.	1813	3	149
Morrow, Gideon	95	Middle Mt.	1842	4	102
Morrow, James	412	Middle Mountain	1791	1	150
Morrow, James & David	45	Adj. V. Cooper	1809	2	169
Morrow, James & David	45	Adj. V. Cooper	1809	3	118
Mouse, Joshua	157¼	Middle Mountain	1847	4	263
Mulford, David	93	New Creek	1792	1	231
Mulford, James	95	Cacapon	1793	1	287
Mullen—See Mullin					
Mullen, John	22	Patterson's Cr.	1835	3	346
Mullen, John	90	Patterson's Cr.	1837	3	407
Mullen, John	48	Patterson's Cr.	1838	3	419
Mullen, John et al	161	Town Mill Run	1822	3	230
Mullin—See Mullen					
Mullin, John	232¾	Patterson's Cr.	1852	4	365
Mullin, John	55	Patterson's Cr.	1852	4	366
Mungold, Valentine	96	Middle Mountain	1796	1	388
Murphy, Hugh (Murphey)	67	Abraham's Cr.	1816	3	179
Murphy, Hugh	237	Abraham's Cr.	1789	1	99
Murphy, Hugh	249	Abraham's Cr.	1789	1	86
Murphy, Hugh	172	Abraham's Cr.	1792	1	196
Murphy, Hugh	624	Allegheny	1792	1	193

Name of Grantee	Acres	Local Description	Year	Book	Page
Myers, Francis (Frances)	205	Allegheny Mt.	1789	1	19
Nave, Adam	190	Lost River	1848	4	271
Nebb, Leonard et al (Neff-Neft)	200	Cacapon Mt.	1829	3	253
Neff, Leonard et al (Nebb-Neft)	200	Cacapon Mt.	1829	3	253
Neil, Moses	362	Patterson's Cr.	1789	1	51
Nelson, Richard	283	Horncamp Run	1803	3	78
Nepper—See Nipper					
Nevil, Joseph	367	Stony River	1789	1	77
Nevill, Joseph (Jasper)	400	Abraham's Cr.	1791	1	146
Nevill, Joseph	700	Stoney River	1809	3	113
Nevill, Joseph	700	Stoney River	1809	2	163
Nevill, Joseph	55	Byrn's & McKim's Cor.	1839	4	23
Nevill, Joseph	300	Stony River	1839	4	26
Nevill, Joseph	237	Stony River	1848	4	270
Nevill, Mort. D. et al	119½	Hayes Ridge	1850	4	313
Nevill, Mortimer D. (Neville)	28¼	Stony River	1858	4	435
Newhouse, John Y. et al Heirs	130	Town Fort Run	1845	4	197
Newman, Benjamin P.	857	North Mountain	1850	4	304
Nicholas, Henry	12	Cornwell Creek	1816	3	172
Nicholas, Henry	377	Powder Lick Run	1816	3	171
Nicholas, Henry	367	Town Fort Run	1815	3	167
Nicholas, Henry	269	Town Run	1812	3	139
Nimrod, Jacob et al	52	S. Mill Creek	1835	3	352
Nipper, Nancy (Nepper)	129	Tear Coat Ridge	1844	4	177
Noel, Nicholas	218	Patterson's Cr.	1789	1	52
Noel, Peter	112	Patterson's Cr.	1793	1	319
Noel, Philip	194	Pond Lick	1794	1	322
Norman, Will	408	Looney's Cr.	1789	1	35
Ogden, David	47	Waite's Run	1815	3	163
Oglevie, Thomas (Oglivie)	35	Van Meter's Run	1804	3	96
O'Haver, Mary (Ohaver)	165	Wait's Run	1809	2	162
Ohaver, Mary	165	Wait's Run	1809	3	112
Oldacre, Lucretia	64	Lost River	1789	1	68
Oldacre, Lucy	94	Gr. Cacapon	1794	1	304
Orms, James	223	Scraggs Run	1800	3	21
Orms, James	172	Branch Mountain	1800	3	20
Orndorf—See Ornduff					
Ornduff, David & James (Orndorf)	9a.3r.33p	Zane's Ridge	1846	4	221
Orr—See Ower					
Orr, James	278	Round Knob	1792	1	234
Orrowhood—Arrohood, Arrowhood					
Orrowhood, Joshua	80	Norman's Run	1829	3	260
Osborn, Josiah	30	Lost River	1793	1	277
Owen, Teakman (Ower)	7	Mill Creek	1792	1	200
Ower—See Owen					
Pain—or Pane					
Pain, Evan	310	Baker's Run	1796	1	381
Painter, John	136	Mill Creek	1792	1	244
Pane—or Pain					
Pane, Evan	50	Baker's Run	1800	3	44
Parker, Joseph M.	135	Cove Run	1826	3	251
Parson, John	83	Manning's Run	1800	3	62
Parsons, Thomas	470	Maxwell's Run	1792	1	251
Pearson, Alexander	41	Moses Run	1804	3	99
Peck, James	124	Lost River	1811	3	133
Pepper, William	123	Cove Run	1791	1	140
Perry, Ignatious	575	North River	1792	1	197
Peterson, Jacob	53	Mill Creek	1791	1	136
Peterson, Martin	50	North Mill Cr.	1816	3	176
Peterson, Michael	99	South Branch	1793	1	270
Peterson, Philip	56	South Br. Mt.	1796	1	418
Petteyon—See Pettlejon, Pettleyon, Pettyjohn					

Name of Grantee	Acres	Local Description	Year	Book	Page
Pettlejon, Peter	77	S. Mill Cr.	1800	3	60
Petty, Joseph	184	Town Fork	1789	1	53
Pettyjohn, Peter (Pettleyon)	77	S. Mill Cr.	1800	3	60
Phares, James	93	North Fork-Patterson Cr.	1798	1	531
Pifer, William F.	155	Brake's Mill Run	1850	4	319
Pifer, William F.	74	New Cr. Mt.	1856	4	405
Plumb, John	292	Muddy Run	1789	1	80
Plumb, John	363	Muddy Run	1789	1	81
Poland, Aaron	92	Lick Run	1839	4	24
Pope, Jacob R.	263	Buck Run	1848	4	272
Post, Valentine	51	Mill Creek	1792	1	210
Powers, Martin	31	South Branch	1788	2	151
Powers, Martin	31	South Branch	1788	3	440
Powers, Valentine	78	South Branch	1792	1	202
Powers, Valentine	38½	Limestone Ridge	1852	4	363
Prater—or Prather					
Prater, Joseph (Prather)	45	Walker's Ridge	1800	3	50
Prather, Jeremiah	374	Stony River	1788	1	12
Price, Arjalon	289	Patterson's Cr.	1788	1	5
Pugh, Daniel	537	Mud Lick Run	1792	1	243
Pugh, Hannibal	70	Cor. Geo. Harness	1833	3	315
Pugh, Jacob	142	Sandy Ridge	1799	3	4
Pugh, Jacob	29	Anderson Ridge	1796	1	363
Pugh, Jesse J.	249½	Flat Ridge	1849	4	301
Putman, Peter	50	Thorn Run	1796	1	469
Putman, Peter	278	Patterson's Cr.	1796	1	468
Radcliff, Stephen	123	Looney's Cr.	1791	1	135
Rain—or Raines					
Rain, Robert	100	Slate Run	1797	1	516
Raines, Robert	200	Big Ridge	1796	1	488
Randall, Abel	406	Allegheny	1789	1	91
Randall, Alexander	175	Brushy Run	1788	1	13
Randall, Jacob	122	South Branch	1795	1	330
Rankin, George	245	Patterson's Cr.	1815	3	168
Ray, Benjamin	143	North Branch	1796	1	494
Reed—or Reid					
Reed, Green B.	8¾	Mill Run	1858	4	430
Reed, William	42	Lost River	1836	3	369
Reid, Anthony	64	Adj. A. Clark	1798	1	552
Reid, Anthony	115	Abram's Cr.	1798	1	548
Reid, Sarah (Read) et al	424	Patterson's Cr.	1789	1	42
Reid, Sarah et al	75	Patterson's Cr.	1789	1	41
Renick, George	200	Vanmeter's Run	1804	3	98
Renick, Felix	225	Lost River	1796	1	471
Renick, Jonathan	61	South Branch	1800	3	56
Renick, William	400	Potato Row Mt.	1796	1	470
Rerunsavall—See Rounsaval					
Rerunsavall, Benjamin	127	Mill Run	1789	1	27
Reynolds, Stephen	275	Lost River	1838	3	427
Riggleman, John	53	Mill Creek	1796	1	413
Rimble, Lambert (Kimble)	43	Lit. New Creek	1799	3	19
Risk, A. B. et al	200	Deep Spgs. Run	1852	4	345
Roadcap, Henry & Morton	470	Basore's Mill Rn	1856	4	401
Roberts, David	34	Cove Run	1797	1	519
Roberts, David Jr.	16	Lost River	1800	3	53
Roberts, David Jr.	166	Lost River	1794	1	309
Roberts, David Sr.	42	Lost River	1794	1	310
Roberts, James	10	Salt Spring Run	1851	4	334
Roberts, John et al	270	Patterson's Cr.	1835	3	349
Roberts, Thomas	144	Lost River	1794	1	298
Roberts, Thomas	178	Cove Run	1789	1	14
Robertson—See Robinson					
Robertson, John G.	125	Middle Mt.	1844	4	176

Name of Grantee	Acres	Local Description	Year	Book	Page
Sager, John	355	Gr. Cacapon	1792	1	242
Sagg, Robert	100	South Branch	1790	1	123
Sagg, Robert et al	287	Middle Mountain	1793	1	285
Salts, Thomas	50	Lost River	1796	1	479
Sancescus—See Lancesco, Lancescus					
Sceres, John T. (Sears)	5	Adj. Orrohood	1836	3	380
Schitizer, William	40⅜	Patterson's Cr.	1851	4	333
Scidmore—or Skidmore					
Scidmore, John	302	South Br.	1791	1	152
Scott, Alexander et al	280	Lit. Mountain	1840	4	54
Scott, James	400	Patterson's Cr.	1796	1	426
Scott, John	85	Patterson's Cr. Mt.	1837	3	417
Scott, William N.	42	Looney's Creek	1833	3	312
Sears, John T. (Sceres)	5	Adj. Orrohood	1836	3	380
See—See also Lee					
See, Absolum	62	Cove Mountain	1831	3	282
See, Adam	62	South Fork	1794	1	321
See, Adam Sr.	21	Middle Mt.	1840	4	52
See, George	39½	Cove Run	1831	3	281
See, George	130	Stone Lick	1796	1	443
See, George	51	Byrns Run	1789	1	118
See, George & Edmund	142	Brush Lick Run	1831	3	283
See, George et al	287	Middle Mountain	1793	1	285
See, George Jr. (Lee)	40	Lost River	1792	1	203
See, George Jr. (Lee)	59	Lost River	1792	1	204
See, George Jr.	62	Middle Mountain	1792	1	175
See, George Jr.	80	Middle Mountain	1792	1	176
See, George (Sea)	145 (140)	Little Cove	1796	1	360
See, George Sr.	78	Watt's Branch	1794	1	308
See, Godfrey & Adam Jr.	65	Mid. Mountain	1840	4	49
See, John	80	Lost River	1842	4	91
Sennet, Jacob	94	Shenandoah River	1796	1	370
Seymore—See Seymour					
Seymore, Aaron	65	Looney's Creek	1843	4	150
Seymore, Abel	412	Middle Mt.	1789	1	21
Seymore, Abel	250	Abraham's Cr.	1792	1	180
Seymore, Abel	15	Adj. his own	1799	3	3
Seymore, Abel	300	Lunie's Cr.	1799	3	12
Seymore, Abel	300	Welton Knob	1800	3	27
Seymore, George	70	Looney's Cr.	1809	3	108
Seymore, Isaac V.	2⅞	South Fork	1850	4	312
Seymore, James	80	Adj. J. Welton	1799	3	5
Seymore, Jonathan	200	Looney's Cr.	1837	3	409
Seymore, Joseph	42	Smoke Hill	1789	1	57
Seymore, Richard	339	Looney's Cr.	1789	1	56
Seymore, Richard et al	310	Allegheny Mt.	1794	1	293
Seymore, Thomas	329	Lunie's Creek	1789	1	18
Seymore, Thomas	400	Looney's Cr.	1789	1	32
Seymore, Thomas	341	New Creek	1789	1	38
Seymore, Thomas	240	New Creek	1789	1	39
Seymore, Thomas	103	Abram's Cr.	1794	1	315
Seymore, Thomas	393	Looney's Cr.	1799	3	6
Seymore, Thomas	173	Abraham's Cr.	1809	3	115
Seymore, Thomas	18	Abraham's Cr.	1809	3	116
Seymore, Thomas & Richard	464	Lunis Creek	1789	1	17
Seymore, William	89	Looney's Creek	1794	1	314
Seymore, William	153	Scott's Run	1794	1	296
Seymore, William et al	160	Stony River	1794	1	327
Seymore, William et al	116	Abram's Cr.	1796	1	478
Seymour, George	70	Loomis Creek	1809	2	157
Seymour, Thomas	173	Abram's Creek	1809	2	165
Seymour, Thomas	18	Adj. P. Trout	1809	2	166
Shartiger, William	40⅜	Patterson Cr.	1851	4	333

Name of Grantee	Acres	Local Description	Year	Book	Page
Shell, Daniel	225	Lit. Mountain	1840	4	70
Shell, Daniel	140½	Looney's Cr.	1844	4	174
Shell, Daniel et al	60	Looney's Cr.	1839	4	22
Shell, George	196	Looney's Cr.	1789	1	25
Shell, George	92	Patterson Cr. Mt.	1838	4	11
Shell, George et al	250	Patterson's Cr.	1835	3	345
Shell, John	200	Lit. Mountain	1839	4	34
Shell, John et al Heirs	130	Stoney River	1839	4	37
Shell, John J.	5 1/16	Lost River	1858	4	419
Shell, John J.	18¼	Lost River	1858	4	420
Shell, Philip	160	Lit. Mountain	1840	4	38
Shepherd—Shepperd					
Shepherd, Job	520	North River	1793	1	259
Shepherd, John	420	Patterson's Cr.	1791	1	156
Shepherd, Jonathan	346	Patterson's Cr.	1791	1	148
Shepler, Henry	75¼	Brake's Mill Run	1849	4	292
Shepperd—or Shepherd					
Shepperd, Jonathan	189	Brushy Run	1796	1	405
Shettingburg, William	23	Adj. E. Arnold	1834	3	334
Shields, Peter	70	North Mill Cr.	1796	1	455
Shillingburg, Hugh et al	600	Abram's Creek	1844	4	160
Shillingburg, William	23	Adj. E. Arnold	1834	3	334
Shiner, Frederick	195	Lost River	1793	1	284
Shipes, Asa	36	Branch Mt.	1819	3	204
Ships, Asa (Asia)	36	Branch Mountain	1819	3	204
Shireman, Conrad	67	Upper Cove	1837	3	401
Shireman, George	89	Cove Run	1829	3	262
Shireman, George	130	Upper Cove	1823	3	231
Shoemaker, Elias	25	Adj. his own	1812	3	143
Shoemaker, Elias	32	Mill Cr.	1796	1	416
Shoemaker, George	130	Lost River	1796	1	505
Shoemaker, John	233	Gr. Cacapon	1802	3	74
Shook, David	204	South Branch	1796	1	487
Shook, Herman	58	Middle Mt.	1798	1	551
Shook, Jacob et al	200	Cacapon Mt.	1829	3	253
Shook, Peter	300	Potomac	1796	1	489
Shrader—See Strader					
Shrader, Nicholas	12	Cor. H. Rule	1792	2	153
Shrader, Nicholas	12	Cor. to Henry Rule	1792	4	158
Shreve—See Shreves, etc.					
Shreve, Joseph	191	Wts. Potomac	1800	3	39
Shreve, Joseph	42	Smoke Hill	1789	1	57
Shreves—See Shreve, Shreeve, Sreeve					
Shreves, Joseph	210	South Br.	1789	1	119
Simmons—See Simon, Simons					
Simmons, Christian Sr.	207	Mid. Mountain	1829	3	265
Simmons, George (Simons)	175	Middle Mt.	1850	4	320
Simmons, George	50	Adj. H. Shipless	1795	1	346
Simmons, George et al	90	South Branch	1795	1	344
Simmons, Michael	16	Middle Mt.	1842	4	109
Simmons, Philip	59	South Fork	1795	1	332
Simmons, S. Y.	24½	Scott's Ridge	1856	4	402
Simmons, Sanford Y.	715½	New Cr. Mt.	1845	4	209
Simmons, Sanford Y.	365	Little Mt.	1847	4	257
Simmons, Sanford Y.	267	Mud Lick Run	1852	4	338
Simmons, Sanford Y.	221	Abram's Cr.	1852	4	361
Simmons, Sanford Y.	56	Baker's Run	1853	4	367
Simmons, Sanford Y.	186¼	Patterson's Cr.	1853	4	368
Simmons, Sanford Y.	113	Patterson Cr. Mt.	1853	4	370
Simmons, Sanford Y.	155½	Baker's Run	1855	4	398
Simmons, Valentine	418⅜	Lick Run	1846	4	229
Simmons, Valentine	295	Lost River	1847	4	246
Simmons, Valentine	525	Looney's Cr.	1839	4	33

Name of Grantee	Acres	Local Description	Year	Book	Page
Simmons, Valentine	600	Patterson's Cr.	1839	4	31
Simmons, Valentine	120	Helmick's Gap	1839	4	29
Simmons, Valentine	785	North Mountain	1833	3	306
Simmons, Van	42	Chrisman's Gap	1802	3	76
Simon—See Simmons, Simons					
Simon, George	94	South Fork	1828	3	237
Simon, George	290	Middle Mountain	1829	3	261
Simons—See Simmons, Simon					
Simons, Christian	90	South Branch	1793	1	271
Simons, Michael	80	South Fork	1835	3	350
Simons, Michael	40	South Fork	1850	4	309
Simons, Peter	100	South Branch	1794	1	261
Sims, Elijah	59 (49)	Locust Ridge	1800	3	42
Sims, Elijah	56	Adj. A. Orchard's Line	1800	3	41
Sinnet, Jacob	94	Shenandoah River	1796	1	370
Sion, Adam (Sions)	600	High Knob	1856	4	406
Sites—See (Getts)					
Sites, Abraham	7½	Elkhorn Run	1830	3	278
Sites, Abram	91	Fork Mt.	1826	3	254
Sites, Abram	43	Adj. A. Sites	1844	4	188
Sites, Conrad	48	Spring Run	1840	4	71
Sites, Conrad	103	South Mill Cr.	1845	4	191
Sites, Daniel	193	South Mill Cr.	1842	4	95
Sites, Daniel Jr.	65	Middle Mountain	1838	4	10
Sites, Elizabeth	25	S. Mill Cr.	1845	4	195
Sites, George	206	Mill Creek	1792	1	205
Sites, George	68	South Mill Cr.	1797	1	514
Sites, George	21	South Mill Cr.	1798	1	553
Sites, George	40	S. Mill Cr.	1816	3	184
Sites, George	36	Fork Mtn.	1825	3	247
Sites, George & Abraham	117	Deep Spring Run	1809	2	160
Sites, George & Abraham	117	Deep Spring	1809	3	110
Sites, Jacob	92	S. Mill Creek	1820	3	211
Sites, Jacob	66⅞	South Mill Creek	1846	4	217
Sites, Jacob	234	Fork Mountain	1834	3	326
Sites, Jacob et al	43	Adj. Abram Site's	1844	4	188
Sites, John	50	Salt Petre Knob	1834	3	324
Sites, John Jr.	5½	South Mill Cr.	1840	4	40
Sites, Solomon & Abraham Jr.	55	South Mill Cr.	1845	4	193
Skidmore—or Scidmore					
Skidmore, Andrew	50	North Fork	1849	4	294
Slagle, Jacob	114	Mid Mountain	1792	1	216
Slater, Thomas	51	Lost River	1789	1	29
Slater, William et al	52a.71p.	Lost River	1846	4	224
Slater, William et al	608	Lost River	1852	4	355
Sleeter, Abram	45	Cove Mt.	1851	4	327
Sly, George	33	North Fork	1794	1	297
Smith, Alexander	25	North Branch	1803	3	86
Smith, Alexander	321	Abraham's Cr.	1801	3	63
Smith, Alexander	218	North Branch	1794	1	329
Smith, Alexander et al	1,000	Wram's Creek	1803	3	85
Smith, Daniel and James et al	365	North River	1839	4	28
Smith, Daniel	19½	Patterson's Cr.	1847	4	249
Smith, David	24	Patterson's Cr.	1803	3	82
Smith, David	250	Patterson's Cr.	1794	1	294
Smith, Henry	257	Cross Run	1848	4	275
Smith, Henry	57	North Fork	1848	4	273
Smith, Jacob	45	So. Mill Cr.	1798	1	522
Smith, Jacob	24	S. Mill Cr.	1799	3	13
Smith, Jacob	65	North Fork	1839	4	27
Smith, John (of Sarah) et al	450	Salt Spg. Run	1854	4	378
Smith, John	76	Patterson's Creek	1797	1	507
Smith, John	113	Mud Lick Run	1816	3	189

Name of Grantee	Acres	Local Description	Year	Book	Page
Smith, John	206	Town Mill Run	1816	3	190
Smith, John	142	Mill Run	1820	3	222
Smith, John	5½	South Mill Cr.	1840	4	40
Smith, John	100	Patterson Cr.	1840	4	39
Smith, Robert	184	Burkett's Hole	1795	1	333
Smith, William	107½	Lost River	1850	4	322
Smith, William	106	South Branch	1798	1	535
Snodgrass, James	178	Huckleberry Ridge	1817	3	195
Snodgrass, John	143	Charles Knob Mt.	1843	4	127
Snodgrass, William	258	Looney's Cr.	1838	3	424
Snyder, Charles	72	Cove Mountain	1843	4	143
Snyder, Charles	132	North Mountain	1843	4	142
Snyder, Isaac	355	Cove Run	1837	3	410
Snyder, Isaac	11¾	North Mt.	1858	4	426
Snyder, Isaac	190	Cove Knob	1858	4	425
Snyder, Isaac	75	Big Cove Run	1847	4	250
Snyder, Jacob (Snider)	33	Lost River	1796	1	375
Snyder, John	10	Cove Run	1822	3	229
Snyder, John	59	Middle Mountain	1848	4	274
Snyder, John	46	Lost River	1822	3	228
Snyder, John	60	Mud Lick Run	1818	3	198
Snyder, Mary	33	Upper Cove Run	1843	4	151
Sperry, John	30	North River	1811	3	128
Sperry, Peter	102	North River	1811	3	127
Sperry, Peter	41	North River	1796	1	453
Sphor—See Spore					
Sphor, David et al	161	Town Mill Run	1822	3	230
Spillman, John (Spilman)	118	Mill Cr.	1791	1	159
Spillman, John (Spilman)	234	Mid. Mountain	1791	1	161
Spillman, John	50	South Mill Cr.	1796	1	456
Spillman, John	120	Middle Mountain	1792	1	283
Spore—See Sphor					
Spore, John U.	48	S. Fork	1794	1	302
Sreeve—See Shreeve, Shreve, Shreves					
Sreeve, Benjamin	250	North Fork	1800	3	40
Stambough, Philip	90	Mill Creek	1789	1	55
Starr, John	46	Loony's Creek	1796	1	408
Starr, John	81	Looney's Cr.	1798	1	530
Steffle—See Steiffle					
Steffle, Adam	63	Mill Creek	1796	1	438
Steiffle, Adam	57	Mill Creek	1796	1	430
Sterrett, James	882	Big Cacapon	1834	3	328
Sterrett, James	371	Big Cacapon	1832	3	292
Steward—See Stewart, Stuart					
Steward, Joseph	74	Gr. Cacapon	1796	1	434
Stewart, Archibald	63	Patterson's Cr.	1796	1	442
Stewart, Jeremiah	96	Baker's Mt.	1836	3	365
Stewart, John	5	Wts. Cacapon	1833	3	311
Stingley, George	44	Adj. G. Shells	1812	3	144
Stingley, George	28	Little Mt.	1794	1	312
Stingley, George	323	Looney's Cr.	1816	3	177
Stingley, George	110	Lit. Mountain	1789	1	54
Stingley, Jacob	30	Adj. his land	1796	1	436
Stingley, Jacob	120	Lit. Mountain	1793	1	278
Stingley, John	127	Little Mt.	1847	4	240
Stingley, John & William	150	Walker's Ridge	1829	3	269
Stingley, Thomas	267¼	Patterson's Cr.	1844	4	181
Stingley, Thomas	38¼	Patterson's Cr.	1844	4	180
Stingley, Thomas	18	Patterson's Cr.	1844	4	179
Stingley, Thomas	446	Patterson's Cr.	1844	4	157
Stingley, Thomas et al	250	Patterson's Cr.	1835	3	345
Stingley, William	24	Patterson's Cr.	1816	3	186
Stingley, William	86	Patterson's Cr.	1794	1	307

Name of Grantee	Acres	Local Description	Year	Book	Page
Stingley, William	100	Allegheny Mt.	1796	1	411
Stone, James	278	Lost River	1791	1	132
Stone, James	50	Lost River	1796	1	399
Stone, James	102	Limestone Run	1796	1	410
Stone, Thomas	248	Lost River	1791	1	133
Stone, William	35	Spring Run	1834	3	332
Stone, William	140	Hanging Rock Cr.	1833	3	313
Stonestreet, Elijah	28	North Fork	1834	3	325
Stookey, David	74	Bear Wallow	1798	1	559
Stover, Abraham	223½	South Fork	1852	4	344
Stover, Jacob et al	157	Fork Mountain	1830	3	274
Strader, Christopher	197	Adj. Sethman Ower	1792	1	233
Strader, Nicholas	12	Cor. to Henry Rule	1792	4	158
Stratherman—or Strauderman, Strautherman, Strawderman					
Strautherman—See Stratherman					
Strautherman, Henry	61	Lost River	1836	3	388
Strawderman, See Stratherman					
Strawderman, Adam	41¾	Lost River	1852	4	351
Strawderman, George	39⅝	Kinsey's Run	1849	4	293
Strawderman, George	58⅝	Lost Run	1846	4	219
Strawderman, John	89	Lost River	1841	4	79
Strawderman, John A.	158	Lost River	1796	1	368
Strosnider, Mordecai et al	350	Adj. S. Switzer	1849	4	297
Strout, George	197	Patterson's Cr.	1813	3	150
Struett, James (Sterrett)	882	Big Cacapon	1834	3	328
Stuart—See Stewart					
Stump, George W. et al	2,528	Branch Mt.	1858	4	421
Stump, Jesse	254	Middle Mt.	1847	4	238
Stump, Jesse	50	Adj. J. Simpkins	1832	3	294
Stump, Jesse et al	130	N. Mill Cr.	1824	3	244
Stump, Leonard	33a.1r.14p.	Adj. M. George	1799	3	7
Stump, Leonard Jr.	10	South Fork	1806	2	155
Stump, Leonard Jr.	8	Adj. M. Stump	1806	2	154
Stump, Leonard Jr.	63	So. Branch	1818	3	201
Stump, Leonard Jr.	10	So. Fork	1806	3	106
Stump, Leonard Jr.	8	Adj. M. Stump	1806	3	105
Stump, Leonard Jr.	151	South Fork	1795	1	335
Stuter—See Stutty					
Stutty, Abraham (Stuttee)	45	Cove Mt.	1851	4	327
Surbough, David	103	Lost River	1794	1	318
Swisher—or Sweitzer, Switcher, Switzer					
Swisher, Henry	166½	North River	1850	4	324
Swisher, Nicholas	115	Gr. Cacapon	1796	1	452
Swisher, Nicholas	97	Gr. Cacapon	1792	1	192
Switcher—See Sweitzer, Swisher, Switzer					
Switcher, Michael	100	Adj. F. Godlove	1800	3	38
Switzer—or Sweitzer, Swisher, Switcher					
Switzer, Henry	180	North River	1840	4	69
Switzer, Henry	247	South Fork	1832	3	297
Switzer, Michael	50	Big Ridge	1833	3	316
Switzer, Philip	64	Lost River	1820	3	217
Switzer, Simon (or Samuel)	160	Gr. Cacapon	1838	4	9
Talbert, John et al	168	Patterson's Cr.	1802	3	75
Talbert, Thomas	397	Patterson's Cr.	1791	1	149
Tannihill, William	335	Trough Mt.	1789	1	117
Taylor, George et al	385	Thompson's Run	1800	3	43
Taylor, Parson M.	32	Patterson Cr.	1856	4	411
Taylor, Parsons M. et al	323	Patterson Cr. Mt.	1856	4	410
Terall, Nicholas (Teral)	387	Allegheny Mt.	1789	1	24
Tetrick, Jacob	100	S. Mill Creek	1834	3	331
Tetrick, Jacob	21	S. Mill Creek	1835	3	356
Tevebough, Daniel	59	Adj. McNeil	1791	1	174
Tevebough, Jacob et al	32	East Ridge	1816	3	192

Name of Grantee	Acres	Local Description	Year	Book	Page
Vanmeter, Isaac	307	Allegheny Mt.	1791	1	157
Vanmeter, Isaac	100	Patterson' Cr.	1798	1	526
Vanmeter, Isaac	347	Patterson's Cr.	1798	1	527
Vanmeter, Isaac	256	Patterson's Cr.	1798	1	549
Vanmeter, Isaac	686	High Knob Mt.	1798	1	550
Vanmeter, Isaac et al	385	Thompson's Run	1800	3	43
Vanmeter, Isaac & Jacob	135	South Br.	1789	1	73
Vanmeter, Jacob	183	High Knob Mt.	1836	3	384
Vanmeter, Jacob	374	Thompson's Run	1800	3	47
Vanmeter, Joseph	261	Vanmeter's Mill	1789	1	90
Vanmeter, Joseph	424	Mud Lick	1789	1	89
Vanmeter, Joseph	362	Patterson's Cr.	1789	1	95
Vanmeter, Joseph	415	Hickory Bottom	1789	1	88
Vanmeter, Joseph	507(407)	Vanmeter's Mill	1789	1	71
Vanmeter, William C.	29⅞	Timber Ridge	1858	4	432
Vannort, Cyrus W.	262½(202½)	Pound Mill Run	1852	4	343
Vannost, Cyrus W.	262½(202½)	Pound Mill Run	1852	4	343
Vatch—See Veach, Veatch					
Vatcher, John T.	96	Looney's Cr.	1809	3	114
Vatcher, John T.	96	Looney's Cr.	1809	2	164
Veach—See Vatch, Veatch					
Veach, Henson (Veatch)	92	Conners Cr.	1836	3	367
Veach, Jeremiah	35	Adj. Arrowhood	1844	4	187
Veatch, Vatch, Veach					
Veatch, Henson Sr.	50	Loonus Cr.	1835	3	353
Veatch, John T. (Vatcher)	96	Looney's Cr.	1809	3	114
Veatch, John T.	96	Looney's Creek	1809	2	164
Veatch, William & Jeremiah	52	Looney's Cr.	1823	3	234
Walker, Joseph	161	Patterson's Cr.	1820	3	213
Walker, Joseph	101	Lit. Mountain	1844	4	184
Walker, Mathias	255	Fravel's Run	1844	4	185
Walker, Philip	55	North River	1843	4	152
Ward, Joseph	254	Allegheny Mts.	1789	1	61
Warden, Benjamin	40	Lost River	1842	4	113
Warden, William	46	Lost River	1796	1	387
Warden, William	34	Lost River	1796	1	395
Warden, William	48	Lost River	1796	1	397
Warden, William	43	Lost River	1796	1	422
Warden, William	123	North River	1813	3	158
Watson, Jonathan	60	South Branch	1796	1	481
Wease—See Weese, Weise, Wiese					
Wease, Charles	107	Mill Creek	1846	4	236
Wease, Elijah	74	Mill Creek	1841	4	88
Wease, Elijah	197	Mill Creek	1840	4	55
Wease, Solomon & William	252	Mill Creek	1840	4	74
Wease, William	26	Mill Creek	1840	4	73
Wease, William	24	South Mill Cr.	1839	4	36
Weatherholt, Peter	108	Lost River	1793	1	282
Weatherholt, Peter	50	Lost River	1793	1	281
Webb, Daniel	136	Cove Run	1830	3	277
Webb, George	20⅜	Spring Lick Ridge	1859	4	441
Webb, George	14	Branch Mt.	1860	4	449
Webb, James	1½	North River	1859	4	440
Webb, James	366	North River	1843	4	141
Webb, John	70	Patterson's Cr.	1804	3	94
Weese—See Wease, Weise, Wiese					
Weese, Elijah (Eliza)	96	N. Mill Creek	1838	3	426
Weise—See Wease, Weese, Wiese					
Weise, John	51	Mill Cr.	1796	1	417
Welch, William	45½(55½)	Thorn Run	1851	4	335
Welton, Aaron	97	Flat Bush Run	1829	3	264
Welton, Aaron	137	Looney's Cr.	1829	3	263
Welton, Aaron A. et al	18,557	Stony River	1860	4	443

Name of Grantee	Acres	Local Description	Year	Book	Page
Wilson, John	40	Lost River	1843	4	148
Wilson, John	77	Kinsey's Run	1846	4	234
Wilson, John	150	Chestnut Ridge	1796	1	433
Wilson, John & David (Willson)	238	Mill Mountain	1846	4	235
Wilson, John Jr.	1a.22p.	Kinsey's Run	1846	4	233
Wilson, Joseph	70	Lost River	1843	4	149
Wilson, Thomas	188	Big Run	1820	3	221
Wilson, Thomas	50	Adj. A. Sweitzer	1837	3	398
Wilson, William	21	S. Mill Creek	1836	3	368
Wilson, William	347	South Fork	1840	4	75
Wimer, Abram	160	Welton's Knob	1842	4	120
Windburg, Charles	74	Burkett's Hole	1792	1	256
Windling, Charles	74	Burkett's Hole	1792	1	256
Wise—See also Weise					
Wise, Christian	295	Lost River	1789	1	26
Wise, Henry	98	North River	1832	3	300
Wise, Henry	60a.56p.	South Fork	1845	4	213
Wise, Jacob	71	Branch Mt.	1840	4	53
Wise, John	56	South Br. Mt.	1796	1	441
Wise, Michael	205	Lost River	1792	1	257
Wise, Peter	50	Mill Creek	1796	1	440
Wise, William	21	S. Mill Creek	1836	3	368
Wiseman—or Wisman					
Wiseman, Philip (Wisman)	272	Big Cacapon	1832	3	293
Wisman—See Wiseman					
Wolfe, Adam Jr.	43½	Shook's Run	1850	4	326
Wolfe, Adam Jr.	1,205	Middle Mt.	1850	4	563
Wolford, Jacob et al	68	Looney's Cr.	1815	3	169
Wood—Woods					
Wood, Angus M.	41¾	Lost River	1847	4	261
Wood, Angus M.	95	Lost River	1852	4	350
Wood, Angus M.	75	Cove Run	1859	4	444
Wood, Peter	100	Branch Mountain	1798	1	557
Wood, Richard	389	North River	1789	1	28
Woodard, Thomas	72	Lost River	1794	1	313
Woods—Wood					
Woods, Thomas	304	Cacapon	1792	1	253
Wright, James	129	Kinsey's Run	1791	1	170
Yoakman, Christopher C.	57	Broad Run	1848	4	281
Yoakum, Alfred	205	Looney's Cr.	1857	4	416
Yoakum, Christopher C. (Yoakman)	57	Broad Run	1848	4	281
Zane, Isaac	371	Lost River	1791	1	173

HARRISON COUNTY

Adams, Daniel J.	4,000	Teters Creek	1787	2	120
Adams, Daniel J.	830	Ledding Cr.	1787	2	121
Adams, Daniel J.	5,000	Stone Coal Cr.	1787	2	122
Adams, Daniel J.	1,526	Leading Cr.	1787	2	256
Adams, Daniel J.	1,000	Old Field Fork	1790	3	296
Adams, Daniel J.	1,000	Old Field Fork	1790	3	297
Adams, Daniel J.	1,000	Wts. of Elk	1790	3	298
Adams, Daniel J.	2,500	Wts. of Elk	1790	3	300
Adams, Daniel J.	2,500	Old Field Fork	1790	3	301
Adams, Daniel J.	2,500	Old Field Fork	1790	3	302
Adams, Daniel J.	2,500	Old Field Fork	1790	3	303
Adams, Daniel J.	2,500	Wts. Elk River	1790	3	304

Name of Grantee	Acres	Local Description	Year	Book	Page
Adams, Daniel J.	2,500	Wts. Elk River	1790	3	305
Adams, Daniel J.	1,000	Old Field Fork	1790	3	335
Adams, Josias	8,817	Sycamore Creek	1852	6	561
Adams, Josias	40	Elk Creek	1816	3	570
Adams, Nathaniel	660	Elk Creek	1787	2	68
Adams, Nathaniel	826	Brusky Fork	1801	5	69
Adams, Nathaniel	166	Elk Creek	1787	2	351
Adams, Thomas	1,000	Mill Cr.	1787	2	63
Adams, Thomas	1,000	Mill Creek	1787	2	152
Adams, Thomas	1,000	Mill Creek	1787	2	246
Adams, Thomas	500	Mill Creek	1787	2	247
Adams, Thomas	500	Mill Creek	1787	2	279
Adams, Thomas	1,000	Mill Creek	1787	2	280
Adams, Thomas	500	Mill Creek	1787	2	367
Adams, Thomas	500	Adj. his No. 5	1787	2	368
Alkier, See Alkire					
Alkire, David	30	West Fork	1817	6	296
Allen, John J.	696	Limestone Cr.	1859	6	173
Allen, John J. et al	420	Rooting Cr.	1834	7	53
Allen, John J. et al	825	Elk Creek	1834	7	68
Allen, John et al Heirs	157	Caldwell's Fork	1821	6	193
Allen, Joshua	350	Wts. West Fork	1791	3	413
Allen, Stephen	86	Wts. West Fork	1826	6	46
Allman, William	200	Fink's Run	1805	5	161
Amos, John	75	Quaker's Fork	1838	7	223
Anderson, James	400	Ingan's Run	1788	3	11
Anderson, James	417	Simpson's Cr.	1785	1	45
Anderson, James	356	Simpson Cr.	1787	2	328
Anderson, James	283	Tygert's V. R.	1787	2	329
Anderson, James	234	Booth's Cr.	1786	1	329
Anderson, James	1,000	Simpson's Cr.	1786	1	470
Anderson, James et al	1,000	Canoe Creek	1787	2	301
Anderson, James Jr.	200	Lost Run	1800	4	555
Anderson, John	375	Booth's Creek	1786	2	31
Anderson, Michael	250	Wts. Hughes R.	1788	3	130
Anglin, Adren	525	Elk Creek	1815	5	270
Anglin, William	400	Tygert's V. R.	1786	2	29
Angus, John	3,000	Wts. Hughes River	1786	1	48
Angus, John	4,000	Adj. his 21st Surv.	1786	1	49
Archer, John	2,000	Wts. Wms. River	1794	4	27
Archibald, James	39	Middle Is. Cr.	1820	6	229
Armstead, John B.	59,329	Wts. West Fork	1797	4	557
Armstrong, Abraham	270	Wts. Hughes River	1799	4	512
Armstrong, Paul	255	Wts. Lit. Kanawha	1787	2	222
Arnett, William W. et al Heirs	50	Laurel Fork	1838	7	286
Arnett, William W. et al Heirs	50	Laurel Run	1838	7	287
Arnett, William W. et al Heirs	50	Old Camp Run	1838	7	288
Arnett, William W. et al Heirs	50	Rush Run	1838	7	289
Arnold, George	221	Middle Fork	1788	3	7
Arnold, George	580	Elk Creek	1788	3	8
Arnold, George	1,240	Brown's Cr.	1793	4	13
Arnold, George	400	Reedy Cr.	1801	5	14
Arnold, George	400	Wts. West Fork	1786	2	14
Arnold, George	163	Wts. West Fork	1793	4	14
Arnold, George	150	Elk Creek	1793	4	15
Arnold, George	73	Hacker's Cr.	1793	4	17
Arnold, George	54	Hacker's Cr.	1793	4	18
Arnold, George	75	Wts. Salt Lick	1802	5	25
Arnold, George	100	Geelick Run	1802	5	26
Arnold, George	785	Elk Creek	1788	3	45
Arnold, George	550	Brown's Cr.	1788	3	56
Arnold, George	297	Elk Creek	1801	5	70
Arnold, George	100	Crawford's Run	1801	5	71
Arnold, George	455	Elk Cr.	1801	5	72

Name of Grantee	Acres	Local Description	Year	Book	Page
Banks, Henry	2,000	Indian Fork	1786	1	88
Banks, Henry	735	Rich Mountain	1786	1	89
Banks, Henry	1,000	Sugar Cr.	1795	4	89
Banks, Henry	1,000	Wts. Hughes River	1786	1	90
Banks, Henry	1,000	Sugar Creek	1795	4	90
Banks, Henry	1,000	Sugar Creek	1796	4	91
Banks, Henry	2,000	Indian Fork	1786	1	91
Banks, Henry	1,000	Sugar Cr.	1795	4	92
Banks, Henry	1,035	Jone's Run	1786	1	92
Banks, Henry	1,000	Sugar Creek	1795	4	93
Banks, Henry	2,000	Indian Fork	1786	1	93
Banks, Henry	1,000	Teter's Cr.	1795	4	94
Banks, Henry	1,000	Jone's Run	1786	1	94
Banks, Henry	1,000	Teter's Cr.	1795	4	95
Banks, Henry	2,000	Water's of Hughes	1786	1	95
Banks, Henry	1,000	Teter's Cr.	1795	4	96
Banks, Henry	2,000	Wts. Hughes River	1786	1	96
Banks, Henry	2,000	Wts. Hughes River	1786	1	97
Banks, Henry	500	Wts. Hughes River	1786	1	98
Banks, Henry	1,000	Beaver Creek	1786	1	99
Banks, Henry	1,000	Jone's Run	1786	1	100
Banks, Henry	1,000	Wts. Hughes River	1786	1	101
Banks, Henry	1,000	Beaver Creek	1786	1	102
Banks, Henry	1,000	Valley River	1786	1	103
Banks, Henry	965	Jone's Run	1786	1	104
Banks, Henry	1,000	Teter's Cr.	1795	4	142
Banks, Henry	1,000	Teter's Creek	1795	4	143
Banks, Henry	1,450	Coon's Run	1786	1	270
Banks, Henry	790	Booth Cr.	1786	1	271
Banks, Henry	2,160	Booth's Cr.	1786	1	272
Banks, Henry	500	Stuart's Run	1786	1	273
Banks, Henry	2,000	File's Creek	1786	1	275
Banks, Henry	1,000	Dodson Run	1786	1	276
Banks, Henry	2,000	File's Creek	1786	1	277
Banks, Henry	1,550	Roaring Cr.	1796	4	282
Banks, Henry	500	Hardin Mill Run	1786	1	331
Banks, Henry	500	Stewart's Run	1786	1	332
Banks, Henry	500	Stewart's Run	1786	1	333
Banks, Henry	1,000	Shinn's Run	1786	1	334
Banks, Henry	1,000	Dodson Run	1786	1	336
Banks, Henry	2,000	Glady Fork	1786	1	337
Banks, Henry	2,520	Shin's Run	1786	1	338
Banks, Henry	650	Booth's Cr.	1786	1	339
Banks, Henry	500	Mill Run	1786	1	400
Banks, Henry	500	Mill Run	1786	1	401
Banks, Henry	1,000	Shinn's Run	1786	1	404
Banks, Henry	380	Booth's Cr.	1786	1	405
Banks, Henry	1,785	Valley River	1786	1	406
Banks, Henry	2,000	File's Creek	1786	1	407
Banks, Henry	500	Stewart's Run	1786	1	408
Banks, Henry	2,237	Valley River	1786	1	476
Banks, Henry	500	Mill Run	1786	1	477
Banks, Henry	706	Shinn's Run	1786	1	480
Banks, Henry	500	Mill Run	1786	1	481
Banks, Henry	2,980	Shinn's Run	1786	1	482
Banks, Henry	1,000	Adj. D. Gray's 1st	1786	1	519
Banks, Henry	250	Murphy's Run	1786	1	541
Barkley, Shadrack	400	Brown's Cr.	1802	5	185
Barkley, Thomas	235	Hall's Run	1789	3	180
Barkley, Thomas	131	Simpson's Cr.	1799	4	455
Barkley, William	500	Limestone Cr.	1786	2	1
Barkley, William	500	10 Mile Creek	1786	1	499
Barnes or Barns					
Barnes, Henry	230	Coal Lick Run	1828	6	78

Name of Grantee	Acres	Local Description	Year	Book	Page
Bee, Ephraim	200	Mid. Isl. Cr.	1836	7	105
Bee, Ephraim	91	Middle Island Cr.	1836	7	129
Bee, Ephraim	107	Mid. Isl. Cr.	1836	7	131
Bee, Ephraim	150	Morgan's Run	1837	7	173
Bee, Ephraim	100	Pigeon Run	1838	7	210
Bee, Ephraim	50	Rock Run	1838	7	211
Bee, Ephraim	50	Buckeye Fork	1838	7	212
Bee, Ephraim	100	Buffalo Calf Run	1838	7	213
Bee, Ephraim	100	Buffalo Calf Run	1838	7	214
Bee, Ephraim	150	Long Run	1838	7	215
Bee, Ephraim	150	10 Mile Cr.	1838	7	344
Bee, Ephraim	60	Buffalo Calf Run	1838	7	345
Bee, Ephraim	72	Wts. Mid. Isl. Cr.	1838	7	346
Bee, Ephraim	240	Jocky Camp Run	1838	7	347
Bee, Ephraim	165	Buffalo Calf Run	1842	7	382
Bee, Ephraim	63	Indian Fork	1842	7	383
Bee, Ephraim	124	Indian Fork	1842	7	384
Bee, Ephraim	66	Laurel Run	1842	7	385
Bee, Ephraim	100	England Run	1845	7	493
Bee, Ezekiel	75	Meat House Fork	1827	6	75
Bee, John D.	29	Meat House Fork	1838	7	290
Bee, Josiah	21	Meat House Fork	1842	7	359
Beecham, Abraham	400	Fork Creek	1788	3	99
Beeler, George	500	French Cr.	1791	3	385
Beeler, George	1,000	Tygert's V. R.	1793	3	517
Beers, Eli	12,000	Wts. Hughes R.	1797	4	329
Beesley—or Beasley					
Beesley, William	100	Lit. Kanawha	1816	3	574
Beeson, Jacob	215	Wts. Hughes R.	1788	3	86
Beeson, Jacob	250	Wts. Hughes Run	1788	3	88
Beeson, Jacob	990	Wts. Hughes River	1788	3	121
Beeson, Jacob	250	Wts. Hughes River	1788	3	128
Beeson, Jacob	250	Wts. Hughes R.	1788	3	129
Beeson, Jacob	100	Indian Fields	1797	4	326
Beeson, Jacob	400	Wts. Lit. Kanawha	1799	4	511
Beham—Bacham, Baham, Bahan, Behan, Bohon					
Beham, Lancelot et al	400	Barkeley's Run	1799	4	527
Behan, Lancelot	200	Barkeley's Run	1799	4	463
Behan, Lancelot et al	400	Barkeley's Run	1799	4	527
Behan, Lancelot	100	Otter Cr.	1823	6	2
Bennett, Jacob	183	Coburn's Cr.	1794	4	52
Bennett, John et al	2,000	Wts. Williams R.	1791	3	401
Bennett, Orion A.	125	Flat Run	1844	7	485
Bennett, Richard	400	Jesse Hughes Run	1790	3	321
Bennett, Simon C.	19¾	Buffalo Cr.	1852	6	167
Bennett, W. R.	31	Lime Camp Drain	1851	6	129
Bennett, William	95	Bennett's Run	1817	6	271
Bennett, William R.	100	Isaac's Cr.	1835	7	74
Bennett, William R.	100	Isaac's Cr.	1835	7	76
Bennett, William R.	100	Lambert's Run	1835	7	77
Bennett, William R.	200	Sycamore Run	1842	7	368
Bennett, William R.	190	Robinson's Run	1843	7	418
Bennett, William R.	175	10 Mile Cr.	1844	7	438
Bennett, William R.	540	10 Mile Cr.	1844	7	486
Bennett, William R.	175	McElroy's Fork	1846	7	513
Bennett, William R. et al	480	Indian Run	1844	7	489
Bentley, Thomas	14 tracts	(See Harrison Book 3)	1789	3	276
(Willed to Joseph Howard)					289
Bentley, William	1,000	Roaring Cr.	1790	3	314
Bentley, William	1,000	Wts. Buckhannon R.	1790	3	363
Berley, or Burley					
Berry, Thomas	200	Berry's Run	1786	1	596
Berry, Thomas Jr.	334	Berry's Run	1786	2	52

Name of Grantee	Acres	Local Description	Year	Book	Page
Bibby, John	400	Crooked Bottom	1793	4	57
Bigler, Henry W.	150	Big Run	1838	7	325
Bigler, Jacob	125	Quaker's Fork	1838	7	324
Bigler, Jacob G.	180	Big Run	1838	7	323
Black, John	500	Elk Lick Run	1796	4	219
Blake, Nicholas	1,036	Briscoe's Run	1792	3	433
Boardman, John et al	30,000	Wts. Lit. Kan.	1795	4	160
Boggess, Augustus	11	Jones's Run	1835	7	88
Boggess, Augustus	35	Jones's Run	1835	7	102
Boggess, Benjamin R.	36	Bingamon's Run	1843	7	429
Boggess, Benjamin R. et al	10	Bingamon's Cr.	1859	6	174
Boggess, Caleb	100	Shinn's Run	1819	6	258
Boggess, Caleb	10	Jones' Run	1838	7	348
Boggess, Caleb	7½	Tom's Run	1841	7	355
Boggess, Caleb	727	Cunningham's Run	1843	7	427
Boggess, Caleb	20½	Cunningham's Run	1844	7	463
Boggess, Caleb et al	28	Binghamon's Cr.	1854	6	166
Boggess, John R.	9	10 Mile Cr.	1852	6	137
Boggess, John R.	10	10 Mile Cr.	1853	6	145
Boggess, John R.	60	Hall's Run	1858	6	158
Boggess, John R.	15	Elk Lick	1854	6	163
Boggess, John R. et al	8½	Jones' Run	1852	6	140
Boggess, John W.	100	10 Mile Cr.	1844	7	436
Boggess, John W.	44	Mud Lick Run	1846	7	504
Boggess, John W. et al	2¾	Jones' Run	1853	6	146
Boggess, John W. et al	70	Mud Lick Run	1854	6	151
Bohon—Bacham, Baham, Bahan, Beham					
Bohon, Lancelot (Lanty)	200	Barkeley Run	1799	4	463
Bohon, Lancelot	100	Otter Cr.	1823	6	2
Bohon, Lancelot et al	400	Barkeley's Run	1799	4	527
Boice, Samuel et al	25,000	Wts. Lit. Kanawha	1797	4	293
Boies, Samuel et al	25,000	Wts. Lit. Kanawha	1797	4	293
Bond, Abel	88	Elk Creek	1800	5	192
Bond, Richard	150	Lick Run	1838	7	224
Bond, Richard	110	New Road Fork	1838	7	225
Bond, Richard	100	Old Road Fork	1838	7	226
Bond, Richard	100	Wts. Hughes River	1838	7	227
Bond, Thomas Dr.	2,000	Wts. Buckhannon R.	1786	1	247
Bond, Thomas Dr.	400	Wts. Buckhannon R.	1786	1	248
Bond, Thomas Dr.	1,400	Wts. Buckhannon R.	1786	1	249
Bond, Thomas Dr.	1,000	Wts. of Elk River	1786	1	250
Bond, Thomas Dr.	708	Wts. Buckhannon R.	1786	1	251
Bond, Thomas Dr.	2,000	Wts. Buckhannon R.	1786	1	252
Bond, Thomas Dr.	600	Wts. Buckhannon R.	1786	1	253
Bond, Thomas Dr.	600	Wts. Buckhannon R.	1786	1	254
Bond, Thomas Dr.	600	Wts. Buckhannon R.	1786	1	255
Bond, Thomas Dr.	1,400	Wts. Buckhannon R.	1786	1	256
Bond, Thomas Dr.	1,000	Wts. of Elk	1786	1	257
Bond, Thomas Dr.	1,000	Wts. Buckhannon R.	1786	1	258
Bond, Thomas Dr.	1,400	Wts. Buckhannon R.	1786	1	259
Bond, Thomas Dr.	1,600	Wts. Buckhannon R.	1786	1	260
Bond, Thomas Dr.	400	Wts. Buckhannon R.	1786	1	261
Bond, Thomas Dr.	400	Wts. Buckhannon R.	1786	1	262
Bond, Thomas Dr.	1,000	Wts. of Elk	1786	1	263
Bond, Thomas Dr.	600	Wts. Buckhannon R.	1786	1	264
Bond, Thomas Dr.	1,400	Wts. Buckhannon R.	1786	1	265
Bond, Thomas Dr.	2,000	Wts. Buckhannon R.	1786	1	266
Bond, Thomas Dr.	600	Wts. Buckhannon R.	1786	1	318
Bond, Thomas Dr.	2,000	Wts. Buckhannon R.	1786	1	320
Bond, Thomas Dr.	2,000	Wts. Buckhannon R.	1786	1	321
Bond, Thomas Dr.	1,400	Wts. Buckhannon R.	1786	1	322
Bond, Thomas Dr.	2,000	Wts. Buckhannon R.	1786	1	323
Bond, Thomas Dr.	765½	Wts. Buckhannon R.	1786	1	324
Bond. Thomas Dr.	600	Wts. Buckhannon R.	1786	1	325

Name of Grantee	Acres	Local Description	Year	Book	Page
Bond, Thomas Dr.	600	Wts. Buckhannon R.	1786	1	326
Bond, Thomas Dr.	2,000	Wts. Buckhannon R.	1786	1	340
Bond, Thomas Dr.	2,000	Wts. Buckhannon R.	1786	1	341
Bond, Thomas Dr.	2,000	Wts. Buckhannon R.	1786	1	342
Bond, Thomas Dr.	1,400	Wts. Buckhannon R.	1786	1	409
Bond, Thomas Dr.	2,000	Buckhannon R.	1786	1	410
Bond, Thomas Dr.	1,000	Wts. of Elk	1786	1	411
Bond, Thomas Dr.	2,000	Wts. Buckhannon R.	1786	1	412
Bond, Thomas Dr.	2,000	Buckhannon R.	1786	1	413
Bond, Thomas Dr.	400	Wts. Buckhannon R.	1786	1	414
Bond, Thomas Dr.	1,400	Wts. Buckhannon R.	1786	1	415
Bond, Thomas Dr.	2,000	Wts. Buckhannon R.	1786	1	455
Bond, Thomas Dr.	2,000	Wts. Buckhannon R.	1786	1	456
Bond, Thomas Dr.	2,000	Wts. Buckhannon R.	1786	1	457
Bond, Thomas Dr.	1,600	Wts. Buckhannon R.	1786	1	458
Bond, Thomas Dr.	1,600	Wts. Buckhannon R.	1786	1	459
Bond, Thomas Dr.	1,400	Wts. Buckhannon R.	1786	1	460
Bond, Thomas Dr.	1,400	Wts. Buckhannon R.	1786	1	461
Bond, Thomas Dr.	600	Wts. Buckhannon R.	1786	1	462
Bond, Thomas Dr.	600	Wts. Buckhannon R.	1786	1	463
Bond, Thomas Dr.	1,400	Wts. Buckhannon R.	1786	1	464
Bond, Thomas Dr.	1,000	Wts. Buckhannon R.	1786	1	465
Bond, Thomas Dr.	1,000	Wts. Elk	1786	1	466
Bond, Thomas Dr.	1,000	Wts. of Elk	1786	1	467
Bond, Thomas Dr.	1,000	Wts. of Elk	1786	1	468
Bond, Thomas Dr.	1,000	Wts. of Elk	1786	1	469
Bond, Thomas Dr.	1,600	Wts. Buckhannon R.	1786	1	474
Bond, Thomas Dr.	600	Wts. Buckhannon R.	1786	1	475
Bond, Thomas Jr.	150	Lick Run	1842	7	386
Bonnell, John	57	Mid. Fork	1819	6	267
Bonnell, John	25	Mid. Fork	1819	6	268
Bonnet, Samuel	400	Hacker's Cr.	1786	2	83
Booker, William	2,000	Wts. Wms. River	1792	3	418
Booth, Daniel	337	Rocky Run	1786	1	580
Booth, John	383	Booth Cr.	1786	2	28
Booth, John	2,500	Wts. Hughes River	1797	4	371
Boreman, John	400	Laurel Cr.	1801	5	87
Bozarth, George	187	Peck's Run	1804	5	146
Bozarth, George	160	Fink's Run	1804	5	149
Bozarth, George	120	Wts. Buckhannon R.	1804	5	150
Boyd, John	400	Washburn's Run	1789	3	265
Boyd, Jonathan	110	Laurel Run	1838	7	301
Boyer, or Bayer					
Bradley, Judith et al	1,000	West Fork	1810	5	226
Breaden, George	61	Wts. Tygert Valley	1788	3	89
Brice, Benjamin J.	102	Hillier's Run	1825	6	37
Brice, Benjamin J.	3	Wts. West Fork	1821	6	203
Brice, Benjamin J.	200	Booth's Cr.	1797	4	396
Bricker, Jacob	400	J. Hughes Run	1790	3	319
Briscoe, Robert	365	Bull Creek	1796	4	316
Brooke, Clement et al	40,000	Wts. Lit. Kanawha	1797	4	395
Brown, Edward	224	Hacker's Cr.	1799	4	484
Brown, Israel (Isaac)	1,000	Roaring Creek	1786	1	538
Brown, Israel	1,000	Laurel Cr.	1788	3	1
Brown, Israel	1,000	Laurel Cr.	1788	3	2
Brown, Israel	1,000	Wts. of Elk	1788	3	3
Brown, Israel	280	Elk Creek	1786	2	22
Brown, Israel	1,000	Tygert's V. R.	1786	2	27
Brown, Israel	4,000	Roaring Cr.	1786	2	79
Brown, Israel	500	Wts. West Fork	1786	2	85
Brown, Israel	400	Rooting Creek	1786	2	102
Brown, Israel	2,000	Laurel Cr.	1788	3	160
Brown, Israel	1,000	Laurel Cr.	1788	3	161

Name of Grantee	Acres	Local Description	Year	Book	Page
Brown, Israel	1,000	Wts. of Elk	1788	3	162
Brown, Israel	2,000	Laurel Creek	1789	3	190
Brown, Israel	372	Roaring Cr.	1788	3	191
Brown, Israel	1,000	Laurel Creek	1788	3	203
Brown, Israel	518	Wts. West Fork	1787	2	213
Brown, Israel	1,000	Gregory's Run	1787	2	218
Brown, Israel	1,000	Wts. of Elk	1788	2	526
Brown, John	400	Wts. West Fork	1788	3	30
Brown, Rezin (Raeson)	113	Jacob's Run	1836	7	150
Brown, Rezin	70	Laurel Run	1844	7	439
Brown, Robert	400	Wts. West Fork	1788	3	47
Brownfield, Robert	271¾	Elk Creek	1797	4	380
Browning, Isaac	200	Hall's Run	1790	3	359
Buckherd, George	500	Tygert's V. R.	1786	2	38
Buckley, Joshua	500	Wts. Wms. River	1789	3	185
Bugbee, Abral et al	30,000	Wts. Lit. Kanawha	1795	4	160
Bumgarner, Jacob	372	Hughes River	1813	5	258
Burckhard, George	500	Tygert's V. River	1786	2	38
Burk, John	100	Wts. Lit. Kanawha	1825	6	27
Burke, Solomon	50	Lit. Kanawha	1816	3	564
Burkhart, Peter	109 (159)	Tygert's V. R.	1798	4	429
Burley, Jacob	1,400	Salt Lick Cr.	1799	4	449
Burns, John	150	Bingamon's Cr.	1836	7	118
Burton, William	1,000	Freeman's Cr.	1786	1	428
Burton, William	1,000	Elk Lick Cr.	1786	1	429
Burton, William	1,000	Isaac's Cr.	1786	1	430
Burton, William	1,000	Freeman's Cr.	1786	1	432
Burton, William	1,000	Freeman's Cr.	1786	1	433
Burton, William	1,000	Freeman's Cr.	1786	1	434
Burton, William	1,000	Freeman's Cr.	1786	1	435
Burton, William	1,000	Freeman's Cr.	1786	1	436
Burton, William	1,000	2 Lick Run	1786	1	437
Burton, William	1,000	Freeman's Creek	1786	1	454
Bush, George	27	Wts. West Fork	1824	6	7
Bush, George	1,000	Freeman's Cr.	1788	3	48
Bush, George	28	Wts. West Fork	1805	5	117
Bush, George	850 (854)	Wts. West Fork	1794	4	140
Bush, George	27	Wts. West Fork	1810	5	230
Bush, George et al	240	Jesse Hughes Run	1802	5	193
Butcher, Paulser	150	Wts. West Fork	1804	5	147
Butcher, Paulser	78	Sycamore	1817	3	588
Butcher, Paulser et al	558½	Polk Cr.	1805	5	119
Cain—See Kain					
Cain, Cornelius	100	Cedar Creek	1816	3	565
Caldwell, Alexander	20,000	Wts. Hughes River	1796	4	290
Caldwell, James	1,000	Adj. John Williamson	1794	4	34
Caldwell, James	1,000	Adj. his No. 26th	1794	4	35
Caldwell, James	1,000	Adj. Williamson's 24th	1794	4	36
Caldwell, James	1,000	Wts. Birch River	1794	4	37
Caldwell, James	1,000	Adj. his No. 17th	1794	4	38
Caldwell, James	1,000	Adj. his No. 18th	1794	4	39
Caldwell, James	1,000	Adj. John Williamson	1794	4	40
Caldwell, James	1,000	Adj. his No. 15th	1794	4	41
Caldwell, James	1,000	Wts. Hughes R.	1795	4	167
Caldwell, James	1,000	Wts. Hughes R.	1796	4	193
Caldwell, James	1,000	Wts. Hughes River	1796	4	204
Caldwell, James	1,000	Wts. Hughes River	1796	4	205
Caldwell, James	1,000	Wts. Hughes River	1796	4	229
Caldwell, James	1,000	Wts. Elk River	1787	2	333
Caldwell, James	1,000	Wts. of Elk	1787	2	334
Caldwell, James	1,000	Mill Cr.	1787	2	335
Caldwell, James	1,000	Mill Creek	1787	2	336
Caldwell, James	1,000	Wts. Burch Creek	1787	2	337

Name of Grantee	Acres	Local Description	Year	Book	Page
Claiborne, Richard	1,000 (100)	Wts. Lit. Kanawha	1785	1	8
Claiborne, Richard	1,000	Wts. Lit. Kanawha	1785	1	10
Claiborne, Richard	1,000	Wts. Lit. Kanawha	1785	1	11
Claiborne, Richard	1,000	Wts. Lit. Kanawha	1785	1	15
Claiborne, Richard	1,000	Wts. Lit. Kanawha	1785	1	16
Claiborne, Richard	1,000	Wts. Lit. Kanawha	1785	1	19
Claiborne, Richard	1,000	Wts. Lit. Kanawha	1785	1	20
Claiborne, Richard	1,000	Wts. Lit. Kanawha	1785	1	21
Claiborne, Richard	1,000	Wts. Lit. Kanawha	1785	1	24
Claiborne, Richard	1,000	Wts. Lit. Kanawha	1785	1	25
Claiborne, Richard	1,000	Wts. Lit. Kanawha	1785	1	29
Claiborne, Richard	1,000	Wts. Lit. Kanawha	1785	1	31
Claiborne, Richard	1,000	Wts. Lit. Kanawha	1785	1	32
Claiborne, Richard	1,000	Wts. Lit. Kanawha	1785	1	33
Claiborne, Richard	1,000	Wts. Lit. Kanawha	1785	1	34
Claiborne, Richard	2,000	Indian Fork	1786	1	105
Claiborne, Richard	2,000	Indian Fork	1786	1	106
Claiborne, Richard	2,000	Wts. Hughes River	1786	1	107
Claiborne, Richard	2,000	Wts. Hughes River	1786	1	108
Claiborne, Richard	2,000	Wts. Hughes River	1786	1	109
Claiborne, Richard	2,000	Bone Creek	1786	1	110
Claiborne, Richard	2,000	Bone Creek	1786	1	111
Claiborne, Richard	2,000	Bone Creek	1786	1	112
Claiborne, Richard	2,000	Wts. Hughes River	1786	1	113
Claiborne, Richard	2,000	Wts. Hughes River	1786	1	114
Claiborne, Richard	2,000	Wts. Hughes River	1786	1	115
Claiborne, Richard	2,000	Wts. Hughes River	1786	1	116
Claiborne, Richard	2,000	Bone Creek	1786	1	117
Claiborne, Richard	2,000	Wts. Hughes River	1786	1	118
Claiborne, Richard	2,000	Wts. Hughes River	1786	1	119
Claiborne, Richard	2,000	Wts. Hughes River	1786	1	120
Claiborne, Richard	2,000	Wts. Hughes River	1786	1	121
Claiborne, Richard	2,000	Wts. Hughes River	1786	1	122
Claiborne, Richard	2,000	Bone Creek	1786	1	123
Claiborne, Richard	2,000	Wts. Hughes River	1786	1	124
Claiborne, Richard	2,000	Wts. Hughes River	1786	1	125
Claiborne, Richard	2,000	Wts. Hughes River	1786	1	126
Claiborne, Richard	2,000	Wts. Hughes River	1786	1	127
Claiborne, Richard	2,000	Wts. Hughes River	1786	1	128
Claiborne, Richard	2,000	Wts. Hughes River	1786	1	129
Clair, Thomas	350	Booth's Cr.	1787	2	275
Clare, Thomas	400	Wts. Booth Cr.	1789	3	220
Clare, Thomas	400	Wts. Hughes River	1789	3	255
Clark—or Clarke					
Clark, Alison	430	Polk Creek	1805	5	121
Clark, Alison	350	Leading Cr.	1805	5	122
Clark, Alison	25	Murphy's Run	1809	5	209
Clark, Alison et al	10¾	Elk Creek	1800	5	17
Clark, James B. et al	30,000	Wts. Hughes R.	1795	4	159
Clark, John	500	Wts. Hughes River	1787	2	266
Clark, Johnson	50	Simpson's Cr.	1799	4	488
Clark, Watson	345	Elk Creek	1786	2	107
Clarke, Hezekiah	2,000	French Creek	1794	4	45
Cleland, James	494	Tygert's V. River	1800	5	41
Cleland, James	400	Salt Lick Cr.	1787	2	389
Cline, George	110	Sand Fork	1816	5	273
Cloud, Abner	8,000	Westfall Mill Run	1787	2	171
Cloud, Abner	8,000	Wts. Tygert's R.	1787	2	172
Cloud, Abner	8,000	Tygert's V. R.	1787	2	173
Cloud, Abner	8,000	Wts. Elk River	1787	2	174
Cloud, Abner	8,000	Middle Fork	1787	2	175
Cloud, Abner	1,702	Middle Fork	1787	2	176
Cloud, Abner	1,000	Roaring Cr.	1787	2	177

Name of Grantee	Acres	Local Description	Year	Book	Page
Davison, Hezekiah	270	Simpson's Cr.	1794	4	59
Davison, Hezekiah	5,000	Burkley Run	1787	2	61
Davison, Hezekiah	5,000	Isaac's Cr.	1787	2	62
Davison, Hezekiah	960	Indian Run	1786	1	162
Davison, Hezekiah	146	10 Mile Cr.	1787	2	252
Davison, Hezekiah	200	10 Mile Cr.	1789	3	260
Davison, Hezekiah	5,000	10 Mile Creek	1786	1	315
Davison, Hezekiah	118	Foxgrape Creek	1787	2	327
Davison, Hezekiah	200	Murphy's Run	1786	1	438
Davison, Hezekiah	5,000	10 Mile Cr.	1786	1	444
Davison, Hezekiah	5,000	10 Mile Cr.	1786	1	445
Davison, Hezekiah	400	Elk Creek	1787	2	541
Davison, Isaac	358	Limestone Cr.	1785	1	35
Davison, Isaac	400	Wts. West Fork	1787	2	420
Davison, John	200	Metse's Run	1786	1	506
Davison, John	1,000	Maiden Glade Run	1786	1	551
Davison, John B.	180	Grass Run	1835	7	81
Davison, John B.	370	Sandy Lick Fork	1844	7	484
Davison, Joseph (Josiah)	800	Pleasant Creek	1787	2	264
Davison, Joseph	35	Simpson's Cr.	1801	5	12
Davison, Joseph	200	Simpson's Cr.	1785	1	39
Davison, Joseph	162	Simpson Cr.	1787	2	498
Davison, Joseph	366	Davison's Run	1786	1	505
Davison, Joseph	400	Simpson's Cr.	1786	1	508
Davison, Joseph	142	Simpson's Cr.	1786	1	509
Davison, Josiah	329	Pleasant Cr.	1801	5	65
Davison, Josiah	100	Rock Camp Run	1835	7	80
Davison, Josiah	200	Pleasant Cr.	1796	4	197
Davison, Josiah	400	Wts. West Fork	1789	3	214
Davison, Josiah	400	Stonecoal Lick	1796	4	239
Davison, Josiah	400	Pleasant Cr.	1787	1	388
Davison, Josiah	1,400	Cor. to David Sayre	1801	5	562
Davison, Melville et al	16	Elk Creek	1849	6	108
Davison, Nathan	5	Brusky Fork	1849	6	100
Davison, Nathaniel	260	10 Mile Cr.	1803	5	108
Davison, Nathaniel	285	Limestone Cr.	1800	4	551
Davison, Obadiah	380	Davison's Run	1787	2	263
Davison, Obadiah	400	Davison's Run	1787	2	350
Davison, Obadiah Jr.	1,000	Limestone Cr.	1788	3	92
Davison, Samuel & Andrew	220	Aaron Smith's Run	1811	5	240
Davison, Samuel L. (or S.)	3a.37p.	Mud Lick Run	1835	7	99
Davisson—or Davidson, Davison					
Davisson, Amaziah	130	Mill Run	1787	2	432
Davisson, Hezekiah	200	Leading Cr.	1787	2	330
Dawson, Elijah	100	Buffalo Cr.	1836	7	134
Deakins, Francis	5,000	Bruskey Fork	1787	2	493
Deakins, William	20,000	Wts. Hughes River	1797	4	381
Deakins, William	500	Polk Creek	1787	2	491
Deakins, William	500	Polk Cr.	1787	2	492
Debois—See Dubois					
Debois, Abraham	5,000	Wts. West Fork	1787	2	299
Delaplain, James	1,166	Middle Fork	1787	2	395
Delaplain, James	2,336	Big Sand Run	1787	2	396
Delaplain, James	1,166	Middle Fork	1787	2	397
Delaplain, James	1,166	Big Sandy Run	1787	2	424
Delaplain, James	1,166	Big Sandy Run	1787	2	425
Denham, David B.	65	Sweep Run	1827	6	77
Dent, Dudley E.	115	Buffalo Cr.	1837	7	165
Dent, George	150	Rush Run	1836	7	147
Dent, George	600	Buffalo Creek	1838	7	264
Despard, Burton	53	Tar Kiln Run	1858	6	159
Despard, Burton et al	350	Grass Run	1844	7	461
Despard, Burton et al	335	Job's Lick Run	1844	7	462

Name of Grantee	Acres	Local Description	Year	Book	Page
Despard, Burton et al	293	Mid. Island Cr.	1844	7	470
Despard, Burton et al	250	Dry Fork	1844	7	471
Despard, Burton et al	1,300	Meat House Fork	1844	7	477
Despard, Burton et al	135	Grass Run	1844	7	478
Despard, Burton et al	124	Grass Run	1844	7	482
Despard, Burton et al	82	Grass Run	1844	7	487
Despard, Burton et al	450	Elk Lick Run	1844	7	488
Despard, Burton et al	480	Indian Run	1844	7	489
Despard, Burton et al	870	Bluestone	1845	7	551
Despard, Richard et al	264	Indian Run	1848	7	530
DeValcoulon, Savory	1,500	Mill Creek	1786	1	61
DeValcoulon, Savory	1,500	Mill Creek	1786	1	64
DeValcoulon, Savory	2,000	Mill Creek	1786	1	65
DeValcoulon, Savory	1,500	Mill Creek	1786	1	66
DeValcoulon, Savory	1,000	Mill Creek	1786	1	67
DeValcoulon, Savory	1,500 (6,500)	Mill Creek	1786	1	72
DeValcoulon, Savory	1,500	Mill Creek	1786	1	130
DeValcoulon, Savory	1,500	Mill Creek	1786	1	133
DeValcoulon, Savory	1,500	Adj. Gallatin's 20th Survey	1786	1	134
DeValcoulon, Savory	1,700	Mill Creek	1786	1	137
DeValcoulon, Savory	1,500	Sandy Creek	1786	1	138
DeValcoulon, Savory	1,500	Adj. Gallatin's 8th	1786	1	142
DeValcoulon, Savory	2,000	Adj. J. Allison	1786	1	155
DeValcoulon, Savory	1,500	Mill Creek	1786	1	156
DeValcoulon, Savory	1,500	Adj. Gallatin's 33rd. Surv.	1786	1	160
DeValcoulon, Savory	1,500	Adj. Gallatin's 35th Surv.	1786	1	161
DeValcoulon, Savory	1,500	Adj. Gallatin's 15th	1786	1	163
DeValcoulon, Savory	4,000	Mill Creek	1786	1	184
DeValcoulon, Savory	1,500	Mill Creek	1786	1	220
DeValcoulon, Savory	1,500	Mill Creek	1786	1	221
DeValcoulon, Savory	1,500	Mill Creek	1786	1	222
DeValcoulon, Savory	1,500	Adj. his 62nd Survey	1786	1	223
DeValcoulon, Savory	1,000	Mill Creek	1786	1	293
DeValcoulon, Savory	1,500	Mill Creek	1786	1	296
DeValcoulon, Savory et al	1,500	Lit. Sandy Cr.	1787	2	157
DeValcoulon, Savory et al	1,500	Mill Cr.	1787	2	159
DeValcoulon, Savory et al	1,000	Mill Creek	1786	1	185
DeValcoulon, Savory et al	1,500	Mill Creek	1786	1	186
DeValcoulon, Savory et al	1,700	Mill Creek	1786	1	187
DeValcoulon, Savory et al	6,700	Sandy & Mill Crs.	1787	2	209
DeValcoulon, Savory et al	4,375	Mill Creek	1786	1	237
DeValcoulon, Savory et al	3,500	Mill Creek	1786	1	238
DeValcoulon, Savory et al	4,500	Mill Creek	1786	1	239
DeValcoulon, Savory et al	1,500	Mill Creek	1786	1	240
DeValcoulon, Savory et al	1,600	Mill Creek	1787	2	268
DeValcoulon, Savory et al	1,000	Ohio Riv. Mth. Gr. Kanawha	1787	2	269
DeValcoulon, Savory et al	9,000	Pond Creek	1788	2	548
Devilbiss, John & George	21	West Fork	1815	5	267
Dick—or Dicks					
Dick, Stephen	105	Elk Creek	1801	5	67
Dickenson, Joseph	20	Booth's Cr.	1810	5	231
Dicks—or Dick					
Dicks, Stephen	150	Shook's Run	1791	3	394
Dickson, John	400	10 Mile Cr.	1787	2	242
Dickson, John	600	10 Mile Cr.	1787	2	404
Divier, Hugh & John	1,005	Middle Fork	1786	2	94
Dobson, Thomas	2,000	10 Mile Cr.	1788	2	525
Dobson, Thomas	2,000	10 Mi. Cr.	1788	2	547
Dotson, Hannah et al Heirs	100	Arnold's Cr.	1842	7	411
Dougherty—or Daugherty					
Dougherty, James	200	Barkeley's Run	1797	4	337
Dougherty, James	200	Stilwell's Cr.	1799	4	504
Dougherty, Patrick	500	Wts. of Cheat	1796	4	274

Name of Grantee	Acres	Local Description	Year	Book	Page
Evans, John	400	Goose Cr.	1798	4	352
Evans, John	400	Goose Cr.	1798	4	353
Evans, John	400	Goose Cr.	1798	4	354
Evans, John	400	Salt Lick Cr.	1797	4	406
Evans, John Jr.	400	Goose Cr.	1797	4	405
Evans, Marmaduke et al	1,260	Freeman's Cr.	1816	5	275
Evans, Nancy & Sopiah	400	Wts. West Fork	1788	3	140
Evans, Seth	555	Lost Creek	1787	2	322
Evans, Thomas	170	Buffalo Cr.	1825	6	21
Everitt, Walter	135	Shinn's Run	1825	6	30
Everson, Richard	16	Brown's Run	1848	7	526
Faire, Thomas et al	200	Simpson's Cr.	1821	6	205
Fairlamb—See Farland, Fairland					
Fairlamb, Frederick	2,000	Wts. of Elk	1788	3	80
Fairland—See Fairlamb, Farland					
Falbot, Benjamin	2,910	Wts. Ohio River	1787	2	332
Falley—See Folley, Folly					
Falls, Jacob	420	Wts. West Fork	1787	2	504
Fals, Jacob	420	Wts. West Fork	1787	2	504
Farguson—or Ferguson, Furguson					
Farguson, Robert	335	Limestone Cr.	1792	3	417
Farland—See Fairland, Fairlamb					
Farland, Frederick	2,000	Wts. of Elk	1788	3	80
Farland, Frederick	5,000	Wts. Elk	1787	2	204
Farr, Abraham	1,000	Tygert's V. R.	1788	3	82
Farriss, William	500	Wts. Hughes River	1785	1	36
Faulkner, Robert	500	Dry Fork	1797	4	313
Faw, Abraham	1,000	Tygert's V. River	1788	3	82
Fell, Edward	1,000	Sand Fork	1788	2	522
Feller, John et al	20,000	Wts. Hughes River	1797	4	372
Ferguson—or Farguson, Furguson					
Ferguson, Andrew	40	(Unknown—Grant incomplete)		7	5
Ferguson, John P.	50 (15)	Sycamore Creek	1848	7	535
Ferguson, Robert	500	Wts. Hughes River	1795	4	188
Fin, John O.	400	Bull Cr.	1789	3	172
Findley—See Finley, Finly					
Findley, Adam	50	Simpson's Cr.	1838	7	302
Findley, William	100	Sand Lick Run	1838	7	303
Fink, Daniel	300	French Cr.	1789	3	210
Fink, Daniel	768	Wts. West Fork	1789	3	256
Fink, Daniel	1,000	Brushy Fork	1796	4	284
Fink, Daniel	400	Wts. West Fork	1787	2	470
Fink, Daniel	800	Buffalo Fork	1787	2	496
Fink, Daniel	200	French Cr.	1787	2	508
Fink, Samuel	320	Stone Coal	1787	2	70
Fink, Solomon et al	14,000	Wts. Hughes River	1797	4	227
Finley—See also Findley					
Finley, John	40	Lost Run	1832	7	2
Fleming, James	66	Simmons Cr.	1796	4	222
Fleming, James Jr.	50	Berry's Run	1827	6	66
Fleming, James Sr. (or Jr.)	50	Simpson's Cr.	1827	6	49
Fleming, Solomon S.	103 sq. po.	Town of Shinnston	1849	6	112
Fleming, Thomas	2¼	Wts. West Fork	1831	6	91
Fleming, William	295	Buffalo Cr.	1829	6	80
Fleming, William & Joseph	131	Buffalo Cr.	1822	6	207
Flesher, Adam	100	Polk Creek	1800	5	39
Flesher, Balsher	112	Wts. West Fork	1787	2	471
Flesher, Henry	187	Wts. Lit. Kanawha	1818	6	281
Flesher, Henry	95	Polk Creek	1787	2	440
Flesher, Henry	400	Polk Creek	1787	2	441
Flesher, Henry	400	Wts. West Fork	1787	2	443
Flesher, Henry et al	325 (335)	Wts. West Fork	1805	5	165

Name of Grantee	Acres	Local Description	Year	Book	Page
Flint, Joseph	100	Glade Run	1800	5	38
Flowers, James et al	264	Indian Run	1848	7	530
Flowers, Samuel T.	49	Indian Fork	1842	7	390
Flowers, Samuel T.	60	Sugar Camp Run	1842	7	391
Flowers, Samuel T.	40	Buckeye Run	1842	7	392
Flowers, Samuel T.	40	Tar Kiln Run	1842	7	393
Flowers, Samuel T.	71	Waldo's Run	1842	7	394
Flowers, Samuel T.	100	Wiseman's Run	1842	7	395
Floyd, Henry F.	90	Buffalo Cr.	1838	7	233
Floyd, Henry T.	33	Buffalo Cr.	1835	7	89
Foley, John	445	West Run	1787	2	278
Folly, Frederick	20,000	Wts. Glady Fork	1794	4	32
Folly, Frederick et al	25,000	Wts. Lit. Kanawha	1797	4	293
Fon, Abraham	1,000	Tygert's V. River	1788	3	82
Foranash, Charles	335	Wts. Buckhannon R.	1785	1	38
Foranash, Charles	371	Stony Run	1786	2	100
Ford, Henry G.	220	Pleasant Cr.	1832	7	3
Ford, Standish	4,982	Wts. Elk River	1788	3	150
Ford, Standish	6,581	Laurel Creek	1789	3	151
Ford, Standish	3,568	Wts. Elk River	1789	3	152
Ford, Standish	3,568	Wts. Elk	1789	3	153
Ford, Standish	3,395	Laurel Creek	1789	3	154
Ford, Standish	2,838	Wts. Elk River	1789	3	155
Ford, Standish	1,000	Clover Lick Fork	1796	4	262
Ford, Standish	1,000	Sand Fork	1796	4	263
Ford, Standish	6,000	Indian Fork	1796	4	283
Ford, Standish	1,000	Warrior's Fork	1792	3	440
Ford, Standish	1,000	Oil Creek	1792	3	446
Ford, Standish	666	Adj. his No. 20	1792	3	447
Ford, Standish	666	Clover Lick Fork	1792	3	448
Ford, Standish	666	Clover Lick Fork	1792	3	449
Ford, Standish	1,000	Clover Lick Fork	1792	3	450
Ford, Standish	1,000	Sand Fork	1792	3	451
Ford, Standish	1,000	Warrior's Fork	1792	3	452
Ford, Standish	1,000	Wts. Kanawha	1792	3	453
Ford, Standish	1,000	Wts. of Kanawha	1792	3	454
Ford, Standish	1,000	Sand Fork	1792	3	455
Ford, Standish	1,000	Clover Lick Fork	1792	3	456
Ford, Standish	1,000	Sand Fork	1792	3	457
Ford, Standish	1,000	Clover Lick Fork	1792	3	458
Ford, Standish	1,000	Sand Fork	1792	3	459
Ford, Standish	1,000	Sand Fork	1792	3	460
Ford, Standish	1,000	Sand Fork	1792	3	461
Ford, Standish	1,000	Wts. West Fork	1792	3	462
Ford, Standish	1,000	Warrior's Fork	1792	3	463
Ford, Standish	1,000	Clover Lick Fork	1792	3	464
Ford, Standish	1,000	Clover Lick Fork	1792	3	465
Ford, Standish	1,000	Wts. West Fork	1792	3	466
Ford, Standish	1,000	Wts. West Fork	1792	3	467
Ford, Standish	1,000	Clover Lick Fork	1792	3	468
Ford, Standish	1,000	Wts. West Fork	1792	3	469
Ford, Standish	1,000	Wts. West Fork	1792	3	470
Ford, Standish	2,000	Wts. Elk River	1792	3	471
Ford, Standish	2,000	Wts. of Elk	1792	3	472
Ford, Standish	2,000	Wts. Elk River	1792	3	473
Ford, Standish	2,000	Wts. of Elk	1792	3	474
Ford, Standish	1,000	Wts. West Fork	1792	3	475
Ford, Standish	2,000	Wts. of Elk	1792	3	476
Ford, Standish	2,000	Wts. of Elk	1792	3	477
Ford, Standish	6,000	Wts. of Elk	1792	3	478
Ford, Standish	600	Wts. of Elk	1792	3	479
Ford, Standish	2,000	Wts. of Elk	1792	3	480
Ford, Standish	2,000	Wts. of Elk	1792	3	481

Name of Grantee	Acres	Local Description	Year	Book	Page
Ford, Standish	1,000	Oil Creek	1792	3	482
Ford, Standish	2,000	Wts. of Elk	1792	3	483
Ford, Standish	3,850	Wts. of Elk	1792	3	484
Ford, Standish	2,000	Wts. of Elk	1792	3	485
Ford, Standish	2,000	Wts. of Elk	1792	3	486
Ford, Standish	3,000	Wts. of Elk	1792	3	487
Ford, Standish	1,000	Wts. of Elk	1792	3	488
Ford, Standish	1,000	Wts. of Elk	1792	3	489
Ford, Standish	2,000	Wts. of Elk	1792	3	490
Ford, Standish	1,000	Wts. of Elk	1792	3	491
Ford, Standish	5,000	Wts. of Elk	1792	3	492
Ford, Standish	2,000	Wts. of Elk	1792	3	493
Ford, Standish	2,000	Wts. of Elk	1792	3	494
Ford, Standish	1,000	Wts. of Elk	1792	3	495
Ford, Standish	260	Booth's Cr.	1800	4	535
Ford, Thomas	100	Buckeye Run	1838	7	195
Ford, Thomas	50	Waldo Run	1838	7	337
Forde—See Ford					
Foster, Peregrine et al	300	Worthington's Cr.	1796	4	216
Fox, James H.	8	Davison's Run	1852	6	142
Franklin, Mary et al Heirs	13½	Harmon's Run	1833	7	28
Freeman, Edward	190	Booth Cr.	1791	3	398
Freeman, Samuel	150	Tevebaugh Run	1805	5	120
Friend, Jacob	500	Leading Cr.	1787	2	542
Friend, Jacob & Robert T.	1,000	Tygert's V. R.	1798	4	424
Friend, Jacob Sr.	200	Wts. of Cheat	1787	2	392
Friend, Jacob Sr.	300	Cheat River	1787	2	400
Friend, Jacob Sr.	100	Wts. Cheat River	1787	2	533
Friend, Joseph	200	Leading Cr.	1786	2	23
Friend, Joseph et al	216	Fork Lick	1800	5	50
Fry, George	415	Cleaver's Run	1788	3	83
Fry, George	100	Tygert's V. R.	1788	3	90
Fuls, Jacob	420	Wts. West Fork	1787	2	504
Furbey, Caleb Jr.	50	Rock Lick Fork	1838	7	265
Furguson—or Farguson, Ferguson					
Fussell, Solomon	250	Sand Run	1789	3	169
Gain, Charles	100	Cat Fish Run	1825	6	36
Gain, Charles	13	Ten Mile Cr.	1834	7	43
Gain, Charles	130	10 Mi. Creek	1835	7	82
Gain, Charles	90	Ten Mi. Cr.	1844	7	467
Gain, John Sr.	100	10 Mi. Cr.	1832	7	10
Gallatin—or Gallatine					
Gallatin, Albert	1,500	Mill Creek	1786	1	62
Gallatin, Albert	2,000	Mill Creek	1786	1	63
Gallatin, Albert	6,000	Reedy Cr.	1788	3	102
Gallatin, Albert	1,500	Mill Creek	1786	1	131
Gallatin, Albert	1,500	Sandy Creek	1786	1	143
Gallatin, Albert	1,500	Mill Creek	1786	1	144
Gallatin, Albert	1,840	Mill Creek	1786	1	145
Gallatin, Albert	1,500	Adj. Thomas Evans	1786	1	146
Gallatin, Albert	1,500	Mill Creek	1786	1	147
Gallatin, Albert	1,330	Mill Creek	1786	1	148
Gallatin, Albert	1,830	Mill Creek	1786	1	149
Gallatin, Albert	1,000	Adj. DeValcoulon's 23rd	1786	1	150
Gallatin, Albert	1,200	Sandy Creek	1786	1	151
Gallatin, Albert	1,500	Mill Creek	1786	1	152
Gallatin, Albert	1,500	Mill Creek	1786	1	153
Gallatin, Albert	1,500	Adj. DeValcoulon's 47th	1786	1	154
Gallatin, Albert	1,500	Adj. B. Harrison	1786	1	157
Gallatin, Albert	1,150	Adj. DeValcoulon's 48th	1786	1	158
Gallatin, Albert	1,750	Adj. DeValcoulon's 22nd	1786	1	159
Gallatin, Albert	1,555½	Mill Creek	1786	1	188
Gallatin, Albert	1,500	Adj. DeValcoulon's 46th	1786	1	214

Name of Grantee	Acres	Local Description	Year	Book	Page
Gallatin, Albert	1,500	Mill Creek	1786	1	215
Gallatin, Albert	1,200	Mill Creek	1786	1	216
Gallatin, Albert	500	Freeman's Cr.	1789	3	221
Gallatin, Albert	396	Gnatty Cr.	1789	3	222
Gallatin, Albert	1,500	Mill Creek	1786	1	224
Gallatin, Albert	1,500	Mill Creek	1786	1	225
Gallatin, Albert et al	1,500	Lit. Sandy Cr.	1787	2	158
Gallatin, Albert et al	1,500	Mill Creek	1787	2	159
Gallatin, Albert et al	4,000	Mill Creek	1786	1	184
Gallatin, Albert et al	1,000	Mill Creek	1786	1	185
Gallatin, Albert et al	1,500	Mill Creek	1786	1	186
Gallatin, Albert et al	1,700	Mill Creek	1786	1	187
Gallatin, Albert et al	6,700	Sandy & Mill Crs.	1787	2	209
Gallatin, Albert et al	4,375	Mill Creek	1786	1	237
Gallatin, Albert et al	3,500	Mill Creek	1786	1	238
Gallatin, Albert et al	4,500	Mill Creek	1786	1	239
Gallatin, Albert et al	1,500	Mill Creek	1786	1	240
Gallatin, Albert et al	1,600	Mill Creek	1787	2	268
Gallatin, Albert et al	1,000	Ohio River, Mth. Gr. Kanawha	1787	2	269
Gallatin, Albert et al	9,000	Pond Creek	1788	2	548
Gallion, Hanna et al Heirs	4,408	Wts. Lit. Kanawha	1825	6	17
Garrett, Harrison et al	35	Lambert's Run	1844	7	466
Garrett, Richard et al	9	Camp Run	1858	6	170
Garvice—See Jarvis					
Gawthrop, Enos D.	83	Lost Run	1838	7	193
Gawthrop, Evan H.	158	Sand Lick Run	1838	7	281
Gawthrop, James	200	Lost Run	1793	4	1
Gawthrop, Thomas	16	Lost Run	1838	7	282
Gibbs, Josiah W.	1,000	West Fork	1787	2	69
Gibbs, Josiah W.	1,000	Elk Lick Cr.	1787	2	245
Gibbs, Josiah W.	1,000	Stone Coal Cr.	1787	2	276
Gibbs, Josiah W.	1,000	Wts. West Fork	1787	2	317
Gibbs, Josiah W.	1,000	Skin Creek	1787	2	318
Gibbs, Josiah W.	1,000	Stone Coal Cr.	1787	2	364
Gibbs, Josiah W.	1,000	Skin Cr.	1787	2	365
Gibbs, Josiah W.	1,000	Skin Cr.	1787	2	366
Gibbs, Josiah W.	1,000	Wts. West Fork	1787	2	402
Gibbs, Josiah W.	1,000	Wts. West Fork	1787	2	403
Gibson, John	165	Canoe Lick Run	1787	2	370
Gibson, John	6,000	Teter's Cr.	1787	2	372
Gibson, John	5,000	Cedar Creek	1786	1	591
Gibson, John	10,000	Wts. Little Kanawha	1786	1	592
Gibson, Joseph	1,000	Wts. Buckhannon R.	1788	2	488
Gibson, Joshua	1,700	New Creek	1787	2	484
Gibson, Joshua	2,564	Brusky Fork	1787	2	485
Gibson, Joshua	500	Peeltree Creek	1787	2	486
Gibson, Joshua	500	Wts. West Fork	1787	2	519
Gibson, William	400	Sugar Creek	1788	3	127
Giese, Thomas	8,000	Middle Fork	1786	1	441
Giese, Thomas	5,000	Mill Run	1786	1	442
Giese, Thomas	3,000	Roaring Cr.	1786	1	443
Giese, Thomas	3,000	Roaring Cr.	1786	1	446
Giese, Thomas	3,000	Roaring Cr.	1786	1	447
Giese, Thomas	1,000	Valley River	1786	1	448
Gifford, Abadiah et al	20,000	Wts. Hughes River	1797	4	372
Gifford, John	289	Mud Lick	1786	2	88
Gifford, John Jr.	15½	Mud Lick Run	1820	6	225
Gifford, William	20	Shinn's Run	1826	6	45
Gillispie, Enos	400	Tigert's V. R.	1805	5	118
Giroud, Honore	2,000	Mill Creek	1786	1	235
Giroud, Honore	10,843¾	Sandy Creek	1786	1	300
Glane, Mathew	400	Wts. Hughes River	1785	1	43

Name of Grantee	Acres	Local Description	Year	Book	Page
Glave, Mathew	400	Wts. Hughes R.	1785	1	43
Glove, Mathew	400	Wts. Hughes River	1785	1	43
Glover, John	150	Bingamon's Cr.	1836	7	146
Goff, John T.	80	Wts. Cheat River	1792	3	438
Goff, Salathial	194	Horseshoe Run	1796	4	275
Goff, Waldo P.	198	Davison's Run	1844	7	450
Goff, Waldo P. et al	100	England Run	1838	7	336
Golden, John	270	McElroy's Fork	1811	5	237
Goodrich, John	1,000	Wts. Lit. Kanawha	1797	4	377
Goodwin, John Jr.	400	Booth's Cr.	1786	1	557
Gordon, Mrs. Janette, Wife of Robt. Gordon et al Hrs.	1,030	Tygert's Valley	1808	5	571
Gordon, Janette, Wife of Robt. Gordon et al Hrs.	4,370	Tygert's V. R.	1808	5	572
Gordon, Mrs. Janette, Wife of Robt. Gordon et al Hrs.	2,225	Cor. to Owen Owens	1808	5	573
Gordon, Mrs. Janette, Wife of Robt. Gordon et al Hrs.	1,660	Simpson's Creek	1808	5	575
Gordon, Mrs. Janette, Wife of Robt. Gordon et al Hrs.	3,700	Husted's Fork	1808	5	576
Graham, Nathan & Samuel Jr. et al	20,000	Wts. Hughes River	1797	4	372
Graham, Richard	500	Bull Cr.	1793	4	4
Graham, Richard	500	Reedy Creek	1793	4	5
Graham, Richard	1,000	Bull Cr.	1793	4	6
Graham, Richard	500	Reedy Creek	1793	4	7
Graham, Richard	1,000	Wts. Lit. Kanawha	1793	3	520
Graham, Richard	820	Wts. Lit. Kanawha	1793	3	521
Graham, Richard	500	Reedy Cr.	1793	3	522
Graham, Richard	500	Reedy Cr.	1793	3	523
Graham, Richard	500	Reedy Cr.	1793	3	524
Graham, Richard	1,000	Reedy Creek	1793	3	525
Graham, Richard	500	Reedy Creek	1793	3	526
Graham, Richard	1,000	Poca River	1793	3	527
Graham, Richard	1,000	Poca River	1793	3	528
Graham, Richard	1,000	Poca River	1793	3	529
Graham, Richard	1,000	Bull Cr.	1793	3	530
Graham, Richard	500	Reedy Creek	1793	3	531
Graham, Richard	500	Reedy Cr.	1793	3	532
Graham, Richard	500	Reedy Cr.	1793	3	533
Gray, Nathaniel	500	Big Run	1786	1	74
Gray, Nathaniel	500	Wts. Hughes River	1786	1	75
Gray, Nathaniel	500	Elk Creek	1786	1	76
Greathouse, Michael	25	Berry's Run	1838	7	183
Greathouse, Moses	50	Berry's Run	1838	7	184
Green, Robert	840	Rooting Cr.	1787	2	250
Green, Robert	360	Rooting Cr.	1787	2	282
Greenough, Thomas	1,000	Elk Lick Run	1797	4	315
Greenough, William	1,000	Steer Creek	1797	4	399
Gregory, Joseph	500	Tack's Run	1787	2	417
Griggs, John	1,500	Wts. Lit. Kanawha	1789	3	228
Grubb, Samuel	125	Merrell's Run	1837	7	178
Gump, Peter	145	Mud Lick Fork	1838	7	240
Gump, Philip	140	Owen Davis' Fork	1838	7	241
Gump, William	250	Rush Run	1838	7	304
Hacker, John	200	Hacker's Cr.	1800	5	43
Hacker, John	400	Hacker's Creek	1786	1	593
Hacker, John	150	Hacker's Creek	1786	1	599
Hacker, William	50	Sand Fork	1816	3	563
Hacker, William et al	215	West Fork	1813	5	262
Haddin, David	100	Haddin's M. Run	1791	3	378
Haddix, William	400	Tygert's V. R.	1789	3	257
Haddix, William	400	Tygert's V. R.	1789	3	258

Name of Grantee	Acres	Local Description	Year	Book	Page
Harvey, David	310	Horseshoe Run	1787	2	281
Harvey, David	281	Leading Cr.	1787	2	406
Harvey, David	116	Horseshoe Run	1787	2	407
Harvie, John	1,000	Lee's Creek	1790	3	352
Harvie, John	1,000	Wts. Lit. Kanawha	1790	3	353
Harvie, John	1,000	Sandy Creek	1790	3	354
Harvie, John	1,000	Sandy Creek	1790	3	356
Harvie, John	600	Sandy Cr.	1790	3	357
Harvie, John	1,000	Mill Creek	1790	3	358
Harvie, John	1,000	Lee's Creek	1790	3	360
Harvie, John	1,000	Wts. Lit. Kanawha	1790	3	361
Harvie, John	1,000	Mill Creek	1790	3	367
Harvie, John	1,000	Mill Cr.	1790	3	368
Harvie, John	1,000	Wts. Lit. Kanawha	1790	3	369
Harvie, John	1,000	Mill Creek	1790	3	370
Haskell, Benjamin Dr. et al	100,000	Wts. Lit. Kanawha	1797	4	374
Haskell, Benjamin Dr. et al	100,000	Wts. Lit. Kanawha	1797	4	375
Hastings, John et al	14,000	Wts. Hughes River	1797	4	292
Hathaway, John	161	Wts. Monon. River	1785	1	41
Haverty, Michael	150	Sand Fork	1819	6	245
Hawk, John	200	Freeman's Cr.	1789	3	206
Hawk, Nicholas	400	Clove Run	1787	2	482
Haycock, Jonathan	200	Sand Fork	1787	2	487
Hayhurst, Joseph	145	Buffalo Cr.	1828	6	57
Hayhurst, Joseph	180	Warrior Fork	1837	7	169
Hayhurst, Joseph	190	Buffalo Cr.	1838	7	186
Hayhurst, Joseph	120	Bartholomew's Fk.	1838	7	266
Hayhurst, Joseph	200	Warrior's Fork	1838	7	305
Haymond, Cyrus	17	Wts. West Fork	1850	6	114
Haymond, Daniel et al	364	Mill Fall Run	1809	5	222
Haymond, John	200	Brown's Cr.	1788	3	17
Haymond, John	88	Mill Creek	1801	5	57
Haymond, John	500	Cor. Joel Lowther	1787	2	73
Haymond, John	200	Sycamore Creek	1786	1	314
Haymond, John	871	Wts. Lit. Kanawha	1791	3	411
Haymond, John	23	Elk Creek	1787	2	509
Haymond, John	205	Simpson's Cr.	1799	4	540
Haymond, John et al	10¾	Elk Creek	1800	5	17
Haymond, John et al	130	Coburn's M. Run	1791	3	386
Haymond, Luther	120	Flinderation Run	1849	6	113
Haymond, Luther	116	Indian Run	1851	6	122
Haymond, Luther	64	Indian Run	1851	6	123
Haymond, Luther	137	Flinderation Run	1851	6	124
Haymond, Luther	2¼	Coburn's Cr.	1855	6	161
Haymond, Luther	13	Simpson's Cr.	1838	7	294
Haymond, Luther	9½	10 Mile Cr.	1842	7	370
Haymond, Luther	20	Cherry Run	1842	7	371
Haymond, Luther	35	Wts. West Fork	1843	7	420
Haymond, Luther	4¾	Grove Run	1843	7	422
Haymond, Luther	150	Grass Run	1844	7	453
Haymond, Luther	74	Bussey's Fork	1845	7	496
Haymond, Luther	41	Sycamore Creek	1845	7	497
Haymond, Luther	145	Limestone Cr	1846	7	510
Haymond, Luther	35	10 Mile Cr.	1846	7	511
Haymond, Luther	155	Grass Run	1848	7	533
Haymond, Luther	200	Grass Run	1848	7	538
Haymond, Luther et al	1,090	Gnatty Cr.	1834	7	58
Haymond, Luther et al	645	Stout's Run	1834	7	67
Haymond, Luther et al	270	Brusky Fork	1842	7	372
Haymond, Luther et al	1,300	Meat House Fork	1844	7	477
Haymond, Luther et al	870	Wts. Hughes	1845	7	551
Haymond, Luther & Lewis	105	Buffalo Cr.	1836	7	109
Haymond, Luther & Lewis	250	Elk Horn Fork	1842	7	409

Name of Grantee	Acres	Local Description	Year	Book	Page
Henderson, Alexander	500	Wts. Lit. Kanawha	1787	2	316
Henderson, Alexander	500	Wts. Lit. Kanawha	1787	2	319
Henderson, Alexander	1,000	Wts. of Elk R.	1787	2	352
Henderson, Alexander	500	Wts. Lit. Kanawha	1787	2	353
Henderson, Alexander	500	Wts. Lit. Kanawha	1787	2	354
Henderson, Alexander	1,000	Middle Island Cr.	1787	2	357
Henderson, Alexander	500	Wts. Lit. Kanawha	1787	2	358
Henderson, Alexander	500	Wts. Lit. Kanawha	1787	2	359
Henderson, Alexander	1,000	18 Mi. Cr.	1787	2	360
Henderson, Alexander	1,000	18 Mi. Cr.	1787	2	361
Henderson, Alexander	1,000	Wts. Elk River	1787	2	362
Henderson, Alexander	500	Wts. Lit. Kanawha	1787	2	363
Henderson, Alexander	440	Wts. Lit. Kanawha	1787	2	401
Henkle—or Hinkle					
Henkle, Abraham	156	Duck Creek	1789	3	259
Henrie—or Henry					
Henrie, Daniel	1,498	Briscoe's Cr.	1799	4	464
Henry—or Henrie					
Henry, Daniel	400	Big Run	1799	4	509
Henry, James	2,000	Wts. Hughes River	1786	2	160
Henry, James	2,000	Wts. Hughes R.	1786	2	161
Henry, James	2,000	Wts. Hughes R.	1786	2	162
Henry, James	2,000	Wts. Hughes R.	1786	2	163
Henry, James	2,000	Wts. Hughes R.	1786	2	164
Herdman—See Hardman, Hartman					
Heron, Nelson & Co. et al	5,000	Valley River	1786	1	357
Heron, Nelson & Co. et al	2,000	Tanner's Run	1786	1	360
Heron, Nelson & Co. et al	2,500	Simpson's Cr.	1786	1	361
Heron, Nelson & Co. et al	2,000	Simpson Cr.	1786	1	362
Heron, Nelson & Company et al	2,000	Simpson's Cr.	1786	1	364
Hervey—or Harvey, Harvie					
Hervey, David	118	Horseshoe Run	1787	2	325
Hess, Abraham	200	Bingamon's Cr.	1835	7	84
Hess, Abraham	75	Bingamon's Cr.	1837	7	157
Hess, Abraham & Jeremiah Jr.	150	Big Run	1844	7	472
Hess, Jeremiah	95	Bingamon's Cr.	1835	7	83
Hess, John	174	Wts. West Fork	1787	2	479
Heth, Harry	2,000	Freeman's Cr.	1800	5	11
Hewes—See Hews, Hughes, Hughs					
Hewes, David	132	Simpson's Cr.	1799	4	522
Hewey, David	118	Horseshoe Run	1787	2	325
Hews—See Hewes, Hughes, Hughs					
Hews, David et al	185	Valley River	1800	5	35
Hews, David et al	100	Otter Creek	1800	5	36
Hews, David T.	66 poles	Clarksburg	1842	7	378
Hickman, Sotha	400	Elk Creek	1787	2	431
Hickman, Thomas	35	Indian Run	1851	6	125
Hickman, Thomas	50	Indian Run	1842	7	369
Hickman, Thomas	40	Zack's Run	1842	7	376
Hickman, Thomas	50	Indian Run	1844	7	451
Hickman, Thomas	100	10 Mi. Creek	1848	7	539
Higgins, Jeddiah	50	Clay Lick Fork	1836	7	133
Higgins, Joshua	100	Brush Run	1836	7	132
Higgins, Joshua	296	Camp Run	1838	7	306
Higgins, Judiah	125	Old Camp Run	1838	7	307
Hill, Peter	3,000	Wts. Elk River	1787	2	267
Hill, Philip et al Heirs	100	Wts. Tygert's V.	1798	6	242
Hill, William	48	Wts. Tygert Valley	1800	4	530
Hilton, William	374	Wts. Cheat River	1787	2	248
Hilton, William	150	Wts. Cheat	1787	2	249
Hilton, William	3,300	Tygert's V. R.	1787	2	405
Hilton, William	310	Horseshoe Run	1793	3	541
Hilyard, Charles	850	Polk Creek	1804	5	131

Name of Grantee	Acres	Local Description	Year	Book	Page
Howard, Joseph	5,000	Wts. Tygerts V. R.	1789	3	245
Howard, Joseph	5,000	Tygert's Creek	1789	3	246
Howard, Joseph	5,000	Middle Fork	1789	3	247
Howard, Joseph	3,000	French Creek	1789	3	248
Howard, Joseph	3,000	French Cr.	1789	3	249
Howard, Joseph	5,000	Middle Fork	1789	3	250
Howard, Joseph	1,000	Adj. His 3rd Entry	1789	3	251
Howard, Joseph	5,000	Tygert's V. R.	1789	3	252
Howard, Joseph	1,000	Wts. West Fork	1789	3	253
Howard, Joseph	1,000	Wts. West Fork	1789	3	254
Howard, Joseph	1,000	Adj. his 7th Ent.	1789	3	276
Howard, Joseph	1,000	Wts. West Fork	1789	3	277
Howard, Joseph	1,000	Wts. of West Fk.	1789	3	278
Howard, Joseph	1,000	Wts. West Fork	1789	3	279
Howard, Joseph	5,000	Tygert's Creek	1789	3	280
Howard, Joseph	5,000	Middle Fork	1789	3	281
Howard, Joseph	1,000	Wts. West Fork	1789	3	282
Howard, Joseph	1,000	Wts. West Fork	1789	3	283
Howard, Joseph	1,000	Wts. West Fork	1789	3	284
Howard, Joseph	3,000	Wts. Lit. Kanawha	1789	3	285
Howard, Joseph	3,000	Wts. Lit. Kanawha	1789	3	286
Howard, Joseph	3,000	Wts. Lit. Kanawha	1789	3	287
Howard, Joseph	3,000	Wts. Lit. Kanawha	1789	3	288
Howard, Joseph	3,000	Wts. Lit. Kanawha	1789	3	289
Howard, Samuel	180	Booth Cr.	1796	4	266
Howard, Samuel et al	40,000	Wts. Lit. Kanawha	1797	4	395
Howel, Jeremiah	100	Lit. Kanawha	1816	3	569
Howel, Jonathan	34	Middle Cr.	1819	6	259
Howel, Jonathan	75	Middle Isl. Cr.	1819	6	262
Hoye, John	1,650	Stonecoal Cr.	1802	5	107
Hoye, John	100	Spruce Run	1806	5	170
Hoye, John	400	Wts. Buck. River	1808	5	183
Hoye, John	236	Brushy Fork	1808	5	184
Huffman—See Hoffman					
Huffman, Weeden	57	Lost Creek	1820	6	236
Hughes—See Hewes, Hews, Hughs					
Hughes, Christopher	698	Tygert's V. R.	1788	3	141
Hughes, Christopher	875	Roaring Cr.	1788	3	142
Hughes, Martin	100	Buckeye Fork	1833	7	18
Hughs—See Hewes, Hews, Hughes					
Hughs, Elias	337	Wts. West Fork	1787	2	507
Hughs, Thomas	387	West Fork	1786	2	90
Hughsted—Hustead, Husted					
Hughsted, Robert	400	Booth Cr.	1790	3	339
Hull, James	140	Wts. West Fork	1799	4	525
Hunt, Jesse	280	Wts. West Fork	1789	3	227
Hunt, John W.	2,000	Wts. Gauley River	1795	4	163
Hunt, John W.	2,350	Wts. Gauley R.	1795	4	164
Hunt, John W.	2,000	Wts. Gauley River	1795	4	165
Hunt, John W.	2,350	Wts. Gauley River	1795	4	166
Hunt, John W.	2,000	Wts. Wms. River	1795	4	174
Hunt, John W.	2,000	Wts. Wms. River	1795	4	175
Hunt, John W.	2,000	Wts. Gauley River	1795	4	176
Hunt, John W.	2,000	Wts. of Gauley	1795	4	177
Hunt, John W.	2,350	Wts. Wms. River	1795	4	178
Hunt, John W.	2,350	Wts. Wms. River	1795	4	179
Hunt, John W.	2,350	Wts. Wms. River	1795	4	180
Hunt, John W.	2,000	Wts. Wms. River	1795	4	181
Hunt, John W.	2,350	Wts. Wms. River	1795	4	182
Hunt, Joseph	1,000	Wts. Hughes River	1793	4	23
Hunt, Joseph	1,000	Wts. Hughes River	1793	4	24
Hupp, Everhart	1,000	Lit. Kanawha	1787	2	67
Hurst, Bennett	40	10 Mi. Cr.	1846	7	505

Name of Grantee	Acres	Local Description	Year	Book	Page
Hurst, Meshack	220	Catie's Lick Run	1825	6	18
Hurst, Meshack	50	Johnson's Fork	1825	6	19
Hurst, Meshack	87	10 Mile Cr.	1825	6	20
Hurst, Meshack	100	Limestone Cr.	1838	7	197
Hustead—or Hughsted, Husted					
Hustead, Gilbert	400	Berkeley's Run	1786	1	586
Hustead, John	354	Valley River	1786	1	385
Hustead, Robert et al	100	Booth's Cr.	1826	6	52
Husted—Hughsted, Hustead					
Husted, Jethro et al	20,000	Wts. Hughes River	1797	4	372
Husted, Moses	30	Husted's Fork	1799	4	514
Hutchinson, William H. et al Executors	5,000	Tygert's V. R.	1822	6	564
Hutchison, Robert	500	Wts. of Elk	1787	2	536
Hutson, Evan	85	Buckeye Fork	1838	7	196
Hutson, Morgan et al	295	Lost Run	1847	7	517
Hutson, Winter	200	Elkhorn Run	1843	7	415
Hyde, James	12	Elk Creek	1796	4	268
Ice, Andrew	50	Buffalo Creek	1838	7	236
Ice, Rawley	50	Buffalo Creek	1825	6	22
Ice, Rawley	115	Buffalo Creek	1828	6	55
Ice, Rawley	130	Buffalo Creek	1836	7	123
Ice, Rawley	25	Buffalo Creek	1836	7	140
Ice, Rawley	20	Wts. Buffalo	1836	7	141
Ice, Rawley	450	Wts. Glade Fork	1837	7	153
Ice, Rawley	375	Buffalo Creek	1838	7	545
Ice, Rawley	600	Bartholomew Fk.	1838	7	546
Ice, Rawley & Abraham Jr.	260	Davis Fork	1824	6	25
Ice, Rawley & Oliver P.	250	Bingamon's Cr.	1844	7	455
Israel, Benoni	100	Buckeye Run	1837	7	154
Israel, Benoni	92	Middle Isl. Cr.	1838	7	278
Israel, Benoni et al	250	Blue Stone Br.	1828	6	56
Israel, Isaac	50	Sycamore Creek	1844	7	454
Israel, Isaac	400	Wts. Hughes River	1793	3	552
Israel, Israel	1,010	Wts. Buckhannon	1788	3	95
Israel, Jacob	280	Middle Is. Cr.	1807	5	174
Israel, Jacob	49	Mid. Island Cr.	1810	5	225
Israel, Jacob	2,450	Wts. of Elk	1797	4	403
Jackson, Edward	447	Cove Run	1800	5	8
Jackson, Edward	200	Tygert's V. R.	1788	3	78
Jackson, Edward	2,000	Glady Fork	1801	5	93
Jackson, Edward	5,000	Tygerts V. R.	1787	2	114
Jackson, Edward	470	Sandy Cr.	1788	3	137
Jackson, Edward & J. G.	500	Elk Creek	1801	5	45
Jackson, George	400	Peck's Run	1786	2	96
Jackson, George	1,150	Limestone Cr.	1788	3	149
Jackson, George	915	Wts. Elk Creek	1795	4	162
Jackson, George	500	Limestone Cr.	1802	5	199
Jackson, George	50,000 (5,000)	Wts. Lit. Kanawha	1796	4	296
Jackson, George	400	Cor. to G. Peck Settlement	1786	1	539
Jackson, George	400	Second Big Run	1786	1	565
Jackson, George et al Executors	1,000	Teter's Creek	1798	4	340
Jackson, George et al Executors	550	Teter's Cr.	1798	4	341
Jackson, George et al Executors	1,000	Teter's Cr.	1798	4	342
Jackson, George et al Executors	600	Teter's Cr.	1798	4	343
Jackson, George et al Executors	500	Teter's Cr.	1798	4	344
Jackson, George et al Executors	550	Teter's Cr.	1798	4	345
Jackson, George et al Executors	170 (190)	Hacker's Cr.	1797	4	347
Jackson, George et al Executors	430	Raccoon Cr.	1798	4	349
Jackson, John	450	Wts. Lit. Kanawha	1796	4	276
Jackson, John	1,000	Roaring Cr.	1787	2	454
Jackson, John	500	Wts. Buckhannon R.	1787	2	472
Jackson, John G.	129	Wts. West Fork	1821	6	204

Name of Grantee	Acres	Local Description	Year	Book	Page
Jackson, John G.	850	West Fork	1814	5	264
Jackson, John G. et al	400	Stone Coal	1816	3	568
Jackson, John Jr.	500	Turkey Run	1786	2	10
Jackson, John Jr. et al	300	Lambert's Run	1799	4	507
Jackson, Joshua	9	10 Mi. Cr.	1802	5	200
Jackson, Joshua	500	10 Mile Creek	1786	1	274
Jackson, Joshua	1,000	Oil Creek	1790	3	306
Jackson, Joshua	467	Oil Creek	1790	3	307
Jackson, Joshua	882	Oil Creek	1790	3	308
Jackson, Joshua	800	Oil Creek	1790	3	309
Jackson, Joshua	1,000	Oil Creek	1790	3	310
Jackson, Joshua	600	Oil Creek	1790	3	316
Jackson, Joshua	300	10 Mile Cr.	1786	1	399
Jackson, Joshua	400 (4,000)	Jones' Run	1786	1	402
Jackson, Joshua	500	Catfish	1786	1	403
Jackson, Josiah (Joshua)	448	Adj. his own	1786	1	398
Jackson, Richard	600	Wts. West Fork	1788	2	489
Jackson, Richard	1,000	Adj. his 2nd	1786	1	520
Jackson, Richard	1,000	West Fork	1786	1	521
Jackson, Richard	1,000	West Fork	1786	1	522
Jackson, Richard	1,000	West Fork	1786	1	523
Jackson, Richard	1,000	Wts. West Fork	1788	2	524
Jackson, Samuel	1,050	Oil Creek	1796	4	221
Jackson, William	147	Sycamore Cr.	1803	5	111
Jackson, William et al	761	10 Mile Creek	1811	5	241
Jacobs, Jonathan	76	Buffalo Cr.	1825	6	24
Jacobs, Jonathan	106	Buffalo Cr.	1821	6	194
James, Caleb	2,000	Wts. Buckhannon R.	1788	2	521
James, Samuel	176	Thomson's Run	1793	4	43
Jarvis—or Garvice					
Jarvis, Jesse et al	250	Blue Stone Br.	1828	6	56
Jarvis, John	50	Wts. Mid. Isl. Cr.	1820	6	238
Jarvis, John	177	Morgan's Run	1838	7	242
Jarvis, John Jr.	58	Meat House Fork	1817	3	591
Jeffrey, Joseph	45	Mid. Island Cr.	1819	6	264
Jeffrey, Joseph	75	Middle Isl. Cr.	1819	6	265
Jeffrey, Joseph	110	Pigeon Run	1838	7	335
Jenkins, Joseph	400	Rooting Creek	1796	4	206
Jobson, Joseph	1,000	Wts. Buckhannon River	1788	2	488
John—Johns, See Jones					
John, William	1,000	Wts. Lit. Kanawha	1787	2	142
John, William	1,000	Mill Creek	1787	2	143
John, William	400	Wts. Lit. Kanawha	1787	2	302
Johnson, Abraham	25	Short Creek	1827	6	67
Johnson, Arthur	186	Wts. West Fork	1793	4	12
Johnson, Henry	500	Briscoe's Cr.	1797	4	400
Johnson, John & Abraham	74	Tygert's V.	1816	3	575
Johnson, Joseph	1,000	Wts. Buckhannon R.	1788	2	488
Johnson, William	50	Wts. Hughes River	1838	7	235
Johnson, William	400	10 Mile Creek	1786	1	327
Johnson, William	750	Worthington's Cr.	1797	4	334
Johnson, William	750	Worthington's Cr.	1798	4	356
Johnson, William	2,000	Wts. West Fork	1799	4	456
Johnston, Arthur	100	Wts. West Fork	1799	4	480
Johnston, Peter	440	Otter Creek	1796	4	261
Johnston, Peter	1,500	Worthington's Cr.	1799	4	367
Johnston, Thomas	200	Otter Creek	1796	4	260
Jones—See also, John, Johns					
Jones, Catherind et al	100	England Run	1838	7	336
Jones, Enoch	350	Blue Lick Run	1791	3	407
Jones, George	73	Wolf Pen Run	1842	7	360
Jones, John	47	Meat House Fork	1842	7	361
Jones, Norris	4,000	Bond's Creek	1786	1	50

Name of Grantee	Acres	Local Description	Year	Book	Page
Jones, Samuel	1,250	Wts. West Fork	1799	4	477
Jones, William	1,000	Elk Lick Run	1797	4	306
Joseph, Nathan	90	Mid. Is. Cr.	1819	6	248
Joseph, Nathan	45	Arnold's Cr.	1813	5	257
Judgings, Mary et al	400	Bartley Run	1794	4	64
Judson, Ely	10,000	Cedar Creek	1796	4	280
Juggins, Mary et al	400	Bartley Run	1794	4	64
Kain—See Cain					
Kain, Daniel	400	Lost Creek	1787	2	478
Kain, Michael	400	Stone Coal Creek	1788	3	26
Karn, Michael	400	Stone Coal Cr.	1788	3	26
Kay, William et al Trustee	5,000	Wts. Lit. Kanawha	1786	1	193
Kay, William et al Trustee	5,000	Wts. Lit. Kanawha	1786	1	194
Kay, William et al Trustee	5,000	Wts. of Elk	1786	1	195
Kay, William et al Trustee	5,000	Wts. of Elk	1786	1	196
Kay, William et al Trustee	5,000	Glady Fork	1796	1	197
Kay, William et al Trustee	2,000	Wts. Hughes River	1786	1	198
Kay, William et al Trustee	2,000	Wts. Hughes River	1786	1	199
Kay, William et al Trustee	2,000	Wts. Lit. Kanawha	1786	1	200
Kay, William et al Trustee	3,000	Sand Fork	1786	1	201
Kay, William et al Trustee	5,000 (2,000)	Richard's Cr.	1786	1	243
Kay, William et al Trustee	2,000	Wts. Lit. Kanawha	1786	1	244
Kay, William et al Trustee	2,000	Wts. Hughes River	1786	1	279
Kay, William et al Trustee	10,000	Holley Fork	1786	1	283
Kay, William et al Trustee	10,000	Holley Fork	1786	1	284
Kay, William et al Trustee	2,000	Richard's Cr.	1786	1	285
Kay, William et al Trustee	2,000	Wts. Hughes R.	1786	1	286
Kay, William et al Trustee	2,000	Wts. Hughes River	1786	1	306
Kay, William et al Trustee	2,000	Spruce Creek	1786	1	307
Kay, William et al Trustee	2,000	Buzzard Cr.	1786	1	308
Keith—or Keath, Keeth					
Keith, James	400	Wts. West Fork	1787	2	468
Keith, James et al	215	West Fork	1813	5	262
Kelly, James	68	Simpson's Cr.	1796	4	223
Kelly, John et al	176	Meat House Fork	1827	6	73
Kendall—or Kindall, Kindell					
Kendall, William	50	Dent's Run	1836	7	142
Kennedy, Benjamin & Elisha	20,000	Wts. Hughes River	1799	4	482
Kenney, Mary et al Heirs	100	Arnold's Cr.	1842	7	411
Kents, Nicholas et al	1,500	Crow's Cr.	1788	3	118
Kertley, Francis	186	Tygert V. R.	1789	3	226
Keuetz, Nicholas et al	1,500	Crow's Cr.	1788	3	118
Kidd, David	165	Dotson Run	1786	2	11
Kidd, David	1,000	Eberman's Creek	1786	2	12
Kidd, David	1,000	Eberman's Cr.	1787	2	458
Kidd, David	150	Dodson's Run	1787	2	459
Kimble—See Kendall, Kindall, Kindell					
Kinchelo, Peter (Kenchelo)	400	Caty Lick Run	1787	2	513
Kindall—or Kendall, Kindell					
Kindall, Stephen	50	Buffalo Cr.	1837	7	158
Kindall, Thomas et al	400	Goose Creek	1793	4	9
Kindell—or Kendall, Kimble, Kindall					
Kindell, Elias	300	Dent's Run	1838	7	268
Kindell, Samuel	115	Dent's Run	1838	7	188
Kindell, Samuel Jr.	100	Buffalo Cr.	1836	7	145
Kindell, Samuel Jr.	150	Dent's Run	1838	7	269
Kindell, Zebedee	70	Dent's Run	1836	7	143
Kindell, Zebedee	100	Dent's Run	1838	7	187
King, Nathan	500	Big Steer Cr.	1797	4	393
King, William	200	Warrior's Fork	1838	7	237
King, William W.	21	West Fork	1842	7	364
Kinney, Israel	150	Nutter's Fork	1838	7	194
Kirtley—See Kertley					

Name of Grantee	Acres	Local Description	Year	Book	Page
Ligney, John	2,000	Crow's Creek	1787	2	170
Ligney, John	2,000	Crow's Cr.	1787	2	303
Lilburn, Robert	2,000	Wts. Hughes R.	1786	2	51
Lilburn, Robert	2,000	Wts. Hughes R.	1787	2	56
Lilburn, Robert	2,000	Wts. Hughes R.	1786	2	109
Lilburn, Robert	2,000	Wts. Hughes R.	1787	2	110
Lilburn, Robert	2,000	Wts. Hughes R.	1787	2	111
Lilburn, Robert	2,000	Wts. Hughes R.	1787	2	112
Lilburn, Robert	2,000	Wts. Hughes R.	1787	2	165
Lindley—See Laidley					
Lindley, James	620	Teter's Cr.	1788	3	114
Lindley, James	145	Board Camp Run	1788	3	145
Lindley, James	1,000	Elk Creek	1786	1	547
Lindsay, Mary A. et al	2,000	Wts. Wms. River	1791	3	401
Link, Thomas	37	Simon's Creek	1797	4	312
Lippincott, Samuel	220	Gregorie's Run	1809	5	216
Little. Abel	300	Otter Cr.	1783	4	171
Little, Thomas	15	Wts. Tygert's V.	1826	6	39
Little, Thomas	190	Tygert's V. R.	1809	5	182
Little, Thomas A.	50	Wts. Tygert's V. R.	1810	5	234
Lloyd—or Loyd					
Lockwood, David et al	40,000	Wts. Lit. Kanawha	1796	4	279
Lockwood, Isaac et al	30,000	Wts. Glady Fork	1794	4	33
Lodowick, John	100	Laurel Lick Run	1786	1	363
Loftus, John et al Heirs	791	Cabin Run	1800	4	543
Loftus, Ralph	500	Middle Run	1798	4	422
Loftus, Ralph	100	Middle Run	1798	4	423
Longstreet, Aaron	450	Wts. Cheat River	1799	4	508
Lord, Abner et al	30,000	Wts. Lit. Kanawha	1796	4	288
Lother—See Lowther					
Loughery—or Laughry, Lowery, Lowry					
Loughery, Hiram	125	Tar Kiln Run	1844	7	456
Lowe, Isaac	50	Glade Fork	1838	7	279
Lowry—See Loughery, Lowery					
Lowry, David	220	Mill Run	1786	1	319
Lowry, David	250	Mill Run	1786	1	452
Lowther, Elias	52	Wts. West Fork	1821	6	201
Lowther, Elias	41	Sycamore Cr.	1818	6	276
Lowther, Elias	36	Sycamore Cr.	1818	6	277
Lowther, Elias	20	Wts. West Fork	1818	6	292
Lowther, Elias	120½	West Fork	1816	3	572
Lowther, Elias et al	761	10 Mi. Cr.	1811	5	241
Lowther, Joel	300	Wts. West Fork	1788	3	135
Lowther, Joel	300	Wts. West Fork	1796	4	225
Lowther, William	400	Simpson Cr.	1787	2	72
Lowther, William	200	Hacker's Cr.	1786	2	87
Lowther, William	220	Wts. West Fork	1786	2	101
Lowther, William	400	Hickory Flats	1786	2	104
Lowther, William	400	Washburn's Cr.	1787	2	437
Lowther, William	400	Washburn's Cr.	1787	2	481
Lowther, William	400	Hacker's Cr.	1787	2	510
Lowther, William	400	Wts. West Fork	1786	1	585
Lowther, William	286	Wts. West Fork	1786	1	588
Lowther, William J. (Lother)	275	Cabin Run	1820	6	230
Lowther, William J.	96	Cabin Lick Fork	1825	6	35
Loy—See Lay, Say					
Loyd, Ephriam	5,000	Wts. Gauley	1789	3	157
Loyd, Ephriam	5,000	Wts. of Gauley	1789	3	193
Loyd, Ephraim	4,000	Wts. of Elk R.	1789	3	194
Lynch, Isaac	100	Buffalo Cr.	1838	7	296
Lynch, James	18	Wts. West Fork	1851	6	120
Lynch, John	3,000	Wts. Hughes River	1795	4	122
Lynch, Line	50	Lit. Kanawha	1816	3	576

Name of Grantee	Acres	Local Description	Year	Book	Page
Lynch, Peter	280	10 Mile Cr.	1837	7	170
Lynch, Peter	865	Lime Stone Cr.	1838	7	297
Lynch, Peter	40	10 Mile Cr.	1838	7	298
Lynch, Peter	23	Limestone Cr.	1842	7	399
Lyne—or Lyon, Lyons					
Lyne, John	1,285	Teter's Cr.	1786	2	46
Lyne, John	715	Grass Run	1786	1	68
Lyne, John	8,718¾	Roaring Cr.	1787	2	136
Lyne, John	500	Berry's Run	1789	3	223
Lyne, William Executor et al	5,000	Tygert's V. R.	1822	6	564
Lyon, James M. et al	10a.3r.	Simpson's Cr.	1858	6	171
Lyons—See Lyne, Lyon					
Lyons, William E.	14	Lambert's Run	1834	7	46
Lyons, William E.	40	Wts. West Fork	1834	7	48
Lyons, William E.	75	10 Mile Cr.	1851	6	134
Lyons, William E.	51	Jack Run	1845	7	492
Mace, Henry	57	Dry Fork	1789	3	186
Mace, Isaac	105	Dry Fork	1789	3	224
Mace, John	100	Lit. Kanawha	1816	3	562
Mackie, John	400	Barkeley's Run	1792	3	501
Mackie, John et al	400	Barkeley's Run	1799	4	527
Magee—or McGee					
Magee, James	68	West Fork	1812	5	248
Magee, James	75	Booth's Cr.	1812	5	249
Magill, Charles	1,000	Tygert's V. R.	1787	2	255
Mair, Francis	2,000	Wts. Gauley River	1791	3	362
Malin, Gideon	1,000	West Fork	1787	2	323
Manear—or Minear, Mineer					
Manear, Adam	312	Big Lick Run	1801	5	52
Manear, John Sr.	369	Tygert's Valley	1786	2	78
Manly, Jonathan	80	Brusky Fork	1801	5	66
Marsh, Elijah	100	Grass Run	1834	7	57
Marsh, Isaac	26	10 Mile Cr.	1844	7	457
Marsh, Isaac	45	10 Mile Cr.	1844	7	465
Marsh, Isaac et al	1,100	Wts. Hughes River	1790	3	323
Marsh, Isaac et al	960	Wts. Hughes River	1790	3	324
Marsh, Isaac et al	980	Wts. Hughes River	1790	3	325
Marsh, Isaac et al	960	Wts. Hughes R.	1790	3	326
Marsh, Jesse	114	Grass Run	1843	7	421
Martenah—See Mortenah					
Martin, Augustus J.	60	Indian Run	1850	6	119
Martin, Augustus J.	150	Indian Run	1838	7	332
Martin, Blackley & Joseph	50	Upper Coal Lick	1842	7	400
Martin, Charles	30	Coal Lick Run	1836	7	112
Martin, Charles	400	Mud Lick Run	1788	3	112
Martin, Charles	400	Mud Lick	1788	3	115
Martin, Daniel	150	Sweep Run	1801	5	15
Martin, Daniel	27	Wts. Tygert's V.	1806	5	171
Martin, Edmund & Elizabeth et al	400	Bartley Run	1794	4	64
Martin, Eli	17	Booth's Cr.	1842	7	401
Martin, James	152	Isner's Run	1790	3	366
Martin, Jesse	3½	Booth's Cr.	1834	7	54
Martin, John	500	Lost Creek	1788	3	52
Martin, John	11¼	Sap Run	1853	6	164
Martin, John	388	Booth Creek	1786	1	516
Martin, John	9⅞	Jack Run	1848	7	529
Martin, John H.	5	Mud Lick Run	1834	7	50
Martin, Joseph	50	Cool Lick Run	1836	7	148
Martin, Joseph	46	Bingamon's Cr.	1837	7	156
Martin, Levi	8	Aaron Smith Run	1836	7	108
Martin, Levi	325	10 Mile Creek	1844	7	464
Martin, Levi	65	Barnett's Run	1845	7	498
Martin, Robert	129	Stalnaker's Run	1787	2	500

Name of Grantee	Acres	Local Description	Year	Book	Page
Martin, Robert et al	20,000	Wts. Hughes River	1797	4	372
Martin, Spencer	59	Helen's Run	1824	6	16
Martin, Thomas & M. D.	9	Bingamon's Cr.	1852	6	133
Martin, William	400	Bushy Fork	1794	4	50
Martin, William	200	Bushy Fork	1794	4	63
Martin, William	1,000	Indian Cr.	1799	4	443
Martin, William	400	Wts. Cheat River	1799	4	505
Martin, William et al	40	Valley River	1801	5	95
Martin, William et al	100	Hooppole Run	1801	5	96
Martin, William et al Executors	1,000	Teter's Cr.	1798	4	340
Martin, William et al Executors	550	Teter's Cr.	1798	4	341
Martin, William et al Executors	1,000	Teter's Cr.	1798	4	342
Martin, William et al Executors	600	Teter's Cr.	1798	4	343
Martin, William et al Executors	500	Teter's Cr.	1798	4	344
Martin, William et al Executors	550	Teter's Cr.	1797	4	345
Martin, William et al Executors	170 (190)	Hacker's Cr.	1797	4	347
Martin, William et al Executors	430	Raccoon Cr.	1798	4	349
Mason, Gideon	50	Plumb Run	1837	7	162
Mason, Rebecca et al Heirs	237	Bingamon Cr.	1819	6	255
Mason, Rebecca et al Heirs	100	Long Run	1819	6	256
Mason, Rebecca et al Heirs	100	Coon Run	1816	3	560
Mason, Rebecca et al Heirs	52	Robinson's Run	1816	3	561
Mason, Rebecca et al Heirs	260	West Fork	1817	3	587
Mason, Richard	2,000	10 Mile Cr.	1786	1	56
Mason, Richard	2,000	10 Mi. Creek	1786	1	57
Mason, Richard	5,000	Wts. Buckhannon R.	1786	1	58
Mason, Richard	5,000	Middle Fork	1786	1	59
Mason, Richard	2,000	10 Mile Cr.	1786	1	77
Mason, Richard	2,000	10 Mile Cr.	1786	1	78
Mason, Richard	2,000	Rush Run	1786	1	79
Mason, Richard	3,000	Rush Run	1786	1	80
Mason, Richard	927	10 Mile Cr.	1786	1	81
Mason, Richard	2,000	10 Mile Cr.	1786	1	82
Mason, Robert	300	Bingamon's Run	1832	7	7
Mason, Robert	1,550	Bingamon's Cr.	1836	7	151
Mason, Robert	513	Bingamon's Cr.	1822	6	212
Mason, Robert	29	Bingamon's Cr.	1822	6	213
Mason, Robert	117	Bingamon's Cr.	1822	6	214
Mason, Robert	145	Bingamon's Cr.	1822	6	217
Mason, Robert	70	Bingamon's Cr.	1820	6	232
Mason, Robert	42	Bingamon's Cr.	1820	6	233
Mason, Robert	740	Bingamon Cr.	1819	6	244
Mason, Robert	300	Big Indian Run	1838	7	310
Mason, Robert	550 (500)	Bingamon's Cr.	1842	7	377
Mason, Robert	2,186	Middle Fork & Glade Cr.	1838	7	548
Mason, Robert Sr.	1a.80p.	Bingamon's Cr.	1857	6	156
Matheny, Noah	75	Garden Run	1837	7	179
Mathews—or Matthews					
Mathews, Richard	5,000	Wts. of Elk	1786	2	39
Matson, Enoch	1,000	Wts. Hughes River	1796	4	208
Matthew, Levi B.	140	Meat House Fork	1840	7	350
Matthew, Levi B.	100	Meathouse Fork	1842	7	362
Matthews, Richard	5,000	Wts. of Elk	1786	1	590
Matthews, Sampson	1,000	Hughes River	1803	5	113
Maulsbey—or Maulsby					
Maulsbey, Polly et al Heirs	260	West Fork	1817	3	587
Maulsby, Lawson	100	Middle Fork	1832	7	9
Maulsby, Lawson B.	200	Morgan's Run	1842	7	402
Maulsby, Lawson B.	100	Shingletree Run	1842	7	403
Maulsby, Polly et al Heirs	237	Bingamon Cr.	1819	6	255
Maulsby, Polly et al Heirs	100	Long Run	1819	6	256
Maulsby, Polly et al Heirs	100	Coon Run	1816	3	560
Maulsby, Polly et al Heirs	52	Robinson's Run	1816	3	561

Name of Grantee	Acres	Local Description	Year	Book	Page
McConkey, Jesse	50	Isaac's Creek	1838	7	200
McCraw, Samuel	1,000	Wts. Buckhannon R.	1785	1	73
McCraw, Samuel et al	7,000	Wts. West Fork	1796	4	286
McCraw, Samuel Jr.	1,000	Barkeley's Run	1786	1	233
McCray, Fauquier	300	Wts. Lit. Kanawha	1799	4	503
McCullough, James	49	Elk Creek	1795	4	185
McCullough, John	18	Grisby's Run	1809	5	181
McDonald, James	500	Wts. Hughes River	1786	1	294
McElhany—See McFelhany					
McFarland—See Farland					
McFarland, Daniel	400	Wts. Hughes River	1793	4	29
McFelhany, James	2,500	Brusky Fork	1787	2	206
McGee—or Magee					
McGee, James	50	Booth Creek	1818	6	293
McGee, John C.	97	Joe's Run	1837	7	152
McGee, Thomas (Magee)	100	Booth's Cr.	1818	6	289
McGill—See Magill					
McHanne—See McFelhany					
McHenry, James	3,000	Wts. Lit. Kanawha	1789	3	166
McHenry, James	2,000	Wts. Hughes R.	1789	3	170
McHenry, James	2,918¾	Wts. Hughes R.	1789	3	202
McHenry, James	2,000	Wts. Hughes River	1789	3	204
McIntire, Elizabeth et al Heirs	100	Coon's Run	1816	3	560
McIntire, Elizabeth et al Heirs	52	Robinson's Run	1816	3	561
McIntire, Enoch	75	Bingamon's Cr.	1835	7	91
McIntire, Enoch	12	Bingamon's Cr.	1849	6	104
McIntire, Hanna et al Heirs	237	Bingamon Cr.	1819	6	255
McIntire, Hannah & Elizabeth et al Heirs	260	West Fork	1817	3	587
McIntire, Hannah et al Heirs	100	Coon Run	1816	3	560
McIntire, Hannah et al Heirs	52	Robinson's Run	1816	3	561
McIntire, Hannah et al Heirs	100	Long Run	1819	6	256
McIntire, Jesse	100	Rock Camp Run	1835	7	85
McIntire, Samuel	400	Wts. West Fork	1788	3	81
McIntire, William Jr.	80	Wts. West Fork	1840	7	351
McIntire, Zadoc	230	Lambert's Run	1829	6	86
McIntire, Zadock	80	Lambert's Run	1853	6	148
McIntosh, James	125	Pleasant Cr.	1836	7	135
McKee—or Mackie, McKey					
McKenney, McKenny, McKinney					
McKenney, James	400	Simpson's Cr.	1788	3	84
McKenney, William	367	Simpson's Cr.	1787	2	477
McKenny, John et al	400	Barkeley's Run	1799	4	527
McKewan, Charles	200	Adj. his No. 3	1790	3	311
McKewan, Charles	200	Bull Creek	1790	3	318
McKim, John Jr.	1,930	Wts. Lit. Kanawha	1797	4	407
McKinley, Uriah	38½	Buffalo Cr.	1855	6	162
McKinney—See McKenney					
McKinney, Archibald	400	Otter Creek	1786	1	584
McKnight, Robert et al Trustee	5,000	Wts. Lit. Kanawha	1786	1	193
McKnight, Robert et al Trustee	5,000	Wts. Lit. Kanawha	1786	1	194
McKnight, Robert et al Trustee	5,000	Wts. of Elk	1786	1	195
McKnight, Robert et al Trustee	5,000	Wts. of Elk	1786	1	196
McKnight, Robert et al Trustee	5,000	Glady Fork	1786	1	197
McKnight, Robert et al Trustee	2,000	Wts. Hughes River	1786	1	198
McKnight, Robert et al Trustee	2,000	Wts. Hughes River	1786	1	199
McKnight, Robert et al Trustee	2,000	Wts. Lit. Kanawha	1786	1	200
McKnight, Robert et al Trustee	3,000	Sand Fork	1786	1	201
McKnight, Robert et al Trustee	5,000 (2,000)	Richard's Cr.	1786	1	243
McKnight, Robert et al Trustee	2,000	Wts. Lit. Kanawha	1786	1	244
McKnight, Robert et al Trustee	2,000	Wts. Hughes River	1786	1	279
McKnight, Robert et al Trustee	10,000	Holley Fork	1786	1	283

Name of Grantee	Acres	Local Description	Year	Book	Page
McKnight, Robert et al Trustee	10,000	Holley Fork	1786	1	284
McKnight, Robert et al Trustee	2,000	Richard's Cr.	1786	1	285
McKnight, Robert et al Trustee	2,000	Wts. Hughes River	1786	1	286
McKnight, Robert et al Trustee	2,000	Wts. Hughes River	1786	1	306
McKnight, Robert et al Trustee	2,000	Spruce Creek	1786	1	307
McKnight, Robert et al Trustee	2,000	Buzzard's Cr.	1786	1	308
McLene—McClean, McClain					
McLene, Fergus	200	Wts. Cheat River	1789	3	177
McMicken, John	500	Elk Lick	1799	4	460
McMurtree, William	5,000	French Creek	1786	1	174
McMurtree, William	5,000	French Creek	1786	1	175
McQuain, Alexander	700	Isaac's Cr.	1816	3	558
McQuain, Alexander	174	Horse Run	1816	3	559
McWhorter, Henry et al	1,000	Wts. Buckhannon R.	1804	5	144
Means, Robert	1,000	Glady Fork	1795	4	108
Means, Robert	3,000	Hacker's Creek	1795	4	109
Means, Robert	500	Stewart's Run	1795	4	110
Means, Robert	500	Stewart's Run	1795	4	111
Means, Robert	500	Stewart's Run	1795	4	112
Means, Robert	500	Stewart's Run	1795	4	113
Means, Robert	500	Stewart's Run	1795	4	114
Means, Robert	1,984	Gnatty Creek	1795	4	115
Means, Robert	3,000	French Creek	1795	4	116
Means, Robert	2,000	Glady Fork	1795	4	117
Means, Robert	1,000	Stewart's Run	1795	4	118
Means, Robert	2,000	Gnatty Cr.	1795	4	119
Means, Robert	5,000	Hacker's Cr.	1795	4	120
Means, Robert	2,000	Gnatty Creek	1795	4	121
Means, Robert	2,000	Wts. Gauley River	1791	3	403
Means, Robert	2,000	Wts. of Gauley	1791	3	404
Meek, Isaac	360	Lost Run	1788	3	98
Melone, James	87	Wts. Hughes R.	1819	6	243
Mendinhall, William	500	Wts. of Elk	1789	3	213
Mercer, James	500	Deck's 3rd, Entry	1790	3	327
Mercer, James	500	Adj. Deck's 5th	1790	3	328
Mercer, James	566	Deck's 6th	1790	3	329
Mercer, James	434	Adj. Deck's 7th	1790	3	330
Mercer, James	500	Adj. his 1st	1790	3	331
Mercer, James	500	Adj. Deck's 4th	1790	3	332
Mercer, James	1,000	Tygert's River	1790	3	333
Mercer, James	1,000	Tygert's V. R.	1790	3	334
Mercer, James	1,000	Tygert's V. R.	1790	3	336
Merrifield, Richard	400	Otter Creek	1789	3	275
Metz, Peter	50	Rock Lick Run	1830	6	89
Michael, James	250	Bartholomew Fork	1838	7	308
Michael, James	200	Bartholomew Fork	1838	7	309
Middleton, Henry O.	775	10 Mi. Cr.	1851	6	127
Middleton, Henry O.	940	Elk Creek	1842	7	410
Middleton, Henry O. et al	270	Brusky Fork	1842	7	372
Miller, Elisha	300	Salt Lick Run	1844	7	444
Miller, John et al	1,000	Barkeley's Run	1786	1	245
Miller, Magnus	4,000	Bond's Creek	1786	1	47
Milner, Nathan	3,000	Wts. of Elk	1787	2	156
Milrose, John	1,000	Tygert's Cr.	1800	4	546
Mincer, Philip	50	Wts. Cheat River	1787	2	516
Minear, Manear, Mineer					
Mitchell, John	360	West Fork	1815	5	265
Modesitt, James W.	135	Simpson's Cr.	1833	7	15
Moore, Enoch	100	Lambert's Run	1806	5	166
Moore, Jeptha	75	Lit. Indian Run	1835	7	103
Moore, Richard Jr.	155	Bingamon's Cr.	1823	6	3
Moore, Richard Jr.	114	Bingamon's Cr.	1844	7	468
Moore, Samuel P.	190	Garner's Run	1794	4	65

Name of Grantee	Acres	Local Description	Year	Book	Page
Moore, Stephen	3,300	10 Mile Cr.	1794	4	66
Morehead, George	300	Simpson's Cr.	1786	2	20
Moreland, John	155	Simpson's Cr.	1798	4	447
Morgan, Levi et al	820	Cunningham's Run	1801	5	94
Morgan, William T.	170	Big Mill F. Run	1830	6	93
Morris, George	95	Limestone Cr.	1826	6	53
Morris, Isaac	100	Simpson's Cr.	1799	4	510
Morris, Isaac Sr.	30	Booth's Cr.	1827	6	70
Morris, Robert	3,970	Fink's Fork	1791	3	379
Morris, Robert	3,170	Freeman's Cr.	1791	3	380
Morris, Robert	5,070	Leading Cr.	1791	3	381
Morris, Robert	4,260	Cove Creek	1791	3	390
Morris, Robert	6,848 (6,840)	Leading Cr.	1791	3	391
Morris, Robert	4,000	Cove Cr.	1791	3	392
Morris, Robert	2,720	Fink's Fork	1791	3	393
Morrison, Archibald	52	Wts. West Fork	1799	4	487
Morrison, Hamilton	200	Pond Run	1797	4	333
Morrison, Hamilton	200	Big Run	1797	4	401
Morrison, John	140	Caty Lick Run	1834	7	65
Morrow, Ralph	250	Peddler's Run	1787	2	148
Mortenah, Charles	1,050	Files Creek	1791	3	377
Mount, Thomas	355	Middle Fork	1788	3	125
Moylan, John	1,000	Wts. Lit. Kanawha	1785	1	1
Moylan, John	1,000	Wts. Lit. Kanawha	1785	1	2
Moylan, John	1,000	Wts. Lit. Kanawha	1785	1	3
Moylan, John	1,000	Wts. Lit. Kanawha	1785	1	9
Moylan, John	1,000	Wts. Lit. Kanawha	1785	1	12
Moylan, John	1,000	Wts. Lit. Kanawha	1785	1	13
Moylan, John	1,000	Wts. Lit. Kanawha	1785	1	14
Moylan, John	1,000	Wts. Lit. Kanawha	1785	1	17
Moylan, John	1,000	Wts. Lit. Kanawha	1785	1	18
Moylan, John	1,000	Wts. Lit. Kanawha	1785	1	23
Moylan, John	1,000	Wts. Lit. Kanawha	1785	1	26
Moylan, John	1,000	Wts. Lit. Kanawha	1785	1	27
Moylan, John	1,000	Wts. Lit. Kanawha	1785	1	28
Moylan, John	1,000	Wts. Lit. Kanawha	1785	1	30
Muir, John	140	Lost Run	1802	5	106
Muir, John	410	10 Mile Cr.	1799	4	368
Murphy, David	400	Simpson's Cr.	1786	1	503
Murry, Patrick	990	Wts. Cheat River	1788	3	147
Murry, Patrick	965	Tygert V. River	1788	3	148
Myers, John	400	Sycamore Cr.	1787	2	515
Namor, Patrick W.	300	Mill Stone Run	1788	3	42
Nay, Fielding	25	Bingamon's Cr.	1832	7	12
Nay, Oliver	160	Bingamon's Cr.	1835	7	95
Nay, Oliver	250	Whetstone Run	1838	7	238
Nay, William & Fielding	100	Bingamon's Cr.	1832	7	11
Neal—or Neale, Neel					
Neal, James	1,000	Wts. Lit. Kanawha	1794	4	47
Neal, James	598	Wts. Hughes R.	1788	3	91
Neal, James	200	Teter's Cr.	1788	3	94
Neal, James	352	10 Mile Creek	1788	3	96
Neal, James	400	Limestone Cr.	1788	3	132
Neal, James	383	Wts. West Fork	1788	3	136
Neal, James	400	Teter's Cr.	1788	3	138
Neale, George	50	Booth's Cr.	1830	6	94
Neel—or Neal, Neale					
Neel, James	100	Otter Cr.	1796	4	278
Neely, John	400	10 Mile Cr.	1797	4	416
Neely, Mathew	200	Buckeye Run	1838	7	243
Neely, Mathew	62	Childers' Run	1838	7	244
Neely, Mathew	63	Mid. Isl. Cr.	1838	7	245
Neely, Mathew	90	Morgan's Run	1838	7	246

Name of Grantee	Acres	Local Description	Year	Book	Page
Nelson, Abraham	3,254	Laurel Cr.	1788	3	14
Nelson, Abraham	746	Laurel Cr.	1788	3	16
Nelson, Abraham Jr.	3,000	Wts. of Elk	1788	3	21
Nelson, Abraham Jr.	3,000	Wts. of Elk	1788	3	22
Nelson, Abraham Jr.	3,000	Wts. of Elk	1788	3	23
Nelson, Alexander	2,000	Wts. Buckhannon R.	1786	1	390
Nelson, Alexander (in trust) et al	5,000	Valley River	1786	1	357
Nelson, Alexander (in trust) et al	2,000	Tanner's Run	1786	1	360
Nelson, Alexander (in trust) et al	2,560	West Fork	1786	1	361
Nelson, Alexander (in trust) et al	2,000	Simpson's Cr.	1786	1	362
Nelson, Alexander (in trust) et al	2,000	Simpson's Cr.	1786	1	364
Nelson, Heron & Co. et al	5,000	Valley River	1786	1	357
Nelson, Heron & Co. et al	2,000	Tanner's Run	1786	1	360
Nelson, Heron & Co. et al	2,560	West Fork	1786	1	361
Nelson, Heron & Co. et al	2,000	Simpson Cr.	1786	1	362
Nelson, Heron & Company et al	2,000	Simpson's Cr.	1786	1	364
Nevil, Joseph	86	Shaver's Fork	1788	3	131
Newlin, Cyrus	1,000	Laurel Creek	1787	2	527
Newman, Morris	150	10 Mi. Cr.	1802	5	202
Newman, Morris	100	Kiah's Run	1799	4	523
Newport, James et al Trustee	5,000	Wts. Lit. Kanawha	1786	1	193
Newport, James et al Trustee	5,000	Wts. Lit. Kanawha	1786	1	194
Newport, James et al Trustee	5,000	Wts. of Elk	1786	1	195
Newport, James et al Trustee	5,000	Wts. of Elk	1786	1	196
Newport, James et al Trustee	5,000	Glady Fork	1786	1	197
Newport, James et al Trustee	2,000	Wts. Hughes River	1786	1	198
Newport, James et al Trustee	2,000	Wts. Hughes River	1786	1	199
Newport, James et al Trustee	2,000	Wts. Lit. Kanawha	1786	1	200
Newport, James et al Trustee	3,000	Sand Fork	1786	1	201
Newport, James et al Trustee	5,000 (2,000)	Richard's Cr.	1786	1	243
Newport, James et al Trustee	2,000	Wts. Lit. Kanawha	1786	1	244
Newport, James et al Trustee	2,000	Wts. Hughes River	1786	1	279
Newport, James et al Trustee	10,000	Holley Fork	1786	1	283
Newport, James et al Trustee	10,000	Holley Fork	1786	1	284
Newport, James et al Trustee	2,000	Richard's Cr.	1786	1	285
Newport, James et al Trustee	2,000	Wts. Hughes R.	1786	1	286
Newport, James et al Trustee	2,000	Wts. Hughes River	1786	1	306
Newport, James et al Trustee	2,000	Spruce Creek	1786	1	307
Newport, James et al Trustee	2,000	Buzzard's Creek	1786	1	308
Newsom, John et al	100	Tygert's Valley	1803	5	112
Nichols, Austin	945	Glady Fork	1794	4	31
Nichols, Austin	25,000	Mid. Island Cr.	1796	4	218
Nichols, Austin	100,000	Wts. Lit. Kanawha	1796	4	287
Nichols, Austin et al	30,000	Wts. Lit. Kanawha	1796	4	288
Nichols, John et al	20,000	Wts. Hughes River	1797	4	372
Nicholson, George	7,000	Wts. West Fork	1796	4	286
Nicolson—See Nicholson					
Nixon, George	128	Booth's Cr.	1806	5	154
Nixon, Jesse	13	Booth's Cr.	1834	7	38
Nixon, Jesse	9	Booth's Cr.	1834	7	44
Nixon, Jonathan	385	Booth's Cr.	1787	2	419
Nixon, Robert	40	Booth's Cr.	1811	5	238
Nixon, Sarah et al Ex.	15	Booth's Cr.	1804	5	127
Norman, Granville H. et al	71	Elk Creek	1860	6	160
Norman, Granville H. et al	71	Elk Creek	1860	6	179
Norton, George & Daniel	1,000	Crow's Cr.	1789	3	225
Norton, Philo	25,000	Big Steer Cr.	1801	5	20
Nutter, Christopher	317	Elk Creek	1787	2	463
Nutter, Christopher	83	Elk Creek	1799	4	531
Nutter, Christopher	500	Elk Creek	1786	1	549
Nutter, John	350	Bingamon's Cr.	1838	7	311
Nutter, Mathew	400	Brusky Fork	1786	1	394
Nutter, Thomas	472	Brown's Creek	1788	3	24

Name of Grantee	Acres	Local Description	Year	Book	Page
Nutter, Thomas	1,400	Elk Creek	1795	4	158
Nutter, Thomas	400	Elk Creek	1786	1	267
Nutter, Thomas	1,000	Elk Creek	1786	1	473
Ogden, Ignatius	142	Briscoe's Run	1793	3	555
Ogden, Phebe et al Heirs	237	Bingamon Cr.	1819	6	255
Ogden, Phebe et al Heirs	100	Long Run	1819	6	256
Ogden, Phebe et al Heirs	100	Coon Run	1816	3	560
Ogden, Phebe et al Heirs	52	Robinson's Run	1816	3	561
Ogden, Phebe et al Heirs	260	West Fork	1817	3	587
Orr, Mathew	100	10 Mile Cr.	1838	7	247
Orr, Nicholas	100	10 Mi. Cr.	1826	6	47
Overton, John	3,000	Valley River	1786	1	207
Overton, John	2,000	Valley River	1786	1	208
Overton, John	233	Middle Fork	1786	1	209
Overton, John	2,000	Barkeley's Run	1786	1	287
Overton, John	2,000	Barkley's Run	1786	1	288
Owens, John	400	West Fork	1786	2	21
Owens, John	400	West Fork	1786	1	439
Pack—or Pock					
Pack, Michael	170	Buffalo Creek	1813	5	259
Painter—Panter, Ponter, Pouter					
Panter, Elias	400	Wts. Buckhannon R.	1787	2	348
Parks, Robert	100	James Run	1834	7	45
Parsons, Edward	160	Murphy's Cr.	1804	5	143
Patton, Francis	200	Booth's Cr.	1796	4	259
Patton, Francis	400	Booth's Cr.	1787	2	260
Pauley, John	85	Tygert's V. R.	1787	2	518
Pearcy, Joshua	175	Meat House Fork	1838	7	239
Pearcy, Joshua	190	New Road Fork	1845	7	501
Peatro, Nicholas & Henry	200	Tygert's Valley	1786	1	572
Peck, George	397	Peck's Run	1786	2	97
Peck, John	50	Rock Run	1832	7	8
Pendell—Pennell, Pindell					
Pendell, Thomas	1,000	Mill Creek	1792	3	556
Pennell—Pendell, Pindell					
Pennell, Joseph	5,000	Wts. Elk River	1787	2	65
Pennell, Joseph	3,000	Wts. of Elk	1787	2	157
Pennell, Joseph	3,000	Tygert's V. R.	1787	2	183
Pennell, Joseph	3,000	Wts. of Elk River	1787	2	184
Pennell, Joseph	5,000	Wts. of Elk	1787	2	185
Pennell, Joseph	5,000	Wts. of Elk River	1787	2	186
Pennell, Joseph	4,000	Wts. of Elk River	1787	2	187
Pennell, Joseph	5,000	Wts. of Elk River	1787	2	188
Pennell, Joseph	5,000	Wts. of Elk R.	1787	2	189
Pennell, Joseph	5,000	Wts. of Elk R.	1787	2	203
Pennell, Thomas	3,000	Wts. of Elk River	1787	2	190
Pennell, Thomas	5,000	Wts. Tygert's R.	1787	2	191
Pennell, Thomas	2,244¼	Sugar Cr.	1787	2	192
Pennell, Thomas	2,000	Sugar Cr.	1787	2	193
Pennell, Thomas	2,000	Wts. Elk River	1787	2	194
Pennell, Thomas	2,000	Wts. Elk River	1787	2	195
Pennell, Thomas	5,000	Wts. of Elk R.	1787	2	196
Pennell, Thomas	3,000	Wts. Elk River	1787	2	197
Pennell, Thomas	5,000	Wts. Elk River	1787	2	198
Pennell, Thomas	3,000	Sugar Creek	1787	2	199
Pennell, Thomas	6,000	Wts. of Elk	1787	2	200
Pennell, Thomas	3,000	Wts. of Elk R.	1787	2	201
Pennell, Thomas	2,000	Wts. of Elk R.	1787	2	202
Penton, Abner	2,000	Wts. of Gauley	1789	3	158
Penton, Abner	2,000	Wts. of Elk	1789	3	163
Penton, Abner	2,000	Wts. of Gauley	1789	3	165
Penton, Abner	2,000	Wts. Gauley	1789	3	168
Penton, Abner	3,000	Laurel Cr.	1789	3	195

Name of Grantee	Acres	Local Description	Year	Book	Page
Powers, John	900	Simpson's Cr.	1787	2	261
Powers, John	400	Booth's Cr.	1787	2	436
Powers, Martin	261	Wts. West Fork	1786	2	54
Powers, William et al Heirs	200	Mill Run	1801	5	55
Praham, Nathan & Samuel Jr. et al	20,000	Wts. Hughes River	1797	4	372
Prescott, Roger	710	Wts. Cheat River	1788	3	103
Prescott, Roger	1,920	King's Run	1788	3	104
Prescott, Roger	1,040	Wts. Cheat River	1788	3	105
Preston, Samuel	155	Elk Creek	1788	3	164
Preston, Samuel	240	Lost Cr.	1788	3	198
Preston, Samuel	135	Raccoon Run	1788	3	199
Preston, Samuel	300	J. Hughes Run	1788	3	200
Preston, Samuel	1,600	Jess Hugh's Run	1787	2	251
Preston, Samuel	660	Stone Coal Cr.	1787	2	283
Preston, Samuel et al	460	Lost Creek	1788	3	37
Price, James	15¾	10 Mile Cr.	1849	6	105
Proctor, Thomas	10,000	Adj. James McGinnis	1786	1	182
Proctor, Thomas	3,000	Wts. Hughes River	1786	1	183
Proctor, Thomas	5,000	Sand Fork	1787	2	288
Proctor, Thomas	5,000	Sand Fork	1787	2	398
Proctor, Thomas	1,000	Spruce Creek	1787	2	399
Proctor, Thomas	1,278 (1287)	10 Mile Creek	1798	4	425
Proctor, Thomas	5,000	Wts. Lit. Kanawha	1787	2	430
Proctor, Thomas	5,000	Sand Fork	1787	2	434
Proctor, Thomas	1,000	Richard's Cr.	1787	2	447
Province, Sarah	1,000	Mill Cr.	1788	2	210
Province, Sarah	1,000	Mill Creek	1787	2	270
Province, Sarah	1,500	Wts. Lit. Kanawha	1787	2	390
Prunty, David	100	Otter Cr.	1801	5	98
Prunty, David	85	Lost Run	1808	5	178
Prunty, David	300	Otter Cr.	1789	3	211
Prunty, David et al	185	Valley River	1800	5	35
Prunty, David et al	100	Otter Cr.	1800	5	36
Prunty, John	300	Booth's Cr.	1801	5	89
Prunty, John	200	Duck Creek	1787	2	289
Prunty, John	242	Lost Run	1798	4	357
Prunty, John	1,000	Dick's Creek	1786	1	507
Prunty, John	334	West Fork	1786	1	526
Prunty, John	1,000	Indian Run	1786	1	556
Prunty, John Jr.	54	Lost Run	1808	5	179
Pryor, Joseph	900	10 Mile Cr.	1797	4	394
Pugh, Daniel	2,000	Wts. Tygert's V. R.	1787	2	294
Pugh, Daniel	346	Teter's Cr.	1792	3	423
Pugh, Daniel	860	Simpson's Cr.	1792	3	424
Pugh, Daniel	25	Elk Creek	1792	3	425
Pugh, Daniel	1,000	10 Mile Cr.	1792	3	426
Pugh, Daniel	450	Teter's Cr.	1792	3	427
Pugh, Daniel	210	File's Cr.	1792	3	428
Pugh, Daniel	134¼	Cherry River	1792	3	429
Pugh, Hannibal	790	Maxwell's Run	1816	5	277
Pullen, John S. et al	175	Wts. Hughes R.	1834	7	66
Puller, John S. et al	175	Wts. Hughes R.	1834	7	66
Queen, William C.	50	Gnatty Cr.	1819	6	253
Radabaugh, Adam	47	Coon's Run	1837	7	168
Radcliff, Edward	400	Freeman's Cr.	1787	2	433
Radcliff, John	490	Elk Creek	1786	2	8
Radcliff, John	400	Elk Creek	1786	2	36
Radcliff, John	254	Grigsby's Run	1786	2	93
Radcliff, John	383	Elk Creek	1810	5	219
Radcliff, John	100	Gnatty Cr.	1791	3	402
Radcliff, John	417	Elk Creek	1786	1	555
Radcliff, John	400	Gnatty Creek	1786	1	589

Name of Grantee	Acres	Local Description	Year	Book	Page
Reynolds, James W. H.	375	Rock Camp	1846	7	512
Reynolds, James W. H.	65	Rock Camp Run	1848	7	537
Reynolds, John	50	Lambert's Run	1832	7	13
Reynolds, John	84	Wts. West Fork	1801	5	19
Reynolds, John	145	Lambert's Run	1833	7	23
Reynolds, W. G.	10	Wts. West Fork	1849	6	106
Rhea, John	10,000	Valley River	1786	1	135
Rhea, John	10,000	Valley River	1786	1	136
Rice, Elias	100	Simpson's Cr.	1797	4	397
Richards, Conrad	277	Lost Cr.	1787	2	535
Richards, Isaac	365	Elk Creek	1787	2	499
Richards, Isaac	400	Elk Creek	1793	3	542
Richards, Jacob	150	Sycamore Cr.	1796	4	224
Richards, Jacob	343	Sycamore Cr.	1786	1	269
Richards, Jacob	160	Geelick Run	1799	4	518
Richards, Margaret & Sarah et al	400	Wts. West Fork	1795	4	173
Richardson, Aaron	240	Tygert's V. R.	1786	2	25
Rider, Daniel & J. W.	50	Board Camp Run	1834	7	62
Riffel, Jacob	50	Tygert's V. R.	1791	3	388
Riffel, Jacob	300	Wts. Tygert's V.	1791	3	389
Righter, John	400	Shinn's Run	1794	4	54
Righter, John	200	Shinn's Run	1820	6	226
Righter, John	100	Shinn's Run	1820	6	227
Righter, John	54	Mud Lick Run	1820	6	228
Righter, John	22	Robinson's Run	1815	5	266
Righter, John	88	Shinn's Run	1797	4	404
Righter, John	88	Shinn's Run	1799	4	515
Righter, John	28	Coon's Run	1817	3	583
Riley, Jesse	82	Stout's Run	1829	6	82
Riley, Jesse	2½	Stout's Run	1847	7	514
Rittenhouse, Bennett	4	10 Mile Cr.	1842	7	404
Roberts, William	1,000	Elk Lick Cr.	1797	4	307
Robey, Naomy et al Heirs	200	Mill Run	1801	5	55
Robins, George	9	Buffalo Cr.	1841	7	356
Robinson—or Robison, Robson					
Robinson, Benjamin	285	Jack Run	1800	5	10
Robinson, Benjamin	26	Jones' Run	1824	6	13
Robinson, Benjamin	67	Ten Mile Cr.	1829	6	84
Robinson, Benjamin	287	Lit. Elk Lick	1829	6	85
Robinson, Benjamin	515	10 Mile Creek	1786	1	502
Robinson, Benjamin	350	Robinson's Run	1799	4	436
Robinson, Benjamin	72	10 Mile Cr.	1799	4	541
Robinson, Benjamin et al	1,300	Robinson's Run	1799	4	437
Robinson, David W. et al	10	Bingamon's Cr.	1859	6	174
Robinson, Fernando A. et al	2¾	Jones's Run	1853	6	146
Robinson, Fernando A. et al	70	Mud Lick Run	1854	6	151
Robinson, Frederick A.	10	10 Mile Cr.	1846	7	502
Robinson, Henry	400	Teter's Cr.	1787	2	219
Robinson, James	200	Adj. Wm. Martin	1804	5	135
Robinson, John	1,000	Richard's Cr.	1791	3	415
Robinson, Lot O.	45	Lower Coal Lick	1842	7	405
Robinson, McKenney	89	10 Mi. Cr.	1805	5	163
Robinson, Samuel et al	237	Bingamon's Cr.	1844	7	442
Robinson, William	318	Mud Lick Run	1800	5	9
Robinson, William	1,000	Robinson's Run	1786	2	49
Robinson, William	300	Wts. West Fork	1786	2	50
Robinson, William	30	Big Indian Run	1844	7	445
Robinson, William	140	Wts. West Fork	1786	1	597
Robinson, William	366	Mud Lick Run	1786	1	598
Robinson, William	357	Simpson Cr.	1786	1	602
Robinson, William	700	Bingamon's Cr.	1786	1	603
Robinson, William	400	Wts. West Fork	1786	1	604
Robinson, William Jr.	50	Big Indian Run	1838	7	313

Name of Grantee	Acres	Local Description	Year	Book	Page
Robison—or Robinson, Robson					
Robison, James	184	Buffalo Cr.	1825	6	26
Robson, William	257	Simpson's Cr.	1795	4	186
Roderbaugh, Adam	47	Coon's Run	1837	7	168
Rodgers, Rhodom	57	Jane's Run	1816	3	573
Roe, John	23¾	Lambert's Run	1829	6	83
Roe, Walter	1,600	Wts. Hughes River	1799	4	467
Rogers, Alford	3¾	Caty Lick Run	1852	6	141
Rogers, Alford	30	Robinson's Run	1843	7	435
Rogers, Alfred A. et al	78	Limestone Cr.	1861	6	184
Rogers, Rhodam	104	Jones Run	1801	5	16
Rogers, William et al	400	Mill Cr.	1796	4	270
Rolestone, William (Rolston)	500	10 Mile Cr.	1789	3	184
Rolfe—or Relfe					
Rolfe, John et al	1,000	Wts. Hughes River	1796	4	207
Rolfe, John et al	29,300	Wts. Hughes River	1796	4	241
Root, Joel et al	14,000	Wts. Hughes River	1797	4	227
Roots, Thomas R.	400	Goose Cr.	1799	4	468
Roots, Thomas R.	400	Goose Cr.	1799	4	469
Roots, Thomas R.	400	Goose Cr.	1799	4	470
Roots, Thomas R.	4,000	French Creek	1799	4	471
Rorabaugh—See Radabaugh, Roderbaugh, Rohrbaugh, Royabaugh					
Rorhbaugh, Anthony	140	Turkey Run	1816	3	577
Ross, John	5,000	West Fork	1786	1	171
Ross, John	5,000	Stonecoal Creek	1786	1	172
Rowel, Daniel	10	2nd Isl. below mth. lit. Kanawha	1798	4	427
Rowel, Daniel	17	3rd. Isl. below mth. lit. Kanawha	1798	4	428
Royabaugh, Adam	47	Coon's Run	1837	7	168
Runnion—or Runyan					
Runnion, Henry	400	Wts. West Fork	1786	2	34
Runnion, William	395	Sycamore Creek	1786	1	594
Runyan—See Runnion					
Runyan, Henry	327	Bent of the River Cr.	1786	2	105
Runyan, Henry	100	Little Buffalo Cr.	1786	1	440
Runyan, Henry	182	Coburn's Cr.	1787	2	480
Runyan, Henry	200	Buffalo Creek	1787	2	512
Runyan, Henry	400	Lost Creek	1786	1	595
Rush, George	1,000	Freeman's Cr.	1788	3	48
Russell, Solomon et al (Fussell)	250	Sand Run	1787	3	169
Ryan, Michael	2,000	Middle Fork	1786	2	15
Ryan, Michael	2,000	Middle Fork	1786	2	16
Ryan, Michael	2,000	Middle Fork	1786	2	17
Ryan, Michael	2,000	Middle Fork	1786	2	18
Ryan, Michael	2,000	Middle Fork	1786	2	19
Ryan, Michael	2,000	Tygert's V. R.	1786	2	33
Ryan, Michael	2,000	Middle Fork	1786	2	95
Ryan, Michael	2,000	Valley River	1786	1	386
Ryan, Michael	1,000	Middle Fork	1786	1	575
Ryan, Michael	2,000	Middle Fork	1786	1	576
Ryan, Michael	1,000	Middle Fork	1786	1	577
Ryan, Michael	2,000	Middle Fork	1786	1	578
Ryan, Michael	1,000	Middle Fork	1786	1	579
Ryan, Michael	2,000	Middle Fork	1786	1	581
Ryon, See Ryan					
Sadler, Henry	850	Wilson Mill Run	1788	3	144
Sandy, John	50	Teverbaugh's Cr.	1838	7	248
Sandy, Vincent A.	180	Whetstone Camp Run	1835	7	98
Sandy, William A.	20	West Fork River	1835	7	71
Sandy, William A.	65	Bingamon's Cr.	1835	7	92
Sandy, William A.	195	Teverbaugh's Cr.	1835	7	93
Sapp, John Jr. (Sap)	8	Sapp Run	1836	7	110

Name of Grantee	Acres	Local Description	Year	Book	Page
Sapp, John (Sap)	23	Booth's Cr.	1819	6	251
Saxton—See Sexton					
Say—See Lay, Loy					
Say, Benjamin Dr.	2,500	Wts. of Elk	1786	1	344
Say, Benjamin Dr.	4,000	Bond's Creek	1786	1	206
Sayers—See Sayre, Seayrs, Sears					
Sayers, Jedediah	600	Mitchell's Run	1824	6	11
Sayers, Sarah et al Heirs	237	Bingamon Cr.	1819	6	255
Sayers, Sarah et al Heirs	100	Long Run	1819	6	256
Sayre, Benjamin	200	Arnold's Creek	1825	6	29
Sayre, Daniel	219	Wts. West Fork	1796	4	217
Sayre, Jedediah	200	Pleasant Cr.	1796	4	273
Sayre, Levi	64	Pleasant Cr.	1832	6	98
Sayre, Solomon et al Heirs	100	Arnold's Cr.	1842	7	411
Scheneizel, George	1,682	Wts. Valley River	1787	3	196
Scheneizel, George	1,682	Tygert's V. R.	1787	2	349
Schneider—Shneider, Snider, Snyder, Snydor					
Schoonover, Henry	124	Wts. Lit. Kanawha	1820	6	220
Schoonover, Henry	176	Sand Fork	1816	5	274
Scott, David	500	Wts. Lit. Kanawha	1800	5	31
Scott, David	500	Wts. West Fork	1800	5	46
Scott, David	400	Salt Lick Cr.	1789	3	262
Scott, David	400	Salt Lick Cr.	1789	3	263
Scott, David	500	Salt Lick Cr.	1800	4	558
Scott, Joseph	400	Goose Creek	1797	4	336
Scott, Moses	400	Stewart's Run	1803	5	110
Scott, Moses	46	Stewart's Run	1802	5	191
Sears—See Sayers, Sayre, Seayrs					
Sears, Jedediah	600	Mitchell's Run	1824	6	11
Sears, Sarah et al Heirs	100	Coon's Run	1816	3	560
Sears,Sarah et al Heirs	52	Robinson's Run	1816	3	561
Sears, Sarah et al Heirs	260	West Fork	1817	3	587
Seas, Michael (Cease)	38	Homer's Run	1824	6	9
Seayrs, Jedediah	600	Mitchell's Run	1824	6	11
Sedden, Joseph D. et al	30,000	Wts. Lit. Kanawha	1795	4	160
See—or Lee; also Lea					
See, George	218	Tygert's V. R.	1787	2	448
Sees, Jeremiah	22	Booth's Cr.	1854	6	165
Selden, Joseph D. et al	30,000	Wts. Lit. Kanawha	1795	4	160
Sells, Benjamin	240	Ben's Run	1796	4	269
Sexton—See Saxton					
Sexton, Charles	590	Buffalo Cr.	1791	3	372
Sexton, Meshack	4,000	Middle Fork	1796	4	285
Sexton, Mesheck	400	Stony River	1785	1	44
Sexton, Mesheck	250	Adj. his No. 2	1786	1	246
Sexton, Mesheck	250	Stone Coal Run	1786	1	291
Sexton, Mesheck	800	Stone Coal Run	1786	1	292
Sexton, Mesheck	600	Elk Creek	1786	1	295
Sexton, Mesheck	250	Adj. his No. 3	1786	1	365
Sexton, Mesheck	250	Adj. J. Deals	1786	1	391
Seyers, Jedediah	600	Mitchell's Run	1824	6	11
Shafer—See Shaver					
Shafer, Ann et al Heirs	100	Coon Run	1816	3	560
Shafer, Ann et al Heirs	52	Robinson's Run	1816	3	561
Shafer, Ann et al Heirs	260	West Fork	1817	3	587
Shahan, Richard	200	10 Mile Cr.	1834	7	55
Shallerop—See Shalleross					
Shalleross, Joseph	1,000	Wts. of Elk R.	1787	2	205
Shanklin, Elizabeth	243½	Coburn's Run	1800	5	1
Shannon, Gamble	80	Middle Isl. Cr.	1837	7	176
Sharp, Aaron	50	Wts. West Fork	1826	6	43
Sharp, Aaron	65	Helen's Run	1836	7	127
Sharp, Aaron	94	Gray's Run	1821	6	200

Name of Grantee	Acres	Local Description	Year	Book	Page
Sharp, Uriah	100	Bingamon's Cr.	1835	7	90
Shaver—See Shafer					
Shaver, Ann et al Heirs	237	Bingamon Cr.	1819	6	255
Shaver, Ann et al Heirs	100	Long Run	1819	6	256
Shaver, William Jr.	12	Tygert's V. R.	1834	7	47
Shaw, Samuel	200	Lost Run	1788	3	116
Shepherd, David	600	Round Bottom	1787	2	119
Shepherd, David	400	Wts. Lit. Kanawha	1787	2	258
Shepherd, Hozad (or Hazel) et al	30,000	Wts. Lit. Kanawha	1795	4	160
Shepherd, John M.	1,000	Buckley's Run	1786	1	301
Sherwood, Isaac et al	20,000	Wts. Hughes River	1797	4	372
Sherwood, Samuel & Matthew et al	20,000	Wts. Hughes River	1797	4	372
Sherwood, Stephen	600	Simpson's Cr.	1787	2	66
Sherwood, Stephen	600	Laurel Cr.	1788	3	122
Sherwood, Stephen	900	Sand Fork	1788	3	124
Sherwood, Stephen	210	Simpson's Cr.	1787	2	155
Sherwood, Stephen	524	Simpson Cr.	1787	2	208
Shewman, Joseph	100	Dent's Run	1831	6	90
Shields, John et al Trustee	5,000	Wts. Lit. Kanawha	1786	1	193
Shields, John et al Trustee	5,000	Wts. Lit. Kanawha	1786	1	194
Shields, John et al Trustee	5,000	Wts. of Elk	1786	1	195
Shields, John et al Trustee	5,000	Wts. of Elk	1786	1	196
Shields, John et al Trustee	5,000	Glady Fork	1786	1	197
Shields, John et al Trustee	2,000	Wts. Hughes River	1786	1	198
Shields, John et al Trustee	2,000	Wts. Hughes River	1786	1	199
Shields, John et al Trustee	2,000	Wts. Lit. Kanawha	1786	1	200
Shields, John et al Trustee	3,000	Sand Fork	1786	1	201
Shields, John et al Trustee	5,000 (2,000)	Richard's Cr.	1786	1	243
Shields, John et al Trustee	2,000	Wts. Lit. Kanawha	1786	1	244
Shields, John et al Trustee	2,000	Wts. Hughes River	1786	1	279
Shields, John et al Trustee	10,000	Holley Fork	1786	1	283
Shields, John et al Trustee	10,000	Holley Fork	1786	1	284
Shields, John et al Trustee	2,000	Richard's Cr.	1786	1	285
Shields, John et al Trustee	2,000	Wts. Hughes R.	1786	1	286
Shields, John et al Trustee	2,000	Wts. Hughes River	1786	1	306
Shields, John et al Trustee	2,000	Spruce Creek	1786	1	307
Shields, John et al Trustee	2,000	Buzzard's Cr.	1786	1	308
Shinn, Aaron	15	Shinn's Run	1819	6	250
Shinn, Benjamin	400	Mud Lick Run	1788	3	34
Shinn, Clement	50	Big Rock Camp	1823	6	4
Shinn, Clement	180	Shinn's Run	1801	5	92
Shinn, Clement	100	Rock Camp Run	1838	7	249
Shinn, Clement	26¼	West Fork	1817	3	589
Shinn, Clement et al	295	Lost Run	1847	7	517
Shinn, Edward	50	10 Mile Cr.	1823	6	1
Shinn, Francis	87	10 Mile Cr.	1834	7	63
Shinn, Isaac	70	Simpson's Cr.	1799	4	452
Shinn, Isaac Jr.	100	Elk Run	1823	6	32
Shinn, Jeremiah	14	Lost Run	1859	6	175
Shinn, Jonathan	57	Shinn's Run	1801	5	61
Shinn, Joseph & Riley	18	Catfish Run	1847	7	516
Shinn, Levi	607	Wts. West Fork	1791	3	375
Shinn, Levi	397	Bingamon's Cr.	1786	1	570
Shinn, Moses	9½	Bingamon's Cr.	1853	6	144
Shinn, Moses	150	Lit. Rock Camp	1822	6	219
Shinn, Moses	32	Bingamon's Cr.	1842	7	406
Shinn, Moses et al	350	Mud Lick Run	1809	5	212
Shinn, Restore	50	Rock Camp Run	1838	7	250
Shinn, Samuel & Isaac	626	Simpson's Cr.	1799	4	458
Shinn, Samuel Jr. & George	200	Rock Camp Run	1819	6	249
Shinn, Samuel Jr. & George	122	10 Mi. Cr.	1819	6	252
Shinn, Solomon	63	Mud Lick Run	1834	7	52

Name of Grantee	Acres	Local Description	Year	Book	Page
Smith, John	1,000	Worthington Cr.	1790	3	320
Smith, Joseph	400	Simpson's Cr.	1796	4	317
Smith, Josiah P. & J. L.	73	Ned's Lick Run	1847	7	523
Smith, Josiah P. & J. L.	70	Rock Camp Run	1847	7	524
Smith, Mark	122	Stone Coal Cr.	1809	5	211
Smith, Peter	136	Eisner's Run	1786	2	103
Smith, Samuel	234	Thompson's Run	1793	4	28
Smith, Samuel	1,000	Cedar Creek	1788	3	60
Smith, Samuel	1,200	Wts. Hughes River	1795	4	172
Smith, Samuel	400	Simpson's Cr.	1790	3	364
Smith, Samuel	236	Simpson's Cr.	1790	3	365
Smith, Samuel	2,000	Wts. Buckhannon R.	1793	3	519
Smith, Samuel D.	92	Grass Run	1850	6	115
Smith, Samuel D.	430	Little Rock Camp Run	1848	7	536
Smith, Samuel D. et al	298	Grass Run	1848	7	531
Smith, Samuel Jr.	1,000	Cedar Cr.	1788	3	62
Smith, Samuel Jr.	1,000	Cedar Cr.	1788	3	63
Smith, Samuel Jr.	1,000	Cedar Cr.	1788	3	64
Smith, Samuel Jr.	1,000	Cedar Cr.	1788	3	65
Smith, Samuel Jr.	1,000	Vincent's Cr.	1788	3	66
Smith, Samuel Jr.	1,000	Cedar Cr.	1788	3	67
Smith, Samuel Jr.	1,000	Cedar Cr.	1788	3	68
Smith, Samuel Jr.	1,000	Cedar Cr.	1788	3	69
Smith, Samuel Sr. (or Jr.)	1,000	Vincent Cr.	1788	3	61
Smith, William	100	Adj. his own	1786	2	89
Smith, William A.	2,000	Granny's Cr.	1789	3	215
Smith, William S.	2,000	Wts. of Hughes R.	1795	4	156
Smyth, Smith, Smythe					
Smyth, Richard (Smith)	500	Tygert's V. R.	1795	4	105
Smyth, Richard	7,000	Wts. Cheat River	1795	4	79
Smyth, Richard	7,000	Wts. Cheat River	1795	4	80
Smyth, Richard	2,000	Leading Cr.	1795	4	81
Smyth, Richard	1,155	Wts. Cheat River	1795	4	82
Smyth, Richard	1,781	Wts. of Cheat	1795	4	83
Smyth, Richard	500	Tygert's V. R.	1795	4	97
Smyth, Richard	500	Tygert's V. R.	1795	4	98
Smyth, Richard	500	Tygert's V. R.	1795	4	99
Smyth, Richard	500	Wts. Cheat River	1795	4	100
Smyth, Richard	500	Wts. of Cheat	1795	4	101
Smyth, Richard	500	Wts. of Cheat	1795	4	102
Smyth, Richard	500	Wts. Tygert's V.	1795	4	103
Smyth, Richard	500	Tygert's V. R.	1795	4	104
Smyth, Richard	500	Tygert's V. R.	1795	4	106
Smyth, Richard	500	Tygert's V. R.	1795	4	107
Smyth, Richard	5,015	Barker's Mill Rn.	1795	4	130
Smyth, Richard	7,000	Wts. Leading Cr.	1795	4	131
Smyth, Richard	1,000	Wts. Leading Cr.	1795	4	132
Smyth, Richard	9,431	Wts. Cheat River	1795	4	133
Smyth, Richard	8,306¼	Wts. Cheat R.	1795	4	134
Smyth, Richard	7,000	Wts. Cheat River	1789	4	135
Smyth, Richard	3,458	Leading Cr.	1795	4	136
Smyth, Richard	3,873	Wts. Cheat River	1795	4	137
Smyth, Richard	1,591	Tygert's V. R.	1795	4	138
Smyth, Richard	1,000	Wts. Cheat River	1795	4	139
Smyth, Richard	500	Wts. Cheat River	1795	4	145
Smyth, Richard	500	Tygert's V. R.	1795	4	146
Smyth, Richard	500	Wts. Cheat River	1795	4	147
Smyth, Richard	500	Wts. Cheat River	1795	4	148
Smyth, Richard	500	Wts. Cheat River	1795	4	149
Smyth, Richard	500	Wts. of Cheat R.	1795	4	150
Smyth, Richard	500	Tygert's V. R.	1795	4	151
Smyth, Richard	500	Tygert's V. R.	1795	4	152
Smyth, Richard	500	Tygert's V. R.	1795	4	153

Name of Grantee	Acres	Local Description	Year	Book	Page
Stackhouse, Isaac	400	Thompson's Cr.	1787	2	476
Stackpole, Richard	115	Teverbaugh's Cr.	1838	7	317
Stallman, Lewis	250	Leading Creek	1812	5	251
Stanley, Amgi et al	14,000	Wts. Hughes River	1797	4	227
Starkey, Benjamin	160	Lick Run	1845	7	499
Statler—or Stutler					
Statzer, Jacob	400	Hughes Run	1797	4	332
Stealey, Jacob et al	650	Murphy's Run	1816	3	567
Stealey, John Jr.	2¼	Elk Creek	1816	3	566
Steeckle, Abraham	77	Wts. Cheat R.	1788	3	93
Stephens—See Stevens					
Stephens, Andrew	60	Booth's Cr.	1817	3	590
Stephens, Richard	1,000	Sandy Creek	1798	4	362
Stevens—or Stephens					
Stevens, John	200	Sycamore Cr.	1786	2	48
Stewart, George	400	Simpson's Cr.	1786	2	92
Stewart, Henry W. et al	20,000	Wts. Hughes River	1797	4	372
Stewart, James	57	Hacker's Cr.	1792	3	499
Stewart, James et al	20,000	Wts. Hughes River	1797	4	372
Stewart, John L. (or S.)	32	Coon's Run	1837	7	167
Stewart, Robert G.	80	Buffalo Cr.	1834	7	60
Stewart, William	2,000	Wts. Hughes River	1786	1	189
Stewart, William	5,000	Wts. of Elk	1786	1	190
Stewart, William	5,000	Holley River	1786	1	191
Stewart, William	1,135	Salt Lick Cr.	1786	1	192
Stewart, William	2,000	Wts. of Hughes	1786	1	241
Stewart, William	2,000	Wts. Hughes River	1786	1	242
Stewart, William	5,000	Sand Fork	1786	1	280
Stewart, William	5,000	Wts. of Elk	1786	1	281
Stewart, William	5,000	Sand Fork	1786	1	282
Stewart, William	5,000	Wts. of Elk	1786	1	303
Stewart, William	5,000	Wts. of Elk	1786	1	304
Stewart, William	5,000	Wts. of Elk	1786	1	305
Stewart, William	250	Murphy's Run	1786	1	309
Stewart, William	1,840	Wts. Lit. Kanawha	1797	4	328
Stewart, William	1,238	Buffalo Cr.	1790	3	355
Stewart, William	1,375	Wts. Lit. Kanawha	1786	1	550
Stier, Circus H.	60	Johnson's Fork	1860	6	182
Stier, Madison et al	78	Limestone Cr.	1861	6	184
Stilwell, John	120	Meat House Fork	1837	7	174
Stilwell, John	60	Mid. Isl. Cr.	1837	7	175
Stokely, John	250	Briscoe's Run	1797	4	350
Storms, Jacob	93	Teverbaugh's Run	1809	5	214
Stotts, Elijah	300	Wts. West Fork	1788	3	39
Stotts, Joseph	200	Wts. West Fork	1787	2	514
Stout, Amos H.	175	Buffalo Cr.	1838	7	318
Stout, Benjamin	45	Barnett's Run	1851	6	130
Stout, Benjamin	8	Smith's Run	1858	6	169
Stout, Daniel	850	Brusky Fork	1786	1	392
Stout, Daniel	150	Brusky Fork	1786	1	395
Stout, Daniel	200	Simpson's Cr.	1799	4	451
Stout, Gabriel	50	Buffalo Cr.	1838	7	251
Stout, Hezekiah	40	Cabin Run	1821	6	198
Stout, Hezekiah	70	Sycamore Cr.	1821	6	199
Stout, Hezekiah	50	Stewart's Cr.	1816	5	276
Stout, James	2,000	Laurel Run	1787	2	439
Stout, Job	200	Wts. Hughes R.	1832	7	1
Stout, John W.	150	Barn's Run	1844	7	446
Stout, Jonathan	300	Tygert's Valley	1787	2	469
Stout, Jonathan	300	Elk Creek	1792	3	504
Stout, Jonathan	200	Hacker's Cr.	1792	3	505
Stout, Joseph	1,260	Wts. West Fork	1795	4	168
Stout, Joseph Jr.	185	Tom's Fork	1832	7	4

Name of Grantee	Acres	Local Description	Year	Book	Page
Thompson, Henry	400	Fox Grape Cr.	1799	4	440
Thompson, Henry	186	Tygert's V. R.	1799	4	442
Thompson, Hugh	1,700	Wts. Cheat River	1788	3	74
Thompson, Hugh	400	Caty Lick Run	1787	2	212
Thompson, Hugh	400	Rock Camp Run	1787	2	216
Thompson, Hugh	1,436	Gnatty Cr.	1787	2	520
Thompson, Israel	80	Bingamon's Cr.	1835	7	73
Thompson, Israel	640	Hacker's Cr.	1787	2	211
Thompson, Israel	2,187	Wts. Buckhannon R.	1787	2	220
Thompson, Israel	1,150	Wts. Buckhannon R.	1787	2	221
Thompson, James	400	Foxgrape Cr.	1787	2	409
Thompson, Jethro	200	Lost Creek	1796	4	267
Thompson, John	400	Fox Grape Cr.	1799	4	441
Thompson, William	400	Fox Grape Cr.	1786	2	32
Thompson, William	144	Adj. his own	1786	2	82
Thompson, William	400	Fox Grape Cr.	1786	2	108
Thompson, William	100	Hacker's Cr.	1798	4	426
Thompson, William	400	Wts. Tygert's V.	1792	3	502
Thomson—or Thompson					
Thomson, Eli	5,000	Cedar Creek	1789	3	159
Thomson, Hugh	400	10 Mile Cr.	1787	2	214
Thorn—or Thorne					
Thorn, Ashville B.	12	Wts. West Fork	1860	6	183
Thorn, Ashville B. et al	8½	Jones Run	1852	6	140
Thorne, Ashville B.	20	10 Mi. Cr.	1851	6	126
Thornhill, William	88	Hacker's Cr.	1787	2	473
Thornton, Robert	1,000	Wts. Lit. Kanawha	1799	4	516
Tichenal, David (Tichanal)	75	Wts. West Fork	1834	7	39
Titmus, Samuel	5,000	Wts. Hughes River	1786	1	179
Tobin, Thomas	500	Wts. Hughes River	1787	2	146
Toler, Cornelius et al	1,000	Barkeley's Run	1786	1	245
Towers, George	84 (184)	Elk Creek	1799	4	485
Townsend, James	163	Stewart's Cr.	1819	6	246
Townsend, James	50	Sand Fork	1816	5	272
Triplett, Hedgeman et al	126	Adj. J. Beeson	1799	4	528
Triplett, Hedgman	50	Wts. West Fork	1801	5	58
Triplett, Robert	400	Walker's Cr.	1798	4	475
Triplett, William et al	181	Muskingum Island	1798	4	474
Tucker, John	380	Booth's Cr.	1786	2	37
Tucker, John	400	Booth Creek	1789	3	188
Tucker, John	90	Booth's Cr.	1789	3	266
Tucker, John	2,000	Wts. Steer Cr.	1797	4	304
Tucker, John	2,000	Lee's Cr.	1797	4	308
Tucker, John	2,000	Wts. Steer Cr.	1797	4	309
Tucker, John	2,000	Wts. Steer Cr.	1797	4	310
Tucker, John	2,000	Wts. Steer Cr.	1797	4	311
Tucker, John et al	2,000	Wts. West Fork	1797	4	398
Tucker, Samuel	40	Booth Cr.	1790	3	337
Tucker, William	250	Wts. Hughes River	1788	3	18
Tucker, William Jr.	400	Booth's Cr.	1797	4	327
Tucker, William Jr.	280	Booth Creek	1787	2	422
Tucker, William Sr.	400	Booth's Cr.	1791	3	376
Tucker, William Sr.	396	Booth's Cr.	1786	1	559
Turner, George	1,000	Buzzard Creek	1798	4	411
Turner, George	2,000	Crow's Creek	1797	4	412
Turner, George	1,000	Richard's Cr.	1798	4	413
Turner, George	7,000	Sand Fork	1797	4	414
Turner, George	2,000	Wts. Hughes River	1788	2	545
Tyson, Enos	200	Buffalo Cr.	1801	5	56
Tyson, Enos	860	Glade Run	1788	3	76
Tyson, Enos	400	Wts. Elk River	1791	3	408
Tyson, Enos	493	Sand Run	1792	3	506
Usher, Thomas & Abraham	1,400	Bull Creek	1788	3	119

Name of Grantee	Acres	Local Description	Year	Book	Page
Whiteside, Peter	5,000	Big Sandy Run	1786	1	178
Whiteside, Peter	2,000	10 Mile Creek	1786	1	229
Whiteside, Peter	2,000	10 Mile Creek	1786	1	230
Whiteside, Peter	1,000	10 Mile Creek	1786	1	232
Whitler, Jacob	1,000	Richard's Cr.	1794	4	53
Wickware, John	1,000	Elk Run	1796	4	373
Wickwire, Alpheus	400	Tygert's V.	1787	2	75
Wickwire, John	150	Tygert's V. R.	1802	5	204
Wiley, Robert et al	180	Elk Creek	1834	7	31
Wiley, Robert et al	175	Wts. Hughes R.	1834	7	66
Wiley, Robert Jr. et al	440	Elk Creek	1834	7	40
Wiley, Robert Jr. et al	1,090	Gnatty Cr.	1834	7	58
Wiley, Robert Jr. et al	645	Stout's Run	1834	7	67
Wilkins, John	150	Tygert's V. R.	1809	5	218
Wilkinson, Gabriel	400	Simpson's Cr.	1799	4	438
Wilkinson, Joseph	400	Simpson's Creek	1786	1	605
Wilkinson, Samuel	393	Elk Creek	1786	2	45
Wilkinson, Thomas	148	Simpson's Cr.	1800	5	63
Wilkinson, Thomas	400	Simpson's Cr.	1786	1	268
Williams, Elisha	2,000	Middle Fork	1787	2	369
Williams, Mark	100	10 Mile Cr.	1838	7	191
Williams, Mark	100	10 Mile Cr.	1846	7	506
Williams, Nathaniel et al	30,000	Wts. Lit. Kanawha	1795	4	160
Williams, Thomas & Jeremiah	29	Caty Lick Run	1844	7	458
Williams, William	25	Caty Lick Run	1827	6	69
Williamson, John	1,000	Mill Creek	1787	2	340
Williamson, John	1,000	Mill Cr.	1787	2	341
Williamson, John	1,000	Mill Cr.	1787	2	342
Williamson, John	1,000	Adj. James Caldwell	1787	2	343
Williamson, John	1,000	Adj. James Caldwell	1787	2	344
Williamson, John	1,000	Adj. James Caldwell	1787	2	345
Williamson, John	1,000	Burch Creek	1787	2	346
Williamson, John	1,000	Wts. of Elk	1787	2	380
Williamson, John	1,000	Mill Creek	1787	2	381
Williamson, John	1,000	Wts. of Elk	1787	2	383
Williamson, John	1,000	Wts. of Elk	1787	2	384
Williamson, John	1,000	Mill Cr.	1787	2	385
Williamson, John	1,000	Wts. of Elk	1787	2	386
Williamson, John	1,000	Birch River	1787	2	414
Williamson, John	1,000	Adj. Caldwell's No. 9	1787	2	415
Williamson, John	1,000	Adj. J. Caldwell	1787	2	416
Williamson, John	1,000	Wts. of Elk	1793	3	510
Williamson, John	1,000	Birch Creek	1792	3	511
Williamson, John	1,000	Adj. Caldwell's No. 17	1793	3	512
Williamson, John	1,000	Adj. Caldwell's No. 16	1792	3	513
Williamson, John	1,000	Adj. his No. 14th Entry	1793	3	514
Williamson, John	1,000	Wts. Birch	1793	3	534
Williamson, John	1,000	Wts. of Elk	1793	3	535
Williamson, John	1,000	Adj. Caldwell's No. 18	1793	3	536
Williamson, John	1,000	Adj. his No. 22nd	1793	3	537
Willmoth, Thomas	279	Wts. Cheat	1785	1	37
Wills, John L. (or S.)	3,500	Tygert's V. R.	1791	3	414
Wilson, Benjamin	200	Wts. Tygert's R.	1786	2	86
Wilson, Benjamin	1,010 sq. ft.	Clarksburg	1850	6	118
Wilson, Benjamin	13¾	Elk Creek	1852	6	143
Wilson, Benjamin	500	West Fork	1815	5	268
Wilson, Benjamin	9¾	Simpson's Cr.	1817	6	274
Wilson, Benjamin	124	Cheat River Mt.	1787	2	475
Wilson, Benjamin	175	Eberman's Cr.	1786	1	515
Wilson, Benjamin	799	Wts. Lit. Kanawha	1786	1	548
Wilson, Benjamin	174	Wts. Lit. Kanawha	1786	1	564
Wilson, Benjamin	300	Tygert Valley R.	1786	1	574
Wilson, Benjamin et al	88	Brown's Cr.	1851	6	135

Name of Grantee	Acres	Local Description	Year	Book	Page
Young, Samuel	5,000	Salt Lick Cr.	1786	1	427
Young, Samuel	2,000	Crow's Creek	1786	1	449
Young, Samuel	1,000	Crow's Creek	1786	1	453
Zone, Martin	297	Lost Creek	1791	3	399
Zorn, Martin	297	Lost Creek	1791	3	399

JACKSON COUNTY

Alexander, George	50	Sand Creek	1842	1	121
Alexander, William	10	Letart Falls	1840	1	32
Allen, Sylvester	80	Sandy Cr.	1852	1	438
Anderson, Samuel	50	Cow Run	1842	1	62
Armstrong, James	100	Wts. West Fork	1842	1	63
Armstrong, James	175	Mill Creek	1848	1	311
Armstrong, James	115	Reedy Cr.	1851	1	411
Armstrong, M. B.	330	Elk Fork	1850	1	372
Armstrong, M. B.	85	Adj. Geo. W. Smith	1850	1	373
Armstrong, M. B.	160	Elk Fork	1850	1	382
Armstrong, M. B.	190	Elk Fork	1850	1	383
Armstrong, M. B.	140	Elk Fork	1851	1	422
Baker, James	370	Hanshaw's Run	1850	1	400
Bee, Ephraim	50	Reedy Creek	1841	1	54
Bee, Ephraim	100	Reedy Creek	1841	1	55
Bee, Ephraim	50	Reedy Creek	1842	1	96
Bee, Ephraim	80	Reedy Creek	1842	1	97
Bee, Ephraim	165	Big Sandy Creek	1842	1	98
Bee, Ephraim	100	Reedy Cr.	1842	1	110
Bee, Ephraim	50	Reedy Cr.	1842	1	111
Bee, Ephraim	45	Big Run	1842	1	112
Bee, Ephraim	100	Big Sand Cr.	1845	1	208
Bee, Ephraim	100	Reedy Creek	1847	1	261
Bee, Ephraim	140	Reedy Creek	1847	1	262
Bee, Ephraim	265	Cain's Run	1847	1	263
Bee, Ephraim	100	Reedy Creek	1847	1	268
Bee, Ephraim	500	Reedy Creek	1859	2	470
Bee, Ephraim	467	Middle Fork	1855	1	472
Bee, Ephraim	300	Reedy Creek	1855	1	476
Bee, Ephraim	150	Middle Fork	1847	1	285
Bee, Ephraim	100	Reedy Cr.	1847	1	286
Bee, Ephraim	150	Reedy Cr.	1856	1	501
Bee, Ephraim et al	415	Spring Cr.	1852	1	442
Bee, Ephraim et al	400	Spring Cr.	1852	1	443
Bee, Ephraim et al	400	Middle Fork	1855	1	471
Bee, Ephraim et al	120	Middle Fork	1855	1	474
Bee, Ephraim et al	985	Reedy Creek	1855	1	477
Bee, Ephraim et al	1,000	Reedy Creek	1856	1	500
Bee, Ephraim et al	380	Colt Run	1856	1	510
Bennett, Joseph	100	Cow Run	1847	1	258
Blosser, Robert	100	Reedy Creek	1857	1	521
Board, George	198	Parchment Fork	1846	1	210
Board, George	190	Elk Fork	1849	1	367
Board, George	35	Mill Cr.	1856	1	487
Board, George	85	Mill Creek	1857	1	530
Board, John	93	Frozen Camp Fork	1851	1	405
Board, Thomas	70	Mill Cr.	1847	1	283
Boggess, George W.	100	Pocatalico	1856	1	499
Boggs, Charles C.	30	Reedy Cr.	1842	1	103
Boggs, John L.	70	Reedy Creek	1842	1	99

Name of Grantee	Acres	Local Description	Year	Book	Page
Boggs, William	330	Spring Cr.	1847	1	282
Boggs, William	100	Spring Creek	1851	1	435
Bollen, Joseph	158	Big Mill Creek	1856	1	481
Bonnett, John A.	380	Parchment Fork	1847	1	252
Bonnett, Nicholas H.	24½	Adj. Peter Cleek	1851	1	403
Bowles, Mason	94	Mill Creek	1841	1	38
Bozzle, C. M.	150	Parchment Fk.	1859	2	466
Bozzle, C. M. et al	434	13 Mi. Creek	1859	2	464
Bozzle, Gilbert Jr.	550	Parchment Fork	1851	1	432
Brown, Joseph	70	Sand Creek	1844	1	173
Buckalew, Elias	44½	Mill Creek	1856	1	512
Bumgardner—or Bumgarner					
Bumgardner, Jacob	35	Sand Creek	1852	1	440
Bumgarner, Jacob	30	Reedy Cr.	1841	1	49
Bumgarner, Jacob	70	Reedy Cr.	1844	1	187
Bumgarner, Jacob	50	Reedy Cr.	1848	1	318
Bush, George F.	150	Spring Cr.	1845	1	203
Cain, Alfred	50	Reedy Creek	1848	1	333
Cain, Gamalial et al	125	Chestnut Run	1849	1	345
Cain, John W.	75	Cain's Run	1848	1	332
Calvert, Nathan S.	250	Buckeye Fork	1844	1	143
Carney, Charles	158	Mill Creek	1847	1	249
Carney, Charles	235	Mill Cr.	1847	1	289
Carney, Charles	228	Grass Lick Fork	1848	1	301
Carney, Charles	200	Elk Fork	1848	1	319
Carney, Charles	225	Sycamore Fork	1849	1	344
Carney, Charles	150	Parchment Fork	1851	1	421
Carney, Charles	88	Elk Fork	1856	1	495
Carney, Charles	122½	Elk Fork	1856	1	504
Carney, Enoch	190	Moses' Fork	1847	1	290
Carney, Jesse	25	Parchment Fork	1850	1	378
Carney, Jesse	170	Bear Fork	1850	1	385
Carney, Jesse et al	80	Mill Cr.	1847	1	287
Carney, Weeden	100	Adj. Jess Carney	1844	1	172
Casto, B. F.	40½	Gray's Lick Fk.	1859	2	465
Casto, D. G.	431	Bear Fork	1859	2	467
Casto, David D.	90	John's Run	1846	1	228
Casto, David G.	58	Mill Creek	1852	1	441
Casto, David G.	68	Big Mill Cr.	1855	1	463
Casto, David G.	65	Mill Creek	1856	1	498
Casto, David L.	73½	Bear Fork	1859	2	468
Casto, E. H.	71	Parchment Fork	1855	1	457
Casto, Elmer (Elmore) H.	50	Cox's Fork	1844	1	155
Casto, Elmore H.	100	Cox's Fork	1842	1	64
Casto, Elmore H.	50	Cox's Fork	1847	1	288
Casto, Elmore H.	72	Adj. J. Whitecotton	1850	1	390
Casto, George	56	Mill Creek	1842	1	86
Casto, George Jr.	100	Mill Creek	1850	1	384
Casto, J. J. et al	434	13 Mi. Creek	1859	2	464
Casto, James et al	80	Mill Cr.	1847	1	287
Casto, James C.	80	Mill Cr.	1856	1	493
Casto, John I. (or J.)	100	Mill Creek	1844	1	188
Casto, John M. D.	95	Mill Cr.	1856	1	506
Chancy, Hiram	188	Reedy Cr.	1856	1	509
Chaney, Hiram	188	Reedy Cr.	1856	1	509
Clark, John	100	Parchment Fork	1846	1	211
Cleek, George	100	Parchment Fork	1851	1	424
Cleek, Peter	85	Middle Fork	1842	1	104
Cleek, Peter	150	Laurel Run	1842	1	105
Coleman, Thomas	75	Maise's Bottom	1844	1	145
Coleman, Thomas	120	Washington Run	1844	1	146
Coleman, Thomas	500	Washington Run	1844	1	147
Coleman, Thomas	105	Lit. Sand Cr.	1850	1	375

Name of Grantee	Acres	Local Description	Year	Book	Page
Conrad—See also Coonrod					
Conrad, Peter	48	Reedy Creek	1840	1	33
Coonrod—See also Conrad					
Coonrod, Peter	100	Coonrod's Run	1846	1	219
Coonrod, Peter	50	Coonrod's Run	1847	1	237
Core, A. S.	990	Spring Creek	1853	1	448
Core, Andrew S.	500	Reedy Cr.	1853	1	447
Corley, Reuben B.	396	Turkey Run	1844	1	177
Cottrell, Elijah (Cottrall)	110	Mill Cr.	1848	1	312
Cottrill, Elijah W.	107	Grass Lick Fork	1856	1	513
Cottrill, G. W.	150	18 Mi. Creek	1860	2	473
Cottrill, G. W. & L. L.	90	18 Mi. Creek	1860	2	474
Counts, Isaac	217	Pocatalico	1858	1	540
Cross, Isaac	300	Pond Creek	1844	1	141
Cross, Solomon	82	Cabin Fork	1844	1	139
Cross, Solomon	50	Pond Creek	1844	1	140
Cross, Solomon	150	Pond Creek	1844	1	174
Cunningham, James	837	Bear Fork	1855	1	461
Cunningham, James	895	Wts. Pocatalico	1855	1	462
Curfman, Michael	300	Cain's Run	1846	1	225
Curry, Robert	50	Sand Creek	1835	1	4
Curry, Robert	50	Sand Creek	1835	1	6
Curtis, Lewis	720	Sycamore Fork	1855	1	476
Curtis, Lewis	53	Sycamore Fork	1857	1	528
Curtis, Lewis	30	Sycamore Fork	1857	1	529
Curtis, Lewis et al	1,253	Mill Cr.	1856	1	486
Curtis, Lewis et al	1,953	Pond Creek	1856	1	507
Davis, James	100	Cox's Fork	1847	1	291
Davis, James	190	Cox's Fork	1850	1	420
Davis, James	33	Parchment Fork	1856	1	480
Dawson, Manoah et al	750	Left Hd. Fork	1859	2	461
Dawson, Manoah et al	1,330	18-Mi. Creek	1859	2	462
Debussey, Thomas	110	Pond Creek	1850	1	417
Dennis, Robert D.	80	Peter's Run	1846	1	226
Dernberger, Benjamin (Derenberger)	275	Pond Creek	1849	1	355
Dewees, Samuel	134½	Adj. Solomon Harpole	1849	1	354
Dewees, William	29	Parchment Fork	1842	1	65
Dewees, William	90	Parchment Fork	1848	1	338
Dewees, William	110	Parchment Fork	1848	1	340
Dewitt, Thomas	105	Muse's Bottom	1844	1	186
Dilworth, Anthony	40	Mill Cr.	1851	1	410
Dobson, George W.	300	Crane's Nest Run	1846	1	220
Dryden, John et al	750	Left Hd. Fork	1859	2	461
Dryden, John et al	1,330	18-Mi. Creek	1859	2	462
Duff, John H.	738	Middle Fork	1855	1	479
Enoch, Isaac	50	Hartley's Run	1843	1	132
Enoch, Isaac	100	Reedy Creek	1846	1	221
Enoch, William P.	100	Quilt Fork	1851	1	415
Evans, Ephraim S.	28	Isaac's Run	1848	1	331
Fields, G. W.	238	Flat Fork	1855	1	454
Fisher, John M.	110	Pocatalico Cr.	1846	1	222
Fisher, John M. et al	750	Left Hd. Fork	1859	2	461
Fisher, John M. et al	1,330	18 Mi. Creek	1859	2	462
Fisher, Leonard	168	Middle Fork	1842	1	87
Fisher, Leonard G.	100	Pocatalico	1856	1	503
Fisher, Leonard G.	100	Dudding's Fork	1858	1	543
Fisher, Leonard G.	100	Pocatalico	1858	1	544
Fisher, William	150	Pocatalico	1858	1	535
Fisher, William	102	Dudding's Fork	1858	1	536
Fisher, William Sr.	200	Pocatalico Cr.	1845	1	205
Fitzhugh, Bushrod W.	500	Pond Creek	1850	1	398
Flesher, Demsey	76	Cain's Run	1846	1	218

Name of Grantee	Acres	Local Description	Year	Book	Page
Flesher, Isaac	100	Wts. West Fork	1834	1	2
Flesher, Isaac	5	Opposite Goose Island	1841	1	50
Flinn, John	150	Pond Creek	1844	1	144
Flowers, Alfred	50	Cow Run	1848	1	313
Flowers, Alfred et al	65	Cow Run	1847	1	255
Flowers, Thomas	150	Cow Run	1836	1	11
Flowers, Thomas	50	Cow Run	1842	1	106
Flowers, Thomas	100	Cow Run	1842	1	107
Foglesong, John	38	Grass Lick Fork	1844	1	156
Foglesong, John	57	Grsss Lick Fork	1844	1	157
Ford, James	41	Big Mill Cr.	1849	1	352
Full, Absalom	50	Big Sand Creek	1836	1	12
Full, Absolom	100	Buckeye Fork	1836	1	14
Full, Absolom	25	Big Sand Cr.	1842	1	66
Full, Absolom	25	Big Sand Cr.	1842	1	74
Full, Absolom	75	Sandy Creek	1845	1	196
Full, Absolom (for Reuben Full)	50	Reedy Creek	1836	1	18
Full, Reuben	50	Childers' Fork	1842	1	75
Full, Reuben	102	Childer's Fork	1846	1	224
Gandee, Levi T.	436	Turkey Run	1844	1	179
Gardner, William	187	Lit. Sand Cr.	1844	1	142
Gardner, William	140	Road Fork	1844	1	148
Gardner, William	136	Mall Camp Run	1844	1	175
Gardner, William	240	Lit. Sand Cr.	1844	1	178
Garnes, Joseph	50	Stone Lick Fork	1842	1	76
Garnes, Joseph	50	Stone Lick Fork	1842	1	77
Garnes, Joseph	133	Grass Lick Fork	1856	1	516
Garnes, T. et al	392	Mill Creek	1860	2	471
Given, Henry	127	Reedy Cr.	1846	1	229
Given, Henry	100	Wolfe Pen Run	1847	1	239
Given, Henry	110	Reedy Cr.	1847	1	240
Godfrey, Harry	120	Parchment Fork	1848	1	339
Goff, William R.	190	Spring Cr.	1842	1	78
Good, Francis	358	Middle Fork	1859	1	558
Green—See also Greer					
Green, Edward	50	Mill Creek	1844	1	171
Green, Edward	50	Mill Cr.	1844	1	184
Green, Leonard	600	Grass Lick Fork	1856	1	515
Greer—See also Green					
Greer, John M.	75	Big Horse Run	1849	1	359
Greer, John M.	190	Lit. Spruce Pine	1858	1	551
Hammon, John	190	Middle Fork	1855	1	464
Hanlin, James M.	250	Pond Creek	1842	1	108
Harpold—or Harpole					
Harpold, Solomon	60	John's Run	1844	1	138
Harpold, Solomon	184	Parchment Run	1847	1	242
Harrison, Reuben	100	Pocatalico Cr.	1838	1	25
Harrison, Reuben Jr.	20	Pocatalico	1842	1	67
Harrison, Reuben Jr.	48	Pocatalico	1842	1	68
Harrison, Zebulon	200	18 Mile Cr.	1838	1	24
Harvey, R. T. et al	392	Mill Creek	1860	2	471
Hatcher, Uriah	390	Middle Fork	1859	2	463
Hayward—See Haywood					
Haywood, Joseph (Hayward)	150	Sand Creek	1840	1	30
Haywood, Joseph	50	Sand Creek	1840	1	31
Haywood, Joseph	125	Isaac's Run	1844	1	166
Hickel, G. R. H.	400	Spring Cr.	1853	1	449
Hosher—or Hosier					
Hosher, Frederick	84	Cow Run	1857	1	534
Hosier—or Hosher					
Hosier, Frederick	50	Bee Lick Fork	1847	1	256
Hughes, James	147	Parchment Fork	1847	1	246
Hughes, Job	114½	Cow Run	1847	1	250

Name of Grantee	Acres	Local Description	Year	Book	Page
Lee, Thomas et al	125	Chestnut Run	1849	1	345
Little, David	100	Cow Run	1842	1	69
Litton, Abraham	300	Elk Fork	1850	1	386
Litton, David	196	Elk Fork	1855	1	469
Litton, David	125	Brush Run	1855	1	470
Litton, David	117	Elk Fork	1856	1	494
Lockhart, Isaac	100	Slab Camp Fork	1845	1	198
Mairs, Joseph	40	Cabin Run	1842	1	116
Mairs, Joseph	60	Big Sand Cr.	1842	1	117
Mairs, Joseph	50	Sugar Camp Run	1842	1	122
Mairs, Joseph	100	Straight Fork	1842	1	123
Mairs, Joseph	100	Copper Fork	1842	1	124
Mairs, Joseph	177	Reedy Creek	1842	1	125
Mairs, Joseph	200	Copper Fork	1842	1	126
Mason, Jeptha	50	Parchment Fork	1846	1	232
Mason, Jeptha	25	Parchment Fork	1849	1	357
McDade, Jesse	50	Kessel's Run	1846	1	213
McDade, Samuel	50	Round Knob Run	1847	1	260
McFarland, Ezekiel	60	Goose Island	1845	1	204
McFarland, Ezekiel	70	Turkey Fork	1849	1	362
McFarland, Ezekiel	90	Big Sandy Cr.	1849	1	363
McFarland, Ezekiel	400	Big Sandy Cr.	1849	1	364
McFarland, James C. et al	1,373	Spring Creek	1847	1	279
McFarland, James C. et al	800	Mill Cr.	1847	1	280
McFarland, James C. et al	490	Mill Cr.	1847	1	281
McGraw, Francis	50	Sand Creek	1836	1	15
McGraw, Francis	50	Sand Creek	1841	1	56
McGraw, Francis	25	Brushy Fork	1841	1	57
McKown, John	200	Adj. George Stone	1838	1	28
McMahon, William B. et al	132	Big Sand. Cr	1844	1	163
McMahon, William B. et al	366	Reedy Cr.	1844	1	164
McMahon, William B. et al	131	Cox's Fork	1844	1	193
Middleton, Henry O.	100	Elk Fork	1844	1	149
Middleton, Henry O.	275	Mall Camp Run	1844	1	150
Middleton, Henry O.	300	Nestleroad Fork	1844	1	151
Middleton, Henry O.	150	Elk Fork	1844	1	152
Middleton, Henry O.	625	Billy's Branch	1844	1	153
Middleton, Henry O.	375	Elk Fork	1845	1	199
Middleton, Henry O.	800	Mill Cr	1846	1	233
Middleton, Henry O.	200	Parchment Fork	1846	1	234
Middleton, Henry O.	420	Big Mill Cr.	1847	1	276
Middleton, Henry O.	625	Mill Cr.	1847	1	278
Middleton, Henry O.	300	Mill Cr.	1847	1	292
Middleton, Henry O.	3,400	Reedy Creek	1848	1	307
Middleton, Henry O.	62	Little Mill Cr	1850	1	393
Middleton, Henry O.	240	Mill Creek	1851	1	407
Middleton, Henry O.	1,250	Wts Mill Cr.	1848	1	561
Miller, George S.	225½	Pocatalico	1859	2	458
Mitchell, Robert	100	13 Mile Cr.	1851	1	436
Morrill, D. G.	200	Reedy Creek	1842	1	82
Morrill, Daniel G.	200	Adj. Wm. Gilpin	1841	1	47
Morrill, Daniel G.	100	Reedy Cr	1842	1	60
Morrill, Daniel G.	50	Big Sand Creek	1842	1	100
Morrill, Daniel G.	100	Isaac's Run	1842	1	118
Morrill, Daniel G.	150	Straight Fork	1842	1	119
Morrill, Daniel G.	50	Big Sand Cr.	1846	1	217
Morrill, D. W.	500	Elk Fork	1850	1	392
Morrill, Daniel W.	200	Sycamore Fork	1850	1	387
Morrill, Daniel W.	586½	Mill Cr.	1850	1	391
Neff, Peter	200	Fall Run	1951	1	402
Neff, Peter	720	Mill Creek	1851	1	404
Neff, Peter	780	Parchment Fork	1850	1	416
Neff, Peter	1,500	Mill Creek	1851	1	563

Name of Grantee	Acres	Local Description	Year	Book	Page
Newell, James	62½	Parchment Fork	1844	1	167
O'Conner, Eliza W. et al	879	Reedy Cr.	1857	1	522
O'Conner, Eliza W. et al	150	Reedy Cr.	1857	1	523
O'Conner, Eliza W. et al	700	Reedy. Cr.	1857	1	524
O'Conner, Eliza W. et al	1,000	Reedy Cr.	1857	1	526
O'Conner, Eliza W. et al	753	Reedy Cr.	1857	1	527
Park, Robert	115	Sandy Cr.	1851	1	408
Parker, William W. et al	879	Reedy Creek	1857	1	522
Parker, William W. et al	150	Reedy Cr.	1857	1	523
Parker, William W. et al	700	Reedy Cr.	1857	1	524
Parker, William W. et al	1,000	Reedy Cr.	1857	1	526
Parker, William W. et al	753	Reedy Cr.	1857	1	527
Parson, Charles	200	Mill Cr.	1849	1	350
Parsons, Charles	200	Mill Creek	1860	2	472
Parsons, Charles Sr.	240	Frozen Camp Fork	1850	1	376
Parsons, Charles (son of John)	142	Stone Lick Fork	1845	1	202
Parsons, David W.	168(178)	Mill Creek	1851	1	431
Parsons, George W.	77	Mill Creek	1850	1	379
Parsons, Henry	100	Parchment Fork	1842	1	92
Parsons, Henry	51½	Parchment Fork	1844	1	168
Parsons, Henry	40	Parchment Fork	1848	1	326
Parsons, Joshua	151½	Laurel Fork	1859	2	457
Parsons, Moses	248	Stone Lick Fork	1858	1	552
Parsons, W. W. & Elias	154	Mill Creek	1857	1	532
Parsons, W. W. & Elias	212	Mill Creek	1857	1	533
Parsons, Washington	110	Parchment Fork	1849	1	346
Pfost—See Post					
Pfost, Aaron	100	Stone Lick Fork	1844	1	160
Pfost, Abraham	60	Mill Creek	1847	1	259
Pfost, Abraham	150	Grass Lick Fork	1850	1	369
Pfost, Abraham	55	Grass Lick Fork	1850	1	370
Pfost, Abraham	35	Grass Lick Fork	1850	1	371
Pfost, G. W. et al Heirs	190	Mill Creek	1858	1	553
Pfost, Isaac	48	Grass Lick Fork	1844	1	158
Pfost, Isaac	47	Grass Lick Fork	1844	1	159
Pfost, Isaac	330	Mill Cr.	1847	1	284
Pickrel, Levi Sr.	137½	Reedy Cr.	1842	1	109
Piercy, John	500	Elk Fork	1855	1	466
Piercy, John	272	Wts. Pocatalico	1855	1	467
Piercy, John	105	Frozen Camp Fork	1855	1	468
Post—Also Pfost					
Post, Abraham	50	Grass Lick Fork	1842	1	90
Post, Abraham	25	Grass Lick Fork	1842	1	91
Post, Isaac	44	Grass Lick Fork	1842	1	88
Post, Isaac	40	Grass Lick Fork	1842	1	89
Post, Isaac	240	Mill Creek	1846	1	216
Price, Temperance	140	Parchment Fork	1857	1	525
Pringle, Aaron	100	Grass Lick Fork	1847	1	293
Pringle, John	50	Mill Cr.	1848	1	314
Rader, E. H.	100	Frozen Camp Fork	1856	1	505
Rader, Edward H.	390	Elk Fork	1849	1	366
Rader, Edward H.	375	Frozen Camp Fork	1850	1	388
Rader, Edward H.	61	Elk Fork	1851	1	409
Rader, Edward H.	429	Frozen Camp Fork	1851	1	412
Rader, George W.	400	Mill Creek	1850	1	381
Rader, Michael	25	Mill Cr.	1838	1	29
Rader, Michael	20¼	Mill Creek	1841	1	53
Rains, Thomas	100	Pocatalico	1856	1	517
Rawlings—Rollings, Rollins					
Rawlings, James Sr.	120	Grass Lick Fork	1842	1	93
Rawlings, James Sr.	80	Grass Lick Fork	1842	1	94
Reed, Elihu	190	Sandy Creek	1852	1	437
Reed, Elihu	400	Lit. Sandy Cr.	1852	1	445

Name of Grantee	Acres	Local Description	Year	Book	Page
Reed, Warren	160	Buck Run	1850	1	399
Reed, Warren	121½	Buck Run	1850	1	401
Reed, Warren	30	Sandy Creek	1856	1	482
Reed, Warren et al	200	Lit. Sandy Cr.	1856	1	484
Rhoads—See Rhodes, Rodes					
Rhoads, John W.	88	Elk Fork	1855	1	455
Rhodes—See Rhoads, Rodes					
Riddle, Benjamin Jr. et al	400	Spring Cr.	1852	1	443
Riley, William	292	Pocatalico	1858	1	557
Ritz, Thomas et al	415	Spring Cr	1852	1	442
Rodes—See Rhoads, Rhodes					
Rodes, Benjamin	190	Higby Branch	1855	1	456
Rodes, John W.	112	Elk Fork	1856	1	497
Rodes, Mathias	62	Flat Fork	1855	1	458
Rodes, Mathias & Joseph	390	Flat Fork	1855	1	459
Rollings—Rawlings, Rollins					
Rollings, Benjamin	100	Frozen Camp Fork	1850	1	380
Rollings, James L.	200	Grass Lick Fork	1849	1	365
Rollins—Rawlings, Rollings					
Rollins, James L.	35	Grass Lick Fk.	1860	2	469
Roush, Daniel	32	Adj. Jess Carney	1850	1	397
Saunders, Henry B. Jr. et al	1,000	Reedy Cr.	1844	1	194
Sayer—See Sayre					
Sayer, Joel	390	Clay Lick Run	1841	1	37
Sayers, Elijah	50	Cow Run	1842	1	120
Sayre—or Sayer					
Sayre, Abel	76	Round Knob Run	1847	1	254
Sayre, Abel & Elijah	100	Adj. Elisha Stewart	1858	1	542
Sayre, Daniel	100	Isaac's Run	1842	1	95
Sayre, Daniel	50	Isaac's Run	1847	1	236
Sayre, David	40	Cow Run	1842	1	70
Sayre, David	50	Cow Run	1842	1	79
Sayre, David	140	Cow Run	1847	1	235
Sayre, David	623	Cow Run	1847	1	275
Sayre, David	270	Cow Run	1850	1	374
Sayre, Elijah	50	Parchment Fork	1842	1	71
Sayre, Elijah	100	Parchment Fork	1842	1	72
Sayre, Elijah	50	John's Run	1846	1	231
Sayre, Elijah	160	Parchment Fork	1851	1	434
Sayre, Elijah	84	Mill Cr.	1852	1	444
Sayre, Elijah	100	Parchment Fork	1858	1	545
Sayre, Elijah	166	Parchment Fork	1858	1	546
Sayre, Enoch	200	13-Mi. Cr.	1844	1	169
Sayre, Joel	150	Mill Creek	1840	1	34
Sayre, Joel	150	Mill Creek	1847	1	269
Sayre, Joseph	840	Cow Run	1848	1	324
Sayre, Mark	50	John's Run	1846	1	230
Scarbrough, Robert	191	Mud Lick Fork	1858	1	554
Seaman, George V.	50	Reedy Cr.	1848	1	315
Seaman, S. B.	100	Reedy Cr.	1842	1	80
Seaman, Willet A.	100	Reedy Creek	1836	1	19
Sellers, George	50	Sand Creek	1835	1	3
Sellers, John C.	200	Reedy Creek	1848	1	310
Shamblin, Jesse	100	Mill Creek	1847	1	248
Shamblin, Jesse (Shambling)	50	Mill Cr.	1849	1	351
Shepherd—See Sheppard					
Shepherd, William	100	Big Sand Cr.	1842	1	73
Sheppard, Henry	30	Sandy Creek	1845	1	197
Sheppard, Jonathan Jr.	200	Crane's Nest Run	1848	1	320
Sheppard, William	25	Crooked Run	1835	1	8
Sheppard, William	25	Adj. his own	1836	1	13
Sheppard, William	115	Reedy Creek	1836	1	16
Sheppard, William	90	Reedy Creek	1836	1	17

Name of Grantee	Acres	Local Description	Year	Book	Page
Sheppard, William	25	Crane's Nest Run	1837	1	20
Sheppard, William	100	Crane's Nest Run	1837	1	21
Sheppard, William	25	Adj. Isaac Enoch	1837	1	22
Sheppard, William	100	Sandy Cr.	1842	1	59
Sheppard, William	250	Big Run	1847	1	266
Sheppard, William	80	Crane's Nest Run	1847	1	272
Sheppard, William	80	Reedy Cr.	1847	1	273
Sheppard, William	50	Reedy Cr.	1847	1	274
Sheppard, William	90	Reedy Creek	1848	1	321
Sheppard, William Sr.	50	Big Run	1842	1	58
Sheppard, William Sr.	330	Reedy Cr.	1848	1	322
Sheppard, William Sr.	130	Reedy Cr.	1848	1	323
Sherman, Henry	132	Adj. Col. Muse's Survey	1844	1	154
Shinn, Charles	25	Teaberry Run	1847	1	257
Shinn, Charles et al	65	Cow Run	1847	1	255
Shinn, Samuel	50	Parchment Fork	1849	1	353
Simmons, Martin	160	Cox's Fork	1855	1	465
Simmons, Martin et al	434	13 Mi. Creek	1859	2	464
Simpson, James K.	250	Cherry Tree Fork	1854	1	451
Sinclair, Hugh	100	Cow Run	1834	1	1
Skeen—See Skene, Skine					
Skene—See Skeen, Skine					
Skene, Stephen	147	Middle Fork	1858	1	550
Skine—See Skeen, Skene					
Skine, Frankin	443	Laurel Fork	1855	1	460
Slaughter, Abraham	100	Adj. Slaughter's Old Survey	1838	1	23
Slaughter, Abraham	20	Big Mill Cr.	1850	1	394
Slaven, William	386	Little Sandy Cr.	1850	1	418
Smith, Benjamin H. et al	1,373	Spring Creek	1847	1	279
Smith, Benjamin H. et al	800	Mill Creek	1847	1	280
Smith, Benjamin H. et al	490	Mill Cr.	1847	1	281
Smith, Charles	100	Washington's Run	1844	1	181
Smith, G. W.	964	Big Run	1857	1	531
Smith, George W.	400	Grass Lick Fork	1842	1	83
Smith, George W.	80 (90)	Parchment Fork	1843	1	135
Smith, George W.	140	Parchment Fork	1843	1	136
Smith, George W.	50	Adj. Peter Conrad	1844	1	189
Smith, George W.	182	Wts. West Fork	1845	1	206
Smith, George W.	280	Elk Fork	1848	1	302
Smith, George W.	1,000	Reedy Creek	1849	1	303
Smith, George W.	337	Elk Fork	1848	1	325
Smith, George W.	70	Big Sandy Cr.	1849	1	349
Smith, George W.	300	Elk Fork	1849	1	368
Smith, George W. et al	132	Big Sand Cr.	1844	1	163
Smith, George W. et al	366	Reedy Cr.	1844	1	164
Smith, George W. et al	539	Reedy Creek	1848	1	298
Smith, George W. et al	625	Elk Fork	1848	1	299
Smith, George W. et al	1,189	Mill Creek	1856	1	485
Sommerville—or Summerville					
Sommerville, Andrew	50	Glade Lick Fork	1845	1	207
Sommerville, Andrew Sr.	120	Summerville's Fork	1848	1	335
Sommerville, John	300	Big Sandy Cr.	1849	1	358
Sommerville, Jonathan	50	Reedy Cr.	1842	1	85
Sommerville, Samuel	70	Reedy Creek	1841	1	40
Sommerville, Samuel	50	Reedy Cr.	1842	1	84
Sommerville, Samuel	50	Road Fork	1842	1	127
Sommerville, Samuel	56	Reedy Cr.	1842	1	128
Sommerville, Samuel	100	Brush Run	1842	1	129
Sommerville, Samuel	100	Buckeye Fork	1842	1	130
Sommerville, Samuel	50	Sand Cr.	1844	1	182
Sprague, James	150	Reedy Cr.	1847	1	238
Sprague, James	80	Peggy's Run	1848	1	334
Staats, Calvin	50	Cow Run	1842	1	101

Name of Grantee	Acres	Local Description	Year	Book	Page
Trotter, Preston	34	Parchment Run	1860	2	476
Trotter, Preston	1,029	18 Mi. Creek	1860	2	477
Trotter, Preston	143	Parchment Fork	1860	2	478
Trotter, Preston	74	Sandy Creek	1856	1	483
Trotter, Preston	19	Grass Lick Fork	1856	1	489
Trotter, Preston	31½	Stone Lick Fork	1856	1	490
Trotter, Preston	53½	Mill Creek	1856	1	491
Trotter, Preston	275	Mill Creek	1856	1	492
Trotter, Preston	104	Elk Fork	1856	1	511
Trotter, Preston	60	Elk Fork	1856	1	518
Trotter, Preston	400	Trace Fork	1856	1	519
Trotter, Preston	1,590	Mill Cr.	1858	1	556
Trotter, Preston et al	200	Lit. Sandy Cr.	1856	1	484
Turner, F. B.	780	Wts. Mill Cr.	1858	1	565
Vandine, Isom C.	200	18 Mile Cr.	1851	1	425
Vandine, John S.	22	Mill Creek	1848	1	330
Vantuyl, Thomas	375	Parchment Fork	1847	1	243
Voorheis, Andrew D.	434	Parchment Fork	1846	1	214
Voorheis, Andrew D.	136	Parchment Fork	1846	1	215
Wallace, John et al	1,000	Reedy Cr.	1844	1	194
Washburn, Thomas	100	Sandy Cr.	1841	1	36
Watson, James O.	490	Mill Cr.	1858	1	549
Watson, Thomas G.	1,200	Mill Cr.	1856	1	488
Watson, Thomas G.	2,900	Mill Cr.	1858	1	537
Watson, Thomas G.	2,400	Mill Cr.	1858	1	538
Watson, William H.	200	Parchment Fork	1851	1	413
Watson, William H.	500	Billy's Run	1858	1	539
Waugh, Arthur	100	Parchment Fork	1855	1	475
Waugh, Arthur	23	Parchment Fork	1855	1	478
Waybright, John	119	Elk Fork	1851	1	426
Waybright, John	109	Elk Fork	1851	1	427
Waybright, Michael	167	Elk Fork	1850	1	389
Webster, Samuel S.	30	Lit. Mill Cr.	1850	1	419
Wheeler, Abraham	100	Handshaw's Run	1842	1	131
Whitecotton, James	147	Timber Run	1842	1	161
Whitecotton, James	150	Mill Creek	1844	1	162
Whitham, James	130	Elk Fork	1853	1	450
Whiting, Mathew A.	190	Middle Fork	1859	2	460
Wilson, Benjamin et al	415	Spring Cr.	1852	1	442
Wolf, Abraham	300	13-Mile Cr.	1858	1	541
Wolf, George B. et al	780	Wts Mill Cr.	1858	1	565
Wolf, James R.	85	Spring Cr.	1842	1	81
Woodruff, David	200	Adj. Thos. Evans	1851	1	433
Wright, Benjamin	100	Adj. H. Kyger	1844	1	170
Wright, Benjamin	143	Newel's Run	1844	1	185
Wright, Benjamin	488	Wolfe Creek	1849	1	348
Wright, Benjamin	200	Mill Creek	1852	1	439

JEFFERSON COUNTY

Brown, Jacob B.	21a.2r.30p.	Potomac River	1854	1	514
Brown, Jacob B.	10a.2r.	Adj. Robert Harper	1855	1	501
Brown, Jacob B. et al	39a.2r.	Wts. Potomac	1851	1	512
Brown, S. Howell	5½	Nr. Tn. Bolivar	1852	1	513
Cain—See Kain					
Craighill, William P.	2½	Little Falls	1813	1	494
Davenport, Braxton	1a.3r.18p.	Island Shenandoah R.	1816	1	496
Davenport, Braxton	2a.17p.	Bull Falls	1816	1	498

Name of Grantee	Acres	Local Description	Year	Book	Page
Davenport, Braxton	3a.3r.17p.	Shenandoah River	1816	1	497
Davenport, Braxton	19a.3r.20p.	Bull Falls	1816	1	499
Downey, John	17	Shenandoah River	1810	1	492
Downey, John	51	Adj. Thos. Smith	1810	1	491
Eutler, George	1a.2r.12p.	Potomac River	1833	1	516
Euller—See Eutler, Eutter					
Flagg, Thomas et al	6½	Adj. M. Anderson	1809	1	490
Gibbs, William et al	6½	Adj. Malan Anderson	1809	1	490
Hain, John	5a.3r.26p.	Adj. Wm. Darke	1803	1	482
Harbough, Leonard et al	5¾	Little Falls	1809	1	485
Huffman, John	78a.3r.	Wts. Potomac	1821	1	508
Hurst, James	110a.1r.12p.	Adj. G. Pemberton	1816	1	500
Kain, John	5a.3r.26p.	Adj. Wm. Darke	1803	1	482
Kerney, Anthony (Keroney)	2a.3p.	Adj. Orendorf	1823	1	509
Little, William	6¾	Island Shenandoah River	1809	1	488
Little, William	7½	Island Shenandoah	1809	1	487
Little, William	2½	Little Falls	1809	1	486
Little, William et al	5¾	Little Falls	1809	1	485
McKewan, Charles	71	Wts. Potomac	1809	1	489
McMurran, Joseph	7	Adj. Adam Link	1824	1	510
McPherson, Daniel	11a.1r.34p.	Island Shenandoah R.	1803	1	479
McPherson, John	3	Adj. Gerard Alexander	1803	1	480
Moler, David et al	8a.2r.24p.	Wts. Potomac	1822	1	507
Morgan, Abraham	9a.20p.	Wts. Potomac	1807	1	483
Nesswaner, Jacob et al	39a.2r.	Wts. Potomac	1851	1	512
Nicewarner—See Nesswaner					
Osburn, William	140sq.p.	Adj. Moses Hunter	1803	1	481
Rain, John	5a.3r.26p.	Adj. Wm. Darke	1803	1	482
Snyder, Daniel	455	Shenandoah R.	1833	1	515
Strader—See Strider					
Strider, Henry	13a.21p.	Wts. Potomac	1820	1	506
Strider, Henry	14	Wts. Shenandoah	1820	1	504
Strider, Henry	21a.1r.	Wts. Potomac	1820	1	505
Stubblefield, George	40	Shenandoah River	1834	1	517
Vestal, William	18	Shenandoah River	1809	1	484
Williams, Edward O.	2a.1r.31p.	Cor. to Chapline	1814	1	495
Williams, Edward O.	27a. 36p.	Wts. Potomac	1812	1	493
Worthington, William C., Trustee	8a.1r.25p.	Adj. G. B. Beall	1850	1	511

KANAWHA COUNTY

Adcock, George C.	140	Lick Br.	1829	2	159
Adkins—or Atkins					
Adkins, Sherod	50	Stone Ft. Fk.	1810	1	434
Adkins, William	80	Beech Fork	1810	1	439
Adkinson—See Atkinson					
Adkinson, William	100	Fork Coopers Cr.	1830	2	191
Adkinson, William & John et al	275	Mink Shoals Branch	1830	2	196
Alderson, George	200	Two Mile Cr. Elk	1805	1	358
Alderson, George	50	Campbell's Creek	1805	1	359
Alderson, George	100	Campbell's Creek	1804	1	349
Alderson, George	266	Adj Home tract	1797	1	105
Alderson, George et al	200	Two Mile of Campbell's Creek	1805	1	362
Alexander, Robert et al	5,002	Coal & Kanawha Rivers	1822	2	68
Alls, Adam (Altz)	150	Rock Camp Fk. Tuppers Cr.	1827	2	136
Allford, William et al	65	Trace Fork	1852	2	609
Anderson, Andrew	141	Tyler's Creek	1856	2	627
Anderson, Thomas	212	Lick Branch	1838	2	588

Name of Grantee	Acres	Local Description	Year	Book	Page
Anthony, James	1,341	West S. of New River	1805	1	363
Anthony, James C.	500	Wts. Gauley River	1805	1	356
Anthony, James C.	2,000	So. West Br. Coal R.	1805	1	355
Anthony, James C.	1,000	Wts. Gauley River	1805	1	361
Arbuckle, James & Matthew	200	Wts. Pocatallico River	1800	1	230
Arbuckle, William	333	13 Mile Creek	1798	1	109
Arbuckle, William et al	245	1st Ck. below Tyler's Ck.	1799	1	187
Arbuckle, William et al	200	Tyler's Creek	1799	1	211
Arbuckle, Wm. et al	200	Rt. Hand Fk. of Tylor's Ck.	1799	1	212
Atkins—or Adkins					
Atkins, Berry	100	Beech Fk. of 12 Pole Cr.	1812	1	580
Atkinson—Adkinson					
Atkinson, James	100	S. E. Elk	1838	2	430
Atkinson, James	50	N. W. Elk	1838	2	421
Atkinson, James	45	East Side Elk River	1823	2	87
Atkinson, John	200	Mill Creek	1835	2	285
Atkinson, John	100	Big Sandy Cr.	1838	2	428
Atkinson, Thomas	78	Morris Cr.	1838	2	429
Aultz—See Alls					
Austin, Gad et al	10,000	2¾ Mi. Cr. of Cole	1795	1	55
Austin, John	86	Poplar Fk. Camp Creek	1810	1	400
Austin, John	550	So. Fk. Coal River	1810	1	401
Austin, John	100	Wts. Coal River	1810	1	402
Austin, John	172	Turtle Creek	1810	1	399
Austin, John	359	Coal Riv. & Camp Cr.	1810	1	544
Austin, John	82	Big Creek	1810	1	403
Austin, John	50	Camp Creek	1813	2	542
Austin, John	985	Pond Fork	1813	2	543
Babbett—See Bobbett					
Bagly, Henry	38	Island in Ohio, Pt. P1.	1793	1	16
Bailey, William	330	Big Sandy Creek	1800	1	251
Baker, Abraham	100	East Side Kanawha	1814	2	553
Baker, Michael	100	Tate's Run of Peters Ck.	1800	1	239
Baker, Michael	100	Peters Creek of Gauley	1800	1	243
Ballard, James	150	Trace Fk. of Mud	1829	2	162
Ballard, Fielding	82	Mud River	1815	2	15
Ballard, Philip	200	Adj. Dingess & French	1812	1	583
Ballard, Philip et al	40	Dry Fork of Sandy R.	1812	1	567
Ballard, Philip et al	50	Dry Fork of Sandy R.	1812	1	568
Ballard, Philip et al	16	Dry Fork of Sandy River	1812	1	569
Ballard, Philip et al	950	E. Side Tug Fork, Sandy	1810	1	542
Ballard, Philip et al	100	Dry Fork of Sandy R.	1812	1	570
Ballard, Philip et al	100	Dry Fork of Sandy R.	1810	1	407
Ballard, Philip Sr.	50	Spruce Fork	1822	2	77
Banks, Henry	23,242	Wts. Coal River	1797	1	106
Banks, Henry	10,000	Big Hurricane Creek	1797	1	107
Banks, Henry	500	Adj. Mercer	1822	2	74
Banks, Henry	600	Gauley River	1822	2	73
Banks, Henry	840	West Side New River	1822	2	72
Banks, Henry	7,908	Hd. of Grapevine Run	1800	1	263
Banks, Henry	4,018	Hd. of Grapevine Run	1800	1	264
Banks, Henry	430	West Side New River	1822	2	71
Banks, Henry	8	Mouth of Elk	1822	2	70
Banks, Henry	250	Wts. of Gauley	1822	2	69
Barclay, John	50,000	Between Elk & Gauley	1796	1	493
Barker, Isaac	75	Bull Creek	1814	2	558
Barnett, Hanna	100	Big Huricane Creek	1812	1	576
Barrett, Edward (Barret)	283	Coal River	1796	1	68
Barrett, Edward	150	Mth. Middle Fk. Mud R.	1810	1	437
Barrett, Edward	115	Trace Fork	1812	2	531
Barton, Wilson	40	Big Hurricane	1822	2	79
Beckett, John	150	Hurricane Cr.	1825	2	107
Beckett, Thomas	100	Little & Big Hurricane	1823	2	86

Name of Grantee	Acres	Local Description	Year	Book	Page
Buffington, William et al	258	Four Pole Cr. adj. Savage	1810	1	379
Burks, James	180	Brown's Creek	1837	2	364
Busby, John	55	Paint Creek	1827	2	133
Busby, John	95	Paint Creek	1827	2	127
Busby, John	100	Paint Creek	1830	2	176
Busby, Thomas	45	Paint Creek	1826	2	115
Busby, William	40	Paint Creek	1830	2	179
Busby, William	91	Cabin Creek	1827	2	563
Buster, Thomas S. et al	307	W. Side of Kanawha	1822	2	76
Byram, Benjamin P. et al	845	Grapevine of Poca	1859	2	665
Byram, Benjamin P. et al	770	Frogg's Creek	1860	2	680
Byrnsides, James	120	Left Fk. Coal River	1801	1	284
Byrnsides, James	32	N. Fk. Coal River	1801	1	283
Byrnsides, James	445¼	N. Fk. Coal River	1801	1	282
Byrnsides, James	19	Coal River	1801	1	281
Byrnsides, James	18	Coal River	1801	1	280
Byrnsides, James	54	N. Fork Coal River	1801	1	279
Byrnsides, James	78	N. Fk. Coal River	1801	1	278
Byrnsides, James	115	Mth. Droddy's Cr. Coal R.	1801	1	303
Byrnsides, James	100	Toney's Fk. of Coal Rv.	1801	1	301
Cabell, Napoleon B.	183	Two-Mi. Creek of Elk	1859	2	675
Campbell, John et al	200	Wts. of Gauley River	1800	1	194
Campbell, John et al	400	Cooper's Camp Creek, Gauley	1800	1	190
Campbell, Mason et al	596	Wts. Pocatalico	1847	2	507
Campbell, Robert	6	12 mi. above mo. Elk, C. Is.	1812	1	573
Campbell, Robert	52	Loop Cr. below Falls	1812	1	572
Campbell, Robert	567	Magazine Br. of Elk	1812	1	571
Campbell, Robert et al	500	Lft. Hd. Br. Big Sandy	1800	1	257
Campbell, Robert et al	500	Lft. Fk. Sandy Creek	1800	1	258
Campbell, Robert et al	500	Lft. Fk. Sandy Cr.	1800	1	259
Campbell, Robert et al	500	Wts. Big Sandy Cr.	1800	1	260
Campbell, Robert et al	500	Lft. Fk. Big Sandy Cr.	1800	1	261
Campbell, Robert et al	500	Little Sandy Cr.	1800	1	262
Campbell, Robert et al	500	Little Sandy Cr.	1800	1	231
Can, Daniel M. (or Carr) et al	200	Big Sandy Cr.	1836	2	304
Carlile, John	600	Lft. Fork Davis Cr.	1803	1	333
Carmeans—also Cremeans					
Carmeans, Higgins et al	90	4-Mi. Cr. of Guyandotte	1810	1	444
Carney, Silas	500	Frogg's Creek	1859	2	659
Carney, Silas et al	447	Wts. Pocatalico	1854	2	621
Carney, Silas et al	773	Wts. Frogg's Cr.	1860	2	697
Carpenter, Joseph	240	Trace Fork	1836	2	300
Carpenter, Joseph	269	Trace Fork	1836	2	302
Carpenter, Thomas	100	Wts. Lick Creek	1838	2	385
Carr, Daniel M. (or Can) et al	200	Big Sandy Cr.	1836	2	304
Carroll, William	70	Mill Branch	1796	1	511
Cart, John	56½	Duck Creek	1816	2	33
Cartmill, David et al	210	Paint Creek	1818	2	43
Cartmill, Henry	100	Wts. Big Scary	1824	2	96
Cartop—See Casdorph					
Casdorph, Jacob	150	Two Mile Creek	1800	1	183
Cavender, Charles	100	Indian Cr.	1831	2	199
Cavendish, William H. et al	1,689	Ohio R. Gr. Sandy Adj. McKee	1807	1	370
Chandler, Gardiner L. et al	50,000	Main Fork Big Sandy	1798	1	139
Chandler, John	391	Trace Fork of Mud	1837	2	355
Chandler, John Sr.	170	Lft Fk. of Trace	1831	2	216
Chandler, Richard C.	66	Wts. Big Hurricane	1837	2	339
Chapen, Uriel	30,000	Wts. of Coal, G & S Riv's.	1797	1	96
Chapman, Joshua M.	70	Wts. of Scary Cr.	1827	2	137
Childers, David	200	Morris Creek	1829	2	167
Childers, John	700	Kanawha River	1790	1	1
Childress, James	100	Alum Creek	1844	2	487
Childress, Shadrack	50	Smithers Creek	1810	1	409

Name of Grantee	Acres	Local Description	Year	Book	Page
Christian, Gilbert et al	15,000	Fks. Great Sandy Rv.	1801	1	286
Clap, Thomas	150	E. Side Guyandotte R.	1803	1	339
Clark—See also Cleek, Click					
Clark, Jacob	275	Coal River	1813	2	539
Clark, Jacob	100	Brown's Creek	1812	2	529
Clark, Jacob	100	Brown's Creek	1813	2	538
Clark, Molly	100	Turkey Creek	1813	2	541
Clark, Robert et al	1,000	Big Hurricane	1800	1	272
Clark, William	100	12-Pole Creek	1810	1	419
Clark, William	300	Beech Fork of 12-Pole	1810	1	420
Cleek—See also Clark, Click					
Cleek, Jacob	400	Davis Creek	1807	1	369
Clendinen, Mary et al	5	Kanawha River	1803	1	342
Click—See also Cleek					
Clopton, John	782	Great Kanawha	1796	1	59
Clopton, John	752	Kanawha River	1796	1	60
Clopton, John	896	Kanawha River	1796	1	61
Clopton, John	1,000	Great Kanawha	1796	1	38
Cloyd, Gordon	9,000	Wts. 18-Mile Creek	1797	1	129
Cobb, Boswell L. & Fleming, Jr.	128	Davis Creek	1838	2	398
Cobb, Huet (Hewitt)	100	Big Sandy	1838	2	432
Cobb, William	800	Sandy Creek	1837	2	584
Cobb, William Dr.	200	Big Lick of Sandy	1825	2	105
Cobbs, William	263	N. Bnk. Elk Cor. J. Young	1836	2	295
Cogar, Peter	30	L. Fork of W. Fk.	1836	2	319
Cogswell, Gen. Eli et al	25,000	Wts. Gauley River	1797	1	95
Coleman, Mason	120	Loop Creek	1825	2	106
Coleman, William, et al	50,000	Main Fk. Big Sandy	1798	1	139
Collins, (or Colans) Archibald	150	3-Fks. of Sandy	1856	2	626
Collins, John	200	Loop Creek	1799	1	153
Comstock, Silas et al	4,000	Gauley River	1796	1	69
Connally, John	39	W. Fork Lit. Kan.	1837	2	353
Conner, James	47½	Big Hurricane	1834	2	275
Conner, James	64½	Big Hurricane Cr.	1834	2	280
Conner, William et al	100	Mud River	1813	2	534
Conrod, Robert R., David P. & Elenor M.	600	Teas's Valley	1799	1	123
Cook, Barnabuss	44	Left. Fk. West Fk.	1833	2	261
Cook, Benjamin et al	500	Cor. to A. McCashlin	1800	1	207
Cook, Benjamin et al	550	Wts. Salmon's Creek	1799	1	156
Cook, Benjamin et al	1,000	Muddletepeg Creek	1799	1	157
Cook, Benjamin et al	1,500	Wts. Peter's Crk.	1799	1	158
Cook, Benjamin et al	850	Nr. McKees Meadows	1799	1	159
Cook, Benjamin et al	747	McKee's Meadow Cr.	1799	1	160
Cook, Samuel	87	Middle Fork Davis Cr.	1838	2	400
Cook, Samuel	100	Davis Creek	1836	2	303
Cooper, Leonard	3,000	Wts. of Mud River	1801	1	300
Cooper, Leonard	150	Rt. Fork Ten-Mile Crk.	1799	1	179
Cooper, Leonard	500	Little Sandy Cr.	1836	2	310
Corran, Robert et al	30,000	Elk Riv. abv. Mth. Big Sdy.	1796	1	459
Corran, Robert et al	30,000	Elk Riv. at Blue Crk.	1796	1	457
Corran, Robert et al	40,000	10-Mi. Cr. of Gr. Kan.	1796	1	456
Craig, Adam	1,000	Little Sandy Crk.	1800	1	299
Craig, John W.	13¾	Elk Riv. Adj. Brown	1841	2	452
Crawford, Edward	192	E. Side Muddlethepeg	1805	1	364
Cremeans—or Carmeans					
Cremeans, Noah	140	Trace Fork	1856	2	633
Crew, Obediah	96	Two-Mi. Crk.	1859	2	663
Cummings, Charles	85	Rock Camp	1856	2	632
Cyrus, Frances	100	Price's Mill Cr. Sandy	1810	1	430
Daggs—See also Diggs					
Daggs, Polly	112	Davis Creek	1840	2	443
Daggs, Rhuel	100	Rt. Fk. Smith's Crk.	1812	2	530

Name of Grantee	Acres	Local Description	Year	Book	Page
Donnally, Andrew et al	268	Kanawha R. Adj. Harmon	1804	1	347
Donnally, Andrew Jr.	10	W. Side of Kanawha	1820	2	56
Donnally, Andrew Jr. et al	5	Kanawha River	1803	1	342
Dotson, Elisha	16	Davis Creek	1849	2	521
Dotson, Elisha	37	Davis Creek	1849	2	523
Dotson, Elisha	18	Davis Creek	1849	2	522
Dotson, Elisha	175	Davis Creek	1836	2	311
Dowell, Major et al	100,000	Guyandotte & Mud Riv.	1798	1	108
Drake, Alfred et al	630	Big Sandy Creek	1842	2	457
Droddy, Charles	130	Wts. Pocatalico	1836	2	324
Dryden, John et al	369	Mill Creek	1859	2	664
Dudding, John	50	Big Hurricane	1837	2	348
Dudding, John et al	230	Cow Creek	1847	2	508
Dunbar, Matthew	580	N. W. Elk	1843	2	461
Duncan, John	225	Lft. Fork Fall Creek	1836	2	299
Duncan, William	60	Wts. Crooked Creek	1823	2	92
Duncan, William	100	Wts. Crooked Creek	1823	2	91
Duval, John P.	1,000	Guyandotte River	1799	1	165
Duval, John P.	1,000	Guyandotte River	1799	1	166
Duval, John P.	500	Wts. of Sandy River	1799	1	167
Duval, John P.	1,000	Wts. Guyandotte River	1798	1	168
Duval, John P. et al	366¼	Wts. 12-Pole Creek	1801	1	302
Duval, William	1,000	Adj. lands of Joseph Carroll	1795	1	32
Edgar, George	682	Gauley River	1797	1	136
Edgar, James et al	700	Gauley River	1797	1	135
Edgar, Thomas et al	1,344	Muddlethepeg on Gauley	1800	1	298
Edwards, William H.	43	Paint Creek	1856	2	628
Ellis, Alfred	250	Cow Creek	1847	2	509
Ellis, Alfred et al	230	Cow Creek	1847	2	508
Ellis, Hiram	190	Hiram's Br.	1838	2	392
Ellis, Hiram	37	Big Hurricane Cr.	1833	2	243
Ellis, Hiram	126½	Big Hurricane	1833	2	271
Ellis, James, M.	125	Big Hurricane Cr.	1837	2	343
Ellis, Lewis H.	87	Big Hurricane	1838	2	391
Erskin, Isaac	60	Low Gap Branch	1837	2	335
Estill, William C.	250	Davis Creek	1809	1	378
Estill, William C.	200	Davis Creek	1810	1	384
Estill, Z. F. et al	50	Wts. Mud River	1810	1	381
Estill, Z. F. et al	142	Falls Mud R.	1810	1	380
Etting, Reubin et al	13,765	Marsh Fk. Tohey's Clear Fk.	1796	1	454
Etting, Reubin et al	4,160	Clear Fork of Coal Riv.	1796	1	476
Etting, Reubin et al	174,673	Marsh Fk. Coal Riv.	1796	1	461
Evans, Thomas	1,000	2nd Lft. Fk. Mill Crk.	1801	1	304
Evans, Thomas	1,000	Rt. Hd. Fk. Mill Creek	1801	1	305
Fabern, Robert et al	550	Big Sandy River	1801	1	287
Fally, Frederick et al	50,000	Bear Camp Drain	1797	1	97
Farley, Henry et al	550	Big Sandy River	1801	1	287
Farrall, John (The Greater)	65	Joel's Creek	1833	2	266
Ferguson—See Forguson					
Fife, Thomas	100	3rd Left Fk. Pocatallico	1818	2	36
Finn, William R.	5a.21p	N. E. Side Elk	1835	2	292
Finn, William R. et al	113	Coopers Cr. and Lit. Sandy	1831	2	204
Finn, William R. et al	210	Coopers Cr. & Elk	1831	2	203
Fisher, John	438	Wts. Pocatalico	1859	2	658
Fitzwater, George	250	Peters Creek & Gauley R.	1800	1	195
Fitzwater, George	400	Wts. Meadow Creek	1800	1	205
Fitzwater, George	100	Cor. to Surv. Jms. Foster	1800	1	265
Fitzwater, George et al	100	Below McClung's M. Crk.	1800	1	199
Fletcher, Joseph et al	80	Adj. Surv. Lewis & Wash.	1812	1	566
Ford, James	83	Price's Mill Creek	1810	1	428
Forguson, Samuel	83	Tom's Creek 12-Pole	1810	1	429
Forguson, Samuel	200	12-Pole Creek	1810	1	383
Foster, Ephraim	150	Cooper's Creek	1845	2	490

Name of Grantee	Acres	Local Description	Year	Book	Page
Foster, James	200	Below McClung's M. Crk.	1800	1	192
Foster, Robert et al	200	Rt. Hd. Fk. Peters Ck.	1800	1	235
French, David	4,000	Adj. Fry on Sandy	1802	1	541
French, David et al	200	Mo. Rock Creek	1812	1	581
French, David et al	500	Little Coal River	1810	1	404
French, David et al	150	Spruce Fork of Coal	1810	1	406
French, David et al	600	Spruce Fork of Coal R.	1810	1	395
French, David et al	400	Spruce Fk. of Coal R.	1810	1	396
Frog, William et al	150	Muddlethepeg & Gauley Riv.	1800	1	204
Frog, William et al	150	Peters Crk.	1800	1	201
Frog, William et al	200	Peters Crk. of Gauley	1800	1	202
Frog, William et al	500	Wts. Gauley Riv.	1800	1	246
Frogg, William et al	305	Peters Creek of Gauley	1800	1	241
Frogg, William et al	400	Wts. Peters Ck.	1800	1	240
Frogg, Wm. et al	519	No. Side Gauley R.	1804	1	346
Frogg, William	325	Buffalo Ck.	1800	1	229
Frogg, William	175	Buffalo Crk. of Elk	1800	1	267
Fullerton, William	60	Kanawha River	1797	1	110
Fullerton, William et al	400	Wts. Sandy River	1800	1	221
Galatine—or Gallatine, Gallatin					
Galatine, Albert	3,500	Reedy Creek	1795	1	42
Galatine, Albert	6,000	W. Fork of Lit. Kanawha	1795	1	39
Galatine, Albert et al	1,000	Davis Creek	1795	1	40
Galatine, Albert et al	27	Kanawha River	1795	1	41
Galatine, Albert et al	2,000	Great Kanawha Riv.	1795	1	44
Galatine, Albert et al	2,000	Great Kanawha Riv.	1795	1	45
Galatine, Albert et al	4,000	Coal River	1795	1	46
Galatine, Albert et al	1,900	Kanawha River	1795	1	48
Galatine, Albert et al	744	Kanawha River	1795	1	49
Gallatine, Albert et al	2,000	West Side Gr. Kan. Ad. Jones	1795	1	473
Gallatine, Albert et al	1,250	Adj. their No. 3	1795	1	468
Gallatine, Albert	3,956	Coal River	1796	1	71
Gallatine, Albert	5,676¾	Bet. Big & Lit. Sandy	1795	1	470
Gallatine, Albert	3,000	Grt. Falls Kan. R.	1795	1	469
Gallatine, Albert et al	1,250	Adj. his No. 1	1795	1	472
Gallatine, Albert et al	5,002	Coal & Kan. Rivers	1822	2	68
Gallatine, Albert et al	3,000	Lft. Fk. Davis Creek	1795	1	466
Gallego—See Galleghar					
Galleghar, Joseph	40,000	Cabin Ck. Pt. Ck. & Tonys Fk.	1797	1	131
Gandy, Uriah	144	Lick Fork	1833	2	238
Gandy, William	100	Upper Flat Fork	1836	2	320
Garrett—See Gerrett, Jarrett					
Garrett, Benjamin	76	Wts. 12-Pole Cr.	1810	1	433
Garrett, James C.	75	Trace Fork	1858	2	644
Gary—See Geary					
Gary, Matthew	67	Porters Creek	1835	2	291
Gary, Matthew	30	S. E. Side of Elk	1835	2	290
Gary, Matthew	90	S. E. Side Elk River	1833	2	571
Geary—See also Gary					
Geary (Gaery), Matthew	216	Big Sandy Creek	1851	2	602
Geary, Matthew	100	N. S. Elk	1851	2	603
Geary, Matthew	100	Big Sandy	1851	2	604
Geary, Matthew	285	McClung's Cr. & Elk	1844	2	484
Geary, Matthew	227	Elk & Big Sandy Cr.	1844	2	483
Geary, Matthew	333	Barren Creek & Elk	1844	2	482
Geary, Matthew	152	Laurel Shoal Creek	1844	2	481
Gerrett—Also Garrett, Jarrett					
Gerrett, Eli et al (Jarrett)	80	Surv. for Lewis & G. Wash.	1812	1	566
Gerrett, William (Jarrett)	(25)22	Kan. R. Near Gerrett's	1810	1	410
Giley, Giles et al	20,000	Wts. of Coal Riv.	1797	1	126
Givens, James	218	Elk River	1796	1	62
Glover, John	200	Pocatallico R.	1817	2	35
Goff, John	171	Wts. Pocatalico	1848	2	511

Name of Grantee	Acres	Local Description	Year	Book	Page
Goshorn, William & J. H. et al	134½	Barren Creek	1859	2	666
Goshorn, William & J. H. et al	1,842	No. Side Elk	1859	2	667
Graham, James P.	100	N. W. Side of Elk	1833	2	249
Graham, John	871	Guyandotte R.	1802	1	308
Grass, Edward	50	Bridge Cr. of Mud	1829	2	161
Grass, Edward	95	Bridge Creek	1837	2	336
Grass, Jacob	4	Bet. Paint & Cabin Crs.	1843	2	458
Grass, Jacob	56	Bet. Paint & Cabin Crs.	1843	2	459
Grass, Jacob	50	Trace Fork	1830	2	187
Grass, John	143	Trace Fork	1852	2	611
Grass, John	169	Trace Fork of Mud	1836	2	306
Graves, Francis J.	150	Wts. Mud River	1852	2	610
Gray, Elijah et al	4,000	Gauley River	1796	1	69
Green, Andrew	32	Joe's Creek	1848	2	607
Green, Andrew	40	Rt. Fk. Joe's Cr.	1833	2	267
Green, Andrew	60	Lft. Fk. Joe's Cr.	1833	2	268
Green, Barnabas	50	No. Fk. of Coal River	1810	1	435
Green, George	45	Sang. Creek on Coal	1833	2	253
Green, John	30,000	Lft. Hd. Fk. Big Sdy. R.	1796	1	93
Green, John	16,000	Kan. Riv. adj. lands James, Morris, and Rennick	1796	1	523
Green, John	84,000	Spruce Fk. of Coal R.	1796	1	516
Greenwood, William	102	Mud River	1810	1	424
Griffith, Ephraim	47	Cobbs Creek	1832	2	230
Griffith, Ephraim	37½	Grapevine Branch	1832	2	234
Griffith, John	1,000	Grt. Sandy River	1802	1	319
Griffith, Lemuel, Fallena & Margaret et al	250	Crooked Creek	1856	2	634
Griffith, Lemuel, Fallena & Margaret et al	16	Adj. Henry Wilson	1856	2	630
Griffith, Lemuel, Fallena & Margaret et al	19	Adj. Henry Bailess	1856	2	629
Grim, C. R.	1,000	Big Sandy	1848	2	516
Grinstead, William A. (or H.)	50	Paint Creek	1830	2	195
Grinstead, William H.	100	Paint Creek	1850	2	525
Hale, John P. et al	1,514	Kelly's & Hughes Crs.	1858	2	636
Hale, John P. et al	970	Kelly's Creek	1858	2	637
Hale, John P. et al	1,272	Kelly's Creek	1858	2	639
Hale, John P. et al	1,367	Kelly's Creek	1858	2	641
Hale, John P. et al	1,664	Witcher's Creek	1858	2	640
Hale, John P. et al	266	S. E. Side Elk	1858	2	643
Hale, John P. et al	45¼	Campbell's Creek	1858	2	642
Hale, John P. et al	2,000	Kelly's Creek	1859	2	673
Hale, John P. et al	500	Bell Creek	1859	2	672
Hale, William P. et al	1,300	Witcher's Creek	1858	2	638
Hall, Philip, Assignee	700	W. Br. Gauley	1797	1	137
Hamilton, Arthur	1,640½	Surv. Josh. & John Fry	1798	1	148
Hamilton, John	520	Near Glade Creek	1815	2	11
Hammack, John & Martin Sr.	50	Adj. M. Hammick	1838	2	433
Hammack, William	50	Johnston's Cr. Poca	1827	2	139
Hammacks, John	86	Wts. Elk	1850	2	527
Hammick, Delany	123	No. Bnk. Pocatalico	1838	2	374
Hammick, John	100	Johnston's Cr.	1838	2	434
Hammick, John	180	S. E. Pocataligo	1838	2	394
Handley, Erasmus	10	Big Hurricane	1836	2	388
Handley, Erasmus	32	Hurricane Cr.	1836	2	387
Handley, John	112	Bell Creek & Lit. Scary	1824	2	94
Handley, Samuel	50	Teas Valley	1832	2	228
Haner, Lewis	(82)80	Camp & Big Crs.	1811	1	546
Hanna, Nathan et al	250	No. W. Side Peters Cr.	1811	1	560
Hannah, Samuel	192½	Paint Creek	1850	2	526
Hansford, Aloah	3½	No. East S. Kan.	1831	2	208
Hansford, Alva	75½	Paint Creek	1830	2	181

Name of Grantee	Acres	Local Description	Year	Book	Page
Hansford, Felix	75	Paint Creek	1827	2	138
Hansford, Felix G.	312	Paint & Cabin Crs.	1851	2	601
Hansford, Felix G.	187	Wts. Williams Br.	1836	2	332
Hansford, Felix G.	400	Paint Creek	1855	2	625
Hansford, Felix G.	133	Sugar Camp	1848	2	514
Hansford, Felix G.	139	Paint Creek	1841	2	454
Hansford, Felix G.	200	Paint Creek	1830	2	565
Hansford, Felix G.	300	Kelly's Creek	1832	2	236
Hansford, Felix G.	22	Paint Creek	1831	2	217
Hansford, Felix G.	55	Paint Creek	1831	2	214
Hansford, Felix G.	74	Paint Cr.	1831	2	212
Hansford, Felix G. Heirs	23¼	So. Side of Kan.	1851	2	600
Hansford, Felix G. & John	800	Paint Creek	1836	2	583
Hansford, Gallatin	82½	Paint Creek	1835	2	281
Hansford, James F.	30	Hughes Creek	1857	2	635
Hansford, John	400	Paint Creek	1800	1	220
Hansford, John	530	Paint Creek	1793	1	24
Hansford, John	410	Paint Creek	1818	2	39
Hansford, John	15	E. Side of Kan.	1820	2	54
Hansford, John	197	Paint Creek	1822	2	82
Hansford, John	393a.30p.	Mo. of Paint Creek	1832	2	239
Hansford, John Sr.	15	Cabin Creek	1845	2	494
Hansford, John Sr.	100	Paint Creek	1836	2	312
Hansford, John Sr.	150	Paint Creek	1827	2	126
Hansford, Marshall	100	Paint Creek	1848	2	513
Hany, Henry	184	12-Pole Creek	1810	1	386
Hany, Henry	500	Whites Cr.	1810	1	387
Hardway, Daniel B.	50	Lft. Fk. West Fk.	1833	2	260
Harman, George	174	Null's Br. of 2-Mi.	1835	2	293
Harman, Henry	200	Field's Creek	1818	2	38
Harper, Asa	39¾	Pocatalico	1846	2	503
Harper, Asa	50	So. Bnk. Pocatalico	1843	2	460
Harper, George W.	42½	Wts. of Straight Cr.	1846	2	502
Harreman, John et al	1,790	Teays Valley	1799	1	175
Harreman, John et al	137	Big Hurricane Creek	1799	1	176
Harreman, John et al	828	Teas Valley	1799	1	177
Harriman, John et al	598	Rock Castle Creek	1800	1	214
Harriman, John et al	1,397	Teays Valley & Mud R.	1800	1	219
Harriman, John et al	2,000	Teays Valley	1793	1	532
Harris, John et al	560	Catchum's Crk.	1814	2	559
Harris, John et al	250	Bull Creek	1815	2	560
Harrison, Josiah	150	Burning Spgs. Crk.	1805	1	360
Hartless, Henry	900	Lit. Sandy Cr.	1824	2	100
Harvey—See Harvie					
Harvey, John	95	Buff's Creek	1837	2	345
Harvey, John	25	Rider's Branch	1834	2	278
Harvey, John	60	Big Hurricane Cr.	1837	2	346
Harvey, Robert T. et al	770	Frogg's Creek	1860	2	680
Harvie—also Harvey					
Harvie, John	44¾	Rider's Br.	1834	2	279
Haslet—Hayzlett, Hazelett, Hazlett					
Haslet, Mahala	200	Lft. Fk. Fall Cr.	1836	2	298
Haslet, Mahala	25	Fall Cr. of Coal	1838	2	401
Hatch, Nathaniel	50	Magazine Br.	1829	2	169
Hatton, Samuel	90	Wts. Sandy River	1810	1	425
Hawkins, Elliott et al	250	Cor. Smith & Branaugh	1826	2	124
Hawkins, Martin et al	2,000	Grt. Kan. Riv.	1798	1	140
Haynes, Joseph	242	Pocatalico R.	1838	2	402
Hays, John et al	130	Falling Rock Cr.	1823	2	88
Hays, Peregrine	75	Walnut Fk.	1846	2	497
Hays, Peregrine et al	75	Lft. Fk. of West Fk.	1846	2	498
Hays, Peregrine et al	64	Lft. Fk. West Fk.	1846	2	499
Hays, Peregrine et al	40	Lft. Fork of West Fk.	1846	2	500

Name of Grantee	Acres	Local Description	Year	Book	Page
Hays, Peregrine et al	50	Lft. Fk. of West Fk.	1846	2	501
Hayzlett—Haslet, Hazelett, Hazlett					
Hayzlett, John	250	Falling Creek	1829	2	170
Hazelett, Washington	114	Fall Cr.	1858	2	645
Hazlett, Alexander	100	Price's Mill Creek	1810	1	427
Helmick, Abraham	156	W. Fk. of Little Kan.	1833	2	270
Henderson, James, John & Samuel	400	Mouth Gr. Kanawha	1800	1	196
Henderson, James John & Samuel	1,000	Nr. Mth. Gr. Kanawha	1800	1	234
Henderson, William	208	Buffalo Cr.	1837	2	347
Henley—or Hensley					
Henley, Samuel (or Hensley)	160	Surv. Jacob Clark	1852	2	612
Henry, John	85	Isl. in K. Nr. Mth. Elk	1810	1	398
Henry, Samuel	1,650	No. Fk. Coal Riv.	1800	1	248
Henry, Samuel	350	Mouth No. Fk. Coal R.	1800	1	208
Henry, Samuel	100	Big Hurricane	1814	2	549
Hensley—or Henley					
Hensley, Jonathan R.	305	Brown's Creek	1837	2	366
Hensley, Samuel (or Henley)	160	Adj. Jacob Clark	1852	2	612
Hicks, John et al	500	Little Sandy Creek	1800	1	231
Hicks, John et al	500	Little Sandy Cr.	1800	1	262
Hicks, John et al	500	Wts. Big Sandy Cr.	1800	1	260
Hicks, John et al	500	Lft. Fk. Sandy Cr.	1800	1	259
Hicks, John et al	500	Lft. Fk. Sandy Cr.	1800	1	258
Hicks, John et al	500	Lft. Hd. Br. Big S. Ck.	1800	1	257
Hicks, Robert et al	500	Lft. Fk. Big Sandy Cr.	1800	1	261
Higginbotham, Thomas et al	135	S. E. Elk	1838	2	404
Higginbotham, Thomas et al	265	S. S. Elk	1838	2	403
Hill, Daniel	400	Wts. Pocatalico	1840	2	444
Hill, George	100	So. Fk. of Coal	1813	2	536
Hill, Jacob	432	Wts. Coal River	1836	2	331
Hill, Martin	813	Bell Creek	1859	2	677
Hill, William	75	Crooked Crk.	1860	2	683
Hill, William S.	197	Blue Creek	1860	2	682
Hinchman, John	276	Witchers Creek	1803	1	334
Hine, Noble et al	7,000	Wts. Davis Crk.	1796	1	72
Hogue, William et al	210	Paint Creek	1818	2	43
Hogue, William et al	75	W. Side Kanawha	1818	2	44
Holley, Joseph	62	Trace Fork of Mud	1812	1	577
Holley, Joseph	255	Trace Fork	1837	2	586
Hollingsworth, Samuel	100,000	Bet. Poca & 18-Mi.	1796	1	489
Hollingsworth, Samuel	53,000	Main Fk. Pocatallico	1796	1	486
Hollingsworth, Samuel	47,000	Elk & Pocatallico R.	1796	1	507
Holmes, Joseph	1,000	1st. lge. Cr. below Poca	1798	1	138
Hopkins, Samuel M.	70,202	Ohio R. bet. S. & Guy.	1796	1	509
Hopkins, Samuel M.	50,000	Ohio, Guy. & Mud Rs.	1796	1	513
Hopkins, Samuel M.	200,000	Left Hand Fk. Poca	1796	1	504
Houchings, Henry	325	Brown's Cr.	1837	2	365
Hubbard, Davis	200	Frog's Creek	1828	2	146
Hubbard, John	125	Rocky Step Br.	1823	2	84
Hubbard, Sally	74	Little Hurricane Cr.	1821	2	64
Hubbard, Sally	443	Scary Creek	1821	2	66
Hubbard, Thomas	183	Scary Creek	1821	2	65
Huddleston, Daniel	17½	Loop Creek	1809	1	375
Huddleston, Daniel et al	200	Rt. hd. fk. Peters Cr.	1800	1	235
Huddleston, David	27	Adj. his own on K. R.	1810	1	411
Huddleston, Job	168	Kanawha nr. Boomer Br.	1830	2	198
Huddleston, Job	205	Laurel Creek	1800	1	255
Huddleston, Job	195	Laurel Creek	1800	1	256
Huddleston, Job	50	Armstrong's Cr.	1813	2	546
Huddleston, John	100	W. Side of Kan.	1813	2	545
Huddleston, John	50	Armstrong Creek	1810	1	412
Huddleston, John	50	Loop Creek	1815	2	7
Huddleston, Nathan	200	Wts. Laurel Cr.	1801	1	295

Name of Grantee	Acres	Local Description	Year	Book	Page
Lamme, Nathan	2,437	18-Mile Crk.	1799	1	170
Lam, Jonathan et al (Lane)	10,000	Two-Mile	1795	1	55
Lancaster, Thomas et al	7,000	Wts. Davis Crk.	1796	1	72
Lane—See Lam					
Langley, Thomas G.	1,000	Sandy Cr.	1800	1	293
Lankford, Robert	150	Mud River	1811	1	547
Lee, George et al	200	Mth. Campbell's Cr.	1826	2	113
Lemasters, Benjamin	100	Peters Creek	1800	1	222
Lewis, James A. et al	630	Big Sandy Creek	1842	2	457
Lewis, John	250	McKees Meadows Br.	1799	1	172
Lewis, John D.	300	Little Blue Crk.	1844	2	488
Lewis, Robert	50	Adj. his own	1810	1	388
Lewis, Thomas	1,437½	E. Side Big Hurricane	1801	1	296
Lewis, Thomas	43	2nd I. in O. R. abv. mth. Kanawha R.	1796	1	75
Lewis, Warner Washington	15,000	Fks. Gr. Sandy	1801	1	289
Likins, Lickens, Likens, Lykens					
Lickens, Andrew	50	Loop Creek	1828	2	149
Lickens, Andrew	10	Murphy's Br.	1828	2	143
Lickens, Andrew Sr.	10	Wts. Loop Cr.	1828	2	142
Likens—or Lickens, Likins, Lykens					
Likens, Andrew	20	Main Loop Cr.	1829	2	174
Likens, Andrew Jr.	30	Loop Creek	1830	2	180
Likens, Andrew Sr.	40	Main Loop Creek	1829	2	175
Likins, Lickens, Likens, Lykens					
Likins, Peter	100	Witcher's Creek	1815	2	21
Lively, James	92	Cobbs Creek	1831	2	209
Lively, M. A.	54	Crooked Creek	1859	2	701
Lively, Randolph	118	W. Side Coal Riv.	1806	1	367
Lour, Peter	90	E. Side Sandy Riv.	1810	1	416
Low—or Lowe					
Low, Bradley	44	Johnson's Creek	1841	2	450
Low, William	100	Johnson's Creek	1841	2	451
Lowe, Bradley	88	John's Creek	1836	2	321
Lykens, Lickens, Likens, Likins					
Lykens, Peter	66/100a.	Adj. Huddleston, Kan. R.	1830	2	177
Lykens, Peter et al	300	Smith's Creek	1832	2	237
Lynn, John	103	Sugar Camp Fk.	1831	2	200
Madison, Susanna S. & A. S.	2,000	War Creek	1793	1	7
Madison, Susanna S. & A. S.	2,000	Sandy River	1793	1	8
Madison, Susanna S. & A. S.	1,000	Camp Creek	1793	1	9
Madison, Susanna S. & A. S.	400	Hurricane Creek	1793	1	10
Madison, Susanna S. & A. S.	2,000	Sunfish Creek	1793	1	11
Madison, Susanna S. & A. S.	3,000	Mill Creek	1793	1	12
Madison, Susanna S. & A. S.	1,000	12-Pole Creek	1793	1	13
Madison, Susanna S. & A. S.	1,000	Mud River	1793	1	14
Madison, Susanna S. & A. S.	1,000	Burning Creek	1793	1	15
Mahony, Polly (Polly Mahoney)	21	Crooked Cr.	1831	2	210
Manning, William	80	Island Cr.	1827	2	135
Manville, James et al	10,000	Two Mile	1795	1	55
Marks, Evan	30	Lft. Fork	1836	2	318
Martin, Benjamin	85,600	So. W. Side G. Kan.	1796	1	481
Martin, Benjamin	12,300	Between Elk, Gauley	1795	1	479
Martin, Benjamin	9,100	Wts. Gauley R.	1795	1	478
Martin, Deoclesian	30	R. Fk. Pocatalico	1836	2	294
Martin, Deoclesian	100	Pocatalico River	1851	2	599
Martin, Diocletian	81	Rt. Fk. Poca	1858	2	654
Martin, Diocletian	20	Rt. Fk. Poca	1858	2	653
Martin, Diocletian	420	Rt. Fk. Poca	1858	2	652
Martin, Diocletian	264	Rt. Fk. Poca	1858	2	651
Matthews, James Wm.	2,000	Pocatallico, 18-Mi.	1804	1	352
Matthews, Joseph et al	15,000	Fks. Gr. Sandy Riv.	1801	1	286
Maupin, John D.	62½	Davis & Smith Cr.	1838	2	414

Name of Grantee	Acres	Local Description	Year	Book	Page
Morris, Leonard et al	190	Abv. Mth. Bell Cr.	1810	1	446
Morris, Levi	191¼	Kanawha R. Adj. Donally	1830	2	567
Morris, Malan	40½	Big Hurricane	1834	2	273
Morris, Thomas Hrs.	302	Big Hurricane Cr.	1837	2	342
Morris, William	1,200	Teas Valley	1796	1	67
Morris, William	360	Elk River	1791	1	2
Morris, William	660	Kan. Riv.	1793	1	25
Morris, William	250	Hd. Kelley's Creek	1800	1	218
Morris, William	100	Hd. School Hse. Br.	1798	1	150
Morris, William	100	Cane Br. of New R.	1800	1	181
Morris, William	100	Kelley's Creek	1798	1	120
Morris, William	608	New River	1834	2	573
Morris, William et al	2,000	Teas Valley	1793	1	532
Morris, William et al	598	Rock Castle Cr. Br.	1800	1	214
Morris, William et al	1,397	Teays Valley, Mud R.	1800	1	219
Morris, William et al	400	Wts. Sandy River	1800	1	221
Morris, William et al	1,790	Teays Valley	1799	1	175
Morris, William et al	137	Big Hurricane Creek	1799	1	176
Morris, William et al	828	Teas Valley	1799	1	177
Morris, William Jr.	200	No. East Side K.	1798	1	151
Morris, William, Jr. & Sr. et al	100	Morris Creek	1800	1	182
Morrison, George M. et al	500	Wts. 2-Mi. Creek	1860	2	694
Morrison, George M. et al	150	2-Mile Creek	1860	2	693
Morrison, George M. et al	862	Bell Creek	1860	2	691
Morrison, George M. et al	1,000	Bell Creek	1860	2	690
Morrison, George M. et al	5,917	Campbell's Creek	1860	2	689
Morrison, George M. et al	523	Campbell's Creek	1860	2	688
Morrison, George M. et al	2,915	Campbell's Creek	1860	2	686
Morton, Mary et al	4,058	No. W. Side Gr. K.	1801	1	315
Moss, John	145	Kanawha River	1796	1	64
Muncey—See Moncey					
Moxey—See Maxey					
Mynes, Andrew	95	Hurricane Creek	1838	2	395
Mynes, Andrew	30	Big Hurricane	1836	2	296
Mynes, Andrew	25	Brown's Creek	1837	2	334
Mynes, Andrew	150	Big Hurr. Creek	1833	2	245
Mynes, Andrew	40	Big Hurr. Creek	1837	2	351
Mynes, Thomas	48	Big Hurr. Creek	1833	2	251
Mynes, Thomas	26	Big Hurricane	1833	2	248
Neal—or Neel					
Neal, Charles et al	67	Adj. Alderson's	1815	2	13
Neal, Samuel	45	Sine Cr. Br. of Peters	1812	1	586
Neel, William et al	1,000	Island Creek	1793	1	452
Neely, William et al	598	Rock Castle Cr.	1800	1	214
Neely, William et al	1,397	Teays Valley & Mud R.	1800	1	219
Newgin, John	100	Lft. Fk. Peters	1801	1	288
Newman, Peyton	100	Wts. Big Sandy	1810	1	414
Nicholas—See Nichols					
Nicholas, George W.	50	Trace Fork of Mud	1836	2	309
Nicholas, Jacob et al	200	Big Sandy Cr.	1836	2	304
Nicholas, John	70	Mud River	1818	2	49
Nicholas, John	19	Rock Camp	1836	2	308
Nicholas, Samuel et al	65	Trace Fork of Mud	1852	2	609
Nichols—See Nicholas					
Nichols, Austin	50,000	Wts. Coal River	1798	1	113
Nichols, Austin et al	3,289½	Poca, Adj. Hollingsworth	1797	1	130
Nichols, George W.	100	Trace Fork of Mud	1838	2	383
Nichols, James	150	Wts. Peters Creek	1800	1	200
Nichols, Solomon	50	W. Fk. L. Kan.	1841	2	448
Niler—See Nyler					
Norton, Philo et al	2,000	Coal River	1795	1	35
Norton, Philo et al	50,000	Davis Creek	1795	1	51
Norton, Philo et al	26,000	Coal River	1795	1	54
Noyes, Isaac	33	Adj. Clopton	1834	2	442

Name of Grantee	Acres	Local Description	Year	Book	Page
Shrewsbury, Joel et al	113	Coopers Cr.	1831	2	204
Shrewsbury, Joel Jr. et al	210	Coopers Cr. Elk	1831	2	203
Sigman, William B.	200	Frogg's Cr. of Poca	1859	2	676
Sinnett, Abel P.	223	N. W. Elk	1848	2	510
Sinnett, Abel P. et al	1,842	No. Side Elk	1859	2	667
Sinnett, Abel P. et al	134½	Barren Creek	1859	2	666
Sisson, Henry C. et al	985	Wts. Pocatallico	1859	2	662
Skiles, Jacob	32,097	Bet. Elk, Gauley	1797	1	528
Skiles, Jacob	420	Kanawha River	1793	1	29
Skiles, Jacob	40,000	Hd. Kelley's Crk.	1798	1	146
Skiles, Jacob	1,000	Adj. More, McKee, Ohio	1803	1	344
Slack, Greenberry et al	630	Big Sandy Creek	1842	2	457
Slack, John	50	Blue Creek, Elk	1835	2	287
Slack, John et al	200	2-Mi. of Campbell's	1805	1	362
Slaughter, Andrew et al	75	W. Side Kan.	1818	2	44
Slaughter, Andrew et al	80	Adj. Lewis & G. Wash.	1812	1	566
Slaughter, Charles D. et al	90	Wts. Elk	1824	2	98
Slaughter, Goodrich et al	67	Adj. Alderson's	1815	2	13
Slaughter, Reuben	75	Below Gr. Kan. Falls	1802	1	321
Slaughter, Reuben	500	Pocatallico River	1802	1	316
Slaughter, Reuben	200	Two-Mile Cr.	1835	2	283
Slaughter, Reubin	400	Two Mill Cr.	1792	1	449
Slaughter, Reubin	65	Elk River	1798	1	119
Slaughter, Reubin et al	2,000	Gr. Kan. R.	1798	1	140
Slaughter, Reubin et al	268	Kan. R. adj. Harmon	1804	1	347
Smiley, Samuel	150	Lft. Fk. Sandy	1814	2	551
Smiley, Samuel et al	300	Mill Cr. Sandy R.	1811	1	550
Smiley, Samuel et al	200	Lft. Fork Sandy	1811	1	549
Smith, Abraham	50	Toney's Fork	1837	2	368
Smith, Abraham	123	Trace Fk.	1837	2	367
Smith, Abram	70	Trace Fork	1850	2	596
Smith, Allen M.	220	W. Side Coal	1831	2	221
Smith, Allen M.	352	Wts. Coal R.	1838	2	418
Smith, Allen M.	100	Forks Coal R.	1838	2	417
Smith, Anthony	100	S. E. Elk, Porter's Cr.	1838	2	416
Smith, Benjamin H. et al	596	Wts. Pocatalico	1847	2	507
Smith, Conrad	65	Island Kan. below Elk	1796	1	65
Smith, Hezekiah et al	7,000	Wts. Davis Creek	1796	1	72
Smith, James	200	Beech Fk. 12 Pole Cr.	1806	1	368
Smith, James	250	Wts. Guyandotte R.	1810	1	426
Smith, James et al	150,000	Gauley River	1796	1	63
Smith, Joseph	30	Davis Creek	1860	2	695
Smith, Judith et al	4,058	No. W. Side Gr. K.	1801	1	315
Smith, Nathan et al	70	Adj. Lands of L. Wash.	1830	2	185
Smith, Nathan et al	330	Adj. L. Wash.	1826	2	122
Smith, Ralph	100	Porter's Creek	1838	2	419
Smith, Ralph et al	135	S. E. Elk	1838	2	404
Smith, Ralph et al	265	S. S. Elk	1838	2	403
Smith, Richard	40,000	Raccoon Fk. Cabin Cr.	1796	1	501
Smith, Richard	38,277½	Guyandotte, Coal R.	1796	1	498
Smith, Richard	54,800	Lft. Hand Fk. of Coal	1796	1	499
Smith, Samuel	120,000	Coal & Mud Rivers	1796	1	512
Smith, Samuel	25,000	13 & 18 Mile Crks.	1797	1	104
Smith, Samuel	31,000	Wts. Sandy River	1797	1	98
Smith, Samuel	10,000	Old Towne Crk.	1797	1	99
Smith, Samuel	35,000	Sandy Creek	1796	1	80
Smith, Samuel	15,000	Elk River	1796	1	81
Smith, Sameul	31,000	Mid. Fk. Mud R.	1797	1	132
Smith, Samuel	33,000	So. W. Fk. Mud R.	1797	1	133
Smith, Stoddard et al	20,000	Wts. of Coal River	1797	1	126
Smith, Thomas	100	20-Mile Creek	1800	1	237
Smith, Thomas	189	N. W. Side Elk	1854	2	619
Smith, Thomas	100	20-Mile Creek	1812	2	532
Smith, Thomas	90	Big Creek Elk	1838	2	422

Name of Grantee	Acres	Local Description	Year	Book	Page
Smith, William et al	773	Wts. Frogg's Cr.	1860	2	697
Smith, William S.	788	W. Side Gr. K.	1799	1	178
Snider—See Snidow, Snyder, Sydnor					
Snider, Christian	500	W. Bank Guyandotte	1798	1	164
Snidow, Christian	35	Mth. Gr. Guyandotte	1808	1	371
Snodgrass, James	100	Wts. Mud River	1810	1	394
Snyder—Snider, Snidow, Sydnor					
Snyder, Daniel B.	200	N. S. Elk	1845	2	495
Snyder, John	1,084	Queen Shoals Elk	1837	2	363
Snyder, John	3,000	No. W. Side Elk	1860	2	687
Snyder, William G. et al	10,378-1/3	Rt. Hd. Fk. Sandy	1798	1	111
Spencer, John	1,500	Adj. Mercer, Ohio R.	1801	1	312
Spencer, John	3,000	Mill Cr., Ohio R.	1801	1	311
Spurlock, Charles	90	4 Mi Cr. Guyand.	1810	1	444
Spurlock, Richard H.	210	Davis Creek	1852	2	614
Stack, John et al	200	2-Mi. Campbell's Creek	1805	1	362
Stacker—See Stacher, Starcher					
Stacker, Daniel	84	W. Fork L .Kanawha	1825	2	101
Stacker, Philip (Stacher)	171	W. Fk. L. Kanawha	1822	2	75
Stanley, Zachariah et al	1,000	Big Hurricane Crk.	1798	1	144
Starcher—See Stacher, Stacker					
Starcher, Daniel	60	Lft. Fk. West Fk. L. K.	1833	2	256
Starke, John	200	Slaughter's Crk.	1815	2	16
Starke, John	150	Slaughter's Creek	1815	2	14
Starke, John	25	Cabin Cr. Isl. in K. R.	1809	1	374
Starke, Wyatt	100	Slaughters Creek	1799	1	154
Stebbins, William Jr.	2,000	Big Sandy	1848	2	519
Steele, John	27,000	Bet. Elk, Kelly Cr.	1796	1	518
Steele, John	19,500	Bet. Kelly, Bell Crs.	1796	1	520
Steele, John	63,500	Bet. Big, Lit. Sandy	1796	1	526
Steele, John	9,500	No. Side Elk River	1796	1	515
Steele, John	20,000	Elk River	1796	1	83
Steele, John	20,000	Elk River	1796	1	84
Steele, John	10,278	Elk River	1796	1	66
Stephens—See Stephons, Stevens					
Stephens, Absolam	34	Little Hurr. Cr.	1823	2	83
Stephens, John	75	Peters Creek	1800	1	197
Stephens, Thomas et al	560	Catchum Creek	1814	2	559
Stephens, Thomas et al	200	Abv. Mth. Pocatallico	1828	2	144
Stephenson, Elijah	100	Tackett's Crk.	1819	2	52
Stephenson, James	225	Trace Fork	1812	1	575
Stephenson, John	125	Trace Fork	1812	1	574
Stephons—See Stephens, Stevens					
Stephons, Thomas Jr.	180	Trace Fork	1814	2	555
Stephons, Thomas Jr.	390	Little Coal R.	1814	2	556
Stevens—See Stephens, Stephons					
Stevens, Levi, et al	25,000	Wts. Gauley River	1797	1	95
Stevens, Thomas	350	No. Fork Coal	1814	2	557
Stevens, Thomas et al	250	Bull Creek	1815	2	560
Stewart—See Stuart					
Stewart, Alexander	609	Elk Creek	1793	1	17
Stewart, Alexander	200	Elk Creek	1793	1	23
Stewart, Alexander	374	Huff Creek	1793	1	22
Stewart, Alexander	500	Keun Creek	1793	1	20
Stewart, Alexander	1,391	Clear Creek	1793	1	21
Stewart, Alexander	300	Huff Creek	1793	1	18
Stewart, Alexander	500	Clear Creek	1793	1	19
Stiles—See Styles					
Stiles, Isaiah	50	Blue Creek	1822	2	78
Stockton, Aaron et al	300	Smith Creek	1832	2	237
Stockton, Aron	900	Smithers Creek	1832	2	569
Stockton, John	748	Bull Creek	1845	2	492
Stockwell, Mark, Executor	590	No. Side Gauley	1803	1	322
Stone, David et al	7,000	Wts. Davis Crk.	1796	1	72

Name of Grantee	Acres	Local Description	Year	Book	Page
Stone, John	144	Wts. Guyandotte R.	1810	1	408
Straughan, James I.	105	Brown's Creek	1837	2	338
Strickling, Ephraim	100	N. W. Bank Elk	1833	2	254
Strickling, Ephraim	69	Middle Fk. Sandy	1838	2	376
Strobia, John	1,000	Kanawha River	1796	1	76
Strollings, Jacob	50	Narrows E. S. Guyan.	1810	1	393
Stuart—See Stewart					
Stuart, Benjamin	250	Forks Guyandotte R.	1793	1	31
Stuart, Benjamin	500	Elk Creek	1793	1	30
Stump, Michael	183	W. Fk. L. Kan.	1841	2	447
Stump, Michael	116	3-Fks. Big Sandy	1841	2	446
Stump, Michael	100	Three Fks. Sandy	1838	2	373
Sturdivant, John et al	7,000	Wts. Davis Cr.	1796	1	72
Styles—See also Stiles					
Styles, Samuel G. and William	260	Pocatallico R.	1835	2	284
Swan—Also Swann					
Swan, James	2,132	Abv. Gr. Falls Kan. R.	1803	1	325
Swan, James	1,295	Big Hurricane Cr.	1803	1	326
Swan, James	695	Wts. Mud River	1803	1	328
Swan, James	1,130	Wts. Guyandotte	1803	1	327
Swan, James	1,100	Big Hurricane Cr.	1803	1	329
Swan, James	990	Wts. Kanawha River	1803	1	331
Swan, James	734	Wts. Mud R.	1803	1	330
Swan, James	529	Wts. Mud River	1803	1	335
Swann, Thomas B. et al	1,842	No. Side Elk.	1859	2	667
Swann, Thomas B. et al	134½	Barren Creek	1859	2	666
Swift, Jonathan	100,000	Rt. Hd. Fk. B. Sandy	1797	1	128
Swindler, Reuben	150	Teas Valley	1837	2	356
Syares—Also Syars, Syres					
Syares, Elijah (Syars)	61	Poplar Fk.	1823	2	89
Sydnor, William G. et al	10,378-1/3	Rt. Hd. Fk. Sandy R.	1798	1	111
Syres (or Syars) Elijah	180	Big Hurricane	1837	2	350
Tabourn, Robt. et al	550	Wts. of Big Sandy	1801	1	287
Tackett, Lewis	468	Lft. Hd. Fk. of Mud	1799	1	216
Tackett, Lewis	700	Big Hurricane	1800	1	215
Tanner, Samuel	380	Spring Creek	1825	2	109
Taylor, George K.	80,000	Main Fk. Big Sandy	1797	1	103
Taylor, George K.	94,600	Wts. Big Sandy Cr.	1796	1	91
Taylor, George K.	213,000	Sandy, Guyand.	1796	1	88
Taylor, George K.	187,000	Lft. Fk. Big Sandy	1796	1	89
Taylor, George K.	91,000	Old Towne & Big Mill	1796	1	90
Taylor, James	30,000	16-18-Mi. & L. Guyand.	1797	1	94
Taylor, John	32	Mud Lick Fk. Coal R.	1836	2	313
Taylor, John	100	Long Branch	1836	2	329
Taylor, Mathew	322½	Pocatalico Crk.	1799	1	121
Taylor, Phinehas	1,000	Coal River	1795	1	53
Teas—or Tease					
Teas, Thomas	300	Big Hurr. Cr.	1800	1	268
Teas, Thomas	398	Big Hurr. Cr.	1800	1	252
Teas, Thomas et al	598	Rock Castle of Mud	1800	1	214
Teas, Thomas et al	1,397	Teays Valley & Mud	1800	1	219
Teas, Thomas et al	1,790	Teays Valley	1799	1	175
Teas, Thomas et al	828	Teas Valley	1799	1	177
Teas, Thomas et al	137	Big Hurricane Cr.	1799	1	176
Tease—or Teas					
Tease, James T. et al	200	Tackett's Cr.	1833	2	255
Thomas, Joseph	135	Crooked Cr. Coal R.	1810	1	438
Thomas, Joseph	54	Falls Creek	1833	2	241
Thomas, Joseph	172	Alum Lick Br.	1810	1	443
Thomas, Zachariah B.	110	E. Side Kanawha	1818	2	42
Thomas, Zachariah B.	45	Falls, Kanawha	1818	2	41
Thompson, Robert	193	Lft. Fk. Witchers Cr.	1803	1	336
Thompson, Robert	120	Witchers Crk.	1803	1	337
Thompson, William	34½	Fuquas Creek	1832	2	232

Name of Grantee	Acres	Local Description	Year	Book	Page
Ward, William	500	Guyandotte River	1798	1	114
Ward, William	500	Guyandotte River	1798	1	149
Ward, William et al	515	Rt. Fk. Peters Cr.	1800	1	236
Warner, Reuben Jr. et al	7,000	Wts. Davis Crk.	1796	1	72
Warren, Stephen et al	20,000	Wts. Coal River	1797	1	126
Weaver, George et al	100	Mud River	1813	2	534
Welch, George	600	Indian Creek	1799	1	161
Welch, George	100	Elk River	1800	1	253
Welch, Jacob	100	Camp Creek	1816	2	26
Welch, Jacob	50	Coal River	1816	2	27
Welch, James	52,000	Wts. Gauley River	1799	1	173
Welch, James	4,879¼	Wts. Teter's Creek	1797	1	100
Welch, James et al	366¼	Wts. 12-Pole	1801	1	302
Welch, James et al	10,378-1/3	Rt. Hd. Fk. Sandy R.	1798	1	111
Welch, John	300	Head Laurel & Glade	1812	1	582
Welch, John (or Jacob)	50	Coal River	1816	2	25
Wheeler, Alexander	67	Clymer's Creek	1819	2	50
Wheeler, Edward	100	Wts. Mud R.	1858	2	650
White, John P.	74	Jordan's Creek	1836	2	326
White, William	100	Trace Fork	1812	1	588
White, William C.	75	Brown's Creek	1858	2	648
White, William C.	25	Brown's Creek	1858	2	649
Williams, Andrew J.	179	Trace Fork	1858	2	646
Williams, Andrew J.	153	Trace Fork	1858	2	647
Williams, Jonathan	85	Trace Fork	1812	1	578
Williams, Thomas	20,000	Wts. Gauley River	1799	1	174
Wilson, David	38	Davis Creek	1844	2	486
Wilson, David	87	Davis Creek	1844	2	485
Wilson, David	200	Davis Creek	1838	2	372
Wilson, David Jr.	173	Davis Creek	1838	2	427
Wilson, George et al	167	Tyler's Creek	1837	2	333
Wilson, James R. et al	200	Tackett's Cr.	1833	2	255
Wilson, John	186	Coal River	1815	2	3
Wilson, John	200	Campbell's Cr.	1815	2	17
Wilson, John et al	307	W. Side Kanawha	1822	2	76
Wilson, John Sr. Heirs	200	Davis Creek	1838	2	371
Wilson, Robert	210	Wts. McClung's Meadow Cr.	1893	1	338
Wilson, Samuel B.	104	Tackett's Cr. Coal R.	1842	2	456
Wilson, Samuel B.	270	Tackett's Creek	1836	2	330
Wilson, Stephen	1,000	Guyandotte, Adj. Myers	1798	1	531
Wilson, William	93,000	Bet. Elk, Gauley Rs.	1795	1	483
Wilson, William S.	279	Fuquay's Cr.	1859	2	678
Wiltcher, Daniel	10	Guyandotte R.	1810	1	432
Windsor, Benjamin & Charles	35	Hughes Creek	1828	2	148
Wishon, John	130	6-Mile Creek of Guy'd.	1810	1	418
Wood—Woods					
Wood, Henry	100	Half-Mi. below mth. Coal	1810	1	397
Wood, Henry	100	Brown's Cr.	1815	2	18
Wood, Henry	200	Coal River	1815	2	19
Wood, Henry Sr., H. M. & Valentine	800	Coal River	1815	2	12
Wood, Nehemiah	250	Gr. Sandy River	1801	1	314
Wood, Tandy	76	So. Br. Brown's Cr.	1810	1	448
Wood, William	100	Trace Fork	1812	1	590
Wood, William	100	Bryan's Fk. Brown's Cr.	1812	1	591
Woodden—or Wooden					
Woodden, John	250	Gauley River	1796	1	79
Wooden, John	500	McMillion's Creek	1808	1	372
Woods—also Wood					
Woods, Milton	199½	Walker's Fork	1845	2	491
Work, Andrew et al	30,000	Elk River Mth. Big Sandy	1796	1	459
Work, Andrew et al	30,000	Elk River, Blue Cr.	1796	1	457
Work, Andrew et al	40,000	10-Mile Cr. of Gr. K.	1796	1	456
Wright, John et al	167	Tyler's Creek	1837	2	333
Wyatt, Matthew P.	9,247	Cabin Creek	1859	2	684

Name of Grantee	Acres	Local Description	Year	Book	Page
Wyatt, Matthew P.	29	Cabin Creek	1838	2	441
Wyatt, Matthew P. et al	248½	Cabin Creek	1838	2	440
Wyatt, Reuben	60	Big Hurricane Cr.	1837	2	344
Young, Benjamin S.	390	Cooper's Creek	1849	2	520
Young, Charles	50	Falling Rock Cr.	1828	2	147
Young, Conrad	100	Peters Creek	1800	1	297
Young, Edward	2,000	Gauley River	1795	1	33
Young, Edward	2,700	Gauley River	1795	1	34
Young, George	100	Blue Creek	1820	2	57
Young, George W.	220	Big Hurricane Cr.	1837	2	341
Young, Henry, Adm.	2,000	Betw. Pocatallico & 18 Mi.	1804	1	352
Young, Jacob	20	Big Hurricane	1832	2	229
Young, Jacob	52	Big Hurricane	1837	2	360
Young, James	25	Big Hurricane	1833	2	252
Young, James	25	Big Hurricane	1833	2	250
Young, John	50	Big Hurricane	1833	2	244
Young, John	100	Elk R. Adj. J. Osborne	1800	1	210
Young, John	180	No. Side Elk	1825	2	102
Young, John	200	Gr. Kan. River	1792	1	3
Young, John et al	90	Wts. Elk	1824	2	98
Young, John D.	150	Wts. Elk River	1829	2	165
Young, John Sr.	50	Leatherwood Cr. of Elk	1829	2	157
Young, Lewis	120	Leatherwood Cr. of Elk	1838	2	423
Young, Lewis et al	100	W. Side Elk	1829	2	164
Young, Robert	400	Buffalo Cr., Elk	1800	1	276
Young, Robert	100,000	Coal, Mud Rivers	1795	1	495
Young, Robert et al	100,000	Fks. Gr. Sandy	1800	1	270
Young, Robert et al	142,236¼	Rt. Fk. Big Sandy	1800	1	271
Young, Samuel	43	Wts. Elk	1838	2	424
Young, William	40	Mill Cr., Elk	1828	2	141

LEWIS COUNTY

Alexander, Vincent	65	Simms Run	1838	1	420
Alkire, David	100	Wts. West Fork	1831	1	148
Alkire, James	150	Skin Creek	1838	2	28
Alkire, John et al	208	Weston & Fairmont T'Pk.	1860	2	484
Alkire, Nicholas	223	Fink's Fork	1838	2	27
Alkire, Nicholas	177	Fink's Fork	1838	2	26
Alkire, Nicholas	500	Sand Fork	1840	2	32
Alkire, Nicholas	435	Dry Fork	1840	2	33
Alkire, Nicholas	140	Fink's Fork	1837	1	288
Alkire, Nicholas & John	12	Hacker's Creek	1858	2	473
Allen, James	100	Skin Creek	1830	1	136
Armstrong, Alexander	100	Bone Creek	1838	1	392
Armstrong, John I. P.	100	Mud Lick Run	1838	1	421
Armstrong, John I. P.	142	Sand Fork	1820	1	39
Armstrong, John I. P. et al	114	Fritzes' Run	1838	1	422
Armstrong, John I. P. et al	106	Sand Fork	1838	2	25
Armstrong, Mathias B.	36	Sand Fork	1843	2	156
Armstrong, Mathias B. et al	120	West Fork	1842	2	82
Armstrong, Mathias B. et al	180	Fritz's Run	1842	2	81
Arnold, Elijah Tr.	200	Goose Pen	1844	2	216
Arnold, Elijah Tr.	900	Ben's Run	1844	2	217
Arnold, George	590	Freeman's Creek	1820	1	47
Arnold, George	826	Freeman's Creek	1820	1	48
Arnold, George I.	168	Cap Run	1844	2	188

Name of Grantee	Acres	Local Description	Year	Book	Page
Arnold, George I.	61	Stone Coal	1858	2	475
Arnold, George I.	500	Oil Creek	1857	2	468
Arnold, George I.	325	Turkey Run	1852	2	434
Arnold, George I.	257	Two Lick Run	1854	2	458
Arnold, George I.	1,733	Butcher's Fork	1851	2	427
Arnold, George I.	150	Adj. David Bennett	1851	2	412
Arnold, George I.	23	Buck Hill	1851	2	420
Arnold, George I.	6	Hackers Creek	1850	2	402
Arnold, George I.	1,000	Hog Camp	1849	2	374
Arnold, George I.	1,314	Crooked Fork	1849	2	378
Arnold, George I.	185	Fritz's Run	1849	2	375
Arnold, George I.	456	Stone Coal	1849	2	377
Arnold, George I.	70	Lick Run	1848	2	361
Arnold, George I.	200	Aquilla Run	1850	2	380
Arnold, George I.	500	Adj. Cox & Weybright	1850	2	381
Arnold, George I.	383	Wts. Buckhannon R.	1847	2	341
Arnold, George I.	614	Wts. West Fork	1847	2	340
Arnold, George I.	150	Hacker's Creek	1847	2	334
Arnold, George I.	52	Adj. S. Bonnett	1844	2	292
Arnold, George I.	150	Polk Creek	1844	2	291
Arnold, George I.	500	Poplar Lick	1844	2	200
Arnold, George I.	120	West Fork	1842	2	97
Arnold, George I.	50	Oil Creek	1842	2	87
Arnold, George I.	154	Mud Lick	1842	2	83
Arnold, George I. et al	1,500	Laurel Fork	1844	2	214
Arnold, George I. et al	210	Skin Creek	1852	2	435
Arnold, George I. et al	500	Turkey Run	1850	2	395
Arnold, George I. et al	280	Oil Creek	1846	2	322
Arnold, George I. et al	71	Stone Coal	1844	2	290
Arnold, George I. et al	100	Pringle's Fork	1844	2	245
Arnold, George I. et al	500	Strait Fork	1844	2	241
Arnold, George I. et al	285	Barn's Run	1844	2	199
Arnold, George I. et al	120	West Fork	1842	2	82
Arnold, George I. et al	180	Fritz's Run	1842	2	81
Arnold, George I. (or J.)	95	Jonathan's Run	1844	2	187
Arnold, George I. & Wm. E.	2,800	Canoe Run	1844	2	244
Arnold, George I. & Wm. E.	350	Wild Cat Run	1847	2	342
Arnold, George I. & Wm. E. et al	520	Rocky Fork	1844	2	223
Arnold, Isaac	25	Owen's Fork	1842	2	68
Arnold, James	534	Mill Stone	1820	1	38
Arnold, James	430	Left Fork of Steer Cr.	1820	1	36
Arnold, James	311	Freeman's Creek	1820	1	37
Arnold, James	468	Freeman's Creek	1819	1	31
Arnold, James	278	Leading Creek	1819	1	30
Arnold, James	500	Fink's Fork	1819	1	13
Arnold, James	200	Leading Creek	1819	1	14
Arnold, James	122	Leading Creek	1819	1	15
Arnold, James I.	50	Cedar Creek	1841	2	52
Arnold, James I.	18	Cedar Creek	1841	2	51
Arnold, James J.	80	Cedar Creek	1831	1	155
Arnold, James J.	50	Cedar Creek	1833	1	205
Arnold, James W.	150	Horn Creek	1831	1	168
Arnold, Porter M.	125	Rocky Fork	1844	2	224
Arnold, William E.	100	Adj. George Jackson	1847	2	319
Arnold, William E.	223	Adj. Carper & Westfall	1847	2	343
Arnold, William E.	130	Oil Creek	1849	2	376
Arnold, William E. et al	1,460	Leading Cr.	1845	2	296
Arnold, William E. & George I. et al	600	Rush Run	1847	2	333
Bailey—See Bayley					
Ball, Agilla W.	23	Rush Run	1838	1	393
Ball, McFarlin	50	Mill Run	1842	2	69
Barnhous—or Barnhouse, Bennhouse					
Barnhous, John	70	Steer Creek	1831	1	167
Barnhouse, Kesia	60	Wts. Cedar Cr.	1834	1	222

Name of Grantee	Acres	Local Description	Year	Book	Page
Bayley, Charles B.	110	Calf Run	1850	2	400
Beall—See Beel					
Beall, George H.	50	Big Root	1843	2	159
Beall, George H.	57	Big Root	1844	2	167
Beall, George H.	50	Wts. Little Kan.	1837	1	299
Beall, George H.	50	Stinking Cr.	1837	1	298
Beall, George H.	50	Wts. Lit. Kanawha	1838	1	411
Beall, Henry	100	Rowels Run	1844	2	289
Beall, Townsend	50	Wts. Lit. Kanawha	1837	1	297
Bee, Asa	21	Hughes River	1838	1	409
Bee, Asa	50	Hughes River	1838	1	410
Beel—See also Beall					
Beel, George	50	S. Side Lit. Kan.	1833	1	216
Bennett, David	33	Skin Creek	1847	2	321
Bennett, David	609	Sand Fork	1847	2	320
Bennett, David	54	Fall Run	1847	2	331
Bennett, David	100	Bennett's Run	1847	2	330
Bennett, David	115	Stone Coal	1847	2	332
Bennett, David	322½	Big Lick	1847	2	339
Bennett, David	200	Laurel Fork	1847	2	338
Bennett, David	104	Adj. J. Wilson	1850	2	398
Bennett, James	700	Sand Fork	1848	2	349
Bennett, James	1,678	Glady Fork L. Kan.	1848	2	355
Bennett, James	1,164	White's Camp Fork	1848	2	354
Bennett, James	100	Raccoon Run	1852	2	436
Bennett, J. M.	430	Polk Cr.	1851	2	407
Bennett, J. M.	1,500	Leather Bark	1861	2	491
Bennett, J. M. et al	700	Wts. Buckhannon R.	1850	2	383
Bennett, J. M. et al	300	Wts. Buckhannon R.	1850	2	382
Bennett, J. M. et al	79	Leading Cr.	1861	2	489
Bennett, John	100	Skin Creek	1820	1	46
Bennett, Jonathan M.	310	Sugar Camp	1854	2	459
Bennett, Jonathan M.	500	Adj. Banks Survey	1850	2	404
Bennett, Jonathan M.	1,130	Wts. Lit. Kanawha	1848	2	365
Bennett, Jonathan M.	850	Big Swamp	1848	2	353
Bennett, Jonathan M.	730	Laurel Fork	1847	2	344
Bennett, Jonathan M.	930	Laurel Fork	1847	2	336
Bennett, Jonathan M.	1,990	French Creek	1847	2	329
Bennett, Jonathan M.	133	Leatherbark	1847	2	328
Bennett, Jonathan M.	122	Hacker's Creek	1847	2	327
Bennett, Jonathan M.	1,100	Crooked Run	1847	2	318
Bennett, Jonathan M.	103	Wts. West Fork	1846	2	315
Bennett, Jonathan M.	463	Wts. West Fork	1846	2	316
Bennett, Jonathan M. et al	1,000	Wts. Little Kanawha	1848	2	366
Bennett, Jonathan M. et al	50	Leading Creek	1846	2	309
Bennett, Jonathan M. et al	106	Wts. Lit. Kanawha	1844	2	255
Bennett, Jonathan M. et al	100	Big Root	1844	2	256
Bennett, Jonathan M. et al	500	Yellow Creek	1844	2	257
Bennett, Jonathan M. et al	400	Flat Fork	1844	2	258
Bennett, Jonathan M. et al	1,500	Laurel Fork	1844	2	214
Bennett, Joseph	75	Mill Run	1844	2	225
Bennett, Lewis M.	50	Wts. Steer Creek	1844	2	288
Bennhouse—See Barnhous, Barnhouse					
Bennhouse, Solomon D.	50	S. W. Br. Lit. Kanawha	1833	1	217
Benson, Robert A. et al	1,460	Leading Cr.	1845	2	296
Berlin, George W. et al	300	Grand Camp	1851	2	413
Berlin, George W. et al	140½	Wts. Buckhannon R.	1851	2	414
Berlin, George W. et al	90	Wts. Buckhannon R.	1851	2	415
Berry, William	250	Salt Lick	1821	1	60
Berry, William	100	Salt Lick Creek	1820	1	44
Bezle, Isaac	25	L. K. R.	1829	1	131
Bland, Theodore G. et al	177	Bear Fork	1844	2	197
Bland, Theodore G. et al	200	Philip's Run	1844	2	196
Bland, Thomas	480	Murphy's Creek	1838	1	389

Name of Grantee	Acres	Local Description	Year	Book	Page
Bland, Thomas	800	Hughes River	1842	2	98
Bland, William J.	175	Wts. Steer Creek	1844	2	181
Bland, William J. et al	175	Trace Fork	1845	2	305
Bland, William J. et al	1,000	Tanner's Fork	1845	2	304
Bland, William J. et al	148	Buck Run	1844	2	228
Bland, Wm. J. et al	20	Wts. West Fork	1844	2	227
Bogarth, Valentine	200	Hughes River	1833	1	193
Boggs, Andrew	300	Bear Garden	1831	1	161
Boggs, William	83	Steer Creek	1824	1	78
Boilon (or Boiton), Thomas	60	Sand Fork	1838	1	423
Boilon, Thomas	20	Indian Fork	1838	2	24
Boilon, Thomas	50	Indian Fork	1838	2	23
Boilon, Thomas et al	520	Rocky Fork	1844	2	223
Bond, William T. et al	140½	Wts. Buckhannon R.	1851	2	414
Bond, William T. et al	90	Wts. Buckhannon R.	1851	2	415
Bond, William T. et al	300	Grand Camp	1851	2	413
Bond, William T. et al	190	Ten-Mile Cr.	1851	2	432
Bonnett, Jesse	100	Wolf Pen	1840	2	42
Bonnett, Samuel B.	17	Hacker's Creek	1850	2	397
Bonwell, Samuel (Bonnett)	100	Laurel Lick	1836	1	272
Booher, Jacob	300	Fink's Fork	1832	1	189
Boon, Jacob	125	Bear Fork	1844	2	186
Bouse, Jesse (Boise)	115	McCord Run	1848	2	367
Bozarth, George	159	Fink's Run	1819	1	25
Bozarth, George	58	Fink's Run	1818	1	6
Bozarth, George	150	Fink's Run	1818	1	8
Brannan, George	85	Laurel Creek	1837	1	291
Brannon, Grandes	100	Farmer's Fork	1828	1	109
Brannon, Jesse	100	Cedar Creek	1828	1	113
Brannon, John	190	Middle Run	1850	2	389
Brannon, John et al	300	Grand Camp	1851	2	410
Brannon, Samuel M.	50	Spring Fork	1842	2	62
Brannon, Samuel M.	47	Cedar Creek	1838	2	21
Brannon, Samuel M.	100	Mark's Ford	1836	1	281
Brannon, Thomas	100	Cedar Creek	1826	1	96
Brannon, Thomas H.	100	Stinking Creek	1847	2	317
Brannon, Thomas H.	150	Wts. Lit. Kanawha	1838	2	20
Brannon, Thomas H.	36	Wts. Lit. Kanawha	1829	1	132
Brown, John J.	200	Leading Creek	1834	1	218
Brown (or Broun), Wm. C. et al	800	Dry Run	1844	2	226
Burk, John	150	Cedar Creek	1834	1	248
Burr, Elldridge G.	300	Buckhannon River	1844	2	201
Burress, Archable	50	Wts. Lit. Kanawha	1830	1	138
Bush, Abraham	50	Wts. Lit. Kanawha	1838	2	22
Bush, Abraham	100	Wts. Lit. Kanawha	1836	1	283
Bush, Adam	9	Leading Creek	1837	1	292
Bush, Adam	27	Sanging Run	1837	1	293
Bush, George	80	Buckhannon River	1818	1	3
Bush, George	100	Stone Coal	1818	1	4
Bush, George W.	100	Wolf Run	1848	2	362
Bush, Henry	15	Leading Cr.	1837	1	295
Bush, Henry	85	Horn Creek	1838	1	334
Bush, Jacob	23	Horn Creek	1838	1	337
Bush, Jacob	50	Stone Lick	1838	1	336
Bush, Jacob	218	Horn Creek	1838	1	335
Bush, Jacob	200	Leading Creek	1831	1	157
Bush, Jacob H.	100	Horn Creek	1832	1	185
Bush, Jacob H.	29	Second Big Run	1843	2	157
Bush, John	70	Tanner's Fork	1833	1	198
Bush, John	25	Tanner's Fork	1837	1	294
Bush, Michael G.	750	Sand Fork	1847	2	337
Bush, Michael G.	100	Canoe Run	1836	1	267
Bush, Michael G.	110	Waters W. Fork	1842	2	88

Name of Grantee	Acres	Local Description	Year	Book	Page
Campbell, Charles T. (or F.) S.	86	Peck's Run	1836	1	261
Carmack, Evan	50	Adj. Fisher	1844	2	287
Cline, George	100	Leading Creek	1833	1	212
Cline, John	112	Leading Creek	1828	1	105
Collins, Cline	100	Sand Fork	1843	2	129
Collins, George	100	Leading Cr.	1828	1	110
Collins, Isaac S.	50	Leading Creek	1842	2	63
Collins, Isaac S.	150	Leading Creek	1842	2	64
Collins, Isaac S.	125	Yellow Creek	1842	2	65
Collins, Robert et al	75	Polk Creek	1822	1	63
Collins, Robert W.	110	Salt Lick	1821	1	61
Collins, Robert W.	250	Salt Lick	1819	1	32
Collins, Robert W.	10	Wts. West Fork	1819	1	16
Collins, Robert W.	50	Geelick Run	1819	1	11
Collins, Robert W.	430	Salt Lick	1819	1	24
Collins, Robert W. et al	130	Salt Lick	1818	1	5
Collins, William	44½	Stewart Cr.	1842	2	70
Collins, William	25	Stuart Creek	1842	2	71
Conley, George	140	West Fork	1833	1	191
Connally, Thomas C.	40	Dry Run	1843	2	151
Connally, Thomas C.	40	Dry Run	1843	2	150
Connally, Thomas C.	200	Wts. Lit. Kanawha	1844	2	206
Conrad—Coonrad					
Conrad, Currence B.	100	Big Ellis	1838	1	425
Conrad, Currence B.	350	Sand Fork	1838	1	424
Conrad, Currence B.	60	Jesuit Run	1854	2	457
Conyers, Enoch	100	Cedar Creek	1837	1	328
Coonrod—or Conrad					
Coonrod, Jacob	50	Dusk Camp	1840	2	46
Cox, David S.	100	Cedar Creek	1834	1	231
Cox, Isaac Jr.	100	Freeman's Creek	1840	2	49
Cox, Isaac P.	38	Buck Lick	1837	1	306
Cox, Isaac P.	200	Smoke Camp	1828	1	116
Cox, Isaac P. and Philip Jr.	400	Freeman's Creek	1840	2	43
Cox, John S.	50	Horn Creek	1842	2	118
Cox, Philip	100	Spruce Fork	1843	2	158
Cox, Philip Jr.	63	Horn Creek	1845	2	298
Cox, Philip Jr.	125	Leading Creek	1834	1	245
Cox, Philip Jr.	50	Leading Creek	1838	1	346
Cox, Philip Jr.	200	Isaac's Branch	1838	1	395
Cox, Philip Jr.	50	Fink's Fork	1838	1	396
Cox, Philip Jr.	100	Spring Fork	1844	2	246
Cox, Philip Jr.	67	Wts. Lit. Kanawha	1844	2	285
Cox, Philip Jr.	50	Mill Stone	1840	2	34
Cox, Philip Jr. et al	265	Bloody Run	1838	1	434
Cox, William F. & George K.	45	Bone Creek	1842	2	119
Cox, William Floyd and George K.	80	Wts. Hughes Riv.	1842	2	99
Crawford, Robert	300	Indian Cap Run	1838	1	384
Crawford, William	300	McCord's Run	1842	2	89
Crites, William	87	Mud Lick	1831	1	139
Cutright, Abraham	125	French Creek	1823	1	69
Cutright, Abraham	157	French Creek	1831	1	163
Cutright, Lot et al	25	French Creek	1845	2	297
Davis, William	40	Stone Coal	1823	1	71
Davisson, Israel	100	Spruce Creek	1843	2	131
Deen, John	5	W. Side Buckhn. R.	1848	2	346
Deen, Lare	10	Peck's Run	1846	2	313
Depew, Henry	78	No. Side Lit. Kan.	1821	1	62
Despard, Burton	7,990	Wts. Buckhn. R.	1844	2	175
Despard, Burton	262	Sand Fork	1844	2	176
Despard, Burton	200	Yellow Creek	1844	2	284
Despard, Burton	426	Adj. Camden	1844	2	283
Despard, Burton	500	Pine Creek	1844	2	252

Name of Grantee	Acres	Local Description	Year	Book	Page
Despard, Burton	438	Big Root	1844	2	253
Despard, Burton	1,500	Wts. W. Fork	1844	2	254
Despard, Burton	1,200	Nigh Cut Run	1844	2	251
Despard, Burton	1,000	Trace Fork	1844	2	250
Despard, Burton	400	Skin Creek	1850	2	392
Despard, Burton et al	79	Leading Cr.	1861	2	489
Despard, Burton et al	1,000	Wts. Lit. Kanawha	1848	2	366
Diss Debar, I. H.	1,405	Fink's Fork	1853	2	447
Diss Debar, I. H.	1,464	Back Fork	1853	2	446
Diss Debar, I. H.	2,507	Freeman's Creek	1853	2	445
Diss Debar, I. H.	1,131	Walnut Fork	1853	2	444
Dobbens, John	100	O'Brians Fork	1824	1	84
Dobbins, John	200	Steer Creek	1828	1	118
Dobins, John & Samuel	150	Plantation Fork	1819	1	18
Duvall, George T. et al	280	Oil Creek	1846	2	322
Edmiston, Matthew	850	Wts. Buckhannon R.	1850	2	390
Fetty, E.	100	Big White Oak	1859	2	480
Fetty, E. et al	33	Polk Creek	1852	2	437
Fetty, Esaias	50	Polk Creek	1859	2	481
Fisher, Charles	107	Crawford Fork	1828	1	120
Fisher, George	200	Washburn Run	1823	1	68
Fisher, George et al	100	Polk Creek	1820	1	35
Fisher, George Jr.	200	Middle Run	1842	2	86
Fisher, George Jr.	195	Murphy's Creek	1834	1	246
Fisher, Michael	150	Sand Run	1824	1	74
Fisher, Michael	100	Laurel Fork	1838	1	398
Fisher, Philip	100	Tanner's Fork	1833	1	206
Fisher, Philip	47	Tanner's Fork	1837	1	326
Fisher, Philip	150	Tanner's Fork	1847	2	325
Flesher, Henry	85	Polk Creek	1844	2	282
Flesher, John	50	Hacker's Creek	1834	1	238
Flesher, John	3a.3r.12p.	Birch Ridge	1838	1	412
Flesher, John (of Henry)	3	W. Side W. Fk. Riv.	1847	2	323
Flesher, Solomon	40	Polk Creek	1842	2	104
Fling, John	100	Wts. Lit. Kanawha	1837	1	323
Furr, Bushrod	50	Paddy's Run	1844	2	218
Furr, Bushrod	100	Spruce Fork	1843	2	133
Furr, Bushrod	100	Crooked Run	1843	2	132
Furr, Bushrod et al	191	Duck Run	1843	2	136
Furr, Shelton	300	Fink's Fork	1838	2	18
Gainer, Bryan	65	Tanner's Fork	1842	2	72
Galford, James H.	6½	Rt. Hd. Fk. West Fk.	1861	2	490
Gibson, Jacob	50	Salt Lick	1836	1	256
Gibson, Jacob & James	185	Salt Lick Creek	1819	1	17
Gibson, Nicholas	256	Salt Lick	1821	1	54
Gibson, Nicholas et al	130	Salt Lick Creek	1820	1	43
Gibson, Nicholas et al	700	Salt Lick Cr.	1820	1	42
Gibson, William	100	Skin Creek	1848	2	356
Goff, Alexander	150	Wts. Lit. Kanawha	1826	1	101
Goff, George G.	250	Leading Creek	1832	1	174
Goff, George G.	60	Wts. Lit. Kanawha	1827	1	129
Goff, George G.	150	Leading Creek	1835	1	253
Goff, George G.	50	Leading Creek	1835	1	254
Goff, George G.	50	Stinker's Creek	1836	1	275
Goff, George G.	50	Leading Cr.	1838	1	349
Goff, George G.	100	Big Run, Leading Cr.	1838	1	348
Goff, George W. & Hiram A.	180	Stinking Cr.	1838	1	413
Goff, Strawther	34	Adj. his own	1838	2	17
Goff, Strawther	66	Wts. Lit. Kanawha	1837	1	300
Goff, Thomas	200	Sycamore Run	1844	2	168
Gould, William O. et al	100	Pringle's Fork	1844	2	245
Green, John	155	Steer Creek	1819	1	20
Green, John	95	Steer Creek	1819	1	19
Hacker, John T.	250	Buffalo Lick	1838	1	414

Name of Grantee	Acres	Local Description	Year	Book	Page
Hacker, Jonathan	2a.3r.28p.	Stillhouse Run	1826	1	97
Hackert—or Heckert					
Hackert, Daniel	50	Leading Cr.	1830	1	135
Halbert—or Holbert					
Halbert, Thomas	100	Wts. Lit. Kanawha	1830	1	137
Hall, John	100	Horn Creek	1838	1	343
Hall, John	50	Horn Creek	1845	2	301
Hall, Jona T.	20	McLaine's Run	1837	1	312
Hall, Joseph	300	Polk Creek	1824	1	79
Hall, Joseph	400	Skin Creek	1820	1	45
Hall, Joseph	500	Skin Creek	1818	1	2
Hall, Mary	100	Freeman's Creek	1832	1	172
Hall, Richard	150	McCan Run W. Fk.	1831	1	151
Hall, Richard	100	McCan's Run	1838	1	333
Halmick, Jacob B. et al	12	Wts. Hughes, Wolf Run	1859	2	482
Hardman, George W.	100	Pine Creek	1843	2	135
Hardman, George W.	50	Big Root	1843	2	134
Hardman, John	100	Skin Creek	1826	1	93
Hardman, Thomas	91	Cedar Creek	1840	2	31
Harris, William	100	Bee Run	1819	1	28
Hawkins, John	40	Murphy's Creek	1856	2	452
Hawkins, John	54	Murphy's Creek	1850	2	387
Hawkins, John	87	Murphy's Creek	1850	2	386
Hawkins, John	364	Middle Run	1849	2	371
Hawkins, John	10	Polk Creek	1849	2	370
Hawkins, John	75	Murphy's Creek	1849	2	373
Hawkins, John	14	Murphy's Creek	1849	2	372
Hawkins, John	100	Bush Fork	1844	2	205
Haymond, Luther	830	Hog Camp Fork	1851	2	423
Haymond, Wilson	120	Salt Lick	1837	1	327
Haymond, Wilson M.	100	Left Hand Fk.	1837	1	310
Haymond, Wilson M.	130	Wts. Lit. Kanawha	1842	2	122
Hays, Ebenezer	380	Adj. Maxwell	1838	2	13
Hays, John H.	25	Adj. J. Straley	1842	2	105
Hays, John H.	50	Hacker's Cr.	1844	2	166
Hays, John H.	25	Wts. Still Run	1844	2	165
Hays, Peregrine	180	Mill Stone	1842	2	58
Hays, Peregrine	100	Mill Stone	1842	2	59
Hays, Peregrine	133	Bull Fork	1843	2	160
Hays, Peregrine	380	Sycamore Run	1844	2	281
Hays, Peregrine et al	256	Mill Stone	1844	2	236
Hays, Peregrine et al	197	Bull Fork	1843	2	161
Hays, Peregrine et al	149	Daniel's Run	1844	2	259
Hays, Peregrine et al	95	Daniel's Run	1844	2	260
Hays, Samuel L.	460	Wts. Lit. Kanawha	1838	2	14
Heckert—or Hackart					
Heckert, Adam	300	Bloody Run	1837	1	313
Heckert, Adam	50	Leading Cr.	1838	1	385
Heckert, Henry E.	50	Bloody Run	1838	1	427
Heckert, Henry E.	150	Horn Creek	1838	1	436
Heckert, Henry E.	19	Leading Cr.	1838	1	426
Heckert, Henry E.	57	Horn Creek	1838	1	399
Heckert, John	50	Leading Cr.	1828	1	119
Heckert, Peter	80	Leading Cr.	1828	1	121
Hickel, Sanford A.	100	Calf Run	1838	1	350
Hinzman, Abraham	238	Lick Fork	1856	2	466
Hinzman, Henry	80	Hacker's Cr.	1836	1	278
Hinzman, Thomas C.	150	Three-Lick	1855	2	461
Hoffman—or Huffman					
Hoffman, John et al Heirs	100	Leading Cr.	1838	1	416
Hoffman, John S.	500	Horn Creek	1844	2	233
Hoffman, John S. et al	95	Daniel's Run	1844	2	260
Hoffman, John S. et al	149	Daniel's Run	1844	2	259

Name of Grantee	Acres	Local Description	Year	Book	Page
Jackson, George A.	40	Bet. Middle, So. Fk.	1853	2	450
Jackson, George W.	18	Wts. Buckhannon R.	1850	2	405
Jackson, George W.	112	Adj. Hurley	1851	2	425
Jackson, Henry	493	Big Sand Run	1842	2	84
Jackson, Jacob I.	24	Stone Coal Cr.	1842	2	57
James, Allon	340	Glady Fork	1824	1	83
Jeffries, James	40	Hughes Run	1832	1	180
Johnson—or Johnston					
Johnson, Elizabeth et al Heirs	175	Wts. Lit. Kanawha	1842	2	75
Johnson, Levi	100	Wts. Lit. Kanawha	1842	2	74
Johnson, Richard	271	Skin Creek	1837	1	325
Johnson, Richard	66	Stone Coal	1859	2	479
Johnson, Richard	306	Canoe Run	1844	2	261
Johnson, Richard et al	71	Stone Coal	1844	2	290
Johnson, William	75	Skin Creek	1838	1	386
Johnston—or Johnson					
Johnston, Perry H.	56	Big Skin Creek	1859	2	483
Johnston, Richard	70	Skin Creek	1848	2	358
Johnston, Richard	220	Skin Creek	1821	1	56
Johnston, Richard et al	57	Skin Creek	1838	2	12
Jones, Samuel	50	Bear Run Lit. Kan.	1834	1	233
Keener, Thomas	50	Steer Creek	1830	1	133
Keeth, James	150	Skin Creek	1822	1	64
Keller, John	200	Wts. Lit. Kanawha	1838	1	400
Kniseley, Washington	25	Leading Creek	1838	1	347
Lacy, Richmond T. et al	800	Wts. Buckhannon R.	1844	2	179
Lacy, Richmond T. et al	640	Wts. Buckhannon R.	1844	2	178
Lacy, Richmond T. et al	518	Indian Camp	1844	2	177
Lance, Henry	200	Big Run	1842	2	106
Law, Asa	40	Sycamore Lick	1859	2	477
Law, Asa	145	Adj. his own	1859	2	478
Linch—or Lynch					
Linch, George	50	E. Side Cedar Cr.	1834	1	223
Linch, George	50	Pine Narrows	1833	1	213
Linch, Levi	68	Wts. Lit. Kanawha	1825	1	88
Linger, Philip M. et al	250	Stone Coal	1857	2	469
Lorentz—or Lorrentz					
Lorentz, Jacob	30	Fick's Run	1836	1	263
Lorentz, Jacob	164	Peck's Run	1836	1	265
Lorentz, Jacob Jr. & Philip A. et al	200	Leading Creek	1856	2	465
Lorentz, Jacob Jr. & Philip A. et al	700	Camp Run	1856	2	464
Lorentz, John	100	Cider Creek	1835	1	255
Lorrentz, Jacob	674	Cutright Run	1826	1	92
Lowther, Daniel S. & Wm. et al	264	Abv. Mth. Stinking Cr.	1848	2	379
Lowther, Elias	200	Bone Creek	1831	1	145
Lowther, Elias et al	130	Salt Lick	1818	1	5
Lowther, Robert	180	W. Fk. Riv.	1824	1	76
Lowther, Wm. & Daniel et al Heirs	300	Freeman's Creek	1838	2	5
Lowther, Wm. & Daniel et al Heirs	61	Freeman's Creek	1838	2	6
Lowther, Wm. & Daniel et al Heirs	567	Polk Creek	1838	2	7
Lowther, Wm. & Daniel et al Heirs	100	Leading Cr.	1838	1	416
Lynch—or Linch					
Lynch, Adam	84	Mud Lick	1843	2	138
Lynch, George	25	Wts. Lit. Kanawha	1838	2	8
Lynch, George	50	Wts. Lit. Kanawha	1838	2	9
Lynch, George	50	Cedar Creek	1836	1	266
Lynch, George et al	191	Duck Run	1843	2	136
Lynch, George Jr.	200	Spruce Run	1843	2	137
Lynch, George Jr.	427	Bear Run	1842	2	56
Lynch, George Jr.	122	Duck Run	1842	2	55
Lynch, George Jr. et al	200½	Burks Run	1845	2	299
Lynch, Levi	30	Sand Fork	1844	2	280
Mace, Jacob	250	Wts. Lit. Kanawha	1828	1	112
Manier, Michael	100	Sand Fork	1844	2	279

Name of Grantee	Acres	Local Description	Year	Book	Page
Marks, Hiram	50	Cedar Creek	1843	2	144
Marks, Hiram	25	Adj. Morgan Marks	1837	1	317
Marks, Morgan	150	Cedar Creek	1836	1	264
Marks, Morgan	31	Paddy's Run	1837	1	316
Marks, Morgan	100	Cedar Creek	1836	1	268
Marks, Morgan	93	Adj. his own	1837	1	314
Marks, Morgan	35	Hd. Steer Creek	1837	1	315
Marsh, George I. et al	250	Stone Coal	1857	2	469
Martin, Stephen	338	Peck's Run	1826	1	94
Matthews, Joseph	125	Murphy's Creek	1858	2	471
Matthews, Joseph	126	Middle Run	1855	2	463
Maxwell, Levi	500	Polk Creek	1844	2	207
Maxwell, Levi	65	Glick Run	1844	2	238
Maxwell, Levi	105	Leading Creek	1844	2	239
Maxwell, Levi	272½	Crawford's Fork	1842	2	67
Maxwell, Lewis	120	Stone Coal	1831	1	169
Maxwell, Lewis	100	Sand Fork	1838	1	364
Maxwell, Lewis	150	Tom's Fork	1838	1	366
Maxwell, Lewis	62	Tom's Fork	1838	1	365
Maxwell, Lewis	150	Indian Fork	1838	1	369
Maxwell, Lewis	110	Robert's Fork	1838	1	368
Maxwell, Lewis	50	Fink's Fork	1838	1	367
Maxwell, Lewis	105	Indian Fork	1838	1	371
Maxwell, Lewis	139	Freeman's Cr.	1838	1	372
Maxwell, Lewis	150	Tom's Fork	1838	1	370
Maxwell, Lewis	110	Freeman's Cr.	1838	1	376
Maxwell, Lewis	100	Allum Fork	1838	1	373
Maxwell, Lewis	155	Allum Fork	1838	1	374
Maxwell, Lewis	150	Freeman's Cr.	1838	1	375
Maxwell, Lewis	125	Alum Fork	1838	1	378
Maxwell, Lewis	100	Beech Lick	1838	1	377
Maxwell, Lewis	188	Robert's Fork	1838	1	379
Maxwell, Lewis	255	Freeman's Creek	1838	1	439
Maxwell, Lewis	161	Allum Fork	1838	1	441
Maxwell, Lewis	52	Ranson Run	1838	1	440
Maxwell, Lewis	50	Isaac's Run	1838	1	442
Maxwell, Lewis	32	Leading Creek	1838	1	443
Maxwell, Lewis	2,200	Kincheloe Creek	1852	2	438
Maxwell, Lewis	600	Back Fork	1852	2	439
Maxwell, Lewis	1,500	Fink's Fork	1852	2	440
Maze, Benniah	120	Yellow Creek	1837	1	290
Maze, Joseph et al	50	Leading Creek	1846	2	309
McCall, John C. Heirs	9,938	Sand Run	1844	2	209
McCally, Henry	100	Crooked Run	1842	2	125
McCally, Henry	100	Wolf Fork	1842	2	126
McCally, James	186	Burnett's Run	1838	1	390
McCally, James	1,346	Haney Camp Run	1838	1	391
McCally, James	48	Wts. West Fork	1838	1	387
McCally, James W.	50	Sand Fork	1843	2	139
McCan, Daniel	100	Fink's Fork	1829	1	130
McCartney, John	200	West Fork	1821	1	55
McGee, John	100	Grass Run	1844	2	272
McGee, John	100	Road Fork	1844	2	273
McGee, John	200	Sand Fork	1851	2	408
McGee, John	60	Stone Coal	1851	2	409
McGee, John et al	800	Dry Run	1844	2	226
McGee, John et al	3,347	Wts. Lit. Kanawha	1844	2	240
McGee, John et al	180	Daniel's Run	1844	2	274
McGee, John et al	2,100	Skin Creek	1844	2	275
McGee, John et al	120	Leading Creek	1844	2	276
McGee, John et al	40	Leading Creek	1844	2	277
McGrew, James C. et al	3,347	Wts. Lit. Kanawha	1844	2	240
McGrew, James C. et al	180	Daniel's Run	1844	2	274
McGrew, James C. et al	2,100	Skin Creek	1844	2	275

Name of Grantee	Acres	Local Description	Year	Book	Page
McGrew, James C. et al	120	Leading Creek	1844	2	276
McGrew, James C. et al	40	Leading Creek	1844	2	277
McHenry, Isaac	100	Ellis Fork	1838	2	4
McKinley, Alexander	75	Wts. West Fork	1843	2	146
McKinley, Anna et al	264	Abv. Mth. Stinking Cr.	1849	2	379
McKinley, Wm. & Anna et al Heirs	567	Polk Creek	1838	2	7
McKinley, Wm. & Anna et al Heirs	61	Skin Creek	1838	2	6
McKinley, Wm. & Anna et al Heirs	100	Leading Cr.	1838	1	416
McKinley, Wm. & Anna et al Heirs	300	Freeman's Creek	1838	2	5
McKisic, Andrew	50	Ward's Run	1821	1	58
McNamar, David	50	Sand Fork	1848	2	368
McNamar, Elijah	50	Lit. Kan. Riv. Adj. own	1836	1	241
McNemar, David	90	Butcher's Fork	1844	2	278
McNemar, William	100	Stone Coal	1853	2	451
McQuain—or McQuane					
McQuain, Alexander	200	Cove Creek	1832	1	178
McQuain, Charles I.	100	Cove Creek	1832	1	177
McQuane, Alexander	50	Wts. Leading Cr.	1834	1	239
McWhorter, John	482	Rush Run	1853	2	442
McWhorter, Mansfield	6½	Wts. McKinnies Run	1861	2	488
Mearbeck, Samuel	100	French Creek	1828	1	106
Middleton, Henry O.	1,600	Sand Run	1841	2	50
Middleton, Henry O.	28	Wts. Lit. Kanawha	1844	2	173
Middleton, Henry O.	73	Yellow Creek	1844	2	174
Middleton, Henry O.	54	Wts. Lit. Kanawha	1844	2	171
Middleton, Henry O.	95	Wts. Lit. Kanawha	1844	2	172
Middleton, Henry O.	187	Yellow Creek	1844	2	169
Middleton, Henry O.	297	Straight Creek	1844	2	170
Middleton, Henry O.	976	Wts. Grass Run	1843	2	147
Middleton, Henry O.	929	Wts. Lit. Kanawha	1843	2	148
Middleton, Henry O.	107	Steer Creek	1843	2	143
Middleton, Henry O.	101	Wts. Steer Cr.	1843	2	141
Middleton, Henry O.	128	Owens Run	1843	2	142
Middleton, Henry O.	1,141	Wts. Middle Run	1843	2	140
Middleton, Henry O.	276	Owen's Run	1842	2	111
Middleton, Henry O.	185	Spruce Run	1842	2	108
Middleton, Henry O.	236	Wts. Lit. Kanawha	1842	2	109
Middleton, Henry O.	4,000	Wts. Buckhannon R.	1842	2	110
Middleton, Henry O.	221	Owen's Run	1842	2	107
Middleton, Henry O.	1,608	Big Sand Run	1842	2	91
Middleton, Henry O.	1,000	Wts. Buckhannon River	1842	2	90
Middleton, Henry O. et al	900	Turkey Run	1842	2	127
Mills, Samuel	100	Salt Lick	1821	1	59
Mills, Samuel et al	50	N. Side Lit. Kanawha	1824	1	81
Mitchell, George C.	39	Beech Run	1842	2	123
Mitchell, George C.	135	Round Bottom	1842	2	102
Mitchell, John et al	150	Rush Run	1838	1	415
Mitchell, John W.	220	Wolf Pen Fork	1842	2	101
Mitchell, John W.	80	Wolf Pen	1842	2	124
Moody, Robert	805	Elk Lick	1832	1	171
Moore, Benjamin	50	Cedar Creek	1831	1	150
Moore, Charles J.	43	Hughes Fork	1853	2	448
Moore, Charles J. et al	300	Grand Camp	1851	2	410
Moneypenny, James	200	Murphy's Creek	1834	1	250
Moneypenny, James	150	Stone Lick	1838	1	401
Moneypenny, James	277	Murphy's Cr.	1838	1	332
Moneypenny, James	150	Limestone	1838	1	437
Moneypenny, Thomas	100	Leading Creek	1832	1	181
Moneypenny, William	100	Leading Creek	1833	1	201
Moneypenny, William	100	Leading Creek	1838	2	3
Morgan, Alfred	25	Wts. Buckhannon R.	1851	2	421
Morgan, Charles S. et al	285	Barn's Run	1844	2	199
Morgan, Charles S. et al	500	Strait Fork	1844	2	241

Name of Grantee	Acres	Local Description	Year	Book	Page
Morgan, Charles S. et al	1,215	Sycamore Fork	1844	2	204
Morrison, William	90	Hacker's Creek	1838	1	402
Murphy, John	2,000	S. Fk. Hughes Riv.	1819	1	12
Murphy, John	1,000	Leather Bark	1819	1	10
Nicholas, Isaac	127	Wts. Polk Cr.	1834	1	227
Nicholas, John	100	Dry Fork Polk Cr.	1834	1	226
Nicholas, John	100	Polk Cr.	1834	1	225
Norman, James	45	Steer Creek	1831	1	153
Norman, James	50	Steer Run	1837	1	324
Norman, James N.	100	S. W. Side Lit. Kan.	1834	1	224
Norman, Semore	25	Steer Creek	1831	1	156
Norris, John	50	Third Run	1849	2	369
Norris, Melton (or Milton)	500	Cedar Creek	1842	2	113
Norris, William & Melton	100	Cedar Creek	1842	2	112
Norris, William & Milton	100	Cedar Creek	1847	2	324
Osburn, Joseph	30	Leading Creek	1842	2	61
Osburn, Joseph Sr. & Archibald et al	226	Walnut Fork	1853	2	453
Ours, Nicholas	6	Buckhannon River	1818	1	7
Parker, W. W. et al	700	Wts. Buckhannon R.	1850	2	383
Peterson, David S.	27	Polk Creek	1852	2	433
Peterson, Jesse L.	400	Cow Run	1848	2	359
Peterson, Jesse L.	86	Wts. Lit. Kanawha	1848	2	360
Peterson, Jesse L. et al	12	Bet. Wts. Hughes, Wolf	1859	2	482
Powers, Benoni T.	10	Sand Fork	1848	2	363
Powers, Benoni T.	90	Ward's Run	1850	2	393
Powers, William	100	Alum Fork Lead	1838	1	403
Randolph, W. E. et al	569	Fink's Fork	1851	2	429
Ratcliff, Jesse	100	Polk Creek	1831	1	159
Reager—or Reger					
Reager, Abraham	85	Big Run	1822	1	67
Reager, Abraham & Isaac	80	Wash Run	1824	1	89
Reager, Henry & Saul	800	Bridge Run	1824	1	85
Reger, Philip Jr.	13	Wts. Buckhannon R.	1831	1	166
Rice, Jothem	325	Mud Lick	1848	2	350
Rice, Thomas Jefferson	100	Wts. Lit. Kan.	1844	2	198
Riddle—or Riddel					
Riddle, Benjamin	50	Wts. Lit. Kan.	1836	1	276
Riddle, Benjamin	100	Tanner's Fork	1838	1	341
Riddle, Benjamin	83	Tanner's Fork	1838	1	342
Riddle, Benjamin	100	Farmer's Fork	1838	1	404
Riddle, Benjamin	180	Leading Creek	1826	1	100
Riddle, Benjamin (Riddel)	100	Stinking Creek	1844	2	222
Riddle, Benjamin	100	Leading Creek	1840	2	35
Riddle, Hiram et al	244	Spruce Fork	1842	2	94
Riddle, Hiram et al	300	Spruce Fork	1842	2	95
Riddle, John	89	Wts. Hughes Riv.	1833	1	208
Riddle, John	200	Wts. Lit. Kan.	1823	1	72
Riddle, John G.	50	Tanner's Fork	1842	2	114
Riddle, John G.	100	Big Run	1845	2	300
Riffle, Francis	50	Wts. Lit. Kanawha	1826	1	99
Riffle, Jacob	200	O'Brian's Fork	1819	1	33
Riffle, Martin	50	Cedar Creek	1833	1	209
Rinehart, John (or Ruichart)	150	Hackers Creek	1834	1	247
Robison, Joseph H.	25	Wts. Lit. Kanawha	1837	1	318
Roger, Abraham	50	Big Run	1832	1	186
Rohrbough, Nathaniel	100	Wts. Buckhannon R.	1838	1	362
Rollings, Bernard J.	300	E. Side Buckhannon R.	1837	1	285
Rowan, Steven H.	1,000	Barnes' Run	1844	2	263
Rowan, Steven H.	990	Indian Fork	1844	2	262
Ruichart, John (or Rinehart)	150	Hacker's Crk.	1834	1	247
Schoolcraft, Aaron	50	Wts. Leading Cr.	1843	2	162
Schoonover, Henry	100	Ellis Fork	1846	2	308
Schoonover, Henry	52	Sand Fork	1846	2	307
Schoonover, Solomon	100	Duck Run	1834	1	249

Name of Grantee	Acres	Local Description	Year	Book	Page
Sharp, Hezekiah D.	69	Mare Run Freeman's Cr.	1836	1	269
Sharp, Timothy	100	Limestone	1836	1	270
Shock, Alexander	50	Steer Creek	1842	2	78
Shock, Jacob	95	Wts. Lit. Kanawha	1842	2	60
Shock, Jacob	40	Steer Creek	1828	1	103
Shock, Jacob	87	Steer Creek	1828	1	102
Shock, Jacob	40	Steer Creek	1824	1	77
Shock, Jacob	213	Steer Creek	1819	1	23
Shreve, John B.	300	Big Sand Run	1842	2	85
Simon, Christian	100	Wts. Buckhannon R.	1818	1	9
Simpson, Allen	4	Buck Hill	1846	2	310
Sirk, Isaac	200	Cedar Creek	1833	1	197
Sleeth, Alexander K.	70	Leading Creek	1838	2	2
Sleeth, Alexander K.	30	Stone Coal	1837	1	304
Sleeth, George W.	100	Leading Cr.	1838	1	361
Sleeth, Henry W.	50	Fink's Fork	1838	2	1
Sleeth, John et al	75	Polk Creek	1822	1	63
Sleeth, Nicholas C.	25	Leading Cr.	1837	1	302
Sleeth, Thomas I.	100	Nicholas Run	1840	2	44
Smith, Abram	35	Mud Lick	1848	2	364
Smith, Abram	83	Skin Creek	1838	1	380
Smith, Abram	5½	Stone Coal	1838	1	381
Smith, Augustin I. et al	900	Turkey Run	1842	2	127
Smith, Augustine I. (or J.)	500	Big Sand Run	1842	2	116
Smith, Augustin I. (or J.) et al	500	Turkey Run	1850	2	395
Smith, Augustin I. (or J.) et al	640	Wts. Buckhannon R.	1844	2	178
Smith, Augustin I. (or J.) et al	518	Indian Camp	1844	2	177
Smith, Augustin J. (or I.) et al	800	Wts. Buckhannon R.	1844	2	179
Smith, Chilton	222	Adj. David Wolf	1851	2	426
Smith, Chilton	80	Sand Fork	1850	2	406
Smith, David	24	Hacker's Creek	1850	2	403
Smith, Elijah	100	S. Fk. Hughes R.	1833	1	211
Smith, Hannah	148	Hughes River	1833	1	196
Smith, John	300	Leading Creek	1825	1	90
Smith, John	50	Leading Creek	1828	1	108
Smith, John	150	Leading Cr.	1828	1	117
Smith, John	75	Horn Creek	1838	1	360
Smith, John	150	Leading Creek	1838	1	359
Smith, John	100	Horn Creek	1836	1	280
Smith, Joseph T.	50	Bear Garden	1831	1	158
Smith, Joshua	95	Mth. Steer Creek	1831	1	149
Smith, Joshua	150	Spruce Fk. Hughes R.	1842	2	115
Smith, Levi	100	Wts. Hughes River	1833	1	194
Smith, Levi	106	Spruce Fork	1838	1	358
Smith, Levi J. et al	190	Ten-Mile Cr.	1851	2	432
Smith, Samuel	75	Pine Creek	1844	2	190
Snider, David et al	197	Bull Fork	1843	2	161
Snyder, William H.	100	Stewart's Cr.	1845	2	293
Snyder, William H.	200	Stewart's Cr.	1844	2	294
Snyder, William H.	100	Burk's Run	1844	2	295
Snyder, William H.	50	Middle Fork	1842	2	77
Snyder, William H.	50	Middle Fork	1843	2	145
Snyder, William H. et al	200½	Burk's Run	1845	2	299
Somerville, Robert	37	Bone Cr.	1838	1	417
Somerville, Robert	63	Bone Creek	1840	2	36
Spriggs, Edward G. et al	150	Rush Run	1838	1	415
Springston—or Springstone					
Springston, John	50	Leading Creek	1844	2	264
Springstone, John	25	Elias's Run	1838	1	339
Squires, Asa	140	Salt Lick	1822	1	65
Squires, Asa	250	O'Brian's Fork	1822	1	66
Squires, Asa	300	O'Brians Fork	1820	1	41
Squires, Elijah et al	130	Salt Lick Creek	1820	1	43

Name of Grantee	Acres	Local Description	Year	Book	Page
Stump, Michael	145	Lft. Fk. Steer Cr.	1831	1	147
Stump, Michael	34	Wts. Lit. Kanawha	1832	1	182
Stump, Michael	100	Bee Run Lit. Kan.	1834	1	232
Stump, Michael	100	White Oak	1844	2	193
Stump, Michael	120	Wts. Steer Creek	1844	2	192
Stump, Michael	50	Wts. Steer Creek	1844	2	194
Stump, Michael	128	Wts. Steer Creek	1844	2	195
Stump, Michael	200	Owen's Fork	1842	2	76
Stump, Michael	275	Sycamore Fork	1843	2	152
Stump, Michael	155	Sycamore Fork	1843	2	155
Stump, Michael	64	Wts. Lit. Kan.	1843	2	154
Stump, Michael	50	Wts. Lit. Kanawha	1843	2	153
Stump, Michael	104	Leading Creek	1836	1	260
Stump, Michael et al	177	Bear Fork	1844	2	197
Stump, Michael et al	200	Philip's Run	1844	2	196
Stump, Michael Jr.	79	Steer Creek	1819	1	26
Stump, Michael Jr.	169	Wts. Steer Creek	1831	1	152
Stump, Michael Jr.	125	Wts. Steer Creek	1831	1	154
Stump, Michael Jr.	80	Steer Creek	1832	1	188
Stump, Michael Jr.	70	"B" Crk. Lit. Kan.	1834	1	228
Summers, George et al	250	Stone Coal	1857	2	469
Suttle, Strawther I.	45	Sand Fork	1840	2	47
Suttle, Strawther I.	55	Kincheloe's Creek	1840	2	48
Swisher, Lewis D.	90	Aquilla's Run	1842	2	93
Talbert—Tolbert, Tolbott					
Talbert, David (Tolbert)	125	Big Run	1832	1	183
Talbert, Samuel B. (or T.)	303	Sugar Camp	1851	2	430
Talbert, Samuel T.	415	French Creek	1851	2	431
Talbert, Samuel T.	282	Bennett's Run	1838	1	445
Talbert, Samuel T.	200	Potter's Run	1838	1	446
Talbert, Samuel T.	95	Adj. Sam. Wilson	1838	1	447
Talbert, Samuel T.	156	Grand Camp	1850	2	385
Talbert, Samuel T.	1,550	Laurel Fork	1847	2	345
Talbott, John	3	Adj. Henry Butcher	1851	2	422
Talbott, John	1,200	Wts. Hughes River	1838	1	418
Talley, William L.	150	Bear Garden	1831	1	160
Tallman, James	89	Ellis Fork	1838	1	352
Tallman, James	100	Stewart's Creek	1838	1	351
Tallman, James	90	Stuart's Creek	1838	1	448
Tavenner, Cabell	265	Washburn's Run	1838	1	397
Tavenner, Cabell	800	Stone Coal	1844	2	208
Tavenner, William C. et al Heirs	250	Stone Coal	1857	2	469
Tharp, Hezekiah D.	41	Wts. Freeman's Cr.	1838	1	405
Tharp, Hezekiah D.	100	Adj. Surv. Evans Arnold	1836	1	277
Tharp, Timothy	62	Elk Lick	1836	1	257
Tharp, Timothy	150	Bear Fork	1842	2	103
Tharp, Timothy	100	Bone Creek	1838	1	383
Tharp, Timothy	25	Elk Lick	1838	1	388
Tharp, Timothy	100	Bone Creek	1838	1	382
Tharp, Timothy	185	Bone Creek	1838	1	356
Tharp, Timothy	50	Bone Creek	1838	1	357
Tharp, Timothy	50	Spruce Fork	1838	1	355
Tharp, Timothy	30	Main Spring Run	1838	1	353
Tharp, Timothy	106	Spruce Fork	1838	1	354
Tharp, Timothy	185	Horn Creek	1844	2	265
Tharp, Timothy et al	265	Bloody Run	1838	1	434
Thompson, Adrian	136	Steer Creek	1828	1	114
Thompson, Adrian A.	175	Owen's Run	1842	2	79
Tolbert—See Talbert					
Tolbert, Samuel F. et al	57	Skin Creek	1838	2	12
Townsend, Ezekiel	100	Wts. Lit. Kanawha	1826	1	98
Townsend, Ezekiel T.	21	Cooper's Run	1837	1	322
Townsend, Ezekiel T.	32	Lit. Kan. Adj. his own	1834	1	236

Name of Grantee	Acres	Local Description	Year	Book	Page
Townsend, Ezekiel T.	50	S. S. Cedar Cr.	1834	1	220
Townsend, Ezekiel T.	50	Cedar Creek	1824	1	75
Townsend, Ezekiel T.	50	Cedar Creek	1836	1	274
Townsend, Solomon B.	80	Wts. Lit. Kanawha	1838	1	435
Tunstill, E. M. et al	226	Walnut Fork	1853	2	453
Tunstill, E. M. et al	33	Polk Creek	1852	2	437
Tunstill, E. M. et al	569	Fink's Fork	1851	2	429
Tunstill, Edward M.	104	Walnut Fork	1853	2	454
Tunstill, Edward M.	70	Walnut Fork	1853	2	455
Vandergrift, Leonard	100	Cedar Creek	1837	1	319
Vannoy, Benjamin G.	150	Tanner's Fork	1844	2	189
Vannoy, Cornelius	100	Wts. Lit. Kanawha	1841	2	41
Waggoner, Jacob	200	Jesse Hughes Run	1832	1	176
Walden, John	100	Yellow Creek	1844	2	269
Walden, John	1,800	Tanner's Fork	1844	2	270
Walden, John	500	Spring Run	1844	2	266
Walden, John	44	Turkey Run	1860	2	487
Walden, John	500	Wts. Lit. Kanawha	1844	2	268
Walden, John	1,000	Yellow Creek	1844	2	267
Walden, John	50	Wts. Lit. Kanawha	1848	2	352
Walden, John	98	Lynn Camp Fork	1848	2	351
Walden, John	1,124	Wts. Leading Creek	1850	2	394
Walden, John	1,300	Skin Creek	1844	2	215
Walden, John et al	1,500	Laurel Fork	1844	2	214
Walker, Travis	140	Hacker's Creek	1828	1	123
Wamsley, Jonathan	423	Stillhouse Run	1831	1	141
Ward, James	180	Buckhannon River	1842	2	92
Ware, Harvey et al	100	Carpenter, Hughes	1837	1	320
Washburn, Alfred N.	75	Bear Run	1852	2	441
Watson, William A.	3	Adj. McCally	1850	2	396
West, Alexander	800	Fink's Fork	1831	1	142
West, John	400	Leading Creek	1832	1	187
Westfall, George	375	Turkey Run	1836	1	282
Westfall, George	15	Laurel Bank	1851	2	416
Westfall, George & Watson	95	Lit. Sand Run	1851	2	418
Westfall, George & Watson	260	Lit. Sand Run	1851	2	419
Westfall, Henry F.	150	Turkey Run	1846	2	314
Westfall, Jacob	100	Cedar Creek	1834	1	230
Westfall, James	400	Leading Creek	1820	1	40
Westfall, Job	25	Wts. Lit. Kan.	1836	1	273
Westfall, Job	75	Wts. Lit. Kanawha	1836	1	259
Westfall, John	150	Laurel Creek	1840	2	45
Westfall, John W.	15	Mud Creek	1846	2	312
Westfall, John W.	5	Stoney Run	1846	2	311
Westfall, John W.	195	Big Sand Run	1842	2	128
Westfall, John W.	80	Wts. Buckhannon R.	1842	2	117
Westfall, Watson	5	Turkey Run	1851	2	417
Westfall, Watson et al	25	French Creek	1845	2	297
Westfall, Wilson	100	East Side Buck. R.	1825	1	87
Weybright, Michael	150	Ward's Run	1832	1	190
Weybright, Michael	50	West Fork	1821	1	57
White, John	200	Polk Creek	1838	1	363
White, John	200	Dry Fork	1850	2	399
White, William	50	Alum Fork	1838	1	407
White, William	50	Butcher's Fork	1838	1	408
Wiant—See Wyant					
Wiant, Henry	125	Leading Creek	1832	1	184
Wiant, Henry Jr.	100	Cedar Creek	1824	1	82
Wiant, Nicholas C.	25	Adj. Brannon	1848	2	348
Wiant, Peter	25	Cleves Run	1833	1	192
Wilkinson, Daniel	200	Freeman's Cr.	1832	1	173
Wilkinson, Lemuel	100	Allum Fork	1832	1	170
Williams, Abraham et al	100	Carpenter & Hughes Fks.	1837	1	320
Williams, John S. (or T.)	60	Three Lick Run	1854	2	456

Name of Grantee	Acres	Local Description	Year	Book	Page
Williams, William D. et al	600	Rush Run	1847	2	333
Willhite, James	50	Glady Fork	1836	1	271
Wilson, Edgar C.	640	Ten-Mile Cr.	1845	2	306
Wilson, Eli	50	Salt Lick	1836	1	258
Wilson, George	100	O'Brian's Fork	1819	1	34
Wilson, John	80	Sand Fork	1838	1	444
Wilson, Joseph	94	Stinking Creek	1837	1	321
Wilson, Joseph	44	Sinking Creek	1834	1	229
Wilson, Joseph	65	Sinking Creek	1834	1	243
Wilson, Samuel	200	Big Skin Creek	1818	1	1
Wilson, Samuel Heirs of	1,550	Sand Fork, Skin Cr.	1846	2	549
Winans, Enos	35	Freeman's Creek	1859	2	476
Woffler, James (or Woofter)	109	Strait's Run	1838	1	406
Wolf, John J.	220	Stuart's Creek	1831	1	140
Wolf, Susannah	25	Stewart's Cr.	1838	1	419
Wood, Thomas S. et al	323	Wts. Lit. Kanawha	1847	2	335
Woofter, James	109	Strait's Run	1838	1	406
Wyant—See also Wiant					
Wyant, Henry	25	Cedar Creek	1844	2	184
Wyant, Henry	25	Cedar Creek	1844	2	185
Yeager, Jonathan	100	Peck Run Buckhan. R.	1831	1	146

LOGAN COUNTY

Abbot, Albert	370	Brown's Branch	1854	4	112
Acord, Robert	55	Breckenridge Fork	1834	1	170
Adams, Dicy	130	Hart's Creek	1854	4	77
Adams, Joseph	30	Hart's Creek	1841	1	407
Adams, Joseph	10	Buck Fork	1854	4	41
Adams, Joseph	14	Buck Fork	1854	4	40
Adams, Joseph	25	Hart's Creek	1842	1	424
Adams, Joseph	25	Hart's Creek	1844	2	154
Adams, Joseph	40	Hart's Creek	1844	2	153
Adams, Joseph	30	Hart's Creek	1844	2	152
Adams, Joseph	80	Buck Fork	1844	2	151
Adams, John W. Jr.	70	Buck Fork	1856	4	306
Adams, John W. Jr.	40	Hart's Creek	1856	4	311
Adkins, Allen & Aaron	119	Big Branch	1857	4	362
Adkins, Anderson	75	Big Fork	1847	2	310
Adkins, Charles	30	Brown's Branch	1852	3	460
Adkins, Charles	80	Hart's Creek	1845	2	195
Adkins, Charles & Isaiah	37	Hart's Creek	1852	3	459
Adkins, Elias	17	Douglass Branch	1843	2	63
Adkins, Elias	33	Low Gap	1843	2	81
Adkins, Elias	20	Wts. Guyandotte	1828	1	67
Adkins, Elias	300	Douglass Branch	1852	3	463
Adkins, Elias	190	Low Gap Branch	1852	3	464
Adkins, Elias & Allen et al	200	Hart's Creek	1856	4	241
Adkins, Enos	230	Douglas Branch	1855	4	214
Adkins, Enos	90	Hart's Creek	1852	3	462
Adkins, Henry	75	Low Gap Branch	1852	3	461
Adkins, Isaac	450	Hart's Creek	1844	2	108
Adkins, Isaac	50	Wts. Guyandotte	1843	2	62
Adkins, Isaac	120	Wts. Guyandotte	1852	3	455
Adkins, Isaac	100	Wts. Guyandotte	1835	1	207
Adkins, Isaac Jr.	130	Big Branch	1852	3	456
Adkins, Isaac Jr.	70	Big Branch	1856	4	290

Name of Grantee	Acres	Local Description	Year	Book	Page
Barker, Anderson	55	Blevins Fork	1837	1	306
Barker, Anderson et al	85	Ugly Creek	1847	2	407
Barker, Anderson & William	331	Limestone	1860	1	494
Barker, Andrew Jr. et al	250	Ugly Creek	1852	3	508
Barker, John	30	Big Creek	1837	1	309
Barker, William	35	Road Fork	1849	3	113
Barr, Amos et al	1,480	Dingess Run	1858	4	447
Belcher, Harvey	44	Cold Spring	1854	4	38
Bennett, Thomas	100	On The River	1832	1	132
Beyley—See Bailey					
Beyley, Thomas	20	Huff Creek	1831	1	118
Bias, Armstrong	25	Spruce Fork	1847	2	314
Bias, James	25	Spruce Fork	1833	1	153
Bias, Obadiah	50	Hewett's Creek	1835	1	196
Bias, Obadiah Jr.	28	Hewitt's Fork	1845	2	223
Bias, Simeon	50	Spruce Fork	1846	2	269
Bird, Benj. V., William A. & D. H.	638	Wts. Big Fork	1850	3	203
Bird, Benjamin V.	100	Williams's Fork	1850	3	202
Blair, Harrison	50	Pigeon Creek	1851	3	294
Blair, John	235	Road Branch	1852	3	479
Blair, John	30	Pigeon Creek	1848	3	6
Blair, John	79	Fork Ridge	1848	3	47
Blair, John	80	Laurel Fork	1843	2	64
Blair, John	92	Pigeon Creek	1848	2	436
Blake, William et al	230	W. Side New Riv.	1830	1	106
Blankenship, Henry	75	Cub Creek	1847	2	318
Blankenship, Henry	18	Reedy Branch	1852	3	436
Blankenship, Henry Jr.	17	Sycamore Fork	1852	3	466
Blankenship, Hiram	50	Rockhouse Fork	1836	1	254
Blankenship, Jonathan B.	46	Peak's Ridge	1848	2	437
Blankenship, William P.	92	14 Mile Creek	1856	4	266
Boggess, John (or Burgess)	25	Wts. Guyandotte	1848	3	5
Bradley, Joshua	50	Marsh Fork	1829	1	88
Bradley, Joshua	150	Marsh Fork	1829	1	90
Brewer, Anthony	13	Wts. Sandy	1855	4	210
Brewer, Anthony	110	Marrowbone Creek	1856	4	242
Brewer, Anthony	140	Marrowbone Cr.	1854	4	70
Brewer, Anthony	34	Marrowbone Cr.	1851	3	394
Brewer, Anthony et al	500	Marrowbone Cr.	1857	4	399
Brewer, Isaac	23	Marrowbone Creek	1852	3	469
Brewer, Isaac	27	Pigeon Creek	1827	1	37
Brewer, Isaac	25	Pigeon Cr.	1834	1	176
Brewer, Isaac	45	Laurel Fork	1833	1	147
Brewer, Isaac	24	Big Laurel	1847	2	312
Brewer, Isaac	42	Marrowbone Cr.	1847	2	311
Brewer, Isaac	30	Marrowbone Cr.	1843	2	82
Brewer, Isaac	42	Burning Creek	1843	2	84
Brewer, Isaac	32	Burning Creek	1843	2	83
Brewer, Isaac	95	Marrowbone Cr.	1843	2	85
Brewer, Isaac	21	Jenney's Creek	1844	2	112
Brewer, Isaac	44	Marrowbone Creek	1844	2	113
Brewer, Isaac	67	Marrowbone Cr.	1849	3	117
Brewer, Isaac	27	Marrowbone Creek	1849	3	116
Brewer, Isaac	46	Marrowbone Creek	1852	3	470
Brewer, Isaac	110	Marrowbone Creek	1854	4	114
Brewer, Isaac	50	Marrowbone Creek	1938	1	332
Brewer, Isaac	25	Marrowbone Creek	1838	1	333
Brewer, Isaac	125	Marrowbone Creek	1836	1	224
Brewer, Isaac	20	Marrowbone Creek	1836	1	228
Brewer, Isaac	89	Marrowbone Creek	1854	4	68
Brewer, Isaac	85	Marrowbone Cr.	1854	4	69
Brewer, Isaac	225	Marrowbone Cr.	1854	4	110
Brewer, Isaac et al	200	Marrowbone Cr.	1855	4	201

Name of Grantee	Acres	Local Description	Year	Book	Page
Brewer, Isaac Jr.	47	Marrowbone Cr.	1848	2	446
Brewer, Isaac Jr.	340	Marrowbone Cr.	1854	4	117
Brewer, Isaac Jr.	175	Marrowbone Cr.	1854	4	118
Brewer, Isaac Jr. et al	65	Jenney's Cr.	1850	3	208
Brewer, James	15	Buck's Br.	1850	3	177
Brewer, James	45	Marrowbone Cr.	1860	2	483
Brewer, James	160	Marrowbone Cr.	1854	4	67
Brewer, James	20	Marrowbone Cr.	1854	4	66
Brewer, Johnson	24	Laurel Fork	1847	2	413
Brewer, Johnson	144	Moses' Fork	1861	2	524
Brewer, Johnson	43	Road Fork	1855	4	126
Brewer, Johnson	15	Trace Fork	1855	4	127
Brewer, Johnson	35	Mill Branch	1852	3	471
Brewer, Lewis	75	Marrowbone Cr.	1850	3	193
Brewer, Lewis	140	Marrowbone Cr.	1850	3	194
Brewer, Lewis	45	Marrowbone Creek	1844	2	114
Brewer, Lewis	80	Marrowbone Cr.	1847	2	313
Brewer, Lewis	75	Marrowbone Cr.	1836	1	227
Brewer, Lewis et al	4,450	Pigeon Creek	1857	4	576
Brewer, Samuel	69	Marrowbone Creek	1847	2	412
Brewer, Samuel	103	Jenney's Creek	1844	2	115
Brewer, Samuel	7	Neeley's Branch	1850	3	219
Brewer, Samuel	116	Marrowbone Creek	1851	3	300
Brewer, Samuel	400	Cane Br.	1854	4	83
Brewer, Samuel	30	Marrowbone Creek	1853	4	16
Brewer, Samuel	70	Marrowbone Cr.	1855	4	213
Brewer, Samuel	87	Marrowbone Cr.	1858	4	422
Brewster—or Bruster					
Brewster, Comfort	19	Elk Fork	1848	3	101
Brewster, Comfort	35	5 Mile Fork	1848	3	84
Brewster, James	55	Rockhouse	1851	3	393
Brooks, William	25	Clear Fork	1852	3	450
Brooks, William	89	Clear Fork	1852	3	449
Brown, James	13	Huff Creek	1843	2	45
Brown, James	69	Huff Creek	1843	2	49
Brown, James	25	West Fork	1834	1	159
Brown, James	7	Huff's Cr.	1846	2	279
Brown, James	35	Huff's Creek	1846	2	278
Brown, James	45	Huff's Creek	1852	3	477
Brown, James	100	Pond Fork	1838	1	331
Brown, James	35	W. Fork Coal	1829	1	94
Brown, Moses	20	Hart's Creek	1852	3	476
Brown, Moses	92	Wts. Guyandotte	1850	3	241
Brown, Moses	25	Guyandotte River	1835	1	206
Brown, Moses	275	Hart's Creek	1856	4	264
Brown, Thomas W.	50	Spruce Fork	1827	1	41
Brown, Thomas W.	84	Crawley Cr.	1826	1	4
Brown, William	25	West Fork	1834	1	175
Browning, Edmond	25	Island Creek	1834	1	173
Browning, Edmond Jr.	53	Cow Creek	1851	3	380
Browning, Edmond Jr.	30	Cow Creek	1851	3	379
Browning, Edmund Jr.	35	Cow Creek	1845	2	196
Browning, Edmund Jr. et al	48	Cow Creek	1851	3	391
Browning, Edward	150	Hand Creek	1825	1	2
Browning, Francis	20	Island Creek	1842	2	43
Browning, Francis	25	Rockhouse	1834	1	174
Browning, Francis	116	Vance's Branch	1856	4	272
Browning, Francis	47	Hart's Creek	1856	4	271
Browning, Francis	39	Trace Fork	1851	3	305
Browning, Francis et al	50	Pine Creek	1826	1	3
Browning, James	190	Kiah's Fork	1856	4	243
Browning, James	11	Cow Creek	1846	2	305
Browning, James	12	Cow Creek	1846	2	297

Name of Grantee	Acres	Local Description	Year	Book	Page
Browning, James	77	Spruce Hollow	1859	1	484
Browning, Jesse	85	Pigeon Creek	1855	4	228
Browning, Jesse	85	Pigeon Creek	1855	4	227
Browning, Jesse	80	Pigeon Creek	1855	4	226
Browning, Jesse Jr.	17	Island Creek	1844	2	111
Browning, Jesse Jr.	39	Island Creek	1844	2	109
Browning, Jesse Jr.	18	Island Creek	1844	2	110
Browning, Jesse Jr.	9½	Rockhouse Fork	1842	1	416
Browning, Jesse Jr. & Edmund Jr.	101	Rockhouse Fork	1842	1	418
Browning, Jesse Jr. & Edmund Jr.	20	Rockhouse	1842	1	417
Browning, John	140	Cane Fork	1858	4	407
Browning, John	100	Cane Fork	1858	4	406
Browning, John R.	160	Pine Creek	1855	4	563
Browning, John R.	250	Pine Fork	1855	4	142
Browning, Mary E.	47	Trace Fork	1856	4	273
Browning, Nathaniel	40	Buffalo Cr.	1851	3	381
Browning, Nathaniel	70	Huff's Creek	1851	3	383
Browning, Nathaniel	14	Lick Branch	1851	3	382
Browning, Nathaniel et al	350	Brushy Fork	1855	4	204
Browning, Nathaniel et al	200	Brushy Fork	1855	4	200
Browning, Oliver	209	Buffalo Creek	1852	3	478
Browning, Reace	34	Island Creek	1847	2	392
Browning, Reace	32	Middle Fork	1847	2	390
Browning, Reace	16½	Island Creek	1842	2	40
Browning, Reace	50	Island Creek	1842	2	42
Browning, Reace	13	Island Creek	1842	2	41
Browning, Reace	30	Island Creek	1847	2	391
Browning, Reace	170	Island Creek	1851	3	307
Browning, Reace	95	Island Creek	1851	3	306
Browning, Reace et al	42	Island Creek	1841	1	404
Browning, Thomas E.	34	Island Creek	1860	1	504
Browning, Thomas E.	112	Island Creek	1860	1	503
Browning, Thomas E. & John R.	79	Ben Creek	1849	3	154
Browning, Thomas E. & John R.	43	Spring Fork	1849	3	153
Browning, William	18	Wts. Guyandotte	1842	1	425
Browning, William	23	Wts. Guyandotte	1834	1	172
Browning, William Jr.	112	Horse Pen Fork	1856	4	307
Browning, William Jr.	130	Browning Fork	1856	4	308
Browning, William Jr.	1,174	Gilbert's Creek	1859	1	498
Browning, William Jr.	216	Wts. Guyandotte	1845	2	222
Browning, William Jr.	31	Rum Creek	1848	3	4
Browning, William Jr.	78	Horse Pen	1856	4	314
Brumfield, John	75	Ugly Creek	1849	3	115
Brumfield, John	50	Wts. Guyandotte	1835	1	210
Brumfield, John H. et al	300	Sand Creek	1852	3	497
Brumfield, John H. et al	260	Buck Lick	1850	3	213
Brumfield, John H. et al	42	Wts. Guyandotte	1850	3	214
Brumfield, John H. et al	80	Sugar Camp	1850	3	215
Brumfield, John H. et al	20	Wts. Guyandotte	1850	3	278
Bruster—See Brewster					
Bruster, Comfort	15	Pigeon Creek	1837	1	273
Bryan, Cyrus P.	17	Wts. Guyandotte	1851	3	303
Bryan, Cyrus P.	4	Pigeon Roost	1851	3	304
Bryan, George E.	28	Laurel Branch	1859	1	472
Bryan, Hugh	50	Road Branch	1850	3	178
Buchannon, Alexander	14	Wts. Guyandotte	1844	2	156
Buchannon, Alexander	20	Wts. Guyandotte	1844	2	155
Buchannon, Thomas	30	Spice Creek	1853	4	20
Buchannon, Henry & Thomas	120	Deep Ford Br.	1851	3	302
Burgess, John	49	Mud Lick	1848	3	46
Burgess, John (or Boggess)	25	Wts. of Guyandotte	1848	3	5
Burgess, Tandy	10	Wts. Guyandotte	1832	1	134
Burgess, William Jr.	29	Buffalo Cr.	1852	3	475

Name of Grantee	Acres	Local Description	Year	Book	Page
Butcher, Allen	93	Smokehouse Br.	1851	3	292
Butcher, James	125	Smokehouse	1856	4	278
Butcher, James	40	Smokehouse	1856	4	277
Butcher, James	20	Smokehouse	1856	4	276
Butcher, Joshua	570	Marsh Fork	1858	4	583
Butcher, Joshua	20	Smokehouse	1852	3	472
Butcher, Joshua	80	Canoe Branch	1842	2	15
Butcher, Joshua	20	Crawley Creek	1828	1	70
Butcher, Joshua	23	Smokehouse	1843	2	86
Butcher, Joshua	35	Brown's Run	1844	2	116
Butcher, Joshua	90	Smokehouse	1844	2	117
Butcher, Joshua	25	Trace Fork	1844	2	118
Butcher, Joshua	17	Cabin Branch	1844	2	119
Butcher, Joshua	70	White Oak Fork	1852	3	473
Butcher, Joshua	50	Bear Wallow Branch	1852	3	474
Canada, Samuel	18	Turnip Patch Br.	1851	3	308
Canterberry—or Canterbury					
Canterberry, David	30	Rockhouse	1845	2	198
Canterberry, David	13	Horse Creek	1845	2	197
Canterberry, Felix W.	20	Big Fork	1845	2	199
Canterberry, Samuel	50	Wts. Guyandotte	1827	1	46
Canterbury, Ezekiel	60	Coal Spring	1855	4	177
Canterbury, Ezekiel	56	Laurel Fork	1856	4	251
Canterbury, Ezekiel	28	Eldridge Branch	1853	4	22
Canterbury, Felix W.	19	Big Fork	1847	2	417
Canterbury, Felix W.	10	Big Fork	1847	2	415
Canterbury, Felix W.	48	Big Fork	1847	2	416
Canterbury, Griffin	125	Rum Creek	1855	4	206
Canterbury, Griffin	20	Wts. Guyandotte	1834	1	164
Canterbury, John	65	Clear Fork	1850	3	269
Canterbury, Joseph	38	Little Laurel	1851	3	311
Canterbury, Samuel Jr.	35	Wts. Guyandotte	1851	3	312
Canterbury, Samuel Jr.	13	Wts. Guyandotte	1844	2	122
Canterbury, Thompson & William	125	Jack's Branch	1847	2	368
Carter, Barnabus	65	Hoover's Fork	1854	4	62
Cartright, Elijah	22	Trace Fork	1848	3	52
Cartright, Elijah	21	Trace Fork	1848	3	51
Cartright, Elijah	25	Dingess Branch	1851	3	313
Cartright, Elijah	15	Trace Fork	1849	3	155
Cartright, Elijah	9	Trace Fork	1843	2	52
Cartright, Moses	10	Trace Fork	1838	1	339
Cartright, Moses	38	Trace Fork	1854	4	48
Cartright, Moses	4½	Trace Fork	1844	2	158
Cartright, Moses	13	Trace Fork	1844	2	104
Cartright, Moses	19	Muzle Fork	1845	2	200
Cartright, Moses A.	185	Trace Fork	1854	4	143
Cartright, Moses A.	64	Right Hd. Fork	1848	3	53
Cartright, Thomas P.	22	Trace Fork	1841	1	388
Cartright, Thomas P.	36	Lick Fork	1846	2	285
Cartright, Thomas P.	68	Lick Fork	1848	2	433
Cartright, Thomas P.	28	Trace Fork	1843	2	54
Cartright, Thomas P.	13	Trace Fork	1843	2	53
Cartright, Thomas P.	8	Pigeon Creek	1827	1	51
Cecil, Samuel	1,100	Wts. Sandy	1854	4	120
Chaffin—or Chaffins					
Chaffin, Nathan	92	Rockhouse	1847	2	370
Chaffin, Pleasant	490	Rockhouse Fork	1860	2	485
Chaffin, Pleasant	154	Rockhouse	1858	4	409
Chaffin, William	125	Marrowbone Creek	1852	3	489
Chaffin, William	46	Marrowbone Cr.	1847	2	339
Chaffin, William	900	Marrowbone Creek	1850	3	562
Chaffin, William	15	Marrowbone Cr.	1860	2	485
Chaffin, William	70	Jenney's Creek	1847	2	387

Name of Grantee	Acres	Local Description	Year	Book	Page
Christion—or Christian					
Christion, James P.	28	Elk Creek	1848	3	54
Christion, James P.	59	Elk Creek	1848	3	12
Christion, James P.	98	Leatherwood Cr.	1851	3	314
Christion, James P.	37	Leatherwood Cr.	1851	3	315
Christion, James P.	20	Elk Creek	1852	3	485
Clark—or Clarke					
Clark, Carter F. (or T.)	90	Wts. Sandy	1836	1	236
Clark, Carter T.	80	Pigeon Creek	1827	1	50
Clark, Carter T.	60	Big Branch	1849	3	123
Clark, Carter T.	206	Den Branch	1849	3	122
Clark, George W.	55	Big Branch	1850	3	225
Clark, George W.	265	Pigeon Creek	1850	3	224
Clark, George W.	100	Big Branch	1850	3	223
Clark, George W.	225	Big Branch	1850	3	222
Clark, George W.	200	Big Branch	1850	3	221
Clark, George W.	25	Wts. Sandy	1856	4	250
Clark, George W.	600	Conley's Fork	1856	4	571
Clark, Henry P.	75	Pigeon Creek	1850	3	220
Clark, Henry P.	50	Little Laurel	1855	4	221
Clark, Henry P.	200	Pigeon Creek	1856	4	230
Clark, Henry P.	25	Big Branch	1855	4	222
Clark, John B.	80	Big Branch	1848	3	50
Clark, John B.	56	Pigeon Creek	1841	1	401
Clark, John B.	50	Pigeon Creek	1841	1	400
Clark, John B.	170	Pigeon Creek	1837	1	307
Clark, Joseph M. & Henry P.	480	Aldridge Branch	1854	4	45
Clark, Thomas	36	Laurel Fork	1847	2	430
Clark, Thomas	14	Aldridge Branch	1844	2	103
Clark, Thomas	77	Panther Branch	1850	3	175
Clark, Thomas	30	Laurel Fork	1852	3	481
Clark, Thomas	190	Fork Ridge	1851	3	309
Clark, Thomas	44	Laurel Fork	1848	3	104
Clark, Thomas K.	76	Panther Branch	1856	4	332
Clark, Thomas K.	32	Fork Ridge	1856	4	331
Clark, Thomas K.	150	Mill Stone	1856	4	333
Clark, Thomas K.	69	Laurel Fork	1856	4	330
Clark, Thomas K.	78	Lick Branch	1856	4	329
Clarke—or Clark					
Clarke, Carter T.	71	Pigeon Creek	1841	1	402
Clarke, Carter T.	78	Wts. Sandy	1841	1	390
Clarke, George W.	1,099	Big Branch	1860	2	476
Clarke, John B.	21	Pigeon Creek	1841	1	403
Clarke, John B.	85	Pigeon Creek	1835	1	217
Clarke, John B.	30	Wts. Sandy River	1838	1	338
Clarke, Samuel	50	Laurel Fork	1846	2	262
Clarke, Samuel	40	Hd. Jack's Br.	1846	2	261
Clendenen, Robert A.	48	Philip's Branch	1844	2	120
Clendenen, Robert A.	20	Spruce Fork	1837	1	272
Clendenen, Robert A.	170	Spruce Fk. Lit. Coal	1842	1	441
Clendenen, Robert A. et al	100	Sycamore Fork	1842	2	25
Clendenen, Robert A. et al	50	Left Hd. Fk. Mud	1842	1	442
Cline, Christian	65	Toney's Fork	1851	3	310
Cline, Christian	150	4 Pole Creek	1855	4	220
Cline, David	28	Gilbert's Creek	1850	3	263
Cline, David	33	Gilbert's Creek	1858	4	408
Cline, Henry	59	Long Pole	1845	2	201
Cline, Jacob	225	Grapevine Creek	1854	4	61
Cline, Jacob	25	Gilbert's Creek	1852	3	482
Cline, James	17	Wts. Sandy	1838	1	337
Cline, James	47	Muzzle Fork	1850	3	245
Cline, John	60	War Creek	1853	4	18
Cline, John	50	Long Pole	1845	2	202

Name of Grantee	Acres	Local Description	Year	Book	Page
Cline, Michael	15	Wts. Sandy	1850	3	264
Cline, Michael Jr.	35	Long Pole Cr.	1850	3	257
Cline, Michael Jr.	21	Huff's Creek	1845	2	225
Cline, Peter	26	Gilbert's Creek	1835	1	201
Cline, Peter	15	Horse Pen	1831	1	116
Cline, Peter	32	Gilbert's Cr.	1845	2	226
Cline, Peter Jr.	54	Horse Pen Fork	1835	1	214
Cline, Thomas	84	Gilbert's Creek	1856	4	358
Cline, Thomas	37	Gilbert's Creek	1846	2	300
Cline, William	40	Tug Fork	1828	1	71
Cline, William	74	Wts. Sandy	1847	2	319
Cline, William	40	Alum Creek	1847	2	340
Cline, William	71	Left Hd. Fork	1861	2	461
Cline, William	24	Wts. Sandy	1850	3	179
Cline, William	50	Alum Creek	1859	1	491
Cline, William	45	Alum Creek	1859	1	490
Cline, William	85	Grants Branch	1859	1	489
Cline, William	43	Laurel Branch	1859	1	488
Cline, William	62	Alum Creek	1851	3	395
Cline, William	35	Big Branch	1851	3	396
Cline, William	10	Wts. Sandy	1838	1	336
Cline, William	220	Alum Creek	1855	4	202
Cline, William	230	Big Branch	1855	4	190
Cline, William	45	Alum Creek	1855	4	188
Cline, William	56	Alum Creek	1855	4	189
Coleman, James	12	Elk Creek	1836	1	245
Coleman, Moses	21	Pigeon Creek	1833	1	151
Coleman, Richard D.	14	Wts. Sandy	1853	4	13
Collins, Levi	75	Ugly Creek	1849	3	118
Collins, Levi	75	Limestone Branch	1854	4	44
Collins, William	23	Wts. Sandy	1844	2	121
Collins, William	78	Hickory Gap Fork	1852	3	491
Collins, William	54	Ben Creek	1852	3	490
Collins, William	24	Spring Fork	1850	3	255
Collins, William	68	Ben Creek	1850	3	252
Collins, William	156	Gulph Fork	1850	3	261
Conley—or Conly					
Conley, Baley	8½	Back Fork	1847	2	338
Conley, Garland Jr.	32	Smokehouse	1853	4	12
Conley, Henry	50	Buck Fork	1852	3	554
Conley, Henry	25	Vance Branch	1848	3	14
Conley, William	48	Spruce Fork	1843	2	69
Conly—or Conley					
Conly, Henry	25	Hart's Creek	1834	1	193
Cook—or Cooke					
Cook, David	40	Clear Fork	1833	1	141
Cook, James Jr.	126	Rock Castle	1847	2	395
Cooke, Andrew L.	43	Turkey Creek	1850	3	265
Cooke, Andrew L.	68	Turkey Creek	1850	3	256
Cooke, David	71	Toney's Fork	1849	3	156
Cooke, David	47	Toney's Fork	1848	3	56
Cooke, Jacob	26	Big Bottom Fork	1841	1	389
Cooke, James	100	Elkins Branch	1848	3	55
Cooke, James	73	Marsh Fork	1847	2	414
Cooke, James Jr.	41	Camp Branch	1852	3	438
Cooke, James Jr.	39	Clear Fork	1852	3	439
Cooke, James Jr.	244	Rock Castle Fork	1852	3	480
Cooke, James Jr.	20	Pen Branch	1852	3	440
Cooke, James Jr.	63	Coon Fork	1852	3	441
Cooke, James Jr.	42	Rockcastle Fork	1847	2	337
Cooke, James Jr. & Josiah	349	Rock Castle Fork	1852	3	442
Cooke, James Sr.	145	Marsh Fork	1850	3	262
Cooke, John	20	Clear Fork	1845	2	224

Name of Grantee	Acres	Local Description	Year	Book	Page
Cooke, John Jr.	39	Sand Lick	1855	4	181
Cooke, John Jr.	50	Elk Creek	1855	4	180
Cooke, John Jr.	15	Cub Creek	1852	3	483
Cooke, John Jr.	9	Road Branch	1852	3	484
Cooke, John Jr.	5	Huff's Cr.	1849	3	124
Cooke, John Jr.	23	Trace Fork	1849	3	126
Cooke, John Jr.	20	Stone Coal	1849	3	125
Cooke, John Jr.	50	Elk Creek	1844	2	124
Cooke, Mitchell	165	Dry Branch	1851	3	280
Cooke, Sylvester	62	Marsh Fork	1849	3	119
Cooke, Thomas	60	Clear Fork	1835	1	218
Cooke, Thomas	30	Dry Branch	1834	1	179
Cooke, Thomas	20	Huff Creek	1845	2	203
Cooke, Thomas	25	Huff's Creek	1845	2	204
Cooke, Thomas Jr.	63	Low Gap Branch	1851	3	279
Cooke, William	26	Laurel Fork	1849	3	120
Cooke, William A.	32	Clear Fork	1848	3	11
Cooke, William A.	238	Skin Fork	1843	2	46
Cooke, William D.	111	Laurel Fork	1852	3	448
Cooke, William D.	31	Stagger Weed Hollow	1846	2	274
Cooke, William & Mitchell	300	Wts. Big Fork	1849	3	121
Cornett—or Cornut					
Cornett, David	144	4 Pole Cr.	1860	2	477
Cornut, David (Cornett)	123	4 Pole Creek	1860	1	508
Cox, Montgomery	1,230	Ugly Creek	1860	2	496
Cozart, Peter G.	75	Laurel Fork	1836	1	249
Crain, (or Cram) Harvey	1,000	Marsh Fork	1860	1	502
Cram (Crain) Harvey	1,000	Marsh Fork	1860	1	502
Cummings—or Cummins					
Cummings, William	50	Spruce Fork	1837	1	267
Cummings, William	50	6 Mi. Cr.	1833	1	158
Cummins—or Cummings					
Cummins, William	25	Turtle Creek	1829	1	86
Cummins, William	50	Spruce Fork	1836	1	255
Cummins, William	75	Wts. Mud	1838	1	340
Curry, Barnabus	23	Island Creek	1844	2	162
Curry, Barnabus	50	Rich Creek	1842	1	419
Curry, Barnabus	31	Cow Creek	1844	2	160
Curry, Barnabus	24	Island Creek	1844	2	161
Curry, Barnabus	44	Cow Creek	1844	2	159
Curry, Barnabus	17	Cow Creek	1846	2	298
Curry, Barnabus & Robert	25	Mill Creek	1826	1	12
Curry, Eli	22	Pigeon Creek	1855	4	215
Curry, John	25	Cow Creek	1837	1	308
Curry, Robert	25	Island Creek	1826	1	16
Curry, William	31	Rockhouse Fork	1860	2	484
Curry, William	36	Rockhouse	1847	2	335
Dalton, John	34	Francis Fork	1857	4	365
Dalton, William	38	Kiah's Fork	1847	2	342
Dalton, William	25	Hart's Cr.	1847	2	341
Dalton, William	16	Kiah's Fork	1857	4	364
Dalton, William	44	Kiah's Fork	1857	4	363
Damron, Samuel	50	Cane Fork	1837	1	292
Damron, Samuel et al	224	Lit. Hart's Creek	1846	2	258
Damron, Samuel et al	47	12 Pole Cr.	1846	2	259
Damron, Samuel et al	93	12 Pole	1845	2	191
Damron, Samuel et al	44	12 Pole	1845	2	190
Damron, Samuel et al	72	Francis's Creek	1845	2	193
Damron, Samuel et al	74	12 Pole	1845	2	192
Damron, Samuel et al	265	Bohemin Fork	1850	3	236
Daniels, Ezekiel	75	Back Creek	1832	1	128
Daniels, Zekieal	25	Tug Fork	1831	1	117
Davis, George	18	Pigeon Creek	1845	2	241

Name of Grantee	Acres	Local Description	Year	Book	Page
Davis, George	17	Pigeon Creek	1845	2	242
Davis, George	82	Pigeon Creek	1847	2	418
Davis, George	70	Marrowbone Creek	1850	3	206
Davis, George	80	Marrowbone Creek	1850	3	205
Davis, Henry	11	Pigeon Creek	1848	2	439
Davis, Henry	19	Old House Branch	1848	3	57
Davis, William	40	Old House Branch	1847	2	400
Davis, William	38	Wts. Sandy	1852	3	493
Davis, William Jr.	25	Wts. Sandy	1842	1	428
Davis, William Jr.	49	Old Field Branch	1842	1	427
Dempsey—or Dempsie					
Dempsey, Andrew	10	Lick Branch	1848	3	85
Dempsey, James	36	Mud Fork	1854	4	121
Dempsey, James	34	Mud Fork	1854	4	122
Dempsey, James	18	Mud Fork	1842	1	426
Dempsey, James	19	Mud Fork	1844	2	127
Dempsey, John	109	Mud Fork	1856	4	237
Dempsey, John	79	Mud Fork	1856	4	236
Dempsey, John	75	Copper's Mine Fk.	1836	1	260
Dempsey, John	60	Mud Fork	1846	2	282
Dempsey, John et al	170	Francis' Fork	1850	3	231
Dempsey, John et al	94	Trace Branch	1850	3	232
Dempsey, John et al	165	Francis' Fork	1850	3	233
Dempsey, John et al	650	Francis' Fork	1850	3	226
Dempsey, John et al	260	Francis' Fork	1850	3	227
Dempsey, John et al	55	12 Pole	1850	3	228
Dempsey, John et al	160	12 Pole	1850	3	230
Dempsey, John et al	630	Hart's Creek	1850	3	229
Dempsey, John Jr.	42	Lick Branch	1855	4	166
Dempsey, John Jr.	19	Ben Creek	1855	4	167
Dempsey, John Jr.	60	Wts. Sandy	1855	4	165
Dempsey, John Jr.	200	Wts. Sandy	1855	4	168
Dempsey, John Jr.	100	Ben Creek	1859	1	475
Dempsey, John Jr.	1,191	Turkey Creek	1860	2	475
Dempsey, John & Joseph	100	Trace Fork	1841	1	394
Dempsey, John Sr.	50	Island Creek	1861	2	463
Dempsey, John Sr.	48	Island Creek	1861	2	463
Dempsey, Joseph	38	Trace Fork	1846	2	299
Dempsey, Joseph	54	Trace Fork	1850	3	180
Dempsey, Joseph	42	Trace Fork	1834	1	195
Dempsey, Joseph	25	Trace Fork	1834	1	191
Dempsey, Joseph	35	Middle Fork	1834	1	192
Dempsey, Joseph	105	Rock House	1829	1	97
Dempsey, Lewis	58	Burning Creek	1855	4	129
Dempsey, William	27	Middle Fork	1848	3	59
Dempsey, William A.	5	Pigeon Creek	1858	4	411
Dempsey, William A.	27	Den Branch of Laurel	1848	3	60
Dempsey, William A.	30	Laurel Fork	1848	3	17
Dempsey, William A.	19	Lick Branch	1850	3	266
Dempsey, William A.	43	Laurel Branch	1851	3	317
Dempsey, William A.	73	Trace Fork	1850	3	246
Dempsey, William A. et al	125	Big Fork	1852	3	506
Dempsey, William B.	84	Henderson's Fork	1856	4	315
Dempsie—or Dempsey					
Dempsie, Joseph	50	Ben's Creek	1827	1	39
Dempsie, Joseph	25	Cow Creek	1827	1	38
Dempsie, Joseph (Dempie)	45	Tug Fork	1827	1	28
Deskins, James	5,100	Miller's Creek	1850	3	560
Deskins, James & John	286	Miller's Creek	1852	3	548
Deskins, John	183	Wts. Sandy	1835	1	453
Deskins, John Jr.	1,100	Road Branch	1848	3	103
Dial, Andrew	185	Doland's Branch	1852	3	495
Dial, Andrew	40	Ugly Creek	1852	3	494

Name of Grantee	Acres	Local Description	Year	Book	Page
Duncan, Mark P.	50	Lick Branch	1855	4	144
Duncan, Mark P.	55	Trace Fork	1854	4	105
Duncan, Mark P.	100	Trace Fork	1852	4	104
Duncan, Mark P.	22	Trace Fork	1848	3	58
Duncan, Mark P.	32	Farley's Fork	1848	3	15
Duncan, Mark P.	68	Flat Ridge	1847	2	403
Duncan, Mark P.	31	Farley's Fork	1842	2	26
Duty, Ellison C.	22	Rockhouse Fork	1862	2	465
Duty, George W.	32	Pigeon Creek	1854	4	87
Duty, George W.	45	Pigeon Creek	1849	3	127
Duty, George W.	130	Pigeon Creek	1862	2	465
Duty, George W.	120	Pigeon Creek	1862	2	466
Duty, George W.	350	Rockhouse Fork	1862	2	467
Duty, George W.	46	Rhode Branch	1846	2	286
Duty, George W.	9	Trace Fork	1843	2	55
Edwards, Leonard	50	Marsh Fork	1829	1	87
Elkin—or Elkins					
Elkin, Daniel	20	Spruce Fork	1838	1	329
Elkin, Daniel	30	Beech Fork	1848	3	61
Elkin, Darby K.	60	Wts. Guyandotte	1853	4	23
Elkin, Harvey & Andrew	55	Hart's Creek	1855	4	169
Elkin, Isaiah	46	Huff Creek	1859	1	501
Elkin, Isaiah	194	Elk Creek	1860	2	486
Elkin, James & Martin	47	Rt. Hd. Fk. Hewitt's Cr.	1847	2	344
Elkin, Joel	16	Island Branch	1852	3	405
Elkin, Marvel	20	Big Creek	1837	1	269
Elkin, Marvil	320	Piney Fork	1858	4	405
Elkin, Mathias	29	Hart's Creek	1859	1	493
Elkin, Mathias	9	Hart's Creek	1857	4	397
Elkin, Mathias	25	Hart's Creek	1857	4	398
Elkin, Reace W.	90	Dry Branch	1852	3	406
Elkin, Reace W. et al	48	Wts. Guyandotte	1852	3	409
Elkin, Reace W. et al	55	Wts. Guyandotte	1852	3	410
Elkin, Richard	18	Pigeon Roost	1848	3	62
Elkin, Richard Jr. et al	35	Sugar Branch	1850	3	237
Elkin, Richard Jr. et al	260	Buck Lick	1850	3	213
Elkin, Richard Jr. et al	42	Wts. Guyandotte	1850	3	214
Elkin, Richard Jr. & Melton et al	20	Wts. Guyandotte	1850	3	278
Elkin, Robert	160	Rock House	1857	4	381
Elkin, Uriah W.	220	Sand Lick	1856	4	316
Elkin, William	4	Laurel Fork	1847	2	420
Elkin, William	21	Laurel Fork	1847	2	419
Elkin, William	48	Huff's Creek	1850	3	195
Elkin, William	20	Laurel Fork	1837	1	271
Elkin, Zacheus & Robert Jr.	250	Hewitt's Fork	1854	4	106
Elkins—or Elkin					
Elkins, Archibald	23	Wts. Guyandotte	1843	2	56
Elkins, Elijah et al	100	Pond Fork	1829	1	99
Elkins, Elizaha	50	Hewitt's Cr.	1826	1	5
Elkins, Harvey	18	Hart's Cr.	1836	1	242
Elkins, Harvey	25	Hart's Creek	1836	1	234
Elkins, Richard	18	Hart's Creek	1828	1	59
Elkins, Richard Jr. et al	80	Sugar Camp	1850	3	215
Elkins, Robert	70	Rockhouse	1837	1	268
Elkins, William	33	Laurel Fork	1833	1	143
Elkins, William	75	Laurel Fork	1833	1	157
Elkins, Zacheous (Zacheus)	30	Pond Fork	1834	1	181
Elkins, Zachrus (Zacheus)	20	Hewitt's Fork	1838	1	369
Ellis, Evan	61	Island Creek	1844	2	164
Ellis, Evan	34	Island Creek	1834	1	180
Ellis, Evan	20	Island Creek	1846	2	273
Ellis, Evan	55	Island Creek	1849	3	160
Ellis, Evan	15	Little Creek	1849	3	159

Name of Grantee	Acres	Local Description	Year	Book	Page
Ellis, Even (Evan)	50	Island Cr.	1826	1	13
Ellis, Henry	10	Island Creek	1846	2	270
Ellis, Henry	14	Little Creek	1842	2	2
Ellis, Henry	79	Huff's Creek	1849	3	158
Ellis, Henry	100	Huff's Creek	1849	3	149
Ellis, Jacob D.	41	Buck Creek	1846	2	271
Ellis, Jacob D.	105	Beech Fork	1846	2	272
Ellis, Jacob D.	54	Marsh Fork	1848	2	447
Ellis, Jacob D.	38	Trace Branch	1852	3	555
Ellis, Jacob D.	37	Beech Fork	1852	3	556
Ellis, Jacob D.	42	Briar Fork	1852	4	3
Ellis, Jacob D.	20	Hurricane Br.	1852	4	2
Ellis, Jacob D.	36	Lick Fork	1852	4	4
Ellis, Jacob D. et al	63	Pigeon Creek	1844	2	163
Ellis, James	75	Island Creek	1852	3	422
Ellis, James	96	Island Creek	1858	4	426
Ellis, Loyd	147	Gilbert's Cr.	1851	3	322
Ellis, Loyd	212	White Oak Br.	1851	3	321
Ellis, Madison	27	Horse Pen Fork	1848	2	443
Ellis, Philip	50	Island Creek	1827	1	54
Ellis, Squire	45	Island Creek	1842	1	429
Ellis, Squire	34	Island Creek	1855	4	130
Ellis, Squire & James	275	Island Creek	1858	4	425
Ellis, William	200	Fork Ridge	1856	4	234
Ellis, William	25	Dingess Run	1856	4	233
Ellis, William	20	Pine Creek	1837	1	270
Ellis, William & Philip Jr.	75	Fork Ridge	1856	4	235
Ellis, Zatter C.	40	Mill Creek	1851	3	320
Ellis, Zatter C.	50	Island Creek	1851	3	319
Ellis, Zatter C.	68	Island Creek	1851	3	318
English, Thomas Dunn	3,920	Jenny's Cr.	1854	4	561
English, Thomas Dunn	440	Sand Creek	1856	4	231
English, Thomas Dunn	488	Pigeon Roost	1853	4	7
English, Thomas Dunn	235	Ugly Creek	1856	4	232
English, Thomas Dunn	120	Wts. Guyandotte	1854	4	46
English, Thomas Dunn	300	Big Ugly	1854	4	58
English, Thomas Dunn	500	Big Ugly	1854	4	59
English, Thomas Dunn	880	Marrowbone Creek	1854	4	60
English, Thomas Dunn	1,380	Jenny's Creek	1854	4	76
Estep, Cornelius	80	Tug Fork	1829	1	89
Estep, Owen	45	Hewitt's Fork	1844	2	165
Estep, Samuel	20	Huff Creek	1831	1	119
Estep, Shadrack	41	Jack's Branch	1846	2	268
Evans, Henry P.	260	Marrowbone Cr.	1854	4	95
Evans, Henry P.	26	Laurel Branch	1850	3	217
Evans, Henry P.	66	Neeley's Branch	1850	3	216
Evans, Pyrrhus	160	Bent Branch	1856	4	336
Evans, Pyrrhus	79	Bark Camp Branch	1855	4	132
Evans, Richard	65	Marrowbone Cr.	1856	4	335
Evans, Richard	50	Marrowbone Creek	1855	4	131
Evans, Richard	20	Big Branch	1851	3	397
Evans, Richard	25	Wts. Sandy	1837	1	265
Evans, Richard	76	Sartain Branch	1849	3	110
Evans, Talton (Tarlton)	105	Laurel Fork	1860	2	479
Evans, Tarlton	50	Laurel Fork	1851	3	324
Evans, William	85	Big Fork	1851	3	323
Farley, Henry	65	Elk Fork	1854	4	88
Farley, Henry	648	Sugar Creek	1854	4	97
Farley, Henry	58	Davis Branch	1849	3	162
Farley, Henry	45	Sugar Tree Creek	1849	3	161
Farley, Henry	50	Elk Fork	1850	3	198
Farley, Henry	26	Trace Fork	1844	2	145
Farley, Henry	21	Trace Fork	1843	2	90

Name of Grantee	Acres	Local Description	Year	Book	Page
Farley, Henry	20	Dan's Branch	1843	2	91
Farley, Henry	60	Pigeon Creek	1827	1	47
Farley, Henry	17	Sandy River	1842	2	3
Farley, Henry & William	150	Pigeon Creek	1826	1	445
Farley, Jesse	39	Buffalo Creek	1853	4	31
Farley, John	43	Buffalo Creek	1855	4	223
Farley, Madison	27	Indian Creek	1847	2	345
Farley, Nimrod	50	Spruce Fork	1834	1	171
Farley, Nimrod	80	Spruce Fork	1833	1	140
Farley, Thomas	67	Buffalo Cr.	1849	3	128
Farley, Thomas	69	Buffalo Cr.	1849	3	129
Farley, Thomas	23	Buffalo Creek	1854	4	96
Farley, William Jr.	100	Mud Fork	1855	4	133
Farley, William Jr.	39	Mud Fork	1860	2	492
Farmer, Jeremiah	25	Cane Fork	1845	2	235
Farmer, Jeremiah	19	Crawley's Creek	1844	2	166
Farmer, Jeramiah	38	Cane Patch Fork	1837	1	266
Farmer, Jeremiah	45	Crawley's Creek	1848	3	19
Farmer, Jeremiah	50	Crawley's Creek	1854	4	39
Farmer, Jeremiah	50	Smokehouse	1856	4	317
Fenwick, James et al	21	Pigeon Creek	1846	2	292
Fenwick, James et al	11	Wts. Sandy	1846	2	293
Fenwick, James et al	27	Pigeon Creek	1846	2	294
Fenwick, James et al	55	Pigeon Creek	1846	2	295
Fenwick, James et al	27	Pigeon Creek	1847	2	358
Fenwick, James et al	44	Slick Rock	1847	2	359
Ferguson, James H. et al	300	Sand Creek	1852	3	497
Ferral—or Ferrel, Ferrell--or Terrell					
Ferral, John et al	180	Tug Fork	1827	1	40
Ferrel, John	38	Tug Fork	1834	1	166
Ferrell, Elijah	185	Pigeon Creek	1852	3	424
Ferrell, Elijah	40	Pigeon Creek	1852	3	425
Ferrell, Elijah (or Terrell)	85	Pigeon Creek	1836	1	261
Ferrell, Elijah et al	63	Pigeon Creek	1844	2	163
Ferrell, Evans	75	Pigeon Creek	1852	3	423
Ferrell, Evans	430	Pigeon Creek	1859	4	449
Ferrell, John	150	Spruce's Branch	1849	3	163
Ferrell, Richard	225	Pigeon Creek	1836	1	454
Ferrell, Samuel	238	Big Ugly	1857	4	395
Fletcher, John	65	Tug Fork	1841	1	412
Floyd, George	2,200	Pigeon Creek	1858	4	579
Floyd, George	4,300	Miller's Creek	1858	4	581
Floyd, George R. C.	12,804	Big Branch	1860	2	511
Fry, Admiral S.	57	Isaac's Branch	1856	4	247
Fry, Admiral S.	157	Big Ugly	1860	1	495
Fry, Baptist	50	Ugly Creek	1850	3	197
Fry, Christian T.	23	Douglass Branch	.854	4	108
Fry, Christian T.	110	Green Shoal Cr.	.854	4	107
Fry, Christian T.	150	Wts. Guyandotte	855	4	153
Fry, Christian T.	45	Green Shoal	1855	4	154
Fry, Christian T.	39	Brown's Branch	1856	4	337
Fry, Hamilton	45	Ugly Creek	1843	2	72
Fry, Hamilton	20	Laurel Fork	1844	2	128
Fry, Hamilton	44	Ugly Creek	1850	3	181
Fry, Hamilton	30	Big Branch	1850	3	182
Fry, Hamilton	33	Ugly Creek	1850	3	196
Fry, Hamilton	50	Ugly Creek	1860	1	497
Fry, Hamilton	230	Big Ugly	1860	1	496
Fry, Hamilton	44	Ugly Creek	1852	3	498
Fry, Hamilton	260	Ugly Creek	1856	4	256
Fry, Hamilton	32	Pigeon Roost	1838	1	367
Fry, Hamilton	700	Ugly Creek	1856	4	255
Fry, Isaac et al	85	Ugly Creek	1847	2	407

Name of Grantee	Acres	Local Description	Year	Book	Page
Fry, John	25	Green Creek	1843	2	73
Fry, John	50	Wts. Guyandotte	1845	2	251
Fry, John	10	Queen Shoal Creek	1828	1	62
Fry, John	20	Wts. Guyandotte	1850	3	184
Fry, John	30	Big Branch	1850	3	183
Fry, John	44	Green Shoal Creek	1852	3	499
Fry, John	25	Gum Shoal Creek	1835	1	219
Fry, John Jr.	125	Big Ugly	1861	2	522
Fry, Joseph	112	Ugly Creek	1848	2	440
Fry, Joseph	50 (or 15)	Ugly Creek	1851	3	384
Garten, Elijah A.	175	Hart's Creek	1857	4	371
Garten, Elijah A.	675 (657)	Hart's Creek	1856	4	574
Garten, Elijah A. et al	770	Hart's Creek	1856	4	275
Goare—or Gore					
Goare, Eli	62	Wts. Guyandotte	1848	3	20
Goare, Eli	60	Wts. Guyandotte	1852	3	407
Goare, Eli et al	122	Wts. Guyandotte	1852	3	408
Goare, John	65	Marsh Fork	1856	4	338
Goare, John	40	Marsh Fork	1849	3	130
Goare, John et al	300	Coal Creek	1856	4	339
Goare, Joseph	84	Clear Fork	1835	1	221
Goare, Joseph	135	Beech Fork	1843	2	47
Goare, Joseph et al	66	Keesee's Branch	1837	1	290
Goare, Levi	5¾	Big Fork	1849	3	131
Goddard, John H.	500	Island Creek	1861	2	521
Godfrey, Armer L.	13	Rockham Branch	1854	4	124
Godfrey, Burgess	108	Bluff Mountain	1827	1	27
Godfrey, Burgess et al	87	Flat Top Mt.	1827	1	26
Godfrey, Thomas	10	Huff's Creek	1851	3	281
Godfrey, Thomas	19	Huff Creek	1851	3	284
Godfrey, Thomas	30	Huff's Creek	1845	2	206
Goff, John B.	1,000	Pigeon Creek	1859	4	593
Gore—or Goare					
Gore, Joseph	90	Marsh Fork	1827	1	42
Gore, Joseph	55	Camp Branch	1828	1	66
Gore, Joseph	20	Wts. Guyandotte	1830	1	107
Grayham, Luke	84	Devil's Fork	1848	3	63
Green, Joshua	143	Big Fork	1853	4	14
Griffith, Ephraim	820	Horse Creek	1847	2	454
Griffith, Ephraim	84	Brushy Fork	1847	2	320
Griffith, Ephraim	74	Horse Creek	1847	2	321
Griffith, Ephriam	126	Sulphur Spring	1847	2	372
Grimmit, John	36	Wts. Guyandotte	1848	3	64
Gunoe, Andrew	29	Clear Fork	1850	3	270
Hager, Andrew	40	Trace Fork	1826	1	15
Hager, Benjamin	69	Hewitt's Fork	1843	2	74
Hager, Benjamin	185	Hewitt's Creek	1847	2	373
Hager, James	75	Wts. Mud	1836	1	263
Hager, James	50	Wts. Mud	1838	1	364
Hager, James	25	Luke Fork	1838	1	363
Hager, James	25	Ballard's Fork	1838	1	362
Hager, James	25	Wts. Mud River	1836	1	232
Hager, James Jr.	50	Wts. Mud	1842	2	29
Hager, James Jr.	50	Wts. Mud River	1840	1	383
Hager, John	68	Spruce Fork	1843	2	76
Hager, John	70	Little Coal River	1842	1	437
Hager, John	25	Turtle Creek	1838	1	318
Hager, Robert	95	Spruce Fork	1847	2	374
Hager, Robert	25	Spruce Fork	1847	2	323
Hager, Robert	50	6 Mile Creek	1843	2	92
Hager, Robert	14	6 Mile Cr.	1843	2	93
Hager, Robert	50	6 Mi. Creek	1847	2	366
Hager, Robert	50	Six Mile Cr.	1837	1	278

Name of Grantee	Acres	Local Description	Year	Book	Page
Haner, Lewis	13½	Big Creek	1827	1	45
Haner, Noah	15	Big Creek	1837	1	279
Haner, Noah	500	Limestone Branch	1854	4	75
Haner, Noah	20	Limestone Branch	1852	3	507
Haner, Noah	25	Limestone Guyandotte	1842	1	438
Haner, Noah	25	Wts. Guyandotte	1842	1	430
Haner, Noah et al	235	Big Ugly Cr.	1852	3	529
Haner, Noah & William et al	250	Ugly Creek	1852	3	508
Hank, Caleb	300	Skin Fork	1830	1	102
Harper, Joseph	60	Clear Fork of Cole	1831	1	109
Harvey, Henry	80	Lick Branch	1848	3	24
Harvey, Henry	5½	Clear Fork	1848	3	66
Harvey, John	120	Cedar Creek	1848	3	23
Harvey, Joshua	19	Clear Fork	1848	3	22
Harvey, William	12	Clear Fork	1831	1	123
Harvey, William	25	Clear Fork	1848	3	21
Harvey, William	50	Clear Fork	1836	1	235
Harris, Bernice	35	Left Hand Fork	1848	3	86
Harris, Joseph	50	Spruce Fork	1847	2	349
Harrison, Charles	100	Sparr's Branch	1836	1	258
Harrison, Charles	40	Spruce Fork	1843	2	75
Hatfield, Aly	75	Ben Creek	1850	3	247
Hatfield, Aly	89	Mate's Creek	1859	1	461
Hatfield, Aly	330	Ben Creek	1859	1	460
Hatfield, Aly	72	Ben Creek	1859	1	462
Hatfield, Aly	66	Ben Creek	1842	2	8
Hatfield, Aly	450	Ben Creek	1859	1	463
Hatfield, Aly	50	Mate's Creek	1859	1	464
Hatfield, Aly Jr.	30	Ben Creek	1856	4	341
Hatfield, Aly Jr.	150	Ben Creek	1856	4	340
Hatfield, Aly, Joseph and Aly Jr.	390	Ben Creek	1861	2	525
Hatfield, Aly, Joseph and Aly Jr.	470	Ben Creek	1861	2	526
Hatfield, Andrew	21	Ben Creek	1845	2	207
Hatfield, Andrew	25	Ben Creek	1845	2	208
Hatfield, Andrew	50	Ben Creek	1852	3	501
Hatfield, Andrew	108	Beech Fork	1852	3	502
Hatfield, Eli	46	Ben's Creek	1841	1	409
Hatfield, Eli	50	Mate's Creek	1835	1	222
Hatfield, Ephraim	84	Beech Creek	1855	4	155
Hatfield, Ephraim	215	Mate's Creek	1836	1	225
Hatfield, Ephraim	125	Meadow Branch	1851	3	399
Hatfield, Ephraim	70	Murphy's Branch	1851	3	398
Hatfield, Ephraim	20	Mate's Creek	1861	2	459
Hatfield, Ephraim	24	Straight Fork	1846	2	257
Hatfield, Ephraim	45	Mate's Creek	1846	2	256
Hatfield, George	333	Mate's Creek	1861	2	457
Hatfield, George	333	Meadow Fork	1861	2	460
Hatfield, Jacob	190	Browning Fork	1859	1	465
Hatfield, Jacob	71	Browning Fork	1859	4	450
Hatfield, James	98	Mate's Creek	1859	4	452
Hatfield, James	75	Mate's Creek	1859	4	451
Hatfield, Joseph	54	Spring Fork	1852	3	500
Hatfield, Joseph Jr.	30	Ben Creek	1844	2	171
Hatfield, Thomas	25	Road Fork	1850	3	248
Hatfield, Thomas	23	Shirkey Fork	1848	3	87
Hatfield, Thomas	125	Horsepen	1854	4	71
Hatfield, Thomas	63	Horse Pen	1841	1	399
Hatfield, Thomas	42	Island Creek	1857	4	379
Hatfield, Thomas	660	Horse Pen	1857	4	380
Hatfield, Valentine	35	Horse Pen	1848	3	26
Hatfield, Valentine	43	Browning Fork	1841	1	397
Hatfield, Valentine	114	Camp Fork	1859	4	454
Hendrix, Francis	33	Cane Fork	1836	1	239

Name of Grantee	Acres	Local Description	Year	Book	Page
Hendrix, Francis	12	Clear Fork	1834	1	182
Henley—See Hensley, Hensly					
Henley, Robert (Hensley)	75	Paint Ridge	1851	3	325
Hensley, Daniel	50	Pigeon Creek	1848	3	25
Hensley, Daniel	8	Rockhouse Fork	1848	3	65
Hensley, Daniel Jr.	15	Rockhouse	1851	3	326
Hensley, Robert	59	Smokehouse	1842	2	9
Hensley, Robert	45	White Oak	1842	2	27
Hensley, Robert	80	Trace Branch	1855	4	134
Hensley, Stephen	20	Big Laurel	1855	4	135
Hensley, William	25	Pigeon Creek	1848	3	67
Hensly—See Henley, Hensley					
Hensly, Robert	50	Smokehouse	1838	1	312
Hill, Lorenzo D.	45	Cane Fork	1845	2	238
Hill, Lorenzo D.	50	Buck Fork	1842	2	4
Hill, Lorenzo D.	40	Rockhouse	1842	2	5
Hill, Lorenzo D.	160	Turtle Lick	1844	2	167
Hill, Lorenzo D.	450	Slab Fork	1844	2	168
Hill, Lorenzo D.	60	Flat Creek	1844	2	169
Hill, Lorenzo D.	150	Francis's Fork	1844	2	450
Hill, Lorenzo D.	100	Mile Branch	1849	3	132
Hill, Lorenzo D.	290	Cane Fork	1851	3	567
Hill, Lorenzo D.	250	Pretty Branch	1856	4	294
Hill, Lorenzo D.	185	Cane Fork	1856	4	280
Hill, Lorenzo D.	430	Canoe Branch	1851	3	387
Hill, Lorenzo D.	650	Cane Patch Fork	1851	3	385
Hill, Lorenzo D.	140	Hart's Creek	1851	3	386
Hill, Lorenzo D. et al	25	Cane Fork	1845	2	239
Hill, Lorenzo D. et al	50	12 Pole Cr.	1844	2	170
Hill,Lorenzo D. (Lorenzo D. Chambers)	400	Rum Creek	1856	4	279
Hinchman, Burwell S.	85	Big Branch	1847	2	322
Hinchman, Burwell S.	50	Spruce Fork	1847	2	346
Hinchman, Cyrus	25	Wts. Guyandotte	1834	1	183
Hinchman, Hiram	58½	Wts. Guyandotte	1832	1	138
Hinchman, James H.	218	Rich Creek	1847	3	27
Hinchman, James H.	129	Rich Creek	1862	2	468
Hinchman, James H.	1,040	Rich Creek	1862	2	469
Hinchman, John K.	24	Spruce Fork	1844	2	129
Hinchman, John K.	42	Hager's Branch	1847	2	324
Hinchman, John K.	23	Wts. Guyandotte	1831	1	114
Hinchman, John K.	25	Spruce Fork	1847	2	348
Hinchman, John K.	50	Hager's Branch	1847	2	347
Hinchman, Milton	11½	Rich Creek	1842	2	6
Hinchman, Ulysses	115	Sand Lick	1858	4	401
Hinchman, Ulysses	900	Madison Creek	1858	4	578
Hinchman, Ulysses	125	Guyandotte	1855	4	145
Hinchman, Ulysses	75	Madison Cr.	1840	1	374
Hinchman, Ulysses	62	Big Fork	1852	3	503
Hinchman, Ulysses	240	Madison Creek	1852	3	504
Hinchman, Ulysses	80 (or 8)	Rich Creek	1852	3	505
Hinchman, Ulysses	125	Big Branch	1851	3	378
Hinchman, Ulysses	69	Slab Fork	1842	2	7
Hinchman, Ulysses	28	Big Fork	1842	2	22
Hinchman, Ulysses et al	30	Laurel Fork	1848	3	10
Hinchman, Ulysses et al	125	Big Fork	1852	3	506
Hinchman, William	68	Long Shoal	1849	3	133
Hinchman, William	100	Wts. Guyandotte	1841	1	395
Hinchman, William	25	Rich Creek	1837	1	277
Hopkins, Henry S.	60	Rock Creek	1829	1	79
Howard, Robert G. et al	43	Pigeon Creek	1859	1	480
Howerton, John	213	Barker's Fork	1847	2	408
Hurley, Ashbury	18	Knox Creek	1850	3	185

Name of Grantee	Acres	Local Description	Year	Book	Page
Jamison—or Jemison					
Jamison, John J. (Jemison)	64	Buffalo Cr.	1843	2	57
Jamison, John J. (Jemison)	73	Buffalo Cr.	1848	3	28
Jarrel, Daniel	50	Pond Fork	1829	1	96
Jarrel, John	40	Pond Fork	1829	1	93
Jarrel, John	60	Pond Fork	1829	1	95
Jarrel, Lemuel	10	Clear Fork	1828	1	74
Jarrel, Lemuel	40	Clear Fork	1828	1	75
Jarrell, Daniel	25	Camp Branch	1840	1	380
Jarrell, Daniel	20	Pond Fork	1840	1	379
Jarrell, Daniel	25	Pond Fork	1845	2	228
Jarrell, Elijah	40	Pond Fork	1845	2	227
Jarrell, Elijah	23	Pond Fork	1833	1	148
Jarrell, Elijah	20	Laurel Fork	1840	1	378
Jarrell, Elijah	20	Pond Fork	1840	1	377
Jarrell, Elijah	12	Pond Fork	1840	1	376
Jarrell, John	17	Pond Fork	1838	1	360
Jarrell, John	33	West Fork	1833	1	146
Jarrell, Landon	25	Bull Creek	1835	1	215
Jarrell, Simeon	25	Laurel Fork	1840	1	375
Jarrell, Simon Jr.	42	Spruce Fork	1833	1	145
Jeffrey, Milton I. (or J.)	46	Spruce Fork	1852	3	509
Jimison—See Jamison, Jemison					
Johnson, George	25	McDonald Fork	1846	2	307
Jones, John	23	Clay Bank Br.	1849	3	164
Jones, John	39	Clay Bank Branch	1852	4	5
Jones, John G.	25	Spruce Fork	1837	1	287
Jones, John G.	22	Hewitt's Fork	1847	2	405
Jones, John G.	9	Hewitt's Fork	1847	2	406
Justice, James	25	White Oak Branch	1852	3	546
Justice, James	140	White Oak	1856	4	257
Justice, James	184	Wts. Guyandotte	1850	3	199
Justice, Thomas	55	Briar Branch	1856	4	258
Kesinger, Wilson	25	Spruce Fork	1845	2	229
King, Patrick H.	500	Copper Mine Fork	1861	2	523
Kirk, Hugh	57	12 Pole Creek	1861	2	505
Kirk, Hugh	55	Laurel Fork	1848	2	448
Kirk, Joseph M.	49	Wts. Sandy River	1850	3	200
Lackey, Daniel	30	Rockhouse	1847	2	350
Lackey, Daniel	20	Laurel Fork	1848	2	434
Lackey, Daniel	8½	Laurel Fork	1848	2	435
Lackey, Daniel	60	Marrowbone Creek	1859	1	459
Lackey, Daniel	17	Laurel Fork	1835	1	458
Lackey, Daniel	20	Rockhouse	1851	3	329
Lackey, Daniel	15	Aldridge Br.	1851	3	328
Lackey, Daniel	25	Sugar Camp Br.	1851	3	327
Lackey, Daniel	170	Laurel Fork	1854	4	50
Lackey, Daniel	28	Big Kill Br.	1856	4	342
Lackey, Daniel	25	Rockhouse	1854	4	49
Laird, John A.	500	12 Pole Creek	1861	2	499
Laird, Samuel	500	Trace Fork	1861	2	500
Lambert, Hiram	175	Big Fork	1852	3	512
Lambert, Hiram	45	Big Fork	1852	3	513
Lambert, Samuel	133	Briar Fork	1847	2	376
Lambert, Samuel	72	Trace Fork	1847	2	353
Lambert, Samuel	64	Marsh Fork	1847	2	352
Lambert, Stephen	73	Buck Fork	1854	4	65
Lambert, Stephen	32	Wolfe Pen	1854	4	72
Laster—See Lester					
Lawson, Anthony	700	Wts. Guyandotte	1856	4	263
Lawson, Anthony	1,111	Big Ugly	1856	4	261
Lawson, Anthony	3,300	Big Ugly Creek	1856	4	322
Lawson, Anthony	950	Beech Branch	1856	4	323

Name of Grantee	Acres	Local Description	Year	Book	Page
Lawson, Lewis B.	14	Freeze Fork	1851	3	333
Lawson, Lewis B.	17	Trace Fork	1851	3	335
Lawson, Lewis B.	30	Rockhouse	1851	3	334
Lawson, William B.	75	Blevin's Fork	1860	2	488
Lechinett, Louis (Luchinett)	13	Gilbert Creek	1853	4	26
Lester—or Laster					
Lester, Joseph	85	Big Ben	1848	3	29
Lester, Joseph	20	Huff's Creek	1831	1	121
Lester, Joseph	37	Huff Creek	1852	3	416
Lester, Joseph	59	Cub Fork	1852	3	417
Lester, Joseph	319	Huff's Creek	1852	3	568
Lester, Joseph	33	Huff's Cr.	1836	1	251
Lester, Joseph	19	Trace Branch	1845	2	211
Lester, Joseph	40	Cub Fork	1845	2	212
Lester, Joseph	16	Huff Creek	1845	2	210
Lester, Pleasant	40	Big Branch	1852	3	549
Lester, Pleasant	27	Huff Creek	1845	2	213
Lester, Thomas	35	Wts. Sandy	1852	3	510
Lester, William	20	Sycamore Creek	1837	1	280
Lewis, James A. et al	875	Wts. New River	1830	1	108
Lilley—or Lilly					
Lilley, Robert	100	Guyandotte	1842	2	10
Lilly, Robert	108	Hart's Creek	1851	3	287
Lilly, Robert	160	Brown's Branch	1851	3	286
Lilly, Robert	125	Lilly's Branch	1851	3	285
Linegar, (Linager) Amos	200	N. Side Wolf Pen	1827	1	24
Linvill—or Linville, Lonville					
Linvill, Preston	25	Little Cole	1832	1	130
Linville, Preston P.	17	Pond Fork	1841	1	384
Linville, Preston P.	25	Bull Creek	1836	1	246
Linville, Preston P.	18	Robinson's Cr.	1836	1	256
Linville, Thomas (Lonville)	75	Jack's Branch	1847	2	378
Linville, Thomas	7	Pond Fork	1841	1	411
Linville, Thomas	18	Bull Creek	1841	1	410
Lockhart, Bird	125	Long Pole Creek	1852	3	511
Lonville—See Linvill, Linville					
Lonville, Thomas	75	Jack's Branch	1847	2	378
Lowe, James M.	35	Marrowbone Cr.	1855	4	192
Lowery, John	25	Clare Fork	1835	1	200
Lucas, Charles	170	Big Ugly	1856	4	281
Lucas, Charles	45	Green Shoal	1850	3	201
Lucas, Charles	75	Gum Shoal Cr.	1858	4	427
Lucas, George	20	Cabin Branch	1838	1	344
Lucas, Ira	93	Hart's Creek	1860	2	487
Lucas, Price	50	Hart's Creek	1843	2	99
Lucas, Price	75	Hart's Creek	1848	3	68
Lucas, Ralph	50	Ugly Creek	1845	2	244
Lucas, Ralph	50	Gum Shoal Br.	1838	1	346
Lucas, Ralph	25	Wts. Guyandotte	1838	1	345
Luchinett—See Lechinett					
Lusk, Eli	20	Huff Creek	1832	1	135
Lusk, Eli	35	Huff Creek	1845	2	214
Lusk, Eli	38	Huff Creek	1852	3	452
Lusk, Eli	216	Nelson's Branch	1852	3	451
Lusk, Gordon	100	Pad's Fork of Huff	1852	3	453
Lusk, Reace T.	75	Briar Fork	1847	2	377
Lusk, Reace T. et al	47	Indian Creek	1847	2	351
Luske, Reace T.	25	Briar Creek	1845	2	230
Mainard—See Maynard					
Mainard, William	31	Buffalo Creek	1849	3	168
Marcum, Gideon	31	12 Pole Creek	1861	2	503
Marcum, Gideon	158	12 Pole Cr.	1861	2	501
Marcum, Gideon	425	Laurel Fork	1857	4	376

Name of Grantee	Acres	Local Description	Year	Book	Page
Marcum, Gideon D.	65	Laurel Fork	1857	4	377
Marcum, Gideon D.	148	Laurel Fork	1851	3	347
Marcum, Gideon D.	100	Laurel Fork	1851	3	348
Marcum, Gideon D.	110	Laurel Fork	1857	4	378
Marcum, Jacob	140	Marrowbone Cr.	1854	4	85
Marcum, Jacob	95	Laurel Fork	1854	4	84
Marcum, Jacob	82	Breeding Fork	1854	4	101
Marcum, Jacob	6	Laurel Fork	1845	2	209
Marcum, Jacob	178	Laurel Fork	1848	3	30
Marcum, Jacob	270	Laurel Fork	1848	3	92
Marcum, Jacob	18	Marrowbone Creek	1848	3	91
Marcum, Jacob	70	Breeding Fork	1849	3	167
Marcum, Jacob M.	130	Breeding Fork	1849	3	166
Marcum, Moses	225	Laurel Fork	1835	1	452
Marcum, Moses Jr.	14	Laurel Fork	1851	3	345
Marcum, Moses Jr.	65	Laurel Fork	1851	3	346
Marcum, Moses M.	65	Alex's Branch	1861	2	462
Marcum, Thomas	60	Buffalo Creek	1838	1	359
Marcum, Thomas	65	Buffalo Creek	1838	1	352
Marcum, William	100	Laurel Fork	1835	1	213
Maroney—See Meroney					
Marshall, Allen	44	Big Fork	1847	2	326
Marshall, James	132	Big Fork	1847	2	380
Mason, Edward	28	Gilbert's Cr.	1836	1	250
Mason, Polly A.	160	Huff Creek	1860	2	489
Massey, Henry	110	Dry Creek	1834	1	167
Massey, William	70	Marsh Fork	1834	1	168
Maynard—See Mainard					
Maynard, Alvis	270	Mill Stone	1855	4	211
Maynard, Avis (or Alvis)	50	Pigeon Roost	1855	4	209
Maynard, Moses S.	25	Pigeon Creek	1854	4	79
Maynard, Moses S.	23	Pigeon Creek	1854	4	98
Maynard, Richard	250	Lick Creek	1854	4	111
Maynard, William	150	Buffalo Creek	1843	2	59
Maynard, William C.	148	Buffalo Creek	1854	4	99
McComas, Patrick K.	47	Crooked Creek	1852	3	551
McComas, Patrick K.	144	Crooked Creek	1852	3	550
McComas, Sally et al Heirs	45	White Oak	1846	2	280
McComas, Sarah et al	165	Mill Creek	1847	2	409
McCoy, Asa	820	Pigeon Creek	1856	4	572
McCoy, Asa	290	Pigeon Creek	1856	4	248
McCoy, Hiram	175	Rock House	1857	4	374
McCoy, Randolph	83	Rock House Fk.	1827	1	22
McCoy, Samuel	75	Slick Rock Branch	1860	2	491
McGinnis, Pyrrhus	25	Marsh Fork	1842	2	20
McGinnis, Pyrrhus	46	Wts. Guyandotte	1842	2	21
McGinnis, Pyrhus	25	Tug Fork	1826	1	17
McGowan, John A.	500	Island Creek	1861	2	518
McDonald, Charles & Lewis	36	Peach Creek	1850	3	174
McDonald, Edward	120	Peach Creek	1851	3	340
McDonald, Edward	30	Wts. Guyandotte	1851	3	341
McDonald, Gordon	60	Buffalo Creek	1842	1	420
McDonald, Gordon	80	Rock House	1849	3	139
McDonald, Gordon	100	Wts. Guyandotte	1856	4	343
McDonald, Gordon	300	Huff's Creek	1856	4	344
McDonald, Harchilese	40	Peach Tree	1827	1	56
McDonald, John	10	Paint Ridge	1853	4	24
McDonald, John	340	Crooked Creek	1853	4	17
McDonald, John	75	Crooked Creek	1853	4	10
McDonald, John	35	Crooked Creek	1852	3	514
McDonald, John & Edward	100	Crooked Creek	1836	1	259
McDonald, Jonas	13	12 Pole Cr.	1844	2	131

Name of Grantee	Acres	Local Description	Year	Book	Page
McDonald, Jonas	24	12 Pole Cr.	1844	2	130
McDonald, Jonas	25	Laurel Fork	1844	2	125
McDonald, Joseph	60	Clear Fork	1833	1	152
McDonald, Joseph	125	Clear Fork	1837	1	285
McDonald, Joseph	100	Clear Fork	1837	1	286
McDonald, Joseph	73	Huff's Creek	1848	3	33
McDonald, Joseph	235	Clear Fork	1851	3	288
McDonald, Joseph	1,300	Reedy Branch	1851	3	564
McDonald, Joseph et al	100	Leatherwood Creek	1838	1	372
McDonald, Lewis	207	Elk Creek	1848	2	438
McDonald, Lewis	39	Cub Creek	1848	3	34
McDonald, Lewis	59	Peach Creek	1850	3	239
McDonald, Lewis	60	Sand Lick Branch	1851	3	343
McDonald, Lewis	97	Peach Creek	1851	3	342
McDonald, Lewis & Charles et al	280	Peach Creek	1856	4	356
McDonald, Lewis & Charles et al	200	Dingess Run	1856	4	357
McDonald, Lewis E.	17	Wts. Guyandotte	1848	3	69
McDonald, Stephen	68	Mill Creek	1849	3	140
McDonald, Stephen	80	Huff's Creek	1828	1	77
McDonald, William	124	Adj. Lewis McDonald	1831	1	115
McDonald, William	70	Reedy Branch	1837	1	283
McDonald, William	55	Cub Creek	1837	1	284
McDonald, William	80	Reedy Branch	1837	1	282
McDonald, William	200	Elk Lick	1833	1	450
McDonald, William	100	Big Bottom Fork	1845	2	245
McDonald, William	75	Rockhouse	1844	2	149
McDonald, William W.	1,023	Rockhouse Branch	1860	2	495
McDonald, William W.	1,900	Rockhouse Branch	1860	2	494
McDonald, William W.	100	Big Spring Branch	1847	2	381
McDonald, William W.	175	Middle Fork	1855	4	187
McDonald, William W.	139	Sand Lick	1855	4	185
McDonald, William W.	225	Big Spring	1855	4	184
McDonald, William W.	58	Rockhouse	1849	3	138
McDonald, William W.	174	Big Spring	1855	4	183
McDonald, William W.	25	Rockhouse	1851	3	375
McDonald, William W.	667	Rockhouse Br.	1855	4	568
McDonald, William W. & Gordon	5	Huff's Creek	1847	2	329
McKinney, Jordon	88	Barker's Ridge	1848	2	441
McKinney, Jordon	123	Lost Ridge	1848	2	442
McKinney, Joseph	360	Big Fork	1847	2	379
McKinney, Oscar et al	79	Toney's Fork	1852	4	6
McNealy—See McNeeley, McNeely					
McNealy, George et al	100	Pond Fork	1829	1	99
McNeeley, James	9½	Spruce Fork	1844	2	174
McNeeley, Joseph	9	Spruce Fork	1847	2	327
McNeeley, Joseph	9	Spruce Fork	1844	2	132
McNeeley, Joseph	33	Spruce Fork	1843	2	100
McNeeley, Joseph	52	Spruce Fork	1852	3	517
McNeeley, Joseph	20	Spruce Fork	1852	3	516
McNeeley, Joseph et al	40	Spruce Fork	1844	2	184
McNeeley, Peter	18	Buffalo Br.	1852	3	518
McNeeley, Peter	23	Pigeon Creek	1854	4	123
McNeeley, Samuel	150	Wts. Guyandotte	1855	4	149
McNeeley, Samuel	75	Wts. Guyandotte	1846	2	301
McNeeley, Thomas	100	Stone Coal	1855	4	148
McNeeley, William	16	Pigeon Roost Br.	1852	3	520
McNeeley, William	75	Hewitt's Fork	1852	3	519
McNeeley, William	38	Buck Fork	1847	2	328
McNeely—See McNealy, McNeeley					
McNeely, James	30	Spruce Fork	1838	1	326
McNeely, Richard	10	Beech Fork	1838	1	325
McNeely, William	40	Beech Fork	1838	1	327

Name of Grantee	Acres	Local Description	Year	Book	Page
McNeely, William	22	Beech Fork	1838	1	328
McVey, James	80	Barker's Ridge	1826	1	19
McVey, James	55	Flat Top Mountain	1827	1	25
McVey, James et al	87	Flat Top Mountain	1827	1	26
Mead—or Meade					
Mead, John	150	Marrowbone Creek	1861	2	503
Mead, Samuel	15	Millers Creek	1835	1	203
Mead, William	50	Tug Fork	1827	1	49
Meade, Benjamin et al	200	Cane Fork	1856	4	320
Meade, James	18	Big Laurel	1847	2	424
Meade, Samuel	21	Mill Branch	1848	3	3
Meade, Samuel et al	70	Laurel Fork	1852	3	521
Meade, William B.	230	Marrowbone Cr.	1851	3	350
Meade, William B.	85	Cub Branch	1851	3	349
Meade, William B.	25	Laurel Fork	1850	3	207
Meade, William B.	67	Big Laurel	1854	4	89
Meade, William B.	31	Jenny's Creek	1854	4	90
Meade, William B.	70	Big Laurel	1847	2	422
Meade, William B.	37	Big Laurel	1847	2	421
Meade, William B.	106	Marrowbone Cr.	1847	2	423
Meade, William B.	219	Jenny's Creek	1848	2	445
Meade, William B. et al	65	Jenney's Creek	1850	3	208
Meade, William Jr.	38	Henley's Branch	1848	3	2
Meadows, Banister	180	Clear Fork	1848	2	432
Meadows, Banister	13	Clear Fork	1852	3	454
Meadows, Edmund	145	Parris Creek	1834	1	169
Meadows, Ephraim	83	Mill Branch	1853	4	11
Meadows, Ephraim	57	Big Fork	1853	4	8
Meadows, Sally	50	Wolf Pen	1827	1	23
Meroney, John et al	230	W. Side New River	1830	1	106
Merret, Obadiah	200	Ugly Creek	1836	1	231
Messer, Reuben	100	Gap Branch	1855	4	193
Messer, Stephen	107	Marrowbone Cr.	1848	2	431
Milam—Milem					
Milam, John	75	Elkhorn	1828	1	73
Milem, James	60	Elkhorn Cr.	1831	1	120
Miller, Abraham	50	Adj. Ballard	1826	1	11
Miller, Daniel	25	Turtle Creek	1835	1	223
Miller, Ezekiel	50	Turtle Creek	1838	1	323
Miller, Ezekiel	33	Spruce Fork	1842	2	14
Miller, James J.	6,300	12 Pole Creek	1861	2	527
Miller, James J. (or I.)	2,330	12 Pole Creek	1859	2	509
Miller, John	100	Wts. Mud River	1838	1	317
Miller, John	50	Turtle Creek	1838	1	324
Miller, Moses	31	Turtle Creek	1834	1	185
Miller, Moses	40	6 Mi. Creek	1834	1	184
Miller, Robert	100	Marshes of Cole	1828	1	60
Miller, W. C. et al	35	Sugar Branch	1850	3	237
Miller, William C. et al	42	Wts. Guyandotte	1850	3	214
Miller, William C. et al	80	Sugar Camp	1850	3	215
Miller, William C. et al	260	Buck Lick	1850	3	213
Miller, Zadock	80	Wts. Mud	1844	2	148
Mills, Robert	52	Flat Top Mt.	1847	2	404
Mitchell, James	50	Turtle Creek	1838	1	322
Mitchell, John	53	Big Fork	1851	3	339
Mitchell, John	167	Big Fork	1850	3	209
Mitchell, John D.	48	Cub Fork	1851	3	337
Mitchell, John D.	59	Rum Creek	1851	3	338
Mitchell, Jordan D.	69	Rum Creek	1851	3	336
Montgomery, Henry	150	Ingram's Branch	1830	1	104
Moore, John	25	Tony's Fork	1850	3	249
Moore, Thomas	25	Wts. Guyandotte	1827	1	34

Name of Grantee	Acres	Local Description	Year	Book	Page
Morgan, Anthony	13	Cub Creek	1848	3	70
Morgan, David	32	Cub Creek	1846	2	275
Morgan, George	35	Indian Creek	1847	2	354
Morgan, Isaac	30	Cub Creek	1842	1	435
Morgan, Isaac	28	Elk Creek	1848	2	444
Morgan, Isaac	38	Road Branch	1846	2	291
Morgan, Isaac	55	Big Fork	1843	2	77
Morgan, Isaac	75	Big Fork	1843	2	78
Morgan, Isaac	105	Indian Creek	1852	3	515
Morgan, Isaac et al	180	Hewitt's Fork	1850	3	254
Morgan, Milton et al	47	Indian Creek	1847	2	351
Morgan, Thomas	25	Huff Creek	1831	1	126
Morgan, Thomas	115	Elkhorn	1831	1	122
Morgan, Thomas	10	Cub Fork	1834	1	187
Mounts, Alexander	47	Beech Creek	1846	2	288
Mounts, Alexander	60	Foundation Fork	1855	4	170
Mounts, Alexander	28	Beech Creek	1854	4	80
Mounts, Alexander	60	Beech Creek	1851	3	344
Mounts, David	100	Tug Fork	1832	1	133
Mounts, David	156	Beech Creek	1846	2	289
Mounts, William	18	Beech Creek	1846	2	290
Mullins, Andrew J.	26	Pigeon Branch	1844	2	135
Mullins, Andrew J.	9	Spruce Fork	1844	2	136
Mullins, Andrew J.	7	Spruce Fork	1844	2	134
Mullins, Boyd W.	1,400	Spruce Fork	1852	3	435
Mullins, Boyd W.	29	Spruce Fork	1855	4	157
Mullins, Boyd W.	10	Spruce Fork	1855	4	156
Mullins, Boyd W.	49	Sang Run	1855	4	158
Mullins, Boyd W.	12	Spruce Fork	1842	2	35
Mullins, Boyd W.	45	Spruce Fork	1842	2	36
Mullins, Boyd W.	19	Spruce Fork	1844	2	133
Mullins, Boyd W.	25	Sang Camp	1838	1	370
Mullins, Boyd W.	20	Sang Camp	1838	1	371
Mullins, Hiram	248	Laurel Fork	1858	4	431
Mullins, Hiram	32	Spruce Fork	1858	4	432
Mullins, Hiram	60	Spruce Fork	1858	4	433
Mullins, Hiram	30	Laurel Fork	1858	4	434
Mullins, Hiram	38	Spruce Fork	1851	3	353
Mullins, Hiram	64	Brushy Fork	1851	3	354
Mullins, Hiram	49	Adkins Fork	1851	3	355
Mullins, Hiram	40	Laurel Fork	1851	3	356
Mullins, Hiram	19	White Oak	1842	2	37
Mullins, Hiram	16	Brushy Fork	1844	2	137
Mullins, Hiram	14	Garr's Fork of Spruce	1844	2	138
Mullins, Hiram	7	Adkins' Fork	1844	2	139
Mullins, Hiram	41	Spruce Fork	1847	2	425
Mullins, Hiram et al	200	Brushy Fork	1855	4	200
Mullins, Hiram et al	350	Brushy Fork	1855	4	204
Mullins, John	31	Big Fork	1849	3	135
Mullins, John	36	Big Fork	1849	3	136
Mullins, John	24	Big Fork	1849	3	169
Mullins, John S.	85	Rock Castle Fork	1852	3	443
Mullins, John S.	46	Big Fork	1851	3	352
Mullins, Milton	43	Wts. Guyandotte	1848	3	89
Mullins, Nathaniel	120	Spruce Fork	1838	1	351
Mullins, Nathaniel	25	Wts. Guyandotte	1826	1	6
Mullins, Nathaniel et al	150	Spruce Fork	1831	1	127
Mullins, Peter	50	Trace Fork	1859	1	466
Mullins, Peter	50	Trace Fork	1844	2	173
Mullins, Peter	34	Hoover's Fork	1854	4	100
Mullins, Peter	37	Hart's Creek	1853	4	28
Mullins, Peter	50	Hart's Creek	1849	3	109
Mullins, Peter	35	Hoover's Fork	1857	4	396

Name of Grantee	Acres	Local Description	Year	Book	Page
Mullins, Peter	12	Trace Fork	1857	4	394
Mullins, Peter	75	Ivy Branch	1857	4	393
Mullins, Peter	35	Trace Fork	1857	4	391
Mullins, Peter	30	Trace Fork	1856	4	359
Mullins, Spencer A.	84	Wts. Guyandotte	1849	3	165
Mullins, Spencer A.	95	Wts. Guyandotte	1849	3	137
Mullins, Spencer A.	900	Sand Creek	1855	4	147
Mullins, Spencer A.	43	Mile Branch	1855	4	146
Mullins, Spencer A.	470	Smokehouse	1859	1	468
Mullins, Spencer A.	125	Smokehouse	1859	1	467
Mullins, Thomas	58	4 Pole Cr.	1848	3	31
Mullins, William	200	Slab Fork	1848	3	90
Mullins, William	48	Big Fork	1848	3	32
Mullins, William	420	Ben's Creek	1860	2	480
Mullins, William et al	41	Big Fork	1851	3	351
Muncey, James	33	Tug Fork	1834	1	186
Muncey, James	45	Marrowbone Cr.	1836	1	248
Muncey, Samuel	25	Stone Coal Cr.	1858	4	435
Muncey, Samuel	200	Jenny's Cr.	1858	4	436
Murphy, Andrew	158	Mate's Creek	1849	3	141
Murphy, Herendon	20	Mate's Creek	1847	2	325
Murphy, Herendon	65	Mate's Creek	1852	3	428
Murphy, Herndon	25	Mate's Creek	1844	2	175
Murphy, John	25	Mate's Creek	1835	1	212
Murphy, John & Andrew	125	Mate's Creek	1857	4	370
Murphy, John et al	180	Tug Fork	1827	1	40
Murphy, Joseph	25	Mate's Creek	1851	3	400
Music, Cummins	2	Pigeon Creek	1849	3	134
Music, Cummins	19	Pigeon Creek	1855	4	207
Music. Cummins	200	Pigeon Creek	1855	4	208
Nelson, Granville	10	Pond Fork	1838	1	356
Nelson, Jordan	57	Ant's Fork	1855	4	136
Nelson, Joseph	25	Jack's Branch	1838	1	358
Nelson, William	25	Pond Fork	1838	1	357
Nelson, Wilson (or William)	30	Hewitt's Fork	1846	2	267
Nester, Daniel	107	Brown's Branch	1854	4	102
Nester, Daniel	120	Brown's Branch	1856	4	267
Newton, Thomas	45	Big Bottom	1829	1	100
Newton, Thomas	30	McDonald Meet. H.	1829	1	98
Nibert—Nighbert					
Nibert, George W.	80	Camp Creek	1847	2	330
Nicholls, William T. et al	72	Francis' Creek	1845	2	193
Nicholls, William T. et al	74	12 Pole	1845	2	192
Nicholls, William T. et al	44	12 Pole	1845	2	190
Nicholls, William T. et al	47	12 Pole Cr.	1846	2	259
Nicholls, William T. et al	224	Lit. Harts Cr.	1846	2	258
Nicholls, Wm. T. et al	93	12 Pole	1845	2	191
Nighbert—See Nibert					
Nighbert, George W.	90	Laurel Branch	1851	3	357
Nighbert, James et al	66	Wts. Guyandotte	1856	4	318
Osburn, Solomon et al	41	Big Fork	1851	3	151
Oten, William	56	Trace Fork	1852	3	522
Oten, William (or Oaten)	17	Trace Fork	1857	4	366
Painter, Charles	20	Huff's Creek	1852	3	523
Parsley—See Pasley, Passley					
Parsley, John (or Passley)	49	Sandy River	1860	2	481
Parsley, John	87	Big Branch	1849	3	142
Parsley, Moses (or Passley)	62	Aldridge Branch	1847	2	389
Parsley, Moses	15	Sand Gut	1855	4	194
Parsley, William	145	Burning Creek	1854	4	33
Parsley, William	110	Burning Creek	1854	4	34
Parsley, William	135	Burning Creek	1854	4	35
Parsley, William et al	1,075	Burning Creek	1858	4	423

Name of Grantee	Acres	Local Description	Year	Book	Page
Pinnell, Francis R.	50	Wts. Guyandotte	1832	1	129
Pinnell, Francis R. et al	150	Spruce Fork	1831	1	127
Pinnell, George M. et al	25	Wts. Guyandotte	1833	1	155
Pinnell, George M. et al	20	Banks of River	1833	1	154
Price, Tuncel	10	Spruce Fork	1841	1	406
Price, Tunsel	95	Spruce Fork	1846	2	264
Prince, David M.	120	Big Laurel	1856	4	283
Pucket, Jesse	41	Muncy Fork	1855	4	216
Pugh, William	345	Big Branch	1861	2	504
Pugh, William	420	Big Branch	1858	4	448
Ratcliff, Richard	1,340	Stafford's Branch	1859	1	483
Reiley, Frances	500	12 Pole Creek	1861	2	519
Riffe, Gabriel	70	Wts. Guyandotte	1848	3	94
Riffe, Peter (Rife)	20	Wts. Tug Fork	1828	1	65
Riffe, Peter	23	Hurricane Fork	1856	4	309
Riffe, Peter et al	66	Guyandotte Wts.	1856	4	318
Robertson—Robinson, Robison					
Robertson, Edwin	41	Mud Fork	1844	2	140
Robinett, Sampson	25	Big Fork	1842	2	38
Robinett, Sampson	40	Big Fork	1827	1	35
Robinson—Robertson, Robison					
Robinson, David	94	Conley's Creek	1849	3	144
Robinson, David	22	Low Gap Branch	1846	2	303
Robinson, David	150	Rich Creek	1851	3	402
Robinson, David	20	Island Creek	1846	2	302
Robison—Robertson, Robinson					
Robison, David	7	Island Creek	1854	4	42
Robison, David	14	Island Creek	1854	4	43
Robison, David	92	Kiah's Fork	1857	4	382
Robison, David	50	Rich Creek	1842	2	44
Robison, David et al	42	Island Creek	1841	1	404
Roman, Isom	63	Mill Stone Branch	1856	4	295
Roman, Isom	56	Pigeon Creek	1848	3	75
Roman, Isom	8	Elk Fork	1856	4	296
Roman, Isom	42	Middle Fork	1848	3	93
Roman, Isom	45	Pigeon Creek	1858	4	437
Rowe, John	38	Ugly Creek	1838	1	350
Runyon, Alexander	40	Trace Fork	1838	1	348
Runyon, Alexander	10	Trace Fork	1838	1	349
Runyon, Alexander	39	Trace Fork	1842	1	423
Runyon, Alexander	42	Pigeon Creek	1844	2	106
Runyon, Alexander	97	Pigeon Creek	1844	2	105
Runyon, Alexander	820	Laurel Fork	1861	2	508
Runyon, Alexander	32	Riff's Branch	1848	3	37
Runyon, Alexander	30	Riff's Branch	1848	3	36
Runyon, Alexander	47	Riff's Branch	1848	3	74
Runyon, Alexander	10	Trace Fork	1848	3	73
Runyon, Alexander	57	Riff's Branch	1849	3	143
Runyon, Alexander	20	Riff's Branch	1851	3	359
Runyon, Alexander	219	Trace Fork	1850	3	558
Runyon, John et al	70	Laurel Fork	1852	3	521
Russell, James	25	Spruce Fork	1838	1	347
Rutherford, Elliott	43	Beech Creek	1852	3	524
Salsbury, Jeremiah (Solsbury)	210	Big Fork	1847	2	383
Samuels, Isaac I. (or J.) et al	300	Sand Creek	1852	3	497
Sandridge, Elizabeth	95	Wts. Sandy	1852	3	430
Sartain, John	25	Marrowbone Creek	1847	2	356
Sartain, John	57	Marrowbone Cr.	1847	2	382
Sartain, John	50	Flat Hollow	1854	4	36
Sartain, John	23	Coal Springs	1848	3	38
Sartain, John et al	200	Marrowbone Cr.	1855	4	201
Sartain, John et al	300	Stone Coal Cr., Sandy	1856	4	339
Scaggs, Joseph	90	Wts. Guyandotte	1856	4	351

Name of Grantee	Acres	Local Description	Year	Book	Page
Scaggs, Joseph	134	Camp Creek	1856	4	352
Scarborough, John W.	125	Tony's Fork	1828	1	61
Sedgebeer (or Sedgebur) Joseph	100	Lick Branch	1858	4	403
Sedgebeer, Joseph	800	Dingess Run	1858	4	446
Shannon, James	30	Big Fork	1852	3	445
Shannon, James	50	Mill Creek	1852	3	447
Shannon, James	120	Turkey Creek	1852	3	446
Shannon, James	25	Big Fork	1852	3	444
Shannon, James	50	Big Fork	1844	2	185
Shannon, James	108	Turkey Creek	1844	2	186
Shannon, James	34	Indian Creek	1846	2	281
Shannon, James H.	25	Big Fork	1836	1	226
Shannon, Lain	30	Cub Creek	1844	2	182
Shealds, William	25	Big Fork	1852	3	437
Short, Benjamin	130	Pretty Ridge	1851	3	366
Short, Benjamin	100	Big Fork	1853	4	15
Short, Samuel et al	265	Bohemin Fork	1850	3	236
Short, Samuel et al	72	Francis' Creek	1845	2	193
Short, Samuel et al	74	12 Pole	1845	2	192
Short, Samuel et al	93	12 Pole	1845	2	191
Short, Samuel et al	44	12 Pole	1845	2	190
Short, Samuel et al	47	12 Pole Cr.	1846	2	259
Short, Samuel et al	224	Little Hart's Cr.	1846	2	258
Shumate, Daniel	50	Sand Lick	1828	1	76
Shumate, Daniel	40	Sand Lick	1829	1	82
Simpkins, Eli	90	Pine Creek	1856	4	345
Sizemore, Edward	75	Big Fork	1845	2	247
Sizemore, George J (or I.)	36	Big Fork	1852	3	552
Sizemore, John	128 (178)	Big Fork	1852	3	527
Sizemore, Owin	74	Big Fork	1852	3	526
Sleater, James	81	Wts. Sandy	1844	2	180
Smith, Aly	20	Rock House	1851	3	403
Smith, Aly	170	Rockhouse	1855	4	172
Smith, Aly	190	Rockhouse	1855	4	171
Smith, Aly	118	Rockhouse	1855	4	173
Smith, Aly	45	Rockhouse	1855	4	174
Smith, Ezekiel	400	Thomas Ridge	1826	1	18
Smith, George	23	Marsh Fork	1844	2	183
Smith, George et al	40	Spruce Fork	1844	2	184
Smith, John	42	Gilbert's Creek	1851	3	363
Smith, John	100	Wts. Tug Fork	1827	1	33
Smith, John	20	Ben Creek	1836	1	230
Smith, John	40	Horse Pen Fork	1836	1	229
Smith, Larken	57	Horse Pen Fork	1856	4	260
Smith, Larkin	350	Horse Pen	1857	4	392
Smith, Larkin	41	Horse Pen	1848	3	78
Smith, Parrish	100	Adj. Rich	1826	1	20
Smith, Thomas	21	Horse Pen	1841	1	386
Smith, William	850	Crawley's Creek	1854	4	86
Smith, William	20	Crawley's Creek	1853	4	27
Smith, William	31	Big Fork	1843	2	51
Smith, William et al	250	Hart's Creek	1846	2	452
Smoot, Charles A.	90	Cane Fork	1851	3	404
Smoot, Charles A.	100	Cane Patch	1851	3	411
Smoot, Charles A. et al	86	Spruce Fork	1843	2	95
Smoot, William	60	Little Coal	1845	2	252
Solsbury—See Salsbury					
Spalden—Spaldin, Spaulding					
Spalden, William R.	19	Anderson Fork	1854	4	119
Spaldin, Charles	38	Bark Camp	1851	3	364
Spaldin, Charles	25	Jenny's Creek	1851	3	365
Spar, John	125	Spruce Fork	1834	1	165

Name of Grantee	Acres	Local Description	Year	Book	Page
Trent, Smith	170	Horse Pen	1857	4	402
Tyree, Richard F.	600	Laurel Creek Cliffs	1827	1	446
Tyree, Richard F.	3,500	Loop of New River	1827	1	448
Vanater, Vanatter, Vannatter, Vernatter					
Vanater, John	75	Hewitt's Cr.	1835	1	208
Vanatter, John	37	Hewitt's Creek	1843	2	97
Vanatter, John	22	6 Mi. Creek	1833	1	142
Vanatter, Samuel	55	Road Fork	1849	3	145
Vanatter, Theodore	42	Sand Lick	1855	4	175
Vance, Abner	50	Elk Creek	1859	1	473
Vance, Abner	63	Elk Creek	1859	1	474
Vance, Abner	29	Elk Creek	1849	3	111
Vance, Abner	80	Elk Creek	1858	4	404
Vance, Abner	6	Turkey Pen	1855	4	176
Vance, Abner Jr.	30	Hart's Creek	1852	3	539
Vance, Abner Jr.	25	Hart's Creek	1834	1	190
Vance, Abner Jr.	25	Hart's Creek	1837	1	301
Vance, Abner Jr.	20	Rich Creek	1842	2	24
Vance, Abner Jr.	55	Hart's Creek	1847	2	385
Vance, Abner Jr.	75	Rich Creek	1848	3	97
Vance, Abner Jr.	247	Hart's Creek	1856	4	270
Vance, Abner Jr.	260	Hart's Creek	1856	4	269
Vance, Jackson	50	Pretty Branch	1861	2	506
Vance, John	10	Horse Pen	1837	1	302
Vance, John	25	Conley's Branch	1837	1	303
Vance, Levi	98	Rich Creek	1855	4	197
Vance, Levi	54	Browning Fork	1855	4	198
Vance, Levi	58	Conley's Fork	1855	4	199
Vance, Levi	56	Rich Creek	1859	1	479
Vance, Levi	30	Rich Creek	1859	1	478
Vance, Mary	47	Cane Fork	1858	4	445
Vance, Mary	11	Cane Fork	1858	4	444
Vance, Mary	90	Mare Branch	1855	4	224
Vance, Meken	20	Hart's Creek	1852	3	538
Vance, Meken	35	Hart's Creek	1844	2	147
Vance, Paris	14	Trace Fork	1852	3	537
Vance, Pearis	70	Trace Fork	1858	4	442
Vance, Polly & William (son)	33	Trace Branch	1855	4	225
Vance, Richard	60	Smokehouse	1833	1	150
Vance, Richard	25	Smokehouse	1834	1	189
Vance, Richard	25	Hart's Creek	1837	1	299
Vance, Richard	43	Trace Branch	1858	4	443
Vance, Richard Jr.	13	Trace Fork	1850	3	192
Vance, Richard Jr.	47	12 Pole	1850	3	191
Vance, Susannah	16	Cow Creek	1847	2	401
Vance, Wesley	25	Hart's Creek	1838	1	361
Vandle, Edw. D. alias Dillon Vandle	180	Adj. his own	1831	1	111
Vannatter—Vanater, Vanatter, Vernatter					
Vannatter, James	16	Camp Fork	1862	3	536
Varney, Alexander	30	Rockhouse	1844	2	189
Varney, Andrew	80	Pigeon Creek	1859	4	455
Varney, Andrew	50	Rockhouse Fork	1836	1	253
Varney, Andrew	23	Rockhouse	1843	2	60
Varney, Andrew	59	Rockhouse Fork	1847	2	384
Varney, Andrew	480	Pigeon Creek	1855	4	152
Varney, Andrew	45	Pigeon Creek	1855	4	151
Varney, Andrew	50	Rockhouse	1855	4	140
Varney, Andrew	60	Murphy's Branch	1855	4	139
Varney, Andrew	25	Pigeon Creek	1852	3	431
Varney, Andrew et al	125	Pigeon Creek	1852	3	432
Varney, Andrew et al	52	Rockhouse Fork	1826	1	21
Varney, Henry	25	Elk Fork	1851	3	373
Varney, Henry	30	Rockhouse	1851	3	374

Name of Grantee	Acres	Local Description	Year	Book	Page
Varney, Henry	35	Rockhouse	1859	1	470
Varney, Henry	109	Rockhouse	1859	1	469
Varney, John H.	50	Mate's Creek	1856	4	355
Varney, John H.	7	Meadow Branch	1856	4	354
Varney, Samuel	90	Rockhouse	1858	4	441
Venters, John	50	Cane Patch Fk. 12 Pole	1835	1	204
Vernatter—Vanater, Vanatter, Vannatter					
Vernatter, John	73	Hewitt's Fork	1847	2	331
Vernatter, John	38	Hewitt's Fork	1847	2	361
Vernatter, John	25	Left Hand Fork	1847	2	333
Vernatter, John	18	Buck Lick	1847	2	332
Vickers, Charles	50	Spruce Fork	1837	1	300
Walker, Jacob et al	79	Toney's Fork	1852	4	6
Wall—or Walls					
Wall, Francis	50	Hewitt's Creek	1827	1	32
Wall, Jacob	20	Jim's Branch	1847	2	402
Wall, Jacob	20	Hewitts Fork	1846	2	277
Wall, Jacob	30	Tomblin Branch	1846	2	276
Wallace, Henry	10	Round Bottom Guyandotte	1842	1	436
Walls—See also Wall					
Walls, Erastus G.	25	Wts. Mud River	1856	4	238
Walls, Joseph	50	Reedy Branch	1845	2	217
Ward, Evermont et al	830	Pigeon Creek	1854	4	78
Ward, Evermont et al	1,800	Big Ugly Creek	1855	4	564
Ward, Evermont et al	4,000	Pigeon Creek	1858	4	585
Ward, Evermont et al	2,280	Rich Creek	1856	4	573
Ward, Evermont et al	1,450	Buffalo Creek	1858	4	589
Ward, Evermont et al	2,240	Island Creek	1858	4	591
Ward, Evermont et al	48	Wts. Guyandotte	1852	3	409
Ward, Evermont et al	122	Wts. Guyandotte	1852	3	408
Ward, Evermont et al	55	Wts. Guyandotte	1852	3	410
Ward, Evermont et al	500	Waters Guyandotte	1856	4	312
Ward, Evermont et al	500	Dingess Run	1856	4	262
Ward, Evermont et al	1,000	Pigeon Creek	1858	4	417
Ward, Evermont et al	1,260	Pigeon Creek	1858	4	416
Ward, Evermont et al	840	Dingess Fork	1858	4	421
Ward, Evermont et al	1,300	Island Creek	1858	4	418
Webb, Thomas	15	Pigeon Creek	1852	3	543
Webb, Thomas	36	Pigeon Creek	1848	3	80
Webb, Thomas	62	Mill Stone	1848	3	42
Webb, Thomas	20	Pigeon Creek	1848	3	43
Webb, Thomas et al	335	Buffalo Cr.	1856	4	310
Welch, Jacob	100	Big Creek	1826	1	7
Westgate, Lorenzo S.	8	Clear Fork	1830	1	105
White, Arthur	44	Elk Fork	1844	2	107
White, Arthur	55	Elk Fork	1837	1	298
White, Arthur	49	Elk Fork	1848	3	98
White, Arthur	35	Elk Fork	1852	3	433
White, Arthur	11	Elk Fork	1852	3	434
White, Benjamin	37	Laurel Fork	1861	2	506
White, Grayson	12	Back Lick Fork	1850	3	276
White, Grayson	22	Middle Fork	1850	3	275
White, Grayson	28	Rock House	1850	3	277
White, Grayson	80	Laurel Branch	1851	3	372
White, Grayson	150	Spice Creek	1851	3	371
White, Grayson	25	Spice Creek	1851	3	370
White, H. S. et al	200	Dingess Run	1856	4	357
White, H. S. et al	280	Peach Creek	1856	4	356
White, Hiram	42	Mill Creek	1843	2	98
White, Hiram	116	Mill Creek	1847	2	367
White, Hiram	100	Mill Creek	1847	2	386
White, Hiram	62	Hewitt's Fork	1845	2	254
White, Isaac	49	Coon Branch	1847	2	364

Name of Grantee	Acres	Local Description	Year	Book	Page
White, James	50	Spruce Fork	1829	1	78
White, James	40	Elk Branch	1827	1	29
White, James Jr.	75	Elk Fork	1835	1	220
White, James Jr.	35	Rockhouse	1843	2	61
White, James Jr.	25	Elk Fork	1835	1	199
White, James Sr.	100	Whites Branch	1853	4	9
White, John	50	Pigeon Creek	1837	1	294
White, John	60	Pigeon Creek	1859	1	471
White, John Jr.	25	Elk Fork	1848	3	100
White, John Sr.	107	Hell Creek	1856	4	319
White, John Sr.	100	Pigeon Creek	1856	4	303
White, Mastin	50	Mill Creek	1837	1	293
White, Peter	50	Rock House	1848	3	99
Wiley, Hezekiah	25	Cane Fork	1835	1	205
Williams—See also Williamson					
Williams, Benjamin Jr. (Williamson)	100	Wts. Sandy	1837	1	297
Williams, Eli (Williamson)	20	Pigeon Creek	1857	4	369
Williamson—See also Williams					
Williamson, Alden	63	Laurel Fork	1841	1	387
Williamson, Aly (Elias)	77	Laurel Fork	1853	4	29
Williamson, Aly (Elias)	60	Salt Lick Branch	1853	4	30
Williamson, Benjamin	265	Wts. Sandy	1857	4	385
Williamson, Benjamin	68	Wts. Sandy	1857	4	386
Williamson, Benjamin	400	Wts. Sandy	1857	4	384
Williamson, Benjamin	150	Wts. Sandy River	1857	4	383
Williamson, Benjamin	125	Wts. Sandy	1835	1	198
Williamson, Benjamin Jr.	14	Ben Creek	1849	3	112
Williamson, Benjamin Jr.	232	Sugar Tree Br.	1844	2	187
Williamson, Benjamin Jr.	48	Wts. Sandy	1844	2	188
Williamson, Elias (Aly)	236	Turkey Creek	1848	3	107
Wilson, Anthony	25	Wilson's Branch	1827	1	55
Wilson, Patrick	500	Island Creek	1861	2	520
Woodram, Balt	30	Pond Fork	1847	2	362
Workman, Abijah	86	Hart's Creek	1854	4	82
Workman, Abijah	78	Hart's Creek	1855	4	217
Workman, Abijah	100	Hager Branch	1851	3	415
Workman, Abijah	40	Cane Patch	1851	3	414
Workman, Abijah	75	Hart's Creek	1852	3	542
Workman, Abraham	25	Wts. Little Coal	1838	1	313
Workman, Abraham	22	Jacks Branch	1842	2	23
Workman, Henry	49	Wiley's Branch	1847	2	363
Workman, Henry	25	12 Pole Creek	1848	3	82
Workman, James	50	W. Fork	1831	1	110
Workman, John	60	Spice Hollow	1848	3	83
Workman, John	22	Pond Fork	1840	1	382
Workman, John	40	Hoover's Fork	1846	2	296
Workman, Joseph	35	Pond Fork	1834	1	161
Workman, Joseph	100	Pond Fork	1833	1	156
Workman, Joseph	40	W. Fork	1834	1	162
Workman, Joseph	100	Laurel Fork	1833	1	149
Workman, Joseph	25	Pond Fork	1833	1	144
Workman, Joseph	50	Pond Fork	1837	1	296
Workman, Joseph	45	Pond Fork	1837	1	295
Workman, Joseph	25	Cow Creek	1840	1	381
Workman, Joseph et al	375	Still Run	1850	3	210
Workman, Joseph et al	35	Big Fork	1850	3	211
Workman, Joseph et al	340	Big Fork	1850	3	212
Workman, Joseph et al	84	Barker's Ridge	1850	3	260
Workman, Joseph et al	60	Barker's Ridge	1850	3	258
Workman, Joseph et al	120	Slab Fork	1850	3	259
Workman, Joseph et al	100	Pond Fork	1829	1	99
Workman, Josephus	40	Smokehouse	1852	3	541

Name of Grantee	Acres	Local Description	Year	Book	Page
Workman, Moses	26	Hart's Creek	1848	3	81
Workman, Moses	200	Sand Lick	1829	1	84
Workman, Moses & John	100	Hart's Creek	1841	1	408
Workman, Obadiah	37	Henderson's Br.	1847	2	388
Workman, Obadiah	44	Hart's Creek	1854	4	103
Workman, Obediah	25	Hart's Creek	1852	3	540
Young, Nathan	12	Big Fork	1849	3	172
Young, Nathan	15	Elk Creek	1843	2	101
Young, Nathan	37	Elk Creek	1843	2	102
Young, Nathan	68	Elk Creek	1844	2	141
Young, Nathan	20	Elk Creek	1844	2	142
Young, Nathan	12	Wts. Guyandotte	1852	3	545
Young, Nathan	48	Big Fork	1852	3	544
Young, Nathan et al	50	Leatherwood	1844	2	123

MARION COUNTY

Allen, G. R. C. Executor					
Wm. Eldridge dec'd., et al	100	White Day Cr.	1854	1	118
Amos, John	4	Davies Run	1849	1	66
Anderson, James	25	Cor. to J. O. Watson	1859	1	171
Anderson, Samuel	13	Booth's Cr.	1844	1	13
Arnett, Pinckney B.	45	Paw Paw Cr.	1844	1	15
Ashcroft, William et al	382	Davies Fork	1847	1	48
Athey, Jacob O. (Atha)	32	Dunkard Mill Run	1844	1	14
Baker, George	200	Dent's Cr.	1849	1	73
Barker, David Jr. et al	38½	Tigert's V. Riv.	1858	1	166
Batson, Chas. W.	10	Plum Run	1849	1	67
Batton, John	12	Piles Fork	1853	1	114
Beattie—or Beatty, Beaty					
Beatty, James C.	79	Buffalo Creek	1847	1	47
Beaty, James C.	22	Piles Fork	1851	1	100
Billingsley, David S.	26	Glade Run	1855	1	145
Blackshire, Morgan	28	Wts. W. Fk. Riv.	1846	1	38
Boggess, Lindsay Jr.	50 sq. po.	Town Fairmont	1846	1	34
Boggess, Thomas L.	1¼	Mill Fall Run	1856	1	149
Booth, James	16	Tigert's Valley Riv.	1844	1	16
Byard, Samuel	6	Adj. Isaac Rice	1859	1	173
Campbell, Dennis D.	150	Buffalo Cr.	1851	1	99
Campbell, Geo. W.	100	Adj. Campbell	1853	1	111
Campbell, George W.	45	Buffalo Creek	1851	1	134
Campbell, George W.	49	Buffalo Cr.	1851	1	89
Conaway, John	30	Piles Fork	1846	1	31
Conway, Jeremiah	107	Buffalo Creek	1848	1	57
Conway, William	225	Whetstone	1849	1	68
Copeland, William	220	Turkey Run	1845	1	22
Corothers—or Corrothers					
Corothers, John W.	2¾	Adj. his own	1857	1	154
Corothers, Robert M. et al	39½	Bingamon Cr.	1860	1	175
Corrothers, Robert	6⅛	Bingamon Cr.	1859	1	167
Corrothers, Samuel	125	White Day Creek	1851	1	133
Cunningham, Daniel	75	Owen Day Fork	1850	1	82
Cunningham, David	40	Buffalo Cr.	1854	1	126
Cunningham, Enoch	243	Buffalo Cr.	1848	1	55
Cunningham, Enoch	23	Teverbaugh Cr.	1848	1	56
Cunningham, Enoch	25	Teverbaugh Cr.	1850	1	83

Name of Grantee	Acres	Local Description	Year	Book	Page
Cunningham, Richard	100	Buffalo Cr.	1854	1	94
Cunningham, Richard et al	44	Buffalo Cr.	1854	1	124
Davis, Squire W.	55	Bingamon Cr.	1851	1	95
Doolittle, Thomas	100	White Day Creek	1848	1	61
Downs, Emory	60	Buffalo Cr.	1847	1	46
Efaw, David	200	Flat Run	1846	1	33
Fetrick, Josephus (Tetrick)	13	L. Bingamon Cr.	1848	1	54
Fleming, William C. et al	6½	Ice's Run	1858	1	162
Floyd, Henry T.	50	Buffalo Cr.	1846	1	35
Galliheu—or Gallihue					
Galliheu, Henry (Gallihen)	140	White Day Creek	1855	1	138
Garlow, Alfred E.	21	Wts. Valley River	1850	1	86
Gump, James	29	Rush Run	1853	1	112
Hains, Abraham	75	Dudley's Fork	1850	1	79
Hall, Ashbel G.	11¼	Adj. Pitcher Land	1857	1	159
Hanway, John	250	Llewellyn Run	1847	1	40
Hanway, John	280	Piles Fork	1847	1	41
Hanway, John	440	Flat Run	1847	1	43
Hanway, John et al	200	Flat Run	1846	1	42
Hanway, John et al	40	White Day Creek	1848	1	53
Hanway, John et al	115	Piles Fork	1846	1	29
Hanway, John et al	224	Piles Fork	1846	1	28
Hanway, John et al	485	Piles Fork	1842	1	562
Hanway, John et al	375	Flat Run	1842	1	563
Harris, John	14	Prickett's Creek	1845	1	21
Hayhurst, Joseph	11	Buffalo Cr.	1853	1	115
Hays, Jefferson	80	White Stone	1846	1	36
Heldreth, William L.	111	Long Run	1854	1	116
Hensill, Smith M.	36	Tigert's Valley R.	1848	1	58
Hess, Abraham	185	Bingamon's Cr.	1849	1	69
Hess, Abraham	28¾	Bingamon Cr.	1859	1	168
Hess, Abraham et al	382	Davies Fork	1847	1	48
Hess, Abraham et al	39½	Bingamon Cr.	1860	1	175
Hess, Abraham & Jeremiah	370	Bingamon Cr.	1845	1	24
Hess, Enoch	71	Big Run	1853	1	113
Hess, Enoch	16½	Bingamon Cr.	1859	1	170
Hess, Jeremiah Jr.	44	Bingamon Cr.	1845	1	26
Hess, Jeremiah Jr. et al	102	Benjamin Creek	1843	1	3
Hibbs, Isaac	7a.1r.35p.	Dent's Run	1861	1	177
Higgins, Nathan	20	Camp Run	1859	1	172
Hollen, Bazzel et al	38 sq. po.	Tn. Palatine	1857	1	158
Hull, John	32	Wts. Monon. Riv.	1846	1	37
Ice, Fielden R.	5½	Dunkard's Mill Run	1859	1	169
Ice, Rawley	42	Buffalo Cr.	1851	1	97
Ice, Rawley et al	130	Brush Run	1851	1	90
Jolliff, Zadock	1¾	Buffalo Cr.	1849	1	70
Johnson, James	35	Adj. Barnabus Johnson	1855	1	142
Johnston, Henry H.	150	Flat Run	1851	1	101
Kendall, Stephen	85	Dent's Run	1850	1	77
Kendall, Zebadee	64	Dent's Run	1950	1	85
Kerns, Elijah	100	Whetstone	1850	1	76
Kidwell, Zedekiah	25	Flat Run	1847	1	50
Kidwell, Zedekiah Jr.	61	Piles Fork	1843	1	6
Kindall, Samuel Jr.	72	Dent's Run	1849	1	62
Knotts, Thomas	4½	Booth Cr.	1855	1	146
Leyman, Daniel	76½	Prickett's Creek	1858	1	163
Linn, Benjamin	11½	River Run	1856	1	150
Linn, Benjamin	21¾	Valley River	1854	1	128
Linn, John	23	Glady Creek	1843	1	9
Little, Thomas A.	3¾	Tigart's Valley	1848	1	59
Marsteller, Burr P.	8	Adj. Nuzum	1848	1	60
Martin, George W. et al	102	Benjamin Creek	1843	1	3
Martin, Jacob G.	53	Teverbaugh Cr.	1850	1	80

Name of Grantee	Acres	Local Description	Year	Book	Page
Martin, Jesse B.	7½	Buffalo Creek	1857	1	155
Mason, John W.	65	Drapes Run	1842	1	1
Mason, Robert	1½	Bingamon Cr.	1849	1	63
McDougal, Francis M.	6½	Ice's Run	1858	1	162
McDougal, Wm.	394	Flaggy Meadow Run	1847	1	39
Meredith, Thos. et al	40	White Day Creek	1848	1	53
Merrill, Harrison	50	Bingamon Cr.	1851	1	98
Merrill, John	89	Buffalo Cr.	1851	1	96
Metheny, Noah T.	32	Buffalo Creek	1854	1	136
Metz, Henry Heirs	100	Piles Fork	1843	1	4
Metz, Lameck	10	Piles Fork	1847	1	44
Metz, Leonard	128	Piles Fork	1844	1	17
Moore—See Moor					
Moor, Richard	50	Bingamon Cr.	1851	1	106
Moran, Otho et al	120	Mud Lick	1854	1	120
Moran, Robert	650	White Day Creek	1855	1	139
Moran, Robert	110	Grassy Run	1855	1	140
Moran, Robert	100	Big Lick Run	1855	1	144
Morgan, Albert	10	Paw Paw Creek	1854	1	122
Morgan, Albert	125	Piles Fork	1851	1	103
Morgan, Albert	107	Piles Fork	1851	1	102
Morgan, Charles	110	Pickett's Cr.	1855	1	143
Morgan, David	40	Johnson's Run	1855	1	148
Morgan, David	9	Cherry Run	1854	1	121
Morgan, David et al	120	Mud Lick	1854	1	120
Morgan, James Jr.	17½	White Day Cr.	1849	1	71
Morgan, Joseph E.	29	Mill Fall Run	1851	1	107
Morgan, Joseph E.	1¾	Buffalo Cr.	1851	1	105
Morgan, Morgan	8	Johnson's Run	1855	1	147
Morris, James T.	10	Booth's Creek	1843	1	2
Musgrave, Jonathan	4a.1r.	Minister's Run	1857	1	153
Nipton, Henry	25	Paw Paw Cr.	1846	1	32
Parish, Edward	60	Flat Run	1845	1	20
Parish, Michael	26	Teaverbough Cr.	1845	1	23
Rex, Eli	48	Mods Run	1844	1	18
Rice, Isaac	150	Piles Fork	1854	1	132
Robinson, Joshua	1a.3r.28p.	Adj. Joseph Martin	1859	1	174
Robison, John M.	100	White Day Cr.	1854	1	119
Robison, John M. et al	100	White Day Cr.	1854	1	118
Rowan, George W.	23	Wts. W. Fk. Riv.	1854	1	130
Rowan, George W. et al	130	Brush Run	1851	1	90
Ryan, George M.	1a.36p.	Booth's Cr.	1861	1	176
Sapp, Joseph B.	82¾	White Day Creek	1856	1	152
Satterfield, Levi	105	Dent's Run	1854	1	123
Shaver, James	27	Warrier's Fork	1854	1	129
Shaver, James	100	Warrior's Fork	1849	1	74
Shrader, Ludwell	46	Wolf Pit Run	1858	1	161
Shup (Shupp) George	28	Dent's Run	1851	1	91
Simpson, J. L. et al	38 sq. po.	Tn. Palatine	1857	1	158
Sine, Alfred F.	130	Piles Fork	1854	1	125
Sine, Moses	97	Piles Fork	1844	1	11
Sine, Moses	50	Piles Fork	1844	1	10
Snodgrass, Elisha	3½	Paw Paw Creek	1844	1	12
Snodgrass, Elisha	19	Buffalo Cr.	1854	1	117
Sterling, Joseph M.	140	Johnson's Run	1855	1	141
Straight, John M.	3	Finch's Run	1843	1	5
Strode, John F. et al	38½	Tigert's V. River	1858	1	166
Sturm, John	57	Teverbaugh Cr.	1845	1	27
Sturms, Daniel	17½	Teverbaugh Cr.	1849	1	64
Sturms, John et al	44	Buffalo Cr.	1854	1	124
Swisher, Joseph	20	Little Creek	1854	1	127
Talkington, Isaac	42½	Plum Run	1850	1	81
Tetrick, Josephus	13	L. Bingamon Cr.	1848	1	54

Name of Grantee	Acres	Local Description	Year	Book	Page
Tetrick, Peter	3½	Teverbaugh Cr.	1850	1	78
Thomas, George Heirs	50	Flat Run	1851	1	92
Thomas, Isaac	48	Flat Run	1847	1	51
Thomas, Isaac Jr.	69½	Flat Run	1845	1	25
Tower, E. W.	261	Piles Fork	1846	1	30
Tower, E. W.	100	White Day Cr.	1847	1	45
Tower, E. W.	70	Piles Fork	1851	1	93
Tower, E. W. et al	115	Piles Fork	1846	1	29
Tower, E. W. et al	224	Piles Fork	1846	1	28
Tower, Edwin W.	300	Bingamon Creek	1847	1	52
Tower, Edwin W.	625	White Day Creek	1858	1	164
Tower, Edwin W.	3¼	Piles Fork	1857	1	157
Tower, Edwin W. et al	200	Flat Run	1846	1	42
Tower, Edwin W. et al	485	Piles Fork	1842	1	562
Tower, Edwin W. et al	375	Flat Run	1842	1	563
Travis, Oliver	3½	Little Creek	1856	1	151
Underwood, David F.	24	Merrill's Run	1854	1	135
Watson, George Sr.	3	Buffalo Cr.	1847	1	49
Watson, Thomas G.	32 p.	Town of Palatine	1850	1	75
West, Jonathan	70½	Grassy Run	1858	1	165
White, James L.	31	Buffalo Creek	1851	1	104
White, James S. & Mary Ann	69	Hess's Run	1849	1	65
Wilson, Edgar C.	107	Wickwire Cr.	1844	1	19
Wilson, Edgar C.	650	Pricketts Creek	1853	1	110
Wilson, Edgar C.	1,000	Mud Lick Run	1854	1	137
Wilson, Edgar C.	650	Prickett's Creek	1857	1	156
Wilson, Thomas T.	4	Adj. Land of Vangilder	1854	1	131
Wood, Lewis W.	65	Flaggy Meadow Run	1850	1	84
Youst, Aaron	150	Piles Fork	1849	1	72
Youst, David	17	Piles Fork	1852	1	109
Youst, Leonard	5½	Piles Fork	1858	1	160
Youst, Leonard	300	Buffalo Creek	1851	1	108

MARSHALL COUNTY

Baker, Daniel	50	Rocky Fork	1838	1	179
Bane, Mordicai et al	73	Grave Creek	1843	1	242
Bills, William	50	Fish Creek	1838	1	202
Buchanan, William B.	65	Wheeling Cr.	1838	1	235
Burge, Elijah	100	Whetstone	1838	1	203
Burley, James L.	20a.2r.7p.	Grave Creek	1860	1	292
Caldwell, Alexander	340	Wts. Fish Creek	1838	1	180
Caldwell, E. H.	9¼	Hart's Fork	1854	1	277
Caldwell, Elbert H.	18a.101p.	Fish Creek	1853	1	275
Caldwell, Elbert H.	45	Laurel Run	1854	1	278
Caldwell, Elbert H.	3	Grave Creek	1851	1	272
Caldwell, Elbert H.	11	Big Grave Creek	1850	1	269
Caldwell, Elbert H.	13½	Grave Creek	1849	1	267
Caldwell, Elbert H.	292	Hart's Run	1848	1	264
Caldwell, Elbert H.	200	Fishing Creek	1846	1	258
Campbell, Edward	1a.93p.	Jim's Run	1855	1	282
Campbell, James	75	Whetstone Cr.	1838	1	204
Carroll, Thomas	29½	Wheeling Creek	1849	1	266
Clarke, Lawrence	24	Bogg's Run	1838	1	181
Coe, Philip	26¾	Big Grave Creek	1847	1	259
Covalt, Abraham (Covatt)	180	Fish Creek	1838	1	206

Name of Grantee	Acres	Local Description	Year	Book	Page
Pierce, Arthur	370	Big Grave Creek	1838	1	191
Pyle, John	100	Sugar Camp	1838	1	215
Reed, Joseph	133	Fish Creek	1838	1	217
Reed, Joseph	100	Laurel Run	1838	1	218
Reed, Samuel	12¾	Fish Creek	1838	1	219
Reed, Samuel	244	Laurel Run	1838	1	220
Rine, George	74¾	Long Run	1856	1	283
Rine, Lazarus Jr.	52	Coon's Run	1838	1	192
Rine, Lazarus Jr.	100	Whetstone	1838	1	193
Sharp, Ransaler	20	Boggs Island	1842	1	241
Sharpe, Pearley	500	Wts. Fish Creek	1838	1	194
Shepherd, Benjamin	44	Big Grave Creek	1847	1	260
Sims, Tompson	35	Sims Run	1853	1	274
Smally, John	100	Whetstone	1838	1	221
Sockman, Henry	165	Fish Creek	1838	1	190
Sockman, Henry Sr.	150	Piney Fork	1840	1	238
Steenrod, Lewis et al	540	Grave Creek	1838	1	200
Stewart, Jesse	300	Sugar Camp Run	1838	1	222
Thomas, Elias	286	Whetstone	1838	1	223
Thompson, Moses	100	Wheeling Creek	1838	1	195
Venus, Samuel et al	500	Lynn Camp Cr.	1838	1	234
Venus, Samuel et al	680	Fish Creek	1838	1	233
Woods, R. B.	50	Wheeling Cr.	1855	1	279
Woods, Robert C.	167	Grave Creek	1838	1	201
Woods, Robert C.	21	Fish Creek	1840	1	236
Woods, Robert C.	80	Fish Creek	1840	1	237
Woods, Robert C.	76	Coon's Run	1850	1	271
Woods, Robert C. et al	540	Grave Creek	1838	1	200
Woods, Robert et al	680	Fish Creek	1838	1	233
Workman, Stephen	100	Rocky Fork	1838	1	196
Workman, Stephen	149	Long Run	1838	1	225
Workman, William	37	Whetstone	1838	1	226
Wykert, Henry C.	13½	Fish Creek	1856	1	285
Wykert, Nicholas	100	Whetstone	1838	1	224
Yoho, Isaac	100	Rocky Fork	1838	1	197
Yoho, William	50	Whetstone	1838	1	198
Young, Aaron	100	Lynn Camp	1838	1	227

*MASON COUNTY

* Grants dated prior to formation of Mason County (1804) may have been in some other county, or state.

Abott, William	62½	13 Mi Cr.	1847	2	102
Alexander, William	3,274½	Cor. to Wilkinson	1791	1	293
Allin, William	55	10 Mi. Creek	1850	2	180
Allin, William	42	Rocky Fork	1851	2	184
Allin, William	52	10 Mi. Creek	1849	2	149
Amoss, Delila et al	45	18 Mi. Creek	1850	2	173
Ball, Daniel R. et al	1	Point Pleasant	1849	2	142
Ball, Isaac M.	50	Wts. Lit. Guyan	1832	1	523
Ball, Isaac M.	253	Adj. G. McCallister	1832	1	524
Ball, James	154	Old Town Creek	1842	2	50
Ball, James	116	Old Town Creek	1842	2	51
Ball, Thomas	46	Cor. Michael Blessing	1845	2	85

Name of Grantee	Acres	Local Description	Year	Book	Page
Barnet, William	50	Ten Mile Cr.	1825	1	411
Barnett, John	226	Spring Fork	1851	2	186
Barnett, John	154	10 Mi. Creek	1851	2	185
Barnett, John	70	Cooper's Fork	1849	2	158
Barnett, John	75	13 Mi. Creek	1849	2	147
Barnett, William	100	10 Mi. Creek	1846	2	98
Barr, Isaac et al	7,000	Wts. Licking Cr.	1792	1	314
Bateman, William et al	300	Mill Stone	1838	2	40
Bateman, William et al	100	16 Mi. Creek	1838	2	39
Beal, John W.	680	Adj. Thomas Morrison	1849	2	150
Behan, Isaac	10½	Adj. Pick's Line	1851	2	200
Black, Jacob	38	Head Lit. Guyan	1835	1	554
Black, Jacob	100	Rock Camp	1830	1	487
Boram, Jacob	100	16 Mi. Cr.	1835	2	18
Boyd, John	1,000	Wts. Ohio	1791	1	301
Bozel, Gilbert (Bozzell)	100	Big Mill Creek	1841	2	38
Bradburn, Joseph	50	Adj. Henry Banks	1826	1	434
Brown, Mathew D.	194	Reedy Creek	1826	1	450
Brown, Mathew D.	257	16 Mi. Creek	1823	1	394
Brown, Mathew D.	590	Brown's Cr.	1847	2	103
Brown, Mathew D. et al	340	Plantation Cr.	1828	1	474
Brown, Mathew D. et al	330	18 Mi. Creek	1828	1	475
Brown, Mathew D. et al	305	5 Mi. Creek	1844	2	76
Brown, Susanna Heirs	250	25 Mi. Creek	1818	1	341
Brown, William Winston Heirs	330	18 Mi. Cr.	1828	1	475
Brown, William Winston Heirs	340	Plantation Cr.	1828	1	474
Bryan, Andrew	175	Big Hurricane	1837	2	21
Byram, Benjamin P.	190	Adj. Henry Banks	1850	2	172
Byram, Benjamin P.	80	Adj. Arbuckle	1845	2	88
Byram, Benjamin P.	218	13 Mi. Creek	1849	2	138
Byram, Benjamin P.	94	Cor. to J. Dunn	1850	2	183
Byram, Benjamin P.	35	Rocky Fork	1858	2	259
Cahill, Edward	500	25 Mi. Cr.	1827	1	454
Cantrell—or Cantrill					
Cantrell, John et al	500	Rock Castle Cr.	1843	2	65
Cantrell, John et al	222	Rock Castle Cr.	1844	2	68
Cantrell, John et al	33	Adj. J. Cantrell	1845	2	90
Cantrell, John et al	600	5 Mi. Creek	1834	1	547
Cantrill, John	80	Adj. A. Fisher	1837	2	24
Cantrill, John	209	13 Mi. Creek	1812	1	323
Cantrill, John	100	Big Mill Cr.	1820	1	359
Cantrill, John	190	10 Mi. Creek	1822	1	375
Carney, Jesse	116	Adj. Geo. W. Smith	1826	1	428
Carney, Thomas et al	261	Cox's Fork	1824	1	408
Carter, Lucy et al	43	3 Mi. Creek	1818	1	344
Carter, Mary Heirs, et al	43	3 Mi. Creek	1818	1	344
Cartwright, Joel	130	13 Mi. Creek	1854	2	224
Cartwright, Joel	50	Adj. J. Tillis	1850	2	174
Casdorph, Thomas	72	2 Mi. Creek	1831	1	501
Casto, Daniel	50	Wts. Mill Cr.	1823	1	381
Casto, James et al	200	Big Mill Cr.	1819	1	355
Casto, John Sr. et al	200	Adj. G. W. Smith	1823	1	380
Casto, Jonathan	100	Mill Cr.	1827	1	456
Casto, William	100	Big Mill Cr.	1820	1	363
Casto, William	60	Big Mill Cr.	1827	1	471
Churchill, William & John	11,415	Wts. Ohio	1792	1	309
Clag, James	100	Wts. Guyandotte	1825	1	424
Clag, Joseph	100	Knife Branch	1835	2	11
Clark, William	123	Mill Path	1823	1	388
Clark, William	100	Cross Creek	1823	1	389
Clark, William	77	Adj. Military Surv.	1819	1	352
Clark, William N. (Clerk)	200	Buffalo Cr.	1827	1	455
Clay, Johnson	20	Wts. Guyan	1830	1	489

Name of Grantee	Acres	Local Description	Year	Book	Page
Frazer—See also Frazier					
Frazer, Samuel (or Frazier)	50	Wts. Lit. Hurricane Cr.	1815	1	332
Frazier—See also Frazer					
Frazier, Allen	55½	25-Mile Cr.	1833	1	536
Frazier, Allen	190	Big Hurricane	1843	2	59
Frazier, Samuel (Frazer)	100	Adj. his own	1837	2	22
Frazier, William	200	25-Mi. Cr.	1843	2	58
French, James	40	16-Mi. Cr.	1824	1	401
French, James	60	16-Mi. Cr.	1827	1	460
Gandy, Uriah Jr.	100	Reedy Cr.	1820	1	357
Garns, Joseph	100	Grass Lick Fork	1823	1	387
Garns, Joseph	100	Stone Lick Fork	1823	1	386
Gibbs, Jacob K. et al	125	W. Creek	1846	2	91
Gibbs, Jacob K. et al	300	West Creek	1842	2	46
Gibson, Alexander	60	Big Hurricane Cr.	1831	1	505
Gilmore, John C.	390	Adj. George Cooper	1846	2	92
Givenden, John (Gividen, Jividen)	184	Mud Lick	1851	1	316
Gray, Jacob	134	13 Mi. Creek	1849	2	151
Gray, James	182	Adj. Joplin	1849	2	143
Greenlee, Alexander	100	13 Mi. Creek	1832	1	518
Greenlee, Alexander	50	13 Mi. Creek	1832	1	522
Greenlee, Clark	112	Rocky Fork	1857	2	246
Greenlee, Clark	18	13 Mi. Creek	1856	2	242
Greenlee, Clark	85½	13 Mi. Creek	1856	2	243
Greenlee, Clark	30	Gallipolis Island	1856	2	245
Greenlee, Edward	50	Rocky Fork	1846	2	95
Greenlee, Edward	85	10 Mi. Creek	1849	2	161
Greenlee, Edward	290	Adj. John Dunn	1850	2	171
Greenlee, Henry	140	13 Mi. Creek	1856	2	244
Greenlee, Henry	250	Adj. R. Greenlee	1847	2	117
Greenlee, John	150	Crossroads	1820	1	361
Greenlee, John	50	Cooper's Fork	1830	1	493
Greenlee, John	100	Rocky Fork	1832	1	509
Greenlee, Maurice	20	13 Mi. Creek	1832	1	515
Greenlee, Morgan	75	10 Mi. Creek	1849	2	144
Greenlee, Morgan	50	10 Mi. Creek	1849	2	145
Greenlee, Morgan	500	Adj. Cooper Surv.	1850	2	170
Greenlee, Morgan	500	Adj. Cooper	1850	2	169
Greenlee, Morris	59	13 Mi. Creek	1820	1	362
Greenlee, Neelee	210	13 Mi. Cr.	1854	2	233
Greenlee, Neely	50	13 Mi. Creek	1844	2	77
Greenlee, Robert Sr.	43	Rocky Fork	1857	2	247
Greenlee, Samuel	112½	13 Mi. Creek	1826	1	445
Greenlee, William	250	Ten Mi. Creek	1832	1	520
Greenlee, William	190	10 Mi. Cr.	1842	2	56
Greenlee, William	500	Adj. Arbuckle	1842	2	55
Greer, James et al	640	13 Mi. Creek	1860	2	266
Greer, James et al	279	13 Mi. Creek	1860	2	264
Greer, John	100	Three Mile Cr.	1830	1	494
Greer, John	100	3 Mi. Cr.	1815	1	330
Greer, John	125	3 Mi. Creek	1852	2	208
Greer, John	60	Cor. to Cooper	1851	2	189
Greer, John	200	Cor. to Cantrell	1851	2	187
Greer, John	83	Cow Run	1850	2	176
Greer, John	200	Adj. Henry Wilson	1850	2	177
Greer, John	100	Cow Run	1844	2	79
Greer, John	130	3 Mi. Creek	1844	2	78
Greer, John M.	570	Cow Run	1856	2	241
Greer, John M.	33	Cow Run	1856	2	239
Greer, Samuel	125	3 Mi. Creek	1851	2	188
Gregg, Jane et al	475	Five Mi. Creek	1827	1	459
Grey, Jacob	280	Mud Lick	1857	2	254
Grim, Joseph	50	10 Mi. Creek	1831	1	502

Name of Grantee	Acres	Local Description	Year	Book	Page
Jackson, Edward H.	75	Adj. J. Sears	1823	1	393
Jackson, Edward H.	200	Sycamore Fork	1821	1	372
Jackson, John	119	Grass Lick	1824	1	403
Jackson, John	180	Grass Run	1824	1	407
Jackson, John	50	Trace Run	1825	1	418
Jackson, John et al	200	Adj. G. W. Smith	1823	1	380
Jackson, John et al	261	Cox's Fork	1824	1	408
Jamison, John	1,000	Licking Creek	1792	1	319
Jeffers, James	690	Adj. N. Yeager	1849	2	163
Jeffers, James	325	13 Mi. Creek	1854	2	235
Jeffers, Jas.	50	Adj. Yeager	1847	2	106
Jeffers, James (Jeffries)	75	13 Mi. Cr.	1843	2	60
Jeffries—See Jeffers					
Jenkins, Calvin	100	Bear Fork	1832	1	513
Jenkins, Calvin	50	Rt. Hd. Fk. Lit. Guyan	1835	1	559
Jividen—See Givenden, Gividen					
Jones, Andrew	10	10 Mi. Cr.	1835	1	558
Jones, Davis	50	25 Mi. Cr.	1837	2	20
Jones, Davis	50	Big Hurricane Cr.	1832	1	529
Jones, John et al	118	Hurricane Cr.	1826	1	438
Jones, Jonathan	117	25 Mi. Creek	1827	1	462
Jones, William et al	200	Adj. Banks Surv.	1851	2	191
Jones, William et al	200	25 Mi. Cr.	1833	1	537
Jones, William et al	100	2nd Gr. Br. Big Kan. Riv.	1833	1	544
Jordan, James L.	100	18 Mi. Creek	1832	1	516
Jordan, James L.	50	18 Mi. Creek	1832	1	517
Jordan, James Y.	129	Wts. Lit. Guyan	1832	1	519
Jorden, John	50	Adj. John Holdway	1832	1	528
Jorden, Jonathan	50	18 Mi. Cr.	1833	1	541
Jorden, Jonathan	100	18 Mi. Cr.	1833	1	539
Jorden, William N.	245	Adj. Harraman	1845	2	87
Kessel, George et al	200	Big Mill Cr.	1819	1	355
Kessel, Jonathan W.	30	Mill Creek	1828	1	478
Kilgore, Thomas	130	18 Mi. Creek	1832	1	525
Kilgore, Thomas	359	18 Mi. Creek	1835	1	549
King, James	150	5 Mi. Creek	1835	1	552
Knap—See Knopp					
Knap, George	100	Big Mill Cr.	1834	1	546
Knap, Moses	104	13 Mi. Cr.	1819	1	349
Knight, George R. et al	641	Adj. A. Long	1842	2	52
Knopp—See Knap					
Knopp, John	19	Crooked Creek	1855	2	236
Kruzan, Isaac	145	Cow Run	1827	1	463
Lawrey—See Lowery, Lowrey, Lowry					
Lee, Henry	11,415	Wts. Ohio	1792	1	310
Lee, John	642	Cooper's Fork	1847	2	118
Lee, Joseph	226	Little Buffalo	1838	2	30
Lemasters, George	200	Yeager's Fork	1844	2	81
Lemasters, George	100	3 Mi. Creek	1844	2	80
Lewis, Andrew Colonel	712	12 Mi. Creek	1824	1	395
Lewis, Ann et al	115	Rock Castle	1835	1	550
Lewis, Benjamin Jr.	150	Trace Fork	1816	1	339
Lewis, John	30	Adj. Andrew Lewis	1842	2	48
Lewis, Thomas et al	4,661	Wts. Ohio	1792	1	312
Little, David et al	100	Middle Rock Fork	1826	1	432
Lockhart, John O.	150	Big Buffalo	1835	2	14
Long, Gideon	100	Cow Run	1823	1	384
Long, Samuel	50	Wts. Mill Cr.	1827	1	464
Long, Samuel	50	Mill Cr.	1827	1	465
Love, Charles	50	Pond Fork	1825	1	420
Lowry, John (Lowrey)	296	Cow Run	1847	2	116
Mace, Paul	100	Parchment Fork	1826	1	448

Name of Grantee	Acres	Local Description	Year	Book	Page
Morgan, Charles et al	5,000	Wts. Ohio	1792	1	311
Morgan, Ralph et al	7,000	Wts. Licking Cr.	1792	1	314
Nelson, George	1,000	Licking Creek	1791	1	302
Nessleroad, John	100	Adj. G. Washington	1820	1	360
Nottingham, Francis et al	100	25 Mi. Creek	1831	1	503
Nottingham, Sampson	100	Wts. Lit. Guyan	1835	1	561
Newcomb, Carter	400	Big Buffalo	1835	1	560
Newell, Jacob	40	13 Mi. Creek	1821	1	367
Newell, Jacob	50	Adj. W. Barnett	1850	2	181
Newell, Jacob	10	Middle Fork	1837	2	26
O'Connor, William et al	500	18 Mi. Creek	1849	2	165
Oldacre, Henry	½	Cor. to Matthews	1842	2	43
Oldacre, John	591	Jake's Branch	1812	1	324
Ours, Nicholas	120	Big Mill Cr.	1823	1	392
Owsley, Thomas	2,207¾	Wts. Licking Cr.	1792	1	316
Owsley, Thomas	1,254¼	Wts. Licking Cr.	1792	1	315
Pare, Thomas	50	25 Mi. Cr.	1833	1	540
Parker, Edwin L. et al	279	13 Mi. Creek	1860	2	264
Parker, Hugh	160	Mud Lick	1857	2	253
Parker, W. W. et al	640	13 Mi. Creek	1860	2	266
Parker, William W. et al	500	18 Mi. Creek	1849	2	165
Parkhurst, Aaron	290	Lit. Buffalo	1840	2	33
Parson—See Parsons, Pearsons, Persons					
Parson, William	125	13 Mi. Creek	1861	2	275
Parsons, A. F.	560	13 Mi. Creek	1858	2	256
Parsons, George	100	Big Sand Creek	1825	1	419
Parsons, Henry	78	Parchment Fork	1825	1	421
Patterson, William Sr.	40	Turkey Run	1831	1	507
Payne, Edward et al	3,000	Wts. Ohio	1792	1	313
Payne, Henry et al	5,000	Wts. Ohio	1792	1	311
Pearsons—See Parson, Parsons, Persons					
Pearsons, John	90	Mill Cr.	1823	1	382
Persons—See Parson, Parsons, Pearsons					
Persons, Charles Sr.	100	Big Mill Cr.	1819	1	347
Persons, George	100	Grass Lick	1821	1	370
Persons, George	16	Big Mill Cr.	1819	1	350
Persons, George	84	Big Mill Cr.	1815	1	334
Persons, John et al	165	Big Mill Cr.	1824	1	398
Persons, Joseph	5½	Adj. G. Washington	1812	1	326
Persons, William	150	Big Mill Cr.	1813	1	329
Persons, William	92	Sycamore Fork	1812	1	327
Persons, William Louther	100	Big Mill Cr.	1818	1	340
Poge, Robert	400	Licking Creek	1791	1	303
Post, Isaac	130	Grass Lick	1827	1	467
Potts, Thomas et al	300	Mill Stone	1838	2	40
Potts, Thomas et al	100	16 Mi. Creek	1838	2	39
Prosser, Wm.	290	Crab Creek	1831	1	500
Prowse, Samuel	100	5 Mi. Creek	1846	2	100
Pruit, Granville	41	13 Mi. Creek	1823	1	391
Pruit, Robert	93	13 Mi. Cr.	1823	1	390
Pullin, Charles C.	5	Adj. John Cantrell	1851	2	193
Pullins, James	355	Adj. Morris Surv.	1844	2	72
Pullins, James et al	255	Adj. W. Stephenson	1830	1	497
Pullins, James et al	115	Rock Castle	1835	1	550
Pullins, James et al	300	10 Mi. Creek	1835	1	553
Putney, Richard	495	Buffalo Creek	1835	2	13
Putney, Richard E.	100	Big Buffalo	1835	2	15
Ray—See Wray					
Reader, Abraham	350	Elk Fork	1824	1	400
Reader, James et al	140	Elk Fork	1828	1	479
Reader, James et al	177	Mill Cr.	1819	1	348
Reader, Michael	105	Big Mill Creek	1826	1	436
Reader, Michael	181	Elk Fork	1826	1	435

Name of Grantee	Acres	Local Description	Year	Book	Page
Shelton, Wetherstone	90	Deborah's Br.	1837	2	23
Shinn, Nehemiah	190	13 Mi. Creek	1859	2	260
Shinn, Samuel	150	Round Knob Run	1825	1	422
Shrewsberry, Joel et al	54	Mill Creek	1830	1	492
Shrewsbury, Joel et al	346	Narrows below Lit. Cr.	1836	2	19
Sissen, Wilson C.	½	Point Pleasant	1849	2	167
Smith, Bur'l S.	304	Rocky Fork	1857	2	251
Smith, Burwell S.	90	Poplar Fork	1857	2	249
Smith, Burwell S.	92	13 Mi Creek	1851	2	195
Smith, Dianna et al	475	5 Mi. Creek	1827	1	459
Smith, Gideon H.	107	13 Mi. Creek	1856	2	238
Smith, Gideon H.	50	13 Mi. Creek	1856	2	237
Smith, Isaac	50	Yeager's Fork	1848	1	122
Smith, Isaac	50	13 Mi. Creek	1848	2	123
Smith, Isaac E.	9	13 Mi. Creek	1854	2	228
Smith, Isaac E.	20	13 Mi. Creek	1854	2	227
Smith, James	43	13 Mi. Creek	1854	2	234
Smith, James et al	300	13 Mi. Creek	1854	2	230
Smith, Jesse	125	Kilgore Cr.	1840	2	31
Smith, John	75	Wts. Lit. Guyan	1840	2	32
Smith, Jonas	75	Arbuckle's Creek	1828	1	485
Smith, Nathan	9	Point Pleasant	1848	2	136
Smith, Nathan	182	Allen's Creek	1854	2	226
Smith, Nathan	109	Allen's Creek	1854	2	225
Smith, Nathan	150	Bear Branch	1827	1	451
Smith, Nathan et al	105	Jenny's Run	1830	1	488
Smith, Samuel	100	13 Mi. Creek	1821	1	371
Smith, Samuel	100	13 Mi. Creek	1818	1	342
Smith, Samuel	150	Rocky Fork	1846	2	93
Smith, Samuel	100	13 Mi. Cr.	1843	2	63
Smith, William	100	Wts. Mud River	1833	1	538
Smith, William	50	S. W. Cor. Robt. Forth	1833	1	533
Snow, James	600	Isaac Branch	1840	2	35
Staats, Calvin	50	Cow Run	1851	2	194
Staats, Calvin et al	91	Cow Run	1860	2	265
Starcher, Jacob	40	Big Mill Cr.	1819	1	353
Stephenson, Charles	55¼	10 Mi. Creek	1852	2	207
Stephenson, Charles	90	Adj. Henry Banks	1846	2	96
Stephenson, Charles	120	10 Mi. Creek	1849	2	148
Stephenson, James L.	70	Adj. George Cooper	1851	2	197
Stephenson, James L.	190	10 Mi. Creek	1846	2	97
Stephenson, William	178	Adj. Charles Pullins	1844	2	69
Stephenson, William	125	Adj. H. Cooper	1825	1	415
Stephenson, William	150	8 Mi. Creek	1835	1	551
Stevens, John B. Sr.	60	Crab Cr.	1838	2	29
Stevens, Robert A. O. & J. B. Jr.	45	Brush Fork	1838	2	28
Stevens, Rob. O. A. & J. B. Jr.	85	Crab Cr.	1838	2	27
Stewart, William	140	13 Mi. Creek	1853	2	219
Summerville, Samuel	200	Old Town Cr.	1828	1	472
Summerville, Samuel et al	641	Adj. A. Long	1842	2	52
Summerville, Thomas	486	Old Town Cr.	1842	2	53
Swallow, Hiram H. et al	164	Adj. Samuel Roush	1853	2	210
Swan, Richard	1½	Mill Run	1857	2	248
Swan, Richard	26	8 Mile Island	1844	2	70
Swope, George	200	Big Mill Cr.	1812	1	328
Swope, George	750	Big Sandy Cr.	1819	1	354
Swope, George	118	Adj. Harrison's	1825	1	410
Taylor, James M. et al	500	18 Mi. Creek	1849	2	165
Templeton, John	50	25 Mi. Creek	1832	1	514
Thornton, George	40	Adj. Simon Grimm	1849	2	152
Thornton, George	36	10 Mi. Creek	1854	2	231
Tillinghost, Nicholas V.	3,274½	Wts. Ohio	1791	1	300
Tillis, Joshua	50	13 Mi. Creek	1849	2	146
Tillis, Richard	100	13 Mile Cr.	1857	2	250

Name of Grantee	Acres	Local Description	Year	Book	Page
Trotter, Preston	1,000	18 Mi. Creek	1848	2	126
Tucker, Thomas	100	Buffalo Creek	1835	2	1
Utt, Merriman	420	13 Mi. Creek	1849	2	140
Vanbibber, Jesse	50	13 Mi. Cr.	1826	1	443
Vandoozer—or Vandozer					
Vandoozer, Hezekiah	80	Little Buffalo	1840	2	36
Wallice, Thomas (Wallace)	200	Cor. J. Crisman	1828	1	469
Warden, James	100	Rockhouse Hollow	1832	1	511
Warner, Bowdidge, Jr.	310	Mud Lick	1857	2	255
Waugh, A. et al	640	13 Mi. Creek	1860	2	266
Waugh, Arthur (Arther)	230	13 Mi. Creek	1860	2	268
Waugh, Arthur	40	13 Mi. Creek	1860	2	267
Waugh, Arthur	342	13 Mi. Creek	1861	2	269
Waugh, Arthur	55	13 Mi. Creek	1851	2	196
Waugh, Arthur	1¼	13 Mi. Cr.	1853	2	220
Waugh, Arthur	319½	13 Mi. Cr.	1853	2	221
Waugh, Arthur	50	13 Mi. Creek	1853	2	222
Waugh, Arthur	45	13 Mi. Creek	1853	2	223
Waugh, Gorey	130	Rocky Fork	1844	2	75
Weaver, John J.	13¼	Wolf's Bar	1860	2	263
Weaver, John J. et al	164	Adj. Samuel Roush	1853	2	210
Wells, Samuel	1,000	Licking Cr.	1791	1	308
Wetzel, William E. et al	558	18 Mi. Creek	1861	2	272
Wetzel, William E. et al	618	18 Mi. Creek	1860	2	274
Wetzel, Lewis	¼	Point Pleasant	1850	2	182
Wethers, Jacob (Withers)	100	Flat Foot Creek	1832	1	510
Wiley, Robert	150	18 Mi. Cr.	1826	1	439
Wiley, Thomas	100	Big Hurricane Cr.	1824	1	409
Williams, John	161	Lees Creek	1792	1	318
Williams, John	686	Lee's Creek	1792	1	307
Wilson, Henry	150	Mud Lick	1850	2	179
Wilson, Washington et al	600	Adj. Simon Grim	1850	2	168
Withers—See Wethers					
Wolf, Abram	190	13 Mi. Creek	1858	2	258
Wolf, James R.	75	Joe's Run	1827	1	468
Wood, Silas et al	416	Little Buffalo	1840	2	34
Wray, Creed T.	518	Adj. Jesse George	1849	2	157
Wright, Benjamin	100	Cow Run	1821	1	369
Wright, Benjamin	200	Washington Run	1821	1	368
Wright, Benjamin Sr.	100	Washington Run	1820	1	358
Wright, Benjamin Sr.	100	Washington Run	1820	1	356
Yauger—See also Yeager					
Yauger, William	3	10 Mi. Creek	1850	2	175
Yauger, William	323½	10 Mi. Creek	1852	2	203
Yeager—or Yauger					
Yeager, Nicholas	42	10 Mi. Creek	1828	1	470
Yeager, Nicholas	85	Ten Mile Cr.	1825	1	414
Yeager, Nicholas	123	Rush Hollow	1824	1	402

McDOWELL COUNTY

Bagby, Robert B. et al	1,033	Clear Fork	1860	1	469
Bagby, Robert B. et al	467	Horse Creek	1860	1	468
Barnett, James Jr.	231	Dock Branch	1860	1	466
Beavers, Alexander D.	80	Snake Root Fork	1862	1	530
Beavers, Alexander D. et al	1,500	Mud Lick Fork	1860	1	464
Beavers, James W.	155	Dalton Branch	1861	1	490

Name of Grantee	Acres	Local Description	Year	Book	Page
Beavers, James W.	19	Trace Branch	1861	1	508
Beavers, Robert (of Alex)	148	Bandy Branch	1861	1	507
Bentley, James B.	83	Harman's Branch	1860	1	474
Bentley, James B.	80	Huff's Branch	1860	1	455
Brewster—See Bruster					
Brewster, William Sr.	35	Dry Fork	1861	1	511
Brittain, Rufus	500	Big Creek	1861	1	570
Brittain, Rufus et al	541	Dry Fork	1861	1	489
Bruster—See Brewster					
Bruster, William Sr.	115	Dry Hollow	1861	1	512
Bruster, William Sr.	65	Dry Fork	1862	1	537
Bruster, William Sr.	48	Dry Fork	1862	1	538
Cartright, Moses A.	450	Sugar Camp Branch	1861	1	522
Cartright, Moses A. et al	935	Little Cub Branch	1861	1	521
Cartright, Moses A. et al	750	Sand Lick Creek	1861	1	523
Cecil, Samuel	94	Cucumber Creek	1860	1	478
Cecil, Samuel et al	260	Whitley's Branch	1862	1	527
Chambers, Joannah	240	Big Slouch	1861	1	493
Charles, John	540	Dry Fork	1861	1	503
Cline, Adam	67	Panther Creek	1861	1	494
Cline, John A.	68	Waters Tug Riv.	1861	1	496
Cline, John Sr.	217	Sugar Camp	1861	1	502
Cline, Michael	97	Branches Spice-Laurel	1861	1	495
Cline, Michael (of Mike)	171	Horse Creek	1860	1	457
Collins, Edward	46	Bradshaw Creek	1860	1	458
Collins, Jacob	90	Dry Fork	1861	1	514
Collins, John (of John)	50	Ben's Ridge	1861	1	491
Collins, William (of John)	80	Crane Creek	1861	1	492
Cox, James O.	9,998	Panther Creek	1861	1	564
Cox, Montgomery	682	Wts. Tug River	1860	1	470
Cox, Montgomery	564	Wts. Dry Fork	1860	1	472
Cox, Montgomery	600	Coon Branch	1860	1	471
Doak, James R. et al	1,250	Mud Hole Branch	1862	1	525
Doak, James R. et al	260	Dry Fork	1862	1	526
George, Harvey et al	130	Dry Fork	1862	1	529
Gibson, Sarah	324	Huff's Branch	1860	1	475
Harman, D. H.	86	Dry Fork	1860	1	473
Harrison, Henry	800	Kewee Creek	1861	1	568
Harrison, John C.	85	Twin Branch	1862	1	535
Harrison, John C.	88	Panther Fork	1862	1	536
Harrison, John C.	522	Long Branch	1861	1	497
Harrison, John C.	111	Bradshaw Creek	1862	1	540
Harrison, John C. et al	500	Panther Creek	1860	1	460
Harrison, John C. et al	4,610	Panther Fork	1860	1	562
Harrison, John C. et al	1,600	Wts. Dry Fork	1860	1	461
Hicks, John T.	3,500	Elkhorn Fork	1860	1	477
Hicks, John T.	2,100	Huff's Creek	1860	1	476
Jackson, Joseph Jr. et al	4,610	Panther Fork	1860	1	562
Jackson, Joseph Jr. et al	500	Panther Creek	1860	1	460
Jackson, Joseph Jr. et al	1,600	Wts. Dry Fork	1860	1	461
Justus, Hiram	1,030	White Oak Fork	1862	1	531
Justus, Hiram	50	Panther Creek	1862	1	532
Justus, Joab Sr.	45	Panther Creek	1862	1	534
Justus, Joab Sr.	30	Middle Fork	1862	1	533
King, Franklin	300	Panther Creek	1861	1	498
Lambert, Philip	670	Clear Fork	1860	1	560
Lambert, Philip	35	Clear Fork	1861	1	513
Lambert, Philip	240	Camp Branch	1861	1	499
Lawson, Anthony et al	935	Little Cub Branch	1861	1	521
Lawson, Anthony et al	750	Sand Lick Creek	1861	1	523
Marrs, David W.	106	South Fork Elkhorn	1861	1	487
Marrs, David W.	206	South Fork Elkhorn	1861	1	488
Mitchell, A. P.	390	Laurel Branch	1861	1	518

Name of Grantee	Acres	Local Description	Year	Book	Page
Mitchell, A. P.	360	Jed Branch	1861	1	517
Moore, Isaac Q.	1,800	Indian Grave Br.	1861	1	572
Murphy, Henry	140	Wts. Tug	1861	1	501
Murphy, Quanten A.	890	Jacob's Fork	1860	1	479
Murphy, Quanten A.	370	Jacob's Fork	1860	1	480
Murphy, Quanten A.	90	Big Creek	1861	1	500
Murphy, Quanten A. et al	325	Jacob's Fork	1860	1	481
O'Dell, Hugh L.	138	North Fork	1861	1	485
Parker, Anderson	226	South Fork	1861	1	516
Parker, Edwin L. et al	1,033	Clear Fork	1860	1	469
Parker, Edwin L. et al	467	Horse Creek	1860	1	468
Parker, Edwin L. et al	1,000	Crane Creek	1860	1	467
Payne, George W.	9	Clear Fork	1861	1	482
Payne, George W.	18	Clear Fork	1861	1	509
Payne, George W.	100	Reedy Springs Br.	1862	1	528
Payne, George W. et al	800	Hd. Crane Creek	1860	1	465
Payne, George W. et al	1,250	Mud Hole Branch	1862	1	525
Payne, George W. et al	260	Dry Fork	1862	1	526
Payne, George W. et al	130	Dry Fork	1862	1	529
Payne, John D.	70	Hurricane Br. Dry Fork	1861	1	505
Payne, John D.	500	Ring's Branch	1861	1	504
Payne, Louis	90	Bark Camp	1861	1	506
Peery, Archibald	190	Dry Fork	1861	1	515
Perry, Thomas A. et al	541	Dry Fork	1861	1	489
Smith, Abraham	70	Elkhorn Branch	1861	1	520
Smith, Abraham	162	North Fork	1861	1	519
Smith, Robert et al	260	Whiteley's Branch	1862	1	527
Steel, Andrew	100	Wts. Tug Riv.	1860	1	463
Steel, Reuben	50	Harman's Branch	1860	1	459
Steel, Samuel	50	Lick Branch	1860	1	462
Trent, Smith	630	Huff's Creek	1861	1	484
Wallis, Henry T.	250	John's Branch	1862	1	539
Walrond, John	39	Bartley's Creek	1862	1	524
Walrond, John	113	Big Branch	1861	1	510
Webb, John F. et al	1,000	Crane Creek	1860	1	467
White, Benjamin et al	325	Jacob's Fork	1860	1	481
Wilhite, Alfred	150	Big Creek	1861	1	486
Williams, Benjamin W.	411	Panther Creek	1859	1	456
Williams, Benjamin W.	169	Camp Branch	1861	1	483
Williams, Benjamin W. et al	1,500	Mud Lick Fork	1860	1	464
Williams, Benjamin W. et al	800	Hd. Crane Creek	1860	1	465

MERCER COUNTY

Anderson, Jabez	175	Lick Creek	1852	1	358
Anderson, James C.	80	Tom's Run	1852	1	361
Anderson, James C. et al	40	Tom's Run	1851	1	352
Anderson, William H.	100	Joshua's Run	1852	1	363
Bailey, James M.	160	Flat Top Mt.	1847	1	306
Bailey, John	90	Wts. Blue Stone	1858	1	434
Bailey, John Madison et al	12	Beaver Creek	1849	1	325
Bailey, Mastin	120	Flat Top Mt.	1847	1	304
Bailey, Micajah	60	White Mouth	1847	1	302
Bailey, Micajah	100	Wide Mouth	1847	1	301
Belcher, Asa	100	Laurel Creek	1853	1	390
Blankenship, Andrew J. et al	75	Flat Top Mt.	1847	1	305

Name of Grantee	Acres	Local Description	Year	Book	Page
Blankenship, Lewis	72	Laurel Creek	1847	1	303
Boling, Charles A.	100	Richland Creek	1858	1	435
Brian, Henly C.	250	Camp Creek	1854	1	393
Brown, Allen et al	270	Lick Creek	1851	1	344
Brown, Allen et al	320	Horse Ford	1851	1	343
Brown, Allen et al	40	Tom's Run	1851	1	352
Brown, Evan H.	200	Lick Creek	1851	1	340
Brown, John W.	140	Tom's Run	1857	1	420
Burgess, James M. et al	200	Richland Creek	1849	1	320
Burnside, George A.	100	Tom's Run	1860	1	451
Byer, George	40	Laurel Creek	1853	1	378
Byer, George	60	Laurel Creek	1853	1	379
Byer, George	40	Bull Falls of New R.	1855	1	398
Calfee, James et al	12	Beaver Creek	1849	1	325
Campbell, Thomas S. & Isaac	300	Culbertson's Bottom	1853	1	385
Caperton, Augustus W. J.	335	Laurel Creek	1853	1	384
Carner, Johnston	75	Lick Creek	1852	1	359
Cauley—or Cawley					
Cawley, Berry	66	Lick Creek	1858	1	433
Cawley, John	120	Rock Lick	1850	1	330
Cawley, John	90	Lick Fork	1858	1	432
Chapman, Henley et al	330	Brush Creek	1851	1	346
Chapman, Henley et al	1,750	Blue Stone	1851	1	549
Christian, John H.	50	Laurel Creek	1851	1	351
Christian, John H.	50	Wts. Laurel	1851	1	350
Clarke, Rufus	110	Bet Lick & Horse Ford	1851	1	345
Clendenin, Archibald S.	80	East River	1843	1	290
Clendenin, Robert G.	50	East River	1848	1	311
Cook, David	216	Wts. New River	1853	1	380
Cook, David	25	Adj. G. Farley	1848	1	307
Cook, Ephriam	185	Tom's Run	1853	1	367
Cook, George	170	Big Pipestem	1855	1	405
Cook, Madison	120	Big Pipestem	1855	1	404
Cooper, Charles	20	12 Mi. Fork	1851	1	353
Davis, John W.	50	12 Mi. Fork	1851	1	347
Dunlap, John Robert	980	Blue Stone	1860	1	559
Ellis, James	235	Pipe Stem	1839	1	276
Ellis, James	150	3 Mi. Branch	1860	1	448
Ellison, Asa M.	30	Tom's Run	1854	1	396
Ellison, Asa M.	50	Tom's Creek	1848	1	308
Ellison, James	50	Camp Branch	1860	1	447
Ellison, Larkin T.	150	Tom's Run	1851	1	341
Eskridge, George et al	75	Lick Creek	1852	1	357
Farley, Andrew Jr.	100	Tom's Run	1852	1	364
Farley, Archibald	50 (15)	Adj. Drewry Farley	1838	1	283
Farley, Drewey Sr.	18	Tom's Run	1849	1	327
Farley, Gideon	50	Tom's Run	1854	1	392
Farley, Gideon	100	Clay Rock Branch	1857	1	417
Farley, Gideon	10	Little Pipestem	1850	1	332
Farley, Gideon	20	Adj. Robt. Gore	1842	1	286
Farley, James	90	Tom's Run	1853	1	370
Farley, Joel	160	Little Pipestem	1857	1	419
Farley, Levi	190	Cat Log, Wts. New Riv.	1848	1	309
Farley, Levi	100	Pipestem	1853	1	368
Farley, Melvin	50	Camp Branch	1853	1	381
Farley, Melvin	50	Pipestem	1857	1	418
Farley, Wilson	50	Pipestem	1853	1	369
Foley, Richard B.	350	Bluff Fork	1858	1	436
French, William H. et al	2,000	Brush Creek	1849	1	326
Gartin, Elijah A.	96	Joshua's Run	1852	1	360
Gore, Henry	65	Bull Falls	1857	1	421
Gunnow—or Gunnoe					
Gunnow, William	390	Leatherwood	1842	1	289

Name of Grantee	Acres	Local Description	Year	Book	Page
Hall, David	1,300	Laurel Fork	1850	1	557
Hall, David	2,830	Wolf Creek	1852	1	553
Hall, David	80	Glady Fork	1849	1	314
Hall, David	100	Brush Creek	1849	1	316
Hall, David	230	Brush Creek	1849	1	319
Hall, David et al	2,000	Brush Creek	1849	1	326
Hall, David et al	330	Brush Creek	1851	1	346
Hall, David et al	1,750	Blue Stone	1851	1	549
Hartwell, Andrew D.	100	Old Flat Top	1853	1	388
Harvey, Thomas	100	Lit. Pipestem	1850	1	328
Henton—or Hinton					
Henton, John	412	Meadow Creek	1840	1	279
Hinton, Avis	325	Madam's Creek	1850	1	336
Hinton, Avis	100	Pinch Gut	1850	1	338
Hinton, Avis	150	Madam's Creek	1850	1	337
Hinton, Even	475	Madam's Creek	1850	1	335
Hinton, Even	325	Madam's Creek	1858	1	424
Hopkins, Jonathan	105	Dry Fork	1853	1	372
Hopkins, Jonathan	100	Dry Fork	1857	1	423
Hopkins, Reuben	50	Big Pipestem	1858	1	431
Hopkins, Reuben	50	Lick Creek	1857	1	422
Hopkins, Reuben	100	Tom's Run	1854	1	391
Houchin, Bennet	60	Tallowry Mountain	1855	1	400
Houchin, Granvill	140	Wts. Blue Stone	1855	1	399
Hunt, Samuel	100	Tom's Run	1853	1	382
Hurst, William	100	Richland Creek	1856	1	410
Hurt, Robert	25	Tom's Run	1851	1	348
Hurt, Robert	45	Tom's Run	1853	1	383
Karnes, Madison et al	200	Richland Creek	1849	1	320
Keaton, Joseph	60	Big Pipestem	1859	1	439
Keaton, Joseph	70	Little Pipestem	1859	1	438
Keaton, Joseph	160	Little Pipestem	1850	1	329
Keaton, Leroy	100	Tom's Run	1851	1	342
Keaton, Leroy	100	Tom's Run	1855	1	402
Kinney, Nicholas C. et al	75	Lick Creek	1852	1	357
Landcraft, Grandison C.	200	Wts. New River	1855	1	406
Layne, Moses W.	100	Tom's Run	1850	1	331
Lilley, John	50	Madam's Creek	1841	1	282
Lilley, John	150	Madam's Creek	1841	1	281
Lilley, Robert	30	Pinch Gut	1841	1	280
Marshall, James	100	Bear Wallow	1846	1	300
Marshall, James	150	Flat Top Mt.	1849	1	324
Marshall, James	50	Big Fork	1849	1	323
Marshall, James	161	Wts. East River	1855	1	397
Marshall, William	50	Flat Top Mt.	1846	1	299
Martin, David	74	Tom's Run	1859	1	440
Martin, David	44	Tom's Run	1852	1	365
Martin, Hutson	129	Wts. Bluestone	1859	1	441
Martin, John	100	Piny Flat	1860	1	450
Martin, John	190	Brush Creek	1854	1	394
Martin, John	62½	Tom's Run	1860	1	449
Martin, Lorenzo D. et al	200	Laurel Creek	1852	1	362
McComas, Eli	100	Crane Creek	1859	1	442
McKenzie—McKinzie					
McKenzie, Alexander	225	12 Mile Fork	1845	1	293
McKenzie, John et al	140	Brush Creek	1860	1	446
McKinzie, Alexander	40	East River	1853	1	389
McKinzie, Alexander (McKenzie)	50	12 Mi. Fork	1853	1	386
McKinzie, John (McKenzie)	100	Wts. East River	1857	1	413
McKinzie, John A.	75	Stoney Ridge	1853	1	374
McKinzie, John A. (McKenzie)	40	12-Mi. Fork	1853	1	373
McNutt, Robert B.	150	Wts. East River	1853	1	371
McNutt, Robert et al	500	Lick Creek	1857	1	415

Name of Grantee	Acres	Local Description	Year	Book	Page
McNutt, Robert et al	1,000	Wts. Blue Stone	1857	1	416
Meador, Green W.	40	Blue Stone	1840	1	278
Meador, James P.	75	Wts. Blue Stone	1858	1	426
Meadows, Jeremiah	128	Leatherwood	1842	1	288
Means, Hugh	60	Lick Creek	1844	1	291
Means, Hugh	150	Isom's Branch	1846	1	294
Means, Hugh	60	Tom's Run	1851	1	349
Michie, Thomas J. et al	75	Lick Creek	1852	1	357
Middleton, Henry O.	240	East River	1845	1	292
Mills, Benjamin	50	12 Mi. Fork	1848	1	310
Neely, Harrison	40	Wts. Blue Stone	1860	1	452
Neely, Harrison	100	Wts. Blue Stone	1860	1	453
Neely, Harrison	115	Wts. Blue Stone	1857	1	414
Neely, John	50	Jarrell's Branch	1860	1	443
Neely, John	550	Pipestem	1838	1	284
Neely, John Sr.	125	Knob Ridge	1856	1	409
Newkirk, Stephen	85	Anderson's Falls	1857	1	412
Oney—See Owney					
Owney, William	300	East River	1849	1	321
Owney, William et al	200	12 Mi. Fork	1854	1	395
Pack, Josephas B.	75	Big & Lit. Pipestem	1859	1	437
Pack, Rufus	3	Island New River	1583	1	377
Pearis, Charles W.	175	Lick Creek	1849	1	312
Pendleton, Albert G.	590	Brush Creek	1839	1	277
Pendleton, Albert G. et al	320	Horse Ford	1851	1	343
Pendleton, Albert G. et al	270	Lick Creek	1851	1	344
Pennington, Parkeson F.	65	3 Mi. Branch	1856	1	408
Pennington, Parkeson F.	65	Sycamore Fork	1858	1	425
Pennington, William	125	White Oak	1849	1	318
Perdue—Perdew, Perdiew					
Perdue, David K. (Perdew)	500	Coal Branch	1853	1	387
Perdue, Zachariah (Perdiew)	450	Wts. Blue Stone	1849	1	315
Perdue, Zachariah et al	375	Blue Stone	1849	1	317
Peters, Elijah	150	Brush Creek	1849	1	313
Phillips, William	65	2 Mi. Branch	1856	1	407
Pine, Ballard	200	Tom's Run	1855	1	403
Pine, Ballard S.	120	Tom's Run	1860	1	445
Rolyson, Joseph	75	Madam's Creek	1842	1	287
Scott, Samuel	190	Camp Creek	1855	1	401
Shrewsbury, William	75	Richland Creek	1849	1	322
Smith, John et al	375	Wts. Blue Stone	1849	1	317
Snider, John	90	Jarrell's Branch	1860	1	444
Stewart, Elias	100	12 Mi. Fork	1850	1	339
Stewart, Robert	100	12 Mi. Fork	1853	1	376
Straley—or Straly					
Straley, Charles D. & H. W.	400	Scaggs Branch	1861	1	454
Straley, Charles D. & H. W. et al	140	Brush Creek	1860	1	446
Straley, Charles D. & H. W. et al	200	12 Mi. Fork	1854	1	395
Straley, Charles D. & W. H.	45	Stoney Ridge	1853	1	375
Straly, Chas. D. & W. H.	100	12 Mi. Fork	1850	1	334
Straly, Chas. D. & W. H.	50	12 Mi. Fork	1850	1	333
Thomas, Samuel	75	Wts. East River	1858	1	427
Thomas, Samuel	75	Wts. East River	1858	1	430
Vermillion, James R. et al	200	Laurel Creek	1852	1	362
White, Benjamin	55	5 Mi. Fork	1851	1	354
White, Benjamin et al	500	Lick Creek	1857	1	415
White, Benjamin et al	1,000	Wts. Blue Stone	1857	1	416
White, Thomas	129	Payne's Fork	1838	1	285
White, William & Andrew	1,930	Flat Top Mt.	1856	1	411
Wiley, Vincent	160	Lick Creek	1852	1	366
Wiley, Vincent	100	Lick Creek	1852	1	356
Wiley, Vincent	100	Lick Creek	1851	1	355
Woods, John H.	200	Lick Creek	1862	1	428

MONONGALIA COUNTY

Name of Grantee	Acres	Local Description	Year	Book	Page
Adkins, Edward	300	Mill Run	1793	4	394
Adkins, Edward	289	Beaver Creek	1788	4	6
Albin, John	390	Pedlar's Run	1785	2	4
Aldridge, John	80	Wts. Cheat River	1792	4	235
Alexander, Robert	200	Jim's Run	1793	4	148
Allen, Joshua	350	Wts. West Fork	1784	1	140
Allin, John	390	Pedlar's Run	1785	2	4
Allison, John	1,000	Salt Lick Creek	1786	2	519
Allison, John	1,000	Wts. Elk River	1786	2	521
Allison, John	1,000	Wts. Elk River	1786	2	520
Allison, John	1,000	Wts. Elk River	1786	2	420
Allison, John	1,000	Grannies Creek	1786	2	417
Allison, John	1,000	Big Sandy Creek	1784	1	336
Allison, John	1,000	Big Sandy Creek	1784	1	337
Allison, John	1,000	Big Sandy Creek	1784	1	267
Allison, John	1,000	Big Sandy Creek	1784	1	264
Allison, John	1,000	Big Sandy Creek	1784	1	266
Allison, John	1,000	Big Sandy Creek	1784	1	265
Allison, John	1,000	Sandy Creek	1784	1	262
Allison, John	500	Mill Creek	1787	3	441
Allison, John	500	Mill Creek	1787	3	440
Allison, John	500	Mill Creek	1787	3	442
Allison, John	500	Mill Creek	1787	3	444
Allison, John	500	Mill Creek	1787	3	446
Allison, John	500	Mill Creek	1787	3	447
Allison, John (or Joseph)	1,000	Duck Creek	1786	2	416
Allison, Joseph	1,000	Wts. Elk River	1786	2	407
Allison, Joseph (or John)	500	Duck Creek	1786	2	408
Allison, Joseph (or John)	1,000	Adj. his 2nd Entry	1786	2	409
Alton, Benjamin	520	Miracles' Run	1837	7	555
Alton, Joseph	190	Pawpaw Creek	1838	7	39
Alton, Samuel	440	Dunkard Creek	1837	7	547
Alton, Samuel	50	Dunkard Creek	1835	7	473
Alton, Samuel	46½	Dunkard Creek	1835	7	474
Ambers, John et al	75	Unknown	1822	6	248
Ammons, Joshua (Ammous)	90	Day's Run	1838	6	290
Amos, James	27	Amos' Run	1825	7	286
Anderson, Charles G.	100	Dunkard Creek	1827	7	312
Anderson, James	400	Simon's Creek	1784	1	139
Anderson, James	400	Simson's Creek	1784	1	186
Anderson, James	500	Hacker's Creek	1785	2	185
Anderson, James et al	1,000	Freeman's Creek	1784	1	367
Anderson, John	100	Day's Run	1828	7	332
Anderson, Joseph	1,000	Buffalo Creek	1786	3	243
Anderson, Joseph	1,000	Buffalo Creek	1786	3	242
Anderson, Levi	18	Dunkard Creek	1829	7	344
Anderson, William	1,000	Wts. Cheat River	1787	3	464
Anderson, William	1,000	Stratler's Run	1787	3	279
Anderson, William	1,000	Decker's Creek	1787	3	431
Anderson, William	2,000	Wts. Cheat Riv.	1787	3	450
Anderson, William et al	300	Cor to C. Donalson	1792	4	276
Anthony, Carrol	400	Dunkard Bottom	1787	3	376
Archer, John	200	Mill Run	1793	4	338
Archer, John	364	Little Sandy Creek	1786	3	87
Armot, Thomas	2,200	White Day Creek	1787	3	350
Armot, Thomas	1,200	Wts. Monon River	1787	3	259
Armstrong, John	1,000	Dunkirk's Creek	1787	3	420
Armstrong, John	1,000	Dunkert Creek	1787	3	343
Armstrong, John	1,000	Dunkert's Creek	1787	3	342
Armstrong, John	1,000	Dunkert's Creek	1787	3	339
Armstrong, John	1,000	Decker's Creek	1791	4	188
Armstrong, William	100	Dunker's Creek	1789	4	63

Name of Grantee	Acres	Local Description	Year	Book	Page
Bankman, John or Henry	128	Pedlar's Run	1804	5	522
Banks, Henry	4,500	Pine Swamps	1802	5	439
Banks, Henry	1,000	Little Sandy	1784	1	277
Banks, Henry	1,000	Little Sandy Creek	1784	1	279
Banks, Henry	1,000	Little Sandy Creek	1784	1	278
Banks, Henry	1,000	Tevebaugh's Run	1796	5	4
Banks, Henry	600	Judy's Mill Run	1822	6	247
Banks, Henry	5,000	Buffalo Creek	1787	3	296
Banks, Henry	2,000	Wts. Cheat River	1787	3	295
Banks, Henry	5,000	Adj. his 39th Sur	1787	3	297
Banks, Henry	4,000	Bingamon's Creek	1787	3	298
Banks, Henry	5,000	Adj. his 38th Surv	1787	3	299
Banks, Henry	5,000	Buffalo Creek	1787	3	300
Banks, Henry	1,000	Mill Creek	1785	2	170
Banks, Henry	820	White Day Creek	1785	2	171
Banks, Henry	3,350	Leading Creek	1784	1	387
Banks, Henry	1,920	Leading Creek	1784	1	388
Banks, Henry	2,720	Leading Creek	1784	1	389
Banks, Henry	6,400	Wts. Hughes River	1784	1	391
Banks, Henry	2,560	Horn Creek	1784	1	390
Banks, Henry	2,900	Wts. Hughes River	1784	1	392
Banks, Henry	1,120	Wts. Hughes River	1784	1	393
Banks, Henry	3,840	Wts. Hughes River	1784	1	394
Banks, Henry	960	Sand Fork	1784	1	396
Banks, Henry	1,875	Sand Fork	1784	1	397
Banks, Henry	1,310	Wts. Hughes River	1784	1	395
Banks, Henry	960	Sand Fork	1784	1	493
Banks, Henry	960	Sand Fork	1784	1	492
Banks, Henry	6,400	Wts. Hughes River	1784	1	491
Banks, Henry	7,680	Wts. Hughes River	1784	1	489
Banks, Henry	2,420	Wts. Hughes River	1784	1	490
Banks, Henry	2,560	Leading Creek	1784	1	488
Banks, Henry	1,040	Leading Creek	1784	1	486
Banks, Henry	2,080	Wts. Hughes River	1784	1	487
Banks, Henry	2,560	Cove Creek	1784	1	485
Banks, Henry	1,640	Wts. Booth Creek	1785	2	320
Banks, Henry	922	Coburn's Creek	1785	2	323
Banks, Henry	1,000	Buffalo Creek	1785	2	321
Banks, Henry	100	Buffalo Creek	1785	2	334
Banks, Henry	972	Coburn's Creek	1785	2	322
Banks, Henry	150	Buffalo Creek	1785	2	324
Banks, Henry	2,000	Buffalo Creek	1785	2	333
Banks, Henry	100	Buffalo Creek	1785	2	335
Banks, Henry	150	Buffalo Cr.	1785	2	337
Banks, Henry	150	Buffalo Cr.	1785	2	336
Banks, Henry	150	Buffalo Cr.	1785	2	339
Banks, Henry	150	Buffalo Cr.	1785	2	338
Banks, Henry	100	Buffalo Creek	1785	2	342
Banks, Henry	100	Buffalo Cr.	1785	2	340
Banks, Henry	150	Buffalo Creek	1785	2	341
Banks, Henry	150	Buffalo Creek	1785	2	343
Banks, Henry	150	Buffalo Creek	1785	2	344
Banks, Henry	150	Buffalo Creek	1785	2	346
Banks, Henry	150	Buffalo Creek	1785	2	345
Banks, Henry	100	Buffalo Creek	1785	2	348
Banks, Henry	100	Buffalo Creek	1785	2	347
Banks, Henry	150	Buffalo Creek	1785	2	349
Banks, Henry	2,000	Buffalo Creek	1785	2	350
Banks, Henry	100	Buffalo Creek	1785	2	351
Banks, Henry	150	Buffalo Creek	1785	2	352
Banks, Henry	150	Buffalo Creek	1785	2	354
Banks, Henry	150	Buffalo Creek	1785	2	353
Banks, Henry	319	3-Forks	1787	3	322

Name of Grantee	Acres	Local Description	Year	Book	Page
Banks, Henry	150	Buffalo Creek	1785	2	117
Banks, Henry	150	Buffalo Creek	1785	2	115
Banks, Henry	150	Buffalo Creek	1785	2	118
Banks, Henry	820	Booth's Creek	1785	2	121
Banks, Henry	150	Buffalo Creek	1785	2	116
Banks, Henry	1,000	Little Sandy Cr.	1784	1	351
Banks, Henry	1,000	Little Sandy	1784	1	350
Banks, Henry	1,000	Lit. Sandy Creek	1784	1	348
Banks, Henry	1,000	Little Sandy	1784	1	349
Banks, Henry	1,000	Lit. Sandy Creek	1784	1	347
Banks, Henry	5,000	Adj. his 40th Surv.	1787	3	353
Banks, Henry	2,560	Leading Creek	1786	3	1
Banks, Henry	2,000	Buffalo Creek	1787	3	393
Banks, Henry	5,000	Bingamon's Cr.	1787	3	394
Banks, Henry	5,000	Buffalo Creek	1787	3	395
Barckley—Barkley					
Barckley, Thomas	400	Wts. West Fork	1784	1	382
Barckley, Thomas	328	Davison Run	1784	1	305
Barckley, Thomas	311	Wts. West Fork	1784	1	383
Bare, John	10	Adj. Heirs J. Madison	1839	7	73
Bare, Michael	50	Miracle's Run	1828	7	333
Barker, James	400	Indian Creek	1792	4	312
Barker, James	28	Cor. John Barker	1824	6	263
Barker, John	386	Scott's Run	1787	3	396
Barker, John Jr.	42	Cor. to A. Cox	1822	6	249
Barker, Joseph Jr.	400	Indian Creek	1792	4	313
Barker, Joseph Jr.	400	Indian Creek	1792	4	310
Barker, Zachariah	300	Indian Creek	1800	5	388
Barker, Zachariah	150	Indian Creek	1798	5	177
Barker, Zachariah	43	On Pennsylvania Line	1821	6	238
Barkley—Barckley					
Barkley, Thomas	400	Simpson's Creek	1787	3	438
Barkley, Thomas	257	———— Creek	1787	3	511
Barkley, Thomas Jr.	212	Simpson's Creek	1787	3	510
Barkshire, Ralph et al	260	Robinson's Run	1811	6	94
Barley, William	62	3-Forks Creek	1819	6	220
Barnes—also Barns					
Barnes, Henry	474	Willis' Run	1799	5	267
Barnes, Henry	319	3-Forks	1787	3	322
Barnes, Henry	400	Adj. Springer	1801	5	428
Barnes, Henry	270	Wts. Monon. River	1809	6	40
Barnes, Henry	125	Wts. Monon. River	1796	4	492
Barnes, Henry et al	500	Adj. Jesse Bailes	1799	5	255
Barnes, James	200	Plum Run	1799	5	263
Barnes, Jesse	82	Strawberry Glades	1792	4	325
Barnes, Thomas	317	Buffalo Creek	1795	4	481
Barnes, Thomas	100	Adj. Richland Price	1802	5	443
Barnes, Thomas	381	Buffalo Creek	1785	1	539
Barnes, Thomas	338	Buffalo Creek	1785	1	538
Barnes, Thomas	365	Wts. Monon. River	1795	4	473
Barnes, Uz	400	Buffalo Creek	1787	3	168
Barnes, Uz	260	Plum Run	1787	3	184
Barnes, Uz et al	500	Rock Camp	1799	5	274
Barnett, Solomon	100	Plum Run	1838	7	40
Barns, Henry	400	Prickett's Creek	1789	4	93
Barrackman, John	128	Pedlar's Run	1804	5	522
Barrett, Frances et al	300	Sandy Creek	1799	5	276
Barrett, Frances et al	400	Sandy Creek	1799	5	277
Bartlett, Thomas	200	Wts. Tigert's V. Riv.	1785	2	11
Bartlett, William	600	Elk Creek	1785	2	258
Bartley, James	91	Dunkard Creek	1828	7	330
Barton, Daniel	311	Dunker's Creek	1787	3	249
Barton, William	1,400	Wts. Little Kanawha	1786	3	25

Name of Grantee	Acres	Local Description	Year	Book	Page
Claiborne, Richard Esq.	1,000	Stewart's Creek	1785	1	413
Claiborne, Richard Esq.	1,000	Adj. John Maylan's 29th	1785	1	510
Claire, Thomas	400	Booth's Creek	1783	1	39
Clare, Thomas	400	Wts. Salt Lick Cr.	1785	1	460
Clare, Thomas	400	Lick Run	1786	3	163
Clare, Thomas	400	Pringle's Run	1787	3	164
Clare, Thomas	405	Sandy Creek	1792	4	289
Clare, Thomas	1,000	Worthington Creek	1784	1	370
Clare, Thomas	1,000	Wts. Lit. Kanawha	1785	2	228
Clare, Thomas	400	Wts. Lit. Kanawha	1785	2	227
Clare, Thomas	126	Coburn's Creek	1784	1	184
Clare, Thomas	375	Laurel Run	1783	1	43
Clare, Thomas	195	James Ferry Run	1785	2	158
Clare, Thomas	394	Joe's Run.	1785	2	128
Clark—Clarke					
Clark, Abisha	100	Dunkard Creek	1825	7	284
Clark, Abisha	230	Dunkard Creek	1836	7	498
Clark, James	400	Sandy Creek	1784	1	171
Clark, Samuel	40	Adj. T. Moore	1798	5	214
Clark, Samuel	65	Flat Run	1843	7	137
Clarke, Abisha	70	Middle Fork	1837	7	545
Clause, John (or Henry)	1,400	Dr. Say's 2nd Entry	1788	4	5
Clear, Edwin	100	Dunkard's Creek	1841	7	105
Cleg—Clegg or Clagg					
Cleg, Alexander	342	Miracle's Run	1785	2	168
Clegg, Alexander	279¾	Dunker's Creek	1785	2	189
Cleland—Clelland					
Cleland, James	400	Salt Lick Creek	1795	4	463
Cleland, James	400	Pappaw Creek	1796	4	540
Cleland, James	400	Cor. to John Jessy	1796	4	491
Cleland, James	350	Wts. Cheat River	1786	3	127
Cleland, Patrick	112	Buffalo Creek	1831	7	376
Clelland—See Cleland					
Clelland, James	100	Buffalo Creek	1799	5	192
Clemens, John	420	Piles Fork	1842	7	112
Clouse—See Clause					
Clutter, Peter	277	Wts. Cheat River	1796	4	507
Clutter, Samuel	76	Adj. J. Crane's	1817	6	165
Clutter, Samuel	27	Cor. to his land	1817	6	162
Coburn, James	400	Decker's Creek	1787	3	328
Coburn, James	692	Decker's Creek	1795	4	479
Coburn, James	160	Lick Run	1787	3	283
Coburn, James	400	Coburn's Creek	1784	1	91
Coburn, James	228	Coburn's Creek	1784	1	126
Coburn, James	400	Coburn's Creek	1784	1	128
Coburn, Jonathan (Cobus)	300	Wts. Monon. River	1786	3	246
Cochran—also Cockran, Cohorn					
Cochran, James	400	Monon. River	1796	5	107
Cochran, James	250	Monon. River	1796	5	110
Cochran, James	250	Bingamon Cr.	1793	4	341
Cochran, John	400	Scott's Run	1791	4	186
Cochran, Nathaniel	100	Wts. Monon. River	1793	4	373
Cochran, Nathaniel	300	Teverbaugh's Run	1796	4	512
Cock, Andrew	340	Snake Creek	1784	1	193
Cockran—also Cochran, Cohorn					
Cockran, James	151	Wts. Monon. River	1784	1	146
Cockran, John	400	Booth's Creek	1784	1	343
Cohom—See Cohorn					
Cohorn, Nathaniel (Cohom)	150	Wts. West Fork	1784	1	154
Colbreath, James	500	3-Forks Creek	1792	4	280
Colbreath, James	500	3-Fk. Creek	1792	4	278
Colbreath, James	500	Muddy Creek	1792	4	281
Colbreath, James	500	Muddy Creek	1792	4	279

Name of Grantee	Acres	Local Description	Year	Book	Page
Colbreath, James	500	3-Forks Creek	1792	4	282
Colbreath, James	500	Adj. his 2nd Entry	1792	4	283
Colbreath, James	500	Adj. his 3rd Entry	1792	4	284
Colbreath, James	500	Adj. East Side 3rd Ent	1792	4	285
Colbreath, James	1,000	3-Forks Creek	1792	4	287
Colbreath, James	500	3-Forks Creek	1792	4	286
Colbreath, James	500	3-Forks Creek	1792	4	288
Cole, Draper	4	Dent's Run	1857	7	242
Collins, Isaac	1¾	Dunkard Creek	1860	7	262
Collins, Isaac	62	Kellum's Fork	1828	7	327
Collins, James	202	Wts. Monon. River	1797	5	132
Collins, John	400	Craft's Run	1791	4	211
Combs—See Cooms					
Compton, William	1,375	Dunkard's Creek	1793	4	371
Conaway, Charles et al	150	David's Run	1827	7	305
Conaway, Jeremiah	45¼	Buffalo Creek	1813	6	112
Conaway, John & Charles	223	Buffalo Creek	1823	6	262
Conner, Eliza	200	Adj. James Conner	1792	4	274
Conner, James	72	Cor. to his Settlement	1791	4	261
Conner, James	400	Wts. Cheat River	1784	1	148
Conner, John Jr.	328	Sandy Creek	1784	1	125
Conner, John Sr.	365	Big Sandy Creek	1784	1	90
Conner, Robert	300	Wts. Cheat	1784	1	127
Conway—See Conaway					
Cook, William	200	Dunkard's Cr.	1791	4	230
Coombs—See Cooms					
Cooms, Philip	33	Wts. Monon. River	1829	7	346
Cooms, Philip	2½	Adj. J. Tichenor	1835	7	471
Cooper, Frederick	96	Wts. Cheat R.	1784	1	101
Cooper, John et al	400	Sandy Creek	1809	6	49
Copenhaver, Isaac et al	100	M. Morgan's Run	1833	7	421
Copin T. (or L.)	100	Adj. Richard Field	1799	5	256
Coplin, Benjamin	362	Elk Creek	1785	2	177
Corbley—Corbly					
Corbley, Andrew	25	Dunkard's Creek	1838	6	289
Corbly, John	100	Dunkard's Creek	1838	6	283
Corder—See Carder, Carter					
Corder, Joseph	100	Wickware's Corner	1819	6	217
Core—See Cory, Koar					
Core, Christopher	20	Rudolph's Run	1831	7	375
Core, Michael	200	Adj. John Haught	1796	4	514
Cory, John	200	Tygert's V. River	1799	5	320
Cotheal, Isaac (Cottreal)	400 (460)	Miracle's Run	1797	5	124
Cotton, William	110	Adj. Peter Meirs	1837	7	544
Counts, Jacob	400	Muddy Creek	1784	1	224
Courtney, Michael	25	Robinson Run	1799	5	258
Cox, Abraham	441	Indian Creek	1797	5	47
Cox, Abraham et al	120	Charlie's Run	1801	5	417
Cox, Andrew	100	Dunkard Creek	1831	7	367
Cox, Isaac et al	1,000	Wts. Lit. Kanawha	1785	1	536
Cox, Isaac et al	100 (1,000)	Leading Creek	1785	1	537
Cox, Isaac et al	1,000	Adj. C. Rose's 9th	1785	1	531
Cox, Isaac et al	1,000	Adj. Crossley Roses 1st	1785	1	529
Cox, Jefferson	100	Dunkard Creek	1836	7	525
Cox, John et al	1,000	Adj. S. Young's 1st	1785	1	530
Cox, Moses	1½	Adj. Geo. Gallaspie	1838	7	41
Cox, Thomas	4	Adj. S. Grubb	1828	7	337
Craft, Thomas	400	Wts. Sandy Creek	1784	1	464
Craighead, George	300	Wts. Cheat River	1802	5	466
Craighead, George	736	Wickware's Creek	1802	5	487
Crain—or Crane					
Crain, Joseph (or Crane)	500	Wts. Lit. Kan.	1785	1	507
Crane, John	500	Worthington Creek	1785	1	508

Name of Grantee	Acres	Local Description	Year	Book	Page
Crane, Jonathan	54	Decker's Creek	1817	6	171
Crane, Samuel	50	Adj. Wm. Beggs	1799	5	240
Crane, Samuel	200	Muddy Creek	1799	5	193
Crane, Samuel	900	Wts. Cheat River	1808	6	35
Cratser, Simon	261	Adj. W. Robinson	1799	5	202
Cresap, Eliz. & Sarah et al	400	Bull Creek	1785	1	535
Cresap, Eliz. & Sarah et al	400	Crooked Run	1785	1	534
Cresap, Eliz. & Sarah et al	400	Decker's Creek	1785	1	533
Cresap, Eliz. & Sarah et al	400	French Creek	1785	1	532
Criss, Henry	50	Adj. Wm. Biggs	1793	4	392
Criss, Lewis	400	Sandy Creek	1793	4	379
Cross, George	34	Dunkard Creek	1851	7	221
Crossley, John	350	Muddy Creek	1802	5	484
Crouch, John Jr.	76	Adj. E. Petty	1789	4	79
Crouch, Joseph	85	Tygert's V. River	1786	3	160
Crow, Robert	347	Plum Run	1789	4	131
Crow, Robert	276	Plum Run	1789	4	106
Crow, Robert	259	Buffalo Creek	1787	3	282
Crow, Robert	253	Slack's Run	1788	4	1
Crowze, Elizabeth	400	Aron's Creek	1784	1	313
Crull, David	400	Aaron's Creek	1785	2	147
Crull, Henry	200	Wts. Cheat River	1784	1	78
Crull, Henry	200	Decker's Cr.	1789	4	57
Cumberlidge—See Cumbridge					
Cumbridge, George F.	15	Dunkard's Creek	1860	7	260
Cunningham, George	7	West's Run	1836	7	500
Cunningham, George	50	Decker's Creek	1829	7	355
Cunningham, George	214	Laurel Run	1820	6	225
Cunningham, George	100	Wts. Cheat River	1828	7	335
Cunningham, John	80	Drake Run	1837	7	556
Cunningham, Margaret	400	Maple Run	1790	4	159
Cunningham, Margaret	100	Decker's Creek	1786	3	241
Cunningham, Mark	275	West's Run	1788	4	41
Cunningham, Mark	200	Wts. of Cheat	1786	3	240
Cunningham, Patrick	2,000	Salt Lick Creek	1787	3	169
Currant, James	400	Wickware's Cr.	1789	4	84
Currant, James	385	Adj. John Wickware	1810	6	81
Currant, Martin	42	Adj. John Wickware	1806	6	306
Curry, David	20	Big Sandy	1818	6	189
Cushman, David	327	Adj. Thomas Cushman	1787	3	285
Cushman, Isaac	168	Lit. Sandy Creek	1800	5	383
Cushman, Isaac	250	Lit. Sandy Creek	1800	5	339
Cushman, Mary	50	Sandy Creek	1787	3	183
Cushman, Thomas	400	Sandy Creek	1783	1	38
Darling, James	20	Dunkard Creek	1856	7	240
Darling, William	150	Wts. Cheat River	1801	5	421
Darling, William	106	Wts. Cheat River	1804	5	515
Darling, William	400	Wts. Cheat	1785	2	282
Daugherty—or Dougherty					
Daugherty, John	205	Wts. Cheat River	1784	1	172
Daugherty, William	500	Pringle's Run	1796	4	510
Davey, Alexander W.	1,000	Roaring Creek	1788	4	35
Davey, Alexander W.	1,000	Roaring Creek	1788	4	31
Davey, Alexander W.	1,000	Roaring Creek	1788	4	28
Davey, Alexander W.	1,000	Roaring Creek	1788	4	25
Davey, Alexander W.	1,000	Roaring Creek	1788	4	15
Davies—also Davis					
Davies, William	100	Big Sandy Creek	1785	2	486
Davies, William	200	Big Sandy Creek	1785	2	485
Davies, William	200	Big Sandy Creek	1785	2	489
Davies, William	100	Big Sandy Creek	1785	2	488
Davies, William	200	Big Sandy Creek	1785	2	487
Davies, William	748	Big Sandy Creek	1785	2	490

Name of Grantee	Acres	Local Description	Year	Book	Page
Davies, William	200	Big Sandy Creek	1785	2	492
Davies, William	200	Big Sandy Creek	1785	2	493
Davies, William	200	Big Sandy Creek	1785	2	495
Davies, William	200	Big Sandy Creek	1785	2	491
Davies, William	200	Big Sandy Creek	1785	2	494
Davis, Bela	200	Decker's Creek	1846	7	172
Davis, Belah	100	Decker's Creek	1835	7	479
Davis, Belah	100	Dripping Springs	1841	7	91
Davis, Benjamin	400	Muddy Creek	1793	4	409
Davis, Elijah	100	Wickware's Creek	1824	7	272
Davis, Elijah	75	Wickware's Creek	1835	7	481
Davis, Eugenious	95	Dripping Springs	1851	7	220
Davis, John	2,000	Quarry Run	1800	5	363
Davis, John	400	Adj. J. Dower's	1800	5	364
Davis, John	700	Morgan's Run	1800	5	365
Davis, John	2,000	Sandy Creek	1800	5	367
Davis, John	2,000	Wts. Dunker's Cr.	1793	4	369
Davis, John	12¼	3-Forks Creek	1815	6	139
Davis, John	400	Big Sandy Creek	1817	6	154
Davis, John	500	Wts. Cheat River	1788	3	486
Davis, John et al	1,270	Roaring Creek	1800	5	366
Davis, John et al	200	Bingamon's Creek	1800	5	398
Davis, John et al	314¼	Dunker's Run	1800	5	396
Davis, John et al	800	Adj. Jacob Tetrick	1801	5	429
Davis, John et al	400	Wts. Yohogania R.	1793	4	408
Davis, Jonathan et al	1,505	Roaring Creek	1799	5	252
Davis, Joseph	400	Simpson Creek	1784	1	211
Davis, Joseph	400	Tygert's Valley R.	1785	2	148
Davis, Joshua	119	Snowy Creek	1796	5	12
Davis, Owen	131	Morgan's Run	1787	3	459
Davis, Owen	391	Carter's Run	1784	1	345
Davis, Owen	124	West Run	1784	1	340
Davis, Reuben	540	Wts. Tygert's V.	1819	6	216
Davis, Robert	175	Wts. Monon. River	1791	4	223
Davis, Robert	78	Wts. Monon. River	1791	4	250
Davis, Thomas	268	Wts. Monon. River	1784	1	342
Davis, Thomas	400	Wts. West Fork	1784	1	339
Davis, Weightman et al	260	Robinson's Run	1811	6	94
Davis, William	334	Wts. West Fork	1784	1	308
Davis, William	400	Little Sandy	1785	2	484
Davis, William	200	Little Sandy	1785	2	483
Davis, William B.	120	Piles Fork	1842	7	111
Davis, William (or Davies)	200	Big Sandy	1785	2	482
Davison—or Davisson					
Davison, Daniel	370	Washburn's Camp Run	1784	1	307
Davison, Daniel	600	Limestone Creek	1784	1	309
Davison, Daniel	400	Limestone Cr.	1784	1	481
Davison, Davis	400	Little Sandy Cr.	1785	1	504
Davison, Hezekiah	330	Booth's Creek	1784	1	115
Davison, John	1,000	Wts. Elk River	1786	3	97
Davison, Reuben	540	Wts. Tygert's V.	1819	6	216
Davisson—or Davison					
Davisson, Andrew	400	Elk Creek	1783	1	55
Davisson, Andrew	330	Wts. Monon. River	1784	1	112
Davisson, Daniel	400	Elk Creek	1783	1	53
Davisson, Hezekiah	400	Ten-Mile Creek	1784	1	384
Davisson, Isaac	370	Wts. West Fork	1783	1	50
Davisson, John	150	Wts. West Fork	1783	1	57
Davisson, Joseph	334	Davisson's Run	1784	1	198
Dawner—See also Downer					
Dawner, John et al	300	Cor. to C. Donalson	1792	4	276
Dawson, Charles	326	Flaggy Meadow Run	1784	1	325
Dawson, Thomas	190	Scott's Run	1787	3	424

Name of Grantee	Acres	Local Description	Year	Book	Page
Dawson, Thomas	307¾	Scott's Mill Run	1784	1	326
Dawson, William	225	Scott's Run	1784	1	282
Dawson, William Jr.	100	Scott's Run	1798	5	92
Deakins, Francis	429	Glade Creek	1802	5	444
Deakins, Francis & William	1,000	Stone Hill	1785	2	463
Deakins, Francis & William	926	Wts. Cheat River	1785	2	467
Deakins, Francis & William	192	Salt Lick Cr.	1785	2	465
Deakins, Francis & William	1,696	Limestone Hill	1785	2	464
Deakins, Francis & William	520	Wts. Cheat River	1785	2	468
Deakins, Francis & William	244	Wts. Cheat R.	1785	2	466
Deakins, Francis & William	287	Salt Lick Creek	1785	2	469
Deakins, Francis & William	897	Big Is. Cheat River	1785	2	470
Deakins, Francis & William	354	Glade Creek	1785	2	473
Deakins, Francis & William	114	Glade Creek	1785	2	471
Deakins, Francis & William	11,209	Adj. his 300 A. Tract	1796	5	561
Deakins, Francis & William	108	Adj. Andrew Miller	1797	5	86
Deakins, Francis & William	10,050	Wolf Creek	1796	4	494
Deakins, Francis & William	1,100	Adj. his 558 A. Tract	1794	4	423
Deakins, Francis & William	560	Salt Lick Creek	1794	4	422
Deakins, Francis & William	2,000	Adj. J. Goff	1794	4	421
Deakins, Francis & William	771	Laurel Run	1794	4	420
Deakins, Francis & William	634	Wts. Cheat River	1785	2	474
Deakins, Francis & William	222	Glade Creek	1785	2	472
Deakins, Francis & William	908	Glade Creek	1785	2	475
Deakins, Francis & William	146	Glade Creek	1785	2	476
Deakins, Francis & William	6,000	Wts. Yohogania	1789	4	549
Deakins, Francis & William	100	Adj. Robert Hooker	1796	4	538
Deakins, Francis & William	300	Salt Lick Creek	1785	2	478
Deakins, Francis & William	326	Salt Lick Creek	1785	2	477
Deakins, Francis & William	190	Wts. of Cheat River	1785	2	480
Deakins, Francis & William	897	———— River	1785	2	479
Deakins, Francis & William	279	Wts. Cheat River	1787	3	382
Deakins, Francis & William	1,000	Beaver Creek	1787	3	403
Deakins, Francis & William	1,000	Sandy Creek	1787	3	367
Deakins, Francis & William	141	Salt Lick Creek	1785	2	481
Deakins, Francis & William	1,500	Hd. Wts. Yohogania R.	1784	1	92
Deakins, Francis & William	337	Sandy Creek	1787	3	379
Deakins, Francis & William	314	Horseshoe Road	1787	3	456
Deakins, Francis & William	82	Salt Lick Creek	1787	3	455
Deakins, Francis & William	1,200	Dunkard's Bottom	1790	4	170
Deakins, Francis & William	1,800	Yohogania	1790	4	171
Deakins, Francis & William	500	Muddy Creek	1790	4	167
Deakins, Francis & William	509	Horse Run	1790	4	168
Deakins, Francis & William	122	Cheat River	1790	4	169
Deakins, Francis & William	793	Mill Run	1790	4	165
Deakins, Francis & William	41	Wts. Cheat River	1790	4	166
Deakins, Francis & William	663	Sandy Creek	1787	3	310
Deakins, Francis & William	499	Glade Creek	1786	3	102
Deakins, Francis & William	1,185	Horse Shoe Run	1786	3	103
Deakins, Francis & William	1,000	Beaver Creek	1787	3	363
Deakins, Francis & Wm.	280	Buffalo Lick	1788	4	43
Deakins, Francis & Wm.	783	Buffalo Cr.	1788	4	45
Deakins, Francis & Wm.	374	Wts. Cheat River	1788	4	44
Deakins, Francis & Wm.	437	Buffalo Lick	1788	4	46
Deakins, Francis & Wm.	103	Wts. Cheat River	1788	4	50
Deakins, Francis & Wm.	300	Buffalo Lick Cr.	1788	4	49
Deakins, Francis & Wm.	363	Buffalo Lick Cr.	1788	4	51
Deakins, Francis & Wm.	617	Wts. Cheat River	1789	4	124
Deakins, Francis & Wm.	113	Wolf Creek	1793	4	367
Deakins, Francis & Wm.	100	Dunkard Bottom	1793	4	368
Deakins, Francis & Wm.	400	2nd Cor. to Hicks Surv.	1794	4	419
Deakins, Francis & Wm.	83	Horse Shoe Road	1785	1	527
Deakins, Francis & Wm.	1,094	Horse Shoe Run	1784	1	354

Name of Grantee	Acres	Local Description	Year	Book	Page
Deakins, Francis & Wm.	500	Glade Creek	1784	1	353
Deakins, Francis & Wm.	281	Wolf Creek	1784	1	352
Deakins, Francis & Wm.	269	Wts. Yohogania	1784	1	280
Deakins, Francis & Wm.	882	Wolf Creek	1784	1	286
Deakins, Francis & Wm.	238	Wolf Creek	1784	1	283
Deakins, Francis & Wm.	558	Wolf Creek	1784	1	285
Deakins, Francis & Wm.	1,000	Yohogania River	1784	1	178
Deakins, William	450	Sandy Creek	1787	3	368
Deakins, William	442	Sandy Creek	1787	3	364
Deakins, William	212	Sandy Creek	1787	3	369
Deakins, William	138	Buffalo Run	1787	3	370
Deakins, William	680	Big Sandy Creek	1787	3	383
Deakins, William	432	Sandy Creek	1787	3	399
Deakins, William	594	Little Sandy Creek	1787	3	398
Deakins, William	1,227	Cor. D. Severns	1787	3	405
Deakins, William Jr.	300	Adj. F. Deakin's	1797	5	96
Deakins, William Jr.	200	Wts. Potomac	1788	4	48
Deakins, William Jr.	100	Adj. F. & W. Deakins	1788	4	54
Deakins, William Jr.	500	Slab Swamps	1787	3	404
Deakins, William Jr.	200	Wts. Yohogania	1787	3	401
Deakins, Wm. & Francis	315	Buffalo Lick Cr.	1793	4	329
Deakins, Wm. & Francis	152	Wolf Creek	1793	4	330
Dearing, Henry	50	Wts. Cheat River	1796	5	27
Dearing, Henry	200	Adj. Anthony Moreley	1796	5	15
Dearing, Henry	100	Dunker's Creek	1796	5	13
Dearing, Henry	80	Adj. Amos Roberts	1796	5	9
Dearing, Henry	200	Little Sandy Cr.	1796	5	7
Dearing, Henry	146	Briery Mt.	1796	5	6
Dearing, Henry	200	Elk Run	1796	5	5
Dearing, Henry	424	Salt Lick Creek	1800	5	345
Dearing, Henry et al	400	Wts. Yohogania R.	1793	4	408
Dearing, Henry et al	50	Booth's Cr.	1800	5	343
Deberry, John	100	Wts. Cheat River	1805	5	553
Decker, Susannah	165	Decker's Creek	1787	3	176
Deerduff, Jacob	250	Sandy Creek	1789	4	137
Demoss, Charles	50	3-Forks Creek	1834	7	440
Demoss, James	260	3-Forks Creek	1832	7	399
Denny, James	172	Buffalo Creek	1787	3	344
Denny, James	400	Adj. D. Scott	1788	4	22
Dent, John	306	Meadow Run	1798	5	213
Dent, John	44	Goose Creek	1800	5	334
Dent, John	400	3-Forks Creek	1796	4	496
Dent, John	650	Wts. Monon. River	1796	4	498
Dent, John	300	Wts. Cheat River	1796	4	497
Dent, John	400	Scott's Run	1786	3	135
Dent, John	363	Scott's Mill Run	1783	1	45
Dent, John	392	Booth's Creek	1784	1	183
Dent, John	450	Booth's Creek	1809	6	39
Dewitt, John	100	Adj. Matheny	1825	7	277
Des-Essart, Peter Poinset	1,200	Wts. West Fork	1785	1	459
DeValcoulon, Savery	1,500	Mill Creek	1785	2	280
Devers, James	100	Short Creek	1821	6	245
Dick, Alexander	4,000	Cedar Creek	1785	1	398
Dodridge, Philip	400	Decker's Creek	1786	3	86
Dodridge, Philip	500	Dunker's Creek	1786	3	125
Dodridge, Philip	400	Dunker's Creek	1786	3	221
Donalson, Charles	300	Martin's Run	1784	1	94
Donalson, Charles	268	Sandy Creek	1789	4	127
Donalson, James	200	Morgan's Run	1796	4	527
Donham—Dunham					
Donham, David	200	Dunkard's Cr.	1791	4	209
Doolittle, Moses	100	Wts. Monon. River	1796	4	535
Doolittle, Moses	160	Booth's Creek	1796	4	474

Name of Grantee	Acres	Local Description	Year	Book	Page
Dunn, James	128	Lick Run	1859	7	257
Dunn, James	17	Wts. Cheat River	1861	7	264
Dunn, Thomas	320	Adj. C. Gallagher	1843	7	148
Dunn, Thomas	75	Wts. Cheat River	1838	7	44
Dunn, Thomas	162	Lick Run	1838	7	43
Dunwoody, James	400	Wts. Lit. Sandy Cr.	1785	2	175
Dunwoody, James	236	Sandy Creek	1785	2	163
Dutchman, Jacob & George	100	Cor. to B. Weaver	1796	4	536
Duvall, John P.	150	Island in Ohio R.	1784	1	364
Duvall, John P.	480	Above Letart Falls	1784	1	360
Duvall, John P.	21	Island Ohio River	1784	1	362
Duvall, John P.	343	Wts. of Elk	1784	1	116
Duvall, John P.	400	Pringle's Run	1786	3	74
Duvall, John Pierce	400	Stone Lick	1784	1	197
Dyer, Edward	206	Hazel Run	1799	5	189
East, Robert	200	Buffalo Creek	1803	5	499
Eastburn, Esther	2,000	Adj. W. Tilton	1785	2	256
Eastburn, Esther	1,000	Warrier Fork	1787	3	423
Eastburn, George	1,000	Cor. J. Eastburn	1787	3	426
Eastburn, Hannah	1,000	Warrier Fork	1787	3	421
Eastburn, Jonathan	1,000	Warrier Fork	1787	3	422
Easton, David	2,000	Wts. of Cheat	1794	4	434
Eddy, Alexander	200	Pappaw Creek	1815	6	128
Eddy, Alexander	322	Miracle's Run	1809	6	70
Eddy, Alexander Jr.	2¼	Adj. John Downer	1841	7	100
Eddy, Alexander Jr.	62	Paw Paw Creek	1841	7	99
Eddy, David	72	Paw Paw Creek	1841	7	102
Eddy, Gawin	48	Indian Creek	1825	7	279
Eddy, Gawin (The Third)	100	Papa Creek	1829	7	341
Eddy, Isaac	147	Pappa Creek	1828	7	323
Eddy, Margaret	5a3r37p	Adj. James Barker	1831	7	383
Eddy, Michael	100	Furtney's Fork	1829	7	353
Eddy, Michael	20	Pap Paw Creek	1841	7	101
Eddy, Michael	49	Paw Paw Creek	1841	7	107
Eddy, Michael Jr.	60	Forks Lit. Paw Paw Cr.	1838	6	295
Edwards, Isaac	435	Andrew Davisson's Run	1784	1	484
Edwards, Isaac	400	Andrew Davisson's Run	1784	1	162
Eldridge, Daniel	1,000	Wts. Monon River	1797	5	88
Eldridge, Thomas	153	Deep Hollow	1814	6	121
Eldridge, Thomas et al	229	Wts. Cheat River	1810	6	89
Ellicott, Evan T & Andrew	41	Wts. Cheat	1846	7	173
Elliott, Abraham et al., Hrs.	354	Roaring Creek	1797	5	87
Ellis, Rowland	148	Sandy Creek	1793	4	399
England, John	73	Little Sandy Creek	1801	5	423
England, Samuel et al	100	Wts. Cheat River	1846	7	174
Evans, Dudley	100	Little Creek	1809	6	65
Evans, Dudley	296	Dunkard Creek	1809	6	66
Evans, Dudley	480	3-Fork Creek	1789	4	81
Evans, Dudley	340	Big Sandy Creek	1797	5	74
Evans, Dudley	1,700	3-Forks Creek	1797	5	129
Evans, Dudley	100	Swamp Run	1800	5	400
Evans, Dudley	80	Swamp Run	1799	5	238
Evans, Dudley	270	3-Forks Creek	1803	5	498
Evans, Dudley	73	Adj. John Stewart	1798	5	206
Evans, Dudley et al	2,000	Dunker's Creek	1797	5	34
Evans, Dudley et al	300	Monon River	1799	5	249
Evans, Edward	400	Wts. Monon River	1785	2	186
Evans, Enoch	7	West Run	1835	7	478
Evans, James	130	Plum Run	1838	6	296
Evans, James	600	Laurel Run	1851	7	222
Evans, John	1,000	Papaw's Creek	1798	5	219
Evans, John	489	Buffalo Cove	1800	5	399
Evans, John	372	3-Fork Lick	1789	4	82

Name of Grantee	Acres	Local Description	Year	Book	Page
Ford, Standish	4,000	Adj. his 54th Entry	1785	2	199
Ford, Standish	2,492	Adj. his 14th	1785	2	200
Ford, Standish	4,000	Adj. his 41st Ent.	1785	2	201
Ford, Standish	4,100	Wts. Little Kanawha	1785	2	209
Ford, Standish	4,000	Adj. his 10th	1785	2	202
Ford, Standish	100	Glade Run	1805	5	556
Ford, Standish	1,400	Coburn's Creek	1796	4	502
Ford, Standish	5,000	Little Pawpaw	1787	3	419
Ford, Standish	1,100	Adj. Laidley & Peters	1787	3	427
Ford, Standish	1,000	Big Sandy Creek	1787	3	429
Ford, Standish	1,000	Big Sandy Creek	1787	3	428
Ford, Standish	1,000	Booth's Creek	1787	3	338
Ford, Standish	300	White Day Creek	1787	3	337
Ford, Standish et al	500	Coburn's Run	1792	4	362
Forde, Standish	500	Doll's Run	1792	4	361
Forde, Standish	1,000	Hellons Run	1787	3	409
Forde, Standish	200	White Day Creek	1787	3	410
Forde, Standish	433	McDonald's Run	1787	3	413
Forde, Standish	1,000	Helms Run	1787	3	412
Forde, Standish	1,370	3-Forks Creek	1787	3	411
Forde, Standish	262	Cor. to his last Surv.	1787	3	414
Forde, Standish	1,000	White Day Creek	1787	3	415
Forde, Standish	4,000	Booth's Creek	1787	3	416
Forde, Standish et al	670	Wts. Tygert's Valley	1829	7	356
Forde, Standish et al	210	Indian Creek	1792	4	350
Forde, Standish et al	100	Adj. J. Prickett	1792	4	351
Forde, Standish et al	284	Dunker Creek	1792	4	353
Forde, Standish et al	442	Dunker's Creek	1792	4	352
Forde, Standish et al	138	Day's Run	1792	4	354
Forde, Standish et al	246	Dunker Creek	1792	4	355
Forde, Standish et al	500	Slatter's Run	1792	4	356
Forde, Standish et al	406	Mitchell's Run	1792	4	357
Forde, Standish et al	500	Hurst's Run	1792	4	358
Forde, Standish et al	500	Indian Creek	1792	4	360
Forde, Standish et al	500	Hurt's Run	1792	4	359
Forde, Standish et al	500	Dunkard's Creek	1792	4	364
Forde, Standish et al	500	Coburn's Run	1792	4	363
Forde, Standish et al	500	Dunker's Creek	1792	4	298
Forde, Standish et al	500	Dunker's Creek	1792	4	303
Forde, Standish et al	500	Dunker's Creek	1792	4	304
Foreman, Joseph et al	229	Wts. Cheat River	1810	6	89
Foreman, Richard	45½	Adj. James Conner	1809	6	80
Foreman, Richard	400	Wts. Cheat River	1802	5	453
Foreman, Robert et al	150	Muddy Creek	1800	5	424
Forgoson, John	400	Decker's Creek	1786	3	110
Fort, Jacob	450	Sandy Creek	1784	1	366
Fortney—See Furtney					
Frank, Michael	400	Wts. Monon River	1785	2	193
Frazee—See also Frazer					
Frazee, Ephraim	343	Sandy Creek	1784	1	188
Frazee, Hezekiah	441	Wts. Cheat River	1786	3	107
Frazer, David	400	Sandy Creek	1784	1	160
Frazer, Samuel (Frazee)	400	Sandy Creek	1788	3	492
Frederick, John	95	Booth's Creek	1833	7	435
Freeland, Elija	100	Piles Fork Buffalo	1838	6	282
Freeland, Elijah	125	Johnny's Run	1846	7	184
Freeland, Elizah	100	Buffalo Creek	1799	5	264
Freeland, John	65	Piles Fork	1835	7	485
Freeland, John	31	Adj. E. Blackshire	1842	7	128
Freeland, John	160	Piles Fork of Buffalo	1838	6	281
Freeland, John	150	Piles Fork	1831	7	364
Freeland, John	100	Piles Fork	1835	7	489
Freeland, Stephen	156	Buffalo Creek	1838	6	297

Name of Grantee	Acres	Local Description	Year	Book	Page
Gibbs, William	1,000	Adj. Wm. Tilton's 2nd	1785	2	208
Gibbs, William	1,000	Wts. West Fork	1786	2	397
Gibbs, William	1,000	Adj. John Malan's	1786	2	399
Gibbs, William	1,000	Wts. Little Kanawha	1785	2	81
Gibbs, William	1,000	Adj. Tilton's 3rd Ent.	1785	2	80
Gibbs, William	1,000	Adj. Tilton's 7th	1785	2	82
Gibbs, William	1,000	Adj. Tilton's First	1785	2	45
Gibbs, William	1,000	Wts. Lit. Kanawha	1786	2	513
Gibbs, William	1,000	Wts. West Fork	1786	2	514
Gibbs, William	1,000	Leading Creek	1786	2	516
Gibbs, William	1,000	Wts. Lit. Kanawha	1786	2	512
Gibbs, William	1,000	Leading Creek	1786	2	442
Gibbs, William	1,000	Land Fork of Lit. K.	1786	2	441
Gibson, John	260	Adj. Philip Woolridge	1796	5	30
Gibson, John	1,000	Mth. Tygert's Creek	1785	2	242
Gibson, John	1,000	Wts. Lit. Kanawha	1785	2	251
Gibson, Thomas	400	Wts. Cheat River	1799	5	271
Gibson, Thomas	50	Sandy Creek	1796	5	59
Giles, Aaron	36	Buffalo Corner	1819	6	208
Gilkerson, John	445	Wts. Monon. River	1788	3	542
Gilkey, David	310	Scott's Run	1787	3	172
Gillaspie—Gillispie					
Gillaspie, George	400	Wts. Monon. River	1785	1	453
Gillingham, James	500	Rt. Fk. Bargain	1791	4	243
Gillingham, James	1,000	Bingamon's Cr.	1791	4	242
Gillingham, James	500	Bingamon's Cr.	1791	4	241
Gillispie, George	400	Wts. Cheat River	1793	4	374
Gillispie, James	38	Wts. Cheat River	1804	5	507
Gillispie, John	1,000	Nauls Creek	1798	5	99
Giroud—See Gerard, or Jarart					
Giroud, Honore	3,000	Wts. Elk River	1785	1	456
Given, Frederick et al	400	Indian Creek	1792	4	322
Glen, Thomas	200	Stone Coal	1796	5	60
Glover, Isaac	100	Piles Fork	1845	7	163
Glover, Nehemiah	260	Unknown	1819	6	212
Glover, Peter	85	Piles Fork	1848	7	207
Glover, Samuel	250	Piles Fork	1846	7	185
Glover, Samuel	100	Buffalo Creek	1834	7	449
Glover, William	80	Dunkard Creek	1835	7	477
Glover, William	127	Dunkard Creek	1838	6	298
Gochenaur, John	100	Dunkard Creek	1829	7	357
Goff, Byram	38	Adj. Thomas Clare	1827	7	310
Goff, James	30	Wts. Cheat River	1796	4	541
Goff, John T.	868	Wts. Yohogania	1787	3	362
Goff, John T.	1,000	Wts. Yohogania	1787	3	354
Goff, John T.	500	Maryland Line	1792	4	290
Goff, John T.	160	Wts. Yohogania	1788	4	8
Goff, John Turton	1,000	Yohogania River	1787	3	302
Goff, Salathiel	152	Wts. Cheat River	1787	3	330
Goff, Salathiel	1,000	Yohogania	1785	2	76
Goff, Salathiel	250	Wts. Cheat River	1784	1	130
Goff, Salathiel	355	Wts. Cheat River	1784	1	124
Goff, Salathiel	250	Wts. Cheat River	1784	1	109
Goff, Salathiel & James	1,000	Wts. Yohogania	1787	3	392
Goff, Thomas James	800	Toley's Meadows	1787	3	301
Goff, Thomas James	310	Forks Cheat River	1784	1	131
Golding, John	400	Scott's Run	1787	3	263
Goodall, Park et al	2,000	Buffalo Creek	1805	4	531
Goodwin—See Goodwine					
Goodwine, John	400	Lost Run	1784	1	482
Gooseman—See Guseman					
Gooseman, Abram	400	Hellon's Run	1789	4	100
Gordon, Philip	130	Booth's Creek	1796	4	476

Name of Grantee	Acres	Local Description	Year	Book	Page
Hammilton, William	400	Adj. Nathan Lewis	1783	1	16
Hammilton, William	200	Laurel Run	1783	1	15
Hampton, Jacob	400	Tygert's Valley R.	1789	4	77
Hampton, Jacob	80	Wts. Tygerts V.	1807	6	25
Hampton, Jacob	400	Wts. Tygert's Valley	1796	4	515
Haney—See Hayned					
Harkness, Robert	400	Sandy Creek	1790	4	158
Hanna, William	400	Wts. Cheat River	1790	4	176
Hannah, John	1,000	Oil Creek	1787	3	165
Hannah, John	1,800	Wts. Elk River	1787	3	166
Hannah, John	1,000	Wts. Elk River	1787	3	167
Hannah, William	3,000	Oyl Creek	1786	3	4
Hannah, William	2,000	Wts. Elk River	1786	3	3
Hannon—See Hennon					
Hansher, William	400	Salt Lick Creek	1785	2	207
Hanway, David	2,000	Sandy Creek	1788	4	18
Hanway, David	255	Wts. Monon River	1788	3	489
Hanway, James et al	31	Adj. J. Harris	1801	5	432
Hanway, Jesse	334	Decker's Creek	1796	5	111
Hanway, Jesse	96	Decker's Creek	1796	5	109
Hanway, Jesse	310	Sandy Creek	1796	5	69
Hanway, Jesse	880	Decker's Creek	1800	5	340
Hanway, Jesse	248	3-Forks Creek	1804	5	310
Hanway, John	67	Swamp Run	1832	7	398
Hanway, John	150	Sandy Creek	1832	7	397
Hanway, John	9	Prickett's Creek	1835	7	482
Hanway, John	10	Day's Run	1846	7	175
Hanway, John	4½	Adj. Wm. Stewart	1842	7	134
Hanway, John	44	Kellum's Fork	1842	7	115
Hanway, John	450	Adj. John Ogden	1838	7	50
Hanway, John	300	Adj. David Piles	1838	7	51
Hanway, John	60	Dunkard's Creek	1838	7	1
Hanway, John	40	Adj. John Nuzum	1836	7	520
Hanway, John	35	Wts. Tygert's Valley	1836	7	513
Hanway, John	230	Day's Run	1835	7	490
Hanway, John et al	16	Indian Creek	1850	7	216
Hanway, John et al	1,200	Morgan's Run	1834	7	436
Hanway, John et al	260	Buffalo Creek	1846	7	182
Hanway, John et al	80	Piles Fork	1846	7	181
Hanway, John et al	500	Statler's Run	1844	7	150
Hanway, John et al	235	Buffalo Creek	1842	7	123
Hanway, John et al	500	PawPaw Creek	1841	7	81
Hanway, John et al	600	3-Forks Creek	1838	7	36
Hanway, John et al	400	3-Forks Creek	1838	7	31
Hanway, John et al	90	Drake's Run	1838	7	25
Hanway, John et al	670	Wts. Tygert's Valley	1829	7	356
Hanway, John Jr.	300	Pedlar's Run	1822	6	252
Hanway, John Jr.	48	Adj. L. Ridgeway	1822	7	282
Hanway, Rachael et al Heirs	120	Adj. Rob't Minis	1797	5	73
Hanway, Samuel	1,200	Prickett's Creek	1821	6	243
Hanway, Samuel	130	Cor. to W. Kinkade	1821	6	244
Hanway, Samuel	1,914	Decker's Creek	1820	6	223
Hanway, Samuel	400	Brush Lick	1820	6	222
Hanway, Samuel	300	Glady Run	1819	6	204
Hanway, Samuel	394	Salt Lick Creek	1787	3	180
Hanway, Samuel	367	Flat Run	1787	3	177
Hanway, Samuel	384	Buffalo Creek	1787	3	179
Hanway, Samuel	400	Wts. Cheat River	1787	3	319
Hanway, Samuel	1,000	Wts. Lit. Kanawha	1787	3	317
Hanway, Samuel	400	Wts. Lit. Kanawha	1788	3	490
Hanway, Samuel	175	Adj. J. Boyles	1791	4	255
Hanway, Samuel	600	White Day Creek	1813	6	116
Hanway, Samuel	21¼	Hellen's Fork	1813	6	115

Name of Grantee	Acres	Local Description	Year	Book	Page
Hanway, Samuel	400	Wickware's Creek	1813	6	114
Hanway, Samuel	100	Glade Run	1832	7	413
Hanway, Samuel	170	West Run	1789	4	60
Hanway, Samuel	1,000	Wickware's Creek	1789	4	56
Hanway, Samuel	1,000	Big Sandy Creek	1787	3	332
Hanway, Samuel	2,000	Steer Creek	1786	3	37
Hanway, Samuel	4,000	Big Steer Creek	1786	3	32
Hanway, Samuel	2,000	Big Steer Creek	1786	3	28
Hanway, Samuel	4,000	Steer Creek	1786	3	39
Hanway, Samuel	4,000	Steer Creek	1786	3	38
Hanway, Samuel	1,000	Tygert's V. River	1785	2	17
Hanway, Samuel	1,000	Big Sandy Creek	1785	2	19
Hanway, Samuel	1,000	Wts. West Fork	1784	1	357
Hanway, Samuel	400	Cedar Creek	1784	1	355
Hanway, Samuel	195	Adj. Enoch Moore	1784	1	331
Hanway, Samuel	348	Wts. Monon River	1784	1	379
Hanway, Samuel	1,000	Wts. Tygert's Valley	1785	1	543
Hanway, Samuel	1,000	Tygert's V. River	1785	2	231
Hanway, Samuel	3,220	Tygert's V. River	1785	2	262
Hanway, Samuel	5,000	Cherry Tree Fork	1785	2	265
Hanway, Samuel	10,000	Wts. Elk River	1785	2	263
Hanway, Samuel	615	Wts. Elk River	1785	2	267
Hanway, Samuel	440	Wts. Elk River	1785	2	266
Hanway, Samuel	1,000	Salt Lick Creek	1785	2	264
Hanway, Samuel	344	Wts. Elk River	1785	2	268
Hanway, Samuel	1,000	Davis's Run	1785	2	269
Hanway, Samuel	5,000	Sand Lick Fork	1785	2	270
Hanway, Samuel	2,560	Cherry Tree Fork	1785	2	271
Hanway, Samuel	5,400	Sand Lick Fork	1785	2	272
Hanway, Samuel	146	Decker's Creek	1800	5	352
Hanway, Samuel	1,000	Sandy Creek	1800	5	351
Hanway, Samuel	400	Adj. Wm. Postlewait	1805	5	549
Hanway, Samuel	228	Doll's Run	1805	5	550
Hanway, Samuel	32¾	Adj. A. Hardin	1805	5	548
Hanway, Samuel	546	Scott's Mill Run	1804	5	518
Hanway, Samuel	15	Isl. Monongalia River	1805	5	535
Hanway, Samuel	60	Adj. D. Scott's	1822	7	281
Hanway, Samuel et al	340	Little Sandy Cr.	1796	5	23
Hanway, Samuel et al	500	Sandy Creek	1788	4	32
Hanway, Samuel et al	100	Adj. J. Barker	1799	5	259
Hanway, Samuel et al	181	White Day Creek	1822	6	251
Hanway, Samuel et al	500	3-Forks Creek	1823	6	260
Hanway, Samuel et al	648	Decker's Creek	1788	3	532
Hanway, Samuel et al	500	Dunker's Creek	1792	4	304
Hanway, Samuel et al	500	Dunker's Creek	1792	4	303
Hanway, Samuel et al	500	Dunker's Creek	1792	4	298
Hanway, Samuel et al	18	Cheat River	1815	6	126
Hanway, Samuel et al	61	Adj. Moore & Ridgeway	1815	6	125
Hanway, Samuel et al	1,000	Decker's Creek	1813	6	110
Hanway, Samuel et al	246	Dunker Creek	1792	4	355
Hanway, Samuel et al	138	Day's Run	1792	4	354
Hanway, Samuel et al	406	Mitchell's Run	1792	4	357
Hanway, Samuel et al	500	Slatter's Run	1792	4	356
Hanway, Samuel et al	500	Hurst's Run	1792	4	358
Hanway, Samuel et al	500	Indian Creek	1792	4	360
Hanway, Samuel et al	500	Hurt's Run	1792	4	359
Hanway, Samuel et al	500	Coburn's Run	1792	4	362
Hanway, Samuel et al	500	Doll's Run	1792	4	361
Hanway, Samuel et al	500	Dunkard's Creek	1792	4	364
Hanway, Samuel et al	500	Coburn's Run	1792	4	363
Hanway, Samuel et al	5,000	White Day Creek	1805	5	545
Hanway, Samuel et al	1,149	Moody Creek	1802	5	450
Hanway, Samuel et al	1,000	Salt Lick Creek	1785	2	275

Name of Grantee	Acres	Local Description	Year	Book	Page
Hendricks, James	500	Mill Creek	1787	3	443
Hendricks, James	500	Mill Creek	1787	3	445
Hendricks, James	500	Mill Creek	1787	3	448
Hendricks, Joseph (or James)	1,000	Tate's Creek	1786	2	421
Hennon—or Hannon					
Hennon, Jeremiah	57	Adj. Jacob Lemley	1845	7	166
Hennon, Matthew	400	Dunkard Creek	1786	3	130
Henrie, Aaron	35	Adj. Wm. Dawson	1798	5	176
Henry, Aaron	76	Indian Creek	1787	3	355
Henry, Aaron	400	Scott's Run	1787	3	361
Henry, Otho	13½	Meadow Run	1832	7	417
Henshaw, William	400	Salt Lick Creek	1784	1	369
Henshaw, William	400	Salt Lick Creek	1784	1	368
Hepburn, William	922	Coburn's Creek	1785	1	496
Hepburn, William	922	Coburn's Creek	1785	1	497
Herford—See Hurford					
Hess, Jemima	400	West's Run	1811	6	92
Hevner, Nicholas	400	Scott's Run	1793	4	393
Hewes—See Hews, Hughes, Hughs					
Hewes, Josiah et al	1,000	Sand Fork	1786	3	235
Hewes, Josiah et al	1,000	Wts. Lit. Kanawha	1786	3	236
Hewes, Josiah et al	1,000	Adj. C. Rose's 7th	1786	3	237
Hewes, Josiah et al	1,000	Wts. Lit. Kanawha	1786	3	238
Hewes, Vincent	63	Johnnycake Run	1829	7	340
Hews, Josiah et al	1,000	Adj. S. Young's 10th	1786	3	133
Hews, Josiah et al	1,000	Leading Creek	1786	3	132
Hews, Josiah et al	1,000	Sand Fork	1786	3	137
Hickman, Joshua	28	Glady Creek	1827	7	315
Hickman, Joshua	4¼	Wts. Monon. River	1819	6	213
Highly—or Hiley					
Highly, Peter	77	Miracle's Run	1828	7	331
Higned, Barney	123	Scott's Run	1792	4	349
Hilegas—also Hillegas					
Hilegas, Michael	1,000	Wts. West Fork	1786	2	318
Hilegas, Michael	1,000	Dunker's Ck.	1786	2	319
Hiley—or Highly					
Hiley, George	273	Dunker's Creek	1785	2	187
Hill, Robert	400	Wts. Monon. River	1784	1	232
Hill, Robert	10	Adj. John Stealey	1799	5	269
Hill, Wm.	350	Hellen's Run	1796	5	2
Hillegas—or Hilegas					
Hillegas, Michael	1,000	Wts. Lit. Kanawha	1786	2	508
Hillegas, Michael	1,000	Dunkard's Creek	1786	2	511
Hillegas, Michael	1,000	Wts. West Fork	1786	2	509
Hillegas, Michael	1,000	Adj. Gibb's 8th	1786	2	510
Hillegas, Michael	905	Adj. Hillegas's 3rd	1785	2	300
Hillegas, Michael	1,000	Land Fork	1786	2	387
Hillegas, Michael	1,000	Adj. Reed & Ford 5th	1786	2	388
Hillegas, Michael	595	Adj. C. Rose	1785	2	389
Hillegas, Michael	1,000	Sand Fork	1786	2	390
Hillegas, Michael	1,000	Stuart's Creek	1786	2	391
Hilliam, Phinehas	400	Dunkard's Creek	1784	1	284
Hindgarden—or Hindgardner					
Hindgarden, Samuel	50	Dunkard Creek	1836	7	523
Hirons, Thomas	100	Grassy Run	1832	7	420
Hite, George	136	Sandy Creek	1800	5	353
Hite, George	200	Tygert's V. R.	1799	5	294
Hite, George	500	Dunker's Creek	1806	5	539
Hite, Mathias	177	Sandy Creek	1799	5	103
Hite, Mathias	200	Buffalo Creek	1800	5	301
Hixenbaugh, Abraham & Geo. Jr.	150	Briar Run	1842	7	133
Hixenbaugh, George Sr.	50	Adj. A. Hixenbaugh	1838	7	3

Name of Grantee	Acres	Local Description	Year	Book	Page
Ice, Frederick	12	Cole Run	1820	6	226
Ice, Jesse	87	Buffalo Creek	1825	7	276
Ice, Jesse	20	Buffalo Creek	1824	6	264
Ice, John	400	Buffalo Creek	1793	4	336
Ice, William	400	Buffalo Creek	1786	3	117
Inskeep, John F. et al	300	Dunkard Creek	1853	7	230
Irwin, James	50	Adj. David Morgan	1796	4	523
Irwin, John	500	Mericle's Run	1796	5	18
Isborn—See Osborne, Ozborne					
Isborn, John et al	81	Wts. Monon River	1796	4	477
Isener, Michael	190	Wts. Tygert's Valley	1785	2	155
Jackson, George	220	Elk Creek	1784	1	216
Jackson, Josiah et al	1,200	Morgan's Run	1834	7	436
Jackson, Samuel	40	Wts. Cheat River	1807	6	11
Jackson, Samuel	910	Ice's Ferry	1810	6	73
Jacobs, Benjamin	98	Coburn's Creek	1841	7	82
Jacobs, Benjamin	41	Coburns Creek	1841	7	83
Jacobs, Benjamin	18	Laurel Run	1836	7	519
Jacobs, Jacob	112	Teverbaugh's Run	1796	4	546
Jacobs, Jacob	88	Adj. L. Flowers	1791	4	190
Jacobs, Jacob	270	Teverbaugh's Run	1791	4	208
Jacobs, Jacob	250	Decker's Creek	1787	3	191
Jacoe, Reuben	180	Cor. to Thomas Berry, Jr.	1809	6	56
James—See Janes (Jones)					
James, Enoch	400	Wts. Monon River	1784	1	206
James, Enoch	1,000	Wts. Monon River	1784	1	165
Janes—See James—also Jones					
Janes, William	5	Swamp Run	1815	6	131
Jarart—Gerard, Giroud—also Jarrett					
Jarart, Aaron	400	Middle Fork	1790	4	160
Jarrett, William et al	18	Cheat River	1815	6	126
Jarrett, William N.	147½	Papa Run	1819	6	202
Jarrett, William N.	70	Craft's Run	1824	6	266
Jarrett, William N.	400	Laurel Hill	1826	7	302
Jarrett, William N.	20	Adj. Isaac Harrow	1827	7	320
Jarrett, William N.	60	Adj. Jemima Hass	1812	6	102
Jarrett, William N.	16¾	Adj. John Stealy	1814	6	122
Jarrett, William N.	38	Morgan's Run	1817	6	158
Jarrett, William N.	100	Wts. Cheat River	1809	6	59
Jarrett, William N.	20	Ridgway's Survey	1809	6	61
Jarrett, William N. et al	150	Adj. Newman Wade	1818	6	194
Jarrett, William N. et al	61	Cors. Moore & Ridgway	1815	6	125
Jarrett, William N. et al	164	Big Laurel Run	1808	6	30
Jarrett, William N. et al	1,000	Big & Lit. Laurel	1806	6	5
Jarrett, Wm. N.	24	Adj. Jacob Jones	1806	6	9
Jarrett, Wm. N.	160	Ice's Ferry	1804	6	4
Jeffers, Dennis	26	Roaring Creek	1818	6	177
Jeffs, James	300	Adj. his orig. Surv.	1806	6	7
Jeffs, John	56	Booth's Creek	1816	6	145
Jenkins—See also Jinkins					
Jenkins, Bartholomew	400	Slack's Run	1787	3	173
Jenkins, Bartholomew	94	Quarry Run	1787	3	289
Jenkins, Bartholomew	304	Wts. Cheat River	1782	1	7
Jenkins, Bartholomew	178	3-Forks Creek	1787	3	181
Jenkins, Bartholomew	251	Wts. Cheat River	1787	3	210
Jenkins, Bartholomew	200	Wts. Cheat River	1787	3	201
Jenkins, Eaven	250	Big Sandy	1791	4	221
Jenkins, Evan	800	Dunker's Creek	1809	6	45
Jenkins, George	200	Cor. to Wm. Norris	1789	4	129
Jenkins, James	496	Wts. Cheat River	1798	5	231
Jenkins, Joseph	400	West Run	1782	1	4
Jenkins, Joshua	400	Coburn's Creek	1784	1	452
Jenkins, Philip (Jinkins)	400	Booth's Creek	1788	3	537

Name of Grantee	Acres	Local Description	Year	Book	Page
Lemasters, Isaac	200	Buffalo Creek	1825	7	289
Lemasters, Lewis	100	Flat Run	1836	7	505
Lemasters, Shelton	140	Mahon's Run	1838	7	11
Lemasters, Thomas	38	Buffalo Creek	1836	7	529
Lemley—See Lemly, Lumley					
Lemley, George	300	Dunkard Creek	1841	7	562
Lemley, George	110	Dunkard Creek	1838	7	53
Lemley, George	115	Elk Lick Fork	1834	7	454
Lemley, George	66	Adj. Wm. Cotton	1838	7	54
Lemley, Jacob	100	Dunkard Creek	1841	7	90
Lemley, Samuel	151	Dunkard Creek	1856	7	238
Lemley, Samuel	9½	Dunkard Creek	1856	7	237
Lemly, Jacob	6	Adj. David Shockley	1852	7	226
Lemmon—See Leamon, Lemon					
Lemmon, Richard	1,000	Big Steer Creek	1785	2	545
Lemmon, Richard	1,000	Big Steer Creek	1785	2	544
Lemmon, Richard	1,000	Big Steer Creek	1786	2	538
Lemmon, Richard	1,000	Big Steer Creek	1785	2	543
Lemmon, Richard	1,000	Big Steer Creek	1786	2	539
Lemmon, Richard	1,000	Big Steer Creek	1786	2	540
Lemmon, Richard	1,000	Big Steer Creek	1786	2	542
Lemmon, Richard	1,000	Big Steer Creek	1786	2	541
Lemmon, Richard	1,000	Big Steer Creek	1786	2	537
Lemmon, Richard	1,000	Big Steer Creek	1786	2	536
Lemmon, Richard	1,000	Big Steer Creek	1786	2	535
Lemmon, Richard	1,000	Big Steer Creek	1785	2	534
Lemmon, Richard	1,000	Big Steer Creek	1786	2	531
Lemmon, Richard	1,000	Big Steer Creek	1786	2	530
Lemmon, Richard	1,000	Big Steer Creek	1786	2	532
Lemmon, Richard	1,000	Big Steer Creek	1786	2	529
Lemmon, Richard	1,000	Big Steer Creek	1786	2	528
Lemmon, Richard	1,000	Big Steer Creek	1786	2	533
Lemon—See Leamon, Lemmon					
Lemon, George	355	Crab Orchard Creek	1785	2	165
Lenham—See Lanham					
Lenham, Lucy	100	Booth's Creek	1797	5	125
Lewellen, John	40	Morgan's Run	1845	7	168
Lewellen, Samuel	391	Papaw Creek	1785	2	230
Lewellen, Samuel	300	Wts. of Cheat	1783	1	32
Lewellin, John	316	Wts. Cheat	1784	1	371
Lewellin, Samuel	400	Papa Creek	1783	1	36
Lewellin, Samuel	350	Indian Creek	1783	1	20
Lewellin, Samuel	400	Indian Creek	1783	1	19
Lewis, Benjamin	80	Day's Run	1845	7	169
Lewis, Benjamin	100	Day's Run	1828	7	328
Lewis, Philip	207	Scott's Mill Run	1784	1	301
Lewis, Richard	240	Amos Camp Run	1847	7	187
Leyming—Liming, Lyming					
Leyming, John	54	Prickett's Creek	1835	7	466
Ligney—See Signey					
Liming, Reason	1a. 1r.	Dunkard Creek	1859	7	266
Liming, Reason	4a. 1r.	Scott's Run	1858	7	265
Liming, Reason	3¾	Scott's Run	1855	7	245
Linch—See Lynch					
Linch, William	1,000	Adj. his 3rd	1786	2	448
Linch, William	500	Adj. his 1st Entry	1786	2	524
Linch, William	1,000	Adj. his 1st Survey	1786	2	523
Linch, William (Lynch)	500	Wts. Little Kanawha	1786	3	7
Lindsay, Levi	300	Dunkard's Creek	1789	4	86
Lindsay, William	153	Reed Island	1784	1	213
Lindsay, William et al	200	Adj. his Settlement	1798	5	211
Lindsey, Levi	1,000	Day's Run	1789	4	89
Lindsey, Mary	1,000	Wts. Lit. Kanawha	1790	4	177
Line, Henry	50	Adj. A. Braden	1801	5	408

Name of Grantee	Acres	Local Description	Year	Book	Page
Linn—See also Lynn					
Linn, John	36	Adj. Wm. Pettyjohn	1817	6	166
Linn, William	60	Glady Creek	1827	7	321
Little, Absolom	400	Glady Creek	1786	3	136
Little, Absolom (Litel) et al	400	Plum Run	1799	5	233
Little, Adonijah	400	Wts. Monon River	1787	3	208
Little, John	100	Papa Run	1787	3	284
Little, Stokely	85	Wts. Monon River	1799	5	290
Lockhard, George	190	Piles Fork	1842	7	113
Lockett—Lackett—or Sackett					
London, Bartholomew	100	Muddy Creek	1786	3	220
London, Bartholomew	500	Muddy Creek	1786	3	218
London, Bartholomew	400	Crab Tree Creek	1784	1	118
Long, Levi	50	Decker's Creek	1815	6	136
Long, Levi et al	150	Adj. Newman Wade	1818	6	194
Longwell, James	100	Papaw Creek	1789	4	117
Lott, Richard P.	294	Sandy Creek	1826	7	291
Lough—Low, Lowe					
Lough, Robert & Joseph	106	Meadow Run	1821	6	234
Loure, Joshua	395	Wts. Monon River	1802	5	472
Love, Samuel et al	500	Fks. Flat Run	1788	4	39
Low—or Lough, Lowe					
Low, Abraham	400	Indian Creek	1796	5	24
Low, Joshua	108	Wolf Pen Ridge	1784	1	151
Low, Nathan	388	Sandy Creek	1784	1	152
Lowe, Joshua	395	Birchfield Run	1788	3	536
Lowe, Joshua	395	Wts. Monon River	1802	5	472
Lowe, Philip	35	Spring Run	1831	7	379
Lowe, Philip	20	Wts. Monon River	1831	7	391
Lowry—See Loure					
Lowry, Joseph	420	Scott's Run	1818	6	188
Lowther, Joseph	156	Washburn's Run	1784	1	377
Loy—See Say					
Lucas, Roberson	400	White Day Cr.	1787	3	358
Luman, Joshua	150	Buffalo Creek	1801	5	420
Lumley—See Lemley					
Lumley, George	66	Adj. Wm. Cotton	1838	7	54
Lumley, George	110	Dunkard Creek	1838	7	53
Lumpkins, Charles	75	Craft's Run	1805	6	304
Lumpkins, Charles	56	Craft's Run	1798	5	209
Lusby, Josiah	1,400	Prickett's Creek	1787	3	349
Lusby, Josiah	2,000	Glade Creek	1787	3	348
Lyming—See Leyming, Liming					
Lyming, John	54	Pricketts Creek	1835	7	466
Lynch—See also Linch					
Lynch, Cornelius	1,500	Dunker's Creek	1798	5	93
Lynch, Cornelius	1,100	Farrows Run	1798	5	95
Lynch, Cornelius	400	3 Forks Creek	1798	5	94
Lynch, Patrick	40	Adj. David Sears	1800	5	357
Lynn—See Linn					
Lynn, Levi	400	Big Beaver Dam	1784	1	166
Lyon—Also Line					
Macabee, Zadock T.	27	Booth's Creek	1840	7	78
Maddera—See Maudeera					
Maddera, Nicholas	312	Dunkard's Creek	1800	5	348
Maddera, Nicholas, (Madeera) et al	200	Buffalo Cr.	1809	6	77
Madison, James	1,000	Buffalo Cr.	1791	4	258
Magill—See also McGill					
Magill, Charles	78	Adj. Thomas Laidley	1797	5	131
Malone, Thomas	220	Prickett's Creek	1835	7	492
Manear—Menier, Minear					
Manear, David	123	Clay Lick Run	1784	1	110
Manear, Jonathan	200	Wts. Cheat River	1784	1	103
Manear, William	200	Adj. R. Powell	1799	5	201

Name of Grantee	Acres	Local Description	Year	Book	Page
McCleery, William (McCleary)	147	Sandy Creek	1797	5	41
McCleland, Alexander	200	3-Forks Creek	1818	6	176
McCleland, John	384	Decker's Creek	1786	3	109
McColley, John	400	Hughes Creek	1786	2	449
McColley, John	400	Bone Creek	1786	3	22
McColum—See McCollum					
McColum, Daniel	352	Sandy Creek	1791	4	256
McCollum, James	365	Adj. John Judy	1782	1	3
McCord, John	10	Day's Run	1848	7	208
McCoy, William	300	Raccoon Creek	1799	5	295
McCrae, F. (McCrea)	18	Meadow Run	1808	6	28
McCrea, F. (McCrae)	140	Glady Creek	1800	5	303
McCreary—McCleary, McCleery					
McCreary, William et al	875	Wts. Elk River	1786	2	411
McCreary, William et al	3,000	Adj. J. Allison	1786	2	410
McCreary, Wm. et al	2,000	Duck Creek	1786	2	414
McCreary, Wm. et al	2,000 (5,000)	Wts. Elk River	1785	2	413
McCreary, Wm. et al	2,000	Wts. Elk River	1786	2	412
McCreary, Wm. et al	3,873	Wts of Elk River	1786	2	522
McCreary, Wm. et al	1,000	Wts. of Elk River	1786	2	462
McCreary, Wm. et al	2,000	Wts. of West Fork	1786	2	460
McCreary, Wm. et al	5,000	Wts. of Elk River	1786	2	461
McCreary, Wm. et al	3,000	Wts. of Elk River	1785	2	459
McCreary, Wm. et al	2,000	Wts. Lit. Kanawha	1786	2	446
McCreary, Wm. et al	5,000	Wts. of Elk River	1786	2	447
McCurdy, Benjamin	60	Papaw Creek	1847	7	193
McDanal, Uriah & Nancy	232	Flat Run	1828	7	329
McDaniel—See McDanal					
McDaniel, Nancy	8½	Flat Run	1838	7	42
McDaniel, William	100	Pleasant Creek	1796	4	534
McDaniel, William	155	Wts. Tygert's Valley	1802	5	457
McDiffit—McDavid, McDavit					
McDiffit, John	100	Piles Fork	1842	7	122
McDonald, James et al	1,000	Big Sandy Creek	1786	3	104
McDowell, Hugh	1,000	Decker's Creek	1785	2	114
McDowell, Hugh	1,000	Decker's Creek	1785	2	113
McDowell, Hugh	1,000	Decker's Creek	1785	2	112
McElfresh, Joshua	18	Wts. Monon River	1833	7	432
McFarland, John	351	Adj. W. Stewart	1798	5	179
McFarland, John	581	Reedy Creek	1787	3	158
McFarland, John	419	Leading Creek	1784	1	69
McFarland, John	400	Reedy Creek	1784	1	72
McFarland, John	1,000	Wts. Lit. Kanawha	1784	1	71
McFarland, John	86	Wts. of Cheat	1784	1	74
McFarland, John	400	Indian Creek	1784	1	81
McGee, James	78 perches	Adj. A. Hawthorne	1816	6	143
McGee, Thomas	220	Coburn's Cr.	1795	4	461
McGee, Thomas	200	Coburn's Creek	1789	4	59
McGill—See Magill					
McGill, Charles	234	Wts. Cheat	1794	4	431
McGill, Charles	62	Adj. his own	1807	6	24
McGill, Charles	400	Buffalo Creek	1796	4	518
McGill, Joseph	100	Plum Run	1835	7	475
McGraw—See also McGrew					
McGraw, Leonard	20	Lick Run	1854	7	231
McGrew, Patrick	143	Big Sandy Creek	1807	6	21
McGrew, Patrick	9	Adj. R. Foreman	1807	6	22
McGrew, Patrick	154 (454)	Adj. his original Surv.	1807	6	23
McIntire, Alexander	200	Little Sandy Cr.	1797	5	67
McIntire, James et al	200	Bingamon's Creek	1799	5	297
McKinley, Thomas	550	Papaw Creek	1799	5	300
McKinley, Thomas	30	Scott's Run	1800	5	302
McKinley, Thomas	43	Adj. James Harow	1808	6	32

Name of Grantee	Acres	Local Description	Year	Book	Page
Miers, Peter (Myers)	425	Adj. D. Barton	1818	6	193
Miers, Solomon	50	Pedlar's Run	1826	7	297
Milburn, John Jr.	206	Dunker Creek	1812	6	97
Miller, Andrew	91¾	Wts. Cheat River	1787	3	390
Miller, Jacob	1½	West Run	1847	7	188
Miller, Jane & Margaret	400(365)	Meadow Run	1791	4	187
Miller, Jesse	6	Pumpkin Run	1836	7	504
Miller, John	400	Wts. Monon River	1793	4	395
Miller, John Sr.	100	Wts. Cheat River	1784	1	144
Miller, Rebecca et al	181	White Day Creek	1822	6	251
Miller, Thomas	158	Booth's Creek	1789	4	58
Miller, Thomas	400	Wts. Monon River	1789	4	91
Miller, Thomas	640	Booth's Creek	1807	6	18
Miller, Thomas	242	Coburn's Creek	1784	1	111
Miller, Thomas	232	Glady Fork	1801	5	431
Miller, Thomas et al	496	3-Forks Creek	1796	4	482
Miller, Thomas et al	48	Wts. Cheat River	1802	5	478
Miller, Thomas et al	5,000	White Day Creek	1805	5	545
Miller, Thomas et al	500	White Day Creek	1798	5	203
Miller, Thomas et al	992	White Day Creek	1798	5	210
Miller, Thomas et al	615	Booth's Creek	1798	5	208
Mills, James	156	Narules Run	1785	1	503
Mills, Thomas	360	Cor. Richard Cain	1784	1	77
Miln—Milne					
Miln, Edmund et al	1,000	Leading Cr.	1786	3	132
Miln, Edmund et al	1,000	Adj. S. Young's 10th	1786	3	133
Miln, Edmund et al	1,000	Adj. W. Gibb's 9th	1786	3	134
Miln, Edmund et al	1,000	Sandy Fork	1786	3	137
Milne, Edmund	1,000	Walker Creek	1787	3	293
Milne, Edmund	1,000	Slate Creek	1787	3	375
Milne, Edmund et al	1,000	Sand Fork	1786	3	235
Milne, Edmund et al	1,000	Wts. Lit. Kanawha	1786	3	236
Milne, Edmund et al	1,000	Adj. C. Rose's 7th	1786	3	237
Milne, Edmund et al	1,000	Wts. Lit. Kanawha	1786	3	238
Minear—Manear, Menier					
Minear, David	105	Buffalo Creek	1786	3	75
Minear, David	260	Wts. Cheat River	1786	3	30
Minear, David (Manear)	52	Licking Creek	1786	3	78
Minear, Philip	200	Booth's Creek	1850	7	215
Minford, Jacob	200	Deep Hollow Run	1802	5	483
Minis—See also Minnis					
Minis, Robert (Minnis)	400	Decker's Cr.	1791	4	217
Minis, Robert (Minnis) et al	400	Wts. of Cheat	1789	4	144
Minnis—or Minis					
Minnis, Robert	18½ (8½)	Adj. McFarland's	1805	5	555
Minnis, Robert	548½	Sandy Creek	1803	5	502
Minnis, Robert	1,000	Adj. W. Anderson	1787	3	457
Minnis, Robert	1,000	Muddy Creek	1787	3	433
Minnis, Robert	500	Wts. Monon River	1788	3	514
Minnis, Robert	500	3-Fork Creek	1788	3	513
Minnis, Robert	200	Raccoon Creek	1788	3	505
Minnis, Robert	500	Wts. of Monon River	1787	3	467
Minnis, Robert	500	Wts. of Monon River	1788	3	468
Minnis, Robert et al	200	Buffalo Creek	1809	6	77
Minnis, Robert (Minis)	200	Wts. West Fork	1788	4	14
Minnis, Robert (Minis)	200	Wts. West Fork	1788	4	13
Minnis, Robert (Minis)	100	Buffalo Creek	1788	4	12
Minnis, Robert (Minis)	400	Adj. A. Harrison	1788	4	11
Minnis, Robert (Minis)	101	Laurel Run	1800	5	382
Minnis, Robert (Minis) et al	68	Aaron's Creek	1795	4	457
Minnis, Robert (Minis)	181	Pritchett Creek	1793	4	386
Minnis, Robert (Minis)	400	Plum Run	1793	4	385

Name of Grantee	Acres	Local Description	Year	Book	Page
Minor, Alexander	92	Dunkard Creek	1832	7	407
Minor, Elinor et al	400	Sandy Creek	1799	5	277
Minor, Elinor et al	300	Sandy Creek	1799	5	276
Minor, Lancaster	24¼	Day's Run	1855	7	246
Minor, Samuel	272	Day's Run	1829	7	339
Minor, Samuel	80	Day's Run	1800	5	362
Minor, Samuel	33	Dunkard's Creek	1838	7	56
Minthorn, Jacob (Minthous)	200	Deep Hollow Run	1802	5	483
Mitchell, John	148	Mine Run (Orange Co.)	1784	1	365
Molisee, Henry	100	Decker's Creek	1837	6	279
Moody—See Mudy					
Moody, Robert	200	Decker's Creek	1793	4	415
Moody, Robert	32	Decker's Creek	1793	4	416
Moody, Robert	243	Joe's Run	1787	3	434
Moore—See also More					
Moore, Daniel	49	Adj. Jacob Brookover	1848	7	210
Moore, David	400	Hazle Run	1784	1	322
Moore, Enoch	195	Muddy Creek	1784	1	332
Moore, Jacob	134½	Stateler's Run	1838	7	57
Moore, James	240	Wts. Cheat River	1785	1	404
Moore, John	45	Day's Run	1842	7	126
Moore, Philip	48	Stateler's Run	1838	7	12
Moore, Thomas	800	Sandy Creek	1784	1	189
Moore, Thomas	150	Big Sandy Creek	1784	1	119
Moore, Thomas	400	Sandy Creek	1784	1	316
Moore, William	30	Adj. Cannon's Surv.	1837	7	553
Moran, Hezekiah	170	White Day Creek	1826	7	300
Moran, Robert	170	White Day Creek	1855	7	233
More—also Moore					
More, John	45	Day's Run	1842	7	126
More, Michael	400	Slater's Run	1791	4	184
More, Philip	48	Statler's Run	1838	7	12
More, William	30	Adj. Cannon's Surv.	1837	7	553
Morehead, John	1,000	Vails Creek	1786	2	392
Morgan, Achilles	60	Buffalo Creek	1819	6	214
Morgan, Charles	400	Miracle's Run	1809	6	33
Morgan, Charles S. et al	150	David's Run	1827	7	305
Morgan, Daniel	300	Miracle's Run	1809	6	34
Morgan, David	1,000	Muddy Creek	1786	3	120
Morgan, David	30	Mud Lick	1834	7	453
Morgan, David	361	Junction W. Fork	1784	1	70
Morgan, David	50	Adj. Wm. Morgan	1819	6	221
Morgan, David Jr.	30	Prickett's Creek	1834	7	456
Morgan, Evan	160	Coburn's Creek	1784	1	143
Morgan, Evan	25	Adj. Benj. Drago	1803	5	500
Morgan, Evan B. et al	258	Hust's Run	1808	6	29
Morgan, Evans	100	Adj. John Miller	1791	4	248
Morgan, Hugh	200	Wts. Cheat River	1796	4	495
Morgan, Hugh	400	Wts. Cheat River	1784	1	192
Morgan, Jacob	15	Little Creek	1826	7	294
Morgan, Jacob	68	Wts. Monon. River	1834	7	451
Morgan, James	400	Wts. Cheat River	1784	1	194
Morgan, James	270	Cheat River	1805	5	557
Morgan, James	400	Dunker's Bottom	1792	4	308
Morgan, James	400	Wts. Monon River	1791	4	265
Morgan, James Jr.	15½	Buffalo Lick Run	1809	6	58
Morgan, James Sr.	20	Prickett's Creek	1836	7	512
Morgan, James Sr.	58	Prickett's Creek	1836	7	511
Morgan, John	97	Pickett's Creek	1825	7	290
Morgan, Morgan	400	Plum Run	1795	4	459
Morgan, Morgan	366	Little Creek	1786	3	232
Morgan, Morgan	361	W. Fk. of Little Cr.	1786	3	219
Morgan, Morgan	58	Adj. Aug. Smith	1809	6	48

Name of Grantee	Acres	Local Description	Year	Book	Page
Morgan, Morgan Sr.	400	Dunker's Mill Run	1791	4	205
Morgan, Stephen	400	Indian Creek	1791	4	197
Morgan, Tacquill	200	Cor. Abraham Low	1801	5	409
Morgan, Taguill	208	Adj. M. Morgan	1791	4	200
Morgan, William	400	Wts. Cheat	1783	1	25
Morgan, William	40	Wts. Cheat	1784	1	175
Morgan, William	143	Wts. Cheat River	1793	4	406
Morgan, William	400	Hether Big Run	1786	3	93
Morgan, William	66	Wts. Cheat River	1791	4	178
Morgan, William	100	Wts. Cheat River	1788	3	488
Morgan, William	66	Wts. Cheat River	1791	4	260
Morgan, Zackquel	220	Decker's Creek	1784	1	87
Morgan, Zacquill	400	Indian Creek	1793	4	383
Morgan, Zebulon	100	Prickett's Creek	1835	7	493
Morris—See Morriss					
Morris, Isaac	392	Mud Lick Run	1791	4	193
Morris, John	332	Sandy Creek	1784	1	321
Morris, Richard	150	Sandy Creek	1787	3	303
Morrison, James	400	Wts. of West Fork	1784	1	271
Morriss—See also Morris					
Morriss, Ezekiel	50	Doll's Run	1831	7	368
Morriss, John	600	Adj. Henry Banks	1787	3	357
Morriss, Richard	35	Piles Fork	1835	7	461
Morriss, Richard	400	Sandy Creek	1783	1	41
Moyers, Solomon	120	Pedlar's Run	1836	7	509
Moylan—See Maylan					
Mudy—See Moody					
Mudy, Robert	280	Adj. his Settlement	1789	4	111
Muir, John	1,000	Wts. Elk River	1796	5	20
Mulcher—or Melcher					
Mulcher, Isaac (Melcher)	1,000	Wts. Lit. Kanawha	1786	2	365
Mulcher, Isaac (Melcher)	800	Wts. Lit. Kanawha	1785	2	366
Mulcher, Isaac (Melcher)	1,400	Wts. Lit. Kanawha	1786	2	364
Mulcher, Isaac (Melcher)	1,400	Adj. J. Underwood	1786	2	368
Mulcher, Isaac (Melcher)	1,000	Wts. Lit. Kanawha	1786	2	369
Mulcher, Isaac (Melcher)	1,000	Wts. Lit. Kanawha	1785	2	367
Mulcher, Isaac (Melcher)	1,000	Wts. Lit. Kanawha	1786	2	370
Mumford, Edward	5,280	Wts. West Fork	1784	1	372
Murdock, George	2,000	Laurel Run	1787	3	512
Muri, Joseph	1,400	Adj. J. Mayland	1786	2	404
Muri, Joseph	1,400	Adj. S. Young	1786	2	405
Murphey—or Murphy					
Murphey, Harrison	212	Prickett's Creek	1837	7	543
Murphey, Harrison et al	112	Prickett's Creek	1827	7	309
Murphey, Marshall	100	Adj. Wm. Poe	1838	7	34
Murphy, Hugh Jr.	102	Adj. Gideon Howard	1796	4	486
Murphy, James	200	Adj. R. Evans	1791	4	249
Murphy, Marshall	110	Adj. Wireman's Surv.	1832	7	402
Murphy, William	170	Dunkard Creek	1837	6	271
Murphy, William Sr.	364	Murphy's Run	1785	2	156
Musgrave—or Musgrove					
Musgrave, Samuel	394	PawPaw Creek	1789	4	107
Musgrave, Zebulon	100	Prickett's Creek	1835	7	493
Musgrove, David	6	Poppy Creek	1822	6	250
Myers—Meirs, Meyers, Miers					
Myers, Charles	310	Adj. M. Yoakam	1787	3	454
Myers, Charles	54	Wts. Monon River	1787	3	417
Myers, Charles	198	Sugar Creek	1787	3	465
Myers, Jacob	250	Laurel Run	1834	7	450
Myers, Jacob	25	Dunkard Creek	1809	6	75
Myers, James	92	Indian Creek	1836	7	494
Myers, John et al	240	Hazle Run	1831	7	373
Myers, Peter (Miers)	425	Adj. D. Barton	1818	6	193

Name of Grantee	Acres	Local Description	Year	Book	Page
Myers, Solomon	120	Pedlar's Run	1836	7	509
Neal, James	400	Wts. Lit. Kanawha	1785	2	127
Neal, James	300	Stillwell's Creek	1785	2	162
Neal, James	500	Wts. Lit. Kanawha	1786	2	433
Neal, James	500	Wts. Lit. Kanawha	1786	2	378
Neal, James	400	Gnatty Creek	1784	1	200
Neal, James	800	Wts. Lit. Kanawha	1785	2	246
Neal, Joseph	400	Robinson's Run	1787	3	174
Neely, Thomas	1,000	Day's Run	1788	4	19
Nelson, Alexander	297	1st Isl. below Mth. L. Kan.	1786	3	8
Nelson, Alexander & Co.	269	2nd Isl. below Mth. L. Kan.	1786	3	9
Nelson, Joseph	100	Wts. Monon River	1797	5	45
Neusome—See Newsome, Nuzum					
Nevel, Henry	200	Muddy Creek	1798	5	178
Newport, James et al	5,000	Reedy Creek	1786	2	518
Newport, James et al	5,000	Reedy Creek	1786	2	403
Newsome—See Neusom, Nuzum					
Newsome, John et al	100	Tygert's V. River	1803	5	494
Nolan—See Nowland					
Nolan, Joshua	90	Elk Lick Fork	1828	7	334
Noose—Noos, Nuse, Nusz					
Noose, Jacob Sr.	300	Decker's Creek	1800	5	375
Noose, Jacob	88	Adj. Jacob Vankirk	1800	5	373
Norris—or Norriss					
Norris, David	100	Wts. Tygert's River	1813	6	113
Norris, David	200	White Day Creek	1799	5	248
Norris, William	400	Wts. of Cheat River	1782	1	5
Norriss, George	115	Tygert's V. River	1832	7	416
Notts—or Notz					
Notts, Absolom (Notz)	60	3-Fork Creek	1812	6	98
Notz, Absolem	296	Sandy Creek	1800	5	385
Notz, Absolem (Not)	500	Cove Run	1803	5	489
Notz, Absolom (Notts)	60	3-Fork Creek	1812	6	98
Nowland—See Nolan					
Nowland, John	200	King Run of Dunker	1792	4	387
Nuse—Noose, Noos, Nusz					
Nuse (Noose), Jacob et al	150	Camp Springs	1787	3	425
Nusz, Jacob (Noose)	732	Hughes Run	1789	4	74
Nusz, Jacob (Noose) et al	68	Aaron's Creek	1795	4	457
Nusz, Jacob Jr. (Noose)	34	Adj. James Coburn	1795	4	464
Nusz, Jacob Jr. (Noose)	192	Adj. S. Hanway	1795	4	462
Nuter—See also Nutter					
Nuter, Christopher	300	Suds Run	1783	1	23
Nutter—See Nuter					
Nutter, John	142	Simpson's Creek	1785	2	178
Nutter, John	400	Simpson's Creek	1784	1	385
Nutter, Matthew	283	Elk Creek	1783	1	21
Nuzum—Neusome, Newsome					
Nuzum, George	100	Prickett's Creek	1836	7	495
Nuzum, John	170	Wts. Tygert Valley	1829	7	350
Nuzum, Richard B.	12	Tygert's V. River	1841	7	89
Oakley, John	782	Wts. Yohogania	1788	3	529
Ochiltree, Isaac et al	150	Laurel Run	1836	7	527
Ogden, Aaron	1,000	Sandy Creek	1788	3	498
Ogden, John	1,000	Sandy Creek	1788	3	499
Oglesby, James	500	Bull Creek	1784	1	234
Oglesby, James	500	French Creek	1784	1	235
Olinphant, John & Andrew et al	168¼	Mason & Dixon Line	1805	5	559
Oliphart, John & Andrew et al	168¼	Cheat River	1805	5	559
Orr, John et al	200	Wooley's Mill Run	1787	3	366
Orr, John et al	1,000	Sand Creek	1787	3	377
Orr, John et al	200	Adj. J. Robinett	1787	3	365
Orr, William	660	Wts. Cheat River	1788	3	548
Orson, George	328	West's Run	1784	1	270

Name of Grantee	Acres	Local Description	Year	Book	Page
Payne, William G.	172	Dillon's Run	1809	6	79
Payne, William G. et al	2,000	Buffalo Creek	1805	5	531
Payne, William G. et al	575	Adj. James Morgan	1802	5	441
Payne, William G. et al	164	Big Laurel Run	1808	6	30
Payne, William G. et al	1,000	Big & Lit. Laurel	1806	6	5
Peace, Phillip	176	Poppaw Creek	1785	1	498
Peacock, Thomas et al	400	White Day Creek	1794	4	444
Peck, Jacob	295	Galloway's Run	1784	1	182
Pendell—Pindell, Pindle					
Pendell, Jacob et al	50	Wts. Monon. River	1798	5	215
Pennick, Garrett	1,000	Wts. Lit. Kanawha	1785	2	363
Pennick, Garrett	1,000	Wts. Lit. Kanawha	1785	2	362
Pentecost, Dorsey	3,000	Wts. Hughes River	1784	1	257
Pentecost, Dorsey et al	1,000	Wts. Hughes River	1784	1	250
Pentecost, Dorsey et al	1,000	Wts. Hughes River	1784	1	252
Pentecost, Dorsey et al	1,000	Wts. Hughes River	1784	1	251
Pentecost, Dorsey et al	1,000	Wts. Hughes River	1784	1	256
Pentecost, Dorsey et al	1,000	Wts. Hughes River	1784	1	254
Pentecost, Dorsey et al	1,000	Wts. Hughes River	1784	1	255
Pentecost, Dorsey et al	1,000	Wts. Hughes River	1784	1	253
Pentecost, Dorsey et al	1,000	Wts. Hughes River	1784	1	466
Pentecost, Dorsey et al	1,000	Wts. Hughes River	1784	1	465
Pentecost, Dorsey et al	1,000	Wts. Hughes River	1785	1	468
Pentecost, Dorsey et al	1,000	Wts. Hughes River	1784	1	471
Pentecost, Dorsey et al	1,000	Wts. Hughes River	1784	1	470
Pentecost, Dorsey et al	1,000	Wts. Hughes River	1784	1	472
Pentecost, Dorsey et al	1,000	Wts. Hughes River	1784	1	473
Pentecost, Dorsey et al	1,000	Wts. Hughes River	1784	1	474
Pentecost, Dorsey et al	1,000	Wts. Hughes River	1784	1	475
Pentecost, Dorsey et al	1,000	Wts. Hughes River	1784	1	477
Pentecost, Dorsey et al	1,000	Wts. Hughes River	1784	1	476
Pentecost, Dorsey et al	1,000	Wts. Hughes River	1784	1	480
Pentecost, Dorsey et al	1,000	Wts. Hughes River	1784	1	479
Pentecost, Dorsey et al	1,000	Wts. Hughes River	1784	1	478
Pentecost, Dorsey et al	1,000	Wts. Hughes River	1784	1	258
Pentecost, Dorsey et al	1,000	Wts. Hughes River	1784	1	259
Pentecost, Dorsey et al	1,000	Wts. Hughes River	1784	1	260
Pentecost, Dorsey et al	1,000	Wts. Hughes River	1784	1	261
Pentecost, Dorsey et al	1,000	Wts. Hughes River	1784	1	334
Pentecost, Dorsey et al	1,000	Hughes River	1784	1	333
Pentecost, Dorsey et al	1,000	Wts. Hughes River	1784	1	335
Perviance—also Purviance					
Perviance, Sam'l & Robt. et al	2,000	Duck Creek	1786	2	414
Perviance, Sam'l & Robt. et al	2,000	Wts. Elk River	1786	2	412
Perviance, Sam'l & Robt. et al	2,000(5,000)	Wts. of Elk	1785	2	413
Perviance, Samuel & Robt. et al	3,000	Adj. J. Allison	1786	2	410
Perviance, Samuel & Robt. et al	875	Wts. Elk River	1786	2	411
Peters, Henry	80	Adj. H. Tucker	1796	4	499
Peters, Robert et al	136	Booth Creek	1796	5	29
Pettit, Samuel	437	Scott's Run	1787	3	466
Pettyjohn, John	400	Wts. Tygert's Valley	1795	4	471
Pettyjohn, John	708	Wts. Tygert's V. Rivers	1784	1	215
Pettyjohn, John	400	Wts. Yohogania	1784	1	99
Pettyjohn, John	330	Wts. Yohogania	1784	1	95
Pettyjohn, John	200	Tygert's V. River	1787	3	356
Pettyjohn, John Jr.	200	Wts. Tygert's Valley	1794	4	442
Pettyjohn, John Sr.	100	Wts. Tygert's Valley	1800	5	331
Pettyjohn, Richard et al	400	Plum Run	1799	5	233
Pettyjohn, William	200	Wts. Tygert's V. R.	1785	2	194
Pettyjohn, William	100	Wts. Tygert's V. River	1799	5	291
Pettyjohn, William	400	Laurel Run	1793	4	382
Pettyjohn, William	100	Tygert's Valley R.	1796	4	544
Pettyjohn, William	390	Laurel Run	1787	3	397

Name of Grantee	Acres	Local Description	Year	Book	Page
Pindle, Thomas	250	Wts. Monon River	1785	2	133
Pindle, Thomas	175	Meadow Run	1787	3	385
Plum—See also Flum					
Plum, Jacob et al	75	Unknown	1822	6	248
Plum, John	300	Coburn's Creek	1786	3	119
Plum, John S.	22	Wts. Cheat River	1852	7	228
Plume, John (Plum)	200	Coburn's Fort	1797	5	75
Plummer, Robert	265	Booth's Creek	1785	1	528
Plummer, Robert	500	Booth's Creek	1784	1	483
Plummer, Robert	413	Booth's Creek	1784	1	312
Plummer, Robert	400	Booth Creek	1784	1	327
Poe, Francis	90	Wickware's Creek	1832	7	406
Poe, James A.	190	Wickwire's Creek	1838	7	58
Poe, Jonathan	100	Wickware's Creek	1825	7	287
Poe, Jonathan	90	Wickwire's Creek	1838	7	16
Poe, Jonathan	90	Wickwire's Creek	1838	7	15
Poe, Stephen H. (or W.)	90	Wickwire's Creek	1838	7	13
Poe, William	8½	Flat Run	1843	7	143
Poe, William	65	Wickwire's Creek	1832	7	425
Poe, William G.	75	Wickwire's Creek	1838	7	14
Pollock, James	400	Dunkirk's Creek	1785	2	150
Pollock, John	400	Robinson's Run	1785	2	239
Polsley, Jacob	138½	Wts. Monon River	1799	5	289
Ponket—See Pouket					
Pope, Joseph Sr.	400	Booth's Creek	1794	4	439
Popino, Elizabeth	500	Scott's Run	1792	4	236
Porter, David	400	Sandy Creek	1784	1	196
Potter, Russell	182	Sandy Creek	1799	5	268
Pouket, Isaac et al	400	Little Cr.	1789	4	73
Powell, Aaron	100	Cor. to John Manear	1793	4	411
Powell, C.	37	Day's Creek	1836	7	510
Powell, Isaac	12	Jones' Run	1856	7	234
Powell, Moses et al	200	Adj. his Settlement	1798	5	211
Powell, Richard	170	3-Forks Creek	1793	4	410
Powell, Richard	400	Decker's Creek	1788	3	506
Powell, Thomas	278	Sandy Creek	1788	4	27
Power, Magon	400	Elk Creek	1784	1	223
Powers, Morgan	400	Glady Creek	1785	2	301
Prather, James	400	3-Fork Lick	1784	1	181
Price, Caleb	80	Meadow Run	1810	6	84
Price, Caleb P.	250	Papaw Creek	1827	7	317
Price, Caleb P.	4	Robison Run	1845	7	165
Price, Charles P. et al	245	Laurel Run	1831	7	372
Price, Isaac	1,000	Papaw Creek	1804	5	516
Price, Isaac	1,000	Cor. to Thomas Laidley	1820	6	228
Price, Isaac I. (or J.)	4	Flaggy Run	1847	7	194
Price, John	22	Adj. T. Pindell	1818	6	178
Price, John	13	PawPaw Creek	1838	7	59
Price, John	20	Adj. Thomas Pindell	1838	7	60
Price, William	150	Statler's Run	1838	7	18
Price, William	37	Statler's Run	1838	7	17
Pricket, Isaac et al	400	Little Cr.	1789	4	73
Pricket, John	400	Wts. Monon River	1786	3	6
Prickett, Jacob	385	Wts. Monon River	1786	3	212
Prickett, Jacob	400	Wts. Monon River	1796	5	1
Prickett, Jacob	120	Prickett's Cr.	1794	4	433
Prickett, Jacob	180	Prickett's Cr.	1791	4	199
Prickett, John	376	Wts. Monon River	1794	4	430
Prickett, John	400	Wts. Tygert's V. R.	1791	4	198
Prickett, Josiah	373	Wts. Monon River	1786	3	108
Prickett, Josiah	22½	Wts. Monon River	1806	6	8
Pride, William	122	Hd. of Ralston	1797	5	44
Printer, William A.	1,000	Dunkard Creek	1787	3	381

Name of Grantee	Acres	Local Description	Year	Book	Page
Province, Sarah	96	Mill Creek	1784	1	275
Province, Sarah	1,000	Mill Creek	1784	1	346
Province, Sarah	400	Mill Creek	1784	1	375
Province, Sarah	333	Adj. his Improvement	1784	1	295
Province, Sarah	375	Mill Creek	1784	1	293
Province, Sarah	1,000	Mill Creek	1784	1	276
Province, Sarah (Provine)	270	Dunkard Creek	1799	5	285
Prunty, John	318	10 Mi. Creek	1785	2	252
Purdy, John	364	Horner Run	1785	2	167
Purviance—also Perviance					
Purviance, Samuel & Rob't et al	1,000	Wts. Hughes River	1785	1	468
Purviance, Samuel & Rob't et al	1,000	Wts. Hughes River	1784	1	334
Purviance, Samuel & Robt. et al	1,000	Wts. Hughes River	1784	1	333
Purviance, Sam'l & Robt. et al	1,000	Wts. Hughes River	1784	1	478
Purviance, Sam'l & Robt. et al	1,000	Wts. Hughes River	1784	1	477
Purviance, Sam'l & Robt. et al	1,000	Wts. Hughes River	1784	1	475
Purviance, Sam'l & Robt. et al	1,000	Wts. Hughes River	1784	1	476
Purviance, Sam'l & Robt. et al	1,000	Wts. Hughes River	1784	1	474
Purviance, Sam'l & Robt. et al	1,000	Wts. Hughes River	1784	1	473
Purviance, Sam'l & Robt. et al	1,000	Wts. Hughes River	1784	1	470
Purviance, Sam'l & Robt. et al	1,000	Wts. Hughes River	1784	1	471
Purviance, Sam'l & Robt. et al	1,000	Wts. Hughes River	1784	1	472
Purviance, Sam'l & Robt. et al	1,000	Wts. Hughes River	1784	1	466
Purviance, Sam'l & Robt. et al	1,000	Wts. Hughes River	1784	1	465
Purviance, Sam'l & Robt. et al	1,000	Wts. Hughes River	1784	1	254
Purviance, Sam'l & Robt. et al	1,000	Wts. Hughes River	1784	1	255
Purviance, Sam'l & Robt. et al	1,000	Wts. Hughes River	1784	1	256
Purviance, Sam'l & Robt. et al	1,000	Wts. Hughes River	1784	1	253
Purviance, Sam'l & Robt. et al	1,000	Wts. Hughes River	1784	1	251
Purviance, Sam'l & Robt. et al	1,000	Wts. Hughes River	1784	1	252
Purviance, Sam'l & Robt. et al	1,000	Wts. Hughes River	1784	1	250
Purviance, Sam'l & Robt. et al	1,000	Wts. Hughes River	1784	1	335
Purviance, Sam'l & Robt. et al	1,000	Wts. Hughes River	1784	1	479
Purviance, Sam'l & Robt. et al	1,000	Wts. Hughes River	1784	1	480
Purviance, Sam'l & Robt. et al	2,000	Wts. Lit. Kanawha	1786	2	446
Purviance, Sam'l & Robt. et al	5,000	Wts. Elk River	1786	2	445
Purviance, Sam'l & Robt. et al	5,000	Wts. of Elk River	1786	2	447
Purviance, Sam'l & Robt. et al	1,000	Wts. of Elk River	1786	2	462
Purviance, Sam'l & Robt. et al	2,000	Wts. of West Fork	1786	2	460
Purviance, Sam'l & Robt. et al	5,000	Wts. of Elk River	1786	2	461
Purviance, Sam'l & Robt. et al	3,000	Wts. of Elk River	1785	2	459
Purviance, Sam'l & Robt. et al	3,873	Wts. of Elk River	1786	2	522
Purviance, Sam'l & Robt. et al	1,000	Wts. Hughes River	1784	1	258
Purviance, Sam'l & Robt. et al	1,000	Wts. Hughes River	1784	1	260
Purviance, Sam'l & Robt. et al	1,000	Wts. Hughes River	1784	1	261
Purviance, Sam'l & Robt. et al	1,000	Wts. Hughes River	1784	1	259
Quandrill, John	1,000	Sandy Creek	1788	3	500
Ragnet, Nicholas	1,300	Reedy Creek	1787	3	275
Ragnet, Nicholas	1,100	Reedy Creek	1787	3	273
Ragnet, Nicholas	600	Wts. Lit. Kanawha	1787	3	271
Ragnet, Nicholas	1,000	Wts. Lit. Kanawha	1787	3	270
Ragnet, Nicholas	1,400	Adj. Dr. Say's 3rd	1787	3	258
Ragnet, Nicholas	1,000	Wts. Lit. Kanawha	1787	3	257
Ragnet, Nicholas	1,400	Wts. Lit. Kanawha	1787	3	197
Ragnet, Nicholas	1,300	Adj. his 3rd Survey	1787	3	195
Ragnet, Nicholas	1,400	Adj. J. Moylan	1787	3	196
Ragnet, Nicholas	1,300	Walker's Branch	1787	3	193
Ragnet, Nicholas	1,300	Adj. Dr. Say's 6th	1787	3	194
Ragnet, Nicholas (Claudius Paul)	1,400	Adj. Dr. Says 4th	1787	3	274
Raguet—or Ragnet					
Rainey, Ann	1,000	Wts. Elk River	1787	3	346
Rainey, John	1,000	Wts. Elk River	1787	3	170
Ramsey, Andrew	57	Wts. Cheat River	1793	4	425

Name of Grantee	Acres	Local Description	Year	Book	Page
Ramsey, Andrew	100	Wts. Cheat River	1789	4	132
Ramsey, Andrew	100	Wts. Cheat River	1788	3	502
Ramsey, Charles	100	Adj. T. Butler	1799	5	183
Ramsey, John	3½	Scott's Run	1841	7	98
Ramsey, John	388	Wts. Cheat River	1809	6	50
Ramsey, John	400	Scott's Mill Run	1784	1	298
Ramsey, John	348	Ice's Place	1784	1	133
Ramsey, John et al	273	Wts. Cheat River	1796	4	490
Ramsey, John et al	1,000	Adj. Crossley Roses 1st	1785	1	529
Ramsey, John et al	1,000	Adj. S. Young's 1st	1785	1	530
Ramsey, John et al	1,000	Adj. C. Rose's 9th	1785	1	531
Ramsey, John et al	1,000	Wts. Lit. Kanawha	1785	1	536
Ramsey, John et al	100 (1,000)	Leading Creek	1785	1	537
Ramsey, John Jr.	185	Wts. Cheat River	1791	4	269
Ramsey, William	112	Adj. John Ramsey	1809	6	55
Ramsey, William	82	Adj. John Ramsey	1809	6	53
Randal—or Randall					
Randal, James	51	Robinson's Run	1799	5	198
Randall, Abel	127	Black Fork	1785	2	298
Ratcliff, John	349	Elk Creek	1784	1	289
Ray—also Rea					
Ray, George S. et al	24	Dunkard Creek	1848	7	204
Ray, Thomas P.	3,000	Wts. Cheat River	1837	7	541
Ray, Thomas P.	3,000	Laurel Run	1832	7	423
Ray, Thomas P. et al	500	3-Forks Creek	1823	6	260
Ray, Thomas P. et al	600	3-Forks Creek	1838	7	36
Ray, Thomas P. et al	400	3-Forks Creek	1838	7	31
Ray, William et al	5,000	Reedy Creek	1786	2	518
Ray, William et al	5,000	Reedy Creek	1786	2	403
Rea—also Ray					
Rea, Adley	185½	Booth's Creek	1793	4	333
Redman, John et al	5,000	Reedy Creek	1786	2	518
Redman, John et al	5,000	Reedy Creek	1786	2	403
Reed & Ford	1,000	Adj. Tilton's 4th	1785	2	59
Reed & Ford	1,000	Adj. Wm. Gibb's 1st	1785	2	32
Reed & Ford	1,000	Adj. Wm. Gibb's 3rd	1785	2	57
Reed & Ford	1,000	Adj. Wm. Gibb's 7th	1785	2	26
Reed & Ford	1,000	Adj. Wm. Tilton's 8th	1785	2	27
Reed & Ford	1,000	Adj. Wm. Tilton	1785	2	24
Reed & Ford	1,000	Adj. Wm. Gibb's 8th	1785	2	25
Reed & Ford	1,000	Adj. Wm. Teter's	1785	2	21
Reed & Ford	1,000	Adj. Wm. Gibb's	1785	2	22
Reed & Ford	1,000	Adj. Wm. Gibb's 6th	1785	2	23
Reed & Ford	8,000	French Creek	1786	3	17
Reed & Ford	2,000	French Creek	1786	3	16
Reed, Francis	400	Wts. West Fork	1785	2	179
Reed, Francis	555	Crooked Run	1787	3	458
Reed, George	160	Laurel Run	1816	6	173
Reed, George	147	Big Sandy Creek	1784	1	330
Reed, John	1,000	Steer Creek	1786	3	44
Reed, John	1,000	Steer Creek	1786	3	43
Reed, John	1,000	Steer Creek	1786	3	45
Reed, John	1,000	Steer Creek	1786	3	47
Reed, John	1,000	Steer Creek	1786	3	49
Reed, John	1,000	Steer Creek	1786	3	46
Reed, John	1,000	Steer Creek	1786	3	48
Reed, John	1,000	Steer Creek	1786	3	51
Reed, John	1,000	Steer Creek	1786	3	54
Reed, John	1,000	Steer Creek	1786	3	50
Reed, John	1,000	Steer Creek	1786	3	53
Reed, John	1,000	Steer Creek	1786	3	52
Reed, John	1,000	Steer Creek	1786	3	55
Reed, John	1,000	Steer Creek	1786	3	56

Name of Grantee	Acres	Local Description	Year	Book	Page
Scott, David et al	400	Indian Cr.	1792	4	322
Scott, David Jr.	950	Monon River	1800	5	321
Scott, David Jr.	400	Wts. Monon River	1794	4	436
Scott, David Sr.	500	Pappa Creek	1796	4	542
Scott, Hannah	400	Wts. Monon River	1797	5	89
Scott, Hannah	400	Pappa Creek	1797	5	49
Scott, Jacob	400	Scott's Run	1791	4	185
Scott, Jacob	200	Wts. Monon River	1791	4	204
Scott, Jacob	400	Indian Creek	1799	5	229
Scott, Jacob	182	Adj. Robert Davis	1798	5	205
Scott, Jacob	5	Adj. Isaac Lemaster	1827	7	313
Scott, Jemima	400	West Run	1791	4	247
Scott, John	400	Wts. of Cheat	1784	1	75
Scott, John	389	Wts. of Cheat	1784	1	76
Scott, John	93	Muddy Creek	1805	5	543
Scratcher—See Seratcher, Seratiher					
Scrip, William	70	Adj. J. Jacobs	1796	5	19
Sears, David & Daniel	400	Lewis Run	1789	4	118
See—See Lee					
Selser—Selson, Sulser					
Selson, John (or Selsor)	75	Wts. Kanawha	1786	2	276
Sepott, George	60	Adj. Wm. Biggs	1792	4	316
Seratiher, Simon	300	Prickett's Creek	1788	3	485
Seratiher, Simon	400	Prickett's Creek	1788	3	487
Severans—Severns, Soverns					
Severans, Absolom	100	Wts. Cheat River	1792	4	320
Severans, Absolom	200	Muddy Creek	1792	4	319
Severans, Joseph	118	Sandy Creek	1792	4	317
Severans, Joseph	82	Sandy Creek	1792	4	318
Severns, Daniel	141	Adj. his Settlement	1798	5	217
Sevour, Robert	400	Sandy Creek	1795	4	456
Shackleford, Benjamin	1,353	Adj. W. Johnston	1796	5	21
Shacklesworth, Philip	374	Tom's Run	1787	3	204
Shafer, Aaron	80	Adj. Thomas Dunn	1847	7	195
Shafer, David	81	Adj. Dolly Horner	1846	7	176
Shafer, David & Henry	200	Bee Run	1837	7	542
Shafer, Dennis M.	2	Adj. John Camp	1859	7	258
Shafer, Henry	50	Lick Run	1844	7	153
Shahan—See Shehan					
Shahan, William	125	Horse Run	1835	7	486
Sharp, Aaron	150	Mill Run	1832	7	403
Shaw, Alexander	152	Adj. A. Severns	1815	6	134
Shaw, Alexander	32	Adj. Elisha Biggs	1815	6	132
Shaw, James et al	273	Wts. Cheat River	1796	4	490
Shaw, Samuel	272	Adj. J. Parker	1818	6	186
Sheath, John	100	Wts. Cheat	1807	6	17
Shehan—also Shahan					
Shehan, George Jr.	62	Sandy Creek	1819	6	205
Shiel—also Shields, Shiele					
Shiel, Dr. Hugh	961	Sand Fork	1786	3	269
Shiel, Hugh	1,000	Wts. Lit. Kanawha	1786	3	268
Shiel, Hugh	1,000	Wts. Lit. Kanawha	1786	3	267
Shields, John et al	5,000	Reedy Creek	1786	2	403
Shields, John et al	5,000	Reedy Creek	1786	2	518
Shiele—Shiel, Shields					
Shiele, Dr. Hugh	1,000	Adj. Wm. Gibb's 3rd	1786	3	148
Shiele, Dr. Hugh	1,000	Wts. Lit. Kanawha	1786	3	143
Shin—or Shinn					
Shin, Benjamin	400	Simpson's Cr.	1785	2	183
Shin, Benjamin	226	Simpson's Cr.	1785	2	182
Shinn, George	96	Dunker's Creek	1801	5	411
Shinn, George	81	Dunkard's Creek	1787	3	309
Shinn, Levi	400	Wts. Monon River	1784	1	174

Name of Grantee	Acres	Local Description	Year	Book	Page
Smith, Benjamin F.	15	Day's Run	1857	7	243
Smith, Benjamin F.	76	Jake's Run	1857	7	244
Smith, Charles	260	Wts. Monon. River	1790	4	174
Smith, George	33	Adj. Amos Smith	1838	7	62
Smith, Henry	400	Buffalo Creek	1792	4	307
Smith, Henry	339	Decker's Creek	1784	1	64
Smith, Hester & William	28	Adj. Amos Smith	1809	6	37
Smith, Hester & William	17	Adj. Thomas Lazelle	1809	6	38
Smith, Jacob	64	Adj. Wm. Hamilton	1819	6	219
Smith, Jacob	371	Adj. Ezekiel Jones	1802	5	480
Smith, Jacob C.	250	Morriss Run	1831	7	392
Smith, John	244	Wts. Elk River	1800	5	361
Smith, John	129	Indian Creek	1807	6	26
Smith, John	456	Adj. J. Snodgrass	1810	6	72
Smith, John	250	Little Sandy Creek	1799	5	243
Smith, John	400	Indian Creek	1796	4	528
Smith, John	200	Wts. Elk River	1796	4	543
Smith, Samuel	30	Muddy Creek	1800	5	368
Smith, Thomas	400	Pawpaw Creek	1795	4	468
Smith, William	400	Wts. Lit. Kanawha	1785	2	243
Smith, William	1,000	Adj. his Settlement	1785	2	151
Smith, William	400	Adj. Beeson's	1785	2	152
Smith, William	1,000	Wts. Lit. Kanawha	1785	2	153
Smith, William	1,000	Wts. Lit. Kanawha	1785	2	235
Smith, William	400	Adj. Robt. Thornton	1785	2	234
Smith, William	1,000	Adj. his Settlement	1785	2	137
Smith, William	400	Settlement on Ohio R.	1785	2	138
Smith, William	343	Robinson Run	1785	2	141
Smith, William A.	400	Wts. Monon River	1789	4	66
Smith, William A.	300	Sandy Creek	1789	4	67
Smith, William A.	300	Sandy Creek	1789	4	98
Smith, William A.	400	Wts. Monon River	1789	4	99
Smith, William et al	403	Adj. Geo. Smith	1815	6	129
Smith, William S.	1,893½	Raccoon Creek	1795	4	446
Smith, William S.	1,225	Adj. Wm. McCleery	1795	4	447
Smith, William S.	2,446½	Adj. Benjamin Reeder	1795	4	467
Snider—See Snyder, Sydnor					
Snider, Agnes et al Heirs	334	Adj. Benj. Wilson	1809	6	41
Snider, George	400	Dog Run	1789	4	80
Snider, George	286	Dunkard's Creek	1785	2	259
Snider, George	300	Day's Run	1789	4	130
Snider, Jesse	236	3-Forks Creek	1800	5	349
Snider, John	250	Crooked Run	1784	1	138
Snider, John et al	120	Charlie's Run	1801	5	417
Snider, Rudolph	369	Hart's Run	1786	3	252
Snider, Rudolph	184	Doll's Run	1787	3	155
Snither—Smither (or Snider)					
Snither, George	300	Day's Run	1789	4	130
Snither, George	400	Dog Run	1789	4	80
Snodgrass, Charles	95½	Adj. John Smith	1811	6	90
Snodgrass, Charles	200	Pappa Creek	1793	4	407
Snodgrass, Charles	285	Farrow's Run	1789	4	109
Snodgrass, Elisha	37	Farrow's Run	1831	7	361
Snodgrass, William	300	Farrow's Run	1785	2	169
Snodgrass, William	130	Adj. James Longwell	1798	5	216
Snyder—Snider, Sydnor					
Snyder, George	200	Day's Run	1793	4	384
Snyder, John Jr.	200	Teverbaugh's Creek	1800	5	332
Sole, Jacob Jr.	100	Dunkard Creek	1827	7	306
Sole, John	100	Dunkard Creek	1831	7	370
Sole, John	100	Dunkard Creek	1832	7	404
Sole, John	100	Adj. J. Davis	1827	7	308

Name of Grantee	Acres	Local Description	Year	Book	Page
Soverns—Severans, Severns					
Soverns, Absolom	400	Sandy Creek	1785	1	499
Soverns, Daniel	400	Sandy Creek	1785	1	506
Soverns, Daniel	409	Sandy Creek	1784	1	209
Soverns, Daniel Jr. et al	100	Sandy Creek	1817	6	174
Soverns, Joseph	400	Sandy Creek	1785	1	505
Soverns, Joseph	300	Sandy Creek	1784	1	136
Spencer, John	1,000	Adj. David Meredith	1796	4	488
Spencer, John	331	Wts. Cheat River	1800	5	387
Spencer, John	100	Big Run	1798	5	151
Spencer, John	2,000	Wts. Cheat River	1798	5	152
Spencer, John	731½	3-Forks Creek	1798	5	98
Spencer, John	2,000	Wts. Cheat River	1798	5	97
Spencer, John	2,000	Morgan Run	1800	5	359
Spencer, John	346	Morgan Run	1800	5	360
Sperry, Nicholas	200	Beaver Creek	1800	5	391
Spicer—or Spiser					
Spicer, Randolph (Spiser)	649	Tygert's V. River	1810	6	85
Spiser, Randolph	282	Tygert's V. River	1804	5	511
Spiser, Randolph (Spicer)	649	Tygert's V. River	1810	6	85
Sprawn, Frederick	25	Adj. I. Cashman	1806	6	1
Spregler, Jacob	189	Stone Coal Lick	1784	1	378
Springer, John	391	Wts. Monon River	1789	4	113
Springer, John	66	Adj. Jacob Upton	1799	5	266
Springer, John	256½	Gyer's Run	1797	5	40
Springer, Nathan	400	Pricket's Creek	1786	3	94
Springer, Nathan	171	Prickett's Creek	1791	4	201
Spurgen—Spurgens, Spurger, Spurgins					
Spurgen, James	324	Pickett's Cr.	1786	3	230
Spurgens, William	174	Little Sandy Cr.	1785	1	408
Spruger, James (Spurgen)	400	Big Sandy Creek	1785	1	501
Spruger, William (Spurgen)	400	Sandy Creek	1785	1	500
Spurgins, William	126	Sandy Creek	1785	1	406
Sriver—See Shriver					
Sriver, Adam	130	Crooked Run	1816	6	153
Staats—or Statts					
Stafford, James	105	Little Creek	1796	5	63
Stafford, James	354	Wts. of Cheat	1784	1	63
Stafford, James	150	Laurel Run	1796	4	500
Stafford, James	50	Wts. Cheat River	1793	4	417
Stafford, James	370	Buffalo Creek	1787	3	190
Stafford, James H.	15	Wts. Cheat River	1843	7	147
Stafford, James H.	20	Wts. Cheat River	1836	7	522
Stafford, James S.	12	Wts. Cheat River	1833	7	429
Stafford, Seth	5	Adj. Lemuel John	1829	7	354
Stafford, Seth	85	Wts. Cheat River	1827	7	311
Stahley—Stealey, Stealy, Steeley					
Stanley, John	16	Adj. D. Crull	1793	4	380
Statler—See Strotler					
Statler, George	180	Dunker's Creek	1787	3	315
Statler, John	400	Dunkard Creek	1798	5	226
Statler, Michael	200	Dunker's Creek	1796	5	26
Statler, Michael	200	Decker's Creek	1809	6	43
Statts, Elizah	400	Wts. Monon River	1785	2	181
Stead—or Stedd					
Stealey—Stahley, Stealy, Steeley					
Stealey, John	400	Sycamore Fork	1796	4	516
Stealey, John	38	Adj. W. Tannihill	1798	5	170
Stealy, John	94	Laurel Run	1798	5	181
Stealy, John	900	Sandy Creek	1798	5	180
Stealy, John	828	Cor. to Wm. Worth	1798	5	182
Stealy, John	500	Decker's Creek	1815	6	138
Stealy, John	144	Decker's Creek	1816	6	144
Stealy, John	2,573	Papaw Creek	1799	5	239

Name of Grantee	Acres	Local Description	Year	Book	Page
Taylor, Wildie	500	Wts. Cheat River	1788	3	491
Taylor, Wildie	180	Adj. Morgan	1806	6	3
Taylor, Wildy	50	Wts. Cheat River	1797	5	65
Tazey, Caleb	23½	Adj. Philip Lewis	1834	7	445
Tebbs—See Tibbs					
Tennant, Adam	110	Statler's Run	1832	7	410
Tennant, Adam Sr.	18	Day's Run	1846	7	177
Tennant, Nimrod	110	Upper Run	1829	7	345
Tennant, Peter	100	Statler's Run	1823	6	261
Tennant, Peter	100	Miracle's Run	1835	7	472
Tennant, Peter	100	Statler's Run	1829	7	352
Tennant, Richard	100	Dunkard Creek	1799	5	187
Tennant, Richard	400	Dunker Creek	1792	4	311
Tennant, Richard B.	44	Statler's Run	1838	7	20
Tennant, Richard D.	120	Upper Run	1829	7	351
Tennant, Richard D.	68	Doss Run	1832	7	409
Tennant, Richard D.	100	Slater's Fork	1844	7	154
Terrell—See Ferrell, Parrell					
Tetre, Jacob	200	Adj. Wm. Deakins	1793	4	328
Tetrick, George	500	Teverbaugh's Run	1787	3	276
Tetrick, Henry Jr.	200	Bingamon Cr.	1793	4	342
Tetrick, Jacob	200	Bingamon's Cr.	1791	4	203
Thomas, Evan	400	Simpson's Creek	1785	2	2
Thomas, Evan	317	Booth's Creek	1784	1	177
Thomas, Ezekiel	393	Booth's Creek	1783	1	58
Thomas, Ezekiel	400	Booth's Creek	1783	1	54
Thomas, Ezekiel	1,000	Booth's Creek	1783	1	22
Thomas, Ezekiel	400	Thomas Run	1784	1	310
Thomas, George	120	Flat Run	1841	7	86
Thomas, George	80	Flat Run	1831	7	393
Thomas, Isaac	150	Miracle's Run	1841	7	104
Thomas, Isaac	25	Flat Run	1838	7	21
Thomas, Isaac	50	Miracle's Run	1831	7	390
Thomas, Israel	160	Flat Run	1841	7	95
Thomas, John	3,300	Buffalo Creek	1786	3	2
Thomas, Joseph Jr.	300	Flat Run	1841	7	88
Thomas, Nathan	400	Indian Creek	1791	4	180
Thomas, William	295	Cor. to J. Brookover	1837	6	276
Thomas, William	32	Miracle Run	1848	7	209
Thomas, William	110	Miracle Run	1843	7	145
Thomas, William Sr.	5½	Miracle Run	1841	7	87
Thomas, William (Wheelright)	54	Miracle Run	1851	7	85
Thompson, Gervis	50	Muddy Creek	1796	4	503
Thompson, Henry	400	Mth. Peel Run	1785	2	3
Thompson, Israel	1,000	Aaron's Creek	1787	3	287
Thompson, Israel	400	Indian Creek	1786	3	33
Thompson, James	90	Adj. Jacob Zinn	1803	5	490
Thompson, James M.	63	Scott's Run	1810	6	82
Thompson, John	400	Fox Grape Creek	1785	2	184
Thompson, John	26	Adj. James Bowlsbey	1809	6	74
Thompson, Joseph	400	Stewart's Fork	1785	2	154
Thompson, Joseph et al	2,000	Buffalo Creek	1805	5	531
Thompson, William	400	Fox Grape Creek	1784	1	303
Thorn, Benjamin	7	Wts. Monongalia	1821	6	241
Tibbs, Catherine	500	Coburn's Cr.	1792	4	275
Tibbs, Francis	140	Adj. S. Troy	1794	4	432
Tibbs, Francis	400	Wts. Monon. River	1790	4	175
Tibbs, Francis Sr.	6¾	1st Isl. in Cheat R.	1800	5	350
Tibbs, James	100	Adj. John Reed	1800	5	354
Tibbs, James	300	Wts. Cheat River	1803	5	488
Tibbs, James	9¼	Meadow Run	1821	6	240
Tibbs, James	640	Decker's Creek	1787	3	182
Tibbs, Joseph	500	Coleman's Lick	1792	4	273

Name of Grantee	Acres	Local Description	Year	Book	Page
Tichnell, Jonathan	16	Adj. Tichnell's Land	1817	6	159
Tidball, James	573	Papaw Creek	1800	5	392
Tidball, James	437	Papaw Creek	1800	5	393
Tidball, Joseph	2,666	Lit. Sandy Cr.	1796	5	112
Tilton, William	2,170	Adj. his 24th	1785	2	71
Tilton, William	4,000	Adj. his 52nd.	1785	2	94
Tilton, William	120	4 Mi. Bel. Mth. Lit. Kan.	1785	2	96
Tilton, William	4,000	Wts. Lit. Kanawha	1785	2	95
Tilton, William	1,840	Wts. Lit. Kan.	1785	2	97
Tilton, William	1,000	Adj. Reed & Ford's 9th	1785	2	98
Tilton, William	548	Adj. Tilton's 14th	1785	2	99
Tilton, William	680	Adj. his 62nd	1784	2	100
Tilton, William	2,000	Wts. Lit. Kanawha	1785	2	102
Tilton, William	866	Wts. Lit. Kanawha	1785	2	103
Tilton, William	300	Adj. his 63rd	1785	2	101
Tilton, William	9,000	Adj. his 18th	1785	2	104
Tilton, William	4,000	Wts. Lit. Kanawha	1785	2	105
Tilton, William	1,000	400p S. W. Gibb's 3rd	1785	2	107
Tilton, William	780	Adj. his 6th	1785	2	106
Tilton, William	1,000	Adj. Gibb's 9th	1785	2	108
Tilton, William	1,000	Adj. Gibb's 2nd	1785	2	109
Tilton, William	1,000	Wts. Lit. Kanawha	1785	2	110
Tilton, William	2,000	Wts. Lit. Kanawha	1787	3	278
Tilton, William	1,055	Adj. his 66th Entry	1785	2	29
Tilton, William	565	Wts. Lit. Kanawha	1785	2	28
Tilton, William	1,000	Adj. Gibb's 4th Survey	1785	2	31
Tilton, William	1,240	Wts. Lit. Kanawha	1785	2	30
Tilton, William	1,000	Adj. Reed & Ford's 7th	1785	2	33
Tilton, William	4,000	Wts. Lit. Kanawha	1785	2	34
Tilton, William	1,000	Adj. his 48th	1785	2	226
Tilton, William	1,000	Adj. Wm. Gibb's 7th	1785	2	223
Tilton, William	1,100	Adj. his 35th	1785	2	224
Tilton, William	1,055	Adj. his 70th	1785	2	221
Tilton, William	1,000	Adj. Gibb's 5th	1785	2	222
Tilton, William	5,001	Adj. his 70th Entry	1785	2	206
Tilton, William	1,830	Adj. his 20th	1785	2	205
Tilton, William	4,000	Adj. his 8th Surv.	1785	2	204
Tilton, William	2,945	Adj. his 59th Surv.	1785	2	203
Tilton, William	1,000	Walker's Creek	1785	2	311
Tilton, William	2,000	Wts. Lit. Kanawha	1785	2	496
Tilton, William	2,000	Adj. his 49th	1785	2	66
Tilton, William	5,134	Grape Creek	1785	2	67
Tilton, William	4,000	Adj. his 31st Survey	1785	2	69
Tilton, William	4,000	Adj. his 36th Surv.	1785	2	68
Tilton, William	2,000	Adj. his 39th	1785	2	64
Tilton, William	4,000	Adj. his 20th	1784	2	65
Tilton, William	4,000	Adj. his 6th	1785	2	62
Tilton, William	4,000	Adj. his 5th	1785	2	63
Tilton, William	840	Wts. Lit. Kanawha	1785	2	58
Tilton, William	5,220	Adj. his 22nd	1785	2	56
Tilton, William	2,160	Adj. his 16th	1785	2	61
Tilton, William	3,760	Adj. his 15th	1785	2	54
Tilton, William	1,000	Walker's Fork	1785	2	55
Tilton, William	1,508	Adj. his 67th Surv.	1785	2	50
Tilton, William	2,400	Adj. his 44th Surv.	1785	2	51
Tilton, William	1,880	Wts. Lit. Kanawha	1785	2	52
Tilton, William	2,300	Adj. his 14th	1785	2	53
Tilton, William	4,500	Wts. West Fork	1785	2	48
Tilton, William	4,000	Adj. his 38th Surv.	1785	2	44
Tilton, William	4,000	Adj. his 11th Surv.	1785	2	49
Tilton, William	1,000	Adj. Wm. Gibb's 1st	1785	2	47
Tilton, William	1,000	Adj. Wm. Gibb's 6th	1785	2	46
Tilton, William	4,000	Adj. his 42nd Surv.	1785	2	43

Name of Grantee	Acres	Local Description	Year	Book	Page
Tilton, William	3,937	Wts. Little Kan.	1785	2	42
Tilton, William	2,000	Adj. his 69th Surv.	1785	2	40
Tilton, William	1,990	Adj. his 24th Surv.	1785	2	41
Tilton, William	4,000	Adj. his 46th Surv.	1785	2	37
Tilton, William	1,934	Wts. Lit. Kanawha	1785	2	39
Tilton, William	10,000	Wts. Lit. Kanawha	1785	2	38
Tilton, William	4,219	Adj. his 58th Surv.	1785	2	36
Tilton, William	5,500	Adj. his 19th Entry	1785	2	35
Tilton, William Esq.	4,000	Adj. his 44th Surv.	1785	2	70
Timmerman, John	50	Glade Creek	1823	6	257
Tingle, William	76	Connor's Run	1796	4	532
Tingle, William et al	500	White Day Creek	1798	5	203
Tingle, William et al	615	Booth's Creek	1798	5	208
Tingle, William et al	992	White Day Creek	1798	5	210
Tingle, William et al	48	Wts. Cheat River	1802	5	478
Titsoard, Leonard (Titsword)	373	Decker's Creek	1789	4	88
Titsoard, Leonard (Titsword)	404	Decker's Creek	1789	4	96
Tomlinson, Joseph	539	Adj. Isaac Williams	1785	2	78
Tomlinson, Joseph	580	Letart's Falls	1785	1	451
Toothman—See Tuthman					
Toothman, Adam	96	Plum Run	1837	7	550
Toothman, Adam	250	Plum Run	1837	7	549
Toothman, Adam	116	Plum Run	1831	7	385
Tower, E. W.	350	Piles Fork	1846	7	563
Tower, E. W.	115	Laurel Run	1848	7	211
Tower, E. W.	100	Buffalo Creek	1846	7	178
Tower, Edwin W.	62	Wickwire's Creek	1841	7	93
Tower, Edwin W.	200	Buffalo Creek	1839	7	75
Tower, Edwin W.	1,661	Decker's Creek	1857	7	565
Tower, Edwin W.	100	Wts. Cheat River	1852	7	229
Tower, Edwin W.	19	Cheat River	1852	7	227
Tower, Edwin W.	914	Decker's Creek	1851	7	217
Tower, Edwin W.	125	Piles Fork	1847	7	191
Tower, Edwin W.	150	White Day Creek	1847	7	198
Tower, Edwin W.	4	Adj. Benj. Hamilton	1843	7	146
Tower, Edwin W.	463	Decker's Creek	1857	7	249
Tower, Edwin W.	4	Booth's Creek	1856	7	235
Tower, Edwin W. et al	300	Dunkard Creek	1853	7	230
Tower, Edwin W. et al	500	Statler's Run	1844	7	150
Tower, Edwin W. et al	400	Booth's Creek	1847	7	199
Tower, Edwin W. et al	1,000	Decker's Creek	1851	7	564
Tower, Edwin W. et al	500	PawPaw Creek	1841	7	81
Trader, Arthur	200	Wts. Monon. River	1786	3	227
Trader, Arthur	322	Pebbles Mill Run	1789	4	139
Travis, Champion	1,200	Wts. Lit. Kanawha	1785	2	296
Travis, Champion	1,200	Wts. Lit. Kanawha	1785	2	295
Tremley, John	145	Sandy Creek	1818	6	184
Trickett, Joseph	89	Decker's Creek	1790	4	164
Trinkett, Joseph	89	Decker's Creek	1790	4	164
Trippett, Topliff	200	Dunkard's Cr.	1838	7	22
Triplett, Hedgeman (Hodgman)	20	Morgan's Run	1787	3	262
Triplett, Hedgeman (Hodgman)	200	Davis's 3rd Entry	1785	2	5
Triplett, Hedgeman	500	Salt Lick Creek	1785	2	317
Triplett, Hedgman	50	Adj. J. Hays	1806	6	6
Triplett, Hedgman et al	431	Oil Creek	1785	1	541
Triplett, Hodgman	200	Lit. Sandy Cr.	1785	2	73
Triplett, Hodgman	1,000	Wts. Elk River	1785	2	377
Triplett, Hodgman et al	1,000	Nauls Creek	1785	2	425
Triplett, Hodgman et al	569	Tate's Creek	1785	2	74
Triplett, Hodgman et al	1,000	Salt Lick Creek	1785	2	275
Triplett, Hodgman et al	8,000	O'Brians Creek	1785	2	274
Triplett, Hodgman et al	2,000	Duck Creek	1785	2	273
Triplett, Joseph	89	Decker's Creek	1790	4	164

Name of Grantee	Acres	Local Description	Year	Book	Page
Vandervort—also Vandevort					
Vandervort, Nicholas	400	White's Run	1788	3	541
Vandevort, Jonah	950	Tibb's Run	1847	7	200
Vandiver, William	702	Decker's Creek	1787	3	407
Vandruff, John	220	Wts. Monon. River	1786	3	126
Vankirk, Jacob	200	Adj. Henry Crull	1793	4	400
Vanmeter—or Vanmetre					
Vanmeter, Isaac	156	Glade Creek	1786	3	88
Vanmeter, Isaac	400	Wts. Yohogania	1786	3	229
Vanmeter, Joseph	2,456	Steer Creek	1792	4	240
Vanmetre, Isaac	126	Sunny Glade Cr.	1785	2	373
Varner, William	37	PawPaw Creek	1841	7	106
Varner, William	160	Papaw Creek	1845	7	161
Vincent, Francis	1,000	Big Steer Creek	1786	2	548
Vincent, William	400	Adj. Abraham Sisco	1799	5	236
Von Emrath, Henry	1,400	Cor. to T. Boom	1787	3	378
Wade—also Waid					
Wade, Alexander	346	Wickwire's Creek	1786	3	233
Wade, Alexander	366½	Scott's Run	1789	4	116
Wade, Alexander	200	Dunkard's Creek	1838	6	287
Wade, Alexander Jr.	29	Dunkard Creek	1846	7	180
Wade, Alexander Jr.	210	Dunkard's Creek	1842	7	130
Wade, Alexander Jr.	130	Dunkard Creek	1845	7	162
Wade, Alexander Jr.	950	Piles Fork	1842	7	124
Wade, Alexander Jr. et al	80	Piles Fork	1846	7	181
Wade, Alexander Jr. et al	260	Buffalo Creek	1846	7	182
Wade, Elisha	232	Dunker Creek	1787	3	462
Wade, George	220	Boilstones Run	1784	1	153
Wade, George Jr.	87	Adj. James Pollock	1786	3	121
Wade, George R.	4	Adj. Joseph Wade	1832	7	414
Wade, Hezekiah	275	Crooked Run	1787	3	460
Wade, Hosea	6	Scott's Run	1838	7	69
Wade, John	46	Robinson's Run	1800	5	374
Wade, Margaret et al	400	Dunker's Creek	1792	4	300
Wade, Thomas	270	Dunkard Creek	1837	7	534
Wade, Thomas	347	Dunkars Creek	1784	1	155
Wade, Thomas	46	Dunkard Creek	1831	7	394
Wade, Thomas Case	284	Dunker's Creek	1786	3	89
Wade, Wenmon	374	Dunker's Creek	1786	3	152
Waggoner—also Wagoner, Wagner					
Waggoner, Susanna et al	207	Wts. W. Fork	1801	5	430
Wagner, Jacob	80	Adj. S. Cratzer's	1820	6	227
Wagoner, Jacob	25	Tygert's V. River	1816	6	152
Waid—also Wade					
Waid, George Sr.	380	Adj. his own	1788	3	494
Walden—also Walton					
Walden, Mary et al	400	Sandy Creek	1799	5	277
Walden, Mary et al	300	Sandy Creek	1799	5	276
Walker, Alpheus D.	100	Tibb's Run	1847	7	196
Walker, James	50	Adj. J. Scott	1821	6	242
Walker, James	210	Prickett's Creek	1800	5	384
Walker, James	400	Wts. Monon. River	1786	3	225
Walker, James	365	Papaw Creek	1799	5	227
Walker, John	100	Adj. Chas. Gallagher	1819	6	197
Wall, James	90	Cheat River	1815	6	124
Walsh, John	100	Unknown	1816	6	151
Walton—or Walden					
Walton, Thomas et al	250	Coburn's Creek	1835	7	484
Ward, Sylvester	142	Adj. his own	1788	4	7
Warley—See also Worley					
Warley, Brace	71	Dunker's Creek	1787	3	318
Warley, Brace (Brice)	330	Dunker Creek	1792	4	324
Warman, Francis	238	Wts. Cheat River	1782	1	6

Name of Grantee	Acres	Local Description	Year	Book	Page
Wireman, Christian	656	Wickware's Creek	1787	3	352
Wireman, Christian	1,000	Decker's Creek	1787	3	175
Wireman, Christian	2,000	Steer Creek	1787	3	171
Wireman, Christian	2,000	Adj. Lands S. Hanway	1786	3	101
Wireman, Christian	1,500	Dunker Creek	1792	4	365
Wireman, Christian	1,493	Buffalo Run	1797	5	122
Wireman, Christian	1,788	Wts. Buffalo	1797	5	123
Wireman, Christian	1,500	Bingamon's Cr.	1797	5	70
Wireman, Christian	1,939	Bingamon's Cr.	1797	5	71
Wireman, Christian	1,815	Buffalo Creek	1797	5	39
Wireman, Christian	1,731	Buffalo Creek	1797	5	38
Wireman, Christian	1,000	Dunker's Creek	1792	4	299
Wireman, Christian	2,000	Wickware's Creek	1788	3	539
Wireman, Christian	2,000	Wickware's Creek	1788	3	483
Wireman, Christian	1,000	Decker's Creek	1787	3	316
Wisby—See Wesbey					
Wise, George	250	Dunkard's Creek	1810	6	71
Wise, George	50	Dunkard's Creek	1837	6	277
Wise, James	120	Adj. Hixenbaugh & Nolan	1837	6	278
Wise, Levi	175	Dunkard Creek	1838	7	65
Wise, Levi	22½	Dunkard Creek	1837	7	538
Woley—See Warley, Worley					
Wolf—See also Woolf					
Wolf, George	300	Cor. to Jacob Counts	1804	5	529
Wolf, Jacob	65	Adj. Reuben Adkins	1796	4	537
Wolf, Jacob	156	Muddy Creek	1819	6	209
Wolf, Jacob	50	Muddy Creek	1802	5	448
Wolf, John	274	Wts. Elk	1783	1	30
Wolf, Lewis	54	Sandy Creek	1817	6	168
Wolf, Louis	40	Adj. Jeff Hanway	1805	5	551
Wolf, Rees	134	Bruin's Run	1793	4	388
Wood—or Woods					
Wood, John	324	Lost Run	1784	1	158
Wood, John	400	Wts. Monon. River	1783	1	29
Wood, Thomas	1,000	State Creek	1786	2	423
Wood, Thomas	1,000	Wts. Lit. Kanawha	1786	2	422
Wood, Thomas	1,000	Walker's Creek	1785	2	424
Woodroff—Woodruff, Woodrough					
Woodrough, Erastus Sr.	30	Dunkard Creek	1847	7	197
Woodrow, Abraham et al	533	Cor. to Asa Hall	1809	6	78
Woods—or Wood					
Woods, Robert	16½	Adj. Francis Burwell	1801	5	425
Woods, Thomas	1,000	Walker's Creek	1787	3	256
Woods, William	178	Adj. James Pindle	1808	6	31
Woodyard, Samuel	325	Wickware's Creek	1836	7	524
Woolf—also Wolf					
Woolf, Francis	300	3-Fork Creek	1789	4	95
Worall—also Worral					
Worall, Samuel Jr.	338	Sandy Creek	1784	1	320
Workman, William	6½	Adj. W. A. Smith	1819	6	203
Worley—See also Warley					
Worley, Anthony	400	Wts. Sandy Creek	1784	1	358
Worley, Anthony Jr. (Worlley)	400	Beaver Creek	1793	4	389
Worley, Brice (Brace)	330	Dunker Creek	1792	4	324
Worley, David A.	250	Dunkard Creek	1849	7	214
Worley, Joshua	400	Sandy Creek	1784	1	363
Worral—See also Worall					
Worral, Samuel Sr.	400	Sandy Creek	1784	1	319
Worth, William	1,000	Adj. Wm. Pettyjohn	1794	4	404
Worth, William	1,000	Adj. Wm. Pettyjohn	1794	4	405
Wright—See Rite					
Yager—also Yeager					
Yager, Peter	8	Dunkard Creek	1839	7	74

MONROE COUNTY

Name of Grantee	Acres	Local Description	Year	Book	Page
Alexander, Michael	83	Swope's Knob	1820	1	348
Alexander, Michael	90	Swope's Knob	1818	1	302
Alexander, Michael	130	Swope's Knob	1815	1	259
Alexander, Michael	84	Laurel Creek	1840	2	147
Alexander, Michael & Matthew	90	Swope's Knob	1830	1	443
Alexander, Michael & Matthew	593	Laurel Creek	1820	1	579
Alexander, Michael & Matthew	195	Adj. John Beckett	1828	1	435
Alexander, Michael & Matthew	220	Swope's Knob	1826	1	405
Alford—See Olford, Alfred					
Alford, Henry	130	Wolf Creek	1818	1	298
Alford, Henry	67	Wolf Creek	1818	1	299
Alford, John	155	Wolf Creek	1826	1	419
Alford, John	55	Wolf Creek	1830	1	445
Alford, Joseph	47	The Sinks	1804	1	69
Alfred, George	35	Big Creek	1809	1	188
Allen, George	100	Indian Draught	1836	1	550
Allen, George	100	Indian Draught	1824	1	393
Allen, George Jr.	93	Indian Draught	1848	2	313
Allen, George Jr.	1a.107p.	Indian Draught	1836	1	527
Allen, Jacob C.	250	Indian Draught	1835	1	520
Allen, Jacob C.	4½	Indian Draught	1849	2	331
Allen, Jacob C.	85	Slate Run	1849	2	329
Allen, Jacob C.	42	Slate Run	1839	2	148
Allen, Jacob C.	48	Stony Creek	1858	3	130
Allen, William	50	Stoney Creek	1830	1	444
Allen, William	196	Indian Draught	1836	1	559
Amiss, Lewis et al	192	Rick Creek	1814	1	251
Anderson, James	72	Indian Draught	1830	1	453
Andrews, John	85	Middle Run	1827	1	421
Anthony, James C.	3,000	Turkey Creek	1805	1	131
Arbuckle, Charles	56	Wolf Creek	1801	1	9
Arbuckle, Mathew	94	Whack's Improvement	1800	1	2
Arbuckle, Mathew	216	Indian Creek	1800	1	4
Arbuckle, Mathew	490	Crooked Run	1800	1	3
Armantrout, Abraham	28	Adj. his own	1846	2	249
Armantrout, Abraham	50	Potts Creek	1851	2	414
Armantrout, Abraham	150	Potts Creek	1851	2	415
Arnett—Arnot, Arnott					
Arnett, Henry	26	Indian Creek	1811	1	216
Arnett, Henry	36	Drooping Lick	1809	1	169
Arnold, Moses	32	Pott's Creek	1851	2	413
Arnot, Henry	68	Laurel Creek	1816	1	273
Arnot, Henry	12	Back Creek	1816	1	272
Arnott, Henry	50 perches	Laurel Creek	1862	3	212
Arnott, Henry Jr.	20	Back Creek	1839	2	144
Arnott, Henry Jr.	12½	Laurel Creek	1836	1	565
Arnott, John Jr.	47	2nd Creek	1820	1	334
Arnott, William	10	Swope's Knob	1850	2	361
Ayers, Anderson (or Andrew)	32	Hungart's Creek	1856	3	79
Baker, Adam	40	Dunlap Creek	1810	1	203
Baker, David	100	Dunlap Creek	1815	1	263
Baker, David	37	Dunlap's Creek	1816	1	279
Baker, David	67	Dunlap Creek	1822	1	361
Baker, Jacob	293	Sweet Spgs. Mt.	1826	1	407
Baker, Jacob & David	161	Pott's Creek	1823	1	387
Baker, John	93	Peters Mountain	1860	3	167
Ballard, Baldwin	40	Rich Creek	1858	3	121
Ballard, Elijah	88	Turkey Run	1805	1	103
Ballard, James	100	Hand's Creek	1836	1	556
Ballard, James Jr.	175	Stinking Lick	1847	2	304
Ballard, Thomas	45	Felties Run	1805	1	121
Ballard, Thompson	90	Stinking Lick	1841	2	169
Ballard, William	110	Bee Branch	1849	2	337

Name of Grantee	Acres	Local Description	Year	Book	Page
Ballard, William	50	Indian Creek	1806	1	140
Ballard, William Jr.	50	Indian Creek	1850	2	365
Ballard, Willis	286	Stinking Lick	1847	2	305
Ballard, Willis	14½	Indian Creek	1843	2	196
Ballard, Willis	280	Bee Branch	1853	3	4
Barton, Joel	13	New River Hill	1854	3	35
Baylie, George	61	Laurel Creek	1801	1	14
Beamer, Philip	300	Cabin Draft	1835	1	589
Bean—or Been					
Beard, Jesse	73	Hungart's Creek	1838	2	73
Beard, Jesse	250	Elk Knob	1838	2	72
Beard, Jesse et al	161	Big Creek	1838	2	74
Beard, Jesse et al	600	Hungart's Creek	1838	2	75
Beard, Jesse et al	1,450	Big Creek	1838	2	76
Beckner, Emanuel	202	Pott's Creek	1846	2	250
Beckner, Matthew	89	Pott's Creek	1851	2	398
Been—or Bean					
Been, William	70	Dropping Lick Cr.	1843	2	194
Been, William	17	Dropping Lick Cr.	1843	2	193
Been, William	70	Dropping Lick Cr.	1843	2	192
Been, William	13	Pott's Creek	1859	3	150
Beirne, Andrew	4a.60p.	2nd Creek	1836	2	16
Beirne, Andrew	30	Devil's Creek	1836	1	543
Beirne, Andrew	7	2nd Creek	1836	1	571
Beirne, Andrew & George	7½	Devil's Creek	1820	1	344
Beirne, Andrew Sr.	1a.20p.	The Sinks	1840	2	150
Black, William	5½	The Sinks	1816	1	274
Bland—or Blann					
Bland, George W.	11½	Dropping Lick	1860	3	178
Bland, George W.	14	Turkey Creek	1854	3	30
Bland, George W.	45	Ft. Peter's Mt.	1854	3	31
Blann, Robert	25	2nd Creek	1820	1	341
Blann, Robert	134	Turkey Creek	1838	2	92
Blanton, John et al	70	2nd Creek	1812	1	237
Boggess, Abraham	5	Dropping Lick	1845	2	234
Boggess, Abraham	16	Dropping Lick	1844	2	218
Bolinger, William	45	Turkey Creek	1838	2	69
Bostic—or Bostick					
Bostic, David	3	Carpenter's Run	1861	3	196
Bostic, David et al	50	Laurel Creek	1844	2	217
Bostic, John	19	Humphreys Run	1857	3	100
Bostic, Joshua	20	Big Run	1844	2	216
Bostic, Reuben	90	Second Creek	1847	2	299
Bostic, William	45	Second Creek	1847	2	280
Bostick—or Bostic					
Bostick, William	100	Laurel Creek	1838	2	126
Boyd, Patrick	110	Broad Run	1809	1	186
Boyd, Patrick	110	Broad Run	1814	1	246
Boyd, Patrick	1,813	Broad Run	1802	1	573
Boyd, Patrick et al	300	Hungert's Creek	1820	1	329
Boyer, Adam	88	2nd Creek	1809	1	180
Bradford, Joseph	25	Paint Bank Branch	1853	3	23
Bradford, Joseph	25	Paint Bank Branch	1853	3	22
Bragg, Thomas	97	Little Wolf Creek	1847	2	291
Brown, Anderson	31	Dropping Lick	1837	2	47
Brown, Anderson	4¼	Dropping Lick	1861	3	204
Brown, Garet (Garrett)	10	Kessinger's Run	1858	3	115
Brown, Garret (Garrett)	123	Stoney Creek	1851	2	425
Brown, John	102	Bradshaw Run	1833	1	480
Broyles, Allen	37	Adj. J. Dickinson	1832	1	471
Broyles, Simeon	100	Rich Creek	1842	2	172
Bruffy, George W.	45	Pot's Creek	1851	2	402
Bruffy, George W.	79	Pott's Creek	1849	2	339

Name of Grantee	Acres	Local Description	Year	Book	Page
Buckland, James	55	Big Creek	1859	3	161
Buckland, James	45	Big Creek	1859	3	162
Buckland, James	100	Big Creek	1862	3	214
Buckland, John	43	Pauley Creek	1855	3	49
Buckland, John	60	Laurel Creek	1849	2	338
Buckland, John	11¾	Laurel Creek	1834	1	512
Buckland, John et al	130	Laurel Creek	1850	2	388
Buckland, John & Francis	89	Pauley Creek	1850	2	359
Buckland, John & Francis	35	Adj. Wm. Meadows	1860	3	163
Buckland, John Jr.	130	Laurel Creek	1838	2	70
Buckland, Peter	95	Adj. Sivers	1856	3	65
Buckland, Reyburn	93	Pauley's Creek	1844	2	230
Buckland, Richard	152	Turkey Foot	1852	2	440
Burdit—or Burdet, Burdette					
Burdit, Giles et al (Burdet)	30	Matt's Branch	1822	1	354
Burdit, Willis (Burdet)	6	Wolf Creek	1818	1	300
Burke, William	71	Fitz's Run	1836	2	15
Burke, William	2¼	Fitz's Run	1836	2	14
Burns, Andrew	77	Back Creek	1802	1	27
Burns, William	689	Cove Creek	1856	3	69
Busby, Isaac	70	Wts. Greenbrier	1809	1	179
Butcher, Joshua	48	Stinking Lick	1822	1	374
Butler, Powell	200	Wts. New River	1843	2	195
Butt, Shannon	187	Hungert's Creek	1861	3	197
Byrnside, James M.	152	Adj. Thomas Walker	1851	2	397
Byrnside, John	1,000	Indian Creek	1812	1	577
Cabell, John	1,240	Turkey Creek	1802	1	17
Cabell, John	1,850	Dropping Lick	1806	1	141
Cales—See also Kales					
Cales, Archibald	50	Adj. John Sims	1862	3	215
Cales, Archibald	72	Adj. Chapman Hale	1862	3	216
Cales, James	50	Wolf Creek	1836	1	537
Cales, James	25	Wolf Creek	1836	1	536
Cales, James Sr.	65	Adj. Archibald Cales	1861	3	200
Calloway, James	58	Clens Run	1814	1	247
Calloway, Joshua	4½	Bradshaw Run	1827	1	422
Calloway, Joshua	170	Indian Creek	1850	2	362
Calloway, Joshua	4½	Bradshaw Run	1827	1	434
Calloway, Vincent	31	Chimney Ridge	1842	2	175
Calloway, Zacharias	96	Rich Creek	1808	1	159
Campbell, Andrew	300	Devil's Creek	1812	1	223
Campbell, Calvin S.	104	Dunlap Creek	1854	3	27
Campbell, Calvin S.	280	Peters Mountain	1860	3	168
Campbell, Calvin S.	75	Dunlap Creek	1860	3	169
Campbell, Calvin S.	20	Back Creek	1859	3	153
Campbell, Calvin S.	140	Dunlap Creek	1856	3	84
Campbell, Calvin S.	58	Dunlap Creek	1856	3	83
Campbell, Clemens J.	77	Peters Mt.	1859	3	140
Campbell, Clemens J.	193	Peters Mt.	1859	3	139
Campbell, Clemens J.	11	Wts. Greenbrier	1856	3	82
Campbell, Clemens J.	50	Wts. Greenbrier	1856	3	81
Campbell, Isaac et al	259	Bradshaw Run	1846	2	267
Campbell, James et al	259	Bradshaw Run	1846	2	267
Campbell, Jesse S.	272	Indian Creek	1856	3	75
Campbell, Robert D.	187	Indian Creek	1846	2	272
Campbell, Thomas	50	Indian Creek	1836	1	568
Campbell, Thomas	50	Indian Creek	1838	2	125
Campbell, Thomas & Isaac	100	Indian Creek	1836	1	569
Campbell, Thomas S. & Isaac	53	Indian Creek	1845	2	241
Cantley, John	68	Wts. New River	1838	2	68
Canterberry, Anderson	74	Indian Creek	1847	2	302
Canterberry, Joshua	16	Back Creek	1836	2	10
Caperton, Hugh	180	Little Mountain	1838	2	57

Name of Grantee	Acres	Local Description	Year	Book	Page
Cornwell, William	200	Laurel Creek	1811	1	220
Cornwell, William	37	3 Lick Fork	1811	1	219
Cornwell, Wm.	683	Little Mountain	1805	1	132
Coulter, James M.	52½	Rich Creek	1843	2	197
Counts, Charles	47	Dunlap's Creek	1837	2	26
Counts, Charles et al (Countz)	200	Back Creek	1838	2	117
Counts, William	116	Devil's Creek	1834	1	487
Counts, William	200	Devil's Creek	1854	3	33
Counts, William	28	2nd Creek	1830	1	442
Cox, John D.	205	Big Creek	1861	3	206
Crawford, Gedion	450	Elk Lick	1803	1	56
Crawford, Thomas Jr.	2	Blue Lick	1849	2	332
Creed, Matthew	100	Indian Creek	1803	1	59
Crews, Thomas D.	100	Dropping Lick	1860	3	175
Croser—Crosier, Crosor					
Croser, Andrew	122	Turkey Creek	1818	1	288
Croser, Andrew	97	Turkey Creek	1817	1	283
Crosier, Andrew D.	70	Pott's Creek	1849	2	340
Crosier, George & Thomas	60	Pott's Creek	1851	2	412
Crosier, James S.	6¼	Turkey Creek	1850	2	355
Crosier, James S.	43	Turkey Creek	1850	2	354
Crosier, John	45	Pott's Creek	1851	2	407
Crosier, Thomas M.	10	Pott's Creek	1859	3	155
Crosier, William	100	Pott's Creek	1838	2	93
Crosier, William	200	Wts. Pott's Creek	1842	2	176
Crosier, William H.	30	Pott's Creek	1858	3	111
Crosor—Croser, Crosier					
Crosor, Andrew	88	2nd Creek	1812	1	233
Crutchfield, Robert	40	Lick Run	1805	1	116
Crow, John	140	Adj. A. Kitchen	1826	1	404
Cummins, Hugh	200	Paint Branch Run	1844	2	232
Cummins, Hugh	120	Pott's Creek	1832	1	473
Cummins, Hugh	40	Pott's Creek	1832	1	472
Cummins, John et al	195	Indian Creek	1838	2	129
Cummins, John Jr.	21	Indian Creek	1850	2	384
Cummons, Woodson	100	Indian Creek	1830	1	448
Curry, James	200	Indian Creek	1809	1	181
Dameron, John	47	Snake Run	1819	1	327
Dameron, John	113	Dunlap Creek	1819	1	326
Dammeron, John (Dameron)	60	Snake Run	1824	1	388
Daugherty—or Dougherty					
Daugherty, George W.	78	Laurel Creek	1860	3	187
Deboy, Coonrod	95	Wolf Creek	1805	1	133
Deboy, John	42	Swope's Knob	1823	1	380
DeCamp, Zachariah	27	Indian Creek	1810	1	193
Delormer, John	150	Snake Run	1823	1	386
Diamond, Alfred K.	218	Powley Creek	1852	3	1
Dick, David	12	Adj. J. Kincaid	1807	1	146
Dickerson, Jesse	100	Hand's Creek	1835	1	525
Dickison, Jacob	30	Rich Creek	1843	2	189
Dickison, Jacob	39	Rich Creek	1841	2	156
Dixon, Thomas E.	60	Second Creek	1859	3	137
Donahoe—See Donohoe					
Donahoe, Thomas	278	Paint Bank Run	1837	2	29
Donaldson, William	25	Back Creek	1836	1	555
Donnally, Patrick	36	Wolf Creek	1805	1	114
Donohoe—See Donahoe					
Donohoe, James S.	100	Pott's Creek	1847	2	295
Donohoe, Thomas	50	Pott's Creek	1846	2	271
Donohoe, William E.	50	Pott's Creek	1846	2	266
Dougherty—See Daugherty					
Dougherty, Andrew J.	150	Laurel Creek	1857	3	90
Dougherty, Henry	160	Caperton's Run	1814	1	250

Name of Grantee	Acres	Local Description	Year	Book	Page
Douglass, Henry	1a.30p.	The Sinks	1804	1	66
Douglass, Henry	570	2nd Creek	1804	1	67
Douty, Henry	900	Wts. Indian Creek	1806	1	136
Douty, Henry	700	Indian Creek	1806	1	135
Douty, Henry	500	Indian Creek	1806	1	134
Drummond, John	49	Ewings Run	1845	2	236
Dunbar, John	2	Turkey Creek	1848	2	323
Dunbar, John A.	88	Pott's Creek	1846	2	251
Dunbar, Jonathan	100	Swope's Knob	1803	1	60
Dunbar, Mathew et al	170	Broad Run	1819	1	304
Dunbar, Robert S.	40	Pott's Creek	1853	3	19
Dunbar, William M. & J. M.	31	Pott's Creek	1853	3	21
Dunbar, William M. & J. M.	104	Pott's Creek	1853	3	20
Dunbar, William T.	61	Pott's Creek	1851	2	409
Dunbar, William T.	148	Pott's Creek	1851	2	410
Dunbar, William T.	72	Pott's Creek	1851	2	408
Dunbar, William T.	70	Pott's Creek	1849	2	341
Dunlap, Robert et al (Heirs)	200	Adj. T. Wyatt	1826	1	398
Dunlap, Robt. & James et al	917	Wolf Creek	1828	1	437
Dunn, James	10	Peter's Mt.	1844	2	229
Dunn, James P.	56	Adj. W. Pennington	1855	3	38
Eads, William et al	12½	Reaburn's Mt.	1840	2	151
Eggleston, Richard C.	50	Dunlap's Creek	1859	3	136
Ellis, Evan	3	Wolf Creek	1859	3	142
Ellis, Jacob et al	17	Wolf Creek	1821	1	346
Ellis, Jacob & Joseph	130	Wolf Creek	1819	1	318
Ellis, James	187	Wolf Creek	1820	1	333
Ellis, John	6	Wolf Creek	1844	2	219
Ellis, Joshua	24	Wolf Creek	1855	3	45
Ellis, Joshua	24	Wolf Creek	1855	3	46
Ellis, Owen	110	Wolf Creek	1810	1	207
Ellis, Owen Jr.	125	Wolf Creek	1819	1	317
Ellis, Philip	150	Wolf Creek	1812	1	227
Ellison, James	320	Indian Creek	1804	1	80
Ellison, John	162	Hand's Creek	1836	2	9
Ellison, John	60	Hans Creek	1803	1	53
Ellison, John	15	Elk Lick	1855	3	56
Ellison, John	6½	Blue Lick	1852	2	445
Ellison, John	33	Hand's Creek	1836	2	1
Ellison, William et al	195	Indian Creek	1838	2	129
Erritt, Michael	100	Pott's Creek	1810	1	205
Erskine, William	3	Indian Creek	1855	3	48
Estill, Isaac	123	Dropping Lick	1806	1	142
Evans, or Evens, Evins					
Evans, James	12	Hand's Creek	1841	2	168
Evans, James	73	Hand's Creek	1836	2	17
Evans, John	42	Rich Creek	1853	3	18
Evens, Thomas	100	Hand's Creek	1847	2	282
Evins, James	40	Peter's Mt.	1823	1	381
Evins, James	73	Hand's Creek	1835	1	521
Ewing, Joseph	32	Turkey Creek	1822	1	358
Ewing, William	210	Swope's Knob	1801	1	10
Farley, Joseph	70	Mott's Branch	1823	1	379
Farley, Matt	97	Buffalo Branch	1810	1	202
Farley, Matt & James Jr.	186	Wts. New River	1822	1	365
Farley, Matthew	36	Adj. Francis Farley	1807	1	144
Farley, Samuel	90	Bet. New & G'br. Rs.	1826	1	411
Farley, Samuel	15	Mth. Greenbrier	1826	1	412
Figget, Figgett, Figgot					
Figget, William T.	24	Pott's Creek	1852	2	426
Figget, William T.	33	Pott's Creek	1852	2	427
Figgett, William T.	24	Pott's Creek	1860	3	179
Figgot, Gibbon G.	117	Pott's Creek	1856	3	61

Name of Grantee	Acres	Local Description	Year	Book	Page
Fincher—See Tincher					
Fincher, James et al	123	Leeches Branch	1827	1	581
Fisher, Isaac	52	Slaty Run	1816	1	275
Fisher, James A.	25	Wolf Creek	1852	2	430
Fisher, James A.	50	Wolf Creek	1850	2	386
Fisher, Leonard	12	Lick Run	1812	1	234
Fisher, Philip	50	Adj. John Brown	1808	1	161
Fisher, Philip	12	Pott's Creek	1807	1	156
Fisher, St. Clair	75	Wolf Creek	1850	2	391
Fisher, William	50	Wolf Creek	1843	2	191
Fisher, William	87	Wolf Creek	1834	1	499
Fisk, Henry	110	Dunlap's Creek	1812	1	225
Fleshman, Abraham	88	Cedar Run	1827	1	424
Fleshman, Andrew	42	Peter's Mt.	1849	2	342
Fleshman, Andrew L.	11¾	Rich Creek	1853	3	5
Fleshman, John	60	Scott's Branch	1815	1	262
Fleshman, John	87	Rich Creek	1841	2	157
Fleshman, John	14	Chimney Ridge	1842	2	170
Fleshman, John	2	Little Mountain	1842	2	171
Fleshman, Jonathan	170	Rich Creek	1861	3	209
Fleshman, Michael	125	Indian Creek	1845	2	244
Fleshman, Thomas	32	Dry Fork	1835	1	517
Fleshman, Thomas	30	Rich Creek	1841	2	155
Flint, Benjamin	13	Kelly's Creek	1855	3	59
Fluke, Jacob	130	Adj. Thomas Meadows	1856	3	71
Fluke, Jacob	132	Hungard's Creek	1852	3	2
Foard—See Ford					
Foard, Allison	42	Elbow Branch	1852	2	444
Foard, James A.	100	Big Wolf Creek	1859	3	144
Foard, James A.	25	Stoney Creek	1859	3	145
Foard, James A.	100	Wolf Creek	1859	3	146
Foard, William Sr.	100	Stoney Creek	1859	3	147
Foard, William Sr.	350	Guinn's Branch	1859	3	148
Folden, James	75	Dry Run	1833	1	476
Folder, James	75	Dry Run	1833	1	476
Ford—See Foard					
Ford, William Jr.	25	Stoney Creek	1846	2	270
Forelander, Lewis	150	Rainbow Run	1804	1	61
Foster, E. M.	27	The Knobs	1858	3	120
Foster, Grigsby	68	Bet. Little & Peters Mts.	1805	1	127
Foster, James	9	Dropping Lick	1826	1	403
Foster, John	60	Wolf Creek	1850	2	360
Fowler, Thomas	110	Below Mth. Indian Cr.	1857	3	91
Foy, Thomas	124	Peters Mountain	1860	3	164
Fraley, Frederick	11	Indian Creek	1803	1	55
Frayley, Frederick	11	Indian Creek	1803	1	55
Fridley, Thomas	164	Pott's Creek	1846	2	252
Fulkiner, Samuel	200	Middle Mountain	1854	3	32
Fulkiner, Samuel	150	Cove Creek	1856	3	66
Fulkiner, Samuel	149½	Cove Creek	1856	3	77
Furguson, John	143	Brush Creek	1858	3	108
Fury, Robert	41	Second Creek	1857	3	97
Fury, Robert	50	Laurel Creek	1837	2	41
Fury, Robert	80	Laurel Creek	1837	2	42
Fury, Robert	50	Laurel Creek	1844	2	220
Fury, Robert	100	Laurel Creek	1847	2	294
Fury, Thomas	80	Laurel Creek	1858	3	131
Gabbard, John	40	Swope's Knob	1804	1	62
Garten—or Gartin					
Garten, Griffith	46	Bradshaw Run	1831	1	459
Garten, Nathaniel	14	Swope's Knob	1827	1	425
Garten, Thompson	64	Wolf Creek	1836	1	572
Gartin, Elijah	215	Laurel Creek	1804	1	73

Name of Grantee	Acres	Local Description	Year	Book	Page
Graham, William	146	Wolf Creek	1803	1	49
Graham, William	80	Wolf Creek	1828	1	440
Graham, William	200	Kelliers Creek	1810	1	189
Graham, William & David	43	Adj. Coonrad Kellar	1802	1	26
Graham, William et al	917	Wolf Creek	1828	1	437
Green, Jesse	11	The Sinks	1817	1	282
Gregory, Ira A.	78	Little Mountain	1860	3	166
Grey, James et al Heirs	96	Turkey Creek	1826	1	400
Grimmet ———— et al	600	Hungert's Creek	1838	2	75
Grimmet, Jacob	200	Hungard's Creek	1860	3	190
Grimmet, Jacob	200	Big Creek	1859	3	156
Grimmet, John	305	Big Creek	1860	3	165
Grimmet, John	78	Hungard's Creek	1860	3	173
Grimmet, Joseph	90	Big Creek	1838	2	77
Grimmet, Joseph	300	Big Creek	1855	3	50
Grimmet, Joseph	123	Peter's Knob	1855	3	57
Groves, Jacob	200	Laurel Creek	1844	2	221
Groves, Jacob	50	Laurel Creek	1838	2	114
Groves, Jacob et al	75	Laurel Run	1837	2	32
Hall, Benjamin	1a.25p.	Union	1802	1	34
Hall, Benjamin	295	Crooked Run	1808	1	153
Hall, John Jr.	90	Dropping Lick	1805	1	92
Hall, Samuel	75	Ft. Peters Mt.	1809	1	167
Halstead, Alexander	418	Indian Creek	1835	1	591
Halstead, Benjamin	110	Wts. Indian Creek	1833	1	483
Halstead, Benjamin	3	Indian Creek	1847	2	292
Halstead, Benjamin	168	Indian Creek	1822	1	367
Halstead, John	40	Indian Creek	1804	1	76
Ham—See Hayne					
Hayne, John (Ham)	50	Wolf Creek	1819	1	306
Hayne, Samuel (Ham)	19	The Sinks	1802	1	19
Hamilton, Samuel	1½	The Sinks	1849	2	333
Handley—See also Hanley					
Handley, Archibald	5	Adj. his own	1827	1	429
Handley, Archibald et al Heirs	96	Turkey Creek	1826	1	400
Handley, Isaac	7	Indian Creek	1819	1	319
Handley, John	31	Dropping Lick	1812	1	232
Handley, William	618	Bradshaw Run	1827	1	428
Handley, William	120	Bradshaw Run	1828	1	439
Handley, William	83	Griffith's Creek	1838	2	128
Handley, William	206½	Pott's Creek	1819	1	305
Handley, William	48	Laurel Creek	1834	1	587
Hank, Caleb	21	Turkey Creek	1838	2	66
Hank, Caleb	74	Dropping Lick	1838	2	67
Hank, Jehu	500	Dropping Lick	1846	2	253
Hanley—See also Handley					
Hanley, Archibald	5	Adj. his own	1827	1	429
Hanley, Archibald	3	Turkey Creek	1837	2	44
Hanley, Archibald et al	96	Turkey Creek	1826	1	400
Hanley, Samuel	77	Indian Creek	1835	1	524
Hanley, William	120	Bradshaw Run	1828	1	439
Hanley, William	618	Bradshaw Run	1827	1	428
Harbert, William	80	Dunlap Creek	1817	1	284
Haregro, Jane	58	Foot Peters Mt.	1815	1	256
Haregro, Jane	68	Clen's Run	1815	1	257
Harvey—See Harvie					
Harvey, Allen L.	143	Adj. H. McDaniel	1855	3	47
Harvey, Benjamin	450	Indian Creek	1805	1	104
Harvey, James	120	Indian Creek	1843	2	209
Harvey, James	70	Indian Creek	1836	2	3
Harvey, John	70	Hand's Creek	1834	1	511
Harvey, Jonathan W. et al	100	Stinking Lick	1838	2	85
Harvey, William	24	Dropping Lick	1860	3	174

Name of Grantee	Acres	Local Description	Year	Book	Page
Harvie—See Harvey					
Harvie, John et al	459	Indian Creek	1805	1	113
Harvie, Nicholas	39	Fitz's Run	1805	1	112
Harvie, Nicholas	490	Indian Creek	1805	1	108
Haynes, George W.	1a.56p.	Wolf Creek	1862	3	213
Haynes, James M.	1a.56p.	2nd Creek	1837	2	33
Haynes, James M. et al	110	2nd Creek	1837	2	31
Haynes, Joseph et al	123	Leeches Branch	1827	1	581
Haynes, William	53	Peter's Mt.	1820	1	336
Heatley, Francis	55	Wts. New River	1809	1	198
Hedrick, George W.	6	Hungart's Creek	1861	3	205
Hedrick, Moses	38	Hungart's Creek	1843	2	198
Hedrick, Moses	53	Adj. Philip Meadows	1857	3	85
Hefner, Henry	17½	Wolf Creek	1819	1	316
Hefner, Henry et al	30	Matt's Branch	1822	1	354
Helms, L. W.	25	Pott's Creek	1861	3	210
Henchman, Joseph	½	Laurel Creek	1838	2	65
Henchman, William	68	Kelly's Creek	1848	2	310
Henchman, William	25	Kelly's Creek	1848	2	316
Henderson, Sarah	117	Turkey Creek	1802	1	8
Herbert, William	185	Dunlap Creek	1818	1	292
Herbert, William	56	Dunlap Creek	1817	1	285
Herbert, William	80	Dunlap Creek	1817	1	284
Herbert, William	190	Snake Branch	1816	1	278
Herbert, William	70	Snake Run	1813	1	243
Herbert, William	23	Snake Run	1822	1	351
Herbert, William	10	Snake Run	1822	1	352
Hickenbotham, Hickenbottom, Higginbotham					
Hickenbotham, Andrew W.	110	Second Creek	1858	3	113
Hickenbottom, James	159	Big Devil's Creek	1807	1	147
Hickinbottom, Thomas	110½	Dunlap Creek	1820	1	330
Hickinbottom, Thomas	106	2nd Creek	1820	1	331
Higginbotham, John G. & E. J.	90	Cove Creek	1846	2	254
Higginbotham, Moses	50	Back Creek	1838	2	82
Higginbotham, Moses	50	Back Creek	1844	2	222
Hinchman, John	174	Wolf Creek	1831	1	456
Hinchman, William	97	Wolf Creek	1852	2	435
Hinchman, William	150	Wts. Greenbrier	1810	1	200
Hinchman, William	200	Kelly's Creek	1837	2	54
Hinton, John	1a.18p.	Laurel Creek	1837	2	30
Hoake—See Hoke					
Hoake, Christopher	240	Laurel Creek	1815	1	258
Hogshead, Charles	94	Plank Cabin Draught	1816	1	266
Hogshead, John	25	2nd Creek	1837	2	27
Hogshead, John	45	Wolf Creek	1807	1	148
Hogshead, John	80	The Sinks	1807	1	154
Hogshead, John	18¾	Adj. Robt. Young	1808	1	162
Hogshead, John	5	Wolf Creek	1809	1	174
Hogshead, John	60	Carpenter's Run	1816	1	265
Hogshead, John	50	Dunlap Creek	1818	1	290
Hogshead, John	88	2nd Creek	1834	1	509
Hogshead, John B.	295	Laurel Creek	1846	2	269
Hogshead, John B.	81	Laurel Creek	1846	2	268
Hogshead, John B. et al	100	Carpenter's Run	1835	1	523
Hoke—See Hoake					
Hoke, C. C.	100	Cove Creek	1858	3	117
Hoke, C. C.	100	Carpenter's Run	1858	3	118
Hoke, Christopher C.	480	Cove Creek	1857	3	89
Hoke, Henry	50	Second Creek	1844	2	233
Hoke, Henry	68	Laurel Creek	1848	2	315
Hoke, Henry et al	100	Carpenter's Run	1835	1	523
Hoke, William	500	Kate's Mountain	1827	1	430
Hoke, William	20	Adj. his own	1826	1	413

Name of Grantee	Acres	Local Description	Year	Book	Page
Hoke, William	164	Laurel Creek	1830	1	452
Hoke, William	435	Laurel	1840	2	153
Hoke, William	116	Carpenter's Run	1826	1	410
Hoke, William & Henry Jr.	100	Laurel Creek	1850	2	377
Hoke, William Jr.	336	Archer's Run	1850	2	376
Hoke, William Jr.	200	Archer's Fork	1860	3	171
Hoke, William Jr.	177	Laurel Creek	1860	3	170
Hoke, William Sr.	35	Laurel Creek	1850	2	368
Hoke, William Sr.	165	Laurel Creek	1850	2	367
Hoke, William Sr.	150	Carpenter's Run	1853	3	15
Hoke, William Sr.	32	Carpenter's Run	1853	3	16
Hoke, William Sr.	68	Carpenter's Run	1853	3	17
Hollerin, William et al	217	2nd Creek	1821	1	350
Holsapple, Henry	18	Carpenter's Run	1861	3	195
Holsapple, Henry	100	Carpenter's Run	1841	2	160
Holsapple, Henry	57	Laurel Creek	1847	2	278
Holsapple, Henry	98	Laurel Creek	1847	2	277
Holsapple, Henry	29	Laurel Creek	1850	2	369
Holsapple, Philip	50	Carpenter's Run	1837	2	39
Houchins, John	95	Hand's Creek	1836	1	538
Hull, Henry	136	2nd Creek	1805	1	96
Hull, John A. J.	99	Dunlap's Creek	1853	3	6
Hull, John A. J. & Henry	100	Second Creek	1858	3	122
Hull, John et al	200	Back Creek	1838	2	117
Humphreys, Jacob C.	6	Indian Creek	1837	2	22
Humphreys, Jacob C.	25	Hand's Creek	1837	2	28
Humphreys, Jacob C.	730	Fitz's Run	1837	2	48
Humphreys, Jacob C.	180	Indian Creek	1846	2	248
Humphreys, James et al	215	Laurel Creek	1847	2	290
Humphreys, John	302	Second Creek	1813	1	242
Humphreys, John	1,035	2nd Creek	1805	1	575
Humphreys, John D.	400	Pott's Creek	1838	2	100
Humphreys, Samuel C.	40	Hand's Creek	1843	2	199
Humphreys, Samuel C.	90	Indian Creek	1843	2	208
Humphreys, William	57	Paint Bank Branch	1838	2	80
Humphreys, William	44	Pott's Creek	1838	2	81
Humphreys, William	90	Pott's Creek	1842	2	179
Hundley, William	404	Hungard's Creek	1838	2	118
Hunt, Samuel C.	172	Stinking Creek	1822	1	360
Hunter, James	35	Stinking Lick	1844	2	213
Hunter, James	49	Brush Creek	1844	2	212
Hunter, Samuel	375	Hans Creek	1805	1	97
Hunter, Samuel	88	Hans Creek	1805	1	98
Hutchinson, Alexander	470	Indian Creek	1810	1	190
Hutchinson, David	48	Rich Creek	1813	1	239
Hutchinson, Isaac et al	192	Rich Creek	1814	1	251
Hutchinson, John	1,720	Second Creek	1855	3	42
Hutchinson, Samuel I. (or J.)	75	Clem's Run	1842	2	173
Hutchinson, Samuel J.	40	Peter's Mt.	1842	2	174
Hutchison, Andrew	10	Hand's Creek	1838	2	99
Hutchison, Andrew	50	Hand's Creek	1850	2	390
Hutchison, William C.	70	Wts. Greenbrier	1852	2	434
Jarred, David	144	Adj. Moses Gwin	1804	1	84
Jarred, David	100	Wts. Greenbrier	1807	1	157
Jarvis, Field	126	Pott's Creek	1822	1	373
Jarvis, Field A.	100	Ewings Run	1838	2	83
Jarvis, Field A.	11½	Little Mountain	1851	2	421
Jarvis, Field W.	25	Pott's Creek	1855	3	36
Jarvis, Field W.	19	Pott's Creek	1855	3	37
Jarvis, John	617	Ewings Run	1822	1	372
Jarvis, John	243	Pott's Creek	1848	2	322
Jarvis, John	25	Adj. Hugh Cummings	1851	2	416
Jarvis, Washington	36	Trout Run	1849	2	343

Name of Grantee	Acres	Local Description	Year	Book	Page
Jarvis, Washington	136	Pott's Creek	1849	2	334
Jarvis, Washington	49	Price's Mt.	1851	2	417
Johnson—See Johnston					
Johnson, Caleb	26	Wolf Creek	1826	1	406
Johnson, James	1½	Adj. Coffman's Tract	1861	3	199
Johnson, Jacob	14	Wolf Creek	1838	2	130
Johnson, Jacob	40	Dry Run	1838	2	132
Johnson, Richard	20	Turkey Creek	1828	1	438
Johnson, Robert	48	Wolf Creek	1819	1	320
Johnson, Thomas R.	25	Turkey Creek	1841	2	161
Johnson, William	160	Wolf Creek	1820	1	345
Johnson, William B.	20	Adj. W. Hinchman	1855	3	55
Johnston—or Johnson					
Johnston, Richard	20	Dropping Lick	1804	1	78
Johnston, Robert	36	Lobs Knobs	1805	1	130
Johnston, Thomas	25	Adj. John McNutt	1803	1	57
Jones, Elisha & T J.	500	Wolf Creek	1838	2	101
Jones, Valentine	50	Snake Run	1813	1	244
Jones, William Sr.	3½	The Sinks	1815	1	253
Kales—See also Cales					
Kales, James	16	Wolf Creek	1850	2	383
Kean, David	165	Dunlap's Creek	1808	1	165
Kean, David	720	Dunlap's Creek	1808	1	164
Kearns, Henry	37	Hungart's Creek	1849	2	351
Keatley—also Keatly					
Keatley, James	31	Wts. New River	1844	2	227
Keatley, James	19	Indian Creek	1836	1	564
Keatley, James	114	Stinking Lick	1860	3	189
Keatley, Wilson	4	Indian Creek	1852	2	436
Keatly, Henry	1¾	Stinking Lick	1850	2	385
Keatly, Henry	244	Ash Branch	1850	2	389
Keaton, John (or Johnson)	5½	Indian Creek	1849	2	335
Keaton, Thompson	14	Hand's Creek	1838	2	55
Kellar, Coonrod	7	Kiln Branch	1810	1	208
Kelly, Henry	100	Little Creek	1836	2	19
Keppers, Wm. & John	233	Keeney's Knob	1826	1	399
Kertley, Henry	114	Stinking Lick	1860	3	189
Kessinger, James	29	Humphrey's Run	1849	2	347
Kessinger, James H.	70	Indian Creek	1849	2	346
Kessinger, James H.	10	Wiseman Mt.	1848	2	324
Kessinger, Mathias	50	Wts. Greenbrier	1850	2	356
Kessinger, Mathias et al	21	Wts. Greenbrier	1852	2	439
Kincaid, Mary et al Heirs	96	Turkey Creek	1826	1	400
Kincaid, Mathew	20	Hungard's Creek	1851	2	403
Kitchen, Alexander	14	2nd Creek	1815	1	260
Kitchen, Alexander	35	2nd Creek	1813	1	238
Knox, Robert	277	2nd Creek	1805	1	109
Lanius, John W.	120	Second Creek	1857	3	94
Lanius, John W.	125	Big Branch	1857	3	95
Larew, John M.	5½	Hand's Creek	1857	3	96
Larkins, James	50	The Sinks	1811	1	215
Lawrence, John	400	Indian Creek	1835	1	522
Lawrence, John	100	Fitz Run	1836	2	5
Legg, Edmund P.	77	Peters Mt.	1858	3	132
Lemmon, John	65	Wolf Creek	1825	1	397
Lewellen, Anderson A.	48	Second Creek	1847	2	284
Lewellen, Anderson A.	2	Second Creek	1847	2	283
Lewis, John	40	2nd Creek	1809	1	199
Lewis, John	90	Cove Creek	1810	1	209
Lewis, John	184	Laurel Creek	1810	1	210
Lewis, John	250	Laurel Creek	1810	1	212
Lewis, John	50	Dunlap Creek	1816	1	267
Lewis, John B.	9	Dunlap's Creek	1851	2	401

Name of Grantee	Acres	Local Description	Year	Book	Page
Lewis, Wilson	170	Adj. I. McDaniel	1822	1	364
Lively, Benjamin	114	Laurel Creek	1802	1	22
Lively, Benjamin	48	Laurel Creek	1802	1	21
Lively, Benjamin	163	Laurel Creek	1835	1	533
Lively, Benjamin	111	Bradshaw Run	1848	2	318
Lively, Benjamin	213	Bradshaw Run	1848	2	311
Lively, Benjamin	11¾	Laurel Creek	1834	1	508
Lively, Benjamin Sr.	2½	Bradshaw Run	1838	2	89
Lively, Benjamin Sr.	3¾	Bradshaw Run	1838	2	131
Lively, Benjamin Sr.	200	Jonnicake Fork	1836	1	539
Lively, Henry	16½	Swope's Knob	1847	2	297
Lively, Joseph	79	Blue Lick	1838	2	102
Lively, Joseph Jr.	8	Blue Lick	1838	2	103
Lively, Joseph Sr.	93	Stoney Creek	1834	1	506
Lively, Thomas	30	Blue Lick Run	1837	2	49
Lively, William M.	22	Laurel Creek	1851	2	404
Lively, Wilson	210	Elk Lick	1847	2	308
Lowdermilk, John	46	Turkey Creek	1820	1	343
Lowe, Joshua	80	Indian Creek	1848	2	317
Lowe, Joshua	50	Laurel Creek	1831	1	465
Lowe, Joshua Jr.	230	Indian Creek	1838	2	90
Lowe, Matthew	10	Swope's Knob	1836	1	528
Lowe, Matthew	30	Hungart's Creek	1858	3	104
Lynch, John	14	Adj. Robt. Reed	1809	1	171
Macarty, John	5½	The Sinks	1824	1	394
Maddox, William	42	Indian Draft	1805	1	120
Maddy—or Mady					
Maddy, Eber W.	420	Little Wolf Creek	1850	2	370
Maddy, Eber W.	300	Wolf Creek	1852	2	437
Maddy, Jacob	81	Licking Creek	1834	1	496
Maddy, Jacob	6½	Indian Creek	1834	1	498
Maddy, Jacob	60	Dropping Lick	1831	1	457
Maddy, Jacob	100	Beck Creek	1832	1	468
Maddy, Jacob	20	Back Creek	1832	1	474
Maddy, Jacob	98	Slaty Run	1838	2	143
Maddy, Jacob	3a.70p.	Indian Creek	1837	2	20
Maddy, Jacob	38	Dropping Lick	1837	2	25
Maddy, Jacob	8	Adj. J. Grimmit	1844	2	223
Maddy, Jacob et al	161	Big Creek	1838	2	74
Maddy, Jacob et al	1,450	Big Creek	1838	2	76
Maddy, Jacob et al	600	Hungert's Creek	1838	2	75
Maddy, Jacob et al	290	Indian Creek	1830	1	450
Maddy, John C.	53	Indian Creek	1848	2	326
Maddy, Joseph	400	Tom's Run	1850	2	371
Maddy, Joseph F. & Eber W.	75	Jacob Howard Deadning	1850	2	378
Mady—or Maddy					
Mady, John	22	Indian Creek	1812	1	230
Mady, William	94	Indian Creek	1802	1	35
Maggart, Henry	45	Wolf Creek	1822	1	353
Maggart, Samuel	17	Indian Creek	1836	2	11
Mahan, Andrew et al (Nahan)	75	Laurel Run	1837	2	32
Mahan, John	36	Devil's Creek	1811	1	217
Mahan, John	70	Turkey Creek	1838	2	64
Malcolm, Samuel	3	The Sinks	1819	1	314
Man—Mann					
Man, Adam	18	Indian Creek	1802	1	25
Mann, Adam	28	Slaty Run	1838	2	104
Mann, Adam Jr.	34	Indian Creek	1834	1	500
Mann, Archibald	50	Indian Creek	1841	2	166
Mann, Archibald	2	Bond's Run	1850	2	387
Mann, Jacob	30	Indian Creek	1832	1	36
Mann, Jacob	155	Wts. Indian Creek	1805	1	100
Mann, James et al	100	Stinking Lick	1838	2	85

Name of Grantee	Acres	Local Description	Year	Book	Page
Mann, James Sr. & Henly	100	Stinking Lick	1847	2	306
Mann, Jefferson T. et al	130	Laurel Creek	1850	2	388
Mann, John	5¼	Indian Creek	1838	2	62
Mann, Moses	22	Indian Creek	1831	1	455
Mann, William T.	107	Indian Creek	1819	1	325
Mann, William T.	1a.20p.	Swope's Knob	1834	1	491
Mathews, William	126	Back Creek	1804	1	74
McCorkle, Samuel (McCorcle)	29	Adj. J. Newman	1856	3	72
McDaniel, Isaac	165	Adj. Wilson Lewis	1822	1	366
McDaniel, Thomas	200	Stinking Lick	1805	1	117
McDaniel, William	3	Indian Creek	1822	1	357
McDaniel, William	44	Indian Creek	1822	1	356
McDaniel, William	151	Adj. I. McDaniel	1822	1	355
McDaniel, William	169	Adj. John Pack	1820	1	340
McDaniel, William	4	Island New River	1836	2	6
McDowell, James	174	Wolf Creek	1808	1	160
McDowell, John	56	2nd Creek	1807	1	158
McGehee, Lively	368	Hans Creek	1805	1	95
McGraw, Andrew	60	Eagle Branch	1858	3	129
McGraw, Henry	100	Hungert's Creek	1819	1	309
McMahan, Cornelius	20	Rich Creek	1843	2	202
McNear—See McNeer					
McNear, Richard & Anderson	27	Hand's Creek	1838	2	84
McNeer, Andrew et al	48	Buffalo Run	1856	3	63
Meadows, Anderson P.	10¾	Brush Creek	1861	3	208
Meadows, Anthony	20	Kate's Path	1834	1	494
Meadows, Anthony	195	Adj. C. Hale	1856	3	73
Meadows, Anthony	44	Adj. Thomas Wyatt	1850	2	381
Meadows, Anthony	25	Wolf Creek	1850	2	380
Meadows, Anthony	23	Wolf Creek	1847	2	300
Meadows, Anthony	80	Wolf Creek	1844	2	228
Meadows, Anthony	266	Wolf Creek	1834	1	505
Meadows, Anthony	107	Wolf Creek	1836	2	4
Meadows, Anthony	210	Adj. Wm. Pack	1859	3	152
Meadows, Anthony	83	New River Hill	1858	3	123
Meadows, Anthony et al	82	Adj. I. Milburn	1846	2	260
Meadows, Francis Jr.	50	Wts. Greenbrier R.	1834	1	488
Meadows, John	136	Howard's Branch	1834	1	490
Meadows, John	12	Adj. R. Roach	1834	1	493
Meadows, Joshua	52½	Adj. John Meadows	1834	1	501
Meadows, Nathan	5	Adj. Joseph Grimmet	1860	3	176
Meadows, Nathan	8	2 Islands in Greenbrier	1860	3	177
Meadows, Nathan	73	Adj. James Siers	1856	3	68
Meadows, Nathan	18	Adj. Anthony Meadows	1856	3	67
Meadows, Robert	76	Wolf Creek	1847	2	293
Meadows, St. Clair	62	Adj. James Ferrell	1854	3	29
Meadows, St. Clair	50	Wolf Creek	1850	2	379
Meadows, St. Clair	8½	Spruce Run	1856	3	76
Meadows, Thomas	83	Howard's Branch	1851	2	405
Meadows, Thomas	75	Wts. Greenbrier	1852	2	438
Meadows, Thomas & Mathias et al	21	Wts. Greenbrier	1852	2	439
Meadows, William	25	Adj. Francis Meadows	1857	3	101
Meadows, William	140	Adj. Reuben Roach	1860	3	172
Mentz, Robert C. L.	190	Cove Creek	1860	3	184
Meredith, Junior	60	Wolf Creek	1848	2	325
Meredith, Junior	50	Wolf Creek	1836	1	560
Messy, Jacob	200	Sinks	1801	1	12
Middleton, Henry O.	21,000	Little Devil's Cr.	1858	3	456
Middleton, Henry O.	2,450	Griffith's Creek	1858	3	454
Milburn, Henry	18	Wts. Greenbrier	1859	3	149
Milburn, Isaac	100	Adj. D. Boardman	1834	1	489
Milburn, Isaac	100	Wolf Creek	1834	1	504
Millburn, Isaac	20	Indian Creek	1821	1	347

Name of Grantee	Acres	Local Description	Year	Book	Page
Miller—or Millar					
Miller, Anderson	22½	Handy Creek	1849	2	330
Miller, Andrew	42	Wolf Creek	1818	1	295
Miller, Andrew	1,067	Wolf Creek	1818	1	296
Miller, George	144	Painter's Run	1805	1	94
Miller, Henry	46	Indian Creek	1836	1	551
Miller, Jacob	14	Rich Creek	1805	1	129
Miller, Jacob	100	Dropping Lick	1841	2	159
Miller, Jacob	16½	Turkey Creek	1833	1	477
Miller, James Sr. (Millar)	110	Wolf Cr.	1800	1	5
Miller, John	15	Dropping Lick	1846	2	255
Miller, Jonathan	105	Wolf Creek	1841	2	158
Miller, Moses	113	Indian Creek	1842	2	185
Miller, Peter	71	Hungart's Creek	1842	2	186
Miller, Peter	7	Swope's Knob	1831	1	463
Miller, Peter et al	165	Hungart's Creek	1842	2	187
Miller, Valentine	3¼	Swope's Knob	1826	1	420
Miller, Thomas	68	Dropping Lick	1805	1	107
Minter, Jesse	116	Snake Run	1809	1	175
Montgomery, Ann	55	2nd Creek	1810	1	211
Morgan, Aaron	3	Turkey Creek	1843	2	200
Morgan, Aaron	27	Little Mountain	1843	2	201
Morris, John B.	42	Rich Creek	1837	2	50
Moss, George	50	Dunlap's Creek	1831	1	466
Moss, Henry	300	Dunlap's Creek	1816	1	280
Moss, Henry	64	Dunlap Creek	1818	1	291
Moss, Henry W.	30	Little Mountain	1822	1	362
Moss, Moses	.50	Laurel Creek	1841	2	154
Mottesheard, Daniel	100	Pott's Creek	1851	2	392
Mottesheard, Daniel S.	55	Second Creek	1844	2	211
Nahan, Andrew et al (Mahan)	75	Laurel Run	1837	2	32
Neal—or Neel, Neele					
Neal, Ephraim	215	Devil's Creek	1861	3	207
Neel, Abner	50	Little Mountain	1859	3	138
Neel, Abner	22	Peters Mountian	1861	3	202
Neel, Abner H.	41	Second Creek	1858	3	116
Neel, Ephraim	30	Dunlap Creek	1859	3	151
Neel, Ephraim	215	Devil's Creek	1861	3	207
Neel, Henry	24	Swope's Knob	1818	1	297
Neel, Jacob	10	Peter's Mt.	1858	3	128
Neel, John	16	Dunlop Creek	1809	1	197
Neel, John O.	65	Second Creek	1843	2	210
Neel, Joseph	25	Second Creek	1820	1	338
Neel, Owen	27	2nd Creek	1809	1	173
Neel, Thomas	4	Second Creek	1859	3	154
Neel, William	50	2nd Creek	1834	1	502
Neel, William H.	50	Second Creek	1851	2	394
Neel, William Jr.	200	Second Creek	1851	2	393
Neele, Thomas	8½	2nd Creek	1834	1	497
Neele, Thomas et al	50	2nd Creek	1846	2	261
Neely, John	12	New River Ridge	1822	1	368
Nelson, James	170	Adj. Nickell Perry	1807	1	150
Nelson, John W.	350	Cove Creek	1861	3	192
Nelson, John W.	300	Cove Creek	1861	3	193
Newman, Jonathan	3¾	Adj. Jacob Johnson	1838	2	121
Nickel—Nickle					
Nickel, Andrew	179	2nd Creek	1846	2	247
Nickle, Andrew	469	Second Creek	1846	2	246
Nickle, Andrew	1a.135p.	2nd Creek	1841	2	164
Nickle, Andrew	84	Laurel Creek	1838	2	105
Nickle, Andrew	5½	Adj. his own	1832	1	469
Nickle, George	4¼	Adj. A. Bierne	1833	1	479
Nickle, Thomas	100	Swope's Knob	1802	1	28

Name of Grantee	Acres	Local Description	Year	Book	Page
Noble, Joshua H. et al	48	Buffalo Run	1856	3	63
Nolan—Noland, Nowlan					
Nolan, John	45	Hungard's Creek	1851	2	399
Noland, (or Nowlan) John	143	Hungard's Creek	1855	3	52
Noland, John	45	Hungard's Creek	1851	2	399
Noland, John	133	Hungart's Creek	1845	2	238
Noland, John	355	Hungart's Creek	1845	2	239
Noland, John	70	Hungard's Creek	1843	2	204
Noland, John	130	Hungard's Creek	1843	2	203
Noland, John	159	Hungard's Creek	1838	2	119
Noland, John	310	Hungard's Creek	1838	2	120
Noland, John	54	Hungard's Creek	1858	3	133
Noland, John et al	165	Hungart's Creek	1842	2	187
Noland, Joseph & John Jr.	175	Hungard's Creek	1862	3	219
Nowlan—Nolan, Noland					
Nowlan, John	143	Hungard's Creek	1855	3	52
Nowlan, John	355	Hungart's Creek	1845	2	239
Nowlan, John	133	Hungart's Creek	1845	2	238
Nowlan, John	54	Hungard's Creek	1858	3	133
Nowlan, Joseph	175	Hungard's Creek	1862	3	219
Nutter, David	110	Broad Run	1801	1	13
Olford—See Alford, Alfred					
Olford, Joseph (Alford)	47	The Sinks	1804	1	69
Pack, Loami	19	Brush Creek	1838	2	106
Pack, Samuel	60	Rush Creek	1804	1	71
Pack, Samuel et al Heirs	200	Adj. T. Wyatt	1826	1	398
Pack, William	190	Adj. John Pack	1836	2	8
Pancoast, David	2	Bull Falls	1832	1	470
Parker, Brownlee	66	Big Run	1846	2	257
Parker, Brownlee	100	Second Creek	1848	2	321
Parker, Brownlee H.	96	Laurel Creek	1861	3	203
Parker, Jesse	120	Laurel Creek	1847	2	285
Parker, Joseph	122	Laurel Creek	1857	3	92
Parker, Joseph	3½	Cove Creek	1860	3	188
Parker, Joseph	45	Laurel Creek	1857	3	93
Parker, Joseph	130	Laurel Creek	1844	2	226
Parker, Joseph	240	Second Creek	1847	2	287
Parker, Joseph	100	Second Creek	1847	2	286
Parker, Joseph	290	Rich Creek	1804	1	86
Parker, William	119	Second Creek	1846	2	256
Patterson, Mathew	14	Griffith's Branch	1803	1	47
Patterson, Thomas	32	Kelly's Creek	1853	3	14
Patterson, Thomas	84	Knob Lick	1848	2	319
Patton, James N.	308	Second Creek	1838	2	122
Patton, James N.	1,363	Second Creek	1838	2	123
Patton, James N.	135	Cove Creek	1837	2	38
Patton, Napoleon	70	Pott's Creek	1855	3	43
Patton, Tristam	150	Flat Mountain	1820	1	342
Patton, William	127	Pott's Creek	1847	2	301
Patton, William	68	Pott's Creek	1847	2	298
Patton, William	75	Pott's Creek	1854	3	26
Patton, William M.	94	Pott's Creek	1855	3	44
Peck, Benjamin B.	14	Indian Creek	1838	2	91
Peck, Elisha G.	107	Scott's Branch	1853	3	24
Peck, Jacob	166	Rich Creek	1837	2	34
Peck, Jacob	23	Rich Creek	1810	1	196
Pence, David	52	Indian Creek	1855	3	40
Pence, David	23	Indian Creek	1834	1	492
Pennington, Highland	94	Adj. S. Hunter	1851	2	400
Pennington, Wheeler	80	New River Ridge	1815	1	261
Pennington, Wheeler	100	New River Hill	1837	2	23
Pennington, Wheeler	38	Adj. Allen Survey	1855	3	39
Pennington, William	60	Adj. Wm. Wyley	1860	3	183

Name of Grantee	Acres	Local Description	Year	Book	Page
Perry, Addison	23	Lick Run	1844	2	225
Perry, Daniel	440	The Sinks	1804	1	82
Perry, Daniel	426	2nd Creek	1802	1	31
Perry, John	310	Adj. Coonrod Kellar	1801	1	11
Peters, Christian	45	Indian Draft	1806	1	138
Peters, Christian	105	Rich Creek	1804	1	85
Peters, Christian	150	Scott's Branch	1804	1	81
Peters, Christian	100	Rich Creek	1809	1	182
Peters, Christian et al	390	Rich Creek	1809	1	185
Peters, Christian et al	357	Brush Creek	1809	1	184
Peters, Conrad	19	Butcher's Run	1848	2	309
Peters, Conrad	47	Brush Creek	1842	2	182
Peters, John	275	Rich Creek	1810	1	195
Peters, John Sr.	85	Adj. B. Abbott	1855	3	41
Phillips, Nehemiah	125	Brush Creek	1842	2	181
Pine, Absolum	45	Adj. James Pine	1819	1	323
Prett—See Pritt					
Pritt, Thomas (Prett)	150	Carpenter's Run	1840	2	152
Pritt, James	81	Carpenter's Run	1844	2	224
Prose—or Pross					
Prose, Paul	35	Lick Run	1819	1	310
Pross, Paul	100	Hungard Creek	1802	1	18
Quigley, Joseph	97	Turkey Creek	1808	1	163
Raburn—See also Reaburn					
Raburn, Charles	176	Laurel Creek	1858	3	112
Rains, Jackson Heirs	70	Panther Run	1861	3	194
Ray, John	24	Dropping Lick	1804	1	68
Raynes, William	100	Indian Creek	1845	2	245
Reaburn—See also Raburn					
Reaburn, Charles	158	Laurel Creek	1836	1	549
Reaburn, Charles	111	Laurel Creek	1838	2	107
Read, Benjamin	475	Cove Creek	1837	2	43
Reed, John et al	50	Laurel Creek	1844	2	217
Reynolds, Thomas	206	Plank Cabin Draft	1816	1	271
Reynolds, Thomas	115	2nd Creek	1810	1	191
Rice, William	345	Wts. Rich Creek	1803	1	54
Ruth, Joseph	44	Dunlap Creek	1824	1	389
Ruth, Joseph	6	Dunlap Creek	1824	1	395
Roach, Isaac	58	Fit's Run	1846	2	265
Roach, Michaelberry	74	Adj. Reuben Roach	1833	1	484
Roach, Reuben R.	67	Pauley's Creek	1834	1	507
Roach, Reuben R.	50	Pauley's Creek	1833	1	485
Robinson, John	43	Rich Creek	1811	1	214
Roles—or Rolls					
Roles, Mordicai	175	Bradshaw Run	1823	1	378
Roles, Mordecai	81	Indian Creek	1835	1	514
Rolls, Mordicai	175	Bradshaw Run	1823	1	378
Rolyson, Charles K.	100	Adj. M. Kessinger	1858	3	126
Rolyson, Charles K.	350	Adj. Wm. Meadows	1858	3	127
Rookstool, Peter	380	Laurel Creek	1851	2	406
Rookstool, Peter	250	Hungart's Creek	1860	3	182
Rookstool, Peter	130	Hungart's Creek	1858	3	110
Rose, Jackson	165	Adj. Moses Arnett	1846	2	258
Rose, Jackson	22	Prices Mt.	1851	2	418
Rose, Jackson	150	Camp Branch	1851	2	419
Rose, William	7	Back Creek	1838	2	108
Ross, John	129	Kelly's Creek	1836	1	534
Ross, John	100	Kelly's Creek	1819	1	322
Ross, John	61	Kelly's Creek	1838	2	86
Ross, John	45	Kelly's Creek	1852	2	429
Rowan, Boston	100	Pott's Creek	1836	1	529
Rowan, Boston	5½	Pott's Creek	1851	2	423
Rowan, Boston	199	Peter's Mt.	1851	2	411

Name of Grantee	Acres	Local Description	Year	Book	Page
Rowan, Boston	50	Pott's Creek	1836	2	2
Rowan, Boston	115	Pott's Creek	1853	3	12
Rowan, Boston	1	Paint Bank Branch	1853	3	13
Rowan, Charles	317	Paint Bank Branch	1822	1	376
Rowan, Charles	60	Pott's Creek	1830	1	451
Rowan, Charles	12	Paint Bank Branch	1830	1	449
Rowan, Charles L.	100	Peter's Mt.	1851	2	422
Rowan, Stewart et al	173	Peter's Mt.	1836	1	562
Rowan, W. A. & C. L.	216	Paint Bank Branch	1838	2	87
Rowan, William	35	Pott's Creek	1847	2	275
Rowan, William	240	Pott's Creek	1847	2	276
Rowan, William A.	200	Pott's Creek	1856	3	64
Rowan, William A.	20	Pott's Creek	1838	2	88
Rowin, Charles	317	Paint Bank Branch	1822	1	376
Sams, John B.	50	Cove Mountain	1842	2	188
Sams, John B.	200	Cove Mountain	1860	3	185
Sams, John et al	110	2nd Creek	1837	2	31
Sams, Joseph H.	50	Laurel Creek	1856	3	70
Sams, Joseph H.	195	Cove Creek	1856	3	74
Saunders, Fleming	176	Jonicake Fork	1848	2	327
Saunders, Holeman	42	Mat's Branch	1850	2	372
Scarbrough, John	116	Back Creek	1805	1	110
Sciers, John	67	Hungart's Creek	1845	2	237
Scott, James	92	Broad Run	1805	1	123
Scott, James	44	The Sinks	1820	1	337
Scott, James K.	137	Hungard's Creek	1855	3	53
Scott, James K.	134	Hungard's Creek	1859	3	160
Scott, Matthew	470	The Sinks	1830	1	584
Scott, Thomas	58	Stinking Lick	1822	1	370
Scott, Thomas	114	Stinking Lick	1822	1	371
Scott, William	140	Hungart's Creek	1856	3	80
Scott, William	100	Adj. Joseph Gwinn	1858	3	105
Shanklin, Richard et al	170	Wolf Creek	1803	1	48
Shanklin, Richard et al	120	Swope's Knob	1809	1	176
Shanklin, Richard et al	112	Turkey Creek	1807	1	143
Shanklin, Richard V.	30	Indian Creek	1841	2	167
Shanklin, Richard V.	3a.66p.	Indian Creek	1843	2	190
Shanklin, William	100	2nd Creek	1836	1	540
Shawver, John	100	Paint Bank Run	1841	2	163
Shawver, John et al	173	Peter's Mt.	1836	1	562
Shelton, John	45	Pott's Creek	1838	2	109
Shepherd, John	44	Pott's Creek	1849	2	349
Shiers, George W.	33	Drooping Lick	1846	2	274
Shiers, Richard	73	Peter's Mt.	1811	1	213
Shoemate, Daniel	97	Rich Creek	1803	1	46
Shoemate, Daniel et al	390	Rich Creek	1809	1	185
Shultz, John	58	Rich Creek	1836	1	561
Shultz, John	7	Rich Creek	1849	2	344
Shultz, John	23	Rich Creek	1838	2	94
Shultz, John	100	Rich Creek	1837	2	35
Shumaker, Paul	132	2nd Creek	1804	1	83
Siers, Jesse	20	Adj. James Siers	1844	2	231
Siers, John	67	Hungart's Creek	1845	2	237
Sims, John	9¾	Rich Creek	1838	2	134
Sims, John	20	Peter's Mountain	1838	2	133
Sims, John	24	Rich Creek	1827	1	432
Sims, John	16	Rich Creek	1826	1	402
Sims, John	14½	Rich Creek	1835	1	519
Sims, John	15	Rich Creek	1835	1	515
Sims, John	20	Indian Creek	1818	1	287
Sims, John	50	Adj. Isaac Beasley	1858	3	125
Skeggs—or Skaggs					
Skeggs, John	9	Wolf Creek	1827	1	431

Name of Grantee	Acres	Local Description	Year	Book	Page
Smith, Anderson	112	Elk Run	1842	2	180
Smith, Jacob	100	Indian Creek	1807	1	155
Smith, Jacob	170	Indian Creek	1805	1	111
Smith, Jacob	38	Pott's Creek	1819	1	303
Smith, John	14	Second Creek	1809	1	168
Smith, John	57	Stoney Run	1805	1	122
Smith, Joseph	18	Second Creek	1849	2	348
Smithson, Thomas	25	Wolf Creek	1815	1	252
Snapp, Joseph H.	115	Hungard's Creek	1853	3	3
Sowards, Solomon	180	Hans Creek	1805	1	124
Spar, George	19	2nd Creek	1812	1	231
Steel—See Steele					
Steel, John M.	23	Pott's Creek	1853	3	10
Steel, John M.	43	Pott's Creek	1853	3	9
Steel, John M.	40	Pott's Creek	1858	3	119
Steel, Nelson G.	100	Pott's Creek	1858	3	114
Steel, Thomas	140	Peter's Mountain	1802	1	24
Steele, Benjamin F. et al	82	Adj. I. Millburn	1846	2	260
Steele, Samuel	14	Peter's Mt.	1833	1	478
Stephenson, Samuel	50	Wolf Creek	1807	1	145
Stodghill, James	58	Rich Creek	1836	1	545
Stodghill, James	23	Panther's Run	1836	1	526
Stodghill, James & Wm.	120	Blue Lick Run	1836	1	554
Stodghill, Jesse	90	Hand's Creek	1831	1	462
Stodghill, John	525	Stoney Creek	1824	1	392
Stodghill, Samuel	111	Hand's Creek	1837	2	37
Stodghill, William	18	Hand's Creek	1846	2	259
Stone, John	140	Dunlap Creek	1820	1	328
Stone, William	95	Indian Creek	1847	2	279
Stuart, Archibald	88	Rich Creek	1816	1	281
Stuart, Thomas	64	Indian Creek	1811	1	218
Summers, John et al	73½	Dunlap Creek	1827	1	433
Sumpter, John T.	100	Pott's Creek	1853	3	8
Sumpter, John T.	71½	Turkey Creek	1853	3	7
Swan, James	1,400	Indian Creek	1803	1	38
Swan, James	1,000	Indian Creek	1803	1	45
Swan, James	1,050	Hans Creek	1803	1	44
Swan, James	1,140	Hans Creek	1803	1	43
Swan, James	3,000	2nd Creek	1803	1	42
Swinney, Archibald	17	Rich Creek	1849	2	336
Swinney, Delaney & Archibald	70	Rich Creek	1843	2	205
Swinney, James	75	Wts. New River	1810	1	204
Swinney, James	31	Adj. Frank Farley	1822	1	375
Swinney, Vincent	79	Adj. B. B. Noble	1859	3	141
Swope, James & John	113	Hands Creek	1830	1	441
Swope, John	130	Hand's Creek	1850	2	382
Swope, John	25	Hand's Creek	1837	2	51
Swope, John	508	Stinking Lick	1861	3	191
Swope, Jonathan	97	Wolf Creek	1839	2	145
Swope, Jonathan et al	17	Wolf Creek	1821	1	346
Tackett, Nimrod	52	Laurel Creek	1836	2	7
Tackett, Nimrod	2a.72p.	Indian Creek	1836	1	510
Tackett, Nimrod	52	Indian Creek	1802	1	29
Tackett, Nimrod	50	Turkey Creek	1819	1	321
Tackett, Nimrod	10	Turkey Creek	1836	1	531
Taylor, Abel	108	Big Creek	1838	2	136
Taylor, John	15	Wts. Greenbrier	1809	1	170
Taylor, John	100	2nd Creek	1810	1	192
Taylor, John	100	Hungard's Creek	1838	2	135
Tennis, John	140	Laurel Creek	1802	1	20
Tennis, John et al Heirs	96	Turkey Creek	1826	1	400
Terry, Thomas	20	Wts. Greenbrier	1809	1	172
Thomas, Adam	4½	Adj. his own	1818	1	286

Name of Grantee	Acres	Local Description	Year	Book	Page
Thomas, Adam	475	Cor. to Wilson (Now Caperton)	1828	1	582
Thomas, Richard	25	Swope's Knob	1836	2	12
Thomas, Richard	60	Indian Draught	1847	2	303
Thomas, Richard	14	Swope's Knob	1836	1	566
Thompson—Also Thomson					
Thompson, John et al	138	Carpenter's Run	1805	1	119
Thompson, John et al	171	2nd Creek	1805	1	118
Thompson, Logan	100	Brush Creek	1847	2	307
Thomson—or Thompson					
Thomson, David	25	Rich Creek	1813	1	241
Thrasher, Robert	71	Blue Lick	1843	2	206
Tiffany, Hugh Sr.	20	Rich Creek	1838	2	110
Tincher, James	100	Kelly's Creek	1838	2	124
Tincher, James	120	Kelly's Creek	1836	1	535
Tincher, James et al	123	Leeches Branch	1827	1	581
Tincher, John	316	Wolf Creek	1838	2	137
Tincher, William	45	Wolf Creek	1837	2	46
Toler—See Towler					
Towler, Richard (Toler)	5	Bull Falls	1838	2	146
Tygart, John	48	Dunlap's Creek	1838	2	71
Upton, Loyd	68	Swope's Knob	1832	1	467
Upton, Meredith	17	Indian Draught	1835	1	518
Vance, Adam	101	Second Creek	1841	2	162
Vance, Adam	10	Carpenter's Run	1807	1	149
Vance, Adam	3	Carpenter's Run	1861	3	198
Vance, Adam J.	125	Carpenter's Run	1860	3	186
Vance, Henry R.	60	Laurel Creek	1855	3	51
Vance, Jacob	136	Maple Spring Run	1838	2	138
Vance, John D.	133	Maple Spring Branch	1855	3	58
Vance, Philip	58	Holesapple Mt.	1841	2	165
Vanstavern, Cornelius	11	2nd Creek	1847	2	289
Vanstavern, Cornelius	185	Second Creek	1847	2	288
Vanstavern, Cornelius et al	215	Laurel Creek	1847	2	290
Vass, Boswell	10	Bradshaw Run	1838	2	139
Vass, Jane	303	Devil's Creek	1837	2	52
Vass, Sarah E.	136	Dropping Lick	1861	3	211
Vawter, Elliott	70	Dunlap's Creek	1852	2	428
Vawter, James	33	Hand's Creek	1844	2	214
Vawter, James	407	Hand's Creek	1845	2	242
Vawter, John H.	634	Hand's Creek	1836	1	558
Vawter, William Sr.	214	Hans Creek	1805	1	93
Venable, Samuel W.	70	Indian Creek	1810	1	194
Vincent, Joseph	62	Kelly's Creek	1815	1	254
Waide, Samuel	65	Elk Lick Run	1836	1	563
Walker, Andrew	2½	The Sinks	1819	1	315
Walker, Daniel	47	Paint Bank Valley	1851	2	424
Walker, Thomas	50	Wts. New River	1838	2	111
Walker, Thomas Sr.	29	Wts. New River	1838	2	112
Walters, Harmon	100	Stony Creek	1857	3	103
Wantz, Philip	50	Houshapple Mt.	1831	1	460
Warren—or Wearen					
Warren, Cornelius H.	83	Brush Creek	1846	2	264
Warren, Cornelius H. (Wearen)	40	Butcher's Run	1845	2	243
Warren, Thornton F.	92	Brush Creek	1853	3	11
Webb, James	140	Pott's Creek	1849	2	345
Webb, James et al	50	Second Creek	1846	2	261
Webb, Warren H.	281	Jonicake Fork	1848	2	328
Wheeler, Anderson	100	Indian Draught	1845	2	235
Wheeler, James R.	106	Hungard's Creek	1856	3	62
Wheeler, James R.	366	Hungard's Creek	1859	3	159
Wheeler, Sarah et al	434	Hungard's Creek	1860	3	458
Wheeler, William R.	38	Hungard's Creek	1859	3	158

Name of Grantee	Acres	Local Description	Year	Book	Page
Wheeler, William R.	137	Big Creek	1859	3	157
Wheeler, William R. et al	434	Hungard's Creek	1860	3	458
White, Charles	139	Hans Creek	1804	1	75
Wickle—Wycle, Wykle					
Wickle, Philip	162½	Back Creek	1803	1	37
Wickline, Andrew J.	50	Second Creek	1858	3	135
Wickline, Daniel	30	Dunlap Creek	1837	2	36
Wickline, Daniel et al	73½	Dunlap Creek	1827	1	433
Wickline, Elijah	53	Peter's Mountain	1857	3	87
Wickline, Elijah	318	Dunlap Creek	1857	3	86
Wickline, Elijah	50	Carpenter's Run	1830	1	446
Wickline, Elijah	96	Second Creek	1851	2	395
Wickline, George	88	Dropping Lick	1816	1	276
Wickline, George	70	Dropping Lick	1805	1	105
Wickline, George	9	Dropping Lick	1852	2	442
Wickline, George Jr.	120	Dropping Lick	1838	2	113
Wickline, George Sr.	14	Dropping Lick	1853	3	25
Wickline, Jacob	50	2nd Creek	1837	2	53
Wickline, Jacob	52	Top Allegheny Mt.	1837	2	40
Wickline, Jacob	46	Dunlap Creek	1816	1	277
Wickline, Jacob	108	Dunlap Creek	1824	1	390
Wickline, Jacob	25	Dunlap's Creek	1850	2	374
Wickline, Jacob Jr.	95	Wolf Creek	1806	1	139
Wickline, Jacob Sr.	20	2nd Creek	1812	1	224
Wickline, Jacob Sr. & Jacob Jr.	90	Dunlop Creek	1805	1	115
Wickline, William Z.	140	Second Creek	1858	3	134
Wiley—Wilie, Willey					
Wiley, Andrew	240	Cove Creek	1846	2	263
Wiley, Thomas	97	Indian Creek	1802	1	30
Wiley, Thomas	220	Laurel Creek	1846	2	262
Wilie, Cochran & Andrew	535	Laurel Creek	1856	3	78
Willey, Eber	23	Slate Run	1839	2	149
Williams, Felix Jr.	60	Rich Creek	1842	2	177
Williams, Felix Jr.	123	Clem's Branch	1842	2	178
Williams, Felix	140	Rich Creek	1802	1	6
Williams, Felix	135	Clem's Run	1814	1	249
Williams, Felix	100	Rich Creek	1814	1	248
Williams, John L. et al	85	Rich Creek	1838	2	56
Willis, Malen H.	65	Wolf Creek	1850	2	357
Wilson, Andrew	150	Price Mountain	1848	2	312
Wilson, Henry	100	Dunlap's Creek	1816	1	264
Wilson, Mathew	60	Pott's Creek	1849	2	350
Wilson, William	4	Wts. New River	1812	1	228
Wilson, William et al	138	Carpenter's Run	1805	1	119
Wilson, William et al	171	2nd Creek	1805	1	118
Wiseman, Isaac	38	Michael's Knob	1823	1	385
Wiseman, Isaac	11	Mitchell's Mt.	1826	1	415
Wiseman, Isaac	100	Dropping Lick	1804	1	65
Wiseman, John R.	5¼	Adj. Robt. Nickle	1836	1	570
Wiseman, Joseph	90	Pott's Creek	1852	2	443
Wiseman, Owen	47	Michael's Knob	1823	1	384
Wiseman, Owen	32	Indian Creek	1838	2	63
Wiseman, Richard	76	Adj. Wm. Pack	1858	3	124
Wiseman, William	78½	Laurel Branch	1803	1	39
Wood—or Woods					
Wood, Bailey Jr.	100	Hungert's Creek	1819	1	311
Wood, John	117	Dropping Lick	1826	1	409
Wood, John	80	Dropping Lick	1826	1	408
Woodram, John & Bird	231	Spruce Run	1847	2	296
Woods—or Wood					
Woods, James	72	Wolf Creek	1823	1	383
Woods, John	265	Pheasant Run	1823	1	382
Woods, John	10½	Dropping Lick	1822	1	369

Name of Grantee	Acres	Local Description	Year	Book	Page
Woodson, Edwin W. et al	259	Bradshaw Run	1846	2	267
Wyant, Elijah M.	28	Hungart's Creek	1857	3	99
Wyant, Elijah M.	80	Pauley's Creek	1850	2	375
Wyant, Elijah M.	110	Hungard's Creek	1855	3	54
Wyant, Elijah M.	130	Pauley Creek	1852	2	441
Wyant, Peter B.	19	Poplar Hollow	1857	3	88
Wycle—also Wickle, Wykle					
Wycle, George C.	95	Little Wolf	1850	2	373
Wylie, Andrew	137	The Sinks	1834	1	586
Wylie, James	437	Paint Bank Branch	1834	1	486
Wylie, James	375	Pott's Creek	1836	1	557
Wylie, James	110	Pott's Creek	1836	1	547
Wylie, James	60	Adj. Wm. Wylie	1819	1	324
Wylie, James	99	Pott's Creek	1848	2	320
Wylie, James	59	Pott's Creek	1838	2	142
Wylie, James	30	Little Mountain	1838	2	141
Wylie, James	20	Peter's Mt.	1838	2	140
Wylie, James	200	Pott's Creek	1834	1	503
Wylie, James	800	Paint Bank Valley	1818	1	289
Wylie, John	346	Pott's Creek	1812	1	222
Wylie, John	60	Pott's Creek	1822	1	377
Wylie, John	171	Pott's Creek	1818	1	301
Wylie, John & James	100	Pott's Creek	1809	1	178
Wylie, John & James	460	Pott's Creek	1809	1	177
Young, Henry J.	100	Back Creek	1857	3	98
Young, James	29	The Sinks	1812	1	221
Young, James	13	Sinks	1802	1	7
Young, James	35	2nd Creek	1802	1	32
Young, Jane	19	Hand's Creek	1805	1	126
Young, Nicholas	134	Pott's Creek	1837	2	24
Young, Nicholas	100	Pott's Creek	1832	1	475
Young, Robert	81	Hans Creek	1809	1	166
Young, Robert	53½	Brushy Mt.	1850	2	364
Young, Robert	400	Adj. A. Griffiths	1802	1	16
Young, Robert	800	Eagle Branch	1802	1	15
Young, William	300	Laurel Creek	1857	3	102

MORGAN COUNTY

Name of Grantee	Acres	Local Description	Year	Book	Page
Alderton, David	20	Adj. James King	1849	1	334
Alderton, David	83	Big Run	1833	1	265
Alderton, Jacob	117	Adj. David Alderton	1833	1	266
Allabaugh, George et al	20	Sleepy Creek	1844	1	314
Ash, Jacob	92	Sleepy Creek	1841	1	294
Ash, Jacob	84	Sleepy Creek	1843	1	312
Aullabaugh. George et al	20	Sleepy Creek	1844	1	314
Baker, Isaac et al	74	Sidling Hill	1855	1	364
Barney, Joshua C.	724a.1r.29p.	Sleepy Creek	1836	1	279
Barney, William et al	293½	Cacapon Mt.	1828	1	243
Bechtol, Aaron et al	920	Dry Run	1845	1	315
Biggerstaff, Isaac	100	Adj. S. Biggerstaff	1823	1	228
Bohrer, Adam	9½	Sleepy Creek	1840	1	291
Boyles, James	17a.3r.15p.	Wts. Potomac	1832	1	260
Breathed, John W. et al	920	Dry Run	1845	1	315
Brosius, Jacob	35	Sidling Hill	1838	1	282
Brosius, Jacob et al	151	Cacapon Creek	1838	1	284
Bruce, Charles K. et al	400	Conoloway Hill	1845	1	321

Name of Grantee	Acres	Local Description	Year	Book	Page
Bruner—also Brunnar					
Bruner, Henry	32a.1r.	Cacapon Creek	1838	1	289
Bruner, Henry et al	73⅝	Cacapon Creek	1830	1	252
Bruner, Henry et al	97	Sidling Hill	1833	1	262
Buck, Isiah	50	Sleepy Creek	1833	1	264
Buck, Josiah (or Isaiah)	187	Spring Ridge	1842	1	304
Burk, Elizabeth	59½	Warm Springs Run	1825	1	230
Burk, John	124	Sir John's Run	1851	1	350
Burk, John	11½	Capt. John's Run	1827	1	241
Burk, John et al	56	Warm Springs Run	1826	1	232
Burnett, Henry	73⅝	Cacapon Creek	1830	1	252
Burney, Joshua C.	724a.1r.29p.	Sleepy Creek	1836	1	279
Cann, Jacob	100	Great Cacapon	1843	1	309
Cann, Jacob	100	Sidling Hill	1843	1	308
Cann, Jacob	139	Cacapon Mt.	1860	1	373
Cann, Jacob	9	Little Mountain	1856	1	367
Cann, Jacob	317	Sidling Hill	1856	1	368
Cann, Jacob	275	Cacapon Mt.	1856	1	369
Cann, Jacob	12¼	Sidling Hill	1853	1	356
Cann, Jacob	94	Cacapon Creek	1851	1	351
Cann, Jacob	134	Sidling Hill	1850	1	344
Cann, Jacob	22¼	Cacapon Creek	1850	1	343
Cann, Jacob	56	Cacapon Creek	1850	1	342
Cann, Jacob	76	Cacapon Mt.	1850	1	341
Cann, Jacob	510	Cacapon Mt.	1849	1	337
Cann, Jacob	140	Cacapon Creek	1847	1	329
Catlett, George	150	Adj. Tidball's	1843	1	310
Catlett, Pheby	6½	Capt. John's Run	1827	1	238
Catlett, William	9	Cacapon Creek	1840	1	292
Catlett, William G.	1a.22p.	Cacapon Creek	1847	1	326
Catlett, William G.	140	Cacapon Creek	1847	1	330
Catlett, William G. et al	222	Road Ridge	1849	1	339
Caton, Richard	38a.2r.	Sidling Hill	1843	1	306
Caton, Richard	125	Sidling Hill	1843	1	305
Caton, Richard	185	Sidling Hill	1840	1	293
Clark, Isaac Jr.	13a.3r.	Sleepy Creek	1845	1	322
Colston, Edward et al	777a.1r.2p.	Meadow Branch	1835	1	278
Courtney, Christian	296	Sleepy Creek	1842	1	301
Cross, Gassaway	250¾	Conoloway Hill	1827	1	236
Cross, Lemuel	12	Cacapon Creek	1838	1	288
Cross, William et al	400	Conoloway Hill	1845	1	321
Crowl, George	5⅝	Sleepy Creek	1829	1	250
Crowl, George et al	346	Sleepy Creek	1841	1	397
Davis, Henry	14a.3r.	Sidling Hill	1849	1	333
Dawson, Abraham	61	Great Cacapon	1826	1	233
Dawson, Abraham	147	Great Cacapon	1826	1	234
Dawson, Isaac Jr.	14¼	Cacapon Mountain	1833	1	274
Dawson, John	148	Cacapon Creek	1847	1	331
Dawson, John	21a.3r.	Warm Spgs. Ridge	1850	1	346
Dawson, John	14¼	Rock Gap Run	1855	1	363
Dawson, John T. & H. R.	178	Sidling Hill	1850	1	338
Dawson, William	34	Sidling Hill	1851	1	348
Dill, Joshua	8	Sleepy Creek	1856	1	370
Doling, William	30	Great Cacapon	1827	1	237
Duckwall, Middleton	21a.3r.	Sleepy Creek	1852	1	352
Dyche, Peter	35	Spring Ridge	1843	1	307
Dyche, Peter et al	26	Conoloway Hill	1849	1	340
Easter, Wesley J.	40	Grindstone Mt.	1847	1	328
Faris (Farris) Aaron	64	Adj. Gassaway Cross	1833	1	270
Faris, Aaron et al	158¾	Cor. Gassaway Cross	1833	1	269
Fauver—or Fauber, Fawver					
Fauver, Henry	18½	Denmitt's Run	1823	1	226
Fawver, Isaac et al	118	Wilcott's Run	1851	1	349

Name of Grantee	Acres	Local Description	Year	Book	Page
Pendleton, Philip C. et al	777a.1r.2p.	Meadow Branch	1835	1	278
Rankin, Samuel	71	Adj. Wm. Rankin	1833	1	272
Rankin, Samuel	21	Sleepy Creek	1833	1	275
Rankin, Samuel	21	Mountain Run	1823	1	227
Rankin, Samuel	24½	Sleepy Creek	1830	1	253
Rankin, Samuel Sr.	57	Sleepy Creek	1843	1	311
Rankin, Simeon	20	Sleepy Creek	1833	1	273
Rankin, Simeon	82	Sleepy Creek	1841	1	298
Reichard, Jacob	12	Sleepy Creek	1825	1	229
Reynolds, George	18	Sidling Hill	1838	1	285
Reynolds, George	166	Adj. Barret & Reynolds	1838	1	283
Reynolds, George et al	151	Cacapon Creek	1838	1	284
Reynolds, George et al	35	Sidling Hill	1838	1	282
Reynolds, Rezin	77	Sidling Hill	1850	1	347
Rooney, Michael	142a.3r.24p.	Third Hill	1853	1	357
Rooney, Michael	4a.16pchs.	Sleepy Creek	1849	1	335
Shade, Adam	420	Sleepy Creek	1852	1	355
Sherrard, John	245	Rock Gap Run	1834	1	267
Sherrard, John et al	331½	Adj. A. Johnson	1834	1	276
Shockey, Basil E.	8	Sleepy Creek	1853	1	359
Smith, Jacob	17	Indian Run	1833	1	263
Smith, James et al	158¾	Cor. Gassaway Cross	1833	1	269
Smith, Valentine	43	Adj. Gassaway Cross	1830	1	251
Smith, William	22	Sleepy Creek	1827	1	242
Smith, William	484	Indian Run	1837	1	280
Spealman—or Speelman					
Spealman, Peter	350	Sleepy Creek	1841	1	299
Spealman, Peter	23	Little Mountain	1845	1	319
Spealman, Peter et al	293½	Cacapon Mountain	1828	1	243
Steinback, Adam	14	Sidling Hill	1845	1	320
Swaim—also Swim					
Swaim, Mathias	28a.2r.	Sleepy Creek	1838	1	281
Tedrick—or Tetrick (See Fedrick)					
Waugh, Archibald et al	20	Sleepy Creek	1844	1	314
Yost, Peter	32½	Sleepy Creek	1842	1	303
Young, John	25	Cacapon Creek	1830	1	255
Young, John	70½	Adj. Martin Bilmire	1832	1	258
Young, John	13	Adj. Shears	1845	1	318
Young, John	3¾	Cacapon Creek	1829	1	246
Young, John et al	26	Conoloway Hill	1849	1	340
Ziler, George et al	73⅝	Cacapon Creek	1830	1	252
Ziler, George et al	97	Sidling Hill	1833	1	262

NICHOLAS COUNTY

Alderson, J. A.	140	Strange Creek	1857	2	391
Alderson, J. A. et al	400	Skiles Run	1860	2	399
Alderson, James A. et al	500	Peter's Creek	1851	2	561
Alderson, Joseph A.	500	Meadow Creek	1856	2	343
Alderson, Joseph A.	50	Adj. John Groves	1855	2	337
Alderson, Joseph A.	180	Mill Creek	1860	2	402
Alderson, Joseph A.	250	Hominy's Creek	1848	2	196
Alderson, Joseph A.	250	Anglin's Creek	1848	2	195
Alderson, Joseph A.	250	Anglin's Creek	1848	2	231
Alderson, Joseph A.	250	Hominy Creek	1848	2	230
Alderson, Joseph A. et al	1,000	Anglin's Creek	1851	2	274
Alderson, Joseph A. et al	275	Anglin's Creek	1851	2	275

Name of Grantee	Acres	Local Description	Year	Book	Page
Duffield—also Dufield					
Duffield, George	150	Wts. Birch River	1829	1	257
Duffield, John & George	72	Wts. of Elk River	1826	1	197
Duffield, John L.	31½	Wts. Birch	1827	1	225
Duffield, John M. et al	90	Bee Run	1833	1	354
Duffield, John Sr. et al	100	Wts. Birch	1823	1	110
Duffield, John W. et al	77	Buffalo Creek	1830	1	272
Duffield, Robert	81	Stoney Creek	1823	1	483
Duffield, Robert	175	Laurel Patch	1823	1	123
Duffield, Robert	200	Stroud's Creek	1822	1	64
Duffield, Robert	100	Britch Clout Shoals	1832	1	334
Duffield, Robert G.	91	Strange Creek	1828	1	237
Duffield, Robert Sr. et al	100	Wts. of Birch	1823	1	110
Dufield—Also Duffield					
Dufield, Henry	80	Wts. Birch	1833	1	361
Dufield, Henry	220	Mth. Birch River	1826	1	201
Dufield, John L.	140	Strange Creek	1833	1	370
Dufield, John Sr.	100	Wts. Birch River	1826	1	212
Dufield, Robert et al	440	Scott's Mountain	1837	1	519
Dufield, Robert Sr.	60	Wts. Elk River	1833	1	374
Dufield, Robert Sr. et al	315	Laurel Creek	1820	1	12
Dufield, Robert Sr. et al	184	Indian Grave	1820	1	13
Dufield, Thomas et al	218	Anthony's Creek	1837	1	505
Duffy, Francis	30	Peter's Creek	1848	2	224
Duffy, Frances et al	80	Peter's Creek	1859	2	367
Duffy, John	230	Wts. Elk	1841	2	50
Duffy, John et al	200	Grannyshee Fork	1847	2	187
Duffy, John et al	14	Muddlethepeg	1844	2	136
Duffy, John et al	572	Wts. Gauley	1838	2	10
Duffy, John et al	608	Wts. Gauley	1838	2	9
Duffy, John & Philip et al	80	Adj. John Grove	1848	2	200
Dunbar, John	59	Laurel Creek	1826	1	192
Dunbar, John	150	Peter's Creek	1829	1	253
Dunbar, John	50	Laurel Creek	1835	1	425
Dunbar, Jonathan	140	Laurel Creek	1828	1	243
Dunbar, Jonathan	50	Adj. John Grose	1829	1	255
Dunbar, Jonathan	140	Laurel Creek	1828	1	238
Dunbar, Jonathan	93	Adj. C. W. King	1820	1	16
Dunn, George	1,000	Peters Creek	1821	1	38
Dunn, George	300	Wts. of Meadow.River	1847	2	177
Dyer—See also Dyre					
Dyer, James	20	Wts. Elk	1841	2	73
Dyer, James	105	Sand Run	1841	2	75
Dyer, James	100	Bolair Hill	1841	2	74
Dyer, James Jr.	100	Wts. William River	1838	2	4
Dyer, James Jr.	125	Wts. Gauley	1838	2	3
Dyer, James R.	25	Adj. Burne Duffy & Co.	1851	2	278
Dyer, James R.	150	Laurel Creek	1851	2	280
Dyer, James R.	360	Brushy Meadow Creek	1851	2	279
Dyer, James R.	40	Wts. of Elk	1851	2	296
Dyer, James R. et al	175	Laurel Creek	1851	2	281
Dyre—also Dyer					
Dyre, James Jr.	180	Wts. William River	1849	2	243
Eagle—and Eagles					
Eagle, David	40	Adj. James Robinson	1857	2	353
Eagles, Enoch	95	Elk River	1847	2	180
Eagles, Enoch	285	Big Laurel	1850	2	262
Edwards, William H.	3,400	Buffalo Creek	1857	2	392
Edwards, William H.	3,500	Buffalo Creek	1857	2	393
Edwards, William H.	2,000	Strange Creek	1857	2	396
Edwards, William H.	4,600	Buffalo Creek	1857	2	394
Edwards, William H.	5,000	20 Mi. Creek	1857	2	566
Edwards, William H.	10,000	20 Mi. Creek	1857	2	569

Name of Grantee	Acres	Local Description	Year	Book	Page
Edwards, William H.	3,800	Road Fork	1857	2	579
Edwards, William H.	10,000	Big Buffalo	1857	2	580
Edwards, William H.	24,000	Big Buffalo Creek	1857	2	583
Edwards, Wm. H.	11,000(1,100)	Wts. Buffalo	1857	2	575
Edwards, Wm. H.	2,700	Wts. Big Buffalo	1857	2	577
Edwards, William H. et al	500	Meadow Creek	1851	2	563
Ellison, William	100	Little Birch	1838	2	27
Ewing, Allen	250	Jerrie's Fork	1841	2	71
Ewing, Elisha	125	Groves Creek	1848	2	225
Ewing, James	50	Adj. Jones	1854	2	333
Ewing, Margaret	73	Flat Fork	1848	2	207
Ewing, Moses	220	Glade Creek	1823	1	125
Ewing, Moses	50	Sugar Camp	1823	1	124
Ewing, Moses	190	Peter's Creek	1832	1	337
Ewing, Moses et al	112	Peter's Creek	1836	1	475
Farr, Wesley	150	Buffalo Creek	1852	2	314
Faulkner, Jacob	76	Muddletypeg	1839	2	29
Fitzwater, George	370	Laurel Creek	1821	1	535
Fitzwater, Isaac	50	Jones' Fork	1822	1	80
Fitzwater, Isaac	305	Peter's Creek	1829	1	260
Fitzwater, Isaac	30	Peter's Creek	1829	1	247
Fitzwater, Isaac C.	100	20 Mi Creek	1831	1	540
Fitzwater, Isaac C.	125	Peter's Creek	1840	2	37
Fitzwater, James S.	150	Blue Knob Creek	1851	2	270
Fitzwater, John	220	Wts. Elk River	1842	2	87
Fitzwater, John	290	McKee's Creek	1829	1	250
Fitzwater, John (son of George)	130	Wts. of Elk	1847	2	182
Fitzwater, John (son of Thomas)	70	Blue Knob Creek	1851	2	297
Fitzwater, Squire	200	Salmon's Creek	1860	2	405
Fitzwater, William	50(80)	Cor. to Rob't McKee	1832	1	313
Fitzwater, William G. et al	170	Young's Creek	1826	1	204
Fitzwater, William G.	34	Otter Creek	1829	1	256
Foster, Andrew	15¼	Adj. Henry Miller	1862	2	378
Foster, James A.	25	Laurel Creek	1854	2	328
Foster John	50	Meadow Creek	1850	2	289
Foster, John	100	Wts. Gauley	1834	1	392
Foster, John	75	Wts. of Gauley	1858	2	370
Foster, Nathaniel	75	Wts. of Gauley	1847	2	181
Foster, Nathaniel	200	Anglin's Creek	1827	1	221
Foster, Nathaniel	125	Wts. Meadow River	1826	1	207
Foster, Nathaniel et al	170	Young's Creek	1826	1	204
Foster, Presley	25	Gauley River	1857	2	352
Foster, Sarah Ann & E. C. et al	1,183¼	Wts. of Gauley	1845	2	147
Foster, Sarah Ann & E. C. et al	1,183¼	Wts. of Gauley	1845	2	148
Foster, Sarah Ann & E. C. et al	1,183¼	Enoch's Run	1845	2	146
Foster, Turley	70	20 Mi. Creek	1821	1	44
Fowler, John C. et al	145	Wts. of Birch River	1861	2	375
Fox, Mahala	75	Cane Branch	1832	1	310
Fox, William M. et al	38	Cane Branch	1831	1	293
Frale, John	58	Fish Pot Shoal	1835	1	414
Frale, John et al	250	Wts. Elk River	1835	1	420
Frame, Andrew B.	123 (125)	Wts. Elk River	1835	1	428
Frame, David	100	Powell's Creek	1838	1	526
Frame, David Jr.	100	Wts. Birch	1823	1	132
Frame, William	56	Powell's Creek	1860	2	407
Frame, William B. (Son of James)	100	Wts. of Elk	1846	2	174
Frele, John et al	250	Elk River	1835	1	420
Friend, Andrew P.	200	Wts. Elk River	1836	1	462
Friend, Andrew P.	144	Buffalo Creek	1822	1	86
Friend, Andrew P.	198	Wts. of Elk River	1822	1	87
Friend, Israel A.	167	Wts. of Elk River	1835	1	453
Friend, Jonathan	100	Upper Rock Camp	1832	1	323
Friend, Mary	38	Wts. of Elk	1822	1	66

Name of Grantee	Acres	Local Description	Year	Book	Page
Hutchison—or Hutchinson					
Hutchison, David C. (or Daniel)	150	Buffalo Creek	1832	1	343
Hutchison, E. R.	140	Buffalo Creek	1834	1	404
Hutchison, E. R.	50	Buffalo Creek	1834	1	403
Hutchison, E. R.	90	Peters Creek	1832	1	344
Hutchison, E. R.	60	Peter's Creek	1832	1	342
Hutchison, E. R.	300	Cliffs of Gauley	1832	1	341
Hutchison, Jacob	150	McMillion's Creek	1854	2	327
Hutchison, Jacob	100	McMillion's Creek	1825	1	174
Hutchison, Joseph	74	McMillion's Creek	1832	1	338
Hutchison, Joseph	80	Glade Creek	1853	2	318
Hutchison, Joseph et al	50	Muddlethepeg	1826	1	198
Hutchison, Samuel	150	Peters Creek	1822	1	78
Hutchison, William	100	Peter's Creek	1839	2	32
Hutchison, William	196	Glade Creek	1856	2	339
Hutchison, William	75	Wts. of Gauley	1839	2	31
Hutchison, William	650	Wts. Gauley	1839	2	33
Hutchison, William	400	Beaver Creek	1842	2	95
Hutchison, William	400	Wts. Elk River	1837	1	503
Hutchison, William et al	570	Wts. Gauley	1844	2	132
Hutchison, William et al	250	Wts of Elk	1841	2	79
Jackson, Jesse	58	Little Birch	1836	1	455
James, Jesse	50	Little Elk Creek	1829	1	264
James, Jesse	50	Laurel Creek	1826	1	193
James, Joseph	50	Peter's Creek	1823	1	126
James, Joseph	80	Adj. Benj. Hamrick	1837	1	520
James, Lewis	80	Wts. of Gauley	1860	2	400
James, Samuel	75	Peters Creek	1826	1	199
Johnson, James	40	Laurel Creek	1834	1	407
Johnson, John	50	Wts. of Elk	1851	2	300
Johnson, John	75	Wts. Laurel Creek	1821	1	57
Johnson, John et al	100	Beech Creek	1820	1	18
Jones, Henry	50	Mumblethepeg Creek	1849	2	244
Jones, John W.	275	Beaver Creek	1844	2	134
Jones, John W.	700	Wts. Gauley	1851	2	282
Jones, Lewis	94	McKee's Creek	1835	1	421
Jones, Lewis	80	Wts. of Gauley	1860	2	400
Jones, Thomas	175	Glade Creek	1823	1	120
Keenan, Andrew	40	Peter's Creek	1835	1	423
Keenan, Andrew	25	Peter's Creek	1835	1	416
Keenan, Andrew	46	Peter's Creek	1846	2	168
Keenan, Robert	100	Peter's Creek	1829	1	258
Keenan, Robert	12	Peter's Creek	1841	2	78
Keenan, Robert	100	Peter's Creek	1842	2	96
Keenan, Robert	45	Peter's Creek	1843	2	114
Keenan, Robert	50	Peter's Creek	1846	1	169
Keenan, Robert	125	Laurel Fork	1848	2	227
Keenan, Robert	300	Panther Mountain	1850	2	251
Keenan, Robert et al	100	Peter's Creek	1841	2	63
Keenan, Samuel B. et al	112	Cane Branch	1831	1	294
Keenan, Samuel B. et al	38	Cane Branch	1831	1	293
Keener, John	30	Wts. Elk	1821	1	49
Keester, John	100	S. S. Gauley	1834	1	406
Kelly, James et al	38	Cane Branch	1831	1	293
Kelly, James et al	112	Cane Branch	1831	1	294
Kelly, Robert et al	572	Wts. Gauley	1838	2	10
Kelly, Robert et al	608	Wts. Gauley	1838	2	9
Kelly, Robert et al	380	Muddlethepeg	1823	1	142
Kelly, Robert et al	2,000	Beaver Creek	1822	1	59
Kelly, Robert & Hamilton et al	450	Williams River	1840	2	38
Kincade—or Kincaid					
Kincade, James	100	Wts. New River	1831	1	296
Kincaid, John	100	Wts. Gauley	1820	1	34

Name of Grantee	Acres	Local Description	Year	Book	Page
Kincaid, Mathew & James	73	Wts. Gauley	1820	1	35
King, Charles W.	130	Wts. Gauley	1822	1	68
Knight, John	100	Wts. Birch River	1824	1	154
Kyre, John	50	Wts. Birch	1826	1	191
Kyre, John	50	Wts. Birch River	1822	1	478
Kyre, Lewis	40	First Creek	1822	1	71
Kyre, Lewis	50	First Creek	1822	1	72
Legg, Eli	7	Laurel Creek	1849	2	233
Legg, Elijah	100	Laurel Creek	1834	1	408
Legg, John	175	Spread Shoal Run	1847	2	189
Legg, William	200	Sycamore Creek	1842	2	91
Legg, William Jr.	21	Laurel Creek	1849	2	232
Lewis, Thomas A.	800	Stroud's Creek	1842	2	98
Lewis, Zachariah et al	1,183¼	Wts. Gauley	1845	2	148
Lewis, Zachariah et al	1,183¼	Wts. Gauley	1845	2	147
Lewis, Zachariah et al	1,183¼	Enoch's Run	1845	2	146
Liekens, James et al	4	Wts. Holly	1835	1	448
Lightner—also Lytner					
Lightner, Elijah	80	Peter's Creek	1825	1	173
Likens—See Liekens					
Lilly, David	30	20 Mi. Creek	1822	1	88
Lilly, David	60	20 Mi. Creek	1824	1	144
Lilly, Elizabeth et al	1,050	Big Laurel	1846	2	164
Linch, Isaac	100	Laurel Run	1842	2	101
Linch, John	150	Wts. of Elk	1842	2	102
Livesay, Valentine	50	McKees Creek	1859	2	368
Long, Jacob	50	Little Buffalo Creek	1832	1	339
Long, Jacob N.	180	Buffalo Waters	1835	1	434
Long, James	77	Wts. Elk River	1823	1	130
Long, James	300	Long Run	1832	1	340
Lough—See Lowe					
Lough, Adam	500	Ben's Run	1823	1	129
Lytner—See also Lightner					
Lytner, Elijah et al	112	Peter's Creek	1836	1	475
Mace, Henry (Mase)	45	Otter Creek	1830	1	271
Mahan, Jacob M.	100	Flat Woods Run	1822	1	74
Malcom—also Malcomb, Malcolm					
Malcom, Joseph	168	Sugar Camp	1823	1	111
Martin, Samuel et al	100	Anglin's Creek	1825	1	175
Martin, Samuel et al	200	Adj. Thomas Hall	1825	1	171
Martin, Samuel V.	250	Lion's Fork	1847	2	191
Martin, Samuel V. et al	175	Laurel Creek	1851	2	281
Martin, Willis	25	Adj. John Mason	1841	2	60
Masterson, Thomas	25	Hawk's Nest	1830	1	268
Masterson, Thomas	2½	Turn Pike Road	1833	1	379
Masterson, Thomas	32	Turn Pike Road	1833	1	372
Mathews, Thomas & Mason et al	2,100	Wts. Birch River	1859	2	359
McAlgen—See McColgan, McOlgen					
McAlgen, David (McColgan-McOlgen)	198	Wts. of Two Run	1853	2	319
McAlgin, David (McColgan-McOlgen)	100	Wts. of Elk	1840	2	39
McAneany—See McAneary					
McAneary, John (McAneany)	2,000	Powell's Creek	1859	2	358
McAneary, John (McAneany)	300	Wts. of Birch River	1859	2	360
McAneary, John (McAneany)	1,500	Wts. Birch River	1857	2	389
McClung, Anthony	105	Philip's Run	1849	2	245
McClung, Edward	23	Adj. Wm. McClung	1833	1	363
McClung, James C.	91	Wts. Gauley	1857	2	395
McClung, James C.	325	Anglin's Creek	1859	2	369
McClung, James C.	88	Wts. Gauley	1857	2	398
McClung, James C.	180	Meadow River	1851	2	301
McClung, John	175	McMillon's Creek	1849	2	239

Name of Grantee	Acres	Local Description	Year	Book	Page
McClung, Joseph	70	Philip's Run	1830	1	282
McClung, Joseph & Anthony	50	Muddlethepeg	1836	1	468
McClung, Mathew	20	Anglin's Creek	1848	2	216
McClung, Mathew	110	Laurel Creek	1848	2	215
McClung, Samuel	770	Mumblethepeg	1834	1	548
McClung, Samuel	375	Philip's Run	1830	1	245
McClung, Samuel N.	50	Philip's Run	1828	1	244
McClung, William	1,000	Wts. Gauley	1827	1	214
McClung, William Sr.	189	Anglin's Creek	1820	1	10
McClung, William Sr.	188	Anglin's Creek	1820	1	11
McClung, William Sr.	284	Anglin's Creek	1820	1	7
McClung, William Sr.	537	Anglin's Creek	1820	1	8
McClung, William Sr.	224	Peter's Creek	1820	1	477
McClung, William Sr.	287	Peter's Creek	1820	1	476
McClung, William Sr.	218	Anglin's Creek	1820	1	9
McClure, Charles	500	Elk & Gauley	1833	1	346
McClogan—See also McAlgen, McOlgen					
McColgan, David	174½	Leatherwood Creek	1836	1	493
McColgan, David	21	Rock Camp	1836	1	492
McColgan, David	70	Wts. Elk River	1836	1	495
McCoy, Andrew et al	50	Muddlethepeg	1826	1	198
McCoy, Andrew H.	825	Brush Fork	1842	2	107
McCoy, Moses	30	Bear Run	1835	1	417
McCoy, William	250	Wts. Elk River	1835	1	429
McCoy, William et al	250	Gulf Shoal	1835	1	413
McCutcheon, James P. & Robert	200	Hominy Creek	1848	2	221
McDermott—See McDurmot					
McDurmot, Addison	340	Adj. John Stephenson	1858	2	357
McElwain—See McLevane					
McGraw, Martin	100	Big Creek	1824	1	167
McKee, John et al	450	Williams River	1840	2	38
McLaughlin, Addison	175	Wts. Little Birch	1837	1	496
McLaughlin, Addison	240	Wts. Little Birch	1837	1	497
McLaughlin, Addison	100 (190)	Wts. Little Birch	1837	1	498
McLaughlin, Addison	420	Carpenter's Run	1837	1	502
McLaughlin, Addison	900	Wts. Birch River	1838	2	23
McLaughlin, Addison	230	Wts. Birch River	1838	2	24
McLaughlin, Addison	570	Wts. Gauley	1838	2	26
McLaughlin, Addison	95	Anthony's Creek	1841	2	82
McLaughlin, Addison	20	Poplar Run	1842	2	92
McLaughlin, Addison	75	Anthony's Fork	1847	2	188
McLaughlin, Addison	75	Anthony's Creek	1848	2	228
McLaughlin, Addison	100	Cobin Run	1848	2	229
McLaughlin, Addison et al	600	Wts. Gauley	1838	2	25
McLaughlin, James	120	Birch River	1851	2	302
McLaughlin, James	200	Poplar Run	1854	2	330
McLevane—McElwain					
McLevane, George	50	Laurel Creek	1835	1	409
McLevane, George et al	250	Gulf Shoal	1835	1	413
McLevane, George M. et al	250 (150)	Laurel Creek	1835	1	426
McMahan, Jacob et al	100	Flat Woods Run	1824	1	161
McMillion, James	100	Buffalo Creek	1838	2	7
McMillion, James	41	Muddlethepeg	1838	2	6
McMillion, James	175	McMillion's Creek	1834	1	399
McMillion, James	120 (126)	Mumblethepeg Creek	1834	1	393
McMillion, James	211	Mumblethepeg	1834	1	398
McMillion, James et al	150	Glade Creek	1823	1	140
McNutt, Jas.	69	Bridge Fork	1829	1	262
McNutt, Joseph	50	Bridge Fork	1823	1	114
McNutt, Joseph	22	Sand Lick	1823	1	112
McNutt, Joseph	9	Kincaid Branch	1823	1	113
McOlgen—See also McAlgen, McColgan					
McOlgen, David	198	Wts. of Two-Run	1853	2	319

Name of Grantee	Acres	Local Description	Year	Book	Page
Middleton, Henry O. et al	600	Wts. Gauley	1838	2	25
Miller, Francis et al	1,050	Big Laurel	1846	2	164
Miller, James	100	Wts. of Elk River	1848	2	204
Miller, James	150	Adj. John Given	1841	2	77
Miller, John	35	Wts of Elk	1822	1	91
Miller, John	200	Bear Run	1836	1	454
Miller, John Jr.	95	Grassy Creek	1824	1	157
Miller, Thomas	34	Adj. his own	1836	1	458
Miller, Thomas	100	Wts. of Holly	1834	1	387
Mollohon—also Molohon					
Mollohon, Charles	50	Wts. of Holly	1835	1	419
Mollohon, George	246	Mill Creek	1832	1	316
Molohon—also Mollohon					
Molohon, Charles	287	Holly Creek	1835	1	427
Molohon, George	150	Wts. Elk River	1826	1	202
Molohon, George G. et al	140	Holly Creek	1835	1	424
Molohon, James	82	Holly Creek	1827	1	222
Molohon, James	25	Back Fork	1828	1	233
Molohon, James F. et al	140	Holly Creek	1835	1	424
Molohon, John	100	Stillhouse Run	1835	1	430
Morris, Edward B.	83	Wts. of Gauley	1860	2	404
Morris, George	62	Point Mountain	1836	1	460
Morris, Henry	75	Line Creek	1841	2	59
Morris, Henry	50	Peter's Creek	1823	1	97
Morris, Henry	50	Line Creek	1820	1	21
Morris, John	75	Peter's Creek	1838	2	12
Morris, John	150	Line Creek	1822	1	81
Morris, John	130	Peter's Creek	1836	1	470
Morris, John	40	Peter's Creek	1836	1	461
Morris, William B.	90	Peter's Creek	1850	2	263
Morris, William B.	125	Beech Run	1843	2	111
Morris, William B.	64	Otter Creek	1843	2	110
Morris, William B.	65	Peters Creek	1838	2	19
Morris, William D.	100	Peter's Creek	1833	1	353
Morrison, William	85	Wts. Elk	1835	1	441
Morrison, William	500	Big Flat Woods Run	1835	1	445
Morrison, William	100	Adj. John Huffman	1835	1	447
Mosberger, John	28	Rose's Run	1830	1	277
Mosberger, John	104	Strange Creek	1833	1	351
Mosberger, John et al	50	Wts. Elk River	1833	1	325
Murphy, James C.	75	Wts. Birch River	1823	1	106
Murphy, James G.	70	Wts. Elk	1820	1	19
Murphy, James G.	140	Wts. Birch	1826	1	194
Murphy, John J.	275	Snake Creek	1835	1	449
Murphy, John J.	105	Strange Creek	1833	1	377
Murphy, Morris	50	Big Otter Creek	1832	1	321
Murphy, Morris et al	100	Otter Creek	1831	1	288
Murphy, Thomas	100	Otter Creek	1828	1	235
Murphy, W. H. & David	175	Brushy Fork	1833	1	376
Murphy, William	100	Strange Creek	1824	1	162
Murphy, William	200	Buffalo Creek	1828	1	239
Neff, Henry	110	McKee's Creek	1838	2	1
Neil, Andrew	255	Little Elk Creek	1837	1	514
Neil, James G.	50	Peter's Creek	1835	1	443
Neil, James G.	60	Wts. Gauley	1828	1	230
Neil, James G.	57	Peter's Creek	1835	1	438
Neil, James G.	135	S. S. Gauley	1830	1	281
Neil, James G.	100	Laurel Fork	1850	2	256
Neil, James G. et al	200	Grannyshee Fork	1847	2	187
Neil, James G. et al	1,050	Big Laurel	1846	2	164
Neil, James G., Samuel & Andrew	300	Big Laurel	1851	2	306
Neil, Jeremiah	100	Sycamore Creek	1842	2	105
Neil, Jeremiah	320	Sycamore Creek	1838	2	13

Name of Grantee	Acres	Local Description	Year	Book	Page
Neil, Jeremiah	22	20 Mi Creek	1830	1	283
Neil, John	5	20 Mi Creek	1838	1	528
Neil, Jonathan	223	Sycamore	1840	2	44
Neil, Robert	40	Peter's Creek	1851	2	304
Neil, Robert	250	Peter's Creek	1841	2	67
Neil, Samuel	145	Adj. John Brown	1836	1	494
Neil, Samuel	240	Peter's Creek	1821	1	536
Neil, Samuel	50	Powell's Creek	1856	2	347
Neil, Samuel	100	Wts. Gauley	1820	1	2
Neil, Samuel	60	Teter's Creek	1827	1	219
Neil, Samuel	704	Wts. Gauley	1827	1	218
Neil, Samuel	33	Teter's Creek	1827	1	220
Neil, Samuel	105	Charlie's Ford	1827	1	226
Neil, Samuel	100	20 Mi Creek	1843	2	123
Neil, Samuel	236	Big Laurel Creek	1851	2	303
Neil, Samuel	40	Line Creek	1822	1	83
Neil, Samuel & Andrew	300	Big Laurel	1847	2	186
Nichols, Alexander	100	20 Mi Creek	1838	2	8
Nichols, Alexander	200	Blue Knob Creek	1849	2	241
Nichols, Hugh	350	Wts. Elk River	1836	1	544
Nichols, James	50	Brushy Meadow Cr.	1849	2	240
Nichols, James	50	Bell Creek	1821	1	41
Nichols, James	25	Pearsons Branch	1836	1	459
Nichols, James	50	Peter's Creek	1836	1	464
Nichols, James	50	Bell Creek	1822	1	481
Nichols, William	200	Big Sycamore	1838	1	527
Nichols, William Jr.	100	20 Mi Creek	1843	2	116
Nichols, William Jr.	75	20 Mi Creek	1843	2	117
Nichols, Zephamiah	100	Wts. Elk River	1826	1	209
Niel, James G.	60	Wts. Gauley	1828	1	230
Night, John	100	Wts. Birch River	1824	1	154
North, John A.	400	Adj. David Jamison	1825	1	182
North, John A.	328	Laurel Cr.	1851	2	305
Nutter, David	50	Hominy Creek	1828	1	232
Nutter, Grandison	30	Adj. David Nutter	1841	2	56
Nutter, William	50	Laurel Creek	1834	1	402
O'Dell, Jacob et al	100	Wts. Gauley	1825	1	170
O'Dell, Jacob Sr.	100	Hominy Creek	1848	2	226
O'Dell, Jeremiah	53	Anglin's Creek	1831	1	304
O'Dell, Jeremiah	400	Adj. Noah Davis	1824	1	166
O'Dell, Jeremiah	47	Laurel Creek	1823	1	105
O'Dell, Jeremiah	100	20 Mi. Creek	1821	1	45
O'Dell, Jeremiah	114	Anglin's Creek	1820	1	31
O'Dell, Jeremiah	300	McClung's Ferry	1820	1	30
O'Dell, Jeremiah	100	McClung's Ferry	1820	1	29
O'Dell, Jeremiah	50	Peters Creek	1820	1	28
O'Dell, Jeremiah	100	Summersville & Lewisburg Rd.	1834	1	388
O'Dell, Jeremiah	50	Laurel Creek	1848	2	217
O'Dell, Jeremiah et al	100	Anglin's Creek	1825	1	175
O'Dell, John	50	Wts. Gauley	1825	1	176
O'Dell, John W. & Jerry	79	Laurel Creek	1858	2	373
O'Dell, Miriam	100	Hominey Creek	1834	1	389
O'Dell, Sylvanus	50	Adj. Edward Hughes	1821	1	48
Parker, Henry	55	Grannies Creek	1830	1	273
Parkhill, John H.	1,750	Mth. Cherry River	1856	2	346
Patterson, James et al	150	Wts. New River	1822	1	62
Patterson, John & Thomas	200	Gauley Mt.	1824	1	164
Pearson—Pierson					
Pearson, Jonathan	100	Peter's Creek	1826	1	185
Pearson, Jonathan et al	100	Diader Run	1823	1	116
Pennington, Jesse	87	Young's Creek	1826	1	186

Name of Grantee	Acres	Local Description	Year	Book	Page
Perine—Perrine					
Perine, Lewis	100	Wts. Elk River	1845	2	139
Perrine, Joseph	43	Wts. of Elk	1822	1	96
Perkins, David & Elias	150	Flat Woods Run	1837	1	521
Pierson—See Pearson					
Pierson, David	32½	Peter's Creek	1841	2	61
Pierson, David	100	Wts. Elk	1845	2	144
Pierson, David et al	100	Peter's Creek	1841	2	63
Pierson, Joseph	100	Smith's Branch	1844	2	138
Pierson, Joseph	80	Adj. R. Campbell	1844	2	129
Pierson, Joseph	200	Wts. Elk River	1857	2	388
Pierson, Joseph	100	Peter's Creek	1820	1	530
Pitzenbarger, Peter	120	Anglin's Creek	1837	1	506
Pitzenbarger, Peter	85	Anglin's Creek	1851	2	307
Prians—See Perine, Perrine					
Price, Henry M. et al Heirs	360	McCort's Mill	1842	2	99
Price, Henry M. et al Heirs	1,000	Wts. Holly River	1842	2	100
Price, James	460	Anglin's Run	1823	1	143
Pritt, James	100	Wts. Holly	1834	1	390
Propst, Noah	63	Adj. Cary & Cris	1856	2	345
Rader, Anthony	134	Peters Creek	1838	1	525
Rader, Anthony	10	Peters Creek	1855	2	336
Rader, Anthony	65	Peter's Creek	1855	2	335
Rader, Anthony (of George)	60	Peter's Creek	1837	1	509
Rader, George	100	Bucks Garden Creek	1822	1	93
Rader, Henry	110	Wts. Holly	1837	1	522
Rader, John et al	40	Conner's Sugar Camp	1834	1	397
Rader, Samuel	50 (51)	Mumblethepeg Creek	1833	1	385
Rader, Samuel	125	Meadow Creek	1848	2	219
Rader, Senit	85	Laurel Creek	1841	2	62
Rader, Senit	100	Peter's Creek	1842	2	103
Rader, Senit	100	Buck's Garden	1842	2	104
Ratlif—Ratliff					
Ratlif, Solomon	100	Big Laurel	1842	2	93
Ratliff—Ratlif					
Ratliff, William D.	41	Wts. Elk River	1847	2	183
Reib—Reip					
Reib, Peter	125	Mill Creek	1852	2	310
Reip—Reib					
Renick, Avis	5	Adj. Grose's	1860	2	408
Renick, William Sr.	200	Cherry River	1825	1	181
Reynolds, Thomas J.	108	Adj. Michael Kern	1860	2	410
Reynolds, William	100	Anglin's Creek	1823	1	103
Rion—Rine—Ryan					
Rion, Edward	55	Peter's Creek	1836	1	463
Rion, Edward	260	Peter's Creek	1820	1	22
Rion, Edward	100	Peter's Creek	1823	1	99
Rion, Edward	100	Second Creek	1823	1	109
Rippetoe, James	15 (15½)	Otter Creek	1842	2	97
Roberts, Henry D.	450	Wts. Birch River	1831	1	292
Robinson, Haymond & J. H.	100	Robinson's Fork	1857	2	387
Robinson, James et al	107	McKee's Creek	1824	1	145
Robinson, James et al	380	Muddlethepeg	1823	1	142
Robinson, James et al	300	Muddlethepeg	1823	1	115
Robinson, James	200	Muddlethepeg	1823	1	100
Robinson, John H.	200	Peter's Creek	1851	2	293
Robinson, John H.	50	Blue Knob Creek	1851	2	285
Robinson, John H.	500	Buffalo Creek	1851	2	284
Robinson, John H.	135	Pine Run	1851	2	283
Robinson, John H.	68	Robinson's Fork	1841	2	81
Robinson, John H.	115	Mumblethepeg	1841	2	80
Robinson, John H.	3,000	Buck's Garden	1851	2	564
Robinson, John H.	220	Peter's Creek	1856	2	342

Name of Grantee	Acres	Local Description	Year	Book	Page
Young, Mathias	50	Adj. Joseph James	1824	1	153
Young, Robert et al	150	Wts. New River	1822	1	62
Young, Robert et al	134	Gauley Mountain	1823	1	141

OHIO COUNTY

Name of Grantee	Acres	Local Description	Year	Book	Page
Adams, John	400	Mid. Island Creek	1800	3	251
Adison, Alexander	600	Mid. Island Creek	1791	2	334
Alexander, Joseph	400	Mid. Island Creek	1791	2	335
Allen, William	50	Fish Creek	1828	4	42
Allen, William	58	Camp Run	1831	4	87
Alley, Elijah	130	Fish Creek	1828	4	41
Allison, Mary et al	278	Wheeling Creek	1811	3	387
Anderson, Joseph	250	Grave Creek	1832	4	104
Anguish, David	102	Cedar Run	1833	4	106
Ankrom, Aaron	420	Mid. Island Creek	1811	3	386
Archer, James Jr.	37	Fish Creek	1804	3	312
Armspoker, Jonas	315	Cross Creek	1786	1	376
Atkinson, John	324	Adj. D. Harris	1786	1	347
Ault, Mathias	100	Buffalo Creek	1788	2	207
Babb, Thomas	400	Buffalo Creek	1788	2	215
Bacon, Jabez	1,000	Mid. Island Cr.	1787	2	109
Bacon, Jabez	1,000	Middle Island Cr.	1787	2	108
Bacon, Jabez	1,000	Mid. Island Cr.	1787	2	111
Bacon, Jabez	1,000	Mid. Island Cr.	1787	2	113
Bacon, Jabez	1,000	Mid. Island Cr.	1787	2	110
Bacon, Jabez	1,000	Mid. Island Cr.	1787	2	112
Bacon, Jabez	1,000	Mid. Island Creek	1787	2	117
Bacon, Jabez	1,000	Mid. Island Creek	1787	2	118
Bacon, Jabez	1,000	Mid. Island Creek	1787	2	119
Bacon, Jabez	922	Mid. Island Creek	1787	2	121
Bacon, Jabez	156	Mid. Island Creek	1787	2	124
Bacon, Jabez	1,000	Mid. Island Creek	1787	2	35
Bacon, Jabez	1,000	Mid. Island Creek	1787	2	34
Bacon, Jabez	922	Mid. Island Creek	1787	2	33
Bacon, Jabez	1,000	Mid. Island Creek	1787	2	29
Bacon, Jabez	1,000	Mid. Island Creek	1787	2	28
Bacon, Jabez	1,000	Mid. Island Creek	1787	2	27
Bacon, Jabez	1,000	Mid. Island Creek	1787	2	25
Bacon, Jabez	1,000	Mid. Island Creek	1787	2	26
Bacon, Jabez	1,000	Mid. Island Creek	1787	2	21
Bacon, Jabez	1,000	Mid. Island Creek	1787	2	22
Bailey—See Bayley, Bealy					
Bailey, James	18½	Island Ohio River	1812	3	392
Bailey, William	1,000	McElroy's Fork	1787	1	531
Bain—see also Bane					
Bain, John	400	Short Creek	1786	1	264
Baker Daniel	50	Whetstone Run	1836	4	153
Baker, Samuel	1,000	Mid. Island Creek	1787	1	512
Bancker—also Banker					
Bancker, Florence	1,000	Middle Island Creek	1788	2	260
Bancker, Florence	1,000	Mid. Island Creek	1788	2	263
Bancker, Florence	1,000	Mid. Island Creek	1787	1	463
Bancker, Florence	1,000	Island Creek	1787	2	1
Bancker, Florence	1,000	Middle Island Creek	1787	2	4
Bancker, Florence	1,000	Mid. Island Cr.	1787	1	464

Name of Grantee	Acres	Local Description	Year	Book	Page
Biggs, Benjamin	400	Short Creek	1785	1	110
Biggs, Joseph	100	Buffalo Creek	1806	3	322
Biggs, Joseph	115	Buffalo Creek	1785	1	119
Biggs, William	145	Buffalo Creek	1786	1	374
Biggs, Zacheus	83	Buffalo Creek	1799	3	214
Biggs, Zacheus	50	Buffalo Creek	1799	3	163
Billeter, Noah	400	Grave Creek	1832	4	102
Birkhead, Abram S.	300	Mid Island Creek	1811	3	391
Black, James	500	Cross Creek	1787	2	60
Black, James	125	Little Wheeling Cr.	1787	2	10
Black, John	400	Wheeling Creek	1793	2	429
Blackburn, John	400	Tomlinson's Run	1794	2	495
Blackburn, John et al	400	Tomlinson's Run	1796	3	80
Blackford, Zepheniah	390	Fish Creek	1786	1	345
Blackmore, James	72	Adj. State Line	1791	2	339
Blackmore, John	1,500	Mid Island Creek	1799	3	203
Blackmore, William	100	Wts. of Ohio	1796	3	96
Blackwell, Robert	4,375	Fishing Creek	1786	1	161
Blackwell, Robert	5,500	Fishing Creek	1786	1	160
Blackwell, Robert	4,000	Fish Creek	1786	1	158
Blackwell, Robert	1,125	Fishing Creek	1786	1	159
Blackwell, Robert	1,000	Fish Creek	1786	1	178
Blackwell, Robert	4,000	Fish Creek	1786	1	157
Bland—See also Blane					
Blane, John	306	Wheeling Creek	1787	1	491
Boggs, John	400	Adj. Wm. Machan	1786	1	257
Boggs, John	400	Cor. James Caldwell	1786	1	255
Boggs, John	250	Wts. of Ohio	1793	2	489
Boggs, John	10	Island Ohio River	1796	3	116
Boggs, William	400	Moore's Run	1795	3	14
Bonam, London et al	400	Cross Creek	1802	3	283
Bonner, William	239	Buffalo Creek	1786	1	357
Bonnett—See also Burnett (Burnet)					
Bonnett, Lewis & John Jr.	400	Wheeling Creek	1811	3	378
Bonnett, Lewis	400	Wheeling Cr.	1787	1	436
Book, Jacob & Michael	270	Wt. Pigeon Creek	1786	1	361
Bowman, Samuel	700	Grave Creek	1831	4	82
Bowman, Samuel	300	Lick Run	1831	4	83
Boxton, Edward (Baxter-Baxton)	400	Cross Creek	1786	1	363
Boyce, Richard	1,000	Adj. James Johnson	1791	2	365
Bradford, David	400	Grave Creek	1787	2	65
Braxton, Edward	400	Cross Creek	1786	1	363
Brice, John	24	Little Wheeling Cr.	1795	3	17
Britton, Samuel et al	800	Proctor's Run	1788	2	161
Brown, Joseph Sr.	84	King's Creek	1796	3	113
Brown, Josias	400	Peter's Run	1794	2	431
Brown, Richard	260	Holliday's Cove	1788	2	156
Brown, Robert	49½	Short Creek	1803	3	295
Brown, William	23	Peters Run	1821	4	20
Bruce, Samuel	400	Buffalo Creek	1786	1	318
Bruin, Bryan	400	Grave Creek	1800	3	218
Bruin, Bryan	500	Grave Creek	1800	3	217
Bruin, Bryan	400	Grave Creek	1800	3	219
Bruin, Bryan	200	Grave Creek	1800	3	221
Bruin, Bryan	400	Grave Creek	1800	3	220
Bruin, Bryan	200	Wheeling Creek	1800	3	223
Bruin, Bryan	272	Wheeling Creek	1800	3	224
Bruin, Bryan	500	Fish Creek	1800	3	228
Bruin, Bryan	200	Grave Creek	1800	3	222
Bruin, Bryan	500	Fish Creek	1800	3	226
Bruin, Bryan	314	Fish Creek	1800	3	225
Bruin, Bryan	500	Fish Creek	1800	3	227
Bruin, Peter B.	200	Fish Creek	1788	2	268

Name of Grantee	Acres	Local Description	Year	Book	Page
Bruin, Peter B.	500	Grave Creek	1788	2	265
Bruin, Peter B.	540	Grave Creek	1788	2	266
Bruin, Peter B.	400	Fish Creek	1788	2	267
Bruin, Peter B.	475	Grave Creek	1788	2	269
Bruin, Peter B.	500	Grave Creek	1788	2	270
Bruin, Peter B.	500	Fish Creek	1788	2	272
Bruin, Peter B.	440	Grave Creek	1788	2	273
Bruin, Peter B.	125	Fish Creek	1788	2	274
Bruin, Peter B.	400	Fish Creek	1788	2	275
Bruin, Peter B.	320	Grave Creek	1788	2	276
Bruin, Peter B.	470	Grave Creek	1788	2	163
Buchanan, J. & S.	5¼	Wheeling Creek	1855	4	167
Buchanan—See also Buckhannon					
Buchanan, James	400	Wheeling Creek	1789	2	242
Buchanan, James	400	Wheeling Creek	1789	2	245
Buchanan, Samuel	23	Wheeling Creek	1815	3	427
Buchanan, William	13¼	Wheeling Creek	1851	4	164
Buchanan, William	292	Wheeling Creek	1788	2	170
Buchanan, William	500	Wheeling Cr.	1787	1	453
Buchanan, William et al	1,000	Wheeling Creek	1810	3	373
Buchanan, William et al	380	Wheeling Creek	1810	3	374
Buchanan, William et al	278	Wheeling Creek	1811	3	387
Buchannan, John	200	Fishing Creek	1815	3	410
Buckhannon, Samuel	75	Wheeling Creek	1797	3	179
Buckhannon, Samuel	1,000	Turkey Run	1793	2	492
Buckhannon, Samuel	1,000	Turkey Run	1793	2	491
Buffington, Thomas	329	Fish Creek	1786	1	382
Buffington, Thomas	400	Fish Creek	1786	1	415
Bukey, John	187	Wheeling Creek	1787	1	493
Bukey, John	220	Short Cr.	1807	3	349
Burch, Jesse et al	691¾	Grove Creek	1819	4	3
Burch, Jesse et al	1,000	Fish Creek	1820	4	10
Burch, Jesse et al	920a.110pchs.	Adj. his own	1820	4	11
Burch, Jesse et al	356a.144p.	Lit. Prison Run	1820	4	13
Burch, Jesse et al	931	Fish Creek	1820	4	12
Burk, James	200	Buffalo Creek	1791	2	337
Burley, Jacob	40	Fish Creek	1832	4	91
Burley, James	600	Long Run	1830	4	48
Burley, James	275	Long Run	1830	4	50
Burnett, Anthony	1,000	Mid. Island Cr.	1792	2	357
Burnett, Lewis (Bonnett)	400	Wheeling Creek	1787	1	436
Burnit, Anthony (Barnett)	1,000	Middle Island Creek	1792	2	357
Burrows, William W.	400	Fishing Creek	1798	3	160
Caldwell, Alexander	370	Middle Island	1796	3	68
Caldwell, Alexander	260	Mid Island Creek	1795	2	549
Caldwell, Alexander	264¾	Mid Island Creek	1803	3	286
Caldwell, Alexander	260	Bowman's Run	1831	4	76
Caldwell, Alexander	300	Lynn Camp	1831	4	77
Caldwell, Alexander	475	Fish Creek	1817	3	440
Caldwell, Alexander	200	Fish Creek	1824	4	34
Caldwell, James	1,000	Mid Island Creek	1795	2	521
Caldwell, James	1,000	Mid Island Creek	1795	2	522
Caldwell, James	1,000	Mid Island Creek	1795	2	523
Caldwell, James	1,000	Mid Island Creek	1795	2	527
Caldwell, James	1,000	Fishing Creek	1795	2	535
Caldwell, James	400	Wheeling Creek	1784	1	47
Caldwell, James	400	Wheeling Creek	1784	1	55
Caldwell, James	400	McKinley's Run	1784	1	56
Caldwell, James	500	Pleasant Fork	1784	1	74
Caldwell, James	500	Pleasant Fork	1784	1	88
Caldwell, James	1,000	Mid Island Creek	1795	2	520
Caldwell, James	1,000	Fishing Creek	1795	2	519
Caldwell, James	1,000	Pleasant Fork	1795	2	518

Name of Grantee	Acres	Local Description	Year	Book	Page
Caldwell, James	1,000	Mid Island Creek	1795	2	517
Caldwell, James	382	Buffalo Creek	1782	1	11
Caldwell, James	231	Mid Island Creek	1796	3	126
Caldwell, James	1,000	Mid Island Cr.	1795	3	29
Caldwell, James	1,000	Mid Island Cr.	1795	3	27
Caldwell, James	1,000	Mid Island Creek	1795	3	26
Caldwell, James	1,000	Fishing Creek	1795	3	24
Caldwell, James	1,000	Mid Island Cr.	1795	3	23
Caldwell, James	1,000	Mid Island Cr.	1795	3	22
Caldwell, James	1,000	Mid Island Cr.	1795	3	21
Caldwell, James	1,000	Mid Island Cr.	1795	3	20
Caldwell, James	1,000	Mid Island Cr.	1795	3	19
Caldwell, James	1,000	Middle Island Creek	1788	2	277
Caldwell, James	1,000	Island Creek	1786	1	286
Caldwell, James	1,000	Mid. Island Cr.	1786	1	285
Caldwell, James	1,500	Mid. Island Creek	1803	3	285
Caldwell, James	1,500	Island Creek	1803	3	284
Caldwell, James	1,000	Middle Island Cr.	1786	1	209
Caldwell, James	1,000	Middle Island Cr.	1786	1	203
Caldwell, James	1,000	Middle Island Cr.	1786	1	199
Caldwell, James	1,000	Pleasant Fork	1784	1	89
Caldwell, James Jr.	400	Middle Island Cr.	1788	2	179
Caldwell, James Jr.	100	Wheeling Creek	1788	2	206
Caldwell, James Jr.	1,000	Middle Island Creek	1788	2	205
Caldwell, James Jr.	345	Mid. Island Creek	1796	3	129
Caldwell, James Jr.	830	Buffalo Run	1798	3	207
Caldwell, James Jr.	576	Mid. Island Cr.	1801	3	268
Caldwell, James Jr.	400	Little Wheeling Cr.	1786	1	295
Caldwell, John	740	Mid. Island Creek	1793	2	413
Caldwell, John	400	Middle Island Creek	1794	2	462
Caldwell, John	600	Wts. of Ohio River	1788	2	184
Caldwell, John	400	Long Reach	1788	2	181
Caldwell, John	1,000	Mid. Island Creek	1795	3	25
Caldwell, John	1,000	Mid. Island Cr.	1795	3	28
Caldwell, John	1,000	Mid. Island Cr.	1795	3	30
Caldwell, John	1,000	Mid. Island Cr.	1795	3	31
Caldwell, John	1,000	Mid. Island Cr.	1795	3	33
Caldwell, John	1,000	Mid. Island Creek	1795	3	36
Caldwell, John	1,000	Mid. Island Cr.	1795	3	34
Caldwell, John	1,000	Mid. Island Cr.	1795	3	38
Caldwell, John	1,000	Mid. Island Cr.	1795	3	43
Caldwell, John	718	Mid. Island Creek	1793	2	480
Caldwell, John	419	Mid. Island Creek	1793	2	479
Caldwell, John	823	Mid. Island Creek	1793	2	481
Caldwell, John	1,200	Mid. Island Creek	1793	2	482
Caldwell, John	352	Mid. Island Creek	1793	2	483
Caldwell, John	34	Long Reach	1793	2	484
Caldwell, John	333	Mid. Island Creek	1793	2	485
Caldwell, John	315	Mid. Island Creek	1793	2	486
Caldwell, John	1,000	Mid. Island Creek	1795	2	524
Caldwell, John	1,000	Pleasant Fork	1795	2	526
Caldwell, John	1,000	Pleasant Fork	1795	2	525
Caldwell, John	1,000	Mid. Island Creek	1795	2	528
Caldwell, John	1,000	Pleasant Fork	1795	2	530
Caldwell, John	1,000	Fishing Creek	1795	2	529
Caldwell, John	1,000	Fishing Creek	1795	2	531
Caldwell, John	1,000	Mid. Island Creek	1795	2	532
Caldwell, John	1,000	Mid. Island Creek	1795	2	533
Caldwell, John	1,000	Mid. Island Creek	1795	2	534
Caldwell, John	1,000	Mid. Island Creek	1795	2	536
Caldwell, John	400	Pleasants Fork	1784	1	77
Caldwell, John	400	Pleasants Fork	1784	1	76
Caldwell, John	400	Pleasants Fork	1784	1	90

Name of Grantee	Acres	Local Description	Year	Book	Page
Cook, John A.	322	White Oak Run	1787	2	248
Cook, Thomas	334	Cross Creek	1789	2	319
Cornwell, Nathan et al	1,500	Cross Creek	1780	1	2
Coulter, Edward	25	Wheeling Creek	1834	4	126
Coutz, Martin	400	———— Branch	1799	3	230
Cowan, Alexander	196a.6p.2r.	Tomlinson's Run	1789	2	239
Cowan, Hugh & William	400	Tomlinson's Run	1789	2	238
Cowan, John	256a.1r.6p.	Tomlinson's Run	1789	2	247
Cox, Friend	400	Adj. George Cox	1786	1	390
Cox, Friend	308	Wts. Buffalo Creek	1786	1	381
Cox, Friend	1,155	Long Run	1830	4	65
Cox, Friend	130	Koons Run	1830	4	67
Cox, Friend	195	Long Run	1830	4	68
Cox, George	400	Cor. to Friend Cox	1786	1	365
Cox, Isaac	390	Pleasant Fork	1787	2	72
Cox, Isaac	13¾	Castleman's Run	1852	4	165
Cox, Israel	258	Buffalo Creek	1786	1	377
Cox, Peter (or Porter)	200	Buffalo Creek	1786	1	367
Cragg—See also Craig					
Cragg, James	400	Little Wheeling Creek	1787	1	433
Cragg, James	88	Little Wheeling Creek	1787	1	400
Cragg, James	400	McKimms Fork	1788	2	173
Craig—also Cragg					
Craig, Mary	20¾	Wheeling Creek	1831	4	74
Craig, Mary	87a.3r.	Wheeling Creek	1834	4	128
Craig, William	400	Middle Island Cr.	1787	1	451
Cravens, Nehemiah	1,000	Mid. Island Creek	1805	3	320
Cravens, Nehemiah	800	Wheeling Creek	1803	3	282
Cravens, Nehemiah	425	Wheeling Creek	1803	3	280
Cravens, Nehemiah	386	Wheeling Creek	1803	3	281
Cresap, Eliz. & Sarah et al	400	Wts. of Ohio	1791	2	328
Cresap, Elizabeth & Sarah et al	400	Long Reach	1785	1	105
Cresap, Elizabeth & Sarah et al	400	Long Reach	1785	1	128
Cresap, Michael	990	Adj. Robert Wood	1811	3	379
Croghan, William	300	Adj. David Rogers	1796	3	82
Croghan, William	500	Hogg Run	1796	3	81
Croghan, William	400	Hogg Run	1796	3	102
Crow, Frederick	174	Fish Creek	1809	3	363
Crow, Peter	400	Wheeling Creek	1796	3	92
Curry, Robert	220	Short Creek	1785	1	141
Curtis, James	360	Buffalo Creek	1786	1	298
Curtis, Philo	1,000	Mid Island Creek	1787	1	516
Curtis, Salathial	18	Wheeling Creek	1815	3	414
Custard, John	194	Mill Creek	1798	3	198
Davenport—See also Devenport					
Davenport, John	1,000	Mid. Island Creek	1787	1	518
Davenport, John	6,949	Mid. Island Creek	1793	2	444
Davenport, John	9,568	Mid. Island Creek	1793	2	445
Davey, Alexander M. (or W.)	2,000	Mid. Island Creek	1788	2	217
Davey, Alexander W.	340	Wheeling Creek	1787	2	36
Davis, Benjamin	400	Cross Creek	1786	1	366
Davis, Benjamin	62	Cross Creek	1787	2	127
Davis, Benjamin	289	Cross Creek	1787	2	128
Davis, Cephus	95	Bennett's Run	1838	4	156
Davis, James et al	400	Mid. Island Cr.	1801	3	261
Davis, James et al	660	Mid. Island Cr.	1801	3	262
Davis, Samuel	400	Grave Creek	1787	1	509
Davisson, Daniel	1,000	Robinson's Fork	1790	2	330
Dawson, Robert	22a.2r.28p.	Mill Creek	1787	2	147
Dehart, Cornelius	196	Fish Creek	1822	4	21
Dehart, Cornelius	100	Fish Creek	1820	4	14
Delevan, Nathaniel	1,000	Wheeling Creek	1787	1	504

Name of Grantee	Acres	Local Description	Year	Book	Page
Ferril—also Ferrell					
Ferril, George	160	Grave Creek	1801	3	249
Feay, George	250	Peter's Run	1809	3	362
Ferrell—also Ferril					
Ferrell, Jared	1,000	Graves Creek	1793	2	458
Fink, Jacob	400	Wheeling Cr.	1789	2	236
Finley, Agnes	400	Short Creek	1787	1	536
Fish, Benjamin	600	Bowman's Run	1831	4	80
Fish, Benjamin	400	Grave Creek	1831	4	81
Fish, Benjamin	514½	Fish Creek	1809	3	364
Fitch, Asahal	1,000	Middle Island Cr.	1787	2	15
Fleming, John et al	400	Wheeling Creek	1786	1	356
Fleming, Nathaniel	750	Harmon's Creek	1796	3	120
Fleming, Peter	100	Wheeling Creek	1794	2	496
Floyd, Gabriel J. et al	1,000	Grove Creek	1818	3	441
Floyd, Gabriel J. et al	1,000	Fish Creek	1818	3	442
Floyd, Gabriel J. et al	1,000	Fish Creek	1818	3	447
Floyd, Gabriel J. et al	1,000	Grave Creek	1818	3	446
Floyd, Gabriel J. et al	1,000	Fish Creek	1818	3	445
Floyd, Gabriel J. et al	1,000	Grave Creek	1818	3	444
Floyd, Gabriel J. et al	1,000	Wheeling Creek	1818	3	443
Fout, Andrew	380	Buffalo Creek	1785	1	175
Fout, Andrew	320	Buffalo Creek	1785	1	174
Fowler, Edward	400	Little Wheeling Cr.	1785	1	136
Frazer—also Frazier					
Frazer, Samuel	440	Little Wheeling Cr.	1787	1	447
Frazier, Samuel Jr.	13½	Wheeling Creek	1819	4	1
Furman, Reuben et al	345	Short Creek	1785	1	108
Fulton, Samuel	200	Adj. John Wilson	1788	2	183
Fulton, Samuel	400	Wts. of Ohio	1788	2	180
Gallihar—also Gallagher					
Gallihar, James	147	Grave Creek	1833	4	107
Gallion, Nathan	500	Wheeling Creek	1803	3	289
Galloway, Equilla	500	Sugar Tree Creek	1786	1	244
Gamble, Robert	9½	Adj. John Law	1812	3	394
Garby—also Gorby					
Garby, Ebenezer (Gorby)	60	Fish Creek	1830	4	54
Garby, Jesse (Gorby)	50	Prison Run	1836	4	145
Garner, Joshua	138	Long Run	1830	4	55
Garner, Joshua	200	Rocky Fork Run	1830	4	56
Garner, Joshua	230	Long Run	1831	4	84
Garner, Joshua	84	Buffington's Run	1831	4	85
Garrett, William	350	Buffalo Creek	1785	1	122
Garrison, James	400	Short Creek	1792	2	376
Garvin, David	13½	Wheeling Creek	1844	4	160
George, William (The Elder)	400	McElroy's Fork	1815	3	412
George, William (The Younger)	400	McElroy's Fork	1815	3	413
Gibbs, William	200	———— Creek	1786	1	418
Gibson, John	400	Buffalo Creek	1782	1	10
Gibson, Robert	145	Buffalo Creek	1793	2	434
Gilispy—Glaspy, Gillispie					
Gilispy, James	300	Buffalo Creek	1788	2	185
Giloriass, Robert	365	Buffalo Creek	1783	1	17
Gist, Independent & States	1,000	Mid. Island Creek	1809	3	360
Gist, Independent & States	1,000	Mid. Island Creek	1809	3	359
Gist, Independent & States	629	Mid. Island Creek	1809	3	358
Gist, Independent & States	1,000	Kim's Fork	1809	3	356
Gist, Independent & States	570	Kim's Fork	1809	3	357
Glaspy—See also Gilispy, Gillispie					
Glaspy, Ann	200	Wheeling Creek	1788	2	162
Glass, Samuel	400	Buffalo Creek	1786	1	303
Glenn, William	1,000	Grave Creek	1786	1	210
Goddard, John	165	Mid. Island Creek	1795	2	554

Name of Grantee	Acres	Local Description	Year	Book	Page
Harrison, Mary A. et al	1,000	Fish Creek	1818	3	442
Harrison, William Jr.	400	Buffalo Creek	1786	1	263
Harrison, William Sr.	368	Short Creek	1786	1	250
Harron—See Heron					
Hart, John	2,000	Fishing Creek	1786	1	162
Harvey, Benjamin	260	Buffalo Creek	1819	4	2
Harvey, Henry	400	Buffalo Creek	1785	1	130
Hawley—or Howley					
Hawley, Elijah	1,000	Mid. Island Creek	1792	2	351
Hawley, Elijah	1,000	Mid. Island Creek	1792	2	350
Hawley, Elijah	1,000	Mid. Island Creek	1792	2	352
Hawley, Elijah	1,000	Mid. Island Creek	1792	2	355
Hawley, Elijah	1,000	Mid. Island Creek	1792	2	354
Hawley, Elijah	1,000	Mid. Island Creek	1792	2	353
Hawley, Ephriam and Israel	1,000	Mid. Island Creek	1792	2	356
Hawthorn, William	300	Wheeling Creek	1788	2	191
Haycock—See Hecock					
Hays, James	300	Fishing Creek	1815	3	428
Hays, James	100	Fishing Creek	1815	3	429
Hays, John	400	King's Creek	1793	2	490
Hays, John	200	Harder's Run	1794	2	470
Hecock, Asa (or Avah)	1,000	Mid. Island Cr.	1787	2	23
Hedges, Aaron	198	Buffalo Creek	1788	2	158
Hedges, Charles	230	Short Creek	1786	1	358
Hedges, Joseph	300	Short Creek	1785	1	140
Hedges, Silas	384	Buffalo Creek	1785	1	165
Hedges, Silas	337	Buffalo Creek	1786	1	164
Hedges, Solomon	385	Buffalo Creek	1783	1	20
Hedges, Solomon	21	Buffalo Creek	1786	1	304
Hedges, Solomon Jr.	10	Buffalo Creek	1786	1	307
Henderson, John	100	Harmon's Creek	1798	3	183
Henderson, John	45	Cross Creek	1798	3	182
Henderson, John	400	Adj. Jacob Walker	1798	3	184
Henderson, John	50	Walker's Run	1798	3	147
Henderson, John	186	Merman's Creek	1796	3	93
Henderson, John et al	500	Mid. Island Creek	1798	3	185
Henderson, John et al	500	Mid. Island Creek	1798	3	186
Henderson, John et al	1,000	Mid. Island Creek	1798	3	149
Henry, Daniel	500	Mid. Island Creek	1788	2	271
Henry, Daniel	1,000	Middle Island Cr.	1788	2	164
Heron—or Harron					
Heron, William (Harron)	1,000	Mid. Island Creek	1787	1	510
Higgins, Robert	89	Buffalo Creek	1794	2	471
Higgins, Robert	400	Buffalo Creek	1794	2	472
Hillard—or Hilliard (also see Willard)					
Hillard, Isaac	1,000	Mid. Island Cr.	1787	1	465
Hillard, Isaac	1,000	Middle Island Creek	1787	1	459
Hillard, Isaac	4,000	Wheeling Creek	1789	2	308
Hillard, Isaac	4,000	Grave Cr.	1789	2	306
Hillard, Isaac	4,000	Wheeling Creek	1789	2	307
Hillard, Isaac	1,000	Mid. Isl. Cr.	1787	2	2
Hillard, Isaac	1,000	Grave Creek	1794	2	469
Hillard, Isaac	1,000	Wheeling Creek	1794	2	466
Hilliard—also Hillard (See also Willard)					
Hilliard, Isaac	1,000	Mid. Island Creek	1788	2	259
Hilliard, Isaac	9,000	Fishing Creek	1797	3	141
Hilliard, Isaac	12,000	Sugar Tree Creek	1797	3	143
Hilliard, Isaac	5,000	Fishing Creek	1797	3	142
Hilliard, Isaac	1,000	Mid. Island Creek	1787	1	497
Hitchcock, Caleb	1,000	Mid. Island Creek	1787	1	506
Hodgdon, Samuel	1,000	Mid. Island Cr.	1786	1	182
Hodgdon, Samuel et al	1,000	Mid. Island Cr.	1786	1	315
Hodgdon, Samuel et al	1,000	Mid. Island Creek	1786	1	267

Name of Grantee	Acres	Local Description	Year	Book	Page
Hukle, Richard	100	Adj. Henry Baker	1804	3	304
Hull, John	215	Pigeon Creek	1787	1	422
Hulslander—or Houslander					
Hulslander, John	10	Glanns Run	1833	4	115
Humphrey, David	400	Buffalo Creek	1787	1	471
Humphrey, George	280	Little Wheeling Cr.	1787	1	485
Humphrey, George	400	Buffalo Creek	1787	1	475
Humphrey, George	225	Wheeling Creek	1809	3	361
Humphrey, George	132	Wheeling Creek	1809	3	366
Humphrey, John	385	Buffalo Creek	1787	1	486
Humphrey, John	400	Fish Creek	1792	2	384
Humphrey, Robert	400	Little Wheeling Cr.	1787	1	398
Hust, Joseph	341	Short Creek	1785	1	107
Huston—See also Houston					
Huston, William	400	Little Wheeling Cr.	1786	1	290
Ingram, Abraham	250	Wolf Run	1834	4	136
Israel, Isaac (In Trust)	750	Mid. Island Cr.	1801	3	258
Israel, Isaac (In Trust)	400	Stutts Run	1801	3	259
Israel, Isaac	400	Mid. Island Creek	1793	2	381
Jackson, David	1,000	Mid. Island Creek	1787	2	11
Jackson, David	1,000	Middle Island Creek	1787	2	90
Jackson, David	1,000	Wheeling Creek	1787	1	500
Jackson, Stephen	1,000	Middle Island Creek	1787	2	86
Jacob, Gabriel	220	Short Creek	1799	3	210
Jacobs, David	122	Fishing Creek	1815	3	423
Jacobs, John Jeremiah et al	1,193	Grave Creek	1784	1	31
Jacobs, John Jeremiah et al	811	Near Fish Creek	1784	1	30
Jacobs, John Jeremiah & Mary	400	Proctor's Run	1784	1	83
Johnson, Benjamin	250	Holliday's Cove	1786	1	419
Johnson, Benjamin et al	359	Island in Ohio River	1786	1	334
Johnson, Benjamin Jr.	500	McLeving Creek	1786	1	420
Johnson, William	225	Long Reach	1787	2	123
Johnson, William	500	Long Reach	1787	2	103
Johnston, Benjamin	86½	Harder's Run	1788	2	250
Johnston, Benjamin Jr.	440	King's Creek	1787	2	146
Johnston, James	400	Long Reach	1799	3	206
Johnston, James C. et al	1,000	Fish Creek	1818	3	442
Johnston, James C. et al	1,000	Grave Creek	1818	3	441
Johnston, James C. et al	1,000	Wheeling Creek	1818	3	443
Johnston, James C. et al	500 (1500)	Fish Creek	1818	3	448
Johnston, James C. et al	1,000	Fish Creek	1818	3	447
Johnston, James C. et al	1,000	Grave Creek	1818	3	446
Johnston, James C. et al	1,000	Fish Creek	1818	3	445
Johnston, James C. et al	1,000	Grave Creek	1818	3	444
Johnston, Robert	400	Wts. Ohio	1788	2	155
Johnston, William et al	400	Tomlinson's Run	1796	3	80
Jones, Abraham et al	400	Fishing Creek	1815	3	411
Jones, David	100	Grave Creek	1788	2	257
Jones, David	400	Graves Creek	1786	1	249
Jones, David	1,000	Grave Creek	1786	1	261
Jones, David	5	Grave Creek	1809	3	372
Jones, David	400	Grave Creek	1800	3	239
Jones, Ignatius	300	Cross Creek	1790	2	326
Jones, John	174	Adj. John Lemon	1788	2	196
Jones, John	400	Adj. R. Pumphrey	1788	2	176
Jones, Morgan	400	Grave Creek	1785	1	133
Jones, Morgan	1,000	Grave Creek	1787	2	63
Jones, Morgan	945	Grave Creek	1787	2	66
Jerome, Augustus S.	255	Wheeling Creek	1837	4	154
Kays—See Keys					
Kellar—or Keller					
Kellar, Francis	200	Buffalo Creek	1787	2	55

Name of Grantee	Acres	Local Description	Year	Book	Page
Lawrence, Benjamin	500	Mid. Island Cr.	1786	1	320
Lay—See Say					
Lay, Benjamin	1,000	Fishing Creek	1788	2	221
Leatherman, Conrad	1,000	Middle Island Creek	1787	1	401
Leatherman, Conrad	1,000	Mill Run	1787	2	102
Leatherman, Conrad	1,000	Mill Run	1787	2	82
Leatherman, Conrad	1,000	Mill Run	1787	2	75
Leatherman, Conrad	1,000	Mill Run	1787	2	74
Leatherman, Margaret	1,000	McElroy's Fork	1787	1	492
Lee, John	1,000	Middle Island Creek	1787	1	413
Lee, John	389	Mid. Island Creek	1803	3	287
Lee, John	400	Mid. Island Cr.	1801	3	260
Lee, John	349	Mid. Island Creek	1801	3	256
Lee, John	450	Mid. Island Creek	1796	3	167
Lee, John	1,000	Purcell's Lick	1785	1	155
Lee, John	400	Mid. Island Creek	1787	2	68
Lee, John	1,000	Mid. Island Creek	1787	2	45
Lee, John	389	Mid. Island Creek	1787	2	44
Lee, John	364	Mid. Island Creek	1787	2	43
Lee, John	170	Wheeling Creek	1793	2	457
Leet, William	500	Gut Run	1789	2	305
Leiman—Seimor, Simmons, Simeon, Simons					
Leiman, Paul et al (Leimor)	4,000	Fish Creek	1786	1	177
Leiman, Paul et al (Leimor)	7,000	Fishing Creek	1786	1	179
Leiman, Paul et al (Leimor)	4,000	Fish Creek	1786	1	180
Leiman, Paul et al (Leimor)	4,000	Fishing Creek	1786	1	189
Leiman, Paul et al (Leimor)	4,000	Fish Creek	1786	1	188
Leiman, Paul et al (Leimor)	4,000	Fish Creek	1786	1	190
Lemon, John	100	Fish Creek	1833	4	120
Lewis, John et al	400	Mid. Island Cr.	1801	3	261
Lewis, John et al	660	Mid. Island Cr.	1801	3	262
Link, Jacob	400	Wheeling Cr.	1789	2	236
Linn, Moses	69	Buffalo Creek	1786	1	238
Lockett—Lackett, Sackett					
Lockwood, Ephriam	1,000	Grave Creek	1787	1	414
Lockwood, Ephriam	200	Wheeling Creek	1788	2	213
Lockwood, Isaac	2,000	Mid. Island Creek	1793	2	442
Logan, John	978	Mid. Island Creek	1791	2	349
Logan, William	150	Buffalo Creek	1787	1	435
Loland, John	260	King's Creek	1796	3	86
Long, Robert	1,000	Mid. Island Creek	1792	2	369
Long, Robert	1,000	Mid. Island Creek	1792	2	370
Lounsberry, Joshua	3,000	Mid. Island Creek	1789	2	324
Lynn, Isaac	300	McKinley's Run	1793	2	487
Maddin, Thomas	24	Harmon's Creek	1796	3	87
Maddin, Thomas	200	Harmon's Creek	1793	2	425
Maddin, Thomas	400	Cross Creek	1789	2	310
Madison, James	500	Fishing Creek	1787	1	412
Madison, James	500	Fishing Creek	1787	2	5
Madison, James	500	Fishing Creek	1787	2	6
Madison, James	500	Fish Creek	1798	3	199
Magruder, Ninian Beall	1,000	Little Wheeling Cr.	1785	1	114
Main—See Mane					
Mane, Henry	250	Whetsell Run	1796	3	72
Manning, Mary et al	321¼	Grave Creek	1823	4	28
Marklin, William	200	Big Wheeling Cr.	1787	1	525
Marklin, William	250	Big Wheeling Cr.	1787	1	523
Marlow, Peter	60	Wheeling Creek	1831	4	71
Marquis, William	400	King's Creek	1789	2	563
Marshall, Samuel	185	Cross Creek	1788	2	160
Marshall, Samuel	145	Buffalo Creek	1789	2	282
Marshall, Samuel	1,000	Cross Creek	1789	2	281

Name of Grantee	Acres	Local Description	Year	Book	Page
McConnell, Samuel	400	Wheeling Creek	1788	2	210
McConnell, William	100	Wolf Run	1836	4	152
McConnell, William	200	Wharton's Run	1836	4	150
McConnell, William	100	Wheeling Creek	1836	4	151
McCord, Thomas	19	Pike Island	1845	4	162
McCoy, Alexander	400	Wheeling Creek	1787	2	254
McCoy, Alexander et al	400	Wheeling Creek	1814	3	408
McCoy, Angus	200	Mill Creek	1789	2	241
McCoy, James	340	Wheeling Creek	1816	3	431
McCoy, James	14a.37p.	Wheeling Creek	1817	3	436
McCoy, James	34	Wheeling Creek	1798	3	161
McCoy, Joseph	200	Adj. Geo. Stricker	1812	3	393
McCoy, Joseph	69	Mid. Island Creek	1811	3	385
McCoy, Robert (or George)	400	Wheeling Creek	1787	1	470
McCreery—McCleery, McCreary					
McCreery, William	17	Wheeling Creek	1809	3	354
McCreary, William	48	Wheeling Creek	1820	4	17
McCullock—McCollock, McCollock					
McCullock, Abraham	300	Adj. J. McCullock	1784	1	65
McCullock, George	300	Buffalo Creek	1784	1	61
McCullock, John	300	Short Creek	1784	1	64
McCullock, John	200	Short Creek	1784	1	60
McCune, Joseph	1,000	Wheeling Cr.	1792	2	373
McCutcheon, Hugh	75	Wheeling Creek	1819	3	452
McDonald, Charles	117	Big Grave Creek	1787	1	511
McDonald, Charles	1,000	Big Grave Creek	1787	2	13
McDonald, John W.	400	Adj. State Line	1787	2	131
McDowell, Nathaniel	300	Little Wheeling Cr.	1787	1	429
McFarland, Daniel	3,000	McElroy's Fork	1796	3	110
McFarland, Daniel	3,000	McElroy's Fork	1796	3	112
McFarland, Daniel	3,000	McElroy's Fork	1796	3	109
McFarland, Daniel	400	Wolf Run	1796	3	108
McFarland, Daniel	300	Grave Creek	1796	3	107
McFarland, Daniel	300	Grave Creek	1796	3	106
McFarland, Daniel	300	Grave Creek	1796	3	105
McFarland, Daniel	300	Grave Creek	1796	3	104
McFarland, Daniel	200	Adj. John Wilson	1791	2	363
McFarland, James (or John)	400	Pleasant Fork	1788	2	193
McFarland, John	1,000	Pleasant Run	1797	3	127
McFarland, John	400	Pleasant Run	1797	3	178
McFarland, John	400	Mid. Island Creek	1788	2	216
McGehan, Duncan	400	Tomlinson's Run	1789	2	299
McGuire, Edward	300	Wheeling Creek	1787	1	399
McGuire, Edward	350	Fish Creek	1787	1	481
McGuire, Edward	350	Wheeling Creek	1787	1	489
McGuire, Francis	137	Prather's Run	1796	3	122
McGuire, Francis	100	Buffalo Creek	1793	2	430
McGuire, Francis	32	Cross Creek	1797	3	175
McGuire, Francis	400	Buffalo Creek	1787	1	426
McGuire, Hugh	400	Arnold's Fork	1803	3	290
McGuire, Hugh	100	Adj. Wm. Craig	1804	3	311
McGuire, Hugh	120	Mid. Island Creek	1796	3	98
McGuire, Hugh	155	Fish Creek	1796	3	97
McGuire, Hugh	110	Wheeling Creek	1797	3	137
McGuire, Thomas	185	Wts. Bufflao Cr.	1787	1	394
McIntire, John	300	Buffalo Creek	1787	1	397
McIntire, John	600	Fishing Creek	1796	3	168
McIntire, John	100	Buffalo Creek	1792	2	371
McIntire, John	142	Buffalo Creek	1792	2	372
McIntire, John	400	Fish Creek	1788	2	186
McIntire, William	332	Wheeling Creek	1798	3	162
McKey, James	500	Grave Creek	1787	2	59

Name of Grantee	Acres	Local Description	Year	Book	Page
Nichols, Richard	1,000	Mid. Island Creek	1787	1	499
Nichols, Richard	1,000	Middle Island Cr.	1787	1	501
Nichols, Richard	1,000	Mid. Island Creek	1787	1	498
Nichols, Richard	1,000	Fish Creek	1793	2	385
Nichols, Richard	1,000	Mid. Island Creek	1792	2	362
Norton, Isaac	1,000	Mid. Island Creek	1787	2	3
Norton, Isaac	1,000	Wheeling Creek	1787	1	458
Norton, Isaac	1,000	Mid. Island Creek	1787	1	496
Ogle, Alexander	320	Buffalo Creek	1783	1	29
Ogle, Benjamin	400	Buffalo Creek	1786	1	380
Ogle, James	1,000	Fish Creek	1797	3	165
Ogle, James	1,000	Fish Creek	1797	3	166
Ogle, James	1,000	Fishing Creek	1804	3	306
Ogle, James et al	200½	Wolf Run	1835	4	141
Ogle, Joseph	260	Buffalo Creek	1783	1	28
Oglesby, James	500	Mid. Island Cr.	1785	1	185
Oglesby, James	500	Mid. Island Cr.	1785	1	186
O'Neal, Constantine	380	Grave's Creek	1787	1	539
Orr, Thomas	400	Wheeling Creek	1787	1	537
Owings, Richard	500	Sugar Tree Creek	1786	1	236
Owings, Richard	500	McKinnon's Fork	1786	1	245
Owings, Richard	500	Sugar Tree Creek	1786	1	242
Owings, Richard	500	Mid. Island Creek	1786	1	247
Owings, Richard	500	Sugar Tree Creek	1786	1	246
Owings, Richard	500	Sugar Tree Creek	1786	1	248
Owings, Richard	500	Buffalo Creek	1782	1	16
Owings, Richard	500	Sugar Tree Creek	1786	1	317
Owings, Richard	500	Sugar Creek	1786	1	327
Owings, Richard	500	Mid. Island Cr.	1786	1	328
Owings, Samuel	270	Proctor's Run	1784	1	70
Owings, Samuel	400	Grave Creek	1784	1	69
Owings, Samuel	400	Grave Creek	1784	1	71
Owings, Samuel	400	Mid Island Cr.	1785	1	229
Owings, Samuel	500	Mid. Island Cr.	1785	1	230
Owings, Samuel	400	Fish Creek	1785	1	232
Owings, Samuel	600	Mid. Island Cr.	1785	1	231
Owings, Thomas	500	Proctor's Run	1784	1	72
Owings, Thomas	500	Proctor's Run	1784	1	73
Owings, Thomas	500	Grave Creek	1787	2	38
Owings, Thomas	500	Grave's Creek	1787	1	535
Page, Nathaniel	500	Proctor's Run	1809	3	365
Page, Robert	119	Buffalo Creek	1788	2	220
Palson, Isaac	50	Long Run	1830	4	51
Parks, Robert	172a.35p.	Herman's Creek	1794	2	468
Parr, Nathan	175	Adj. David Shepherd	1797	3	169
Parr, Stephen	395	Wts. Ohio River	1787	1	494
Parriott, John	3¼	River Hill	1833	4	112
Parriott, John et al	100	Fish Creek	1834	4	137
Patrick, Peter	150	Fish Creek	1819	4	8
Patterson, John	400	Buffalo Creek	1782	1	12
Patterson, William	313	Fishing Creek	1787	2	106
Patterson, William	1,000	Proctor's Run	1789	2	314
Patterson, William	1,000	Cor. George Stricker	1789	2	313
Patterson, William	1,000	Fish Creek	1789	2	312
Pearce—See Pierce					
Pearce, Mathew	2,000	Mid. Island Creek	1794	2	412
Pearce, Mathew	2,000	Mid. Island Creek	1794	2	411
Pearce, Mathew	2,000	Mid. Island Creek	1794	2	410
Pearce, Mathew	1,000	Mid. Island Creek	1794	2	409
Pearce, Mathew	2,000	Mid. Island Creek	1794	2	408
Pearce, Mathew	2,000	Mid. Island Creek	1794	2	407
Pearce, Mathew	2,000	Mid. Island Creek	1794	2	406
Peck, Abel	1,249	Mid. Island Creek	1792	2	360

Name of Grantee	Acres	Local Description	Year	Book	Page
Pentacost—or Penticost					
Pentacost, Dorsey	400	Tomlinson's Run	1789	2	228
Pentacost, Dorsey	400	Tomlinson's Run	1789	2	280
Pentacost, Dorsey	400	Tomlinson's Run	1789	2	286
Pentacost, Dorsey	400	Tomlinson's Run	1789	2	287
Pentacost, Dorsey	400	Hardin's Run	1789	2	291
Pentacost, Dorsey	400	Tomlinson's Run	1789	2	292
Pentacost, Dorsey et al	200	Buffalo Creek	1791	2	343
Penticost, Dorsey	350	Grave Creek	1788	2	192
Penticost, Dorsey	350	Little Grave Creek	1788	2	214
Penticost, Dorsey et al	578	Buffalo Creek	1787	2	9
Penticost, Dorsey et al	300	Buffalo Creek	1787	1	441
Perine—or Perrine					
Perine, James	57	Fish Creek	1805	3	317
Perine, James	142	Adj. Obidiah Peden	1805	3	319
Perine, James	80	Adj. Obidiah Peden	1805	3	318
Perine, William	263	Fish Creek	1803	3	294
Perine, William	130	Mid. Island Creek	1807	3	336
Perine, William	200	Mid. Island Creek	1807	3	335
Perine, William	1,000	Mid. Island Creek	1807	3	337
Perine, William	1,000	Mid. Island Creek	1807	3	334
Perine, William	150	Fish Creek	1803	3	291
Perine, William	187½	Fish Creek	1803	3	292
Perrine, William	301	Grave Creek	1810	3	371
Perrine, William	222	Fish Creek	1815	3	417
Persons—See Pierson					
Persons, Baldwin	250	Cross Creek	1790	2	331
Persons, Baldwin	400	Buffalo Creek	1786	1	375
Persons, Baldwin	250	Cross Creek	1786	1	391
Peterson, John	45	Buffalo Creek	1801	3	250
Pettit, Alexander	385	Jake's Run	1802	3	265
Pettit, Alexander	100	Wheeling Creek	1802	3	264
Phillips, John (or William)	5,000	Fishing Creek	1787	1	479
Phillips, John	2,000	Fishing Creek	1787	1	478
Phillips, John	2,000	Fishing Creek	1787	1	480
Phillips, John	4,000	Fishing Creek	1787	1	477
Phillips, Phebe	273	Wheeling Creek	1784	1	82
Pickering, Timothy et al	1,000	Mid. Island Creek	1786	1	268
Pickering, Timothy et al	1,000	Mid. Island Cr.	1786	1	315
Pickering, Timothy et al	1,000	Middle Island Creek	1786	1	267
Pickering, Timothy et al	1,000	Mid. Island Cr.	1786	1	233
Pickering, Timothy et al	1,000	Mid. Island Cr.	1786	1	194
Pickering, Timothy et al	1,000	Mid. Island Creek	1786	1	193
Pickering, Timothy et al	1,000	Mid. Island Cr.	1786	1	184
Pickering, Timothy et al	1,000	Mid. Island Creek	1786	1	192
Pickering, Timothy et al	1,000	Island Creek	1786	1	182
Pickering, Timothy et al	1,000	Mid. Island Cr.	1786	1	183
Pierce—See also Pearce					
Pierce, Lewis	343	Buffalo Creek	1787	2	132
Pierson—See Persons					
Platt, Alexander S.	1,000	Mid. Island Creek	1792	2	358
Platt, Alexander S.	1,000	Mid. Island Creek	1792	2	359
Poage, George	512	Graves Creek	1787	2	53
Poage, Robert	190	Wheeling Creek	1796	3	114
Pollard, William	2,000	Fishing Creek	1787	2	97
Porter, Andrew	3,000	Fishing Creek	1786	1	352
Prather, Charles	451	Adj. Van Swearinger	1797	3	140
Prather, Charles	20	Buffalo Creek	1793	2	437
Price—See also Grice					
Pumphrey, Rachel et al	400	Wheeling Creek	1814	3	408
Pumphrey, Reazon	400	Buffalo Creek	1787	2	69
Pumphrey, Reazon	400	Adj. James Harrison	1787	2	67
Pumphrey, Washington	3¾	Wheeling Creek	1847	4	163

Name of Grantee	Acres	Local Description	Year	Book	Page
Roberts, Jonathan	80	Grave Creek	1809	3	355
Roberts, Richard	200	McElroy's Fork	1811	3	380
Roberts, William J.	400	Big Grave Creek	1787	1	455
Robinson, Aaron	460	Buffalo Creek	1786	1	167
Robinson, Andrew	400	Wheeling Creek	1787	2	40
Robinson, Andrew	68	Wheeling Cr.	1787	1	448
Robinson, Andrew	211	Wheeling Creek	1801	3	243
Robinson, Andrew	868	Wheeling Creek	1801	3	244
Robinson, Andrew	225	Grave Creek	1798	3	191
Robinson, Andrew	211	Wheeling Creek	1787	1	534
Robinson, Andrew	400	Wheeling Creek	1787	1	543
Robinson, Edward	400	Buffalo Creek	1785	1	142
Robinson, John	24¼	Wheeling Creek	1809	3	352
Rodacker, Henry	40	Fish Creek	1832	4	103
Rogers, Abraham	105	Buffalo Creek	1788	2	209
Rogers, Andrew	79	Buffalo Creek	1809	3	347
Rogers, Nichols (Nicholas)	230	Buffalo Creek	1788	2	157
Rolfe—Relfe, Rolph					
Rolfe, John et al	1,000	Mid. Island Creek	1798	3	148
Rolph—See Relfe, Rolfe					
Rolph, John	670	Mid. Island Creek	1794	2	419
Rolph, John	200 (900)	Mid. Island Creek	1794	2	428
Rolph, John	330	Mid. Island Creek	1794	2	465
Rolph, John	500	Mid. Island Creek	1794	2	417
Rolph, John	831	Mid. Island Creek	1793	2	416
Rolph, John	200	Mid. Island Creek	1793	2	415
Rolph, John	400 (460)	Mid. Island Creek	1793	2	414
Roquet—Ragnet, Raquet					
Roquet, Nicholas	1,000	Fishing Creek	1787	2	138
Row, Jacob	300	Wheeling Creek	1787	1	456
Rulong, Aaron et al	660	Mid. Island Cr.	1801	3	262
Rulong, Aaron et al	400	Mid. Island Cr.	1801	3	261
Russell, Alexander	1,000	McElroy's Fork	1787	2	81
Russell, Alexander	1,000	McElroy's Fork	1787	2	80
Russell, Alexander	1,000	McElroy's Fork	1787	1	404
Rutherford, Robert	1,000	Wts. Ohio	1787	2	20
Rutherford, Robert	2,000	Mid. Island Creek	1787	2	126
Rutherford, Thomas	1,000	Harden's Run	1779	1	1
Rutherford, Thomas	500	Short Creek	1779	1	6
Ryan—also Rine, Rion					
Ryan, James	137	Short Creek	1789	2	321
Ryan, James	400	Wheeling Creek	1784	1	38
Ryan, John	100	Long Run	1830	4	58
Ryan, Lazerus Jr.	100	Long Run	1830	4	57
Sackett—Lackett, Lockett					
Sackett, Cyrus	1,000	Fish Creek	1791	2	367
Salters—See Saulters					
Sanford, Ezekel	1,000	Mid. Island Creek	1787	1	507
Sanford, Ezekiel	1,000	Mid. Island Creek	1787	2	12
Sanford, Hezekiah	1,000	Mid. Island Cr.	1787	2	16
Sanford, Hezekiah	1,000	Mid. Island Creek	1787	2	88
Sanford, Hezekiah	1,000	Mid. Island Creek	1787	2	91
Sanford, Hezekiah	1,000	Grave Creek	1787	1	508
Sanford, Samuel	1,000	Mid. Island Creek	1787	1	505
Sanford, Samuel	1,000	Mid. Island Creek	1787	1	514
Satchele—or Satchill					
Satchele, John	422½	Harden's Run	1787	2	142
Saulters, James	10	Boggs Run	1805	3	324
Say, Benjamin	1,000	Fishing Cr.	1788	2	221
Scott, John	34½	Bennett's Run	1838	4	157
Scott, John	11	Wheeling Creek	1838	4	155
Scott, Robert	400	Fish Creek	1800	3	229
Sear, David	300	Fish Creek	1788	2	190

Name of Grantee	Acres	Local Description	Year	Book	Page
Seimor—Leiman, Simeon, Simmons, Simons					
Seimor, Paul et al	4,000	Fish Creek	1786	1	190
Seimor, Paul et al	4,000	Fishing Creek	1786	1	189
Seimor, Paul et al	4,000	Fish Creek	1786	1	188
Seimor, Paul et al	7,000	Fishing Creek	1786	1	179
Seimor, Paul et al	4,000	Fish Creek	1786	1	180
Seimor, Paul et al	4,000	Fish Creek	1786	1	177
Semple, William	1,000	Pleasant Fork	1785	1	131
Shaw, John	330	Round Bottom	1803	3	274
Shepherd, Abraham	700	Turkey Run	1788	2	218
Shepherd, Abraham	1,000	Turkey Run	1788	2	222
Shepherd, David	400	Adj. Michael Cresap	1786	1	251
Shepherd, David	1,000	Mid. Island Creek	1786	1	266
Shepherd, David	42	Short Creek	1788	2	182
Shepherd, David	400	Mid. Island Creek	1786	1	348
Shepherd, David	475	Mid. Island Cr.	1786	1	350
Shepherd, David	220	Wheeling Creek	1787	1	541
Shepherd, Moses	1,050	Gunstaf's Run	1806	3	328
Shepherd, Moses	600	Wheeling Creek	1803	3	298
Shepherd, Moses	1,441	Wheeling Creek	1803	3	296
Shepherd, Moses	2,000	Wheeling Creek	1803	3	297
Shepherd, Moses	200	Turkey Run	1797	3	136
Shepherd, Moses	1,416	Wheeling Creek	1803	3	293
Shepherd, William	925	Wheeling Creek	1788	2	224
Shepherd, William	1,000	Wheeling Creek	1788	2	223
Simmons—Leiman, Seimor, Simeon, Simons					
Sinclair, William Sr.	530	Hardin's Run	1787	2	253
Smith, Ezra et al	3,000	Mid. Island Creek	1793	2	438
Smith, Forgus	24	Cross Creek	1794	2	513
Smith, George	400	Buffalo Creek	1786	1	296
Smith, Henry	250	Grave Creek	1797	3	134
Smith, James	400	Wheeling Creek	1784	1	44
Smith, James	76	Grave Creek	1797	3	135
Smith, James	90	Wheeling Creek	1786	1	354
Smith, James	150	Sancoe's Run	1811	3	390
Smith, Levi	30	Wheeling Creek	1835	4	143
Smith, Levi	100	Wheeling Creek	1835	4	142
Smith, Ralph	400	McElroy's Fork	1813	3	406
Smith, Ralph	196	McElroy's Fork	1813	3	405
Smith, Samuel et al	278	Wheeling Creek	1811	3	387
Smith, Samuel Sr.	1,000	Wheeling Creek	1788	2	200
Smith, Samuel Sr.	400	Wheeling Cr.	1788	2	199
Smith, Samuel Sr.	400	Wheeling Creek	1788	2	198
Smith, Samuel Sr.	400	Wheeling Creek	1788	2	195
Smith, Samuel Sr.	1,000	Grave Creek	1788	2	189
Smith, Samuel Sr.	1,000	Wheeling Creek	1788	2	188
Smith, Samuel Sr.	400	Wheeling Creek	1788	2	187
Smith, Samuel Sr.	1,000	Big Wheeling Creek	1788	2	174
Sockman, Henry	64	Grave Creek	1833	4	117
Sparr—or Spawr					
Sparr, John (Spawr)	400	Short Creek	1786	1	322
Spear, Alexander	1,000	McElroy's Fork	1787	1	528
Sprigg, Zachariah	39	Wheeling Creek	1786	1	306
Sprigg, Zachariah	150	Short Creek	1786	1	262
Sprigg, Zachariah	300	Short Creek	1784	1	49
Stanford, Hezekiah	1,000	Grave Creek	1787	1	508
Steenrod, Daniel	190	Adj. Archie Woods	1815	3	421
Stephenson, Charles	400	Buffalo Creek	1786	1	369
Stephenson, George	342	Buffalo Creek	1787	2	105
Stewart, John et al	400	Wheeling Creek	1814	3	408
Stout, Samuel	2,600	Fishing Creek	1794	2	421
Strain, Samuel	400	Cor. to George Brown	1795	2	551
Straver, John	100	Fish Creek	1822	4	22

Name of Grantee	Acres	Local Description	Year	Book	Page
Stricker—or Striker					
Stricker, Elizabeth	400	Mid. Island Cr.	1786	1	332
Stricker, Elizabeth et al	85	Mid. Island Creek	1786	1	325
Stricker, Elizabeth et al	900	Mid. Island Creek	1786	1	335
Stricker, George	600	Fish Creek	1788	2	204
Stricker, George	1,000	Adj. Thomas Wells	1788	2	203
Stricker, George	1,000	Adj. John Stricker	1788	2	194
Stricker, George	1,000	Proctor's Run	1788	2	178
Stricker, George	250	Mid. Island Creek	1787	2	120
Stricker, George	500	Proctor's Run	1787	2	116
Stricker, George	250	Mid. Island Cr.	1787	2	115
Stricker, George	250	Long Reach	1787	2	92
Stricker, George	200	Adj. John Boggs	1787	2	96
Stricker, George	500	Mid. Island Creek	1787	2	94
Stricker, George	500	Mid. Island Creek	1787	2	61
Stricker, George	400	Wts. Ohio River	1787	2	56
Stricker, George	500	Proctor's Run	1787	2	24
Stricker, George	1,700	Mid. Island Creek	1794	2	514
Stricker, George	400	Mid. Island Creek	1797	3	139
Stricker, George	235	Cor. John Boggs	1785	1	215
Stricker, George	148	Mid. Island Cr.	1801	3	257
Stricker, George	400	Fish Creek	1803	3	277
Stricker, George	200	Bogg's Run	1804	3	302
Stricker, George	500	Mid. Island Cr.	1787	1	524
Stricker, George et al	200	Buffalo Creek	1791	2	343
Stricker, John	200	Mid. Island Cr.	1786	1	314
Stricker, John	1,000	Fish Creek	1789	2	289
Stricker, John	1,000	Fish Creek	1789	2	290
Stricker, John	1,000	Fish Creek	1789	2	288
Stricker, John	1,000	Fish Creek	1789	2	285
Stricker, John	1,000	Fish Creek	1789	2	284
Stricker, John	1,000	Fish Creek	1789	2	283
Stricker, John	1,000	Fish Creek	1789	2	279
Stricker, John	500	Pleasant Fork	1789	2	234
Stricker, John	1,000	Fish Creek	1789	2	233
Stricker, John	1,000	Fish Creek	1789	2	232
Stricker, John	1,000	Fish Creek	1789	2	231
Stricker, John	1,000	Fish Creek	1789	2	229
Stricker, John (Striker)	600	Mid Island Creek	1786	1	416
Stricker, John	1,000	Fish Creek	1789	2	226
Stricker, John	163	Pleasant Fork	1789	2	225
Stricker, Lawrence	400	Stull's Run	1788	2	166
Striker, John	600	Mid Island Creek	1786	1	416
Stroup, Conrad	500	Wheeling Creek	1787	1	432
Stroup, Conrad	500	Wheeling Creek	1787	1	403
Stroup, Conrad	200	Wheeling Creek	1787	2	37
Stroup, Conrad	500	Wheeling Creek	1787	1	474
Summers, Walter	195	Wheeling Creek	1787	1	431
Sutherland, David	600	Mid Island Creek	1786	1	308
Swan, Charles	400	Fish Creek	1786	1	360
Swearinger—or Swearingen					
Swearinger, Andrew	400	Wts. Ohio	1793	2	386
Swearinger, Van	514	Wts. Ohio	1793	2	379
Swearinger, Van	400	Wts. Ohio River	1787	1	408
Swearinger, Van	370	Short Creek	1787	1	540
Swearinger, Van et al	800	Adj. J. Nessly	1789	2	317
Tallant, Henry	2 9/10	Wheeling Creek	1853	4	166
Teal, Charles	100	Cross Creek	1799	3	202
Terrel—or Terril					
Terrel, John	152¼	Big Grave Creek	1796	3	74
Terril, George	160	Grave Creek	1801	3	249
Thomas, Charles	100	Jeffers Run	1815	3	415
Thompson, Hugh	2,000	Mid Island Creek	1789	2	293

Name of Grantee	Acres	Local Description	Year	Book	Page
Warren—See Warun					
Warton, Robert	200	Wheeling Creek	1796	3	78
Warun—or Warren					
Warun, James (Warren)	1,000	Middle Island Creek	1787	1	513
Warun, James (Warren)	1,000	Middle Island Creek	1787	1	527
Washington, Lund	1,000	Shirtees Creek	1779	1	5
Washington, Lund	2,000	Rockhouse Creek	1779	1	4
Waterbury, John et al	3,000	Mid Island Creek	1793	2	438
Webster, John Lee	270	Harmon's Creek	1786	2	32
Webster, John Lee	200	King's Creek	1787	2	30
Webster, John Lee	470	Harmon's Creek	1787	2	31
Weed, Smith	2,000	Mid. Island Cr.	1793	2	441
Wellman—See Willman					
Wells—See also Wills					
Wells, Absolom	200	Buffalo Creek	1786	1	368
Wells, Absolom	400	Buffalo Creek	1786	1	370
Wells, Alexander	200	Mingo Bottom	1780	1	3
Wells, Alexander	160	Mingo Bottom	1794	2	459
Wells, Alexander et al	1,500	Cross Creek	1780	1	2
Wells, Benjamin	400	Buffalo Creek	1782	1	8
Wells, Benjamin	400	Cross Creek	1782	1	14
Wells, Charles	400	Buffalo Creek	1782	1	7
Wells, Charles	400	Buffalo Creek	1782	1	15
Wells, Charles	200	Adj. Robert Woods	1800	3	240
Wells, Charles	400	Buffalo Creek	1786	1	343
Wells, Charles	400	Cross Creek	1794	2	467
Wells, Charles	530	Buffalo Creek	1794	2	476
Wells, Charles	103	Cross Creek	1794	2	477
Wells, Charles	77	Buffalo Creek	1794	2	493
Wells, Duket	246	Middle Island	1808	3	344
Wells, John	146	Cross Creek	1785	1	214
Wells, Joseph	400	McKinnon's Fork	1786	1	341
Wells, Nicholas	500	Mid. Island Creek	1809	3	350
Wells, Richard	400	Cross Creek	1787	2	136
Wells, Thomas	700	Sancoes Run	1799	3	231
Wells, Thomas	190	Cow Run	1815	3	430
Wells, William	800	Mid. Island Creek	1807	3	338
Wells, William	450	McElroy's Fork	1813	3	398
Wertz, Anna et al	4,000	Fishing Creek	1845	4	161
Whetzel—Whitsel, Whitsell, Whitzell					
Whetzel, John	500	Wheeling Cr.	1787	1	450
White, Andrew	400	Wheeling Creek	1789	2	298
White, Jemimia	206	Short Creek	1794	2	473
Whitsel, John	500	Wheeling Creek	1788	2	197
Whitsel, John	1,000	Wheeling Creek	1787	1	428
Whitsel, John	350	Wheeling Creek	1787	1	495
Whitsell—Whetzel, Whitsel, Whitzell					
Whitsell, Martin	350	Wheeling Creek	1787	1	406
Whitzell, Martin	400	Shell's Run	1801	3	252
Wiggins, Edward	300	Cross Creek	1787	2	48
Wiggins, Edward	400	Cross Creek	1787	2	129
Wikert—Wykart, Wykert					
Wikert, Nicholas	100	Fish Creek	1820	4	15
Willard—See Hillard or Hilliard					
Willard, Isaac	4,000	Grave Creek	1789	2	306
Willard, Isaac	4,000	Wheeling Creek	1789	2	307
Willard, Isaac	4,000	Wheeling Creek	1789	2	308
Willard, Isaac	1,000	Middle Island Creek	1787	2	2
Williams, Isaac	400	Grave Creek	1787	2	58
Williams, Isaac	90	Grave Creek	1787	2	134
Williams, Isaac	400	Grave Creek	1787	2	137
Williams, Jeremiah	2,000	Mid Island Creek	1796	3	76
Williams, Jeremiah	500	Mid Island Creek	1796	3	77

Name of Grantee	Acres	Local Description	Year	Book	Page
Williams, Jeremiah	100	Adj. David McClure	1796	3	84
Williams, Jeremiah	200	Proctor's Run	1811	3	384
Williams, Jeremiah	890	Purcell's Run	1803	3	288
Williams, Jeremiah	1,000	Fishing Creek	1806	3	325
Williams, Jeremiah	650	Rows Run	1806	3	326
Williams, Jeremiah	150	Adj. Hugh Willson	1806	3	327
Williams, Jeremiah	630	Fishing Creek	1810	3	367
Williams, Jeremiah	520	Fishing Creek	1810	3	368
Williams, Jeremiah	500	Fishing Creek	1810	3	369
Williams, Lewis	400	Wheeling Cr.	1784	1	117
Williams, Peter	1,000	Mid Island Creek	1792	2	361
Williams, Thomas	145	Wheeling Creek	1802	3	270
Williams, William	400	Buffalo Creek	1787	1	425
Williams, William	100	Long Run	1833	4	113
Williamson, David	300	Fishing Creek	1786	1	292
Williamson, David	300	Fishing Creek	1786	1	300
Williamson, David	300	Fishing Creek	1786	1	301
Williamson, David	280	Wheeling Creek	1786	1	302
Williamson, David	399	Graves Creek	1786	1	310
Williamson, David	400	Short Creek	1786	1	355
Williamson, John	140	Peace & Plenty Island	1793	2	395
Williamson, John	400	Long Reach	1793	2	396
Williamson, John	250	Wheeling Creek	1787	2	62
Williamson, Moses	105	Wheeling Creek	1785	1	144
Williamson, Moses Jr.	150	Wheeling Creek	1786	1	211
Williamson, Moses Sr.	400	Wheeling Creek	1785	1	135
Williamson, Thomas	300	Wheeling Creek	1785	1	137
Willman, John Vowels	172	Buffalo Creek	1786	1	240
Wills—See also Wells					
Wills, Alexander	72	Buffalo Creek	1791	2	333
Wills, Alexander	51	Buffalo Creek	1792	2	387
Wills, Charles (See Wells)	24	Buffalo Creek	1788	2	172
Wills, Charles	530	Buffalo Creek	1794	2	476
Wills, Charles	103	Cross Creek	1794	2	477
Wills, Charles	400	Buffalo Creek	1786	1	343
Wills, Charles Sr.	1,000	Long Reach	1815	3	416
Wills, John	114	Cross Creek	1787	2	70
Willson—or Wilson					
Willson, Joseph	400	Wheeling Creek	1787	1	442
Willson, William	57	Wheeling Creek	1793	2	404
Wilson, Benjamin	225	Fishing Creek	1815	3	424
Wilson, John	392	Adj. S. Fulton	1784	1	68
Wilson, John	108	Adj. J. Atkinson	1784	1	66
Wilson, Thomas	445	Bonnets Run	1793	2	455
Wilson, Thomas	400	Adj. Wm. McMahan	1796	3	119
Wilson, Thomas	400	Grave Creek	1796	3	118
Wilson, Thomas	400	Wheeling Creek	1796	3	115
Wilson, Thomas	340	Mid. Island Creek	1796	3	94
Wilson, William	383	Harmon's Creek	1796	3	95
Woods, Alexander Q.	400	Fish Creek	1834	4	125
Woods, Andrew	410	Wheeling Creek	1808	3	346
Woods, Andrew	509	Middle Island Creek	1786	1	235
Woods, Andrew & Archibald	1,300	Wheeling Creek	1790	2	329
Woods, Andrew P.	400	Fish Creek	1824	4	32
Woods, Andrew P.	1,000	Fish Creek	1824	4	35
Woods, Archibald	170	Bogg's Run	1804	3	301
Woods, Archibald	740	Mid. Island Creek	1808	3	345
Woods, Archibald	2,000	Mid. Island Creek	1797	3	177
Woods, Archibald	450	Long Reach	1803	3	276
Woods, Archibald	400	Adj. Thomas Gains	1787	2	104
Woods, Archibald	21,000	Mid. Island Creek	1796	3	71
Woods, Archibald	1,000	Mid. Island Creek	1795	3	52
Woods, Archibald	1,000	Mid. Island Creek	1795	3	53

Name of Grantee	Acres	Local Description	Year	Book	Page
Wynkoop, Henry et al	4,000	Fish Creek	1786	1	190
Yates—or Yeats					
Yates, Richard	400	Wheeling Creek	1785	1	139
Yates, Richard	400	Adj. James Roney	1783	1	18
Yates, Richard	155	Wheeling Creek	1786	1	440
Yates, Richard	304	Wheeling Creek	1787	1	439
Yates, Richard	400	Lit. Wheeling Cr.	1787	1	437
Yates, Richard	365	Wheeling Creek	1787	1	438
Yeats—or Yates					
Yeats, Thomas	38½	McGraw's Run	1813	3	401
Yeats, Thomas	445	Wheeling Creek	1815	3	422
Yoho, George Jr.	63	Whitstone Run	1830	4	63
Yoho, Henry	21	Fish Creek	1803	3	272
Yoho, Henry	389	Fish Creek	1804	3	313
Yoho, Jacob	100	Rocky Fork Run	1830	4	64
Yoho, Lewis	100	Rocky Fork Run	1830	4	53
Yoho, William	50	Rocky Fork Run	1830	4	62
Young, James et al	400	Harrison's Run	1788	2	252
Young, John Jr.	2,658	Fishing Creek	1786	1	282
Zane—See also Lane					
Zane, Andrew	40	Adj. J. Tomlinson	1797	3	131
Zane, Andrew	246	Grave Creek	1797	3	130
Zane, Ebenezer	285	Wheeling Island	1800	3	241
Zane, Ebenezer	285	Island Ohio River	1786	1	272
Zane, Ebenezer	54	Island Ohio River	1787	2	133
Zane, Ebenezer	1,000	Grave Creek	1785	1	120
Zane, Ebenezer	260	Adj. Robt. Woods	1785	1	121
Zane, Ebenezer	400	Wheeling Creek	1784	1	34
Zane, Ebenezer	280	Gland's Run	1784	1	33
Zane, Ebenezer	400	Wheeling Creek	1784	1	32
Zane, Elizabeth	400	Short Creek	1787	1	473
Zane, Isaac Sr.	400	Grave Creek	1784	1	100
Zane, John	400	Buffalo Creek	1782	1	9
Zane, John	400	Grave Creek	1784	1	101
Zane, Jonathan	140	Wheeling Creek	1784	1	42
Zane, Salis	400	Wheeling Creek	1784	1	67

PENDLETON COUNTY

Adamson, William	216	Seneca Creek	1858	3	490
Alt—also Ault					
Alt, Jacob	425	North Mill Creek	1856	2	465
Alt, William	2¾	Mill Creek	1839	3	101
Amick—See Emick, Emmick					
Amiss, Geo. W.	33	Snowy Mountain	1847	3	317
Amiss, George W.	48	Strait Creek	1847	3	318
Anderson, William	2,525	South Fork	1849	3	596
Arbacast, Arbocast, Arbogast, Armagush, Armocast, Armogast					
Arbacast, Daniel	41	Crab Apple Bottom	1825	4	243
Arbocast, Adam	100	Greenbrier Waters	1812	2	373
Arbocast, David	15	Crab Bottom	1812	2	372
Arbocast, David	60	South Branch	1796	1	273
Arbocast, George	3½	Crab Bottom	1823	4	216
Arbocast, John	20	Crab Apple Bottom	1802	2	187
Arbocast, John	28	Crab Bottom	1799	1	541
Arbocast, Michael	20	Crab Bottom	1796	1	327

Name of Grantee	Acres	Local Description	Year	Book	Page
Arbogast—See various spellings, Arbacast, etc.					
Arbogast, Daniel	73	Lantz Mountain	1840	3	115
Arbogast, Emanuel	58	Hunting Ground	1842	3	194
Arbogast, Emanuel	81	Backbone Mt.	1838	3	74
Arbogast, David	55	Crab Bottom	1837	4	539
Arbogast, George	186	Crab Apple Bottom	1812	2	374
Arbogast, George	12	Crab Apple Bottom	1800	2	59
Arbogast, Henry	9	Crab Bottom	1815	2	431
Arbogast, Jacob & Ephriam et al	115	South Branch	1838	3	85
Arbogast, Michael & Henry	125	Roaring Spring	1809	2	294
Armagush—See Arbacast, Arbocast, Arbogast, Armocast, Armogast					
Armagush, John et al	95	High Knob	1801	2	114
Armantrout, D. H. & C. H.	60	North Mill Creek	1838	3	73
Armantrout, Daniel H.	332	North Mill Creek	1838	3	72
Armentrout, Daniel H.	78	South Branch	1836	4	511
Armocast—See Arbacast, etc. for variations in spelling					
Armocast, Adam	59	Crab Apple	1789	1	2
Armocast, Michael	139	Crab Apple Bottom	1790	1	10
Armogast—See Arbacast, etc. for variations in spelling					
Armogast, John	171	Crab Apple Branch	1790	1	9
Armstrong, Amos	210	Bull Pasture	1820	5	178
Armstrong, Garret	5	Bull Pasture	1824	4	236
Armstrong, James	10	Wts. Mowrah's Run	1823	4	224
Armstrong, Jared	1a.1rd.	Bull Pasture	1841	3	152
Armstrong, Jaret	21	Bull Pasture	1836	4	496
Armstrong, John	266	Bull Pasture	1801	2	120
Armstrong, John	42	Bull Pasture	1817	5	30
Armstrong, John T.	286	Bull Pasture	1845	3	565
Armstrong, Thomas	58	Bull Pasture	1827	4	287
Armstrong, William	80	Bull Pasture River	1797	1	344
Baker, John	29	Buffalo Run	1824	4	233
Balser, Susannah	23	South Branch	1825	4	241
Bangee—or Banjay, Banjoy					
Bangee, Elizabeth	11	South Fork	1836	4	516
Banjay, Joseph (Banjoy)	168	Waggoner's Run	1838	3	21
Banninger—See Benninger					
Barkeley, Obid	25	Peter's Mountain	1837	4	545
Barker, Scely	50	Peter's Run	1821	5	203
Barrer—See Borrer					
Bashe—or Boshe					
Bashe, Beat Lewis	160	Waldron's Mountain	1796	1	317
Bashe, Beat Lewis	130	South Branch	1797	1	433
Bashe, Beat Lewis	97	South Branch	1791	1	28
Baulton—See Boulton					
Beath, James	35	Crab Run	1825	4	250
Beath, James M., J. A. & J. P.	78	Crab Run	1846	3	290
Beath, John P., J. M. & J. A.	2¾	Crab Run	1846	3	291
Beath, John	96	Bull Pasture	1804	2	223
Bell, David	28	Bull Pasture	1801	2	139
Bell, James	59	Straight Creek	1838	3	16
Bell, Joseph	430	Bunner's Run	1801	2	143
Bell, Joseph	100	Straight Creek	1798	1	456
Bell, Joseph	150	Straight Creek	1795	1	225
Bennet—or Bennett, Bennit					
Bennet, Joseph	30	Big Run	1827	4	288
Bennet, Thomas	65	North Fork	1801	2	121
Bennett, John	80	North Fork	1804	2	202
Bennett, John	68	False Gap	1799	1	486
Bennett, John	36	Horse Ridge	1796	1	358
Bennett, John	50	North Fork	1796	1	333
Bennett, John	42	North Fork	1793	1	88
Bennett, John	54	Walnut Bottom	1793	1	87
Bennett, John Sr.	153	Walnut Bottom Run	1793	1	80

Name of Grantee	Acres	Local Description	Year	Book	Page
Bush, Michael	23	North Fork	1796	1	292
Bush, Michael	60	Reed's Creek	1796	1	332
Butcher, Nicholas	35	North Mill Creek	1800	2	45
Buzzard, Lewis	37	North Mill Creek	1821	5	191
Buzzard, Lewis	25	Mill Creek	1820	5	180
Buzzard, Lewis	15	North Mill Creek	1816	5	6
Buzzard, Lewis	25	North Mill Creek	1814	2	413
Buzzard, Michael	85	North Fork	1793	1	104
Calep—or Caless, Callip, Colip, Collip					
Calep, John	278	Mill Creek	1819	5	88
Calep, John	40	South Branch	1797	1	354
Caless—See Calep, Callip, Colip, Collip					
Calihan, Charles	51	Bull Pasture	1817	5	27
Caller, John or Jacob	112	Dry Run	1817	5	20
Callip—See Calep, Caless, Colip, Collip					
Callip, John	55	Mill Creek	1793	1	107
Cammel—See Campbell					
Campbell, James	75	Bull Pasture	1801	2	102
Campbell, James (Cammel)	29	Duff Run	1828	4	318
Campbell, James B.	8	Jackson's River	1846	3	283
Campbell, John	50	Adj. Samuel Campbell	1849	3	364
Campbell, Samuel	100	Bull Pasture	1809	2	298
Campbell, Samuel	50	Bull Pasture	1809	2	296
Campbell, Thomas	37	Jackson's River	1829	4	339
Campbell, Thomas et al	177	Little Mountain	1849	3	391
Campher, Ethamus	184	Horse Run	1838	3	22
Campher, Ethanus	59	High Knob	1843	3	214
Campher, Ethanus	260	Broad Run	1849	3	369
Campher, Jacob (Camphir)	69	Cowger's Mt.	1843	3	213
Cann—also Conn					
Cann, Michael (Conn)	400	North Mill Creek	1791	1	31
Cann, Michael (Conn)	120	Brushy Run	1800	2	20
Capito, Daniel	30	Big Run	1805	2	242
Capito, Daniel	7	South Branch	1815	2	432
Capito, Daniel	60	South Branch	1799	1	509
Capito, Daniel	90	Adj. Samuel Morril's	1799	1	412
Capito, Daniel	10	Adj. Dyer's	1820	5	135
Caplinger—also Chaplinger					
Caplinger, Adam	40	South Branch	1831	4	374
Caplinger, George (Chaplinger)	45	South Fork	1791	1	15
Caplinger, George	40	South Branch	1797	1	390
Caplinger, George (Chaplinger)	90	South Branch	1794	1	128
Carlile, John et al	500	Crab Run	1825	4	249
Carper, Abraham	104	South Branch	1791	1	23
Carr, Adam	26	Sawmill Run	1843	3	212
Carr, Adam	530	North Fork	1832	4	382
Carr, Adam	260	North Fork	1850	3	405
Carr, Jacob	180	Seneca Creek	1803	2	192
Carr, Jacob	96	North Fork	1794	1	113
Carr, Jacob	80	North Fork	1797	1	431
Carr, Jacob	20	Seneca Creek	1800	2	60
Carr, Jacob	65	Long Bottom	1801	2	147
Casner—or Cosner					
Casner, Adam	90	Mill Creek	1821	5	211
Casner, Adam	57	South Branch	1799	1	533
Casner, John	28	Mill Creek	1792	1	76
Casner, John	16	Brushy Run	1820	5	169
Casner, John et al	31	Brushy Run	1820	5	170
Casner, Paul	54	Cor. to Grenault	1846	3	287
Casner, Paul	35	North Mill Creek	1848	3	352
Cassle—also Castle					
Cassle, Henry	50	Smith's Creek	1798	1	459
Cassle, Valentine	145	Smith's Creek	1796	1	326

Name of Grantee	Acres	Local Description	Year	Book	Page
Conrod, Jacob	360	North Fork	1799	1	497
Conrod, Jacob	182	Conrad's Run	1792	1	64
Conrod, Jacob	37	North Fork	1794	1	144
Conrod, Jacob	643	North Fork	1799	2	479
Conrod, Jacob	160	Buffalo Hill	1794	1	143
Conrod, Jacob	50	Reed's Creek	1792	1	63
Conrod, Jacob	61	Skidmore Run	1791	1	27
Conrod, Laban	271	Skidmore's Gap	1839	3	102
Conrod, Sampson	116	Buffalo Hills	1829	4	335
Conrod, Ulrich	40	Black Thorn	1794	1	219
Conrod, Ulry	2,730	South Branch Potomac	1834	4	554
Conrod, Ulry	388	Conrod's Gap	1839	3	103
Conrod, Ulry	45	Brushy Mountain	1846	3	296
Conrod, Ulry	4	Hage Gap	1849	3	368
Cook, John	50	South Branch	1815	2	417
Cook, Nicholas	55	Friend's Gap	1824	4	234
Cookholts—(See Gougal)					
Cosner or Casner					
Cosner, Adam	184	Mill Creek	1835	4	487
Cosner, George	250	Mill Creek	1835	4	486
Cosner, John	94	Brushy Run	1829	4	334
Cosner, Paul	90	Spring Run	1832	4	381
Cosner, Samuel & Philip	233	Mill Creek	1835	4	481
Couchran—or Cochran					
Couchran, James	100	South Fork	1827	4	290
Coulter, Thomas J.	12	Bull Pasture	1836	4	535
Coulter, Thomas J.	52	Bull Pasture	1836	4	533
Cow, John	24	Buffalo Run	1797	1	455
Cowan, John	25	Buffalo Run	1802	2	165
Cowgar—or Cogar					
Cowgar, Henry et al	77	South Branch	1831	4	367
Cowgar, Henry & John	40	South Fork	1822	4	176
Cowgar, John	35	South Fork	1825	4	245
Cowgar, John	25	South Branch	1817	5	26
Cowgar, John	29	Black Thorn	1796	1	300
Cowgar, John	13	South Fork	1810	2	329
Cowgar, John	43	South Fork	1822	4	179
Cowger, Henry	576	South Branch	1836	4	561
Cowger, Henry	150	Sweedlin's Hill	1839	3	104
Cowger, Henry	115	South Fork Mt.	1838	3	23
Cowger, Henry	32	South Fork	1810	2	316
Cowger, Job & George	102	South Fork	1848	3	340
Cowger, John	60	Black Thorn	1810	2	313
Cowger, John	50	South Fork	1797	1	373
Coyl or Coil, Coyle					
Coyl, Andrew	50	Mallow's Run	1793	1	85
Coyl, Jacob Sr.	50	South Branch	1791	1	26
Cragg, or Gragg					
Cragg, William	37	North Fork	1799	1	527
Crousehorn—Crosehorn, Croushorn					
Crousehorn, Jacob	22	South Branch	1819	5	121
Crousehorn, Jacob	23	Jackson's River	1841	3	154
Crummet, Christopher	20	South Fork	1810	2	320
Crummet, Daniel	6	Black Thorn	1846	3	293
Crummet, Daniel	16	Black Thorn	1846	3	292
Crummet, Eli et al	360	Crummet's Run	1858	2	484
Crummet, Frederick	60	Black Thorn	1802	2	186
Crummet, Frederick	40	Crummet's Run	1798	1	506
Crummet, Frederick	45	Black Thorn	1819	5	92
Crummet, George	12	Crummet's Run	1846	3	295
Crummet, George	32	Crummet's Run	1846	3	294
Crummet, George	33	South Fork	1823	4	205
Crummet, George	35	South Fork	1820	5	153

Davis, William	26	Lit. Walnut Bottom	1796	1	311
Davison, John	44	Bull Pasture	1797	1	428
Day, John	34	Spruce Gap	1826	4	273
Day, John	130	South Fork	1820	5	149
Day, Leonard	19	Harper's Gap Run	1843	3	216
Day, Leonard	20	North Fork	1843	3	215
Day, Nathan	30	Buffalo Run	1840	3	139
Day, Nathan	77	Stony Run	1842	3	196
Day, Samuel	150	North Fork	1796	1	361
Day, Samuel	150	North Fork	1796	1	322
Day, William	196	South Branch	1848	3	341
Dean, George	25	Canoe Run	1823	4	208
Dean, Samuel	6	North Mill Creek	1850	3	395
Dean, Samuel et al	217	Trumbo's Gap	1838	3	55
Dever, John & Hugh	50	Little Fork	1800	2	32
Devericks, John	465	Cow Pasture	1805	2	253
Devericks, John	23	Shaw's Fork	1825	4	254
Devericks, Thomas	300	Shaw's Fork	1800	2	46
Dice, George	200	Cor. to Waggoner	1814	2	414
Dice, George	75	South Fork	1794	1	120
Dice, George	25	Dice's Run	1793	1	110
Dice, Isaac H.	5	South Branch	1855	3	468
Dice, Jacob	11	South Fork	1848	3	354
Dice, Jacob	11	South Fork	1848	3	353
Dice, John	325	Cedar Knob	1820	5	140
Dice, John (of George)	50	Roaring Creek	1838	3	68
Dice, John (of George)	140	Seneca Creek	1837	4	546
Dice, John (of George)	73	Swamp Run	1834	4	454
Dice, John Jr.	50	South Fork	1827	4	291
Dice, John & Jacob	100	South Fork	1833	4	425
Dice, John & Reuben	8	South Branch	1817	5	15
Dice, John & Reuben	10	South Fork	1817	5	14
Dice, Mathias	210	South Fork	1804	2	200
Dice, Mathias	26	Rough Run	1797	1	383
Dice, Reuben	130	Peter's Mt.	1842	3	197
Dice, Reuben	21	Peters Run	1851	3	438
Dickenson—Dickeson, Dickinson					
Dickenson, Henry	56	Horse Run	1838	3	76
Dickenson, Henry	238	South Fork	1850	3	396
Dickenson, Henry	460	Horse Run	1844	3	245
Dickenson, Samuel et al	53	South Fork	1831	4	371
Dickeson, Robert et al	175	South Fork	1820	5	148
Dickeson, Samuel	75	Horse Run	1819	5	105
Dickeson, Samuel	57	Sugar Run	1820	5	151
Dickinson, Henry	80	Paddins Gap	1832	4	386
Dickinson, Henry	90	South Fork	1834	4	435
Dingler, Michael	80	Brushy Run	1795	1	195
Doggy—See Daggy					
Dolley, Andrew	7	North Fork	1818	5	83
Dolley, Andrew	18	North Fork	1818	5	84
Dolley, John	140	North Fork	1803	2	199
Dolly, Andrew et al	490	Long Run	1850	3	424
Dolly, John Jr.	74	North Fork Mt.	1837	4	541
Donnan—or Dunnon					
Donnan, Peter	40	South Branch	1797	1	348
Dosher—See Dasher					
Dosher, Rebecca et al	148	Six Mile Lick	1851	3	441
Douglas, James	15	South Fork	1800	2	55
Douglas, Robert	60	Cow Pasture	1801	2	111
Douglas, Thomas	118	Cow Pasture	1797	1	341
Dove, Jacob	10	Panther's Run	1846	3	297
Draes—or Drais					
Draes, Jacob (Drais)	50	South Fork	1795	1	240
Drais, Jacob (Davis)	177	Middle Mt.	1796	1	544
Drais, Jacob (Draes)	50	South Fork	1795	1	240

Name of Grantee	Acres	Local Description	Year	Book	Page
Edmond, Thomas	30	Adj. Harris & Leach	1817	5	28
Edmond, Thomas	18	Bull Pasture	1818	5	43
Edmond, Thomas	50	Bull Pasture	1820	5	184
Edmond, Thomas	90	Bull Pasture	1815	2	441
Edmund, Thomas	50	Cow Pasture	1808	2	270
Eleyard, Henry	58	Shaw's Ridge	1846	3	299
Emick—or Amick, Emmick					
Emick, Henry	28	Black Thorn	1805	2	248
Emick, Henry	7	Black Thorn	1799	1	417
Emick, Henry	60	Black Thorn	1799	1	480
Emick, Henry	45	Dry Run	1807	2	272
Emick, Henry	10	Adj. J. Pitsenbarger	1799	2	35
Emick, Henry	32	Adj. his former lands	1799	2	36
Emick, Henry	100	South Fork	1799	2	41
Emick, Henry Jr.	74	Brandywine Gap	1818	5	66
Emick, Henry & Nicholas	40	Mill Run Gap	1796	1	260
Emick, Henry Sr.	25	Swadley's Run	1818	5	72
Emick, Jacob	80	Swadley's Run	1820	5	173
Emick, Nicholas	90	South Branch	1793	1	84
Emick, Nicholas	27	Mill Run Gap	1796	1	262
Emmick—See Amick, Emick					
Emmick, Henry	70	Black Thorn	1804	2	224
Emmick, Henry	60	Adj. Jacob Props	1804	2	226
Emmick, Henry	16	South Branch	1804	2	225
Erbock—or Erbough					
Erbock, Joseph	168	Entry Ridge	1799	1	537
Erbock, Joseph	57	South Branch	1795	1	231
Erbock, Joseph	7	South Branch	1796	1	255
Erbock, Joseph	8	South Branch	1796	1	294
Ervine—See Erwin					
Erwin, Edward	77	Black Thorn	1792	1	61
Erwin, Edward	150	Black Thorn	1792	1	60
Erwin, George	8	Cow Pasture	1804	2	203
Erwin, George	60	Cow Pasture	1811	2	345
Erwin, John	290	Bull Pasture	1805	2	259
Erwin, John D.	84	Cow Pasture	1834	4	438
Erwin, John D.	90	Bull Pasture	1851	3	432
Erwin, William (Ervine)	32	Cow Pasture	1836	4	534
Evans, John	100	Bull Pasture	1803	2	195
Evick, Eve	27	South Branch	1802	2	163
Evick, Eve	30	Straight Creek	1802	2	159
Evick, Francis	50	South Branch	1797	1	347
Evick, Francis et al	180	South Branch	1795	1	173
Evick, Francis et al	80	South Branch	1794	1	136
Evick, George	25	South Branch	1794	1	162
Eye, Christian	41	Black Thorn	1834	4	455
Eye, Christian	110	Mill Run	1820	5	154
Eye, Christian	50	Black Thorn Run	1822	4	174
Eye, Christopher	90	Stoney Run	1797	1	346
Eye, George	50	Black Thorn	1811	2	353
Eye, Henry	258	South Fork	1833	4	416
Eye, Henry et al	300	Road Run	1836	4	493
Eye, Jacob	22	Buffalo Run	1834	4	449
Eye, Jacob	138	Long Mountain	1842	3	188
Eye, Jacob	20	Buffalo Run	1854	3	462
Eye, Jacob Jr.	45	South Fork	1823	4	218
Eye, Jacob Jr.	200	Black Thorn	1822	4	201
Eye, Jacob Jr.	121	South Fork Mountain	1831	4	368
Eye, John	35	Black Thorn	1830	4	347
Eye, John (Son of George)	23	Stuffle's Run	1850	3	408
Eye, William	91	South Fork Mt.	1850	3	407
Eyeman—See also Eymon					
Eyeman, Henry	11	North Fork	1815	2	430

Name of Grantee	Acres	Local Description	Year	Book	Page
Eymon, Emanuel	130	Mill Creek	1829	4	341
Feasle—or Feisel					
Feisel, Michael	50	South Fork	1797	1	442
Feisel, Michael	55	Sweedlin Run	1797	1	343
Fifthorn—See Fitchorn, Peithorn					
Fisher, Absolom	100	South Branch	1811	2	355
Fisher, Charles	63	South Branch	1792	1	73
Fisher, Charles	40	Mill Creek	1796	1	310
Fisher, George	43	North Mill Creek	1796	1	296
Fisher, George Jr.	40	Mill Creek	1800	2	66
Fisher, George Jr.	40	South Branch	1798	1	475
Fisher, George Jr.	10	South Branch	1798	1	462
Fisher, George Jr.	44	South Branch	1795	1	175
Fisher, George Jr.	60	Mill Creek	1792	1	62
Fisher, George Jr.	40	South Branch	1800	2	18
Fisher, John	67	Buffalo Run	1791	1	24
Fisher, John	18	Meadow Run	1802	2	161
Fisher, John	100	Salt Peter Cave	1809	2	299
Fisher, John	280	South Branch	1800	2	3
Fisher, John	23	Buffalo Run	1817	5	19
Fisher, John Jr.	57	Buffalo Run	1832	4	388
Fisher, John Sr.	22	South Branch	1826	4	285
Fisher, John Sr.	20	So. Branch	1822	4	189
Fisher, John Sr.	60	Long Mountain	1822	4	190
Fisher, Philip	95	South Fork	1796	1	274
Fisher, Philip	120	South Fork	1796	1	276
Fisher, Philip	7	Yarkey's Run	1827	4	295
Fisher, Philip Jr.	200	South Fork	1802	2	156
Fisher, Philip Jr.	30	Six Mile Lick	1797	1	389
Fisher, William	104	South Fork	1840	3	120
Fitchorn—Fifthorn—also Peithorn					
Fitchorn, Philip	76	Mill Creek	1799	2	1
Fitzbarger—See also Pitzbarger, or Pitsenbarger, Pitzenbarger					
Fitzbarger, Abraham	75	Black Thorn	1802	2	170
Fleischer—also Flesher					
Fleischer, Henry	65	South Branch	1797	1	451
Flesher, Andrew	110	South Branch	1826	4	283
Flesher, Andrew	1,345	South Branch	1858	2	481
Flesher, Andrew	35	South Branch	1852	3	445
Flesher, Conrad	50	Straight Creek	1804	2	228
Flesher, Conrod	42	Crab Apple Bottom	1796	1	308
Flesher, George	105	South Branch	1826	4	272
Flesher, Henry	154	Bull Pasture	1836	4	503
Flesher, Henry	65	Bull Pasture River	1810	2	311
Flesher, Henry et al	105	South Branch	1800	2	21
Flesher, Henry J.	50	Straight Creek	1846	3	300
Flesher, Henry Jr.	150	Bull Pasture	1802	2	175
Flesher, Jehu (or John)	3½	Flesher's Run	1827	4	292
Flesher, John	142	Straight Creek	1827	4	293
Flesher, John	67	Straight Creek	1827	4	294
Flesher, Joseph et al	122	Bull Pasture Mt.	1840	3	133
Flynn, George (Plyman)	100	Black Thorn	1802	2	157
Fox, George	45	Crab Bottom	1820	5	168
Fox, Michael	35	Crow Bottom	1801	2	90
Fox, Michael	28	Crab Bottom	1796	1	359
Friend, Jacob	42	Richardson's Run	1798	1	469
Friend, Jacob	56	Richardson's Run	1796	1	291
Friend, Jacob	83	Lick Run	1793	1	91
Fritze—or Fritzer					
Fritzer, John	59	Brushy Run	1797	1	382
Froshour, Jacob	100	South Mill Creek	1800	2	81
Fuls—See Full, Fults					
Full, George	85	Salt Block Run	1796	1	242

Name of Grantee	Acres	Local Description	Year	Book	Page
Full, George	70	Mallow's Run	1795	1	232
Full, George	55	South Branch	1801	2	91
Full, Jacob	73	South Branch	1838	3	25
Fuls—See Full, Fults					
Fuls, Philip	82	Mill Creek	1793	1	90
Fuls, Philip	100	South Branch	1796	1	280
Fults—See Full, Fuls					
Fults, Philip	13	Mill Creek	1793	1	89
Gady, Nicholas (Judy)	20	South Branch	1795	1	185
Gall, George	56	Jackson's River	1811	2	360
Gall, John	50	Jackson's River	1804	2	220
Gambill—Gamble, Gammel					
Gambill, Robert	675	Adj. Jacob Simmons	1849	3	420
Gamble, John	30	Black Thorn	1796	1	282
Gammel, William (Gamble)	39	Big Run	1792	1	47
Gardner, George	60	Straight Creek	1793	1	86
Gilmore, Alexander	603	Jackson River	1847	3	583
Gisemore, Bernherd	50	Buffalo Run	1799	1	516
Gougal, Andrew (Cookholts)	50	Reed's Creek	1791	1	19
Gragg—or Cragg					
Gragg, Samuel	105	Seneca Creek	1795	1	202
Gragg, William	37	North Fork	1799	1	527
Gragg, William	1	North Fork	1800	2	71
Gragg, William	37	South Branch	1810	2	331
Graham—or Grayham					
Grayham, Isaac	10	Mill Creek	1843	3	217
Grayham, Isaac	72	South Mill Creek	1838	3	65
Grayham, Isaac	80	North Mill Creek	1838	3	64
Grayham, Isaac & Barbara	318	Reed's Creek	1841	3	219
Grayham, Jacob	169	Mill Creek	1849	3	383
Grayham, James	90	Mallow's Run	1798	1	403
Grayham, James	50	Reed's Creek	1842	3	185
Greenwalt, Adam	85	Mill Run	1834	4	447
Greenwalt, George	12	Adj. L. Mallows	1829	4	337
Greenwalt, George	160	Mallow's Run	1799	1	418
Greenwalt, George	30	South Branch	1821	5	202
Greenwalt, George	115	Mallow's Gap	1821	5	201
Greenwalt, George Jr.	100	Mallow's Run	1799	1	532
Greenwalt, George Jr.	50	Mallow's Run	1815	2	415
Grim, John	15	Jackson's River	1820	5	179
Gum, Abraham	29	South Branch	1818	5	54
Gum, Abraham	140	Straight Creek	1804	2	229-A
Gum, Adam	3	Crab Bottom	1823	4	215
Gum, Isaac	150	Bark Creek	1804	2	235
Gum, Isaac	100	Crab Apple Bottom	1802	2	168
Gum, Jacob	95	Crab Apple	1800	2	75
Gum, Jacob	218	Crab Apple Bottom	1790	1	4
Gum, Jacob	2¾	Crab Apple Bottom	1802	2	176
Gum, John E. et al	182	Jackson's River	1836	4	505
Gum, John E. & Isaac	100	Back Creek	1832	4	407
Gum, John E. & Isaac	167	Back Creek	1838	3	15
Gum, Otho	43	E. Side Bark Mt.	1838	3	14
Gum, Peter	4	Crab Bottom	1843	3	218
Gwin, Andrew	223	Shaw's Ridge	1841	3	182
Gwin, Joseph	400	Calf Pasture	1809	2	295
Hagler—See also Haigler					
Hagler, William Sr.	23	North Fork	1827	4	299
Haigler, James W.	790	Roaring Creek	1850	3	599
Haigler, John	10	Reed's Creek	1857	3	481
Haigler, John	20	Reed's Creek	1857	3	480
Haigler, John	680	Reed's Creek	1847	3	578
Haigler, John	250	Roaring Creek	1835	4	461
Haigler, John	22	Seneca Creek	1850	3	412

Name of Grantee	Acres	Local Description	Year	Book	Page
Haigler, John	34	Roaring Creek	1850	3	411
Haigler, John	5	Seneca Creek	1850	3	413
Hainer—See also Heener, Hiner					
Hainer, John (Heener)	40	South Fork	1803	2	193
Hall, David	260	Buffalo Meadow Run	1797	1	436
Hall, Peter Sr.	18	Crab Bottom	1817	5	21
Hall, Thomas	30	New Cut Road	1796	1	319
Hall, Thomas	165	South Fork	1801	2	112
Hallin—See Hollen					
Hallin, Joseph (Hollen)	58	South Fork	1834	4	445
Halterman, Barbary (Daughter)	40	Straight Creek	1829	4	343
Halterman, Charles	200	Straight Creek	1797	1	372
Halterman, Charles	15	Straight Creek	1796	1	290
Ham, William	180	Bull Pasture	1815	2	425
Hamer—See also Hammer					
Hamilton, Gawen	163	Seneca Creek	1795	1	229
Hamilton, Gawen	120	South Fork	1797	1	355
Hamilton, Gawen	158	Seneca Creek	1795	1	230
Hamilton, Gawin	270	South Branch	1797	1	395
Hamilton, Gawin	40	South Branch	1799	1	489
Hamilton, Gawin	27	Buffalo Run	1794	1	119
Hamilton, Gawin	92	North Fork	1794	1	117
Hamilton, Gawin	200	South Fork	1802	2	135
Hamilton, Gawin et al	80	South Branch	1794	1	136
Hamilton, Gawin et al	180	South Branch	1795	1	173
Hammer, Balser (Hamer)	170	Coil's Creek	1795	1	182
Hammer, Balser (Hamer)	40	South Branch	1796	1	252
Hammer, Balser	280	South Branch	1804	2	233
Hammer, Balser (Hamer)	27	Crab Apple Bot.	1809	2	290
Hammer, Elias	42	Adj. Ulry Conrod	1854	3	463
Hammer, George	40	South Branch	1822	4	188
Hammer, George	43	Buffalo Gap	1823	4	206
Hammer, George	37	Buffalo Run	1829	4	338
Hammer, George	196	Buffalo Run	1827	4	300
Hammer, George	100	South Branch	1816	2	445
Hammer, George	16	Collick Mt.	1831	4	370
Hammer, George (of Balser)	75	Crab Apple Bottom	1832	4	404
Hammer, George (of Balser)	90	Crab Apple Bottom	1832	4	397
Hammer, George & Henry	40	South Branch	1819	5	103
Hammer, George Jr.	100	Cottle's Mountain	1837	3	2
Hammer, Jacob	18	South Branch	1847	3	321
Hammer, Jacob	80	Back Creek	1837	3	1
Hammer, Jacob et al	288	Crab Bottom	1837	4	543
Hammer, John C.	312	South Branch	1848	3	342
Hanson, A. et al	177	Little Mountain	1849	3	391
Harhold—See Harholt					
Harholt, George et al	50	South Fork	1843	3	234
Harman, Andrew	205	Bull Pasture	1830	4	359
Harman, Andrew	7	Bull Pasture	1828	4	321
Harman, Barbara (Widow)	80	Roaring Spring	1810	2	343
Harman, George	41	Bull Pasture	1836	4	530
Harman, George	80	Bull Pasture	1840	3	146
Harman, Isaac	38	Harper's Gap Run	1843	3	223
Harman, Isaac	50	North Fork	1800	2	56
Harman, Joel	46	North Fork Mt.	1843	3	222
Harman, Joel et al	116	Harper's Run	1843	3	224
Harman, Joshua	120	North Fork Mt.	1843	3	221
Harman, Joshua et al	56	South Branch	1849	3	371
Harman, Moab (Noah)	63	South Branch	1846	3	311
Harman, Noah	19	Road Run	1829	4	328
Harman, Noah	295	Shaw's Run	1846	3	305
Harman, Noah	318	Brushy Run	1829	4	327

Name of Grantee	Acres	Local Description	Year	Book	Page
Harman, Noah	350	Roaring Creek	1836	4	492
Harman, Reuben & Noah	84	Horse Camp Road	1823	4	211
Harman, Solomon & Isaac	41	Adj. Reuben Harman	1845	3	271
Harman, Thomas & Jonas	244	Adj. Noah Harman	1845	3	272
Harold, Andrew Jr.	158	Dry Run	1847	3	315
Harold, John	75	Stony Run	1809	2	304
Harold, John	50	Stony Run	1813	2	391
Harper, Adam	20	North Fork	1796	1	289
Harper, Adam	100	Dry Run	1796	1	258
Harper, Adam	72	Ragged Bottom	1791	1	20
Harper, Adam Jr.	45	Crab Bottom	1795	1	169
Harper, Elias	65	Seneca Creek	1819	5	132
Harper, George	1,425	South Branch	1842	3	552
Harper, Jacob	46	North Fork	1795	1	204
Harper, Jacob	60	Laurel Run	1795	1	200
Harper, Jacob	23	South Branch	1797	1	452
Harper, Jacob	7½	Roaring Ridge	1827	4	296
Harper, Jacob	18	Roaring Ridge	1822	4	180
Harper, Jacob Jr.	32	Roaring Ridge	1822	4	184
Harper, Jacob Jr.	23	North Fork	1817	5	17
Harper, Jacob Sr.	30	North Fork	1818	5	58
Harper, Jesse	94	Roaring Ridge	1831	4	373
Harper, Jesse W.	10	Seneca Creek	1853	3	455
Harper, Jesse W.	9	Bear Wallow	1849	3	370
Harper, Leonard	10	South Branch	1841	3	164
Harper, Leonard	83	North Fork	1828	4	322
Harper, Leonard	1,800	North Fork	1856	2	460
Harper, Leonard et al	4	North Fork	1836	4	526
Harper, Levi et al	116	Harper's Run	1843	3	224
Harper, Nicholas	280	South Branch	1795	1	196
Harper, Nicholas	150	South Branch	1799	1	508
Harper, Nicholas	140	South Branch	1796	1	298
Harper, Nicholas	95	South Branch	1796	1	253
Harper, Nicholas	30	Dry Run	1809	2	303
Harper, Nicholas et al	165	Laurel Run	1820	5	172
Harper, Nicholas et al	105	South Branch	1800	2	21
Harper, Phillip	118	North Fork	1796	1	265
Harper, Phillip	40	North Fork	1821	5	213
Harper, Phillip	26	North Fork	1796	1	297
Harper, Phillip	45	North Fork	1800	2	44
Harper, Phillip & Jacob	122	North Fork	1797	1	391
Harper, Phillip Jr.	28	North Fork	1815	2	416
Harper, Solomon	28	Adj. Briggs	1827	4	297
Harper, Solomon	27	Briggs Run	1840	3	121
Harper, Sylvanus	118	Seneca Creek	1851	3	428
Harpole, Michael	70	South Branch	1794	1	134
Harpole, Nicholas	19	Mill Creek	1794	1	115
Harris—or Harriss					
Harris, James	25	Tom's Run	1802	2	128
Harris, James	50	Skidmore Run	1802	2	126
Harris, William	6	Bull Pasture Mt.	1810	2	312
Harris, William	50	Bull Pasture Mt.	1810	2	310
Harris, William	8	Bull Pasture	1819	5	95
Harriss, James	150	Reed's Creek	1794	1	213
Harter, Peter R.	30	Sweedlin's Run	1846	3	312
Harter, Simeon	29	Sweedlin Valley	1853	3	457
Hartman, Henry	12	3-Lick	1816	5	5
Hartman, Henry	83	Thorny Meadow Run	1846	3	302
Hartman, Henry et al	31	Brushy Run	1820	5	170
Hartman, Henry et al	74	Brushy Run	1830	4	355
Heavener, Heavenor, Heavner, Hevener, Heviner, Hevinor, Hevner, Hevnor, Hivner					
Heavener, Jacob Jr. et al	182	Jackson's River	1836	4	505
Heavenor—See Heavener for variations in spelling					

Name of Grantee	Acres	Local Description	Year	Book	Page
Heavnor, George	58	South Fork	1830	4	357
Heavner—See Heavener for variations in spelling					
Heavner, Christian	98	South Fork	1837	3	7
Hederick, Charles	44	Skidmore Run	1791	1	14
Hederick, Charles	120	Skidmore Run	1798	1	402
Hederick, John	40	South Branch	1797	1	438
Hederick, John	140	South Branch	1797	1	449
Hederick, John	17	Skidmore Run	1793	1	95
Hedrick—Also Hederick					
Hedrick, Adam Jr.	300	Adj. Geo. Coil	1843	3	225
Hedrick, Adam Sr.	28	Wilmuth's Ridge	1838	3	57
Hedrick, Charles	42	Mill Creek	1840	3	122
Hedrick, Charles	13	Long Ridge	1809	2	291
Hedrick, Charles	50	Tract Hill	1795	1	192
Hedrick, Charles Sr.	16	Skidmore Run	1792	1	68
Hedrick, Eve	880	South Branch	1859	2	486
Hedrick, Frederick	53	North Fork	1801	2	131
Hedrick, Henry	20	South Branch	1807	2	274
Hedrick, Jacob	60	Tract Hill	1818	5	50
Hedrick, John	40	Mill Creek	1818	5	48
Hedrick, John	55	South Branch	1835	4	485
Hedrick, John	95	Mill Run	1811	2	359
Hedrick, John & Adam	55	Wiatt's Run	1812	2	380
Hedrick, John & Charles	2	South Branch	1801	2	107
Hedrick, John & Henry	40	Thorny Meadow Run	1802	2	162
Hedrick, Reuben	5	Buffalo Hill	1850	3	439
Hedrick, Reuben et al	1¾	Wyatt Run	1857	3	479
Hedrick, Samuel	44	North Mill Creek	1838	3	58
Hedrick, Solomon	72	Harper's Gap	1849	3	365
Hedrick, Solomon & Jonas et al	293	Shook Spring	1852	3	446
Hedrick. Zebulon	21	Mill Creek	1840	3	111
Hefner, Jacob	386	Back Creek	1837	3	5
Hefner, John D.	600	Stony Run	1862	2	507
Hefner, Peter (Heffner)	58	South Fork	1838	3	80
Heffner—also Hefner					
Heffner, Christian	17	South Fork	1835	4	471
Heffner, Peter	125	Camp Run	1835	4	476
Heffner, Zebulon	104	South Fork	1845	3	270
Heifly—See Hively					
Heifly, Michael	30	South Fork	1810	2	317
Heifly. Michael	25	South Fork	1810	2	318
Heinaker—or Hynocker					
Heiner—See also Heener, Hiner					
Heiner, John (Heener-Hiner)	40	South Fork	1803	2	193
Heiser—See Hiser, Hizer					
Heiser, Charles	50	South Fork	1797	1	379
Helsel—or Heltzel					
Helsel, Philip H. (Heltzel)	105	South Fork	1834	4	451
Hendrick, John	468	South Branch	1833	4	424
Hendrick, William	40	Stony Lick Run	1829	4	329
Henkle—or Hinkle					
Henkle, Abraham	177	North Fork	1814	2	409
Henkle, Abraham	40	North Fork	1794	1	154
Henkle, Caleb	94	South Branch	1847	3	320
Henkle, Caleb	50	South Fork	1842	3	199
Henkle, Elias & Abraham	100	North Fk. Mtn.	1797	1	376
Henkle, Isaac	50	Dry Run	1796	1	302
Henkle, Isaac	40	North Fork	1794	1	140
Henkle, Isaac	30	North Fork	1794	1	125
Henkle, Isaac	95	North Fork	1794	1	139
Henkle, Isaac	296	North Fork	1820	5	580
Henkle, Jesse	25	Brigg's Run	1815	2	435
Henkle, Jesse	242	South Branch	1810	2	449

Name of Grantee	Acres	Local Description	Year	Book	Page
Henkle, Joab & Wesley	192	North Fork	1848	3	345
Henkle, Justice	35	North Fork	1795	1	208
Henkle, Justice	136	North Fork	1791	1	34
Henkle, Michael	589	North Fork	1813	2	452
Henkle, Michael	332	North Fork	1816	5	579
Henkle, Michael	250	North Fork	1816	5	577
Henkle, Moses	100	North Fork	1797	1	385
Henkle, Moses	320	Senaca Creek	1791	1	21
Henkle, Moses	170	Roaring Springs	1793	1	67
Henkle, Moses	103	Seneca Creek	1792	1	48
Henkle, Moses	100	Walnut Bottom	1791	1	38
Henkle, Moses	400	South Branch	1800	2	17
Henkle, Paul	50	North Fork	1794	1	166
Henkle, Paul	50	North Fork	1798	1	415
Henry, John et al	380	Cow Pasture	1816	2	443
Hevener—See Heavener for variations in spelling					
Hevener, George	5	South Branch	1821	5	193
Heviner—See Heavener for variations in spelling					
Heviner, Christian	72	South Fork	1824	4	238
Hevinor—See Heavener for variations in spelling					
Hevinor, Frederick	15	Brandywine Run	1796	1	306
Hevinor, Frederick	160	South Fork	1796	1	312
Hevner—See Heavener for variations in spelling					
Hevner, Adam	30	Crab Apple Bottom	1800	2	47
Hevner, Amos & Uriah	150	Back Creek	1842	3	205
Hevner, Cutlip	210	Camp Run	1799	1	524
Hevner, Henry	84	South Fork	1837	3	10
Hevner, Henry	35	Straight Creek	1845	3	277
Hevner, Jacob	30	Crab Bottom	1819	5	114
Hevner, Jacob	84	South Branch	1799	1	528
Hevner, Jacob	200	South Fork	1846	3	288
Hevner, Jacob Jr.	670	Middle Mountain	1848	3	333
Hevner, Nicholas	80	South Fork	1812	2	384
Hevner, Peter	27	Adj. his father's land	1822	4	181
Hevner, William	102	Mallow Run	1850	3	409
Hevnor—See Heavener for variations in spelling					
Hicks, John	230	Bull Pasture	1818	5	68
Hide—or Hidy, Hyde, Hydee					
Hide, John	20	Crab Apple Bottom	1802	2	172
Hidy—Hide, Hyde, Hydee					
Hidy, Jacob	413	Crab Bottom	1847	3	573
Hille—See Hilly					
Hill, John	99	Mill Creek	1791	1	35
Hill, John et al	200	Spring Lick	1796	1	269
Hilly, Frederick	77	South Branch	1809	2	281
Hinegardner, Goodlove	140	Crab Run	1836	4	536
Hiner—See Heener, Heiner					
Hiner, Alexander	50	Bull Pasture	1818	5	44
Hiner, Alexander	14	Buck Spring	1830	4	348
Hiner, Bailey & George I.	22	Black Thorn	1845	3	260
Hiner, George	35	Bull Pasture	1844	3	252
Hiner, Harman	118	Black Thorn	1818	5	81
Hiner, Harman	80	Black Thorn	1818	5	82
Hiner, John	76	Bull Pasture River	1822	4	199
Hiner, John	600	Bull Pasture	1804	2	216
Hiner, John	120	Bull Pasture	1833	4	431
Hiner, John	93	Bull Pasture	1835	4	468
Hiner, John (Heiner-Heener)	40	South Fork	1803	2	193
Hiner, John et al	140	Calf Pasture	1808	2	269
Hiner, Joseph	24	Black Thorn	1826	4	255
Hiner, Joseph	4	Black Thorn	1841	3	160
Hiner, Joseph Jr.	380	Black Thorn	1855	2	458
Hiner, Josiah	50	Bull Pasture	1845	3	279

Name of Grantee	Acres	Local Description	Year	Book	Page
Hiner, Josiah	81	Black Thorn	1849	3	392
Hiner, Samuel	100	Shaw's Ridge	1845	3	261
Hiner, Young J. & Bailey	22	Black Thorn	1845	3	260
Hinkle—Henkle					
Hinkle, Abraham	65	North Fork	1819	5	127
Hinkle, Abraham et al	165	Laurel Run	1820	5	172
Hinkle, Joseph	95	South Branch	1795	1	198
Hinkle, Joseph	21	Wilkinson's Run	1795	1	199
Hinkle, Justus	75	Eberman's Run	1801	2	123
Hinkle, Justus	7¾	North Fork	1801	2	134
Hinkle, Michael	552	North Fork	1832	4	378
Hinkle, Moses	70	North Fork	1809	2	283
Hinkle, Moses	160	North Fork	1795	1	215
Hinkle, Moses	100	Reed's Run	1798	1	479
Hinkle, Moses	76	South Branch	1797	1	434
Hiser—See Heiser, Hizer					
Hiser, Charles	85	South Fork	1844	3	240
Hiser, Charles	35	South Fork	1844	3	241
Hiser, Charles	60	Adj. Johnson & Keister	1817	5	18
Hiser, Charles	400	South Fork	1838	3	81
Hiser, Charles	50	South Fork	1797	1	379
Hiser, Charles	8	South Branch	1819	5	100
Hiser, Charles	46	South Branch	1830	4	352
Hiser, Daniel H.	50	Cream Creek	1846	3	301
Hiser, Daniel H. & Fred'k Sr.	300	Brushy Mt.	1851	3	434
Hiser, Frederick	36	Rocky Mountain	1823	4	210
Hiser, Frederick	50	South Branch	1830	4	345
Hiser, Frederick	33	South Branch	1841	3	169
Hiser, Frederick	20	Rocky Mt.	1822	4	182
Hiser, Frederick	6	Cream Creek	1841	3	170
Hiser, Frederick Sr.	68	Cream Creek	1856	3	474
Hively—See also Heifly					
Hively, Amos	68	South Fork	1840	3	123
Hively, Amos	64	South Fork Mt.	1850	3	410
Hively, Henry (or Kee)	41	Adj. Wm. Anderson	1845	3	278
Hively, John	69	South Fork	1840	3	124
Hively, John	158	South Fork	1824	4	228
Hively, John	213	Buffalo Gap	1836	4	563
Hively, John	8½	South Branch	1817	5	16
Hively, John et al	89	Broad Run	1846	3	304
Hively, John Sr.	146	South Fork	1841	3	165
Hively, Kee W.	26	South Fork	1850	3	406
Hively, Michael	30	So. Fork	1810	2	317
Hively, Michael	65	South Fork	1820	5	165
Hively, Michael	25	So. Fork	1810	2	318
Hively, Michael	312	South Fork	1841	3	162
Hivner—See Heavener for variations in spelling					
Hivner, Jacob	386	Back Creek	1837	3	5
Hizer—See Heiser, Hiser					
Hizer, Charles	46	South Branch	1830	4	352
Hizer, Daniel H. & Frederick Sr.	300	Brushy Mt.	1851	3	434
Hodge, Jeremiah	14	Cow Pasture	1820	5	156
Hodge, John	264	Shaw's Fork	1850	3	394
Hodge, William	100	Shaw's Fork	1838	3	31
Hole—See Holl or Hull					
Hole, Peter (Hull)	56	Adj. Barnet Lance	1790	1	8
Holl, George (Hull)	9	Jackson's River	1800	2	72
Hollaway, John	52	South Fork	1832	4	401
Hollaway, Lewis	24	South Fork	1832	4	393
Hollen, Joseph	58	South Fork	1834	4	445
Hollen, William et al	135	Buffalo Run	1845	3	259
Hollingsworth, Levi	3,530	Mill Creek	1795	1	227
Hollingsworth, Levi	1,300	Mallow's Run	1795	1	226

Name of Grantee	Acres	Local Description	Year	Book	Page
Hollingsworth, Levi	82,710	North Fork	1795	1	573
Hollingsworth, Levi	52,757	South Fork	1795	1	586
Hollingsworth, Levi	11,580	South Mill Creek	1795	1	576
Hollingsworth, Levi	11,435	North Fk. Mountain	1795	1	582
Hollingsworth, Levi	4,050	Dry Run	1795	1	588
Hollingsworth, Levi	8,980	South Branch	1795	1	592
Hollingsworth, Levi	4,230	Reed's Creek	1795	1	590
Hollingsworth, Levi	7,900	South Fork	1795	1	594
Hook, Robert S.	94	Bull Pasture	1845	3	262
Hoope, John Jr.	3,000	Straight Creek	1796	1	581
Hoover—See Hamer, Hammer—also Hover					
Hoover, Benjamin	240	Brushy Fork	1840	3	126
Hoover, Daniel	144	Cowger's Mt.	1842	3	186
Hoover, Daniel et al	89	Broad Run	1846	3	304
Hoover, George A.	11	South Fork	1853	3	456
Hoover, George	25	Heitzell Run	1796	1	263
Hoover, Heiness	38	South Branch	1829	4	330
Hoover, Henry	60	Crab Apple Bottom	1818	5	59
Hoover, Hiness	40	South Branch	1841	3	148
Hoover, Jacob	50	Rich Hollow	1796	1	277
Hoover, Jacob	122	South Fork	1797	1	454
Hoover, Jacob I. (or J.)	347	Straight Fork	1840	3	125
Hoover, Jacob Jr.	50	South Fork	1815	2	421
Hoover, Jacob Jr.	50	Broad Run	1797	1	448
Hoover, Jacob Sr.	10	Powder Run	1843	3	220
Hoover, Jacob Sr.	90	Brushy Fork	1813	2	392
Hoover, Lawrence	55	Black Thorn	1794	1	137
Hoover, Michael	28	Adj. his own	1810	2	315
Hoover, Michael	55	South Fork	1802	2	155
Hoover, Michael	136	South Fork	1795	1	223
Hoover, Michael	389	Spring Branch	1796	1	241
Hoover, Michael	18	South Fork	1799	1	521
Hoover, Michael	150	Hoover's Run	1799	1	487
Hoover, Peter	56	Slifer Lick	1820	5	160
Hoover, Peter	24	South Fork	1799	1	536
Hoover, Peter	490	South Fork	1801	2	113
Hoover, Peter	50	Broad Run	1799	1	513
Hoover, Peter	140	South Fork	1799	1	416
Hoover, Peter	80	Smith Creek	1798	1	399
Hoover, Peter	95	South Fork	1796	1	303
Hoover, Peter	80	South Branch	1809	2	277
Hoover, Peter et al	140	Calf Pasture	1808	2	269
Hoover, Samuel	16	Buffalo Hill	1851	3	431
Hoover, Samuel	36	Buffalo Run	1836	4	532
Hoover, Sebastian	1,200	Little Fork	1803	2	189
Hoover, Sebastian	9¾	Little Fork	1791	1	37
Hoover, Sebastian	120	South Branch	1796	1	315
Hoover, Sebastian	24	South Fork	1794	1	129
Hoover, Sebastian	28	South Fork	1794	1	131
Hoover, Sebastian	180	South Fork	1794	1	123
Hoover, Sebastian	150	South Fork	1794	1	150
Hoover, Sebastian	478	South Fork	1803	2	197
Hoover, Sebastian et al	280	Black Thorn	1826	4	263
Hoover, Sebastian et al	150	Black Thorn	1826	4	274
Hoover, Sebastian et al	90	Black Thorn	1827	4	302
Hoover, Solomon	66	Lick Run	1851	3	433
Hoover, Thomas	81	South Fork	1835	4	473
Hoover, Wm. & Daniel	545	Cowger's Lit Mountain	1846	3	303
Hoover, William et al	120	Broad Run	1851	3	435
Hoover, Zack. & Daniel (of Wm.) et al	23	Broad Run	1838	3	90
Hopkins, Cyrus	25	Reed's Creek	1853	3	460
Hopkins, Cyrus	100	Seneca Creek	1851	3	443

Name of Grantee	Acres	Local Description	Year	Book	Page
Hopkins, Cyrus	714	Adj. John Kellar	1851	3	426
Hopkins, Cyrus	73	Reed's Creek	1849	3	367
Hopkins, Cyrus	130	Reed's Creek	1849	3	366
Hopkins, Cyrus et al	100	Reed's Creek	1853	3	453
Hopkins, John & Cyrus	227	Reed's Creek	1836	4	565
Hopkins, John Jr.	77	Reed Creek	1833	4	408
Hotom, John	60	North Mill Ck	1819	5	125
Hotom, John	12	Brushy Run	1818	5	64
Hotom, John	125	Mill Creek	1791	1	41
House, Jacob	110	South Fork	1796	1	246
Hover—See Hoover					
Hover, George	25	Heitzell's Run	1796	1	263
Huffman, Burget	75	South Fork	1794	1	165
Huffman, Burgett	248	South Branch	1799	1	477
Huffman, Daniel	67	North Mountain	1829	4	340
Huffman, Henry	50	Black Thorn	1804	2	218
Huffman, Henry	85	So. Fork	1825	4	248
Huffman, Henry	36	Black Thorn	1827	4	301
Huffman, Henry Jr.	68	Black Thorn	1827	4	298
Huffman, Laban	90	Seneca Creek	1845	3	280
Huffman, Michael	18	Black Thorn	1812	2	370
Huffman, Michael	275	Stuffel's Run	1822	4	203
Huffman, Solomon	55	North Fork Mt.	1836	4	507
Huffman, Solomon	78	Seneca Creek	1849	3	390
Hull—See Hole, Holl					
Hull, Adam	160	Laurel Fork	1833	4	413
Hull, Adam	9	Crab Bottom	1812	2	388
Hull, Adam	50	Crab Bottom	1812	2	387
Hull, Adam	55	Crab Apple Bottom	1799	1	526
Hull, Adam	615	South Branch	1833	4	549
Hull, Felix H. & G. W.	250	Crab Run	1841	3	180
Hull, Frederick K.	200	Middle Mountain	1848	3	343
Hull, Frederick K.	75	Middle Mountain	1848	3	344
Hull, Frederick K.	35	Back Mountain	1848	3	355
Hull, Frederick K.	16	Middle Mt.	1838	3	26
Hull, Frederick K.	42	Bear Camp	1838	3	27
Hull, Frederick K.	29	North Fork	1841	3	156
Hull, Frederick K.	243	Laurel Fork	1843	3	209
Hull, Frederick K.	98	Middle Mt.	1843	3	208
Hull, Frederick K.	400	Back Creek	1841	3	191
Hull, Frederick K.	75	Crab Bottom	1838	3	62
Hull, Frederick K.	60	Middle Mt.	1838	3	60
Hull, Frederick K.	137	Riffle's Old Road	1838	3	61
Hull, Frederick K.	175	Back Creek	1836	4	506
Hull, Frederick K. et al	661	Laurel Fork	1838	3	59
Hull, George	9	Jackson's River	1800	2	72
Hull, George	78	Crab Apple Bottom	1797	1	450
Hull, George	8	Crab Apple Bottom	1802	2	180
Hull, Henry	65	South Fork	1811	2	358
Hull, Henry	90	South Fork	1810	2	335
Hull, Henry	53	South Fork	1845	3	273
Hull, Henry	45	Crab Bottom	1824	4	229
Hull, Henry	5	Crab Bottom	1822	4	194
Hull, Henry	3	Crab Bottom	1822	4	193
Hull, Henry	2a.40p.	South Fork	1818	5	49
Hull, Henry	100	South Fork	1836	4	512
Hull, Jacob	90	Camp Run	1809	2	279
Hull, Jacob	110	Camp Run	1809	2	280
Hull, Jacob	70	Crab Bottom	1797	1	444
Hull, Jacob	100	Big Run	1838	3	28
Hull, Jacob	70	Little Back Mt	1838	3	29
Hull, Jacob	50	Camp Hollow	1838	3	100

Hull, Jacob	70	Middle Mountain	1838	3	99
Hull, Jacob	183	Laurel Fork	1841	3	157
Hull, Jacob	57	Back Creek	1843	3	206
Hull, Jacob	180	Bear Camp Ridge	1843	3	207
Hull, Jacob	40	Middle Mountain	1838	3	63
Hull, Peter	390	Bull Pasture	1802	2	173
Hull, Peter	27	Crab Bottom	1808	2	276
Hull, Peter	65	Crab Bottom	1809	2	297
Hull, Peter	50	Laurel Fork	1800	2	25
Hull, Peter	7	Crab Apple Bottom	1800	2	24
Hull, Peter	120	Laurel Fork	1800	2	26
Hull, Peter	30	Riffel's Old Road	1800	2	30
Hull, Peter	90	Crab Apple Bottom	1800	2	31
Hull, Peter	150	Crab Bottom	1810	2	339
Hull, Peter	75	Crab Bottom	1796	1	284
Hull, Peter	100	Crab Bottom	1796	1	328
Hull, Peter	320	North Fork	1797	1	392
Hull, Peter	23	South Fork	1797	1	447
Hull, Peter	84	Crab Apple Bottom	1799	1	510
Hull, Peter	570	Bull Pasture	1804	2	230
Hull, Peter	114	Crab Apple Bottom	1790	1	7
Hull, Peter	198	South Branch	1790	1	6
Hull, Peter	24	Bull Pasture	1838	3	30
Hull, Peter	33	Bull Pasture	1841	3	179
Hull, Peter	5	Crab Bottom	1838	3	79
Hull, Peter	2¼	Duff's Run	1836	4	495
Hull, Peter	4¼	Bull Pasture	1834	4	432
Hull, Peter	500	Bull Pasture	1833	4	427
Hull, Peter	48	Back Creek	1833	4	428
Hull, Peter	585	South Fork	1801	2	138
Hull, Peter	40	Wts. Greenbrier	1801	2	137
Hull, Peter	80	Laurel Fork	1801	2	119
Hull, Peter	75	Wts. Greenbrier	1801	2	118
Hull, Peter	130	Cart Mill's Run	1801	2	117
Hull, Peter A.	275	Back Creek	1836	4	564
Hull, Peter & Adam	200	Bark Creek	1805	2	237
Hull, Peter A. Heirs	60	South Branch	1840	3	110
Hull, Peter A. & Jacob	135	Laurel Run	1838	3	98
Hull, Peter et al	145	Crab Apple Bottom	1796	1	318
Hull, Peter et al	500	Crab Run	1825	4	249
Hull, Peter (Hole)	56	Adj. Barnet Lance	1790	1	8
Hull, Peter Jr.	25	Bull Pasture	1818	5	39
Hull, Peter Jr.	4	Crab Run	1818	5	38
Hull, Peter Jr.	60	Bull Pasture	1818	5	37
Hull, Peter Jr.	2a.40p.	Bull Pasture	1818	5	36
Hull, Peter Jr.	32	Bull Pasture	1815	2	422
Hull, Peter K.	15	Bull Pasture	1836	4	497
Hull, Peter K. & G. W.	280	Strait Fork	1838	3	78
Hull, Peter K. & Geo. W.	680	North Fork	1836	4	498
Hull, Peter Maj.	6½	Crab Bottom	1837	3	11
Hull, Peter Sr.	190	Crab Bottom	1811	2	346
Hull, Peter Sr.	18	Crab Bottom	1817	5	21
Hull, Peter Sr.	118	Crab Bottom	1816	5	3
Hull, William	4	Crab Bottom	1820	5	157
Hull, William Jr.	55	South Branch	1826	4	284
Hull, William R.	8½	Bull Pasture	1834	4	433
Hyde—or Hide, Hidy, Hydee					
Hyde, John	20	Crab Apple Bottom	1802	2	172
Hyde, John	4	Crab Apple Bottom	1802	2	174
Hydee—Hide, Hidy, Hyde					
Hydee, Jacob	9	Crab Bottom	1826	4	265
Hydee, John (Hyde)	4	Crab Apple Bottom	1802	2	174
Hynocker, Christian (Heinaker)	53	South Branch	1798	1	461

Name of Grantee	Acres	Local Description	Year	Book	Page
James, William	20	Straight Creek	1796	1	279
James, William	75	Straight Creek	1796	1	278
Jeffers, James	256	North Mill Creek	1838	3	32
Jeffers, James	25½	North Mill Creek	1835	4	464
Johns, Isaac	104	Shaw's Fork	1833	4	410
Johns, James	28	Shaw's Fork	1828	4	316
Johns, James Jr.	64	Shaw's Fork	1837	4	544
Johns, James Jr.	17	Shaw's Fork	1833	4	421
Johns, Jeremiah	165	Shaw's Fork	1833	4	417
Johns, Robert	100	Shaw's Fork	1833	4	422
Johns, William	30	Cow Pasture	1805	2	255
Johnson, Andrew	92	North Fork	1792	1	65
Johnson, Andrew	107	North Fork	1792	1	50
Johnson, Andrew	76	North Fork	1792	1	45
Johnson, Andrew	81	North Fork	1792	1	44
Johnson, James	5	South Fork	1845	3	263
Johnson, James	77	Straight Creek	1809	2	285
Johnson, James	150	South Branch	1820	5	141
Johnson, James Hrs. et al	100	Reed's Creek	1853	3	453
Johnson, Jesse	37	Jackson's River	1798	1	503
Johnson, Richard	20	Smith Creek	1799	1	517
Johnson, Richard	140	Smith's Creek	1797	1	419
Jones, Henry	50	Cow Pasture	1798	1	463
Jones, Henry	11	Cow Pasture	1798	1	460
Jones, Henry	140	Cow Pasture	1801	2	145
Jones, Henry	120	Trout Fork	1801	2	101
Jones, Henry	30	South Branch	1801	2	97
Jones, Henry	35	South Branch	1801	2	96
Jones, Henry	12	South Branch	1801	2	95
Jones, John	45	Cow Pasture	1809	2	306
Jones, John	9	Strait Creek	1836	4	528
Jones, Joseph	350	Crab Run	1823	4	204
Jones, Joseph	179	Crab Run	1838	3	82
Jones, Samuel Sr.	38	Shaw's Fork	1846	3	313
Jones, Thomas	46	Bull Pasture Mt.	1822	4	198
Jones, Thomas	66	Bull Pasture	1840	3	140
Jones, Thomas et al	105	Stormy Run	1826	4	260
Jordan or Jurdon					
Jordan, Andrew	333	South Fork	1811	2	348
Jordan, Andrew	6	Purgatory Knob	1811	2	356
Judy, Amos	275	Dry Run	1849	3	384
Judy, Amos et al	4	North Fork	1836	4	526
Judy, George	120	North Mill Creek	1838	3	56
Judy, George	25	Mill Creek	1834	4	444
Judy, Henry	40	North Fork	1800	2	51
Judy, Henry	6	Adj. Heath's Land	1810	2	314
Judy, Henry	100	Spruce Mountain	1800	2	80
Judy, Henry,	90	North Mill Creek	1804	2	219
Judy, Henry	39	Dry Run	1795	1	190
Judy, Henry	36	North Fork	1793	1	105
Judy, Henry et al	56	South Branch	1849	3	371
Judy, Henry Jr.	50	Dry Run	1802	2	178
Judy, Henry Sr.	55	North Fork	1796	1	250
Judy, Jacob & George	28	Mill Creek	1836	4	510
Judy, Margaret (Widow)	9	South Branch	1812	2	381
Judy, Martin	165	North Fork	1848	3	346
Judy, Martin Sr.	13	North Fork	1852	3	449
Judy, Nicholas	35	North Mill Creek	1805	2	240
Judy, Nicholas	48	South Branch	1794	1	149
Judy, Nicholas	20	South Branch	1795	1	185
Jurdon or Jordan					
Jurdon, Andrew Sr.	170	Adj. Botkin's	1821	5	210

Name of Grantee	Acres	Local Description	Year	Book	Page
Jurdon, James	60	Bull Pasture Mt.	1823	4	221
Jurdon, John	30	South Fork	1822	4	195
Kanester, Kanister, Keester, Keister, Kenester, Kester, Knestrick					
Kanester, Frederick	138	South Fork	1835	4	463
Kanester, Frederick	138	South Fork	1833	4	426
Kanister—See Kanester for variations in spelling					
Kanister, Frederick	1	South Fork	1836	4	523
Kee, Aaron	23	South Branch	1815	2	434
Kee, Aron	25	South Branch	1813	2	406
Keeper, Jacob	235	Banniger's Gap	1794	1	151
Keeper, Jacob	80	South Fork	1797	1	339
Keester or Kanester, Kanister, Keister, Kenester, Kester, Knestrick					
Keester, Frederick	18	Brandywine River	1793	1	83
Keester, Frederick	9	South Fork	1793	1	82
Keester, James	60	Broad Run	1795	1	171
Keester, James	250	Horse Run	1795	1	174
Keister or Kanester, Kanister, Keester, Kenester, Kester, Knestrick					
Keister, Frederick	54	Adj. Frank Houser	1843	3	226
Keister, Frederick	110	Brandywine Gap	1799	1	483
Keister, Frederick	5	South Fork	1840	3	112
Keister, Frederick	195	Horse Run	1834	4	457
Keister, Frederick Jr.	50	South Branch	1799	1	519
Keister, George	58	South Fork Mtn.	1833	4	420
Keister, George	60	South Fork	1810	2	319
Keister, George et al	217	Trumbo's Gap	1838	3	55
Keister, George Sr.	145	Horse Run	1838	3	83
Keister, George Sr.	460	South Fork	1834	4	550
Keister, James	148	Horse Run	1844	3	247
Keister, James	30	Horse Run	1799	1	492
Keister, James	246	South Fork	1831	4	362
Keister, James et al	120	Broad Run	1851	3	435
Keister, John	63	Brandywine	1840	3	127
Keister, John	724	L. Fork	1852	2	455
Keister, John	55	South Fork	1844	3	246
Keister, John	117	Dry Run	1849	3	385
Keister, John D.	57	South Fork	1858	3	489
Keister, Malinda	196	Horse Run	1859	3	491
Kellar, Adam	128	East Side Allegheny	1851	3	427
Kellar, John	86	Horse Camp Run	1846	3	285
Kellar, John	130	Horse Camp Run	1846	3	286
Kelley, George	100	Dry Run	1796	1	261
Kenester—Kanester, Kanister, Keester, Keister, Kester, Knestrick					
Kenester, Frederick	22	South Fork	1812	2	371
Keeslin—or Keesling					
Keslin, John	60	Bull Pasture	1817	5	34
Kester—Kanester, Kanister, Keester, Keister, Kenester, Knestrick					
Kester, Frederick	45	Stagger Hollow	1819	5	113
Kester, Frederick	55	Adj. John Davis	1819	5	112
Kester, George	45	South Fork	1819	5	104
Key, Aaron	120	Buffalo Hill	1800	2	7
Keykendahl—or Curkindaul					
Kile, Absolom	15	Upper Tract	1859	3	496
Killingsworth, Richard	100	Bull Pasture	1799	1	525
Killingsworth, William	30	Bull Pasture Mt.	1828	4	319
Kimmel, George	50	Gragg's Run	1804	2	214
Kincade—Kinkead					
Kincade, Thomas	63	Crab Bottom	1822	4	172
King, Jacob	40	Adj. George Mallow	1821	5	209
King, Jacob	143	North Mill Creek	1805	2	249
King, Jacob	50	South Fork	1809	2	287
Kinkead,—See Kincade					
Kinkead, Peter H. et al	661	Laurel Fork	1838	3	59

Name of Grantee	Acres	Local Description	Year	Book	Page
Kinkead, Thomas	596	Crab Apple Bottom	1837	4	568
Kinkead, William P.	52	Adj. Jacob Hull	1848	3	334
Kiser, David	50	South Fork	1844	3	264
Knap, Moses et al	100	Bull Pasture	1798	1	470
Knestrick—Kanester, Kanister, Keester, Keister, Kenester, Kester					
Knestrick, Frederick	20	South Branch	1821	5	197
Knestrick, Frederick	190	South Branch	1820	5	139
Knestrick, Fredrick	4½	South Branch	1819	5	119
Kuykendahl—or Curkindaul					
Kyle—See Kile					
Lamb, Noah	31	South Fork	1841	3	128
Lambert, George	60	Dry Run	1800	2	48
Lambert, John	110	Judy's Knob	1800	2	49
Lambert, John Jr.	200	Dry Run	1798	1	498
Lambert, John Jr.	50	North Fork	1852	3	450
Lance—See also Lantz					
Lance, Joseph et al	95	High Knob	1801	2	114
Landes, Jesse	5	North Mill Creek	1854	3	467
Lantz,—See Lance					
Lantz, Joseph	96	North Fork	1801	2	124
Lantz, Joseph	85	Crab Apple Bottom	1797	1	375
Lantz, Joseph	80	Crab Bottom	1797	1	432
Laugh—See Lough					
Laurence—See also Lawrence					
Laurence, William	100	Pounding Mill Run	1800	2	63
Lawman, David	43	Smith Creek	1843	3	211
Lawrence—See also Laurence					
Lawrence, William	21	Adj. McCoy & Friend	1797	1	338
Layne, Joseph	10	Crab Run	1841	3	183
Leach—also Leech					
Leach, John	53	Bull Pasture	1818	5	42
Leaterson,—See also Peterson					
Leaterson, Charles	20	South Branch	1802	2	127
Lee, Charles C. et al	3,450	Wts. Greenbrier R.	1851	3	430
Leech—also Leach, Leetch					
Leech, John (Leetch)	17	Cow Pasture	1801	2	110
Leech, John	30	Bull Pasture	1810	2	344
Leezer, Joseph (Leazer)	100	Black Thorn	1798	1	410
Life, Christian	48	Jackson's River	1817	5	35
Life, John	50	Crab Bottom	1801	2	103
Life, Martin	94	Crab Apple Bottom	1800	2	70
Life, Samuel	6	Crab Bottom	1819	5	101
Lightner, Adam	3	Jackson's River	1838	3	33
Lightner, John et al	36	Jackson River	1831	4	375
Lofland, Dorman	96	South Fork	1816	5	1
Lofland, Dorman	210	Head of ——Drain	1800	2	99
Lofland, Dorman	88	Horse Camp Run	1800	2	88
Lofland, Dorman	140	Big Run	1800	2	89
Lofland, Dorman	75	Big Run	1800	2	87
Lofland, Smith	200	Big Run	1801	2	140
Lofland, Smith et al	900	North Fork	1801	2	142
Lofland, Smith et al	1,100	South Fork	1801	2	141
Lough—or Laugh					
Lough, Adam	10	South Branch	1813	2	401
Lough, George	10	South Branch	1800	2	28
Lough, Isaac	57	South Fork	1835	4	483
Lough, John (of Adam)	380	Bee Ridge	1834	4	434
Lough, John	200	South Fork	1819	5	116
Lough, John	84	Stony Gap	1822	4	178
Lough, John	20	South Branch	1825	4	242
Lough, John Sr.	60	South Fork	1813	2	403
Lough, John W.	614	Buffalo Run	1860	2	490
Lough, William	1)	Entry Mtn.	1845	3	274

Name of Grantee	Acres	Local Description	Year	Book	Page
McCoy, Oliver	230	Bull Pasture	1797	1	349
McCoy, Oliver	300	Buffalo Run	1797	1	340
McCoy, Oliver	3¼	South Branch	1795	1	170
McCoy, Robert	120	Black Thorn	1800	2	9
McCoy William	100	Bull Pasture	1812	2	362
McCoy, William	98	Bull Pasture	1812	2	385
McCoy, William	57	Bull Pasture	1812	2	386
McCoy, William	60	Smith's Creek	1822	4	170
McCoy, William	200	Straight Creek	1798	1	457
McCoy, William	175	Crab Run	1800	2	8
McCoy, William	712	Buffalo Gap	1851	3	429
McCoy, William Sr.	120	Bull Pasture	1828	4	320
McCoy, William Sr.	3¾	Bull Pasture Mt.	1828	4	314
McCullock, McCulloch, McCulloh					
McCullock, Robert	29,895	Seneca Creek	1796	1	360
McCulloh, Robert	8,665	North Fork	1796	2	474
McCulloh, Robert	14,870	North Fork	1796	2	477
McCulloh, Robert	270	Buffalo Gap	1802	2	152
McCulloh, Robert	500	Thorny Meadow Run	1802	2	151
McCulloh, Robert	150	South Branch	1802	2	150
McCulloh, Robert	2,430	Buffalo Gap	1796	1	316
McCulty, James	43	Mill Creek	1836	4	520
McCulty, James	190	Mill Creek	1835	4	479
McDaniel—See McDannel					
McDannel, Archibald	70	Crab Run	1804	2	232
McDonnel—or McDannel, McDonald					
McGlaughland, James	9	South Fork	1805	2	243
McGloughlin—See McGlaughland					
McKenney, James	200	Bull Pasture	1802	2	136
McKindley—McKenley, McKinley					
McKinley, Peter	246	South Branch	1798	1	466
McKinley, Peter	200	Canoe Run	1794	1	114
McKonkey, Jacob	72	South Branch	1794	1	156
McLaughlin—See McGlaughland					
McMaghen, John (McMahan)	105	Bogard's Cabin	1798	1	411
McMahan—See McMaghen					
McMullen, Duncan	70	Adj. Harpole's	1810	2	330
McMullen, Isaac Sr.	100	South Branch	1830	4	358
McMullen, John	276	South Fork	1832	4	409
McMullen, John	19	Adj. Johnson	1820	5	142
McMullen, William	26	South Branch	1821	5	196
McNeil, Paul & C. C. See, Hrs.	596	Wts. Greenbrier	1853	3	452
McNeil, Paul et al	3,450	Wts. Greenbrier R.	1851	3	430
McQueen, Alexander	52	Black Thorn	1799	2	34
McQueen, Alexander	50	Jackson's Mountain	1794	1	148
Meeker, John	115	Crab Run	1800	2	86
Mefford, John	115	Straight Creek	1799	1	515
Mefford, John	96	Straight Creek	1802	2	184
Meyers—See Mayers, Moyers, Myers					
Meyers, Martin et al	1,800	Sounding Knob	1832	4	406
Michael,—See also Matchel, Mitchel, Mitchell					
Michael, William	40	Crab Apple Bottom	1798	1	502
Michael, William	5	Crab Apple Bottom	1802	2	179
Miller, Adam	32	Crab Apple Bottom	1830	4	354
Miller, Adam G. et al	288	Crab Bottom	1837	4	543
Miller, Conrad	45	Mill Run	1828	4	312
Miller, Conrod	100	Mallow's Run	1797	1	336
Miller, Conrod	35	Mallows Run	1829	4	326
Miller, George	30	Mallow's Run	1797	1	443
Miller, George	26	Rocky Mountain	1809	2	289
Miller, George	60	Full's Run	1797	1	345
Miller, George	83	Powder Run	1848	3	357
Miller, George	50	North Fork	1802	2	158

Name of Grantee	Acres	Local Description	Year	Book	Page
Peithorn, Philip	76	Mill Cr.	1799	2	1
Pennington, Richard et al	50	Cor. to Minness & Nelson	1814	2	408
Pennington, Richard Jr.	100	Bull Pasture	1811	2	349
Pennington, Richard Jr.	30	South Branch	1804	2	234
Pennington, Richard Jr.	70	Crab Apple Bottom	1799	2	39
Perien, Henry	200	Richardson's Run	1791	1	36
Perrine—See Perien					
Peterson, Charles (Leterson)	20	So. Branch	1802	2	127
Peterson, William	170	North Fork	1795	1	207
Peterson, William	166	Skidmore's Run	1791	1	39
Phares—See Pharis					
Phares, Johnson	198	North Fork	1795	1	210
Phares, Johnson	92	North Fork	1795	1	187
Phares, Johnson	400	North Fork	1794	1	122
Phares, Johnson	50	North Fork	1798	1	465
Phares, Johnson	28	Dry Run	1798	1	458
Phares, Johnson	75	North Fork	1798	1	408
Phares, Robert	25	Buffalo Hills	1794	1	163
Phares, Robert	130	Skidmore Run	1793	1	81
Pharis—See Phares					
Pharis, Johnston	24	North Fork	1795	1	209
Pitsenbarger, Pitsenberger, Pitsinbarger—See also Fitzbarger, Pitzenbarger					
Pitsenbarger, Jacob	80	Sink Hole Mt.	1840	3	130
Pitsenbarger, Jacob	18	Sink Hole Mt.	1840	3	131
Pitsenbarger, Washington A	88	Black Thorn	1850	3	421
Pitsenberger, John	14	Black Thorn	1852	3	451
Pitsenberger, John	64	Black Thorn	1825	4	253
Pitsenberger, John	66	Dry Run	1825	4	252
Pitsinbarger, John	24	Black Thorn	1834	4	437
Pitzenbarger, Abraham	75	Black Thorn	1802	2	170
Poop—Pope or Pupp					
Pope, John Sr.	47	Rough Run	1856	3	476
Pope, John	17	Sweedlin Hill	1835	4	466
Pope, John (Pup)	12	Rough Run	1823	4	219
Pope, Peter Jr.	30	Rough Run	1838	3	37
Pope, Peter (Poop)	5	Rough Run	1805	2	263
Price, Lewis	210	South Branch	1800	2	85
Price, Lewis	140	South Branch	1800	2	98
Props—or Propst					
Props, Adam (alias Probbs)	23	South Branch	1813	2	395
Props, Adam	17	Black Thorn	1819	5	124
Props, Adam	150	South Fork	1812	2	361
Props, Adam	60	Black Thorn	1813	2	394
Props, Daniel	4½	Black Thorn Fork	1822	4	171
Props, Daniel	120	South Fork	1824	4	235
Props, Daniel	20	Black Thorn	1816	5	4
Props, Frederick	15	Marks Run	1795	1	236
Props, Frederick	140	South Fork	1804	2	221
Props, George	78	South Fork	1810	2	324
Props, George	10	South Fork	1810	2	325
Props, George	3½	South Fork	1811	2	352
Props, Henry	80	South Fork	1797	1	384
Props, Henry	60	South Fork	1796	1	271
Props, Henry	32	Adj. his former land	1818	5	85
Props, Henry	45	South Fork	1818	5	86
Props, Henry	90	Black Thorn	1810	2	323
Props, Jacob	80	Sink Hole Mountain	1799	2	2
Props, Jacob	12	South Fork	1820	5	155
Props, Jacob	145	Little Fork	1819	5	129
Props, Jacob	45	Props Knob	1819	5	128
Props, John	50	Adj. Widow Props	1810	2	322
Props, John	25	Long Mountain	1820	5	162
Props, John	172	S. Branch	1798	1	464

Name of Grantee	Acres	Local Description	Year	Book	Page
Props, John	30	Brandywine Gap	1818	5	79
Props, John	165	Buffalo Run	1817	5	31
Props, Leonard	110	Canon's Run	1820	5	161
Props, Leonard	140	Black Thorn	1796	1	313
Props, Leonard	70	South Fork	1793	1	78
Props, Leonard	50	Dry Run	1807	2	275
Props, Leonard	12	Miller's Run	1810	2	326
Props, Leonard Jr.	32	Miller's Run	1813	2	405
Props, Leonard Sr.	70	Black Thorn	1795	1	228
Props, Leonard Sr.	30	South Fork	1796	1	270
Props, Leonard Sr.	120	South Fork	1828	4	325
Props, Leonard Sr.	290	Adj. M. Props	1813	2	390
Props, Michael	45	Props Run	1798	1	404
Props, Michael	65	South Fork	1794	1	142
Props, Michael	45	Props Run	1804	2	209
Props, Sophia	119	South Fork	1794	1	164
Props, Sophia	40	South Branch	1799	1	534
Propst—or Props					
Propst, Adam	155	Lick Run	1834	4	450
Propst, Adam Sr.	36	Black Thorn	1836	4	494
Propst, Daniel (of Daniel)	68	Mill Run	1859	3	492
Propst, Daniel et al	10	Town of Franklin	1836	4	529
Propst, Daniel (of Henry)	50	South Fork	1843	3	231
Propst, Daniel (of Henry)	20	Propst's Knob	1836	4	531
Propst, David	31	Buffalo Run	1834	4	446
Propst, Eli	104	Mill Gap	1833	4	430
Propst, Eli (of Daniel)	39	South Fork	1835	4	477
Propst, Eli (of Daniel)	175	South Fork	1836	4	513
Propst, Eli (of Daniel)	12	Sink Hole Mt.	1838	3	50
Propst, Elias (of Daniel)	214	Mill Run	1851	3	442
Propst, George	2	South Fork Mt.	1845	3	267
Propst, George (of Frederick)	55	East Branch	1847	3	323
Propst, George Sr.	13	Swadlin Ridge	1838	3	47
Propst, George Sr.	58	Owen Run	1838	3	48
Propst, Henry (of Henry)	50	Rexroad Mt.	1844	3	248
Propst, Henry Sr.	201	South Fork	1836	4	508
Propst, Henry Sr.	2	South Fork	1836	4	515
Propst, Jacob (of Geo., of Leonard)	7	Black Thorn	1839	3	106
Propst, Jacob (of Henry)	20	Propst Gap	1833	4	412
Propst, Jacob, S. H. & Wm. A.	79	Miller's Run	1850	3	418
Propst, Jacob & Samuel	95	Dry Run	1837	3	4
Propst, Jacob Sr.	159	Little Fork	1838	3	43
Propst, Jacob Sr.	95	Briery Branch	1833	4	414
Propst, Jacob Sr.	94	Lit. Fork	1834	4	456
Propst, John	85	Mill Run	1845	3	276
Propst, John	178	Miller's Run	1850	3	414
Propst, John G.	396	Slipper Run	1862	3	503
Propst, John (of George)	8	Black Thorn	1844	3	249
Propst, John (of George)	10	South Fork	1853	3	458
Propst, John (of George, of Frederick)	30	Black Thorn	1838	3	51
Propst, John (of Jacob)	3	Sink Hole Mt.	1833	4	411
Propst, John (of Jacob)	35	Mill Run	1839	3	107
Propst, John (of Jacob)	17	Adj. Jacob Probst	1832	4	385
Propst, John (of Jacob)	65	Mill Gap	1832	4	383
Propst, John Sr.	96	South Fork Mt.	1834	4	443
Propst, John Sr.	78	South Fork	1840	3	129
Propst, John Sr.	1,500	South Fk. & Long Run	1841	3	178
Propst, Jonas	86	Miller's Run	1850	3	399
Propst, Jonas	185	Miller's Run	1847	3	331
Propst, Leonard & Daniel	188	Propst Run	1850	3	417
Propst, Levi	2¼	Black Thorn	1860	3	502
Propst, Levi	340	Dry Run	1858	3	487

Name of Grantee	Acres	Local Description	Year	Book	Page
Rexroad, Zachariah	12	South Branch	1819	5	130
Rexrode—or Rexroad					
Rexrode, George	53	South Branch	1795	1	239
Rexrode, George	145	Black Thorn	1812	2	367
Rexrode, George Jr.	14	Black Thorn	1812	2	368
Rexrode, John	28	Crab Run	1805	2	260
Rexrode, John	28	Crab Bottom	1805	2	256
Rexrode, John	66	Crab Bottom	1804	2	212
Rexrode, Leonard	40	Swadley Run	1800	2	13
Rexrode, Zachariah	130	South Fork	1796	1	356
Rexrode, Zachariah Jr.	200	Trout Rock	1796	1	330
Riggleman, Jacob	135	South Mill Creek	1850	3	400
Riggleman, Reuben	74	Six Mile Creek	1849	3	373
Rimer—or Rymer					
Rimer, George	65	Strait Creek	1810	2	336
Roberts, John	96	South Branch	1803	2	198
Roberts, John	100	South Branch	1803	2	191
Roberts, John	28	Cor. to Skidmore	1798	1	507
Roberts, John	169	Dry Run	1800	2	11
Rogers, Hanna et al	240	Reed's Creek	1817	5	9
Rollman—Rolman, Roolman, Ruleman					
Rollman, Christian	125	South Fork	1796	1	423
Rollman, Christian Sr.	87	Cow Pasture	1800	2	10
Rollman, Justus	47	Mill Run	1799	1	514
Rolman, Christian	13	South Fork	1828	4	313
Rolman, Christian Jr.	37	Bull Pasture	1819	5	111
Rolman, Christian Jr.	102	Bull Pasture	1819	5	110
Roolman, Christian Jr.	100	South Fork	1797	1	439
Root, Jacob	39	South Branch	1792	1	70
Root, Jacob	23	Laurel Run	1792	1	71
Root, Jacob	70	North Fork	1792	1	72
Roy, Joseph	222	Harper's Gap	1792	1	54
Roy, Joseph	31	Seneca Creek	1792	1	56
Roy, Joseph	80	North Fork	1798	1	401
Roy, Joseph	35	North Fork	1798	1	398
Ruddle, James	37	Buffalo Hill	1841	3	177
Ruleman, Rollman, Rolman, Roolman					
Ruleman, Christian	40	Deep Run	1836	4	509
Ruleman, Christian	3a.1r.30p.	South Fork	1830	4	353
Ruleman, Christian	17	Falling Springs	1830	4	349
Ruleman, Christian	47	South Fork	1805	2	244
Ruleman, Christian	100	South Fork	1838	3	91
Ruleman, Christian Jr.	100	Bull Pasture	1812	2	376
Ruleman, Christian Jr.	230	South Fork	1813	2	398
Ruleman, Jacob	225	South Fork	1861	2	494
Rymer—also Rimer					
Rymer, William	38	Straight Creek	1851	3	440
Samuels, Larkin	44	South Branch	1847	3	314
Secafoos—Sycafoos, Sycafooze, Sycafuse, Zycafoose					
Secafoos, Peter	55	Crab Apple Bottom	1800	2	73
See, C. C. & Paul McNeil, Hrs.	596	Wts. Greenbrier	1853	3	452
Settington—Sitlington, Sittington					
Settington, John	425	Bull Pasture	1819	5	134
Settington, John	145	Crab Run	1820	5	176
Settington, John	17	Straight Creek	1820	5	177
Settington, John	8	Bull Pasture	1820	5	175
Severn, Lewis (Sivern)	170	South Branch	1802	2	153
Seybert—Sybert					
Seybert, Jacob	247	Straight Creek	1842	3	204
Seybert, Jacob	440	Straight Creek	1840	3	145
Seybert, Jacob	350	Straight Creek	1815	2	426
Seybert, Jacob	7	Straight Creek	1810	2	337
Seybert, Jacob	100	Straight Creek	1800	2	5

Name of Grantee	Acres	Local Description	Year	Book	Page
Toops, John	172	South Branch	1798	1	464
Towberman, Henry	76	Rocky Gap	1822	4	187
Towberman, Peter (Toberman)	155	Shenandoah Mt.	1833	4	415
Townsend, Davis & Benjamin	55	Back Creek	1843	3	210
Tremble—or Trimble					
Tremble, James	16	Strait Creek	1838	3	20
Tremble, James	34	Strait Creek	1838	3	19
Trimble, James et al	115	Bull Pasture Run	1827	4	286
Trimble, James Sr.	15	Strait Creek	1818	5	74
Trimble, John	40	Crab Bottom	1819	5	108
Trimble, John	39	Strait Creek	1838	3	40
Trops, Frederick (Props)	15	Marks Run	1795	1	236
Troxell, John	115	North Mill Creek	1794	1	220
Trumbo—or Trumbow					
Trumbo, Esther	28	Heavenor's Run	1820	5	150
Trumbo, George	450	South Fork	1819	5	93
Trumbo, George	60	South Fork	1809	2	307
Trumbo, George	225	South Fork	1796	1	420
Trumbo, John	30	South Fork	1815	2	437
Trumbo, Levi	28	South Fork	1820	5	143
Trumbo, Levi	139	South Fork	1838	3	39
Trumbo, Levi	35	South Branch	1832	4	387
Trumbo, Levi	42	Backbone Hollow	1839	3	108
Trumbo, Mary et al	148	Six Mile Lick	1851	3	441
Trumbo, Michael	218	South Fork	1836	4	499
Trumbo, Saulsberry	57	Sweedlin Hill	1841	3	161
Trumbo, Saulsberry	175	South Fork	1835	4	465
Trumbo, William	1,160	South Fork	1835	4	558
Trumbo, William	14	South Fork	1822	4	186
Trumbo, William	8	South Fork	1822	4	185
Trumbow—also Trumbo					
Trumbow, Andrew et al	77	South Branch	1831	4	367
Turnbull, James	45	Straight Creek	1804	2	222
Turnipseed, Jacob	100	South Branch	1798	1	504
Valentine, James et al	156	Back Creek	1846	3	284
Vance, Jesse	56	North Fork	1842	3	202
Vance, John Sr.	120	Harper's Run	1818	5	63
Vance, Robert	25	Roaring Ridge	1826	4	280
Vance, Robert	8	Roaring Knob	1835	4	475
Vandervender—Vandevender, Vandeventer					
Vandervender, George	280	Black Thorn	1804	2	217
Vandevender, or Vandervender, Vandeventer					
Vandevender, Adam	80	Adj. his Land	1819	5	122
Vandevender, Henry	86	Adj. Roberts' Survey	1825	4	247
Vandevender, Isaac	44	Smoke Hole	1795	1	191
Vandevender, Jacob	230	Black River	1795	1	189
Vandevender, Peter	70	South Fork	1794	1	121
Vandeventer or Vandervender, Vandevender					
Vandeventer, Isaac	200	South Branch	1800	2	57
Vandeventer, Jacob	200	Long Run	1800	2	61
Vannamon, Peter	10	Buffalo Hill	1796	1	324
Vannamon, Peter	86	Buffalo Hill	1794	1	146
Vannamon, Peter (Nanimon)	46	Buffalo Hill	1796	1	314
Varner or Verner					
Varner, Conrad	154	Flesher's Run	1799	1	535
Varner, George Jr.	16	South Fork	1826	4	279
Varner, George Jr.	12	South Fork	1844	3	254
Varner, George Sr.	39	Shaw's Ridge	1845	3	269
Varner, George Sr.	33	Brushy Fork	1832	4	402
Varner, John	85	South Branch	1797	1	380
Varner, John	82	South Fork	1817	5	11
Varner, Joseph	37	Brushy Fork	1822	4	191
Varner, Joseph	70	Brushy Fork	1818	5	80

Name of Grantee	Acres	Local Description	Year	Book	Page
White, Jacob et al	228	Middle Mtn.	1843	3	232
White, John	50	Crab Bottom	1797	1	377
White, John	342	North Fork	1838	3	44
White, John Sr.	315	Crab Apple Bottom	1837	4	569
White, John Sr.	410	Straight Fork	1840	3	135
White, Thomas	36	Gaudy Creek	1848	3	347
White, Thomas	52	Seneca Road	1853	3	454
Whitecotton, James Sr.	79	Seneca Creek	1795	1	180
Whiteman, William	60	South Fork	1793	1	160
Wilfong—also Willfong					
Wilfong, Daniel	127	Laurel Fork	1843	3	237
Wilfong, Elias	180	Adj. Adam Stephenson	1835	4	482
Wilfong, Henry	130	Adj. Daniel Wilfong	1835	4	478
Wilfong, Henry	45	Brushy Fork	1834	4	442
Wilfong, Henry	48	Greenbrier Road	1833	4	423
Wilfong, Henry	20	Brushy Fork	1817	5	8
Wilfong, Henry	60	Broad Run	1796	1	257
Wilfong, Jacob	12	Smith Creek	1818	5	60
Wilfong, Jacob	76	Smith's Creek	1818	5	61
Wilfong, Jacob	135	Smith's Creek	1818	5	62
Wilfong, Michael	280	Brushy Fork	1795	1	224
Wilkinson, George	354	North Fork	1792	1	59
Willfong—See also Wilfong					
Willfong, Elias	40	Adj. his own	1836	4	514
Wilson, Alebab	17	Bull Pasture Mt.	1823	4	226
Wilson, Charles	48	Little River	1791	1	40
Wilson, Isaac	10	Little River	1827	4	309
Wilson, James	94	Adj. Sweedlin	1827	4	310
Wilson, James	306	Sweedlin Valley	1862	3	505
Wilson, James et al	100	Bull Pasture	1798	1	470
Wilson, John E.	382	South Branch	1860	2	492
Wilson, John E.	40	Bull Pasture	1841	3	167
Wilson, John E. & Samuel (of Wm)	68	Carlisle's Run	1842	3	189
Wilson, Samuel	43	Bull Pasture	1828	4	315
Wilson, Samuel	40	Bull Pasture Mt.	1812	2	365
Wilson, Samuel	14	Bull Pasture	1812	2	364
Wilson, Samuel	130	Bull Pasture	1821	5	208
Wilson, Samuel & Isaac	180	Bull Pasture	1818	5	40
Wilson, Samuel Sr.	339	Bull Pasture Mt.	1840	3	134
Wilson, William	200	Bull Pasture	1805	2	264
Wilson, William	40	Bull Pasture	1820	5	183
Wilson, William	67	Bull Pasture	1820	5	182
Wimer—or Winner, Wymer					
Wimer, Amos et al	94	Hunting Ground	1842	3	203
Wimer, George	13	Straight Creek	1799	2	38
Wimer, George	130	Straight Creek	1799	2	37
Wimer, Henry (Winner)	334	Strait Fork	1837	3	3
Wimer, Jacob	250	Dry Run	1799	1	496
Wimer, Philip	6	Crab Bottom	1809	2	305
Wimer, Philip	100	Dry Run	1838	3	45
Wimer, Philip	2½	Dry Run	1847	3	327
Wimer, Philip	36	Backbone Mt.	1800	2	15
Wimer, Philip	130	Dry Run	1796	1	243
Wimer, Philip	3	Dry Run	1847	3	326
Wimer, Philip	48	Dry Run	1796	1	266
Wimer, Philip	100	Dry Run	1796	1	267
Wimer, Philip et al	82	Black Thorn	1857	3	483
Winner—or Wimer, Wymer					
Winner, Henry (Wimer)	334	Strait Fork	1837	3	3
Winner, Philip (Wimer)	100	Dry Run	1838	3	45
Wise, Adam	390	South Fork	1845	3	559
Wise, Martin	50	Brushy Run	1841	3	151
Wise, Martin	790	North Mill Creek	1861	2	503

Name of Grantee	Acres	Local Description	Year	Book	Page
Wise, Martin	40	Mill Creek	1822	4	183
Wise, Martin et al	60	North Mill Creek	1819	5	117
Wise, Sebastian	10	North Mill Creek	1796	1	256
Wood—or Woods					
Wood, Isaac	260	Brushy Run	1795	1	206
Wood, John	34	Brushy Run	1799	1	531
Wood, John	85	Bull Pasture	1796	1	363
Wood, Thomas	30	Buffalo Hills	1820	5	152
Woods, Thomas	25	South Branch	1827	4	308
Woolf—or Wolf					
Woolf, Philip	65	Black Thorn	1799	2	33
Wornstoff—See Warnsturf					
Wymer—or Wimer, Winner					
Wymer, Amos et al	19	Back Hunting Ground	1843	3	238
Wymer, Henry	6	Back Hunting Ground	1843	3	239
Yager—See Yeager					
Yager, George	144	Bull Pasture	1797	1	342
Yeager, John	50	Wts. Greenbrier	1809	2	300
Zycafoose—Secafoos, Sycafoos, Sycafoose, Sycafuse					
Zycafoose, Sampson	120	East Side Allagh. Mt.	1840	3	138
Zycafoose, Sampson	2	Snowy Mt.	1839	3	109
Zycafoose, Sampson et al	251	Laurel Fork	1840	3	137

PLEASANTS COUNTY

Browse, Thomas	152	French Creek	1857	1	216
Campbell, Robert	10⅛	Bull Creek	1855	1	214
Galloway, William K. & Moses	919	Sugar Tree Creek	1859	1	218
Martin, Abner	13	Cedar Run	1861	1	219
Smith, John (of James)	51	Coal Run	1856	1	215

POCAHONTAS COUNTY

Adams, Edward L.	565	Clover Creek	1834	1	161
Adams, Edward L.	100	Old Field Fork	1850	1	414
Adkison, Barnet	200	Swago Creek	1834	1	172
Alderman, Daniel	50	Beaver Lick Creek	1827	1	74
Aldridge—or Auldridge					
Aldridge, Samuel	78	Old Field Fork	1843	1	329
Arbogast, Adam	40	Mill Stone Run	1852	1	490
Arbogast, Benjamin	50	Allegheny Mountain	1833	1	145
Arbogast, Benjamin	42	Sitlington Creek	1824	1	9
Arbogast, Emanuel et al	511	Wts. Greenbrier	1854	1	527
Arbogast, Jacob H.	110	Wts. Greenbrier	1838	1	246
Arbogast, Jacob H.	1¼	Adj. Adam Arbogast	1838	1	245
Arbogast, Jacob H.	3½	Wts. of Greenbrier	1838	1	261
Arbogast, Jacob H. et al	1,307	Wts. Greenbrier	1858	2	38
Arbogast, John	14	Setlington Creek	1848	1	380
Arbogast, Moses	130	Adj. Patton's Survey	1843	1	315

Name of Grantee	Acres	Local Description	Year	Book	Page
Arbogast, Moses	366	Wts. Greenbrier	1852	1	489
Arbogast, Moses H.	6	Wts. Greenbrier	1854	1	546
Arbogast, William & Benjamin	46	Little Run	1835	1	175
Arbogast, William & Benjamin	70	Little River	1834	1	169
Auldridge—See Aldridge					
Auldridge, John	8	Stony Creek	1849	1	392
Auldridge, Samuel	17	Buckeye Mt.	1848	1	379
Auldridge, Samuel	132	Old Field Fork	1837	1	233
Auldridge, Thomas	100	Wts. Greenbrier	1835	1	176
Auldridge, Thomas	168	Old Field Fork	1843	1	314
Auldridge, Thomas	214	Wts. of Elk	1837	1	232
Baxter, William	116	Stony Creek	1836	1	207
Beal, George et al	726	Slaty Fork	1849	1	403
Beard, Joseph	30	Wts. Greenbrier	1853	1	496
Beard, Josiah	32	Wts. Greenbrier	1853	1	521
Beard, Josiah et al	1,093	Wts. Greenbrier	1858	2	562
Beard, Samuel W.	10	Beaver Lick Creek	1851	1	471
Beverage, Henry	9	Deer Creek	1851	1	481
Bible, Jacob	218	Cooper's Run	1838	1	256
Bible, Jacob	186	Allegheny Mt.	1838	1	257
Bible, Jacob	47	Deer Creek	1852	1	491
Blair, Thomas C.	190	Mill Stone Run	1852	1	487
Blair, William	250	Bruffy's Creek	1828	1	102
Blair, William	30	Droop Mt.	1834	1	165
Blair, William	140	Droop Mt.	1828	1	103
Blair, William	650	Wts. Cherry River	1849	1	393
Blair, William	540	Cranberry Creek	1841	1	300
Blair, William	180	Wts. Cranberry	1836	1	220
Blair, William	220	Stomping Creek	1836	1	199
Boggess, William	40	Robins Fork	1856	2	4
Boggs, William	242	Robins Fork	1832	2	578
Boggs, William	40	Robins Fork	1856	2	4
Boggs, William	6	Spring Creek	1854	1	541
Boggs, William	180	Spring Creek	1854	1	542
Boggs, Wm. E. & Fielden	400	Kinnison's Run	1835	1	174
Bradshaw, John	50	Little Back Creek	1836	1	218
Bradshaw, John	266	Naps Creek	1826	1	71
Bradshaw, John	104	Naps Creek	1825	1	38
Bradshaw, William	17	Little Levels	1825	1	31
Bridges, James	100	Indian Draught	1835	1	180
Brock, Thomas	60	Stony Creek	1825	1	33
Brown, Josiah	133	Wts. Elk River	1826	1	57
Brown, Josiah	150	Adj. John Sharp	1828	1	110
Brown, Josiah	132	Indian Draught	1828	1	108
Bruffey—or Bruffy					
Bruffey, John	90	Bruffy's Creek	1847	1	377
Bruffy, James	25	Cheat Mountain	1844	1	345
Brufly, James	158	Adj. Patrick Bruffy	1844	1	344
Bruffy, James	1,200	Greenbrier River	1850	1	418
Bruffy, John	735	Little Sinking Creek	1840	1	292
Bruffy, John	260	Cove Run	1852	1	485
Bruffy, John	120	Droop Mt.	1853	1	503
Bruffy, William	90	Brush Run	1855	1	557
Burner, Allen C.	250	Wts. Greenbrier	1858	2	36
Burner, George	18	Wts. Greenbrier	1854	1	544
Burner, Joshua	100	Wts. of Greenbrier	1837	1	244
Burnside, Robert	70	Adj. Thomas Hill	1853	1	502
Burnside, Robert	1,000	Wts. Greenbrier	1853	1	522
Buzzard, Eli	216	Galford's Creek	1837	1	236
Buzzard, Eli	4	Sitlington's Creek	1837	1	234
Buzzard, Henry	95	Old Field Fork	1848	1	381
Buzzard, Henry et al	234	Old Field Fork	1853	1	505
Buzzard, Reuben	125	Setlington's Creek	1850	1	413

Name of Grantee	Acres	Local Description	Year	Book	Page
Buzzard, Solomon	16	Setlington's Creek	1835	1	177
Cackley, Jacob F. et al	1,000	Wts. Elk	1851	1	446
Cackley, Jacob F. et al	2,900	Wts. Elk	1851	1	454
Cackley, William	36	Near Huntersville	1833	1	143
Cackley, William H. et al	57	Roundhill	1859	2	45
Callison—See Kelison, Kellison					
Callison, Anthony	175	Fryer's Knob	1833	1	134
Callison, Anthony	79	Droop Mountain	1824	1	6
Callison, James Sr.	200	Droop Mountain	1823	1	3
Callison, Josiah	20	Coal Run	1851	1	448
Callison, Josiah	47	Trump Run	1851	1	449
Campbell, Samuel B. et al	1,307	Wts. Greenbrier	1858	2	38
Casebolt, Jefferson	95	Wts. of Greenbrier	1833	1	137
Casebolt, Thomas	9½	Locust Creek	1838	1	276
Casebolt, Thomas	46½	Locust Creek	1827	1	75
Cassel—or Cassell					
Cassel, James	75	Wts. Greenbrier	1857	2	23
Cassel, James	165	Wts. Greenbrier	1857	2	26
Cassel, James	66	Wts. Greenbrier	1854	1	540
Cassel, Samuel	30	Wts. Greenbrier	1854	1	538
Cassel, Samuel	115	Allegheny Run	1857	2	25
Cassel, William	227	Allegheny Run	1835	1	198
Cassell, Jacob	33	Wts. Greenbrier	1836	1	197
Cassell, Samuel	280	Wts. Greenbrier	1847	1	373
Cassell, William	104 sq p.	Allegheny Run	1850	1	417
Cassell, William	320	Wts. Greenbrier	1857	2	21
Clark—or Clarke					
Clark, Alvin et al	1,093	Wts. Greenbrier	1858	2	562
Clark, Sheldon	600	Wts. Cherry River	1840	1	288
Clark, Sheldon	700	Spring Creek	1849	1	387
Clark, Sheldon	1,355	Wts. Cherry River	1860	2	567
Clark, Sheldon	2,760	Tea Cr. and Wms. Riv.	1850	1	408
Clark, Sheldon	440	Spice Run	1849	1	388
Clark, Sheldon	400	Ewings Run	1853	1	518
Clark, Sheldon et al	2,100	Sinking Creek	1840	1	287
Clark, Sherman H.	4¼	Spice Run	1855	1	553
Clark, Sherman H.	1,200	Spice Run	1855	1	554
Clarke—or Clark					
Clarke, John J. (or I.)	300	Beaver Lick Creek	1836	1	191
Clarke, Sheldon	72	Cherry River	1834	1	159
Clarke, Sheldon	372	Spring Creek	1832	1	160
Clarke, Sheldon	206	Sinking Creek	1836	1	196
Clarke, Sherman W.	110	Wts. Greenbrier	1853	1	516
Cleek—or Click					
Cleek, John & William et al	49	Knaps Creek	1858	2	31
Cleek, William	400	Yew Mountain	1851	1	447
Cleek, William	13	Knaps Creek	1844	1	343
Cleek, William & John	78	Brown's Mt.	1844	1	342
Cleek, William et al	1,632	Cochran's Creek	1856	2	551
Click—or Cleek					
Click, Michael	100	Naps Creek	1833	1	136
Clutter, Joseph	280	Droop Mt.	1848	1	378
Clunon, Timothy	285	Laurel Run	1856	2	2
Cochran, James	145	Old Field Fork	1828	1	106
Cochran, James	18	Wts. of Greenbrier	1833	1	138
Cochran, Jesse et al	430	Wts. Greenbrier	1852	1	495
Cochran, Thomas Jr.	200	Buckeye Mt.	1824	1	23
Cockran, John Sr.	90	Mountain Lick	1847	1	372
Cockley—See Cackley					
Collins, Benjamin	18	Adj. his own	1846	1	361
Collins, Benjamin et al	195	Coal Run	1854	1	537
Collins, Benjamin et al	220	Cheat Mt.	1853	1	524
Collins, Charles	28	Wts. Creenbrier	1836	1	203

Name of Grantee	Acres	Local Description	Year	Book	Page
Collins, Charles	24	Wts. Greenbrier	1836	1	217
Collins, John	290	Wts. Greenbrier	1851	1	452
Collins, John	70	Dinwiddie Run	1851	1	453
Collins, William	130	Sandy Lick	1851	1	482
Colaw, George (Colow)	950	Wts. Greenbrier	1854	1	548
Colaw, George et al (Colow)	2,070	Wts. Greenbrier	1858	2	42
Colter—or Coulter					
Colter, George I. (or J.)	280	Spruce Run	1856	2	8
Conrad, Solomon	150	Deer Creek	1838	1	277
Conrad, Solomon	60	Deer Creek	1826	1	59
Coulter—or Colter					
Coulter, Charles	230	Spice Run	1855	1	555
Coulter, George J.	125	Oldham Run	1853	1	510
Craig, George E.	84	Knap's Creek	1845	1	354
Craig, George E.	3¾	Brown's Mt.	1845	1	352
Craig, George E.	1¼	Brown's Mt.	1845	1	351
Cunningham, Zadock	2	Trout Run	1854	1	547
Cunningham, Zadock	336	Wts. Greenbrier	1854	1	545
Curry, John	500	Allegheny Run	1851	1	451
Curry, John	377	Wts. Greenbrier	1851	1	450
Curry, Robert	1,025	Wts. Cheat River	1854	1	551
Dilly, Andrew	4½	Thorny Creek	1851	1	483
Dilly, Andrew	22	Thorny Creek	1854	1	535
Dilly, Andrew	94	Old Field Fork	1860	2	49
Dilly, John	88	Adj. Wm. Moore	1845	1	349
Dilly John	22	Thorny Creek	1845	1	350
Dilly, Martin	12	Adj. his own	1844	1	338
Dilly, Martin	64½	Brown Creek	1827	1	76
Dilly, Martin	100	Thorny Creek	1824	1	13
Dilly, Martin	100	Adj. William Cleek	1844	1	337
Dilly, Martin	2½	Adj. Wanless	1844	1	335
Dimmock, Charles et al	2,900	Wts. Elk	1851	1	454
Duffield, Andrew	350	Stony Creek	1850	1	406
Duncan, Henry	150	Stony Creek	1833	1	157
Duncan, William	225	Indian Draught	1835	1	179
Echols, John	9,000	Elk & Greenbrier	1856	2	549
Edmiston, George et al	28,500	Wts. Williams River	1860	2	564
Edmiston, George M. G. & James	2,050	Tea Creek & Lit. Laurel	1850	1	407
Edmiston, George M. G. et al	5,450	Wts. Williams & Gauley	1850	1	405
Edmiston, James	320	Mill Stone Run	1852	1	486
Edmiston, James et al	430	Wts. Greenbrier	1852	1	495
Edmiston, James & George M. G. et al	4,100	Williams River	1850	1	416
Edmiston, James & George M. G. et al	5,943	Brier Knob	1850	1	415
Ervin, James R.	3,900	Old Field Fork	1858	2	37
Ervin, James R.	1,000	Tea Creek	1856	2	13
Ervine, Edward	200	Duncan's Run	1834	1	168
Ervine, Edward	33	Adj. S. Nottingham	1835	1	188
Ervine, Edward	7	Adj. Hartman Lee	1835	1	189
Ewing, William	18	Stony Creek	1851	1	455
Farnsworth, Alexander R. L.	96	Laurel Run	1850	1	411
Farnsworth, Levi	136	Stamping Creek	1826	1	63
Flemmon, John R. F.	235	Dry Fork	1853	1	520
Flesher, Benjamin et al	4,400	Wts. Greenbrier	1859	2	48
Floyd, William H.	350	Spring Fork	1851	1	426
Floyd, William H.	350	Big Spring Fork	1851	1	430
Francisco, Charles C. et al	2,600	Wts. Williams River	1851	1	423
Friel, John	30	Thorny Creek	1835	1	181
Friel, Joseph	66	Wts. Greenbrier	1825	1	40
Friel, Josiah	400	Laurel Creek	1852	1	488
Galford, Allen	375	Wts. Greenbrier	1857	2	29
Galford, Allen	50	Spring Run	1854	1	536

Name of Grantee	Acres	Local Description	Year	Book	Page
Galford, Allen et al	195	Coal Run	1854	1	537
Galford, John	75	Sitlington's Creek	1833	1	156
Galford, John	10	Sitlington's Creek	1836	1	219
Galford, John	76	Setlington Creek	1838	1	269
Galford, Thomas	154	Elk Lick Run	1861	2	53
Galford, Thomas	29	Setlington's Creek	1836	1	202
Galford, William	62	Setlington Creek	1838	1	270
Galford, William	42	Setlington's Run	1836	1	216
Gammon, Elizabeth A. et al	460	Brush Run	1854	1	550
Gatewood, Andrew M.	16	Sitlington Creek	1828	1	115
Gatewood, Andrew M.	144	Sitlington Creek	1828	1	114
Gatewood, Samuel V.	1,000	Big Spring Fork	1853	1	515
Gatewood, Samuel V.	1,000	Big Spring Fork	1853	1	514
Gatewood,Warwick	700	Big Spring Fork	1851	1	476
Gay—See Guy					
Gay, George	900	Wts. Williams River	1848	1	383
Gay, John	385	Stony Creek	1837	1	240
Gay, Samuel M.	108	Big Knob	1849	1	394
Gay, Samuel M.	500	Indian Draft	1835	1	186
Gay, Samuel M.	265	Brushy Lick Run	1833	1	154
Gay, Samuel M.	416	Wts. of Elk River	1838	1	248
Gay, Samuel M.	100	Beaver Creek	1837	1	242
Gay, Samuel M. (or G.)	14	Adj. Jacob Waugh	1826	1	55
Gay, Samuel M. & John	384	Old Field Fork	1840	1	291
Gay, William	275	Indian Draught	1838	1	268
Geiger, Michael	42	Unicorn Ridge	1854	1	549
Gibson, David	210	Old Field Creek	1827	1	79
Gibson, David	8	Old Field Creek	1841	1	299
Gibson, David	1,000	Old Field Fork	1851	1	438
Gibson, John	47½	Old Field Fork	1828	1	105
Gibson, John	1¾	Rich Mountain	1833	1	131
Gibson, John & David	200	Warricks Run	1826	1	67
Gibson, William	77	Naps Creek	1834	1	162
Gibson, William	23	Clover Creek	1861	2	56
Gibson, William	220	Old Field Fork	1860	2	50
Gibson, William	200	Knaps Creek	1836	1	223
Gilliland, John	125	Naps Creek	1826	1	50
Gilliland, John	50	Brown's Mt.	1834	1	164
Gilliland, Robert	240	Indian Draught	1827	1	62
Gilmer, Alexander	454	Setlington's Creek	1858	2	559
Gilmore, Alexander	454	Setlington's Creek	1858	2	559
Griffin, Abraham	227	Stony Creek	1836	1	210
Griffin, Jonathan	17	Thorny Creek	1833	1	135
Griffin, Jonathan I. (or J.)	300	Bruffy's Mt.	1852	1	494
Grimes, Arthur	35	Johnny Creek	1827	1	77
Grimes, Arthur	78	Thorny Creek	1846	1	370
Grimes, Arthur & Charles	170	Thorny Creek	1843	1	310
Grimes, Charles	100	Knaps Creek	1844	1	330
Grimes, Charles	52	Adj. his own	1843	1	318
Grimes, Henry	145	Adj. James Sharp	1844	1	332
Gum, John E.	220	Setlington Creek	1838	1	267
Gum, William	200	Wts. Greenbrier	1851	1	437
Guy—see Gay					
Guy, Samuel M. (or G.)	14	Adj. Jacob Waugh	1826	1	55
Hamilton, William	980	Greenbrier Mt.	1855	1	556
Hamilton, William	1,730	Wts. Greenbrier	1857	2	555
Hanna—or Hannah					
Hanna, David Sr.	200	Wts. of Greenbrier	1823	1	1
Hannah, David	10½	Wts. Greenbrier	1853	1	504
Hannah, David	75	Field Fork	1828	1	109
Hannah, David et al	304	Oldham Run	1856	2	7
Hannah, David et al	2,216	Leatherwood	1853	1	498
Hannah, David & John	200	Old Field Fork	1846	1	368

Name of Grantee	Acres	Local Description	Year	Book	Page
Holden, James	107	Naps Creek	1835	1	195
Houchen, John	136	Adj. George Burner	1844	1	336
Houchen, John	41	Mountain Lick	1837	1	231
Houchen, Moses	140	Mountain Lick	1837	1	230
Hudson, Elijah	70	Sitlington's Creek	1834	1	163
Hudson, Elijah	68	Setlington's Creek	1838	1	264
Hughart, John P. K.	1,000	Leatherwood	1853	1	523
Hughes, John	243	Dry Fork	1834	1	171
Hughes, Milburn	8	Little Levels	1826	1	49
Irvin—or Irwin					
Irvin, John	114	Dougherty's Run	1832	1	128
Irwin—or Irvin					
Irwin, John	66	Adj. John McCarty	1825	1	39
Johnson, Elizabeth	180	Alder Lick Run	1838	1	283
Johnson, Elizabeth	84	Alder Lick Run	1838	1	284
Johnson, John Jr.	26	Wts. Greenbrier	1825	1	30
Jones, Hieskill	135	Sterm Run	1838	1	262
Jorden—Jordin, Jourdin					
Jorden, Isaac	2	Adj. H. M. Moffett	1844	1	331
Jordin, John	42	Little Levels	1827	1	85
Jordin, John	24	Wts. Greenbrier	1828	1	111
Jordin, John M. et al	360	Wts. Greenbrier	1851	1	442
Jourdin, John M. et al	65	Stamping Creek	1853	1	525
Kee, Andrew	44	Adj. Geo. Kee	1851	1	459
Kee, George	94	Burks Mountain	1835	1	187
Kee, George	174	Wts. Greenbrier	1826	1	70
Kee, John	100	Adj. Geo. Kee	1851	1	460
Kee, Joshua B.	92	Wts. Greenbrier	1844	1	346
Keer—or Kerr					
Keer, Robert B. (Kerr)	8	Saulsberry Run	1857	2	16
Kelison—See Kellison, Callison					
Kelison, Daniel	94	Droop Mt.	1826	1	65
Kelison, Daniel	100	Droop Mountain	1824	1	7
Kellison—See Callison, Kelison					
Kellison, Daniel	74	Fryer's Hole	1849	1	395
Kellison, Daniel	380	Fryer's Hole	1849	1	396
Kellison, David	340	Tyger's Knob	1835	1	173
Kellison, Edward	55	Wts. of Greenbrier	1837	1	241
Kellison, Edward	180	Wts. of Greenbrier	1832	1	130
Kellison, Jacob & Sheldon	35	Spring Creek	1857	2	17
Kellison, James	375	Wts. of Greenbrier	1824	1	5
Kellison, James	480	Sinking Creek	1840	1	286
Kellison, James et al	304	Oldham Run	1856	2	7
Kellison, William	2½	Island Greenbrier R.	1856	2	9
Kellison, William	40	Wts. Greenbrier	1843	1	316
Kelly, John	30	Naps Creek	1827	1	90
Kelly, John	35	Wts. Greenbrier	1825	1	34
Kelly, John	56½	Naps Creek	1825	1	35
Kennison, Jacob	13	Buckeye Mt.	1844	1	339
Kerr—or Keer					
Kerr, David W.	35	Adj. Brush's Line	1843	1	319
Kerr, David W.	100	Deer Creek	1843	1	321
Kerr, David W.	873	Deer Creek	1861	2	51
Kerr, Robert B.	470	Deer Creek	1861	2	52
Kerr, William	19	Adj. John Sutton	1843	1	317
Lamb, Alexander R.	245	Wts. of Greenbrier	1838	1	249
Lamb, Thomas	28	Adj. his own	1836	1	201
Layne, Douglas B.	800	Wts. Elk	1851	1	461
Layne, Douglas B. et al	2,900	Wts. Elk	1851	1	454
Lee—Also See					
Lewis, James Jr.	100	Asahel's Ridge	1825	1	41
Lewis, Samuel et al	2,600	Wts. William River	1851	1	423
Lightner, Peter	54	Mill Run	1844	1	334

Name of Grantee	Acres	Local Description	Year	Book	Page
Moore, Isaac	87	Naps Creek	1827	1	73
Moore, Isaac	128	Mill Run	1826	1	68
Moore, Isaac	730	Mill Run	1828	1	116
Moore, Isaac	32	Stony Creek	1837	1	235
Moore, Isaac & Robert	400	Adj. M. Harold	1838	1	273
Moore, James	48	Knaps Creek	1844	1	340
Moore, James C.	114	Mill Run	1858	2	40
Moore, James C.	42	Adj. Wm. Moore	1847	1	376
Moore, James E.	10	George's Run	1851	1	462
Moore, John	2	Marling's Branch	1858	2	33
Moore, John	50	Thorney Creek	1827	1	83
Moore, Levi	55	Naps Creek	1823	1	2
Moore, Moses	54	Knaps Creek	1854	1	533
Moore, Robert	5	Indian Draught	1825	1	29
Moore, Robert	108	Indian Draught	1838	1	250
Moore, Samuel W. et al	525	Laurel Creek	1838	1	271
Moore, William	50	Wts. Greenbrier	1833	1	146
Moore, William	12	McCutcheon's Run	1840	1	290
Morrison, Absolom	194	Frier's Hole	1827	1	84
Morrison, Absolom	120	Fryer's Knob	1836	1	194
Morrison, Alexander	45	Fryer's Knob	1849	1	389
Morrison, Alexander	80	Rush Run	1833	1	144
Morrison, Thomas	20	Fryer's Knob	1849	1	398
Morrison, Thomas	14	Adj. D. Kelison	1838	1	272
Mullinax, John & George	511	Wts. Greenbrier	1854	1	527
Nicholas, Thomas	82	Wts. Greenbrier	1835	1	185
Nichols, Samuel	59	Laurel Gap	1824	1	19
Nichols, William	120(122)	Douthard's Creek	1826	1	64
Nichols, William	7½	Douthard's Creek	1826	1	61
Nottingham, William	270	Setlington's Creek	1843	1	311
Nottingham, William	6	Adj. Paul McNeil	1843	1	312
Nottingham, William	50	Saulberry Run	1837	1	227
Oldham, Joseph	216	Wts. Greenbrier	1825	1	36
Oldham, William R. et al Hrs.	100	Wts. Greenbrier	1851	1	424
Philips, Frederick	14	Deer Creek	1846	1	363
Piles, Francis	80	Beaver Lick Creek	1827	1	94
Piles, James	116	Beaver Lick Creek	1827	1	95
Piles, James	75	Beaver Lick Creek	1827	1	91
Piles, James	100	Beaver Lick Creek	1827	1	89
Poage, George (Poge)	325	Stomping Creek	1827	1	93
Poage, George	3	Little Levels	1846	1	369
Poage, George W.	550	Beaver Lick Creek	1850	1	409
Poage, Thomas R. & Wm.	445	Stomping Creek	1827	1	92
Poage, William Jr.	67	Naps Creek	1826	1	51
Poage, Woods	33	Wilson Survey	1851	1	463
Poage, Woods	6½	Laurel Run	1854	1	529
Price, James A.	50	Buck's Mt.	1833	1	142
Price, James A.	14	Clover Lick	1856	2	12
Price, James A.	85	Naps Creek	1833	1	139
Price, James A.	210	Clover Creek	1845	1	356
Price, James A.	620	Clover Creek	1849	1	399
Price, James A.	113	Wts. Greenbrier	1851	1	464
Rankin, James & Thomas J.	556	Laurel Run	1850	1	419
Rider, Alexander	218	Laurel Run	1850	1	410
Rider, Alexander W.	1,810	Cochran's Creek	1856	2	553
Rider, George	42	Naps Creek	1828	1	113
Rodgers, James	300	Swago Creek	1836	1	211
Ruckman, Agnes F. et al	226	Brown's Mt.	1842	1	307
Ruckman, David L.	108	Stephen Hale Run	1849	1	404
Ruckman, John H.	200	Wts. Greenbrier	1864	2	57
Ruckman, John H.	2,400	Wts. Greenbrier	1851	1	465
Ruckman, John H.	245	Beaver Dam Creek	1851	1	466
Ruckman, John H.	610	Adj. Samuel Ruckman	1851	1	467

Name of Grantee	Acres	Local Description	Year	Book	Page
Ruckman, John H.	25	Wts. Williams River	1853	1	513
Ruckman, John H.	¾	Buckeye Mountain	1849	1	391
Ruckman, John H.	60	Stamping Creek	1849	1	400
Ruckman, Nancy F.	44	Knaps Creek	1854	1	531
Sampson, Alford	110	Brown's Creek	1856	2	5
Sanders, Charles J. (or S.)	75	Thorny Creek	1844	1	348
Sebert or Seybert					
Sebert, Abraham	6½	Little Levels	1825	1	28
Sebert, Joseph	250	Swego Creek	1830	1	124
Sebert, Joseph & Lantz et al	1,200	Middle Mountain	1854	1	530
Sebert, Joseph & Lantz et al	800	Cochran's Creek	1854	1	528
Sebert, Lantz et al	400	Douthard's Creek	1854	1	532
See—or Lee					
See, George & Jacob et al	2,300	Big Spring Fork	1836	1	190
See, Jacob W.	1,000	Adj. Jacob Slaven	1847	1	371
Seybert or Sebert					
Seybert, Andrew et al	4,400	Wts. Greenbrier	1859	2	48
Seybert, Isaac et al	3,980	Wts. Little River	1859	2	47
Sharett, Elizabeth	41	Knaps Creek	1838	1	252
Sharett, Elizabeth et al	226	Brown's Mt.	1842	1	307
Sharp, Alexander W.	12	Clover Lick Creek	1851	1	472
Sharp, Alexander W.	18	Clover Lick Creek	1851	1	473
Sharp, James	198	Beaver Lick Creek	1825	1	32
Sharp, James	256	Old Field Fork	1828	1	101
Sharp, John	238	Lewis Lick Run	1828	1	107
Sharp, John	348	Setlington Creek	1838	1	282
Sharp, John	70	Adj. Thomas Wilson	1851	1	474
Sharp, John	36	Naps Creek	1827	1	97
Sharp, John	12	Sitlington's Creek	1837	1	228
Sharp, John	5	Sitlington's Creek	1837	1	229
Sharp, John Jr.	30½	Setlington Creek	1827	1	98
Sharp, Robert	200	Thorny Creek	1843	1	313
Sharp, William (Son of Wm.)	600	Slaty Fork	1851	1	434
Sharp, William	185	Wts. Elk River	1826	1	52
Sharp, William	44	Naps Creek	1834	1	167
Sharp, William	10	Brown's Creek	1835	1	178
Sharp, William	280	Clover Creek	1835	1	182
Sharp, William & J. W.	250	Wts. Elk	1855	1	552
Sheets, Jacob	290	Wts. Greenbrier	1857	2	24
Simmons, Nicholas	45	Wts. Greenbrier	1861	2	55
Simmons, Nicholas	36	Wts. Greenbrier	1847	1	374
Simmons, Nicholas	82	Wts. Greenbrier	1835	1	148
Skeen, William	13	Naps Creek	1858	2	39
Skeen, William	350	Big Spring Fork	1851	1	435
Skeen, William	400	Ewings Run	1854	1	543
Skeen, William	644	Droop Mountain	1858	2	557
Slaven—or Slavens					
Slaven, Elizabeth A. et al Hrs.	460	Brush Run	1854	1	550
Slaven, Jacob G.	46	Wts. Greenbrier	1841	1	298
Slaven, Jacob G.	150	Adj. John Slaven	1838	1	280
Slaven, Jacob G.	570	Back Allegheny	1851	1	468
Slaven, Jacob G. Hrs.	460	Brush Run	1854	1	550
Slavens, John Sr.	348	Greenbrier Mt.	1825	1	25
Slavens, William	262	Greenbrier Mt.	1825	1	26
Smith, Augustus W.	100	Back Creek	1827	1	96
Smith, Jesse	150	Brushy Lick Run	1837	1	237
Smith, John	220	Clover Lick	1838	1	266
Snyder, Mary et al	575	Tee Creek	1855	1	560
Staton, Daniel	42	Buffalo Run	1842	1	209
Sutton, Jacob G.	22	Setlington Creek	1838	1	260
Sutton, S. S. & W. W.	208	Hendrix Run	1838	1	259
Tallman, Benny et al	450	Leatherbark Creek	1838	1	275
Tallman, Benny et al	220	Cheat Mt.	1853	1	524

Name of Grantee	Acres	Local Description	Year	Book	Page
Tallman, William W.	147	Deer Creek	1838	1	274
Taylor, Ludy	4¼	Setlington's Creek	1836	1	204
Taylor, Ludy	53	Setlington's Creek	1836	1	206
Tharp, Margaret	165	Wts. Greenbrier	1828	1	112
Townsend or Townson					
Townsend, Solomon	33	Spring C. Run	1826	1	66
Townson or Townsend					
Townson, James (Townsend)	88	Deer Creek	1830	1	117
Vanrenen, Elizabeth et al	575	Tee Creek	1855	1	560
Vanrenon, Cornelius	42	Stony Creek	1858	2	41
Varner, Isabella et al	575	Tee Creek	1855	1	560
Varner, John	140	Crooked Fork	1838	1	263
Varner, John	166	Old Field Fork	1846	1	367
Varner, Philip	100	Adj. Hull's	1833	1	132
Varner, Solomon	64	Little River	1836	1	200
Wade, Stuart	4	Knap's Creek	1849	1	401
Wanless, Andrew	215	Trout Run	1842	1	302
Wanless, Andrew	29	Wts. Greenbrier	1851	1	469
Wanless, Andrew	865	Greenbrier Mt.	1851	1	480
Wanless, John	115	Brown's Mt.	1833	1	141
Wanless, Leaven	86	Naps Creek	1832	1	129
Wanless, Leven	18	Thorny Creek	1845	1	357
Wanless, Ralph	14	Brown Mt.	1844	1	333
Wanless, William	94	Wts. Greenbrier	1851	1	445
Wanless, William	334	Wts. Greenbrier	1851	1	444
Wanless, William	80	Wts. Greenbrier	1825	1	43
Wanless, William	125½	Wts. Greenbrier	1825	1	42
Wanless, William	28	Wts. Greenbrier	1825	1	44
Warwick, Benjamin	47	Woods Run	1830	1	121
Warwick, John W.	17	Glade Run	1849	1	402
Warwick, John W.	200	Gauley Mountain	1861	2	54
Warwick, Robert C.	46	Deer Creek	1836	1	205
Waugh, John	114	Thorny Creek	1838	1	253
Waugh, Robert	55	Adj. Martin Dilly	1843	1	322
Waugh, Samuel	167	Thorny Creek	1824	1	16
Waugh, Samuel	63	Thorny Creek	1824	1	17
Waugh, Samuel	20	Thorny Creek	1824	1	18
Waugh, William	2	Adj. his own	1844	1	341
Waugh, William	310	Leatherbark Creek	1837	1	226
White, John V.	3	Stomping Creek	1836	1	192
White, John V.	73	Stomping Creek	1836	1	193
Whiting, Ebenezer	25	Droop Mt.	1852	1	492
Whiting, Samuel	85	Droop Mt.	1838	1	278
Whiting, Samuel Jr.	50	Old Fork Creek	1838	1	279
Wilfong, George	148	Leatherbark	1853	1	508
Wilfong, George	200	Adj. Charles Collins	1838	1	285
Wilfong, George	27	Adj. his own	1846	1	366
Wilfong, George	80	Wts. Greenbrier	1846	1	365
Wilfong, Henry	150	Adj. Solomon Varner	1831	1	126
Wilfong, Henry	160	Palsey Ridge	1831	1	127
Wilfong, Henry, & Wm. G. & G. W.	454	Leather Bark	1856	2	11
Wood, Samuel	2a.109p.	Mill Creek	1827	1	72
Woodall, William J. (Wooddell)	250 (256)	Little Mtn.	1859	2	46
Woodell, Alexander	100	Naps Creek	1824	1	15
Woodell, John W.	20	Deer Creek	1841	1	297
Yeager, Andrew	42	Wts. Greenbrier	1854	1	534
Yeager, Andrew	18	Wts. Greenbrier	1854	1	539
Yeager, Andrew	74	Cor. to Adam Arbogast	1849	1	385
Yeager, Andrew	1,800	Wts. Greenbrier	1857	2	28
Yeager, Andrew	20	Wts. Greenbrier	1842	1	306
Yeager, Jacob	125	Adj. Jacob Wilfong	1838	1	254
Yeager, Jacob	282	Adj. Lewis Lunceford	1838	1	255
Yeager, Jacob	325	Little River	1833	1	150

Name of Grantee	Acres	Local Description	Year	Book	Page
Yeager, Jacob	17	Palsey Ridge	1833	1	152
Yeager, Jacob	246	Allegheny Mtn.	1836	1	212
Yeager, Jacob	50	Adj. his own	1828	1	100
Yeager, John	34	Deer Creek	1849	1	386
Yeager, John	19	Deer Creek	1856	2	14
Yeager, John	370	Wts. Greenbrier	1853	1	509
Yeager, John	33	Deer Creek	1836	1	208
Yeager, John et al	28,500	Wts. Williams R.	1860	2	564
Yeager, John et al	575	Tee Creek	1855	1	560
Young, George et al	348 (248)	Stony Creek	1849	1	390

PRESTON COUNTY

Abbot, Jerrid T.	500	Cheat River	1859	1	277
Adams, George R.	90	Wts. of Cheat	1852	2	480
Albrite, Daniel	107	Pine Swamps	1838	2	249
Annan, Joseph A.	35	Cheat River	1860	1	300
Armstrong, Isaac	198	Big Sandy Cr.	1845	2	358
Armstrong, Isaac	109	Little Sandy Cr.	1841	2	306
Armstrong, Isaac et al	126	Sandy Creek	1828	2	119
Armstrong, Thomas	100	Little Sandy Cr.	1843	2	326
Arthur, William	130	Little Sandy Cr.	1849	2	436
Ashburn, Aaron	24	Decker's Creek	1860	1	292
Ashburn, Aaron	29	Decker's Creek	1847	2	386
Ashby, Nathan	85	Elsey's Run	1831	2	136
Ashby, Nathan	48	Wts. Cheat	1826	2	103
Ashby, Nathan	112	Snowy Creek	1823	2	76
Ashby, Nathan	200	Snowy Creek	1822	2	70
Ashby, Nathan	260	Beaver Dam Run	1821	2	62
Ashby, William	50	Wts. Yohogania	1851	2	457
Baldwin, Israel	88	Snowy Creek	1860	1	296
Baldwin, Israel	42	Adj. Claiborne Survey	1858	1	259
Baldwin, Israel	23	York's Run	1836	2	196
Baldwin, Israel	200	3 Forks Creek	1828	2	108
Baldwin, Israel	245	Raccoon Creek	1845	2	343
Baldwin, Israel	280	Roaring Creek	1854	2	499
Baldwin, Israel	500	3 Forks Creek	1855	2	504
Baldwin, Israel	10¾	Adj. B. Fairfax	1858	2	490
Baldwin, Israel	380	Pine Swamp	1851	2	450
Baldwin, Israel	52	Snowy Creek	1850	2	443
Baldwin, Israel	445	Adj. John Trembly	1848	2	408
Baldwin, Israel	350	Snowy Creek	1845	2	354
Beavers, Thomas	167	Buffalo Creek	1858	1	233
Bee, Asey	360	3 Forks Creek	1822	2	68
Benson, Joseph N.	132	Beaver Creek	1860	1	299
Bishoff, John	207	Roaring Creek	1837	2	229
Bishoff, John et al	600	Roaring Creek	1828	2	117
Bishoff, John Jr.	54	Dougherty's Run	1830	2	132
Bishoff, Joseph	160	Dougherty's Run	1826	2	99
Bishoff, William	45	Roaring Creek	1858	1	255
Bishoff, William	236	Roaring Creek	1839	2	298
Bishop, Henry	128	Station Run	1856	2	505
Bishop, John	100	Draper's Run	1823	2	73
Bishop, John	50	Adj. Henry Lewis	1821	2	63
Blaney, John H.	100	Bull Run	1853	2	488
Blaney, Jonathan	123	Bull Run	1834	2	167

Name of Grantee	Acres	Local Description	Year	Book	Page
Boger, Samuel	157	Adj. Wm. Ashby	1860	1	288
Boger, Samuel	3	Adj. John Boger	1848	2	397
Boger, Samuel	250	Sandy Creek	1849	2	437
Boger, Samuel	80	Adj. John Fike	1860	1	289
Boger, Samuel	35	Little Sandy Creek	1861	1	309
Boger, Samuel	354	Little Sandy Cr.	1860	1	302
Boger, Samuel	5	Pancheon Hill	1860	1	301
Boger, Samuel	18	Adj. Jesse Spurgen	1860	1	293
Boger, Samuel	88	Little Sandy Creek	1860	1	294
Bolyard, Lewis	86	Sandy Creek	1838	2	279
Bond, Joshua	50	Wts. Cheat	1838	2	280
Bowermaster, Simon E.	9	Big Sandy Creek	1844	2	327
Brandon, William	120	Wts. Cheat	1838	2	251
Brandon, William	50	Big Sandy Creek	1832	2	140
Brown, Ashford	7¼	Adj. Field's Survey	1851	2	475
Brown, George	40	Raccoon Creek	1826	2	97
Brown, Joseph	62	Dougherty's Run	1853	2	491
Brown, Joseph et al	400	Wts. of Cheat	1844	2	334
Brown, Joseph et al	393¾	Wts. of Cheat	1844	2	335
Brown, Samuel B.	31	Lit. Sandy Creek	1820	2	60
Brown, Thomas	16	Green's Run	1842	2	320
Brown, Thomas	490	Adj. D. Parsons	1856	2	515
Brown, William	720	3 Forks Creek	1851	2	469
Brown, William	350	3 Forks Creek	1851	2	454
Brown, William G.	540	Dillins Creek	1858	1	262
Brown, William G. et al	1,491	Cheat River	1858	1	244
Brown, William G. et al	50	Decker's Creek	1842	2	322
Brown, William G. et al	400	Adj. Thomas Johnson	1853	2	486
Brownfield, Charles	81	Buffalo Creek	1838	2	281
Bucklew, Jonas	54	Salt Lick Creek	1836	2	205
Bucklew, Philip	100	Salt Lick Creek	1825	2	87
Buckelew, William	44	Wts. of Cheat	1838	2	240
Bunker, Edward C.	300	Decker's Creek	1858	1	232
Byrne, Charles et al	32	Buckhorn Run	1824	2	80
Byrne, John P.	200	Wts. of Cheat	1838	2	250
Byrne, John P.	125	Bull Run	1857	1	229
Byrne, John P.	40	Sandy Creek	1851	2	446
Byrne, John P.	16	Big Sandy Creek	1851	2	448
Byrne, John P.	230	Big Sandy Creek	1847	2	385
Byrne, John P. et al	73	Bull Run	1858	1	260
Byrne, John P. et al	1,491	Wts. of Cheat River	1858	1	244
Byrne, John P. et al	1,000	Maple Run	1841	2	314
Byrne, John P. et al	365	Wts. of Cheat	1842	2	317
Byrne, John P. et al	50	Decker's Creek	1842	2	322
Byrne, John P. et al	600	Yougaheny River	1854	2	494
Byrne, John P. et al	130	Bull Run	1852	2	485
Byrne, John P. et al	400	Adj. Thomas Johnson	1853	2	486
Byrne, John P. et al	580	Adj. Wm. Dunn	1851	2	447
Byrne, John P. et al	382	Bull Run	1847	2	383
Byrne, John P. et al	382	Bull Run	1848	2	407
Byrne, Samuel	53	Little Sandy Cr.	1834	2	174
Cale, Jacob	15	Wts. Cheat	1841	2	308
Calvert, Enoch	114	Buffalo Creek	1822	2	71
Casad, Nathan	133	Lick Run	1833	2	159
Chitister, William	200	Big Sandy Creek	1837	2	226
Chitister, William	122	Big Sandy Cr.	1846	2	372
Chitister, William Jr.	20	Adj. James McGraw	1851	2	458
Collins, Elephalet	40	Big Sandy Creek	1859	1	279
Collins, Elephalet	14	Sandy Creek	1859	1	282
Collins, Eleplet	130	Sandy Creek	1845	2	344
Compton, Edmund H.	277	Bull Run	1841	2	309
Conley, Charles	5	Sandy Creek	1854	2	496
Conley, John	240	Lick Run	1834	2	180

Name of Grantee	Acres	Local Description	Year	Book	Page
Conley, William et al	35	Hether Run	1861	1	304
Connaught, Henry	150	Horse Shoe Run	1858	1	249
Conner, Joab G.	105	Cheat River	1858	1	264
Conner, Michael	67	Pringle's Run	1834	2	177
Conner, Michael et al	41	Lick Run	1838	2	238
Conner, William Jr.	40	Sandy Creek	1838	2	278
Cook, Thomas	97	Buffalo Creek	1858	1	245
Crain—See Crane					
Crain, Samuel	67	Muddy Creek	1824	2	78
Crain, Samuel et al	17	Muddy Creek	1823	2	75
Crane, Jacob	615	Snowy Creek	1859	1	263
Crane, Jacob	514	Snowy Creek	1859	1	266
Crane, Jacob	30	Adj. S. Titchenell	1841	2	302
Crane, Jacob	100	Dougherty's Run	1833	2	153
Crane, John	776	Muddy Creek	1858	1	256
Crane, John	500	Wts. Cheat	1838	2	282
Crane, John	491	Muddy Creek	1838	2	270
Crane, John & Calvin	346	Salt Lick Creek	1836	2	207
Crane, John et al	130	Muddy Creek	1858	1	261
Crane, Smith	86	Dougherty's Run	1848	2	409
Crane, William B. et al	150	Snowy Creek	1857	2	546
Crawford, James	21	Lit. Sandy Creek	1848	2	410
Crawford, James G.	81	Sandy Creek	1848	2	401
Criss, Isaac	120	Little Sandy Cr.	1834	2	173
Criss, Isaac	91	Little Sandy Creek	1834	2	185
Criss, Jacob	180	Muddy Creek	1836	2	211
Cresap, C. J. P. etal	40	Cheat River	1860	1	297
Cresap, C. J. P. et al	35	Hether Run	1861	1	304
Cunningham, William et al	492	Yohogania River	1838	2	248
Cupp, William	150	Pine Swamps	1837	2	225
Cuppel—or Cuppett					
Cuppel, John Jr. (Cuppett)	80	Glade Run	1833	2	157
Cuppel, John Jr. (Cuppett)	6	Lit. Sandy Cr.	1833	2	152
Cuppett, Daniel	155	Sandy Creek	1847	2	381
Dalrymple, John A.	1,961	Cheat River	1860	1	298
Dalrymple, John A.	350	Big Wolfe Creek	1861	1	305
Dalton, Nimrod (Danton)	145	Sandy Creek	1838	2	252
Danton, Nimrod (Dalton)	145	Sandy Creek	1838	2	252
Darby, Daniel	12	Wts. of Cheat River	1854	2	500
David, J. W.	53	Buffalo Creek	1858	1	246
Deal, Henry	367	Little Sandy Creek	1834	2	166
Deal, Henry	328	Buffalo Cr.	1837	2	221
Deberry, Samuel	54	Beaver Creek	1846	2	361
Denison, James	63½	Big Sandy Creek	1832	2	141
Dennison, James	170	Caniday Fork	1836	2	209
Dewit, Henry	100	Salt Lick Creek	1825	2	86
Dille, John A.	7	Cheat River	1860	1	295
Dille, John A.	910	Sandy Creek	1856	2	524
Dodge, Austin	100	Wts. of Cheat	1857	2	531
Dorsey, Caleb	13½	Laurel Run	1853	2	492
Drabell, John R.	176	Laurel Run	1858	1	257
Durant, William	95	Wts. of Cheat	1847	2	396
Eliason, Jeremiah (Ellison)	61	Adj. Claiborne	1838	2	254
Elliott, Mary et al	50	German Settlement	1858	1	231
Elliott, William	61½	Drape's Run	1824	2	83
Elliott, William	90	Roaring Creek	1824	2	84
Elliott, William	23	Drape's Run	1824	2	81
Elliott, William	80	Wts. Cheat River	1825	2	94
Elliott, William et al	520	Pine Swamps	1826	2	98
Ellison, Jeremiah (Eliason)	61	Adj. Claiborne	1838	2	254
Evans, David	51	Adj. J. Yotter	1848	2	399
Everley, Peter	81	Big Sandy Creek	1838	2	253
Everly, Henry	55	Wts. of Cheat	1848	2	411

Name of Grantee	Acres	Local Description	Year	Book	Page
Everly, Lewis	150	Muddy Creek	1838	2	283
Everly, Peter	54	Big Sandy Creek	1845	2	353
Fairfax, Buckner	96	Muddy Creek	1834	2	165
Fairfax, Buckner	200	Lit. Sandy Cr.	1822	2	69
Fairfax, Buckner	6½	Wts. of Cheat	1851	2	459
Fairfax, Buckner	120	Elsey's Run	1851	2	461
Fairfax, Buckner	50	Elsey's Run	1851	2	460
Fairfax, Buckner	600	Wts. of Cheat	1851	2	462
Fairfax, Buckner	1,000	Martin's Run	1838	2	570
Fairfax, Buckner	190	Adj. John Ralston	1828	2	111
Fairfax, Buckner	116	Adj. Wm. Conner	1828	2	109
Fairfax, Buckner	116	Little Sandy Cr.	1838	2	284
Fairfax, Buckner	350	3 Forks Creek	1836	2	197
Fairfax, Buckner	78	Elsey's Run	1859	1	267
Fairfax, Buckner	800	Cheat River	1859	1	265
Fairfax, Buckner	125	3 Forks	1859	1	269
Fairfax, Buckner	420	Glade Run	1859	1	270
Fairfax, Buckner	3,350	Adj. Laidley Survey	1859	1	272
Fairfax, Buckner	100	Field's Creek	1846	2	365
Fairfax, Buckner	570	Cheat River	1859	1	268
Fairfax, Buckner et al	2,000	Wts. of Cheat	1846	2	362
Fairfax, Buckner et al	1,400	Elsey's Run	1842	2	572
Fairfax, Buckner et al	41	Lick Run	1838	2	238
Fairfax, Buckner et al	16	Adj. Peter Matheny	1847	2	384
Fairfax, Buckner et al	1,600	Wts. Cheat River	1842	2	574
Fairfax, William	450	3 Forks Creek	1828	2	113
Falkinstine, Samuel	13	Adj. D. Goodwin	1848	2	420
Fear, Joseph	119	Adj. D. Evans	1848	2	400
Feathers, Jacob	20	Green's Run	1831	2	137
Feathers, James	100	Roaring Creek	1835	2	190
Feathers, John	123	Roaring Creek	1857	2	538
Felton, John	210	Wts. Cheat	1838	2	256
Fields, Hiram	100	Paint Bank Run	1836	2	195
Fields, Israel B. & Elizabeth	100	Cheat River Hill	1859	1	285
Fike, John	388	Sandy Creek	1848	2	412
Fitchenall, Stephen	110	Wts. of Cheat	1825	2	93
Flinn, Peter et al	240(340)	Snowy Creek	1844	2	336
Foreman, Joseph	165	Muddy Creek	1838	2	239
Foreman, Joseph Jr.	60	Muddy Creek	1838	2	255
Forman, Joseph	272	Muddy Creek	1838	2	277
Forman, Joseph	165	N. E. Bank Muddy Cr.	1838	2	239
Forman, Richard	500	Coiner's Run	1838	2	275
Forman, Richard	100	Huckleberry Run	1838	2	285
Forman, Robert	112	Wts. Cheat	1838	2	276
Forman, William	75	Muddy Creek	1849	2	432
Forman, William	52	Wts. Cheat	1847	2	387
Fortney, Joshua	46	Raccoon Creek	1827	2	104
Frankhouser, Peter	200	Sandy Creek	1857	2	539
Frazer, Isaac	100	Little Sandy Creek	1854	2	497
Freeland, James	100	Nettle Ridge	1834	2	171
Funk, Jacob	783	Wts. of Cheat	1856	2	525
Funkhouser—or Frankhouser					
Gabel, William (Gable)	500	Muddy Creek	1824	2	85
Gabel, William (Gable)	300	Muddy Creek	1825	2	90
Gandy, Levi	138	3 Forks Creek	1823	2	74
Gandy, Owen	160	3 Forks Creek	1846	2	367
Gandy, Samuel	55	Laurel Run	1819	2	58
Garner, Alfred	36	Wts. Cheat	1841	2	312
Gibson, Levi	5½	Sovereign's Run	1848	2	415
Gibson, Robert	36	Big Sandy Creek	1830	2	127
Glenn, Elias B.	95	Big Sandy	1838	2	257
Glover, Benjamin et al	467	Sandy Creek	1827	2	105
Glover, William	30	Sandy Creek	1850	2	441

Name of Grantee	Acres	Local Description	Year	Book	Page
Hersman, Mark C.	80	Canady Fork	1838	2	288
Hill, Joseph	74	Big Sandy Creek	1834	2	163
Hill, Joseph	140	Sandy Creek	1838	2	287
Hill, Joseph	128	Big Sandy Creek	1838	2	258
Holme, John M.	17	Snowy Creek	1861	1	306
Hooten, A. L. et al	40	Cheat River	1860	1	297
Hoye, John (Hoy)	72	Potomac River	1844	2	337
Hoye, John (Hoy)	36	Beaver Creek	1844	2	332
Hoye, John	180	Laurel Run	1844	2	339
Hoye, John	655	Madison Run	1844	2	340
Hoye, John	3,000	Laurel Run	1844	2	569
Hoye, John	280	Wts. of Cheat	1848	2	406
Hoye, John	560	Snowy Creek	1847	2	388
Hoye, John	180	Beaver Creek	1847	2	373
Hoye, John	27	Little Sandy Creek	1831	2	133
Hoye, John	74	Sandy Creek	1842	2	316
Hoye, John	500	Wts. of Yohogania	1843	2	323
Huddleson, Jonathan	28½	Decker's Creek	1860	1	290
Ingle, Adam	96	Adj. John Thomas	1838	2	289
Jackson, Samuel	86	Nettle Ridge	1833	2	158
James, Isaac	220	Adj. Daniel Griffy	1839	2	297
Jefferes—or Jeffers					
Jefferes, Abraham et al	30	Roaring Creek	1825	2	89
Jefferes, Abraham et al	173	Roaring Creek	1825	2	88
Jeffers, or Jefferes					
Jeffers, Abraham et al	520	Pine Swamps	1826	2	98
Jeffers, Amos	121	Beaver Creek	1846	2	360
Jenkins, Evan et al	32	Sovern's Run	1836	2	206
Jenkins, Evan, John & Graham	95	Wts. of Cheat	1848	2	421
Jenkins, Graham	130	Wts. of Cheat	1857	2	541
Jenkins, James	8¾	Big Sandy Creek	1837	2	213
Jenkins, James	8½	Wts. of Cheat River	1855	2	501
Jenkins, John	22	Sovern's Run	1846	2	368
Jenkins, Jonathan	17	Big Sandy Creek	1825	2	101
Jenkins, Thomas	11	Sandy Creek	1825	2	91
Johnson, Andrew	210	Morgan's Run	1825	2	96
Johnson, Wick et al	860	Big Sandy Creek	1837	2	231
Jones, Laura M.	943	Adj. Alex. Turney	1856	2	522
Jones, Laura M.	499	Wts. of Cheat	1856	2	523
Jones, Laura M.	1,106	Wts. of Cheat	1856	2	527
Kelly, John	12	Adj. D. Wolf	1848	2	417
Kelly, John	25	Beaver Creek	1837	2	232
Kelly, William J.	20	3 Forks Creek	1856	2	514
Kelsey, Robert	400	Wts. Cheat	1839	2	300
Knotts, Absolom	41	Big Sandy Creek	1834	2	178
Ladd, John H.	268	Dougherty's Run	1841	2	301
Lawson, Alexandria	100	Wts. Cheat	1839	2	299
Lawson, Benjamin	105	Big Sandy Creek	1845	2	352
Lawson, Benjamin	50	Big Sandy Creek	1845	2	350
Lawson, Benjamin	100	Big Sandy Creek	1834	2	160
Lawson, Joshua	16	Wts. of Cheat	1851	2	473
Leach, Jesse	200	Dougherty's Run	1830	2	122
Leach, Jesse	109	Muddy Creek	1830	2	131
Lemon—or Semon					
Lemon, James (Semon)	100	Lit. Sandy Cr.	1820	2	59
Lewis, John	120	Dougherty's Run	1857	2	532
Line—or Sine					
Line, Henry et al	520	Pine Swamps	1826	2	98
Lipscomb, Fielding	50	Cheat River	1860	1	303
Lister, George (Sisler)	48	Muddy Creek	1845	2	349
Liston, Abraham	40	Adj. Jacob Cole	1836	2	203
Liston, Abraham	3½ (3¼)	Wts. of Cheat	1856	2	508
Ludington, Horace	286	Little Sandy Cr.	1834	2	172

Name of Grantee	Acres	Local Description	Year	Book	Page
Nines, Elias	44	Salt Lick Creek	1858	1	235
Nines, Elias	50	Salt Lick Creek	1858	1	236
Nines, Elias	500	Salt Lick Creek	1858	1	234
Owens, Thomas	43	Cor. Fisher	1858	1	241
Owens, Thomas	1,900	Horse Shoe Run	1858	1	240
Owens, Thomas	50	Horse Shoe Run	1858	1	239
Owens, Thomas	465	Adj. Rudolph Heckart	1858	1	238
Owens, Thomas	114	Horse Shoe Run	1858	1	237
Owens, Thomas	500	Buffalo Creek	1857	2	533
Owens, Thomas	300	Salt Lick Creek	1856	2	506
Parsons, David	70	Bunyon's Run	1838	2	292
Patton, Caleb A.	207	Roaring Creek	1837	2	228
Pearce, George	83	Canady's Fork	1838	2	262
Pearce, Jesse	106	Canady's Fork	1838	2	261
Pearse, George	84	Big Sandy Creek	1834	2	162
Pell, Hezekiah	84	Wts. Cheat	1838	2	260
Pell, Hezekiah	10	Wts. Cheat	1832	2	139
Percy, James et al	1,578	Snowy Creek	1856	2	518
Poston, John H.	10	Mill Race	1852	2	484
Potter, John & William	120	Adj. I. Baldwin	1857	2	548
Price, James A. et al	54½	Morgan's Run	1838	2	273
Prunty, John Jr.	100	Big Sandy Creek	1837	2	235
Purinton, D. B.	616	Buffalo Creek	1858	1	248
Purinton, Orpheus	565	Buffalo Creek	1858	1	243
Radabough—See Rodebough					
Ravenscraft, Abner	9	Cheat River	1857	1	217
Readhaver—See Rodehaver					
Reshal—See Rishel					
Ridgeway, Elihue	55	Big Sandy Creek	1833	2	145
Rinehart, Thomas	100	Adj. Wm. Wiles	1851	2	452
Ringer, Coonrod	12	Muddy Creek	1859	1	283
Ringer, Jacob	6½	Sandy Creek	1858	1	253
Ringer, Jacob et al	467	Sandy Creek	1827	2	105
Ringer, Lewis	240	Mill Run	1849	2	440
Rishel, John	98	Little Sandy Creek	1828	2	118
Rishel, John (Reshal)	10	Adj. John Morris	1838	2	237
Robertson, James	139	Horse Shoe Run	1838	2	244
Robinson, William	100	Adj. L. Vansickle	1848	2	402
Robinson, William	528	Little Sandy Creek	1847	2	395
Rodebough, George et al	73	Bull Run	1858	1	260
Rodebough, George et al	130	Bull Run	1852	2	485
Rodebough, George et al	580	Adj. Wm. Dunn	1851	2	447
Rodehaver, Rodeheaver, Rodehafer					
Rodehaver, Jacob	64	Little Sandy Creek	1820	2	61
Rodehaver, John	297	Spring Run	1836	2	212
Rodehaver, John	5	Crab Orchard	1859	1	274
Rodeheaver, Rodehaver, Rodehafer					
Rodeheaver, Samuel (Readhaver)	5¾	Brandonville	1838	2	243
Rodeheaver, Samuel	176	Little Sandy Creek	1832	2	142
Rogers, Archibald	30	3 Forks Creek	1859	1	286
Royse, John	19	Wts. Cheat River	1826	2	102
Royse, John	162	Little Sandy Creek	1834	2	176
Royse, John et al	393¾	Wts. of Cheat	1844	2	335
Royse, John et al	400	Wts. of Cheat	1844	2	334
Royse, Moses	15	Sandy Creek	1849	2	438
Royse, Moses	50	Big Sandy Creek	1838	2	246
Royse, Moses	200	Little Sandy Creek	1838	2	245
Sanderson, Joseph	72	Muddy Creek	1825	2	77
Sargent, David	68	Big Sandy Creek	1837	2	230
Schletter, Henry	210	Horse Shoe Run	1857	1	221
Schletter, John H.	140	Horse Shoe Run	1857	1	220
Scott, David	174	Hazel Run	1848	2	422
Scott, John	63	Big Sandy Creek	1827	2	106

Name of Grantee	Acres	Local Description	Year	Book	Page
Scott, Thomas	125½	Big Sandy Creek	1846	2	364
Scott, Thomas et al	316	Sandy Creek	1848	2	416
Sease, David (Seese)	235	Sandy Creek	1851	2	474
Sell, Enos	250	Horse Shoe Run	1857	1	223
Sell, Henry J.	100	Horse Shoe Run	1857	1	222
Semon or Lemon					
Semon, James (Lemon)	100	Lit. Sandy Creek	1820	2	59
Serpell, Jane P.	338	Salt Lick Creek	1857	1	230
Shackleford, Joseph	150	3 Forks Creek	1838	2	271
Shafer—Shaffer, Shaver					
Shafer, Daniel Acres	150	Sandy Creek	1837	2	224
Shafer, John	100	Big Sandy Creek	1834	2	188
Shaffer, Benjamin & Elias	200	Snowy Creek	1845	2	359
Shaffer, Harriett et al	50	German Settlement	1858	1	231
Shaffer, Henry	900	Crites' Mill Road	1856	2	526
Shaffer, John Jr.	97	Horse Shoe Run	1857	1	224
Shahan—See Shehan, Strahan					
Shahan, George	105	Big Sandy Creek	1838	2	263
Shahan, George	84	Sandy Creek	1838	2	294
Shahan, John	34	Little Sandy Cr.	1838	2	296
Shahan, Reuben	18	Sandy Creek	1849	2	430
Shehan, David	45	Little Sandy Cr.	1833	2	147
Shehan, Jones	45	Little Sandy Creek	1833	2	144
Shehan, Joshua	50	Big Sandy Creek	1836	2	208
Shaver—or Shafer, Shaffer					
Shaver, Benjamin	101	Salt Lick Creek	1846	2	363
Shaw, Alexander	100	Parker's Run	1830	2	130
Shaw, Benjamin	43	Little Sandy Creek	1833	2	151
Shaw, Benjamin	68	Old Lewis Survey	1848	2	398
Shaw, Benjamin	19	Little Sandy Creek	1828	2	112
Shaw, Benjamin	20	Muddy Creek	1828	2	110
Simer, David P.	98½	Brain's Run	1824	2	79
Simpson, John	60	Sandy Creek	1838	2	291
Simpson, Samuel	120	Old Field Lick	1838		293
Sinclair,Alexander	18	Sandy Creek	1857	2	536
Sine—See Line					
Sisler, George(Lister)	48	Muddy Creek	1845	2	349
Sisler, Jacob	70	Worley's Run	1834	2	184
Smith or Smyth, Smythe					
Smith, Aaron	500	Little Sandy Creek	1836	2	191
Smith, George (of A.)	50	Adj. Amos Hawley	1856	2	521
Smith, George (of A.)	1,108	Horse Shoe Run	1856	2	519
Smith, George (of A.)	250	Adj. Henry Fortney	1856	2	520
Smith, George (of A.)	105	Adj. S. Squires	1856	2	517
Smith, George (of A.)	26	Cheat River	1858	1	242
Smith, George (of Alexander)	275	Muddy Creek	1850	2	445
Smith, Henry	8	Sandy Creek	1849	2	435
Smith, Jacob	17	Crab Orchard	1860	1	291
Smith, Jacob Sr.	100	Big Sandy Creek	1834	2	189
Smith, Jehu	85	Lit. Sandy Creek	1847	2	376
Smith, Joseph M.	38	Adj. J. Cale	1848	2	418
Smith, Nathan M.	50	Parker's Run	1861	1	308
Smith, Samuel	67	Little Sandy Creek	1828	2	114
Smith, William	50	Parker's Run	1845	2	347
Smith, William	11	Brown's Run	1847	2	375
Smythe or Smith					
Smythe, Jacob	530	Big Sandy Creek	1828	2	120
Snyder, Abraham	100	Nettle Ridge	1836	2	193
Snyder, Jacob	183	Nettle Ridge	1836	2	198
Spark, Samuel	1¼	Adj. Deakins	1837	2	215
Spurgeon—Spurgin					
Spurgeon, Jesse	93	Laurel Run	1834	2	164
Spurgeon, Jesse	240	Buffalo Run	1837	2	233

Name of Grantee	Acres	Local Description	Year	Book	Page
Turney, Henry	25½	Beaver Creek	1847	2	390
Uenstol, John (Umpstott)	35	Sandy Creek	1837	2	234
Umpstott, John (Uenstol)	35	Sandy Creek	1837	2	234
Vanmeter, David & Janet et al	492	Yohogania River	1838	2	248
Vansickle, David	84	Peter Fike's Mill	1833	2	148
Vansickle, David	100	Buffalo Run	1834	2	170
Vansickle, Lewis	120	Buffalo Creek	1834	2	179
Wall, Charles	112	Adj. James Walls	1838	2	268
Walls, Charles	217	Big Sandy Creek	1845	2	357
Walls, George	40	Sandy Creek	1858	1	252
Walls, James	103	Big Sandy Creek	1838	2	267
Walls, Solomon	36	Wts. Cheat	1847	2	379
Warman, James	160	Adj. Wm. Dunn	1845	2	346
Watring, Frederick	233	Adj. John D. Stemple	1857	1	226
Watring, Frederick et al	200	Wts. of Potomac	1851	2	470
Watring, Jacob	53	Horse Shoe Run	1849	2	429
Watring, Jacob P.	198	Cheat River	1858	1	247
Watring, John A.	½	German Settlement	1858	1	250
Watring, John C. & Daniel	160	Adj. D. Stemple	1851	2	465
Watring, Nicholas	138	Horse Shoe Run	1858	1	251
Watring, Peter	100	Horse Shoe Run	1858	1	254
Watts, William	100	Big Sandy Creek	1834	2	186
Weaver, Willima (Weever)	85	Dunkard's Creek	1836	2	202
Welch, John	281	Muddy Creek	1847	2	380
Wheeler, Henry H.	90	Horse Shoe Run	1857	1	227
Wheeler, Smith et al	123	Sandy Creek	1856	2	528
Wheeler, William	98	Adj. Jacob Watring	1844	2	333
Wheeler, William	56	Wts. Yohogania	1844	2	330
White, Henry	47	Adj. Baldwin Vanmeter	1852	2	483
White, John	78	Wts. of Cheat	1851	2	466
White, John	110	Glade Run	1851	2	467
White, John Jr.	55	Briery Run	1851	2	468
Wile, Henry Jr.	79	Salt Lick Creek	1836	2	200
Wile, Henry L.	26	Wts. of Cheat	1856	2	507
Wile, William J. (or I.)	38	Wts. of Cheat	1856	2	511
Wilhelm, Solomon	22	Roaring Creek	1854	2	498
Wilkins, John	47	Little Sandy Cree	1834	2	175
Willey, Waitman T. et al	580	Adj. Wm. Dunn	1851	2	447
Williams, William	100	Martin's Run	1825	2	92
Willitts, Jesse	9	Glade Run	1827	2	107
Wilman, William	100	Cheat River	1857	1	228
Wilson, E. C.	141	3 Forks Creek	1857	1	225
Wilson, E. C.	250	Sandy Creek	1859	1	275
Wilson, E. C. et al	600	Yougaheny River	1853	2	494
Wilson, Edgar C.	600	Decker's Creek	1842	2	318
Wilson, Edgar C.	413	Deckard's Creek	1854	2	495
Wilson, Norval	500	Wts. of Cheat	1857	2	534
Wolf, Augustine	150	Hoyle's Run	1851	2	449
Wolf, David	96	Adj. Dugan's Line	1830	2	124
Wolf, Joseph	180	Salt Lick Creek	1830	2	123
Yatter—or Yotter					
Yotten, Joseph	112	Laurel Run	1847	2	391
Yotter—or Yatter					
Yotter, Joseph	112	Laurel Run	1847	2	391
Yotter, Joseph	18	Adj. Evans	1848	2	404
Yotter, Joseph	240	Little Sandy	1848	2	405
Zinn, George D.	28	Preston Glades	1839	2	295
Zinn, Henderson B.	75	Decker's Creek	1843	2	325
Zinn, Henderson B.	133	Decker's Creek	1846	2	370
Zinn, William B.	274	3 Forks Creek	1838	2	269
Zinn, William B.	10	Adj. J. Fairfax	1842	2	319
Zweyer, John	70	Sovern Run	1846	2	369

PUTNAM COUNTY

Name of Grantee	Acres	Local Description	Year	Book	Page
Alford, William	336	Rock Camp	1859	1	372
Arbough, Henry	50	Lick Creek	1855	1	328
Atkinson, John W.	180	18 Miles Creek	1858	1	360
Beckett, William	155	Buzzard's Branch	1856	1	338
Bias—See Byas					
Billups, Peter	15	Trace Fork	1856	1	332
Billips, S. L.	47	Harvey's Creek	1857	1	352
Bowyer, John	1,030	18 Mile Creek	1854	1	323
Bowyer, John	115	Poplar Fork	1853	1	322
Brown, John J. et al	2,000	18 Mile Creek	1859	1	379
Buck, Robert	490	18 Mile Creek	1860	1	386
Byas, Absolom	100	Trace Fork	1859	1	375
Byram, Benjamin P.	980	Pocataligo	1860	1	385
Byram, Benjamin P.	2,750	18 Mile Creek	1856	1	337
Byram, Benjamin P.	220	Buffalo Creek	1851	1	315
Byram, Benjamin P. et al	2,000	18 Mile Creek	1859	1	379
Carpenter, Andrew	91	Lick Creek	1855	1	330
Carpenter, Lewis	55	Lick Creek	1857	1	353
Carpenter, Lewis	34	Trace Fork	1857	1	354
Clendenen, William	116	18 Mile Creek	1858	1	363
Crago, James et al	190	18 Mile Creek	1860	1	390
Crago, Sarah	200	Pocataligo	1860	1	387
Cyrus, James S. (Cyres)	99	Big Hurricane Cr.	1857	1	345
Dodd, James (Dood)	260	Climer's Creek	1856	1	331
Dudding, John et al (Dodding)	264	Cow Creek	1849	1	311
Duke, George W.	92	Panther Creek	1852	1	319
Ellis, Alfred A.	14	Poplar Fork	1858	1	365
Ellis, Alfred et al	264	Cow Creek	1849	1	311
Fisher, Leonard C.	157	18 Mile Creek	1858	1	362
Givenden—or Gividen, Jividen					
Givenden, John	184	Mud Lick	1851	1	316
Gividen—or Givenden, Jividen					
Gividen, Ezekiel	99	18 Mile Creek	1857	1	348
Good, George	220	Buffalo Creek	1854	1	325
Grass, Edward Jr.	117	Gum Hollow	1858	1	356
Grass, Edward Jr.	420	Bridge Creek	1857	1	347
Grass, William	7	Trace Fork	1859	1	374
Grass, William	78	Trace Creek	1859	1	373
Grass, William et al	511	Lick Creek	1856	1	334
Grass, William et al	492	Trace Fork	1856	1	333
Hale, John P. et al	5,938	Poca River	1859	1	369
Harmon, John A.	521	18 Mile Creek	1858	1	357
Harmon, Thomas A.	170	Lick Creek	1857	1	341
Harvey, R. T.	429	Trace Creek	1859	1	366
Harvey, R. T. et al	2,000	18 Mile Creek	1859	1	379
Harvey, Robert T. et al	190	18 Mile Creek	1860	1	390
Harvey, Robert T. et al	196	18 Mile Creek	1860	1	391
Harvey, Robert T. & J. C. B.	1,250	Luke's Branch	1849	1	312
Hedrick, Henry	200	18 Mile Creek	1860	1	384
Hedrick, John	287	18 Mile Creek	1859	1	380
Hensley, Benjamin	1,428	Pocataligo	1861	1	393
Hensley, James A.	34	Lick Creek	1851	1	317
Henson, John Sr.	218	Turkey Branch	1859	1	382
Higginbotham, George W.	100	18 Mile Creek	1860	1	392
Higginbotham, James et al	196	18 Mile Creek	1860	1	391
Higginbotham, James & William	295½	18 Mile Creek	1860	1	388
Hill, Aaron et al	186	18 Mile Creek	1858	1	358
Hill, William	432	18 Mile Creek	1857	1	349
Hutten, Joseph	100	Pocataligo	1858	1	361
Jenkins, Samuel K.	470	Adj. George Bowers	1853	1	321

Name of Grantee	Acres	Local Description	Year	Book	Page
Jividen—Givenden, Gividen					
Jividen, Ezekiel	113	18 Mile Creek	1859	1	383
Matthews, William	43	Sycamore Creek	1857	1	355
McCallister, A. J. et al	511	Lick Creek	1856	1	334
McCallister, James	240	Trace Fork	1859	1	370
McCallister, James	190	Trace Fork	1859	1	368
McCallister, Joseph	15	Trace Fork	1859	1	367
McMullen, William A. et al	5,938	Poca River	1859	1	369
Mines or Mynes					
Mines, Levi	45	Adj. Isaac Mines	1851	1	314
Mourning, Joshua	61	Pigeon Roost	1857	1	350
Mynes or Mines					
Mynes, Levi	140	Adj. Isaac Mynes	1852	1	320
Paul, Hugh	135	Lick Creek	1857	1	340
Paul, James	92	Lick Creek	1857	1	351
Paul, Lee	140	Long Hollow	1857	1	342
Paul, Thomas	112	Rider's Branch	1855	1	326
Pfost, Jonathan	292½	18 Mile Creek	1855	1	327
Ray, John E.	190	18 Mile Creek	1859	1	371
Rayburn, Bennett	286	13 Mile Creek	1859	1	381
Roberts, Alexander B.	33	Brown's Creek	1850	1	313
Russel, John	100	18 Mile Creek	1858	1	359
Sanders, Russel	200	Pocataligo Creek	1852	1	318
Sanders, Russel	36	Pocataligo	1856	1	335
Sanders, Russel	149	Pocataligo	1856	1	336
Short, William D. et al	1,000	Null's Branch	1858	1	364
Sigman, Jacob M.	580	18 Mile Creek	1859	1	376
Steward, James et al	1,000	Null's Branch	1858	1	364
Thomas, John C.	20	18 Mile Creek	1859	1	377
Thomas, John C.	88	18 Mile Creek	1859	1	378
Thompson, R. N. B. et al	492	Trace Fork	1856	1	333
Thompson, R. N. B. et al	511	Lick Creek	1856	1	334
Vickers, Thomas A. et al	186	18 Mile Creek	1858	1	358
Webb, Edward	37	Sycamore Creek	1857	1	346
Webb, Edward	295	Sycamore Creek	1857	1	343
Webb, Edward	12	Sycamore Creek	1857	1	344
Wheeler, John	85	Kelly's Branch	1857	1	339
Whittington, William	40	18 Mile Creek	1854	1	324
Young, Amos H.	539	Harvey's Creek	1855	1	329

RALEIGH COUNTY

Beckett, John H. (Beckert)	246¼	Sand Lick	1861	1	7
Beckett, John H. (Beckert)	468¾	Paint Creek	1861	1	5
Harper, Jacob	485	Marsh Fork	1856	1	451
Harper, Jacob	80	Paint Creek	1856	1	3
Jerral, James	13a.8r.	Marsh Fork	1860	1	4
McGinnis, Achiles	88¼	Crab Orchard	1855	1	1
McGinnis, Pyrrhus	555½	Marsh Fork	1854	1	450
Riffe, Henry M.	1,791⅜	Marsh Fork	1862	1	454
Smith, Canady	125½	Paint Creek	1861	1	6
Williams, John	70	Paint Creek	1856	1	2
Williams, John	195¾	Paint Creek	1861	1	8
Wilson, Andrew Sr.	1,500	Marsh Fork	1857	1	452

RANDOLPH COUNTY

Name of Grantee	Acres	Local Description	Year	Book	Page
Adams, Richard Jr. et al	50,000	Birch River	1800	2	250
Alexander, Alexander	1,000	Burgoo Creek	1794	1	272
Alexander, Alexander	1,000	Burgoo Creek	1794	1	273
Alexander, Alexander	1,000	Wts. of Elk	1794	1	274
Alexander, Alexander	1,000	Burgoo Creek	1794	1	275
Anderson, Alen	120	Stuart Run	1849	1	546
Anderson, William	100	Wts. Valley River	1841	3	306
Angell, Israel	1,000	Mill Creek	1791	1	156
Anglin, Adrian	100	Leatherwood	1813	2	478
Arbogast, John	63½	Haddin's Run	1836	3	201
Arbogast, John	72	Stuart's Run	1836	3	208
Arbogast, John	69	Stuart's Run	1842	3	342
Armentrout, Aaron	600	Rich Mountain	1842	3	349
Armentrout, Christopher	200	Dry Fork	1851	4	10
Armentrout, Christopher	205	Rich Mountain	1840	3	298
Armentrout, Christopher	500	Laurel Fork	1840	3	289
Armentrout, Christopher	190	Rich Mountain	1840	3	297
Armentrout, Christopher	320	Dry Fork	1844	3	387
Armentrout, Christopher	218	Dry Fork	1792	1	208
Armentrout, Christopher et al	702	Middle Mountain	1857	4	405
Armentrout, Christopher et al	660	Dry Fork	1853	3	563
Armstead, William et al	2,000	Wts. of Cheat	1795	1	362
Armstrong, William D.	30	Cassadie's Fork	1860	4	493
Armstrong, William D.	108	Cassiday's Fork	1859	4	478
Armstrong, William D.	84	Cassiday's Fork	1859	4	477
Armstrong, William D. et al	124	Cassadie's Fork	1860	4	505
Armstrong, William D. et al	171	Cassadie's Fork	1860	4	507
Armstrong, William D. et al	160	Cassadie's Fork	1860	4	485
Arnold, George	261	Sugar Creek	1793	1	260
Arnold, James	400	Cove Creek	1795	1	358
Arnold, James	455	Cove Run	1801	2	309
Arnold, James	455	Fork Lick	1800	2	305
Arnold, James	761	Wts. Tygert's Valley	1800	2	277
Arnold, James	1,000	Glady Fork	1800	2	272
Arnold, James	200	Fork Ridge	1800	2	266
Arnold, James	300	Buffalo Lick Creek	1800	2	265
Arnold, James	135	Dry Fork	1799	2	177
Arnold, James	1,550	Sandy Creek (Gandy)	1792	1	213
Arnold, Jonathan	97	Gandy Creek	1852	4	120
Arnold, Jonathan	500	Roaring Creek	1852	4	157
Arnold, Jonathan	1,000	Middle Fork	1856	4	366
Arnold, Jonathan	370	Roaring Creek	1858	4	436
Arnold, Jonathan	416	Leatherwood	1850	1	542
Arnold, Jonathan	3,080	Sugar Creek	1851	4	517
Arnold, Jonathan	983	Roaring Creek	1850	2	612
Arnold, Jonathan	100	Gandy Creek	1850	1	458
Arnold, Jonathan	787	Leatherwood	1851	1	493
Arnold, Jonathan	770	Roaring Creek	1850	1	527
Arnold, Jonathan et al	52	Shaver's Mtn.	1851	4	50
Arnold, Jonathan et al	600	Black Fork	1851	4	74
Arnold, Jonathan et al	692	Rich Mountain	1851	4	75
Arnold, Jonathan et al	104	Cheat Mountain	1852	4	104
Arnold, Jonathan et al	2,297	Dry Fork	1852	4	113
Arnold, Jonathan et al	233	Mill Run	1852	4	119
Arnold, Jonathan et al	382	Wts. Holly	1852	4	149
Arnold, Jonathan et al	390	Wts. Buckhannon	1852	4	135
Arnold, Jonathan et al	400	Shaver's Fork	1852	4	167
Arnold, Jonathan et al	300	Shaver's Fork	1853	4	241
Arnold, Jonathan et al	2,447	Middle Fork	1853	4	214
Arnold, Jonathan et al	228	Big Run	1852	4	184
Arnold, Jonathan et al	3,000	Wts. Middle Fork	1853	4	258

Name of Grantee	Acres	Local Description	Year	Book	Page
Banks, Henry	1,000	Rock Camp Creek	1790	1	88
Banks, Henry	1,000	Burgas Creek (Burgoo)	1790	1	87
Barnhouse, Solomon	406¾	Sugar Creek	1826	3	97
Barns, Asa et al	26,622	Old Field Fork	1797	1	438
Barr, James et al	400	Wts. Buckhannon	1789	1	51
Barr, James et al	1,920	Middle Fork	1789	1	50
Barr, James et al	1,920	Middle Fork	1789	1	49
Barr, James et al	1,920	Middle Fork	1789	1	48
Barr, James et al	1,920	Middle Fork	1789	1	46
Barr, James et al	1,920	Middle Fork	1789	1	47
Barr, Ozias & Peter	20,000	Wts. Cheat	1796	2	44
Barton, Jeremiah & Jane	1,000	Gauley River	1799	2	168
Barton, Richard W. et al	600	Black Fork	1851	4	74
Baxter, George	500	Raccoon Creek	1788	1	3
Beall, Alexander	875	Shaver's Run	1790	1	77
Beall, Brooke	500	Wts. Cheat	1788	1	23
Beall, Brooke	500	Barker's Settlement	1789	1	27
Beall, William M.	800	Harmon's Run	1798	2	151
Beard, David	267	Leading Creek	1793	1	271
Beckley, John et al	21,401	Wts. Elk	1798	2	160
Beckley, John et al	38,742	Wts. Elk	1798	2	159
Bell, Broke	125	Wts. Valley River	1793	1	256
Bell, Broke	500	Wts. Valley River	1793	1	255
Bell, Broke	493	Wts. Valley River	1793	1	254
Bell, Broke	382	Valley River	1793	1	253
Bell, Broke	500	Wts. of Cheat	1793	1	279
Bell, William	237	Bowling Run	1816	2	506
Benet—Bennett					
Benet, Mary et al	314	Stone Coal	1791	1	131
Bennett, David & J. M.	2,190	Lick Run	1850	1	529
Bennett, Jacob S.	60	Sugar Creek	1838	3	273
Bennett, James	1,500	Adj. J. Sponogle	1853	4	244
Bennett, Jonathan M. & David et al	1,990	Wts. Buckhannon River	1850	1	469
Bennett, Jonathan M. et al	990	Back Fork Elk	1854	4	277
Bennett, Jonathan M. et al	540	Point Mountain	1858	4	442
Bennett, Jonathan M. et al	2,200	Fall Run	1854	4	548
Bennett, Jonathan M. et al	1,990	Ten Mile Creek	1850	2	610
Bennett, Jonathan M. et al	500	Wts. Buckhannon River	1850	1	463
Berlin, Frederick	211	Clover Run	1857	4	401
Berlin, Frederick et al	1,000	Adj. Adam Harper	1857	4	560
Berlin, Frederick et al	5,000	Clover Run	1857	4	567
Berlin, George W.	2,500	Leading Creek	1850	2	604
Berlin, George W.	1,650	Dry Fork	1849	3	582
Bickle, Christian	75	Wts. Holly	1820	2	519
Bickle, Jacob	155	Shaver's Mt.	1794	1	324
Bingham, Samuel	95½	Eberson's Creek	1793	3	74
Bishop, Samuel G.	219	Leading Creek	1820	3	28
Bishop, Samuel G.	250	Leading Creek	1820	3	27
Blackman, David	3¼	Leading Creek	1857	4	421
Blackman, David	1,000	Black Fork	1852	4	185
Blackman, David	5	Wts. Tygert's Valley	1836	3	195
Blackman, David	88	Wts. Valley River	1838	3	274
Blackman, David	9	Wts. Cheat	1850	1	476
Blackman, David	90	Black Fork	1850	1	477
Blackman, David	43½	Leading Creek	1851	1	494
Blagg, Samuel et al	50,000	Wts. Cheat	1797	2	62
Bliss, George et al	114,000	Wts. Monon. River	1797	2	61
Bogard, Cornelius	243	Adj. James Westfall	1793	1	259
Bogard, Cornelius et al	100,000	Middle Fork	1796	1	374
Boggess, Caleb Jr. et al	1,895	Wts. Elk	1852	4	109
Boggess, Caleb Jr.	500	Wts. Buckhannon River	1850	1	463
Boggess, Caleb Jr.	790	Jenk's Fork	1851	1	495
Boggs, Francis	164	Wts. Elk	1813	2	471

Name of Grantee	Acres	Local Description	Year	Book	Page
Chenoweth, Archibald	185	File's Creek	1852	4	187
Chenoweth, Elijah & Thomas	22	Pond Lick Run	1860	4	494
Chenoweth, Elijah & Thomas	150	Pond Lick Run	1851	1	515
Chenoweth, Everest	50	Thompson Run	1850	1	480
Chenoweth, Gabriel	110	Eberman's Creek	1838	3	275
Chenoweth, Hickman	150	Leading Creek	1850	4	168
Chenoweth, Lemuel	840	Middle Fork River	1851	1	496
Chenoweth, Lemuel et al	628	Cheat Mtn.	1851	4	524
Chenoweth, Lemuel et al	100	Roaring Creek	1860	4	502
Chenoweth, Lemuel et al	692	Rich Mountain	1851	4	75
Chenoweth, Marshall	120	Chenoweth Creek	1859	4	462
Chenoweth, William P.	100	Eberman's Creek	1838	3	247
Clark, Daniel	25	Wts. Valley River	1803	2	343
Clark, Robert	229	Tygert's Valley River	1794	1	322
Clark, William	82	Adj. C. Myers	1793	1	270
Clark, William	98	Wts. Valley River	1794	1	319
Clark, William	124	Wts. Cheat	1791	1	114
Clifton, Charles F. & E. B.	235	Wts. Holly	1851	1	497
Clifton, James W.	280	Back Fork	1850	2	592
Clifton, John Jr.	154	Wts. Elk	1816	2	517
Cloud, Abner Jr.	334	Tygert's Valley R.	1790	1	105
Cloud, Abner Jr.	345	Grassy Creek	1790	1	104
Cloud, Abner Jr.	347	Grassy Creek	1790	1	107
Cloud, Abner Jr.	580	Grassy Creek	1790	1	106
Cloud, Abner Jr.	360	Grassy Creek	1790	1	108
Coberly, Aaron	75	Shaver's Fork	1856	4	368
Coberly, Aaron	30	Shaver's Fork	1861	4	509
Coberly, Aaron et al	220	Shaver's Fork	1856	4	355
Coberly, Aaron or James et al	90	Shaver's Fork	1861	4	513
Coberly, James	144	Shaver's Fork	1852	4	117
Coberly, James	100	Hay Stack Knob	1842	3	344
Coberly, Jesse	51¾	Wts. of Cheat	1852	4	118
Coberly, Jesse	26	Little Black Fork	1856	4	374
Coberly, Jesse	26	Little Black Fork	1856	4	434
Coberly, Joseph	30	Leading Creek	1841	3	304
Coberly, Levi	50	Wts. Cheat River	1822	3	47
Coberly, Levi	15	Shaver's Fork	1857	4	392
Coberly, William H.	470	Pheasant Run	1858	4	578
Coberly, William H.	61¾	Wilmouth Run	1861	4	512
Coberly, William H. (Coberley)	114½	Isner's Run	1850	2	599
Coberly, William H. et al	29	Leading Creek	1858	4	438
Coberly, William H. et al	280	Casadie's Fork	1859	4	466
Cocke, Bowler	2,000	Valley Fork	1799	2	180
Cocke, Bowler	2,000	Adj. M. Gratz	1799	2	181
Cocke, Bowler	2,000	Valley Fork	1799	2	182
Cocke, Bowler	2,000	Valley Fork	1799	2	183
Cocke, Bowler	2,000	Adj. Simon Nathan	1799	2	184
Cocke, Bowler	2,000	Valley Fork	1799	2	185
Cocke, Bowler	2,000	Valley Fork	1799	2	187
Cocke, Bowler	2,000	Valley Fork	1799	2	186
Cocke, Bowler	2,000	Cor. Nathan Survey	1799	2	188
Cocke, Bowler	2,000	Adj. S. Nathan	1799	2	189
Cocke, Bowler	2,000	Valley Fork	1799	2	190
Cocke, Bowler	2,000	Valley Fork	1799	2	191
Cocke, Bowler	2,000	Valley Fork	1799	2	179
Cocke, Bowler	2,000	Valley Fork	1799	2	167
Cocke, Bowler	2,000	Valley Fork	1799	2	121
Cocke, Bowler	4,000	Valley Fork	1799	2	120
Cocke, Bowler	2,000	Adj. M. Gratz	1799	2	119
Cocke, Bowler	2,000	Adj. Nathan's	1799	2	118
Cocke, Bowler	2,000	Valley Fork	1799	2	117
Coffman, George C. et al	22	Raccoon Creek	1826	3	104
Coil, George	100	Dry Fork	1795	1	329

Name of Grantee	Acres	Local Description	Year	Book	Page
Fisher, Jacob	30	Wts. Holly	1816	2	498
Fisher, Jacob	20	Wts. Holly	1818	2	548
Fisher, Solomon et al	304	Wts. Holly	1850	2	590
Fisk, Solomon et al	26,622	Old Field Fork	1797	1	438
Flack, James	8,162½	Wts. Cheat	1800	2	281
Flanagan—Flannagan, Flannigan					
Flanagan, Ebenezer	480	Dry Fork	1852	4	153
Flanagan, Ebenezer	370	Dry Fork	1819	3	10
Flanagan, Ebenezer	134	Dry Fork	1816	2	493
Flanagan, Ebenezer Jr.	150	Dry Fork	1848	3	465
Flanagan, Jacob	60	Dry Fork	1852	4	154
Flanagan, Jacob	140	Dry Fork	1852	4	155
Flanagan, Jesse	140	Dry Fork	1856	4	370
Flanagan, John	21	Dry Fork	1815	2	490
Flanagan, John	390	Dry Fork	1851	4	530
Flanagan, Robert et al	60	Dry Fork	1852	4	136
Flanagan, Robert et al	60	Dry Fork	1854	4	266
Flanagan, Silas	40	Points Knob	1851	4	14
Flanagan, William	10	Dry Fork	1852	4	152
Flannagan, John	89	Dry Fork	1834	3	176
Flannagan, John	127¼	Dry Run	1837	3	222
Flannagan, Robert	25	Dry Fork	1851	4	92
Flannagan, Robert	250	Dry Fork	1851	4	38
Flannigan, Ebenezer	440	Dry Fork Cheat	1799	2	173
Fogerson, Ferguson, Forgason, Forgerson, Forgison, Forguson					
Fonshee, Francis	1,000	Wts. Buckhannon	1791	1	152
Ford, Standish	1,000	Wts. of Buckhannon	1800	2	215
Ford, Standish	25,000	Shaver Fork	1800	2	249
Ford, Standish	1,000	Wts. Buckhannon	1800	2	244
Ford, Standish	1,000	Wts. Buckhannon	1800	2	243
Ford, Standish	1,000	Middle Fork	1800	2	242
Ford, Standish	1,000	Middle Fork	1800	2	241
Ford, Standish	1,000	Middle Fork	1800	2	240
Ford, Standish	1,000	Middle Fork	1800	2	238
Ford, Standish	1,000	Middle Fork	1800	2	239
Ford, Standish	1,000	Middle Fork	1800	2	236
Ford, Standish	1,000	Middle Fork	1800	2	237
Ford, Standish	1,000	Bean Camp Run	1800	2	235
Ford, Standish	1,000	Middle Fork	1800	2	234
Ford, Standish	1,000	Middle Fork	1800	2	233
Ford, Standish	1,000	Wts. Buckhannon	1800	2	232
Ford, Standish	1,000	Wts. Buckhannon	1800	2	231
Ford, Standish	1,000	Wts. Buckhannon	1800	2	230
Ford, Standish	1,000	Wts. Buckhannon	1800	2	229
Ford, Standish	1,000	Wts. Buckhannon	1800	2	227
Ford, Standish	1,000	Wts. Buckhannon	1800	2	228
Ford, Standish	1,000	Middle Fork	1800	2	226
Ford, Standish	1,000	Middle Fork	1800	2	222
Ford, Standish	1,000	Middle Fork	1800	2	224
Ford, Standish	1,000	Middle Fork	1800	2	225
Ford, Standish	1,000	East Fork	1800	2	216
Ford, Standish	1,000	Middle Fork	1800	2	217
Ford, Standish	1,000	Middle Fork	1800	2	218
Ford, Standish	1,000	Middle Fork	1800	2	219
Ford, Standish	1,000	Middle Fork	1800	2	220
Ford, Standish	1,000	Middle Fork	1800	2	221
Ford, Standish	1,061	Buchannon River	1800	2	211
Ford, Standish	1,061	Buchannon River	1800	2	210
Ford, Standish	1,061	Buchannon River	1800	2	209
Ford, Standish	1,061	Buchannon River	1800	2	207
Ford, Standish	1,061	Buchannon River	1800	2	208
Ford, Standish	1,061	Buchannon River	1800	2	204
Ford, Standish	1,061	Buchannon River	1800	2	205

Name of Grantee	Acres	Local Description	Year	Book	Page
Ford, Standish	1,061	Buckannon River	1800	2	206
Ford, Standish	1,061	Buchannon River	1800	2	202
Ford, Standish	1,061	Buchannon River	1800	2	203
Ford, Standish	1,061	Buchannon River	1800	2	201
Ford, Standish	1,061	Buchannon River	1800	2	198
Ford, Standish	1,061	Buchannon River	1800	2	199
Ford, Standish	1,061	Buchannon River	1800	2	200
Ford, Standish	1,061	Buchannon River	1800	2	197
Ford, Standish	1,061	Buchannon River	1800	2	196
Forgason—or Ferguson, Forgerson, Forgison, Forguson					
Forgason, James	24	Wts. Cheat	1807	2	392
Forgason, James	101 (107)	John's Run	1809	2	413
Forgason, Robert	50	Wts. Cheat	1825	3	90
Forgason, Robert	65	Clover Run	1831	3	139
Forgerson—See Ferguson					
Forgerson, Robert (Fogerson)	50	Wts. Cheat	1825	3	88
Forgison, James	60	Clover Run	1801	2	323
Forguson, James	227	Shaver's Fork	1801	2	294
Forinash, Charles	94	Wts. Buchannon	1801	2	290
Fornelson, Charles	155	Adj. his own	1789	1	38
Foster, George	46	Dry Fork	1796	1	393
Foushee, Francis	1,000	Wts. Buckhannon	1791	1	152
Fowler, Alexander	500	Middle Fork	1796	1	441
Fowler, Alexander	500	Middle Fork	1796	1	443
Fowler, Alexander	500	Middle Fork	1796	1	444
Fowler, Alexander	500	Middle Fork	1796	1	442
Frame, David	32	Wts. Elk	1813	2	472
Frame, David	317	Raccoon Creek	1804	2	352
Frame, James	50	Camp Run	1817	2	535
Frame, James	100	Wts. Elk	1817	2	534
French, David	2,000	Wts. Cheat	1797	2	57
Friend, Andrew	73	Bear Creek	1817	2	518
Friend, Elizabeth Heirs	125	Otter Creek	1822	3	45
Friend, Jacob Jr. & R. T.	200	Wts. Cheat	1793	1	267
Friend, Joseph	300	Miller's Bottom	1816	2	513
Friend, Joseph	675	Grassy Fork	1816	2	511
Friend, Joseph et al	900	Wts. Elk	1816	2	512
Friend, Joseph et al	166	Dry Run	1802	2	319
Friend, Joseph et al	200	Clover Run	1802	2	317
Friend, Joseph et al	262	Licking Creek	1802	2	318
Friend, Joseph et al	273	Bull Run	1802	2	316
Friend, Joseph et al	100	Salt Lick	1819	3	7
Friend, R. T. & Jacob Jr.	400	Sugar Creek	1793	1	268
Friend, Robert	100	Cherry Tree Fork	1793	1	266
Gainer—See Garner					
Gainer, Cornelius & George	50	Sugar Creek	1839	3	282
Gainer, George W.	145	Pond Lick Run	1849	1	544
Gainer, George W.	26	Leading Creek	1849	1	543
Gainer, George W.	146	Darling's Fork	1851	4	64
Gainer, George W.	219	Leading Creek	1851	4	16
Gainer, George W.	175	Leading Creek	1835	3	168
Gainer, George W.	6	Rock Lick Run	1851	4	15
Gale, George et al	11,100	Laurel Fork	1796	1	403
Gale, George et al	2,520	Black Water	1796	1	404
Gale, George et al	7,000	Dry Fork	1796	1	405
Gale, George et al	100,000	Wts. Gauley	1796	1	406
Gale, George et al	28,702	Black Fork	1796	1	402
Gallatin, Albert	5,400	Dry Run	1796	2	12
Gandy, Uriah	190	Cravens Run	1790	1	67
Gandy, Uriah	190	Craven's Run	1795	1	371
Garner—See Gainer					
Garner, Cornelius & George	50	Sugar Creek	1839	3	282
Garner, George W.	175	Leading Creek	1835	3	168

Name of Grantee	Acres	Local Description	Year	Book	Page
Harman, Samuel	176	Horse Camp Run	1844	3	384
Harman, Solomon	222	Horse Camp Run	1845	3	398
Harness—See Harris					
Harness, George	111	Dry Fork	1794	1	306
Harness, George	1,358	Dry Fork	1794	1	317
Harness, George	414	Valley River	1796	2	126
Harness, George	1,303	Dry Fork	1789	1	36
Harness, George	480	Dry Fork	1789	1	35
Harness, George et al	100,000	Wts. Gauley	1796	1	406
Harness, George et al	7,000	Dry Fork	1796	1	405
Harness, George et al	2,520	Black Water	1796	1	404
Harness, George et al	11,100	Laurel Fork	1796	1	403
Harness, George et al	28,702	Black Fork	1796	1	402
Harness, John	200	Cor. to P. Yoakam	1796	1	419
Harness, John	86	Black Water Cr.	1796	1	421
Harness, John	171	Black Water Cr.	1796	1	422
Harness, John	500	Black Water Cr.	1796	1	426
Harness, John	185	Black Water Cr.	1795	1	376
Harness, John	130	Black Water Cr.	1795	1	352
Harness, John	107	Black Water Cr.	1800	2	273
Harness, John	166	Big Ridge	1789	1	34
Harper, Adam	120	Clover Run	1835	3	185
Harper, Amby	2a.3r.18p	Top of Allegheny	1860	4	503
Harper, Daniel	14½	Leading Creek	1858	4	460
Harper, Henry	60½	Wood's Run	1838	3	276
Harper, Henry	550	Glady Fork	1851	4	232
Harper, Henry	100	Shaver Run	1826	3	98
Harper, Henry	11	Wts. Valley River	1833	3	162
Harper, Henry Jr.	19	Tigert's Valley River	1846	3	429
Harper, Henry Jr.	5½	Valley River	1846	3	418
Harper, John	590	Shaver Fork	1857	4	415
Harper, Jonathan W.	910	Clover Run	1857	4	569
Harper, Jonathan W.	14	Clover Run	1857	4	422
Harper, Moses	78	Big Run	1857	4	395
Harper, Moses	65	Top of Cheat Mt.	1859	4	463
Harper, Moses	150	Strader Spring	1823	3	71
Harper, Moses	176	Horse Camp Run	1852	4	207
Harper, Moses	(160½)165	Cheat Mountain	1852	4	139
Harris—See Harness					
Harris, Charles	600	Wts. Monon River	1792	1	239
Harris, John	15	Glady Creek	1824	3	111
Harris, William	100	Wts. Elk	1815	2	487
Harris, William	238	Beaver Run	1816	2	494
Harsh, Andrew	220	Clay Lick Run	1848	3	466
Harsh, Jacob	74	Teter's Creek	1843	3	364
Harshaw, William	250	Teters Creek	1791	1	150
Hart, Edward	200	Wts. Tygert's Valley	1804	2	350
Hart, Edward	115	King's Run	1809	2	426
Hart, Edward	2½a.7p.	Adj. Solomon Ryan	1796	1	381
Hart, Elijah M.	58	King's Run	1857	4	402
Hart, Hugh S.	240	Cheat Mountain	1857	4	396
Hart, Hugh S.	215½	Isner Run	1850	1	487
Hart, Hugh S. et al	214½	Shavers Fork	1858	4	450
Hart, Hugh S. et al	214½	Shaver's Fork	1858	2	569
Hart, James M.	24	Wts. Tygert Valley	1834	3	173
Hart, John M.	130	Tygert's Valley River	1820	3	26
Hart, John S. et al	150	Clover Run	1846	3	426
Hart, Joseph	300	Leonard Fork	1851	4	27
Hart, Joseph	4¾	Wts. Valley River	1852	4	198
Hart, Joseph	160	Stone Coal Ridge	1843	3	358
Hart, Joseph et al	700	Middle Fork	1851	4	527
Hart, Milton	100	Mine Lick Run	1853	4	225
Hart, Milton	30	Rich Mountain	1856	4	353

Name of Grantee	Acres	Local Description	Year	Book	Page
Hart, Milton	200	Dry Fork	1852	4	176
Hart, Milton	65	Wts. Valley River	1852	4	175
Hart, Milton et al	499	Roaring Creek	1851	1	498
Hart, Milton et al	139	Roaring Creek	1851	4	523
Hart, Milton et al	29	Leading Creek	1858	4	438
Hart, Milton et al	280	Casadie's Fork	1859	4	466
Hart, Milton et al	240	Wts. Valley River	1845	3	405
Hart, Milton et al	300	Dry Fork	1854	4	300
Hart, Milton et al	40	Leading Creek	1854	4	298
Hart, Milton et al	200	Dry Fork Cheat	1854	4	275
Hart, Milton et al	200	Shaver's Fork	1854	4	265
Hart, Milton et al	112	Shaver's Fork	1853	4	264
Hart, Milton et al	658	Cheat Mountain	1852	4	104
Hart, Milton et al	250	Dry Fork	1856	4	356
Hayse, George	50	Leading Creek	1835	3	184
Headley, Isaac	169	Wts. Tygert's Valley	1820	3	33
Hearn, John	500	Teter's Creek	1792	1	149
Heath—See Heth					
Heath, Andrew & Isaac	1,000	Wts. of Elk	1797	2	125
Hebb, Reuben	48a.2r.20p.	Cove Settlement	1837	3	226
Hebb, Reuben	45	Raccoon Creek	1839	3	283
Heckart—See Hackart, Heckhart					
Heckart, Adam	110	Laurel Creek	1807	2	398
Heckhart, John	200	Yohogania River	1826	3	101
Helmack, Jacob	40	Wts. Tygert's V.	1804	2	367
Henderson, Alexander (or Rob't.) et al	1,920	Middle Fork	1789	1	46
Henderson, Robert et al	1,920	Middle Fork	1789	1	48
Henderson, Robert et al	1,920	Middle Fork	1789	1	49
Henderson, Robert et al	1,920	Middle Fork	1789	1	50
Henderson, Robert et al	400	Wts. Buchannon River	1789	1	51
Henderson, Robert et al	1,920	Middle Fork	1789	1	47
Henkel—See Henkle, Hinkle					
Henkel, Jonas	139	Shaver Fork	1850	2	596
Heth—also Heath					
Heth, Henry et al	50,000	Wts. of Gauley	1797	2	67
Hiar—Higher, Hire, Hyre					
Hiar, Jacob	400	Jackson's Run	1793	3	75
Hickman, Mary P. et al	1,000	Wts. Elk	1789	1	13
Hickman, Mary P. et al	1,000	Wts. Elk River	1789	1	12
Hickman, Mary P. et al	1,000	Wts. Elk River	1789	1	11
Hickman, Mary P. et al	1,000	Wts. of Gauley	1789	1	17
Hickman, Mary P. et al	1,000	Wts. of Elk	1789	1	15
Hickman, Mary P. et al	1,000	Rock Camp Creek	1789	1	16
Hickman, Mary P. et al	1,000	Wts. Elk River	1789	1	14
Hicks, John et al	65,734	Wts. Gauley	1797	2	145
Higbee, Charles	100,000	Wts. Gauley	1796	1	429
Higher, Hiar, Hire, Hyre					
Higher, Peter et al	142	Pound Bottom Run	1795	1	363
Hill, George	49	Wts. Valley River	1852	4	138
Hines, Matthew	75	Sand Creek	1819	3	17
Hines, Matthew et al	262	Licking Creek	1802	2	318
Hines, Matthew et al	200	Clover Run	1802	2	317
Hines, Matthew et al	273	Bull Run	1802	2	316
Hines, Matthew et al	166	Dry Run	1802	2	319
Hines, Matthew et al	900	Wts. Elk	1816	2	512
Hinkle—See Henkel					
Hinkle, Annanias	1	Craven's Run	1860	4	500
Hinkle, Annanias	100	Beaver Creek	1845	3	401
Hinkle, J. & A.	125	Wts. Cheat	1840	3	293
Hinkle, Jonas	40	Tygert's Valley R.	1817	2	524
Hinkle, Justus	100	Adj. B. Hornbeck	1817	2	522
Hire, Hiar, Higher, Hyre					

Name of Grantee	Acres	Local Description	Year	Book	Page
Hollister, Austin	2,732	Leatherwood	1857	4	563
Hollister, Austin	840	Wts. Elk	1858	4	576
Hollister, Austin	5,938	Wts. Williams River	1858	4	575
Holmes, John et al	100,000	Wts. Gauley	1796	1	406
Holmes, John et al	7,000	Dry Fork	1796	1	405
Holmes, John et al	2,520	Black Water	1796	1	404
Holmes, John et al	11,100	Laurel Fork	1796	1	403
Holmes, John et al	28,702	Black Fork	1796	1	402
Homan, Sithman	102	Dry Fork	1794	1	282
Homan, Sithman	170	Bill's Creek	1794	1	283
Homan, Sithman	300	Tom's Run	1792	1	207
Homan, Sythman	330	Dry Fork	1804	2	364
Hooker, John et al	114,000	Wts. Monon. River	1797	2	61
Hornbeck, Benjamin	200	Leading Creek	1809	2	420
Hornbeck, Benjamin	25	Valley River	1809	2	425
Hornbeck, Benjamin	100	Leading Creek	1809	2	424
Hornbeck, Benjamin	100	Leading Creek	1809	2	423
Hornbeck, Benjamin	91	Tygert's Val. Riv.	1813	2	475
Hornbeck, John	11¼	Wts. Valley River	1851	4	31
Hough, John & Oliver	400	Wts. Buckhannon R.	1790	1	80
Hough, John & Oliver	400	Wts. Buckhannon R.	1790	1	81
Hough, John & Oliver	400	Wts. Buckhannon R.	1790	1	82
Hough, John & Oliver	400	Wts. Buckhannon R.	1790	1	83
Hough, John & Oliver	400	Wts. Buckhannon R.	1790	1	84
Hough, John & Oliver	400	Wts. Buckhannon R.	1790	1	79
Hovatter—See Hoalten, Hoatten, Holler					
Howell, Henry W.	360	Mill Creek	1855	4	334
Howell, Henry W.	1,200	Middle Mountain	1855	4	331
Howell, Henry W.	1,360	Middle Fork	1855	4	329
Howell, Jeremiah B. et al	304	Wts. of Holly	1850	2	590
Howell, William	15	Wts. of Cheat	1810	2	444
Howley, Ezra	10,000	Wts. of Cheat	1797	2	43
Hoye—or Hoy					
Hoye, John	300	Buffalo Lick	1847	3	457
Hoye, John	185	Black Fork	1844	3	390
Hoye, John	520	Shaver's Fork	1843	3	359
Hoye, John	80	Teter's Creek	1803	2	327
Hoye, Paul	2,400	Dry Fork	1796	1	386
Hubble, Richard	25,000	Wts. of Cheat	1797	2	122
Huff, William	50	Wts. Tygert's Valley	1816	2	507
Huffman—See Hoffman					
Huffman, Alexander	50	Laurel Creek	1819	3	8
Huffman, Christopher	40	Horse Camp	1791	1	133
Huffman, Israel	50	Sugar Creek	1833	3	155
Huffman, Israel	50	Lick Run	1833	3	156
Huffman, John	50	Glade's Run	1837	3	224
Huffman, John	34	Glade Run	1842	3	336
Huffman, Michael et al	100	Wts. Valley River	1832	3	150
Huffman, Michael et al	400	Wts. Tygert's Val.	1828	3	125
Huffman, Weeden et al	2,190	Lick Run	1850	1	529
Hughart, John P. K.	1,000	Leatherwood	1857	4	391
Hulicks, Mine	200	Clover Run	1790	1	64
Hulicks, Mine	250	Forks of Cheat	1790	1	66
Hunt, Ralph	400	Tetter's Creek	1791	1	162
Hunt, Ralph	400	Sugar Creek	1791	1	161
Hunt, Ralph	400	Wts. Tygert's River	1791	1	160
Hunt, Ralph	400	Sugar Creek	1791	1	158
Hunt, Ralph	400	Sugar Creek	1791	1	159
Hunt, Ralph	400(4)	Sugar Creek	1791	1	157
Hunt, Ralph	400	Sugar Creek	1791	1	154
Hunt, Ralph	400	Mill Creek	1791	1	163
Hunt, Ralph	400	Sugar Creek	1791	1	164
Hunt, Ralph	400	Mill Creek	1791	1	165

Name of Grantee	Acres	Local Description	Year	Book	Page
Hutton, Moses	186	Mill Creek	1855	4	327
Hutton, Moses	100	Mill Run	1820	3	34
Hutton, Moses	500	Shaver Run	1850	2	613
Hutton, Moses	671	Riffle Run	1851	1	521
Hutton, Moses	18	Riffle Run	1850	2	612
Hutton, Moses	500	Mitchell's Run	1855	4	322
Hutton, Moses et al	2,918	Middle Fork	1853	4	545
Hutton, Moses et al	8	Wts. Valley River	1861	4	511
Hutton, Moses et al	1,422½	Schoolcraft Run	1855	4	554
Hyland, Francis et al	65,734	Wts. Gauley River	1797	2	145
Hyre—Hiar, Higher, Hire					
Hyre, Abel	350	Leading Creek	1850	1	536
Hyre, Abel et al	156	Clever's Run	1851	4	4
Hyre, Abel et al	270	Leading Creek	1850	1	492
Hyre, Abraham	135	Leading Creek	1850	1	538
Hyre, Abraham	40	Thompson's Run	1856	4	390
Hyre, William	832	Wts. Buckhannon	1851	1	501
Hyre, William	500	Wts. Buckhannon	1851	1	512
Ingram, Abraham	26½	Wts. of Cheat R.	1811	2	451
Inskeep, John et al Adm.	1,000	Swamp Run	1805	2	372
Inskeep, John et al Adm.	4,000	Valley River	1805	2	371
Isner, Allen	190	Isner's Run	1850	2	589
Isner, Asahel	50	Wts. Cheat	1825	3	95
Isner, Asahel	50	Wts. Cheat	1836	3	210
Isner, Henry	330	Shaver's Fork	1851	4	96
Isner, Henry	50	Wts. Cheat	1849	1	552
Isner, Henry	50	Wts. Cheat	1849	1	553
Isner, Henry Jr.	50	Wts. Cheat	1836	3	212
Isner, Henry & William	35	Shaver's Fork	1855	4	309
Isner, Henry & William et al	500	Shaver's Fork	1852	4	174
Isner, Isaiah et al	250	Isner's Run	1851	4	46
Isner, Isaiah et al	124	Isner's Run	1852	4	200
Isner, Jacob	180	Hornbeck Run	1857	4	403
Isner, Jefferson et al	44	Shaver's Fork	1852	4	177
Isner, Jehu	100	Cross Run	1850	2	588
Isner, Michael	104	Wts. of Cheat	1798	2	162
Isner, Selathial & William	88	Shaver's Fork	1852	4	121
Isner, Thomas	164	Adj. Michael Isner	1798	2	164
Isner, William	1	Mill Creek	1854	4	299
Isner, William	100	Cross Run	1848	3	458
Isner, William	58	Chenoweth Creek	1855	4	328
Jackson, David	800	Wts. Buckhannon R.	1804	2	347
Jackson, Edward	2,000	Middle Fork	1797	2	56
Jackson, Edward	1,200	Middle Fork	1797	2	143
Jackson, Edward	2,000	Middle Fork	1797	2	144
Jackson, Edward	800	Fink's Run	1802	2	313
Jackson, Edward	250	Wts. Buchannon	1808	2	406
Jackson, Edward	56,000	Wts. Valley River	1796	1	400
Jackson, Edward	2,000	Wts. Buchannon	1801	2	289
Jackson, Edward et al	50,000	Wts. Valley River	1796	1	373
Jackson, Edward et al	311	Wts. Valley River	1793	1	280
Jackson, Edward et al	136	Wts. Valley River	1802	2	326
Jackson, Edward et al	196	Little Black Fork	1801	2	296
Jackson, Edward et al	246	Wts. Tygert's Valley	1801	2	295
Jackson, Edward et al	247	Teter's Creek	1801	2	288
Jackson, Elizabeth (Widow)	3,000	Wts. Buckhannon	1806	2	567
Jackson, George	300	Big Fork	1804	2	351
Jackson, George	1,400	Childer's Run	1801	2	300
Jackson, George	200	Reagor's Run	1800	2	268
Jackson, George et al	500	Shaver Mt.	1798	2	94
Jackson, George et al	564	Shaver Mt.	1798	2	92
Jackson, George et al	564	Shaver Mt.	1798	2	93
Jackson, George et al	564	Shaver Mt.	1798	2	90

Name of Grantee	Acres	Local Description	Year	Book	Page
Jackson, George et al	564	Shaver Mt.	1798	2	91
Jackson, George et al	629	File's Creek	1797	2	87
Jackson, George et al	564	Shaver Mt.	1798	2	88
Jackson, George et al	745	Shaver Mt.	1798	2	85
Jackson, George et al	500	Eberman's Creek	1798	2	84
Jackson, George et al	629	Eberman's Creek	1797	2	86
Jackson, Henry	400	Radcliff's Run	1807	2	388
Jackson, Henry	264	Valley River	1805	2	368
Jackson, Henry	900	Fink's Run	1804	2	355
Jackson, Henry	800	Peck's Run	1804	2	344
Jackson, Henry	150	Teter's Creek	1800	2	270
Jackson, Henry	1,000	Wts. Buckhannon R.	1801	2	275
Jackson, John	600	Wts. Buckhannon R.	1800	2	310
Jackson, John	400	Turkey Creek	1804	2	354
Jackson, John et al	277	Sandy Creek	1804	2	353
Jackson, Samuel	100	Adj. John Rodabaugh	1804	2	360
Jackson, Samuel	1,350	Wts. Buckhannon R.	1804	2	361
Jackson, Samuel	100	Peck's Run	1804	2	359
Jackson, Samuel	145	Eberman's Creek	1804	2	348
Jackson, Samuel	400	Peck's Run	1800	2	308
James, John	200	Wts. Tygert's Valley	1801	2	320
James, John	200	Wts. Tygert's Valley	1801	2	314
James, John H.	83	Wts. Cheat	1836	3	199
James, Otho W.	190	Wts. Cheat	1850	1	485
James, Samuel	200	Sugar Creek	1792	1	227
James, Thomas	185	Wts. Cheat	1850	1	484
Jarvis, Granville E. et al	861	Licking Creek	1853	4	249
Jarvis, Granville E. et al	306	Middle Fork	1850	2	586
Jeter, Joseph et al	500	Middle Fork	1838	3	277
Johns—See Jones, Jons					
Johns, Joseph et al	1,040	Haddix Creek	1853	4	544
Johnson, James et al	660	Dry Fork	1853	3	563
Johnson, John	76½	Teter's Creek	1841	3	315
Johnson, John et al	1,268	Clover Run	1844	3	391
Johnson, John et al	293	Clover Run	1842	3	357
Johnson, John et al	453	Clover Run	1841	3	312
Johnson, Robert	114	Dry Fork	1852	4	189
Johnson, Robert et al	125	Dry Fork	1854	4	306
Johnson, Robert et al	130	Dry Fork	1854	4	307
Johnson, Robert et al	300	Black Fork	1848	3	462
Johnson, Robert et al	190	Wts. of Cheat	1848	3	461
Johnson, Robert et al	130	Dry Fork	1847	3	440
Johnson, Robert et al	584	Dry Fork	1847	3	439
Johnson, Robert et al	266	Dry Fork	1847	3	438
Jones—See Johns, Jons					
Jones, Benjamin	500	Stuart's Run	1790	1	101
Jones, Benjamin	250	Fork Lick	1791	1	122
Jones, Solomon	53¾	Tom's Run	1836	3	197
Jones, Thomas A.	9a.3r.20p.	Tygert's Valley	1825	3	94
Jones, William	50	Wild Cat Ridge	1847	3	450
Jons, Benjamin	500	Stuart's Run	1790	1	101
Joseph, Joseph et al	277	Sandy Creek	1804	2	353
Journeay, John	8,000	Middle Fork	1790	1	76
Kaighn, John et al	400	Wts. Buckhannon	1789	1	51
Kaighn, John et al	1,920	Middle Fork	1789	1	50
Kaighn, John et al	1,920	Middle Fork	1789	1	49
Kaighn, John et al	1,920	Middle Fork	1789	1	48
Kaighn, John et al	1,920	Middle Fork	1789	1	47
Kaighn, John et al	1,920	Middle Fork	1789	1	46
Kalame—See Callam, Collum					
Kalar, Jacob et al	790	Shaver Fork	1857	4	562
Kaler, Daniel	100	Wts. Cheat	1846	3	419
Kanan, Joseph	312	Cor. to J. Stalnaker	1794	1	307

Name of Grantee	Acres	Local Description	Year	Book	Page
Kannamon, Joseph	300	Wts. Tygert V. River	1792	1	231
Kee, Aaron	1,440	Wts. Buckhannon R.	1810	2	430
Keller—See Kelly					
Keller, Adam	270	Gulf Hill	1852	4	150
Keller, Jacob et al	436	Glady Fork	1838	3	272
Kelley, Abel H.	350	Pond & Wolf Runs	1856	4	558
Kelley, Abel H.	150	Laurel Run	1849	1	554
Kelley, Dolbear	150	Pond Lick Run	1855	4	316
Kelley, Harrison & Asa	450	Schoolcraft Run	1852	4	234
Kelley, William	100	Eberman's Creek	1803	2	341
Kelly, Abel H.	380	Cheat Mountain	1851	4	80
Kelly, Dolbear	59	Panther Hill	1851	4	79
Kelly, Dolbear	240	Adj. Wm. Kelly	1851	4	65
Kelly, Harrison et al	100	Mine Lick Run	1853	4	225
Kelly, Harrison et al	200	Shaver's Fork	1854	4	265
Kelly, Harrison et al	40	Leading Creek	1854	4	298
Kelly, Harrison et al	250	Dry Fork	1856	4	356
Kelly, John	125	Shaver's Fork	1856	4	376
Kelly, John	360	See Run	1856	4	379
Kelly, John C.	190	Wts. of Cheat	1850	2	594
Kelly, Samuel	200	Teter's Creek	1790	1	103
Kennedy, James et al	1,100	Peck's Run	1804	2	349
Kertley, Francis	400	Valley River	1789	1	45
Kidd, James	110	Tygert's V. River	1800	2	264
Kidd, James	110	Tygert's V. River	1800	2	267
Kingan, John	300	Teter's Creek	1800	2	271
Kittle, Abraham	100	Adj. H. P. Row	1793	1	249
Kittle, Abraham	107	Glady Creek	1794	1	310
Kittle, Abraham I.	25	Whitman's Run	1822	3	58
Kittle, Abram	214	Wts. Tygert's Valley	1796	1	382
Kittle, Jacob	40	Wts. Tygert's Valley	1804	2	366
Kittle, Martin D.	27	Adj. Wm. Davison	1840	3	294
Kittle, Richard	8	Adj. his own	1809	2	412
Koontz—See Coontz					
Lacy, Josiah et al	1,000	Wts. of Cheat	1797	2	42
Lamb, Granville	1,500	Middle Fork	1857	4	428
Lamb, Granville	100	Wts. Valley River	1852	4	159
Lambert, James H.	120	Red Creek	1860	4	499
Lambert, James H.	19½	Red Creek	1857	4	429
Lamberton, John	106,029	Black Fork	1796	1	378
Lancisco, Henry	160	Camp Run	1790	2	24
Lantz, Joseph H. et al	75	Dry Fork	1852	4	201
Layne, Douglas B. & A. C.	2,738	Wts. Gauley	1851	4	67
Leary, John	166	Cross Run	1851	4	2
Leary, Samuel	90	Chenoweth's Creek	1856	4	352
Lee—or See					
Lee, Adam (See)	30	Tygert's V. Riv.	1812	2	463
Lee, Adam (See)	540	Wts. Elk	1797	2	69
Lee, Charles et al (See)	200,000	Wts. Elk	1795	1	341
Lee, Charles et al (See)	100,000	Wts. Cheat	1795	1	359
Lee, George H. et al (See)	582	Wts. Buchannon R.	1850	2	608
Lee, George H. et al (See)	888	Wts. Holly	1850	2	609
Lee, Henry (See)	6,200	Wts. Elk	1796	2	29
Lee, Henry (See)	7,760	Wts. Elk	1796	2	28
Lee, Henry (See)	4,050	Wts. Elk	1796	2	15
Lee, Henry (See)	3,000	Wts. Elk	1796	2	14
Lee, John H. (See)	150	Leading Creek	1841	3	308
Lee, John H. (See)	100	Leading Creek	1850	2	587
Leonard, John A.	250	Sandy Creek	1843	3	366
Lewis, David	3,003	Wts. Valley River	1792	1	212
Lewis, John Banks	84	Adj. D. McClain	1794	1	334
Linch—or Lynch					
Linch, John	80	Milford's Bottom	1843	3	360

Name of Grantee	Acres	Local Description	Year	Book	Page
McCrum, Robert	4½	Valley River	1827	3	121
McElwaine—Mucklewaine					
McGee—See Magee					
McGee, Adam	390	Teter's Creek	1847	3	451
McKinney, Anna et al	6,747	Middle Fork	1838	3	568
McQuain, John	190	Shaver's Fork	1857	4	404
McQuarter—See McQuirter					
McQuirter, Henry et al	300	Back Fork	1811	2	449
McVicker, Archibald	50	Wts. Valley River	1840	3	295
Means—See Mears					
Mears, Henry et al	250	Elk River	1809	2	420
Menear—See Minear					
Menear, David	200	Clover Fork	1792	1	223
Messenburgh—Messenbird, Messenburg					
Messenbird, George	9,870	Wts. Gauley	1796	1	425
Middleton, Henry O.	1,000	White Oak Run	1847	3	76
Middleton, Henry O.	190	Laurel Run	1844	3	394
Middleton, Henry O.	800	Middle Fork	1845	3	404
Middleton, Henry O.	99	Adj. his own	1846	3	406
Middleton, Henry O.	1,190	Middle Fork	1851	4	521
Miller, Andrew	170	Wts. Cheat	1789	1	31
Miller, Andrew	76	Goff's Sugar Camp Run	1838	3	268
Miller, Francis	100	Elk River	1815	2	482
Miller, Henry	15	Wts. Valley River	1825	3	84
Miller, Henry	50	Leading Creek	1801	2	299
Miller, John	230	Wts. Cheat	1794	1	313
Miller, John et al	300	Back Fork	1811	2	449
Miller, Levi	400	Joe's Run	1843	3	367
Miller, Robert	100	Fork Lick	1820	3	30
Minear—See Menear					
Minear, David	42	Wts. Cheat	1800	2	284
Minear, Enoch	82	Wts. Cheat	1850	2	606
Minear, Enoch	100	Mill Run	1848	3	463
Minear, Isaac	95	Wts. Tygert Valley	1819	3	19
Mitchell, George	200	Wts. Valley River	1821	3	39
Mitchell, John	230	Tygert's Valley R.	1819	3	5
Mitchell, John	60	Wts. Tygert's V. R.	1806	2	385
Moore, Daniel	42	Sugar Creek	1822	3	55
Moore, David	48	Shaver's Fork	1851	4	54
Moore, David	58½	Shaver's Fork	1851	4	55
Moore, David	11½	Island, Shaver's Fork	1851	4	56
Moore, Henry C.	20,867	Wts. Elk	1857	2	553
Moore, Henry C.	146	Wts. Holly	1852	4	123
Moore, Henry C.	770	Wts. Elk	1851	4	23
Moore, Henry C.	295	Doddrill's Ridge	1851	4	22
Moore, Henry C.	50a.3r.	Point Mt.	1858	4	444
Moore, Henry C.	43	Point Mt.	1858	4	446
Moore, Henry C.	164	Point Mt.	1858	4	445
Moore, Henry C.	690	Big Run	1848	4	447
Moore, Henry C.	76	Point Mt.	1858	4	448
Moore, Henry C. et al	190	Wts. Elk	1857	4	414
Moore, Henry C. et al	382	Wts. Holly	1852	4	149
Moore, Henry C. et al	1,517	Sugar Creek	1851	4	518
Moore, Henry C. et al	750	Leatherwood	1859	4	579
Moore, James	60	Haddix Creek	1851	4	53
Moore, James et al	105	Shaver's Fork	1857	4	418
Moore, James et al	315	Shaver's Fork	1858	4	572
Moore, James et al	428	Shaver's Fork	1858	4	571
Moore, Rachel et al	400	Glady Creek	1816	2	492
Moore, Samuel P.	711	Cheat Mt.	1797	2	83
Moore, Samuel P.	711	Cheat Mt.	1797	2	82
Moore, Samuel P.	711	Cheat Mt.	1797	2	81
Moore, Samuel P.	500	Eberman's Creek	1797	2	79

Name of Grantee	Acres	Local Description	Year	Book	Page
Parker, Edwin L. et al	1,000	Adj. Adam Harper	1857	4	560
Parsons, Abraham	250	Shaver's Fork	1852	4	130
Parsons, Abraham	70	Shaver's Fork	1853	4	239
Parsons, Abraham	600	Black Fork	1849	3	481
Parsons, Abraham et al	85	Shaver's Fork	1852	4	131
Parsons, Charles	200	Brush Fork	1791	1	128
Parsons, Charles	400	Wts. Buckhannon	1789	1	37
Parsons, Jacob W.	332	Dry Fork	1851	4	231
Parsons, Jacob W.	100	Wts. Cheat	1851	4	6
Parsons, James	400	Wts. Cheat	1851	1	506
Parsons, James	140	Otter Creek	1847	3	444
Parsons, James	68	Wts. Cheat	1809	2	416
Parsons, James	300	Wts. Cheat	1801	2	304
Parsons, James W.	252	Dry Run	1850	2	586
Parsons, James W.	50	Wts. Cheat	1850	2	595
Parsons, James W.	4a.2r.28p.	Wts. Cheat	1850	2	605
Parsons, Job Jr.	240	Shaver's Fork	1851	4	68
Parsons, Jonathan	205	Mill Run	1790	1	39
Parsons, Jonathan	205	Mill Run	1790	1	73
Parsons, Solomon	100	Wts. Cheat	1841	3	324
Parsons, Ward	200	Wts. Cheat	1851	4	83
Parsons, Ward	50	Wts. Cheat	1852	4	132
Parsons, Ward	400	Shaver's Fork	1852	4	133
Parsons, William	50	Wts. Cheat	1809	2	421
Patterson, Joseph	187,000	Middle Fork	1797	2	50
Patton, James et al	1,100	Peck's Run	1804	2	349
Patton, Robert Jr.	3,150	Adj. Wm. Stewart	1796	2	27
Paul, Hugh et al	50,000	Wts. Tygert's Valley	1798	2	152
Paul, Hugh et al	23,000	Wts. of Elk	1797	2	39
Paul, Hugh et al	40,000	Wts. Wms. River	1797	2	38
Payne—Paine, Pane					
Payne, William G.	1,500	Wts. Gauley	1802	2	328
Payne, William G.	1,000	Wts. Elk	1802	2	329
Payne, William G.	1,000	Wts. Gauley	1802	2	330
Pearce, Samuel	122	Bill's Creek	1803	2	340
Pearcy—or Piercy					
Pearcy, Jacob	150	Isner's Run	1837	3	218
Pearcy, Jacob	100	Isner's Run	1837	3	219
Pearcy, Jacob Jr.	65	Isner's Run	1851	4	40
Pearcy, Jacob Jr. et al	250	Isner's Run	1851	4	46
Pearcy, Jacob Jr. & Patterson	14¼	Isner's Run	1851	4	44
Pearcy, Jacob & Patterson	175	Middle Fork	1851	4	45
Peck, George	76	Horse Camp Run	1793	1	258
Penfields, Samuel	15,000	Laurel Fork	1797	2	41
Pennington, John & V. B.	400	Dry Fork	1852	4	160
Pennington, Nathaniel	58	Dry Fork	1853	4	223
Pennington, Nathaniel	110	Dry Fork	1853	4	224
Perkins, James et al	50,000	Wts. Cheat	1797	2	62
Peters, Henry	800	Middle Fork	1800	2	261
Pfost—or Post					
Phares, Benjamin	100	Adj. John Phares	1840	3	296
Phares, Benjamin	435	Middle Fork	1852	4	178
Phares, Benjamin J. et al	865	Jones' Run	1861	2	560
Phares, Jacob et al	390	Gandy Creek	1851	1	505
Phares, Jesse	7	Leading Creek	1852	4	147
Phares, Jesse	13	Leading Creek	1852	4	146
Phares, Jesse F.	144	Three Forks	1858	4	452
Phares, Jesse F. et al	160	Cassadie's Fork	1860	4	485
Phares, John	385	Craven's Run	1851	4	532
Phares, John M.	287	Bow Run	1857	4	570
Phares, John M.	94½	Leading Creek	1851	1	503
Phares, John M.	100	Cleaver's Run	1859	4	476
Phares, John M.	28	Bow Run	1857	4	430

Name of Grantee	Acres	Local Description	Year	Book	Page
Phares, John M. et al	96	Roney's Run	1853	4	215
Phares, John M. & Washington	95	Leading Creek	1851	4	5
Phares, William	200	Leading Creek	1848	3	78
Phares, William	125	Roney's Run	1851	1	504
Philips—or Phillips					
Philips, Henry	50,029	Wts. Elk River	1795	1	338
Philips, Henry	14,845	Dry Run	1795	1	339
Philips, Henry	19,000	Glady Branch	1795	1	340
Philips, Isaac	211	Glady Creek	1792	1	237
Phillips, Henry	6,000	Dry Fork	1795	1	453
Phillips, Jesse	25	Glady Creek	1825	3	86
Phillips, John J.	150	Glady Creek	1831	3	140
Phillips, Thomas	140	Roaring Creek	1822	3	65
Phillips, Thomas	400	Wts. Tygert's Valley	1822	3	64
Phillips, Thomas	164	Adj. his own	1792	1	204
Phillips, Thomas Jr.	25	Beaver Creek	1838	3	243
Pickett, George	500	Eberman's Creek	1794	1	300
Pickett, George	500	Shaver's Mtn.	1794	1	299
Pickett, George	500	Shaver's Mtn.	1794	1	298
Pickett, George	37,047	Wts. of Elk	1797	2	49
Pickett, George	711	Wts. of Cheat	1794	1	295
Pickett, George	711	Shaver Mtn.	1794	1	296
Pickett, George	355	Glady Fork	1794	1	297
Pickett, George	122,000	Elk River	1799	2	178
Pickett, Heathcoat	61	Wts. of Cheat	1793	1	276
Piercy or Pearcy					
Piercy, Addison	163	File's Creek	1852	4	134
Piercy, Addison et al	43	Middle Fork	1851	4	97
Piercy, Addison et al	469	Middle Fork	1851	4	98
Piercy, Addison et al	190	Dry Fork	1851	4	37
Piercy, Addison et al	400	Dry Fork	1851	4	41
Piercy, Addison et al	200	Dry Fork	1851	4	43
Piercy, Addison et al	400	Dry Fork	1851	4	42
Piercy, Jacob Jr. et al	124	Isner's Run	1852	4	200
Piercy, Patterson	155	Shaver's Fork	1854	4	295
Pifer, Jacob	100	Mill Run	1850	2	606
Plunkett, David et al	1,900	Black Fork	1794	1	284
Poffinberry—Buffenbarger, Pufenbarry					
Poffinberry, Peter (Buffenbarger)	103	Wts. Dry Fork	1796	2	5
Poling, Barnet P.	50	Brushy Fork	1838	3	255
Poling, Elisha & James	133	Cove Run	1838	3	256
Poling, Elisha & Martin	100	Glade Run	1824	3	112
Poling, John J. & Barnet	200	Whitman's Run	1827	3	122
Poling, Jonathan	139	Lick Run	1843	3	369
Poling, William	85	Sugar Creek	1821	3	37
Pool, Joseph	1,000	Roaring Creek	1811	2	459
Post, Barbara	27	Beech Run	1805	2	383
Powers, James	150	Indian Run	1854	4	294
Powers, Thomas J. et al	100	Little Black Fork	1860	4	489
Powers, Valentine	400	Slab Camp	1795	1	350
Price, Joseph C.	211	Teter's Creek	1841	3	323
Price, Joseph C.	88½	Teter's Creek	1841	3	322
Price, William	125	Sugar Creek	1821	3	40
Prince, James et al	21,401	Wts. Elk	1798	2	160
Prince, James et al	38,742	Wts. Elk	1798	2	159
Prindle, James et al	400	Glady Creek	1816	2	492
Pritt, John	70	Hickory Run	1841	3	327
Pritt, John	100	Wts. Valley River	1837	3	229
Pritt, John	21	Hickory Run	1841	3	328
Pritt, John M.	58	Wts. Valley River	1839	3	284
Pritt, William S.	188	File's Creek	1852	4	124
Propst, John	50	Hadden's Run	1842	3	346
Pufenbarry—Buffenbarger					

Name of Grantee	Acres	Local Description	Year	Book	Page
Scott, Thomas B.	64	Wilmoth's Run	1851	1	513
Scott, Thomas B. et al	2,918	Middle Fork	1853	4	545
Scott, Thomas B. et al	500	See Run	1856	4	363
See—or Lee					
See, Alam (Lee)	750	Wts. Tygert's Valley	1821	3	35
See, Adam (Lee)	24	Wts. Tygert's V. R.	1819	3	9
See, Adam (Lee)	140	Wts. Valley River	1831	3	136
See, Adam (Lee)	250	Wts. Valley River	1796	1	428
See, Adam et al (Lee)	3,650	Tygert's V. River	1845	3	396
See, Anthony B. (Lee)	494	Stuart's Run	1844	3	373
See, Charles C. (Lee)	1,500	Hadden Mill Run	1837	3	567
See, Charles C. (Lee)	770	Cheat Mtn.	1845	3	400
See, Charles C. (Lee)	474	Wts. Valley River	1844	3	392
See, Charles C. (Lee)	21	Wts. V. River	1844	3	386
See, Charles C. (Lee)	587	Wts. V. River	1844	3	374
See, Charles C. (Lee)	191	Wts. V. River	1850	1	468
See, Charles C. (Lee)	790	Wts. V. River	1850	1	467
See, Charles C. (Lee)	100	Wts. V. River	1837	3	230
See, Charles C. Heirs et al (Lee)	448	Wts. V. River	1844	3	372
See, Jacob W. (Lee)	440	Clay Lick Run	1851	4	59
See, Jacob W. (Lee)	760	Mill Run	1851	4	58
See, Michael (Lee)	100	Wts. Valley River	1800	2	246
See, Michael (Lee)	200	Wts. Valley River	1805	2	377
Selby, Samuel (The 3rd)	800	Shaver Fork	1798	2	96
Selby, Samuel (The 3rd) et al	1,000	Pheasant Run	1798	2	97
Sexton, Charles	200	Clover Run	1790	1	65
Seymore—Seymour					
Seymore, John	303	Wts. Cheat	1840	3	290
Seymore, William	95	Big Swamp	1800	2	257
Seymour, John et al	702	Middle Mtn.	1857	4	405
Shaffer—See Shaver					
Shaffer, Daniel	50	Brushy Fork	1842	3	354
Shanklin, Robert S.	200	Adj. Gabriel Chenoweth	1817	2	533
Shaver—Shaffer					
Shaver, John	50	Brushy Run	1837	3	233
Shaw, William	483	Wts. Monon. River	1796	2	16
Shearer, Antona	220	Wts. Valley River	1801	2	303
Sheffey, Hugh W.	2,780	Back Fork Elk	1859	4	470
Shelton, William J.	136¾	Middle Fork	1858	4	459
Sheveront, Eliza et al	125	King's Run	1832	3	151
Shipley, Joseph	4,000	Roaring Creek	1805	2	373
Shirk, Joab	164	Horse Camp Run	1844	3	385
Shobe, Leonard	50	Dry Fork	1793	1	269
Shobe, Leonard	200	Dry Fork	1791	1	86
Shobe, Martin (Little)	44	Dry Fork	1815	2	485
Shobe, Rodolph	112	Black Water Creek	1791	1	151
Shobe, Rodolph	239	Dry Fork	1790	1	63
Shobe, Rodolph	200	Spruce Run	1800	2	254
Shobe, Rodolph	250	Dry Fork	1800	2	255
Shock—See also Shook					
Shock, Henry	'50	Wts. Elk	1817	2	525
Shock, Henry	32	Wts. Elk	1818	2	546
Shock, Jacob	152	Wts. Elk	1817	2	527
Shook—See also Shock					
Shook, Jacob	289	Big Lime Stone	1799	2	174
Shook, Jacob	50	Dry Fork	1792	1	206
Shreeves—Shreve, Shreves, Shrieve					
Shreeves, James	77	Wts. Valley River	1851	4	71
Shreve, John et al	171	Cassadie's Fork	1860	4	507
Shreve, Joseph	122	Dry Fork	1789	1	43
Shreve, Joseph	420	Horse Camp Run	1789	1	42
Shreve, Joseph et al	200	Wolf Creek	1804	2	357
Shreves, John et al	124	Cassadie's Fork	1860	4	505

Name of Grantee	Acres	Local Description	Year	Book	Page
Smith, John	105	Leading Creek	1794	1	312
Smith, Jonathan	343	Glady Creek	1789	1	24
Smith, Jonathan	400	Sugar Creek	1792	1	146
Smith, Samuel et al	50	Tygert's V. River	1813	2	464
Smith, William	52	Wts. Valley River	1793	1	251
Smith, William	2,000	Sugar Creek	1800	2	278
Smith, William	140	Glady Creek	1798	2	161
Smith, William S.	1,000	Teter's Creek	1796	1	389
Smith, William S.	1,000	Big Sandy Creek	1796	1	447
Smith, William S.	1,000	Teter's Creek	1796	1	448
Smith, William S.	1,000	Wts. Tygert's Valley	1796	2	1
Smith, William S.	1,000	Teter's Creek	1796	2	2
Smith, William S.	1,000	Teter's Creek	1796	2	4
Smith, William & Samuel	94	Tygert's V. River	1811	2	450
Smoot, Thomas	200	Wts. Monon. River	1792	1	224
Smoot, Thomas	224	Wts. Monon. River	1792	1	225
Smyth—Smith					
Smyth, Richard	18,300	Wts. Elk River	1796	1	388
Smyth, Richard	22,104½	Wts. Cheat River	1795	1	348
Smyth, Richard	10,800	Wts. Elk River	1795	1	349
Smyth, Richard	31,000	Wts. Cheat River	1795	1	346
Smyth, Richard	1,000	Wts. Gauley	1793	1	247
Smyth, Richard	10,000	Wts. Cheat River	1795	1	347
Snelson, James A.	348	Whitman's Creek	1858	4	456
Snelson, Thomas N.	175	Whitman's Creek	1858	4	454
Snider—Snyder, Sydnor					
Snider, Daniel	42	Wts. Cheat	1822	3	59
Snider, David	100	Leading Creek	1836	3	209
Snider, David	70	Wts. Cheat	1822	3	61
Snider, David	30	Wts. Cheat	1822	3	60
Snider, Frederick	350	Stuart's Run	1848	3	83
Snider, Jacob	135	Stuart's Run	1842	3	343
Snider, John	65	Dry Fork	1849	1	570
Snider, John	13	Dry Fork	1852	4	202
Snider, John	46½	Dry Fork	1854	4	268
Snider, John	165	Dry Fork	1849	3	479
Snider, John	265	Darby Run	1844	3	571
Snider, John	177	Rich Mountain	1858	4	449
Snider, John et al	800	Dry Fork	1851	4	522
Snyder—Snider, Sydnor					
Snyder, Henry & William	1,000	Burgoo Run	1857	4	394
Snyder, John	6¾	Stuart's Run	1850	1	540
Snyder, John	279½	Stuart's Run	1850	1	540
Snyder, John	154	Stewart Run	1851	1	509
Snyder, John et al	1,025	Dry Fork	1853	4	542
Southerland, William	1,000	Wts. Cheat	1793	1	326
Southerland, William	1,000	Wts. Cheat	1793	1	325
Spicer, Randolph	1,250	Big Sandy Creek	1808	2	405
Sponaugle—Sponoggle					
Sponaugle, Sydney	406	Dry Fork	1853	4	250
Sponoggle, Jacob	1,200	Adj. Coal	1853	4	230
Sproul, John	106	Wts. Tygert's Valley	1800	2	258
Stalnaker, Andrew	50	Maiden Glades	1831	3	144
Stalnaker, Andrew	95	Wts. V. River	1831	3	133
Stalnaker, Andrew Jr.	50	Glade Run	1824	3	110
Stalnaker, Asbury	57	Log Lick Run	1851	4	48
Stalnaker, Asbury	93	Thompson Run	1851	4	47
Stalnaker, Asbury	123	Leading Creek	1856	4	385
Stalnaker, Asbury	33	Thompson Run	1849	3	482
Stalnaker, Archibald	50	Wts. Valley River	1836	3	200
Stalnaker, Boston	152	Valley River	1799	2	193
Stalnaker, Ferdinand et al	494	Back Fork	1838	3	270
Stalnaker, Garretson	225	Cheat Run	1851	1	518

Name of Grantee	Acres	Local Description	Year	Book	Page
Triplett, Milton	186	Leading Creek	1858	2	570
Triplett, Milton	186	Rock Lick Run	1858	4	451
Triplett, Philadelphai R.	195	Laurel Lick Run	1851	4	32
Troutwine, Frederick	89	Tygert's V. River	1812	2	460
Tucker, John et al	1,000	Wts. Cheat	1798	2	115
Turner, James	15	Stony Run	1823	3	69
Valentine, George	150	Brushy Fork	1842	3	345
Valentine, Henry	100	Brushy Fork	1842	3	352
Vanbibber, Andrew	7,150	Wts. Elk	1793	1	264
Vanbibber, Andrew	2,850	Big Run	1793	1	263
Vanbibber, Andrew	2,850	Big Run	1793	1	262
Vanbibber, Andrew	7,150	Wts. Elk	1793	1	265
Vance, James	365	Dry Fork	1853	4	257
Vance, John	50	Wts. Cheat	1816	2	499
Vance, John Jr.	383	Summerfield Run	1808	2	402
Vance, Robert	496	Branch Road	1808	2	403
Vanscoy, Aaron (Vanschoy)	67	Leading Creek	1801	2	287
Vanscoy, Aaron	117	Spring Stone Run	1841	3	309
Vanscoy, Aaron	48	Leading Creek	1844	3	382
Vanscoy, George W.	138	Bow Run	1852	4	182
Vanscoy, James	100	Leading Creek	1846	3	424
Vanscoy, Jonathan	80	Panther Knob	1846	3	425
Vanzandt, William L.	1,000	Leatherwood	1853	4	208
Vick, William	117	Pheasant Run	1856	4	389
Wadsworth, Theodore, et al	26,622	Old Field Fork	1797	1	438
Walcott, Alexander	100,000	Wts. Elk	1796	2	30
Walcott, Alexander	100,000	Wts. Gauley	1796	2	31
Walcott, Alexander	100,000	Wts. Cheat	1797	2	128
Walker, John	50	Dry Fork	1835	3	166
Walker, Joseph	100	Dry Fork	1817	2	530
Walker, Joseph	500	Laurel Fork	1835	3	189
Walker, Joseph	150	Dry Fork	1835	3	170
Walsh, Robert	500	Middle Fork	1792	1	136
Walsh, Robert	500	Middle Fork	1792	1	138
Walsh, Robert	500	Middle Fork	1792	1	135
Walsh, Robert	500	Middle Fork	1792	1	137
Wamesley—Wamsley, Warmsley, Wormsley, Womesley					
Wamesley, James	270	Slate Lick Run	1794	1	323
Wamsley—See Wamesley					
Wamsley, Andrew M.	10	Wts. Valley River	1852	4	163
Wamsley, Jacob S. & S. L.	50	Wts. Elk	1857	4	435
Wamsley, Jacob S. & S. L.	386	Wts. Elk	1856	4	357
Wamsley, James	42	Valley River	1810	2	437
Wamsley, Jesse	100	Haddon's Run	1836	3	193
Wamsley, Jesse	500	Wts. Valley River	1841	3	301
Wamsley, Jesse	50	Haddon's Run	1836	3	192
Wamsley, John	200	Tygert's Valley R.	1816	2	516
Wamsley, John C.	25	Louck's Run	1854	4	286
Wamsley, Jonathan	31	Shaver's Run	1813	2	473
Wamsley, Joseph	50	Riffle Run	1837	3	238
Wamsley, Joseph	50	Wts. Valley River	1849	1	566
Wamsley, Matthew	50	Wts. Valley River	1852	4	162
Wamsley, Matthew	100	Wts. Tygert's Valley	1810	2	435
Wamsley, Samuel	110	Pound Run	1845	3	574
Wamsley, Samuel	40	Valley River	1816	2	515
Wamsley, Solomon	200	Mill Run	1841	3	300
Wamsley, Thomas	112	Riffle's Run	1819	3	15
Wamsley, William	75	Adj. his own	1791	1	130
Wamsley, William et al	100,000	Middle Fork	1796	1	374
Ward, Adonijah B.	20	Rattlesnake Run	1858	4	441
Ward, Adonijah B.	130	Rattlesnake Run	1851	4	25
Ward, Adonijah B.	265	Shaver's Fork	1854	4	291
Ward, Adonijah B.	220	Rattlesnake Run	1854	4	288
Ward, Adonijah B.	300	Rattlesnake Run	1850	1	541

Name of Grantee	Acres	Local Description	Year	Book	Page
Ward, Adonijah B. et al	1,000	Rich Mtn.	1856	4	364
Ward, Casper et al	100	Little Black Fork	1860	4	489
Ward, George W.	63½	Rattlesnake Run	1857	4	406
Ward, Jacob	220	Adj. his own	1812	2	462
Ward, Jacob	535	Wts Cheat	1850	2	601
Ward, Jacob	440	Big Lick Run	1846	3	573
Ward, Jesse C.	10½	Wts. Valley River	1860	4	506
Ward, Jonas	222	Adj. Geo. Lee	1796	1	398
Ward, Levi	200	Rattlesnake Run	1835	3	565
Ward, Levi	118	Tygert's Valley R.	1818	2	552
Ward, Levi	195	Rattlesnake Run	1841	3	318
Ward, Levi	116	Tygert's Valley R.	1819	3	4
Ward, Levi et al	400	Roaring Creek	1850	1	470
Ward, Levi S.	50	File's Creek	1853	4	219
Ward, Levi S.	118	File's Creek	1861	4	516
Ward, Levi S.	82	Adj. John Wood	1861	4	514
Ward, Mathew L.	72	Rattlesnake Run	1859	4	465
Ward, Peter H. et al	85	Shaver's Fork	1852	4	131
Ward, Sylvester	238	Thorny Flats	1796	1	394
Ward, Sylvester	984	Stony Run	1790	1	68
Ward, Washington G.	800	Valley River	1841	3	316
Ward, Washington G.	14	Wilson's Orchard	1848	3	460
Ward, Washington G. & Wm L.	2,714	Middle Fork	1851	1	514
Ward, Whitman	900	Leading Creek	1851	4	62
Ward, William L.	2,640	Currence's Mill Creek	1854	4	279
Ward, William L.	100	Near Prong, Mid Fk. R.	1854	4	272
Ward, William L.	1,150	Wts. Tygert's V.	1853	4	221
Ward, William L. et al	980	Mill Creek	1851	4	29
Ward, William L. et al	500	Middle Fork	1851	4	28
Ward, William L. et al	1,990	Ten Mile Creek	1850	2	610
Ware, George W. et al	200	Windy Run	1836	3	204
Ware, Hiram	100	Wts. Valley River	1833	3	157
Ware, Jacob S.	25	Windy Run	1849	1	565
Ware, Richard	100	Valley River	1825	3	92
Ware, Richard et al	100	Wts. Valley River	1832	3	150
Ware, Richard et al	400	Wts. Tygert's Valley	1828	3	125
Ware, William et al	75	Wts. Valley River	1826	3	99
Warmsley, Wamesley, Wamsley Wormsley, Womesley					
Warner, James	272	Wts. Tygert's Valley	1825	3	87
Warner, John	900	Mitchell Run	1856	4	373
Watson, James	35,000	Black Fork	1797	2	95
Watson, James	15,000	Black Fork	1797	2	89
Watson, Josiah	50,000	Wts. Cheat	1796	1	427
Watts, Henson et al	166	Dry Fork	1854	4	270
Wease, Weese, Wees					
Wease, George	50	Branch Road	1805	2	369
Wease, Jacob	100	King's Run	1805	2	370
Webly, William C.	127	Shaver's Fork	1851	1	510
Wees, Wease, Weese					
Wees, George	200	Isner's Run	1831	3	134
Wees, Jacob Jr.	50	King's Run	1818	2	542
Wees, Jacob M.	50	Wts. Cheat	1853	4	240
Wees, Jacob M.	24	Shaver's Fork	1857	4	397
Wees, Jacob M.	65	Shaver's Fork	1857	4	399
Wees, Jacob M.	15	Shaver's Fork	1857	4	398
Wees, William	2¼	Dobson's Run	1854	4	301
Weese, Wease, Wees					
Weese, Jacob et al	100	Eberman's Creek	1837	3	239
Weese, Jacob W. Jr.	50	Wts. Cheat	1836	3	211
Weese, Zirus	375	Wts. Valley River	1842	3	333
Weese, Zirus	200	Wts. Cheat	1850	2	602
Welch, James	99,995½	Wts. Elk	1797	2	53
Welch, James et al	50,000	Wts. Valley River	1796	1	373

Name of Grantee	Acres	Local Description	Year	Book	Page
Wilmoth, George W.	50	Leading Creek	1836	3	214
Wilmoth, James M.	100	Log Lick Run	1850	1	533
Wilmoth, Jonathan	100	Wts. Cheat	1822	3	50
Wilmoth, Levi N.	100	Rattlesnake Run	1842	3	338
Wilmoth, Levi N.	20	Wts. Cheat	1852	4	183
Wilmoth, Levi N.	175	Rattlesnake Run	1852	4	193
Wilmoth, Levi N.	380	Collett's Run	1851	4	8
Wilmoth, Levi N.	184	Shaver Mtn.	1855	4	315
Wilmoth, Levi N.	140	Shaver Mtn.	1856	4	378
Wilmoth, Levi N.	70	Bickle's Knob	1850	1	472
Wilmoth, Levi N.	38	Wts. Cheat	1850	1	473
Wilmoth, Levi N.	250	Shaver Fork	1858	4	574
Wilmoth, Levi N. et al	220	Shaver Fork	1856	4	355
Wilmoth, Levi N. et al	174	Rattlesnake Run	1856	4	371
Wilmoth, Nicholas	200	Wts. Cheat	1822	3	49
Wilmoth, Nicholas	63	Wts. Cheat	1802	2	331
Wilmoth, Thomas (Witmouth)	130	Wts. Cheat	1801	2	292
Wilmoth, William et al	310	Glady Fork	1830	3	129
Wilson, Archibald	76	Beaver Creek	1853	4	252
Wilson, Benjamin	400	Bill's Creek	1792	1	238
Wilson, Benjamin	150	Dotson's Run	1795	1	337
Wilson, Benjamin	145	Eberman's Creek	1803	2	346
Wilson, Edwin D. (Ewin)	9	Wts. Valley River	1851	4	101
Wilson, Francis	500	Middle Mtn.	1792	1	141
Wilson, Francis	500	Middle Mtn.	1792	1	142
Wilson, George	118	Adj. J. Crouch	1794	1	305
Wilson, Henry	120	Raccoon Creek	1839	3	286
Wilson, Henry	143	Raccoon Creek	1839	3	287
Wilson, Henry et al	861	Licking Creek	1853	4	249
Wilson, Josiah D.	2,730	Back Fork	1854	4	551
Wilson, Josiah D. et al	2,270	Wts. Back Fork	1854	4	283
Wilson, Josiah D. et al	1,000	Wts. Back Fork	1854	4	281
Wilson, Josiah D. et al	1,600	Sugar Creek	1855	4	337
Wilson, Lewis et al	130	Dry Fork	1847	3	440
Wilson, Lewis et al	266	Dry Fork	1847	3	438
Wilson, Lewis et al	40	Middle Fork	1850	2	593
Wilson, Lewis et al	306	Middle Fork	1850	2	586
Wilson, Lewis or John et al	584	Dry Fork	1847	3	439
Wilson, Moses	50	Bill's Creek	1809	2	410
Wilson, Moses	100	Tom's Run	1811	2	453
Wilson, Robert	300	Bull Run	1790	1	74
Wilson, Stephen	1,765	Wts. Cheat	1793	1	248
Wilson, Thomas	278	Raccoon Creek	1818	2	541
Wilson, Thomas	100	Raccoon Creek	1822	3	54
Wilson, Thomas	200	Mud Gut Run	1800	2	214
Wilson, Thomas	40,000	Wts. Buckhannon	1795	1	351
Wilson, Thomas	60,000	Middle Fork	1795	1	353
Wilson, Thomas	125	Bull Run	1839	3	288
Wilson, Thomas et al	22	Raccoon Creek	1826	3	104
Wilson, William	36	Sugar Creek	1809	2	411
Wilson, William	100	Raccoon Creek	1812	2	461
Wilson, William	270(207)	Teter's Creek	1811	2	457
Wilson, William	250	Sugar Creek	1807	2	390
Wilson, William	305	Barker's Settlement	1807	2	389
Wilson, William	700	Wts. Valley River	1805	2	376
Wilson, William	100	Beaver Creek	1805	2	375
Wilson, William	110	Raccoon Creek	1805	2	374
Wilson, William	39	Wts. Tygert's Valley	1803	2	337
Wilson, William	180	Tom's Run	1802	2	335
Wilson, William	245	Elk Lick Fork	1802	2	334
Wilson, William	592	Leading Creek	1802	2	332
Wilson, William	450	Bill's Creek	1802	2	333
Wilson, William	54	Wts. Valley River	1802	2	325
Wilson, William	408	Bill's Creek	1801	2	301

RITCHIE COUNTY

Name of Grantee	Acres	Local Description	Year	Book	Page
Amos, Henry	17	Indian Creek	1852	1	282
Ayres—or Ayers					
Ayres, Baccus	108	Indian Creek	1847	1	85
Ayers, Barnes et al (Bacus)	200	Indian Creek	1850	1	174
Ayers, John et al	246	North Fk. of Hughes	1854	1	341
Bays, Richard et al	185	Galaspie Run	1844	1	27
Bee, Asa	400	Otter Slide	1848	1	93
Bee, Asa	251	Lick Run	1852	1	266
Bee, Asa & Zebulon	300	South Fork Hughes	1851	1	217
Bee, Ephriam	295	North Fk. Hughes	1844	1	25
Bee, Ephriam et al	617	South Fk. & Sugar Camp	1860	1	445
Bee, Zebulon	162	Otter Slide Creek	1859	1	428
Bell, John et al	153	Goose Creek	1859	1	440
Bell, John H.	88	Leatherbark	1859	1	438
Bell, Samuel et al	200	Goose Creek	1857	1	382
Blair, J. B.	177	Spruce Creek	1851	1	231
Blair, J. B.	350	North Fk. Hughes	1850	1	179
Blair, J. B. et al	100	Spruce Creek	1851	1	247
Blair, Jacob B.	135	Grass Run	1850	1	178
Blair, Jacob B.	2,000	Leatherbark	1851	1	233
Blair, Jacob B.	175	Cane Run	1851	1	234
Blair, Jacob B.	300	Spruce Creek	1851	1	232
Blair, Jacob B.	780	North Fk Hughes	1851	1	246
Blair, Jacob B.	123	Grass Run	1851	1	193
Blair, Jacob B.	162	Leatherbark	1851	1	194
Blair, Jacob B.	100	McFarland Run	1850	1	192
Blair, Jacob B.	115	Laurel Run	1850	1	191
Blair, Jacob B.	1,401	Leatherbark	1850	1	181
Blair, Jacob B.	30	North Fk. Hughes	1852	1	257
Blair, Jacob B.	500	Dutchman's Run	1852	1	270
Blair, Jacob B.	795	Sheep Run	1858	1	402
Blair, Jacob B.	100	Lowther's Run	1850	1	491
Blair, Jacob B.	100	McFarland's Run	1850	1	492
Blair, Jacob B. et al	100	McFarland's Run	1850	1	153
Blair, Jacob B. et al	100	McFarland's Run	1850	1	150
Blair, Jacob et al	100	McFarland's Run	1850	1	154
Blue, Samuel	330	North Fk. Hughes	1848	1	106
Blue, Samuel	130	North Fk. Hughes	1844	1	17
Blue, Samuel	500	Straight Fork	1849	1	122
Blue, Samuel et al	773	Goose Creek	1849	1	120
Blue, Samuel et al	1,000	N. F. Hughes	1848	1	87
Bollinger, John et al	167	Long Run	1860	1	460
Bond, William P.	206	Brown's Run	1847	1	83
Boys, Richard et al	185	Galaspie Run	1844	1	27
Brown, John & Thomas	199	Goose Creek	1849	1	123
Bukey, Spencer T.	50	Slab Creek	1849	1	126
Bukey, Spencer T.	450	Lamb's Run	1849	1	125
Bukey, Spencer T.	105	Slab Creek	1849	1	124
Butcher, George W.	167	Spruce Creek	1852	1	265
Butcher, Henry	230	South Fk. Hughes	1852	1	269
Butcher, Henry B. et al	100	N. Fk. Hughes	1854	1	346
Cain, Cornelius G.	148	South Fk. Hughes	1858	1	417
Calhoon, Allen	25	Bunnel's Run	1853	1	338
Carpenter, William	16	Bond's Creek	1857	1	389
Carpenter, William	250	North Fk. Hughes	1853	1	323
Chapman, Warner W.	74	North Fk. Hughes	1851	1	249
Clark, Isaac	656	McFarland Run	1850	1	188
Clayton, A. A. et al	198	Spruce Creek	1860	1	486
Cline, Eli	74	North Fk. Hughes	1847	1	64
Cline, Eli	100	North Fk. Hughes	1849	1	127
Clouse, Samuel	16½	North Fk. Hughes	1852	1	295

Name of Grantee	Acres	Local Description	Year	Book	Page
Collins, George	120	Bone Creek	1846	1	40
Collins, Jacob	103	Brown's Run	1849	1	129
Collins, Jacob	29	North Fk. Hughes	1849	1	128
Collins, John	32	Bond's Creek	1855	1	357
Collins, John	248	Bond's Creek	1857	1	393
Collins, John	311	Bond's Creek	1857	1	392
Collins, John	130	Yellow Bank Run	1850	1	190
Collins, John	182	Bond's Creek	1849	1	133
Collins, John	197	Bunnel's Run	1849	1	132
Collins, John	112	Big Run	1847	1	76
Collins, John	276	Bond's Creek	1849	1	130
Collins, John	429	North Fk. Hughes	1849	1	131
Collins, John et al	438	Calhoun Run	1850	1	187
Collins, Josiah	88	Buck Run	1855	1	359
Collins, Josiah	54	North Fk. Hughes	1851	1	222
Collins, Josiah	30	Short Run	1851	1	223
Collins, Josiah	24	Bond's Creek	1849	1	134
Collins, Josiah	64	Wolf Pen Run	1848	1	109
Collins, Joshua et al	154	North Fk. Hughes	1853	1	339
Collins, William	100	North Fk. Hughes	1847	1	66
Collins, William	189	North Fk. Hughes	1847	1	79
Collins, William	10	North Fk. Hughes	1847	1	75
Collins, William	124	North Fk. Hughes	1850	1	160
Collins, William	85	Nat's Run	1858	1	403
Collins, William et al	100	N. Fk. Hughes	1848	1	112
Collins, William et al	970	Nat's Run	1850	1	161
Conwell, John	15	N. Fk. Hughes	1856	1	376
Conwell, John	127	N. Fk. Hughes	1856	1	374
Cook, John	48	White Oak Creek	1858	1	395
Cook, John	563	White Oak Creek	1858	1	394
Copelin, David (Coplin)	100	Alum Cave Run	1852	1	302
Core, A. S.	827	So. Fork Hughes	1859	1	441
Core, Andrew S.	269	Galaspie's Run	1853	1	309
Core, Andrew S.	60	Dry Run	1853	1	310
Core, Andrew S.	420	Spruce Creek	1853	1	315
Core, Andrew S.	147	Straight Fork	1853	1	312
Core, Andrew S.	52	Spruce Creek	1853	1	311
Core, Andrew S.	250	Slab Creek	1853	1	329
Cox, David	30	Buck Run	1856	1	373
Cox, Isaac N.	31	Lost Run	1851	1	235
Cox, Isaac N. et al	200	South Fk. Hughes	1851	1	224
Cox, Isaac N. et al	275½	Wolf Pen Fork	1853	1	330
Cox, Philip Jr. et al	1,000	Slab Creek	1852	1	259
Cox, Philip Jr. et al	1,200	Cane's Run	1853	1	303
Cross, John	18	North Fk. Hughes	1857	1	380
Cunningham, Benjamin	50	Leatherbark	1851	1	218
Cunnnigham, Harrison B.	67	Leatherbark	1850	1	146
Cunningham, Harrison B.	28	Leason's Fork	1850	1	145
Cunningham, John R.	36	South Fk. Hughes	1859	1	437
Cunningham, William	94	Bond's Creek	1854	1	348
Daugherty—See Dougherty					
Daugherty, Jacob et al	15	Dry Run	1856	1	375
Davisson, Samuel	100	Spruce Creek	1852	1	284
Dawson, Levy	150	Hasher's Run	1850	1	169
Deem, Commodore P.	284	Long Run	1851	1	198
Deem, Commodore P.	178	Weaver's Fork	1851	1	195
Deem, Commodore P.	204	Laurel Run	1851	1	196
Deem, Commodore P.	287	North Fk. Hughes	1851	1	197
Deem, Commodore P.	67	Cabin Run	1848	1	90
Deem, Marshall	37	So. Fk. Hughes R.	1853	1	336
Deem, Philip	66	Cabin Run	1848	1	89
Dennison, A. J. et al	500	Dutchman's Run	1860	1	446
Dixon, David	25	North Fk. Hughes	1858	1	418

Name of Grantee	Acres	Local Description	Year	Book	Page
Hardman, James	100	Spring Fork	1850	1	168
Hardman, James S.	27	Grass Run	1854	1	354
Hardman, James S.	55	Leatherbark	1854	1	349
Hardman, Thomas	104	Grass Run	1852	1	262
Harris, John	2,400	Goose Creek	1848	1	86
Harris, John Sr.	15	North Fk. Hughes	1850	1	148
Harris, Thomas M.	400	Butcher's Fork	1844	1	16
Harris, Thomas M. et al	933	Otter Slide Cr.	1853	1	325
Haydon, Henry	87	Bone Creek	1852	1	294
Haydon, Henry	4	Bone Creek	1852	1	293
Haymond, Daniel	100	Straight Run	1852	1	256
Haymond, Daniel	150	Bond's Run	1848	1	115
Haymond, Luther	445	Bond's Run	1848	1	116
Haymond, William C.	15	North Fk. Hughes	1861	1	484
Haymond, William C.	175	Spring Run	1848	1	104
Haymond, William C.	112	North Fk. Hughes	1851	1	240
Hill, Daniel B.	394	Leatherbark	1851	1	239
Hill, Daniel B.	65	Leatherbark	1851	1	238
Hitchcox, M. M. & Wm. L.	271	Husher's Run	1858	1	405
Hitchcox, Michael M.	200	Husher's Run	1850	1	147
Hitchcox, Waldo P.	990	Husher's Run	1854	1	355
Hitchcox, William	293	Husher's Run	1851	1	236
Hitchcox, William L.	140	Whitney's Run	1851	1	199
Hoff, John	100	Bone Creek	1854	1	347
Hoover, Michael et al	262	Devil Hole Creek	1850	1	176
Hoover, Thomas	600	Devil Hole Creek	1848	1	88
Hoover, Thomas	96	Indian Run	1850	1	175
Hoover, Thomas	18	Dog Run	1850	1	170
Hoover, William	100	Indian Creek	1851	1	243
Hughes, Joseph	175	Bunnel's Run	1860	1	480
Jackson, B. W. et al	100	Spruce Creek	1851	1	247
Jackson, B. W. et al	179	McFarland's Run	1852	1	258
Jackson, Henry	70	Bear Run	1849	1	117
Jackson, Henry J.	580	North Fk. Hughes	1851	1	211
Jackson, Henry J.	616	South Fk. Hughes	1849	1	118
Jackson, Henry J.	30	North Fk. Hughes	1851	1	210
Jackson, Henry J.	260	South Fk. Hughes	1851	1	250
Jackson, Henry J.	124	McFarland's Run	1852	1	288
Jackson, Henry J.	4,102	Bare Run	1853	1	332
Jackson, Henry J.	390	South Fk. Hughes	1855	1	360
Jackson, Henry J.	100	McFarland's Run	1858	1	411
Jackson, Henry J.	1,100	McFarland's Run	1858	1	412
Jackson, William S. et al	200	South Fk. Hughes	1851	1	224
Jarvis, E. J.	75	Bunnel's Run	1852	1	297
Jarvis, E. J. et al	970	Nat's Run	1850	1	161
Jarvis, E. J. et al	154	North Fk. Hughes	1853	1	339
Jarvis, Edward J.	143	Bunnel's Run	1861	1	481
Johnson, William F.	2	Oil Spring Run	1861	1	483
Johnston, Robert	2,685	South Fk. Hughes	1859	1	423
Jones, Edmund B.	45½	Left Fk. Hughes	1861	1	487
Jones, Elizabeth	25	Arnold's Creek	1847	1	77
Jones, Jacob et al	710	Buffalo Run	1846	1	36
Jones, Jacob et al	624	Goose Creek	1846	1	37
Jones, Jacob et al	50	Goose Creek	1846	1	60
Jones, Jacob et al	28	North Fk. Hughes	1848	1	91
Jones, Jacob et al	288	Cabin Run	1848	1	92
Jones, James B.	14	McKim's Fork	1855	1	366
Jones, James B.	136	Wolf Run	1855	1	367
Jones, James R.	26	Indian Creek	1856	1	371
Jones, James R.	25	Indian Creek	1852	1	296
Kerkendall, Nimrod	108	Slab Creek	1854	1	352
Kerkendall, Nimrod	68	Isaac's Fork	1852	1	274
Kerkendall, Nimrod	435	Slab Creek	1852	1	273

Name of Grantee	Acres	Local Description	Year	Book	Page
Maxwell, Lewis	271	Grass Run	1847	1	57
Maxwell, Lewis	76	Wolf Pen Fork	1847	1	56
Maxwell, Lewis	87	Spruce Creek	1847	1	58
Maxwell, Lewis	364	Leatherbark	1847	1	54
Maxwell, Lewis	99	Leatherbark	1847	1	55
Maxwell, Lewis	160	Spruce Creek	1847	1	53
Maxwell, Lewis	160	Spruce Creek	1847	1	52
Maxwell, Lewis	120	Leatherbark	1847	1	51
Maxwell, Lewis	100	Spruce Creek	1847	1	50
Maxwell, Lewis	200	Leatherbark	1847	1	82
Maxwell, Lewis	46	Leatherbark	1847	1	63
Maxwell, Lewis	100	South Fk. Hughes	1847	1	62
Maxwell, Lewis	200	Spruce Creek	1847	1	59
Maxwell, Lewis	233	Wolf Pen Fork	1846	1	45
Maxwell, Lewis	542	Spruce Creek	1846	1	44
Maxwell, Lewis	65	Spruce Creek	1846	1	43
Maxwell, Lewis	313	Grass Run	1844	1	29
Maxwell, Lewis	77	Branch Indian Cr.	1844	1	24
May, David, Adm.	2,836	Goose Creek	1859	1	422
McDonald, Alexander	64	Spruce Creek	1856	1	369
McDonald, Alexander H.	100	Spruce Creek	1852	1	300
McGregor, David	100	Galaspie's Run	1859	1	430
McGregor, David	100	Laurel Run	1858	1	415
McGregor, David	40	Galaspie's Run	1853	1	314
McGregor, David	270	Silver Run	1849	1	119
McGregor, David et al	970	Dutchman's Run	1860	1	447
McGregor, David et al	390	Laurel Run	1858	1	416
McGregor, David et al	118	McFarland's Run	1856	1	370
McKinney, James	37	North Fk. Hughes	1852	1	298
McKinney, James & William P.	200	North Fk. Hughes	1844	1	26
Melon—Mellon, Millon					
Melon, John W.	(57)67	McFarland Run	1857	1	386
Melon, John W.	112	McFarland Run	1853	1	333
Melon, John W. et al	118	McFarland Run	1856	1	370
Melon, John W. et al	400	Galaspie's Run	1858	1	400
Middleton, George et al	185	Galaspie Run	1844	1	27
Middleton & Richard	185	Galaspie Run	1844	1	27
Millon, Marcus (Mellon)	125	Arnold's Creek	1847	1	81
Mitchell, John W.	100	Beach Fork	1846	1	46
Mitchell, John W.	198	Laurel Fork	1852	1	276
Mitchell, John W.	113	Slab Creek	1852	1	283
Mitchell, John W.	65	Beech Fork	1854	1	344
Mitchell, John W. et al	116	Slab Creek	1854	1	353
Mitchell, Josiah	50	Beech Fork	1850	1	155
Mitchell, Josiah	49½	South Fk. Hughes	1850	1	202
Mitchell, William	150	Spruce Creek	1848	1	105
Mitchell, William	149	Alum Fork	1849	1	143
Mitchell, William T. et al	275½	Wolf Pen Fork	1853	1	330
Moats, William	8	Adj. T. Harris	1851	1	237
Morgan, Charles S.	50	Goose Creek	1846	1	60
Morgan, Charles S.	710	Buffalo Run	1846	1	36
Morgan, Charles S. et al	624	Goose Creek	1846	1	37
Morgan, Charles S. et al	288	Cabin Run	1848	1	92
Morgan, Charles S. et al	28	N. Fork Hughes	1848	1	91
Mount—or Mounts					
Mount, Ezekiel	85	Goose Creek	1859	1	442
Mounts, Benjamin	125	Goose Creek	1848	1	94
Moyers, Lewis, Jr.	600	McFarland's Run	1849	1	121
Mullenax, Coonrod et al	262	Devil's Hole Cr.	1850	1	176
Mullenia, Coonrod et al	262	Devil's Hole Cr.	1850	1	176
Murphy, Purviance	81	South Fk. Hughes	1854	1	340
Musgrave, David	147	Stuart's Run	1851	1	226
Neal, Daniel R.	227	Bond's Creek	1856	1	368
Neal, Daniel R.	200	North Fk. Hughes	1844	1	11

Name of Grantee	Acres	Local Description	Year	Book	Page
Purviance, Robert Jr. et al	169	So. Fk. Hughes	1860	1	468
Purviance, Robert Jr. et al	793	So. Fk. Hughes	1860	1	467
Purviance, Robert Jr. et al	793	Laurel Run	1860	1	466
Purviance, Robert Jr. et al	1,409	So. Fk. Hughes	1860	1	465
Purviance, Robert Jr. et al	525	So. Fk. Hughes	1860	1	463
Purviance, Robert Jr. et al	607	So. Fk. Hughes	1860	1	462
Purviance, Robert Jr. et al	587	So. Fk. Hughes	1860	1	461
Rexroad, Henry	63	Dog Run	1844	1	22
Rexroad, Henry	14	Back Run	1844	1	20
Rexroad, Noah	50	North Fk.Hughes	1844	1	28
Rexroad, Solomon	42	Lick Run	1844	1	21
Richard & Middleton	185	Galaspie Run	1844	1	27
Riggs, Matthew	69½	Straight Run	1851	1	228
Right, Harrison	214	Spruce Creek	1855	1	365
Right, James	14	Spruce Creek	1855	1	364
Rogers, John B.	244½	Leatherbark	1859	1	434
Rogers, John B.	50	Leatherbark	1860	1	443
Rogers, Samuel G. et al	(176) 106	Indian Creek	1857	1	381
Rollins, Jeremiah	66	Dry Fork	1844	1	19
Ruby, Lloyd (Ruly)	8	Hughes River	1847	1	70
Ruly, Lloyd (Ruby)	8	Hughes River	1847	1	70
Rush, William	31	Big Run	1849	1	137
Rush, William	45	North Fk. Hughes	1854	1	343
Sinnett, Abel	100	Indian Creek	1858	1	409
Sinnett, George	334	King Knob Run	1853	1	319
Sinnett, Henry	205	Indian Creek	1853	1	327
Sleeth, David W.	55	Leatherbark	1850	1	156
Sleeth, David W.	38	Leatherbark	1850	1	157
Sleeth, David W.	69	South Fk. Hughes	1850	1	158
Sleeth, David W.	35	Leatherbark	1850	1	159
Sleeth, David W.	235	Grass Run	1851	1	215
Sleeth, David W.	61	Grass Run	1852	1	255
Sleeth, Granville W.	100	Leatherbark	1850	1	163
Smith, Jacob H.	1,990	King's Run	1852	1	264
Smith, James L.	134	Spruce Creek	1858	1	404
Smith, James L.	82	Spruce Creek	1858	1	407
Smith, Levi	100	Spruce Creek	1848	1	97
Smith, Nathaniel	151	Spruce Creek	1858	1	401
Somerville—or Summerville					
Somerville, James W.	260	Big Run	1858	1	406
Sommerville, Robert L.	128	Wolf Pen Run	1851	1	242
Springer, Job	500	McFarland's Run	1850	1	144
Spurgeon, James	100	Gallaspie's Run	1846	1	39
Stanley, John	100	Plum Run	1852	1	290
Starkey, Lorenzo D.	660	Slab Creek	1860	1	459
Starr, John	113	So. Fk. Hughes	1850	1	172
Starr, John	144	Indian Creek	1846	1	49
Stenchcomb—or Stinchcomb					
Stenchcomb, Thomas	100	Grass Run	1848	1	107
Stenchcomb, Thomas et al	200	Bear Run	1848	1	110
Stinchcomb, Thomas	200	Spruce Fork	1852	1	287
Stinchcomb, Thomas	160	Straight Fork	1852	1	286
Stinchcomb, Thomas	1,118	Grass Run	1852	1	277
Stinchcomb, Thomas et al	179	McFarland's Run	1852	1	258
Stinchcomb, Thomas et al	126	Straight Creek	1857	1	387
Summerville—or Somerville					
Summerville, Robert	200	Bone Creek	1860	1	478
Summerville, Robert	250	Bone Creek	1851	1	229
Summerville, Robert	900	Bone Creek	1848	1	96
Swisher, Jacob et al	153	Goose Creek	1859	1	440
Tenant, Samuel et al	200	Goose Creek	1857	1	382
Terry, James H.	200	Goose Creek	1844	1	23
Tharp, Timothy	985	Bone Creek	1848	1	98
Tharp, Timothy	149	Stone Lick Fork	1851	1	206

Name of Grantee	Acres	Local Description	Year	Book	Page
Tharp, Timothy	426	Leatherbark Fork	1852	1	278
Tharp, Timothy	170	Bone Creek	1853	1	320
Tharp, Timothy	23	Bone Creek	1853	1	321
Thaw, Clemont E.	135	Husher's Run	1852	1	285
Underwood, John R. et al	75	Lamb's Run	1852	1	291
Valentine, George	143	Long Run	1849	1	141
Valentine, George	158	Cain's Run	1849	1	142
Valentine, George	85	Long Run	1851	1	230
Valentine, George et al	75	Lamb's Run	1852	1	291
Valentine, Wm. A. & H. et al	407	Lamb's Run	1859	1	435
Walker, William et al	933	Otter Slide	1853	1	325
Ward, Martin C.	100	Bone Creek	1860	1	477
Wass, Harrison et al	15	Dry Run	1856	1	375
Wass, John et al	116	Slab Creek	1854	1	353
Watson, Wilson	88	Bone Creek	1855	1	356
Webb, John	214	Stone Creek	1853	1	308
Webb, John	532	McFarland's Run	1852	1	263
Webb, John A.	230	Indian Creek	1851	1	221
Webb, William	198	Indian Creek	1850	1	173
Westfall, John W.	693	Spruce Creek	1851	1	244
Westfall, John W.	125	Slab Creek	1851	1	245
Westfall, John W.	203	Straight Fork	1853	1	307
Westfall, John W.	30	South Fk. Hughes	1861	1	482
Wigner, John G.	10	No. Fk. Hughes	1858	1	408
Williams, George H. et al	587	So. Fk. Hughes	1860	1	461
Williams, George H. et al	607	So. Fk. Hughes	1860	1	462
Williams, George H. et al	525	So. Fk. Hughes	1860	1	463
Williams, George H. et al	192	Cave Run	1860	1	464
Williams, George H. et al	1,409	So. Fk. Hughes	1860	1	465
Williams, George H. et al	793	Laurel Run	1860	1	466
Williams, George H. et al	793	So. Fk. Hughes	1860	1	467
Williams, George H. et al	169	So. Fk. Hughes	1860	1	468
Williams, George H. et al	434	McFarland's Run	1860	1	469
Williams, George H. et al	300	Indian Creek	1860	1	470
Williams, George H. et al	745	So. Fk. Hughes	1860	1	471
Williams, George H. et al	500	Long Run	1860	1	472
Williams, George H. et al	506	Leatherbark	1860	1	473
Williams, George H. et al	¾	Smithville	1860	1	474
Williams, William T.	200	Slab Creek	1858	1	413
Wilson, A. J.	535	Straight Fork	1852	1	301
Wilson, A. J.	70	Beeson's Run	1853	1	328
Wilson, A. J.	300	Poplar Lick	1857	1	390
Wilson, A. J. et al	438	Calhoun Run	1850	1	187
Wilson, Alexander	100	Dutchman's Run	1847	1	71
Wilson, Archibald J.	87	Long Run	1847	1	80
Wilson, Archibald J.	1,000	Leatherbark	1850	1	183
Wilson, Archibald J.	300	Spruce Creek	1850	1	184
Wilson, Archibald J.	70	Wolf Pen Fork	1850	1	185
Wilson, Archibald J.	15	Long Run	1852	1	268
Wilson, Bassil H.	45	No. Fk. Hughes	1860	1	485
Wilson, J. M. Jr.	21	Buck Run	1849	1	140
Wilson, John M.	224	Long Run	1849	1	138
Wilson, John M.	336	Spring Run	1850	1	189
Wilson, John M. Sr.	100	Goose Creek	1848	1	108
Wilson, Joseph et al	214	Strait Creek	1860	1	479
Wilson, Josiah D.	355	Spruce Creek	1852	1	253
Wilson, Josiah D.	100	No. Fk. Hughes	1852	1	254
Wilson, Josiah D.	405	Grass Run	1852	1	494
Wilson, Josiah D.	960	Indian Creek	1852	1	493
Wilson, William	100	Dutchman's Run	1847	1	74
Wilson, William S. et al	96	Slate Creek	1853	1	306
Wright—See Right					
Wyre, Archibald	152	Spruce Fork	1850	1	186
Yater, Joseph	78	Buck Run	1849	1	139
Zinn, Otho P.	20	So. Fk. Hughes	1852	1	292

ROANE COUNTY

Name of Grantee	Acres	Local Description	Year	Book	Page
Adkins, Davidson et al	1,000	Little Pigeon	1861	1	527
Bee, Ephriam	600	Little Spring Cr.	1859	1	512
Bennett, Jonathan M. et al	640	Big Sandy	1859	1	514
Brown, James H. et al	5,450	Wts. Big Sandy	1859	1	503
Chapman, Henry B. et al	6,163	Wts. Pocataligo	1858	1	500
Chapman, Henry et al	1,000	Little Pigeon	1861	1	527
Duval, George W.	280	Reedy Creek	1859	1	506
Duval, George W.	150	Reedy Creek	1859	1	505
Duval, Lewis L.	327	Waters Pocotaligo	1859	1	507
Duval, Lewis L.	260	Flat Fork	1859	1	508
Duval, Lewis L.	50	Flat Fork	1859	1	509
Duval, Lewis L.	125	Higby	1859	1	516
Duval, Lewis L.	250	Reedy Creek	1860	1	524
Goshorn, W. F. & J. H. et al	5,450	Wts. Big Sandy	1859	1	503
Harper, Epperson	328	Pocataligo River	1860	1	525
Jones, George W.	119	Higby Creek	1860	1	519
Kyger, Hugh et al	51	Spring Creek	1859	1	513
Kyger, Hugh et al	400	Charles Fork	1860	1	518
Lorentz, Jacob	390	Big Sandy	1859	1	517
Lorentz, John et al	640	Big Sandy	1859	1	514
Neal, Daniel R.	225	Bear Fork	1858	1	499
Neal, Daniel R.	145	Billy's Run	1858	1	497
Neal, Daniel R.	175	Billy's Run	1858	1	498
Parker, Wm. W. & S. H. et al	640	Big Sandy	1859	1	514
Riddle, Benjamin	74	Spring Creek	1860	1	523
Riley, George W.	125	Flat Fork	1860	1	526
Riley, George W.	100	Wts. Pocataligo	1859	1	511
Riley, George W. & William	150	Reedy Creek	1859	1	510
Simmons, James & Jonathan	400	Little Spring Creek	1860	1	522
Sinnett, Able P.	315	Big Sandy	1859	1	502
Sinnett, Abel P. et al	5,450	Wts. Big Sandy	1859	1	503
Smith, Benjamin H. et al	6,163	Wts. Pocataligo	1858	1	500
Smith, Benjamin H. & G. W.	4,225	Big Sandy	1859	1	515
Smith, G. W. et al	51	Spring Creek	1859	1	513
Smith, G. W. et al	400	Charles Fork	1860	1	518
Stewart, John W.	70	Reedy Creek	1858	1	501
Stewart, John W.	9a.28p.	Reedy Creek	1860	1	520
Swann, Thomas B. et al	5,450	Wts. Big Sandy	1859	1	503
Tompkins, C. H. et al	32	Spring Creek	1859	1	504
Tompkins, C. H. et al	186	Spring Creek	1860	1	521
Wolf, Joseph B. et al	32	Spring Creek	1859	1	504
Wolf, Joseph B. et al	186	Spring Creek	1860	1	521

TAYLOR COUNTY

Armstrong, A. et al	104	3 Forks Creek	1859	1	447
Armstrong, Adolphus et al	65½	Valley River	1853	1	430
Armstrong, Adolphus	16¾	Sandy Creek	1857	1	441
Asbury, John	9½	Adj. Harrison Fletcher	1856	1	440
Bartlett, Robert	161¾	Sand Lick Run	1846	1	398
Bartlett, Robert	20½	Sand Lick Run	1849	1	415
Bartlett, Robert	71	Sand Lick Run	1849	1	416
Bartlett, Robert	7½	Flagg Run	1857	1	442
Behen, Lancelott T.	10	Shelby Run	1849	1	413
Blue, William	4¾	3 Fork Creek	1848	1	407

TUCKER COUNTY

Name of Grantee	Acres	Local Description	Year	Book	Page
Allender, George et al	112	Shaver's Fork	1859	1	497
Arnold, Jonathan	4,430	Big Spring	1860	1	498
Arnold, Jonathan	850	Horse Shoe Run	1858	1	465
Arnold, Jonathan	124	Horse Shoe Run	1858	1	464
Arnold, Jonathan	310	Black Fork	1858	1	463
Arnold, Jonathan	475	Coburn Run	1858	1	461
Arnold, Jonathan	174	Black Fork	1858	1	462
Arnold, Jonathan	1,588	Horse Shoe Run	1858	1	460
Arnold, Jonathan	150	Horse Shoe Run	1859	1	495
Arnold, Jonathan et al	4,680	Black Fork	1858	1	466
Arnold, Jonathan et al	768½	Black Fork	1858	1	467
Arnold, Jonathan et al	79	Dry Fork	1858	1	468
Arnold, Jonathan et al	1,637	Black Fork	1858	1	469
Arnold, Jonathan et al	1,543	Maxwell's Run	1858	1	470
Arnold, Jonathan et al	1,340	Dry Fork	1858	1	472
Arnold, Jonathan et al	257	Horse Shoe Run	1859	1	493
Arnold, Jonathan et al	1,483	Horse Shoe Run	1859	1	494
Arnold, Jonathan et al	1,117	Dry Fork	1858	1	589
Boner—or Bonner					
Boner, Solomon	50	Dry Fork	1859	1	487
Boner, Solomon & S. H. et al	980	Red Creek	1858	1	473
Brown, Bernard L. et al	431	Clover Run	1858	1	477
Brown, Bernard L. et al	1,543	Maxwell's Run	1858	1	470
Brown, Bernard L. et al	1,340	Dry Fork	1858	1	472
Brown, Bernard L. et al	1,637	Black Fork	1858	1	469
Butcher, Reuben S.	50	Nail Run	1858	1	481
Byrne, John P.	2,500	Licking Creek	1858	1	482
Campbell, Geo. G.	286	Clover Run	1859	1	490
Carr, Enos et al	768	Black Fork	1861	1	506
Cassin, Tabitha M.	1,327	Horse Shoe Run	1858	1	593
Collett, Hugh P.	150	Wts. Cheat	1859	1	486
Collett, Hugh P. et al	176	Dry Fork	1858	1	476
Collett, Hugh P. et al	300	Dry Fork	1858	1	475
Crawford, Bushrod W. et al	431	Clover Run	1858	1	477
Deakins, William F.	3,160	Horse Shoe Run	1858	1	594
Deakins, William F.	512	Horse Shoe Run	1858	1	546
Deakins, William F.	125	Clover Run	1859	1	496
Deakins, Wm. F.	1,000	Coburn's Run	1858	1	478
Deakins, Wm. F.	560	Horse Shoe Run	1858	1	479
Dobbins, Geo. W. & W. B.	26,000	Black & Dry Runs	1857	1	586
Dobbins, George W.	768½	Black Fork	1857	1	449
Dobbins, George W. & W. B.	420	Black Fork	1857	1	448
Ewin, William	1,250	Clover Run	1858	1	480
Ewin, William	860	Black Fork	1859	1	492
Ewin, William	6,940	Wts Cheat	1857	1	584
Fitzwater, James P.	160	Clover Run	1857	1	450
Flanagan, Jacob	78½	Dry Fork	1860	1	499
Goff, David et al	257	Horse Shoe Run	1859	1	493
Goff, David et al	1,483	Horse Shoe Run	1859	1	494
Harper, Adam	1,100	Clover Run	1857	1	591
Harper, Jonathan W.	18	Island in Cheat Rv.	1857	1	459
Harper, Jonathan W.	23	Cheat River	1857	1	458
Hart, Milton	118	Dry Fork	1860	1	501
Hart, Milton et al	176	Dry Fork	1858	1	476
Hart, Milton et al	300	Dry Fork	1858	1	475
Hart, Milton et al	239	Back Bone Mt.	1857	1	456
Hoffman, John S.	2,513	Black Fork	1860	1	504
Hoffman, John S. et al	4,680	Black Fork	1858	1	466
Hoffman, John S. et al	768½	Black Fork	1858	1	467
Hoffman, John S. et al	79	Dry Fork	1858	1	468

TYLER COUNTY

Name of Grantee	Acres	Local Description	Year	Book	Page
Ankrom, Nelson	100	Sancoe's Run	1843	2	308
Ankrom, Nelson	100	Sugar Run	1852	2	443
Ankrom, Nelson	100	McKim's Creek	1841	2	229
Ankrom, Nelson	100	Big Run	1842	2	254
Ankrom, Nelson	115	McKim's Fork	1842	2	253
Ankrom, Richard (Son of Jacob)	150	Canoe Run	1820	1	40
Ankrom, Richard (Son of Jacob)	200	Middle Island Cr.	1820	1	39
Ankrom, Richard Jr.	100	Purgatory Run	1817	1	7
Ankrom, William C.	212	Rush Run	1846	2	348
Ankrom, William et al	42	Sugar Tree Creek	1847	2	376
Archbold, Samuel	50	Long Run	1837	1	416
Archbold, Samuel	50	Long Run	1837	1	415
Archbold, Samuel	100	Long Run	1847	2	363
Archer, William	162	Sanco's Run	1835	1	359
Ash, John	100	Foster's Run	1820	1	54
Ash, John	422	Foster's Run	1852	2	446
Ash, John	278	Sancoe Run	1844	2	337
Ash, John Sr.	12	Sancho's Run	1851	2	409
Ash, Peter D. & Anthony	61	Sancho Creek	1853	2	456
Ash, William	111	Sancoe's Run	1847	2	369
Ashby, John W.	50	Lynn Camp Run	1832	1	306
Ashby, William et al Heirs	50	Lynn Camp Run	1838	2	105
Asher, Henry	100	Indian Creek	1830	1	212
Asher, Henry	100	Indian Creek	1830	1	220
Baker, John et al	117(717)	Indian Creek	1838	2	138
Baker, John et al	156	Indian Creek	1838	2	139
Baker, Mashack (of Evin)	25	Adj. James Smith	1840	2	197
Baker, Meshack	238	Big Run	1839	2	171
Baker, William	30	Indian Creek	1854	2	470
Bailey, James	191	Middle Island Cr.	1834	1	330
Bailey, James	200	Middle Island Cr.	1819	1	26
Bales, Adin	100	Fallen Timber Run	1838	2	94
Bales, Adin	60	Fallen Timber Run	1838	2	95
Bamings, Asa	200	Laurel Run	1838	2	93
Banning, Asa	200	Laurel Run	1838	2	93
Barker, John Jr	100	Indian Creek	1819	1	23
Bartlett, M. D.	141	Long Run	1856	2	492
Bartrug, Peter	250	Fish Creek	1824	1	116
Bates, Adan	60	Fallen Timber Run	1838	2	95
Bierd, Isaac (Byard)	50	Knob Fork	1826	1	139
Bills, Thomas	100	Brush Run	1847	2	370
Bland, David	54	Fishing Creek	1841	2	207
Bogard, John	100	Lynn Camp Run	1832	1	288
Bogard, John	100	Rocky Run	1826	1	147
Bogard, John	100	Little Fishing Cr.	1828	1	163
Boiles, Phebe et al	170	Fish Creek	1822	1	87
Boiles, Phebe et al	465	Sugar Run	1822	1	88
Bond, Barney B.	30	Purgatory Creek	1854	2	472
Bond, Barney B.	3	Mid. Island Cr.	1854	2	473
Bond, Barney Butler et al Heirs	200	Jefferson Run	1849	2	396
Bond, Barney Butler et al Heirs	8	Purgatory Run	1849	2	395
Bond, Barney et al Heirs of	200	Purgatory Run	1845	2	338
Bond, John	100	Purgatory Run	1834	1	335
Bond, John		(See Tyler No. 2, P. 338)	1843	2	299
Bond, John	100	Purgatory Run	1841	2	220
Bond, Thomas (of Benjamin)	100	Short Run	1853	2	451
Bond, Thomas	45	Short Run	1843	2	298
Bond, Thomas	200	Bond's Upper Run	1817	1	13
Booker, Henry	100	Indian Creek	1820	1	55
Booker, Henry	200	Indian Creek	1817	1	3
Booker, Henry	100	Weekly's Run	1838	2	107
Booth, James	200	Fishing Creek	1822	1	92
Booth, James	100	Fishing Creek	1818	1	16

Name of Grantee	Acres	Local Description	Year	Book	Page
Boreman, William I. et al	321	McKim's Fork	1846	2	357
Boreman, William I. (or J.)	574	Muddy Creek	1852	2	422
Boreman, William I. (or J.) et al	118	Mid. Island Creek	1852	2	423
Boreman, William I. (or J.) et al	100	McKim's Fork	1846	2	361
Boreman, William J.	1,012½	Pt. Pleasant Creek	1859	2	511
Boreman, William J. et al	94	Davis Run	1851	2	408
Bowls, Isaac G.	100	Middle Island Cr.	1851	2	427
Bowman, James	50	Sugar Run	1832	1	296
Bowman, James	50	Sugar Run	1832	1	291
Bowman, Silas	100	Fish Creek	1832	1	294
Boyles—See Boiles					
Brooks, Nicholas	30	Fishing Creek	1828	1	169
Browse, Nicholas	157	Mid Island Cr.	1842	2	284
Browse, Thomas	1,450	Middle Island	1838	1	431
Browse, Thomas	74	Middle Island	1838	2	19
Browse, Thomas	2,750	Wts. Mid Island	1838	2	18
Browse, Thomas et al	256	Fishing Creek	1838	2	100
Browse, Thomas et al	370	Fishing Creek	1838	2	35
Buckhannon, John	126	Fishing Creek	1839	2	170
Buckhannon, John	250	Lower Long Run	1838	2	106
Buckhannon, John	100	Fishing Creek	1835	1	380
Buckman, James (Ruckman)	135	Fishing Creek	1837	1	407
Bullman, John	70	Middle Island Cr.	1819	1	33
Bullman, John	100	Sugar Creek	1842	2	285
Byard, Isaac	100	Knob Fork	1829	1	203
Byard, Isaac	449	Little Fishing Creek	1842	2	283
Byard, Isaac	100	Knob Fork	1840	2	199
Byard, Isaac	50	Knob Fork	1826	1	139
Caldwell, Alexander	500	Rocky Run	1836	1	392
Caldwell, Alexander	300	Rocky Run	1830	1	226
Caldwell, Alexander	50	Proctor's Run	1830	1	229
Caldwell, Alexander	250	Proctor's Run	1830	1	228
Caldwell, Alexander	190	Lynn Camp	1830	1	227
Caldwell, Alexander	400	Lynn Camp	1831	1	233
Caldwell, Alexander	250	Proctor's Run	1831	1	234
Caldwell, Alexander	200	Fish Creek	1831	1	232
Caldwell, Alexander	350	Lynn Camp Run	1832	1	275
Caldwell, Elbert H.	100	Fish Creek	1838	1	443
Caldwell, William	75	Church's Fork	1828	1	177
Calvert, Thomas C.	425	Lynn Camp Run	1838	2	135
Campbell, Joseph et al	164	Fishing Creek	1824	1	120
Cardis, Frederick (Cordes)	18	Sancho Creek	1858	2	509
Carney—See Karney					
Carney, Solomon	285	Rocky Run	1833	1	322
Carney, Solomon et al	100	Rocky Run	1833	1	321
Carrell—See Caril, Carrill					
Carrill, Samuel	25	Buffalo Run	1828	1	175
Carrill, Samuel (Carrell)	100	Buffalo Run	1828	1	180
Christen, John	20	Pursley's Run	1857	2	502
Church, Hannah	50	Church's Fork	1842	2	256
Church, Henry	75	Fish Creek	1821	1	72
Church, Henry	100	Fish Creek	1821	1	71
Church, Henry	100	Fish Creek	1820	1	47
Church, Henry	196	Fish Creek	1820	1	49
Church, Henry	80	Church's Fork	1831	1	252
Church, Henry	50	Proctor's Run	1832	1	271
Church, Henry	100	Church's Fork	1828	1	189
Church, Henry	100	Fish Creek	1837	1	414
Church, Henry	46	Little Fishing Cr.	1838	2	36
Church, Henry Jr.	80	Church's Fork	1842	2	255
Clark, Abisha	215	Fish Creek	1841	2	218
Clark, Ebenezer	325	Proctor's Run	1838	2	109
Clark, Ebenezer	20	Little Fishing Creek	1838	2	108

Name of Grantee	Acres	Local Description	Year	Book	Page
Cochran, Friend	67	Sheet's Run	1848	2	392
Cochran, James	120	Mowrey's Run	1838	2	134
Cochran, Samuel	50	Crow's Run	1839	2	172
Cochran, Samuel et al	405	Rock Run	1848	2	389
Cochran, Thomas	250	Tom's Run	1827	1	151
Coen, Isaac	100	Pine Run	1838	2	150
Coen, Peter	100	Rocky Run	1838	2	149
Coen, Peter	100	Lit. Fishing Cr.	1834	1	340
Collins, Henry B.	296	McKim's Fork	1852	2	439
Collins, Henry et al	250	McKim's Fork	1842	2	279
Conaway, Abraham J.	5a.3r.32.	Foster's Run	1854	2	480
Conaway, Alpheus	12	Middle Island Creek	1858	2	510
Conaway, Alpheus	34	Wheeler's Run	1851	2	411
Conaway, Alpheus et al	409	Short Run	1855	2	490
Conaway, Andrew D. (Conway)	59	Bond's Run	1835	1	362
Conaway, Andrew D.	23	Wheeler's Run	1850	2	403
Cook, Richard	100	Little Fishing Cr.	1830	1	218
Cook, Richard	22	Little Fishing Cr.	1828	1	168
Cooper, John	200	Proctor's Run	1832	1	281
Corbley, Andrew	200	Purgatory Run	1844	2	332
Corbley, Andrew	300	Purgatory Run	1841	2	224
Corbley, Andrew	140	Long Run	1842	2	257
Corbly, Elizabeth et al	170	Fish Creek	1822	1	87
Corbly, Elizabeth et al	465	Sugar Run	1822	1	88
Cordes—See Cardis					
Cornell, Aaron	33a.2r.24p.	Middle Island Cr.	1861	2	517
Cornell, John	100	Sugar Tree Creek	1850	2	406
Covalt—or Covault					
Covalt, Abraham	15	Long Drain	1832	1	302
Covalt, James	54	Pursley's Run	1857	2	503
Covault, Abraham (Covalt)	225	Pursley Run	1838	2	165
Cox, Abraham et al	100	Sheet's Run	1838	2	119
Cox, David	72	Fishing Creek	1844	2	331
Cox, Friend	313	Whetstone Branch	1838	1	446
Cox, Friend	100	Whetstone Creek	1838	1	445
Cox, Friend	200	Narrow's Run	1838	1	447
Cox, Friend	235	Wts. Whetstone	1838	1	448
Cox, Friend	200	Proctor's Run	1836	1	396
Cox, Friend	50	Lit. Fishing Cr.	1844	2	324
Craig, John	100	Buffalo Creek	1851	2	428
Cumbrage—See Cumbridge					
Cumbrage, Isaac	118	Jefferson Run	1852	2	444
Cumbridge, Isaac	33	Big Camp Mistake	1855	2	484
Cumbridge, Isaac	16	Big Camp Mistake	1855	2	482
Cunningham, James	100	Pine Fork	1828	1	186
Curtis, David	3,000	McElroy's Fork	1820	1	48
Dancer, Jesse A.	126	Buffalo Creek	1851	2	407
Davis, Absolom	50	McKim's Fork	1846	2	356
Davis, Alexander	58	McKim's Creek	1855	2	487
Davis, Alexander	50	McKim's Fork	1847	2	368
Davis, Charles & Simon	104	Camp Mistake Run	1852	2	425
Davis, John	100	Wheeler's Run	1835	1	391
Davis, John Sr.	85	Camp Mistake Run	1849	2	397
Davis, John Sr.	223	Big Camp Mistake	1846	2	349
Davis, Jonathan	100	McKim's Fork	1825	1	130
Davis, Jonathan	50	McKim's Fork	1838	2	21
Davis, Jonathan	50	McKim's Fork	1842	2	278
Davis, Jonathan et al	94	Davis Run	1851	2	408
Davis, Jonathan et al	321	McKim's Fork	1846	2	357
Davis, Jonathan et al	100	McKim's Fork	1846	2	361
Davis, Robert et al	74	McKim's Creek	1853	2	457
Dawson, Elisha	50	Bond's Run	1835	1	360
Debolt, Benjamin	180	Shidler's Run	1838	2	40

Name of Grantee	Acres	Local Description	Year	Book	Page
Grigg—or Gragg, Gregg					
Grigg, Thomas Sr.	60	Middle Island Cr.	1851	2	431
Grigg, Thomas Sr.	50	Middle Island Cr.	1852	2	441
Guthry—Guthrey, Guttery					
Guthry, Robert	100	Proctor's Run	1831	1	260
Guttery, Robert (Guthrey)	70	Fishing Creek	1838	2	78
Hall, Ephraim	40	Proctor's Run	1831	1	240
Hallam, Michael	100	Big Run	1842	2	244
Hallam, Michael	90	Sugar Tree Creek	1849	2	399
Hallam, Michael et al	68	Big Run	1853	2	459
Hammond, John	100	McKim's Fork	1842	2	258
Hammond, John	148	McKim's Fork	1846	2	358
Hammond, John et al	405	Rock Run	1848	2	389
Hammond, John P.	443	Broad Run	1842	2	288
Handlin—See Hanlin					
Handlin, John	250	Brush Run	1842	2	261
Hanes, Calvin et al	605	Short Run	1853	2	455
Hanes, Galvin et al	409	Short Run	1855	2	490
Hanes, Nathan	200	Short Run	1837	1	405
Hanlin—See Handlin					
Hanlin, John	400	McKim's Fork	1838	2	15
Hardman, Harrison H. et al	100	Muddy Creek	1842	2	230
Hardman, Harrison H et al	350	Middle Island Cr.	1842	2	243
Harris, Anthony	200	Knob Fork	1830	1	213
Hart, James	90	Lower Long Run	1844	2	333
Hart, John	100	Little Fishing Cr.	1842	2	260
Hart, John	70	Little Fishing Cr.	1842	2	259
Hart, William	253	Long Drain	1843	2	309
Hartley, Peter	28	Middle Island Cr.	1851	2	417
Hayes—also Hays					
Hayes, James	100	Fishing Creek	1820	1	41
Hayes, James	100	Ten Mile Fork	1820	1	42
Hays, Edmund	38	Fishing Creek	1843	2	300
Hays, John E.	25	Fishing Creek	1838	2	52
Hays, Levi	100	Wts. Fishing Creek	1828	1	184
Headley, Anthony	100	Pine Fork	1843	2	316
Headley, Caleb	265	Fishing Creek	1846	2	355
Headley, Caleb	125	Fishing Creek	1838	2	153
Headley, Caleb	70	Fishing Creek	1838	2	157
Heckman, Jacob (Heekman)	100	Rock Camp Run	1831	1	248
Heekman—See Heckman, Hickman					
Hendershott, Joseph	100	Shidler's Run	1838	2	156
Hickenbotham—See Higginbotham					
Hickenbotham, Isaac	50	Fishing Creek	1828	1	190
Hickenbothom, Isaac	100	Fishing Creek	1828	1	183
Hickman, David	100	Pine Fork	1836	1	394
Hickman, David	469	Little Camp Mistake	1835	1	375
Hickman, David	100	Pine Fork	1834	1	355
Hickman, David	25	Pine Fork	1834	1	354
Hickman, David	66	Pine Fork	1834	1	353
Hickman, David	200	Elk Fork	1838	2	97
Hickman, David	345	Long Run	1838	2	96
Hickman, David	400	Sugar Tree Creek	1838	2	50
Hickman, David	134	Walnut Fork	1838	2	51
Hickman, David	2,000	Point Pleasant Cr.	1842	2	287
Hickman, David	145	Thomas Run	1842	2	286
Hickman, David	300	Pt. Pleasant Creek	1840	2	193
Hickman, David	220	Piney Fork	1840	2	195
Hickman, David	215	Elk Fork	1840	2	194
Hickman, David	58	Shinango Run	1838	2	155
Hickman, David	65	Middle Island Creek	1852	2	438
Hickman, David	1,675	Middle Island Cr.	1848	2	384
Hickman, David	300	Camp Mistake Run	1846	2	345

Name of Grantee	Acres	Local Description	Year	Book	Page
Hickman, David	360	Kelches Run	1846	2	346
Hickman, David	140	Big Camp Mistake	1846	2	347
Hickman, David et al	225	Big Camp Mistake Run	1838	2	49
Higginbotham—See Hickenbotham					
Higginbotham, William	100	Rock Camp Run	1833	1	317
Higginbotham, William	100	Fish Creek	1833	1	318
Higginbotham, William	104	Fishing Creek	1818	1	14
Higginbotham, William	100	Fishing Creek	1818	1	19
Higgins, Jonathan	100	Lynn Camp Run	1832	1	301
Higgins, William	100	Proctor's Run	1828	1	166
Highley, Barbara	30	Buffalo Run	1830	1	198
Hill, Eliza	100	McKim's Fork	1843	2	301
Hill, Horace & R. T.	217	McKim Creek	1856	2	494
Hill, James	150	Wts. Pt. Pleasant Run	1838	2	22
Hill, James et al	100	Pursley Run	1838	2	29
Hill, Rowland T.	1a.3r.20p.	McKim's Fork	1857	2	500
Hill, Thomas	50	McKims Fork	1842	2	233
Hill, Thomas	50	McKim's Fork	1841	2	221
Hill, Thomas et al	250	McKim's Fork	1842	2	279
Hisham, Jesse (Hissam)	125	Sheet's Run	1838	2	154
Hisham, Jesse (Hissam)	150	Buffalo Creek	1834	1	356
Hissam—See Hisham					
Hoge, Isaac	1,765	Fishing Creek	1844	2	334
Hoge, Isaac	1,100	Fish Creek	1844	2	335
Hoge, Isaac	58	Indian Creek	1855	2	489
Hoge, Isaac Jr.	900	Fishing Creek	1840	2	202
Horner, Charles	100	Fish Creek	1831	1	259
Horner, Isaac	200	Fish Creek	1821	1	78
Horner, Isaac Jr.	78	Buffalo Run	1840	2	200
Horner, John	50	Fish Creek	1832	1	312
Horner, John W.	80	Indian Creek	1851	2	414
Horner, John W.	83	Walnut Fork	1851	2	413
Horner, John W.	636	Indian Creek	1852	2	445
Horner, John W. et al	17	Indian Creek	1851	2	415
Horner, William	95	Church's Fork	1847	2	366
Hubbert, Bement et al (Hubburt)	100	Long Reach	1826	1	146
Huggins, Abijah	100	Proctor's Run	1832	1	297
Huggins, Abijah	100	Wolf Run	1843	2	310
Huggins, John Jr.	30	Proctor's Run	1832	1	305
Hustage—See Husted					
Hustage, John (Hustid)	27	Indian Creek	1851	2	416
Husted, John (Hustead)	53	Coal Bank Run	1852	2	440
Hustid—Hustage, Hustead, Husted					
Ice, Abraham	20	Archer's Fork	1842	2	262
Ice, Abraham	50	Carpenter's Fork	1834	1	342
Ice, Abraham	50	Carpenter's Fork	1835	1	366
Ice, Abraham	50	Archer's Fork	1835	1	370
Ice, Abraham	100	Archer's Fork	1828	1	195
Ice, Aden B.	50	Cutting Timber Run	1835	1	381
Ice, William	100	Archer's Fork	1828	1	171
Ingle, J. J.	100	Sancho Creek	1856	2	493
Ingle, John I.	100	Gorrell's Run	1839	2	173
Ingraham, Silas	2,737	Four Mile Fork	1843	2	317
Ingram—See Ingraham					
Ireland, John	150	Camp Mistake Run	1838	2	55
Ireland, John et al	125	Camp Mistake	1838	2	14
Jacobs, John C.	200	Fishing Creek	1822	1	90
Jacobs, Jonathan	50	Fishing Creek	1838	2	111
Jarrett, Justice	100	Canoe Run	1830	1	216
John, David	200	Walnut Fork	1838	2	53
John, David	200	Walnut Fork	1838	2	54
John, David	50	Indian Creek	1854	2	476
Johnson, Henry	100	Lynn Camp Run	1832	1	314

Name of Grantee	Acres	Local Description	Year	Book	Page
Lantz, Alexander	60	Fishing Creek	1848	2	390
Lantz, Alexander	40	Buffalo Run	1838	2	24
Lantz, Alexander	30	Fishing Creek	1838	2	25
Lantz, Alexander	110	Wyatt's Run	1838	2	26
Lantz, Alexander	120	Buffalo Run	1838	2	27
Lantz, John	600	Fish Creek	1843	2	307
Lantz, John	66	Long Drain	1831	1	253
Lantz, John	30	Fish Creek	1833	1	261
Lantz, John	200	Long Drain	1823	1	104
Lantz, Lott	200	Rocky Fork	1825	1	123
Lantz, William	2,300	Fish Creek	1840	2	196
Larey, John B. (Lacy)	250	Point Pleasant Fk.	1835	1	364
Larue, Isaac	400	Middle Island Cr.	1821	1	74
Larue, Isaac	320	Middle Island Creek	1838	2	11
Lauck, Richard W. et al	310	Purgatory Run	1847	2	365
Lawson, Thomas R.	200	Long Run	1850	2	426
Leason, William	115	Buffalo Run	1828	1	172
Leazure or Leezer, Lezer					
Leep, Alvey	80	Proctor's Run	1838	1	444
Leep, Gabriel	280	Proctor's Run	1830	1	210
Leep, John	150	Fishing Creek	1828	1	178
Leep, Robert	200	Long Run	1837	1	411
Leep, Robert	54	Long Run	1838	2	113
Leeper, Henry P.	100	Brush Run	1847	2	373
Leezer, or Leazure, Lezer					
Leezer, Christian	100	Fish Creek	1824	1	114
Leezer, Christian	100	Church's Fork	1828	1	179
Leezer, Daniel	100	Hd. Wts. Fish Creek	1824	1	109
Lefever—see also Lafever					
Lefever, George	100	McKim's Fork	1842	2	263
Lemaster—See Lamasters, Lemasters—also Lancaster					
Lemaster, Isaac	50	Rocky Run	1838	2	141
Lemaster, John	135	Lynn Camp Run	1835	1	388
Lemasters, Achilles	100	Rocky Run	1838	2	82
Lemasters, James	50	Upper Big Run	1838	2	114
Lemasters, Samuel	85	Rocky Run	1833	1	320
Lewis, Jacob	50	Sheet's Run	1826	1	141
Lewis, Jacob	50	Cedar Run	1835	1	382
Lezer or Leazure, Leezer					
Lezer, Christian	100	South Fk. Fish Cr.	1821	1	75
Lezer, Christian	95	Church's Fork	1842	2	265
Lezer, Christian	55	Church's Fork	1842	2	264
Lients, George	110	Little Fishing Cr.	1848	2	391
Lieuts, George	110	Little Fishing Cr.	1848	2	391
Little, Thomas	100	Long Drain	1831	1	250
Little, William	200	Knob Fork	1825	1	121
Little, William	200	Long Drain	1823	1	99
Little, William	100	Fish Creek	1823	1	98
Little, William Jr.	100	Knob Fork	1839	2	180
Little, William Jr.	100	Knob Fork	1839	2	181
Loe—See Lowe					
Loe, David	100	Fishing Creek	1839	2	179
Long, George	200	Rocky Run	1841	2	225
Long, George	42	Sancoe's Run	1849	2	393
Long, George	83	Sugar Creek	1844	2	322
Long, Samuel J.	120	Steel's Run	1838	2	80
Long, Samuel J.	25	Steel's Run	1838	2	81
Long, Wilson	50	Brushy Fork	1847	2	364
Lonan—See also Looman					
Lonon, John	35	Wheeler's Run	1852	2	442
Looman—See Lonan					
Looman, John	100	McKim's Fork	1846	2	359
Looman, John	50	McKim's Fork	1841	2	206

Name of Grantee	Acres	Local Description	Year	Book	Page
Minor, John Jr.	50	Proctor's Run	1832	1	309
Minor, Theophilus	200	Fish Creek	1831	1	245
Moore, Isaac	100	Foster's Run	1848	2	382
Moore, Isaac	50	Sancoe's Run	1848	2	383
Moore, Peter	140 (120)	Janet's Run	1841	2	204
Moore, Peter	100	Jarret's Run	1838	2	57
Morgan, Aaron et al	500	Fishing Creek	1819	1	32
Morgan, Archilles	300	Fishing Creek	1819	1	30
Morgan,Achilles et al	245	Hupp's Run	1838	1	436
Morgan, Elija	335	Fishing Creek	1838	1	435
Morgan, Elijah	50	Fishing Creek	1838	2	85
Morgan, Elijah	340	Upper Run	1838	2	84
Morgan, Elijah	144	Fishing Creek	1842	2	266
Morgan, Elisha	120	Fishing Cr.	1838	1	428
Morgan, Elisha	150	Fishing Creek	1837	1	413
Morgan, Eliza et al	93	Fishing Creek	1838	1	438
Morgan, Eliza et al	177	Fishing Creek	1838	1	437
Morgan, Hiram J.	115	Fish Creek	1838	2	117
Morgan, Hugh & James	80	Fishing Creek	1828	1	158
Morgan, Jacob (of Aaron)	25	Fishing Creek	1838	2	115
Morgan, James	25	Pickenpaw Run	1835	1	387
Morgan, John G.	150	Buffalo Run	1838	2	118
Morgan, Joseph M.	90	Sugar Tree Creek	1847	2	375
Morgan, Morgan	100	Fishing Creek	1822	1	91
Morgan, Morgan	16	Fishing Creek	1838	1	429
Morgan, Nathan	150	Richwood Run	1838	2	116
Morgan, Richard	35	Fishing Creek	1830	1	199
Morgan, Uriah et al	164	Fishing Creek	1824	1	120
Morgan, Zaquell	200	Fishing Creek	1831	1	265
Morris, Abraham	50	Pitt's Run	1841	2	216
Morris, Jacob	50	Rocky Fork	1831	1	258
Morris, James	50	Proctor's Run	1832	1	313
Morris, James	50	Fish Creek	1831	1	242
Morris, James	50	Fish Creek	1831	1	244
Morris, Jonathan	100	Rocky Fork	1831	1	246
Murphy, Massey & Marie et al	245	Hupp's Run	1838	1	436
Musgrove, James	9a.70p.	Mid. Island Creek	1854	2	479
Musser, David	50	Sugar Creek	1838	2	56
Musser, David et al	42	Sugar Tree Creek	1847	2	376
Musser, William	100	Davis Run	1842	2	280
Myers, Frederic D.	100	Morgan's Run	1843	2	303
Myers, Jacob et al	465	Sugar Run	1822	1	88
Myers, John et al	465	Sugar Run	1822	1	88
Myers, Joseph	200	Fish Creek	1822	1	89
Myers, Peter et al	170	Fish Creek	1822	1	87
Newman, Alexander et al	500	Laurel Run	1838	2	132
Orr, Robert C.	19	McElroy's Fork	1857	2	501
Orr, Robert C. et al	255	McElroy's Creek	1857	2	498
Owens, Isaac	36	McKim's Fork	1857	2	508
Owens, Isaac et al	68	Big Run	1853	2	459
Owens, John	265	McKim's Fork	1837	1	425
Owens, John et al	112	Long Run	1838	2	28
Owens, John Jr.	1,000	Big Run	1835	1	373
Owens, Joseph	18	McKim's Run	1849	2	398
Owens, Joseph H.	7	McKim's Fork	1856	2	496
Owens, Thomas	100	I. D. Well's Run	1849	2	394
Pain or Payne					
Pain, Ebenezer	80	Fish Creek	1828	1	176
Patrick, Daniel	150	Church's Fork	1841	2	211
Patrick, George	200	Church's Fork	1841	2	219
Patrick, John Heirs of	100	Church's Fork	1841	2	203
Paugh, Jackson	30	Proctor's Run	1842	2	268
Pedan, John (or James)	175	Adj. Arch Woods	1838	2	59

Name of Grantee	Acres	Local Description	Year	Book	Page
Peden, James	125	Lit. Fishing Cr.	1845	2	339
Pigot, Edward	105	Arnold's Creek	1837	1	417
Pills—or Pitts					
Pills, Zachariah	200	Buffalo Run	1825	1	128
Pitts, William	50	Big Run	1842	2	238
Porter, Nevin	93	Pursley's Run	1857	2	504
Postlewait, Absolom	90	Lynn Camp Run	1838	2	89
Postlewait, Absolom	150	Lynn Camp Run	1832	1	289
Postlewait, Edmund	100	Lynn Camp Run	1834	1	326
Postlewait, Emanuel	100	Fishing Creek	1832	1	304
Postlewait, Isaac	50	Rocky Fork	1826	1	136
Postlewait, Isaac	50	Rocky Fork	1834	1	328
Postlewait, Isaac	100	Lynn Camp Run	1832	1	310
Postlewait, Isaac	100	Lynn Camp Run	1832	1	298
Postlewait, Richard	100	Rocky Fork	1834	1	325
Postlewait, Richard	50	Rock Fork	1826	1	138
Postlewait, Richard	50	Rocky Run	1832	1	307
Postlewait, Richard et al	100	Rocky Run	1833	1	321
Postlewait, William	50	Rocky Fork	1834	1	327
Postlewait, William	50	Rocky Fork	1830	1	202
Postlewait, William	50	Rocky Fork	1832	1	285
Pratt, William	100	McElroy's Fork	1843	2	312
Price, Samuel	50	Sugar Camp Run	1838	2	58
Price, William	200	Fishing Creek	1828	1	173
Prunty, John (son of David)	100	Fishing Creek	1826	1	149
Reed, Levi et al	500	Laurel Run	1838	2	132
Rhodes, Bazil et al (Roads)	67	Middle Island	1838	2	98
Rice, John	205	Little Fishing Cr.	1843	2	293
Rice, William & Eli	22	Buffalo Creek	1854	2	471
Riggs, Bazell	200	Wts. of Ohio	1818	1	20
Riggs, Bazil	66	Middle Island Creek	1835	1	390
Riggs, Bazil	50	Adj. S. Thomas	1837	1	418
Riggs, Elmer	100	2 Lick Run	1842	2	236
Riggs, Elmer	100	Wolf Pen Fork	1838	2	63
Riggs, Mathew	200	Short Run	1847	2	380
Riggs, Milton	50	Rigg's Run	1847	2	379
Riggs, Milton	100	Rocky Run	1838	2	12
Right—See Wright					
Right, Abraham	125	Church's Fork	1842	2	251
Rine, Lazerus Jr.	160	Proctor's Run	1830	1	225
Ripley, John	86	Foster's Run	1836	1	403
Ripley, John	100	Pitt's Run	1834	1	352
Ripley, Lewis	41	Middle Island	1824	1	115
Roberts, John	65	Fish Creek	1841	2	205
Roberts, John	100	Knob Fork of Fish Cr.	1824	1	111
Roberts, John	50	Long Drain	1832	1	283
Roberts, Noah	124	Hiley's Fork	1844	2	321
Roberts, Simeon	200	Rush Run	1841	2	217
Roberts, Stephen	75	So. Fk. Fish Cr.	1824	1	107
Roberts, Stephen	100	Fish Creek	1828	1	192
Robeson, Albicon	300	Sugar & Laurel Cks.	1845	2	209
Robinson, William	126	Proctor's Run	1844	2	320
Ruckman, James	135	Fishing Creek	1837	1	407
Ruckman, James	78	Lit. Fishing Cr.	1837	1	422
Rush, Bethel	450	Lynn Camp Run	1838	2	143
Ruth, Bethel	80	Lynn Camp Run	1838	2	144
Rush, Charles	25	Fishing Creek	1834	1	332
Rush, Charles	100	Lynn Camp Run	1838	2	8
Rush, Charles	300	Rush's Run	1838	2	9
Rush, Charles	100	Shidler's Run	1838	2	160
Rush, Charles	100	Rush Run	1838	2	161
Rush, Paul	50	Adj. Henry Church	1838	2	162
Rush, Peter	18	Fishing Creek	1838	2	60

Name of Grantee	Acres	Local Description	Year	Book	Page
Smith, Ralph (of James)	8½	Sancho Run	1852	2	424
Smith, Ralph (of James)	30	Middle Island Creek	1848	2	387
Smith, Ralph (of James)	50	Adj. James Smith	1840	2	198
Smith, Thomas	100	Nutter's Fork	1838	2	124
Smith, Thomas	100	Big Camp Mistake Run	1838	2	125
Smith, Thomas	1,000	Flint Run	1842	2	234
Smith, Thomas	200	Cedar Run	1838	2	90
Snodgrass, Thomas H	50	Fishing Creek	1838	2	64
Snodgrass, Washington	110	Lower Long Run	1838	2	65
Sole—also Soles					
Sole, John	104	Fish Creek	1844	2	328
Sole, John	215	Church's Fork	1841	2	227
Sole, Peter	161	Rock Camp Run	1843	2	292
Sole, Peter	161	Rock Camp Run	1842	2	271
Sole, Peter	100	Church Fork	1826	1	144
Soles, John	100	Fish Creek	1824	1	112
Soles, John	30	Church's Fork	1831	1	238
Soles, Peter	50	Rock Run	1832	1	299
Soles, Peter	50	Lit. Fishing Creek	1832	1	282
Soles, Peter Jr.	100	Church's Fork	1830	1	196
Sowers, Frederick	12	Field's Creek	1842	2	249
Spencer, Richard	46	Indian Creek	1855	2	481
Spencer, Richard	260	Indian Creek	1850	2	404
Springer, Uriah	25	Reeder's Run	1841	2	215
Srieve—See Shrieve, Shrieves					
Stanbury, Archibald C.	100	Fishing Creek	1826	1	135
Starkey, Levi	73	Morris Run	1853	2	454
Starkey, Samuel	50	Ten Mile Fork	1828	1	167
Stead—See also Steed					
Stead, John	90	Arnold's Creek	1821	1	67
Stealey—or Stealy					
Stealey, James	50	Foster's Run	1846	2	360
Stealey, James	353	Wheeler's Run	1844	2	329
Stealey, James et al	118	Middle Island Cr.	1852	2	423
Stealey, John	100	Adj. Robt. Gorrill's	1822	1	93
Stealey, William	21	Jefferson's Run	1852	2	447
Stealy, James	173	Point Pleasant Fk.	1837	1	427
Stealy, James	27	Mid. Island Cr.	1837	1	426
Steed—See Stead					
Steed, Elijah	105	Sheet's Run	1842	2	289
Steed, Jesse	100	Canoe Run	1830	1	214
Steel, Adam	100	Fishing Creek	1834	1	331
Steel, Thomas	50	Sugar Camp	1826	1	143
Steel, Thomas	400	Little Fishing Cr.	1835	1	372
Steel, Thomas	100	McKim's Fork	1838	2	30
Steel, Thomas	50	Sugar Camp	1826	1	142
Steel, Thomas	200	McKim's Fork	1842	2	270
Steel, Thomas	200	McKim's Fork	1848	2	386
Stephen—or Stephens, Stevens					
Stephen, Apollo	50	Fishing Cr.	1842	2	290
Stephens, Apolo	30	Fishing Creek	1834	1	334
Stephens, Apollo et al	370	Fishing Creek	1838	2	35
Stephens, Apollo et al	300	Piney Fork	1838	2	123
Stephens, Apollo et al	60	Pine Fork	1838	2	163
Stephens, Apollo et al	256	Fishing Creek	1831	2	100
Stephenson, James M.	2,800	McKim's Fork	1838	1	430
Stephenson, James M.	300	Arnold's Creek	1844	2	327
Stephenson, James M. et al	100	Pursley's Run	1838	2	29
Stevens—Stephen, Stephens					
Stevens, Stacy	50	Fishing Creek	1838	2	122
Stewart, Noble	6½	Pursley's Run	1842	2	272
Stewart, Noble	59	Pursley Run	1854	2	469
Stewart, William	70	Lynn Camp Run	1838	2	146

Name of Grantee	Acres	Local Description	Year	Book	Page
Stiles, Thomas	100	Long Drain	1831	1	250
Stonekey, Henry (Stoneking)	50	Church's Fork	1842	2	235
Stoneking, Henry	50	Indian Creek	1843	2	296
Stoneking, Henry	50	Church's Fork	1842	2	235
Stoneking, Henry et al	17	Indian Creek	1851	2	415
Stoneking, Jacob	150	Fish Creek	1838	2	3
Stoneking, Jacob	100	Fish Creek	1840	2	201
Stoneking, Jacob	100	Fish Creek	1839	2	183
Stork, Mason et al	15	Low Head Island	1853	2	460
Stottlemire, David	200	Fish Creek	1839	2	191
Stout, Nathaniel	117	Steed's Run	1838	2	66
Stout, Nathaniel	40	Pine Fork	1831	1	235
Straight—Strait, Streight					
Straight, Jasper or Joseph	100	Brush Run	1827	1	153
Straight, Jasper	100	Crow's Run	1827	1	157
Strait—Straight, Streight					
Strait, Jasper	87	Brush Run	1838	2	147
Strait, Jasper or Joseph	50	Fishing Creek	1838	1	441
Streight—Straight, Strait					
Stull, Enoch	50	Foster Run	1851	2	419
Suman—Shooman, Shuman					
Suman, William	50	Hartley's Run	1838	2	91
Swan, William	740	Middle Island Creek	1839	2	192
Swan, William	50	Bond's Run	1842	2	281
Swan, William et al	100	Muddy Creek	1842	2	230
Sweeney, John	22	McElroy's Creek	1857	2	499
Swisher, Jacob	100	Fishing Creek	1818	1	15
Swisher, Jacob	100	Fishing Creek	1818	1	17
Syare, H. T. (Sayre)	118	Rush Fork	1841	2	208
Talkington, Jacob	20	Ten Mile Fork	1838	2	68
Talkington, Jacob	20	Ten Mile Fork	1838	2	70
Talkington, Jacob	40	Benjamin's Run	1838	2	69
Talkington, Jacob	20	Barker's Run	1838	2	71
Taylor, Isaac	50	Fish Creek	1823	1	106
Taylor, John	57	Sheet's Run	1842	2	291
Thomas, Adam	150	Arnold's Creek	1835	1	371
Thomas, Charles	200	Bond's Upper Run	1821	1	65
Thomas, Charles	23	Middle Island Cr.	1817	1	5
Thomas, Ellis	160	Thomas Run	1827	1	155
Thomas, Elton	50	Middle Island Cr.	1823	1	101
Thomas, Francis	400	Adj. Travis Scott	1819	1	37
Thomas, Jacob	200	Baker's Run	1845	2	344
Thomas, Jacob	100	Big Run	1829	1	207
Thomas, Jacob	100	Indian Creek	1832	1	270
Thomas, Saul	100	Wts. of Ohio	1819	1	27
Thomas, Saul	100	Long Reach	1817	1	2
Thomas, Saul	100	Long Reach	1817	1	1
Thomas, Saul et al	20	Banks of Ohio River	1819	1	34
Thistle, George T. et al	115	Pt. Pleasant Run	1838	2	33
Thistle, Sampson	600	Narrows Run	1845	2	343
Toncray, Hiram et al	300	Piney Fork	1838	2	123
Toncray, Hiram et al	60	Pine Fork	1838	2	163
Tuel, Christopher et al	15	Indian Creek	1853	2	460
Tucker, Henry	70	Nutter's Fork	1832	1	278
Tustin, Jacob	60	Indian Creek	1843	2	319
Twibell—or Twible, Twybell					
Twibell, David	100	Lit. Fishing Cr.	1832	1	292
Twibell, David	50	Fishing Creek	1835	1	367
Twibell, John	200	Wts. of Fish Creek	1821	1	63
Twibell, John	150	Little Fishing Cr.	1830	1	215
Twibell, Josiah	200	Rocky Fork	1831	1	256
Twible—or Twibell, Twybell					
Twible, Martha (Twybell)	100	Little Fishing Cr.	1820	1	52

Name of Grantee	Acres	Local Description	Year	Book	Page
Twybell, Martha (Twible)	100	Little Fishing Cr.	1820	1	52
Twybell—or Twibell, Twible					
Ullom, Stephen	100	Bear Run	1842	2	274
Underwood, Ellis	100	Big Camp Mistake	1834	1	333
Underwood, Ellis	110	McElroy's Fork	1843	2	314
Underwood, Ellis et al	125	Camp Mistake	1838	2	14
Underwood, Dixon & Hugh	60	McElroy's Fork	1823	1	97
Underwood, William	100	Big Camp	1825	1	132
Underwood, William	100	Jefferson Run	1843	2	306
Underwood, William et al	225	Big Camp Mistake Run	1838	2	49
Vandegrift, Samuel	120	Sancoe Run	1850	2	402
Vandegrift, Samuel	180	Sancoe's Fork	1842	2	232
Vandegrift, Samuel	81¼	Sancho's Run	1853	2	462
Vandergrift, Samuel	18¾	Middle Island Creek	1853	2	464
Vandergrift, Samuel	170	Sancho's Run	1853	2	463
Vandergrift, Samuel et al	310	Purgatory Run	1847	2	365
Vance, Joseph	120	Fishing Creek	1838	1	439
Varner, Ashbury	50	Sancho Creek	1851	2	434
Verdin, John	100	Wts. of Ohio	1832	1	284
Villers, James	150	Ash Camp Run	1842	2	275
Villers, James	85	Long Drain	1832	1	308
Wade—or Waid					
Wade, George (Alias Waid)	100	Fish Creek	1824	1	108
Wade, George	75	Lick Run	1839	2	190
Wade, George	25	Fish Creek	1839	2	189
Wade, John	100	Fish Creek	1839	2	188
Wade, Joseph	50	Narrows Run	1839	2	187
Waid—or Wade					
Waid, George	40	Sugar Run	1831	1	231
Waid, Hezekiah Jr.	100	Fish Creek	1828	1	187
Warley—See Worley					
Watkins, John	125	Dulin's Run	1837	1	409
Watson, William	100	Grassy Lick	1823	1	100
Watson, William	100	Lynn Camp Run	1838	2	164
Way, Thomas	40	Buffalo Creek	1860	2	513
Way, William	100	Elk Fork	1860	2	514
Weakley—or Weakly, Weekley, Weekly					
Weakley, Elizabeth	65	Muddy Creek	1835	1	374
Weakley, Richard	50	Muddy Creek	1835	1	389
Weakley, Richard	50	Muddy Creek	1838	2	74
Weakly, Thomas	100	Indian Creek	1830	1	219
Weekley, Richard et al	100	Big Run	1838	2	101
Weekly, James	100	Indian Creek	1817	1	6
Weekly, Levi (Weekley)	100	Muddy Creek	1819	1	35
Welch, John	50	Pine Fork	1828	1	182
Wells,—See also Willis, Wills					
Wells, Benjamin	10	Thomas's Run	1838	2	31
Wells, Butler et al	100	Long Reach	1826	1	146
Wells, Drucilla et al	177	Fishing Creek	1838	1	437
Wells, Drucilla et al	93	Fishing Creek	1838	1	438
Wells, Duckett (Wills)	359	Pitt's Run	1841	2	223
Wells, Duckett (Wills)	100	Jefferson Run	1844	3	336
Wells, Duckett et al (Wills)	100(130)	Indian Creek	1837	1	399
Wells, Duckett et al (Wills)	100	Muddy Creek	1842	2	230
Wells, Eli	457	Wts. of Ohio	1838	2	32
Wells, Eli	75	Sugar Tree Fork	1847	2	381
Wells, John	150	Fish Pot Run	1843	2	315
Wells, John	50	Middle Island Cr.	1817	1	8
Wells, John D.	50	Middle Island	1826	1	140
Wells, John D.	85	McKim's Fork	1826	1	145
Wells, John D.	65	McKims Form	1837	1	401
Wells, Nicholas	100	Thomas Run	1838	2	72
Wells, Oliver P.	50	Middle Island	1851	2	420

Name of Grantee	Acres	Local Description	Year	Book	Page
Wells, Ralph	440	McKim's Creek	1847	2	377
Wells, Thomas	150	Sancoe Run	1819	1	36
Wells, William	600	Long Run	1817	1	4
Wells, William	200	Cane's Run	1819	1	22
Wells, William	50	McElroy's Fork	1825	1	131
Wells, William T. & Salman	480	Pursley's Creek	1851	2	435
Wells, Zadock C. et al (White)	350	Middle Island Cr.	1842	2	243
West, James G	155	State Road Run	1838	2	126
West. James G.	145	State Road Fork	1838	2	128
West, James G.	190	Richwood Run	1838	2	127
West, James G.	50	Fishing Creek	1835	1	358
West, James G.	148	Richwood Run	1835	1	369
West, John	50	Pine Fork	1828	1	182
West, Samuel	100	Pine Fork	1827	1	150
West, Thomas	50	Pine Fork	1828	1	188
Wheeler, Samuel	140	Middle Island Cr.	1817	1	11
White, Jane	200	Indian Creek	1831	1	264
White, Reazin	50	Lit. Fishing Creek	1838	2	148
White, Zadock C.	100	Indian Run	1838	2	129
White, Zadock C. et al (Wells)	350	Middle Island Cr.	1842	2	243
Wilcox, Stephen C.	74	Purgatory Run	1854	2	467
Wiley—See Willey					
Wiley, Henry	50	Fishing Creek	1829	1	205
Williams, Francis E.	200	Lit. Fishing Cr.	1832	1	295
Williams, Jeremiah	500	Dolin's Run	1832	1	287
Williams, Jeremiah Jr.	100	Little Fishing Cr.	1839	2	186
Williams, Jeremiah Jr.	200	Proctor's Run	1832	1	290
Williams, Lewis	167	Proctor's Run	1832	1	277
Williams, Lewis	200	Narrow's Run	1835	1	376
Williams, Lewis et al	115	Point Pleasant Run	1838	2	33
Williams, Lewis et al	500	Fishing Cr.	1819	1	32
Williamson, Anderson	115	Big Buffalo Run	1834	1	341
Williamson, Anderson	13	Big Buffalo	1854	2	474
Williamson, David H.	170	Buffalo Creek	1851	2	436
Williamson, James	300	Thomas's Run	1837	1	408
Williamson, James C.	610	Long Reach	1819	1	28
Williamson, Thomas C.	11a.20p.	Adj. C. Parker	1861	2	518
Willey—See Wiley					
Willey, James	184	Fishing Creek	1823	1	96
Willey, James	100	Fishing Creek	1820	1	51
Willey, James	200	Fishing Creek	1820	1	50
Willey, James	100	Fishing Cr.	1820	1	53
Willey, James	166	Fishing Creek	1828	1	165
Willey, James	100	Old State Road	1831	1	263
Willey, James	50	Fishing Creek	1833	1	319
Willey, James	100	Fishing Creek	1833	1	323
Willey, James Sr.	50	Fishing Cr.	1841	2	214
Willis—See Wells, Wills					
Willis, Notly	184	Mud Lick Run	1850	2	405
Wills—See also Wells, Willis					
Wills, Oliver P.	50	Middle Island	1851	2	420
Wills, Duckett et al (Wells)	100(130)	Indian Creek	1837	1	399
Wilson, John	650	Mid. Island Creek	1838	2	34
Wise, Jackson	350	Dulin's Run	1838	2	7
Wise, Jackson	100	Dulin's Run	1838	2	6
Wood—Woods					
Wood, James Jr.	100	Lynn Camp Run	1832	1	300
Wood, James Sr.	100	Sorrill Run	1832	1	286
Wood, William	18	Little Fishing Cr.	1842	2	276
Woods, Andrew	300	Middle Island Cr.	1820	1	60
Woods, James Sr.	200	Sorrel Run	1832	1	311
Woods, Robert C.	800	Dry Run	1832	1	276
Woods, Robert C.	800	Proctor's Run	1833	1	324

Name of Grantee	Acres	Local Description	Year	Book	Page
Woods, Robert C.	1,200	Middle Island Cr.	1839	2	185
Woods, Robert C.	500	Lynn Camp	1822	1	94
Woods, Robert C. et al	266	Proctor's Run	1832	1	315
Workman, Andrew	50	Long Run	1838	2	92
Workman, Andrew	100	Fishing Creek	1830	1	197
Worley, David	100	Long Drain	1831	1	239
Worley, David	100	Fish Creek	1820	1	45
Worley, David	42	Fish Creek	1823	1	105
Wright—See Right					
Wright, Daniel	100	Indian Creek	1838	2	131
Wright, Jonathan	50	Indian Creek	1838	2	130
Wyatt, Augustus B.	177	Fishing Creek	1826	1	137
Wyatt, John	40	Pine Fork	1831	1	237
Wyatt, Sacker	100	Fishing Creek	1824	1	113
Wyatt, Sacker	100	Richwood Run	1838	2	73
Wyatt, Sacker	45	Fishing Creek	1828	1	164
Wykart, Francis	150	Proctor's Run	1830	1	224
Wykart, Nicholas	200	Whetstone Run	1835	1	361
Wykart, Nicholas	100	Proctor's Run	1830	1	223
Yoho, Henry	75	Fishing Creek	1820	1	59
Yoho, Henry Jr.	200	Proctor's Run	1832	1	274
Yoho, George	62	Fishing Creek	1822	1	84
Yoho, George	36	Whetstone	1835	1	383

UPSHUR COUNTY

Bennett, David	100	White Camp Fork	1852	1	522
Bennett, J. M., et al	700	Kanawha Run	1852	1	528
Berlin, George W.	30	French Creek	1852	1	523
Bond, Charlotte T. et al, Heirs	1,950	Panther Fork	1852	1	529
Camden, Richard P. et al	700	Kanawha Run	1852	1	528
Core, John O.	9	French Creek	1853	1	527
Hefner, Nimrod D.	100	White Camp Fork	1852	1	524
Hinkle, Job	21a.3r.5p.	Adj. John Lewis	1860	1	542
Hire, John D.	79¾	Fink's Run	1856	1	521
Jamison, William (Jemison)	553	Middle Fork	1859	1	541
Loudin, William	661	Herod's Run	1854	1	531
Loudin, William S.	140	Ten-Mile Creek	1859	1	538
Magruder, Allan B.	200	French Creek	1853	1	526
Magruder, Allan B.	300	Millseat Run	1853	1	525
Marple, Moses	150	Peck's Run	1860	1	539
Middleton, Henry O.	127	Buckhannon River	1860	1	543
Morgan, Alfred	140	Wts. Buckhannon River	1856	1	520
Pebbles, James G.	524	French Creek	1858	1	540
Peebles—See Pebbles					
Peterson, Jesse L. & H. M.	496	Cow Run	1855	1	519
Simons, John	76½	Pringle Fork	1859	1	536
Strader, Asa, et al	200	Buckhannon River	1852	1	530
Trimble, John & Porterfield	334	Grand Camp Branch	1859	1	537
Westfall, Henry F.	½	Jaw Bone Run	1857	1	535
Westfall, Henry F.	5¼	Adj. E. J. Colerider	1854	1	533
Westfall, Henry F.	79	Middle Fork	1854	1	532
Westfall, Watson, et al	200	Buckhannon River	1852	1	530
Wilson, Edgar C.	300	10-Mile Branch	1855	1	534

WAYNE COUNTY

Name of Grantee	Acres	Local Description	Year	Book	Page
Adkins, Alexander	36	Bowen's Creek	1852	2	80
Adkins, Alexander	75	Beech Fork	1857	2	265
Adkins, Andrew	300	12 Pole	1846	1	86
Adkins, Andrew	27	Beech Fork	1850	1	397
Adkins, Andrew	50	12 Pole	1850	1	398
Adkins, Andrew	275	Adkins' Branch	1856	2	201
Adkins, Andrew	38	Beech Fork	1861	2	343
Adkins, Archibald	400	Beech Fork	1845	1	33
Adkins, Archibald	130	12 Pole	1845	1	34
Adkins, Attison	5	12 Pole	1856	2	203
Adkins, Charles	400	Beech Fork	1853	2	92
Adkins, Charles	30	Beech Fork	1854	2	137
Adkins, Charles	21	Beech Fork	1859	2	302
Adkins, Charles	50	Beech Fork	1861	2	338
Adkins, Charles	25	Beech Fork	1861	2	340
Adkins, Charles	107	Mill Branch	1862	2	357
Adkins, Charles et al	185	Beech Fork	1845	1	39
Adkins, Elijah	500	Beech Fork	1846	1	87
Adkins, George	500	Cove Creek	1845	1	38
Adkins, George	100	12-Pole	1849	1	259
Adkins, George	265	Cove Creek	1856	2	200
Adkins, George	5	12 Pole	1858	2	276
Adkins, Henry	75	12 Pole	1857	2	219
Adkins, Henry	255	Francis Creek	1857	2	220
Adkins, Henry	75	Blue Lick	1857	2	221
Adkins, Henry	235	Trough Fork	1857	2	222
Adkins, Henry	140	Wts. Cove Creek	1857	2	223
Adkins, Henry	600	Little Laurel	1857	2	224
Adkins, Henry et al	100	Hezekiah's Fork	1850	2	7
Adkins, Hezekiah	400	Beech Fork	1846	1	88
Adkins, Hezekiah	80	Beech Fork	1849	1	306
Adkins, Hezekiah	80	12 Pole	1850	1	426
Adkins, Hezekiah	40	12 Pole	1855	2	124
Adkins, Hezekiah	40	12 Pole	1855	2	125
Adkins, Hezekiah Jr.	65	12 Pole	1848	1	208
Adkins, Hiram	285	12 Pole	1847	1	187
Adkins, Hiram	20	Beech Fork	1853	2	93
Adkins, Isaiah	35	12 Pole	1845	1	42
Adkins, Isaiah	25	12 Pole	1845	1	43
Adkins, Jacob	37½	Beech Fork	1846	1	89
Adkins, Jacob	65	Beech Fork	1846	1	139
Adkins, Jacob	40	12 Pole	1847	2	249
Adkins, Jacob	200	Beech Fork	1857	2	250
Adkins, Jacob	60	12 Pole	1857	2	251
Adkins, Jacob	10	12 Pole	1860	2	313
Adkins, Jesse Jr.	50	12 Pole	1845	1	40
Adkins, Jesse Jr.	50	12 Pole	1847	1	188
Adkins, Jesse Jr.	25	Beech Fork	1854	2	142
Adkins, John	135	Wts. Beech Fork	1847	1	192
Adkins, John	10	Grassy Lick	1858	2	285
Adkins, John	6	Bowen's Creek	1858	2	286
Adkins, John	16	Bowen's Creek	1858	2	287
Adkins, John	180	Beech Fork	1858	2	288
Adkins, John R.	80	Beech Fork	1858	2	291
Adkins, Littleberry	25	Beech Fork	1845	1	41
Adkins, Littleberry	200	Beech Fork	1847	1	193
Adkins, Littleberry	45	Beech Fork	1853	2	88
Adkins, Millington	50	Lick Creek	1857	2	284
Adkins, Owen	50	Rich Creek	1846	1	84
Adkins, Owen	120	Lick Creek	1849	1	276
Adkins, Owen	70	Cynthia Branch	1850	1	349

Name of Grantee	Acres	Local Description	Year	Book	Page
Blaus, Hiram	43	Laurel Creek	1844	1	28
Blaus, Hiram	30	Lick Creek	1845	1	32
Bloss, Or Blaus					
Bloss, Hiram	45	Laurel Creek	1847	1	150
Bloss, Hiram	120	12 Pole Creek	1851	2	68
Bloss, Hiram	180	Laurel Creek	1858	2	271
Bloss, Isaac	150	Big Lynn	1850	1	376
Booten, Stephen	10	12 Pole	1850	2	9
Bowen, Alderson	85	Beech Fork	1846	1	82
Bowen, Alderson	600	Bowen's Creek	1846	1	95
Bowen, Hugh	45	Cave Branch	1862	2	358
Bowen, Hugh et al	380	2 Mile Creek	1859	2	523
Bowen, James E.	65	Beech Fork	1846	1	96
Bowen, James E.	40	Beech Fork	1850	1	399
Brian—See Bryans					
Bromley—or Brumley					
Bromley, John	225	Lost Creek	1849	1	344
Brown, William	110	12 Pole	1857	2	267
Brumfield, Allen T.	30	Laurel Creek	1848	1	232
Brumfield, Allen T.	50	Laurel Creek	1847	1	153
Brumley—or Bromley					
Brumley, John	350 (35)	Mill Creek	1843	1	10
Brumley, John	65	Mill Creek	1846	1	77
Brumley, John	80	12 Pole	1846	1	97
Brumley, John	175	Mill Creek	1848	1	212
Brumley, John	80	Mill Creek	1854	2	150
Brumley, John	25	Mill Creek	1854	2	152
Brumley, John	25	Mill Creek	1854	2	153
Brumley, John	115	Horse Creek	1860	2	317
Brumley, John et al (Bromley)	180	12 Pole	1849	1	343
Brumley, John et al	1,450	Mill Creek	1843	1	9
Brumley, John et al	325	Mill Creek	1845	1	51
Brumley, John et al	1,666	Lost Creek	1850	1	420
Brumley, John et al	165	Moses' Fork	1850	1	435
Brumley, John et al	225	Bull Creek	1850	1	436
Brumley, John et al	525	12 Pole	1850	1	437
Brumley, John et al	475	Camp Creek	1850	1	438
Brumley, John et al	70	Drag Creek	1852	2	74
Brumley, John et al	190	Henry Smith Branch	1854	2	145
Brumley, John et al	1,000	Drag Creek	1860	2	316
Brumley, John et al	1,050	Mill Creek	1854	2	515
Brumley, John et al	1,600	Horse Creek	1856	2	517
Bryans, William O.	90	Little Lynn	1851	2	16
Buffington, William	125	Greenbrier Trace	1847	1	201
Burchet, Meredith	70	Cove Creek	1860	2	308
Buskirk, James V.	110	Buskirk's Fork	1851	2	50
Campbell, James	50	Big Hurricane	1849	1	277
Canterbury, R. F. et al	700	Big Laurel	1850	1	444
Canterbury, Reuben F.	215	Trough Fork	1850	1	440
Carroll, James	350	Big Hurricane	1847	1	152
Carson, William A.	250	Beech Fork	1846	1	76
Cassady, John	12½	Mill Creek	1850	1	423
Chafin, Stanley	50	Bull Creek	1849	1	325
Chafin, Stanley	90	Bull Creek	1850	1	354
Chafin, Stanley	33	Tug Fork	1847	1	157
Childers, Benjamin	100	Bowen's Creek	1846	1	102
Childers, Benjamin	200	Bowen's Creek	1846	1	103
Childers, Benjamin	20	Bowen's Creek	1854	2	154
Childers, Benjamin	25	Bowen's Creek	1858	2	263
Childers, Benjamin	25	Bowen's Creek	1858	2	264
Cissle—See also Sciscle					
Cissle, Kenzy B.	125	Blue Lick	1848	1	214
Clark, A. F.	125	Brush Creek	1860	2	352

Name of Grantee	Acres	Local Description	Year	Book	Page
Clay, Caleb	22	Camp Creek	1850	1	400
Copley—See Coply					
Copley, Anthony	100	Horse Creek	1849	1	260
Copley, Anthony	143	Dingess Branch	1850	2	1
Copley, Cyrus	85	Drag Creek	1851	2	70
Copley, Henry (or Henly)	190	12 Pole	1850	1	402
Copley, Ira	190	McComas Branch	1850	1	350
Copley, Ira	75	Poplar Lick	1859	2	295
Copley, Ira	33	Horse Creek	1861	2	344
Copley, Ira & James Jr.	25	Tug River	1856	2	209
Copley, James Jr.	60	Horse Creek	1850	1	353
Copley, James Jr. et al	700	12 Pole	1857	2	521
Copley, Thomas	25	Tug Fork	1849	1	336
Copley, Thomas	95	Bull Creek	1849	1	337
Copley, Thomas Jr.	250	Tug Fork	1847	1	194
Copley, Thomas Jr.	45	Tug Fork	1847	1	196
Copley, William H.	65	Horse Creek	1847	1	158
Copley, William H. et al	70	Drag Creek	1852	2	74
Copley, William Jr.	18	Camp Creek	1849	1	328
Copley, William Sr.	50	Drag Creek	1849	1	326
Copley, William Sr.	16	Tug Fork	1849	1	327
Coply or Copley					
Coply, James Jr.	62½	Horse Creek	1849	1	309
Coply, James Sr.	185	Tug Fork	1850	1	401
Coply, William H.	250	Tug Fork	1849	1	310
Cox, John	65	12 Pole Creek	1843	1	7
Cox, John	40	Billey's Branch	1850	2	2
Cox, John	185	Brush Creek	1855	2	163
Crabtree, Hiram	140	Tabour's Creek	1843	1	8
Crabtree, Hiram	60	Hurricane Creek	1846	1	143
Crabtree, Hiram	75	Panther Branch	1854	2	140
Crabtree, Hiram	25	Big Hurricane	1861	2	332
Crabtree, Solomon	6	Big Hurricane	1853	2	89
Cremans, Hiram (Cremeans)	13	Bowen's Creek	1858	2	266
Cremeans—Cremans					
Crum, Adam Jr.	40	Moore's Fork	1860	2	318
Crum, Adam Jr.	40	Venter's Branch	1860	2	319
Crum, David	50	Moses Fork	1845	1	47
Crum, David	15	12 Pole	1850	1	366
Crum, David	18	Moses Fork	1850	1	367
Crum, Frederick	175	Wiley's Branch	1846	1	144
Crum, Frederick	80	Pomeroy Branch	1848	1	213
Crum, Frederick	15	Bull Creek	1856	2	191
Crum, Frederick	60	Bull Creek	1856	2	192
Crum, Joel	110	Moore's Fork	1857	2	252
Crum, William	50	12 Pole	1846	1	98
Crum, William	50	Turkey Creek	1846	1	99
Crum, William	50	Spruce Branch	1846	1	100
Crum, William	12	Silver Creek	1846	1	101
Crum, William	25	Bull Creek	1849	1	308
Crum, William	75	Bull Creek	1850	1	355
Crum, William	140	Trough Fork	1850	1	365
Crum, William	40	Lick Branch	1850	1	403
Crum, William	46	Silver Creek	1850	1	404
Crum, William	42	Bull Creek	1851	2	18
Crum, William	75	Tug River	1856	2	181
Crum, William	160	Wagon Lick Fork	1856	2	182
Crum, William	85	Bull Creek	1856	2	183
Crum, William	50	Bull Creek	1856	2	184
Crum, William	28	Bull Creek	1856	2	185
Crum, William	45	Bull Creek	1856	2	186
Crum, William	20	Bull Creek	1856	2	190
Crum, William	100	Bull Creek	1856	2	194

Name of Grantee	Acres	Local Description	Year	Book	Page
Ferguson, Samuel Jr.	90	Rush Creek	1857	2	235
Ferguson, William & James	133	Moses' Fork	1860	2	326
France, Jesse	130	Peter Cave Branch	1851	2	20
Frasher, Frasier, Frasure, Frazier					
Frasher, Hasten	25	Mill Creek	1848	1	236
Frasher, John	225	Boyd Branch	1849	1	286
Frasher, John	150	Mill Creek	1849	1	302
Frasher, John et al	210	Milam's Creek	1849	1	311
Frasher, John et al	375	Camp Creek	1851	2	19
Frasher, John et al	175	Mill Creek	1851	2	55
Frasher, John L.	17	Mill Creek	1860	2	325
Frasher, John L. et al	700	Drag Creek	1853	2	90
Frasher, John L. et al	32	Mill Creek	1860	2	331
Frasher, Martin	45	Mill Creek	1849	1	304
Frasier, Frasher, Frasure, Frazier					
Frasier, John Sr.	25	Adj. John Thomas	1849	1	261
Frasure, Frasher, Frasier, Frazier					
Frasure, John	45	Bull Creek	1846	1	106
Frasure, John et al	50	Drag Creek	1845	1	72
Frasure, Martin et al	20	Mill Creek	1847	1	151
Frazier, Frasher, Frasier, Frasure					
Frazier, Hasten	25	Mill Creek	1848	1	236
Frazier, John et al	30	Tug Fork	1847	1	181
Friley, Stephen	250	Camp Creek	1848	1	254
Friley, Stephen	140	Turkey Camp	1849	1	257
Fry, David	33	Spring Branch	1846	1	107
Fry, James Jr.	40	Beech Creek	1847	1	197
Fry, Jesse	125	Bartrum's Branch	1855	2	146
Fry, Jesse	12	Rich Creek	1855	2	149
Fry, Johnson et al	125	12 Pole	1852	2	67
Gilkerson, Gilkinson, Guilkison					
Gilkison, Ira	35	Beech Fork	1859	2	301
Gilkison, Ira	12	Beech Fork	1861	2	341
Gilkison, John et al	150	Powder Mill Creek	1843	1	2
Gilkison, Morris	125	12 Pole	1845	1	46
Gilkison, Morris	80	Beech Fork	1847	1	159
Gilkison, Morris et al	185	Beech Fork	1845	1	39
Gilkison, Morris	75	Beech Fork	1859	2	303
Grizzle, John	75	Big Hurricane	1847	1	160
Hammon, Jesse	75	Burchett's Branch	1848	1	235
Hampston—See Hampton					
Hampston, Henry Jr.	100	Mill Creek	1849	1	312
Hampton—See Hampston					
Hampton, Henry Sr.	60	Mill Creek	1847	1	200
Hampton, Reuben	75	Mill Creek	1847	1	156
Harris, Lawrence	50	Camp Creek	1853	2	81
Harris, Reuben	125	Camp Creek	1850	1	356
Harris, Reuben	25	12 Pole	1850	1	443
Harris, Reuben	135	Camp Creek	1853	2	82
Harris, Samuel	100	Lick Creek	1857	2	231
Heater, Hiram	195	Cove Creek	1851	2	40
Henkle—See Hinkle					
Henkle, George B.	180	Laurel Fork	1847	1	186
Herald, James R.	38	Sweet Water	1851	2	47
Hill, Lorenzo D.	100	Hezekiah Creek	1844	1	30
Hinkle—See Henkle					
Hinkle, George B.	550	Lick Fork	1850	1	417
Hinkle, George B.	160	Rich Creek	1848	1	215
Hinkle, George B.	130	12 Pole	1850	2	8
Hobbs, Arthur	150	Camp Creek	1849	1	256
Hobbs, James M.	50	Camp Creek	1844	1	27
Hobbs, James M.	210	Camp Creek	1852	2	76
Holt, John W.	55	Murphy Branch	1851	2	48

Name of Grantee	Acres	Local Description	Year	Book	Page
Holt, Nathan	8	Mill Creek	1849	1	281
Holt, Nathan et al	90	Trace Fork	1848	1	248
Holt, Nathan et al	1,666	Lost Creek	1850	1	420
Holt, Nathan et al	165	Moses's Fork	1850	1	435
Holt, Nathan et al	225	Bull Creek	1850	1	436
Holt, Nathan et al	525	12 Pole	1850	1	437
Holt, Nathan et al	475	Camp Creek	1850	1	438
Holt, Nathan et al	1,000	Drag Creek	1860	2	316
Holt, Nathan et al	1,600	Horse Creek	1856	2	517
Holt, Nathaniel	20	Mill Creek	1849	1	287
Hooser, Sintha Ann (Sinthan)	100	Big Hurricane	1848	1	237
Isaacks—See Isaacs					
Isaacs, Fielding	110	Joel's Branch	1849	1	278
Isaacs, Samuel (Isaacks)	25	12 Pole	1853	2	100
Jackson, Elijah	28	Wolf Pen Fork	1851	2	49
Jarrel—or Jarrell					
Jarrel, John	75	Mill Creek	1847	1	161
Jarrell—or Jarrel					
Jarrell, Harrison	65	Rich Creek	1851	2	66
Jarrell, John	35	Mill Creek	1853	2	104
Jarrell, John et al	250	Raccoon Branch	1850	1	378
Jarrell, John et al	65	Mill Creek	1853	2	105
Jarrell, Samuel	220	Missouri Branch	1851	2	21
Jarrell, Samuel & Harrison	192	Milam's Creek	1846	1	113
Jarrell, Samuel et al	190	Henry Smith Branch	1854	2	145
Johnson, Eli	115	Drag Creek	1849	1	313
Kenyon, Nelson	700	Crane's Nest	1858	2	278
Kirk, Alpha M.	45	Milam's Creek	1850	1	383
Kirk, John	40	Stone Coal	1848	1	216
Kirk, John	60	Tug Fork	1851	2	61
Kirk, Joseph M.	165	Stone Coal	1848	1	217
Kirk, Joseph M.	38	Tug Fork	1849	1	314
Lambert, Elijah	125	Mill Creek	1848	1	218
Lambert, Isaac	60	Mill Creek	1849	1	315
Lambert, John	360	Joel's Branch	1849	1	288
Loar, Harman et al	125(134)	Tug Fork	1847	1	175
Loar, Harman	330	Hurricane	1844	1	26
Low, Car	140	Brush Creek	1846	1	114
Low, Car	38	Rich Creek	1850	1	427
Low, Car	50	12 Pole	1860	2	310
Low, Garrett	27	Jenny's Creek	1851	2	22
Low, Jacob	10	12 Pole	1849	1	263
Low, Jacob	110	12 Pole	1850	1	409
Low, William	75	Lick Log	1847	1	198
Low, William	40	12 Pole	1849	1	262
Lucas, Ezekiel	75	Brush Creek	1848	1	207
Lucas, Vincent	75	Bowen's Creek	1849	1	305
Luster, Elihu et al	65	Big Lynn Cr	1858	2	258
Lycan—See Lycans					
Lycan, Andrew	130	Mill Creek	1854	2	115
Lycans, Goodwin	130	Hurricane	1850	1	384
Lycans, Peyton N.	30	Big Hurricane	1851	2	23
Lycans, Peyton N.	90	Panther Branch	1853	2	94
Mainard, George	300	12 Pole Creek	1849	1	292
Mainard, George	66	Missouri Branch	1852	2	71
Mainard, James	75	Hezekiah's Creek	1847	1	162
Mainard, James	270	12 Pole	1851	2	24
Mainard, James	195	Queen Camp Fork	1851	2	42
Mainard, James	85	Trough Fork	1855	2	134
Mainard, James	290	Milam Creek	1857	2	226
Mainard, James Jr.	90	Hezekiah's Creek	1850	1	386
Mainard, James Sr.	110	Kern's Creek	1850	1	385
Mainard, Jesse	145	12 Pole	1851	2	43

Name of Grantee	Acres	Local Description	Year	Book	Page
Mainard, Jesse Sr.	50	12 Pole	1857	2	269
Mansfield, J. J.	58	Rockhouse Fork	1860	2	314
Mansfield, Joseph J.	54	2 Mile Creek	1860	2	315
Marcum, Carter F.	50	Hezekiah's Fork	1855	2	136
Marcum, Jacob	180	Bull Fork	1855	2	147
Marcum, Jacob	100	Stone Coal	1860	2	349
Marcum, Jacob Jr.	50	Goard Branch	1851	2	27
Marcum, James H. et al	875	12 Pole	1858	2	273
Marcum, John C.	130	Jenny's Creek	1849	1	316
Marcum, John C.	300	Mud Lick Fork	1850	1	411
Marcum, John C.	100	Mud Lick Fork	1848	1	238
Marcum, John C.	22	Jenny's Creek	1848	1	239
Marcum, John C. Sr.	50	Mud Lick	1846	1	115
Marcum, Joseph	100	Tug Fork	1846	1	138
Marcum, Joseph	155	Stone Coal	1849	1	289
Marcum, Joseph	115	Stone Coal	1854	2	117
Marcum, Joseph	105	Bridge Branch	1855	2	126
Marcum, Joseph	125	Stone Coal	1855	2	127
Marcum, Joseph Jr.	125	Stone Coal	1848	1	220
Marcum, Joseph Jr.	80	Tug Fork	1848	1	251
Marcum, Joshua	60	Jenny's Creek	1849	1	290
Marcum, Joshua	250	Jenny's Creek	1858	2	272
Marcum, Moses	130	Moses Fork	1851	2	25
Marcum, Peter	200	Mill Creek	1850	1	430
Marcum, Stephen S. et al	340	Mill Creek	1843	1	6
Marcum, William W.	100	Spruce Branch	1850	1	410
Marcum, William W.	37	Moses Fork	1851	2	26
Marcum, William W.	45	Jenny's Creek	1857	2	239
Marcum, William W.	23	Jenny's Creek	1861	2	353
Marcum, William W.	2,000	Turkey Camp Branch	1857	2	520
Martin, Jesse et al	150	Powder Mill Creek	1843	1	2
Massey, Bazzle D.	50	Beech Fork	1856	2	196
Massey, Bazzle D.	45	Beech Fork	1856	2	197
Massey, Bazzle D.	350	Beech Fork	1856	2	198
Mathew—See Mathews, Mathias					
Mathew, Daniel	25	Sycamore Creek	1853	2	91
Mathew, Daniel	100	12 Pole	1857	2	280
Mathews—See Mathew, Mathias					
Mathews, Forester	30	Sycamore Creek	1849	1	264
Mathias—See Mathew, Mathews					
Mathias, Daniel	16	Rich Creek	1849	1	340
May, Granville P.	95	12 Pole	1849	1	291
May, Jacob	30	12 Pole	1848	1	219
May, Jacob	45	12 Pole	1850	1	442
Mayo, William J.	40	Beech Fork	1855	2	164
Mays, Robert	35	Steer Branch	1858	2	290
Mays, William J.	40	Beech Fork	1855	1	164
McCann, Richard W.	25	12 Pole	1855	2	135
McDyer, John et al	700	Big Laurel	1850	1	444
McHenry, John et al	1,600	Horse Creek	1856	2	517
Mead—See Meed					
Meed—or Mead					
Meed, Benjamin	25	12 Pole	1858	2	305
Meed, Solomon (Mead)	80	12 Pole	1849	1	338
Meed, Solomon	110	Blue Water	1857	2	268
Miller, William C. et al	115	Beech Fork	1850	1	352
Mills, Thomas	125	Beech Fork	1846	1	116
Mills, Thomas	220	Beech Fork	1846	1	117
Monsey—or Munsey					
Monsey, William (Munsey)	80	Jenny's Creek	1856	2	187
Morrison, Asa	15	Beech Fork	1851	2	63
Morrison, James	290	Beech Fork	1846	1	142
Morrison, James	17	Beech Fork	1853	2	95

Name of Grantee	Acres	Local Description	Year	Book	Page
Morrison, James	12	Beech Fork	1859	2	300
Morrison, James R.	28	Beech Fork	1859	2	299
Morrison, Naaman C.	60	Beech Fork	1858	2	279
Morrison, Naaman C. (Naman)	10	Beech Fork	1861	2	345
Munsey, William (Monsey)	80	Jenny's Creek	1856	2	187
Mutter, Isaac	60	12 Pole	1851	2	44
Mutter, Lewis	25	12 Pole	1849	1	339
Napier, Edmund	75	Brush Creek	1855	2	172
Napier, Edmund	9	Big Lynn	1850	1	370
Napier, Moses F.	30	Lick Run	1848	1	242
Napier, Patrick	65	Big Lynn	1845	1	61
Napier, Patrick	160	Brush Creek	1846	1	119
Napier, Patrick	45	Big Lynn	1847	1	163
Naiper, Patrick	70	Stone Coal	1853	2	84
Napier, Robert	180	Big Lynn	1847	1	154
Napier, Thomas F.	60	Big Lynn	1845	1	62
Napier, Thomas F. et al	500	Big Lynn	1846	1	108
Napier, William	25	Beech Branch	1848	1	243
Napier, William	300	Big Lynn	1853	2	108
Nelson, Isaac	125	Hezekiah Creek	1845	1	67
Nelson, Isaac Sr.	70	Hezekiah's Creek	1851	2	28
Nelson, Isaac et al	50	Hezekiah's Fork	1851	2	54
Nelson, Samuel	15	Big Laurel	1856	2	211
Nelson, William	25	Laurel Fork	1846	1	118
Nelson, William	60	Laurel Creek	1852	2	72
Nelson, William C. et al	115	Beech Fork	1850	1	352
Nichols, William T. et al	25	Crow's Nest Branch	1843	1	16
Nichols, William T. et al	160	12 Pole Creek	1843	1	17
Nichols, William T. et al	90	Parker's Creek	1843	1	20
Nichols, William T. et al	30	Parker's Creek	1845	1	31
Nichols, William T. et al	60	12 Pole	1843	1	15
Nichols, William T. et al	140	12 Pole	1843	1	18
Nichols, William T. et al	370	Milam Creek	1843	1	19
Nichols, William T. et al	70	Blue Water	1843	1	21
Nichols, William T. et al	250	12 Pole	1843	1	22
Nixon, William	33	Camp Creek	1851	2	65
Nixon, William	230	Camp Creek	1857	2	346
Noe, William	40	12 Pole	1849	1	265
Noe, William	300	12 Pole	1856	2	210
Osburn, Edmund	69	12 Pole	1851	2	29
Osburn, John	50	12 Pole	1843	1	14
Osburn, John	116	Peter Cave Branch	1845	1	58
Osburn, John Jr.	240	Brush Creek	1850	1	387
Osburn, John Jr. (son of Thomas)	50	Wolf Creek	1855	2	170
Osburn, John Sr.	300	12 Pole	1847	1	166
Osburn, John Sr.	100	Camp Creek	1847	1	167
Osburn, John Sr.	25	Camp Creek	1847	1	168
Osburn, John Sr.	375	Little Lynn	1847	1	184
Osburn, John Sr.	125	12 Pole	1847	1	185
Osburn, John Sr.	40	Bartrum Fork	1849	1	266
Osburn, John Sr.	25	Little Lynn	1851	2	30
Osburn, Leander	30	Trace Branch	1847	1	164
Osburn, Leander	110	Trace Branch Fork	1847	1	165
Osburn, Thomas	100	Wolf Creek	1848	1	244
Osburn, Thomas	100	Wolf Creek	1848	1	252
Osburn, Thomas	45	Trace Fork	1854	2	158
Pack—See Parks					
Pack, Andrew	90	Camp Creek	1850	1	431
Pack, Andrew & George	60	Camp Creek	1850	1	357
Pack, Bartley	25	Tug Fork	1856	2	212
Pack, Charles	13	Hezekiah Fork	1855	2	128
Pack, David	50	Camp Creek	1858	2	259
Pack, George	100	Trough Fork	1849	1	341
Pack, George	200	Trough Fork	1858	2	275

Name of Grantee	Acres	Local Description	Year	Book	Page
Pack, George Jr.	55	Camp Creek	1848	1	245
Pack, James & George	290	Trough Creek	1858	2	274
Pack, James & Samuel	50	Big Laurel	1850	1	388
Pack, Samuel	25	Trough Branch	1855	2	122
Page, Samuel	16	Laurel Creek	1845	1	44
Page, Samuel	100	12 Pole	1846	1	120
Page, Samuel	25	12 Pole	1847	1	202
Page, Samuel	15	12 Pole	1849	1	294
Page, Samuel	95	12 Pole	1849	1	295
Parks—See Pack					
Parks, James S.	80	Hurricane	1858	2	256
Parks, James S.	120	Big Hurricane	1858	2	257
Parks, Robert H.	100	Big Hurricane	1861	2	355
Parks, Shelton	190	Hurricane	1846	1	75
Parks, Shelton	300	Tabor's Creek	1847	1	171
Parsley—See Pasley					
Parsons, Thomas	25	12 Pole	1858	2	260
Pasley, Jesse	140	Jenny's Creek	1850	1	412
Pasley, Jesse	85	Jenny's Creek	1856	2	188
Pasley, Jesse	200	Mud Lick Fork	1856	2	189
Pasley, Jesse	100	Jenny's Creek	1856	2	202
Pasley, Jesse	200	Silver Creek	1860	2	327
Pauley, Hyram	130	Blue Lick Branch	1848	1	240
Perry, Arnold	35	12 Pole	1849	1	293
Perry, Arnold	210	12 Pole	1850	1	359
Perry, Arnold	135	Rich Creek	1850	2	3
Perry, George	65	12 Pole	1849	1	267
Perry, George	90	Long Branch	1849	1	268
Perry, George	90	Long Branch	1851	2	53
Perry, Jesse	100	12 Pole	1857	2	240
Perry, Nathan	55	Honey Trace Branch	1849	1	317
Perry, Nathan	110	Crane's Nest	1859	2	304
Pinson, William	50	Rich Creek	1847	1	170
Porter, Alexander	114	12 Pole	1849	1	320
Porter, Alexander	100	Big Branch	1857	2	241
Porter, Patrick	40	Blue Lick Branch	1847	1	169
Porter, Patrick	215	Blue Lick	1855	2	165
Porter, Samuel	45	Sycamore Creek	1857	2	254
Pratt, John	50	Meeting House Br.	1851	2	39
Pratt, John	45	Lick Branch	1859	2	298
Price, John	135	Rock Camp Branch	1847	1	172
Price, William	65	Camp Creek	1850	1	351
Prichard—See Prichett					
Prichett, William	150	Beech Fork	1846	1	83
Preston, Isaac	35	Lick Log Branch	1849	1	319
Preston, Isaac	55	Lick Log Branch	1852	2	77
Preston, Henry	41	12 Pole	1860	2	320
Preston, Thomas	225	12 Pole	1849	1	318
Preston, Thomas et al	373	Rich Creek	1855	2	169
Queen, Absolom et al	300	12 Pole	1857	2	238
Queen, Absolom et al	275	Parker's Creek	1857	2	519
Queen, James	450	Hezekiah's Fork	1847	1	173
Queen, John	125	Hurricane Fork	1846	1	121
Queen, John	150	12 Pole	1850	1	428
Queen, John	75	Dalton Fork	1855	2	161
Queen, John H.	50	12 Pole	1857	2	228
Queen, John H.	45	12 Pole	1858	2	261
Queen, Walter	30	12 Pole	1845	1	65
Queen, Walter	395	12 Pole	1849	1	346
Queen, Walter	90	Indian Lick	1857	2	227
Ramey, James	80	Crouch Fork	1858	2	270
Ratcliff—See Ratliff					
Ratcliff, William	30	Lost Creek	1853	2	86

Name of Grantee	Acres	Local Description	Year	Book	Page
Ratcliff, William & G. C.	110	Spring Branch	1850	1	429
Ratcliff, William & G. C.	80	Cyntha's Branch	1854	2	143
Ratcliff, William & G. C.	135	Rich Creek	1854	2	144
Ratcliff, William & G. C.	45	Bull Creek	1855	2	171
Ratcliff, Thompson	50	Mill Creek	1843	1	5
Ratliff, Thompson et al	340	Mill Creek	1843	1	6
Ratliff, William	65	Tug Fork	1847	1	176
Ratliff, William	50	Tug Fork	1847	1	177
Ratliff, William et al	125(134)	Tug Fork	1847	1	175
Reed, Thomas	100	Wolf Creek	1848	1	246
Robertson, John	130	Robertson's Branch	1851	2	56
Robertson, Johnson (or Joseph)	65	Mill Creek	1849	1	282
Robertson, Richard	175	Mill Creek	1848	1	221
Robertson, Richard et al	175	Mill Creek	1851	2	55
Roman, James	150	12 Pole	1849	1	296
Ross, Covington	70	Lynn Creek	1845	1	63
Ross, Covington	70	Camp Creek	1846	1	122
Ross, Covington	125	Road Fork	1846	1	123
Ross, Covington	30	12 Pole	1850	1	360
Ross, Covington	42	Little Lynn Branch	1858	2	281
Ross, Henry	125	Beech Fork	1847	1	174
Ross, Henry	80	12 Pole	1855	2	139
Ross, Hugh	700	Cove Creek	1859	2	294
Ross, James M.	45	Big Lynn Creek	1857	2	242
Ross, James M.	10	12 Pole	1857	2	243
Ross, James M.	7	12 Pole	1857	2	244
Ross, James M.	60	Lynn Creek	1861	2	342
Ross, Madison	70	Bartrum Fork	1845	1	64
Ross, Madison	90	12 Pole	1846	1	140
Ross, Madison	130	Bartrum Fork	1846	1	141
Ross, Madison	30	12 Pole	1849	1	321
Ross, Madison	60	Bartrum Fork	1849	1	322
Ross, Madison	30	Big Lynn Fork	1849	1	323
Ross, Robert	20	Little Lynn	1859	2	292
Ross, Robert	150	Little Lynn	1859	2	293
Ross, Robert et al	550	Beech Fork	1852	2	73
Ross, Robert et al	125	Cove Creek	1855	2	173
Ross, Robert et al	1,625	Beech Fork	1851	2	513
Salmons, William	60	Moses' Fork	1856	2	205
Samuels, John et al	550	Beech Fork	1852	2	73
Samuels, John et al	125	Cove Creek	1855	2	173
Samuels, John et al	1,625	Beech Fork	1851	2	513
Sciscle—See Cissle					
Sciscle, Kinsey B.	75	Camp Branch	1846	1	125
Seashole, John (Seasholl)	4,590	12 Pole	1846	1	447
Selbe, Charles	230	Trace Fork	1845	1	73
Selbee, Charles	100	Mill Creek	1854	2	119
Sellards—See Sollards, Sullards					
Sellards, Jemima	40	12 Pole	1848	1	247
Shelton, Thomas M.	45	Lick Creek	1850	1	421
Shelton, Thomas M.	120	Lick Creek	1850	1	422
Short, Samuel et al	60	12 Pole Creek	1843	1	15
Short, Samuel et al	25	Crow's Nest Branch	1843	1	16
Short, Samuel et al	160	12 Pole	1843	1	17
Short, Samuel et al	140	12 Pole	1843	1	18
Short, Samuel et al	370	Milam Creek	1843	1	19
Short, Samuel et al	90	Parker's Creek	1843	1	20
Short, Samuel et al	70	Blue Water	1843	1	21
Short, Samuel et al	250	12 Pole	1843	1	22
Short, Samuel et al	30	Parker's Creek	1845	1	31
Short, Samuel et al	400	Wts. 12 Pole	1845	1	36
Short, Samuel et al	600	12 Pole	1845	1	37
Short, Samuel Sr.	75	Rich Creek	1855	2	159
Short, Samuel Sr.	75	Rich Creek	1855	2	160

Name of Grantee	Acres	Local Description	Year	Book	Page
Wiley, Hezekiah	50	12 Pole	1856	2	199
Wiley, Hezekiah et al	100	Hezekiah's Fork	1850	2	7
Wiley, John N.	120	Laurel Creek	1851	2	52
Wiley, Thomas	160	Cove Creek	1846	1	137
Wiley, Thomas	100	Spring Branch	1849	1	342
Wiley, Thomas	25	Spring Branch	1854	2	118
Wiley, William	80	Cove Creek	1860	2	329
Wiley, William	50	Cove Creek	1860	2	330
Wiley, William	129	Cove Creek	1850	1	394
Williams, William	135	Bear Branch	1850	1	413
Williamson, James	110	12 Pole	1846	1	136
Williamson, James	75	12 Pole	1850	1	414
Williamson, James	100	Brush Creek	1859	2	296
Wilson, Alexander	14	Mill Creek	1848	1	225
Wilson, Alexander	95	Big Hurricane	1848	1	226
Wilson, Alexander	35	Mill Creek	1846	1	132
Wilson, Alexander Jr.	12½	Lick Fork	1849	1	274
Wilson, Allen	65	12 Pole	1846	1	147
Wilson, Allen	325	Deep Hole Branch	1848	1	227
Wilson, Anderson	456	12 Pole	1847	1	199
Wilson, Anderson	95	12 Pole	1850	2	6
Wilson, Anderson et al	90	Trace Fork	1848	1	248
Wilson, Andrew (or Anderson)	25	Billy's Branch	1850	2	15
Wilson, Charles	20	Mill Creek	1846	1	130
Wilson, Charles	30	Tug Fork	1846	1	131
Wilson, Charles	25	Mill Creek	1850	1	395
Wilson, David	6	Mill Creek	1854	2	120
Wilson, David	20	Brumley Branch	1854	2	121
Wilson, Jackson	175	Mill Creek	1848	1	230
Wilson, Jackson	45	Laurel Branch	1850	1	396
Wilson, Jackson	35	Mill Creek	1851	2	58
Wilson, James	40	Mill Creek	1843	1	3
Wilson, Leander	175	Mill Creek	1846	1	133
Witcher, Daniel	180	Hezekiah's Fork	1847	1	191
Witcher, Daniel	100	12 Pole	1848	1	249
Witcher, Daniel	80	12 Pole	1848	1	250
Wicther, Daniel	240	Hezekiah's Fork	1851	2	41
Witcher, Daniel	220	Hezekiah's Fork	1853	2	107
Witcher, Daniel	90	12 Pole	1853	2	110
Witcher, Daniel	125	Alum Branch	1857	2	247
Wooton, Thomas A.	20	Big Lynn Creek	1855	2	148
Workman, Abagail	25	12 Pole	1861	2	354
Workman, Alderson	10	12 Pole	1860	2	322
Workman, Joseph	140	12 Pole	1850	1	415
Workman, Pleasant Jr.	65	Mill Creek	1849	1	275
Workman, Pleasant Sr.	55	12 Pole	1849	1	298
Workman, Stephen	150	12 Pole	1846	1	134
Workman, Stephens	350	12 Pole	1846	1	135
York, John	22	Camp Creek	1851	2	38
York, Joseph D.	140	Lost Creek	1849	1	324
York, Joseph D.	195	Lick Creek	1850	1	416
York, Joshua & John	110	Camp Creek	1858	2	262

WEBSTER COUNTY

Strong, William F., et al	1,500	Adj. Hughart & Snyder	1864	1	359
Wallace, Mathew, et al	1,500	Cor. to Hugart & Snyder	1864	1	359
Warwick, John W., et al	1,500	Adj. Hugart & Snyder	1864	1	359

WETZEL COUNTY

Name of Grantee	Acres	Local Description	Year	Book	Page
Ally, Elijah	360	Fishing Creek	1849	1	36
Anderson, William	40	Little Fishing Cr.	1858	1	167
Ankrom, Arthur	366	Fishing Creek	1852	1	120
Boreman, William J.	150	Fishing Creek	1849	1	62
Boyers, Josiah	600	Little Fishing Cr.	1849	1	37
Calvert, Albert G.	6¼	Lynn Camp Run	1858	1	149
Calvert, Albert G.	16 (16¾)	Fish Creek	1858	1	147
Church, Henry Jr.	345	Fish Creek	1852	1	110
Church, Henry Jr.	50	Rush Run	1852	1	109
Church, Henry Jr.	50 (55)	Church Fork	1848	1	17
Church, Samuel	240	Fish Creek	1852	1	115
Church, Samuel	80	Fish Creek	1849	1	38
Clark, Isaac	60	Fish Creek	1848	1	16
Cockran, James	190	Fishing Creek	1849	1	108
Cockran, James	45	Fishing Creek	1848	1	10
Copenhaver, James W.	50	South Fork	1848	1	15
Cox, Friend	48	Little Fishing Cr.	1852	1	119
Delaney, Moses	50	Fishing Creek	1849	1	39
Edgell, Elias	178	Fishing Creek	1858	1	158
Ferrell, James P.	45	Church's Fork	1859	1	176
Ferrell, James P.	5½	Church's Fork	1859	1	177
Freeland, James P.	50	Pickenpaw Run	1848	1	13
Glover, Amos	75	Adj. James Vilar's	1853	1	129
Gooch, Stephen T.	300	Fallen Timber Run	1849	1	28
Hall, Ephraim	100	Proctor's Run	1850	1	78
Hamrick—or Hemrick					
Hamrick, Alexander (Hemrick)	100	Church Fork	1852	1	112
Hamrick, Amos (Hemrick)	354	Church Fork	1852	1	116
Hanan, George N.	50	Fish Creek	1851	1	94
Hanan, George N., et al	200	Church Fork	1849	1	46
Hays, Edmund W.	12	Fishing Creek	1854	1	142
Hays, James, Sr.	14½	Fishing Creek	1855	1	144
Hays, John E.	40	Fishing Cr.	1852	1	113
Hemrick—See Hamrick					
Headly, Caleb	100	Fishing Creek	1848	1	5
Hendershot, Phebe, et al Heirs	46	Lit. Fishing Creek	1858	1	165
Hendershot, Phebe et al, Heirs	141	Rush Run	1858	1	166
Hickman, David	305	10 Mile Fork	1849	1	86
Higginbotham, Haymond	300	Willy Fork	1850	1	93
Higginbotham, Isaac & Samuel	420	Fishing Creek	1849	1	30
Hindgardner, Michael	145	Rush Run	1849	1	40
Hitchcock, Joshua	100	Fishing Creek	1850	1	79
Hoge, Isaac	100	Fishing Creek	1849	1	174
Hoge, Isaac	825	Fishing Creek	1859	1	168
Hoge, Isaac	444	Fishing Creek	1860	1	185
Hoge, Isaac	93	Long Drain	1858	1	152
Hoge, Isaac	850	Fishing Creek	1856	1	145
Hoge, Isaac	1,300	Fishing Creek	1855	1	143
Hoge, Isaac	1,447	Fish Creek	1854	1	138
Hoge, Isaac	38	Fish Creek	1852	1	127
Hoge, Isaac	130	Whetstone Creek	1852	1	128
Hoge, Isaac	232	Lynn Camp	1852	1	105
Hoge, Isaac	300	Fishing Creek	1851	1	103
Hoge, Isaac	400	Draper's Fork	1851	1	104
Hoge, Isaac	500	Pine Fork	1849	1	85
Hoge, Isaac	1,000	Crow's Run	1850	1	77
Hoge, Isaac	75	Narrows Run	1849	1	60
Hoge, Isaac	500	Fishing Creek	1848	1	21
Hoge, Isaac	45	Fish Creek	1849	1	61
Hoge, Isaac	260	Fishing Creek	1849	1	64
Hoge, Isaac	230	Fishing Cr.	1849	1	63
Hoge, James M.	450	Lynn Camp	1852	1	121

Name of Grantee	Acres	Local Description	Year	Book	Page
Horner, Charles et al	61	Railroad Fork	1858	1	154
Horner, Charles et al	16	Church Fork	1858	1	151
Horner, J. W. et al	2,800	Fishing Creek	1851	1	96
Horner, John W. et al	2,200	Big Fishing Cr.	1850	1	76
Horner, John W. et al	400	Fishing Creek	1851	1	95
Hostutler, John	106	Church Fork	1854	1	139
Hostutler, John	60	Fish Creek	1849	1	41
Hostutler, John	20	Church Fork	1848	1	18
Hostutler, John	25	Church Fork	1848	1	19
Hostutler, Nathaniel	45	Fish Creek	1858	1	148
Hostutler, Nathaniel	550	Fish Creek	1848	1	14
Hustutler—Hostutler					
Ice, Adin B.	250	Fishing Creek	1858	1	155
Ice, Andrew	100	Fishing Creek	1848	1	26
Ice, Isaac	45	Fishing Creek	1850	1	8
Ice, John	86	Fishing Creek	1858	1	146
Ice, John Jr.	60	Fishing Creek	1853	1	131
Ice, John Jr.	50	Fishing Creek	1850	1	9
Joliff, Hezekiah (Jolliff)	100	Fishing Creek	1850	1	89
Kenney, James W. et al	16	Church Fork	1858	1	151
Kenney, James W. et al	61	Railroad Fork	1858	1	154
King, Jeremiah	21	Fishing Creek	1859	1	169
King, John	71	Fishing Creek	1858	1	162
King, William	100	Fishing Creek	1850	1	66
Lantz, Alexander	1,170	Fishing Creek	1858	1	157
Lantz, Alexander	1,567	Fishing Creek	1853	1	135
Lantz, Alexander	350	Reader's Run	1849	1	31
Lauck, R. W.	800	Fishing Creek	1852	1	125
Lauck, R. W.	140	Fishing Creek	1852	1	122
Lauck, R. W. et al	2,800	Fishing Creek	1851	1	96
Lauck, Richard W.	500	Fishing Creek	1852	1	124
Lauck, Richard W.	200	Fishing Creek	1852	1	123
Lauck, Richard W.	150	Shenango Run	1848	1	20
Lauck, Richard W. et al	400	Fishing Creek	1851	1	95
Lauck, Richard W. et al	2,200	Big Fishing Cr.	1850	1	76
Leazer, John	100	Fish Creek	1848	1	6
Leep, Mary Ann	46	Fishing Creek	1858	1	165
Leep, Mary Ann et al, Heirs	141	Rush Run	1858	1	166
Lemly, George	344	Long Drain	1849	1	59
Lieuts, Francis D.	225	Fishing Creek	1859	1	171
Long, Samuel J.	34½	Fishing Creek	1859	1	170
Long, Samuel J.	530	Mod's Run	1850	1	80
Louck—See Lauck					
Lowe, Levi M.	68	Fishing Creek	1859	1	173
Lowe, Levi M.	100	Fishing Creek	1850	1	90
Manion, Patrick	100	10-Mile Fork	1858	1	156
Marriner—See Merriner					
Marshall, James	188	Adj. Peter Sole	1848	1	22
Martin, Job H.	50	Fishing Creek	1854	1	136
Martin, John	400	Fishing Creek	1849	1	54
Martin, John	400	Fishing Creek	1849	1	55
Martin, John	60	Fishing Creek	1849	1	56
Martin, John	5¾	Fishing Creek	1860	1	179
Martin, Presley	700	Fishing Creek	1851	1	97
Martin, Presley M.	1,000	Fishing Creek	1849	1	44
Martin, Presley M.	100	Pine Fork	1849	1	87
McCoy, Charles P.	200	Fishing Cr.	1850	1	67
McCoy, Charles P.	200	Pine Fork	1850	1	68
McCoy, Charles P.	42	Fishing Cr.	1850	1	73
McCoy, Charles P.	90	Fishing Cr.	1850	1	74
McCoy, Charles P.	150	Pine Fork	1850	1	75
Merriner, Mathew (Marriner)	100	Church Fork	1849	1	42
Millburn, John	350	Brush Run	1849	1	33

Name of Grantee	Acres	Local Description	Year	Book	Page
Starkey, Levi Jr.	100	Ten Mile Fork	1849	1	29
Stottlemire, David	300	Long Drain	1852	1	118
Stottlemire, David	212	Long Drain	1858	1	164
Stottlemire, Joseph Jr.	114	Fish Creek	1848	1	25
Stout, John	140	Fishing Creek	1854	1	141
Strait, Levi et al	50	Fishing Creek	1849	1	35
Suman—or Shuman					
Suman, William	110	Little Fishing Cr	1849	1	51
Talkington, David	100	10 Mile Creek	1848	1	7
Talkington, Jessie	200	10 Mile Fork	1858	1	161
Talkington, Samuel	100	10 Mile Creek	1848	1	12
Tucker, Thomas	700	Fishing Creek	1849	1	53
Tucker, Thomas	200	Reader's Run	1850	1	83
Ullom, Alfred	100	Bear Run	1851	1	102
Ullom, Stephen (Ulom)	110	Fish Creek	1854	1	140
Vickers, John	33	Fish Creek	1850	1	82
Vilars, James	275	Fish Creek	1853	1	133
Villers—Vilars					
West, James G.	3,079	Fishing Creek	1853	1	513
West, P. G.	16½	Fishing Creek	1858	1	160
West, P. G.	200	Fishing Creek	1858	1	159
West, Perry G.	650	Fishing Creek	1850	1	92
Wilson, William	230	Fishing Creek	1861	1	189
Wyatt, Alpheus	250	Fishing Creek	1858	1	163
Wyatt, Augustus	140	Fishing Creek	1853	1	134
Wyatt, Sacker	100	Fishing Creek	1858	1	153

WIRT COUNTY

Atkinson, John P.	167	Adj. H. Depue	1851	1	208
Baker, Elisha et al	382	Straight Creek	1859	1	351
Baker, Elisha et al	1,096	Straight Creek	1858	1	341
Baker, Morton	150	Dayley's Run	1852	1	239
Barnes, Israel	196	Tucker's Creek	1854	1	278
Barnes, Israel	51	Tucker's Creek	1853	1	267
Beauchamp, Alfred	94	Lee Creek	1855	1	296
Bee, Ephraim	230	2 Lick Run	1851	1	236
Bell, Silas & George	98	Straight Creek	1855	1	294
Belt, Asa et al	284	Strait Creek	1851	1	226
Bennett, Arnold W.	70	Tucker Creek	1850	1	200
Bennett, Elkanah	25	Slate Creek	1854	1	277
Bennett, J. M. et al	1,000	Spring Creek	1851	1	211
Boggs, Charles C.	132	Hicks Run	1851	1	221
Boggs, John L.	30	Reedy	1851	1	222
Boggs, M. D. W.	64	Spring Creek	1851	1	223
Boice, John	332	Tucker's Creek	1855	1	288
Brummage, William J. (Brumage)	182	Straight Creek	1858	1	343
Buel, Hiram	100	Adj. Tilton's Surv. No. 31	1857	1	320
Buel, Lauraine	140	Reedy Creek	1861	1	374
Buffington, William	542	Adj. D. R. Neal	1851	1	209
Bumgarner, Joseph et al	83	Reedy	1858	1	342
Bumgarner, Jacob	50	Summerville Run	1852	1	238
Bumgarner, Jacob	55	Summerville Run	1851	1	227
Burns, Israel	196	Tucker Creek	1854	1	278
Butcher, Rolla et al	2,234	Spring Creek	1858	1	515
Clark, James	248	Adj. Wm. P. Rathbone	1857	1	321

Name of Grantee	Acres	Local Description	Year	Book	Page
Clark, James	66	Spring Creek	1857	1	330
Coe, F. A. P.	40	Island Run	1851	1	224
Coe, George W.	50	Island Run	1851	1	212
Conrad, Peter	7	Reedy	1859	1	364
Copen, Thompson	140	Standing Stone	1855	1	290
Copen, Thompson	606	Standing Stone	1855	1	289
Corley, R. B.	34	Adj. D. Pickering	1850	1	201
Corley, R. B.	104	Adj. James Naylor	1850	1	202
Courtney, Mason	45	Tucker's Creek	1858	1	344
Crawford, Calvin	100	Road Run	1851	1	228
Crawford, J. Watson	50	Bridge Run	1859	1	350
Creel, B. W. et al	24	Adj. Ephraim Sayre	1860	1	376
Curfman, Michael	80	Reedy	1859	1	361
Daggett, George L.	126	Tucker Creek	1851	1	198
Davis, Samuel C.	19	Spring Creek	1855	1	297
Dent, Alpheus et al	378	Rock Run	1859	1	363
Dent, James E.	606	Standing Stone	1855	1	299
Depew, David & Hiram	200	Vincent Run	1854	1	287
Donnally, Dryden et al	24	Adj. Ephraim Sayre	1860	1	376
Dulin, A. H.	44	Rock Run	1853	1	266
Dulin, A. H.	100	Rock Run	1851	1	197
Enoch, A. et al	257	Goose Creek	1850	1	205
Enoch, Abraham	460	Adj. Jesse C. Roach	1857	1	336
Enoch, Abraham	108	Adj. Wm. Buffiington	1853	1	263
Enoch, Abraham	11	Spring Creek	1856	1	314
Enoch, David Jr.	63	Ripple Run	1857	1	331
Enoch, David	200	Ripple Run	1854	1	272
Enoch, Isaac (the 3rd)	63	Reedy	1856	1	306
Enoch, Isaac (the 3rd)	120	Reedy	1856	1	307
Enoch, Isaac (the 3rd)	50	Reedy	1856	1	308
Enoch, T. J.	114	Ripple Run	1856	1	309
Enoch, William L.	100	Goose Creek	1853	1	254
Evans, Jonathan	81	Slate Creek	1858	1	348
Fisher, C. W.	95	Standing Stone	1859	1	365
Fought, Alfred	12	Silver Run	1854	1	275
Fought, Alfred et al	98	Adj. Robert Barnes	1858	1	338
Garrison, A. M. et al	216	Standing Stone	1859	1	359
Gates, James D.	200	Tucker Creek	1852	1	240
Graham, E. T. et al	383	Reedy	1853	1	256
Hall, John P.	121	Spring Creek	1858	1	375
Hall, John P. et al	200	Spring Creek	1860	1	369
Hall, John P. et al	266	Spring Creek	1858	1	346
Hall, John P. et al	198	Spring Creek	1859	1	355
Hall, John P. et al	115	Spring Creek	1859	1	356
Hammon, Michael	112	Lee Creek	1858	1	337
Harris, John	163	Reedy	1853	1	258
Hickman, Abraham	210	Spring Creek	1858	1	345
Hickman, Gerry et al	2,234	Spring Creek	1858	1	515
Hollaran, John (Hollaron)	88	Tucker's Creek	1854	1	279
Hollaran, John (Hollaron)	52	Tucker's Creek	1854	1	280
Hopkins, E. C.	375	Slate Creek	1860	1	367
Hull, James F. et al	216	Standing Stone	1859	1	359
James, George C.	738	Slate Creek	1859	1	352
Kearfman, Michael	80	Reedy	1859	1	361
King, Thomas	69	Lynn Camp Run	1852	1	248
Kyger, Hugh et al	260	2 Run	1861	1	377
Kyger, Hugh et al	50	Upper 2 Run	1861	1	378
Lang, George	39	Tucker's Creek	1856	1	315
Leazier, B. F.	64	Lick Run	1859	1	349
Lee, Joshua et al	200	Spring Creek	1860	1	369
Lee, Joshua et al	115	Spring Creek	1859	1	356
Lee, Joshua et al	198	Spring Creek	1859	1	355
Lee, Joshua et al	266	Spring Creek	1858	1	346

WOOD COUNTY

Name of Grantee	Acres	Local Description	Year	Book	Page
Chancellor, John C.	200	Chevauxdefrize Creek	1842	2	257
Chancellor, Thomas	100	Brush Run	1815	1	157
Chancellor, Thomas	564	Indian Creek	1838	2	130
Chancellor, Thomas	½	Mth. Lit. Kanawha	1859	3	494
Chapman, A. J. et al	500	Bull Creek	1842	2	273
Chapman, M.	384	Walker's Creek	1842	2	266
Chapman, M.	36	Adj. D. Kincheloe	1845	2	329
Chapman, M. C.	300	Lee Creek	1842	2	265
Chapman, Mathias	340	Worthington's Cr.	1822	1	265
Chapman, Mathias et al	200	Reedy Creek	1804	1	38
Chapman, Warner W.	330	Potato Run	1842	2	264
Clark, John & John W.	200	Sandy Creek	1840	2	173
Cline, Abraham	100	Bull Creek	1815	1	172
Cline, William	100	State Road Creek	1817	1	197
Cline, William	100	Goose Creek	1817	1	198
Coe, E. G.	100	Brushy Fork	1851	3	4
Coe, E. G. & B. E.	554	Sandy Creek	1851	3	5
Cole, A. N. et al	54	Killer's Island	1859	3	488
Collins, Henry	106	Adj. James R. Jones	1841	2	195
Collins, Henry	100	Wts. of Hughes	1838	2	152
Collins, Henry B. et al	200	Wts. Hughes River	1841	2	196
Collins, John	660	Pond Creek	1841	2	192
Collins, John	50	Adj. Jacob Collins	1841	2	183
Collins, Joseph	138	Buck Fork	1841	2	194
Collins, Wm.	135	Sugar Camp Run	1841	2	186
Compton, James et al	200	Wts. Hughes River	1817	1	199
Compton, Thomas	250	Bull Creek	1814	1	155
Connell, Richard	50	Wts. Lit. Kanawha	1838	2	147
Conrad—or Coonrad					
Conrad, Jacob	50	Unknown	1817	1	194
Cook, James	142	Adj. H. Farsons	1861	3	513
Cook, Paul	142	Worthington's Creek	1841	2	179
Coonrad—See Conrad					
Coonrad, Christopher	50	Reedy Creek	1820	1	241
Coonrad, John	83	Reedy Creek	1820	1	238
Cooper, Lemuel et al	298	Cow Run	1860	3	498
Cooper, Valentine	100	Tygert's Creek	1809	1	69
Cooper, Valentine	133	Cor. to Paul Armstrong	1802	1	18
Copen, Thompson	100	Tucker's Creek	1837	2	102
Copen, Thompson	100	Stone Creek	1838	2	133
Coplin, David	8	Walker's Creek	1858	3	477
Coplin, David	738	Stillwell Creek	1855	3	46
Corbit, James	116	Spring Creek	1835	2	81
Cork, Jacob	11	Walker's Creek	1859	3	492
Cork, Jacob	120	Stillwell Creek	1851	3	8
Cork, Jacob et al	200	Stillwell Creek	1844	2	292
Cork, Jacob et al	65	Stillwell Creek	1844	2	294
Cork, Jacob et al	335	Stillwell Creek	1844	2	293
Cox, James	100	Reedy Creek	1851	2	442
Cozad, David	270	Wts. Lit. Kanawha	1838	2	153
Creel, Alexander H.	83	Tygert's Creek	1833	2	49
Creel, B. W	64	Walker's Creek	1858	3	481
Creel, Bushrod W.	620	Walker's Creek	1837	2	101
Creel, Bushrod W.	800	Berries' Run	1838	2	157
Creel, Bushrod W	100	Wts. Lit. Kanawha	1842	2	251
Creel, Bushrod W.	912	Stillwell Creek	1844	2	286
Creel, Bushrow W.	900	Stillwell Creek	1844	2	313
Creel, Bushrod W.	750	Flint Run	1846	2	336
Creel, Bushrod W.	965	Walker's Creek	1855	3	43
Creel, George W. et al	100	Walker's Creek	1838	2	454
Creel, John B.	100	Wts. Lit. Kanawha	1837	2	89
Creel, John B.	190	Walker's Creek	1835	2	83
Creel, John B. et al	100	Wts. Lit. Kanawha	1837	2	452

Name of Grantee	Acres	Local Description	Year	Book	Page
Creel, John Buckner et al	170	Stillwell's Cr.	1811	1	129
Creel, John Buckner et al	300	Stillwell Creek	1811	1	116
Crispin, E. et al Heirs	190	Adj. H. Farson	1854	3	29
Crispin, Ephraim	175	Goose Creek	1852	3	19
Cross, John et al	495	Brushy Fork	1859	3	490
Cross, Nimrod	200	Rock Camp Run	1842	2	242
Culp, Ephraigm	160	Indian Creek	1842	2	250
Darnel, Hosier	97	Greves Run	1848	2	378
Davis, Jesse	89	Tigert's Creek	1819	1	228
Davis, Jesse	100	Tygert's Creek	1828	2	34
Davis, Joseph et al	275	Tygert's Creek	1834	2	62
Davis, Label	100	Stillwell Creek	1847	2	362
Dawkins, John	36	Wts. Little Kanawha	1840	2	170
Dawkins, John	37	Adj. John Barnett	1837	2	112
Deavingburger—Derenburger, Devinburger					
Deavingburger, George (Derenburger)	50	Lee Creek	1825	2	11
Deem, Abraham	80	Goose Creek	1846	2	337
Deem, Abraham	25	Slate Creek (State)	1815	1	164
Deem, Abraham et al	124	Lick Run	1859	3	484
Deem, Adam (the 2nd)	100	Wts. Hughes River	1838	2	123
Deem, Adam	253	Wts. Hughes River	1837	2	100
Deem, Adam (Deems)	300	Wts. Hughes River	1815	1	160
Deem, Alexander	121	Slate Creek	1859	3	497
Deem, Haymond B.	171	Tygert's Creek	1852	3	20
Deem, Hiram	25	Little Tygert's Cr.	1838	2	134
Deem, Hiram	18	Tygart's Creek	1856	3	452
Deem, Jacob	135	Slate Creek	1830	2	40
Deem, Jacob	50	Tiger's Creek	1815	1	165
Deem, Jacob	100	Slate Creek	1811	1	118
Deem, Jacob	300	Tigert's Creek	1807	1	54
Deem, Jacob	50	Adj. Bentley	1820	1	247
Deem, Jacob	100	Slate Creek	1820	1	248
Deem, Jacob Sr.	100	Grass Run	1820	1	246
Deem, Jonathan	122	Slate Creek	1857	3	463
Deem, Myranda & James	188	Mud Lick Run	1854	3	38
Deem, Myranda & James	231	Slate Creek	1860	3	499
Deem, Peter	35	Tygert Creek	1842	2	225
Deem, Peter	60	Tygert's Creek	1841	2	182
Deem, Peter	116	Buck Run	1844	2	298
Deem, Peter	22	Tygert's Creek	1847	2	357
Deem, Peter	100	Ratcliff's Run	1847	2	356
Deem, Philip	150	Wts. Hughes River	1841	2	180
Deem, William	203	Tygert's Creek	1859	3	496
Deem, William	75	Adj. J. Deem	1842	2	224
Deem, William	307	Tygert's Creek	1854	3	39
Deem, William	460	Tygert's Creek	1857	3	459
Deem, William	100	Tygert's Creek	1847	2	353
Deem, William	562	Tygert's Creek	1847	2	358
Deem, William	95	Mud Lick Run	1850	2	417
Deem, William	180	Slate Creek	1857	3	461
Deem, William & Alexander	100	Slate Creek	1857	3	460
Derenburger, Deavingburger, Devinburger					
Devaughan, Asa	162	Neal's Run	1834	2	72
Devaughan, Reuben	221	Walker's Creek	1855	3	44
Devaughan, Thompson	229	Walker Creek	1854	3	47
Devaughan, William	50	Walker's Creek	1844	2	299
Devaughan, William	39	Adj. T. Devaughan	1855	3	42
Devaughan, William Jr. et al	45	Goose Creek	1858	3	478
Devaughan, William	50	Coalbank Run	1847	2	355
Devinburger, Deavingburger, Derenburger					
Devinburger, George	76	Lee Creek	1851	2	434
Dickinson, Josiah S.	280	Cave Run	1848	2	377

Name of Grantee	Acres	Local Description	Year	Book	Page
Die or Dye					
Die, Reuben	68	Little Kanawha	1804	1	35
Die, Reuben	100	Chestnut Run	1810	1	109
Die, Reuben	150	Burning Springs	1810	1	108
Die, Reuben	100	Wts. Lit. Kanawha	1810	1	110
Dodridge, Philip et al	500	Pond Run	1804	1	44
Dotson, Emanuel	100	State Road Run	1815	1	171
Dotson, Emanuel	100	Buck Run	1818	1	211
Dotson, Emanuel	44	Buck Run	1818	1	212
Dotson, Emanuel	56	Buck Run	1820	1	230
Dotson, John	100	Dotson's Run	1837	2	90
Dotson, John	289	Sugar Camp Run	1837	2	93
Dotson, John	100	Bunnell's Run	1838	2	145
Dotson, John et al	200	Straight Run	1837	2	92
Dotson, Richard	100	Long Run	1821	1	250
Dotson, Richard	300	Wts. of Hughes	1804	1	45
Dotson, Richard et al	200	Adj. Edmund Dotson	1817	1	201
Dotson, Solomon	100	Wts. Hughes River	1843	2	276
Dotson, Thomas	25	Wts. Hughes River	1837	2	91
Dotson, William	50	Cabin Run	1822	1	263
Dotson, William	100	Cabin Run	1818	1	216
Dotson, William	100	Dotson Run	1815	1	170
Dotson, William B	100	Gum Run	1843	2	277
Dotson, Zachariah	130	Sugar Camp Run	1842	2	223
Douglas, John	180	Goose Creek	1840	2	174
Douglas, John et al	1,000	Briscoe's Run	1802	1	6
Douglass, Ann	40	Millar's Run	1804	1	43
Drake, James	300	Indian Creek	1842	2	253
Drake, James	350	Dog Run	1842	2	252
Drake, James	100	Indian Creek	1837	2	99
Drake, James	100	Indian Creek	1837	2	98
Drake, James	50	Indian Creek	1834	2	58
Drake, James	100	Adj. his own	1834	2	56
Drake, James	100	Indian Creek	1818	1	215
Duffy, Francis	50	Lynn Camp	1809	1	88
Dye—or Die					
Dye, Elijah P.	100	Mud Lick Run	1847	2	354
Dye, Elijah P.	60	Tygert's Creek	1857	3	462
Dye, Henry	100	Lynn Camp Run	1821	1	258
Earl, James	35	Adj. E. Moss	1818	1	210
Emerick, Samuel	117	Wts. Stillwell	1844	2	285
Enoch, Abraham	100	Wts. Hughes River	1838	2	165
Enoch, Abraham	39	Silver Run	1844	2	296
Enoch, Abraham	100	Spring Creek	1845	2	335
Enoch, Abraham	98	Turtle Run	1853	3	25
Enoch, Abraham et al	230	Silver Run	1848	2	382
Enoch, Abraham et al	480	Lick Run	1850	2	394
Enoch, Abraham et al	58	Lick Run	1855	3	451
Enoch, Abraham et al	106	Walker's Creek	1855	3	450
Enoch, Abraham et al	242	Big Run	1855	3	41
Enoch, Abraham (2nd), et al	100	Goose Creek	1837	2	103
Enoch, Isaac	1,800	Reedy Creek	1820	1	251
Enoch, Isaac	40	Cor. to Thomas Pribble	1802	1	24
Enoch, Isaac	600	Reedy Creek	1809	1	68
Enoch, Isaac	200	2nd Left Hand Fork	1810	1	105
Enoch, Isaac	150	Reedy Creek	1812	1	147
Enoch, Isaac	180 (185)	Reedy Creek	1815	1	162
Enoch, Isaac	150	Reedy Creek	1815	1	163
Enoch, Isaac	450	Slate Creek	1816	1	181
Enoch, Isaac	50	Reedy Creek	1825	2	10
Enoch, Isaac	150	Worthington's Creek	1828	2	31
Enoch, Isaac	100	Worthington's Creek	1828	2	32
Enoch, Isaac	488	Wts. Hughes River	1830	2	43

Name of Grantee	Acres	Local Description	Year	Book	Page
Grffiith, David et al Heirs	2,000	Worthington's Creek	1801	1	12
Grffiith, David et al Heirs	2,000	Adj. T. Rutherford	1801	1	11
Grogan, Drury	17	Lee Creek	1848	2	385
Grogan, Thomas G.	73	Lee Creek	1846	2	338
Grogan, Thomas G.	46	Newberry Island	1850	2	391
Haddox, George (Hadden)	100	Wts. Hughes	1838	2	148
Haddox, Rowland	100	Wts. Hughes	1838	2	143
Harness, Solomon et al	300	Bull Creek	1816	1	189
Harper, Henry	142	Worthington Creek	1842	2	237
Harris, Daniel	100	Reedy Creek	1810	1	113
Harris, John	121	Adj. J. Parish	1817	1	200
Harris, John	114	Wts. Hughes	1841	2	207
Harris, John	60	Rock Camp Run	1842	2	228
Harris, John et al	272	Wts. Hughes	1842	2	229
Harris, John & T M.	100	Husher's Run	1842	2	259
Harris, Thomas M. et al	396	Wts. Hughes River	1842	2	255
Hartshorne, William	129	Hughes River	1801	1	9
Hartshorne, William	40	So. Fk. Hughes	1801	1	3
Harwood, John H.	100	Adj. James Lewis	1810	1	102
Harwood, John H.	42	Island Ohio River	1833	2	50
Harwood, John H.	141	Vought's Run	1834	2	59
Haymond, Cyrus	200	Straight Run	1820	1	244
Haymond, Daniel	200	Wts. Hughes	1841	2	199
Haymond, Daniel	300	Brush Run	1841	2	197
Haymond, Mansfield B.	100	Bond's Creek	1836	2	86
Haymond, Thomas et al	350	Cor. to Wm. McCleery	1802	1	20
Haymond, Thomas et al	75	Cor. to C. Carpenter	1802	1	19
Helmick, Jacob	50	Wts. Hughes	1822	1	264
Helmick, Jacob	50	Wts. Hughes	1828	2	35
Henderson, Alex. (of Dumfries)	98	Cow Creek	1811	1	141
Henderson, Alexander	4	Adj. Henderson's 4th	1809	1	71
Henderson, Alexander	102	Lit. Kanawha River	1809	1	74
Henderson, Alexander	50	Lit. Kanawha	1809	1	79
Henderson, Alexander	200	Cow Creek	1809	1	90
Henderson, Alexander	200	Adj. Hitchcock	1811	1	115
Henderson, Alexander	105	Reedy Creek	1812	1	150
Henderson, Alexander	50	Wts. Lit. Kanwaha	1812	1	151
Henderson, George W.	50	Adj. A. Henderson	1845	2	316
Henderson, John G.	162	Adj. Henderson's 5th	1804	1	37
Henderson, John G.	125	Burning Spring Run	1804	1	39
Henderson, John G.	31	Adj. Alex. Henderson	1809	1	72
Henderson, John G.	240	Adj. Henderson's 7th	1809	1	73
Henderson, John G.	100	Spring Creek	1809	1	75
Henderson, John G.	100	Lit. Kanawha River	1809	1	97
Henrie—or Henry					
Henrie, Benjamin	112	Big Run	1808	1	58
Henrie, Daniel et al	600	Cow Creek	1802	1	16
Henrie, Daniel et al	300	Pond Run	1803	1	31
Henrie, Daniel et al Hrs.	83	Big Run	1830	2	37
Henrie, Margaret et al	117	Big Run	1821	1	256
Henry—or Henrie					
Henry, Wm. & Rachael et al Hrs.	340	Big Run	1827	2	20
Henry, Wm. & Rachael et al Hrs.	125	Big Run	1827	2	19
Hickman, Elias (Hickmond)	100	Walker's Creek	1816	1	192
Hickman, Zachariah	72	Walker Creek	1858	3	473
Hindman, John	100	Standing Stone	1823	2	5
Hitchcock—or Hitchcox					
Hitchcock, Caleb	600	Cow Creek	1802	1	16
Hitchcock, Caleb	1a89p.	Ohio River	1801	1	4
Hitchcox, William & M.	100	Adj. J. M. Stephenson	1842	2	258
Hollarn, John	94	Tucker's Creek	1850	2	431
Holloran, John	94	Tucker's Creek	1850	2	431
Hoover, Thomas	126	Dog Run	1844	2	318

Name of Grantee	Acres	Local Description	Year	Book	Page
Hopkins, Thomas B.	450	Adj. John Stokeley	1812	1	149
Howard, Richard	100	Goose Creek	1854	3	37
Howell, Elias	100	Reedy Creek	1846	2	340
Howell, Elias	100	Reedy Creek	1845	2	327
Husher, George	100	State Road Creek	1811	1	120
Husher, George	100	Terrell's Run	1811	1	121
Husher, George	175	Husher's Run	1811	1	122
Husher, George	160	Bond's Creek	1811	1	123
Husher, George	200	Hughes River	1805	1	50
Ingles, William	600	Lee Creek	1804	1	47
Jackson, Jesse	100	Big Run	1803	1	32
Jackson, John J.	53	Wts. of Ohio	1828	2	30
Jackson, John J.	10	Adj. E. Gates	1828	2	33
Jackson, John J. et al	676	Pond Run	1840	2	175
Jackson, William L.	6	Goose Creek	1861	3	503
James George C.	161	Slate Creek	1848	2	386
James, James	110	Ohio River	1819	1	226
Jenne, Lemuel E.	1,000	Pond Creek	1847	2	352
Jett, Peter	50	Tucker's Creek	1842	2	238
Jett, Thomas	690	Adj. J. Stokely	1811	1	130
Jett, Thomas	300	Blaze Run	1811	1	133
Jett, Thomas	300	Tigert's Creek	1811	1	132
Jett, Thomas	1,000	Tigert's Creek	1811	1	131
Jett, Thomas Dr.	100	Adj. his own	1817	1	203
Jett, Thomas Dr.	100	Nr. Mth. Lit. Kanawha	1809	1	96
Jett, Thomas Dr.	310	Adj. James Wilson	1817	1	204
Johnson, Henry	400	Big Run	1803	1	33
Johnson, Henry	300	Bull Creek	1809	1	89
Johnson, Thomas	47	Slate Creek	1858	3	476
Johnson, William	18	Keller's Island	1859	3	489
Johnson, William Jr.	85	Island in Ohio	1856	3	457
Jones, David	265	Stillwell Cr.	1855	3	449
Jones, David	51	Stoneking's Fork	1858	3	467
Jones, David et al Heirs	190	Adj. H. Farson	1854	3	29
Jones, Jacob	884	Walker's Creek	1843	2	280
Jones, Jacob	200	Adj. Henry Farson	1844	2	288
Jones, Jacob	580	Walker's Creek	1844	2	289
Jones, Jacob	500	Goose Creek	1844	2	287
Jones, Jacob	284	Straight Creek	1844	2	307
Jones, Jacob	286	Walnut Fork	1848	2	383
Jones, Jacob et al	782	Walker's Creek	1843	2	281
Jones, Jacob et al	1,210	Stillwell Creek	1844	2	291
Jones, Jacob et al	550	Stillwell Creek	1844	2	295
Jones, Jacob et al	250	Stillwell Creek	1844	2	310
Jones, Jacob et al	80	Stillwell Creek	1844	2	309
Jones, Jacob et al	750	Walker's Creek	1844	2	308
Jones, Jacob et al	400	Worthington Creek	1844	2	311
Jones, Jacob et al	575	Goose Creek	1845	2	333
Jones, James	150	Wts. Hughes	1838	2	149
Jones, James R.	150	Indian Creek	1842	2	243
Jones, James R.	74	Adj. his own	1844	2	306
Jones, Morgan	200	Walker's Creek	1844	2	290
Jones, Morgan	200	Goose Creek	1843	2	279
Keller, Francis	100	Adj. his own	1822	1	270
Keller, Francis	150	Big Run	1820	1	239
Kincheloe, Robert	190	Worthington	1810	1	92
Kincheloe, Robert	200	Stillwell Creek	1810	1	91
King, Stephen	150	Walnut Fork	1837	2	114
Kite, John	50	Tygert Creek	1809	1	85
Laidley, James G.	100	Lit. Kanawha River	1809	1	76
Laidley, James G.	450	Worthington's Cr.	1806	1	52
Laidley, James G. et al	200	Tygert's Creek	1809	1	77
Laird, Adam	100	Laurel Run	1847	2	363
Laisure, Benoni	50	Walker's Creek	1852	3	14

Laisure, John C.	50	Goose Creek	1836	2	85
Laisure, John C.	221	Goose Creek	1846	2	341
Leach, Thomas	300	Wts. Lit. Kanawha	1819	1	225
Leach, Willis	110	Adj. Thomas Creel	1854	3	34
Ledsome, Daniel	50	Wts. Lit. Kanawha	1837	2	118
Lewis, George V. et al	95	Lee Creek	1851	2	435
Lewis, Jonas	500	Little Sandy	1810	1	101
Lewis, Wiatt et al	359	Slate Creek	1852	3	15
Lindsley, Noah et al	500	Pond Run	1804	1	44
Linnett—See Sennett, Sinnett					
Linnett, Patrick	88	Adj. his own	1819	1	222
Lochse, Charles A.	50	Sander's Run	1844	2	282
Lockard, Lockhart, Lockheart					
Lockard, John M.	50	Reedy Creek	1841	2	206
Lockard, John M.	50	Reedy Creek	1841	2	208
Lockhart, Enoch S.	205	Reedy Creek	1850	2	409
Lockhart, Isaac	200	Slab Camp Fork	1832	2	44
Lockhart, John M.	93	Lynn Camp Run	1850	3	410
Lockhart, John O.	120	Elk Run	1851	3	10
Lockhart, John O. et al	95	Lee Creek	1851	2	435
Lockhart, William	87	Gum Run	1850	2	411
Lockheart, John M.	50	Reedy Creek	1834	2	61
Loomis, George et al	495	Brushy Fork	1859	3	490
Lough, Robert	100	Straight Creek	1845	2	326
Lough, Robert	100	Dutchman's Run	1845	2	325
Lowe—See Lough					
Lowman, John	100	Big Run	1822	1	262
Lowther, Elias Jr.	100	Wts. Hughes	1840	2	169
Lowther, Jesse	100	Jug Handle Run	1815	1	158
Maddore, Jesse H. et al	275	Tiger's Cr.	1834	2	62
Maddox, Jesse H. et al	275	Tyger's Creek	1834	2	62
Maley—See Mealie, Mealy					
Maley, James et al	61	Indian Creek	1827	2	28
Maley, John et al	78	Dog Run	1827	2	25
Maley, Lawrence	200	Hughes River	1808	1	57
Maley, William	62	Wts. Hughes	1811	1	128
Mann, William et al	800	Mth. Hughes	1812	1	142
Marsh, Elias	20	Adj. his own	1838	2	154
Marsh, Elias	100	Wolf Pen Run	1838	2	155
Marsh, Elias	130	Wts. Hughes	1838	2	156
Marsh, Elias	250	Adj. his own	1841	2	193
Marsh, Elias	100	Adj. H. B. Collins	1842	2	217
Marsh, Elias et al	200	Wts. Hughes	1841	2	196
Marsh, Enoch	40	Wts. Hughes	1842	2	272
Marsh, Enoch	100	Wts. Hughes	1838	2	150
Marsh, Enoch	50	Wts. Hughes	1838	2	138
Marshall, William	37	Stilwell Creek	1860	3	511
Martin, James	200	Wts. Hughes	1817	1	202
Martin, James	100	Bunnell's Run	1828	2	36
Masters, Jarrett	50	Slate Creek	1847	2	371
McCall, George C.	143	Walker's Creek	1854	3	32
McCleery, William	330	Reedy Creek	1809	1	82
McCleery, William	1,700	Tucker's Creek	1802	1	21
McClintick, William T.	93	Neal's Run	1834	2	78
McClure, James	152	Wts. of Kanawha	1838	2	158
McClure, James	227	Wts. Lit. Kanawha	1838	2	159
McClure, James	287	Williams' Run	1838	2	160
McFarland, Ezekiel	150	Turkey Fork	1819	1	227
McFarland, Ezekiel	130	Lit. Kanawha River	1809	1	81
McFarland, Ezekiel	16	Reedy Creek	1809	1	83
McFarland, Ezekiel	50	Lit. Kanawha	1810	1	95
McFarland, Ezekiel	100	Lynn Camp Run	1816	1	182
McFarland, Ezekiel	600	Wts. Sandy	1816	1	184
McFarland, Ezekiel	50	Wts. Lit. Kanawha	1816	1	183
McFarland, Ezekiel	150	Reedy Creek	1816	1	187

Name of Grantee	Acres	Local Description	Year	Book	Page
Neal, Daniel R. et al	200	Indian Creek	1841	2	198
Neal, Daniel R. et al	230	Silver Run	1848	2	382
Neal, James H.	12	Wts. of Lit. Kan.	1811	1	125
Neal, John et al	170	Adj. Thomas Tavener	1810	1	94
Neale, Alfred	150	Island Ohio River	1850	2	392
Neale, Lewis	50	Bellville Tract	1830	2	38
Newbanks, Levi et al	100	Tucker Creek	1845	2	332
Nicklin, Israel T. et al	580	Long Run	1842	2	234
Nixon, Joshua	205	Bill Bond's Run	1820	1	245
Ott, Fidellis	50	Reedy Creek	1838	2	135
Ott, Lewis	68	Adj. F. Duffy	1826	2	12
Ott, Lewis	30	Lynn Camp Run	1826	2	13
Page, Henry	103	Tygert's Creek	1847	2	365
Parker, Richard	125	Goose Creek	1838	2	127
Parker, Richard	42	Goose Creek	1838	2	132
Parker, Stafford H. et al	200	Williams Fork	1844	2	302
Parker, Stafford H. et al	125	Stoneking Fork	1844	2	284
Parker, Stafford H. et al	375	Wts. Stillwell	1844	2	283
Parkhurst, Aaron	1,500	Slate Creek	1840	2	176
Parkhurst, Aaron	250	Lee Creek	1845	2	321
Parkhurst, Amos F.	500	Pond Creek	1845	2	322
Parkhurst, Amos F. et al	1,000	Bellville Road	1845	2	317
Parkhurst, Freeman	500	Pond Creek	1845	2	319
Paugh, Henry	89	Neal's Run	1860	3	505
Paugh, Henry	103	Slate Creek	1853	3	27
Payne, William G. et al	800	Mth. Hughes	1812	1	142
Perine—See Pryon					
Perine, Isaac	100	Slab Camp Run	1808	1	61
Petty, John	74	Wts. Lit. Kanawha	1834	2	74
Petty, John F.	200	Wts. Lit. Kanawha	1838	2	128
Petty, John F.	100	2-Run	1850	2	427
Petty, John F.	200	2-Run	1850	2	428
Petty, William	100	Wts. Lit. Kanawha	1810	1	106
Phelps, Hugh	200	Lit. Kanawha River	1801	1	5
Phelps, Hugh et al	200	Tygert's Creek	1809	1	77
Phelps, Hugh et al	620	Ohio River	1809	1	80
Phelps, John	200	Neal's Run	1815	1	176
Phelps, John J.	50	Neal's Run	1833	2	51
Phelps, John J.	170	Neal's Run	1846	2	346
Phelps, John J.	50	Neal's Run	1834	2	63
Phelps, Laura & Malissa	100	Neal's Run	1833	2	48
Philip, Benjamin	150	Wts. Hughes River	1838	2	139
Pickering, Daniel	660	Little Creek	1851	3	12
Pickering, Daniel	170	Standing Stone	1838	2	136
Pickering, Lafayette & N. B.	150	Standing Stone	1850	2	422
Pickering, Mary et al	64	Spring Creek	1834	2	450
Pickering, Thomas	20	Cave Run	1850	2	419
Pierpoint, J. W.	150	Adj. S. Blue	1842	2	245
Pierpoint, Joseph W.	300	Indian Creek	1842	2	246
Pierpoint, Joseph W.	400	Indian Creek	1842	2	247
Pierpoint, Joseph W.	900	Wts. Hughes River	1842	2	244
Pool, Henry	80	Slate Creek	1848	2	387
Pool, Thomas	100	Slate Creek	1846	2	343
Pool, Thomas	200	Tucker's Creek	1846	2	342
Prebble—See Pribble					
Prebble, Abraham	100	Walker's Creek	1823	2	7
Pribble, Hedgman	60	Silver Run	1841	2	205
Pribble, Henry	100	Hughes River	1835	2	80
Pribble, Hiram	94	Wts. Hughes River	1848	2	380
Pribble, Thomas	67	Cr. George Foutley	1802	1	23
Price, Charles	95	Wts. L. Kanawha	1847	2	361
Price, Charles	145	Wts. L. Kanawha	1827	2	448
Price, Charles	28a.80p.	Wts. L. Kanawha	1834	2	64
Price, Charles	98	Tygert's Creek	1834	2	77

Name of Grantee	Acres	Local Description	Year	Book	Page
Wells, Isaiah	42	Goose Run	1847	2	364
Wells, Isaiah	59	Hughes Run	1844	2	305
Wells, Levi (Wills)	245	Wts. Lit. Kanawha	1838	2	140
Wells, Levi	50	Bunnell's Run	1817	1	206
Wells, Levi	50	Bunnell's Run	1817	1	205
Wells, Levi	30	Wts. Hughes	1818	1	217
Wells, William	76	Wts. Hughes	1816	1	188
West, James J.	400	Adj. James Nailor	1850	2	424
West, Z. M.	100	Adj. James Nailor	1846	2	351
White, George	200	Pond Creek	1844	2	304
White, George	108	Pond Creek	1852	3	16
Williams, Otho L.	113	Rock Run	1850	2	414
Williams, Samuel L.	60	Pond Run	1811	1	136
Willis, Blackburn	98	Walker's Creek	1856	3	458
Willis, Notley	56	Wts. Hughes	1842	2	232
Willis, Notley	70	Wts. Hughes	1842	2	233
Willis, Notley	130	N. Fk. of Hughes	1842	2	231
Willis, Notley et al	580	Long Run	1842	2	234
Wills, or Wells					
Wills, Isaiah (Wells)	59	Wts. Hughes	1844	2	305
Wilson, Blackburn	98	Walker's Creek	1856	3	458
Wilson, James	435	Neal's Run	1809	1	78
Wilson, Josiah D. et al	335	Stillwell Creek	1844	2	293
Wilson, Josiah D. et al	65	Stillwell Creek	1844	2	294
Wilson, Stephen R.	1,930	Cor. Israel Lacy	1802	1	22
Wilson, Traverse	50	Slate Creek	1830	2	41
Wilson, Travis	50	Shelving Rock Fork	1820	1	235
Wilson, William	190	Mth. Tigert Creek	1802	1	25
Wigner, John & John G	170	Bond's Creek	1842	2	236
Wilfong, George	140	Big Sandy	1826	2	15
Wilfong, Henry	100	Tucker's Creek	1826	2	14
Wilkinson, Joseph	100	Wts. Hughes	1818	1	214
Winding, Benjamin	114	Galispie's Fork	1859	3	493
Wiseman, Caleb	50	Searjeant's Run	1820	1	236
Wiseman, Caleb	100	Buffalo Bottom	1820	1	237
Wiseman, Caleb	50	Lynn Camp Run	1841	2	189
Wiseman, Caleb	50	Camp Run	1838	2	124
Wiseman, Caleb	70	Lynn Camp Run	1850	2	401
Wood, Francis	50	Pond Run	1842	2	262
Wood, James	89	Adj. A. Henderson	1813	1	152
Wood, James	141	Adj. A. Henderson	1834	2	68
Wood, James	276	Adj. G. W. Henderson	1834	2	69
Wood, James	173	Adj. M. Cressap	1834	2	71
Wood, Slias et al	625	Slate Creek	1845	2	334
Woodyard, Alfred et al Hrs.	410	Lynn Camp Run	1850	2	400
Woodyard, Alfred et al Hrs.	290	Tucker's Creek	1850	2	399
Woodyard, George	50	Lynn Camp Run	1841	2	203
Woodyard, James	165	L. C. Run	1850	2	397
Woodyard, James	35	Sugar Camp Run	1850	2	398
Woodyard, James	150	Lynn Camp Run	1838	2	151
Woodyard, James	200	Daily's Run	1812	1	146
Woodyard, James	50	Lynn Camp Run	1842	2	235
Woodyard, Lewis	375	Lynn Camp Run	1850	2	396
Woodyard, Lewis	55	Mud Lick Run	1850	2	395
Woodyard, Lewis	488	Tucker's Creek	1850	2	393

WYOMING COUNTY

Adams, James	105	Big Branch	1860	1	412
Adams, James	25	Salt River	1855	1	273
Allen, John, Jr.	125	Laurel Fork	1858	1	384
Allen, John, Sr.	72	Laurel Fork	1857	1	376
Anderson, John H.	(27) 77	Dry Branch	1853	1	147
Bailey, Eli	244	Tug Fork	1856	1	307
Bailey, Henderson	115	Big Fork	1852	1	64
Bailey, Henderson	82	Rock House Fork	1859	1	390
Bailey, Henderson	75	Rock House Br.	1859	1	391
Bailey, Henderson	119	Big Fork	1860	1	419
Bailey, James	30	Big Fork	1853	1	78
Bailey, James	30	Pigeon Creek	1853	1	79
Bailey, James	135	Big Fork	1860	1	408
Bailey, James O.	50	Milam's Ridge	1855	1	274
Bailey, Joseph P.	100	Big Fork	1854	1	152
Bailey, Joseph P.	40	Old Trace Ridge	1854	1	153
Bailey, Joseph P.	90	Indian Creek	1855	1	297
Bailey, Joseph P.	44	Spider Ridge	1855	1	298
Bailey, Joseph P.	159	Big Fork	1858	1	357
Bailey, Lowdan	142	Strate's Fork of Huff	1853	1	117
Bailey, Lowdan	2½	Big Huff Creek	1854	1	170
Bailey, Reuben B.	66	Big Fork	1854	1	208
Bailey, Rufus	29	Bear Town Fork	1855	1	272
Bailey, Thomas	84	Beasley Fork	1853	1	115
Bailey, Thomas	25	Castle Branch	1853	1	116
Bailey, Thomas	50	Big Huff Creek	1853	1	138
Bailey, Thomas	37	Castle Branch	1854	1	171
Bailey, Thomas	67	Trace Fork	1854	1	172
Bailey, Thomas	85	Big Huff Creek	1854	1	173
Bailey, Thomas	19	Big Huff Creek	1856	1	301
Bailey, Thomas	37	Brushy Fork	1856	1	302
Bailey, Thomas	23	Long Lick Fork	1856	1	303
Belcher, Richard	172	Mill Branch	1861	1	424
Belcher, William A.	38	Rock Castle Fork	1853	1	80
Bishop, Henry	181	Indian Creek	1860	1	423
Bishop, Larkin	40	Indian Creek	1853	1	97
Blankenship, Henry	9	Cub Creek	1852	1	65
Blankenship, Henry	36	Big Fork	1854	1	217
Blankenship, Henry, Jr.	23	Cub Creek	1853	1	77
Blankenship, Wm. H.	122	Spider Ridge	1855	1	254
Blankenship, Claborn	8½	Clear Fork	1853	1	134
Blankenship, Eli	69	Garden Gap Branch	1854	1	176
Blankenship, Eli	20	Swamp Fork	1860	1	420
Brinegar, David, et al	189	Rock Castle Cr.	1861	1	431
Brinegar, Jacob	614	Fork Ridge	1853	1	81
Brinegar, Jacob	110	Rock Castle Fork	1854	1	163
Buchanan, Arthur	117	Pinnacle Fork	1854	1	207
Buchanan, Arthur	128	Pinnacle Fork	1857	1	333
Canterbury, John	105	Clear Fork	1854	1	156
Canterbury, John	130	Clear Fork	1854	1	237
Chambers, James	75	Laurel Fork	1854	1	219
Chambers, Leroy B.	187	Laurel Fork	1854	1	218
Cline, Humphrey	46	Wts. Guyandotte	1856	1	328
Cline, Michael	85	Hardway Branch	1854	1	174
Cline, Michael	120	Johnycake	1854	1	175
Cline, Michael	14	Tug Fork	1857	1	337
Cline, Michael	19	Negro Branch	1857	1	338
Cline, Peter	30	Big Fork	1853	1	106
Cline, Umphrey	17	Wts. Guyandotte	1853	1	105
Cook—or Cooke					
Cook, Elliott	63	Cow Creek	1853	1	107
Cook, Green M.	64	Turkey Fork of Big Fk.	1854	1	194
Cook, Green M.	14	Elkins Branch	1854	1	195

Name of Grantee	Acres	Local Description	Year	Book	Page
Gadd, Wilson T.	230	Black Fork	1855	1	244
Gadd, Wilson T.	64	Pinnacle Fork	1859	1	388
Garretson, Abraham	100	Tommy's Ridge	1860	1	413
Garretson, Hiram J. et al	300	Big Fork	1860	1	414
Gillenwaters, Joseph	100	Reedy Branch	1855	1	271
Gillinwaters, Mary	30	Lester Fork	1860	1	407
Glandon, Jacob	160	Big Fork	1858	1	365
Glandon, Stephen	100	Pigeon Creek	1858	1	364
Graham, Luke	175	Bee Tree Ridge	1855	1	246
Graham, Luke	96	Barker's Ridge	1855	1	249
Graham, Luke	300	Barker's Ridge	1855	1	250
Graham, Luke	93	Milam's Ridge	1855	1	251
Green, Joshua et al	285	Workman's Bear Pen	1854	1	228
Goare, Levi	56	Big Fork of G'dotte	1852	1	49
Goare, Levi	20	Wolfe Pen	1853	1	98
Goare, Levi	76	Dry Branch	1853	1	145
Goare, Levi	42	Wts. of Guyandotte R.	1860	1	399
Goare, Levi	84	Spring Branch	1860	1	400
Goare, Levi	28	Dry Branch	1860	1	406
Goare, Levi	80	Gadd's Fork	1860	1	416
Goare, Levi et al	42	Little Huff Cr.	1860	1	404
Godfrey, Armour L. et al	42	Little Huff Cr.	1860	1	404
Godfrey, Ausker P. (Oscar)	26	Padd's Fork	1860	1	397
Godfrey, Lewis G.	31	Muddy Branch	1860	1	396
Godfrey, Thomas	415	Pinnacle Fork	1854	1	192
Goode, David	46	Rock Castle Creek	1860	1	417
Gunnoe, Andrew	17	Knob Fork	1854	1	236
Gunnoe, Andrew	32	Knob Fork	1854	1	239
Gunnoe, Andrew	35	Clear Fork	1860	1	422
Gore—See Goare					
Hamons, Jesse & Daniel	47	Wild Cat Branch	1858	1	371
Haney, James	45	Meetinghouse Br.	1853	1	148
Harvey, James	6	Clear Fork	1853	1	142
Harvey, James	45	Meetinghouse Br.	1853	1	148
Harvey, Henry	80	Clear Fork	1855	1	275
Harvey, John et al	164	Cedar Creek	1855	1	273
Harvey, Pateson	115	Wall's Branch	1858	1	358
Harvey, William	3	Clear Fork	1858	1	359
Hatfield, John	19	Long Branch	1855	1	245
Hatfield, Phebe et al	208	Wts. of Guyandotte	1855	1	261
Hatfield, Valentine	75	Long Branch	1855	1	284
Hinchman, Ulysses	95	Cabin Creek	1858	1	366
Hinchman, Ulysses	72	Cabin Creek	1856	1	324
Howerton, John	25	Barker's Fork	1855	1	266
Howerton, John	87	Barker's Fork	1855	1	265
Howerton, John	78	Peaks Ridge	1855	1	253
Howerton, John	40	Barker's Fork	1855	1	252
Howerton, John	35	Barker's Fork	1857	1	355
Howerton, John	66	Milam's Ridge	1857	1	356
Hunt, Henry	114	Little White Oak Fk	1854	1	154
Hunt, Henry	76	Big Fork	1855	1	247
Jackson, Henry F.	152	Mill Branch	1857	1	349
James, Valentine et al	208	Wts. Guyandotte R.	1855	1	261
Jestice—or Justice					
Jestice, James	91	Salt River	1856	1	314
Johnston, George	38	Cub Creek	1852	1	54
Johnston, George	66	Cub Creek	1855	1	248
Johnston, George	93	Cub Creek	1855	1	281
Johnston, George	21½	Cub Creek	1855	1	282
Johnston, George	28	Cub Creek	1855	1	290
Johnston, George	22	McDonald's Fork	1858	1	379
Johnston, George	65	Cub Creek	1858	1	380
Johnston, George	68	Mossy Branch	1860	1	409

Name of Grantee	Acres	Local Description	Year	Book	Page
Johnston, George	90	McDonald Fork	1860	1	410
Johnston, George	58	Clay Branch	1860	1	411
Jones, John	194	Slab Fork	1854	1	225
Jones, John et al	80	Slab Fork	1854	1	188
Justice—See Jestice, Jistice					
Justice, James	53	Wts. Guyandotte	1860	1	403
Justice, James	17¼	Wts. Guyandotte	1852	1	59
Justice, James (Jestice)	80	Long Pole Creek	1854	1	178
Justice, James (Jistice)	132	Panther Fork	1860	1	401
Justice, James (Jistice)	86	Long Pole Cr.	1860	1	402
Lain, Alexander (Lane)	52	Big Fork	1857	1	339
Lain, Alfred W. et al (Lane)	285	Workman's Bear Pen Ridge	1854	1	228
Laxton, Thomas	1,071	Rock Castle Creek	1854	1	183
Lester—or Luster					
Lester, Archibald B.	25	Cane Break Br.	1860	1	393
Lester, Archibald B.	35	Lizzard Branch	1860	1	394
Lester, Joseph	55	Huff's Creek	1852	1	55
Lester, Joseph	30	Trace Fork	1853	1	108
Lester, Joseph	212	Milam's Ridge	1854	1	189
Lester, Joseph	36	Little Huff Creek	1854	1	191
Lester, Joseph	145	Brooks Branch	1854	1	238
Lester, Joseph	14	Barker's Fork	1855	1	285
Lester, Joseph	41	Little Huff Cr.	1857	1	351
Lester, Joseph	38	Cub Creek	1860	1	421
Lester, Joseph	180	Cub Creek	1857	1	534
Lester, Maston	38	Musle Creek (Muscle)	1852	1	50
Lester, Maston	119	Muscle Fork	1858	1	383
Lester, Maston	42	Negro Branch	1853	1	110
Lester, Maston	45	Ike Fork	1854	1	166
Lester, Maston	70	Tug Fork	1856	1	327
Lester, Pleasant	80	Big Branch	1854	1	177
Lester, Pleasant	198	Big Branch	1859	1	538
Lester, Thomas	17	Tug Fork	1857	1	350
Lockhart, John	92	Nigger Branch	1860	1	405
Lusk, Eli	57	Barker's Fork	1856	1	315
Lusk, Gordon C.	85	Micajah Ridge	1852	1	62
Lusk, Henry F.	36	Micajah's Ridge	1854	1	193
Lusk, Henry F.	75	Spider Ridge	1854	1	190
Lusk, Reece T.	50	Indian Creek	1853	1	122
Lusk, Reece T.	46	Indian Creek	1855	1	292
Lusk, Reece T.	65	Briar Creek	1855	1	291
Lusk, Reece T.	51	Pinnacle Fork	1855	1	293
Lusk, Reece T.	144	Spider Ridge	1861	1	428
Luster—or Lester					
Marshall, Allen	186	Peak's Ridge	1853	1	101
Marshall, James	284	Milam's Fork	1853	1	99
Marshall, James	58	Cage's Ridge	1853	1	100
McDonald, Andrew J.	285	Clear Fork	1854	1	168
McDonald, Andrew J.	540	Mill Creek	1854	1	169
McDonald, Andrew J.	32	Coon Fork	1854	1	179
McDonald, Isaac E.	220	Cabin Creek	1856	1	317
McDonald, Isaac E.	528	Meeting House Br.	1858	1	535
McDonald, Isaac E. et al	605	Cabin Creek	1856	1	308
McDonald, Joseph	195	Elk Lick	1854	1	180
McDonald, Joseph	344	Clear Fork	1854	1	182
McDonald, Joseph	130	Reedy Branch	1855	1	289
McDonald, Lewis	85	Cabin Creek	1853	1	75
McDonald, Lewis	195	Pinnacle Fork	1853	1	111
McDonald, Lewis	100	Joke's Branch	1853	1	112
McDonald, Lewis	17	Clear Fork	1853	1	113
McDonald, Lewis	110	Indian Creek	1853	1	114
McDonald, Lewis	262	Pinnacle Fork	1854	1	184
McDonald, Lewis	113	Big Fork	1854	1	185

Name of Grantee	Acres	Local Description	Year	Book	Page
McDonald, Lewis	343	Little White Oak	1854	1	186
McDonald, Lewis	40	Big Fork	1854	1	215
McDonald, Lewis	464	Black Fork	1854	1	216
McDonald, William	1,100	Clear Fork	1855	1	524
McDonald, William	860	Double Camp Br.	1856	1	527
McKinney, Powhatan B.	31	Mossman Ridge	1855	1	278
McKinney, Samuel P.	35	Barker's Ridge	1855	1	255
Meadows, Ephraim	53	Big Fork	1856	1	304
Milam—or Milem					
Milam, James A.	21	Wolf Pen	1854	1	232
Milem, George	258	Cabin Creek	1854	1	198
Milem, Russell	162	Barker's Fork	1854	1	167
Mills, Robert	29	Devil's Fork	1855	1	286
Mills, Robert	181	Devil's Fork	1855	1	287
Mitchel—or Mitchell					
Mitchel, Joseph	19	Coe's Creek	1854	1	199
Mitchell, Charter et al	126	Big Fork	1854	1	227
Mitchell, Joseph	67	Big Fork	1854	1	197
Mitchell, Rebecca	13	Big Fork	1855	1	264
Morgan, Anthony	29	Cub Creek	1855	1	277
Morgan, Anthony	36	Cub Creek	1855	1	283
Morgan, Anthony	32	Elk Trace Fork	1855	1	288
Morgan, Anthony	35	Indian Creek	1858	1	375
Morgan, David	24	Cub Creek	1853	1	123
Morgan, David	58	Cub Creek	1855	1	267
Morgan, David	30	Cub Creek	1858	1	373
Morgan, David	82	Cub Creek	1858	1	374
Morgan, George	30	Indian Creek	1853	1	118
Morgan, George	30	Indian Creek	1853	1	136
Morgan, Harvey	35	Indian Creek	1857	1	343
Morgan, Jonathan	35	Indian Creek	1855	1	256
Morgan, Jonathan	98	Wolf Pen	1855	1	257
Morgan, Jonathan	37	Indian Creek	1855	1	258
Morgan, Milton	109	Lick Fork	1856	1	329
Morgan, Milton	40	Indian Creek	1858	1	372
Morgan, Milton	25	Indian Creek	1853	1	88
Mullen—Mullens, Mullins					
Mullen, Sanders	100	Skin Fork	1854	1	234
Mullens, Sanders et al	605	Cabin Creek	1856	1	308
Mullins, John	56	Big Fork	1857	1	344
Mullins, John S.	101	Rock Castle Creek	1853	1	140
Mullins, John S.	60	Cabin Creek	1853	1	144
Mullins, John S. (Mullens)	106	Wts. Cabin Creek	1853	1	146
Mullins, John S.	65	Pretty Ridge	1855	1	300
Osborn—Orsborn, Osburn					
Osborn, Jefferson et al	4,337	Pinnacle Fork	1854	1	204
Osburn, Jefferson et al	255	Spider Ridge	1855	1	296
Pane, James	54	Pinnacle Fork	1854	1	212
Payne—See Pane					
Perdue, Daniel	74	Rock Castle Fork	1853	1	86
Perdue, Daniel	88	Rock Castle Fork	1853	1	87
Perdue, Nathan	65	Skin Fork	1855	1	279
Perdue, Nathan	50	Balden Branch	1857	1	352
Perry, James	52	Wts. Guyandotte	1853	1	141
Philips, Wiley (Willie)	135	Cabin Creek	1852	1	56
Philips, Wiley (Willie)	26	Big Fork	1854	1	240
Philips, Wiley	40	Big Fork	1854	1	241
Philips, William G.	37	Cabin Creek	1861	1	430
Philips, Willie (Wiley)	303	Barker's Fork	1861	1	426
Quicksel, James	102	Big Fork	1858	1	382
Raimey—or Ramey					
Raimey, Mathew	44	Big Fork	1854	1	201
Raimey, Mathew (Ramey)	42	Big Fork	1854	1	205

Portions of the following counties of the present State of Virginia were used in the formation of West Virginia counties.

AUGUSTA COUNTY, VIRGINIA

Name of Grantee	Acres	Local Description	Year	Book	Page
Abbott, Benjamin et al	1,000	Monon. River	1782	1	37
Aberman, or Eberman					
Aberman, Jacob	116	Seneca Creek	1767	1	507
Aberman, Jacob	137	Canoe Run	1771	1	528
Aberman, Jacob	71	South Branch	1772	1	538
Aberman, Jacob et al	54	Buffalo Run	1771	1	534
Aberman, Jacob et al	98	Buffalo Run	1771	1	534
Aberman, Michael	64	South Branch	1767	1	504
Aberman, Michael et al	148	Seneca Creek	1771	1	532
Aberman, William	26	South Branch	1771	1	529
Acerman—Aberman					
Alexander, John	210	Tygert's V. R.	1784	1	110
Anderson, Henry	270	Sidlington's Cr.	1787	1	209
Arbogast, Arbocast, Arbocust, Armagast, Armocast, Armocust, Armogast					
Armagast, Michael	193	Crab Apple Bottom	1790	1	254
Armocust, Michael	174	Crab Apple Bottom	1792	1	279
Badgley, Anthony	80	Mill Creek	1789	1	225
Baker, Humphrey	430	Stalnaker Cr.	1785	1	166
Baker, Samuel	396	Lost River	1756	1	599
Baker, William	386¼	Lost River	1752	1	593
Beard, John	70	Jenning's Branch	1771	1	537
Bell, David	113	Black Thorn	1780	1	5
Bell, James Sr.	80	North Mountain	1791	1	270
Bell, John & James (of David)	92	Black Thorn	1782	1	29
Bell, John & James (of David)	150	Black Thorn	1782	1	30
Beninger, See Paninger, Peninger					
Bennett, John (Bennet)	48	Mud Lick Run	1785	1	160
Bennett, John	87	South Branch	1789	1	240
Bennett, John	135	South Branch	1773	1	563
Bennett, John Sr.	94	South Branch	1791	1	263
Bennett, Joseph	40	South Branch	1791	1	272
Bennett, Joseph	46	Dry Run	1772	1	539
Bennett, Joseph	70	Clover Lick Run	1772	1	539
Bennett, William	55	North Fork	1789	1	241
Bingaman, John	40	Spring Branch	1787	1	190
Bingaman, John	107	Elk Spring	1787	1	191
Blackmore, Nathaniel	300	Shirtee Cr.	1780	1	12
Blake—See Bleak					
Bleak, Thomas	115	Wts. Greenbrier	1783	1	54
Blizzard, John	23	South Branch	1774	1	576
Bodkin, John	140	Black Thorn	1782	1	32
Bodkin, John	140	Black Thorn	1782	1	33
Boffingbarrier, Buffenberger, Buffenberry, Poffenberger, Poffenberry					
Boffingbarrier, George	35	South Branch	1789	1	238
Bogard, or Bogert					
Bogert, Cornelius	380	Tygert's V. River	1784	1	135
Bogert, Cornelius	55	South Branch	1773	1	562
Boughman, Henry	780	Wts. Greenbrier	1759	1	482
Bragg, Joseph	30	Black Thorn	1788	1	211
Breadon, George	200	Tygert's V. River	1785	1	159
Bright, Samuel	150	Black Thorn	1758	1	479
Bright, Samuel	150	Big Run	1770	1	521
Brisk, Robert	358	Brown's Cr.	1783	1	64
Brock, Thomas	290	Stony Creek	1795	1	313
Buckley, Joshua	73	Indian Draught	1796	1	328
Buffenberger, or Boffingbarrier, Buffenberry, Poffenberger, Poffenberry					
Buffington, Jonathan	390	Leading Cr.	1785	1	163
Bumgardner, Godfrey	126	Sugar Gap Run	1773	1	549

Name of Grantee	Acres	Local Description	Year	Book	Page
Holder, Thomas	494	Leading Cr.	1784	1	143
Hole—See Hoal, Hull					
Hole, Peter	97	Riffle's Old Road	1787	1	202
Hollingsworth, Levi	40,000	Wts. Shenandoah	1795	1	319
Hon, Joseph	386¼	Lost River	1750	1	592
Hoover—See Hover					
Hoover, Bastian	70	Black Thorn	1789	1	221
Hoover, Bastin	67	South Branch	1769	1	512
Hoover, Jacob	304	South Branch	1789	1	222
Hoover, Jacob	46	South Branch	1791	1	271
Hoover, Lawrence	128	Black Thorn	1787	1	201
Hoover, Michael	64	South Branch	1791	1	268
Hoover, Michael	50	South Branch	1791	1	278
Hoover, Postel	44	Wts. Potomac	1765	1	498
Hoover, Postel	65	Wts. Potomac	1765	1	498
Hornbarrier, Jacob	229	Richardson's Run	1767	1	502
Hornbeck, Benjamin	270	Leading Cr.	1784	1	116
Hornbeck, Benjamin	157	Leading Cr.	1784	1	118
Hornbeck, Benjamin	277	Leading Cr.	1785	1	156
Hover—or Hoover					
Hover, Bastian	44	South Branch	1773	1	555
Hover, Bastian	45	Black Thorn	1773	1	561
Hull—See Hoal, Hole					
Ingram, Abraham	50	Deer Creek	1794	1	297
Ingram, Abraham	138	Adj. his own	1795	1	317
Isener, Michael	400	Eberman's Run	1784	1	101
Jarvis, Thomas	400	Deer Creek	1783	1	46
Johnson, Andrew	62	Clover Lick	1768	1	509
Johnson, Andrew	30	South Branch	1785	1	162
Johnson, Andrew et al	148	Seneca Creek	1771	1	532
Johnson, Andrew et al	54	Buffalo Run	1771	1	534
Johnson, Andrew et al	98	Buffalo Run	1771	1	534
Johnson, Stephen	190	Wts. Greenbrier	1788	1	212
Johnston, Richard	69	Smith's Creek	1790	1	252
Jones, Benjamin	120	Tygert's V. River	1784	1	136
Jones, Isaac	195	Stony Creek	1794	1	300
Jordan, John	90	Bull Pasture	1773	1	560
Keester—See Keister, Kester, Kister, Knester, Knestrick					
Keister—See Keester, Kester, Kister, Knester, Knestrick					
Kelly, Owen	370	Knap's Creek	1795	1	315
Kelso, James	480	Clover Lick Cr.	1795	1	316
Kester—See Keester, Keister, Kister, Knester, Knestrick					
Kettle, Abraham	288	Tygert's V. River	1785	1	157
Kettle, Abraham	210	Tygert's V. River	1785	1	158
Kinging, John	162	South Branch	1784	1	138
Kirkpatrick, William	200	South Branch	1789	1	253
Kister—See Keester, Keister, Kester, Knester, Knestrick					
Kister, Frederick	35	Walnut Bottom	1757	1	477
Kister, Frederick	57	South Branch	1769	1	515
Knester—See Keester, Keister, Kester, Kister, Knestrick					
Knestrick—See Keester, Keister, Kester, Kister, Knester					
Lackey, James et al	1,000	Wts. Monon. River	1782	1	40
Lambert, John	90	Tygert's V. River	1789	1	235
Lambert, John Sr.	262	Dry Run	1789	1	245
Lambert, Mathias	50	Wts. Tygert's V.	1789	1	244
Lanciscus, Henry	45	South Branch	1773	1	558
Landsdall, William	300	Wts. Greenbrier	1788	1	342
Leith, George	250	Burk Springs	1752	1	594
Lesat, Joseph	96	Black Thorn	1793	1	288
Levit, William	158	Tygert's V. River	1784	1	109
Lewis, John	160	Black Thorn	1794	1	303
Lewis, John et al	1,000	Glady Cr.	1782	1	41
Lewis, Thomas et al	1,750	Horse Run	1766	1	501

Name of Grantee	Acres	Local Description	Year	Book	Page
Simmons, Leonard	27	Bake Oven Run	1783	1	89
Simmons, Leonard	50	South Branch	1789	1	231
Simmons, Leonard	54	South Fork	1793	1	284
Simmons, Leonard	150	Hammer's Run	1795	1	305
Simmons, Leonard	104	South Branch	1767	1	503
Simmons, Leonard (Seimons)	180	South Branch	1787	1	186
Simmons, Mark (Seimons)	91	South Branch	1787	1	188
Simmons, Nicholas	60	South Branch	1770	1	525
Skidmore, Andrew	336	Wts. Tygert's V.	1782	1	31
Skidmore, Edward et al	1,000	Wts. Monon. R.	1782	1	42
Skidmore, John	290	Crab Apple Bottom	1781	1	19
Skidmore, John	170	Mud Lick Branch	1773	1	542
Skidmore, John	237	Peter Reed's Creek	1773	1	547
Skidmore, John et al	400	Colt Springs	1780	1	6
Skidmore, John et al	390	South Branch	1780	1	8
Skidmore, Joseph	19	South Branch	1781	1	20
Skidmore, Joseph	54	Lick Run	1767	1	505
Skidmore, Joseph	97	Walnut Bottom	1767	1	505
Skidmore, Joseph Jr.	150	South Branch	1767	1	507
Skidmore, Thomas	288	Wts. Tygert's V.	1782	1	28
Skidmore, Thomas	102	Leading Cr.	1784	1	103
Slatery, Patrick	300	Indian Draft	1783	1	68
Slavin, John	50	Wts. Greenbrier R.	1795	1	302
Slavins, John	130	Back Creek	1787	1	195
Smith, Abraham	142	Licking Creek	1764	1	495
Smith, Abraham	115	Dry Run	1773	1	541
Smith, Abraham et al	390	South Branch	1780	1	8
Smith, Charles	162	South Fork	1780	1	2
Smith, Charles	76	South Branch	1769	1	512
Smith, Henry	84	South Branch	1796	1	327
Smith, John	230	Stony Creek	1792	1	283
Smith, Mary	130	Mill Creek	1766	1	500
Smith, Nicholas	270	Tygert's V. River	1784	1	148
Smith, Peter	54	South Branch	1767	1	504
Smith, Peter	65	South Branch	1773	1	554
Smith, Robert	25	Dry Run	1785	1	167
Somwalt—or Somvalt, Sumwalt					
Somwalt, George	236	South Branch	1774	1	568
Somwalt, George (Sumwalt)	213	South Branch	1789	1	233
Somwalt, John	31	South Branch	1790	1	256
Springston, Abraham	118	Tygert's V. River	1785	1	155
Stalnaker, Jacob	194	Tygert's V. River	1784	1	106
Stalnaker, Jacob Jr.	120	Tygert's V. River	1784	1	107
Stalnaker, Valentine	150	Adj. J. Stalnaker	1784	1	102
Stephenson, Hugh	1,000	Cross Creek	1774	1	567
Stewart—or Stuart					
Stone, Henry	73	South Branch	1787	1	176
Stone, Henry	63	Scuth Branch	1787	1	184
Stone, Henry	107	Black Thorn	1789	1	217
Stone, Henry	72	Black Thorn	1789	1	220
Stone, Henry	200	Black Thorn	1791	1	269
Stone, Henry	54	Black Thorn	1773	1	552
Stone, Henry	69	Black Thorn	1773	1	552
Stout, George	50	South Branch	1784	1	132
Stout, Hezekiah	92	Back Creek	1785	1	164
Stuart, Isbela et al	1,000	Wts. Mon. River	1782	1	35
Sumwalt—See Somwalt					
Sumwalt, George	236	South Branch	1774	1	568
Sutton, Joseph	150	Brushy Run	1795	1	325
Swadley, Mark	130	Winter Spring	1769	1	517
Swadley, Mark	40	Black Thorn	1769	1	518
Tackett, Christopher	375	Sidlington Cr.	1783	1	76
Tackett, Lewis	297	Sidlington Creek	1783	1	49
Tackett, Lewis	400	Sidlington Creek	1783	1	51

Name of Grantee	Acres	Local Description	Year	Book	Page
Taylor, William	230	Warrick's Creek	1787	1	208
Teter, George	120	South Branch	1773	1	543
Teter, Paul (Teeter)	40	Seneca Creek	1767	1	506
Teter, Paul	53	South Branch	1773	1	557
Teter, Philip	118	Deep Spring	1773	1	542
Thomas, James	375	Lost River	1756	1	598
Thompson, William et al	280	Back Creek	1779	1	11
Trace, Jacob	94	South Branch	1774	1	571
Tremble—or Trimble					
Tremble, James	300	Crab Apple Bottom	1760	1	483
Tremble, James	160	South Branch	1760	1	484
Trimble—or Tremble					
Trimble, James	180	Black Thorn	1756	1	471
Trimble, James	200	South Branch	1757	1	473
Trimble, James	100	Black Thorn	1758	1	478
Trimble, James	450	Limestone Spring	1758	1	479
Trimble, James	300	Crab Apple Bottom	1761	1	481
Trimble, James	140	Black Thorn	1761	1	485
Trimble, James	200	Black Thorn	1761	1	485
Trimble, James	130	South Branch	1761	1	486
Trimble, James	100	South Branch	1761	1	487
Trimble, James	100	Black Thorn	1761	1	487
Trimble, James	330	South Branch	1761	1	488
Trimble, James	100	Black Thorn	1770	1	522
Truby, John et al	262	Tygert's V. River	1784	1	122
Turnin, Ignatius	313	Thorny Creek	1791	1	259
Vannamon—See Venimen					
Venimen—or Vannamon					
Venimen, Peter	128	Town's Creek	1772	1	538
Venimen, Peter	137	Smith's Creek	1773	1	544
Venimen, Peter	136	South Branch	1773	1	545
Venimen, Peter	150	Dry Run	1773	1	548
Venimen, Peter	11	Tom's Run	1773	1	558
Vernor—or Vernon					
Vernor, Adam (Vernon)	117	South Branch	1784	1	100
Vernor, Adam Jr. (Vernon)	46	Brushy Fork	1789	1	216
Viney, Andrew	386¼	Lost River	1750	1	590
Waddle, or—Woddel, Woodell					
Waddle, William	245	Stony Creek	1794	1	293
Wagner—or Wagoner, Waggoner					
Wagner, Adam	54	Fallen Timber	1790	1	255
Wagoner, Ludwick	47	South Branch	1766	1	499
Wagoner, Ludwick	131	South Branch	1773	1	544
Walker, Thomas	80	Wts. New River	1756	1	481
Walker, Thomas	180	Wts. New River	1756	1	482
Ward, William	160	Black Thorn	1781	1	16
Ward, William	35	Black Thorn	1781	1	18
Warden, William	400	Lost River	1750	1	588
Warrick, Jacob	340	Wts. Greenbrier	1783	1	50
Warrick, Jacob	800	Sidlington's Cr.	1783	1	53
Warrick, Jacob	180	Clover Lick	1783	1	66
Warrick, Jacob	354	Sidlington Creek	1783	1	72
Warrick, Jacob	70	Warrick's Creek	1783	1	74
Warrick, Jacob	400	Clover Lick Cr.	1789	1	246
Warrick, Jacob	150	Lick Run	1795	1	306
Warrick, Jacob	180	Greenbrier R.	1795	1	307
Warrick, Jacob	420	Greenbrier R.	1795	1	308
Warrick, Jacob	200	Greenbrier R.	1795	1	309
Warrick, Jacob	520	Allegheny Mt.	1795	1	310
Warrick, Jacob	141	Setlington's Cr.	1795	1	311
Warrick, John	350	Wts. Tygert Valley	1783	1	58
Warrick, John	323	Roaring Spring	1783	1	62
Warrick, William	900	Deer Creek	1783	1	48
Warrick, William et al	370	Beaver Springs	1797	1	335

Name of Grantee	Acres	Local Description	Year	Book	Page
Washington, George					
(Assgn. Posey)	2,813	Shirtee's Creek	1774	1	565
Wees, Weise, Wise					
Wees, Adam et al	254	South Mill Creek	1773	1	545
Weise—Wees, Wise					
Welch, George	23	Stony Lick Run	1771	1	529
Wells, Alexander	200	Hard Bargain Cr.	1780	1	4
Welton, John Jr.	400	Patterson's Cr.	1752	1	596
Westfall, Daniel	200	Tygert's V. River	1784	1	124
Westfall, George	400	Tygert's V. River	1784	1	108
Westfall, Jacob	150	Wts. Tygert's V.	1783	1	79
Westfall, Jacob et al	152	Leading Cr.	1787	1	189
Westfall, James	193	File's Creek	1783	1	82
Westfall, Joel	150	Tygert's V. River	1784	1	134
Westfall, William et al	1,000	Wts. Monon. River	1782	1	35
White, Jacob	100	Eberman's Run	1787	1	204
Whiteman, Henry	146	South Fork	1784	1	85
Whiteman, Henry	220	Brushy Fork	1796	1	330
Wilfong—See Wittfong					
Wimer, Jacob	154	Dry Run	1784	1	96
Wimer, Philip	246	Dry Run	1784	1	98
Wilmoth, Thomas	177	Leading Cr.	1784	1	126
Wilmoth, Thomas	130	Skidmore Run	1768	1	509
Wilson, Benjamin	250	Wts. Monon. River	1784	1	113
Wilson, Benjamin	200	Wts. Monon. River	1784	1	128
Wilson, Benjamin	400	Eberman's Cr.	1784	1	129
Wilson, Benjamin	170	Leading Cr.	1784	1	130
Wilson, Benjamin	150	Eberman's Run	1784	1	131
Wilson, Charles	140	South Branch	1782	1	43
Wilson, John	400	Eberman's Run	1784	1	117
Wilson, John et al	152	Leading Cr.	1787	1	189
Wilson, William	100	Leading Cr.	1784	1	120
Wilson, William	60	Bull Pasture	1784	1	154
Wise—or Wees, Weise					
Wise, Martin	225	Mill Creek	1787	1	179
Wittfong—or Wilfong					
Wittfong, Michael	70	Brushy Fork	1773	1	553
Wittfong, Michael	50	Brushy Fork	1773	1	554
Wolf, Nicholas	100	Beaver Creek	1784	1	147
Wood, James et al	750	South Branch	1750	1	464
Wood, James et al	600	South Branch	1750	1	465
Wood, James et al	2,400	South Branch	1750	1	466
Wood, James et al	330	South Branch	1750	1	468
Wood, James et al	660	South Branch	1750	1	469
Wood, James Jr.	242	Black Thorn	1787	1	178
Woodell—See Waddle, Woddel					
Young, John	375	South Branch	1768	1	508

BATH COUNTY, VIRGINIA

Barbour, James et al, Assignee	400	Wts. Greenbrier	1799	1	72
Barlow, John	100	Wts. Greenbrier	1803	1	125
Barlow, John	160	Stony Cr.	1817	1	167
Barnes, Abraham	178	Wts. Greenbrier	1796	1	25
Barnett, James	150	Wts. Greenbrier	1801	1	112
Barnett, James et al	2,700	Wts. Greenbrier	1799	1	43
Beard, John	66	Locust Creek	1798	1	40
Beard, John	80	Locust Cr.	1809	1	149
Beard, Josiah	1,200	Locust Cr.	1823	1	581
Bird, John	410	Wts. Greenbrier	1800	1	84

Name of Grantee	Acres	Local Description	Year	Book	Page
Boiler—Boiles, Boyles					
Boiler, David	286	Locust Creek	1801	1	114
Boiles—or Boiler, Boyles					
Bolar, John et al	120	Cockran's Creek	1821	1	180
Boyles—or Boiles, Boiler					
Bradshaw, John	200	Knap's Cr.	1811	1	157
Bradshaw, John	200	Knap's Cr.	1812	1	162
Brock, Daniel et al	10	Locust Cr.	1820	1	176
Brown, James et al	400	Beaver Lick Cr.	1804	1	136
Buck, Thomas	195	Wts. Greenbrier	1796	1	26
Buckley, Joshua	67	Wts. Greenbrier	1800	1	99
Burgess, John	96	Wts. Greenbrier	1810	1	151
Burgess, John Jr.	100	Locust Cr.	1803	1	124
Burnside, John	450	Wts. Greenbrier	1801	1	117
Burnside, William	50	Wts. Greenbrier	1822	1	185
Callison, Anthony	240	Locust Cr.	1818	1	170
Callison, Anthony	8	Locust Creek	1823	1	182
Callison, Anthony	58	Trump's Run	1823	1	187
Callison, James	324	Locust Cr.	1801	1	122
Callison, John (Gallison)	50	Wts. Greenbrier	1801	1	88
Carry, Joseph (Cary)	6,000	Knap's Creek	1796	1	10
Casebolt, Henry	123	Wts. Greenbrier	1794	1	3
Casebolt, Henry	132	Wts. Greenbrier	1797	1	46
Casebolt, Henry	177	Wts. Greenbrier	1801	1	111
Casebolt, Henry	100	Wts. Greenbrier	1822	1	184
Casebolt, Thomas	24	Locust Creek	1821	1	181
Cleek, Michael	30	Knap's Creek	1811	1	158
Coberley, Thomas	50	Deer Cr.	1801	1	89
Cochran, John	16	Adj. Wm. Cockley	1823	1	189
Cochran, William	60	Swego Creek	1823	1	188
Collins, John	150	Wts. Greenbrier	1810	1	152
Cooper, James	20	Cartmill Cr.	1810	1	156
Corbit, Samuel	400	Wts. Greenbrier	1799	1	65
Deveis—or Deviase					
Deveis, Abraham	90	Marlin Mountain	1801	1	102
Deviase—or Deveis					
Deviase, Abraham	70	Knap Creek	1795	1	6
Dinwiddie, John	200	Mayes Bottom	1811	1	160
Dizer, Isaac G.	30	Wts. Greenbrier.	1808	1	141
Dizer, Stephen A.	142	Wts. Greenbrier	1804	1	135
Dizer, William	50	Wts. Greenbrier	1804	1	134
Dizer, William	605	Wts. Greenbrier	1809	1	145
Donavan, Sarah & Allen	570	Adj. Jacob Warrick	1821	1	179
Dougherty, Michael et al	160	Knap's Cr.	1801	1	120
Dozier—See Dizer					
Drennen—See Drinen					
Drennen, John	29	Wts. Greenbrier	1809	1	150
Drinen—See Drennen					
Drinen, Thomas et al Heirs	41	Wts. Greenbrier	1817	1	168
Dunlap, James et al	160	Knap's Cr.	1801	1	120
Edmiston, Andrew et al	10	Locust Cr.	1820	1	176
Erwin, Benjamin	80	Wts. Greenbrier	1796	1	12
Erwin, John	300	Wts. Greenbrier	1804	1	137
Ewing, John	200	Lit. Levels	1811	1	161
Ewing, John Sr.	160	Wts. Greenbrier	1800	1	78
Ewing, Joshua	150	Lit. Levels	1797	1	27
Ewing, Joshua	509	Wts. Greenbrier	1794	1	2
Ewing, William	745	Swego Creek	1795	1	4
Francisco, Charles L. et al	120	Cockran's Creek	1821	1	180
French, George et al	3,000	Wts. Greenbrier	1796	1	9
French, George et al	1,000	Wts. Stony Cr.	1796	1	20
Frum, David (Trum)	64	Wts. Greenbrier	1801	1	93
Galford, Thomas	96	Sitlington's Cr.	1796	1	21

Name of Grantee	Acres	Local Description	Year	Book	Page
Galford, Thomas	30	Wts. Greenbrier	1811	1	159
Galford, William	25	Sitlington's Cr.	1817	1	166
Gallagher, Charles (Gallegher)	32,000	Wts. Greenbrier	1796	1	23
Gallagher, Charles	11,000	Sinking Cr.	1796	1	22
Gallison, John (Callison)	50	Wts. Greenbrier	1801	1	88
Gay—See Guy					
Gay, Robert	137	Wts. Greenbrier	1820	1	177
Gay, Robert	40	Clover Lick	1798	1	57
Gay, Robert	100	Wts. Greenbrier	1802	1	108
Gilliland, Samuel	50	Wts. Greenbrier	1797	1	28
Gillespey, James Jr. (or Jacob)	166	Cartmill's Cr.	1801	1	119
Greenbrier Company, The	420	Ewing's Cr.	1800	1	68
Greenbrier Company, The	480	Wts. Greenbrier	1800	1	67
Greenbrier Company, The	312	Mill Creek	1800	1	74
Grimes, John	210	Thorny Cr.	1820	1	173
Grimes, John	21	Lit. Levels	1823	1	193
Guy—See Gay					
Guy. Robert (Gay)	40	Clover Lick Cr.	1798	1	57
Halcomb—See Holcomb, Hulcomb					
Halcomb, Timothy (Holcomb)	218	Wts. Greenbrier	1803	1	132
Hannah, David	32	Adj. John Smith	1802	1	107
Hannah, William	25	Wts. Greenbrier	1821	1	178
Hartman, Isaac	200	Deer Creek	1799	1	63
Hartman, John	75	Cartmill Cr.	1807	1	139
Hatten, John	198	Camp Run	1801	1	94
Hawk, Isaac	20	Locust Creek	1801	1	95
Hawk, Isaac	214	Locust Creek	1803	1	130
Hill, Richard	50	Lit. Sinking Cr.	1822	1	183
Hively, Jacob	113	Knap's Cr.	1801	1	109
Holcomb—See Halcomb, Hulcomb					
Houchin, William (Houchen)	40	Wts. Greenbrier	1797	1	52
Houchin, William	36	Wts. Greenbrier	1797	1	29
Hughes, Millbourn	150	Stamping Cr.	1820	1	174
Hulcomb—See Halcomb, Holcomb					
Hulcomb, Timothy	100	Beaver Lick Cr.	1803	1	131
Hulcomb, Timothy	70	Stamping Cr.	1809	1	148
Hulcomb, Timothy Jr.	300	Stamping Cr.	1810	1	153
Johnson, James	20	Wts. Greenbrier	1804	1	128
Johnson, Thomas & John	265	Wts. Greenbrir	1812	1	163
Johnston, John	485	Wts. Greenbrier	1799	1	61
Jordan, John	36	Lit. Levels	1801	1	121
Jordan, John	28	Locust Cr.	1801	1	113
Keckley, Valentine	88	Knap's Cr.	1797	1	47
Keenan, Patrick	150	Wts. Greenbrier	1819	1	172
Kincaid, Thomas	6,000	Knap's Creek	1796	1	16
Kincaid, Thomas	2,306½	Wts. Greenbrier	1796	1	7
Kinnison, David	260	Adj. James Brindley	1801	1	115
Knox, Jeremiah	1,000	Wts. Greenbrier	1799	1	64
Kuhn, Jacob	30,000	Wts. Greenbrier	1798	1	38
Leacox, David	10	Sinking Cr.	1801	1	92
Legg, John et al	3,000	Wts. Greenbrier	1796	1	9
Legg, John et al	1,000	Wts. Stony Creek	1796	1	20
Lenagar, Isaac	200	Sinking Cr.	1801	1	110
Lewis, James Jr.	4	Lit. Levels	1822	1	186
Lewis, John	132	Stony Creek	1796	1	8
Machum, Samuel	100	Knap's Creek	1801	1	103
Magrath, Patrick	50	Knapp's Cr.	1800	1	79
Massingbird, George (Massinbird) et al	570	Wts. Greenbrier	1799	1	44
Massingbird, George Assignee et al	400	Wts. Greenbrier	1799	1	72
McClanachan, Robert	12,851½	Wts. Greenbrier	1796	1	17
McClure, Arthur	200	Wts Gauley River	1809	1	146
McCollum—or MeCollens					

BOTETOURT COUNTY, VIRGINIA

Name of Grantee	Acres	Local Description	Year	Book	Page
Hog—or Hogg					
Hog, Peter et al	21,941	Wts. Pocatalico	1773	1	597
Hog, Peter et al	51,302	Mth. Gr. Kanawha R.	1772	1	590
Hogg—or Hog					
Horn, Mary et al	28,400	Wts. Lit. Kanawha	1773	1	221
Lewis, Andrew et al	51,302	Mth. Gr. Kanawha R.	1772	1	590
Lewis, Andrew et al	21,941	Wts. Pocatalico	1773	1	597
McDowell, Daniel	1,000	Mill & Muddy Crs.	1774	1	231
McNulty, William et al	28,400	Wts. Lit. Kanawha	1773	1	221
Mercer, George et al	6,788	Wts. Pocatalico	1773	1	595
Murphy, Robert et al	28,400	Wts. Lit. Kanawha	1773	1	221
Muse, George	927	Near Mth. Lit. Kan.	1772	1	588
Muse, George et al	7,276	Pocatalico River	1773	1	225
Muse, George et al	7,794	Mth. Pocatalico River	1773	1	228
Muse, George et al	51,302	Mth. Great Kanawha	1772	1	590
Polson, John et al	51,302	Mth. Gr. Kanawha	1772	1	590
Richardson, David et al	28,400	Wts. Lit. Kanawha	1773	1	221
Savage, Thomas et al	21,941	Wts. Pocatalico	1773	1	597
Self, Frances et al	28,400	Wts. Lit. Kanawha	1773	1	221
Smith, John et al	28,400	Wts. Lit. Kanawha	1773	1	221
Stephen, Adam et al	51,302	Mth. Great Kan. R.	1772	1	590
Stephen, Adam et al	21,941	Wts. Pocatalico	1773	1	597
Stewart, Robert et al	28,400	Wts. Lit. Kanawha	1773	1	221
Stobo, Robert et al	28,400	Wts. Lit. Kanawha	1773	1	221
Thomas, James & A. F. et al	28,400	Wts. Lit. Kanawha	1773	1	221
Vanbraam, Jacob et al	28,400	Wts. Lit. Kanawha	1773	1	221
Wagoner, Andrew et al	51,302	Mth. Gr. Kanawha R.	1772	1	590
Wagoner, Andrew et al	6,788	Wts. Pocatalico	1773	1	595
Washington, George	2,314	3 or 4 mi. below mth. Lit. Kan. R.	1772	1	587
Washington, George	4,395	Lit. Kanawha abv. Gr. Bend in Ohio R.	1772	1	585
Washington, George	2,448	Ohio, 16 mi. below Lit. Kanawha	1772	1	584
Washington, George	7,276	Pocatalico River	1773	1	225
Watts, Napp A. et al	28,400	Wts. Lit. Kanawha	1773	1	221
West, John et al	51,302	Mth. Gr. Kanawha R.	1772	1	590
West, John Jr. et al	6,788	Wts. Pocatalico	1773	1	595
Wilper, John David et al	21,941	Wts. Pocatalico	1773	1	597
Wright, ——— et al	21,941	Wts. Pocatalico	1773	1	597

FREDERICK COUNTY, VIRGINIA

Abrams, Bazil & Elizabeth et al Hrs.	267	Lick Run	1791	2	324
Abrell, John (Abrill)	376	Wts. Opequon	1760	1	499
Abrell, John	89	Wts. Opequon	1757	1	458
Abrell, John	220	Wts. Opequon	1757	1	459
Adams, John	391	Back Creek	1775	2	274
Adams, Thomas	316	Naked Barrens	1753	2	378
Akings, Thomas	116	Tuscarorah Creek	1765	2	489
Alexander, Gerard	863	Long Marsh	1753	1	138
Allen, Robert et al	193	Mill Creek	1762	1	278
Anderson, James	350	Mill Creek	1754	1	150
Andrews, Earnest	256	Wts. Opequon	1760	1	493
Arnold, John	300	Wts. Opequon	1750	1	212
Arnold, John	306	Wts. Opequon	1763	1	340

Name of Grantee	Acres	Local Description	Year	Book	Page
Arnold, Josiah	400	Gr. Cacapon	1752	1	91
Arnold, Richard Sr.	400	Gr. Cacapon	1752	1	85
Ashbridge, George	224	Back Creek	1754	1	158
Ashbridge, George	224	Back Creek	1755	1	206
Ashby, Jesse (Jessy)	487	Limestone Ridge	1761	1	536
Ashcraft, Felix	400	Sleepy Cr.	1766	2	585
Babb, Thomas	179	Wts. Opequon	1754	1	167
Bailey, John	354	Sleepy Creek	1771	2	224
Bailey, John Sr.	200	Sleepy Creek	1769	2	146
Bailey, William (Bayley)	380	Sleepy Creek	1768	2	104
Bailey, William	400	Sleepy Creek	1769	2	150
Bailey, William et al	143	Sleepy Creek	1801	2	348
Baker, Henry	195	Back Creek	1777	2	278
Baldwin, Francis	262	Back Creek	1750	1	33
Baldwin, Francis	6¾	Back Creek	1762	1	304
Baldwin, Francis	327	Drains of Opequon	1766	2	549
Baldwin, Francis	360	Back Creek	1766	2	550
Baldwin, William	411	Back Creek	1768	2	102
Baldwin, William	188	Back Creek	1760	1	517
Baldwin, William	50	Back Creek	1760	1	520
Baldwin, William	278	Middle Creek	1762	1	592
Banner, Gasper	334 3/16	Back Creek	1789	2	311
Barber, Richard	200	Wts. Potomac	1754	1	164
Barrett, James	26	Back Creek	1766	2	587
Barton, Roger	48½	North Mountain	1794	2	344
Barwick, Thomas	391	Warm Spring Run	1748	1	1
Bayle—See Boyle					
Baylis, John	423	Wts. Opequon	1754	1	161
Baylis, John Col.	400	Wts. Opequon	1760	1	482
Beeler, Christopher	333	North Branch	1752	1	77
Beeler, Joseph	751	Wts. Opequon	1769	2	138
Bell, Nathaniel	296	Wts. Mill Creek	1764	2	472
Bell, Nathaniel	262	Mill Creek	1766	2	521
Bell, Nathaniel	59	Mill Creek	1766	2	524
Bickerstaff, William	309	Wts. Potomac	1762	1	258
Blackburn, Robert	500	Wts. Opequon	1768	2	100
Blackford, Joseph	171	Back Creek	1771	2	210
Blair, James	163	Wts. Opequon	1770	2	180
Boarer, Adam	298	Indian Camp Springs	1793	2	340
Boggs, William	243	Back Creek	1766	2	8
Boggs, William	275	Back Creek	1750	1	118
Booth, Caleb	221	Mill Cr.	1763	1	384
Borden, John	213	Wts. Potomac	1760	1	500
Bowen, Henry	103	Back Cr.	1753	1	124
Bower, Henry Jr.	370	Wts. Opequon	1771	2	218
Boyd, John	101	Wts. Opequon	1766	2	592
Boyd, William	200	Mill Creek	1766	2	582
Boyle—or Bayle					
Boyle, James	400	Wts. Potomac	1766	2	533
Boyle, Stephen	100	Sleepy Creek	1767	2	56
Bradford, Peter	100	Wts. Opequon	1764	2	482
Bradford, Peter	323	Middle Creek	1764	2	483
Brance—or Bronse, Brouse					
Breed, Joseph	149	Back Creek	1755	1	204
Breeson, John	281	Back Creek	1770	2	160
Bridges, Joseph	65	Back Creek	1774	2	268
Bridges, Joseph	390	Back Creek	1778	2	286
Brinker, Henry	381	Opequon River	1753	1	135
Briscoe, John Dr.	117	Wts. Opequon	1770	2	162
Briscoe, John Dr.	167	Wts. Opequon	1764	2	471
Briscoe, John Dr.	400	Wts. Opequon	1760	1	473
Briscoe, John Dr.	462	Wts. Opequon	1760	1	487
Britton, Joseph	200	Cacapon	1752	1	69

Name of Grantee	Acres	Local Description	Year	Book	Page
Cunningham, John	157	Wts. Opequon	1774	2	260
Cunningham, Robert	318	Mill Creek	1751	1	52
Cunningham, Robert	450	Mill Creek	1760	1	507
Cunningham, Robert	500	Wts. Opequon	1766	2	546
Cunningham, Robert	314	Mill Creek	1762	1	590
Curry, William	140	Wts. Opequon	1770	2	190
Cusick, Thomas	306	Adj. Daniel Davis	1768	2	88
Dalton, John	400	North Mt.	1752	2	394
Darke, Joseph	380	Elk Branch	1770	2	184
Daugherty—or Dougherty					
Davenport, Adrian & Samuel	400	Mill Branch	1792	2	337
Davis, James	420	Wts. Potomac	1762	1	290
Davis, John	70	Wts. Potomac	1768	2	76
Davis, John	340	Wts. Potomac	1769	2	134
Davis, William	75	Adj. Evert Marsh	1776	2	410
Dawson, Isaac	523	Sleepy Creek	1770	2	192
Dawson, Isaac	160	Sleepy Creek	1760	1	533
Decker, Garrat	380	South Branch	1748	1	9
Decker, Luke	70	Wts. Potomac	1754	1	196
DeMoss, Charles	225	Wts. Opequon	1789	2	303
Dent, Thomas	28	Sleepy Creek	1764	2	462
Dent, Thomas	400	Sleepy Creek	1760	1	486
Dent, Thomas	158	Back Creek	1765	2	488
Dick, C. et al	260	Patterson Cr.	1754	1	165
Dick, Charles et al	300	Patterson Cr.	1754	1	187
Dick, Charles et al	350	Wts. South Br.	1754	1	188
Dickson, James	294	Wts. Potomac	1762	1	575
Dillion—or Dillon					
Dillion, James	56	Back Creek	1775	2	272
Dillion, William	384	Wts. Opequon	1752	2	370
Dillon, Daniel	342	Back Creek	1762	1	254
Dillon, James	56	Back Cr.	1775	2	272
Dillon, Luke	86	Back Creek	1761	1	566
Dillon, William	400	Back Creek	1752	1	101
Dillon, William	384	Wts. Opequon	1752	2	370
Dillon, William	398	Wts. Opequon	1752	1	102
Dodson, John	260	Mill Creek	1754	1	189
Dokes, John	166	Back Creek	1766	2	596
Doster, Thomas	379	Wts. Back Creek	1766	2	578
Dougherty, James	174	Sleepy Creek	1788	2	292
Dougherty, John & James	400	Sleepy Creek	1766	2	543
Douglass, James	442	Wts. Opequon	1766	2	589
Dunbar, James	400	Wts. Opequon	1767	2	46
Dunbar, James	95	Wts. Opequon	1766	2	590
Duncan—Dungan, Dunken, Dunkin					
Duncan, Matthew	209	Tuscarorah Cr.	1756	1	244
Dungan, Helen	233	Cabin Run	1763	2	434
Dunken, Patrick	121	Wts. Opequon	1753	1	133
Dunkin, Matthew	417	Dry Run	1760	1	504
Dunn, Jeremiah	161	Tilhanzey Branch	1768	2	106
Dunn, Jeremiah	162	Back Creek	1770	2	178
Eades, Thomas	145	Gr. Cacapon	1789	2	310
Eastburn, Robinson	400	Wts. Sleepy Creek	1789	2	312
Eaton, Isaac	137	Mill Creek	1766	2	574
Eckstine, Leonard	82	Wts. Opequon	1768	2	90
Eckstine, Leonard	164	Wts. Opequon	1764	2	456
Edwards, David	412	Gr. Cacapon	1752	1	87
Edwards, Jonathan	150	Wts. Opequon	1768	2	92
Edwards, Joseph	400	Great Cacapon	1748	1	2
Edwards, Joseph	375	Cacapon River	1752	1	86
Edwards, Joseph	400	Opequon	1753	1	115
Edwards, Joseph	239	Wts. Opequon	1766	2	534
Edwards, Thomas	400	Cacapon River	1752	1	90

Name of Grantee	Acres	Local Description	Year	Book	Page
Glass, David	114	Wts. Opequon	1761	1	550
Glass, Robert	544	Wts. Opequon	1754	1	178
Glass, Samuel	200	Wts. Opequon	1754	1	184
Glenn, James	155	Adj. Wm. Bayliss	1766	2	436
Glenn, James	247	Tuscarorah Cr.	1766	2	559
Glover, William	355	Wts. Opequon	1760	1	476
Goldsbury, Thomas Manard	407	Shenandoah River	1756	2	392
Golsbary—See Goldsbury					
Goodlett, Robert	100	Sleepy Creek	1767	2	66
Gordon, Charles	184	Wts. Opequon	1768	2	122
Gore, Joshua et al	328	Cacapon Mountain	1827	2	354
Gossett, Mathias	31⅞	Wts. Opequon	1772	2	254
Gossett, Mathias	350	Wts. Opequon	1766	2	516
Graham, John	410	Hite's Marsh	1763	1	322
Grayson, Col. Benjamin	499	Opequon Creek	1754	1	156
Grayson, Col. Benjamin	----	Opequon Cr.	----	1	61
Green, Thomas et al	416	Wts. Opequon	1766	2	520
Griffey, Edward	241	Wts. Opequon	1750	1	176
Griffey, Edward	241	Wts. Opequon	1754	1	193
Griffith, John	392	Back Creek	1766	2	26
Gritton, John	245	Lit. Cacapon	1766	2	525
Grubb, Benjamin	400	So. Fk. of Bull Skin	1751	1	46
Grubb, Samuel & William	431	Bull-Skin	1762	1	268
Hagan, James	183	Wts. Opequon	1763	1	348
Hall, William	486	Elk Branch	1756	1	234
Hall, William	2,236	Howard's Marsh	1764	2	477
Hamlen—or Hamlin					
Hamlen, Thomas	218	Spring Ridge	1762	1	587
Hamlen, Thomas	225	Warm Springs	1762	1	588
Hamlin—or Hamlen					
Hamlin, John	416	Warm Springs	1762	1	589
Hancher, John (Houcher)	172	Wts. Opequon	1766	2	584
Handley, Murty	300	Adj. John Hampton	1749	1	13
Handley, Samuel	343	Wts. Opequon	1770	2	182
Hardwick, Hazell	407	Adj. John Evans	1753	2	402
Harlan—or Harland					
Harlan, James	280	Warm Springs	1768	2	78
Harlan, Moses	174	Wts. Potomac	1766	2	573
Harlan, Stephen	433	North Mt.	1760	2	398
Harland—or Harlan					
Harland, George	441	North Mt.	1760	2	400
Harland, John	234	Wts. Potomac	1766	2	554
Harmison, Thomas	247	Ambrose Run	1766	2	13
Harper, Robert	184	Elk Branch	1763	1	330
Harper, Robert	125	Mouth of Shenandoah	1751	2	362
Harper, Robert	92	Wts. Potomac	1762	1	580
Harrison, Samuel	300	Wts. Opequon	1764	2	459
Hart, Miles	187	Elk Branch	1756	1	235
Hart, Thomas	268	Elk Branch	1754	1	144
Hart, Thomas	49	Elk Branch	1763	1	382
Hart, Thomas Jr.	323	Wts. Potomac	1755	1	210
Hastings, Job	43	Middle Creek	1766	2	552
Haynes, Abraham	882	Dry Branch	1754	1	166
Haynes, Hugh	247	Wts. Opequon	1760	1	484
Haynes, Noah	343 (340)	Long Marsh	1751	1	31
Hays, Elizabeth et al	390	Mill Run	1771	2	230
Hays, Nathan & Theodice, Heirs	112	Wts. Potomac	1791	2	327
Hayton, John et al	100	Vanmeter's Run	1796	2	356
Hayton, John et al	175	Vanmeter's Run	1796	2	347
Hayworth, James	227	Great Spring Br.	1752	1	103
Hazenbeler—or Hotzenbeler					
Hazenbeler, Stephen	394	Wts. Cacapon	1756	1	220
Heaton, Robert	378	Back Creek	1754	1	168
Hedges, Jonas	261	North Mountain	1754	2	388

Name of Grantee	Acres	Local Description	Year	Book	Page
Hedges, Jonas	352	Adj. John Mauzy	1754	2	414
Hedges, Jonas	352	Near Watkins' Ferry	1756	2	418
Hedges, Joshua	391	North Mountain	1754	2	386
Hedges, Solomon	102	New Creek	1760	1	464
Hedges, Solomon	320	New Creek	1760	1	465
Helm—or Helms					
Helm, Meredith	200	Wts. Opequon	1766	2	545
Helm, Meredith Jr.	400	Opequon	1752	1	100
Helm, Thomas Capt.	300	Wts. Opequon	1763	1	366
Helms, Thomas	320	Opequon Cr.	1751	1	55
Helms, Thomas	269	Opequon Cr.	1752	1	63
Henderson, Alexander	248	Cherry Branch	1766	2	34
Henderson, Alexander	336	Wts. Opequon	1767	2	36
Henderson, Alexander	403	Wts. Cacapon	1766	2	38
Henderson, Alexander	275	Gibbon's Branch	1766	2	40
Higginas, Robert	100	Elk Lick	1760	1	494
Higgins—See Higginas					
Higgins, Thomas	600	Capt. John's Run	1751	1	56
Highland, Richard	273	Wts. Opequon	1762	1	567
Hill, John	300	Mill Creek	1760	1	530
Hite, Abraham	362	Henry's Mill Run	1751	1	49
Hite, Abraham	400	Mill Creek	1753	1	122
Hite, Jacob	457	Opequon Creek	1751	1	42
Hite, Jacob	135	Wts. Opequon	1769	2	142
Hite, Jacob	700	Wts. Opequon	1769	2	144
Hite, Jacob	209	Wts. Opequon	1754	1	169
Hite, Jacob et al Ex.	175	Vanmeter's Run	1796	2	347
Hite, Jacob et al Ex.	100	Vanmeter's Run	1796	2	356
Hoge, John	400	Wts. Opequon	1766	2	24
Hogg, John Rev.	393	Wts. Opequon	1754	1	195
Holladay, James	210	Mill Creek	1754	1	190
Hood, Lucas Sr.	133	Sleepy Cr.	1765	2	509
Horner, George	400	Cacapon River	1752	1	67
Hotzenbeler—See Hazenbeler					
Hotzenbeler, Peter	137	Wts. Opequon	1766	2	515
Houcher, John (Hancher)	172	Wts. Opequon	1766	2	584
Houte, George	254	Elk Branch	1763	1	344
Hughes—or Hughs					
Hughes, Hugh	480	Gr. Cacapon	1754	1	154
Hughes, William Jr.	460	Cacapon River	1754	1	151
Hughes, William Sr.	400	Gr. Cacapon	1752	1	83
Hughs—or Hughes					
Hughs, Thomas	419	Wts. Cacapon	1752	1	108
Huls, Josiah	89	Sleepy Cr.	1760	1	521
Huls, Josiah	334	Sleepy Creek	1760	1	522
Huls, Josiah	125	Wts. Potomac	1760	1	527
Huntsbarger, Jacob	214	Elk Branch	1762	1	270
Hyatt, John	659	Wts. Opequon	1761	1	551
Hyatt, John	77	Wts. Opequon	1761	1	554
Hyatt, John Jr.	345	Wts. Opequon	1761	1	546
Hyatt, John Jr	126	Wts. Opequon	1761	1	547
Hyatt, William	184	Opequon Creek	1751	1	41
Hyatt, William	195	Wts. Opequon	1751	1	44
Hyatt, William	400	Deep Hollow	1754	1	173
Jackson, James	95½	Buffalo Lick Run	1771	2	236
Jackson, Robert	116(161)	Back Creek	1768	2	110
Jackson, Robert	276	Back Creek	1766	2	593
Jackson, William	135	Sleepy Creek	1766	2	535
Jenkins—or Jinkins					
Jenkins, Aron	400	Elk Lick	1752	1	109
Jenkins, John (Jinkins)	222	Elk Lick	1789	2	305
Johnson—or Johnston					
Johnson, Hannah (Widow)	186	Wts. Opequon	1751	1	53

Name of Grantee	Acres	Local Description	Year	Book	Page
Johnson, Jacob	55	Tilhanzey Branch	1769	2	136
Johnson, Mary	400	Bullskin	1752	1	82
Johnson, William Sr.	400	Capt. John's Run	1791	2	326
Johnston, George	467	The Marsh	1753	1	211
Johnston, George Capt.	552	Bull Skin	1750	1	20
Johnston, Robert	239	Bullskin Run	1753	1	132
Joliffe—or Jolliffe					
Joliffe, William Jr.	152	Wts. Opequon	1761	1	543
Jolliffe, William	129	Wts. Opequon	1766	2	20
Jolliffe, William	113	Ross Spring Br.	1766	2	22
Jones, Gabriel	400	Drains of Opequon	1751	1	43
Jones, Robert	336	Cherry Br.	1793	2	339
Jones, Thomas	157	Back Creek	1753	1	129
Jones, William	400	Wts. Opequon	1755	1	202
Jones, William	300	Mill Creek	1760	1	488
Joseph, Thomas et al	1,056	Middle Creek	1752	1	104
Julian, George	400	Back Creek	1750	1	119
Julian, Stephen	31	Back Creek	1770	2	152
Kelley, David	144	Mill Creek	1762	1	583
Kennard, Nicholas	400	Wts. Potomac	1751	1	50
Kennedy, John	140	Back Creek	1766	2	594
Kennedy, Robert	56	Back Creek	1768	2	108
Kennedy, Samuel	115	Back Creek	1766	2	9
Kennedy, Thomas	335	Dry Run	1766	2	2
Keyes—See Keys					
Keyes, Gersham	109	Adj. Evert Marsh	1761	2	406
Keys—or Keyes					
Keys, Gersham	420	Wts. Shenandoah	1763	1	308
Keys, Gersham	415	Shenandoah River	1762	2	430
Keys, Humphry	113	Wts. Potomac	1762	1	276
Keywood, John	383	Wts. Opequon	1754	1	179
Keywood, Moses	127	Wts. Opequon	1763	1	314
Keywood, Moses	300	Wts. Opequon	1766	2	571
Kinison—or Kenison, Kennison					
Kinison, Edward	400	Gr. Cacapon	1760	1	505
Kirkendahl, Benjamin	291	South Branch	1748	2	358
Kirkendahl, John	448	South Branch Potomac	1749	1	10
Lafferty, Judeah	72	Adj. T. Rutherford	1760	2	424
Lambert, Moses	291	Elk Creek	1755	1	201
Landon, Thomas	316	Back Creek	1752	1	74
Lanham—See Lonam					
Laramore, James	293	Back Creek	1789	2	313
Larew—Larue, Lerue, LeRue					
Lawson, Thomas	295	Tilhanzey's Branch	1766	2	540
Lee, Charles	1,109	Warm Springs Run	1810	2	349
Lee, Charles	1,614	Wts. Potomac	1810	2	351
Lee, Charles	1,045	Wts. Potomac	1810	2	353
Lerue—Larew, Larue, LeRue					
Lerue, Elizabeth (Lereu)	319	Long Marsh	1766	2	519
Lerue, Isaac	21	Long Marsh	1771	2	202
Lerue, Isaac	100	Sleepy Cr.	1771	2	216
Lerue, Isaac	396	Long Marsh	1761	1	556
Lerue, Isaac et al (Lereu)	416	Wts. Opequon	1766	2	520
Lewis, David	400	Wts. Opequon	1753	1	117
Lewis, David Jr.	164	Mill Creek	1764	2	457
Lewis, Fielding et al	260	Patterson Cr.	1754	1	165
Lewis, Fielding et al	300	Patterson Cr.	1754	1	187
Lewis, Fielding et al	350	Wts. South Br.	1754	1	188
Lewis, Henry	285	Mill Branch	1756	1	213
Lewis, John	400	Mill Creek	1764	2	451
Lilburn, Francis	397	Mill Creek	1756	1	237
Lilburn, Francis	490	Mill Creek	1763	1	370
Lindanwood, George	400	Mill Creek	1768	2	72

Name of Grantee	Acres	Local Description	Year	Book	Page
Smith, William	400	Sleepy Cr.	1760	1	516
Smith, William	400	Sleepy Creek	1766	2	541
Snoddy, William	258	Wts. Opequon	1768	2	126
Snodgrass, David & John	201	Tuscarorah Cr.	1766	2	561
Snodgrass, John	34	Wts. Opequon	1792	2	330
Snodgrass, John	142	Mill Creek	1760	1	503
Snodgrass, Robert & Joseph	250	Back Creek	1766	2	572
Speake, Thomas	309	Lit. Cacapon	1757	1	462
Speake, Thomas Capt.	485	Long Marsh	1770	2	196
Speer, Joseph S.	407	Back Creek	1792	2	333
Spitler, Jacob et al	390	Mill Run	1771	2	230
Springer, Dennis	353	Back Creek	1754	1	182
Springer, Dennis	291	Elk Lick Br.	1756	1	228
Stalnaker, Henry	215	Wts. Mill Cr.	1756	2	588
Stapleton, Charles	380	Mill Creek	1766	2	514
Stephen—See Stephens, Stevens					
Stephen, Adam	813	Wts. Opequon	1753	1	137
Stephen, Adam	386	Wts. Opequon	1765	2	492
Stephen, Alexander Capt.	398	Sleepy Creek	1767	2	42
Stephen, John	272	Pond Bottom	1770	2	198
Stephen, Lewis	799	Limestone Ridge	1752	1	70
Stephens, Dr. Adam	400	Opequon	1752	1	95
Stephens, Dr. Adam	332	Wts. Opequon	1752	1	96
Stephens, Lewis	437	Opequon	1752	1	59
Stephenson, Richard	180	Wts. Opequon	1762	1	571
Sterly, Jacob	504	Wts. Opequon	1763	1	342
Stertyanacre, Henry	215	Wts. Mill Creek	1756	2	588
Stevens—See Stephen, Stephens					
Stevens, Robert	164	Back Creek	1788	2	297
Stewart—See Stuart					
Stewart, Robert	353	Wts. Opequon	1760	1	511
Stockton, Robert	196	Wts. Opequon	1766	2	7
Strode, James	57	Wts. Potomac	1767	2	50
Strode, James	275	Wts. Opequon	1767	2	51
Strode, James	92	Wts. Potomac	1767	2	53
Strode, James	172	Wts. Opequon	1756	1	241
Strode, James	74	Wts. Opequon	1772	2	246
Strode, James	289	Wts. Opequon	1760	1	495
Stroud, Samuel	225	Wts. Opequon	1764	2	473
Stuart—See Stewart					
Stuart, William	147	Back Creek	1762	1	595
Sutton, Abraham	247	Back Creek	1766	2	538
Sutton, Abraham	79	Back Creek	1766	2	539
Swain—See Swame, Swim, Swym					
Swain, John	325	Adj. Gersham Keys	1751	2	446
Swame—See Swain, Swim, Swym					
Swame, Mathias	200	Sleepy Creek	1770	2	200
Swearingen—See Swerengen					
Swearingen, Thomas Capt.	155	Wts. Potomac	1752	1	94
Swearingen, Thomas Capt.	400	Wts. Potomac	1754	1	152
Swearingen, Thomas Capt.	189	Wts. Potomac	1756	1	245
Swearingen, Thomas Capt.	41	Opequon	1763	1	372
Swearingen, Thomas Capt.	324	Jone's Mill Run	1763	1	378
Swearingen, Van	321	Wts. Potomac	1760	1	483
Swearingen, Van	200	Wts. Potomac	1760	1	485
Swearingen, Van Capt.	384	Back Creek	1771	2	222
Swearingen, Van Capt.	234	Back Creek	1764	2	480
Swerengen, Capt. Thomas	478	Potomac River	1750	1	19
Swerengen, Capt. Thomas	97	Wts. Potomac	1765	2	494
Swim—See Swain, Swame, Swym					
Swim, Mathias	159	Sleepy Creek	1766	2	556
Swym—See Swain, Swame, Swim					
Swym, Mathias Jr.	315	Sleepy Creek	1789	2	314
Talbot, Thomas	400	Buffalo Lick Run	1773	2	256

Name of Grantee	Acres	Local Description	Year	Book	Page
Watkins, Evan	Lots 5,6,11,12	Maidstone	1770	2	164
Watson, John	371	Mill Creek	1765	2	493
Watson, Jos. et al Ex.	175	Vanmeter's Run	1796	2	347
Watson, Joseph et al Ex.	100	Vanmeter's Run	1796	2	356
Weisenberger, George	356	Sleepy Creek	1794	2	343
Wells, Tunis	318	Wts. Potomac	1770	2	168
Welton, William	354	Gr. Cacapon	1751	1	27
West, Stephen	413	Wts.Opequon	1764	2	454
West, Stephen	479	Vanmeter's Marsh	1764	2	455
Wharton, Joseph Jr.	4,400	Timber Ridge	1772	2	252
Wharton, Thomas & Joseph	400	Back Creek	1768	2	94
Wharton, Thomas & Joseph	400	Wts. Potomac	1768	2	98
White, David	276	Sleepy Creek	1792	2	334
White, David	200	Sleepy Creek	1793	2	335
White, David	400	Sleepy Creek	1766	2	576
Wilcox, Robert & S. et al Hrs.	267	Lick Run	1791	2	324
Wilkinson, Joseph	400	Back Creek	1763	1	350
Williams, John	270	Wts. Potomac	1760	1	513
Williams, Vinson	400	Patterson's Cr.	1754	1	153
Williams, William	121	Wts. Potomac	1760	1	514
Williams, William	181	Wts. Potomac	1760	1	525
Wilson, John et al	586	Wts. Opequon	1756	1	231
Wilson, Robert	316	Opequon	1754	1	162
Wilson, Thomas	273 (223)	Wts. Opequon	1754	1	183
Wodrow—See Woodrow					
Wolf, Lewis	344	Wts. Opequon	1775	2	276
Wood, Richard	204½	Back Creek	1788	2	300
Woodfin, John	400	Cacapon	1749	1	8
Woodfin, John	316	Wts. Cacapon	1756	1	225
Woodrow, Alexander et al	221	Back Creek	1766	2	10
Wright, James	270	Middle Creek	1762	1	568
Wright, James Sr.	308	Middle Creek	1756	1	221
Wright, John	90	Wts. Potomac	1756	1	229
Wright, John	398	Wts. Potomac	1760	1	512
Wright, John (Right)	231	Adj. D. Osborne	1754	2	390
Wright, William	200	Wts. Potomac	1754	2	382
Wyatt, Thomas	237	Wts. Opequon	1760	1	467
York, Jeremiah	323	Wts. Opequon	1751	1	35
Zane, Isaac Jr.	1,455	Back Creek	1770	2	158

MONTGOMERY COUNTY, VIRGINIA

Adger—See Edgar					
Adger, Thomas	600	Teas Valley	1789	1	376
Adger, Thomas	800	Wts. Hurricane	1789	1	377
Anteny, William	750	Poplar Camp	1791	1	388
Anthony—See Anteny					
Austin, William	2,000	Pipestem Knob	1798	1	526
Austin, William	500	Wts. Mud	1798	1	527
Austin, William	3,080	16-Mile Cr.	1798	1	528
Austin, William	2,000	Gr. Kanawha near Poca	1798	1	529
Austin, William	1,000	Adj. Fry	1798	1	530
Austin, William	2,000	Wts. Guyandotte	1798	1	531
Austin, William	3,210	Wts. Cole	1798	1	532
Austin, William	1,300	Wts. Cole	1798	1	533
Austin, William	3,062¼	Loop Creek	1798	1	591

Name of Grantee	Acres	Local Description	Year	Book	Page
Breckenridge, John et al	904	Guyandotte	1792	1	422
Breckenridge, John et al	340	Guyandotte	1792	1	431
Breckenridge, John et al	970	Lit. Sandy Cr.	1792	1	432
Breckinridge, John	300	Mth. of Mill Cr.	1785	1	7
Byrnsides, James	470	Wts. Cole	1793	1	440
Cains—See Carnes					
Cains, Michael	627	16-Mi. Cr.	1787	1	324
Cains, Michael	475	16-Mile Cr.	1787	1	325
Calloway, John	2,000	Cole River	1789	1	369
Calloway, John	2,000	Wts. Cole	1789	1	371
Carnahan, James	30,000	S. S. Mud	1786	1	280
Carnahan, James (Carnaghan)	30,000	Mud River	1786	1	284
Carnahan, James	2,430	Mud River	1787	1	326
Carnes—See Cains					
Carnes, Michael	708	16-Mile Cr.	1787	1	309
Carnes, Michael	443	16-Mile Cr.	1787	1	310
Carnes, Michael	747	16-Mile Cr.	1788	1	363
Carrington, J. & M. et al (In Trust)	40,000	Mud River	1789	1	368
Carrington, Joseph and Mayo	10,000	Wts. Mud	1789	1	367
Carter, George	400	So. Side New River	1785	1	603
Chapman, Isaac	212	Wts. Cole	1793	1	423
Chapman, Isaac	230	Sycamore Creek	1793	1	424
Chenith—or Chenowith, Chenwith					
Chenith, John	1,000	12-Pole	1786	1	289
Chenowith—See Chenith, Chenwith					
Chenwith—or Chenith, Chenowith					
Chenwith, Thomas	1,000	12-Pole	1786	1	288
Childress, Joseph et al	400	Wts. Mud	1792	1	399
Christian, William et al	930	Paint Cr.	1793	1	456
Clark, Jonah et al Assignees	99,666 2/3	Wts. Guyandotte	1796	1	522
Clinton, Dewit	130,000	Coal R. & Paint Cr.	1796	1	561
Clinton, Dewit	142,000	Huff & Buffalo Crs.	1796	1	564
Cochran, Robert et al	3,000	16 Mi. Below Mth. G. K.	1788	1	358
Crawford, Edward	2,670	Wts. Lit. Guyandotte	1787	1	327
Dillon, Edward	50,096	Clear Fk. & Huff Cr.	1796	1	568
Donnally, Andrew	400	1 Mi. below Cabin Cr.	1792	1	414
Donnally, Andrew	500	Cabin Creek	1792	1	415
Donnally, Andrew et al	75	Gr. K. at Falls	1792	1	417
Doren, John	136	Cole River	1793	1	453
Doren, John	182	Cole River	1793	1	454
Duvall, John P.	5,000	Wts. Cole	1793	1	436
Duvall, John P.	4,220	Guyand. abv. 2nd Falls	1793	1	437
Duvall, John P.	633¾	12-Pole	1793	1	438
Duvall, John P.	900	Cole River	1793	1	439
Duvall, John P.	780¾	Wts. Guyandotte	1793	1	448
Duvall, John P.	2,000	12-Pole Creek	1793	1	449
Duvall, John P.	1,000	Wts. Mud	1793	1	450
Duvall, John P.	1,000	12-Pole	1793	1	451
Duvall, John P.	1,000	Adj. his own	1793	1	452
Duvall, John P.	5,275	12-Pole	1793	1	553
Duvall, William	1,196	Peter Huff's Cr.	1789	1	372
Duvall, William	7,400	Wts. Cole	1792	1	416
Duvall, William et al	20,000	Wts. Mud	1787	1	340
Dwight, Jonathan et al	99,666 2/3	Wts. Guyandotte	1796	1	522
Edgar, See Adger					
Edgar, Thomas	9,730	Pack's Gap	1797	1	574
Elcan, Marcus	1,785	So. Fk. Cole	1789	1	374
Elcan, Marcus	1,240	So. Fk. Cole	1789	1	375
Ely, William (Att'y-in-Fact) et al	99,666 2/3	Wts. Guyandotte	1796	1	522
Finley, John et al	1,999a.3r.23p.	5 Mi. below Mth. Gr. K.	1786	1	278
French, Samuel	496	Poplar Camp Cr.	1791	1	390

Name of Grantee	Acres	Local Description	Year	Book	Page
Glentworth, James	1,000	Wts. Guyandotte	1786	1	201
Goodson, Thomas	300	Wts. Guyandotte	1785	1	8
Goodson, Thomas	2,123	Wts. Guyandotte	1790	1	385
Goodson, William	100	Mth. Guyandotte	1795	1	484
Graham, John	23,800	Above Mth. G. K.	1796	1	519
Grainger, Gideon et al	99,666 2/3	Wts. Guyandotte	1796	1	522
Gratz, Bernard & Michael	1,000	Wts. Guyandotte	1786	1	153
Gratz, Bernard & Michael	1,000	Wts. Guyandotte	1786	1	154
Gratz, Bernard & Michael	1,000	Wts. Guyandotte	1786	1	155
Gratz, Bernard & Michael	1,000	Adj. their No. 70	1785	1	156
Gratz, Bernard & Michael	1,000	Wts. Guyandotte	1786	1	157
Gratz, Bernard & Michael	1,000	Wts. Guyandotte	1786	1	158
Gratz, Bernard & Michael	1,000	Wts. Guyandotte	1786	1	163
Gratz, Bernard & Michael	1,000	Wts. Guyandotte	1785	1	164
Gratz, Bernard & Michael	1,000	Wts. Guyandotte	1786	1	165
Gratz, Bernard & Michael	1,000	Wts. Guyandotte	1786	1	166
Gratz, Bernard & Michael	1,000	Wts. Guyandotte	1786	1	167
Gratz, Bernard & Michael	1,000	Wts. Guyandotte	1786	1	168
Gratz, Bernard & Michael	1,000	Wts. Guyandotte	1786	1	169
Gratz, Bernard & Michael	1,000	Wts. Guyandotte	1786	1	170
Gratz, Bernard & Michael	1,000	Wts. Guyandotte	1786	1	181
Gratz, Bernard & Michael	1,000	Wts. Guyandotte	1786	1	182
Gratz, Bernard & Michael	1,000	Wts. Guyandotte	1786	1	184
Gratz, Bernard & Michael	1,000	Wts. Guyandotte	1786	1	185
Gratz, Bernard & Michael	1,000	Wts. Guyandotte	1786	1	186
Gratz, Bernard & Michael	1,000	Wts. Guyandotte	1786	1	187
Gratz, Bernard & Michael	1,000	Wts. Guyandotte	1786	1	188
Gratz, Bernard & Michael	1,000	Wts. Guyandotte	1786	1	189
Gratz, Bernard & Michael	1,000	Wts. Guyandotte	1786	1	190
Gratz, Bernard & Michael	1,000	Wts. Guyandotte	1786	1	194
Gratz, Bernard & Michael	1,000	Wts. Guyandotte	1786	1	195
Gratz, Bernard & Michael	1,000	Guyandotte	1786	1	215
Gratz, Bernard & Michael	1,000	Guyandotte	1786	1	216
Gratz, Bernard & Michael	1,000	Guyandotte	1786	1	220
Gratz, Bernard & Michael et al	1,000	Wts. Guyandotte	1787	1	311
Gratz, Bernard & Michael et al	1,000	Wts. Guyandotte	1787	1	331
Gratz, Michael	1,000	Wts. Guyandotte	1786	1	159
Gratz, Michael	1,000	Wts. Guyandotte	1786	1	196
Gratz, Michael	1,000	Wts. Guyandotte	1786	1	197
Gratz, Michael	1,000	Wts. Guyandotte	1786	1	198
Gratz, Michael	1,000	Wts. Guyandotte	1786	1	199
Gratz, Michael	1,000	Guyandotte	1786	1	221
Gratz, Michael	1,000	Guyandotte	1786	1	222
Gratz, Michael	1,000	Guyandotte	1786	1	223
Gratz, Michael & Bernard	1,000	Wts. Guyandotte	1786	1	183
Gratz, Michael & Bernard	1,000	Guyandotte	1786	1	217
Gratz, Michael & Bernard	1,000	Guyandotte	1786	1	218
Gratz, Michael & Bernard	1,000	Guyandotte	1786	1	219
Gratz, Michael et al	4,500	7 mi. below Mth Gr. K.	1787	1	230
Gratz, Michael et al	2,000	7 Mi. Below Mth. Gr. K.	1787	1	293
Gratz, Michael et al	4,500	7 Mi. Below Mth. Gr. K.	1787	1	294
Gratz, Michael et al	14,000	7 Mi. Below Mth. Gr. K.	1787	1	295
Gratz, Michael et al	3,248¾	7 Mi. Below Mth. Gr. K.	1787	1	296
Gratz, Michael et al	3,248¾	7 Mi. Below Mth. Gr. K.	1787	1	298
Gratz, Michael et al	3,248¾	7 Mi. Below Mth. Gr. K.	1787	1	299
Gratz, Michael et al	3,248¾	7 Mi. Below Mth. Gr. K.	1787	1	313
Gratz, William et al	2,000	7 Mi. Below Mth. Gr. K.	1787	1	297
Graves, Francis	3,962	Buffalo Cr.	1795	1	498
Greenaugh, William	1,999¾a.32p.	1st Cr. Below Mth. Gr. K.	1786	1	202
Hannah, Nicholas	960	Piney River	1788	1	356
Hannah, Nicholas	920	Piney River	1788	1	357
Hannan, Easem	1,700	Wts. Guyandotte	1795	1	483
Hannan, Thomas (Hannon)	1,000	Wts. Guyandotte	1796	1	520

Name of Grantee	Acres	Local Description	Year	Book	Page
O'Mealy, Michael	12,870	Wts. Cole	1792	1	407
O'Mealy, Michael	22,780	Cole River and Paint Cr.	1792	1	408
O'Mealy, Michael	2,711	Paint Cr.	1792	1	409
O'Mealy, Michael	1,727	Piney River	1792	1	410
O'Mealy, Michael	2,514	Paint Cr.	1792	1	411
O'Mealy, Michael	2,332	Paint Cr.	1792	1	412
Parberry, James	2,000	S. S. Guyandotte	1786	1	279
Parberry, James	1,000	Wts. Cole	1787	1	332
Pearis, George et al	930	Paint Cr.	1793	1	456
Pentecost, Dorsey et al	1,000	Wts. Sandy	1785	1	9
Pentecost, Dorsey et al	1,000	Wts. Guyandotte	1785	1	10
Pentecost, Dorsey et al	1,000	Wts. Guyandotte	1785	1	11
Pentecost, Dorsey et al	1,000	Wts. Guyandotte	1785	1	12
Pentecost, Dorsey et al	1,000	Wts. Guyandotte	1785	1	13
Pentecost, Dorsey et al	1,000	Wts. Guyandotte	1785	1	14
Pentecost, Dorsey et al	1,000	Wts. Guyandotte	1785	1	15
Pentecost, Dorsey et al	750	Sandy Creek	1785	1	16
Pentecost, Dorsey et al	1,000	Wts. Guyandotte	1785	1	17
Pentecost, Dorsey et al	1,000	Wts. Guyandotte	1785	1	18
Pentecost, Dorsey et al	1,000	Wts. Guyandotte	1785	1	19
Pentecost, Dorsey et al	1,000	Wts. Guyandotte	1785	1	20
Pentecost, Dorsey et al	1,000	Wts. Guyandotte	1785	1	21
Pentecost, Dorsey et al	1,000	Wts. Guyandotte	1785	1	22
Pentecost, Dorsey et al	1,000	Wts. Guyandotte	1785	1	23
Pentecost, Dorsey et al	1,000	Sandy Cr.	1785	1	24
Pentecost, Dorsey et al	1,000	Sandy Cr.	1785	1	25
Pentecost, Dorsey et al	1,000	Wts. Guyandotte	1785	1	26
Pentecost, Dorsey et al	1,000	Wts. Sandy	1785	1	27
Pentecost, Dorsey et al	1,000	Wts. Guyandotte	1785	1	28
Pentecost, Dorsey et al	1,000	Wts. Guyandotte	1785	1	29
Pentecost, Dorsey et al	1,000	Wts. Guyandotte	1785	1	30
Pentecost, Dorsey et al	1,000	Wts. Guyandotte	1785	1	31
Pentecost, Dorsey et al	1,000	Wts. Guyandotte	1785	1	32
Pentecost, Dorsey et al	1,000	Wts. Guyandotte	1785	1	33
Pentecost, Dorsey et al	1,000	Wts. Guyandotte	1785	1	34
Pentecost, Dorsey et al	1,000	Wts. Guyandotte	1785	1	35
Pentecost, Dorsey et al	1,000	Wts. Guyandotte	1785	1	36
Pentecost, Dorsey et al	1,000	Wts. Guyandotte	1785	1	37
Pentecost, Dorsey et al	1,000	Wts. Guyandotte	1785	1	38
Pentecost, Dorsey et al	1,000	Wts. Guyandotte	1785	1	39
Pentecost, Dorsey et al	1,000	Wts. Guyandotte	1785	1	40
Pentecost, Dorsey et al	1,000	Wts. Guyandotte	1785	1	41
Pentecost, Dorsey et al	1,000	Wts. Guyandotte	1785	1	42
Pentecost, Dorsey et al	1,000	Wts. Guyandotte	1785	1	43
Pentecost, Dorsey et al	1,000	Wts. Guyandotte	1785	1	44
Pentecost, Dorsey et al	1,000	Wts. Guyandotte	1785	1	45
Pentecost, Dorsey et al	1,000	Wts. Guyandotte	1785	1	46
Pentecost, Dorsey et al	1,000	Wts. Guyandotte	1785	1	47
Pentecost, Dorsey et al	1,000	Wts. Guyandotte	1785	1	48
Pentecost, Dorsey et al	1,000	Wts. Guyandotte	1785	1	49
Pentecost, Dorsey et al	1,000	Wts. Guyandotte	1785	1	50
Pentecost, Dorsey et al	1,000	Wts. Guyandotte	1785	1	51
Pentecost, Dorsey et al	1,000	Wts. Guyandotte	1785	1	52
Pentecost, Dorsey et al	1,000	Wts. Guyandotte	1785	1	53
Pentecost, Dorsey et al	1,000	Wts. Guyandotte	1785	1	54
Pentecost, Dorsey et al	1,000	Wts. Guyandotte	1785	1	55
Pentecost, Dorsey et al	1,000	Wts. Guyandotte	1785	1	56
Pentecost, Dorsey et al	1,000	Wts. Guyandotte	1785	1	57
Pentecost, Dorsey et al	1,000	Wts. Guyandotte	1785	1	58
Pentecost, Dorsey et al	1,000	Wts. Sandy Cr.	1785	1	59
Pentecost, Dorsey et al	1,000	Sandy Cr.	1785	1	60
Pentecost, Dorsey et al	1,000	Sandy Cr.	1785	1	61
Pentecost, Dorsey et al	1,000	Wts. Sandy	1785	1	62

Name of Grantee	Acres	Local Description	Year	Book	Page
Pentecost, Dorsey et al	1,000	Wts. Sandy	1785	1	63
Pentecost, Dorsey et al	1,000	Wts. Sandy	1785	1	64
Pentecost, Dorsey et al	1,000	Wts. Sandy	1785	1	65
Pentecost, Dorsey et al	1,000	Wts. Sandy	1785	1	66
Pentecost, Dorsey et al	1,000	Wts. Sandy	1785	1	67
Pentecost, Dorsey et al	1,000	Wts. Sandy	1785	1	68
Pentecost, Dorsey et al	1,000	Wts. Sandy	1785	1	69
Pentecost, Dorsey et al	1,000	Wts. Sandy	1785	1	70
Pentecost, Dorsey et al	1,000	Wts. Sandy	1785	1	71
Pentecost, Dorsey et al	1,000	Wts. Sandy	1785	1	72
Pentecost, Dorsey et al	1,000	Wts. Sandy	1785	1	73
Pentecost, Dorsey et al	1,000	Adj. Their No. 206	1785	1	74
Pentecost, Dorsey et al	1,000	Wts. Sandy	1785	1	75
Pentecost, Dorsey et al	1,000	Wts. Sandy	1785	1	76
Pentecost, Dorsey et al	1,000	Wts. Sandy	1785	1	77
Pentecost, Dorsey et al	1,000	Wts. Sandy	1785	1	78
Pentecost, Dorsey et al	1,000	Wts. Sandy	1785	1	79
Pentecost, Dorsey et al	1,000	Wts. Sandy	1785	1	80
Pentecost, Dorsey et al	1,000	Wts. Sandy	1785	1	81
Pentecost, Dorsey et al	1,000	Wts. Sandy	1785	1	82
Pentecost, Dorsey et al	1,000	Wts. Sandy	1785	1	83
Pentecost, Dorsey et al	1,000	Wts. Sandy	1785	1	84
Pentecost, Dorsey et al	1,000	Wts. Sandy	1785	1	85
Pentecost, Dorsey et al	1,000	Wts. Sandy	1785	1	86
Pentecost, Dorsey et al	1,000	Wts. Sandy	1785	1	87
Pentecost, Dorsey et al	1,000	Wts. Sandy	1785	1	88
Pentecost, Dorsey et al	1,000	Wts. Sandy	1785	1	89
Pentecost, Dorsey et al	1,000	Wts. Sandy	1785	1	90
Pentecost, Dorsey et al	1,000	Wts. Guyandotte	1785	1	91
Pentecost, Dorsey et al	1,000	Wts. Guyandotte	1785	1	92
Pentecost, Dorsey et al	1,000	Wts. Sandy	1785	1	93
Pentecost, Dorsey et al	1,000	Wts. Sandy	1785	1	94
Pentecost, Dorsey et al	1,000	Wts. Sandy	1785	1	95
Pentecost, Dorsey et al	1,000	Wts. Sandy	1785	1	96
Pentecost, Dorsey et al	1,000	Wts. Guyandotte	1785	1	97
Pentecost, Dorsey et al	1,000	Wts. Sandy	1785	1	98
Pentecost, Dorsey et al	1,000	Wts. Sandy	1785	1	99
Pentecost, Dorsey et al	1,000	Wts. Sandy	1785	1	100
Pentecost, Dorsey et al	1,000	Wts. Sandy	1785	1	101
Pentecost, Dorsey et al	1,000	Wts. Sandy	1785	1	102
Pentecost, Dorsey et al	1,000	Wts. Guyandotte	1785	1	103
Pentecost, Dorsey et al	1,000	Wts. Sandy	1785	1	104
Pentecost, Dorsey et al	1,000	Wts. Sandy	1785	1	105
Pentecost, Dorsey et al	1,000	Wts. Sandy	1785	1	106
Pentecost, Dorsey et al	1,000	Wts. Sandy	1785	1	107
Pentecost, Dorsey et al	1,000	Wts. Sandy	1785	1	108
Pentecost, Dorsey et al	1,000	Wts. Sandy	1785	1	109
Pentecost, Dorsey et al	1,000	Wts. Sandy	1785	1	110
Pentecost, Dorsey et al	1,000	Wts. Sandy	1785	1	111
Pentecost, Dorsey et al	1,000	Wts. Sandy	1785	1	112
Pentecost, Dorsey et al	1,000	Wts. Sandy	1785	1	113
Pentecost, Dorsey et al	1,000	Wts. Sandy	1785	1	114
Pentecost, Dorsey et al	1,000	Wts. Sandy	1785	1	115
Pentecost, Dorsey et al	1,000	Wts. Guyandotte	1785	1	116
Pentecost, Dorsey et al	1,000	Wts. Guyandotte	1785	1	117
Pentecost, Dorsey et al	1,000	Wts. Guyandotte	1785	1	118
Pentecost, Dorsey et al	1,000	Wts. Guyandotte	1785	1	119
Pentecost, Dorsey et al	1,000	Wts. Guyandotte	1785	1	120
Pentecost, Dorsey et al	1,000	Guyandotte Creek	1785	1	121
Pentecost, Dorsey et al	1,000	Sandy Creek	1785	1	122
Pentecost, Dorsey et al	1,000	Guyandotte	1785	1	123
Pentecost, Dorsey et al	1,000	Sandy	1785	1	124
Pentecost, Dorsey et al	1,000	Guyandotte	1785	1	125

Name of Grantee	Acres	Local Description	Year	Book	Page
Preston, John et al	2,000	Wts. Cole	1793	1	425
Preston, John et al	970	Lit. Sandy	1792	1	432
Preston, John & Francis	2,500	Wts. Cole	1787	1	330
Prior, William Sr.	263	Kelly's Place	1788	1	355
Quarrier, Alexander	891	Paint Cr.	1789	1	370
Reid, Andrew	36,356½	Paint Creek	1797	1	577
Reid, Andrew et al	50,000	Loop, Pipe & Arbuckles Cr.	1796	1	566
Reynolds, Richard	920	Wts. Guyandotte	1785	1	191
Richardson, George	1,000	Wts. Guyandotte	1786	1	192
Richardson, George	1,000	Breckenridge's Cr.	1786	1	193
Ross, David et al	20,000	Wts. Mud	1787	1	340
Rutherford, Robert	600	Opposite Pt. Pleasant	1793	1	442
Rutland, Thomas	500	Wts. Cole	1788	1	359
See, Michael	400	Campbell's Bottom	1789	1	380
Semple, William	4,000	Mth. Gr. Kanawha	1786	1	263
Semple, William	8,000	2nd Cr. below Mth. Gr. K.	1786	1	273
Semple, William	2,456	Mth. Gr. K.	1786	1	274
Semple, William	1,888	Mth. Gr. K.	1786	1	275
Semple, William	1,840	Mth. Gr. K.	1786	1	276
Semple, William	3,815¼	Mth. Gr. K.	1786	1	277
Semple, William et al	4,000	Mth. Gr. K.	1786	1	200
Semple, William et al	4,000	Mth. Gr. K.	1786	1	229
Semple, William et al	5,499¾	Mth. G. K.	1786	1	264
Semple, William et al	5,499¾	Mth. Gr. K.	1786	1	265
Semple, William et al	6,998¼	Mth. Gr. K.	1786	1	266
Semple, William et al	5,499a.3r.39p.	Mth. Gr. K.	1786	1	267
Semple, William et al	6,998a.1r.21p.	Mth. Gr. K.	1786	1	268
Semple, William et al	6,998¼a.1r.21p.	Mth. Gr. K.	1786	1	269
Semple, William et al	6,998¼a.1r.21p.	Mth. Gr. K.	1786	1	270
Semple, William et al	5,499¾	Mth. Gr. K.	1786	1	271
Semple, William et al	10,000	Mth. Gr. K.	1786	1	272
Shelton, Abraham	712	Poplar Camp Cr.	1792	1	404
Singer, Casper et al	3,000	16 Mi. below Mth. Gr. K.	1788	1	358
Smith, Philip	877	15 Mi. above Mth. Guyandotte	1795	1	513
Smyth, Richard	21,500	Point Pleasant	1794	1	458
Stewart—or Stuart					
Stewart, Arthur	1,229	Piney River	1792	1	401
Stewart, John et al	50,000	Loop & Pipe Cr.	1796	1	566
Stras, George Frederick	1,280	Piney River	1794	1	455
Stuart—or Stewart					
Stuart, John	331	Little Falls, Kanawha	1796	1	523
Swiger, Casper et al	3,000	16 Mi. below Mth. Gr. K.	1788	1	358
Taylor, Thomas A.	2,200	Paint Creek	1786	1	281
Taylor, Thomas A.	1,000	Cabin Creek	1786	1	285
Taylor, Thomas A.	1,000	Cabin Creek	1786	1	286
Taylor, Thomas Augustus	1,000	Cabin Creek	1786	1	287
Taylor, Thomas Augustus	1,000	Cabin Creek	1786	1	290
Taylor, Thomas Augustus	1,000	Cabin Creek	1786	1	291
Taylor, Thomas Augustus	1,000	Cabin Creek	1786	1	292
Taylor, William T.	3,000	2nd Cr. below Mth. G. K.	1793	1	443
Taylor, William T.	6,000	2nd Cr. below Mth. G. K.	1793	1	444
Toney, John	344	Cole River	1794	1	457
Turner, Francis	700	Horse Creek	1793	1	441
Upton, Thomas	1,400	Wts. Cole	1787	1	333
Upton, Thomas	3,400	Mth. Davis Cr. on G. K.	1787	1	337
Ward, John	3,744	Cole River	1789	1	373
Ward, William et al	190	Wts. Guyandotte	1792	1	419
Ward, William et al	1,000	Wts. Guyandotte	1792	1	420
Ward, William et al	310	Huff's Cr.	1792	1	421
Ward, William et al	904	Guyandotte	1792	1	422
Ward, William et al	340	Guyandotte	1792	1	431
Welch, James	90,000	Big & Lit. Laurel	1797	1	572

Name of Grantee	Acres	Local Description	Year	Book	Page
Welch, James	17,000	Wts. New River	1797	1	575
Welch, John et al	1,999a.3r.23p.	5 mi. below Mth. G. K.	1786	1	278
Whetcraft—or Whetcroft, Whitcraft, Whitcroft					
Whetcroft, William	976	Cole River	1797	1	524
Whetcroft, William	1,000	Cole River	1797	1	525
Whetcroft, William	2,460	Cole River	1797	1	534
Whetcroft, William	3,460	Cole River	1797	1	535
Whetcroft, William	2,355	Cole River	1797	1	536
Whetcroft, William	2,550	Cole River	1797	1	537
Whetcroft, William	1,675	Cole River	1797	1	538
Whetcroft, William	1,225	Cole River	1797	1	539
Whetcroft, William	1,290	Cole River	1797	1	540
Whetcroft, William	1,120	Cole River	1797	1	541
Whetcroft, William	937	Cole River	1797	1	542
Whetcroft, William	1,100	Cole River	1797	1	543
Whetcroft, William	1,200	Cole River	1797	1	544
Whetcroft, William	(1,285) 1,258	Cole River	1797	1	545
Whetcroft, William	850	Cole River	1797	1	546
Whetcroft, William	1,055	Cole River	1797	1	547
Whetcroft, William	1,055	Cole River	7797	1	548
Whetcroft, William	1,150	Cole River	1797	1	549
Whetcroft, William	3,390	Cole River	1797	1	551
Whetcroft, William	2,790	Cole River	1797	1	552
Whetcroft, William	720	Cole River	1797	1	579
Whetcroft, William	1,333	Cole River	1797	1	580
Whetcroft, William	1,050	Cole River	1797	1	581
Whetcroft, William	295	Cole River	1797	1	582
Whetcroft, William	4,125	Cole River	1797	1	583
Whetcroft, William	4,600	Cole River	1797	1	584
Whetcroft, William	2,530	Guyandotte	1797	1	585
Whetcroft, William	2,530	Guyandotte	1797	1	586
Whetcroft, William	2,530	Guyandotte	1797	1	587
Whetcroft, William	2,530	Guyandotte	1797	1	588
Whetcroft, William	4,400	Wts. Guyandotte	1797	1	589
Whetcroft, William	12,114	Cole River	1797	1	590
Whitcraft—or Whetcraft, Whetcroft, Whitcroft					
Whitcroft—or Whetcraft					
Whitcroft, William	1,000	Wts. Cole	1788	1	360
Whitcroft, William	1,300	Paint Creek	1788	1	361
Whitcroft, William	2,890	Cole River	1797	1	550
Williams, Elisha et al	25,000	Wts. Guyandotte	1796	1	522
Williams, Elisha et al	99,666 2/3	Wts. Guyandotte	1796	1	522
Willing, Charles et al	4,500	7 mi. below Mth. G. K.	1787	1	230
Willing, Charles et al	2,000	7 mi. below Mth. G. K.	1787	1	293
Willing, Charles et al	4,500	7 mi. below Mth. G. K.	1787	1	294
Willing, Charles et al	14,000	7 mi. below Mth. G. K.	1797	1	295
Willing, Charles et al	3,248¾	7 Mi. below Mth. Gr. K.	1787	1	296
Willing, Charles et al	2,000	7 Mi. below Mth. Gr. K.	1787	1	297
Willing, Charles et al	3,248¾	7 Mi. below Mth. Gr. K.	1787	1	298
Willing, Charles et al	3,248¾	7 Mi. below Mth. Gr. K.	1787	1	299
Willing, Charles et al	1,000	Wts. Guyandotte	1787	1	311
Willing, Charles et al	3,248¾	7 Mi. below Mth. Gr. K.	1787	1	313
Willing, Charles et al	1,000	Wts. Guyandotte	1787	1	331
Wilson, James	12trs.1,000ea.	Guyandotte	1786	1	203-214
Wilson, James	5trs.1,000ea.	Guyandotte	1786	1	224-228
Wilson, James	31trs.1,000ea.	Guyandotte	1786	1	232-262
Wilson, James et al	1,000	Wts. Guyandotte	1787	1	311
Wilson, James et al	1,000	Wts. Guyandotte	1787	1	331
Wilson, John	25,000	Wts. Mud	1787	1	341
Woodson, Hughes	857	Sun Fish Cr.	1791	1	387
Wynkoop, Benjamin	25,000	Mud River	1787	1	336
Yancey, Tyree	500	Glade Cr.	1788	1	362

RUSSELL COUNTY, VIRGINIA

Name of Grantee	Acres	Local Description	Year	Book	Page
Banks, Henry et al	200,000	Wts. Great Sandy River	1795	1	216
Henry, John et al	150,000	Wts. Great Sandy River	1796	1	217
Morris, Robert	500,000	Wts. Sandy & Guyand	1795	1	199
Morris, Robert	320,000	Sandy Cr.	1795	1	196
Nicholas, Wilson C.	300,000	Sandy Cr. at Roark's Gap	1795	1	201
Nicholas, Wilson C.	300,000	Sandy Cr. at Roark's Gap	1795	1	215
Nicholas, Wilson C. Assn., et al	320,000	Sandy Cr.	1795	1	196
Smyth, Alexander et al	150,000	Wts. Gr. Sandy River	1796	1	217
Smyth, Richard et al	200,000	Wts. Gr. Sandy River	1795	1	216
Swan, James	22,788¼	Clinch & Sandy	1796	1	218
Wolcott—or Walcott					
Wolcott, Alexander	100,000	Wts. Sandy River	1797	1	219
Wolcott, Alexander	350,000	Wts. Gr. Sandy	1797	1	220

TAZEWELL COUNTY, VIRGINIA

Adare—or Odar, O'Dair					
Adare, John	24	Panther Fork	1845	1	245
Adare, William	9	Slate Creek	1845	1	244
Adkins, Isaac	158	Clear Fork	1822	1	90
Adkins, Isaac et al	150	Clear Fork	1804	1	7
Aldridge, James	50	Sand Lick	1854	2	265
Aldridge, James Jr.	121	Brush Top Ridge	1850	2	45
Allen, Robert et al	35	Big Creek	1832	1	128
Altizer, John	159	Back Fork	1850	2	20
Altizer, John	80	Beech Fork	1853	2	193
Altizer, Riley	180	Beech Fork	1853	2	191
Altizer, William	66	Grassy Spring Ridge	1853	2	192
Altizer, William	46	Little Fork Ridge	1846	1	254
Armes—See Arnes					
Armes, Theophilus (Arnes)	64	Dividing Ridge	1850	1	371
Arnes—See Armes					
Arnes, Theophilus (Armes)	170	Laurel Cr.	1849	1	361
Asbery, Smith (Asberry)	125	Indian Creek	1853	2	196
Asbury, William B.	217	Rocky Ridge	1856	2	502
Austin, Samuel W. et al	1,200	Clay & Flat Top Mt.	1860	1	416
Badeau, W. C. et al	2,500	Mill & Sugar Crs.	1858	2	528
Bailey—See Baly					
Bailey, Archibald	24	Bluestone River	1809	1	35
Bailey, George	50	Wts. Bluestone	1820	1	54
Bailey, Gorden	15	Trace Fork	1853	2	210
Bailey, Gorden	20	Tug River	1853	2	215
Bailey, Gordon	23	Lick Branch	1860	1	408
Bailey, Harvey	22	Long Branch	1848	1	323
Bailey, Harvey	50	Long Branch	1848	1	324
Bailey, Harvey et al	100	Wts. Tug	1848	1	320
Bailey, Henry	75	Wts. Bluestone	1820	1	52
Bailey, Henry	150	East River	1820	1	53
Bailey, James	35	Wts. Guyandotte	1821	1	59
Bailey, James	17	Wts. Guyandotte	1822	1	85
Bailey, John	200	Mill Ridge	1810	1	36
Bailey, John	100	Wts. Brush Cr.	1820	1	57
Bailey, Richard	200	Lorton's Lick Br.	1812	1	41
Bailey, Richard	33	Bluestone	1822	1	88

Name of Grantee	Acres	Local Description	Year	Book	Page
Bailey, Samuel	25	Wts. Bluestone	1822	1	87
Bailey, Samuel	49	Bluestone	1822	1	89
Bailey, Z.	100	Chestnut Fork	1855	2	321
Baker, Henry	50	Slate Creek	1853	2	207
Baly—or Bailey					
Baly, James	100	Bluestone River	1804	1	13
Baly, Richard	50	Bluestone River	1803	1	3
Baly, Richard	36	Bluestone River	1803	1	4
Bandy—or Baudy					
Bandy, James	68	Broad & Brushy Spur	1858	2	423
Bandy, James	54	Wts. Sandy	1879	2	444
Bandy, William	92	Little Brushy Ridge	1853	2	204
Bandy, William W.	29	Brushy Fork	1856	2	340
Bandy, William W.	140	Beech Fork	1855	2	344
Barnett, Archibald	240	Thomas White Br.	1853	2	176
Barnett, Archible (Barnet)	170	Dry Fork	1836	1	153
Barnett, Archible	25	Dry Fork	1830	1	123
Barnett, Archible	55	Dry Fork	1830	1	125
Barnett, Archible	82	Dry Fork	1835	1	136
Barnett, James (of Arch)	88	Dry Fork	1856	2	360
Barnett, James	47	Sandy	1825	1	110
Barnett, Joseph	43	Baptist Valley	1854	2	224
Barrett, Robert	388	Vol's Creek	1851	2	80
Barrett, Robert	(100)1,000	Wts. Dry Fork	1850	1	380
Baudy—or Bandy					
Baudy, William	92	Little Brushy Ridge	1853	2	204
Beavers—See Bevers					
Beavers, Alexander	10	Dry Fork	1836	1	158
Beavers, Alexander	50	Dry Fork	1836	1	159
Beavers, Alexander	28	Reedy Spring Br.	1854	2	240
Beavers, Alexander	43	Dry Fork	1847	1	313
Beavers, Alexander D. (of John)	120	Barrenshee Cr.	1858	2	428
Beavers, Alexander Jr.	210	Bill's Branch	1844	1	204
Beavers, Alexander R.	145	Laurel Fork	1862	2	440
Beavers, Alexander R. et al	90	Chinkapin Spur	1850	2	15
Beavers, Alexander (Son of Rolin)	60	Wts. Sandy	1821	1	67
Beavers, James W.	160	Stone Coal	1850	1	377
Beavers, James W.	195	Dry Fork	1850	1	379
Beavers, John	46	Wts. Sandy	1846	1	253
Beavers, Moses	65	Dick's Creek	1825	1	109
Beavers, Moses	110	Dick's Creek	1842	1	193
Beavers, Moses	228	Dick's Creek	1849	1	354
Beavers, Robert	17	Stony Ridge	1834	1	133
Beavers, Robert	60	Dry Fork	1844	1	210
Beavers, Robert Sr.	9	Wts. Dry Fork	1850	2	24
Beavers, William	63	Stony Ridge	1847	1	290
Becclehimer, Isaac	40	Elkhorn	1837	1	162
Beecher, William Jr. (Belcher)	44	Elkhorn	1847	1	302
Beeton, Thomas J.	100	Flat Top Mt.	1852	2	151
Belcher—See Belsher, Belshy, Belshys					
Belcher, Andrew	40	Big & Dry Branch	1854	2	239
Belcher, Benjamin	93	Perry Camp Fork	1852	2	158
Belcher, Benjamin	50	Long Branch	1853	2	182
Belcher, Benjamin	24	Elkhorn	1847	1	272
Belcher, Benjamin	105	Clear Fork	1856	2	336
Belcher, Benjamin	33	Big Creek	1850	1	372
Belcher, Isaac	97	Elkhorn	1858	2	424
Belcher, Isaac et al	10	North Fork	1856	2	364
Belcher, Isom	70	Laurel Fork	1822	1	76
Belcher, Jesse	56	Brush Cr.	1820	1	51
Belcher, Obediah	50	Brush Creek	1823	1	94
Belcher, Peter	155	Elkhorn	1848	1	315
Belcher, Peter	87	Laurel Creek	1857	2	393

Name of Grantee	Acres	Local Description	Year	Book	Page
Bowman, Daniel P.	65	Big Stony Ridge	1852	2	159
Bowman, Daniel P.	33	Horse Pen Cr.	1852	2	160
Bowman, Daniel P.	219	Horsepen Cr.	1855	2	287
Breeding, Alfred et al	70	Bradshaw Creek	1847	1	262
Breeding, Alfred et al	35	Bradshaw Creek	1847	1	263
Breeding, John	138	Long Branch	1855	2	284
Breeding, John	30	Slate Creek	1847	1	291
Breeding, John	85	Fork Ridge	1847	1	304
Brewster—or Bruster					
Brittain, Rufus	316	Rockhouse Spur	1853	2	181
Brittain, Rufus	204	Barrenshe Creek	1858	2	418
Brittain, Rufus	575	Horse Pen Cr.	1854	2	455
Brown, Elizabeth	89	Lit. Stony Ridge	1847	1	289
Brown, George W. G. et al	3,226	Spice & Sand Lick Crs.	1854	2	472
Brown, Jeremiah	88	Laurel Cr.	1851	2	63
Brown, Reece T. et al	50	Laurel Cr.	1833	1	130
Brown, Thomas	46	Big Fork Ridge	1846	1	260
Bruster—or Brewster					
Bruster, Andrew P.	268	Max Camp Br.	1856	2	338
Bruster, Andrew P.	284	Cucumber Cr.	1856	2	339
Bruster, Archibald T.	100	Wts. Dry Fork	1850	2	23
Bruster, Ebenezer	40	Dry Fork	1821	1	64
Bruster, Ebenezer	28	Dry Fork	1836	1	157
Bruster, William	45	Lick Branch	1851	2	97
Bruster, William	60	Cane Break Branch	1851	2	98
Bruster, William	150	Birch Branch	1851	2	99
Burchfield, Noah	134	Dry Fork	1853	2	171
Burk, James et al	1,100	Big & Middle Crs.	1854	2	221
Canada, Ali	44	Panther Cr.	1858	2	425
Canada, Andrew	184	Groundhog Branch	1853	2	183
Canada, Andrew	40	Groundhog Branch	1853	2	184
Cartmill, John	100	Wts. Bluestone	1804	1	8
Cartright, Moses A.	600	Wts. Tug	1860	1	415
Cartright, Moses A.	400	Little Indian Cr.	1860	1	417
Cartright, Moses A.	100	Wts. Tug	1860	1	418
Cazy, D. S.	25	Wts. Clear Fork	1849	1	341
Cecil, James	100	Wts. Clinch & Sandy	1805	1	467
Cecil, Samuel	355	Cucumber Ridge	1859	1	393
Cecil, Samuel et al	144	Big Creek	1851	2	67
Cecil, Samuel et al	175	Sand Lick	1857	2	390
Cecil, Samuel & Wm. P. et al	844	Long Branch	1851	2	78
Cecil, William P.	1,240	Cucumber Ridge	1851	2	68
Cecil, William P. et al	662	Big Creek	1851	2	72
Cecil, William P. & Samuel et al	150	Big Creek	1851	2	69
Chapin, C. O. et al	1,000	Big Spice	1858	2	436
Chapin, C. O. et al	3,000	Wts. Elkhorn	1859	2	538
Charles, George	29	Dry Fork	1842	1	388
Charles, John	29	Dry Fork	1851	2	105
Charles, John	40	Dry Fork	1850	1	382
Charles, John	75	Dry Fork	1862	2	439
Charles, Michael et al	100	Dry Fork	1826	1	120
Christian, Addison	150	Jonathan's Br.	1860	1	411
Christian, Addison	100	Dry Fork	1860	1	412
Christian, Alexander	315	Indian Creek	1851	2	100
Christian, Anthony	74	Big & Little Fork	1853	2	218
Christian, Anthony	277	Big Fork Ridge	1853	2	219
Christian, Daniel Jr. (of John)	103	Red Oak Ridge	1850	2	26
Christian, David	200	Indian Creek	1851	2	81
Christian, John	61	Red Oak Ridge	1850	2	25
Christian, John	305	Red Oak Ridge	1850	2	56
Christian, John	41	Indian Creek	1851	2	102
Christian, John	13	Dry Fork	1834	1	134
Christian, John	30	Dismal Creek	1853	2	205

Name of Grantee	Acres	Local Description	Year	Book	Page
Christian, John et al	100	Dismal Creek	1853	2	211
Christian, Maston	60	Harmon's Br.	1844	1	201
Christian, Maston	50	Jonathan's Br.	1842	1	187
Christian, Maston	23	Sandy Fork	1842	1	188
Christian, Maston	36	Dry Fork	1842	1	191
Christian, Thomas	40	Indian Cr.	1824	1	97
Christian, Thomas	15	Tug River	1826	1	119
Christian, Thomas	77	Dry Fork	1836	1	143
Christian, Thomas B.	140	Indian Creek	1856	2	365
Christian, Thomas S.	214	Spring Fork	1849	1	360
Christian, Thomas S.	266	Belcher Ridge	1850	1	381
Christian, William	196	Indian & Middle Crs.	1851	2	101
Christian, William	231	Dividing Ridge	1850	1	370
Clark, Joseph	100	East River	1810	1	37
Clark, William	31	Wts. Sandy	1851	2	65
Cline, Christian	18	Tug River	1845	1	215
Cline, Christian	102	Bee Branch	1859	1	403
Cline, Christian	276	Long Branch	1859	1	404
Cline, Christian	383	Long Branch	1859	1	405
Cline, Henry	11	Barren Cr.	1846	1	255
Cline, Henry	17	Barren Cr.	1846	1	256
Cline, Henry	25	Tug River	1847	1	293
Cline, Henry	26	Wts. Tug	1855	2	318
Cline, Henry Jr.	74	Snake Root Br.	1856	2	341
Cline, Henry Jr.	38	Snake Root Br.	1859	1	396
Cline, Henry Sr.	50	Lit. Indian Cr.	1857	2	392
Cline, Herndon	68	Clear Fork	1856	2	375
Cline, Herndon	140	Henry's Ridge	1856	2	376
Cline, Herranton	50	Elkhorn	1851	2	104
Cline, Herranton	28	Clear Fork	1850	1	369
Cline, James	72	Bull Creek	1847	1	310
Cline, James	38	Bull Ceek	1847	1	311
Cline, John	5	Wts. Tug	1850	2	153
Cline, John Jr.	13	Day Camp Br.	1856	2	342
Cline, John Jr.	43	Jim & Mudhole Brs.	1856	2	343
Cline, John Sr.	25	Panther Lick	1855	2	317
Cline, John Sr.	179	Grapevine Br.	1857	2	394
Cline, Michael Jr.	90	Tug River	1843	1	196
Cline, Michael Jr.	25	Spice Cr.	1847	1	292
Cline, Michael Jr.	80	Tug River	1848	1	314
Cline, Michael (of Henry)	29	Spice Creek	1850	1	368
Cline, Peter (of Henry)	176	Spice Creek	1860	1	419
Cline, William	30	Pounding Mill Br.	1850	1	366
Cline, William	61	Andrew's Branch	1850	1	367
Cline, William Sr.	23	Fish Trap Shoal	1853	2	214
Coleman, John	159	Bluestone	1821	1	61
Collins, Benjamin	206	Panther Creek	1860	1	410
Collins, Jacob	50	Panther Creek	1847	1	278
Collins, Jacob	82	Panther Creek	1856	2	388
Collins, John	32	Panther Creek	1847	1	279
Collins, John	156	Dry Fork	1856	2	383
Collins, John Sr.	40	Dividing Ridge	1849	1	339
Collins, William	83	Tug River	1849	1	344
Collins, William (of John)	30	Bear Town Br	1857	2	397
Collins, William (of John)	97	Dry Fork	1860	1	407
Compton, John (Cumpton)	88	Tug River	1824	1	106
Compton, John (Cumpton)	56	Tug River	1824	1	107
Compton, John Jr.	350	Blackberry Cr.	1812	1	40
Compton, John Jr.	150	Bluestone	1822	1	77
Compton, John Sr.	30	Bluestone	1822	1	78
Compton, Squire	56	Laurel Creek	1852	2	161
Compton, William	45	Wts. Bluestone	1822	1	86
Cornwell, William K. et al	500	McClure Branch	1858	2	543

Name of Grantee	Acres	Local Description	Year	Book	Page
Dillion—also Dillon					
Dillion, Harvey G.	184	Wts. Elkhorn	1851	2	109
Dillion, Hugh	47	Big Creek	1854	2	228
Dillion, Hugh	12	Big Creek	1854	2	229
Dillion, Hugh (Dillon)	211	Spice Creek	1854	2	243
Dillion, Samuel	55	Brush Cr.	1824	1	102
Dillon—See Dillion					
Dillon, Hugh	61	Long Branch	1852	2	155
Doughten—or Daughten					
Doughten, Jesse	100	Horsepen Ridge	1851	2	110
Doughten, Jesse	41	Horsepen	1851	2	111
Doughten, Jesse	73	Horse Pen	1853	2	187
Doughten, Jesse	100	Horsepen	1853	2	188
Doughten, Jesse	82	Mare Camp Br.	1853	2	189
Doughten, Jesse	35	Camp Branch	1856	2	351
Doughten, Jesse	10	Big Creek	1856	2	352
Doughten, Jesse	82	Max Camp	1856	2	353
Doughten, Jesse	73	Horsepen	1856	2	354
Doughten, Jesse	68	Big Horsepen	1856	2	355
Doughten, Jesse	300	Cucumber Cr.	1856	2	362
Doughten, Jesse	25	Lit. Horsepen	1856	2	363
Doughten, Jesse et al	2,600	Wts. Horsepen	1854	2	463
Doughten, Jesse J.	219	Horsepen	1855	2	272
Doughten, Jesse J.	100	Deskins Branch	1858	2	413
Doughten, Jesse J.	1,031	Jacob's Fork	1858	2	523
Dratt, John et al	1,180	Clear Fork	1858	2	532
Eastep—See Estep					
Ellis, John W.	400	War Creek	1851	2	95
Ellswick, William Sr.	104	Red Oak Ridge	1856	2	335
Estep, Shadrack (Eastep)	23	Lick Branch	1848	1	316
Fay, Eliza T. et al	1,200	Clay & Flat Top	1860	1	416
Fletcher, Nancy	44	Tug River	1844	1	206
Fletcher, Roland	50	Tug River	1818	1	49
Fletcher, Rowland	30	Tug River	1825	1	111
Fletcher, William	34	Tug River	1825	1	112
Fletcher, William	60	Tug River	1825	1	113
Fletcher, William	45	Elkhorn	1825	1	114
Fletcher, William	13	Spice Run	1825	1	115
Flummer, Samuel	15	Wts. Bluestone	1809	1	31
Francisco, Jacob	440	Peeled Chestnut Fk.	1858	2	520
Francisco, Jacob	340	Laurel Creek	1858	2	522
Franklin, Thomas	93	Wts. Blue Stone	1856	2	378
Franklin, Thomas H.	(132)232	Laurel Creek	1854	2	236
French, James	150	Red Oak Ridge	1824	1	95
Gates, Augustus	169	Slate Creek	1857	2	411
Gates, John H.	120	Red Oak Ridge	1853	2	197
Gates, John H.	200	War & Slate Crs.	1859	1	401
George, George P.	464	Flat Top	1858	2	531
George, George P.	39	Claybourn's Ridge	1858	2	416
George, Harvey Sr.	100	Dry Fork	1849	1	340
George, John B.	170	Brush Creek	1824	1	96
George, William O. et al	320	Long Branch	1856	2	346
Gibson, George	70	Dividing Ridge	1848	1	327
Gill, Joseph	13	Wts. Muddy Fk.	1850	2	57
Gillespie, Henry H.	50	Spice Creek	1856	2	374
Gillespie, Nancy et al Heirs	27	Wts. Tug	1852	2	162
Gillespie, Thomas H.	30	Horsepen	1853	2	172
Gillespie, Thomas H.	88	Horse Pen	1858	2	421
Gillespie, Thomas H. et al	282	George's Camp Br.	1855	2	301
Gillespie, Thomas H. et al	566	Big Creek	1855	2	302
Gillespie, Thomas H. et al	104	Jacob's Fork	1858	2	433
Gillespie, Thomas H. et al	600	Cucumber Creek	1856	2	495
Gillespie, William et al	70	Dry Fork	1845	1	219

Name of Grantee	Acres	Local Description	Year	Book	Page
Harman, Daniel H.	150	Jacob's Fork	1858	2	435
Harman, Daniel H. Sr.	34	Stone Coal Br.	1853	2	173
Harman, Daniel Sr.	245	Wts. Bluestone	1803	1	459
Harman, E. F.	300	Laurel Creek	1855	2	304
Harman, E. F. & H. A.	556	Tug & Laurel	1855	2	482
Harman, Elias	100	Bluestone	1805	1	14
Harman, Elias et al	148	East River	1803	1	457
Harman, Elias G. W.	33	Cub Creek	1851	2	82
Harman, Elias G. W.	14	War Creek	1847	1	280
Harman, Elias V.	55	Dry Fork	1851	2	114
Harman, Elias V.	120	Rocky Ridge	1851	2	115
Harman, Elias V.	163	Jacob's Fork	1856	2	361
Harman, Elias V.	230	Dry Fork	1857	2	410
Harman, Elias V. & D. H.	8	Beech Fork	1847	1	264
Harman, Elias V. & D. H.	38	Fork Ridge	1847	1	265
Harman, Elias V. & D. H.	48	Wts. Sandy	1847	1	266
Harman, Erastus et al	(750) 2,250	Fork Ridge	1860	1	480
Harman, Erastus F.	64	Jacob's Branch	1855	2	288
Harman, Erastus F.	272	Long Branch	1855	2	303
Harman, Erastus F. & H. A. et al	50	Lick Creek	1854	2	263
Harman, Erastus F. & Nancy B.	600	Wts. Tug & Guyandotte	1858	2	419
Harman, Erastus F. et al	1,000	Big Spice Cr.	1858	2	436
Harman, Erastus F. et al	3,000	Wts. Elkhorn	1859	2	538
Harman, Erastus F. et al	500	McClure Branch	1858	2	543
Harman, Erastus F. et al	2,000	Big Spice Creek	1858	2	544
Harman, G. W. et al	140	Beech Fork	1887	2	452
Harman, H. A.	101	Bark Camp	1855	2	275
Harman, H. A.	69	Wts. Dry Fork	1855	2	276
Harman, H. A.	62	Mill Branch	1855	2	277
Harman, H. A.	66	Lit. Slate Cr.	1855	2	278
Harman, H. A.	94	Woodley Branch	1855	2	279
Harman, H. A.	119	Bradshaw Fork	1855	2	280
Harman, H. A.	54	Bradshaw Fork	1855	2	283
Harman, H. A.	383	Laurel Creek	1855	2	305
Harman, H. A.	131	Spice Creek	1855	2	306
Harman, H. A.	145	Elkhorn	1855	2	308
Harman, H. A. et al	1,400	Dismal Creek	1851	2	91
Harman, H. A. et al	2,500	Mill & Sugar Crs.	1858	2	528
Harman, Henry B.	50	Clear Fork	1836	1	160
Harman, Henry B. et al	70	Bradshaw Run	1847	1	262
Harman, Henry B. et al	35	Bradshaw Creek	1847	1	263
Harman, Henry D.	208	Tug River	1847	1	286
Harman, Henry D. & D. H.	188	Dry Fork	1849	1	342
Harman, Henry D. et al	150	Lit. Slate Cr.	1851	2	126
Harman, Henry Jr.	400	Wts. Bluestone	1805	1	15
Harman, Henry M.	21	Wts. Dry Fork	1850	2	28
Harman, Henry M.	93	War Ridge	1856	2	345
Harman, Henry M.	200	Dismal Cr.	1856	2	382
Harman, Henry M. et al	100	Dismal Cr.	1853	2	211
Harman, Henry Sr.	49	Dry Fork	1842	1	189
Harman, Hezekiah A.	50	Big Slate Cr.	1851	2	125
Harman, Hezekiah A.	185	Middle Creek	1854	2	269
Harman, Hezekiah A.	125	Little Slate Cr.	1855	2	274
Harman, Hezekiah A.	33	Laurel Fork	1855	2	307
Harman, Hezekiah A.	405	Big Creek	1856	2	498
Harman, Hezekiah A. & E. F. et al	2,000	Lick & Mill Cr.	1854	2	458
Harman, Hezekiah A. & E. F. et al	2,295	Clear Fork	1854	2	476
Harman, Hezekiah A. et al	277	Lit. Cub Cr.	1852	2	163
Harman, Hezekiah A. et al	79	Crane Trace Br.	1855	2	289
Harman, Hezekiah A. et al	30	Big Branch	1855	2	290
Harman, Hezekiah A. et al	131	Panther Cr.	1855	2	291
Harman, Hezekiah A. et al	50	Clear Fork	1855	2	292
Harman, Hezekiah A. et al	66	Moseley's Br.	1855	2	293

Name of Grantee	Acres	Local Description	Year	Book	Page
McGuire—See McGuyer					
McGuire, Cornelius	56	Middle Creek	1851	2	131
McGuire, William (Preacher)	47	Indian Cr.	1824	1	100
McGuire, William (Preacher)	68	Indian Cr.	1824	1	101
McGuyer—See McGuire					
McGuyer, Joseph	115	Indian Cr.	1824	1	98
McGuyer, Joseph	24	Indian Cr.	1824	1	99
Meade,Henry W. & Charles R. et al	100	Sand Lick Cr.	1855	2	273
Michum—or Mitchem					
Michum, Francis	30	Rock House Br.	1850	2	46
Milam, Milham, Milum					
Milam, Allen	47	Bottom Creek	1851	2	85
Milam, Allen	15	Bottom Cr.	1847	1	298
Milam, Allen	10	Bottom Cr.	1847	1	306
Milam, Allen	37	Bottom Cr.	1855	2	328
Milam, Henry	100	Milam Springs Br.	1859	1	398
Milam, James	37	Wts. Tug	1836	1	151
Milam, James	9	Elkhorn	1853	2	169
Milam, John	69	Cedar Cliff	1851	2	83
Milam, John	38	Flat Top Ridge	1851	2	84
Milam, John	62	Wts. Tug	1851	2	132
Milam, John	13	Elkhorn	1836	1	149
Milma, John	100	Fork Ridge	1845	1	242
Milam, John	468	Elkhorn	1856	2	496
Milam, Lewis	55	Elkhorn	1836	1	155
Milam, Lewis	22	Rockhouse Ridge	1845	1	240
Milam, Lewis	81	Little Ridge	1850	1	376
Milam, Louis	50	Elkhorn	1845	1	239
Milam, Russell	50	Wts. Tug	1851	2	133
Milham—or Milam, Milum					
Milham, James A.	38	Elkhorn	1847	1	270
Milum—Milam, Milham					
Milum, Henry	190	Jump Branch	1856	2	384
Mires, John	50	Horse Pen Cove	1850	2	44
Mitchell, John	40	Reedy Ridge	1821	1	70
Mitchell, Moses	268	Grassy Spring Ridge	1853	2	199
Mitchem—or Michum					
Mitchem, Francis (Mitcham)	292	Flat Top Mt.	1850	2	49
Mitchem, Francis	50	Rockhouse Branch	1845	1	226
Mitchem, Isaiah (Mitcham)	101	Adkin's Branch	1855	2	286
Mitchem, Zibia	30	Indian Creek	1815	1	45
Moore, Andrew P.	44	Elkhorn Fork	1851	2	128
Moore, Andrew P	55	Big Creek	1851	2	129
Moore, Andrew P.	232	Wts. Tug	1851	2	130
Moore, Andrew P.	112	Tug River	1854	2	256
Moore, Andrew P.	84	Fork Ridge	1849	1	355
Moore, Andrew P.	900	Laurel Fork	1849	1	356
Moore, Emily (wife of J. S.)	30	Wts. Tug	1858	2	417
Moore, James	42	Wts. Tug	1841	1	183
Moore, John S	108	Wts. Tug	1834	1	132
Moore, John S.	62	Laurel Fork	1836	1	145
Moore, William T. (Moor)	107	Laurel Creek	1848	1	321
Moore, William T.	24	Wts.. Tug	1850	2	58
Moore, William T.	120	Wts. Bluestone	1851	2	73
Moore, William T.	55	Laurel Fork	1836	1	150
Moore, William T.	380	Cabin Creek	1856	2	379
Moore, William T. & A. P.	220	Wts. Bluestone	1841	1	176
Moore, William T. & A. P.	90	Dividing Ridge	1835	1	140
Moore, William T. et al	50	Wts. Tug	1841	1	181
Moore, William T. et al	60	Elkhorn	1841	1	182
Moore, William T. et al	239	Laurel Ridge	1850	1	378
Moore, William T. et al	1,000	Wts. Elkhorn	1856	2	387
Morgan, Abraham	50	Guyandotte	1805	1	23

Pruit—See Prewit, Pruett					
Pruit, John Jr.	100	Wts. Sandy River	1810	1	34
Purdue—See Perdue					
Purdue, David K. (Purdew)	268	Laurel Fork	1854	2	474
Quicksall, Daniel	169	Vol's Creek	1853	2	200
Quicksall, Daniel	156	Dividing Ridge	1850	1	392
Quicksall, Thomas	50	Vol's Creek	1850	2	47
Quicksall, Thomas	75	Beech Fork	1847	1	283
Quicksall, Thomas	142	Wts. Sandy	1847	1	284
Ratliff, Richard Jr.	50	Tug River	1850	2	10
Ratliff, Richard Jr. (of Tug River)	52	Wts. Tug	1854	2	267
Ratliff, William	100	Rock Lick Cr.	1851	2	141
Reed, Jackson	1,000	Horse Creek	1858	2	429
Reed, John L.	1,000	Grape Vine Br.	1857	2	408
Reed, John W.	98	Wts. Sandy	1850	2	8
Reed, John W.	90	Wts. Sandy	1850	2	9
Reed, John W.	42	Crain Ridge	1850	2	18
Reed, John W.	40	Dry Fork	1844	1	213
Reed, John W.	75	Dry Fork	1848	1	329
Reed, John W.	30	Dry Fork	1848	1	330
Reed, John W.	7	Crain Ridge	1848	1	331
Reed, John W.	30	Dry Fork	1848	1	332
Reed, John W.	2,400	Dry Fork	1857	2	518
Riffe, Gabriel (Rife)	76	George's Fork	1853	2	203
Riffe, Gabriel	35	Dry Fork	1824	1	104
Riffe, Gabriel	15	Dry Fork	1824	1	105
Roberts, James	78	Wts. Tug River	1859	1	395
Rose, Bartley	28	Barrenshee Branch	1850	2	60
Rose, Bartley	27	Barrenshee Cr.	1851	2	140
Rowe, Stephen	83	Long Branch	1855	2	310
Rowe, Stephen	165	Grape Branch	1858	2	420
Russell, Daniel	100	Tug River	1850	2	38
Russell, Daniel	45	Tug River	1850	2	39
St. Clair, Alexander et al	200	Board Camp Br.	1852	2	166
Sayers, D. G. et al	74	Dry Fork	1883	2	450
Sayers, D. G. et al	140	Beech Fork	1887	2	452
Scarbury, William	56	Bradshaw Fork	1854	2	270
Seiler, Anthony et al	2,500	Mill & Sugar Camp	1858	2	528
Shannon, Anna E.	342	Wts. Tug River	1852	2	167
Shannon, James	100	Huff Cr.	1805	1	21
Shannon, James	100	Guyandotte River	1805	1	22
Shannon, Lain	34	Wts. Guyandotte	1821	1	69
Shannon, William	100	Indian Cr.	1808	1	27
Shannon, William	120	Wts. Bluestone	1809	1	471
Shields, John	70	Guyandotte River	1822	1	83
Short, William	9	Wts. Sandy	1849	1	357
Short, William	42	Dry Fork	1849	1	358
Siler—See Seiler					
Simmons, John	150	Wts. Bluestone	1805	1	25
Sisson, Emanuel	34	Wts. Bluestone	1804	1	5
Sizemore, John	125	Rocky Ridge	1850	2	61
Sizemore, John	34	Dry Fork	1847	1	309
Sizemore, John	85	Rocky Ridge	1847	1	389
Sluss, Henry	90	Wts. Laurel Fork	1850	2	40
Smith—See Smyth					
Smith, Isaiah et al	50	Lick Creek	1854	2	263
Smith, Isaiah et al	2,000	Lick & Mill Crs.	1854	2	458
Smith, Isaiah et al	2,295	Clear Fork	1854	2	476
Smith, Isaiah	62	Mill Creek	1853	2	195
Smith, John (of Isaiah)	606	Sugar Camp	1856	2	337
Smith, Jonathan et al	1,000	Wts. Elkhorn	1856	2	387
Smith, L. D. et al	(1,500)2,250	Fork Ridge	1860	1	480
Smith, Robert et al	144	Big Creek	1851	2	67
Smith, Robert et al	150	Big Creek	1851	2	69

Name of Grantee	Acres	Local Description	Year	Book	Page
Woosley, Hezekiah	50	Dry Fork	1847	1	312
Woosley, Hezekiah	40	Dry Fork	1849	1	352
Yates, John	70	Wts. Sandy	1851	2	150
Yokill, George	100	Laurel Cr.	1855	2	320
Yokill, George	67	Low Gap Branch	1855	2	329
Yost, William O. et al	1,000	Dry Fork & Tug	1861	1	477
Yost, William O. et al	1,180	Clear Fork	1858	2	536

WYTHE COUNTY, VIRGINIA

Banks, Henry	30,000	Wts. Great Sandy	1796	1	207
Barrell, Joseph et al	50,000	Wts. Guyandotte	1796	1	209
Barrett—See Barrell					
Blanchard, John D.	7,000	Wts. Sandy	1798	1	214
Boothe, David	20,000	Wts. Guyandotte	1796	1	206
Boothe, David	40,000	Wts. Guyandotte	1796	1	208
Clinton, Dewit	142,000	Peter Huff & Buffalo Crs.	1796	1	203
Dillon, Edward	21,212	Wts. New River	1796	1	204
Dwight, Josiah et al	50,000	Wts. Guyandotte	1796	1	209
McGregor, Call	25,000	12 Pole & Guyandotte	1796	1	205
McLaughlin, Duncan et al	12,000	Clinch & Sandy R.	1797	1	212
Moore, Samuel	40,162½	Wts. Sandy R.	1797	1	211
Morgan, David	400	Wts. Sandy R.	1798	1	213
Morris, Robert	500,000	Wts. Sandy & Guyandotte	1795	1	199
Morris, Robert	480,000	Tug & Guyandotte	1795	1	198
Morris, Robert Assignee, et al	320,000	Sandy Cr.	1795	1	196
Nicholas, Wilson C.	300,000	Sandy Cr. Roark's Gap	1795	1	201
Nicholas, Wilson C.	500,000	Bluestone & Guyandotte	1795	1	237
Nicholas, Wilson C.	300,000	Hd. Sand Cr. Roark's Gap	1795	1	215
Nicholas, Wilson C. Asg. et al	320,000	Sandy Cr.	1795	1	196
Patterson, David et al	12,000	Clinch & Sandy	1797	1	212
Pickett, George	40,000	Blue Stone & Tug	1795	1	200
Pollard, Robert	150,000	Wts. Tug River	1795	1	197
Taylor, James	9,260¼	Wts. Guyandotte	1796	1	210
Wilson, Thomas	57,000	Big & Cucumber Crs.	1795	1	202
Wolcott, Alexander	350,000	Wts. Gr. Sandy	1800	1	220

WEST VIRGINIA GRANTS

BARBOUR (W. VA.)

Name of Grantee	Acres	Local Description	Year	Book	Page
Auvil, Daniel M. et al	50	Barker's Mill Run	1866	1	227
Canfield, Isaac	317	Hunter's Fork	1865	1	89
Cleavinger, Edmund	40	Simpson's Creek	1867	1	283
Hall, Charles B. et al	1,920	Valley River	1865	1	84
Harden, Nester	500	Brushy Fork	1867	1	430
Howes, Joseph et al	30	Valley River	1866	1	226
Jarvis, G. E. et al	30	Valley River	1866	1	226
Jarvis, Granville E.	100	Bartlett's Corner	1872	2	92
Jarvis, Granville E.	57¾	Adj. S. Clevenger	1872	2	93
Martin, Henry D.	2½	Cor. to Trahan	1865	1	69
Middleton, H. O. et al	725	Zeb's Creek	1864	1	12
Morgan, Charles S. et al	1,920	Valley River	1865	1	84
Morrall, Lair D.	261	Teter's Creek	1876	2	164
Nester, Jacob	20	Adj. John Huffman	1865	1	53
Nester, James	60	Teter's Creek	1865	1	40
Right, William J. et al	50	Barker's Mill Run	1866	1	227
Shanabarger, Christopher H.	42½	Cove Run	1865	1	69
Smith, Hiram	22	Adj. J. B. Gainer	1868	1	446
Wilmoth, Edmund	300	Sugar Creek	1876	2	161
Wilson, Lewis et al	725	Zeb's Creek	1864	1	12
Zinn, William B.	7	Adj. S. J. Cornwall	1867	1	356
Zinn, William B.	24	Big Sandy Cr.	1867	1	356

BERKELEY (W. VA.)

Ashton, John	307	Sleepy Creek	1866	1	288
Kilmer, John et al	50	North Mountain	1870	2	29
Small, John M. et al	50	North Mountain	1870	2	29

BOONE (W. VA.)

Adkins, Mark	35	Wts. Mud River	1867	1	357
Adkins, Mark et al	250	Big Creek	1867	1	311
Ball, James A.	45	Aunt's Fork	1867	1	360
Ball, James A.	10	Aunt's Fork	1867	1	361
Barker, Russell T.	60 (62)	Spruce Fork	1868	1	542
Bias, E. R.	24	Adj. B. S. Chambers	1868	1	573
Bias, Simeon	211	Jack's Branch	1867	1	330
Brown, James H.	1,000	Coal River	1879	2	180
Brown, James H.	500	Cor. F. J. Jacobs	1879	2	181
Brown, Lorenzo D. & Elijah	35	Lit. Coal River	1868	1	580
Brown, William	115	Wolf Pen	1868	1	579
Clay, M. C.	150	Spruce Fork	1879	2	189
Cooper, Francis	48	Adj. Henry Smith	1868	1	443
Elkin, John E.	28	Hewitt's Cr.	1867	1	357
Elkin, Zaccheus	47	Hewitt's Cr.	1867	1	358
Estep, Stephen B.	100	Wts. Mud River	1867	1	303

Name of Grantee	Acres	Local Description	Year	Book	Page
Estep, Stephen B.	118	Wts. Mud River	1867	1	303
Ferrell, Middleton	34	Lit. Coal River	1868	1	581
Ferrell, William	25	Lit. Coal River	1868	1	578
Fry, George	48	Hewitt's Creek	1867	1	426
Hagar, Lorenzo D.	266	Hewitt's Creek	1866	1	138
Hagar, Robert	37	6-Mile Creek	1870	2	22
Hagar, Robert	40	Mud River	1870	2	22
Harless, James (Harlass)	38	Van Meter's Branch	1867	1	363
Hill, James	100	Big Creek	1866	1	213
Hill, James	27	Big Creek	1866	1	214
Jarrel, Daniel	34	Dry Branch	1868	1	577
Jarrel, Daniel	100	Pond Fork	1868	1	577
Jarrel, Daniel	44	Lit. Coal River	1868	1	580
Jordan, Johnson	268	Tony's Branch	1868	1	447
Kissinger, Wilson	50	Sparr Branch	1870	2	56
Lovejoy, Anderson	20	Wts. of Mud	1867	1	311
Lovejoy, Anderson et al	250	Big Creek	1867	1	311
Miller, William	179	Turtle Creek	1876	2	166
Miller, Zadock	24	Mud River	1870	2	23
Nelson, George W.	260	Laurel Cr.	1870	2	46
Nelson, James	50	Spruce Fork	1868	1	543
Oxley, Thomas L.	266	Horse Creek	1867	1	285
Pauley, Joseph	848	Lit. Coal River	1867	1	361
Pauley, Joseph	31	Jack's Branch	1867	1	362
Perry, William	152	Adj. R. Elkins	1867	1	302
Sansom, Edward	168	Laurel Fork	1867	1	280
Sansone, Edward	168	Laurel Fork	1867	1	280
Stone, Samuel S.	200	Lit. Coal	1879	2	182
Vickars, James	216	Bennett's Branch	1868	1	546
Workman, George & Tunsel	100	Pond Fork of Coal	1867	1	363
Workman, James M.	223	Big Creek	1868	1	552

BRAXTON (W. VA.)

Anawalt, Annanias et al	144	Otter Cr.	1866	1	212
Baxter, F. J. et al	187	Wts. Steer Creek	1868	1	474
Berry, P. B. et al	89	Big Birch River	1868	1	585
Berry, William H.	80	Cedar Creek	1868	1	586
Byrne, Marcellus	723	Shrieve's Run	1870	2	32
Carpenter, John S.	50	Camp Run	1869	1	593
Carpenter, John S.	50	Laurel Creek	1869	1	594
Carr, John et al	187	Wts. Steer Creek	1868	1	474
Conrad, Lemuel	55	Long Run	1867	1	348
Conrad, Lemuel	61	Buck Knob	1867	1	348
Corley, W. L. J.	166	Big Birch River	1867	1	371
Dobbins, Francis M.	171	Wts. Steer Cr.	1867	1	354
Ellison, A. N.	50	Little Birch	1866	1	267
Frame, Milton et al	211	Long Run	1866	1	265
Frame, Milton et al	65	Steer Creek	1866	1	266
Griffin, Leroy A.	240	Laurel Run	1866	1	116
Griffin, Leroy A. et al	144	Otter Cr.	1866	1	212
Hamrick, Nathan Mc. et al	225	Diadda Run	1868	1	463
Hamrick, Seth F.	40	2-Mile Cr.	1867	1	301
Hamrick, Seth F.	125	O'Brian's Fork	1867	1	301
Haymond, M. P.	40	Salt Lick Cr.	1867	1	328
Hughes, Bartlett	75	Strange Creek	1866	1	242
Jackson, Sylvester et al	130	Birch River	1868	1	585

Name of Grantee	Acres	Local Description	Year	Book	Page
Keener, James	90	Wolf Pen	1866	1	242
Long, William A.	30	Coon Creek	1866	1	240
McHamrick, Nathan et al	225	Diadda Run	1868	1	463
Mollohan, George D.	346	Laurel Fork	1867	1	320
Perkins, Elijah	73	Wts. Steer Cr.	1866	1	264
Perkins, Elijah	23½	Cedar Creek	1866	1	265
Perkins, Elijah	88	Wts. of Elk	1868	1	588
Perrine, Joseph H.	75	Strange Creek	1866	1	214
Persinger, Martin et al	200	Road Run	1866	1	217
Pierson, Burton C. et al	225	Diadda Run	1868	1	463
Posey, Alfred et al	200	Road Run	1866	1	217
Riffle, John M.	50	Wts. Birch	1866	1	241
Roberts, John	100	Laurel Run	1868	1	509
Roberts, John et al	100	Laurel Run	1868	1	510
Rodgers, John	30½	Wts. of Elk	1867	1	320
Rodgers, John	50	Rush Fork	1868	1	587
Singleton, F. F.	146	Salt Lick Cr.	1868	1	448
Singleton, French F.	55	Salt Lick Cr.	1868	1	448
Singleton, Uriah W.	40	Long Run	1867	1	310
Singleton, W. K.	61	Salt Lick Creek	1868	1	592
Singleton, William K.	53	Salt Lick	1868	1	587
Singleton, William K.	123	Salt Lick	1868	1	588
Skidmore, Felix et al	211	Long Run	1866	1	265
Skidmore, Felix et al	65	Wts. Steer Creek	1866	1	266
Skidmore, Felix et al	130	Birch River	1868	1	585
Sprigg, John S. et al	100	Laurel Run	1868	1	510
Stout, Sylvester	60	Copen's Run	1874	2	126
Stout, Sylvester	100	L. Kanawha R.	1874	2	127
Sutton, F. J.	83	Carpenter's Fork	1868	1	446
Sutton, F. J.	37	Bear Run	1868	1	591
Sutton, Felix J.	100	Carpenter's Fork	1866	1	266
Tonkins, William	100	Salt Lick Cr.	1867	1	306
William, John et al	89	Big Birch River	1868	1	585
Williams, William	57	Big Run	1868	1	449

CABELL (W. VA.)

Ballard, Perry et al	732	Wts. Mud River	1867	1	294
Black, James C.	18	Trace Cr.	1867	1	297
Black, James C. et al	732	Wts. Mud River	1867	1	294
Himes, Rees C.	474	10 Mi. & Stout Crs.	1866	1	133
Kilgore, George	40	7 Mile Creek	1865	1	93
Morrison, Thompson	10	Cabell Creek	1868	1	543
Samuels, Henry J	50	Mud River	1866	1	130
Samuels, Henry J.	94	Mud River	1866	1	132

CALHOUN (W. VA.)

Arnold, George I. et al	2,590	Anna Maria & Lit. Crs.	1867	1	372
Arnold, James W.	100	Nighcut	1866	1	166
Ayers, Michael A. & A. B.	73	Laurel Creek	1866	1	160
Ball, Jasper	17½	Mill Run	1866	1	163

Name of Grantee	Acres	Local Description	Year	Book	Page
Barr, Alfred	18½	Mill Run	1866	1	153
Bennett, J. M. et al	250	Cor. S. G. Stalnaker	1870	2	6
Bennett, J. M. et al	300	Cor. to M. Jackson	1870	2	6
Bennett, Nelson M.	13¾	Steer Creek	1866	1	198
Betts, Collins et al	160	Big Root Cr.	1868	1	468
Conrad, Anthony	161½	Sycamore	1868	1	508
Cotteral, Thomas	45½	West Fork	1866	1	166
Elliot, Henry	158	Pine Creek	1866	1	158
Elliot, Jabez	105	Pine Creek	1866	1	152
Elliott, Henry	158	Pine Creek	1866	1	161
Farnsworth, Isaac et al	160	Big Root	1868	1	468
Ferrell, H. R.	476½	Lower Leading Cr.	1868	1	531
Ferrell, H. R.	219	Yellow Creek	1868	1	534
Ferrell, Thornton F.	100	Yellow Creek	1866	1	202
Ferrell, Valentine et al	160	Big Root Cr.	1868	1	468
Freed, Jacob	296½	5-Mile Run	1866	1	162
Freed, Jacob et al	450	Leading & Straight Crs.	1866	1	162
Gay, James et al	450	Leading & Straight Crs.	1866	1	162
Hays, Peregrine	500	West Fork	1866	1	156
Hays, Peregrine et al	575	Yellow Creek	1866	1	149
Hoffman, John S.	301	Lower Run	1866	1	223
Hoffman, John S. et al	149	Rowell's Run	1866	1	222
Hoffman, John S. et al	187	Yellow Creek	1866	1	231
Hoffman, John S. et al	2,590	Anna Maria & Lit. Crs.	1867	1	372
Johnson, Peter	100	Burrow's Run	1866	1	159
Knotts, Absolom	200	West Fork	1866	1	167
Laughlin, Robert	186	West Fork	1866	1	173
Lynch, George	140	Daniel & Fall Runs	1866	1	167
Lynch, George	400	Wts. West Fork	1868	1	532
Lynch, George	150	Rowel's Run	1868	1	534
Maze, Joseph	150½	Straight Creek	1868	1	463
Maze, Joseph	260	Leading Cr.	1868	1	516
Norman, Rachael Elizabeth	36½	Leaf Bank	1866	1	154
Norman, Semore & Henry B.	19	Stinson Fork	1866	1	150
Norman, Semore & Henry B.	132	Leading Creek	1866	1	150
Norman, Semore & Henry B.	186	Stinson Fork	1866	1	151
Norman, Semore & Henry B.	350	Leaf Bank	1866	1	154
Norman, Semore & Henry B. et al	575	Yellow Creek	1866	1	149
Norris, Milton et al	149	Rowell's Run	1866	1	222
Norris, Milton et al	187	Yellow Creek	1866	1	231
Rafferty, Patrick et al	250	Adj. Stalnaker	1870	2	6
Rafferty, Patrick et al	300	Cor. to M. Jackson	1870	2	6
Reip, Adam	350	Stinson's Fork	1868	1	533
Sterm, Henry	200	Yellow Creek	1866	1	152
Stump, Alfred	52	Sycamore Fork	1868	1	506
Stump, Jacob J.	21½	Wts. Steer Cr.	1868	1	584
Westfall, J. M.	50	Lick Run	1869	1	598

CLAY (W. VA.)

Lewis, Charles	148¾	Big Laurel	1866	1	130
Schoonover, Daniel	1,500	Wts. of Elk	1865	1	87
Schoonover, William	1,183	Big Laurel Creek	1865	1	61
Schoonover, William	230¾	Wts. Elk River	1865	1	75

DODDRIDGE (W. VA.)

Name of Grantee	Acres	Local Description	Year	Book	Page
Bonnell, Charles	21	Skelton's Run	1867	1	321
Bonnell, Charles	520	Frank's Run	1867	1	321
Donahoe, Michael	276	Arnold's Creek	1866	1	229
Donahoe, Michael	470	Arnold's Creek	1866	1	229
Donahoe, Michael	200	Cherry Camp	1866	1	230
Elliott, Truman	11	Rock Camp	1866	1	216
Hutson, Winter	21½	Adj. his own	1871	2	75
Johnston, Robert	7,150	So. Fk. Hughes R	1866	1	233
Shinn, Josiah H.	79	Long Run	1866	1	209
Snodgrass, Jesse F.	84	Archie's Fork	1865	1	85
Stewart, C. J. (or I.)	350	Arnold's Creek	1865	1	42
Stewart, C. J. (or I.)	590	Arnold's Creek	1865	1	42
Stewart, C. J. (or I.)	240	Arnold's Creek	1865	1	43
Stutler, Isaac	10	Morgan's Run	1867	1	391
Stutler, Isaac	26	Tate's Fork	1867	1	392
Thomas, George	45	Adj. Sandy	1871	2	85

FAYETTE (W. VA.)

Blume, G. M. et al	100	Wts. New River	1867	1	434
Bolling, Martha et al Heirs	131	Butler Spgs. Br.	1871	2	72
Carrington, Charles S.	1,325	Gauley River	1870	2	15
Gray, Cynthia Ann	255	Cane Branch	1873	2	96
Gray, John H.	136	Cain Branch	1867	1	371
Harvey, Morris et al	1,000	New River	1866	1	203
Holliday, Israel E.	110	Mann's Creek	1866	1	169
Hughart, Joseph	200	Glade Cr.	1866	1	253
Lively, Caleb W.	700	Meadow Creek	1866	1	252
Parker, Edwin L.	850	New River & Salt Lick	1866	1	125
Paynter, Anderson et al	1,000	New River	1866	1	203
Riston, Robert	415	Paint Creek	1868	1	476
Sidenstricker, Washington	200	Glade Creek	1873	2	98
Smith, Josiah	116	Buffalo Creek	1871	2	88
Townsend, Benjamin et al	100	Wts. New River	1867	1	434
Tyree, Francis Heirs of	131	Butler Spgs Br.	1871	2	72

GILMER (W. VA.)

Arnold. Maranda	25	Lit. Kanawha	1866	1	202
Arnold, Sarah et al, Heirs	80	Mud Lick	1868	1	540
Beall, Hamilton C	32	Big Crooked Run	1867	1	372
Bennett, J. M.	992	Steer Creek	1875	2	156
Bennett, J. M. et al	27¾	Lit. Crooked Run	1867	1	350
Bennett, J. M. & J. D.	1,000	Lick Run	1867	1	349
Bush, Daniel S.	90	Horn Creek	1866	1	142
Bush, George F.	140	Stinking Cr.	1869	1	591
Bush, John W. et al	240	Stinking Cr.	1870	2	31
Fisher, Charles et al	240	Stinking Cr.	1870	2	31
Gainer, Henson	30	Laurel Fork	1867	1	373
Goff, James R. Heirs of	363	Tanner's Fork	1876	2	163

Name of Grantee	Acres	Local Description	Year	Book	Page
Holt, John et al	27¾	Lit. Crooked Run	1867	1	350
Jackson, Minter	57 (50)	Big Crooked Run	1868	1	536
Jackson, Minter	75	Job's Run	1868	1	536
Jackson, Minter	183	Cedar Creek	1868	1	537
Jackson, Minter	125	Low Gap Run	1868	1	538
Lynch, George et al Heirs	80	Mud Lick	1868	1	540
Lynch, George Jr.	7	Wts. Lit. Kanawha	1868	1	572
McQuain, George H.	18½	Leading Cr.	1868	1	507
McQuain, George H.	50	Leading Cr.	1868	1	508
McQuain, George H.	150	Leading Cr.	1868	1	509
Norris, William P.	53	Grass Run	1867	1	289
Stalnaker, S. G.	78	Job's Run	1870	2	30
Stalnaker, Squire B. & George	51	Piney Run	1868	1	565
Starcher, William	167	Barnes' Run	1868	1	572
Stienbeck, Daniel F.	265	Leading Creek	1870	2	47
Stump, John	93	Steer Creek	1866	1	228
Stump, Michael	224	Owen's Fork	1868	1	503
Stump, Michael	13	Steer Creek	1868	1	507
Wilson, H. N.	46	Tanner	1865	1	18
Yarrington, Elizabeth et al Hrs.	80	Mud Lick	1868	1	540

GRANT (W. VA.)

Neville, M. D.	90¼	Stony River	1869	2	1
Neville, M. D.	100	Abram's Creek	1869	2	1

GREENBRIER (W. VA.)

Caldwell, James R. et al	2,108	Howard's Creek	1866	1	190
Coulter, Thomas S.	117	Slab Camp	1869	2	5
Dennis, Robert F. et al	2,108	Howard's Creek	1866	1	190
Ferrell, William B.	1,800	Little Creek	1868	1	561
Fleshman, John	185	Kenney's Knob	1867	1	278
May, Elijah	70	Buck Lick	1873	2	102
McClung, William & Company	360	Brushy Meadow Cr.	1867	1	429
McDowell, James W.	200	Howard's Creek	1869	1	592
McLung, William & Company	360	Brushy Meadow Cr.	1867	1	429
Nickell, James M.	515	Howard's Creek	1867	1	434
Rucker, John	112	Bear Branch	1869	1	599
Schermerhorn, Eliza L.	1,069	Keeney's Knob	1867	1	376
Schermerhorn, Eliza L.	1,750	Blue Sulphur Spgs.	1867	1	377
Schermerhorn, Eliza L.	781	Lick Creek	1867	1	378
Schermerhorn, Eliza L.	5,277	Lick Creek	1867	1	379
Schermerhorn, Eliza L.	363	Muddy Creek	1867	1	382
Schermerhorn, Eliza L.	26	Adj. Sam'l McClung	1867	1	383
Schermerhorn, Eliza L.	36	Lick Creek	1867	1	383
Schermerhorn, Eliza L.	1,748	Keeney's Knob	1867	1	384
Schermerhorn, Eliza L.	891	Muddy Creek	1867	1	385
Schermerhorn, Eliza L.	26	Adj. Sam'l McClung	1867	1	386
Schermerhorn, Eliza L.	1,865	Muddy Creek	1867	1	387
Schermerhorn, Eliza L.	2,629	Muddy Creek	1867	1	388
Snider, John	250	Brushy Ridge	1869	1	607

HAMPSHIRE (W. VA.)

Name of Grantee	Acres	Local Description	Year	Book	Page
Boseley, Mary & Elizabeth	20	Adj. B. Stuckley	1865	1	46
Brown, James et al	194	So. Branch	1867	1	390
Carskaddon, James	7	Patterson's Cr.	1870	2	35
Cox, Thomas S.	13	Little Capon	1866	1	219
French, William	12¾	Potomac	1871	2	91
Horn, Andrew	31	Middle Ridge	1867	1	270
Johnson, Zachariah	18a.1r.27p.	S. B. Mountain	1866	1	168
Largent, Benjamin F.	125	North River Mt.	1867	1	353
Monroe, John et al	77½	Capon Mt.	1871	2	79
Mulledy, Robert et al	194	So. Branch	1867	1	390
Parsons, Susan	20½	South Branch	1868	1	442
Parsons, Susan et al	212	Jersey Mountain	1877	2	168
Parsons, Susan et al	117	South Branch	1877	2	170
Patterson, Robert	15¼	Adj. Edw. Trickett	1869	1	600
Philips, John W.	19	Break Neck Hill	1879	2	177
Philips, John W.	8	Town Hill	1879	2	178
Philips, John W.	16	Branch Mountain	1879	2	178
Philips, John W.	3⅛	Lit. Cacapon	1879	2	179
Philips, John W. et al	5a.1r.16p.	South Br. Mt.	1879	2	180
Pugh, David et al	77½	Capon Mt.	1871	2	79
Reed, Thomas et al	5a.1r.16p.	So. Branch Mt.	1879	2	180
Sanders, Alexander	34	South Branch	1873	2	105
Smith, Edward M. and Robt. L. et al	117	South Branch	1877	2	170
Smith, Edward M. and Robt. L. et al	212	Jersey Mt.	1877	2	168
Vanortwick, Simeon	241	Ivy Run	1868	1	562
Vanosdall, Cornelius	92½	Spring Gap Mt.	1869	1	606

HANCOCK (W. VA.)

Graham, James (Deed)	Lot No. 4	New Cumberland	1910	2	225
Hobbs, Robert R	27	King's Creek	1912	2	232
Ward, David (Deed)	Lots No. 2 & 3	New Cumberland	1910	2	229

HARDY (W. VA.)

Bean, Joshua	60½	Coburn's Knob	1871	2	78
Burch, Samuel M. et al Heirs	200	Tucker's Run	1867	1	296
Evans, John (of Peter)	84	E. of Mt. Run	1870	2	57
Feller, William H.	10¾	North River	1870	2	59
Harper, Samuel	67¼	Lost River	1870	2	9
High, Frederick S.	670	Branch Mt.	1870	2	8
Landacre, Jesse	883	Big Ridge	1873	2	103
McMechen, S. A. et al	504¼	Fork Mountain	1874	2	132
McMechen, S. A. et al	308	Fork Mountain	1874	2	133
McMechen, Samuel et al	2,707	Deep Spring	1875	2	148
Simmons, Sanford Y.	152½	Patterson's Cr. Mt.	1871	2	81
Sion, Adam	71	Bald Ridge	1867	1	273
Wolf, Adam et al	2,707	Deep Spring	1875	2	148
Wolf, Adam Jr. et al	504¼	Fork Mountain	1874	2	132
Wolf, Adam Jr. et al	308	Fork Mountain	1874	2	133

HARRISON (W. VA.)

JACKSON (W. VA.)

KANAWHA (W. VA.)

Name of Grantee	Acres	Local Description	Year	Book	Page
Alderson, Curtis G.	198	Grapevine Creek	1865	1	31
Belcher, Ali	226	Campbell's Creek	1864	1	10
Belcher, Allen	700	Campbell's Creek	1864	1	9
Belcher, George	3,490	Campbell's Creek	1864	1	3
Belcher, George	300	Campbell's Creek	1864	1	5
Belcher, George	200	8-Mile Creek	1864	1	9
Belcher, George et al	144	Point Lick	1865	1	39
Belcher, George et al	150	Campbell's Creek	1865	1	80
Belcher, Joseph F.	1,590	Blue & Campbell's Crs.	1864	1	11
Dawson, William S.	150	Allen's Fork	1865	1	35
Derrick, Andrew	310	Poca River	1864	1	8
Dryden, John et al	312½	Wilson's Furnace Hol.	1869	2	2
Dryden, John et al	199¼	2-Mile	1869	2	3
Dryden, John et al	400	N. E. Kanawha R.	1866	1	131
Estep, Samuel	600	Blue Creek	1864	1	8
Griffith, Jacob B.	100	Grapevine	1865	1	40
Jones, Henry Heirs	100	Grapevine	1865	1	51
King, George W.	150	Mill Creek	1866	1	128
Lively, M. A.	54	Coal River	1866	1	129
McMullen, William A. et al	400	N. E. Kanawha	1866	1	131
McMullin, William A. et al	312½	Wilson's Furnace Hol.	1869	2	2
McMullin, William A. et al	199¼	2-Mile	1869	2	3
Melton, Thomas	6¼	Elk River	1873	2	99
Morrison, George M. et al	144	Point Lick	1865	1	39
Morrison, George M. et al	150	Campbell's Creek	1865	1	80
Rimmer, Robert	15	Davis Creek	1864	1	10
Taylor, Doddridge	150	Derrick's Cr.	1864	1	7
Thomas, George W. S.	100	Coffman's Fork	1865	1	50
White, Isaac	60	Campbell's Cr.	1865	1	26
Woody, Elizabeth	150	Frogg's Creek	1865	1	67

LEWIS (W. VA.)

Bennett, J. M.	1,500	Leatherbark	1866	1	232
Bennett, J. M. et al	79	Leading Cr.	1866	1	257
Camden, G. D. et al	79	Leading Cr.	1866	1	257
Despard, Burton et al	79	Leading Cr.	1866	1	257
Jackson, Andrew	160	Freeman's Cr.	1867	1	359
Jackson, Andrew	22	Wts. West Fork	1867	1	360
Stalnaker, Charles	30	Hacker's Cr.	1867	1	359
White, Fortunatis	175	Jordan & Kemper	1873	2	123
White, Fortunatis	125	Freeman's Cr.	1867	1	358

LOGAN (W. VA.)

Alderson, Warren	350	Upper Lick	1871	2	89
Allen, Hoffman & Louisa G. et al	490	Gilbert's Creek	1873	2	107
Allen, Hoffman & Louisa G. et al	700	Gilbert's Cr.	1873	2	108
Allen, Hoffman & Louisa G. et al	1,114	Pigeon Creek	1873	2	109

Name of Grantee	Acres	Local Description	Year	Book	Page
Deskins, John W. et al	580	Ben's Creek	1868	1	490
Dingess, Charles F.	147	Messenger Fork	1871	2	79
Dingess, Eliza Heirs	88	12-Pole	1884	2	219
Dingess, John	160	Pine Fork	1868	1	491
Ferrell, Richard Jr.	75	Pigeon Creek	1867	1	366
Ferrell, Richard Jr.	50	Pigeon Creek	1867	1	367
Floyd, George R. C.	6,000	Trace Fork	1871	2	72
Floyd, George R. C.	572	Pigeon Creek	1875	2	145
Floyd, George R. C.	300	Marrowbone	1875	2	146
Goff, John B.	1,400	Pigeon Creek	1866	1	120
Goff, John B. et al	81	Pigeon Creek	1873	2	120
Grimmit, John	25	Lick Branch	1873	2	117
Grimmit, John	80	Guyandotte River	1866	1	206
Hatfield, James	75	Mate's Creek	1877	2	171
Hatfield, James	98	Mate's Creek	1877	2	171
Hill, Lorenzo D.	90	12-Pole Cr.	1868	1	515
Hill, Lorenzo D.	9	Lilley's Branch	1868	1	518
Hill, Lorenzo D.	36	Canoe Branch	1868	1	518
Hinchman, Ulysses	100	Middle Fork	1868	1	550
Justus, Benjamin H.	900	Fork Spur of Mill Cr.	1871	2	70
Justus, Benjamin H.	166	Adj. Steel	1871	2	74
Justus, Benjamin H.	300	Adj. James Ellis	1871	2	74
Lawson, Anthony	1,634	Cow Creek	1870	2	48
Lawson, Anthony	6	Laurel Fork	1867	1	365
Lawson, Anthony	100	Laurel Fork	1867	1	365
Lawson, Anthony	59	Moses' Fork	1867	1	366
Lawson, James M.	700	Sycamore Cr.	1873	2	124
Lechenet, Lewis (Louis) et al	260	Lick & Shoal Brs.	1879	2	182
Lechenet, Louis	190	Adj. Rob't Elkins	1871	2	65
Marcum, Jacob	25	Stone Coal	1875	2	143
Marcum, Jacob M.	50	Laurel Fork	1868	1	490
McCoy, Florina et al Heirs	200	Laurel Fork	1875	2	149
McDonald, William W.	267	Big Spring	1875	2	154
McDonald, William W.	310	Big Huff Cr.	1875	2	155
McNeely, Joseph	29	Cor. B. Mullins	1870	2	49
McNeely, Joseph	25	Op. Meeting House	1870	2	62
McNeely, Joseph et al	200	Op. Lick Branch	1870	2	61
McNeely, Joseph et al	200	Coal River	1879	2	192
Mead, William T.	30	Adj. Robt. Hensley	1879	2	208
Mounts, Michael et al	73	Beech Creek	1868	1	488
Mullins, Andrew J.	50(5)	Spruce Fork	1868	1	556
Mullins, John	70	Op. John Mullins	1871	2	87
Mullins, John	15	Tug Fork	1868	1	474
Mullins, Milton A.	51	Canoe Branch	1868	1	556
Mullins, Milton A.	28	Winding Shoal	1868	1	557
Music, Cumings	180	Pigeon Creek	1866	1	208
Nighbert, George W.	490	Winding Shoals Br.	1871	2	69
Parsley, Rhoda et al Heirs	200	Laurel Fork	1875	2	149
Roman, Isom	290	Pigeon Cr.	1870	2	33
Short, Samuel et al	50	Big Branch	1871	2	70
Short, Samuel et al	100	Pigeon Creek	1871	2	71
Showalter, David	21	Horsepen Fork	1868	1	552
Showalter, David	47	Peet's Branch	1868	1	557
Simpkins, Nancy	85	Lick Fork	1871	2	77
Spaulding, Charles	25	Marrowbone	1884	2	224
Spratt, James	200	Gilbert's Creek	1875	2	144
Spratt, James	260	Long & Lick Brs.	1879	2	204
Spratt, James et al	260	Lick & Shoal Brs.	1879	2	182
Spratt, Robert P.	50	Deep Ford Branch	1879	2	186
Starr, James et al	400	12-Pole Creek	1868	1	461
Steel, George	202	Island Creek	1868	1	554
Steel, Ralph	100	Island Creek	1875	2	143
Steele, L. D. et al	400	Island Creek	1875	2	140

MARION (W. VA.)

MARSHALL (W. VA.)

MASON (W. VA.)

Name of Grantee	Acres	Local Description	Year	Book	Page
Ball, James	26¾	Old Town	1869	1	599
Barnett, Robert Jr.	95	13-Mile	1865	1	73
Barnett, Robert Sr.	700	13-Mile	1865	1	74
Barnett, William	250	13-Mile	1866	1	123
Casto, Joseph	195	13-Mile	1865	1	72
Cossin, Allen et al	91	Cow Run	1867	1	404
Edwards, Ransler	390	13-Mile	1865	1	74
Gilmore, John C. et al	260	3-Mile	1865	1	94
Hawthorne, Pascall et al	558	18-Mile	1865	1	33
Hawthorne, Pascall et al	618	18-Mile	1865	1	34
Hill, Labin	270	Cor. to Robt. Barnett Jr.	1869	2	4
Lewis, Pallas S.	46	3-Mile	1866	1	245
Parsons, William	125	13-Mile	1866	1	136
Pettit, Silas	240	Lit. Kanawha	1866	1	135
Sayre, Laban & Daniel Heirs.	165	Big Spruce	1869	2	5
Sines, Lewis	87	10-Mile	1868	1	589
Smith, J. P. R. B. et al	260	3-Mile	1865	1	94
Staats, Calvin et al	91	Cow Run	1867	1	404
Wetzel, William E.	83	10-Mile	1875	2	139
Wetzel, William E. et al	558	18-Mile	1865	1	33
Wetzel, William et al	618	18-Mile	1865	1	34

McDOWELL (W. VA.)

Bailey, Cloyd	290	Jonny Cake Branch	1868	1	528
Bailey, Eli	34	Panther Cr.	1868	1	450
Bailey, Eli	100	Panther Cr.	1868	1	450
Bailey, Eli	125	Trap Fork	1868	1	452
Bailey, Harvey	2,200	Short Pole & War Cr.	1871	2	68
Bailey, Jackson	66	Panther Creek	1868	1	461
Bailey, Zachariah	133	North Fork	1868	1	500
Beavers, Alexander D.	300	Barrenshee Creek	1866	1	221
Beavers, Alexander D.	100	Clear Fork	1867	1	281
Beavers, Alexander D.	190	Panther Creek	1867	1	292
Beavers, James W.	19	Jacob's Fork	1873	2	95
Beavers, Margaret et al	500	Slate Cr.	1867	1	431
Beavers, Margaret et al	800	Barrenshee Creek	1867	1	432
Beavers, Robert (of Alex)	148	Bandy Br.	1867	1	431
Belcher, Addison	70	Tug & Elkhorn	1866	1	195
Belcher, Benjamin	300	Bill's Branch	1867	1	337
Belcher, Benjamin	60	Elkhorn	1867	1	338
Belcher, Isaac	25	Tug River	1867	1	338
Belcher, Isaac	220	Wts. Tug River	1867	1	339
Belcher, James A.	100	Laurel Creek	1867	1	335
Belcher, Tobias	173	Low Gap Fork	1867	1	335
Belcher, Tobias	86	Elkhorn	1867	1	336
Belcher, Tobias	130	Elkhorn	1867	1	336
Bentley, James B.	175	War Creek	1868	1	547
Bentley, James B.	85	Cub Fork	1868	1	548
Bishop, David	110	Laurel Creek	1868	1	454
Blankenship, Elijah	90	Crane Creek	1867	1	282
Blankenship,, Presley Sr.	95	Panther Cr.	1868	1	438
Brewster—See Bruster					
Bruster, William Sr.	35	Dry Fork	1872	2	93
Bruster, William Sr.	115	Dry Hollow	1872	2	94
Carter, Polly	50	Tug River	1870	2	49
Cartright, Jane	500	Lick Branch	1866	1	248

Name of Grantee	Acres	Local Description	Year	Book	Page
Lawson, Anthony et al	210	Grapevine Branch	1868	1	500
Lee, William R.	300	4-Pole Creek	1867	1	326
Lester, Abner	146	Bare Bottom	1868	1	457
Lester, Elisha	256	Mill Ridge	1867	1	438
Lester, Masten	360	War Creek	1868	1	525
Lester, Thomas M.	43½	Tug River	1866	1	187
Lester, Thomas M.	400	Indian Ridge	1866	1	188
Lester, Thomas M.	50	Greenbrier Ridge	1866	1	189
Lester, Thomas M.	240	Laurel of Elkhorn	1866	1	189
Lester, Thomas M.	41	Day Camp	1866	1	191
Lester, Thomas M.	58	Elkhorn	1866	1	191
Lester, Thomas M.	40	Laurel Creek	1866	1	192
Lester, Thomas M.	96	Bottom Cr. & Laurel	1866	1	192
Lester, Thomas M.	270	Elkhorn & Tug	1866	1	193
Lester, Thomas M.	188	Bottom Cr. & Laurel	1866	1	194
Lester, Thomas M.	284	Tug & Elkhorn	1866	1	194
Lester, Thomas M.	50	Shannon's Branch	1867	1	340
Lester, Thomas M.	200	Wts. Tug	1867	1	340
Lester, Thomas M.	100	Pawpaw Bottom	1868	1	458
Lockhart, Barbara (of Sally)	100	Old Horse Fork	1868	1	542
Marcum, Jacob et al	20	Mill Creek	1867	1	343
Milam, Allen	185	Laurel Creek	1868	1	505
Milam, Allen	50	Bottom Creek	1868	1	506
Milam, Andrew	140	Elkhorn	1867	1	342
Milam, James	123	Belcher Branch	1871	2	75
Milam, John T.	150	Clark's Branch	1871	2	82
Mitchell, A. P.	30	Wts. Tug	1868	1	499
Mitchell, A. P. et al	240	Indian Ridge	1871	2	81
Mitchell, A. P. et al	210	Grapevine Branch	1868	1	500
Mitchell, James P.	40	Elkhorn	1867	1	343
Mitchem, Francis	40	Flat Top Mt.	1868	1	452
Mitchem, Francis	70	Little Flat Top	1868	1	453
Murphy, Herndon	134	Wts. of Tug	1870	2	21
Murphy, John	185	Adkin's Branch	1867	1	347
Osborn, Jessie	322	Wts. of Tug	1868	1	455
Osborn, Wiley	536	Fork Ridge	1868	1	456
Parker, Edwin L.	3,000	Davey Creek	1867	1	279
Payne, John D.	500	Ring's Branch	1867	1	392
Payne, John D.	70	Hurricane Br.	1867	1	393
Payne, John D.	25½	Dry Fork	1868	1	516
Payne, Lewis	90	Bark Camp Br.	1867	1	394
Payne, Simeon L. & J. D.	200	Panther Cr.	1868	1	519
Peery, Henry F.	100	Rockhouse Branch	1868	1	454
Reed, William L.	70	Adj. Andrew Stowers	1870	2	60
Rose, Bartley	300	Bottom Creek	1867	1	292
Rose, Isaac	200	Elkhorn Fork	1867	1	326
Sayers, David G.	500	Bill's Br. & Lick Fk.	1866	1	219
Sayers, David G.	117	Trace Branch	1867	1	318
Sayers, David G. et al	500	Jacob's Fork	1868	1	526
Sayers, David G. et al	(100)500	Panther Fork	1868	1	526
Sayers, David G. et al	100	Panther Creek	1868	1	527
Shannon, James H. et al	20	Mill Creek	1867	1	343
Short, Benjamin	87½	Crane Trace Branch	1868	1	476
Short, Joseph	47	Ring's Branch	1870	2	17
Short, William	50	Tug River	1870	2	28
Short, William	82	Laurel Creek	1870	2	29
Smith, George P. & Zacheus	94	North Fork of Tug	1868	1	457
Smith, Isaiah Jr.	50	Mill Creek	1867	1	341
Smith, John & G. P.	312	Webb Ridge	1868	1	459
Stanley, Margaret	200	Lick Branch	1867	1	427
Totten, James M.	170	Belcher's Branch	1866	1	195
Williams, William	1,030	White Oak Fork	1870	2	63
Williams, William	190	Panther Fork	1868	1	517

MERCER (W. VA.)

Name of Grantee	Acres	Local Description	Year	Book	Page
Bailey, Archibald et al	200	Wide Mouth	1879	2	201
Bailey, Augustus I.	80	Wide Mouth	1879	2	193
Bailey, William A.	50	Wide Mouth	1879	2	202
Barley, Augustus I.	80	Wide Mouth	1879	2	193
Belcher, Madison F.	60	Big Blue Stone	1868	1	504
Cook, Manderville	79	Wts. New River	1868	1	488
Crowel, Nancy, Ballard & John	100	Rich Creek	1879	2	200
Dunlap, John R. et al	1,000	Big Blue Stone	1868	1	480
Ellison, James	30	Big Blue Stone	1868	1	486
English, James W. et al	2,000	Wts. Blue Stone	1868	1	483
Farley, Joel	88	Waters Old House Br.	1868	1	487
Farley, Wilson	70	Wts. Pipestem	1868	1	486
Godfrey, John D et al	200	Wide Mouth	1879	2	201
Houchins, James	162	Big Blue Stone	1868	1	473
Hurst, William	94	Rich Creek	1879	2	191
McComas, Martha (Now Peters)	140	Flat Top	1879	2	199
McKenzie, John A.	86	East River	1868	1	479
Neeley—See Newlee					
Newlee, George B.	125	Lick Creek	1868	1	485
Oney, William	50	East River	1870	2	40
Oney, William	25	12-Mile Fork	1868	1	481
Oney, William	25	Brush Cr.	1868	1	484
Pearis, Samuel P.	356	Tom's Run	1870	2	54
Pearis, Samuel P.	84	Blue Stone	1870	2	55
Pearis, Samuel P.	374	Big Bluestone	1870	2	55
Pearis, Samuel P.	195	Big Pipe Stem	1868	1	482
Pearis, Samuel P.	70	Flat Top Mt.	1868	1	483
Pendleton, A. G. et al	2,000	Wts. Blue Stone	1868	1	483
Peters, Martha	140	Flat Top	1879	2	199
Reed, Elias	200	Rich Creek	1879	2	197
Roles, James	550	Big Pipestem	1868	1	484
Straley, Harrison W. et al	1,000	Big Blue Stone	1868	1	480
Taylor, Sampson	100	Rich Creek	1879	2	190
Walker, Ira W.	100	Wide Mouth	1879	2	194
White, Benjamin et al	2,000	Wts. Blue Stone	1868	1	483
Wimmer, Samuel	200	Rich Creek	1879	2	198

MONONGALIA (W. VA.)

Smith, B. F.	77¼p.	Morgantown	1868	1	445
Youst, Mary (Yost) Devisee of G. Youst	24	Paw-Paw Creek	1866	1	142

MONROE (W. VA.)

Ballard, Lewis, Assignee	100	Lit. Mountain	1870	2	59
Cummins, Austin	100	Peter's Mt.	1868	1	562
Ethell, Sandford	5	Wts. Greenbrier	1867	1	351
Ethell, Sandford	135	Adj. George Alderson	1867	1	351
Miller, James E.	166¾	Cedar Run	1866	1	203
Nowlan, John Sr.	33½	Hungart's Creek	1867	1	352
Wickline, George J.	65	Dunlap's Creek	1874	2	125

MORGAN (W. VA.)

Name of Grantee	Acres	Local Description	Year	Book	Page
Ashton, John	34¾	Sleepy Creek Mt.	1867	1	287
Ashton, John	307	Sleepy Creek	1866	1	288
Bechtol, Aaron	410	Wts. Potomac	1865	1	19
Bechtol, Aaron	140	Spring Run	1865	1	20
Bechtol, Henry C.	34	Spring Run	1865	1	20
Bechtol, Joseph et al	219	Wts. Potomac	1864	1	1
Burk, John	25	Sir. John's Run	1867	1	294
Cann, Jacob	193	Sidling Hill	1864	1	2
Culp, Lewis et al	219	Wts. Potomac	1864	1	1
Duckwall, Middleton	8	Sleepy Creek	1870	2	46
Gross, Dennis	67	Potomac River	1866	1	147
House, William	109	Sidling Hill	1864	1	1
Kesler, Absalom	74	Sidling Hill	1867	1	355
Smith, Elias	15	Cor. McCowan's	1870	2	34
Weber, Gotleib F.	38	Sleepy Creek Mt.	1867	1	405

NICHOLAS (W. VA.)

Alderson, J. A.	4,800	Anglin's Creek	1868	1	456
Bell, Samuel Sr.	156	Peter's Creek	1868	1	437
Conner, Nerius B.	25½	Adj. J. Chapman	1869	1	607
Conner, Nerius B.	48	Glade Creek	1868	1	608
Davis, S. T.	100	Big Birch	1870	2	12
Duffy, Sally & John et al	200	McKee's Creek	1870	2	8
Foster, Andrew	15¼	Adj. H. Miller	1870	2	36
Fowler, John C. et al	145	Wts. Birch River	1868	1	529
Hart, Isaac et al	200	McKee's Creek	1870	2	8
Hooker, Levi J.	900	20-Mile Creek	1866	1	114
Hooker, W. C. et al	145	Wts. Birch River	1868	1	529
Maury, Robert H.	150	Adj. Sam'l Neil	1867	1	407
Maury, Robert H.	4,560	Peter's Creek	1867	1	407
Maury, Robert H.	2,560	Wts. Gauley	1867	1	409
Maury, Robert H.	5,960	Big Sycamore	1867	1	410
Maury, Robert H.	5,450	20-Mile Creek	1867	1	411
Maury, Robert H.	4,150	Peter's Creek	1867	1	413
Maury, Robert H.	4,440	Lit. Elk Cr. & Gauley	1867	1	415
Maury, Robert H.	3,000	20-Mile Creek	1867	1	417
Maury, Robert H.	1,090	Beech Run	1867	1	418
McClung, James C.	180	Adj. J. R. Ramsey	1868	1	491
Patterson, Heirs et al	200	McKee's Creek	1870	2	8
Robinson, J. Haymond	950	Wts. Mumblethepeg	1868	1	497
Williams, Joseph	98	Wts. Gauley	1869	1	603
Williams, Samuel H.	100	Wts. of Gauley	1869	1	604

PENDLETON (W. VA.)

Hoover, William	620	Cor. to Probst	1871	2	83
Hopkins, Cyrus	110	Rud's Creek	1873	2	122

PLEASANTS (W. VA.)

Name of Grantee	Acres	Local Description	Year	Book	Page
Green, Christopher	20	Ohio R. at French Cr.	1870	2	11
Green, Christopher	37	2nd Brother Isl. Ohio	1870	2	11
Green, Christopher	5	1st Brother Isl. Ohio	1870	2	12
Martin, Abner	13	Cedar Run	1865	1	53

POCAHONTAS (W. VA.)

Dorr, Charles P. et al	6,800	Gauley R. & Tee Cr.	1884	2	212
Fickey, Frederick Jr. et al	8,000	Wts. Cheat	1867	1	312
Holt, Homer A. et al	6,800	Gauley R. & Tee Cr.	1884	2	212
Kerr, Robert B.	470	Deer Creek	1873	2	118
Smith, James	15	Wts. Greenbrier	1868	1	567
Thomas, Edward L. et al	8,000	Wts. Cheat	1867	1	312
Wallace, Matthew	130	Greenbrier River	1884	2	215
Warwick, Jacob et al	6,800	Gauley R. & Tee Cr.	1884	2	212

PRESTON (W. VA.)

Abbott, Jerred T.	500	Wts. Cheat	1865	1	58
Baldwin, Israel	52	Laurel Run	1866	1	126
Boger, Samuel	60	Sandy Creek	1865	1	106
Hoffman, John H.	153	Wts. Cheat	1865	1	76
Michael, John	160	Big Sandy Cr.	1865	1	66
Morris, R.	70	Muddy Creek	1866	1	125
Murdock, Godfrey G.	4¼	Lick Run	1865	1	16
Ward, Ulysses	4,850	Snowy Creek	1866	1	114

PUTNAM (W. VA.)

Blankenship, William	557	Hurricane Cr.	1865	1	13
Bowyer, John	420	Poplar Creek	1864	1	4
Burnside, Benjamin & John	124	Mud River	1875	2	150
Byers, Bennett	462	18-Mile Creek	1865	1	94
Chase, Owen G.	124	Adj. J. K. Craig	1866	1	121
Cooper, Thomas	290	18-Mile Cr.	1866	1	254
Estill, H. G.	51	Nr. Alfred Brown	1868	1	566
Hall, Robert M.	42	Cor. to Wm. Frazer	1866	1	146
Hall, Robert M.	448	Hunnicut Branch	1866	1	146
Hensley, F. G.	150	Raccoon Creek	1867	1	291
Hensley, John	150	Wts. Cole River	1867	1	290
Jones, Thomas	100	18-Mile Creek	1865	1	49
Middleton, H. O.	1,137	Poca	1865	1	13
Nicholas, Ephraim	87	Brown's Creek	1867	1	291
Smith, Joseph B.	120	Big Hurricane Cr.	1866	1	254
Summers, M. A.	140	Trace Fork	1866	1	159

RALEIGH (W. VA.)

Name of Grantee	Acres	Local Description	Year	Book	Page
Bryson, Mary E. et al Hrs.	177½	Soak Creek	1867	1	317
Caldwell, E H. et al	714	Shockley's Fork	1867	1	419
Gartner, Allen	150	Sewell Branch	1870	2	23
Hansley—See Hensley					
Hansley, Sarah V.	144¼	Maple Meadow	1867	1	420
Hansley, Stephen M. et al	714	Shockley's Fork	1867	1	419
Harper, Hamilton	505	Sand Lick Cr.	1868	1	478
Harper, Jacob Heirs	214½	Paint Cr.	1866	1	169
Harper, Jacob Heirs	345¾	Paint Cr.	1866	1	170
Hensley—See Hansley					
Mann, William T.	280	Wts. New River	1867	1	278
McGinnis, Evaline et al Hrs.	214½	Paint Cr.	1866	1	169
McGinnis, Evaline et al Hrs.	345¾	Paint Cr.	1866	1	170
McGinnis, Gordon	50¾	Soak Cr.	1868	1	478
McGinnis, Pyrrhus	80a.18p.	Soak Cr.	1867	1	421
McGinnis, Samuel	135	Sand Lick	1867	1	296
Miller, Henry F.	50	Paint Cr.	1868	1	468
Richman, W. C.	39a.58p.	Suell Gut	1869	1	598
Richmond, William C.	150	New River	1871	2	86
Riffe, Henry M.	1,791⅜	Marsh Fork	1867	1	317
Riffe, Henry M. et al	714	Shockley's Fork	1867	1	419
Riffe, Henry M. et al Heirs	177½	Soak Creek	1867	1	419
Turner, John B	78½	Sand Lick	1866	1	172
Turner, John B.	121½	Sand Lick	1866	1	172
Turner, John B.	242	Laurel Branch	1867	1	406
Turner, William	128½	Sand Lick	1866	1	171
Williams, John	195¾	Paint Cr.	1867	1	354

RANDOLPH (W. VA.)

Armstrong, William D.	155	Rich Mountain	1866	1	145
Arnold, Jonathan	60	Beaver Creek	1866	1	140
Arnold, Jonathan et al	421(420)	Shafer Mt.	1868	1	451
Arnold, Jonathan et al	500	Dry Fork	1868	1	539
Arnold, Thomas J. et al	500	Wts. Buckhannon	1866	1	112
Baker, Isaiah et al	444	Whitman's Flats	1867	1	271
Barrett, George W. et al	375½	Cheat Mt.	1867	1	330
Bennett, William	414	Long Run & Jake's Fk.	1866	1	135
Bennett, William	48	Middle Fork	1866	1	255
Brannon, John et al	5,000	Wts. Cheat River	1868	1	495
Brown, B. L. et al	500	Dry Fork	1868	1	539
Buckey, Alpheus et al	200	File's Creek	1873	2	106
Burk, Charles W.	2¾	Leading Cr.	1867	1	315
Coberly, William H. et al	250	Cheat Mountain	1866	1	139
Crouch, Abraham	55	Adj. Andrew Crouch	1866	1	251
Crouch, Abraham	20	Mill Run	1866	1	252
Crouch, Jacob	118	Mill Run	1866	1	250
Crouch, Jacob et al	258	Haddin Mill Run	1867	1	288
Daniels, George H. et al	200	File's Creek	1873	2	106
Fickey, Frederick Jr. et al	2,000	Dry Fork	1883	2	210
Fickey, Frederick Jr. et al	8,000	Wts. Cheat	1867	1	312
Gibson, Alexander et al	87	Rich Mountain	1868	1	532
Goff, Claudius Heirs et al	1,200	Roaring Creek	1866	1	197
Hall, William H. et al Hrs.	1,000	Shaver's Fork	1867	1	331
Hamilton, William Heirs et al	1,000	Shaver's Fork	1867	1	331
Hamilton, William Heirs	500	Wts. Cheat River	1867	1	308

Name of Grantee	Acres	Local Description	Year	Book	Page
Harman, Thomas	55	Dry Fork	1866	1	148
Hart, Milton	127	Roaring Creek	1866	1	143
Hart, Milton et al	250	Cheat Mountain	1866	1	139
Hughes, Draper et al Hrs.	1,200	Roaring Creek	1866	1	197
Hutton, Alfred & Elihu	390	Mill Creek	1867	1	404
Kierans, John et al	5,000	Wts. Cheat River	1868	1	495
Leary, James F. et al	87	Rich Mountain	1868	1	532
Logan, James H.	100	Wts. Cheat	1866	1	110
Logan, James H. et al	500	Wts. Buckhannon R.	1866	1	112
Logan, James H. et al Heirs	500	Wts. Cheat River	1867	1	308
Logan, William E. & J. H.	350	Valley River	1867	1	272
Logan, William E. & James H.	215	Valley River	1866	1	148
Magee, Michael	340½	Cheat Mt.	1867	1	369
Marsteller, Nicholas	100	Shaver's Fork	1873	2	98
McVeigh, W. M. & J. H. et al	5,000	Wts. Cheat River	1868	1	495
Middleton, Henry O.	829	Laurel & Mid. Forks	1866	1	157
Parker, E. L. et al Heirs	1,000	Shaver's Fork	1867	1	331
Phares, Benjamin	1,040	Rich Mountain	1870	2	10
Reel, William C.	31½	Piercy Run	1869	2	3
Rosacrance, Jesse W. et al	258	Haddin's Mill Run	1867	1	288
Rosecrans—See Rosacrance					
Ryan, James	47	Rich Mountain	1866	1	138
Sachs, E. F (Sacks)	350	Middle Fork	1868	1	505
Sacks, Erhart F.	225	Whitman's Flats	1867	1	273
Sacks, Erhart F. et al	444	Whitman's Flats	1867	1	271
Simmons, Daniel W.	100	Cassadie's Fork	1866	1	246
Snyder, John	35	Dry Fork	1870	2	58
Stalnaker, Asbury	30	Leading Creek	1866	1	137
Stalnaker, Hamilton	950	Mill Creek	1866	1	249
Suiter, Jacob B. et al	375½	Cheat Mt.	1867	1	330
Taylor, John	26	Wts. of Cheat	1866	1	247
Taylor, John et al	421(420)	Shafer Mt.	1868	1	451
Thomas, Edward L. et al	2,000	Dry Fork	1883	2	210
Thomas, Edward L. et al	8,000	Wts. Cheat	1867	1	312
Ward, Levi S.	82	Cheat Mountain	1866	1	155
Ward, Levi S.	118	File's Creek	1866	1	156
Wilmoth, Levi N.	109	Wts. Cheat	1867	1	319

RITCHIE (W. VA.)

Clayton, A. A.	51	Leatherbark	1866	1	131
Clayton, A. A. et al	198	Spruce Creek	1864	1	3
Clayton, John S.	40	Leatherbark	1864	1	12
Collins, Josiah	94	Buck Run	1865	1	63
Dotson, Solomon	190	North Fork	1865	1	37
Hall, Smith C. & Cyrus	1,070	Wts. Hughes	1866	1	268
Haymond, William C.	15	Wts. Hughes	1864	1	2
Johnson, William F.	2	Oil Spring Run	1867	1	277
Johnston, Robert	4,100	Otter Slide	1866	1	232
Jones, Edmund B.	45½	North Fork	1865	1	27
Law, A. P. et al	198	Spruce Creek	1864	1	3
Leggitt, James N.	10	Hughes River	1866	1	198
Lowther, James R.	200	Slab Creek	1866	1	113
Merrill, John W.	80½	Goose Creek	1865	1	103
Modesitt, John	95	Leather Bark	1875	2	141
Patton, John C.	1,000	Wts. Hughes	1867	1	334
Pierpoint, Larkin	190	Lit. Straight Fork	1866	1	268
Sharpneck, John	11	Goose Creek	1865	1	21

ROANE (W. VA.)

TUCKER (W. VA.)

TYLER (W. VA.)

Name of Grantee	Acres	Local Description	Year	Book	Page
Hardman, H. H.	96½	McElroy's Fork	1868	1	590
Hoge, Isaac	11a.3r.19p.	Buffalo Creek	1865	1	26
Owens, Isaac	29	Long Run	1865	1	88
Smith, Valentine	34	Narrow's Run	1865	1	99
Steel, Thomas et al	132	Plum Run	1865	1	108
Steel, Thomas et al	200	McKim's Fork	1865	1	109
Underwood, Nattey W.	24a.1r.	McElroy's Fork	1868	1	511
Woodburn, Peter	4¾	Middle Island Cr.	1865	1	5

UPSHUR (W. VA.)

Middleton, Henry O.	1,800	Buckhannon River	1866	1	158
Phillips, S. B.	110	French Creek	1865	1	91

WAYNE (W. VA.)

Adkins, B. F. T. et al	85	Spring Branch	1867	1	374
Adkins, Henry	140	Blue Creek	1870	2	56
Adkins, Thomas J.	10	Camp Branch	1870	2	58
Ball, William	7	Sycamore Creek	1867	1	328
Bloss, Isaac	90	Hezekiah's Fork	1868	1	469
Bloss, Isaac Sr.	75	Big Laurel	1868	1	469
Bloss, Isaac Sr.	70	Hezekiah's Fork	1868	1	470
Bloss, Isaac Sr.	250	Barker's Creek	1868	1	470
Bloss, Isaac Sr.	185	Grassy Branch	1868	1	471
Bloss, Isaac Sr.	275	Trough Fork	1868	1	471
Bloss, Isaac Sr.	80	Hezekiah's Fork	1868	1	472
Bloss, Isaac Sr.	90	12-Pole Cr.	1868	1	475
Clark, A.T.	125	Brush Creek	1867	1	435
Cole, John H. et al	65	Horse Bone	1867	1	325
Copley, William D.	155	Camp Creek	1870	2	25
Cyrus, Louis & Virginia et al Hrs.	25	Mill Creek	1874	2	134
Dameron, Samuel Sr.	600	McComas Branch	1868	1	444
Damron—See Dameron					
Damron, Moses	106	12-Pole	1866	1	244
Damron, Moses Jr.	106	12-Pole	1866	1	243
Defoe, William A.	7	12-Pole	1870	2	14
Defoe, William A. et al	100	Queen Branch	1870	2	13
Elliot, John	35	Lit. Laurel	1870	2	35
Ferguson—See Furgerson					
Ferguson, Charles W.	50	Rocky Branch	1866	1	199
Ferguson, Charles W.	20	2-Mile	1866	1	200
Ferguson, Charles W.	90	12-Pole	1866	1	200
Ferguson, Charles W.	30	2-Mile	1866	1	201
Findley, Hezekiah	113	12-Pole	1870	2	26
Findley, Hezekiah	62	12-Pole	1870	2	27
Finly—See Findley					
Frasher—or Frasier, Frasure, Frazier					
Frasher, William et al	45	Spring Branch	1867	1	374
Frasher, William et al	85	12-Pole	1867	1	374

Name of Grantee	Acres	Local Description	Year	Book	Page
Frasier—See Frasher					
Frasure—See Frasher					
Frazier—See Frasher					
Fry, Andrew	25	Brush Creek	1868	1	541
Fry, Nancy	12	Brush Creek	1868	1	539
Furgurson—See Ferguson					
Furgurson, Edmund et al	19	12-Pole	1868	1	523
Furgurson, Milton J. et al	120	White Oak Br.	1868	1	523
Hoard, C. B. et al	50	Cove Creek	1870	2	52
Hoard, C. B. et al	145	12-Pole	1870	2	52
Hoard, C. B. et al	100	Cove Creek	1870	2	53
Holt, John W.	25	Orchard Branch	1874	2	128
Jarrell, John et al	65	Horse Bone	1867	1	325
Justice, George T.	34	Brush Creek	1867	1	430
Lambert, James W.	70	12-Pole	1868	1	467
Low, Garrett	200	Ginney's Creek	1868	1	541
Low, Jarrett	9	Old Fork	1868	1	553
Lucas, Vincent	220	Bowen's Creek	1866	1	227
Lycans, Jacob (Lylans)	46	Billy's Branch	1869	1	605
Lylans, Jacob	46	Billy's Branch	1869	1	605
Mainard, John et al	100	Queen Branch	1870	2	13
Mansfield, J. J.	124	Brush Creek	1868	1	522
Mansfield, J. J. et al	19	12-Pole	1868	1	523
Mantsfield—See Mansfield					
Marcum, Jacob	115	Bull Creek	1867	1	314
Marcum, Jacob	538	Bark Camp Branch	1869	1	602
Marcum, Jacob M.	430	12-Pole	1869	1	604
Marcum, Jacob M.	200	12-Pole	1869	1	605
Marcum, Van B.	100	Spruce Branch	1869	1	601
Marcum, Van B.	1,375	Moses Fork	1869	1	601
Marcum, Van B.	84	Bark Camp Branch	1869	1	602
Mays, Andrew	95	12-Pole	1867	1	304
Moore, Thomas P.	55	12-Pole	1873	2	100
Napier, Robert	157	Lynn Creek	1867	1	305
Napier, Young et al (Younge)	45	12-Pole	1867	1	374
Nelson, G. M.	25	Big Laurel	1867	1	402
Nixon, William	230	Camp Creek	1867	1	276
Osborn, John	85	Brush Creek	1868	1	465
Osburn, John	25	Wolf Creek	1867	1	375
Osburn, John	25	Wolf Creek	1867	1	376
Parks, Robert H.	100	Big Hurricane Cr.	1868	1	465
Parsley—See Pasley					
Parsley, Jesse et al	100	Lick Fork	1873	2	101
Pasley—See Parsley					
Pasley, Jesse	140	Jennie's Creek	1867	1	310
Pasley, Jessie	75	Ginney's Creek	1868	1	467
Perry, Nathan	125	12-Pole	1873	2	100
Preston, Henry	23	12-Pole	1867	1	304
Preston, William	45	12-Pole	1866	1	260
Preston, William	625	Sycamore Cr.	1866	1	261
Reece, James P. et al Hrs.	25	Mill Creek	1874	2	134
Sellards, James	11	12-Pole	1866	1	199
Shelden, Milton	25	Big Lynn	1874	2	129
Shelden, Milton	32	12-Pole	1874	2	130
Shelden, Milton	15	12-Pole	1874	2	131
Smith, John	35	Beech Fork	1870	2	27
Smith, John	25	12-Pole	1870	2	28
Smith, Marshall Z. et al Hrs.	25	Mill Creek	1874	2	134
Spaulding, Jackson et al	100	Lick Fork	1873	2	101
Spurlock, H. et al	120	White Oak Br.	1868	1	523
Spurlock, Hurston	50	Laurel Creek	1875	2	138
Vinson, William	415	12-Pole	1870	2	36
Vinson, William	500	12-Pole	1870	2	37

Name of Grantee	Acres	Local Description	Year	Book	Page
Wheeler, J. C.	47	Hezekiah Creek	1870	2	51
Wheeler, J. C. et al	50	Cove Creek	1870	2	52
Wheeler, J. C. et al	145	12-Pole	1870	2	52
Wheeler, J. C. et al	100	Cove Cr.	1870	2	53
Wheeler, Joseph C.	17	Big Sycamore	1867	1	425
Wheeler, Joseph C.	220	Sycamore Cr.	1867	1	425
Wheeler, Joseph C.	200	Drift Wood Br.	1867	1	428
Wheeler, Joseph C. Assigne	30	Bartrum's Branch	1869	1	606
Wilson, Elbert S.	161	Billy's Branch	1868	1	464

WEBSTER (W. VA.)

Cochran, William C.	100	Grassy Creek	1867	1	293
Dodrill, Robert (Doddrill)	425	Point Mountain	1867	1	403
Dorr, Charles P. et al	6,800	Gauley R. & Tee Cr.	1884	2	212
Gregory, Currence	350	Big Grassy Cr.	1867	1	276
Gregory, William G. et al	100	Wts. of Elk	1867	1	275
Hamrick, Christopher M. et al	127	Elk River	1870	2	14
Hamrick, James M. et al	100	Wts. Elk	1867	1	275
Holt, Homer A. et al	6,800	Gauley & Tee Cr.	1884	2	212
Linch—or Lynch					
Linch, George et al	127	Elk River	1870	2	14
Lynch, Adam G.	400	Big Grassy Cr.	1867	1	274
Lynch, John Jr.	100	Wts. Elk	1868	1	499
McCort, John B.	50	Camp Run	1867	1	307
McHamrick, Christopher M. et al	127	Elk River	1870	2	14
Miller, G. W. K.	41	Back Fork	1867	1	299
Miller, G. W. K.	291	Back Fork	1867	1	300
Miller, G. W. K.	45	Back Fork	1867	1	316
Miller, Samuel C.	400	Laurel Creek	1876	2	164
Mollohan, Charles	345	Laurel Fork	1867	1	309
Strong, William F. et al	1,500	Gauley Mt.	1866	1	244
Wallace, Matthew et al	1,500	Gauley Mt.	1866	1	244
Warwick, John W. et al	6,800	Gauley & Tee Cr.	1884	2	212
Warwick, John W. et al	1,500	Gauley Mt.	1866	1	244
Woodzell, James	255	Wts. of Gauley	1867	1	284
Woodzell, James	250	Wts. Elk	1867	1	285
Woodzell, James	140	Wts. Elk	1868	1	530
Woodzell, James	175	Spilman Mt.	1868	1	531

WETZEL (W. VA.)

Caldwell, E. H.	67½	Hupp's Creek	1865	1	21
Fluharty, Jacob	300	Pine Fork	1865	1	64
Hall, L. S.	37	Lit. Fishing Cr.	1873	2	104
Hall, L. S.	237½	Fishing Cr.	1868	1	439
Hall, L. S.	92	Fishing Cr.	1868	1	440
Hall, L. S.	1,350	Hupp's Run	1868	1	440
Hall, L. S.	102	Lit. Fishing Cr.	1868	1	441
Hall, L. S.	27	Fishing Cr.	1868	1	513
Hall, L. S.	2,000	Pine Fork	1868	1	513
Hall, L. S.	800	Fishing Cr.	1868	1	514

Name of Grantee	Acres	Local Description	Year	Book	Page
Hall, L. S.	900	Fishing Cr.	1868	1	514
Hall, L. S.	30	Fishing Cr.	1868	1	515
Hall, L. S.	207	Lit. Fishing Cr.	1868	1	589
Hart, Anthony	7	Little Fishing Cr.	1865	1	25
Headlee, Anthony A.	25	Fishing Cr.	1866	1	164
Headlee, Anthony A.	10	Pine Fork	1866	1	165
Hoge, Isaac	81	Fishing Creek	1865	1	38
Hoge, Isaac	58	Hupp's Creek	1865	1	38
Hoge, Isaac	825	Fishing Creek	1865	1	84
Hoge, Isaac	43	Fish Cr.	1866	1	144
Leap, John W.	107½	Doolin Run	1870	2	39
Lieuts, Francis D.	636	Fishing Creek	1864	1	4
Lieuts, George	109½	Little Fishing Cr.	1866	1	218
Louck, R. W.	164	Fishing Creek	1865	1	72
Martin, Benjamin	5¾	North Fork	1865	1	104
Matheny, William A.	24¼	Fishing Cr.	1866	1	245
Morgan, Elihu	34½	Wilson's Run	1865	1	23
Morgan, J. W.	300	Willey's Fork	1868	1	560
Morgan, John W.	215	Fishing Cr.	1868	1	559
Morris, Joseph et al	13¼	Fish Creek	1866	1	174
Murphy, John	151	Fishing Cr.	1867	1	312
Murphy, John	50	Upper Field Run	1868	1	441
Parriott, Samuel A.	373	Fish Creek	1865	1	88
Peterson, William F.	105	Shenango Run	1865	1	95
Peterson, William F.	350	Reeder's Run	1865	1	95
Peterson, William F.	27½	Proctor Run	1865	1	96
Peterson, William F.	128	Fishing Creek	1865	1	96
Peterson, William F.	230	Fishing Cr.	1867	1	324
Peterson, William F.	301	Little Fish Cr.	1867	1	325
Remley, Ulrich et al	13¼	Fish Creek	1866	1	174
Robinson, S. J.	76	Big & Lit. Fish Crs.	1870	2	51
Robinson, S. J.	87	Reader's Run	1868	1	501
Robinson, Samuel J.	40	Church's Fork	1868	1	501
Robinson, Samuel J.	510	Willey's Fork	1868	1	501
Robinson, Samuel J.	125	Church's Fork	1868	1	502
Robinson, Samuel J.	141	Trail's Run	1868	1	502
Snodgrass, Charles W.	28	Lick Run	1865	1	107
Stephens, Stacy	39	Fishing Creek	1865	1	77
Tucker, Thomas	85	Archey's Fork	1867	1	323
Ullom, Alfred	14½	Fish Creek	1866	1	134
Van Horn, George	47	Long Drain	1867	1	283
Wilson, Joseph	100	Fishing Creek	1866	1	215
Woods, Westley	39½	Laurel Run	1871	2	64
Wyatt, Alpheus	250	Fishing Creek	1866	1	163

WIRT (W. VA.)

Adams, P. M.	100	Spring Cr.	1865	1	44
Adams, P. M.	100	Bear Run	1865	1	45
Adams, P. M.	317	Spring Creek	1866	1	224
Anderson, Hiram	56a.102p.	Island Run	1865	1	30
Bailis, Charles	62	Standing Stone	1865	1	6
Bailis, Wilson	59½	Greaves Run	1876	2	162
Blair, J. B.	100	Reedy Creek	1867	1	436
Blair, J. B.	257	Reedy Creek	1867	1	436
Boice, Joseph	16	Tucker's Cr.	1868	1	473
Buel, Laurain	140	Reedy Creek	1866	1	153
Buffington, G. W.	39	Lit. Island Run	1865	1	99

Name of Grantee	Acres	Local Description	Year	Book	Page
Buffington, G. W.	89	Slate Creek	1865	1	100
Buffington, G. W. et al	246	Standing Stone	1865	1	65
Buffington, G. W. et al	246	Standing Stone	1866	1	127
Buffington, George W.	97	Grieves Run	1865	1	47
Cain, James W.	64	Wts. Hughes	1865	1	39
Clark, James	29	Wts. Lit. Kanawha	1865	1	97
Clark, James	217	Spring Creek	1866	1	141
Creel, B. W. et al	24	Wts. Lit. Kanawha	1865	1	15
Deem—See Dihm					
Dihm, George F.	527	Lit. Kanawha	1866	1	126
Donaly, Dryden et al	400	Henderson's Run	1868	1	512
Dovener, R. G.	26	Greaves Run	1876	2	167
Fisher, Charles W.	56	Standing Stone	1865	1	45
Hale, J. W.	50a 2r.15½p.	Two-Run	1866	1	122
Hale, Joseph W.	31	Standing Stone	1865	1	22
Hale, Joseph W. et al	246	Standing Stone	1865	1	65
Hale, Joseph W. et al	246	Standing Stone	1866	1	127
Hall, John P.	121	Spring Cr.	1865	1	48
Harkins, Thomas	600	Slate Creek	1865	1	36
Harner, David	87	Summerville Fork	1868	1	560
Howe, Sarah A.	600	Standing Stone	1866	1	204
Jackson, H. J.	262	Flint Run	1865	1	75
Keyes, Oswell E	3	Standing Stone	1865	1	73
Lee, John B.	100	Reedy	1866	1	214
Lee, John B.	186	Reedy	1866	1	224
Lee, Joshua	500	Spring Creek	1865	1	63
Lee, Thomas	200	Reedy	1866	1	225
Lee, Thomas	418	Reedy	1866	1	225
Lockhart, E. S.	230	Reedy	1865	1	71
Lockhart, Wm. E. et al Hrs.	1,103	Wts. Hughes	1865	1	62
Lyon, E. B.	29	Tucker's Creek	1866	1	123
Mackey, A.	49	Flint Run	1865	1	91
Merrill, John W.	114a.1r.13½p.	Goose Creek	1865	1	105
Mullinax, Sullivan	31	Lee Creek	1865	1	70
Nutter, Humphrey D.	85	Flint Run	1865	1	90
Nutter, Thomas C.	56	Slate Creek	1865	1	25
Nutter, Thomas C. Assgn.	56	State Cr.	1871	2	91
Palmer, Waterman	100	Slate Creek	1865	1	14
Rathbone, J. C.	45p.	Island Kanawha	1865	1	82
Rector, Enoch	100	Slate Creek	1865	1	14
Robinson, James F.	210	Standing Stone	1865	1	46
Rochambeau—See Rockinbo					
Rockinbo, James W. et al	1,103	Wts. Hughes River	1865	1	62
Schock, M. P. et al	400	Henderson's Run	1868	1	512
Scloch, M. P. et al	24	Wts. Lit. Kanawha	1865	1	15
Shock—See Schock, Scloch					
Shock, M. P. et al	24	Wts. Lit. Kanawha	1865	1	15
Stephenson, James M	338	Wts. Lit. Kanawha	1865	1	52
Stephenson, K. B. & J. M.	174	Slate Creek	1865	1	52
Thomas, Anthony	62	Reedy Creek	1868	1	512
Thorn, Michael	13	Lynn Camp Run	1865	1	92

WOOD (W. VA.)

Adams, P. M.	25	Stillwell Creek	1865	1	32
Berry, Thomas P.	55	Shelving Fork	1865	1	59
Berry, Washington	34	Slate Creek	1865	1	83
Blair, J. B. et al	300	Stillwell Cr.	1865	1	81
Blair, J. B. et al	195	Stillwell Cr.	1865	1	82

Name of Grantee	Acres	Local Description	Year	Book	Page
Boise, George et al	32	Wolf Run	1865	1	78
Boise, George et al	185	Slate Cr.	1865	1	78
Boise, Samuel	96	Sandy Creek	1865	1	70
Boise, William	24	Slate Creek	1865	1	79
Boise, William	84	Slate Creek	1865	1	79
Deem, Elliot et al	20	Tygert's Cr.	1866	1	128
Deem, Jacob (the 3d)	133	Tygert's Cr.	1865	1	57
Dovener, R. G.	121	Slate Creek	1865	1	43
Dovener, R. G.	595	Slate Creek	1865	1	44
Farrow, Howard P. et al	180	Tygert's Creek	1865	1	55
Golden, James	42	Slate Creek	1865	1	56
Haven, William et al	180	Tygert's Creek	1865	1	55
Jackson, J. J. et al	300	Stillwell Creek	1865	1	81
Jackson, J. J. et al	195	Stillwell Creek	1865	1	82
Kincheloe, John	15	Lee Creek	1866	1	248
Leach, James	2½	Tygart's Creek	1865	1	24
Leach, James	15¼	Tygart's Creek	1865	1	24
Mayhugh, Walker et al	20	Tygert's Creek	1866	1	128
Rankins, Armstrong	26	Wts. Lit. Kanawha	1865	1	35
Reed, John M.	44	Plum Run	1871	2	80
Riley, J. D. Jr.	18	Walker's Creek	1865	1	56
Snyder, Adam	44	Slate & Tygert Crs.	1865	1	15
Steel, James E.	4	Slate Creek	1865	1	55
Stephenson, James M. & K. B.	48	Camp Run	1865	1	51
Stephenson, K. B. et al	300	Stillwell Cr.	1865	1	81
Stephenson, Kenny B. et al	195	Stillwell Cr.	1865	1	82
Summers, James et al	32	Wolf Pen	1865	1	78
Summers, James et al	185	Slate Creek	1865	1	78
Woodyard, Jacob et al	20	Tygert's Creek	1866	1	128

WYOMING (W. VA.)

Allen, Heirs of John Sr. Dec'd	72	Big Fork	1879	2	187
Belcher, Abram	120	Big Fork	1866	1	178
Belcher, Richard	120	Indian Creek	1868	1	538
Bishop, David et al	114	Indian Ridge	1865	1	102
Bishop, Kier	40	Indian Creek	1868	1	530
Blankenship, Hannah et al Hrs.	72	Big Fork	1879	2	187
Blankenship, Lewis	106	Milam's Fork	1868	1	537
Blankenship, Mary	48	Lick Branch	1867	1	419
Brooks, Isaac Q.	133	Milam's Fork	1866	1	120
Brown, Mathias H.	25	Still House Hollow	1884	2	217
Brown, Mathias H.	25	Huff's Creek	1884	2	218
Buchanan, George	40	Adj. T. Sizemore	1870	2	47
Burgess, Harriet et al Hrs.	72	Big Fork	1879	2	187
Clay, Hiram	189	Big Fork	1865	1	101
Collins, Ann et al Hrs.	72	Big Fork	1879	2	187
Cook, Ballard P. & D. C.	565	Wolf Glade Fork	1865	1	105
Cook, Green M.	62	Lick Fork	1866	1	177
Cook, Isaac	10	Clear Fork	1866	1	240
Cook, John L.	52	Rock Castle	1866	1	180
Cook, Mitchell	112	Rockcastle	1865	1	28
Cook, Richard M.	293	Turkey Creek	1865	1	107
Cook, Richard M.	274	Lit. Marsh Fork	1866	1	119
Cook, Selia	25	Adj. James Shannon	1871	2	78
Cook, Sylvester	50	Glade Fork	1865	1	102
Dare, Goodall	502	Milam's Fork	1866	1	117
Dare, Goodall	97	Milam's Fork	1866	1	118

Name of Grantee	Acres	Local Description	Year	Book	Page
Dare, Goodall	98	Laurel Creek	1879	2	186
Ellis, Henry	25	Wild Cat	1870	2	24
Ellis, Henry	50	Little Huff	1870	2	24
Elswick, George W	65	Camp Branch	1866	1	258
Elswick, William	126	Double Camp	1871	2	87
Elswick, William	200	Shannon's Mill Br.	1884	2	223
Evans, John	120	Little Glade Run	1866	1	116
Garrettson, John	18	Devil's Fork	1868	1	544
Garrettson, John	35	Toney's Ridge	1868	1	544
Garrettson, John	40	Big Fork	1868	1	545
Garrettson, John	130	Gap Ridge	1868	1	546
Green, Joseph et al	114	Indian Ridge	1865	1	102
Green, Joshua	62	Lit. White Oak	1866	1	182
Grimmit, William	50	Unknown	1866	1	179
Gunnoe, Jane et al Hrs	72	Big Fork	1879	2	187
Hammons, Cheed	66	Cabin Creek	1866	1	178
Hatfield, Anderson	87½	Indian Creek	1875	2	142
Hatfield, James	100	Road Branch	1867	1	399
Hatfield, John W.	69	Wolf Pen	1866	1	175
Hill, Martin F.	19	Big Fork	1867	1	399
Howerton, John	100	Big Fork	1867	1	398
Hunt, Henry	43	White Oak & Indian	1866	1	184
Jackson, Henry F.	245	Wolf Pen	1867	1	401
Lambert, Hiram	175	Skin Fork	1870	2	7
Lawson, Anthony	25	Cub Creek	1867	1	364
Lawson, Anthony	50	Cub Creek	1867	1	364
Lester, Joseph D.	58	Lit. Huff Cr.	1884	2	214
Lusk, Adonirane J.	30	Indian Creek	1866	1	208
Lusk, Adonirane J.	65	Indian Creek	1867	1	402
Lusk, Crockett H.	25	Trace Fork	1867	1	400
Lusk, Eli	38	Bear Town Ridge	1866	1	147
Lusk, Rece T	152	Marsh Fork	1866	1	185
Lusk, Rece T.	100	Indian Creek	1866	1	186
Maze, Joseph	30	Big Fork	1866	1	238
Maze, Joseph	86	Big Fork	1866	1	238
Maze, Joseph	73	Big Fork	1866	1	239
McCraw—See McGraw					
McCraw, John	214	Laurel Fork	1866	1	216
McCraw, John	20	Milam's Fork	1868	1	447
McDonald, Edward	80	Mill Creek	1868	1	568
McDonald, Isaac E.	82	Reedy	1875	2	138
McDonald, William et al Hrs.	95	Mill Creek	1868	1	571
McDonald, William Heirs et al	226	Clear Fork	1868	1	566
McGraw—See McCraw					
McGraw, John	220	Milam's Fork	1865	1	100
McGraw, John	65	Laurel Fork	1865	1	110
Moran—See Mourn, Mourne					
Mourn, William	48	Clear Fork	1870	2	25
Mourne, William	176	Shannon's Mill Br.	1866	1	184
Mullins, John S	75	Guyandotte River	1879	2	203
Philips, Willie	40	Big Fork	1870	2	32
Philips, Willie	303	Barkers Ridge	1868	1	576
Phillips, William G.	529	Laurel Branch	1865	1	29
Ramey, Matthew	693	Big Fork	1866	1	257
Ramey, Matthew	187	Panther Branch	1866	1	258
Roach, Juliet et al Heirs	72	Big Fork	1879	2	187
Roberts, James	100	Cabin Creek	1866	1	175
St. Clair, Samuel P.	14	Indian Creek	1866	1	181
St. Clair, Samuel P.	24	Lick Branch	1866	1	181
St Clair, Samuel P.	19	Indian Creek	1866	1	182
Shannon, James H.	79	Clear Fork	1866	1	176
Short, Benjamin	75	Saw Pit Branch	1870	2	61
Sizemore, Calvin	54	Big Fork	1865	1	27

SUPPLEMENT

to

SIMS INDEX TO LAND GRANTS IN WEST VIRGINIA

Note: Grants of Fincastle, Giles and Rockingham counties, as well as a few from other counties, which were not on record in the Auditor's Office at the time the Sims Index to Land Grants in West Virginia was published (1952).

FINCASTLE COUNTY

Name of Grantee	Acres	Local Description	Year	Book	Page
Clay, Mitchell	803	Clover Bottom, Bluestone	1774	1	522
Craik, James	4,232	Great Kenhawa	1772	1	505
French, Matthew	226	Wolf Creek	1790	1	527
Fry, John	1,525	Little Sandy Creek	1772	1	510
Fry, John	2,084	Big Sandy	1772	1	512
Fry, John	4,149	Below mth. Gr. Kenhawa	1772	1	508
Grayson, A. & J. (Assignee)	156	Crab Orchard Fork	1831	1	533
Ingles, William	1,000	Abbs Valley	1774	1	520
Keasler, George	190	Mill Creek of New R.	1790	1	530
Kimberlane, Martin	87	Doak's Mill Run	1790	1	529
McFarlane, James	176	Wolf Creek	1811	1	531
Mercer, George	13,532	Mouth of Gr. Kenhawa	1772	1	502
Neely, James et al	40	New River	1831	1	532
Ogle, James	78	Little Reed Island Cr.	1790	1	528
Phipps, J. & T. Young	102	New River	1833	1	534
Savage, John et al	28,627	Ohio & Big Sandy River	1772	1	514
Washington, George	10,990	Great Kenhawa River	1772	1	499
Washington, George (Assignee of Burwell Bassett)[1]	10,990	Great Kenhawa River	1784	1	524
Young, T. & J. Phipps	102	New River	1833	1	534

Note: Grants made **after** 1776 were from surveys made at the time Fincastle County existed (1772-1776).

[1] General George Washington obtained a grant from the Crown, but being engaged in the Revolutionary War, failed to fulfill the conditions of his grant Burwell Bassett attempted to lay claim to the same tract under a new patent, which was later made to General Washington by the Commonwealth of Virginia, upon an assignment from Bassett

GILES COUNTY

Name of Grantee	Acres	Local Description	Year	Book	Page
Albert, John	3	East Side New River	1842	1	300
Aldridge, William & Samuel Brown, Sr.	50	West Side New River	1813	1	112
Aldridge, William & John Chapman, Jr., Assignee	102	Flat Top Mt.	1811	1	53
Aldridge, William & John Chapman, Jr., Assignee	56	Big Bluestone	1811	1	54
Aldridge, Wm. & John Chapman, Jr.	91	Wolf Cr. Wts. Bluest.	1811	1	59
Aldridge, Wm. & John Chapman, Jr.	104	Wolf Creek Wts. Bluest.	1811	1	61
Aldridge, Wm. and Christian Snidow	250	Flat Top Mt.	1811	1	71
Aldridge, William	156	Turkey Pen Ridge	1812	1	96
Bailey, Archibald	46	Big Laurel Fk. of Guy.	1818	1	197
Beauford, John	81	Big Spring Mt.	1813	1	118
Beirne, Christopher & Albert G. Pendleton	729	Wts Lit Stony Crk.	1851	1	307
Bird, Godfrey	18	Rich Cr. Wts.	1816	1	172
Blake, William	221	Round Bottom	1814	1	124

Name of Grantee	Acres	Local Description	Year	Book	Page
Bolding, William, by John Preston, Attorney, Assignee of Philip Snidow	66	New River	1812	1	109
Bradley, James	177	Keers Fork of Big Stony Crk.	1838	1	292
Bradley, James	43	Potts Mt.	1855	1	311
Bradley, Micajah	168	Fork Mt.—Big Br.	1838	1	293
Brittle, Edw. J.	40	Lit. Laur. Fk. of Guy.	1818	1	201
Brown, George W. & James F. Williams	408	Little Mountain	1835	1	317
Brown, Samuel Sr. & William Aldridge	50	West Side New River	1813	1	112
Burdet, Archibald	16	12 Mile Fk. East Riv.	1835	1	284
Burgess, Hiram	63	Camp Br. of Rich Cr.	1823	1	234
Burgess, Hiram	27	Big Bluestone	1828	1	270
Burk, Wm.	288	West Side New Riv.	1811	1	75
Burk, William Jr. & Thomas Cook	148	Lit. Blue Stone	1816	1	179
Caldwell & Lively (John Caldwell & Peggy Lively)	50	Big Br. of Johns Cr.	1838	1	291
Caldwell, Seth and Eliz. (part of 184 a. tr. conveyed to Geo. and John Stafford)		West End of Buckeye Mt.	1809	1	21
Canterbury, Joel—assigned to John McClaugherty	50	West Side New River	1822	1	214
Caperton, Rhoda	186	West Side New River	1824	1	254
Chambers, Robert—assignee of Jacob Chambers	60	Big Bot. Fk. of Guyand.	1827	1	268
Chapman, Archibald assignee of Geo. Chapman,	125	Joel's Hollow	1810	1	18
Chapman, George	50	West Side New River	1811	1	67
Chapman, Henley	500	S. W. Side New River	1809	1	1
Chapman, Henley	9	Fort Branch	1810	1	15
Chapman, Henley	30	Sinking Cr.	1810	1	16
Chapman, Henley	90	West Side New River	1813	1	116
Chapman, Henley	80	West Side New River	1813	1	120
Chapman, Henley	43 a. 1 r. 8 p.	Adj. patent of Benoist	1823	1	230
Chapman, Isaac	169	Near Turkey Hollow	1817	1	184
Chapman, Isaac & James Johnston	40	West Side New River	1810	1	33
Chapman, John & Joshua Copley	84	West Side New River	1817	1	190
Chapman, John Jr. Assignee of Wm. Aldridge	104	Wolf Cr. of Bluestone	1811	1	61
Chapman, John Jr. Assignee of Wm. Aldridge	56	Big Bluestone	1811	1	54
Chapman, John Jr. Assignee of Wm. Aldridge	91	Wolf Cr. Bluestone	1811	1	59
Chapman, John Jr. Assignee of Wm. Aldridge	102	Flat Top Mt.	1811	1	53

Name of Grantee	Acres	Local Description	Year	Book	Page
Chapman, William	99	West Side New River	1816	1	169
Chapman, William	61	Clear Fork of Cole	1818	1	203
Christian, Thomas	140	Clear Fork of Guyan	1812	1	84
Christian, Thomas	60	Huff and Toney's Fork	1818	1	200
Clay, Henry	12	Wts. of Richland Creek	1816	1	182
Cole, Chapman Jr.	27	South Side of Potts Mt.	1841	1	306
Collins, Mary	50	Knob Mt. and Sink. Cr.	1818	1	201
Cook, James	60	Clear Fork of Guyand.	1818	1	199
Cook, John Jr.	180	Guyandotte River	1811	1	78
Cook, John Jr.	25	S. E. Side of Big Bot. Fk. of Guyandotte	1827	1	264
Cook, John Jr.	32	Elk Br. of Big Bot. Fk.	1827	1	265
Cook, John Jr.	104	Clear Fork of Guyand.	1835	1	285
Cook, John Sr.	170	Lit. Laurel Fork of Guyand.	1810	1	36
Cook, John Sr.	30	Clear Fork of Guyand.	1812	1	86
Cook, Thomas	34	Clear Fork	1812	1	101
Cook, Thomas	75	Toney's Fork of Guyand.	1818	1	195
Cook, Thomas	20	Clear Fork of Guyand.	1822	1	222
Cook, Thomas & William Burk, Jr.	148	Lit. Bluestone	1816	1	179
Cook, William	23	Lit. Laurel Fork	1824	1	246
Copley, Joseph	60	West Side New River	1815	1	128
Copley, Joshua & John Chapman	84	West Side New River	1817	1	190
Copley, Thomas	12	West Side New River	1811	1	57
Corder, Wm. Assignee of John Mullin	80	W. S. New River	1809	1	13
Criner, John	27	Sinking Cr.	1837	1	289
Cryner—also Criner					
Cryner, Andrew	36	Sinking Cr.	1809	1	9
Cubine, William	75	Big Ridge—Opposite Bear Wallow	1824	1	252
Davice, Hiram	80	Flat Top Mt.	1815	1	154
Dillion, John	11	Twelve Mile Fork	1826	1	261
Dillion, John	101	12-Mi. Fk. East Riv.	1826	1	262
Dingess, John	81	East River	1810	1	46
Dingess, Wm. & David French	216	Clear Fork of Guyan	1810	1	28
Duncan, Wm.	50	Drains of Sink. Cr.	1809	1	8
Dunn, Martin	235	East Side New River	1840	1	298
Dunn, Martin	100	Wts. of New River	1844	1	303
Earickson, Matthew	25	Big Bluestone	1816	1	170
Ellison, Asa	46	Toms Run	1823	1	236
Elmore, John & William Huffman	60	Johns Creek	1853	1	310
Farley, Forest (part of 435 a. tr. conv. to Charles King)		Walker's Creek	1826	1	255
Ford, Lewis	25	East Riv. below mth. 12-Mi. Fk.	1823	1	232

Name of Grantee	Acres	Local Description	Year	Book	Page
Frasher, Creed T. (Assigned to David Rutledge)	148	East Side New Riv.	1837	1	290
French, David & William Dingess	216	Clear Fork of Guyand.	1810	1	28
French, David	200	Joel's Hollow	1810	1	31
French, David	500	West Side New River	1810	1	38
Garrel—See Jarrel, Jarrell					
Garrel, Gipson	55	Sycamore Fork of Cole	1824	1	244
Godfrey, Bird	18	Rich Creek	1816	1	172
Gunnoe, Daniel	114	Mill Cr. of Cl. Fk. of G.	1822	1	218
Hale, Charles	50	Mill Cr.	1853	1	309
Hale, Elias	50	Rich Creek	1835	1	283
Handley, Alexander Assignee of Wm. Handley	92	Little Fork Mt.	1817	1	189
Harless—See Hearless					
Harper, John	32	Cole River	1815	1	150
Harper, Joseph	54	Dry Fk. of Clear Fk.	1815	1	148
Harvey—See Harvie					
Harvey, William	100	Laurel Br. of Guyand.	1821	1	212
Harvie—See Harvey					
Harvie, John	100	Wts. of White Stick	1815	1	156
Harvie, John	50	Clear Fork of Guyand.	1812	1	99
Harvie, John & William Wall	17	Clear Fk. of Guyand.	1822	1	215
Harvie, Joshua	27	Clear Fork of Guyand.	1822	1	221
Harvie, William	50	Clear Fork of Guyand.	1821	1	213
Harvie, William	80	Lick Br. of Cl. Fk.	1822	1	214
Harvie, William	50	Clear Fork of Guyand.	1822	1	219
Hearless, Elias	76	Clover Hollow	1822	1	220
Hearless, Martain	110	South Fork of Potts	1822	1	223
Headerick, John	125	Sinking Creek	1815	1	142
Hedrick—See Headerick					
Hinton, John	61	Madam's Cr.	1833	1	279
Hinton, John	62	White Oak Br.	1833	1	280
Hinton, John	135	Madam's Creek	1833	1	281
Holand, Sarah	50	Elk Creek of Guyand.	1814	1	140
Houchens, James	84	War Ridge of Pipestem	1824	1	248
Huffman, Wm. & John Elmore	60	John's Creek	1853	1	310
Hutchinson, James	125	Big & Bee Br.	1838	1	294
Hutchinson, Samuel	40	Pott's Mountain	1825	1	257
Hutchinson, Samuel (Pt in Monroe)	296	Wts. of John's & Pott's Crs.	1838	1	295
Hutchinson, Samuel	20	John's Creek	1825	1	256
Jackson, Joseph	41	West Side of N. Riv.	1816	1	177
Jarrell, Gibson	229	Clear Fork of Cole	1823	1	227
Jarrell, Gibson	38	Clear Fork	1823	1	235
Jarrell, Gibson	55	Sycamore Fk. of Cole	1824	1	244
Jarrell, Lemuel	22	Clear Fk. of Cole	1826	1	259

Name of Grantee	Acres	Local Description	Year	Book	Page
Johnson—See Johnston					
Johnson, James & Isaac Chapman	40	West Side New Riv.	1810	1	33
Johnston—See Johnson					
Johnston, Andrew & David	520	Clear Fork of Guyand.	1812	1	103
Johnston, Andrew & David	84	Bet. New Riv. & Butt Mt.	1809	1	11
Johnston, Chapman	489	South Side Big Mt.	1860	1	313
Johnston, David & Andrew	400	Cub Cr. of Guyand.	1817	1	187
Johnston, David & Andrew	133	West Side New Riv.	1811	1	64
Johnston, David & Andrew	140	Big Spring Mt.	1812	1	107
Johnston, James	55	Fork Ridge of Butt Mt.	1811	1	73
Johnston, William	16	Clear Fk. of Guyand.	1814	1	139
Jones, Jacob	58	Granny's Run	1849	1	305
Kadle, Thomas	20	Bluestone adj. Gottlieves	1832	1	278
Keaton, William	87	Pipe Stem Knobs	1824	1	249
King, Charles (3 Trs.)	435	Walker's Creek	1826	1	255
Kirk, John	180	West Side New Riv.	1812	1	88
Kirk, Lewis	8	S. S. Knob Mt.	1827	1	263
Kirk, Thomas	50	West Side New Riv.	1813	1	114
Lambert, Jeremiah (Pt. in Tazewell)	65	Cor. to his 50 A. Tract	1853	1	308
Lilley, Robert (Assignee of Josiah Meadow)	30	Big Bluestone	1816	1	168
Lilley, William Jr.	20	Big Bluestone	1837	1	288
Lilly—See Lilley					
Lilly, Edmond	56	Big Bluestone	1814	1	131
Lilly, Robert	82	Big Bluestone	1809	1	23
Lively, Peggy & John Caldwell	50	Big Branch of John's Cr.	1838	1	291
Lowery, John	39	Low Gap of Clear Fk.	1824	1	251
Lugar, Geo.	21	Wts. of Sinking Cr.	1816	1	166
Luster, William	60	Big Fk. of Guyand.	1812	1	92
Maupin, Gabriel	70	Richland Cr. of Bluestone	1811	1	69
Maxy—See Moxy					
Maxy, Josiah	55	Big Bluestone	1828	1	271
McClaugherty, Hugh	177	Cove Br. of Bluestone	1836	1	286
McClaugherty, James Jr.	20	Mth. Rich Creek	1812	1	80
McClaugherty, James	85	Opposite Brushy Bottom	1832	1	277
McClaugherty, James & William White	260	Three Knobs	1837	1	318
McClaugherty, John (Assignee of John Mullin, Sr.)	6-1/2	N. S. New River	1809	1	5
McClaugherty, John	187	North East Side New R.	1826	1	260
McClaugherty, John (Assign. of Joel Canterbury)	50	West Side New River	1822	1	214
McDaniel, Henry (Assigned to Geo. Zickefuse)	259	Pipestem on New River	1810	1	43
McDanold—or McDonald					
McDanold, Joseph	250	Huff Cr. of Guyand.	1814	1	134
McDanold, Joseph	150	Cub Creek, of Guyand.	1814	1	136
McDanold, Joseph	50	Turkey Creek, of Guyand.	1814	1	138
McDanold, Joseph	100	Meetinghouse of Guyand.	1815	1	159

Name of Grantee	Acres	Local Description	Year	Book	Page
McDanold, Joseph	282	Huff Cr. of Guyandotte	1815	1	160
McDanold, Joseph	32	Big Bend of Guyand.	1820	1	209
McDanold, Joseph	41	Mill Cr. of Big Bot Fk.	1824	1	240
McDanold, Joseph	36	Mill Cr. of Big Bot. Fk.	1824	1	250
McDanold, Joseph et al (part in Tazewell County)	180	Big Fork of Guyandotte	1821	1	210
McDanold, Lewis	50	Clear Fork of Guyand.	1813	1	111
McDanold, Lewis	101	Clear Fk. of Guyand.	1814	1	132
McDanold, Stephen	50	Mill Cr. of Big Bot. Fk.	1824	1	245
McDonald—See McDanold					
McDonald, Joseph & Lewis (Part in Cabell County)	250	Big Bend Guyand.	1817	1	191
McPherson, Jacob	25	Sinking Cr. Wts.	1827	1	269
McVey, James	380	Flat Top Mt.	1823	1	239
McVey, James	212	Near a Br. of Camp Cr.	1827	1	267
Meador—See Meadow, Meadows, Meddes, Medders					
Meador, Josiah	50	Big Bluestone	1815	1	144
Meadow—See Meador, Meadows, Meddes, Medders					
Meadow, Jesiah	50	Wts. Big Bluestone	1816	1	180
Meadow, Josiah (Assigned to Robt. Lilley)	30	Big Bluestone	1816	1	168
Medders—See Meadow, Meadows, Meador, Meddes					
Medders, Jacob	25	Adj. Caperton on River Hill	1830	1	274
Meddes—See Meadow, Meadows, Meador, Medders					
Meddes, Jacob	138	Christian's Ridge, Odear's Run of New River	1824	1	253
Millirons, David	8	East Side of New River	1827	1	266
Mullins, John (Assigned to Wm. Corder)	80	W. S. New River—cor to Gabriel Moppin	1809	1	13
Mullins, John Sr. (Assigned to McClaugherty, John)	6-1/2	North Side New River	1809	1	5
Mustard, John & Wm.	260	Flat Top Mt., Kimberland Fk.	1847	1	304
Nausamond, John Sr.	240	West Side of New River	1816	1	173
Neeley, John	71	Pipe Stem	1823	1	237
Neeley, John	125	Pipe Stem Knobs	1823	1	238
Newton, Thomas	50	Clear Fork of Guyandotte	1822	1	220
Pack, Samuel Jr.	135	Wts. of Cooper's Creek	1815	1	158
Pack, Samuel Jr.	20	Mth. Pipestem	1830	1	275
Paris—See Peares, Pearis					
Peares, Samuel P.	60	Big Bluestone	1822	1	225
Pearis—See Peares					
Pearis, Charles L.	9	Big Bluestone—Black Lick	1829	1	273
Peck, Benjamin Jr.	89	Big Spring Mt.	1816	1	166
Peck, Jacob	702	Wts. of Bluestone	1812	1	82

Name of Grantee	Acres	Local Description	Year	Book	Page
Peck, Jacob	217	North Side Peter's Mt.	1843	1	301
Pendleton, Albert G. & Christopher J. Beirne	729	Little Stony Cr.	1851	1	307
Peters, John	50	West Side of New Riv.	1840	1	296
Peters, John Sr.	20½	Rich Creek	1861	1	315
Preston, John (Attorney-in-Fact for William Bolding)	65	New River	1812	1	109
Priliman, Nancy and Christian, Wm. & George Snidow	65	New River	1812	1	109
Rutlege, David (Assignee of Creed T. Frasher)	148	East Side New River	1837	1	290
Scarbrough, Isaac	56	White Oak of Cl. Fk. of Coal	1815	1	151
Scarbrough, John W.	170	Toney's Fk. of Coal River	1815	1	146
Scarbrough, Zachariah	26	Clear Fork of Coal	1815	1	152
Shoemate—See Shumate					
Shoemate, Daniel	499	Miller Camp Br. of Coal	1823	1	231
Shoemate, Edmond	67	Brush Cr. of Bluestone	1835	1	282
Shoemate, Edmond	33	East Side of New River	1840	1	297
Shoemate, Hardin	100	East Side of N. R.	1843	1	302
Shoemate, Tolison	67	North East Side of N. Riv.	1840	1	298-A
Shrewsbury, John	58	Below Mth. of Lit. Wolf Cr.	1828	1	272
Shumate—See Shoemate					
Shumate, Thompson (Assignee of Tolison Shumate)	99	Martin Dunn's Ridge	1859	1	312
Smith, James and Samuel	247	Pott's Cr. Mt.	1820	1	207
Smith, Nimrod	190	Wts. East River	1809	1	6
Smith, Wm.	50	South Side East River	1810	1	35
Snidow, Christian	64	West Side New Riv.	1812	1	122
Snidow, Christian & Wm. Aldridge	250	Flat Top Mt.	1811	1	71
Snidow, Philip (Assignee of Wm. Bolding)	65	New River	1812	1	109
Snidow, Wm. & George and Nancy Priliman, formerly Nancy Snidow, heirs of Philip Snidow)	65	New River	1812	1	109
Stafford, Geo. and John Jr.	184	West End of Buckeye Mt.	1809	1	21
Stafford, James (Part of 184 a. tr. conveyed to Geo. and John Stafford)	127	West End of Buckeye Mt.	1809	1	21
Stewart, Alexander	100	South Side of East River	1810	1	48
Stewart, Alexander	86	East River	1811	1	63
Stover, Jacob Jr.	30	Right Hand Fork of White Oak Br. of Clear Fork of Coal River	1824	1	247
Stover, Jacob Sr.	127	Clear Fork of Coal	1824	1	241
Stover, John	21	Lick Creek of Coal River	1826	1	258
Strailey, James	87	West Side of New River near Wallow Hole	1816	1	164

Name of Grantee	Acres	Local Description	Year	Book	Page
Strailey, Jacob	49	West Side New River on Rich Hill	1810	1	41
Toler, David	40	Huff Creek	1816	1	175
Toler, David	60	Huff Creek	1818	1	193
Toler, David	200	Little Laurel Fk. of Guyand.	1810	1	25
Toler, James	50	Clear Fork of Guyandotte	1818	1	194
Toler, Richard	18	Huff Creek	1816	1	186
Toler, Richard	55	Huff Creek	1818	1	196
Toler, Richard	75	Big Fork of Guyandotte	1822	1	216
Toler, William	10	Road Fork of Huff Creek	1818	1	198
Toler, Zachariah H. & Wm. Toler	139	Clear Fork of Guyandotte	1812	1	94
Tracy, William	100	Five-Mile Fork of East Riv.	1811	1	51
Tyree, Richard F. (Part in Greenbrier)	125	Slater's Improvement on New River	1815	1	163
Waddle, Robert	99	Bear Spring of New River	1813	1	119
Walker, Chrispyanous	100	Big Bottom Fk. of Bluestone	1823	1	233
Walker, Thomas	320	West Side of New River	1814	1	126
Wall, William & John Harvie	17	Clear Fork of Guyandotte	1822	1	215
Walls, William	52	Clear Fork of Guyandotte	1819	1	205
Walters, John	45	Sinking Creek of New Riv.	1822	1	216
White, William	147	West Side New River	1837	1	287
White, William & James McClaugherty	260	Three Knobs	1837	1	318
Wiley—See Wilie					
Wiley, James	118	East Side New River	1840	1	299
Wiley, John A. & Esquire	17	New River—south of River Hill	1861	1	314
Wiley, John A.	108	New River, Cor. to Mary Walker	1861	1	316
Wilie—See Wiley					
Wilie, Squire Assignee of Martin Dunn	100	Cor. to T. Shoemate	1844	1	303
Williams, James F. & George W. Brown	408	Little Mountain	1835	1	317
Williams, George (Exec. of Geo. Williams)	73	Cor. to Lucas	1824	1	243
Wilson, Isaiah	30	Wts. of Sinking Creek	1816	1	171
Wilson, James	140	John's Creek	1830	1	276
Yost, John	102	Big Spring Mt.	1814	1	130
Zickefuse, George (Assignee of Henry McDaniel)	259	W. S. New R. on Pipestem	1810	1	43

GREENBRIER COUNTY

Cook, John	54	So. East Side Big Laurel Cr. of Meadow River	1826	6	551
Cook, John	86	Forks of Meadow Cr.	1826	6	552
Cook, John	60	Mead. Cr. Mt. (1 mi. fr. M. C.)	1826	6	553

HARDY COUNTY

Name of Grantee	Acres	Local Description	Year	Book	Page
Chambers, Benjamin	46,783	Bet. So. Fk. of So. Br. and Lost R.	1795	1	578

MONTGOMERY COUNTY

Name of Grantee	Acres	Local Description	Year	Book	Page
Breckenridge, Jno.	1,150	Hd. Wts. of Coal R.	1784	1	605
Farler, Frances	10	On N. R. below Culbertson's Bottom	1785	1	604

OHIO COUNTY

Name of Grantee	Acres	Local Description	Year	Book	Page
Washington, George	587	Round Bottom	1784	1	546

ROCKINGHAM COUNTY

Name of Grantee	Acres	Local Description	Year	Book	Page
Aberman, Jacob	100	N. Fk. So. Br. of Pot.	1787	1	450
Argebright, Martin	256	Adj. Collier & Wright	1787	1	193
Argebright, Martin	120	Adj. Taylor	1784	1	205
Aylor, Anthony	80	Adj. Windleblut, Shanklin	1787	1	254
Barger, Jacob	99	Lick Run-Br. S. Fk. Potomac	1787	1	544
Baxter, George	228	No. Mt. bet. Love, Irons	1786	1	382
Baxter, George	118	Adj. Josiah Davison et al	1786	1	384
Beazley, Jeremiah	48	Bet. Lewis & the Mountain	1784	1	185
Benet, Joseph	127	Southeast si. N. Fk. So. Br.	1781	1	106
Berry, Malechia	159	South side Shenan. R.	1786	1	330
Bible, Adam	180	West's Gap, Shenand River	1787	1	557
Bible, Adam Jr.	113	Dry Riv. Brock's Gap	1787	1	563
Birer, Joseph	55	Custes's Cr.	1787	1	536
Boss—See Poss					
Boss, Nicholas	250	No. si. N. Riv. Shenandoah	1780	1	250
Boswell, George	182	Madison's Gap	1780	1	48
Boswell, George	220	Bet. his land and Mountain	1780	1	108
Boswell, George	400	N. & S. Riv. Shenan, adj. Madison and Frazier	1782	1	141
Bowin, Thomas	100	Round Hill, adj. Green	1784	1	190
Bowman, John	10	Place called the Forest	1787	1	586
Boyer, Ingle	56	Mt. Run, br. of Smith's Cr.	1781	1	87
Boyer, Ingle	200	West side Smith's Cr.	1781	1	91
Boyer, Ingle	316	West side Smith's Cr.	1781	1	139
Breenaman—See Brunaman					
Breenaman, Anthony	31	Wts. Humes Run	1785	1	282
Briggs, Joseph	125	West brs. of Reed's Cr.	1787	1	447
Bright, John	60	Smith's Cr.	1787	1	533
Brown, Peter	158	Bet. Keller and Tanner	1787	1	604

Name of Grantee	Acres	Local Description	Year	Book	Page
Brunaman—See Breenaman					
Brunaman, Anthony	240	Wts. of Humes Run	1785	1	314
Brunk, Jacob	69	So. Br. Brock's Cr.	1785	1	317
Bruster, James	360	Cub Run (4 tracts)	1785	1	337
Bush, Leonard	50	Blind Lick-brs. S. Br. Pot.	1787	1	433
Bush, Michael	40	Branches of Reed's Cr.	1787	1	435
Bush, Michael	13	Adj. his land—Reed Cr.	1787	1	436
Byrd, Andrew	300	So. Si. N. Fk. Shenandoah	1784	1	276
Campbell, Robert	206	Bet. So. Riv. & So. Mt.	1783	1	51
Campfield, Richard	145	Fort Run, No. R. Shenan.	1782	1	136
Caplenger—See Keeplinger					
Caplenger, John	60	N. Si. N. Riv., West's Gap	1780	1	117
Chenveront, Joseph	62	Flat Spring, N. Fk. Pot.	1787	1	397
Circle, Lewis	104	Place called Forrest	1785	1	291
Circle, Lodowick	220	West side Smith's Cr	1784	1	259
Clifton, William	70	East side So. Br. Potomac	1784	1	232
Coger, Jacob	73	Broad Run, S. Fk. P.	1787	1	498
Coil, Gabriel	12	So. Br. P. adj. Shelton's tr.	1781	1	22
Coil, Gabriel Jr.	55	So. Br. Potomac	1787	1	429
Coil, George	100	Swisher's Run Gap	1787	1	401
Collick, Thomas	170	Buffalo Ridge, So. Br. Pot.	1787	1	576
Conrod, George	590	Smith's Cr.	1780	1	124
Conrod, Jacob	46	East side So. Br. Potomac	1784	1	230
Conrod, Jacob	44	So. West si. So. Br.	1787	1	579
Conrod, Peter	260	Boon's Run, br. Shenandoah	1787	1	468
Cowan, Henry	100	Drafts of Smith Cr.	1788	1	629
Cress, George	56	Adj. Logan, Lawrence, Hall et al	1787	1	514
Craig, John	400	So. side his lands	1784	1	228
Crawford, John	363-1/2	Both sides Brira Br.	1781	1	85
Cummins, Moses	220	East side Smith's Cr.	1784	1	236
Cummins, Moses	100	Smith Cr. James' Br.	1784	1	256
Custard, Conrod	40	Brock's Gap, Tunis's Cr.	1780	1	122
Custard, Paul	59	Brock's Gap, adj. Miller	1787	1	443
Davis, John	370	No. Riv. Shen., Mossy Cr.	1784	1	219
Davis, John	62	Opposite Mth. Mossy Cr.	1784	1	220
Davis, John	144	Bet. his & Erwin's land	1787	1	421
Davison, Josiah	196	East si. Love lands	1787	1	399
Davison, Josiah	160	Adj. Geo. Baxter	1787	1	402
Davisson, Josiah	80	Bet. Harrison, Baxter, et al	1787	1	390
Dayger, Gasper	340	Hazel Hollow	1784	1	269
Deck—See Deek					
Deck, Henry	50	East side Custis's Cr.	1784	1	201
Deek, Michael	20	Boon's Run	1787	1	531
Deek, Michael	36	Boon's Run, adj. Kirkley	1787	1	583
Depoy, Isaac	400	Dry Fk. Smith's Cr.	1787	1	484
Dever—See Diver					
Dever, Hugh	120	Beaver Creek	1780	1	6

Name of Grantee	Acres	Local Description	Year	Book	Page
Disponet, Joseph	189	Parting Run, West's Gap	1788	1	631
Diver—See Dever					
Diver, Hugh	210	N. si. N. Riv. Shenand.	1781	1	31
Diver, Hugh	170	W. si. Mossy Cr .	1781	1	33
Diver, James	585	Brira Br.	1781	1	95
Diver, James	122	Adj. Miller, Bowyer, King	1785	1	348
Diver, James	400	Bet. lands Harter and Diver	1785	1	350
Diver, James	83	Timber Ridge	1787	1	610
Diver, James	66	Timber Ridge	1787	1	612
Douglass, Joseph	35	N. Riv. Shenandoah	1780	1	8
Douglass, Joseph	400	N. si. N. Riv. Shenandoah	1780	1	46
Douglass, Joseph	17	Opposite hd. Fisher's Cr.	1781	1	73
Douglass, Joseph	58	Head drafts Fisher's Spring	1781	1	75
Dunkle, John (no plat)	50	So. Fk. So. Br. Potomac	1784	1	280
Dye—See Dyer					
Dye, Roger	55	Wts. So. Fk. Potomac	1785	1	295
Dyer—See Dye					
Dyer, James	173	S. Fk. Potomac	1787	1	518
Dyer, Roger	129	So. Fk. wts. of Potomac	1785	1	356
Elliott, Robert	66	Branches of Cub Cr.	1784	1	223
Ergabright, Adam & James Smith	80	Back Drafts of Cook's Cr.	1780	1	110
Evick, Francis	118	East si. So. Br. Potomac	1787	1	386
Ewins, John	27	Hd. Brs. of Linvil's Cr.	1781	1	41
Farley—See Frailey					
Florney, William	113	Beaver & Brier Creeks	1781	1	69
Fogel, Nicholas	54	Dry Run bet. Peaked Mt. and Shen.	1784	1	177
Ford, Michael	88	West side Brock's Cr.	1780	1	2
Fought, Adam	70	Yeager's br. of Smith Cr.	1787	1	445
Fought, Adam	240	Drafts of Smith Cr.	1787	1	476
Fourman, Andrew	73	Cub Run	1788	1	652
Foy, John	41	Near Boon's Run	1787	1	471
Frailey, Daniel & John Helfrey	66	Ea. si. Smith Cr.	1787	1	424
Frazier, John	62	Adj. Thompson and Kern	1780	1	54
Friend, Jacob	75	Richardson's Run S. Br. P.	1787	1	448
Friend, Jacob	20	Richardson's Lick Run	1787	1	618
Friend, Joseph	69	Bet. S. Fk. Pot and No. Mt.	1787	1	394
Fulk, John	190	Brock's Gap	1787	1	482
Gartin, Uriah	86	Dry riv. br. N. Riv. Shenand.	1781	1	39
Gartin, Uriah	50	East si. Dry River	1787	1	419
Gougle, Andrew	17	Peter Reed's Cr., P.	1787	1	396
Gragg, William	200	Hickory Level, Seneca Cr.	1787	1	606
Graton—See Grayton					
Graton, John	268	Wts. Cook's Creek	1784	1	238
Gray, Jacob	100	N. si. N. Riv. Shenandoah	1787	1	624
Grayton—See Graton					
Grayton, John	508	Bet. N. R. and Naked Cr.	1785	1	324
Hagey, Godfrey	400	Forks of Smith's Cr.	1784	1	240

Name of Grantee	Acres	Local Description	Year	Book	Page
Haine, Gasper	77	Adj. Mathias Kirsh	1787	1	496
Hamilton, James (no description)	62	(Inc. former entry of 38 a. made for Thomas Bates, assignee of Thos. Howell)	1787	1	516
Hanagan, Michael	180	Place called the Forrest	1784	1	278
Harmantrout, Philip	70	No. si. Peaked Mt.	1787	1	540
Harmontrout, Frederick	125	Adj. Craig, Price et al	1786	1	374
Harper, Jacob	48	N. si. So. Br. Pot.	1787	1	388
Harris, John	200	So. east side Long Meadow	1787	1	405
Harrison, Jeremiah	84	Dry Fk. Smith's Cr.	1785	1	297
Harrison, Jno.	100	East si. Dry Fk. Smith's Cr.	1786	1	365
Harrison, John & Jeremiah	340	West si. Smith Cr.	1785	1	332
Harrison, Reuben	198	Big Spring of Smith Cr.	1781	1	132
Harrison, Reuben	88	Smith's Cr.	1787	1	637
Harrison, Thos. & Thos. Hewit	400	East si. Harrison's land	1784	1	182
Harvie, John	200	Entrance of Swift Run Gap	1787	1	415
Heaton, Jonas	22	Bet. his and Green's land	1784	1	258
Heator, Henry	94	Martin's Run, Brock's Gap	1787	1	431
Helfrey, John	100	Smith's Cr.	1784	1	213
Helfrey, John & Daniel Frailey	66	Ea. si. Smith Creek	1787	1	424
Herdman, John	54	Head West Fk. Cook's Cr.	1780	1	4
Herdman, John	141	Peaked Mt. adj. Bunkle's	1784	1	180
Hermon, David	90	Sugar Run of So. Br. Pot.	1787	1	393
Hetrick, Charles	60	On Mt. and So. Br. of Pot.	1787	1	598
Hewit, Thomas & Thomas Harrison	400	East si. Harrison's land	1784	1	182
Hilyard, Cornelius	200	Smith's Cr.	1781	1	77
Hinkincle, Jost	22	Sugar Gap Run	1785	1	301
Hinton, John	210	Muddy Cr.	1782	1	143
Holder, Michael	136	So. side Stony Lick Run	1784	1	196
Hook, William	60	Stoney Lick	1780	1	56
Hook, William Jr.	15	Mill Cr. Run, adj. Purkie	1785	1	303
Hook, William Jr.	112	Adj. Hudlow, Hook, Perkey	1780	1	112
Hopkins, Archibald	134	Br. of Muddy Cr.	1781	1	20
Hopkins, Archibald	128	East side Muddy Cr.	1781	1	89
Hopkins, Archibald	128	East side Muddy Cr.	1781	1	134
Hopkins, Archibald	177	Muddy Cr. adj. Shanklin	1784	1	216
Hopkins, Archibald	150	Muddy Cr. bet Evan's Mill Place	1784	1	274
Hopkins, Archibald Jr.	126	Near No. Mt. adj. Hopkins	1786	1	379
Hopkins, John	96	West si. S. Br. Potomac	1781	1	138
Hopkins, John Jr.	40	West branches Muddy cr.	1784	1	187
Horner, John	57	N. Si. Shenandoah	1787	1	417
Hour, Christopher	280	Dry Fk. Smith Cr.	1781	1	12
Hover, Bostle	46	S. Fk. So. B. P.	1785	1	358
Hudlow, Andrew	34	Stoney Lick Run	1780	1	59
Hudlow, Andrew	12	Pt. bet. and below mth. Scott's Run and N. Riv.	1780	1	127
Huffman, Nicholas	170	Bet. Wood's and Peaked Mt.	1787	1	413

Name of Grantee	Acres	Local Description	Year	Book	Page
Hunter, John	150	No. si. N. Fk. Shenandoah	1780	1	131
Huston, Archibald	100	West si. Stover's Mill Cr.	1784	1	255
Huston, John	97	Bet. Gilbert and Bruster's	1784	1	267
Huston, Nathan	175	So. W. si. Stover's Mill Cr.	1784	1	225
Jameson, Andrew	50	Bet. Keesel & Elliott	1788	1	654
Keepling, John	43	Bet. his and Allstot's	1784	1	169
Keeplinger—See Caplenger, Kislinger					
Keesel, George	250	Adj. Joseph Davis, et al	1787	1	464
Kellor, Lodovick	145	Br. of N. Fk. Shenandoah	1780	1	126
Keplinger—See Caplenger, Kislinger					
Keplinger, Adam	170	On Buffaloe Run	1787	1	600
Keplinger, Christopher	117	Nr. No. Mt. adj. Ketner	1788	1	649
Kester, Conrod	115	Three Lick of Brock's Gap	1780	1	49
Kester, Philip	140	Mill Cr. br. N. Riv. Shenand.	1788	1	658
Kester, Richard	100	Brock's Gap on Mill Run	1787	1	642
Kinkel, Isaac (Kinkell)	85	Sugar Lick Gap	1781	1	65
Kinley, Benjamin	178	Ea. si. Muddy Cr.	1781	1	29
Kinley, Benj.	255	Hd. Linvel Cr., Anthony's Sp.	1781	1	36
Kirk, Matthias	80	Bet. his and Haine's land	1787	1	456
Kirkley, Sinclair	30	Shenandoah R., adj. Dick's	1787	1	528
Kiser, Valentine	11	Draft of Mill Cr. adj. Hook	1787	1	442
Kislinger—See Caplenger, Keeplinger, Keplinger					
Kislinger, Henry	9	Quail Run, adj. Thornhill's	1784	1	184
Laird, David	147	No. River, adj. Beard, et al	1786	1	360
Laird, David	200	Adj. Jaspher Fought	1786	1	362
Laird, James	56	Peaked Mt.	1787	1	490
Lare, Joseph	66	Upper Round Hill	1784	1	211
Laufer, John	190	Smith's Cr.	1784	1	207
Lewis, Sarah	230	So. Riv. Shenand. & So. Mt.	1780	1	61
Lewis, Thomas	90	No. east side Shenandoah	1788	1	656
Loftus, Ralph	51	Brieary Br.	1781	1	44
Lough, Adam	138	Head Br. Switzer Run Gap	1787	1	588
Lough, George	162	Switser's Gap Run of S. B. P.	1787	1	439
Love, Ephraim	108	No. Mt., adj. Baxter's	1786	1	377
Love, Daniel	120	Adj. Cravin's land	1787	1	525
Lowdobark, Joseph	168	Bet. Peaked Mt. & Shenand.	1784	1	272
Mallow, George	185	Ft. of Peaked Mt.	1781	1	93
Matthews, Richard	300	Mold Hill, adj. Miller	1783	1	146
Matthews, Townsend	400	Dr. Fk. Smith's Cr.	1785	1	322
McFarlin, Alexander	278	E. Si. Big Spring, Smith Cr.	1784	1	198
McGill, James	220	So. si. N. Riv. Shennandoah	1781	1	74
McGill, John (MacGill)	242	No. si. N. Riv. Shenandoah	1781	1	100
McNeal, George	46	West's Gap, adj. Fitzwater	1780	1	120
Michael, William	117	Adj. Mann, Price & Long	1785	1	346
Miller, Abraham	200	Brock's Gap	1785	1	352
Miller, Abraham	60	Place called the Forest	1786	1	370
Miller, Abraham	28	Place called the Forest	1787	1	564

Name of Grantee	Acres	Local Description	Year	Book	Page
Miller, David	76	Place called the Forest	1784	1	271
Miller, George	80	Shaver's Riv.	1787	1	480
Miller, Henry	96	Mossy Cr.	1788	1	625
Miller, Isaac (Assignee)	117	Adj. his land	1787	1	437
Miller, Isaac	234	Northeast si. Mole Hill	1787	1	591
Miller, Leonard	140	West side Stover's Mill Cr.	1784	1	243
Miller, Samuel	215	No. east si. Mold Hill	1782	1	148
Minick, John	100	Ft. No. Mt. near Forest	1787	1	594
Moole, Edward	216	Head brs. Smith's Cr.	1787	1	644
Moyer, Michael	45	No. Riv. above Brock's Gap	1788	1	633
Nalle, William	150	Hawksbill, bet. Maggots et al	1780	1	116
Nezlerod, Frederick	83	Ft. N. Mt., adj. Ketner	1788	1	646
Null, George	150	Naked Creek	1787	1	493
Null, Henry	100	West si. his land, Naked Cr.	1788	1	634
Null, Henry	200	So. si. Shenand., adj. Bare	1788	1	635
Orbock, Adam	200	No. Riv. Shenand., at Forest	1787	1	488
Painter, Leonard	50	Ea. si. Custis's Cr.	1784	1	203
Patteson, William	215	Head Dry Beaver Pond Cr.	1784	1	279
Patton, Matthew	42	Both sides S. Fk. S. Br. P.	1787	1	466
Patton, Matthew	58	Adj. R. Dyer on S. Br. P.	1787	1	547
Peebles, Adam	26	Brock's Gap	1787	1	521
Pence, George	215	Cub Run	1783	1	153
Pence, George	90	Drafts of Cub Run	1787	1	619
Pence, William	28	N. W. Si. Shen. adj. Burk	1784	1	160
Pence, William	77	Bet. Peaked Mt. & Shenand.	1785	1	299
Pence, William	13	Bet. Peaked Mt. adj. Breniman	1785	1	306
Perkins, David	70	Tunis's Cr., Brock's Gap	1780	1	130
Petner, John	306	Fort Run br., of No. Riv. S.	1787	1	458
Petner, John	109	Ft. of North Mt.	1787	1	461
Pharis, Johnson	114	East si. N. Fk. Potomac	1787	1	411
Phifer, Adam	250	East si. No. Riv. Shenan.	1787	1	622
Poss—See Boss					
Poss, Nicholas	70	No. east si. No. Riv.	1784	1	253
Powers, Charles	73	No. west side So. Br. Potomac	1784	1	234
Price, Augustine	170	Adj. Persinger and Francis	1781	1	67
Price, Augustine Jr.	22	No. West side. Shenand. R.	1784	1	175
Price, Augustine Sr.	191	Bet. Shen. R. and So. Mt.	1784	1	173
Price, Daniel	85	So. si. Peaked Mt. & Shen.	1783	1	158
Price, Daniel	134	No. west si. Shen. & Peak Mt.	1783	1	164
Price, Daniel	49	No. west si. Shenand. River	1784	1	170
Price, Daniel	25	Bet. Peaked Mt. & Shen.	1785	1	305
Price, David	160	Brock's Gap, Tunis's Cr.	1787	1	511
Price, Henry	23	Peaked Mt. & Shenand. Riv.	1784	1	167
Price, William	200	So. si. Dry Riv. of Shenand.	1786	1	327
Proops, Henry	92	N. west si. S. Fk. S. Br. Pot.	1787	1	499
Props, Frederick	25	Mark's Run of S. Fk. S. Br. P.	1787	1	542
Quinn, James	60	Briery Branch	1787	1	584

Name of Grantee	Acres	Local Description	Year	Book	Page
Rader—See Reder					
Rader, Matthias	100	East si. Brock's Gap—Forest	1785	1	335
Rader, Michael	84	Bet. lands of Bird & Circle	1787	1	451
Rager—See Rader, Reder					
Ragin, Richard	50	Irish Sink Draught	1787	1	486
Ralstone, James	56	No. si. Dry Riv. adj. Frame	1785	1	293
Reeves, Brewer	324	No. west si. Long Meadow	1781	1	16
Reeves, Brewer	256	E. si. Long Meadow	1785	1	354
Reeves, Brewer	174	West side Long Meadow	1787	1	507
Reeves, Bruer	343	No. Riv. Shenan., adj. Moore	1784	1	263
Reeves, Thomas	300	N. west side Long Meadow	1781	1	14
Reder—See Rader					
Reder, Adam	200	No. si. N. Fk. Shenandoah	1780	1	114
Renhart, Adam (Rinhart)	125	Tunis Cr. in Brock's Gap	1787	1	524
Rice, Benijah	220	Dry Fork of Shenandoah	1787	1	641
Richel, George	70	So. Br. of P. adj. Venimon	1787	1	617
Ruble, George	54	Bennett's Run in West Gap	1787	1	509
Ruliman—See Rullman					
Ruliman, Christian	53	N. si. S. Fk. of Potomac	1787	1	503
Rullman, Christian	47	So. si. his land S. Fk. P.	1786	1	372
Runkle, Peter	33	Stony Run, br. of Shenand.	1784	1	261
Runkle, Peter	49	Adj. Peter Conrod's land	1784	1	265
Runyan, John	98	Brock's Gap, Tunis's Cr.	1781	1	79
Runyan, John	98	Brock's Gap, Tunis's Cr.	1780	1	128
Rupe, Martin	35	No. si. Brock's Gap Riv.	1787	1	561
Rush, Charles	343	So. si. Peaked Mt.	1787	1	639
Rutherford, Joseph Jr.	150	Br. of Cub Cr. & Peaked Mt.	1787	1	567
Scelcher, Henry	50	Smith's Cr., adj. Fairfax	1787	1	407
Scheving—See Swing					
Scheving, Godfrey	14	Adj. Rutherford on Cub Run	1787	1	552
Scothorn, Ann	107	Adj. Sample, Harrison	1787	1	453
Scothorn, Joseph	310	Hd. drafts of Smith's Cr.	1786	1	367
Scott, Jacob	150	Bet. Glave's on So. Mt.	1787	1	427
Sellers, Michael	106	W. si. Smith Cr.	1781	1	63
Sellers, Michael	60	Ea. si. Dry Fk. Smith's Cr.	1785	1	319
Selzer, Henry	125	Adj. Ekerly, Harrison, et al	1787	1	608
Shackleford, Henry	93	So. Mt. on Gily's Run	1785	1	285
Shanklin, Thomas	18	Adj. Widow Fulton	1787	1	596
Shiry, Michael	37	Drafts of Curtis's Run	1787	1	513
Shoemaker, Peter	29	Br. of Rock's Cr. (Brock's)	1780	1	10
Shouls, Charles	312	Dry Fk. of Smith Cr.	1781	1	102
Sinate, Patrick	68	Lit. Mt. Clay Hill, S. Br. P.	1781	1	18
Sinks, Daniel	43	N. west si. Shenand. R.	1785	1	288
Skidmore, James	70	Mill Run, S. Br. P.	1787	1	581
Skidmore, John	63	E. si. S. Br. Potomac	1781	1	83
Skidmore, John	23	Reed Cr. of S. Br. P.	1787	1	616
Skidmore, Joseph	41	S. Br. of Potomac	1787	1	441
Skidmore, Joseph	96	Hd. Sharry Meadow Run	1787	1	570

Name of Grantee	Acres	Local Description	Year	Book	Page
Smith, Benjamin	200	Branches of Smith's Cr.	1780	1	52
Smith, Conrod	235	Bet. Smith Cr. & Long Mead.	1781	1	24
Smith, Daniel	88	Drafts of Smith Cr., Dry Fk.	1782	1	144
Smith, Henry	400	East si. Beaver Cr.	1785	1	340
Smith, Henry	328	Near hd. Beaver Cr.	1785	1	343
Smith, Jacob	60	East si. Custis Cr.	1783	1	151
Smith, James & Adam Ergabright	80	Back draft of Cook's Cr.	1780	1	110
Smith, John	150	So. west si. Beaver Cr.	1781	1	81
Smith, John Jr.	32	Buffalo Run, So. B. P.	1784	1	206
Smith, John Sr.	98	West si. S. Br. P., adj. Wilmot	1784	1	252
Smith, Joseph	114	East side Dry River	1781	1	104
Smith, Joseph	22	Dry Riv., adj. Douglass et al	1785	1	310
Smith, William	85	So. west si. Dry R.	1785	1	308
Spencer, Thomas	196	Beaver Cr.	1781	1	26
Stephenson, Ester, (Ex. of Jno. Taylor)	230	No. west si. John Taylor's	1783	1	156
Stephenson, Ester, (Ex. of John Taylor)	184	Bet. two tracts of own land	1787	1	602
Stolp—See Stots					
Stolp, Henry	19	Bet. his and Roberson's land	1785	1	312
Stots—See Stolp					
Stots, Henry	35	No. Riv. Shen. adj. Lares	1784	1	248
Straton, Sariah	82	Ea. si. S. Br. Potomac	1787	1	409
Stratton, Sariah	110	Head Reed's Cr. of S. B. P.	1787	1	478
Stratton, Sariah (Assignee Thos. Lewis, who was Assignee of Henry Banks)	110	Thorny Bottom Run	1787	1	573
Stratton, Sarriah	150	So. Br. Potomac	1787	1	614
Stratton Seraiah	160	Both sides So. Br. P.	1781	1	98
Stubbs, Peter	159	Hungry Run, Brock's Gap	1787	1	506
Swing—See Scheving					
Swing, Godfrey	146	Branches of Cub Run	1787	1	504
Swing, Godfrey	50	Drafts of Cub Run	1787	1	549
Teeter, George	152	Timber Ridge	1787	1	501
Teeter, George	42	N. Fk. So. Br. Potomac	1787	1	555
Teetor, Paul	43	N. Fk. So. Br., Seneca Cr.	1787	1	474
Trumbo, Jacob	100	Brock's Gap	1787	1	434
Vice, John	41	N. W. si. Shen. adj. Price	1784	1	162
Warin, Michael	120	McCoy's and Long Meadow	1781	1	71
West, James	100	Wts. Smith's Cr.	1784	1	246
Whitsel, Henry	104	West's Gap, Mud Lick Br.	1788	1	627
Wilt, Peter	50	North Mt., adj. Hannigar	1796	1	1
Wizel, Peter	300	N. si. No. Riv. Shenandoah	1784	1	244

WYTHE COUNTY

Name of Grantee	Acres	Local Description	Year	Book	Page
Cloyd, Gordon	7,800	East Side of Guyandotte R. at Mth. of P. Huff Cr.	1796	1	238

www.ingramcontent.com/pod-product-compliance
Ingram Content Group UK Ltd.
Pitfield, Milton Keynes, MK11 3LW, UK
UKHW020122290926
15471UKWH00003B/224

9 780806 317144